# A Manual of Environmental Protection Law

## The Pollution Control Functions of the Environment Agency and SEPA

Michael Fry BA, LLM

Solicitor

CLARENDON PRESS · OXFORD
1997

Oxford University Press, Great Clarendon Street, Oxford OX2 6DP
Oxford New York
Athens Auckland Bangkok Bogota Bombay
Buenos Aires Calcutta Cape Town Dar es Salaam
Delhi Florence Hong Kong Istanbul Karachi
Kuala Lumpur Madras Madrid Melbourne
Mexico City Nairobi Paris Singapore
Taipei Tokyo Toronto
and associated companies in
Berlin Ibadan

Oxford is a trade mark of Oxford University Press

Published in the United States
by Oxford University Press Inc., New York

British Library Cataloguing in Publication Data
Data available

Library of Congress Cataloging in Publication Data
Data available
ISBN 0–19–826230–2
ISBN 0–19–826233–7 (Pbk)

1 3 5 7 9 10 8 6 4 2

Typeset by Hope Services (Abingdon) Ltd.
Printed in Great Britain
on acid-free paper by
Biddles Ltd.,
Guildford & King's Lynn

# A MANUAL OF ENVIRONMENTAL PROTECTION LAW

The Pollution Control Functions of the
Environment Agency and SEPA

# Foreword

The office of Secretary of State for the Environment was established in this country in 1970. In the words of Mr Geoffrey Rippon MP, one of the first holders of the office, this was a "world-first in the battle for the environment". As he said:

"I count myself fortunate to be armed with the powers and resources required for a total strategic approach to environmental management, protection and improvement".

That was just before this country became part of the European Community. It would have been difficult to anticipate the enormous effects of that move in fields outside the areas of commerce and trade, with which the Community was thought to be principally concerned. Protection of the environment was not even mentioned as a separate objective in the Treaty as it then stood. The growth in European-based environmental legislation has been dramatic, particularly since the inclusion of specific articles in the Treaty relating to the environment. It is one of the main contributors to the bulk of the statutory material found in this volume.

But even in the purely domestic context, the thought that the powers available in 1970 would remain adequate for "a total strategic approach" has been disproved by experience of subsequent administrations. It is true that students of the old Public Health and Alkali Acts would still find much that is familiar in the current legislation. Many of the old powers and procedures live on under new names. But they do so within a vastly more complex framework, and within a radically different organizational structure. Finding one's way around this material is a daunting task even for the specialist.

The present volume seeks to bring together in one volume the statutory sources of law relating to pollution control—both primary and secondary. The annotations include comprehensive cross-references. It will prove an indispensable companion for those struggling through the tangled thickets of environmental legislation. I am very pleased to have been asked to write this foreword, and I wish it well.

*Sir Robert Carnwath CVO,*
*Justice of the High Court,*
*Chancery Division,*
*November 1996*

# Contents

|                        |     *page* |
|------------------------|-----------:|
| Foreword               |          v |
| Use of the *Manual*    |         xi |
| Abbreviations          |        xii |
| Introduction           |       xiii |

## Part I: Primary Legislation

| | |
|---|---:|
| Rivers (Prevention of Pollution) (Scotland) Act 1951 | 3 |
| Rivers (Prevention of Pollution) (Scotland) Act 1965 | 9 |
| Control of Pollution Act 1974 | 11 |
| Salmon and Freshwater Fisheries Act 1975 | 67 |
| Control of Pollution (Amendment) Act 1989 | 71 |
| Environmental Protection Act 1990 | 83 |
| Water Industry Act 1991 | 229 |
| Water Resources Act 1991 | 267 |
| Clean Air Act 1993 | 333 |
| Radioactive Substances Act 1993 | 381 |
| Environment Act 1995 | 415 |

## Part II: Secondary Legislation

| | |
|---|---:|
| The Surface Waters (Classification) Regulations 1989, S.I. 1989/1148 | 539 |
| The Controlled Waters (Lakes and Ponds) Order 1989, S.I. 1989/1149 | 541 |
| The Trade Effluents (Prescribed Processes and Substances) Regulations 1989, S.I. 1989/1156 | 542 |
| The Control of Pollution (Radioactive Waste) Regulations 1989, S.I. 1989/1158 | 545 |
| The Sludge (Use in Agriculture) Regulations 1989, S.I. 1989/1263 | 547 |
| The Surface Waters (Dangerous Substances) (Classification) Regulations 1989, S.I. 1989/2286. | 554 |
| The Controlled Waters (Lochs and Ponds) (Scotland) Order 1990, S.I. 1990/120 (S.12) | 557 |
| The Surface Waters (Classification) (Scotland) Regulations 1990, S.I. 1990/121 (S.13) | 558 |
| The Surface Waters (Dangerous Substances) (Classification) (Scotland) Regulations 1990, S.I. 1990/126 (S.15) | 560 |
| The Radioactive Substances (Appeals) Regulations 1990, S.I. 1990/2504 | 563 |
| The Environmental Protection (Prescribed Processes and Substances) Regulations 1991, S.I. 1991/472 | 566 |

The Environmental Protection (Applications, Appeals and Registers)
  Regulations 1991, S.I. 1991/507                                        605
The Environmental Protection (Authorisation of Processes)
  (Determination Periods) Order 1991, S.I. 1991/513                      619
The Bathing Waters (Classification) Regulations 1991, S.I. 1991/1597.    622
The Bathing Waters (Classification) (Scotland) Regulations 1991,
  S.I. 1991/1609 (S.144)                                                 626
The Controlled Waste (Registration of Carriers and Seizure of Vehicles)
  Regulations 1991, S.I. 1991/1624                                       630
The Control of Pollution (Radioactive Waste) (Scotland) Regulations 1991,
  S.I. 1991/2539 (S.200)                                                 648
The Environmental Protection (Duty of Care) Regulations 1991,
  S.I. 1991/2839                                                         650
The Surface Waters (Dangerous Substances) (Classification) Regulations
  1992, S.I. 1992/337                                                    653
The Trade Effluents (Prescribed Processes and Substances) Regulations
  1992, S.I. 1992/339                                                    656
The Environmental Protection (Waste Recycling Payments) Regulations
  1992, S.I. 1992/462                                                    657
The Surface Waters (Dangerous Substances) (Classification) (Scotland)
  Regulations 1992, S.I. 1992/574 (S.63)                                 659
The Controlled Waste Regulations 1992, S.I. 1992/588                     662
The Environmental Information Regulations 1992, S.I. 1992/3240           671
The Waste Management Licensing Regulations 1994, S.I. 1994/1056          675
The Surface Waters (River Ecosystem) (Classification) Regulations 1994,
  S.I. 1994/1057                                                         735
The Environmental Protection Act 1990 (Commencement No.15) Order
  1994, S.I. 1994/1096                                                   738
The Transfrontier Shipment of Waste Regulations 1994, S.I. 1994/1137     741
The Waste Management Licensing (Amendment etc.) Regulations 1995,
  S.I. 1995/288                                                          751
The Statutory Nuisance (Appeals) Regulations 1995, S.I. 1995/2644        753
The Environmental Licences (Suspension and Revocation) Regulations
  1996, S.I. 1996/508                                                    757
The Waste Management Regulations 1996, S.I. 1996/634                     759
The Waste Management Licensing (Scotland) Regulations 1996,
  S.I. 1996/916 (S.100)                                                  761
The Special Waste Regulations 1996, S.I. 1996/972                        763
The Environment Act 1995 (Isles of Scilly) Order 1996, S.I. 1996/1030    792
The Statutory Nuisance (Appeals) (Scotland) Regulations 1996,
  S.I. 1996/1076 (S.116)                                                 793
List of regulations relating to the control of injurious substances:
  section 140 of the Environmental Protection Act 1990                   797
List of instruments made, or having effect, under the Clean Air Act 1993 799
List of regulations relating to clean air made under the European
  Communities Act 1972                                                   802

List of instruments made, or having effect, under the Radioactive
   Substances Act 1993                                                                 803
Note of regulations under revision                                                     806

# Part III: Associated Material

Addresses                                                                               811
List of guidance notes: Part I of the Environmental Protection Act 1990    815
List of Waste Management Papers                                                       822
Statutory guidance: Environment Act 1995                                           823
Waste Management: The Duty of Care: A Code of Practice                        824

Index                                                                                   857

# Use of the Manual

The legislation in this *Manual* is up to date to 1 September 1996. In respect of the Environment Act 1995, whilst a large part of the Act is in force, at the time of preparing the *Manual*, certain provisions have not commenced. Prospective amendments made by this Act have been incorporated and noted as such either at the amendment itself or at the end of the section or at the Part concerned.

The *Manual* covers the law of England and Wales and of Scotland. Primary and secondary legislation is set out in Parts I and II respectively, in chronological order. Lists of statutory instruments made under certain provisions are also set out in Part II. Certain statutory instruments, such as those relating to the control of water pollution, which are due shortly to be amended or replaced are not included but are noted at the end of Part II. The index enables statutory provisions relating to a particular matter to be located.

In this *Manual*, the legislation has been annotated to provide, in a convenient form, information on and references to the following points:

1. Statutory definitions and construction of words and phrases;
2. Amendments made to the legislation;
3. Commencement provisions;
4. Secondary legislation made pursuant to powers in the statutes;
5. Cases; and
6. Cross-references to related and other relevant provisions.

To avoid undue repetition the annotations are arranged on the basis of sections, articles or regulations. In section 4 of the Environmental Protection Act 1990, for example, "prescribed process" appears several times in the section; a cross-reference to the definition is set out at the first point in the section where this term appears. Where appropriate the authority for a statement, in the annotations, is placed after a colon. Thus the definition of controlled waters at section 30F of the Control of Pollution Act 1974 is set out as:

"Controlled waters" has the meaning given by s.30A(1) above: s.56(1) below.

Selected cases are noted at certain points; these do not comprise an exhaustive list either of the cases or of legislation which has been the subject of legal proceedings.

In editing the *Manual*, the objective has been to present material in an updated and convenient format. It is to be noted, however, that for the authoritative text, and amendments made to it, reference should be made to the Acts, statutory instruments and other original sources.

# Abbreviations

| | |
|---|---|
| All ER | All England Law Reports |
| APC | Air Pollution Control |
| art. | Article |
| BATNEEC | Best available techniques not entailing excessive cost |
| BPEO | Best practicable environmental option |
| BPM | Best practicable means |
| c. | Chapter |
| COD | Crown Office Digest |
| Crim LR | Criminal Law Review |
| DoE | Department of the Environment |
| EA | Environment Agency |
| EC | European Community |
| Env LR | Environmental Law Reports |
| EU | European Union |
| HMIP | Her Majesty's Inspectorate of Pollution |
| HMIPI | Her Majesty's Industrial Pollution Inspectorate |
| HMSO | Her Majesty's Stationery Office |
| HSE | Health and Safety Executive |
| ISBN | International standard book number |
| IPC | Integrated Pollution Control |
| JEL | Journal of Environmental Law |
| LAAPC | Local Authority Air Pollution Control |
| MAFF | Ministry of Agriculture, Fisheries and Food |
| MRS | Metal recycling site |
| NRA | National Rivers Authority |
| OECD | Organisation for Economic Cooperation and Development |
| OJ | Official Journal of the European Communities |
| p./pp. | page/pages |
| para. | paragraph |
| PPG | Planning Policy Guidance Note |
| pt. | Part |
| reg. | Regulation |
| s./ss. | section/sections |
| SCCR | Scottish Criminal Case Reports |
| SEPA | Scottish Environment Protection Agency |
| sch. | Schedule |
| S.I. | Statutory Instrument |
| SLT | Scots Law Times |
| SNH | Scottish Natural Heritage |
| SO | Scottish Office |
| SSSI | Site of Special Scientific Interest |
| WO | Welsh Office |

# Introduction

The aim of this *Manual is* to provide a collection of the sources of law relating to the pollution control functions of the new Environment Agencies in one reference volume.

On 1 April 1996 responsibilities relating to environmental protection which had previously been exercised by various authorities and persons were transferred to the new Agencies, the Environment Agency in respect of England and Wales and the Scottish Environment Protection Agency, SEPA, in respect of Scotland. The proposal to establish an environment agency had been made by the Prime Minister in a speech on 8 July 1991. Following a consultation process and a further period of time, during which an Environment Agencies' Paving Bill to take preliminary steps to establish new agencies was proposed but not proceeded with, the Environment Bill was introduced into the House of Lords on 1 December 1994. This bill contained proposals to establish the Environment Agency and SEPA along with other matters such as proposals relating to contaminated land, a national air quality strategy and a national waste strategy. Following the passage of the bill through Parliament the royal assent was granted on 19 July 1995.

The Environment Act 1995 makes extensive changes to legislation not only in respect of amendments to existing statutes consequent on the establishment of the new Agencies but also in the enactment of new provisions. As provided in Part I of the Environment Act 1995, the new Agencies have taken over several functions concerning environmental protection. This *Manual* concerns the work of the Agencies relating to integrated pollution control, the control of pollution of water resources, the regulation of controlled waste and of radioactive substances and, in Scotland, air pollution functions previously exercised by local authorities. In addition to annotated primary and secondary legislation, the *Manual* includes a collection of associated material including addresses, references to additional sources and the code of practice relating to the waste management duty of care.

Inevitably, it is not possible to include all relevant legislation and other material in one volume. In respect of secondary legislation, statutory instruments have been selected which concern the operation of the statutes set out in the *Manual*. However, owing to limitations of space, not all instruments relating to pollution control can be included; hence instruments such as the Urban Waste Water Treatment Regulations 1994, S.I. 1994/2841 and S.I. 1984/2842, are not set out. In common with other areas of law there is no fixed boundary defining environmental protection law. There is, for example, a considerable interface between environmental law and law relating to Health and Safety at Work. However, necessarily as a result of limited space, areas of law such as Health and Safety at Work are not included. Readers are advised that it may be necessary to refer to legislation and other material which is not contained in this *Manual*.

In other respects an area wider than the work of the Agencies is covered. Save for the responsibility conferred on SEPA in respect of smoke control areas in Scotland, the Clean Air Act 1993 largely concerns the functions of local authorities and the Secretary of State. This Act is, however, included as it forms part of air pollution legislation. Additionally provisions relating to statutory nuisances under the Environmental Protection Act 1990 and associated secondary legislation are set out in the *Manual*. It is hoped that a balance has been achieved between the somewhat competing objectives of providing a comprehensive guide whilst keeping to a manageable format.

Michael Fry
September 1996

Part I

# Primary Legislation

# Rivers (Prevention of Pollution) (Scotland) Act 1951

## Chapter 66

---

An Act to provide for establishing river purification boards in Scotland and for conferring on or transferring to such boards functions relating to the prevention of river pollution; to make new provision for maintaining or restoring the cleanliness of the rivers and other inland waters and the tidal waters of Scotland in place of the Rivers Pollution Prevention Act 1876, and certain other enactments; and for purposes connected with the matters aforesaid.

[1st August 1951]

---

*The functions previously conferred on river purification authorities under this Act have been transferred to the Scottish Environment Protection Agency, SEPA: Environment Act 1995 (c. 25), s. 21, p. 438 below. SEPA took over its functions under this Act on the transfer date, 1 April 1996: S.I. 1996/139.*

*This Act now comprises the following sections.*

## Part I: Central Authority

1. Duty of Secretary of State in relation to prevention of pollution of rivers and other waters.  4

## Part III: Central Authority

*River Purification authorities[1]*

18. Provision and obtaining of information  4
19. Power to take samples of effluents  5

## Part IV: General

*Miscellaneous Provisions*

32. Expenses  6
35. Interpretation  6
36. Short title, transitional provisions, repeal, commencement and extent  7

*All other parts, sections and schedules of, and to, this Act have been repealed.*

....................................................................................................................................

---

[1] Ss. 18 and 19 now relate to the functions of SEPA.

## PART I: Central Authority

*Duty of Secretary of State in relation to prevention of pollution of rivers and other waters*

**1.** (1) It shall be the duty of the Secretary of State to protect the cleanliness of the rivers and other inland waters and the tidal waters[1] of Scotland[2].

(2)–(4) *Repealed by the Local Government (Miscellaneous Provisions) (Scotland) Act 1981 (c. 23), ss. 31, 41, sch. 4. This amendment came into force on 11 June 1981, the date of the Royal Assent.*

## PART II

*This Part, which related to river purification boards, has been repealed. Prior to the Environment Act 1995 it had been partly repealed. So far as previously unrepealed, this part was repealed by the Environment Act 1995 (c. 25), s. 120, sch. 22, para. 3(2), sch. 24; this amendment came into force on 1 April 1996: S.I. 1996/186. Under the Environment Act 1995, s. 21(3), p. 440 below, river purification boards were dissolved on the transfer date, 1 April 1996: S.I. 1996/139.*

## PART III: Prevention of Pollution

### *River Purification Authorities*[3]

**17.** *Repealed by the Environment Act 1995 (c. 25), s. 120, sch. 22, para. 3(2), sch. 24. This amendment came into force on 1 April 1996: 1996/186.*

*Provision and obtaining of information*

**18.** (1) For the purpose of enabling it[4] to perform the functions[5] conferred on it SEPA[6] may make surveys[7] and gauge and keep records of the flow or volume and other characteristics of any stream[8],[9], and may take steps for the measurement and recording of the rainfall[10] and for the installation and maintenance for these purposes of gauges or other apparatus and works connected therewith, and may take such other steps as may be necessary in order to obtain any information required for the purposes aforesaid.

(2) The Secretary of State may give directions requiring SEPA[11] to exercise all or any of the powers conferred on it[12] by the foregoing subsection and to furnish to him such information obtained in pursuance of the directions at such times and in such form as may be specified in the directions, and it shall be the duty of SEPA to comply with any directions so given.

(3) SEPA[13] shall give reasonable facilities for the inspection of records kept by it[14] of the rainfall or the flow or volume of any stream[15] and for the taking of copies or extracts from such records,

---

[1] "Tidal waters" defined by s. 35(1), p. 7 below.

[2] S. 1 came into force on the date of the Royal Assent, 1 August 1951.

[3] Ss. 18 and 19 now relate to the functions of SEPA.

[4] Word "it" in this subsection substituted by the Environment Act 1995 (c. 25), s. 120, sch. 22, para. 3(3)(a)(i).

[5] "Functions" defined by s. 35(1), p. 6 below.

[6] "SEPA" defined by s. 35(1), p. 6 below. Word "SEPA" substituted by the Environment Act 1995 (c. 25), s. 120, sch. 22, para. 3(3)(a)(ii).

[7] Former words "of their area" repealed by the Environment Act 1995 (c. 25), s. 120, sch. 22, para. 3(3)(a)(iii), sch. 24.

[8] "Stream" defined by s. 35(1), p. 6 below and subsection (6) below.

[9] Former words "in their area" repealed by the Environ-

ment Act 1995 (c. 25), s. 120, sch. 22, para. 3(3)(a)(iii), sch. 24.

[10] Former words "in their area or any part thereof" repealed by the Environment Act 1995 (c. 25), s. 120, sch. 22, para. 3(3)(a)(iii), sch. 24.

[11] Words "SEPA" in this subsection substituted by the Environment Act 1995 (c. 25), s. 120, sch. 22, para. 3(3)(b).

[12] Word "it" substituted by the Environment Act 1995 (c. 25), s. 120, sch. 22, para. 3(3)(b).

[13] Words "SEPA" in this subsection substituted by the Environment Act 1995 (c. 25), s. 120, sch. 22, para. 3(3)(c)(i).

[14] Word "it" substituted by the Environment Act 1995 (c. 25), s. 120, sch. 22, para. 3(3)(c)(ii).

[15] Former words "in their area" repealed by the Environment Act 1995 (c. 25), s. 120, sch. 22, para. 3(3)(c)(iii), sch. 24.

and such facilities shall be available free of charge to all local authorities[1,2] and shall be available to other persons on payment of such reasonable fees as may be determined by[3] SEPA.

**(4)–(5)** *Repealed by the Control of Pollution Act 1974 (c. 40), s. 108(2), sch. 4. This amendment came into force on 31 January 1985: S.I. 1985/70.*

**(6)** Notwithstanding anything in this Act, any controlled waters within the meaning of section 30A of the Control of Pollution Act 1974[4] shall be deemed to be included in the expression "stream" for the purposes of SEPA's[5] powers under this section[6,7].

## Power to take samples of effluents

**19.** **(1)** SEPA[8] shall have a right to obtain and take away samples of water from any stream[9] or of any effluent which is passing from any land[10] or vessel into any stream[11].

**(2)–(2B)** *Repealed by Environment Act 1995 (c. 25), s. 120, sch. 24. This amendment came into force on 1 April 1996: S.I. 1996/186.*

**(3)** Notwithstanding anything in this Act, any controlled waters within the meaning of section 30A of the Control of Pollution Act 1974[12] shall be deemed to be included in the expression "stream" for the purposes of SEPA's[13] powers under this section.

**(4)** In this section[14] any reference to land includes a reference to premises[15,16,17].

*The remainder of this part, formerly comprising sections 20 to 28, has been repealed. It had been partly repealed before the repeal by the Control of Pollution Act 1974 came into force. Sections 20 to 28 were repealed by the Control of Pollution Act 1974 (c. 40), s. 108(2), sch. 4. Except for s. 25(1)(c) and (4) and s. 26(2), (4) and (7) to (9) this amendment came into force on 31 January 1985: S.I. 1985/70; in respect of s. 25(1)(c) and (4) and s. 26(2), (4) and (7) to (9) this amendment came into force on 31 May 1991: S.I. 1991/1173.*

[1] "Local authority" defined by s. 35(1), p. 6 below.
[2] Former words "whose districts are wholly or partly included in the area of the river purification authority" repealed by the Environment Act 1995 (c. 25), s. 120, sch. 22, para. 3(3)(c)(iii), sch. 24.
[3] Words "reasonable fees as may be determined by" substituted by the Local Government (Scotland) Act 1973 (c. 65, s. 135(10), sch. 16, para. 6. This amendment came into force on 16 May 1975: S.I. 1973/2181 (S. 158).
[4] P. 18 below. Words "controlled waters . . . 1974" substituted by the Water Act 1989 (c. 15), s. 190, sch. 25, para. 17. This amendment came into force on 1 September 1989: S.I. 1989/1561.
[5] Word "SEPA's" substituted by the Environment Act 1995 (c. 25), s. 120, sch. 22, para. 3(3)(d).
[6] Subsection (6) inserted by the Control of Pollution Act 1974 (c. 40), s. 108(1), sch. 3, para. 14. This amendment came into force on 4 July 1984: S.I. 1984/853.
[7] SEPA took over its functions under this section on the transfer date, 1 April 1996: S.I. 1996/139. The amendments, including repeals, made to this section by the Environment Act 1995 also came into force on 1 April 1996: S.I. 1996/186.
[8] "SEPA" defined by s. 35(1), p. 6 below. Word "SEPA" substituted by the Environment Act 1995 (c. 25), s. 120, sch. 22, para. 3(4)(a)(i).
[9] "Stream" defined by s. 35(1), p. 6 below and subsection (3) below.
[10] "Land" defined by s. 35(1) below and subsection (4) below.
[11] Former words "in the area of the authority" repealed by the Environment Act 1995 (c. 25), s. 120, sch. 22, para. 3(4)(a)(ii), sch. 24.
[12] P. 18 below. Words "controlled waters . . . 1974" substituted by the Water Act 1989 (c. 15), s. 190, sch. 25, para. 17. This amendment came into force on 1 September 1989: S.I. 1989/1561.
[13] Word "SEPA's" substituted by the Environment Act 1995 (c. 25), s. 120, sch. 22, para. 3(4)(b).
[14] Former words "any reference to an analysis" shall be construed as including a reference to any test of whatever kind, and "analysed" and "analyst" shall be construed accordingly, and repealed by the Environment Act 1995 (c. 25), s. 120, sch. 24.
[15] Subsection (4) inserted by the Rivers (Prevention of Pollution) (Scotland) Act 1965 (c. 13), s. 10(6)(b). This amendment came into force on 2 August 1965: s. 17(7).
[16] This section is extended by the Rivers (Prevention of Pollution) (Scotland) Act 1965 (c. 13), s. 10, p. 9 below.
[17] SEPA took over its functions under this section on the transfer date, 1 April 1996: S.I. 1996/139. The amendments, including repeals, made to this section by the Environment Act 1995 also came into force on 1 April 1996: S.I. 1996/186.

## PART IV: General[1]

**29.** *Repealed by the Control of Pollution Act 1974 (c. 40), s. 108(2), sch. 4. This amendment came into force on 31 January 1985: S.I. 1985/70.*

### Miscellaneous Provisions

**30–31.** *Repealed by the Control of Pollution Act 1974 (c. 40), s. 108(2), sch. 4. This amendment came into force on 31 January 1985: S.I. 1985/70.*

*Expenses*

**32.** (1) Any expenses incurred by the Secretary of State under this Act shall be defrayed out of moneys provided by Parliament.

(2) *Repealed by the Control of Pollution Act 1974 (c. 40), s. 108(2), sch. 4. This amendment came into force on 31 January 1985: S.I. 1985/70.*

**33–34.** *Repealed by the Control of Pollution Act 1974 (c. 40), s. 108(2), sch. 4. This amendment came into force on 31 January 1985: S.I. 1985/70.*

*Interpretation*

**35.** (1) In this Act, unless the context otherwise requires, the following expressions have the meanings hereby respectively assigned to them, that is to say—

"contravention" includes failure to comply with, and "contravene" shall be construed accordingly;

"functions" includes powers and duties;

"land" includes land covered by water;

"local authority" means a council constituted under section 2 of the Local Government etc. (Scotland) Act 1995;[2]

"SEPA" means the Scottish Environment Protection Agency;[3]

"sewage effluent" includes any effluent from the sewage disposal or sewerage works of a local authority;

"sewerage authority" shall be construed in accordance with section 62 of the Local Government etc. (Scotland) Act 1994;[4]

"stream" includes any river, watercourse or inland water (whether natural or artificial) and any tidal waters to which this Act applies, except that it does not include either—

(a) any body of water which does not discharge into a stream; or

(b) any sewer vested in a sewerage[5] authority,

but any reference to a stream includes a reference to the channel or bed of a stream which is for the time being dry;

[1] Part IV, now comprising sections 32, 35, and 36, came into force on the date of the Royal Assent, 1 August 1951.
[2] This definition substituted by the Local Government etc. (Scotland) Act 1994 (c. 39), s. 180(1), sch. 13, para. 38(8)(a). This amendment came into force on 1 April 1996: S.I. 1996/323.
[3] This definition inserted by the Environment Act 1995 (c. 25), s. 120, sch. 22, para. 3(5)(b). This amendment came into force on 1 April 1996: 1996/186.
[4] This definition inserted by the Local Government etc. (Scotland) Act 1994 (c. 39), s. 180(1), sch. 13, para. 38(8)9b). This amendment came into force on 1 April 1996: S.I. 1996/323.
[5] Word "sewerage" substituted by the Local Government etc. (Scotland) Act 1994 (c. 39), s. 180(1), sch. 13, para. 38(8)(c). This amendment came into force on 1 April 1996: S.I. 1996/323.

"tidal waters" means any part of the sea or the tidal part of any river, watercourse or inland water (whether natural or artificial) and includes the waters of any enclosed dock which adjoins tidal waters;

"trade effluent" includes any liquid (either with or without particles of matter in suspension therein) which is discharged from any premises other than surface water and domestic sewage.

*Note: Certain former definitions in this subsection have been repealed by the Water (Scotland) Act 1967 (c. 78), the Local Government (Scotland) Act 1973 (c. 65), the Control of Pollution Act 1974 (c. 40) and the Environment Act 1995 (c. 25).*

(2) *Repealed by the Local Government (Scotland) Act 1973 (c. 65), s. 237(1), sch. 29. This amendment came into force on 16 May 1975: S.I. 1973/2181 (S. 158).*

(3)–(8) *Repealed by the Control of Pollution Act 1974 (c. 40), s. 108(2), sch. 4. This amendment came into force on 31 January 1985: S.I. 1985/70.*

........................................................................................................................................................................

*Short title, transitional provisions, repeal, commencement and extent*

**36.** (1) This Act may be cited as the Rivers (Prevention of Pollution) (Scotland) Act 1951.

(2) *Repealed by the Control of Pollution Act 1974 (c. 40), s. 108(2), sch. 4. This amendment came into force on 31 January 1985: S.I. 1985/70.*

(3) *Repealed by the Statute Law (Repeals) Act 1974 (c. 22), s. 1, sch., pt. XI. This amendment came into force on 27 June 1974, the date of the Royal Assent.*

(4) *Repealed by the Control of Pollution Act 1974 (c. 40), s. 108(2), sch. 4.*

(5) This Act shall extend to Scotland only.

*Schedules 1–3 to this Act were repealed by Control of Pollution Act 1974 (c. 40), s. 108(2), sch. 4; schedule 4 was repealed by the Statute Law (Repeals) Act 1974 (c. 22), s. 1, sch., pt. XI.*

# Rivers (Prevention of Pollution) (Scotland) Act 1965

## Chapter 13

An Act to make further provision for maintaining or restoring the cleanliness of the rivers and other inland waters and of the tidal waters of Scotland; to amend the Rivers (Prevention of Pollution) (Scotland) Act 1951; and for purposes connected with the matters aforesaid.

[2nd June 1965[1]]

*The functions previously conferred on river purification authorities under this Act have been transferred to the Scottish Environment Protection Agency, SEPA: Environment Act 1995 (c. 25), s. 21, p. 438 below. SEPA took over its functions under this Act on the transfer date, 1 April 1996: S.I. 1996/139.*

*This Act now comprises the following sections.*

10. Samples of effluent     9
13. Saving for certain acts done for scientific etc. purposes with consent of Secretary of State or in certain cases of a district board     10
15. Interpretation and construction     10
17. Short title, citation, extent, repeals and commencement     10

*All other sections of, and the schedules to, this Act were repealed by the Control of Pollution Act 1974 (c. 40), s. 180(2), sch. 4. This amendment came into force on 31 January 1985: S.I. 1985/70.*

### Miscellaneous and supplemental

*Samples of effluent*

**10.** (1) In any legal proceedings it shall be presumed, until the contrary is shown, that any sample of effluent taken at an inspection chamber or manhole or other place provided in compliance with a condition imposed under sections 34 to 40 of the Control of Pollution Act 1974[2] in relation to any waters is a sample of what was passing from the land or premises to those waters.

(2) The Scottish Environment Protection Agency (in this section referred to as "SEPA")[3] may agree with the occupier of any land or premises from which effluent is discharged on the point or points at which, in exercise of SEPA's[4] rights under section 19 of the principal Act[5], samples are to be taken of the effluent passing into any waters, and in any legal proceedings it shall be presumed, until the contrary is shown, that any sample of effluent taken at a point fixed under this section is a sample of what was passing from the land or premises to those waters.

---

[1] S. 17(7) of this Act provided that the sections of this Act set out below came into force on 2 August 1965.

[2] P. 11 below. Words "sections 34 . . . 1974" substituted by the Control of Pollution Act 1974 (c. 40), s. 108(1), sch. 3, para. 24. This amendment came into force on 31 January 1985: S.I. 1985/70.

[3] Words "The Scottish . . . 'SEPA')" substituted by the Environment Act 1995 (c. 25), s. 120, sch. 22, para. 6(a)(i).

[4] Word "SEPA's" substituted by the Environment Act 1995 (c. 25), s. 120, sch. 22, para. 6(a)(II).

[5] P. 5 above. "The principal Act" means the Rivers (Prevention of Pollution) (Scotland) Act 1951: s. 15(1) below.

(3)  An agreement under the last foregoing subsection shall have effect in relation to land or premises (notwithstanding any change of occupier), but SEPA[1] or the occupier for the time being may at any time declare that it shall cease to have effect.

(4)  In default of agreement under the foregoing provisions of this section, SEPA may apply to the Secretary of State and the Secretary of State may, after considering any representations made to him by the occupier of the land or premises and any other person who appears to the Secretary of State to be interested, fix the point at which samples are to be taken; and the Secretary of State may from time to time on the application of SEPA or the occupier of the land or premises review and vary any decision taken by him under this subsection.

(5)  SEPA shall maintain a register containing such particulars as the Secretary of State may direct of sampling points fixed under the foregoing provisions of this section, and the register shall be open to inspection at all reasonable hours by any person appearing to SEPA to be interested.

(6)  *This subsection amends section 19 of the Rivers (Prevention of Pollution) (Scotland) Act 1951 (c. 66). Paragraph (a) has been repealed by the Environment Act 1995 (c. 25), s. 120, sch. 24. Paragraph (b) inserts subsection (4) which is set out at p. 5 above.*[2]

*Saving for certain acts done for scientific etc. purposes with consent of Secretary of State or in certain cases of a district board*

**13.**  (1)  In section 9 of the Salmon and Freshwater Fisheries (Protection) (Scotland) Act 1951[3] (saving for certain acts which would otherwise be offences) for the words "where such act relates to salmon" there shall be substituted the words "in the case of an act which relates to salmon and which is not an act specified in paragraph (a) or (b) of section 4 of this Act, with the previous permission in writing".

(2)  *Repealed by the Control of Pollution Act 1974 (c. 40), s. 180(2), sch. 4.*

*Interpretation and construction*

**15.**  (1)  In this Act "the principal Act" means the Rivers (Prevention of Pollution) (Scotland) Act 1951[4] and this Act shall be construed as one with the principal Act.

(2)–(3)  *Repealed by the Control of Pollution Act 1974 (c. 40), s. 180(2), sch. 4.*

(4)  Any reference in this Act to any other enactment shall be construed as a reference to that enactment as amended by or under any other enactment.

*Short title, citation, extent, repeals and commencement*

**17.**  (1)  This Act may be cited as the Rivers (Prevention of Pollution) (Scotland) Act 1965.

(2)  This Act and the Rivers (Prevention of Pollution) (Scotland) Act 1951 may be cited together as the Rivers (Prevention of Pollution) (Scotland) Acts 1951 and 1965.

(3)  This Act shall extend to Scotland only.

(4)–(7)  *Repealed by the Control of Pollution Act 1974 (c. 40), s. 180(2), sch. 4.*

---

[1] Words "SEPA" in subsections (3) to (5) substituted by the Environment Act 1995 (c. 25), s. 120, sch. 22, para. 6(b).
[2] SEPA took over its functions under this section on the transfer date, 1 April 1996: S.I. 1996/139. The amendments made to this section by the Environment Act 1995 also came into force on 1 April 1996: S.I. 1996/186.
[3] 1951 c. 26.
[4] P. 3 above.

# Control of Pollution Act 1974

Chapter 40

*Arrangement of sections*

## Part I: Waste on Land

*Not reproduced*

## Part IA: Abandoned Mines

30Y. Introductory     15
30Z. Mine operators to give SEPA six months' notice of any proposed abandonment     15

## Part II: Pollution of Water

*General provisions*

30A. Waters to which Part II applies     18
30B. Classification of quality of waters     19
30C. Water quality objectives     20
30D. General duties to achieve and maintain objectives etc.     21
30E. Consultation and collaboration     21

*Control of entry of polluting matter and effluents into water*

30F. Pollution offences     21
30G. Prohibition of certain discharges by notice or regulations     22
30H. Discharges into and from sewers etc.     22
30I. Defence to principal offences in respect of authorised discharges     23
30J. Other defences to principal offences     24
31. Control of pollution of rivers and coastal waters etc.     25
31A. Requirements to take precautions against pollution     26
31B. Nitrate sensitive areas     26
31C. Registering of agreement     27
31D. *Repealed*     28
32. *Repealed*     29
33. Control of sanitary appliances on vessels     29

*Consents for discharges*

34. Consents for discharges of trade and sewage effluent etc.     29
35. Reference to Secretary of State of certain applications for consent     31
36. Provisions supplementary to ss. 34 and 35     31
37. Revocation of consents and alteration and imposition of conditions     33
38. Restriction on variation and revocation of consent and of previous variation     34
38A. General review of consents     34
39. Appeals to Secretary of State     35
40. Transitional provisions relating to consents     37

*Ancillary provisions relating to discharges*

41. Registers     38
42A. Exclusion from registers of information affecting national security     39

42B.  Exclusion from registers of certain confidential information                    39
43–45. *Repealed*

*Miscellaneous*

46.    Operations by river purification authorities to remedy or forestall pollution of water    41
46A.   Notices requiring persons to carry out anti-pollution operations             42
46B.   Grant of, and compensation for, rights of entry etc.                         43
46C.   Appeals against works notices                                                44
46D.   Consequences of not complying with a works notice                            45
47.    Duty of river purification authorities to deal with waste from vessels etc.    45
48.    Power of river purification authorities to exclude unregistered vessels from rivers etc.    46
49.    Deposits and vegetation in rivers etc.                                       46
49A.   Enforcement notices as respects discharge consents                           47
49B.   Appeals against enforcement notices                                          47
50.    Investigation of water pollution problems arising from closure of mines       48
51.    Codes of good agricultural practice                                          48
52–54. *Repealed*                                                                   48

*Supplemental*

55.    *Repealed*                                                                   49
55A.   Regulations under this Part                                                  49
56.    Interpretation etc. of Part II                                               49

## Part III: Noise

*Not reproduced*

## Part IV:

*Repealed*

## Part V: Supplementary Provisions

*Legal Proceedings*

85. Appeals to Crown Court or Court of Session against decisions of magistrates' court or
    sheriff                                                                         51
86. *Repealed*                                                                      51
87. Miscellaneous provisions relating to legal proceedings                          51
88. Civil liability for contravention of s. 3(3)                                    52

*Financial provisions*

89. Expenses and receipts of Secretary of State etc.                                53
90. Establishment charges and interest in respect of certain expenses of authorities    53

*Miscellaneous*

91. Rights of entry and inspection etc.                                             54
92. Provisions supplementary to s. 91                                               55
93. Power of authorities to obtain information                                      56
94. Prohibition of disclosure of information                                        56
95. Service of documents on and by certain undertakers                              57
96. Local inquiries                                                                 57
97. Default powers                                                                  58
98. Interpretation of Part V                                                        58

# Part VI: Miscellaneous and General

*Miscellaneous*

 99. Alteration of penalties                                                    59
100. *Repealed*                                                                 59
101. Disposal of waste etc. by Atomic Energy Authority                          59
102. Power to give effect to international agreements                           60
103. *Repealed*                                                                 60

*General*

104. Orders and regulations                                                     60
105. Interpretation etc—general                                                 61
106. General application to Scotland                                            62
107. Application to Isles of Scilly                                             63
108. Minor and consequential amendments of enactments, and repeals             63
109. Short title, commencement and extent                                      63

SCHEDULES

    Schedule 1—*Not reproduced*
    Schedule 1A—Orders designating nitrate sensitive areas: Scotland          64
    Schedules 2–4—*Not reproduced*

# Control of Pollution Act 1974

Chapter 40

---

An Act to make further provision with respect to waste disposal, water pollution, noise, atmospheric pollution and public health; and for purposes connected with the matters aforesaid.

[31st July 1974]

---

## PART I: Waste on Land

This Part is not reproduced.

The waste management licensing provisions of Part II of the Environmental Protection Act 1990, p. 111 below, replace the waste disposal licensing provisions of this Part. The waste management licensing provisions of the 1990 Act were brought into force on 1 May 1994, subject to four transitional provisions, by S.I. 1994/1096, p. 738 below.

*Summary of sections of Part I:*

1–21.  The Environmental Protection Act 1990, s. 162, sch. 16, pt. II provides for the repeal of these sections. Certain sections have not yet been repealed.

22.  *England and Wales*: s. 22(1) and (2) repealed by the Environmental Protection Act 1990; s. 22(3) and (4), as amended, relate to arrangements between an occupier and a local authority for the cleaning of the occupier's land to which the public have access.

*Scotland*: repealed by the Local Government and Planning (Scotland) Act 1982 (c. 43).

23.  *England and Wales*: this section, as amended, relates to the prohibition of parking to facilitate street cleaning.

*Scotland*: repealed by the Local Government and Planning (Scotland) Act 1982 (c. 43).

24.  This section has not been brought into force. It is repealed in part, and the remainder repealed prospectively, by the Litter Act 1983 (c. 35).

25.  Repealed by the Coal Industry Act 1994 (c. 21).

26.  *England and Wales*: repealed by the Water Act 1989 (c. 15).

*Scotland*: this section did not apply in Scotland.

27–30.  The Environmental Protection Act 1990, s. 162, sch. 16, pt. II provides for the repeal of these sections. Certain sections have not yet been repealed.

## PART IA: Abandoned Mines

*This Part extends to Scotland only: s. 30Y(3). It is inserted by the Environment Act 1995 (c. 25), s. 59. S. 59 of the 1995 Act, in so far as the amendments made by the section confer power on the Secretary of State to make regulations, came into force on 12 October 1995: S.I. 1995/2649. Otherwise, this Part is not in force.*

*Introductory*

**30Y.** (1) For the purposes of this Part, "abandonment", in relation to a mine[1],—

(*a*) subject to paragraph (b) below, includes—

    (i) the discontinuance of any or all of the operations for the removal of water from the mine;

    (ii) the cessation of working of any relevant seam, vein or vein-system[2];

    (iii) the cessation of use of any shaft or outlet of the mine;

    (iv) in the case of a mine in which activities other than mining activities are carried on (whether or not mining activities are also carried on in the mine)—

        (A) the discontinuance of some or all of those other activities in the mine; and

        (B) any substantial change in the operations for the removal of water from the mine; but

(*b*) does not include—

    (i) the abandonment of any rights, interests or liabilities by the Accountant in Bankruptcy acting as permanent or interim trustee in a sequestration (within the meaning of the Bankruptcy (Scotland) Act 1985[3]); or

    (ii) any disclaimer under section 178 or 315 of the Insolvency Act 1986[4] (power of liquidator, or trustee of bankrupt's estate, to disclaim onerous property) by the official receiver acting in a compulsory capacity;

and cognate expressions shall be construed accordingly.

(2) In this Part, except where the context otherwise requires—

"acting in a compulsory capacity", in the case of the official receiver, means acting as—

(*a*) liquidator of a company;

(*b*) receiver or manager of a bankrupt's estate, pursuant to section 287 of the Insolvency Act 1986;

(*c*) trustee of a bankrupt's estate;

(*d*) liquidator of an insolvent partnership;

(*e*) trustee of an insolvent partnership;

(*f*) trustee, or receiver or manager, of the insolvent estate of a deceased person;

"the official receiver" has the same meaning as it has in the Insolvency Act 1986 by virtue of section 399(1) of that Act;

"relevant seam, vein or vein-system", in the case of any mine, means any seam, vein or vein-system for the purpose of, or in connection with, whose working any excavation constituting or comprised in the mine was made.

(3) This Part extends only to Scotland.

*Mine operators to give SEPA six months' notice of any proposed abandonment*

**30Z.** (1) If, in the case of any mine[5], there is to be an abandonment[6] at any time after the expiration of the initial period[7], it shall be the duty of the operator of the mine to give notice[8] of the proposed abandonment to SEPA[9] at least six months before the abandonment takes effect.

---

[1] "Mine" defined by s. 105(1), p. 61 below.
[2] For "relevant seam, vein or vein-system" see subsection (2) below.
[3] 1985 c. 66.
[4] 1986 c. 45.
[5] "Mine" defined by s. 105(1), p. 61 below.
[6] "Abandonment" defined by s. 30Y above.
[7] "Initial period" defined by subsection (8) below.
[8] "Notice" defined by s. 105(1), p. 61 below.
[9] "SEPA" means the Scottish Environment Protection Agency: s. 105(1) below.

(2) A notice under subsection (1) above shall contain such information (if any) as is prescribed[1] for the purpose, which may include information about the operator's opinion as to any consequences of the abandonment.

(3) A person who fails to give the notice required by subsection (1) above shall be guilty of an offence and liable—

(a) on summary conviction, to a fine not exceeding the statutory maximum;

(b) on conviction on indictment, to a fine.

(4) A person shall not be guilty of an offence under subsection (3) above if—

(a) the abandonment happens in an emergency in order to avoid danger to life or health; and

(b) notice of the abandonment, containing such information as may be prescribed, is given as soon as reasonably practicable after the abandonment has happened.

(5) Where the operator of a mine is—

(a) the Accountant in Bankruptcy acting as permanent or interim trustee in a sequestration (within the meaning of the Bankruptcy (Scotland) Act 1985[2]); or

(b) the official receiver acting in a compulsory capacity[3],

he shall not be guilty of an offence under subsection (3) above by reason of any failure to give the notice required by subsection (1) above if, as soon as is reasonably practicable (whether before or after the abandonment), he gives to SEPA notice of the abandonment or proposed abandonment, containing such information as may be prescribed.

(6) Where a person gives notice under subsection (1), (4)(b) or (5) above, he shall publish prescribed particulars of, or relating to, the notice in one or more local newspapers circulating in the locality where the mine is situated.

(7) Where SEPA—

(a) receives notice under this section or otherwise learns of an abandonment or proposed abandonment in the case of any mine, and

(b) considers that, in consequence of the abandonment or proposed abandonment taking effect, any land has or is likely to become contaminated land, within the meaning of Part IIA of the Environmental Protection Act 1990[4],

it shall be the duty of SEPA to inform the local authority in whose area that land is situated of the abandonment or proposed abandonment.

(8) In this section—

"the initial period" means the period of six months beginning with the day on which subsection (1) above comes into force;

"local authority" means a council constituted under section 2 of the Local Government etc. (Scotland) Act 1994[5].

## PART II: Pollution of water

### England and Wales

This Part has been repealed by the Water Act 1989 (c. 15), s. 190, sch. 27, pt. I and the Water Consolidation (Consequential Provisions) Act 1991 (c. 60), s. 3, sch. 3, pt. I. Transitional and transitory provisions and savings are set out in Schedule 2 to the 1991 Act.

---

[1] "Prescribed" defined by s. 105(1), p. 61 below.
[2] 1985 c. 66.
[3] "Acting in a compulsory capacity" defined by s. 30Y(2) above.
[4] P. 162 below.
[5] 1994 c. 39.

## Scotland

This Part is set out below. The functions previously conferred on river purification authorities under this Part have been transferred to the Scottish Environment Protection Agency, SEPA: Environment Act 1995 (c. 25), s. 21, p. 438 below. SEPA took over its functions under this Act on the transfer date, 1 April 1996; S.I. 1996/139.

### Amendments to this Part made by the Environment Act 1995

Except where noted, the word "SEPA" in this Part has been substituted by the Environment Act 1995 (c. 25), s. 120, sch. 22, para. 29(2) and (10).

The amendments made to this Part by the Environment Act 1995 came into force on 1 April 1996: S.I. 1996/186. To avoid undue repetition this commencement date is not set out in the footnotes which relate to these amendments.

### Commencement, repeals and source of sections in this Part

**30A–30E.**  Substituted by the Water Act 1989 (c. 15), s. 169, sch. 23, para. 4. Came into force on 1 September 1989: s. 194(3)(e), S.I. 1989/1530.

**30F–30J.**  Inserted by the Environment Act 1995 (c. 25), s. 106, sch. 16, para. 2. Came into force on 1 April 1996: S.I. 1996/186.

**31, 31A–31C.**  Substituted by the Water Act 1989 (c. 15), s. 169, sch. 23, para. 4. Came into force on 1 September 1989: s. 194(3)(e), S.I. 1989/1530.

**31D, 32.**  *Repealed by the Environment Act 1995 (c. 25), s. 120, sch. 22, para. 29(7) (s. 31D), sch. 24 (ss. 31D, 32). This amendment came into force on 1 April 1996: S.I. 1996/186.*

**33.**  Substituted by the Water Act 1989 (c. 15), s. 169, sch. 23, para. 4. Came into force on 31 May 1991: S.I. 1991/1172.

**34–38.**  Substituted by the Water Act 1989 (c. 15), s. 169, sch. 23, para. 4. Came into force on 1 September 1989: s. 194(3)(e), S.I. 1989/1530.

**38A.**  Inserted by the Environment Act 1995 (c. 25), s. 120, sch. 22, para. 29(14). Came into force on 1 April 1996: S.I. 1996/186.

**39–41.**  Substituted by the Water Act 1989 (c. 15), s. 169, sch. 23, para. 4. Came into force on 1 September 1989: s. 194(3)(e), S.I. 1989/1530.

**42A–42B.**  Substituted by the Environment Act 1995 (c. 25), s. 120, sch. 22, para. 29(20) (replaces s. 42). Came into force on 1 April 1996: S.I. 1996/186.

**43–45.**  *These sections did not apply in Scotland.*

**46.**  Substituted by the Water Act 1989 (c. 15), s. 169, sch. 23, para. 5. Came into force on 1 September 1989: s. 194(3)(e), S.I. 1989/1530.

**46A–46D.**  Inserted by the Environment Act 1995 (c. 25), s. 120, sch. 22, para. 29(22). In so far as it confers power on the Secretary of State to make regulations, this amendment came into force on 12 October 1995: S.I. 1995/2649; otherwise it is not in force.

**47–48.**  Substituted by the Water Act 1989 (c. 15), s. 169, sch. 23, para. 5. These sections have not yet come into force.

**49.**  Substituted by the Water Act 1989 (c. 15), s. 169, sch. 23, para. 5. Came into force on 1 September 1989: s. 194(3)(e), S.I. 1989/1530.

**49A–49B.**  Inserted by the Environment Act 1995 (c. 25), s. 120, sch. 22, para. 29(26). Not in force.

**50–51.**  Substituted by the Water Act 1989 (c. 15), s. 169, sch. 23, para. 5. Came into force on 1 September 1989: s. 194(3)(e), S.I. 1989/1530.

**52.**  *This section did not apply in Scotland.*

**53–55.**  *Repealed by the Environment Act 1995 (c. 25), s. 120, sch. 22, para. 29(28), sch. 24. This amendment came into force on 1 April 1996: S.I. 1996/186.*

**55A.**  Inserted by the Natural Heritage (Scotland) Act 1991 (c. 28), s. 27, sch. 10, para. 7(3). Came into force on 1 October 1991: S.I. 1991/2187.

**56.**          Substituted by the Water Act 1989 (c. 15), s. 169, sch. 23, para. 6. Came into force on
1 September 1989: s. 194(3)(e), S.I. 1989/1530.

*Radioactive waste*

The provisions of this Part specified in the Schedule to the Control of Pollution (Radioactive Waste)
(Scotland) Regulations 1991, S.I. 1991/2539, p. 648 below, have effect, without modification, in relation to any radioactive waste as they have effect in relation to effluent or other matter or substance
which is not radioactive waste: reg. 3.

*Waste*

For construction of references to waste see the Waste Management Licensing Regulations 1994, sch.
4, para. 11, p. 718 below.

## General provisions

*Waters to which Part II applies*

**30A.** (1) This part applies to any waters (in this Part referred to as "controlled waters") of any of the
following classes—

(*a*)  relevant territorial waters, that is to say, subject to subsection (5) below, the waters which
extend seaward for three miles[1] from the baselines from which the breadth of the territorial sea adjacent to Scotland is measured;

(*b*)  coastal waters, that is to say, any waters which are within the area which extends landward
from those baselines as far as the limit of the highest tide or, in the case of the waters of any
relevant river or watercourse[2], as far as the fresh-water limit of the river or watercourse,
together with the waters of any enclosed dock which adjoins waters within that area;

(*c*)  inland waters, that is to say, the waters of any relevant loch or pond[3] or of so much of any
relevant river or watercourse as is above the fresh-water limit;

(*d*)  ground waters, that is to say, any waters contained in underground strata[4], or in—

(i)  a well, borehole or similar work sunk into underground strata, including any adit or
passage constructed in connection with the well, borehole or work for facilitating the
collection of water in the well, borehole or work; or

(ii)  any excavation into underground strata where the level of water in the excavation
depends wholly or mainly on water entering it from the strata.

(2) The Secretary of State—

(*a*)  shall deposit maps with SEPA[5] showing what appear to him to be the freshwater limits of
every relevant river or watercourse[6]; and

(*b*)  may from time to time, if he considers it appropriate to do so by reason of any change of
what appears to him to be the fresh-water limit of any river or watercourse, deposit a map
showing a revised limit for that river or watercourse;

and in subsection (1) above "fresh-water limit", in relation to any river or watercourse, means
the place for the time being shown as the fresh-water limit of that river or watercourse in the latest map deposited for that river or watercourse under this subsection.

(3) It shall be the duty of SEPA to keep any maps deposited with it under subsection (2) above
available, at all reasonable times, for inspection by the public free of charge.

[1] "Miles" defined by subsection (4) below.
[2] "Watercourse" defined by s. 56(1), p. 50 below. For the
construction of waters of any river or watercourse see
s. 56(2). For "relevant river or watercourse" see subsection
(4) below.
[3] "Loch or pond" and "relevant loch or pond" defined by
subsection (4) below. See also n. 3, p. 19 below.
[4] "Underground strata" defined by s. 56(1), p. 50 below.

For the construction of waters contained in underground
strata see s. 56(2).
[5] "SEPA" means the Scottish Environment Protection
Agency: s. 105(1) below.
[6] Former words "in the area of that authority" repealed by
the Environment Act 1995 (c. 25), s. 120, sch. 22, para. 29(3),
sch. 24.

**(4)** In this section—

"miles" means international nautical miles of 1,852 metres;

"loch or pond" includes a reservoir of any description;

"relevant loch or pond" means (subject to subsection (5) below) any loch or pond which (whether it is natural or artificial or above or below ground) discharges into a relevant river or watercourse or into another loch or pond which is itself a relevant loch or pond;

"relevant river or watercourse" means any river or watercourse (including an underground river or watercourse and an artificial river or watercourse) which is neither a public sewer nor a sewer[1] or drain[2] which drains into a public sewer.

**(5)** The Secretary of State may by order provide—

(*a*)  that any area of the territorial sea adjacent to Scotland is to be treated as if it were an area of relevant territorial waters for the purposes of this Part;

(*b*)  that any loch or pond which does not discharge into a relevant river or watercourse or into a relevant loch or pond is to be treated for those purposes as a relevant loch or pond[3].

**(6)** The power of the Secretary of State to make an order under subsection (5) above shall be exercisable by statutory instrument subject to annulment in pursuance of a resolution of either House of Parliament; and such an order may—

(*a*)  contain such supplemental, consequential and transitional provision as the Secretary of State considers appropriate; and

(*b*)  make different provision for different cases, including different provision in relation to different persons, circumstances or localities.[4]

*Classification of quality of waters*

**30B. (1)** The Secretary of State may, in relation to any description of controlled waters[5] (being a description applying to some or all of the waters of a particular class or of two or more different classes), by regulations prescribe a system of classifying the quality of those waters according to criteria specified in the regulations[6].

**(2)** The criteria specified in regulations under this section in relation to any classification shall consist of one or more of the following, that is to say—

(*a*)  general requirements as to the purposes for which the waters to which the classification is applied are to be suitable;

(*b*)  specific requirements as to the substances[7] that are to be present in or absent from the water and as to the concentrations of substances which are or are required to be present in the water;

(*c*)  specific requirements as to other characteristics of those waters;

and, for the purposes of any such classification, regulations under this section may provide that the question whether prescribed[8] requirements are satisfied may be determined by reference to such samples as may be prescribed.

[1]  "Sewer" defined by s. 56(1), p. 49 below.
[2]  "Drain" defined by s. 56(1), p. 49 below.
[3]  See the Controlled Waters (Lochs and Ponds) (Scotland) Order, S.I. 1990/120, p. 557 below.
[4]  Case: **section 30A** *Mackenzie v Tractor Shovels Tawse Ltd* [1992] SCCR 71.
[5]  "Controlled waters" has the meaning given by s. 30A(1) above: s. 56(1) below.
[6]  The following regulations have been made under this section:
The Surface Waters (Classification) (Scotland) Regula-

tions 1990: S.I. 1990/121, p. 558 below;
The Surface Waters (Dangerous Substances) (Classification) (Scotland) Regulations 1990: S.I. 1990/126, p. 560 below;
The Bathing Waters (Classification) (Scotland) Regulations 1991: S.I. 1991/1609, p. 626 below;
The Surface Waters (Dangerous Substances) (Classification) (Scotland) Regulations 1992: S.I. 1992/574, p. 659 below.
[7]  "Substance" defined by s. 56(1), p. 49 below.
[8]  "Prescribed" defined by s. 105(1), p. 61 below.

*Water quality objectives*[1]

**30C.** (1) For the purpose of maintaining and improving the quality of controlled waters[2] the Secretary of State may, by serving a notice on SEPA[3] specifying—

(a) one or more of the classifications for the time being prescribed under section 30B above; and

(b) in relation to each specified classification, a date,

establish the water quality objectives for any waters[4] which are, or are included in, waters of a description prescribed for the purposes of that section.

(2) The water quality objectives for any waters to which a notice under this section relates shall be the satisfaction by those waters, on and at all times after each date specified in the notice, of the requirements which at the time of the notice were the requirements for the classification in relation to which that date is so specified.

(3) Where the Secretary of State has established water quality objectives under this section for any waters he may review objectives for those waters if—

(a) five years or more have elapsed since the service of the last notice under subsection (1) or (6) of this section to be served in respect of those waters; or

(b) SEPA[5], after consultation with such persons as it considers appropriate, requests a review;

and the Secretary of State shall not exercise his power to establish objectives for any waters by varying the existing objectives for those waters except in consequence of such a review.

(4) Where the Secretary of State proposes to exercise his power under this section to establish or vary the objectives for any waters[6] he shall—

(a) give notice to SEPA[7] setting out his proposal and specifying the period (not being less than three months from the date of publication of the notice) within which representations with respect to the proposal may be made; and

(b) consider any representations which are duly made;

and if he decides, after considering any such representations, to exercise his power to establish or vary those objectives, he may do so either in accordance with the proposal contained in the notice or in accordance with that proposal as modified[8] in such manner as he considers appropriate.

(5) A notice under subsection (4) above shall be given—

(a) by publishing the notice in such manner as the Secretary of State considers appropriate for bringing it to the attention of persons likely to be affected by it; and

(b) by serving a copy of the notice on SEPA[9].

(6) If, on a review under this section or in consequence of any representations made following such a review for the purposes of subsection (4) above, the Secretary of State decides that the water quality objectives for any waters[10] should remain unchanged, he shall serve notice of that decision on SEPA[11].

---

[1] S. 30C is modified by the following regulations:
The Surface Waters (Dangerous Substances) (Classification) (Scotland) Regulations 1990: S.I. 1990/126, p. 560 below;
The Bathing Waters (Classification) (Scotland) Regulations 1991: S.I. 1991/1609, p. 626 below;
The Surface Waters (Dangerous Substances) (Classification) (Scotland) Regulations 1992: S.I. 1992/574, p. 659 below.
[2] "Controlled waters" has the meaning given in s. 30A above: s. 56(1) below.
[3] "SEPA" means the Scottish Environment Protection Agency: s. 105(1) below.
[4] Former words "within the area of that authority" repealed by the Environment Act 1995 (c. 25), s. 120, sch. 22, para. 29(4)(1), sch. 24.

[5] Word "SEPA" substituted by the Environment Act 1995 (c. 25), s. 120, sch. 22, para. 29(4)(b).
[6] Former words "in the area of a river purification authority" repealed by the Environment Act 1995 (c. 25), s. 120, sch. 22, para. 29(4)(c)(i), sch. 24.
[7] Word "SEPA" substituted by the Environment Act 1995 (c. 25), s. 120, sch. 22, para. 29(4)(c)(ii).
[8] "Modified" defined by s. 105(1), p. 61 below.
[9] Word "SEPA" substituted by the Environment Act 1995 (c. 25), s. 120, sch. 22, para. 29(4)(d).
[10] Former words "in the area of a river purification authority" repealed by the Environment Act 1995 (c. 25), s. 120, sch. 22, para. 29(4)(e)(i), sch. 24.
[11] Word "SEPA" substituted by the Environment Act 1995 (c. 25), s. 120, sch. 22, para. 29(4)(e)(ii).

*General duties to achieve and maintain objectives etc.*

**30D.** **(1)** It shall be the duty of the Secretary of State and of SEPA[1] to exercise the powers conferred on him or it by or under the following provisions of this Part or the provisions of the Rivers (Prevention of Pollution) (Scotland) Acts 1951[2] and 1965[3] and of the Environmental Protection Act 1990[4] in such manner as ensures, so far as it is practicable by the exercise of those powers to do so, that the water quality objectives specified for any waters in a notice under section 30C above, or in a notice under section 83 of the Water Resources Act 1991[5], are achieved at all times.

**(2)** It shall be the duty of SEPA, for the purposes of the carrying out of its functions under the following provisions of this Part or the provisions of the Rivers (Prevention of Pollution) (Scotland) Acts 1951 and 1965, to monitor the extent of pollution in controlled waters[6].

*Consultation and collaboration*

**30E.** In the performance of its[7] functions in relation to waters partly in Scotland and partly in England SEPA[8] shall, in matters of common interest, consult and collaborate with the Environment Agency[9].

## Control of entry of polluting matter and effluents into water

*Pollution offences*

**30F.** **(1)** A person contravenes this section if he causes or knowingly permits any poisonous, noxious or polluting matter or any solid waste matter to enter any controlled waters[10].

**(2)** A person contravenes this section if he causes or knowingly permits any matter, other than trade effluent[11] or sewage effluent[12], to enter controlled waters by being discharged from a sewer[13] or from a drain[14] in contravention of a prohibition imposed under section 30G below.

**(3)** A person contravenes this section if he causes or knowingly permits any trade effluent or sewage effluent to be discharged—

(a) into any controlled waters; or

(b) from land in Scotland, through a pipe, into the sea outside the seaward limits of controlled waters.

**(4)** A person contravenes this section if he causes or knowingly permits any trade effluent or sewage effluent to be discharged, in contravention of any prohibition imposed under section 30G below, from a building or from any plant—

(a) on to or into any land; or

(b) into any waters of a loch or pond[15] which are not inland waters[16].

**(5)** A person contravenes this section if he causes or knowingly permits any matter whatever to enter any inland waters so as to tend (either directly or in combination with other matter which he or another person causes or permits to enter those waters) to impede the proper flow of the waters in a manner leading, or likely to lead, to a substantial aggravation of—

(a) pollution due to other causes; or

[1] "SEPA" means the Scottish Environment Protection Agency: s. 105(1) below.
[2] P. 3 above.
[3] P. 9 above.
[4] Prospective amendment: words "and of the Environmental Protection Act 1990" inserted by the Environmental Protection Act 1990 (c. 43), s. 162, sch. 15, para. 15(2). This amendment has not yet come into force.
[5] P. 272 below. Words "section . . . 1991" substituted by the Water Consolidation (Consequential Provisions) Act 1991 (c. 60), s. 2(1), sch. 1, para. 27(1). This amendment came into force on 1 December 1991: s. 4(2).
[6] "Controlled waters" has the meaning given by s. 30A(1), p. 18 above: S. 56(1) below.
[7] Word "its" substituted by the Environment Act 1995 (c. 250, s. 120, sch. 22, para. 29(5)(a).
[8] "SEPA" means the Scottish Environment Protection Agency: s. 105(1) below. Word "SEPA" substituted by the Environment Act 1995 (c. 25), s. 120, sch. 22, para. 29(5)(b).
[9] Words "Environment Agency" substituted by the Environment Act 1995 (c. 25), s. 120, sch. 22, para. 29(5)(c).
[10] "Controlled waters" has the meaning given by s. 30A(1), p. 18 above: s. 56(1) below.
[11] "Trade effluent" defined by s. 56(1), (3), p. 49 below.
[12] "Sewage effluent" defined by s. 56(1), p. 49 below.
[13] "Sewer" defined by s. 56(1), p. 49 below.
[14] "Drain" defined by s. 56(1), p. 49 below.
[15] "Loch or pond" defined by s. 30A above and s. 56(2), p. 50 below.
[16] "Inland waters" has the meaning given by s. 30A(1), p. 18 above: s. 56(1) below.

(b) the consequences of such pollution.

(6) Subject to the following provisions of this Part, a person who contravenes this section shall be guilty of an offence and liable—

(a) on summary conviction, to imprisonment for a term not exceeding three months or to a fine not exceeding £20,000 or to both;

(b) on conviction on indictment, to imprisonment for a term not exceeding two years or to a fine or to both.

*Prohibition of certain discharges by notice or regulations*

30G. (1) For the purposes of section 30F above a discharge of any effluent[1] or other matter is, in relation to any person, in contravention of a prohibition imposed under this section, if, subject to the following provisions of this section—

(a) SEPA[2] has given that person notice[3] prohibiting him from making or, as the case may be, continuing the discharge; or

(b) SEPA has given that person notice prohibiting him from making or, as the case may be, continuing the discharge unless specified conditions are observed, and those conditions are not observed.

(2) For the purposes of section 30F above a discharge of any effluent or other matter is also in contravention of a prohibition imposed under this section if the effluent or matter discharged—

(a) contains a prescribed[4] substance[5] or a prescribed concentration of such a substance; or

(b) derives from a prescribed process or from a process involving the use of prescribed substances or the use of such substances in quantities which exceed the prescribed amounts.

(3) Nothing in subsection (1) above shall authorise the giving of a notice for the purposes of that subsection in respect of discharges from a vessel[6]; and nothing in any regulations made by virtue of subsection (2) above shall require any discharge from a vessel to be treated as a discharge in contravention of a prohibition imposed under this section.

(4) A notice given for the purposes of subsection (1) above shall expire at such time as may be specified in the notice.

(5) The time specified for the purposes of subsection (4) above shall not be before the end of the period of three months beginning with the day on which the notice is given, except in a case where SEPA is satisfied that there is an emergency which requires the prohibition in question to come into force at such time before the end of that period as may be so specified.

(6) Where, in the case of such a notice for the purposes of subsection (1) above as (but for this subsection) would expire at a time at or after the end of the said period of three months, an application is made before that time for a consent in pursuance of section 34 of this Act[7] in respect of the discharge to which the notice relates, that notice shall be deemed not to expire until the result of the application becomes final—

(a) on the grant or withdrawal of the application;

(b) on the expiration, without the bringing of an appeal with respect to the decision on the application, of any period prescribed by virtue of section 39(2) below[8] as the period within which any such appeal must be brought; or

(c) on the withdrawal or determination of any such appeal.

*Discharges into and from sewers*

30H. (1) For the purposes of section 30F above where—

---

[1] "Effluent" defined by s. 56(1), p. 49 below.
[2] "SEPA" means the Scottish Environment Protection Agency: s. 105(1) below.
[3] "Notice" defined by s. 105(1), p. 61 below.
[4] "Prescribed" defined by s. 105(1), p. 61 below.

[5] "Substance" defined by s. 56(1), p. 49 below.
[6] "Vessel" defined by s. 105(1), p. 61 below.
[7] P. 29 below.
[8] P. 35 below.

(a)  any sewage effluent[1] is discharged as mentioned in subsection (3) or (4) of that section from any sewer[2] or works—

    (i)  vested in a sewerage authority[3]; or

    (ii)  vested in a person other than a sewerage authority and forming (or forming part of) a system provided by him such as is mentioned in section 98(1)(b) of the Local Government etc. (Scotland) Act 1994[4]; and

(b)  the authority or, as the case may be, the person did not cause or knowingly permit the discharge but was bound (either unconditionally or subject to conditions which were observed) to receive into the sewer or works matter included in the discharge,

the authority or person shall be deemed to have caused the discharge.

(2)  A sewerage authority shall not be guilty of an offence under section 30F of this Act by reason only of the fact that a discharge from a sewer or works vested in the authority contravenes conditions of a consent relating to the discharge if—

(a)  the contravention is attributable to a discharge which another person caused or permitted to be made into the sewer or works; and

(b)  the authority either was not bound to receive the discharge into the sewer or works or was bound to receive it there subject to conditions but the conditions were not observed; and

(c)  the authority could not reasonably have been expected to prevent the discharge into the sewer or works;

and a person shall not be guilty of such an offence in consequence of a discharge which he caused or permitted to be made into a sewer or works vested in a sewerage authority if the authority was bound to receive the discharge there either unconditionally or subject to conditions which were observed.

(3)  A person in whom any such sewer or works as is described in subsection (1)(a)(ii) above is vested (such person being in this subsection referred to as a "relevant person") shall not be guilty of an offence under section 30F of this Act by reason only of the fact that a discharge from the sewer or works contravenes conditions of a consent relating to the discharge if—

(a)  the contravention is attributable to a discharge which another person caused or permitted to be made into the sewer or works; and

(b)  the relevant person either was not bound to receive the discharge into the sewer or works or was bound to receive it there subject to conditions but the conditions were not observed; and

(c)  the relevant person could not reasonably have been expected to prevent the discharge into the sewer or works;

and another person shall not be guilty of such an offence in consequence of a discharge which he caused or permitted to be made into a sewer or works vested in a relevant person if the relevant person was bound to receive the discharge there either unconditionally or subject to conditions which were observed.

....................................................................................................................................................................

*Defence to principal offences in respect of authorised discharges*

30I.  (1)  Subject to the following provisions of this section, a person shall not be guilty of an offence under section 30F above in respect of the entry of any matter into any waters or any discharge if the entry occurs or the discharge is made under and in accordance with, or as a result of, any act or omission under and in accordance with—

(a)  a consent in pursuance of section 34 of this Act[5] or under Chapter II of Part III of the Water Resources Act 1991[6] (which makes corresponding provision for England and Wales);

(b)  an authorisation for a prescribed process designated for central control granted under Part I of the Environmental Protection Act 1990[7];

---

[1]  "Sewage effluent" defined by s. 56(1), p. 49 below.
[2]  "Sewer" defined by s. 56(1), p. 49 below.
[3]  "Sewerage authority" defined by s. 56(1), p. 49 below.
[4]  1994 c. 39.

[5]  P. 29 below.
[6]  P. 273 below.
[7]  P. 88 below.

(c)  a waste management or disposal licence;

(d)  a licence granted under Part II of the Food and Environment Protection Act 1985[1];

(e)  section 33 of the Water (Scotland) Act 1980[2] (temporary discharge by authorities in connection with the construction of works);

(f)  any provision of a local Act or statutory order which expressly confers power to discharge effluent into water; or

(g)  any prescribed[3] enactment.

(2)  Nothing in any disposal licence shall be treated for the purposes of subsection (1) above as authorising—

(a)  any such entry or discharge as is mentioned in subsections (2) to (4) of section 30F above[4]; or

(b)  any act or omission so far as it results in any such entry or discharge.

(3)  In this section—

"disposal licence" means a licence issued in pursuance of section 5 of this Act[5];

"local Act" includes enactments in a public general Act which amend a local Act;

"statutory order" means an order, byelaw, scheme or award made under an Act of Parliament, including an order or scheme confirmed by Parliament or brought into operation in accordance with special parliamentary procedure; and

"waste management licence" means such a licence granted under Part II of the Environmental Protection Act 1990[6].

*Other defences to principal offences*

**30J.** (1)  A person shall not be guilty of an offence under section 30F above[7] in respect of the entry of any matter into any waters or any discharge if—

(a)  the entry is caused or permitted, or the discharge is made, in an emergency in order to avoid danger to life or health;

(b)  that person takes all such steps as are reasonably practicable in the circumstances for minimising the extent of the entry or discharge and of its polluting effects; and

(c)  particulars of the entry or discharge are furnished to SEPA[8] as soon as reasonably practicable after the entry occurs.

(2)  A person shall not be guilty of an offence under section 30F above by reason of his causing or permitting any discharge of trade or sewage effluent[9] from a vessel[10].

(3)  A person shall not be guilty of an offence under section 30F above by reason only of his permitting water from an abandoned mine[11] or an abandoned part of a mine to enter controlled waters[12].

(4)  Subsection (3) above shall not apply to the owner or former operator of any mine or part of a mine if the mine or part in question became abandoned after 31st December 1999.

(5)  In determining for the purposes of subsection (4) above whether a mine or part of a mine became abandoned before, on or after 31st December 1999 in a case where the mine or part has become abandoned on two or more occasions, of which—

[1]  1985 c. 48.
[2]  1980 c. 45.
[3]  "Prescribed" defined by s. 105(1), p. 61 below.
[4]  P. 21 above.
[5]  S. 5 is not reproduced; see note at p. 14 above.
[6]  P. 111 below.
[7]  P. 21 above.
[8]  "SEPA" means the Scottish Environment Protection Agency: s. 105(1) below.
[9]  "Trade effluent" and "sewage effluent" defined by s. 56(1), (3), p. 61 below.
[10]  "Vessel" defined by s. 105(1), p. 61 below.
[11]  "Mine" defined by s. 105(1), p. 61 below.
[12]  "Controlled waters" has the meaning given by s. 30A(1), p. 18 above: s. 56(1) below.

(a)  at least one falls on or before that date, and

(b)  at least one falls after that date,

the mine or part shall be regarded as becoming abandoned after that date (but without prejudice to the operation of subsection (3) above in relation to that mine or part at, or in relation to, any time before the first of those occasions which falls after that date).

(6)  Where, immediately before a part of a mine becomes abandoned, that part is the only part of the mine not falling to be regarded as abandoned for the time being, the abandonment of that part shall not be regarded for the purposes of subsection (4) or (5) above as constituting the abandonment of the mine, but only of that part of it.

(7)  A person shall not, otherwise than in respect of the entry of any poisonous, noxious or polluting matter into any controlled waters, be guilty of an offence under section 30F above by reason of his depositing the solid refuse of a mine or quarry[1] on any land so that it falls or is carried into inland waters[2] if—

(a)  he deposits the refuse on the land with the consent of SEPA;

(b)  no other site for the deposit is reasonably practicable; and

(c)  he takes all reasonably practicable steps to prevent the refuse from entering those inland waters.

(8)  A roads authority[3] obliged or entitled to keep open a drain by virtue of section 31 of the Roads (Scotland) Act 1984[4] shall not be guilty of an offence under section 30F above by reason of its causing or permitting any discharge to be made from a drain kept open by virtue of that section unless the discharge is made in contravention of a prohibition imposed under section 30G above[5].

..............................................................................................................................................................................................................

**31.**  *Control of pollution of rivers and coastal waters etc.*

(1), (2) and (3)  *Repealed by the Environment Act 1995 (c. 25), s. 106, sch. 16, para. 3, s. 120, sch. 24. This amendment came into force on 1 April 1996: S.I. 1996/186.*

(4)  Where it appears to the Secretary of State that, with a view to preventing poisonous, noxious or polluting matter from entering any controlled waters[6], it is appropriate to prohibit or restrict the carrying on in a particular area of activities which he considers are likely to result in pollution of the waters, then, subject to subsection (5) below, he may by regulations—

(a)  designate that area; and

(b)  provide that prescribed[7] activities shall not be carried on at any place within the area except with the consent (which shall not be unreasonably withheld) of SEPA[8] and in accordance with any reasonable conditions to which the consent is subject;

(c)  provide that a contravention of the regulations shall be an offence and prescribe the maximum penalty for the offence; and

(d)  make provision for the imposition by SEPA of charges in respect of the consent mentioned in paragraph (b) above.

(5)  It shall be the duty of the Secretary of State, before he makes any regulations under subsection (4) above—

(a)  to publish in the Edinburgh Gazette and in at least one newspaper circulating in the area in question a copy of the proposed regulations and a notice specifying—

(i)  a period of not less than twenty-eight days, beginning with the date on which the notice is first published, within which objections to the proposed regulations may be made, and

---

[1] "Quarry" defined by s. 105(1), p. 61 below.
[2] "Inland waters" has the meaning given by s. 30A(1), p. 18 above: s. 56(1) below.
[3] "Roads authority" defined by s. 105(1), p. 61 below.
[4] 1984 c. 54.
[5] P. 22 above.

[6] "Controlled waters" has the meaning given by s. 30A(1), p. 18 above: s. 56(1) below.
[7] "Prescribed" defined by s. 105(1), p. 61 below.
[8] "SEPA" means the Scottish Environment Protection Agency: s. 105(1) below. Word "SEPA" substituted by the Environment Act 1995 (c. 25), s. 120, sch. 22, para. 29(6)(a).

(ii)  the person to whom such objections may be made; and

(b)  to consider any objections to the proposed regulations which are made within that period and, if such an objection is so made by a prescribed person and is not withdrawn, to cause a local inquiry to be held in pursuance of section 96 of this Act[1] with respect to the proposed regulations;

and the Secretary of State may, after considering any such objections as are mentioned in paragraph (b) of this subsection and the report of any person appointed to hold a local inquiry with respect to the proposed regulations, make the regulations either in the form in which a copy of them was published in pursuance of this subsection or in that form with such modifications[2] as he considers appropriate.

(6)  SEPA may by byelaws make such provision as it[3] considers appropriate for prohibiting or regulating the washing or cleaning, in any controlled waters[4], of things of a kind specified in the byelaws; and a person who contravenes any byelaws made by virtue of this subsection shall be guilty of an offence and liable on summary conviction to a fine not exceeding level 4 on the standard scale[5] or such smaller sum as is specified in the byelaws.

(7)  *Repealed by the Environment Act 1995 (c. 25), s. 106, sch. 16, para. 3, s. 120, sch. 24. This amendment came into force on 1 April 1996: S.I. 1996/186.*

(8)  The maximum penalty prescribed in pursuance of subsection (4) of this section shall not exceed the penalties specified in section 30F(6) above[6].

(9)  In subsection (4) of this section, the reference to the entry of poisonous, noxious or polluting matter into controlled waters shall not include a reference to the entry of nitrate into controlled waters as a result of, or of anything done in connection with, the use of any land for agricultural[7] purposes.

(10)  *Repealed by the Environment Act 1995 (c. 25), s. 106, sch. 16, para. 3, s. 120, sch. 24. This amendment came into force on 1 April 1996: S.I. 1996/186.*

..................................................................................................................................

*Requirements to take precautions against pollution*

31A.  (1)  The Secretary of State may by regulations make provision—

(a)  for prohibiting a person from having custody or control of any poisonous, noxious or polluting matter unless prescribed[8] works and prescribed precautions and other steps have been carried out or taken for the purpose of preventing the matter from entering controlled waters[9];

(b)  for requiring a person who already has custody or control of, or makes use of, any such matter to carry out such works for that purpose and to take such precautions and other steps for that purpose as may be prescribed[10].

(2)  Without prejudice to the generality of the power conferred by subsection (1) above, regulations under that subsection may—

(a)  confer power on SEPA[11]

(i)  to determine for the purposes of the regulations the circumstances in which a person is required to carry out works or take any precautions or other steps; and

---

[1]  P. 57 below.
[2]  "Modifications" defined by s. 105(1), p. 61 below.
[3]  Word "it" substituted by the Environment Act 1995 (c. 25), s. 120, sch. 22, para. 29(6)(b)(i).
[4]  Former words "in its area" repealed by the Environment Act 1995 (c. 25), s. 120, sch. 22, para. 29(6)(b)(ii), sch. 24.
[5]  The current fine at level 4 on the standard scale is £2,500: Criminal Procedure (Scotland) Act 1995 (c. 46), s. 225.
[6]  Words "s. 30F(6) above" inserted by the Environment Act 1995 (c. 25), s. 106, sch. 16, para. 4.

[7]  "Agricultural" defined by s. 56(1), p. 49 below.
[8]  "Prescribed" defined by s. 105(1), p. 61 below.
[9]  "Controlled waters" has the meaning given by s. 30A(1), p. 18 above: s. 56(1) below.
[10]  The following regulation has been made under this section:
The Control of Pollution (Silage, Slurry and Agricultural Fuel Oil) (Scotland) Regulations 1991: S.I. 1991/346.
[11]  "SEPA" means the Scottish Environment Protection Agency: s. 105(1) below.

(ii) by notice[1] to that person, to impose the requirement and to specify or describe the works, precautions or other steps which that person is required to carry out or take;

(b) provide for appeals to the Secretary of State against notices served by SEPA in pursuance of provision made by virtue of paragraph (a) above; and

(c) provide that a contravention of the regulations shall be an offence the penalty for which shall be—

(i) on summary conviction, imprisonment for a term not exceeding three months or to a fine not exceeding £20,000[2] or to both;

(ii) on conviction on indictment, to imprisonment for a term not exceeding two years or to a fine or both.

*Nitrate sensitive areas*

**31B.** (1) Where the Secretary of State considers that it is appropriate to do so with a view to achieving the following purpose, that is to say, preventing or controlling the entry of nitrate into controlled waters[3] as a result of, or of anything done in connection with, the use of any land for agricultural[4] purposes, he may by order designate that land, together with any other land to which he considers it appropriate to apply the designation, as a nitrate sensitive area.

(2) Where any area has been designated as a nitrate sensitive area by an order under this section and the Secretary of State considers that it is appropriate to do so with a view to achieving the purpose mentioned in subsection (1) above, he may, subject to such restrictions (if any) as may be set out in the order, enter into an agreement under which, in consideration of payments to be made by him—

(a) the owner of the dominium utile[5] of any agricultural land in that area; or

(b) where any such owner has given his written consent to the agreement being entered into by any person having another interest in that land, that other person,

accepts such obligations with respect to the management of that land or otherwise as may be imposed by the agreement.

(3) Where it appears to the Secretary of State in relation to any area which is, or is to be, designated by an order under this section as a nitrate sensitive area that it is appropriate for provision for the imposition of requirements, prohibitions or restrictions to be contained in an order under this section (as well as for him to be able to enter into such agreements as are mentioned in subsection (2) above), he may, by a subsequent order under this section or, as the case may be, by the order designating that area—

(a) with a view to achieving the purpose mentioned in subsection (1) above, require, prohibit or restrict the carrying on on or in relation to any agricultural land in that area of such activities as may be specified or described in the order; and

(b) provide for such amounts (if any) as may be specified in or determined under the order to be paid by the Secretary of State, to such persons as may be so specified or determined, in respect of the obligations imposed in relation to that area on those persons by virtue of paragraph (a) above.

(4) Without prejudice to the generality of subsection (3) above, provision contained in an order under this section by virtue of that subsection may—

(a) confer power upon the Secretary of State to determine for the purposes of the order the circumstances in which the carrying on of any activities is required, prohibited or

---

[1] "Notice" defined by s. 105(1), p. 61 below.
[2] The figure of £20,000 substituted by the Environmental Protection Act 1990 (c. 43), s. 145(2). This amendment came into force on 1 January 1991: s. 164(2).
[3] "Controlled waters" has the meaning given by s. 30A(1), p. 18 above: s. 56(1) below.

[4] "Agricultural" defined by s. 56(1), p. 49 below.
[5] Words "the owner of the dominium utile" substituted by the Agricultural Holdings (Scotland) Act 1991 (c. 55), s. 88(1), sch. 11, para. 39. This amendment came into force on 25 September 1991: s. 89(2).

restricted and to determine the activities to which any such requirement, prohibition or restriction applies;

(b) provide for any requirement to carry on any activity not to apply in cases where the Secretary of State has consented to a failure to carry on that activity and any conditions on which the consent has been given are complied with;

(c) apply a prohibition or restriction in respect of any activities to cases where the activities are carried on without the consent of the Secretary of State or in contravention of any conditions subject to which any such consent is given;

(d) provide that a contravention of a requirement, prohibition or restriction contained in the order or in a condition of a consent given in relation to or for the purposes of any such requirement, prohibition or restriction shall be an offence the maximum penalties for which shall not exceed the maximum penalties specified in subsection (6) of section 30F above[1];

(e) provide for amounts paid in pursuance of any provision contained in the order to be repaid at such times and in such circumstances and with such interest as may be specified in or determined under the order;

(f) provide (subject to any regulations under subsection (6) below) for anything falling to be determined under the order by any person to be determined in accordance with such procedure and by reference to such matters and to the opinion of such persons as may be specified in the order.

(5) The Secretary of State shall not make an order under this section except in accordance with any applicable provisions of Schedule 1A to this Act[2].

(6) The Secretary of State may, for the purposes of any orders under this section which require his consent to the carrying on any activity, by regulations make provision with respect to—

(a) applications for any such consent;

(b) the conditions of any such consent;

(c) the revocation or variation of any such consent;

(d) the reference to arbitration of disputes about determinations on any such application;

(e) the imposition of charges where such an application has been made, such a consent has been given or there has been any act or omission in pursuance of any such consent; and

(f) the registration of any such application or consent[3].

*Registering of agreement*

**31C. (1)** An agreement under subsection (2) of section 31B above may—

(a) where the land is registered in the Land Register of Scotland, be registered in that register;

(b) in any other case, be recorded in the appropriate Division of the General Register of Sasines.

(2) An agreement registered or recorded under subsection (1) above shall be enforceable at the instance of the Secretary of State against persons deriving title to the land (including any person acquiring right to a tenancy by assignation or succession) from the person who entered into the agreement; provided that such an agreement shall not be enforceable against a third party who shall have in good faith and for value acquired right (whether completed by infeftment or not) to the land prior to the agreement being registered or recorded as aforesaid, or against any person deriving title from such third party.

---

[1] Words "subsection (6) of section 30F above" substituted by the Environment Act 1995 (c. 25), s. 106, sch. 16, para. 5.
[2] P. 64 below.

[3] See also S.I. 1996/1564 made under the European Communities Act 1972.

(3) Notwithstanding the terms of any agreement registered or recorded under subsection (1) above, the parties to the agreement or any persons deriving title from them may at any time agree to terminate it; and such an agreement to terminate it shall be registered or recorded in the same manner as was the original agreement.

**31D.** *Repealed by the Environment Act 1995 (c. 25), s. 120, sch. 22, para. 29(7), sch. 24. This amendment came into force on 1 April 1996: S.I. 1996/186.*

**32.** *Repealed by the Environment Act 1995 (c. 25), s. 106, sch. 16, para. 3, s. 120, sch. 24. This amendment came into force on 1 April 1996: S.I. 1996/186.*

*Control of sanitary appliances on vessels*

**33.** (1) SEPA[1] may by byelaws make such provision as it[2] considers appropriate for prohibiting or regulating the keeping or use, on any controlled waters[3,4], of vessels of a kind specified in the byelaws which are provided with sanitary appliances; and a person who contravenes any byelaw made by virtue of this section shall be guilty of an offence.

(2) The Secretary of State may by order provide that any byelaws specified in the order which were made by virtue of section 25(1)(c) of the Rivers (Prevention of Pollution) (Scotland) Act 1951[5] (byelaws) shall have effect, with such modifications[6] (if any) as are so specified, as if made by virtue of the preceding subsection[7].

(3) In this section "sanitary appliance" means a water closet or other prescribed[8] appliance (except a sink, bath and a shower-bath) which is designed to permit polluting matter to pass into the water on which the vessel in question is for the time being situated.

(4) A person guilty of an offence by virtue of any of the preceding provisions of this section shall be liable on summary conviction to a fine of an amount not exceeding level 4 on the standard scale[9] or such smaller sum as may be specified in the byelaws.

## Consents for discharges

*Consents for discharges of trade and sewage effluent etc.*

**34.** (1) An application to SEPA[10] for consent in pursuance of this section for discharges of any effluent[11] or other matter shall be accompanied or supplemented by all such information as SEPA[12] may reasonably require; and SEPA may if it thinks fit treat an application for consent for discharges at two or more places as separate applications for consent for discharges at each of those places.

(2) Subject to the following section, it shall be the duty of SEPA in relation to an application for consent[13] made in pursuance of this section—

(a) to give the consent either unconditionally or subject to conditions or to refuse it; and

---

[1] "SEPA" means the Scottish Environment Protection Agency: s. 105(1) below.
[2] Word "it" substituted by the Environment Act 1995 (c. 25), s. 120, sch. 22, para. 29(8)(a).
[3] "Controlled waters" has the meaning given by s. 30A(1), p. 18 above: s. 56(1) below.
[4] Former words "in the area of the authority" repealed by the Environment Act 1995 (c. 25), s. 120, sch. 22, para. 29(8)(b), sch. 24.
[5] 1951 c. 66.
[6] "Modifications" defined by s. 105(1), p. 61 below.
[7] The following order has been made under this section: The Control of Pollution (Continuation of Byelaws) (Scotland) Order 1991, S.I. 1991/1156. This order makes pro-

vision for a byelaw regarding vessels on Loch Lomond and Loch Eck.
[8] "Prescribed" defined by s. 105(1), p. 61 below.
[9] The current fine at level 4 on the standard scale is £2,500: Criminal Procedure (Scotland) Act 1995 (c. 46), s. 225.
[10] "SEPA" means the Scottish Environment Protection Agency: s. 105(1) below.
[11] "Effluent" defined by s. 56(1), p. 49 below.
[12] Words "SEPA" and "SEPA's" in the remainder of this section substituted by the Environment Act 1995 (c. 25), s. 120, sch. 22, para. 29(9)(a).
[13] Words "SEPA ... consent" substituted by the Environment Act 1995 (c. 25), s. 120, sch. 22, para. 29(9)(b)(i).

(*b*) not to withhold the consent unreasonably;

and if within the period of four[1] months beginning with the date when an application for consent is received by SEPA, or within such longer period as may at any time be agreed upon in writing between SEPA and the applicant, SEPA has neither given nor refused the consent nor informed the applicant that the application has been transmitted to the Secretary of State in pursuance of the following section, the applicant may treat the consent applied for as having been refused[2].

(3) If it appears to SEPA that a person has, without SEPA's consent, caused or permitted matter to be discharged[3] in contravention of section 30F(2) to (4)[4] of this Act and that a similar contravention by that person is likely, SEPA may if it thinks fit serve on him an instrument in writing giving its consent, subject to conditions specified in the instrument, for discharges of a kind so specified; but consent given in pursuance of this subsection shall not relate to any discharge which occurred before the instrument giving the consent was served on the recipient of the instrument.

(4) The conditions subject to which SEPA may give its consent in pursuance of this section shall be such reasonable conditions as SEPA thinks fit; and without prejudice to the generality of the preceding provisions of this subsection those conditions may include reasonable conditions—

(*a*) as to the places at which the discharges to which the consent relates may be made and as to the design and construction of any outlets for the discharges;

(*b*) as to the nature, origin, composition, temperature, volume and rate of the discharges and as to the period during which the discharges may be made;

(*c*) as to the provision of facilities for taking samples of the matter discharged and in particular as to the provision, maintenance and use of manholes, inspection chambers, observation wells and boreholes in connection with the discharges;

(*d*) as to the provision, maintenance and testing of meters for measuring the volume and rate of the discharges and apparatus for determining the nature, composition and temperature of the discharges;

(*e*) as to the keeping of records of the nature, origin, composition, temperature, volume and rate of the discharges and in particular of records of readings of meters and other recording apparatus provided in accordance with any other condition attached to the consent;

(*f*) as to the making of returns and the giving of other information to SEPA about the nature, origin, composition, temperature, volume and rate of the discharges; and

(*g*) as to the steps to be taken, in relation to the discharges or by way of subjecting any substance[5] likely to affect the description of matter discharged to treatment or any other process, for minimising the polluting effects of the discharges on any controlled waters[6];

and it is hereby declared that consent may be given in pursuance of this section subject to different conditions in respect of different periods.

(5) A person who, in an application for consent in pursuance of this section, makes any statement which he knows to be false or misleading in a material particular or recklessly makes any statement which is false or misleading in a material particular shall be guilty of an offence and shall be liable—

(*a*) on summary conviction, to a fine not exceeding the statutory maximum;

[1] Word "four" substituted by the Environment Act 1995 (c. 25), s. 120, sch. 22, para. 29(9)(b)(ii).
[2] Words "the applicant . . . refused" substituted by the Environment Act 1995 (c. 25), sch. 22, para. 29(9)(b)(iii).
[3] Former words "in its area" repealed by the Environment Act 1995 (c. 25), s. 120, sch. 22, para. 29(0)(c), sch. 24.
[4] Words "section 30F(2) to (4)" substituted by the Environment Act 1995 (c. 25), s. 106, sch. 16, para. 6.
[5] "Substance" defined by s. 56(1), p. 49 below.
[6] "Controlled waters" has the meaning given by s. 30A(1), p. 18 above: s. 56(1) below.

(*b*)  on conviction on indictment, to a fine or to imprisonment for a term not exceeding two years, or to both[1].

*Reference to Secretary of State of certain applications for consent*

**35.** **(1)**  The Secretary of State may, either in consequence of representations made to him or otherwise, direct SEPA[2] to transmit to him for determination applications for consent in pursuance of the preceding section which are specified in the direction or are of a kind so specified, and it shall be the duty of SEPA to comply with the direction and to inform each relevant applicant that his application has been transmitted to the Secretary of State.

**(2)**  Before determining an application transmitted to him by SEPA in pursuance of this section the Secretary of State may if he thinks fit, and shall if a request to be heard with respect to the application is made to him in accordance with regulations[3] by the applicant or SEPA, cause a local inquiry to be held in pursuance of section 96 of this Act[4] into the application or afford to the applicant and SEPA an opportunity of appearing before and being heard by a person appointed by the Secretary of State for the purpose.

**(3)**  Where in pursuance of the preceding subsection the Secretary of State affords to an applicant and SEPA an opportunity of appearing before and being heard by a person with respect to the application in question, it shall be the duty of the Secretary of State to afford an opportunity of appearing before and being heard by that person to any person who, in pursuance of subsection (1)(c) or (5) of the following section, has made representations relating to the application.

**(4)**  It shall be the duty of the Secretary of State to determine an application transmitted to him by SEPA in pursuance of this section by directing SEPA to refuse its consent in pursuance of the preceding section in consequence of the application or to give the consent either unconditionally or subject to such conditions as are specified in the direction, and it shall be the duty of SEPA to comply with the direction.

*Provisions supplementary to ss. 34 and 35*

**36.** **(1)**  Where SEPA[5] receives an application for consent in pursuance of section 34 of this Act[6] or serves an instrument in pursuance of subsection (3) of that section, it shall, subject to subsections (2A) and (2B) below[7], be the duty of SEPA, before deciding whether to give or refuse consent in pursuance of the application or, as the case may be, after serving the instrument—

(*a*)  to publish in the prescribed[8] form notice of the application or instrument in two successive weeks in a newspaper or newspapers circulating in—

    (i)  the area or areas in which the places are situated at which it is proposed in the application that the discharges should be made or, as the case may be, at which discharges are the subject of consent given by the instrument, and

    (ii)  the area or areas appearing to SEPA to be in the vicinity of any controlled waters[9] which SEPA considers likely to be affected by the discharges,

[1] Subsection (5) substituted by the Environment Act 1995 (c. 25), s. 112, sch. 19, para. 1(2).
[2] "SEPA" means the Scottish Environment Protection Agency: s. 105(1) below.
[3] "Regulations" defined by s. 105(1), p. 61 below.
[4] P. 57 below.
[5] "SEPA" means the Scottish Environment Protection Agency: s. 105(1) below.
[6] P. 29 above.
[7] Words ", subject to subsections (2A) and (2B) below," inserted by the Environment Act 1995 (c. 25), s. 120, sch. 22, para. 29(11)(a).
[8] "Prescribed" defined by s. 105(1), p. 61 below.
[9] "Controlled waters" has the meaning given by s. 30A(1), p. 18 above: s. 56(1) below.

and, not earlier than the day following that on which the first publication of the notice is completed in all relevant areas in pursuance of the preceding provisions of this paragraph, to publish such a notice in the Edinburgh Gazette;

(b) to send copies of the application or instrument to each local authority in whose area, and to each water authority[1] within whose limits of supply[2], it is proposed in the application that a discharge should be made or in whose area, or within whose limits of supply[3], a discharge is the subject of consent given by the instrument and, in the case of an application or instrument relating to coastal waters[4], relevant territorial waters[5] or an application relating to waters outside the seaward limits of relevant territorial waters, to the Secretary of State; and

(c) to consider any written representations relating to the application or instrument which are made to SEPA by any person within the period of six weeks beginning with the date on which the notice of the application or instrument is published in the Edinburgh Gazette.

(2) For the purposes of subsection (1) above, "local authority" means a council constituted under section 2 of the Local Government etc. (Scotland) Act 1994[6], and any place at sea at which it is proposed in an application that a discharge should be made shall be treated as situated at the point on land nearest to that place.

(2A) A person who proposes to make, or has made, an application to SEPA for consent in pursuance of section 34 of this Act may apply to the Secretary of State within a prescribed period for a certificate providing that subsection (1) above shall not apply to that application.

(2B) If the Secretary of State is satisfied that—

(a) it would be contrary to the interests of national security; or

(b) it would prejudice to an unreasonable degree the commercial interests of any person,

not to issue a certificate applied for under subsection (2A) above, he may issue the certificate and, if he does so, subsection (1) above shall not apply to the application specified in the certificate[7].

(3) Where notice of an application is published by SEPA in pursuance of subsection (1)(a) of this section, SEPA shall be entitled to recover the cost of publication from the applicant.

(4) SEPA shall be entitled to disregard the provisions of subsection (1) of this section in relation to an application (except so much of paragraph (b) of that subsection as requires copies of the application to be sent to the Secretary of State) if SEPA proposes to give consent in pursuance of the application and considers that the discharges in question will have no appreciable effect on the water into which they are proposed to be made.

(5) The preceding provisions of this section shall have effect with prescribed modifications[8] in relation to an application which is the subject of a direction in pursuance of subsection (1) of the preceding section.

---

[1] "Water authority" defined by s. 56(1), p. 50 below.

[2] Words ", and to each water authority within whose limits of supply," inserted by the Local Government etc. (Scotland) Act 1994 (c. 39), s. 180(1), sch. 13, para. 95(3)(a)(i). This amendment came into force on 1 April 1996: S.I. 1996/323.

[3] Words ", or within whose limits of supply," inserted by the Local Government etc. (Scotland) Act 1994 (c. 39), s. 180(1), sch. 13, para. 95(3)(a)(ii).

[4] "Coastal waters" has the meaning given by s. 30A(2), p. 18 above: s. 56(1) below.

[5] "Relevant territorial waters" has the meaning given by s. 30A(1), p. 18 above: s. 56(1) below.

[6] 1994 c. 39. Words "council . . . 1994" inserted by the Local Government etc. (Scotland) Act 1994 (c. 39), s. 180(1), sch. 13, para. 95(3)(b). This amendment came into force on 1 April 1996: S.I. 1996/323.

[7] Subsections (2A) and (2B) inserted by the Environment Act 1995 (c. 25), s. 120, sch. 22, para. 29(11)(b).

[8] "Modifications" defined by s. 105(1), p. 61 below.

(6) Where SEPA proposes to give consent in pursuance of section 34 of this Act in consequence of an application in respect of which representations have been made in pursuance of subsection (1)(c) of this section then—

(a) it shall be the duty of SEPA to serve notice of the proposal on the person who made the representations and to include in the notice a statement of the effect of the following paragraph; and

(b) that person may, within the period of twenty-one days beginning with the day on which the notice of the proposal is served on him, request the Secretary of State in accordance with regulations to give a direction in pursuance of subsection (1) of the preceding section in respect of the application; and

(c) it shall be the duty of SEPA not to give consent in consequence of the application before the expiration of that period and, if within that period the said person makes a request in pursuance of the preceding paragraph and serves notice of the request on SEPA, not to give consent in pursuance of the application unless the Secretary of State has given notice to SEPA that he declines to comply with the request;

and in calculating in the case of any application the period of four[1] months mentioned in section 34(2) of this Act or a longer period there mentioned there shall be disregarded any period during which SEPA[2] is prohibited by virtue of paragraph (c) of this subsection from giving consent in consequence of the application.

(7) A consent for any discharges which is given in pursuance of section 34 of this Act is not limited to discharges by a particular person and accordingly extends to the discharges in question which are made by any person.

*Revocation of consents and alteration and imposition of conditions*

37. (1) SEPA[3] may from time to time review any consent given in pursuance of section 34 of this Act[4] and the conditions, if any, to which the consent is subject; and subject to the following section SEPA may, by a notice[5] served on the person making a discharge in pursuance of the consent, revoke the consent if it is reasonable to do so or make reasonable modifications[6] of the said conditions or, in the case of an unconditional consent, provide that it shall be subject to reasonable conditions specified in the notice.

(2) Subject to the following section, the Secretary of State may—

(a) for the purpose of enabling Her Majesty's Government in the United Kingdom to give effect to any Community obligation or to any international agreement to which the United Kingdom is for the time being a party;

(b) for the protection of public health or of flora and fauna dependent on an aquatic environment; or

(c) in consequence of any representations made to him or otherwise,

direct SEPA to serve a notice in pursuance of the preceding subsection containing such provisions as are specified in the direction and it shall be the duty of SEPA to comply with the direction; and if SEPA fails to serve the notice within such period as the Secretary of State may allow he may serve the notice on behalf of SEPA, and it is hereby declared that for the purposes of this Part of the Act a notice served on behalf of SEPA by virtue of this subsection is served by SEPA.

---

[1] Word "four" substituted by the Environment Act 1995 (c. 25), s. 120, sch. 22, para. 29(11)(c).

[2] The Act here contains the wording "to which the application was made". Following the amendments made by the Environment Act 1995 this subsection now refers to SEPA and not, as previously, a river purification authority and accordingly it appears that this wording should be omitted.

[3] "SEPA" means the Scottish Environment Protection Agency: s. 105(1) below.

[4] P. 29 above. Words "SEPA ... Act" substituted by the Environment Act 1995 (c. 25), s. 120, sch. 22, para. 29(12).

[5] "Notice" defined by s. 105(1), p. 61 below.

[6] "Modifications" defined by s. 105(1), p. 61 below.

*Restriction on variation and revocation of consent and of previous variation*

**38.** **(1)** Each instrument signifying the consent of SEPA[1] in pursuance of section 34 of this Act[2] shall specify a period during which no notice in pursuance of subsection (1) or (2)(c) of the preceding section is to be served in respect of the consent without the written agreement of a person making a discharge in pursuance of the consent; and the said period shall be a reasonable period of not less than four[3] years beginning with the day on which the consent takes effect.

**(2)** Each notice served by SEPA in pursuance of subsection (1) or (2)(c) of the preceding section (except a notice which only revokes a consent or conditions) shall specify a period during which a subsequent notice in pursuance of that subsection which alters the effect of the first-mentioned notice is not to be served without the written agreement of a person making a discharge in pursuance of the consent to which the first-mentioned notice relates; and the said period shall be a reasonable period of not less than four[3] years beginning with the day on which the first-mentioned notice is served.

**(3)** SEPA shall be liable to pay compensation to any person in respect of any loss or damage sustained by that person as a result of SEPA's[4] compliance with a direction given in relation to any consent by virtue of section 37(2)(b) of this Act if—

(*a*) in complying with that direction SEPA does anything which, apart from that direction, it would be precluded from doing by a restriction imposed under subsection (1) or (2) above; and

(*b*) the direction is not shown to have been in consequence of—

(i) a change of circumstances which could not reasonably have been foreseen at the beginning of the period to which the restriction relates; or

(ii) consideration by the Secretary of State of material information which was not reasonably available to SEPA at the beginning of that period;

and in this paragraph information is material, in relation to a consent, if it relates to any discharge made or to be made by virtue of the consent, to the interaction of any such discharge with any other discharge or to the combined effect of the matter discharged and any other matter.

**(4)** A restriction imposed under subsection (1) or (2) of this section shall not prevent the service by SEPA of a notice by virtue of section 37(1) or (2)(c) of this Act in respect of a consent given under section 34(3) of this Act if—

(*a*) the notice is served not more than three months after the beginning of the period specified in section 36(1)(c) of this Act[5] for the making of representations with respect to the consent; and

(*b*) SEPA or, as the case may be, the Secretary of State considers, in consequence of any representations received by it or him within that period, that it is appropriate for the notice to be served.

*General review of consents*

**38A.** **(1)** If it appears appropriate to the Secretary of State to do so he may at any time direct SEPA[6] to review—

(*a*) the consents given under section 34 of this Act[7]; or

---

[1] "SEPA" means the Scottish Environment Protection Agency: s. 105(1) below.
[2] P. 29 above.
[3] Word "four" substituted by the Environment Act 1995 (c. 25), s. 120, sch. 22, para. 29(13).
[4] The word "SEPA's" has been substituted here in place of "the authority's". Following the amendments made by the Environment Act 1995 this subsection now refers to SEPA

and not, as previously, a river purification authority although the Act does not make provision for a substitution at this point.
[5] P. 32 above.
[6] "SEPA" means the Scottish Environment Protection Agency: s. 105(1) below.
[7] P. 29 above.

(*b*)  any description of such consents,

and the conditions (if any) to which those consents are subject.

(2)  A direction given by virtue of subsection (1) above—

(*a*)  shall specify the purpose for which; and

(*b*)  may specify the manner in which,

the review is to be conducted.

(3)  After carrying out the review, SEPA shall submit to the Secretary of State its proposals (if any) for—

(*a*)  the modification[1] of the conditions of any consent reviewed pursuant to the direction; or

(*b*)  in the case of any such consent which is unconditional, subjecting the consent to conditions.

(4)  Where the Secretary of State has received any proposal under subsection (3) above in relation to any consent he may, if it appears appropriate to him to do so, direct SEPA, in relation to that consent—

(*a*)  to make modifications of the conditions of the consent; or

(*b*)  in the case of an unconditional consent, to subject the consent to conditions.

(5)  A direction given by virtue of subsection (4) above may direct SEPA to do, in relation to any such consent, only—

(*a*)  any such thing as SEPA has proposed should be done in relation to that consent; or

(*b*)  any such thing with such modifications as appear to the Secretary of State to be appropriate.

*Appeals to Secretary of State*

**39.  (1)**  Any questions as to whether—

(*a*)  SEPA[2] has unreasonably withheld its consent in pursuance of section 30J(4)[3] or 34 of this Act[4] or regulations made by virtue of section 31(4) of this Act[5] or has given its consent in pursuance of the said section 34 or such regulations subject to conditions which are unreasonable; or

(*b*)  a notice served in pursuance of section 37(1) of this Act[6] contains terms (other than a term required by subsection (2) of section 38 of this Act[7]) which are unreasonable; or

(*c*)  the period specified in any instrument or notice in pursuance of subsection (1) or (2) of section 38 of this Act is unreasonable,

shall be determined for the purposes of this Part of this Act by the Secretary of State; but no question relating to a determination of the Secretary of State in pursuance of section 35(4) of this Act[8] shall be referred to him in pursuance of this subsection and any such determination shall be final.

(2)  Provision may be made by regulations as to the manner in which and the time within which a question may be referred or a request may be made in pursuance of the preceding provisions of this section and as to the procedure for dealing with such a reference or request.

[1] "Modification" defined by s. 105(1), p. 61 below.
[2] "SEPA" means the Scottish Environment Protection Agency: s. 105(1) below.
[3] P. 24 above. Words "section 30J(4)" inserted by the Environment Act 1995 (c. 25), s. 106, sch. 16, para. 7.
[4] P. 29 above.
[5] P. 25 above.
[6] P. 34 above.
[7] Words "section 38 of this Act" substituted by the Environment Act 1995 (c. 25), s. 120, sch. 22, para. 29(15)(a).
[8] P. 31 above.

(3) In any case where—

(a) a question as to whether SEPA has unreasonably withheld its consent in pursuance of section 34 of this Act, or has given its consent in pursuance of that section subject to conditions which are unreasonable, is referred to the Secretary of State in pursuance of this section; and

(b) representations relating to the application for the consent in question were made to the authority in pursuance of section 36(1)(c) of this Act[1],

it shall be the duty of the Secretary of State, before he determines the question, to secure that SEPA has served notice of the reference on the persons who made the representations and to take account of any further written representations relating to the application which are received by him from those persons within a prescribed period.

(4) Where a question is referred to the Secretary of State in pursuance of subsection (1) of this section and he determines that the consent in question was unreasonably withheld or that the conditions or terms or period in question are or is unreasonable, he shall give to SEPA such a direction as he thinks fit with regard to the consent, conditions, terms or period and it shall be the duty of SEPA to comply with the direction.

(5) The withholding by SEPA of such a consent as is mentioned in subsection (1) of this section, the conditions subject to which such a consent is given and such period as is[2] so mentioned shall be treated as reasonable for the purposes of this Part of this Act until the contrary is determined in pursuance of subsection (1) of this section except that where a question as to the reasonableness of the conditions of a consent given in pursuance of regulations made by virtue of section 31(4) of this Act is referred to the Secretary of State in pursuance of this section the consent shall be treated for those purposes as unconditional while the reference is pending.

(5A) Subject to subsection (5B) below, where a question is referred to the Secretary of State in pursuance of subsection (1)(b) above, the revocation of the consent or, as the case may be, the modification[3] of the conditions of the consent or the provision that the consent (having been unconditional) shall be subject to conditions, shall not take effect while the reference is pending.

(5B) Subsection (5A) above shall not apply to a reference where the notice effecting the revocation, modification or provision in question includes a statement that in the opinion of SEPA it is necessary for the purpose of preventing or, where that is not practicable, minimising—

(a) the entry into controlled waters[4] of any poisonous, noxious or polluting matter or any solid waste matter, or

(b) harm to human health,

that that subsection should not apply.

(5C) Where the reference falls within subsection (5B) above, if, on the application of the holder[5] or former holder of the consent, the Secretary of State (or other person determining the question referred) determines that SEPA acted unreasonably in excluding the application of subsection (5A) above, then—

(a) if the reference is still pending at the end of the day on which that determination is made, subsection (5A) above shall apply to the reference from the end of that day; and

(b) the holder or former holder of the consent shall be entitled to recover compensation from SEPA in respect of any loss suffered by him in consequence of the exclusion of the application of that subsection;

---

[1] P. 32 above.
[2] Words "period as is" substituted by the Environment Act 1995 (c. 25), s. 120, sch. 22, para. 29(15)(b).
[3] "Modification" defined by s. 105(1), p. 61 below.
[4] "Controlled waters" has the meaning given by s. 30A(1), p. 18 above: s. 56(1) below.
[5] "Holder" defined by subsection (8) below.

and any dispute as to a person's entitlement to such compensation or as to the amount of it shall be determined by a single arbiter appointed, in default of agreement between the parties concerned, by the Secretary of State on the application of any of the parties[1].

(6) At any stage of the proceedings on a reference to the Secretary of State in pursuance of this section he may, and shall if so directed by the Court of Session, state in the form of a special case for the decision of the court any question of law arising in those proceedings.

(7) This section is subject to section 114 of the Environment Act 1995[2] (delegation or reference of appeals).

(8) In this section "the holder", in relation to a consent, is the person who has the consent[3].

*Transitional provisions relating to consents*

**40.** (1) Regulations[4] may provide—

(a) for any consent for discharges which was given in pursuance of the Rivers (Prevention of Pollution) (Scotland) Acts 1951 and 1965[5] to have effect for any of the purposes of this Part of this Act as if given in pursuance of prescribed[6] provisions of section 34 of this Act[7]; and

(b) for any conditions to which such a consent was subject in pursuance of any of those enactments to have effect for any of those purposes as if attached to the consent in pursuance of prescribed provisions of this Part of this Act.

(2) Regulations may provide for the terms of a consent for an outlet which was given in pursuance of the Rivers (Prevention of Pollution) (Scotland) Act 1951 and for conditions to which such a consent was subject in pursuance of that Act or which were imposed with respect to the outlet in pursuance of section 28(4) of that Act—

(a) to have effect, with or without modifications[8], for any of the purposes of this Part of this Act as if the terms or conditions were conditions attached to a consent given in pursuance of section 34 of this Act for discharges from the outlet; or

(b) to be treated, with or without modifications, for any of those purposes in such other manner as may be prescribed.

(3) An application for such a consent as is mentioned in subsection (1) of this section which is pending immediately before the relevant day[9] shall be treated on and after that day as an application for consent in pursuance of section 34 of this Act which was made on the day on which it was actually made.

(4) *Repealed by the Environment Act 1995 (c. 25), s. 120, sch. 22, para. 29(16), sch. 24. This amendment came into force on 1 April 1996: S.I. 1996/186.*

(5) Regulations may provide for any appeal which immediately before the relevant day is pending in pursuance of the Rivers (Prevention of Pollution) (Scotland) Acts 1951 and 1965 to be treated on and after that day as an appeal in pursuance of prescribed provisions of this Part of this Act.

(6) In this section "the relevant day" means 31st January 1985.

---

[1] Subsections (5A) to (5C) inserted by the Environment Act 1995 (c. 25), s. 120, sch. 22, para. 29(15)(c). For the application of these subsections in respect of references under s. 39(1)(b) pending on 1 April 1996, see S.I. 1996/973, reg. 3.
[2] P. 489 below.
[3] Subsections (7) to (8) inserted by the Environment Act 1995 (c. 25), s. 120, sch. 22, para. 29(15)(d).
[4] "Regulations" defined by s. 105(1), p. 61 below.
[5] 1951 c. 66; 1965 c. 13.
[6] "Prescribed" defined by s. 105(1), p. 61 below.
[7] P. 29 above.
[8] "Modifications" defined by s. 105(1), p. 61 below.
[9] "Relevant day" defined by subsection (6) below.

*Ancillary provisions relating to control of discharges*

*Registers*

**41.** (1) It shall be the duty of SEPA[1] to maintain in accordance with regulations[2], registers containing prescribed[3] particulars of or relating to[4]—

(a) any notices of water quality objectives or other notices served under section 30C above[5];

(b) application for consents—

(i) made to SEPA in pursuance of this Part of this Act;

(ii) sent to the Secretary of State in pursuance of section 34 of this Act[6] (as modified[7] by regulations made under section 55 of this Act[8]);

(c) consents given in pursuance of any provision of this Part of this Act[9] and the conditions to which the consents are subject;

(d) samples—

(i) of effluent[10] taken by SEPA in pursuance of section 19 of the Rivers (Prevention of Pollution) (Scotland) Act 1951[11];

(ii) *Repealed by the Environment Act 1995 (c. 25), s. 120, sch. 22, para. 29(17)(b)(ii), sch. 24. This amendment came into force on 1 April 1996: S.I. 1996/186.*

(iii) of water taken by SEPA;

and information produced by analyses of the samples and the steps taken in consequence of the information;

(e) *Repealed by the Environment Act 1995 (c. 25), s. 120, sch. 22, para. 29(17)(b)(iii), sch. 24. This amendment came into force on 1 April 1996: S.I. 1996/186.*

(f) enforcement notices served under section 49A of this Act[12];

(g) directions given by the Secretary of State in relation to SEPA's functions under this Part of this Act;

(h) convictions, for offences under this Part of this Act, of persons who have the benefit of consents under section 34 of this Act;

(j) information obtained or furnished in pursuance of conditions of such consents;

(k) works notices under section 46A[13] of this Act;

(l) appeals under section 46C[14] of this Act;

(m) convictions for offences under section 46D[15] of this Act; and

(n) such other matters relating to the quality of water as may be prescribed[16].

(2) It shall be the duty of SEPA—

(a) to secure that registers maintained by SEPA in pursuance of the preceding subsection are, after such date as is prescribed with respect to the registers, open to inspection by the public free of charge at all reasonable hours; and

---

[1] "SEPA" means the Scottish Environment Protection Agency: s. 105(1) below.

[2] "Regulations" defined by s. 105(1), p. 61 below.

[3] "Prescribed" defined by s. 105(1), p. 61 below.

[4] Words "or relating to" inserted by the Environment Act 1995 (c. 25), s. 120, sch. 22, para. 29(17)(a).

[5] P. 20 above.

[6] P. 29 above.

[7] "Modified" defined by s. 105(1), p. 61 below.

[8] S. 55 is repealed by the Environment Act 1995.

[9] Former words "(except section 40(4) )" repealed by the Environment Act 1995 (c. 25), s. 120, sch. 22, para. 17(b)(i), sch. 24.

[10] "Effluent" defined by s. 56(1), p. 49 below.

[11] P. 5 above.

[12] P. 47 below.

[13] P. 42 below.

[14] P. 44 below.

[15] P. 45 below.

[16] Paragraphs (f) to (n) inserted by the Environment Act 1995 (c. 25), s. 120, sch. 22, para. 17(c).

(*b*) to afford members of the public reasonable facilities for obtaining from SEPA, on payment of reasonable charges, copies of entries in the register;

and, for the purposes of this subsection, places may be prescribed at which any such registers or facilities as are mentioned in paragraph (a) or (b) above are to be available or afforded to the public in pursuance of the paragraph in question[1].

(3)  The Secretary of State may give SEPA directions requiring the removal from any register maintained by it under this section of any specified information which is not prescribed for inclusion under subsection (1) of this section or which, by virtue of section 42A or 42B of this Act, ought to have been excluded from the registers[2].

*Exclusion from registers of information affecting national security*

**42A.** (1)  No information shall be included in a register kept or maintained by SEPA[3] under section 41 of this Act if and so long as, in the opinion of the Secretary of State, the inclusion in such a register of that information, or information of that description, would be contrary to the interests of national security.

(2)  The Secretary of State may, for the purposes of securing the exclusion from registers of information to which subsection (1) of this section applies, give SEPA directions—

(*a*) specifying information, or descriptions of information, to be excluded from their registers; or

(*b*) specifying descriptions of information to be referred to the Secretary of State for his determination;

and no information to be referred to the Secretary of State in pursuance of paragraph (b) of this subsection shall be included in any such register until the Secretary of State determines that it should be so included.

(3)  SEPA shall notify the Secretary of State of any information it excludes from a register in pursuance of directions under subsection (2) of this section.

(4) A person may, as respects any information which appears to him to be information to which subsection (1) of this section may apply, give a notice to the Secretary of State specifying the information and indicating its apparent nature; and, if he does so—

(*a*) he shall notify SEPA that he has done so; and

(*b*) no information so notified to the Secretary of State shall be included in any such register until the Secretary of State has determined that it should be so included.

*Exclusion from registers of certain confidential information*

**42B.** (1)  No information relating to the affairs of any individual or business shall, without the consent of that individual or the person for the time being carrying on that business, be included in a register kept or maintained by SEPA[4] under section 41 of this Act, if and so long as the information—

(*a*) is, in relation to him, commercially confidential[5]; and

(*b*)  is not required to be included in the register in pursuance of directions under subsection (7) of this section;

but information is not commercially confidential for the purposes of this section unless it is determined under this section to be so by SEPA, or, on appeal, by the Secretary of State.

(2)  Where information is furnished to SEPA for the purpose of—

(*a*) an application for a consent under section 34 of this Act[6];

[1] Words "and, . . . question" added by the Environment Act 1995 (c. 25), s. 120, sch. 22, para. 29(18).
[2] Subsection (3) added by the Environment Act 1995 (c. 25), s. 120, sch. 22, para. 29(19).
[3] "SEPA" means the Scottish Environment Protection Agency: s. 105(1) below.
[4] "SEPA" means the Scottish Environment Protection Agency: s. 105(1) below.
[5] "Commercially confidential" defined by subsection (11) below.
[6] P. 29 above.

(b)  complying with any condition of such a consent; or

(c)  complying with a notice under section 93 of this Act[1],

then, if the person furnishing it applies to SEPA to have the information excluded from any register kept or maintained by SEPA under section 41 of this Act, on the ground that it is commercially confidential (as regards himself or another person), SEPA shall determine whether the information is or is not commercially confidential.

(3)  A determination under subsection (2) of this section must be made within the period of fourteen days beginning with the date of the application and if SEPA fails to make a determination within that period it shall be treated as having determined that the information is commercially confidential.

(4)  Where it appears to SEPA that any information (other than information furnished in circumstances within subsection (2) of this section) which has been obtained by SEPA under or by virtue of any provision of any enactment might be commercially confidential, SEPA shall—

(a)  give to the person to whom or whose business it relates notice that that information is required to be included in a register kept or maintained by SEPA under section 41 of this Act, unless excluded under this section; and

(b)  give him a reasonable opportunity—

(i)  of objecting to the inclusion of the information on the ground that it is commercially confidential; and

(ii)  of making representations to SEPA for the purpose of justifying any such objection;

and, if any representations are made, SEPA shall, having taken the representations into account, determine whether the information is or is not commercially confidential.

(5)  Where, under subsection (2) or (4) of this section, SEPA determines that information is not commercially confidential—

(a)  the information shall not be entered on the register until the end of the period of twenty-one days beginning with the date on which the determination is notified to the person concerned; and

(b)  that person may appeal to the Secretary of State against the decision;

and, where an appeal is brought in respect of any information, the information shall not be entered on the register pending the final determination or withdrawal of the appeal.

(6)  Subsections (2), (4) and (7) of section 49B of this Act[2] shall apply in relation to appeals under subsection (5) of this section; but

(a)  subsection (4) of that section shall have effect for the purposes of this subsection with the substitution for the words from ("which may" onwards of the words "(which must be held in private)"; and

(b)  subsection (5) of this section is subject to section 114 of the Environment Act 1995[3] (delegation or reference of appeals etc).

(7)  The Secretary of State may give SEPA directions as to specified information, or descriptions of information, which the public interest requires to be included in registers kept or maintained by SEPA under section 41 of this Act notwithstanding that the information may be commercially confidential.

(8)  Information excluded from a register shall be treated as ceasing to be commercially confidential for the purposes of this section at the expiry of the period of four years beginning with the date of the determination by virtue of which it was excluded; but the person who furnished it may apply to SEPA for the information to remain excluded from the register on the ground that it is still commercially confidential and SEPA shall determine whether or not that is the case.

[1]  P. 56 below.    [2]  P. 47 below.    [3]  P. 489 below.

**(9)** Subsections (5) and (6) of this section shall apply in relation to a determination under subsection (8) of this section as they apply in relation to a determination under subsection (2) or (4) of this section.

**(10)** The Secretary of State may prescribe the substitution (whether in all cases or in such classes or descriptions of case as may be prescribed) for the period for the time being specified in subsection (3) above of such other period as he considers appropriate.

**(11)** Information is, for the purposes of any determination under this section, commercially confidential, in relation to any individual or person, if its being contained in register would prejudice to an unreasonable degree the commercial interests of that individual or person.

............................................................................................................................................

## *Miscellaneous*

*Operations by river purification authorities[1] to remedy or forestall pollution of water*

**46. (1)** Subject to subsection (1B) below[2], where it appears to SEPA[3] that any poisonous, noxious or polluting matter or any solid waste matter is likely to enter, or is or was present in, any controlled waters[4] SEPA[5] may carry out[6] such operations as it considers appropriate—

(*a*) in a case where the matter appears likely to enter such waters, for the purpose of preventing it from doing so; and

(*b*) in a case where the matter appears to be or to have been present in such waters, for the purpose of removing or disposing of the matter or of remedying or mitigating any pollution caused by its presence in the waters or of restoring the waters (including the fauna and flora dependent on the aquatic environment of the waters), so far as it is reasonably practicable to do so, to the state in which they were immediately before the matter became present in the waters;

but nothing in this subsection empowers SEPA to impede or prevent the making of any discharge in pursuance of a consent given by any authority by virtue of section 34 of this Act[7].

**(1A)** In either case mentioned in subsection (1) of this section, SEPA shall be entitled to carry out investigations for the purpose of establishing the source of the matter and the identity of the person who has caused or knowingly permitted it to be present in controlled waters or at a place from which it was likely, in the opinion of SEPA, to enter controlled waters.

**(1B)** Without prejudice to the power of SEPA to carry out investigations under subsection (1A) above, the power conferred by subsection (1) above to carry out operations shall be exercisable only in a case where—

(*a*) SEPA considers it necessary to carry out forthwith any operations falling within paragraph (a) or (b) of subsection (1) above; or

(*b*) it appears to SEPA, after reasonable inquiry, that no person can be found on whom to serve a works notice under section 46A of this Act[8].

**(2)** Where SEPA carries out any operations or investigations[9] in pursuance of this section SEPA shall, subject to the following subsection, be entitled to recover the costs of doing so from any persons who caused or knowingly permitted the matter in question to be present

---

[1] This section now relates to the functions of SEPA.

[2] Words "Subject to subsection (1B) below," substituted by the Environment Act 1995 (c. 25), s. 120, sch. 22, para. 29(21)(a)(i). This amendment is not in force.

[3] "SEPA" means the Scottish Environment Protection Agency: s. 105(1) below.

[4] "Controlled waters" has the meaning given by s. 30A(1), p. 18 above: s. 56(1) below.

[5] Former words "in its area" repealed by the Environment Act 1995 (c. 25), s. 120, sch. 22, para. 29(21)(a)(ii), sch. 24.

[6] Former words "in its area or elsewhere" repealed by the Environment Act 1995 (c. 25), s. 120, sch. 22, para. 29(21)(a)(ii), sch. 24.

[7] P. 29 above.

[8] Subsections (1A) and (1B) inserted by the Environment Act 1995 (c. 25), s. 120, sch. 22, para. 29(21)(b). This amendment is not in force.

[9] Words "or investigations" inserted by the Environment Act 1995 (c. 25), s. 120, sch. 22, para. 29(21)(c). This amendment is not in force.

at the place from which it was likely in the opinion of SEPA to enter the controlled waters or, as the case may be, to be present in the controlled waters.

(3)  No such costs shall be payable by a person—

(*a*)  in so far as he satisfies the court in which it is sought to recover the costs that the costs were incurred unnecessarily; or

(*b*)  for any operations or investigations[1] in respect of water from an abandoned mine or an abandoned part of a mine[2] which that person permitted to reach such a place as is mentioned in the preceding subsection or to enter the controlled waters.

(3A)  Subsection (3)(b) of this section shall not apply to the owner[3] or former operator of any mine or part of a mine if the mine or part in question became abandoned after 31st December 1999.

(3B)  Subsections (5) and (6) of section 30J above[4] shall apply in relation to subsections (3) and (3A) above as they apply in relation to subsections (3) and (4) of that section[5].

(4)  In determining the damage which a person has suffered in consequence of pollution in respect of which operations have been or may be carried out in pursuance of this section, account shall be taken of the extent to which it is shown that the damage has been reduced by operations in pursuance of this section and of the extent to which it is shown that the damage is likely to be so reduced.

*Notices requiring persons to carry out anti-pollution operations*

**46A.**  (1)  Subject to the following provisions of this section, where it appears to SEPA[6] that any poisonous, noxious or polluting matter or any solid waste matter is likely to enter, or to be or to have been present in, any controlled waters[7], SEPA shall be entitled to serve a works notice on any person who, as the case may be,—

(*a*)  caused or knowingly permitted the matter in question to be present at the place from which it is likely, in the opinion of SEPA, to enter any controlled waters; or

(*b*)  caused or knowingly permitted the matter in question to be present in any controlled waters.

(2)  For the purposes of this section, a "works notice" is a notice requiring the person on whom it is served to carry out such of the following operations[8] as may be specified in the notice, that is to say—

(*a*)  in a case where the matter in question appears likely to enter any controlled waters, operations for the purpose of preventing it from doing so; or

(*b*)  in a case where the matter appears to be or to have been present in any controlled waters, operations for the purpose—

(i)   of removing or disposing of the matter;

(ii)  of remedying or mitigating any pollution caused by its presence in the waters; or

(iii) so far as it is reasonably practicable to do so, of restoring the waters, including any flora and fauna dependent on the aquatic environment of the waters, to their state immediately before the matter became present in the waters.

(3)  A works notice—

(*a*)  must specify the periods within which the person on whom it is served is required to do each of the things specified in the notice; and

---

[1] Words "or investigations" inserted by the Environment Act 1995 (c. 25), s. 120, sch. 22, para. 29(21)(d)(i). This amendment is not in force.

[2] "Mine" defined by s. 105(1), p. 61 below. Words "or an abandoned part of a mine" inserted by the Environment Act 1995 (c. 25), s. 120, sch. 22, para. 29(21)(d)(ii). This amendment is not in force.

[3] "Owner" defined by s. 106(9), p. 62 below.

[4] P. 24 above.

[5] Subsections (3A) and (3B) inserted by the Environment Act 1995 (c. 25), s. 120, sch. 22, para. 29(21)(e). This amendment is not in force.

[6] "SEPA" means the Scottish Environment Protection Agency: s. 105(1) below.

[7] "Controlled waters" has the meaning given by s. 30A(1), p. 18 above: s. 56(1) below.

[8] "Operations" defined by s.56(1), p. 49 below.

(*b*)  is without prejudice to the powers of SEPA by virtue of section 46(1B)(a) of this Act.

(4)  Before serving a works notice on any person, SEPA shall reasonably endeavour to consult that person concerning the operations which are to be specified in the notice.

(5)  The Secretary of State may by regulations make provision for or in connection with—

(*a*)  the form or content of works notices;

(*b*)  requirements for consultation, before the service of a works notice, with persons other than the person on whom that notice is to be served;

(*c*)  steps to be taken for the purposes of any consultation required under subsection (4) above or regulations made by virtue of paragraph (b) above; and

(*d*)  any other steps of a procedural nature which are to be taken in connection with, or in consequence of, the service of a works notice.

(6)  A works notice shall not be regarded as invalid, or as invalidly served, by reason only of any failure to comply with the requirements of subsection (4) above or of regulations made by virtue of paragraph (b) of subsection (5) above.

(7)  Nothing in subsection (1) above shall entitle SEPA to require the carrying out of any operations which would impede or prevent the making of any discharge in pursuance of a consent given by SEPA by virtue of section 34 of this Act[1].

(8)  No works notice shall be served on any person requiring him to carry out any operations in respect of water from an abandoned mine[2] or an abandoned part of a mine which that person permitted to reach such a place as is mentioned in subsection (1)(a) above or to enter any controlled waters.

(9)  Subsection (8) above shall not apply to the owner[3] or former operator of any mine or part of a mine if the mine or part in question became abandoned after 31st December 1999.

(10)  Subsections (5) and (6) of section 30J of this Act[4] shall apply in relation to subsections (8) and (9) above as they apply in relation to subsections (3) and (4) of that section.

(11)  Where SEPA—

(*a*)  carries out any such investigations as are mentioned in section 46(1A) of this Act, and

(*b*)  serves a works notice on a person in connection with the matter to which the investigations relate,

it shall (unless the notice is quashed or withdrawn) be entitled to recover the costs or expenses reasonably incurred in carrying out those investigations from that person.

(12)  The Secretary of State may, if he thinks fit in relation to any person, give directions to SEPA as to whether or how it should exercise its powers under this section.

......................................................................................................................................................................

*Grant of, and compensation for, rights of entry etc.*

**46B.** (1)  A works notice[5] may require a person to carry out operations[6] in relation to any land or waters notwithstanding that he is not entitled to carry out those operations.

(2)  Any person whose consent is required before any operations required by a works notice may be carried out shall grant, or join in granting, such rights in relation to any land or waters as will enable the person on whom the works notice is served to comply with any requirements imposed by the works notice.

(3)  Before serving a works notice, SEPA[7] shall reasonably endeavour to consult every person who appears to it—

---

[1]  P. 29 above.
[2]  "Mine" defined by s. 105(1), p. 61 below.
[3]  "Owner" defined by s. 106(9), p. 62 below.
[4]  P. 24 above.
[5]  "Works notice" means a works notice under s. 46A

above: subsection (7) below.
[6]  "Operations" defined by s. 56(1), p. 49 below.
[7]  "SEPA" means the Scottish Environment Protection Agency: s. 105(1) below.

(*a*)  to be the owner[1] or occupier of any relevant land[2], and

(*b*)  to be a person who might be required by subsection (2) above to grant, or join in granting, any rights,

concerning the rights which that person may be so required to grant.

(**4**)  A works notice shall not be regarded as invalid, or as invalidly served, by reason only of any failure to comply with the requirements of subsection (3) above.

(**5**)  A person who grants, or joins in granting, any rights pursuant to subsection (2) above shall be entitled, on making an application within such period as may be prescribed[3] and in such manner as may be prescribed to such person as may be prescribed, to be paid by the person on whom the works notice in question is served compensation of such amount as may be determined in such manner as may be prescribed.

(**6**)  Without prejudice to the generality of the regulations that may be made by virtue of subsection (5) above, regulations by virtue of that subsection may make such provision in relation to compensation under this section as may be made by regulations by virtue of subsection (4) of section 35A of the Environmental Protection Act 1990[4] in relation to compensation under that section.

(**7**)  In this section—

"relevant land" means—

(*a*)  any land or waters in relation to which the works notice in question requires, or may require, operations to be carried out; or

(*b*)  any land adjoining or adjacent to that land or those waters;

"works notice" means a works notice under section 46A of this Act[5].

*Appeals against works notices*

**46C.** (**1**)  A person on whom a works notice[6] is served may, within the period of twenty-one days beginning with the day on which the notice is served, appeal against the notice to the Secretary of State.

(**2**)  On any appeal under this section the Secretary of State—

(*a*)  shall quash the notice, if he is satisfied that there is a material defect in the notice; but

(*b*)  subject to that, may confirm the notice, with or without modification, or quash it.

(**3**)  The Secretary of State may by regulations make provision with respect to—

(*a*)  the grounds on which appeals under this section may be made; or

(*b*)  the procedure on any such appeal.

(**4**)  Regulations under subsection (3) above may (among other things)—

(*a*)  include provisions comparable to those in section 290 of the Public Health Act 1936[7] (appeals against notices requiring the execution of works);

(*b*)  prescribe the cases in which a works notice is, or is not, to be suspended until the appeal is decided, or until some other stage in the proceedings;

(*c*)  prescribe the cases in which the decision on an appeal may in some respects be less favourable to the appellant than the works notice against which he is appealing;

---

[1] "Owner" defined by s. 106(9), p. 62 below.
[2] "Relevant land" defined by subsection (7) below.
[3] "Prescribed" defined by s. 105(1), p. 61 below.
[4] P. 120 below.

[5] P. 42 above.
[6] "Works notice" means a works notice under s. 46A above: subsection (5) below.
[7] 1936 c. 49.

(*d*) prescribe the cases in which the appellant may claim that a works notice should have been served on some other person and prescribe the procedure to be followed in those cases;

(*e*) make provision as respects—

(i)  the particulars to be included in the notice of appeal;

(ii)  the persons on whom notice of appeal is to be served and the particulars, if any, which are to accompany the notice; or

(iii)  the abandonment of an appeal.

(5)  In this section "works notice" means a works notice under section 46A of this Act[1].

(6)  This section is subject to section 114 of the Environment Act 1995[2] (delegation or reference of appeals).

*Consequences of not complying with a works notice*

**46D.**  (1)  If a person on whom SEPA[3] serves a works notice[4] fails to comply with any of the requirements of the notice, he shall be guilty of an offence.

(2)  A person who commits an offence under subsection (1) above shall be liable—

(*a*) on summary conviction, to imprisonment for a term not exceeding three months or to a fine not exceeding £20,000 or to both;

(*b*) on conviction on indictment, to imprisonment for a term not exceeding two years or to a fine or to both.

(3)  If a person on whom a works notice has been served fails to comply with any of the requirements of the notice, SEPA may do what that person was required to do and may recover from him any costs or expenses reasonably incurred by SEPA in doing it.

(4)  If SEPA is of the opinion that proceedings for an offence under subsection (1) above would afford an ineffectual remedy against a person who has failed to comply with the requirements of a works notice, SEPA may take proceedings in any court of competent jurisdiction for the purpose of securing compliance with the notice.

(5)  In this section "works notice" means a works notice under section 46A of this Act[5].

*Duty of river purification authorities[6] to deal with waste from vessels etc.*

**47.**  (1)  It shall be the duty of SEPA[7]—

(*a*) to arrange for the collection and disposal of waste from vessels[8,9] which appears to SEPA to need collection in consequence of the provisions of section 33 of this Act[10]; and

(*b*) to arrange for the provision of facilities for the washing out of prescribed[11] appliances from vessels[12].

(2)  SEPA may arrange for the provision of facilities by way of water closets, urinals and wash basins for the use of persons from vessels[13].

[1] P. 42 above.
[2] P. 489 below.
[3] "SEPA" means the Scottish Environment Protection Agency: s. 105(1) below.
[4] "Works notice" means a works notice under s. 46A above: subsection (5) below.
[5] P. 42 above.
[6] This section now relates to the functions of SEPA.
[7] "SEPA" means the Scottish Environment Protection Agency: s. 105(1) 12. below.
[8] "Vessel" defined by s. 105(1), p. 61 below.
[9] Former words "in its area" repealed by the Environment Act 1995 (c. 25), s. 120, sch. 22, para. 29(23)(a), sch. 24.
[10] P. 29 above.
[11] "Prescribed" defined by s. 105(1), p. 61 below.
[12] Former words "in its area" repealed by the Environment Act 1995 (c. 25), s. 120, sch. 22, para. 29(23)(a), sch. 24.
[13] Former words "in the authority's area" repealed by the Environment Act 1995 (c. 25), s. 120, sch. 22, para. 29(230(b), sch. 24.

(3) A port local authority constituted under Part X of the Public Health (Scotland) Act 1897[1] shall have power to make arrangements with SEPA for the purposes of any of the preceding provisions of this section.

*Power of river purification authorities to exclude unregistered vessels from rivers etc.*

48. (1) Where it appears to SEPA[2] to be appropriate to do so for the purpose of preventing the pollution of inland waters[3,4] SEPA may make byelaws providing that vessels shall not be on any such waters which are specified in the byelaws unless the vessels are registered by SEPA in accordance with the byelaws or are exempted by the byelaws from registration; and a person who causes or knowingly permits a vessel to be on inland waters in contravention of byelaws made by virtue of this subsection shall be guilty of an offence and liable on summary conviction to a fine not exceeding level 5 on the standard scale[6] or such smaller sum as may be specified in the byelaws.

(2) Byelaws made by SEPA in pursuance of the preceding subsection may authorise SEPA to make reasonable charges in respect of the registration of vessels in pursuance of the byelaws; and no charges shall be payable, by persons in or from vessels registered by SEPA in pursuance of the byelaws, in respect of the use by those persons of facilities provided in pursuance of the preceding section by or by arrangement with SEPA.

*Deposits and vegetation in rivers etc.*

49. (1) If without the consent of SEPA[7], which shall not be unreasonably withheld,—

   (a) a person removes from any part of the bottom, channel or bed of any inland waters[8] a deposit accumulated by reason of any dam, weir or sluice holding back the waters and does so by causing the deposit to be carried away in suspension in the waters; or

   (b) any substantial amount of vegetation cut or uprooted in any inland waters, or so near to any such waters that it falls into it, is allowed to remain in the waters by the wilful default of any person,

then, subject to the following subsection, that person shall be guilty of an offence and liable on summary conviction to a fine not exceeding level 4 on the standard scale[9].

(2) Nothing in paragraph (a) of the preceding subsection applies to anything done in the exercise of statutory powers conferred by or under any enactment relating to land drainage, flood prevention or navigation.

(3) Regulations[10] may provide that any reference to inland waters in subsection (1) of this section shall be construed as including a reference to such coastal waters[11] as are prescribed[12] for the purposes of that subsection.

(4) Any question as to whether the consent of SEPA in pursuance of subsection (1) of this section is unreasonably withheld shall be determined by the Secretary of State; and any consent given in pursuance of section 24 of the Rivers (Prevention of Pollution) (Scotland) Act 1951[13] (which is superseded by this section) shall be treated for the purposes of this section as given in pursuance of this section.

---

[1] 1897 c. 38.
[2] "SEPA" means the Scottish Environment Protection Agency: s. 105(1) below.
[3] "Inland waters" has the meaning given by s. 30A(1), p. 18 above: s. 56(1) below.
[4] Former words "in its area" repealed by the Environment Act 1995 (c. 25), s. 120, sch. 22, para. 29(24), sch. 24.
[5] "Vessel" defined by s. 105(1), p. 61 below.
[6] The current fine at level 5 on the standard scale in £5,000: Criminal Procedure (Scotland) Act 1995 (c. 46), s. 225.
[7] "SEPA" means the Scottish Environment Protection Agency: s. 105(1) below.
[8] "Inland waters" has the meaning given by s. 30A(1), p. 18 above: s. 56(1) below.
[9] The current fine at level 4 on the standard scale is £2,500: Criminal Procedure (Scotland) Act 1995 (c. 46), s. 225.
[10] "Regulations" defined by s. 105(1), p. 61 below.
[11] "Coastal waters" has the meaning given by s. 30A(1), p. 18 above: s. 56(1) below.
[12] "Prescribed" defined by s. 105(1), p. 61 below.
[13] 1951 c. 66.

(5) This section is subject to section 114 of the Environment Act 1995[1] (delegation or reference of appeals)[2].

*Enforcement notices as respects discharge consents*

**49A.** (1) If SEPA[3] is of the opinion that the holder of a relevant consent[4] is contravening any condition of the consent, or is likely to contravene any such condition, it may serve on him a notice (an "enforcement notice").

(2) An enforcement notice shall—

(*a*) state that SEPA is of the said opinion;

(*b*) specify the matters constituting the contravention or the matters making it likely that the contravention will arise;

(*c*) specify the steps that must be taken to remedy the contravention or, as the case may be, to remedy the matters making it likely that the contravention will arise; and

(*d*) specify the period within which those steps must be taken.

(3) Any person who fails to comply with any requirement imposed by an enforcement notice shall be guilty of an offence and liable—

(*a*) on summary conviction, to imprisonment for a term not exceeding three months or to a fine not exceeding £20,000 or to both;

(*b*) on conviction on indictment, to imprisonment for a term not exceeding two years or to a fine or to both.

(4) If SEPA is of the opinion that proceedings for an offence under subsection (3) above would afford an ineffectual remedy against a person who has failed to comply with the requirements of an enforcement notice, SEPA may take proceedings in any court of competent jurisdiction for the purpose of securing compliance with the notice.

(5) The Secretary of State may, if he thinks fit in relation to any person, give to SEPA directions as to whether it should exercise its powers under this section and as to the steps which must be taken.

(6) In this section—

"relevant consent" means a consent for the purposes of section 30J(7)(a)[5], 34[6] or 49(1) of this Act; and

"the holder", in relation to a relevant consent, is the person who has the consent in question.

*Appeals against enforcement notices*

**49B.** (1) A person upon whom an enforcement notice has been served under section 49A of this Act may appeal to the Secretary of State.

(2) This section is subject to section 114 of the Environment Act 1995[7] (delegation or reference of appeals etc.).

(3) An appeal under this section shall, if and to the extent a requirement to do so is prescribed[8], be advertised in the manner prescribed.

---

[1] P. 489 below.
[2] Subsection (5) added by the Environment Act 1995 (c. 25), s. 120, sch. 22, para. 29(25).
[3] "SEPA" means the Scottish Environment Protection Agency: s. 105(1) below.
[4] "Holder" and "relevant consent" defined by subsection (6) below.
[5] P. 25 above.
[6] P. 29 above.
[7] P. 489 below.
[8] "Prescribed" defined by s. 105(1), p. 61 below.

**(4)** If either party to the appeal so requests or the Secretary of State so decides, an appeal shall be or continue in the form of a hearing (which may, if the person hearing the appeal so decides, be held, or held to any extent, in private).

**(5)** On the determination of an appeal under this section, the Secretary of State may either quash or affirm the enforcement notice and, if he affirms it, may do so either in its original form or with such modifications[1] as he may in the circumstances think fit.

**(6)** The bringing of an appeal under this section shall not have the effect of suspending the operation of the notice appealed against.

**(7)** The period within which and the manner in which appeals under this section are to be brought and the manner in which they are to be considered shall be as prescribed.

*Investigation of water pollution problems arising from closure of mines*

**50.** SEPA[2] shall have power to carry out studies for the purpose of ascertaining—

    (*a*) what problems relating to the pollution of controlled waters[3] may arise or have arisen in consequence of the abandonment of any mine[4,5] or might arise if any such mine were abandoned; and

    (*b*) what steps are likely to be appropriate for the purpose of dealing with the problems and what the cost of taking those steps would be.

*Codes of good agricultural practice*

**51.** **(1)** The Secretary of State may by order made by statutory instrument approve any code of practice issued (whether by him or by another person) for the purpose of—

    (*a*) giving practical guidance to persons engaged in agriculture with respect to activities that may affect controlled waters[6]; and

    (*b*) promoting what appear to him to be desirable practices by such persons for avoiding or minimising the pollution of any such waters,

and may at any time by such an order approve a modification[7] of such a code or withdraw his approval of such a code or modification[8].

**(2)** A contravention of a code of practice as for the time being approved under this section shall not of itself give rise to any criminal or civil liability, but SEPA[9] shall take into account whether there has been or is likely to be any such contravention in determining when and how it should exercise any powers conferred on it by regulations[10] under section 31A of this Act[11].

**(3)** The Secretary of State shall not make an order under this section unless he has first consulted SEPA.

**53–54.** *Repealed by the Environment Act 1995 (c. 25), s. 120, sch. 22, para. 29(28), sch. 24. This amendment came into force on 1 April 1996: S.I. 1996/186.*

---

[1] "Modifications" defined by s. 105(1), p. 61 below.
[2] "SEPA" means the Scottish Environment Protection Agency: s. 105(1) below.
[3] "Controlled waters" has the meaning given by s. 30A(1), p. 18 above: s. 56(1) below.
[4] "Mine" defined by s. 105(1), p. 61 below.
[5] Former words "in its area" repealed by the Environment Act 1995 (c. 25), s. 120, sch. 22, para. 29(27), sch. 24.
[6] "Controlled waters" has the meaning given by s. 30A(1), p. 18 above: s. 56(1) below.
[7] "Modification" defined by s. 105(1), p. 61 below.
[8] The Water (Prevention of Pollution) (Code of Practice) (Scotland) Order 1992, S.I. 1992/395 approved the Code of Good Practice for the Prevention of Environmental Pollution from Agricultural Activity issued on 6 March 1992. The explanatory note sets out that the Code can be obtained from the Scottish Office Agriculture and Fisheries Department, Pentland House, 47 Robb's Loan, Edinburgh EH14 1TW.
[9] "SEPA" means the Scottish Environment Protection Agency: s. 105(1) below.
[10] "Regulations" defined by s. 105(1), p. 61 below.
[11] P. 26 above.

*Supplemental*

**55.** *Repealed by the Environment Act 1995 (c. 25), s. 120, sch. 22, para. 29(28), sch. 24. This amendment came into force on 1 April 1996: S.I. 1996/186.*

*Regulations under this Part*

**55A.** Regulations[1] made under this Part of this Act may provide that any provision of this Part, except this section and sections 43 to 45, shall have effect with such modifications[2] as may be prescribed[3] for the purpose of enabling Her Majesty's Government in the United Kingdom—

    (a) to give effect to any Community obligation or exercise any related right; or

    (b) to give effect to any obligation or exercise any related right under any international agreement to which the United Kingdom is for the time being a party,

and "related right", in relation to an obligation, includes any derogation or other right to make more onerous provisions available in respect of that obligation[4].

*Interpretation etc. of Part II*

**56.** **(1)** Except where the context otherwise requires, in this Part of this Act—

"agriculture" and "agricultural" have the same meanings as in the Agriculture (Scotland) Act 1948[5];

"coastal waters", "controlled waters", "ground waters", "inland waters" and "relevant territorial waters" have the meanings given by section 30A(1) above[6];

"drain" has the same meaning as in the Sewerage (Scotland) Act 1968[7,8];

"effluent" means any liquid, including particles of matter and other substances in suspension in the liquid;

"micro-organism" includes any microscopic biological entity which is capable of replication;

"operations" includes works[9];

"sewage effluent" includes any effluent from sewage disposal, or sewerage, works vested in a sewerage authority[10];

"sewer" has the same meaning as in the Sewerage (Scotland) Act 1968[11];

"sewerage authority" shall be construed in accordance with section 62 of the Local Government etc. (Scotland) Act 1995[12];

"substance" includes micro-organisms and any natural or artificial substance or other matter, whether it is in solid or liquid form or in the form of a gas or vapour;

"trade effluent" includes any effluent which is discharged from premises[13] used for carrying on any trade or industry, other than surface water and domestic sewage;

---

[1] "Regulations" defined by s. 105(1), p. 61 below.

[2] "Modifications" defined by s. 105(1), p. 61 below.

[3] "Prescribed" defined by s. 105(1), p. 61 below. The following regulation has been made under this section:
The Surface Waters (Dangerous Substances) (Classification) (Scotland) Regulations 1992: S.I. 1992/574, p. 659 below.

[4] S. 55A inserted by the Natural Heritage (Scotland) Act 1991 (c. 28), s. 27, sch. 10, para. 7(3). This amendment came into force on 1 October 1991: S.I. 1991/2187.

[5] 1948 c. 45.

[6] P. 18 above.

[7] 1968 c. 47.

[8] The definition of "drain" inserted by the Environment Act 1995 (c. 25), s. 106, sch. 16, para. 8.

[9] The definition of "operations" inserted by the Environment Act 1995 (c. 25), s. 120, sch. 22, para. 29(29).

[10] The definition of "sewage effluent" substituted by the Local Government etc. (Scotland) Act 1994 (c. 39), s. 180(1), sch. 13, para. 95(5)(a). This amendment came into force on 1 April 1996: S.I. 1996/323.

[11] The definition of "sewer" inserted by the Environment Act 1995 (c. 25), s. 106, sch. 16, para. 8.

[12] The definition of "sewerage authority" substituted by the Local Government etc. (Scotland) Act 1994 (c. 39), s. 180(1), sch. 13, para. 95(5)(a).

[13] "Premises" defined by s. 105(1), p. 61 below.

"underground strata" means strata subjacent to the surface of any land;

"water authority" shall be construed in accordance with section 62 of the Local Government etc. (Scotland) Act 1994[1,2];

"watercourse" includes all rivers, streams, ditches, drains, cuts, culverts, dykes, sluices, sewers, and passages through which water flows except mains and other pipes which belong to the water authority or are used by a water authority or any other person for the purposes only of providing a supply of water to any premises.

(2) In this Part of this Act—

(a) any reference to the waters of any loch or pond or of any river or watercourse includes a reference to the bottom, channel or bed of any loch, pond, river or, as the case may be, watercourse which is for the time being dry; and

(b) any reference to water contained in underground strata is a reference to water so contained otherwise than in a sewer, pipe, reservoir, tank or other underground works constructed in any such strata.

(3) For the purposes of the definition of "trade effluent" in subsection (1) above any premises (whether on land or not) wholly or mainly used (whether for profit or not) for agricultural purposes or for the purposes of fish farming or for scientific research or experiment shall be deemed to be (and in the case of fish farms, always to have been) premises used for carrying on a trade.

(4) *Repealed by the Environment Act 1995 (c. 25), s. 120, sch. 22, para. 29(28), sch. 24. This amendment came into force on 1 April 1996: S.I. 1996/186.*

(5) For the purposes of this Part of this Act a notice imposing conditions with respect to discharges which was given by a river purification authority in pursuance of—

(a) Section 28(4) of the Rivers (Prevention of Pollution) (Scotland) Act 1951[3]; or

(b) section 1(5) of the Rivers (Prevention of Pollution) (Scotland) Act 1965[4],

shall be treated as having given the authority's consent in pursuance of the Act in question for those discharges subject to those conditions.

(6) [5]Except as provided by regulations made under this subsection, nothing in this Part of this Act applies to radioactive waste within the meaning of the Radioactive Substances Act 1993[6]; but regulations may—

(a) provide for prescribed[7] provisions of this Part of this Act to have effect with such modifications[8] as the Secretary of State considers appropriate for the purposes of dealing with such radioactive waste;

(b) make such modifications of the Radioactive Substances Act 1993 and any other Act as the Secretary of State considers appropriate in connection with regulations made under paragraph (a) above.

......................................................................................................................................................

[1] 1994 c. 39.
[2] The definition of "water authority" substituted by the Local Government etc. (Scotland) Act 1994 (c. 39), s. 180(1), sch. 13, para. 95(5)(b).
[3] 1951 c. 66.
[4] 1965 c. 13.
[5] Prospective amendment: Subsection (6) substituted by the Environmental Protection Act 1990 (c. 43), s. 162, sch. 15, para. 17. This amendment has not yet come into force. The present wording of subsection (6) is:
(6) Section 30(5) of this Act shall have effect in relation to this Part of this Act as if for any reference to Part I of this Act there were substituted a reference to this Part of this Act.
The Control of Pollution (Radioactive Waste) Scotland Regulations 1991, S.I. 1991/2539, p. 648 below, are made under s. 30(5) as applied by this subsection.
[6] Words "Radioactive Substances Act 1993" in this subsection substituted by the Radioactive Substances Act 1993 (c. 12), s. 49(1), sch. 4, para. 3. This Act came into force on 27 August 1993: s. 51(2).
[7] "Prescribed" defined by s. 105(1), p. 61 below.
[8] "Modifications" defined by s. 105(1), p. 61 below.

## PART III: Noise

Part III is not reproduced. This Part contains provisions under the following headings:

Periodical inspections by local authorities: s. 57

Construction sites: ss. 60–61

Noise in streets: s. 62

Noise abatement zones: ss. 63–67

Noise from plant or machinery: s. 68

Supplemental: ss. 69–84.

The Environment Act 1995 (c. 25), s. 120, sch. 24 provides for the repeal of sections 58, 58A, 58B, 59 and 59A.

## PART IV: Pollution of the Atmosphere

This Part has been repealed by the Clean Air Act 1993 (c. 11), s. 67(3), sch. 6. The Clean Air Act 1993, which consolidates enactments relating to clean air, including this Part, is at p. 333 below.

## PART V: Supplementary Provisions

### Legal proceedings

*Appeals to Crown Court or Court of Session against decisions of magistrates' court or sheriff*

**85.** **(1)** An appeal against any decision of a magistrates' court in pursuance of this Act (other than a decision made in criminal proceedings) shall lie to the Crown Court at the instance of any party to the proceedings in which the decision was given if such an appeal does not lie to the Crown Court by virtue of any other enactment.

**(2)** In Scotland an appeal against any decision to the sheriff in pursuance of this Act (other than a decision made in criminal proceedings) shall lie to the Court of Session at the instance of any party to the proceedings in which the decision was given if such an appeal does not lie to the Court of Session by virtue of any other enactment.

**(3)** Where a person appeals to the Crown Court or the Court of Session against a decision of a magistrates' court or the sheriff dismissing an appeal against a notice served in pursuance of this Act which was suspended pending determination of that appeal, the notice shall again be suspended pending the determination of the appeal to the Crown Court or Court of Session[1,2].

**86.** *Repealed by the Water Act 1989 (c. 15), s. 190(3), sch. 27, pt. I. This amendment came into force on 1 September 1989: s. 194(3)(g), S.I. 1989/1530.*

*Miscellaneous provisions relating to legal proceedings*

**87.** **(1)** When an offence under this Act which has been committed by a body corporate is proved to have been committed with the consent or connivance of, or to be attributable to any neglect on the part of, any director, manager, secretary or other similar officer of the

[1] This section came into force on 1 January 1976 as respects England and Wales: S.I. 1975/2118, and 18 July 1976 as respects Scotland: S.I. 1976/1080.

[2] **Case: section 85** *R v Canterbury Crown Court, ex parte Kent County Council* [1994] Env LR 192.

body corporate or any person who was purporting to act in any such capacity, he as well as the body corporate shall be guilty of that offence and be liable to be proceeded against and punished accordingly.

Where the affairs of a body corporate are managed by its members the preceding provisions of this subsection shall apply in relation to the acts and defaults of a member in connection with his functions of management as if he were a director of the body corporate.

(2) Where the commission by any person of an offence under this Act is due to the act or default of some other person, that other person shall be guilty of the offence; and a person may be charged with and convicted of an offence by virtue of this subsection whether or not proceedings for the offence are taken against any other person.

(3) [1]Notwithstanding anything in section 331 of the Criminal Procedure (Scotland) Act 1975[2,3], summary proceedings in Scotland for any offence under section 30F of this Act or regulations or byelaws made in pursuance of section 31 of this Act[4] may be commenced at any time within one year from the time when the offence was committed, and subsection (3) of section 331 of the said Act of 1975[5] shall apply for the purposes of this subsection[6] as that subsection applies for the purposes of that section.

(4) Where an appeal against a decision of a relevant authority[7] lies to a magistrates' court[8] by virtue of any provision of this Act, it shall be the duty of the authority to include in any document by which it notifies the decision to the person concerned a statement indicating that such an appeal lies as aforesaid and specifying the time within which it must be brought.

(5) Where on an appeal to any court against or arising out of a decision of a relevant authority in pursuance of this Act the court varies or reverses the decision it shall be the duty of the authority to act in accordance with the court's decision.

(6) A judge of any court and a justice of the peace shall not be disqualified from acting in cases arising under this Act by reason of his being, as one of several ratepayers or as one of any other class of persons, liable in common with the others to contribute to or be benefited by any rate or fund out of which any expenses of a relevant authority are to be defrayed[9,10].

*Civil liability for contravention of s. 3(3)*

**88.** (1) Where any damage is caused by poisonous, noxious or polluting waste which has been deposited on land, any person who deposited it or caused or knowingly permitted it to be deposited, in either case so as to commit an offence under section 3(3) or by virtue of section 18(2) of this Act, is liable for the damage except where the damage—

(*a*) was due wholly to the fault of the person who suffered it; or

(*b*) was suffered by a person who voluntarily accepted the risk thereof[11].

[1] The provision in this subsection relating to England and Wales has been repealed by the Environment Act 1995 (c. 25), s. 106, sch. 16, para. 9(a), sch. 24.
[2] 1975 c. 21.
[3] Words "section 331 of the Criminal Procedure (Scotland) Act 1975" substituted by the Environment Act 1995 (c. 25), s. 106, sch. 16, para. 9(b). This reference is construed as including a reference to s. 136 of the Criminal Procedure (Scotland) Act 1995 (c. 46): Criminal Procedure (Consequential Provisions) (Scotland) Act 1995 (c. 40), s. 2(4).
[4] Words "offence under section 30F . . . section 31 of this Act" substituted by the Environment Act 1995 (c. 25), s. 106, sch. 16, para. 9(c).
[5] Words "subsection (3) of section 331 of the said Act of 1975" substituted by the Environment Act 1995 (c. 25), s. 106, sch. 16, para. 9(d). This reference is construed as including a reference to s. 136(3) of the Criminal Procedure

(Scotland) Act 1995 (c. 46).
[6] Former words "in its application to Scotland" repealed by the Environment Act 1995 (c. 25), s. 106, sch. 16, para. 9(e), sch. 24.
[7] "Relevant authority" defined by s. 98, p. 58 below.
[8] In Scotland a reference to the sheriff is substituted for the reference to the magistrates' court: s. 106(6) below.
[9] This section came into force on 1 January 1976 as respects England and Wales: S.I. 1975/2118, and 18 July 1976 as respects Scotland: S.I. 1976/1080.
[10] **Cases: section 87** *Friel v Initial Contract Services* [1994] SLT 1217; *Woodhouse v Walsall Metropolitan Borough Council* [1994] Env LR 30.
[11] Ss. 3 and 18 are contained in Part I of this Act. Part I is not included in this Manual as it has largely been replaced by Part II of the Environmental Protection Act 1990: see note at p. 14 above. For the equivalent provision in the 1990 Act see s. 73 of that Act at p. 157 below.

(2) The matters which under paragraphs (*a*) to (*c*) of subsection (4) of section 3 of this Act may be proved by way of defence to a charge of committing an offence under subsection (3) of that section may be proved also by way of defence to an action brought by virtue of the preceding subsection (the reference in the said paragraph (*a*) to the charge being construed as a reference to the act alleged to give rise to the liability).

(3) In this section—

"damage" includes the death of, or injury to, any person (including any disease and any impairment of physical or mental condition);

"fault" has the same meaning as in the Law Reform (Contributory Negligence) Act 1945[1]; and

"land" includes such water as is mentioned in section 4(4) of this Act.

(4) For the purposes of the following enactments, namely—

(*a*) the Fatal Accidents Acts 1846 to 1959[2];

(*b*) the Law Reform (Contributory Negligence) Act 1945; and

(*c*) the Limitation Act 1980[3],

and for the purposes of any action of damages in Scotland arising out of the death of, or personal injury to, any person, any damage for which a person is liable under subsection (1) of this section shall be treated as due to his fault.

(5) Subsection (1) of this section is without prejudice to any liability which arises apart from the provisions of this section[4].

## Financial provisions

### Expenses and receipts of Secretary of State etc.

89. (1) There shall be paid out of money provided by Parliament—

(*a*) any expenses incurred by the Secretary of State for the purposes of this Act; and

(*b*) any increase attributable to the provisions of this Act in the sums payable under any other Act out of money so provided.

(2) Any sums received by the Secretary of State by virtue of this Act shall be paid into the Consolidated Fund[5].

### Establishment charges and interest in respect of certain expenses of authorities

90. (1) *England and Wales: Repealed by the Water Act 1989 (c. 15), s. 190(3), sch. 27, pt. I. This amendment came into force on 1 September 1989: s. 194(3)(g), S.I. 1989/1530.*

(1) *Scotland:* Where a sum is payable to SEPA[6] by any person by virtue of this Act in respect of the expenses incurred by SEPA, SEPA shall be entitled to recover from that person such a further sum in respect of its establishment charges as appears to SEPA to be reasonable.

(2) *England and Wales:* Where a sum is payable to a[7]

---

[1] 1945 c. 28.

[2] The reference to the Fatal Accidents Acts includes reference to the Fatal Accidents Act 1976: Fatal Accidents Act 1976 (c. 30), s. 6(1), sch. 1, para. 2.

[3] 1980 c. 58. Words "the Limitation Act 1980" substituted by the Limitation Act 1980 (c. 58), s. 40(2), sch. 3, para. 12. This amendment came into force on 1 May 1981: s. 41(2).

[4] This section came into force on 14 June 1976 as respects England and Wales: S.I. 1976/731, and 1 January 1978 as respects Scotland: S.I. 1977/1587.

[5] This section came into force on 1 January 1976 as respects England and Wales: S.I. 1975/2118, and 18 July 1976 as respects Scotland: S.I. 1976/ 1080.

[6] "SEPA" means the Scottish Environment Protection Agency: s. 105(1) below. Words "SEPA" in this subsection substituted by virtue of subsection (3) below.

[7] Words "Where a sum is payable to" substituted by the Water Act 1989 (c. 15), s. 190(1), sch. 25, para. 48(9). This amendment came into force on 1 September 1989: S.I. 1989/1146.

*Scotland:* Where such a sum or further sum as is mentioned in the preceding subsection is payable to SEPA[1] by any person or a sum is payable to any other

relevant authority[2] by any person by virtue of this Act in respect of expenses incurred by the authority or by virtue of section 36 of the Local Government Act 1974[3] in respect of establishment charges related to such expenses or by virtue of section 193 of the Local Government (Scotland) Act 1947[4] in respect of general expenses related to such expenses, then—

(a) the authority and that person may agree that the sum or further sum[5] shall be paid in instalments; and

(b the authority shall be entitled to receive from that person interest on the sum or further sum[5], or on such portion of it as is for the time being unpaid, at such reasonable rate or rates as the authority may determine[6].

(3) In the application of this section to Scotland, for the references to a water authority there shall be substituted references to SEPA[7,8].

## Miscellaneous

*Rights of entry and inspection etc.*

91. (1) Any person authorised in writing in that behalf by a relevant authority[9] may at any reasonable time—

(a) enter upon any land or vessel[10] for the purpose of—

(i) performing any function[11] conferred on the authority or that person by virtue of this Act, or

(ii) determining whether, and if so in what manner, such a function should be performed, or

(iii) determining whether any provision of this Act or of an instrument made by virtue of this Act is being complied with;

(b) carry out such inspections, measurements and tests on the land or vessel or of any articles on it and take away such samples of the land or articles as he considers appropriate for such a purpose.

(2) If it is shown to the satisfaction of a justice of the peace on sworn information in writing—

(a) that admission to any land or vessel which a person is entitled to enter in pursuance of the preceding subsection has been refused to that person or that refusal is apprehended or that the land or vessel is unoccupied or that the occupier is temporarily absent or that the case is one of emergency[12] or that an application for admission would defeat the object of the entry; and

(b) that there is reasonable ground for entry upon the land or vessel for the purpose for which entry is required,

then, subject to the following subsection, the justice may by warrant under his hand authorise that person to enter the land or vessel, if need be by force.

---

[1] In Scotland "SEPA" is substituted for "water authority" by subsection (3) below.

[2] "Relevant authority" defined by s. 98, p. 58 below.

[3] 1974 c. 7.

[4] 1947 c. 43.

[5] *England and Wales:* "or further sum" repealed by the Water Act 1989 (c. 15), s. 190(3), sch. 27, pt. I. This amendment came into force on 1 September 1989: s. 194(3)(g), S.I. 1989/1530.

[6] Words "such reasonable rate or rates as the authority may determine" substituted by the Local Government, Planning and Land Act 1980 (c. 65), s. 1(2), sch. 2, para. 17.

This amendment came into force on 13 November 1980, the date of the Royal Assent.

[7] Word "SEPA" substituted by the Environment Act 1995 (c. 25), s. 120, sch. 22, para. 29(30).

[8] This section came into force on 1 January 1976 as respects England and Wales: S.I. 1975/2118, and 18 July 1976 as respects Scotland: S.I. 1976/1080.

[9] "Relevant authority" defined by s. 98, p. 58 below.

[10] "Vessel" defined by s. 105(1), p. 61 below.

[11] "Function" defined by s. 98, p. 58 below.

[12] For "emergency" see s. 92(7) below.

(3) A justice of the peace shall not issue a warrant in pursuance of the preceding subsection in respect of any land or vessel unless he is satisfied—

(a) that admission to the land or vessel in pursuance of subsection (1) of this section was sought after not less than seven days notice of the intended entry had been served on the occupier; or

(b) that admission to the land or vessel in pursuance of that subsection was sought in an emergency and was refused by or on behalf of the occupier; or

(c) that the land or vessel is unoccupied; or

(d) that an application for admission to the land or vessel would defeat the object of the entry.

(4) A warrant issued in pursuance of this section shall continue in force until the purpose for which the entry is required has been satisfied.

(5) In the application of this section to Scotland—

(a) *Repealed by the Environment Act 1995 (c. 25), s. 120, sch. 22, para. 29(31), sch. 24. This amendment came into force on 1 April 1996: S.I. 1996/186.*

(b) any reference to a justice of the peace shall include a reference to the sheriff[1,2].

........................................................................................................................................................

*Provisions supplementary to s. 91*

**92.** (1) A person authorised to enter upon any land or vessel[3] in pursuance of the preceding section shall, if so required, produce evidence of his authority before he enters upon the land or vessel.

(2) A person so authorised may take with him on to the land or vessel in question such other persons and such equipment as may be necessary.

(3) Admission to any land or vessel used for residential purposes and admission with heavy equipment to any other land or vessel shall not, except in an emergency[4] or in a case where the land or vessel is unoccupied, be demanded as of right in pursuance of subsection (1) of the preceding section unless a notice[5] of the intended entry has been served on the occupier not less than seven days before the demand.

(4) A person who, in the exercise of powers conferred on him by virtue of the preceding section or this section, enters upon any land or vessel which is unoccupied or of which the occupier is temporarily absent shall leave the land or vessel as effectually secured against trespassers as he found it.

(5) It shall be the duty of a relevant authority[6] to make full compensation to any person who has sustained damage by reason of—

(a) the exercise by a person authorised by the authority of any powers conferred on the person so authorised by virtue of the preceding section or this section; or

(b) the failure of a person so authorised to perform the duty imposed on him by the preceding subsection,

except where the damage is attributable to the default of the person who sustained it; and any dispute as to a person's entitlement to compensation in pursuance of this subsection or as to the amount of the compensation shall be determined by arbitration[7].

(6) A person who wilfully obstructs another person acting in the exercise of any powers conferred on the other person by virtue of the preceding section or this section shall be guilty of

---

[1] This section came into force on 1 January 1976 as respects England and Wales: S.I. 1975/2118, and 18 July 1976 as respects Scotland: S.I. 1976/1080.

[2] **Cases: section 91** *Polymeric Treatments Ltd v Walsall Metropolitan Borough Council* [1993] Env LR 427; *Gotech Industrial and Environmental Services v Friel* [1995] SCCR 22.

[3] "Vessel" defined by s. 105(1), p. 61 below.

[4] For "emergency" see subsection (7) below.

[5] "Notice" defined by s. 105(1), p. 61 below.

[6] "Relevant authority" defined by s. 98, p. 58 below.

[7] For the application of this provision in Scotland, see s. 106(5), p. 62 below.

an offence and liable on summary conviction to a fine not exceeding level 3 on the standard scale[1].

(7) In the preceding section and this section any reference to an emergency is a reference to a case where a person requiring entry to any land or vessel has reasonable cause to believe that circumstances exist which are likely to endanger life or health and that immediate entry to the land or vessel is necessary to verify the existence of those circumstances or to ascertain their cause or to effect a remedy[2,3].

*Power of authorities to obtain information*

**93.** (1) Subject to the following subsection, a relevant authority[4] may serve on any person a notice[5] requiring him to furnish to the authority, within a period or at times specified in the notice and in a form so specified, any information so specified which the authority reasonably considers that it needs for the purposes of any function conferred on the authority by this Act.

(2) Provision may be made by regulations for restricting the information which may be required in pursuance of the preceding subsection and for determining the form in which the information is to be so required.

(3) A person who—

(*a*) fails without reasonable excuse to comply with the requirements of a notice served on him in pursuance of this section; or

(*b*) in furnishing any information in compliance with such a notice, makes any statement which he knows to be false or misleading in a material particular or recklessly makes any statement which is false or misleading in a material particular,

shall be guilty of an offence.

(3A) A person guilty of any offence under this section shall be liable—

(*a*) on summary conviction, to a fine not exceeding the statutory maximum; or

(*b*) on conviction or indictment, to a fine or to imprisonment for a term not exceeding two years, or to both[6].

(4) In the application of this section to Scotland, in subsection (1) the reference to this Act shall include a reference to the Rivers (Prevention of Pollution) (Scotland) Act 1951[7] and a reference to Part II of the Natural Heritage (Scotland) Act 1991[8,9].[10,11]

*Prohibition of disclosure of information*

**94.** (1) If a person discloses information relating to any trade secret used in carrying on a particular undertaking and the information has been given to him or obtained by him by virtue

---

[1] Words "level 3 on the standard scale" substituted by the Criminal Justice Act 1982 (c. 48), ss. 38, 46 as respects England and Wales and the Criminal Procedure (Consequential Provisions) (Scotland) Act 1995 (c. 40), s. 3(1), sch. 1 as respects Scotland. The current fine at level 3 on the standard scale is £1,000: Criminal Justice Act 1991 (c. 53), s. 17 (England and Wales); Criminal Procedure (Scotland) Act 1995 (c. 46), s. 225 (Scotland).

[2] This section came into force on 1 January 1976 as respects England and Wales: S.I. 1975/2118, and 18 July 1976 as respects Scotland: S.I. 1976/1080.

[3] **Case: section 92** *Polymeric Treatments Ltd v Walsall Metropolitan Borough Council* [1993] Env LR 427.

[4] "Relevant authority" defined by s. 98, p. 58 below.

[5] "Notice" defined by s. 105(1), p. 61 below.

[6] Subsection (3) substituted by the Environment Act 1995 (c. 25), s. 112, sch. 19, para. 1(3).

[7] 1951 c. 66.

[8] 1991 c. 28.

[9] Words "and a reference . . . 1991" inserted by the Natural Heritage (Scotland) Act 1991 (c. 28), s. 27, sch. 10, para. 7(4). This amendment came into force on 1 October 1991: S.I. 1991/2187.

[10] This section came into force on 1 January 1976 as respects England and Wales: S.I. 1975/2118, and 18 July 1976 as respects Scotland: S.I. 1976/1080.

[11] **Case: section 93** *JB and M Motor Haulage Ltd v London Waste Regulation Authority* [1993] Env LR 243.

of this Act he shall, subject to the following subsection, be guilty of an offence and liable on summary conviction to a fine not exceeding level 5 on the standard scale.[1]

(2) A person shall not be guilty of an offence under the preceding subsection by virtue of the disclosure of any information if—

(a) the disclosure is made—

    (i) in the performance of his duty, or

    (ii) in pursuance of section 79(1)(b) of this Act, or

    (iii) with the consent in writing of a person having a right to disclose the information; or

(b) the information is of a kind prescribed[2] for the purposes of this paragraph and, if regulations[3] made for those purposes provide that information of that kind may only be disclosed in pursuance of the regulations to prescribed persons, the disclosure is to a prescribed person.

(3) In the application of this section to Scotland, in subsection (1) the reference to this Act shall include a reference to the Rivers (Prevention of Pollution) (Scotland) Act 1951[4] and a reference to Part II of the Natural Heritage (Scotland) Act 1991[5,6,7].

*Service of documents on and by certain undertakers*

**95.** Section 187 of the Water Act 1989[8] (service of documents) shall apply for the purposes of the service of any document required or authorised by virtue of this Act to be served on or by a water undertaker or sewerage undertaker as it applies for the purposes of the service of any document required or authorised by virtue of that Act to be served on or by any person[9].

*Local inquiries*

**96.** (1) The Secretary of State may cause a local inquiry to be held in any case in which he considers it appropriate for such an inquiry to be held either in connection with a provision of this Act or with a view to preventing or dealing with pollution other than air pollution[10] or noise at any place.

(2) Subsections (2) to (5) of section 250 of the Local Government Act 1972[11] (which contain supplementary provisions with respect to local inquiries held in pursuance of that section) shall, without prejudice to the generality of subsection (1) of that section, apply to inquiries in England and Wales in pursuance of the preceding subsection as they apply to inquiries in pursuance of that section[12].

(3) Subsections (2) to (8) of section 210 of the Local Government (Scotland) Act 1973[13] (local inquiries) shall, without prejudice to the generality of subsection (1) of that section, apply to

[1] Words "level 5 on the standard scale" substituted by the Criminal Justice Act 1982 (c. 48), ss. 38, 46 as respects England and Wales and the Criminal Procedure (Consequential Provisions) (Scotland) Act 1995 (c. 40), s. 3(1), sch. 1 as respects Scotland. The current fine at level 5 on the standard scale is £5,000: Criminal Justice Act 1991 (c. 53), s. 17 (England and Wales); Criminal Procedure (Scotland) Act 1995 (c. 46), s. 225 (Scotland).

[2] "Prescribed" defined by s. 105(1), p. 61 below.

[3] "Regulations" defined by s. 105(1), p. 61 below.

[4] 1951 c. 66.

[5] 1991 c. 28.

[6] Words "and a reference ... 1991" inserted by the Natural Heritage (Scotland) Act 1991 (c. 28), s. 27, sch. 11, para. 7(4). This amendment came into force on 1 October 1991: S.I. 1991/2187.

[7] This section came into force on 1 January 1976 as respects England and Wales: S.I. 1975/2118 and, save for subsection (2)(a)(ii), on 18 July 1976 as respects Scotland: S.I. 1976/1080. Subsection (2)(a)(ii) came into force in Scotland on 31 January 1985: S.I. 1986/70.

[8] 1989 c. 15.

[9] This section substituted by the Water Act 1989 (c. 15), s. 190(1), sch. 25, para. 48(10). This amendment came into force on 1 September 1989: S.I. 1989/1146.

[10] Words "other than air pollution" inserted by the Clean Air Act 1993 (c. 11), s. 67(1), sch. 4, para. 2. This amendment came into force on 27 August 1993: s. 68(2).

[11] 1972 c. 70.

[12] Former words "but as if the reference to a local authority in subsection (4) included a reference to a water authority" repealed by the Water Act 1989 (c. 150), s. 190(3), sch. 27, pt. I. This amendment came into force on 1 September 1989: s. 194(3)(g), S.I. 1989/1530.

[13] 1973 c. 65.

inquiries in Scotland in pursuance of subsection (1) of this section as they apply to inquiries held in pursuance of that section[1].[2]

## Default powers

**97.** (1) If the Secretary of State is satisfied that any other relevant authority[3] has failed to perform any functions[4] which it ought to have performed, he may make an order declaring the authority to be in default.

(2) An order made by virtue of the preceding subsection which declares an authority to be in default may, for the purpose of remedying the default, direct the authority (hereafter in this section referred to as "the defaulting authority") to perform such of its functions as are specified in the order and may specify the manner in which and the time or times within which those functions are to be performed by the authority.

(3) If the defaulting authority fails to comply with any direction contained in such an order the Secretary of State may, instead of enforcing the order by mandamus, make an order transferring to himself such of the functions of the authority as he thinks fit.

(4) Where any functions of the defaulting authority are transferred in pursuance of the preceding subsection, the amount of any expenses which the Secretary of State certifies were incurred by him in performing those functions shall on demand be paid to him by the defaulting authority.

(5) Any expenses which in pursuance of the preceding subsection are required to be paid by the defaulting authority in respect of any functions transferred in pursuance of this section shall be defrayed by the authority in the like manner, and shall be debited to the like account, as if the functions had not been transferred and the expenses had been incurred by the authority in performing them; and the authority shall have the like powers for the purpose of raising any money required in pursuance of this subsection as the authority would have had for the purpose of raising money required for defraying expenses incurred for the purposes of the functions in question.

(6) An order transferring any functions of the defaulting authority in pursuance of subsection (3) of this section may provide for the transfer to the Secretary of State of such of the property, rights, liabilities and obligations of the authority as he considers appropriate; and where such an order is revoked the Secretary of State may, by the revoking order or a subsequent order, make such provision as he considers appropriate with respect to any property, rights, liabilities and obligations held by him for the purposes of the transferred functions.

(7) The Secretary of State may by order vary or revoke any order previously made by him in pursuance of this section.

(8) In this section "functions", in relation to an authority, means functions conferred on the authority by virtue of this Act.

(9) This section shall not apply to Scotland[5].

## Interpretation of Part V

**98.** In this Part of this Act—

"functions" includes powers and duties; and

"relevant authority" means—

---

[1] Former words "but as if the reference to a local authority in subsection (7) included a reference to a river purification authority" repealed by the Environment Act 1995 (c. 25), s. 120, sch. 22, para. 29(32), sch. 24.
[2] This section came into force on 1 January 1976 as respects England and Wales: S.I. 1975/2118, and 18 July 1976 as respects Scotland: S.I. 1976/1080.
[3] "Relevant authority" defined by s. 98 below.
[4] "Functions" defined by subsection (8) of this section and s. 98 below.
[5] This section came into force on 1 January 1976: S.I. 1975/2118.

(a)  in England[1], the Secretary of State,[2] a county council,[3] a district council, a London borough council, the Common Council of the City of London, the Sub-Treasurer of the Inner Temple and the Under Treasurer of the Middle Temple[4], and, for the purposes of sections 91 to 93[5] of this Act, a sewerage undertaker[6]; and

(aa)  in Wales, the Secretary of State, a county council or a county borough council and, for the purposes of sections 91 to 93 of this Act, a sewerage undertaker; and[7]

(b)  in Scotland—

    (i)  as respects sections 91 and 92, a council constituted under section 2 of the Local Government etc. (Scotland) Act 1994[8]; and

    (ii)  as respects this Part other than those sections, the Secretary of State, SEPA[9] or a council constituted under section 2 of the Local Government etc. (Scotland) Act 1994[10].[11]

# PART VI: Miscellaneous and General

## Miscellaneous

### Alteration of penalties

**99.** The enactments mentioned in Schedule 2 to this Act[12] shall have effect subject to the provisions of that Schedule (which alter the penalties for the offences to which those enactments relate)[13].

**100.** *Repealed by the Environmental Protection Act 1990 (c. 43), s. 162(2), sch. 16, pt. IX. This amendment came into force on 1 January 1991: s. 164(2). S. 162(5) of the Environmental Protection Act 1990 provides that any regulations made under this section shall have effect as if made under s. 140 of the 1990 Act, p. 200 below.*

### Disposal of waste etc by Atomic Energy Authority

**101.** Without prejudice to the powers of the United Kingdom Atomic Energy Authority apart from this section, the Authority shall have power—

(a)  to engage in the United Kingdom and elsewhere in such activities relating to the treatment or disposal of waste and other matter as the Secretary of State may from time to time specify by notice given to the Authority; and

---

[1] Former words "and Wales" repealed by the Local Government (Wales) Act 1994 (c. 19), s. 22(3), sch. 9, para. 10(4), s. 66(8), sch. 18. This amendment came into force on 1 April 1996: S.I. 1996/396.

[2] Former words "a water authority" repealed by the Water Act 1989 (c. 15), s. 190(3), sch. 27, pt. I. This amendment came into force on 1 September 1989: s. 194(3)(g), S.I. 1989/1530.

[3] Former words "the Greater London Council" repealed by the Local Government Act 1985 (c. 51), s. 102(2), sch. 17. This amendment came into force on 1 April 1986: ss. 1(2), 102(3).

[4] The Waste Regulation and Disposal (Authorities) Order 1985, S.I. 1985/1884, art. 5(1), sch. 2, para. 12 provides that this section shall have effect as if the words ", any authority established by the Waste Regulation and Disposal (Authorities) Order 1985" were inserted here.

[5] P. 54 above.

[6] Words "and, for the purposes . . . undertaker" inserted by the Water Act 1989 (c. 15), s. 190(1), sch. 25, para. 48(11). This amendment came into force on 1 September 1989: S.I. 1989/1146.

[7] Paragraph (aa) inserted by the Local Government (Wales) Act 1994 (c. 19), s. 22(3), sch. 9, para. 10(4). This amendment came into force on 1 April 1996: S.I. 1996/396.

[8] 1994 c. 39.

[9] "SEPA" means the Scottish Environment Protection Agency: s. 105(1) below.

[10] Paragraph (b) substituted by the Environment Act 1995 (c. 25), s. 120, sch. 22, para. 29(33).

[11] This section came into force on 1 January 1976 as respects England and Wales: S.I. 1975/2118, and 18 July 1976 as respects Scotland: S.I. 1976/1080.

[12] Schedule 2 is not reproduced.

[13] This section came into force on 1 January 1976: S.I. 1975/2118.

(*b*) to do anything which appears to the Authority to be appropriate for the purpose of exercising the powers conferred on the Authority by the preceding paragraph[1].

*Power to give effect to international agreements*

**102.** (1) Regulations[2] may provide that any provision of this Act, except this section, shall have effect with such modifications[3] as are prescribed[4] with a view to enabling the Government of the United Kingdom to give effect to any provision made by or under any international agreement to which the government is for the time being a party[5].

(2) The Secretary of State may make, to the Commission established by the Convention for the Prevention of Marine Pollution from Land-based Sources which was signed at Paris on behalf of the Government of the United Kingdom on 4 June 1974[6], such payments towards the expenses of the Commission as he may with the approval of the Treasury determine[7].

**103** *Repealed by the Clean Air Act 1993 (c. 110), s. 67(3), sch. 6. This amendment came into force on 27 August 1993: s. 68(2).*

## General

*Orders and regulations*

**104.** (1) Any power conferred by this Act (except sections[8] 63 and 65(6)) to make an order or regulations[9]—

(*a*) includes power to make different provision by the order or regulations for different circumstances and to include in the order or regulations such incidental, supplemental and transitional provisions as the person making the order or regulations considers appropriate in connection with the order or regulations; and

(*b*) shall be exercisable by statutory instrument except in the case of the powers conferred by section 97 of this Act[10];

and any statutory instrument made by virtue of this subsection, except an instrument containing only regulations made by virtue of section 18 of this Act or an order made by virtue of section 44(5) or 109(2)[11] of this Act, shall be subject to annulment in pursuance of a resolution of either House of Parliament.

(2) No regulations shall be made by virtue of section 18 of this Act and no order shall be made by virtue of section 52[12] of this Act unless a draft of the regulations or order has been approved by a resolution of each House of Parliament[13].

(3) *Repealed by the Water Act 1989 (c. 15), sch. 27, pt. I. This amendment extends to Scotland only. As respects England and Wales this subsection refers to regulations made under s. 31(5) which has now been repealed.*

[1] This section came into force on 1 January 1976: S.I. 1975/2118.

[2] "Regulations" defined by s. 105(1), p. 61 below.

[3] "Modifications" defined by s. 105(1), p. 61 below.

[4] "Prescribed" defined by s. 105(1), p. 61 below.

[5] The following regulations have been made under this section:
The Bathing Waters (Classification) (Scotland) Regulations 1991: S.I. 1991/1609, p. 626 below;
The Waste Management Licensing Regulations 1994: S.I. 1994/1056, p. 675 below.

[6] Cmnd. 7251; Treaty Series No. 64/1978.

[7] This section came into force on 1 January 1976: S.I. 1975/2118.

[8] Former word "59" repealed by the Environment Act 1995 (c. 25), s. 120, sch. 22, para. 29(34), sch. 24.

[9] "Regulations" defined by s. 105(1), p. 61 below.

[10] P. 58 above.

[11] Words "section 44(5) or 109(2)" substituted by the Water Act 1989 (c. 15), s. 169, sch. 23, para. 7. This amendment came into force on 1 September 1989: s. 194(3)(e), S.I. 1989/1530. Whilst this amendment extends to Scotland only, the references omitted by this substitution, s. 33(4), 52 and 53, have been repealed as respects England and Wales.

[12] Former words "or 53" repealed by the Water Act 1989 (c. 15), s. 190(3), sch. 27, pt. I. This amendment came into force on 1 September 1989: s. 194(3)(g), S.I. 1989/1530. This amendment extends to Scotland only: s. 194(8)(d); as respects England and Wales, s. 53 has been repealed.

[13] This section came into force on 12 December 1974; S.I. 1974/2039.

*Interpretation etc—general*

**105.** (1) In this Act—

"the Alkali Act" means the Alkali, &c. Works Regulation Act 1906[1];

"county", "county borough"[2] and "district", except in relation to Scotland, have the same meanings as in the Local Government Act 1972[3];

"mine" and "quarry" have the same meanings as in the Mines and Quarries Act 1954[4];

"modifications" includes additions, omissions and amendments and "modify" and cognate expressions shall be construed accordingly;

"notice" means notice in writing;

"owner", except in relation to Scotland, means the person for the time being receiving the rackrent of the premises in connection with which the word is used, whether on his own account or as agent or trustee for another person, or who would so receive the rackrent if the premises were let at a rackrent;

"premises" includes land;

"prescribed" means prescribed by regulations;

"regulations" means regulations made by the Secretary of State;

"road" (except where the context otherwise requires) has the same meaning as in Part IV of the New Roads and Street Works Act 1991[5];

"roads authority" has the same meaning as in the Roads (Scotland) Act 1984[6];

"SEPA" means the Scottish Environment Protection Agency[7];

"trade effluent" includes any liquid (either with or without particles of matter in suspension in it) which is discharged from premises used for carrying on any trade or industry, other than surface water and domestic sewage, and for the purposes of this definition any premises wholly or mainly used (whether for profit or not) for agricultural or horticultural purposes or for scientific research or experiment shall be deemed to be premises used for carrying on a trade; and

"vessel" includes a hovercraft within the meaning of the Hovercraft Act 1968[8].

(2) Except so far as this Act expressly provides otherwise and subject to the provisions of section 33 of the Interpretation Act 1889[9] (which relates to offences under two or more laws), nothing in this Act—

(*a*) confers a right of action in any civil proceedings (other than proceedings for the recovery of a fine) in respect of any contravention of this Act or an instrument made in pursuance of this Act;

(*b*) affects any restriction imposed by or under any other enactment, whether public, local or private; or

(*c*) derogates from any right of action or other remedy (whether civil or criminal) in proceedings instituted otherwise than under this Act.

[1] 1906 c. 14.
[2] Words "county borough" inserted by the Local Government (Wales) Act 1994 (c. 19), s. 22(3), sch. 9, para. 10(5). This amendment came into force on 1 April 1996: S.I. 1996/396.
[3] 1972 c. 70.
[4] 1954 c. 70.
[5] 1991 c. 22. The definition of "road" inserted by the Roads (Scotland) Act 1984 (c. 54), s. 156(1), sch. 9, para. 74(6) and amended by the New Roads and Street Works Act 1991 (c. 22), s. 168(1), sch. 9, pt. IV, para. 105. The amendment made by the 1991 Act came into force on 1 January 1993: S.I. 1992/2990. This definition applies to Scotland only: Roads (Scotland) Act 1984, s. 157(4).

[6] 1984 c. 54. The definition of "roads authority" inserted by the Roads (Scotland) Act 1984 (c. 54), s. 156(1), sch. 9, para. 74(6). This amendment came into force on 1 January 1985: s. 157(2). This definition applies to Scotland only: s. 157(4).
[7] The definition of "SEPA" inserted by the Environment Act 1995 (c. 25), s. 120, sch. 22, para. 29(35).
[8] 1968 c. 59.
[9] S. 18 of the Interpretation Act 1978 (c. 30) has replaced s. 33 of the Interpretation Act 1889: Interpretation Act 1978, s. 22, sch. 2, pt. I.

(3) Subject to subsections (3A) to (3D) below, this Act shall bind the Crown.

(3A) No contravention by the Crown of any provision made by or under this Act shall make the Crown criminally liable; but the Court of Session may, on the application of—

(*a*) the Scottish Environment Protection Agency; or

(*b*) any other public or local authority charged with enforcing that provision,

declare unlawful any act or omission of the Crown which constitutes such a contravention.

(3B) Notwithstanding anything in subsection (3A) above, any provision made by or under this Act shall apply to persons in the public service of the Crown as it applies to other persons.

(3C) If the Secretary of State certifies that it appears to him, as respects any Crown premises and any powers of entry exercisable in relation to them specified in the certificate, that it is requisite or expedient that, in the interests of national security, the powers should not be exercisable in relation to those premises, those powers shall not be exercisable in relation to those premises; and in this subsection "Crown premises" means premises held or used by or on behalf of the Crown.

(3D) Nothing in this section shall be taken as in any way affecting Her Majesty in her private capacity[1].

(4) References in this Act to any enactment are references to it as amended by or under any other enactment[2].

*General application to Scotland*

**106.** (1) The provisions of this section shall, in addition to any express provision for the application to Scotland of any provision of this Act, have effect for the general application of this Act to Scotland.

(2) *Repealed by the Environment Act 1995 (c. 25), s. 120, sch. 24. This amendment came into force on 1 April 1996: S.I. 1996/186.*

(3) *Repealed by the Local Government (Scotland) Act 1994 (c. 39), s. 180(2), sch. 14. This amendment came into force on 1 April 1996: S.I. 1996/323.*

(4) *Repealed by the Roads (Scotland) Act 1994 (c. 54), s. 156, sch. 9, para. 74(7), sch. 11. This amendment came into force on 1 January 1985: s. 157(2).*

(5) Any question which is required by any provision of this Act to be determined by arbitration shall be determined by a single arbiter appointed, in default of agreement between the parties concerned, by the Secretary of State on the application of any of the parties.

(6) For any reference in this Act to a magistrates' court there shall be substituted a reference to the sheriff.

(7) For any reference in this Act to a port health authority there shall be substituted a reference to a port local authority constituted under Part X of the Public Health (Scotland) Act 1897[3].

(8) For any reference in this Act to the London Gazette there shall be substituted a reference to the Edinburgh Gazette.

(9) In this Act "owner" means the person for the time being entitled to receive or who would, if the same were let, be entitled to receive, the rents of the premises in connection with which the word is used and includes a trustee, factor, tutor or curator, and, in the case of public or municipal property, includes the persons to whom the management thereof is entrusted[4].

---

[1] Subsections (3)–(3D) substituted for s. 105(3), as it had effect in Scotland, by the Environment Act 1995 (c. 25), s. 116, sch. 21, para. 4. S. 105(3), in relation to England and Wales, is not reproduced.

[2] This section came into force on 12 December 1974: S.I.

1974/2039.

[3] 1897 c. 38.

[4] This section came into force on 1 January 1976: S.I. 1975/2118.

*Application to Isles of Scilly*

**107.** This Act shall have effect in its application to the Isles of Scilly with such modifications[1] as the Secretary of State may by order specify, and the Secretary of State may by order vary or revoke any order previously made in pursuance of this section[2].

*Minor and consequential amendments of enactments, and repeals*

**108.** (1) The enactments specified in Schedule 3 to this Act[3] shall have effect subject to the amendments there specified (which are minor amendments and amendments consequential on provisions of this Act).

(2) The enactments mentioned in the first and second columns of Schedule 4 to this Act[4] are hereby repealed to the extent specified in the third column of that Schedule.

(3) The Secretary of State may by order repeal or amend any provision of any local Act passed before this Act (including an Act confirming a provisional order) or of any order or other instrument made under an Act so passed if it appears to him that the provision is inconsistent with, or has become unnecessary or requires alteration in consequence of, any provision of this Act or corresponds to any provision repealed by this Act or relates to trade effluent[5].

*Short title, commencement and extent*

**109.** (1) This Act may be cited as the Control of Pollution Act 1974.

(2) This Act shall come into force on such day as the Secretary of State may by order appoint; and—

(*a*) without prejudice to the generality of section 104(1)(*a*) of this Act, different days may be appointed in pursuance of this subsection for different provisions of this Act and for such different purposes of the same provision as may be specified in the order;

(*b*) any provision appointing a day in pursuance of this subsection may be revoked or varied by an order made by the Secretary of State which comes into force before that day[6].

(3) This Act, except sections [7]100 and 101 and this section, does not extend to Northern Ireland[8].

---

[1] "Modifications" defined by s. 105(1), p. 61 above.
[2] This section came into force on 12 December 1974: S.I. 1974/2039.
[3] Schedule 3 is not reproduced.
[4] Schedule 4 is not reproduced.
[5] "Trade effluent" defined by s. 105(1), p. 61 above.
[6] The commencement dates in respect of Parts IA and II are set out at the beginning of those Parts at pp. 14 and 17 above respectively; the commencement dates in respect of Parts V and VI are set out at the end of each section.
[7] Former words "75, 77" repealed by the Clean Air Act 1993 (c. 11), s. 67(3), sch. 6. This amendment came into force on 27 August 1993: s. 68(2).
[8] This section came into force on 12 December 1974: S.I. 1974/2039.

# SCHEDULES

## SCHEDULE 1A[1]

ORDERS DESIGNATING NITRATE SENSITIVE AREAS: SCOTLAND

### PART I

APPLICATIONS BY SEPA FOR DESIGNATION ORDERS

*Orders made only on application*

1. (1) Subject to sub-paragraph (2) below, the Secretary of State shall not make an order under section 31B of this Act[2] by virtue of which any land is designated as a nitrate sensitive area, except with the consent of the Treasury and on an application which—

   (a) has been made by SEPA[3] in accordance with paragraph 2 below; and

   (b) by virtue of sub-paragraph (2)(a) of that paragraph identifies the controlled waters[4] with respect to which that land is so comprised by the order.

   (2) This paragraph shall not apply to an order which reproduces or amends an existing order without adding any land appearing to the Secretary of State to constitute a significant area to the land already comprised in the areas for the time being designated as nitrate sensitive areas.

*Procedure for applications*

2. (1) SEPA shall not, for the purposes of paragraph 1 above, apply for the making of any order under section 31B of this Act, by which any land would be comprised in the areas for the time being designated as nitrate sensitive areas unless it appears to SEPA—

   (a) that pollution is or is likely to be caused by the entry of nitrate into controlled waters as a result of, or of anything done in connection with, the use of particular land for agricultural[5] purposes; and

   (b) that the provisions for the time being in force in relation to those waters and that land are not sufficient, in the opinion of SEPA, for preventing or controlling such an entry of nitrate into those waters.

   (2) An application under this paragraph shall identify—

   (a) the controlled waters appearing to SEPA to be the waters which the nitrate is entering or is likely to enter; and

   (b) the land appearing to SEPA to be the land the use of which for agricultural purposes, or the doing of anything in connection with whose use for agricultural purposes, is resulting or is likely to result in the entry of nitrate into those waters.

   (3) An application under this paragraph shall be made by serving a notice containing the application on the Secretary of State.

---

[1] This schedule inserted by the Water Act 1989 (c. 15), s. 169, sch. 23, para. 8. This amendment came into force on 1 September 1989: s. 194(3)(e), S.I. 1989/1530.

[2] P. 27 above.

[3] "SEPA" means the Scottish Environment Protection Agency: s. 105(1) above. Words "SEPA" in this schedule substituted by the Environment Act 1995 (c. 25), s. 120, sch. 22, para. 29(2) and (10).

[4] "Controlled waters" has the meaning given by s. 30A(1), p. 18 above: s. 56(1) above.

[5] "Agricultural" defined by s. 56(1), p. 49 above.

# Part II

## Orders Containing Mandatory Provisions Etc.

### *Publication of proposal for order containing mandatory provisions*

**3.** (1)  This paragraph applies where the Secretary of State proposes to make an order under section 31B of this Act[1] which—

(*a*)  makes or modifies[2] any such provision as is authorised by subsection (3)(a) of that section; and

(*b*)  in doing so, contains provision which is not of one of the following descriptions, that is to say—

   (i)  provision reproducing existing provisions without modification and in relation to substantially the same area; and

   (ii)  provision modifying any existing provisions so as to make them less onerous.

(2)  The Secretary of State shall, before making any such order as is mentioned in sub-paragraph (1) above—

(*a*)  publish a notice with respect to the proposed order at least once in each of two successive weeks, in one or more newspapers circulating in the locality in relation to which the proposed order will have effect;

(*b*)  not later than the date on which that notice is first published, serve a copy of the notice on—

   (i)  SEPA;

   (ii)  every local authority[3] whose area includes the whole or any part of that locality; and

   (iii)  in the case of an order containing any such provision as is authorised by section 31B(3)(b) of this Act, such owners[4] and occupiers of agricultural[5] land in that locality as appear to the Secretary of State to be likely to be affected by the obligations in respect of which payments are to be made under that provision;

and

(*c*)  publish a notice in the Edinburgh Gazette which—

   (i)  names every local authority on whom a notice is required to be served under this paragraph;

   (ii)  specifies a place where a copy of the proposed order and of any relevant map or plan may be inspected; and

   (iii)  gives the name of every newspaper in which the notice required by virtue of paragraph (a) above was published and the date of an issue containing the notice.

(3)  The notice required by virtue of sub-paragraph (2)(a) above to be published with respect to any proposed order shall—

(*a*)  state the general effect of the proposed order;

(*b*)  specify a place where a copy of the proposed order and of any relevant map or plan may be inspected by any person free of charge at all reasonable times during the period of forty-two days beginning with the date of the first publication of the notice; and

(*c*)  state that any person may, within that period, by notice to the Secretary of State object to the making of the order.

### *Supply of copies of proposed orders*

**4.**  The Secretary of State shall, at the request of any person and on payment by that person of such charge (if any) as the Secretary of State may reasonably require, furnish that person with a copy of any proposed order of which notice has been published under paragraph 3 above.

---

[1] P. 27 above.
[2] "Modifies" defined by s. 105(1), p. 61 above.
[3] "Local authority" defined by para. 8 below.
[4] "Owner" defined by s. 106(9), p. 62 above.
[5] "Agricultural" defined by s. 56(1), p. 49 above.

## *Modifications of proposals*

**5.** (1) Where notices with respect to any proposed order have been published and served in accordance with paragraph 3 above and the period of forty-two days mentioned in sub-paragraph (3)(b) of that paragraph has expired, the Secretary of State may make the order either in the proposed terms or, subject to sub-paragraph (2) below (but without any further compliance with paragraph 3 above), in those terms as modified in such manner as he thinks fit, or may decide not to make any order.

(2) The Secretary of State shall not make such a modification of a proposed order of which notice has been so published and served as he considers is likely adversely to affect any persons unless he has given such notices as he considers appropriate for enabling those persons to object to the modification.

(3) Subject to sub-paragraph (2) above and to the service of notices of the proposed modification on such local authorities as appear to him to be likely to be interested in it, the modifications that may be made by the Secretary of State include any modification of the area designated by the proposed order as a nitrate sensitive area.

## *Consideration of objections etc.*

**6.** Without prejudice to section 96 of this Act[1], where notices with respect to any proposed order have been published and served in accordance with paragraph 3 above, the Secretary of State may, if he considers it appropriate to do so, hold a local inquiry before deciding whether or not to make the proposed order or to make it with modifications.

## *Consent of Treasury for payment provisions*

**7.** The consent of the Treasury shall be required for the making of any order under section 31B of this Act the making of which does not require the consent of the Treasury by virtue of paragraph 1 above but which contains any such provision as is authorised by subsection (3)(b) of that section.

**8.** In this Part, "local authority" means a council constituted under section 2 of the Local Government etc. (Scotland) Act 1994[2].

---

[1] P. 57 above.
[2] 1994 c. 39. Words "council . . . 1994" substituted by the Local Government etc. (Scotland) Act 1994 (c. 39), sch. 13, para. 95(10). This amendment came into force on 1 April 1996: S.I. 1996/323.

# Salmon and Freshwater Fisheries Act 1975

Chapter 51

An Act to consolidate the Salmon and Freshwater Fisheries Act 1923 and certain other enactments relating to salmon and freshwater fisheries, and to repeal certain obsolete enactments relating to such fisheries.

[1st August 1975[1]]

This Act comprises the following six Parts:

I   Prohibition of certain modes of taking or destroying fish etc.

II   Obstructions to passage of fish

III Times of fishing and selling and exporting fish

IV  Fishing licences

V   Administration and enforcement

VI  Miscellaneous and supplementary.

Sections 4 and 5, from Part I, relating to pollution and the prohibition of the use of noxious substances and other matters, and sections 39 and 43, from Part VI, relating to border rivers and extent, are reproduced below.

## PART I: Prohibition of Certain Modes of Taking or Destroying Fish, etc.

*Poisonous matter and polluting effluent*

**4.** (1)  Subject to subsection (2) below, any person who causes or knowingly permits to flow, or puts or knowingly permits to be put, into any waters containing fish or into any tributaries or waters containing fish, any liquid or solid matter to such an extent as to cause the waters to be poisonous or injurious to fish or the spawning grounds, spawn or food of fish, shall be guilty of an offence[2,3].

(2)  A person shall not be guilty of an offence under subsection (1) above for any act done in the exercise of any right to which he is by law entitled or in continuance of a method in use in connection with the same premises before 18th July 1923, if he proves to the satisfaction of the court

---

[1]  This Act came into force on 1 August 1975: S. 43(4).

[2]  S. 37 and sch. 4, pt. I, as amended by the Magistrates' Courts Act 1980, s. 32(2), provide that the maximum punishment by way of fine or imprisonment which may be imposed on a person convicted of an offence under this section is:

on summary conviction, the prescribed sum and £40 for each day on which the offence continues after a conviction thereof;

on indictment, two years or a fine or both.

The current prescribed sum is £5,000: Criminal Justice Act 1991 (c. 53), s. 17(2).

[3]  The Water Consolidation (Consequential Provisions)

Act 1991 (c. 60), s. 2(1), sch. 1, para. 30(1) provides that:

A person shall not be guilty of an offence under s. 4 of this Act in respect of any entry of matter into any controlled waters (within the meaning of Part III of the Water Resources Act 1991) which occurs—

(a) under and in accordance with a consent under Chapter II of Part III of the Water Resources Act 1991 or under Part II of the Control of Pollution Act 1974 (which makes corresponding provision for Scotland); or

(b) as a result of any act or omission under and in accordance with such a consent.

that he has used the best practicable means, within a reasonable cost, to prevent such matter from doing injury to fish or to the spawning grounds, spawn or food of fish.

(3) Proceedings under this section shall not be instituted except by the Agency[1,2] or by a person who has first obtained a certificate from the Minister[3] that he has a material interest in the waters alleged to be affected[4,5].

*Prohibition of use of explosives, poisons or electrical devices and of destruction of dams etc.*

**5.** **(1)** Subject to subsection (2) below, no person shall use in or near any waters (including waters adjoining the coast of England and Wales to a distance of six nautical miles measured from the baselines from which the breadth of the territorial sea is measured[6]) any explosive substance, any poison or other noxious substance, or any electrical device, with intent thereby to take or destroy fish.

**(2)** Subsection (1) above shall not apply to the use by a person of any substance or device—

(*a*) for a scientific purpose, or for the purpose of protecting, improving or replacing stocks of fish; and

(*b*) with the permission in writing of the Agency[7].[8]

**(3)** No person shall, without lawful excuse, destroy or damage any dam[9], flood-gate or sluice with intent thereby to take or destroy fish.

**(4)** A person who contravenes subsection (1) or (3) above or who, for the purpose of contravening subsection (1) above, has in his possession any explosive or noxious substance or any electrical device, shall be guilty of an offence[10,11].

**(5)** The use of any substance in any waters for a purpose falling within paragraph (a) of subsection (2) above, and with the permission mentioned in paragraph (b) of that subsection, shall not constitute an offence under—

(*a*) section 4 above;

(*b*) any byelaws made under paragraph 31 of Schedule 3 below[12];

[1] "The Agency" means the Environment Agency: s. 41(1). Words "the Agency" substituted by the Environment Act 1995 (c. 25), s. 105, sch. 15, para. 2. This amendment came into force on 1 April 1996: S.I. 1996/186.

[2] Former words "for the area" repealed by the Water Act (c. 15), s. 190(3), sch. 27, pt. I. This amendment came into force on 1 September 1989: s. 194(3)(g), S.I. 1989/1530.

[3] "The Minister" means the Minister of Agriculture, Fisheries and Food: s. 41(1). The functions of the Minister in relation to the area of the Environment Agency, which before 1 September 1989 was the area of the Welsh Water Authority for the purpose of their functions relating to fisheries, have been transferred to the Secretary of State: S.I. 1978/272, S.I. 1978/520, Water Act 1989 (c. 15), s. 141(5), sch. 17, para. 1, Environment Act 1995 (c. 25), s. 105, sch. 15, para. 2.

[4] For provision relating to radioactive substances in respect of the operation of this section see the Radioactive Substances Act 1993 (c. 12), s. 40, p. 404 below, sch. 3, pt. I, para. 4, p. 411 below.

[5] **Cases: section 4** *FJH Wrothwell Ltd v Yorkshire Water Authority* [1984] Crim LR 43; *National Rivers Authority v Welsh Development Agency* [1993] Env LR 407; *CPC (UK) Ltd v National Rivers Authority* [1995] Env LR 131.

[6] Words "to a distance . . . measured" substituted by the Fishery Limits Act 1976 (c. 86), s. 9(1), sch. 2, para. 20. This amendment came into force on 1 January 1977: S.I. 1976/2215.

[7] "The Agency" means the Environment Agency: s. 41(1). Words "the Agency" substituted by the Environment Act 1995 (c. 25), s. 105, sch. 15, para. 2. This amendment came into force on 1 April 1996: S.I. 1996/186.

[8] Former words "for the area" repealed by the Water Act (c. 15), s. 190(3), sch. 27, pt. I. This amendment came into force on 1 September 1989: s. 194(3)(g), S.I. 1989/1530. Former words following para. (b) (which required Ministerial approval for the giving of permission to use noxious substances) repealed by the Environment Act 1995 (c. 25), s. 105, sch. 15, para. 7, sch. 24. This amendment came into force on 1 April 1996: S.I. 1996/186.

[9] "Dam" includes any weir or other fixed obstruction used for the purpose of damming up water: s. 41(1).

[10] S. 37 and sch. 4, pt. I, as amended by the Magistrates' Courts Act 1980, s. 32(2), provide that the maximum punishment by way of fine or imprisonment which may be imposed on a person convicted of an offence under this section is:

on summary conviction, the prescribed sum;

on indictment, two years or a fine or both.

The current prescribed sum is £5,000: Criminal Justice Act 1991 (c. 53), s. 17(2).

[11] For the provisions relating to the exclusion of offences under conservation legislation, including this section, in respect of fish farming see the Fisheries Act 1981 (c. 29), ss. 33, 44, sch. 4, pt. I, para. 3.

[12] Para. 31 of sch. 3 has been repealed by the Water Consolidation (Consequential Provisions) Act 1991 (c. 60), s. 3, sch. 3. Similar provision is made by the Water Resources Act 1991 (c. 57), sch. 25, paras. 6(4) and 7(2). These relate to the power of the Agency to make byelaws for the purpose of regulating the deposit or discharge in waters of liquid or solid matter detrimental to salmon, trout or freshwater fish or the spawn or food of fish. For provisions relating to byelaws made by the Agency see the Water Resources Act 1991, ss. 210, 211 and sch. 25.

(c)  section 85(1) of the Water Resources Act 1991[1];

(d)  section 22(1)(a) of the Rivers (Prevention of Pollution) (Scotland) Act 1951[2].

**(6)**  *Repealed by the Water Act 1989 (c. 15), s. 190(3), sch. 27, pt. I. This amendment came into force on 1 September 1989: s. 194(3)(g), S.I. 1989/1530.*

## PART IV: Administration and enforcement

Sections 31–36 contain provisions relating to the powers of water bailiffs and other persons. These include powers of search (s. 31), power to enter lands (s. 32) and provisions relating to orders and warrants to enter suspected premises (s. 33).

Section 37 and Schedule 4 contain provisions relating to the prosecution and punishment of offences against this Act and the procedure on such prosecutions. Part II of Schedule 4 includes provisions enabling the court by which a person is convicted of an offence against this Act to order the forfeiture of specified objects. In the case of the offence of unlawful possession of any substance or device in contravention of section 5 the court may order the forfeiture of that substance or device.

Section 37A contains provisions relating to fixed penalty notices for offences, under this Act and other specified Acts, which are prescribed by regulations as fixed penalty offences. This section is inserted by the Environment Act 1995 (c. 25), s. 104.

## PART VI: Miscellaneous and Supplemental

*Border rivers and Solway Firth*

**39. (1)**  This Act—

(a)  does not apply to the River Tweed, but

(b)  applies to so much of the River Esk, with its banks and tributary streams up to their source, as is situated in Scotland,

and in this subsection "the River Tweed" means "the river" as defined by the Tweed Fisheries (Amendment) Act 1859[3] and any byelaw amending that definition[4].

**(1A)**  In the application of this Act, under subsection (1)(b) above, to the River Esk in Scotland, references to this Act in sections 31 to 33 and section 36 shall be construed as including references to sections 1, 3 and 18 to 20 of the Salmon and Freshwater Fisheries (Protection) (Scotland) Act 1951[5] as applied to that River by section 21 of that Act[6].

**(1B)**  Sections 31 to 34 and 36(2) of this Act shall, subject to the modifications set out in subsection (1C) below, apply throughout the catchment area of the River Esk in Scotland but a water bailiff shall exercise his powers under those sections as so applied only in relation to an offence—

(a)  against this Act;

(b)  against section 1 of the Salmon and Freshwater Fisheries (Protection) (Scotland) Act 1951; or

(c)  which is deemed to be an offence under this Act by virtue of section 211(6) of the Water Resources Act 1991[7],

---

[1] P. 273 below. Para. (c) substituted by the Water Consolidation (Consequential Provisions) Act 1991 (c. 60), s. 2(1), sch. 1, para. 30(2). This amendment came into force on 1 December 1991: s. 4(1).

[2] S. 22 of the Rivers (Prevention of Pollution) (Scotland) Act 1951 has been repealed.

[3] 1859 c. lxx.

[4] This Act has effect as if in this subsection the reference to this Act includes reference to the Salmon Act 1986 (c. 62), s. 32: s. 32(6)(b) of the 1986 Act.

[5] 1951 c. 26.

[6] Subsection (1A) inserted by the Salmon Act 1986 (c. 62), s. 26(2). This amendment came into force on 7 January 1987: S. 43(1).

[7] 1991 c. 57.

which he has reasonable cause to suspect has been committed in a place to which this Act applies by virtue of subsection (1)(b) above.

(1C) The modifications referred to in subsection (1B) above are—

(a) references in sections 31 to 34 of this Act to "this Act" shall be construed as including references to section 1 of the Salmon and Freshwater Fisheries (Protection) (Scotland) Act 1951 (as applied to the River Esk by section 21 of that Act); and

(b) in section 33—

(i) references to a justice of the peace shall be construed as including references to a sheriff; and

(ii) in subsection (2), the reference to an information on oath shall be construed as including a reference to evidence on oath[1].

(2) Where the minimum size of mesh of nets used for taking salmon prescribed by any provision of this Act or by any byelaw in force in any part of the Solway Firth within England is greater than that which may be lawfully used in the part of the Solway Firth within Scotland, the provision or byelaw shall have effect as if the minimum size of mesh so prescribed in relation to the part of the Solway Firth within England were such as may be so lawfully used as aforesaid in the part of the Solway Firth within Scotland.

(3) The limits of the Solway Firth for the purposes of this section shall be determined by the Minister[2].

(4) *Repealed by the Water Act 1989 (c. 15), s. 190(3), sch. 27, pt. I. This amendment came into force on 1 September 1989: s. 194(3)(g), S.I. 1989/1530.*

(5) Nothing in this section or the Water Resources Act 1991[3] shall authorise the Agency[4] to take legal proceedings in Scotland in respect of an offence against this Act[5].

...................................................................................................................................

*Citation etc.*

**43.** (1) This Act may be cited as the Salmon and Freshwater Fisheries Act 1975.

(2) Subject to section 39 above and subsection (3) below, this Act extends only to England and Wales.

(3) The following provisions of this Act, namely—

section 28(1) and (2) above,

section 39(1), (1A), (1B), (1C), (4) and (5) above[6],

section 42(1) above, so far as it relates to the repeal of section 15 of the Salmon and Freshwater Fisheries Act 1972 and section 18 of the Water Act 1973,

paragraph 3 of Schedule 4 below,

extend to Scotland.

(4) This Act shall come into force on 1st August 1975.

---

[1] Subsections (1B) and (1C) inserted by the Environment Act 1995 (c. 25), s. 105, sch. 15, para. 19. This amendment came into force on 1 April 1996: S.I. 1996/186.

[2] "The Minister" means the Minister of Agriculture, Fisheries and Food: s. 41(1).

[3] P. 267 below. Words "the Water Resources Act 1991" substituted by the Water Consolidation (Consequential Provisions) Act 1991 (c. 60), s. 2(1), sch. 1, para. 30(3). The provision does not expressly state the words to be substituted; in the above text the words "the Water Resources Act 1991" have been substituted for the words "the Water Act 1989". This amendment came into force on 1 December 1991: s. 4(1).

[4] "The Agency" means the Environment Agency: s. 41(1).

Words "the Agency" substituted by the Environment Act 1995 (c. 25), s. 105, sch. 15, para. 2. This amendment came into force on 1 April 1996: S.I. 1996/186.

[5] Subsection (5) inserted by the Salmon Act 1986 (c. 62), s. 41(1), sch. 4, para. 13. This amendment came into force on 7 January 1987: S. 43(1).

[6] Words ", (1A)" inserted by the Salmon Act 1986 (c. 62), s. 26(3); this amendment came into force on 7 January 1987: S. 43(1). Words ", (1B), (1C)" inserted by the Environment Act 1995 (c. 25), s. 105, sch. 15, para. 21; this amendment came into force on 1 April 1996: S.I. 1996/186. Words "(4) and (5)" substituted by the Salmon Act 1986 (c. 62), s. 41(1), sch. 4, para. 14; this amendment came into force on 7 January 1987: S. 43(1).

# Control of Pollution (Amendment) Act 1989

## Chapter 14

*Arrangement of sections*

| | | |
|---|---|---|
| 1. | Offence of transporting controlled waste without registering. | 72 |
| 2. | Registration of carriers. | 73 |
| 3. | Restrictions on power under section 2. | 74 |
| 4. | Appeals against refusal of registration etc. | 75 |
| 5. | Duty to produce authority to transport controlled waste. | 76 |
| 6. | Seizure and disposal of vehicles used for illegal waste disposal. | 77 |
| 7. | Further enforcement provisions. | 79 |
| 8. | Regulations. | 80 |
| 9. | Interpretation. | 80 |
| 10. | Expenses. | 81 |
| 10A. | Application to the Isles of Scilly. | 81 |
| 11. | Short title, commencement and extent. | 81 |

# Control of Pollution (Amendment) Act 1989

An Act to provide for the registration of carriers of controlled waste and to make further provision with respect to the powers exercisable in relation to vehicles shown to have been used for illegal waste disposal.

[6th July 1989[1]]

*The functions previously conferred on waste regulation authorities under this Act have been transferred, in respect of England and Wales, to the Environment Agency and, in respect of Scotland, to the Scottish Environment Protection Agency, SEPA: Environment Act 1995 (c. 25), ss. 2, 21, p. 421/438 below. The new agencies took over their functions under this Act on the transfer date, 1 April 1996: S.I. 1996/139; S.I. 1996/234.*

*Offence of transporting controlled waste without registering*

1. (1) Subject to the following provisions of this section, it shall be an offence for any person who is not a registered carrier of controlled waste[2], in the course of any business of his or otherwise with a view to profit, to transport[3] any controlled waste to or from any place in Great Britain.

(2) A person shall not be guilty of an offence under this section in respect of—

(a) the transport of controlled waste within the same premises between different places in those premises;

(b) the transport to a place in Great Britain of controlled waste which has been brought from a country or territory outside Great Britain and is not landed in Great Britain until it arrives at that place;

(c) the transport by air or sea of controlled waste from a place in Great Britain to a place outside Great Britain.

(3) The Secretary of State may by regulations provide that a person shall not be required for the purposes of this section to be a registered carrier of controlled waste if—

(a) he is a prescribed[4] person or a person of such a description as may be prescribed[5]; or

(b) without prejudice to paragraph (a) above, he is a person in relation to whom the prescribed requirements under the law of any other member State are satisfied.

(4) In proceedings against any person for an offence under this section in respect of the transport of any controlled waste it shall be a defence for that person to show—

(a) that the waste was transported in an emergency[6] of which notice was given, as soon as practicable after it occurred, to the regulation authority[7] in whose area the emergency occurred;

(b) that he neither knew nor had reasonable grounds for suspecting that what was being transported was controlled waste and took all such steps as it was reasonable to take for ascertaining whether it was such waste; or

---

[1] This Act came into force on various dates noted at the sections below.

[2] "Controlled waste" defined by s. 9(1), p. 80 below.

[3] "Transport" defined by s. 9(1), p. 80 below.

[4] "Prescribed" defined by s. 9(1), p. 80 below.

[5] The following regulations have been made under this section:

The Controlled Waste (Registration of Carriers and Seizure of Vehicles) Regulations 1991, S.I. 1991/1624, p. 630 below;

The Controlled Waste Regulations 1992, S.I. 1992/588, p. 662 below;

The Waste Management Licensing Regulations 1994, S.I. 1994/1056, p. 675 below.

[6] "Emergency" defined by subsection (6) below.

[7] "Regulation authority", and its area, defined by s. 9(1), p. 80 below. Words "regulation authority" substituted by the Environmental Protection Act 1990 (c. 43), s. 162, sch. 15, para. 31(2). This amendment came into force on 31 May 1991: S.I. 1991/1319.

(c)  that he acted under instructions from his employer.

(5)  A person guilty of an offence under this section shall be liable on summary conviction to a fine not exceeding level 5 on the standard scale[1].

(6)  In this section "emergency", in relation to the transport of any controlled waste, means any circumstances in which, in order to avoid, remove or reduce any serious danger to the public or serious risk of damage to the environment, it is necessary for the waste to be transported from one place to another without the use of a registered carrier of such waste[2,2A].

*Registration of carriers*

2. (1)  Subject to section 3 below, the Secretary of State may by regulations make provision for the registration of persons with regulation authorities[3] as carriers of controlled waste[4] and, for that purpose, for the establishment and maintenance by such authorities, in accordance with the regulations, of such registers as may be prescribed[5].

(2)  Regulations under this section may—

(a)  make provision with respect to applications for registration;

(b)  impose requirements with respect to the manner in which regulation authorities maintain registers of carriers of controlled waste;

(c)  provide for the issue of a certificate of registration free of charge to a registered carrier of controlled waste both on his registration and on the making of any alteration of any entry relating to him in a register of such carriers;

(d)  provide for such a certificate to be in such form and to contain such information as may be prescribed;

(e)  provide that the provision by a regulation authority to a registered carrier of such copies of a certificate of registration as are provided in addition to the certificate provided free of charge in pursuance of provision made by virtue of paragraph (c) above is to be made subject to the payment of a charge imposed under the regulations.

(3)  Provision contained in any regulations under this section by virtue of subsection (2)(a) above may, in particular, include provision which—

(a)  prescribes the manner of determining the regulation authority to which an application is to be made;

(b)  prescribes the form on which and other manner in which an application is made;

(c)  prescribes the period within which an application for the renewal of any registration which is due to expire is to be made;

(d)  imposes requirements with respect to the information which is to be provided by an applicant to the authority to which his application is made;

(e)  *Without prejudice to the power of regulation authorities to impose a charge in respect of their consideration of any such application, paragraph (e) (power to require them to impose such charges) shall cease to have effect: Environment Act 1995 (c. 25), s. 120, sch. 22, para. 37(2)(a), sch. 24. This amendment is not in force.*

(3A)  Without prejudice to the generality of paragraphs (b) and (d) of subsection (3) above—

---

[1] The current fine at level 5 on the standard scale is £5,000: Criminal Justice Act 1991 (c. 53), s. 17 (*England and Wales*); Criminal Procedure (Scotland) Act 1995 (c. 46), s. 225 (*Scotland*).

[2] S. 1(3) came into force on 16 July 1991; the remainder of this section came into force on 1 April 1992: S.I. 1991/1618.

[2A] Case: section 1 *Cosmick Transport Services v Bedfordshire County Council* [1996] Env LR 78.

[3] "Regulation authority" defined by s. 9(1), p. 80 below. Words "regulation authority/authorities" in this section substituted by the Environmental Protection Act 1990 (c. 43), s. 162, sch. 15, para. 31(2). This amendment came into force on 31 May 1991: S.I. 1991/1319.

[4] "Controlled waste" defined by s. 9(1), p. 80 below.

[5] "Prescribed" defined by s. 9(1), p. 80 below. The following regulations have been made under this section:

The Controlled Waste (Registration of Carriers and Seizure of Vehicles) Regulations 1991, S.I. 1991/1624, p. 630 below;

The Waste Management Licensing Regulations 1994, S.I. 1994/1056, p. 675 below.

The Transfrontier Shipment of Waste Regulations 1994, S.I. 1994/1137, p. 741 below.

(a)　the power to prescribe a form under paragraph (b) of that subsection includes power to require an application to be made on any form of any description supplied for the purpose by the regulation authority to which the application is to be made; and

(b)　the power to impose requirements with respect to information under paragraph (d) of that subsection includes power to make provision requiring an application to be accompanied by such information as may reasonably be required by the regulation authority to which it is to be made[1].

(4) Provision contained in any regulations under this section by virtue of subsection (2)(b) above may, in particular, include provision—

(a)　specifying or describing the information to be incorporated in any register maintained by a regulation authority in pursuance of any such regulations;

(b)　requiring a registered carrier of controlled waste to notify a regulation authority which maintains such a register of any change of circumstances affecting information contained in the entry relating to that carrier in that register;

(c)　requiring a regulation authority, to such extent and in such manner as may be prescribed, to make the contents of any such register available for public inspection free of charge; and

(d)　requiring such an authority, on payment of such charges as may be imposed under the regulations, to provide such copies of the contents of any such register to any person applying for a copy as may be prescribed.

(5) Subsections (2) to (4) above are without prejudice to the generality of subsection (1) above[2].

*Restrictions on power under section 2*

3. (1) Nothing in any regulations under section 2 above shall authorise a regulation authority[3] to refuse an application for registration except where—

(a)　there has, in relation to that application, been a contravention of the requirements of any regulations made by virtue of subsection (2)(a) of that section; or

(b)　the applicant or another relevant person has been convicted of a prescribed[4] offence[5] and, in the opinion of the authority, it is undesirable for the applicant to be authorised to transport[6] controlled waste[7].

(2) Nothing in any regulations under section 2 above shall authorise any regulation authority to revoke any person's registration as a carrier of controlled waste except where—

(a)　that person or another relevant person has been convicted of a prescribed offence; and

(b)　in the opinion of the authority, it is undesirable for the registered carrier to continue to be authorised to transport controlled waste;

but registration in accordance with any regulations under that section shall cease to have effect after such period as may be prescribed or if the registered carrier gives written notice requiring the removal of his name from the register.

(3) Regulations under section 2 above may require every registration in respect of a business which is or is to be carried on by a partnership to be a registration of all the partners and to cease to have effect if any of the partners ceases to be registered or if any person who is not registered becomes a partner[8].

[1] Subsection (3A) inserted by the Environment Act 1995 (c. 25), s. 120, sch. 22, para. 37(2)(b). This amendment came into force partially on 1 February 1996: S.I. 1996/186.
[2] This section came into force on 16 July 1991: S.I. 1991/1618.
[3] "Regulation authority" defined by s. 9(1), p. 80 below. Words "regulation authority" in this section substituted by the Environmental Protection Act 1990 (c. 43), s. 162, sch. 15, para. 31(2). This amendment came into force on 31 May 1991: S.I. 1991/1319.
[4] "Prescribed" defined by s. 9(1), p. 80 below.
[5] For "another relevant person has been convicted of a prescribed offence" see subsection (5) below.
[6] "Transport" defined by s. 9(1), p. 80 below.
[7] "Controlled waste" defined by s. 9(1), p. 80 below.
[8] The following regulations have been made under this section:
The Controlled Waste (Registration of Carriers and Seizure of Vehicles) Regulations 1991, S.I. 1991/1624, p. 630 below;
The Transfrontier Shipment of Waste Regulations 1994, S.I. 1994/1137, p. 741 below.

**(4)** Nothing in any regulations under section 2 above shall have the effect of bringing the revocation of any person's registration as a carrier of controlled waste into force except—

(a) after the end of such period as may be prescribed for appealing against the revocation under section 4 below; or

(b) where that person has indicated, within that period, that he does not intend to make or continue with an appeal.

**(5)** In relation to any applicant for registration or registered carrier, another relevant person shall be treated for the purpose of any provision made by virtue of subsection (1) or (2) above as having been convicted of a prescribed offence if—

(a) any person has been convicted of a prescribed offence committed by him in the course of his employment by the applicant or registered carrier or in the course of the carrying on of any business by a partnership one of the members of which was the applicant or registered carrier;

(b) a body corporate has been convicted of a prescribed offence committed at a time when the applicant or registered carrier was a director, manager, secretary or other similar officer of that body corporate; or

(c) where the applicant or registered carrier is a body corporate, a person who is a director, manager, secretary or other similar officer of that body corporate—

(i) has been convicted of a prescribed offence; or

(ii) was a director, manager, secretary or other similar officer of another body corporate at a time when a prescribed offence for which that other body corporate has been convicted was committed.

**(6)** In determining for the purposes of any provision made by virtue of subsection (1) or (2) above whether it is desirable for any individual to be or to continue to be authorised to transport controlled waste, a regulation authority shall have regard, in a case in which a person other than the individual has been convicted of a prescribed offence, to whether that individual has been a party to the carrying on of a business in a manner involving the commission of prescribed offences[1].

*Appeals against refusal of registration etc.*

**4.** **(1)** Where a person has applied to a regulation authority[2] to be registered in accordance with any regulations under section 2 above, he may appeal to the Secretary of State if—

(a) his application is refused; or

(b) the relevant period from the making of the application has expired without his having been registered;

and for the purposes of this subsection the relevant period is two months or, except in the case of an application for the renewal of his registration by a person who is already registered, such longer period as may be agreed between the applicant and the regulation authority in question.

**(2)** A person whose registration as a carrier of controlled waste[3] has been revoked may appeal against the revocation to the Secretary of State.

**(3)** On an appeal under this section the Secretary of State may, as he thinks fit, either dismiss the appeal or give the regulation authority in question a direction to register the appellant or, as the case may be, to cancel the revocation.

**(4)** Where on an appeal made by virtue of subsection (1)(b) above the Secretary of State dismisses an appeal, he shall direct the regulation authority in question not to register the appellant.

**(5)** It shall be the duty of a regulation authority to comply with any direction under this section.

---

[1] This section, so far as it relates to the making of regulations, came into force on 16 July 1991; otherwise it came into force on 14 October 1991: S.I. 1991/1618.

[2] "Regulation authority" defined by s. 9(1), p. 80 below. Words "regulation authority" in this section substituted by the Environmental Protection Act 1990 (c. 43), s. 162, sch. 15, para. 31(2). This amendment came into force on 31 May 1991: S.I. 1991/1319.

[3] "Controlled waste" defined by s. 9(1), p. 80 below.

(6) The Secretary of State may by regulations make provision as to the manner in which and time within which an appeal under this section is to be made and as to the procedure to be followed on any such appeal[1].

(7) Where an appeal under this section is made in accordance with regulations under this section—

(a) by a person whose appeal is in respect of such an application for the renewal of his registration as was made, in accordance with regulations under section 2 above, at a time when he was already registered; or

(b) by a person whose registration has been revoked,

that registration shall continue in force, notwithstanding the expiry of the prescribed[2] period or the revocation, until the appeal is disposed of.

(8) For the purposes of subsection (7) above an appeal is disposed of when any of the following occurs, that is to say—

(a) the appeal is withdrawn;

(b) the appellant is notified by the Secretary of State or the regulation authority in question that his appeal has been dismissed; or

(c) the regulation authority comply with any direction of the Secretary of State to renew the appellant's registration or to cancel the revocation.

(9) This section is subject to section 114 of the Environment Act 1995[3] (delegation or reference of appeals etc)[4,5].

*Duty to produce authority to transport controlled waste*

5. (1) If it reasonably appears to any duly authorised officer of a regulation authority[6] or to a constable that any controlled waste[7] is being or has been transported in contravention of section 1(1) above[8], he may—

(a) stop any person appearing to him to be or to have been engaged in transporting that waste and require that person to produce his authority or, as the case may be, his employer's authority for transporting that waste[9]; and

(b) search any vehicle[10] that appears to him to be a vehicle which is being or has been used for transporting that waste, carry out tests on anything found in any such vehicle and take away for testing samples of anything so found.

(2) Nothing in subsection (1) above shall authorise any person other than a constable in uniform to stop a vehicle on any road[11].

(3) Subject to the following provisions of this section, a person who is required by virtue of this section to produce an authority for transporting controlled waste shall do so by producing it forthwith to the person making the requirement, by producing it at the prescribed[12] place and within the prescribed period or by sending it to that place within that period[13].

---

[1] The following regulation has been made under this section:
The Controlled Waste (Registration of Carriers and Seizure of Vehicles) Regulations 1991, S.I. 1991/1624, p. 630 below.
[2] "Prescribed" defined by s. 9(1), p. 80 below.
[3] P. 489 below.
[4] Subsection (9) inserted by the Environment Act 1995 (c. 25), s. 120, sch. 22, para. 37(3). This amendment came into force on 1 April 1996: S.I. 1996/186.
[5] S. 4(6) came into force on 16 July 1991; save for s. 4(9) noted at n. 5, the remainder of this section came into force on 14 October 1991: S.I. 1991/1618.
[6] "Regulation authority" defined by s. 9(1), p. 80 below. Words "regulation authority" in this section substituted by the Environmental Protection Act 1990 (c. 43), s. 162, sch. 15, para. 31(2). This amendment came into force on 31 May 1991: S.I. 1991/1319.
[7] "Controlled waste" defined by s. 9(1), p. 80 below.
[8] P. 72 above.
[9] For a person's authority for transporting controlled waste see subsection (6) below.
[10] "Vehicle" defined by s. 9(1), p. 80 below.
[11] "Road" defined by s. 9(1), p. 80 below.
[12] "Prescribed" defined by s. 9(1), p. 80 below.
[13] The following regulation has been made under this section:
The Controlled Waste (Registration of Carriers and Seizure of Vehicles) Regulations 1991, S.I. 1991/1624, p. 630 below.

**(4)** A person shall be guilty of an offence under this section if he—

(*a*) intentionally obstructs any authorised officer of a regulation authority or constable in the exercise of the power conferred by subsection (1) above; or

(*b*) subject to subsection (5) below, fails without reasonable excuse to comply with a requirement imposed in exercise of that power;

and in paragraph (b) above the words "without reasonable excuse" shall be construed in their application to Scotland, as in their application to England and Wales, as making it a defence for a person against whom proceedings for the failure are brought to show that there was a reasonable excuse for the failure, rather than as requiring the person bringing the proceedings to show that there was no such excuse.

**(5)** A person shall not be guilty of an offence by virtue of subsection (4)(b) above unless it is shown—

(*a*) that the waste in question was controlled waste; and

(*b*) that that person did transport[1] it to or from a place in Great Britain.

**(6)** For the purposes of this section a person's authority for transporting controlled waste is—

(*a*) his certificate of registration as a carrier of controlled waste or such a copy of that certificate as satisfies prescribed requirements; or

(*b*) such evidence as may be prescribed that he is not required to be registered as a carrier of controlled waste.

**(7)** A person guilty of an offence under this section shall be liable on summary conviction to a fine not exceeding level 5 on the standard scale[2].[3]

*Seizure and disposal of vehicles used for illegal waste disposal*

**6. (1)** A justice of the peace or, in Scotland, a sheriff or a justice of the peace may issue a warrant to a regulation authority[4] for the seizure of any vehicle[5] if he is satisfied, on sworn information in writing—

(*a*) that there are reasonable grounds for believing—

    (i) that an offence under section 3 of the Control of Pollution Act 1974 or section 33 of the Environmental Protection Act 1991[6] (prohibition on unlicensed deposit, treatment or[7] disposal of waste) has been committed; and

    (ii) that that vehicle was used in the commission of the offence;

(*b*) that proceedings for that offence have not yet been brought against any person; and

(*c*) that the authority have failed, after taking the prescribed[8] steps, to ascertain the name and address of any person who is able to provide them with the prescribed information about who was using the vehicle at the time when the offence was committed.

**(2)** Subject to subsections (3) and (4) below, where a warrant under this section has been issued to a regulation authority in respect of any vehicle, any duly authorised officer of the regulation

---

[1] "Transport" defined by s. 9(1), p. 80 below.

[2] The current fine at level 5 on the standard scale is £5,000: Criminal Justice Act 1991 (c. 53), s. 17) (*England and Wales*); Criminal Procedure (Scotland) Act 1995 (c. 46), s. 225 (*Scotland*).

[3] S. 5(3) and (6), so far as they relate to the making of regulations, came into force on 16 July 1991; otherwise this section came into force on 1 April 1992: S.I. 1991/1618.

[4] "Regulation authority" defined by s. 9(1), p. 80 below. Words "regulation authority" in this section substituted by the Environmental Protection Act 1990 (c. 43), s. 162, sch. 15, para. 31(2). This amendment came into force on 31 May 1991: S.I. 1991/1319.

[5] "Vehicle" defined by s. 9(1), p. 80 below.

[6] P. 116 below. Words "or section 33 of the Environmental Protection Act 1990" inserted by the Environmental Protection Act 1990 (c. 43), s. 162, sch. 15, para. 31(3)(a). This amendment came into force on 31 May 1991: S.I. 1991/1319.

[7] Words "deposit, treatment or" inserted by the Environmental Protection Act 1990 (c. 43), s. 162, sch. 15, para. 31(3)(b).

[8] "Prescribed" defined by s. 9(1), p. 80 below. The following regulation has been made under this section:

The Controlled Waste (Registration of Carriers and Seizure of Vehicles) Regulations 1991, S.I. 1991/1624, p. 630 below.

authority or any constable may stop the vehicle and, on behalf of the authority, seize the vehicle and its contents.

(3) Nothing in this section shall authorise any person other than a constable in uniform to stop a vehicle on any road[1]; and a duly authorised officer of a regulation authority shall not be entitled to seize any property under this section unless he is accompanied by a constable.

(4) A warrant under this section shall continue in force until its purpose is fulfilled; and any person seizing any property under this section shall, if required to do so, produce both the warrant and any authority in pursuance of which he is acting under the warrant.

(5) Where any property has been seized under this section on behalf of a regulation authority, the authority may, in accordance with regulations made by the Secretary of State[2], remove it to such place as the authority consider appropriate and may retain custody of it until either—

(a) it is returned, in accordance with the regulations, to a person who establishes that he is entitled to it; or

(b) it is disposed of by the authority in exercise of a power conferred by the regulations to sell or destroy the property or to deposit it at any place.

(6) Regulations under this section shall not authorise a regulation authority to sell or destroy any property or to deposit any property at any place unless—

(a) the following conditions are satisfied, that is to say—

(i) the authority have published such notice, and taken such other steps (if any), as may be prescribed for informing persons who may be entitled to the property that it has been seized and is available to be claimed; and

(ii) the prescribed period has expired without any obligation arising under the regulations for the regulation authority to return the property to any person; or

(b) the condition of the property requires it to be disposed of without delay[3].

(7) Regulations under this section may—

(a) impose obligations on a regulation authority to return any property which has been seized under this section to a person who claims to be entitled to it and satisfies such requirements for establishing his entitlement, and such other requirements, as may be prescribed;

(b) provide for the manner in which the person entitled to any such property is to be determined where there is more than one claim to it;

(c) provide for the proceeds of sale of any property sold by a regulation authority under the regulations to be applied towards meeting expenses incurred by the authority in exercising their functions by virtue of this section and, in so far as they are not so applied, to be applied in such other manner as may be prescribed;

(d) make provision which treats a person who establishes that he is entitled to a vehicle as having established for the purposes of regulations under this section that he is also entitled to its contents.

(8) Subject to their powers by virtue of any regulations under this section to sell or destroy any property or to dispose of it by depositing it at any place, it shall be the duty of a regulation authority, while any property is in their custody by virtue of a warrant under this section, to take such steps as are reasonably necessary for the safe custody of that property.

(9) Any person who intentionally obstructs any authorised officer of a regulation authority or constable in the exercise of any power conferred by virtue of a warrant under this section shall be

[1] "Road" defined by s. 9(1), p. 80 below.
[2] The following regulation has been made under this section:
The Controlled Waste (Registration of Carriers and Seizure of Vehicles) Regulations 1991, S.I. 1991/1624, p. 630 below.
[3] Subsection (6) substituted by the Environment Act 1995 (c. 25), s. 120, sch. 22, para. 37(4). This amendment came into force on 21 September 1995: S.I. 1995/1983.

guilty of an offence and liable, on summary conviction, to a fine not exceeding level 5 on the standard scale[1],[2].

*Further enforcement provisions*

**7.** (1) Subject to subsection (2) below, the provisions of section 71[3] of the Environmental Protection Act 1990 (powers of entry, of dealing with imminent pollution and to obtain information)[4] shall have effect as if the provisions of this Act were provisions of that Act and as if, in those sections, references to a relevant authority were references to a regulation authority[5].

(2) *Repealed by the Environment Act 1995 (c. 25), s. 120, sch. 22, para. 37(6), sch. 24. This amendment came into force on 1 April 1996: S.I. 1996/186.*

(3) A person shall be guilty of an offence under this subsection if he—

(*a*) fails, without reasonable excuse, to comply with any requirement in pursuance of regulations under this Act to provide information to the Secretary of State or a regulation authority; or

(*b*) in complying with any such requirement, provides information which he knows to be false or misleading[6] in a material particular or recklessly provides information which is false or misleading[6] in a material particular;

and in paragraph (a) above the words "without reasonable excuse" shall be construed in their application to Scotland, as in their application to England and Wales, as making it a defence for a person against whom proceedings for the failure are brought to show that there was a reasonable excuse for the failure, rather than as requiring the person bringing the proceedings to show that there was no such excuse.

(4) A person guilty of an offence under subsection (3) above shall be liable on summary conviction to a fine not exceeding level 5 on the standard scale[7].

(5) Where the commission by any person of an offence under this Act is due to the act or default of some other person, that other person shall also be guilty of the offence; and a person may be charged with and convicted of an offence by virtue of this subsection whether or not proceedings for the offence are taken against any other person.

(6) Where a body corporate is guilty of an offence under this Act (including where it is so guilty by virtue of subsection (5) above) in respect of any act or omission which is shown to have been committed with the consent or connivance of, or to be attributable to any neglect on the part of, any director, manager, secretary or other similar officer of the body corporate or any person who was purporting to act in any such capacity, he, as well as the body corporate, shall be guilty of that offence and shall be liable to be proceeded against and punished accordingly.

(7) Where the affairs of a body corporate are managed by its members, subsection (6) above shall apply in relation to the acts and defaults of a member in connection with his functions of management as if he were a director of the body corporate[8].

(8) *Repealed by the Environment Act 1995 (c. 25), s. 120, sch. 22, para. 37(7), sch. 24. This amendment came into force on 1 April 1996: S.I. 1996/186.*

---

[1] The current fine at level 5 on the standard scale is £5,000: Criminal Justice Act 1991 (c. 53), s. 17 (*England and Wales*); Criminal Procedure (Scotland) Act 1995 (c. 46), s. 225 (*Scotland*).

[2] This section, so far as it relates to the making of regulations, came into force on 16 July 1991; otherwise it came into force on 14 October 1991: S.I. 1991/1618.

[3] P. 156 below. Words "section 71" substituted by the Environment Act 1995 (c. 25), s. 120, sch. 22, para. 37(5). This amendment came into force on 1 April 1996: S.I. 1996/186.

[4] Words "of the Environmental . . . information)" substituted by the Environmental Protection Act 1990 (c. 43), s. 162, sch. 15, para. 31(4)(a). This amendment came into force on 31 May 1991: S.I. 1991/1319.

[5] "Regulation authority" defined by s. 9(1), p. 80 below. Words "regulation authority" in this section substituted by the Environmental Protection Act 1990 (c. 43), s. 162, sch. 15, para. 31(2). This amendment came into force on 31 May 1991: S.I. 1991/1319.

[6] Words "or misleading" inserted by the Environment Act 1995 (c. 25), s. 112, sch. 19, para. 3. This amendment came into force on 1 April 1996: S.I. 1996/186.

[7] The current fine at level 5 on the standard scale is £5,000: Criminal Justice Act 1991 (c. 53), s. 17 (*England and Wales*); Criminal Procedure (Scotland) Act 1995 (c. 46), s. 225 (*Scotland*).

[8] This section came into force on 14 October 1991: S.I. 1991/1618.

*Regulations*

**8.** (1) The powers of the Secretary of State under this Act to make regulations shall be exercisable by statutory instrument subject to annulment in pursuance of a resolution of either House of Parliament.

(2) Regulations made in exercise of any such power may—

(*a*) contain such supplemental, consequential and transitional provision as the Secretary of State considers appropriate; and

(*b*) make different provision for different cases (including different provision for different persons, circumstances or localities)[1].

*Interpretation*

**9.** (1) In this Act—

"controlled waste" has, at any time[2], the same meaning as for the purposes of Part II of the Environmental Protection Act 1990[3,4];

"prescribed" means prescribed by regulations made by the Secretary of State[5];

"regulation authority" means—

(*a*) in relation to England and Wales, the Environment Agency[6]; and

(*b*) in relation to Scotland, the Scottish Environment Protection Agency[7];

and any reference to the area of a regulation authority shall accordingly be construed as a reference to any area in England and Wales or, as the case may be, in Scotland[8].

"road" has the same meaning as in the Road Traffic Act 1988[9];

"transport", in relation to any controlled waste, includes the transport of that waste by road or rail or by air, sea or inland waterway but does not include moving that waste from one place to another by means of any pipe or other apparatus that joins those two places.

"vehicle" means any motor vehicle or trailer within the meaning of the Road Traffic Regulation Act 1984[10].[11]

(2) *Repealed by the Environmental Protection Act 1990 (c. 43), s. 162, sch. 15, para. 31(6), sch. 16, pt. II. This amendment came into force on 1 April 1992: S.I. 1991/2829.*

---

[1] The regulations made under this Act are noted at the appropriate sections of the Act and at s. 9, n. 5 below. S. 8 came into force on 16 July 1991: S.I. 1991/1618.

[2] Words ", at any time," substituted by the Environmental Protection Act 1990 (c. 43), s. 162, sch. 15, para. 31(5)(a)(i). This amendment came into force on 1 April 1992: S.I. 1991/2829.

[3] P. 111 below. Words "for the purposes . . . 1990" substituted by the Environmental Protection Act 1990(c. 43), s. 162, sch. 15, para. 31(5)(a)(ii). This amendment came into force on 1 April 1992: S.I. 1991/2829.

[4] Former definition of "disposal authority" repealed by the Environmental Protection Act 1990 (c. 43), s. 162, sch. 15, para. 31(5)(b), sch. 16, pt. II. This amendment came into force on 31 May 1991: S.I. 1991/1319.

[5] The following regulations have been made under this section:
The Controlled Waste (Registration of Carriers and Seizure of Vehicles) Regulations 1991, S.I. 1991/1624, p. 630 below;

The Controlled Waste Regulations 1992, S.I. 1992/588, p. 662 below;
The Waste Management Licensing Regulations 1994, S.I. 1994/1056, p. 675 below;
The Transfrontier Shipment of Waste Regulations 1994, S.I. 1994/1137, p. 741 below.

[6] The Environment Agency is established by the Environment Act 1995 (c. 25), Part I, p. 420 below.

[7] The Scottish Environment Protection Agency, SEPA, is established by the Environment Act 1995 (c. 25), Part I, p. 438 below.

[8] The definition of "regulation authority" substituted by the Environment Act 1995(c. 25), s. 120, sch. 22, para. 37(8). This amendment came into force on 1 April 1996: S.I. 1996/186.

[9] 1988 c. 52.

[10] 1984 c. 27.

[11] This section came into force on 16 July 1991: S.I. 1991/1618.

*Expenses*

**10.** There shall be paid out of money provided by Parliament—

(*a*) any administrative expenses incurred by the Secretary of State in consequence of this Act; and

(*b*) any increase attributable to this Act in the sums payable out of money so provided under any other Act[1].

*Application to the Isles of Scilly*

**10A. (1)** Subject to the provisions of any order under this section, this Act shall not apply in relation to the Isles of Scilly.

**(2)** The Secretary of State may, after consultation with the Council of the Isles of Scilly, by order provide for the application of any provisions of this Act to the Isles of Scilly; and any such order may provide for the application of those provisions to those Isles with such modifications as may be specified in the order.

**(3)** An order under this section may—

(*a*) make different provision for different cases, including different provision in relation to different persons, circumstances or localities; and

(*b*) contain such supplemental, consequential and transitional provision as the Secretary of State considers appropriate, including provision saving provision repealed by or under any enactment.

**(4)** The power of the Secretary of State to make an order under this section shall be exercisable by statutory instrument; and a statutory instrument containing such an order shall be subject to annulment in pursuance of a resolution of either House of Parliament[2].

*Short title, commencement and extent*

**11. (1)** This Act may be cited as the Control of Pollution (Amendment) Act 1989.

**(2)** This Act shall come into force on such day as the Secretary of State may by order made by statutory instrument appoint; and different days may be so appointed for different provisions and for different purposes[3].

**(3)** *Repealed by the Environment Act 1995 (c. 25), s. 120, sch. 24. This amendment came into force on 1 April 1996: S.I. 1996/186.*

**(4)** This Act shall not extend to Northern Ireland[4].

---

[1] This section came into force on 16 July 1991: S.I. 1991/1618.

[2] This section inserted by the Environment Act 1995 (c. 25), s. 118(1). This amendment came into force on 1 February 1996: S.I. 1996/186.

[3] The provisions of the commencement order relating to this Act, S.I. 1991/1618, are noted at the end of each section.

[4] This section came into force on 16 July 1991: S.I. 1991/1618.

# Environmental Protection Act 1990

## Chapter 43

*Arrangement of sections*

## Part I: Integrated Pollution Control and Air Pollution Control by Local Authorities

*Preliminary*

| | |
|---|---|
| 1. Preliminary | 89 |
| 2. Prescribed processes and prescribed substances | 91 |
| 3. Emission etc. limits and quality objectives | 92 |
| 4. Discharge and scope of functions | 93 |
| 5. *Repealed* | 94 |

*Authorisations*

| | |
|---|---|
| 6. Authorisations: general provisions | 95 |
| 7. Conditions of authorisations | 95 |
| 8. Fees and charges for authorisations | 97 |
| 9. Transfer of authorisations | 98 |
| 10. Variation of authorisations by enforcing authority | 99 |
| 11. Variation of conditions etc.: applications by holders of authorisations | 100 |
| 12. Revocation of authorisation | 102 |

*Enforcement*

| | |
|---|---|
| 13. Enforcement notices | 102 |
| 14. Prohibition notices | 103 |
| 15. Appeals as respects authorisations and against variation, enforcement and prohibition notices | 103 |
| 16–18. *Repealed* | 104 |
| 19. Obtaining of information from persons and authorities | 104 |

*Publicity*

| | |
|---|---|
| 20. Public registers of information | 105 |
| 21. Exclusion from registers of information affecting national security | 106 |
| 22. Exclusion from registers of certain confidential information | 107 |

*Provisions as to offences*

| | |
|---|---|
| 23. Offences | 108 |
| 24. Enforcement by High Court | 109 |
| 25. Onus of proof as regards techniques and evidence | 110 |
| 26. Power of court to order cause of offence to be remedied | 110 |
| 27. Power of chief inspector to remedy harm | 110 |

*Authorisations and other statutory controls*

| | |
|---|---|
| 28. Authorisations and other statutory controls | 111 |

## Part II: Waste on Land

*Preliminary*

29.   Preliminary                                                                           112
30.   Authorities for purposes of this Part                                                 113
31.   *Repealed*                                                                            114
32.   Transition to waste disposal companies etc                                            114

*Prohibition on unauthorised or harmful depositing, treatment or disposal of waste*

33.   Prohibition on unauthorised or harmful deposit, treatment or disposal etc. of waste   116

*Duty of care etc. as respects waste*

34.   Duty of care etc. as respects waste                                                   117

*Waste Management Licences*

35.   Waste management licences: general                                                    119
35A.  Compensation where rights granted pursuant to section 35(4) or 38(9A)                 120
36.   Grant of licences                                                                     121
36A.  Consultation before the grant of certain licences                                     124
37.   Variation of licences                                                                 125
37A.  Consultation before certain variations                                               126
38.   Revocation and suspension of licences                                                 127
39.   Surrender of licences                                                                 129
40.   Transfer of licences                                                                  131
41.   *Repealed*                                                                            131
42.   Supervision of licensed activities                                                    131
43.   Appeals to Secretary of State from decisions with respect to licences                 133
44.   Offences of making false or misleading statements or false entries                    134

*Collection. disposal or treatment of controlled waste*

44A.  National waste strategy: England and Wales                                            134
44B.  National waste strategy: Scotland                                                     136
45.   Collection of controlled waste                                                        137
46.   Receptacles for household waste                                                       139
47.   Receptacles for commercial or industrial waste                                        140
48.   Duties of waste collection authorities as respects disposal of waste collected        141
49.   Waste recycling plans by collection authorities                                       142
50.   *Repealed*                                                                            143
51.   Functions of waste disposal authorities                                               144
52.   Payments for recycling and disposal etc. of waste                                     145
53.   Duties of authorities as respects disposal of waste collected: Scotland               146
54.   *Repealed*                                                                            147
55.   Powers for recycling waste                                                            147
56.   Powers for recycling waste: Scotland                                                  148
57.   Power of Secretary of State to require waste to be accepted, treated, disposed of or
      delivered                                                                             148
58.   Power of Secretary of State to require waste to be accepted, treated, disposed of or
      delivered: Scotland                                                                   148
59.   Powers to require removal of waste unlawfully deposited                                149
60.   Interference with waste sites and receptacles for waste                               150
61.   *Repealed*                                                                            151

*Special waste and non-controlled waste*

62.   Special provision with respect to certain dangerous or intractable waste              151
63.   Waste other than controlled waste                                                     152

*Publicity*

64.  Public registers                                                                                          152
65.  Exclusion from registers of information affecting national security                                      154
66.  Exclusion from registers of certain confidential information                                            154
67.  *Repealed*                                                                                                156

*Supervision and enforcement*

68–70.  *Repealed*                                                                                             156
71.  Obtaining of information from persons and authorities                                                    156
72.  *Repealed*                                                                                                157

*Supplemental*

73.  Appeals and other provisions relating to legal proceedings and civil liability                          157
74.  Meaning of "fit and proper person"                                                                      158
75.  Meaning of "waste" and household, commercial and industrial waste and special waste                     159
76.  Application to the Isles of Scilly                                                                       160
77.  Transition from Control of Pollution Act 1974 to this Part                                              161
78.  This Part and radioactive substances                                                                    162

## Part IIA: Contaminated Land

78A.  Preliminary                                                                                              162
78B.  Identification of contaminated land                                                                     165
78C.  Identification and designation of special sites                                                         166
78D.  Referral of special site decisions to the Secretary of State                                           167
78E.  Duty of enforcing authority to require remediation of contaminated land etc                            168
78F.  Determination of the appropriate person to bear responsibility for remediation                         169
78G.  Grant of, and compensation for, rights of entry etc                                                    170
78H.  Restrictions and prohibitions on serving remediation notices                                          170
78J.  Restrictions on liability relating to the pollution of controlled waters                              173
78K.  Liability in respect of contaminating substances which escape to other land                           173
78L.  Appeals against remediation notices                                                                     175
78M.  Offences of not complying with a remediation notice                                                    176
78N.  Powers of the enforcing authority to carry out remediation                                            176
78P.  Recovery of, and security for, the cost of remediation by the enforcing authority                      177
78Q.  Special sites                                                                                           179
78R.  Registers                                                                                               180
78S.  Exclusion from registers of information affecting national security                                    181
78T.  Exclusion from registers of certain confidential information                                          182
78U.  Reports by the appropriate Agency on the state of contaminated land                                    183
78V.  Site-specific guidance by the appropriate Agency concerning contaminated land                         183
78W.  The appropriate Agency to have regard to guidance given by the Secretary of State                     184
78X.  Supplementary provisions                                                                                184
78Y.  Application to the Isles of Scilly                                                                      185
78YA.  Supplementary provisions with respect to guidance by the Secretary of State                           186
78YB.  Interaction of this Part with other enactments                                                        186
78YC.  This Part and radioactivity                                                                            187

## Part III: Statutory Nuisances and Clean Air

*Statutory nuisances: England and Wales*

79.  Statutory nuisances and inspections therefor                                                            187
80.  Summary proceedings for statutory nuisances                                                             190
80A.  Abatement notice in respect of noise in street                                                         192
81.  Supplementary provisions                                                                                193

81A. Expenses recoverable from owner to be a charge on premises                     194
81B. Payment of expenses by instalments                                             195
82.  Summary proceedings by persons aggrieved by statutory nuisances                196

*Statutory nuisances: Scotland*

83. *Repealed*                                                                       198

*Termination of existing controls over offensive trades and businesses*

84. Termination of Public Health Act controls over offensive trades etc             198

*Application to gases of certain Clean Air Act provisions*

85. *Repealed*                                                                       199

## Part IV: Litter etc

86–99. *Not reproduced*                                                              199

## Part V: Amendment of the Radioactive Substances Act 1960

100–105. *Repealed*                                                                  199

## Part VI: Genetically Modified Organisms

106–127. *Not reproduced*                                                            200

## Part VII: Nature Conservation in Great Britain and Countryside Matters in Wales

This Part, and schedules 6, 7 and 11, are set out in the companion volume, *A Manual of Nature Conservation Law*, edited by Michael Fry ( Oxford, 1995) at page 228

## Part VIII: Miscellaneous

*Other controls on substances, articles or waste*

140. Power to prohibit or restrict the importation, use, supply or storage of injurious
     substances or articles                                                         200
141. Power to prohibit or restrict the importation or exportation of waste          202
142. Powers to obtain information about potentially harmful substances              203
143. *Repealed*                                                                     205
144. Amendments of hazardous substances legislation                                 205
145. Penalties for offences of polluting controlled waters etc                      205

*Pollution at sea*

146–147. *Not reproduced*                                                           205
    148. *Repealed*                                                                 205

*Control of dogs*

149–51. *Not reproduced*                                                            205

*Straw and stubble burning*

152. *Not reproduced*                                                               205

*Environmental expenditure*

153–155. *Not reproduced*                                                           205

# Part IX: General

156.  Power to give effect to Community and other international obligations etc ... 205
157.  Offences by bodies corporate ... 206
158.  Offences under Parts I, II, IV, VI, etc.  due to fault of others ... 207
159.  Application to Crown ... 207
160.  Service of notices ... 207
161.  Regulations, orders and directions ... 208
162.  Consequential and minor amendments and repeals ... 208
163.  Financial provisions ... 209
164.  Short title, commencement and extent ... 209

SCHEDULES

Schedule I—Authorisations for Processes: Supplementary
Provisions ... 211
Part I—Grant of Authorisations ... 211
Part II—Variation of Authorisations ... 213
Schedule 2—Waste Disposal Authorities and Companies ... 215
Part I—Transition to Companies ... 215
Part II—Provisions regulating Waste Disposal Authorities and Companies ... 221
Schedule 2A—Objectives for the purposes of the National Waste Strategy ... 222
Schedule 2B—Categories of waste ... 223
Schedule 3—Statutory Nuisances: Supplementary Provisions ... 224
Schedules 4—*Not reproduced*
Schedule 5—*Repealed*
Schedules 6–11—*Not reproduced*
Schedule 12—Injurious or Hazardous Substances: Advisory Committee ... 227
Schedules 13–16—*Not reproduced*

# Environmental Protection Act 1990

## 1990 Chapter 43

An Act to make provision for the improved control of pollution arising from certain industrial and other processes; to re-enact the provisions of the Control of Pollution Act 1974 relating to waste on land with modifications as respects the functions of the regulatory and other authorities concerned in the collection and disposal of waste and to make further provision in relation to such waste; to restate the law defining statutory nuisances and improve the summary procedures for dealing with them, to provide for the termination of the existing controls over offensive trades or businesses and to provide for the extension of the Clean Air Acts to prescribed gases; to amend the law relating to litter and make further provision imposing or conferring powers to impose duties to keep public places clear of litter and clean; to make provision conferring powers in relation to trolleys abandoned on land in the open air; to amend the Radioactive Substances Act 1960; to make provision for the control of genetically modified organisms; to make provision for the abolition of the Nature Conservancy Council and for the creation of councils to replace it and discharge the functions of that Council and, as respects Wales, of the Countryside Commission; to make further provision for the control of the importation, exportation, use, supply or storage of prescribed substances and articles and the importation or exportation of prescribed descriptions of waste; to confer powers to obtain information about potentially hazardous substances; to amend the law relating to the control of hazardous substances on, over or under land; to amend section 107(6) of the Water Act 1989 and sections 31(7)(a), 31A(2)(c)(i) and 32(7)(a) of the Control of Pollution Act 1974; to amend the provisions of the Food and Environment Protection Act 1985 as regards the dumping of waste at sea; to make further provision as respects the prevention of oil pollution from ships; to make provision for and in connection with the identification and control of dogs; to confer powers to control the burning of crop residues; to make provision in relation to financial or other assistance for purposes connected with the environment; to make provision as respects superannuation of employees of the Groundwork Foundation and for remunerating the chairman of the Inland Waterways Amenity Advisory Council; and for purposes connected with those purposes.

[lst November 1990[1]]

## PART I: Integrated Pollution Control and Air Pollution Control by Local Authorities

*Transfer of functions*

The functions previously conferred on the chief inspector for England and Wales under this Part of this Act have been transferred to the Environment Agency: Environment Act 1995 (c. 25), s. 2 , p. 421 below. The functions previously conferred on the chief inspector for Scotland and, in Scotland, on local authorities as enforcing authorities in relation to the release of substances into the air, under

---

[1] This Act came into force on various dates noted at the Parts or sections below.

this Part have been transferred to the Scottish Environment Protection Agency, SEPA: Environment Act 1995 (c.25), s. 21, p. 438 below. The new agencies took over their functions under this Part on the transfer date, 1 April 1996: S.I. 1996/139; S.I. 1996/234.

*Commencement*

Sections 1, 2, 6–15 and 19–28 came into force on 1 January 1991; s. 3 came into force on 19 December 1990: S.I. 1990/2635.

The amendments made to this Part by the Environment Act 1995 came into force on 1 April 1996: S.I. 1996/186 except where otherwise noted. To avoid undue repetition this commencement date is not set out in the footnotes which relate to these amendments.

*Case: Part I*

Gateshead Metropolitan Borough Council v Secretary of State for the Environment and Northumbrian Water Group plc [1995] Env LR 37.

*Modifications*

For modifications to this Part see the Waste Management Licensing Regulations 1994, sch. 4, para. 8, p. 717 below.

*References*

A list of process and technical guidance notes is at page 815 below.

*Additional references to material not set out in this Manual*

Integrated Pollution Control: *A Practical Guide*. Guidance issued by the Department of the Environment and the Welsh Office. 1996, DoE, ISBN 1 85112 003 3.

Planning Policy Guidance Note 23: Planning and Pollution Control. Department of the Environment, July 1994.

*Note:* the above document was published before the introduction of the Environment Bill into Parliament and the subsequent enactment of the Environment Act 1995. This Act provided for the transfer of functions to the Environment Agency and SEPA noted above.

## Preliminary

*Preliminary*

1. (1) The following provisions have effect for the interpretation of this Part.

(2) The "environment" consists of all, or any, of the following media, namely, the air, water and land, and the medium of air includes the air within buildings and the air within other natural or man-made structures above or below ground.

(3) "Pollution of the environment" means pollution of the environment due to the release (into any environmental medium) from any process of substances which are capable of causing harm to man or any other living organisms supported by the environment.

(4) "Harm" means harm to the health of living organisms or other interference with the ecological systems of which they form part and, in the case of man, includes offence caused to any of his senses or harm to his property; and "harmless" has a corresponding meaning.

(5) "Process" means any activities carried on in Great Britain, whether on premises or by means of mobile plant, which are capable of causing pollution of the environment and "prescribed process" means a process prescribed under section 2(1) below.

(6) For the purposes of subsection (5) above—

"activities" means industrial or commercial activities or activities of any other nature whatsoever (including, with or without other activities, the keeping of a substance);

"Great Britain" includes so much of the adjacent territorial sea as is, or is treated as, relevant territorial waters for the purposes of Part III of the Water Resources Act 1991[1]; or as respects Scotland, Part II of the Control of Pollution Act 1974[2]; and

"mobile plant" means plant which is designed to move or to be moved whether on roads or otherwise.

(7) The "enforcing authority", in relation to England and Wales, is the Environment Agency[3] or the local authority by which[4], under section 4[5] below, the functions conferred or imposed by this Part otherwise than on the Secretary of State are for the time being exercisable in relation respectively to releases of substances into the environment or into the air; and "local enforcing authority" means any such local authority.

(8) In relation to Scotland, references to the "enforcing authority" and a "local enforcing authority" are references to the Scottish Environment Protection Agency (in this Part referred to as "SEPA")[6,7].

(9) "Authorisation" means an authorisation for a process (whether on premises or by means of mobile plant) granted under section 6 below[8]; and a reference to the conditions of an authorisation is a reference to the conditions subject to which at any time the authorisation has effect.

(10) A substance is "released" into any environmental medium whenever it is released directly into that medium whether it is released into it within or outside Great Britain and "release" includes—

(a)    in relation to air, any emission of the substance into the air;

(b)    in relation to water, any entry (including any discharge) of the substance into water;

(c)    in relation to land, any deposit, keeping or disposal of the substance in or on land;

and for this purpose "water" and "land" shall be construed in accordance with subsections (11) and (12) below.

(11) For the purpose of determining into what medium a substance is released—

(a)    any release into—

(i)    the sea or the surface of the seabed,

(ii)    any river, watercourse, lake, loch or pond (whether natural or artificial or above or below ground) or reservoir or the surface of the riverbed or of other land supporting such waters, or

(iii)    ground waters,

is a release into water;

(b)    any release into

(i)    land covered by water falling outside paragraph (a) above or the water covering such land; or

(ii)    the land beneath the surface of the seabed or of other land supporting waters falling within paragraph (a)(ii) above,

is a release into land; and

(c)    any release into a sewer (within the meaning of the Water Industry Act 1991[9] or, in

---

[1] P. 271 below. Words "Part III of the Water Resources Act 1991;" substituted by the Water Consolidation (Consequential Provisions) Act 1991 (c .60), s .2 (1), sch. 1, para. 56(1)(a). This amendment came into force on 1 December 1991: s. 4(2).

[2] P. 16 above.

[3] The Environment Agency is established by the Environment Act 1995 (c. 25), s. 1, p. 420 below.

[4] Words "the Environment Agency or the local authority by which," substituted by the Environment Act 1995 (c .25), s. 120, sch. 22, para. 45(2).

[5] P. 93 below.

[6] SEPA is established by the Environment Act 1995 (c. 25), s. 20, p. 438 below.

[7] Subsection (8) substituted by the Environment Act 1995 (c. 25), s. 120, sch. 22, para. 45(3).

[8] P. 95 below.

[9] 1991 c. 56. Words "the Water Industry Act 1991" substituted by the Water Consolidation (Consequential Provisions) Act 1991 (c. 60), s. 2 (1), sch. 1, para. 56 (1)(b). This amendment came into force on 1 December 1991: s. 4(2), 1968 c. 47.

relation to Scotland, of the Sewerage (Scotland) Act 1968[1]) shall be treated as a release into water;

but a sewer and its contents shall be disregarded in determining whether there is pollution of the environment at any time.

(12) In subsection (11) above "ground waters" means any waters contained in underground strata, or in—

(a)  a well, borehole or similar work sunk into underground strata, including any adit or passage constructed in connection with the well, borehole or work for facilitating the collection of water in the well, borehole or work; or

(b)  any excavation into underground strata where the level of water in the excavation depends wholly or mainly on water entering it from the strata.

(13) "Substance" shall be treated as including electricity or heat and "prescribed substance" has the meaning given by section 2(7) below.

(14) In this Part "the appropriate Agency" means—

(a)  in relation to England and Wales, the Environment Agency [2]; and

(b)  in relation to Scotland, SEPA[3,4].

---

*Prescribed processes and prescribed substances*

2. (1)  The Secretary of State may, by regulations, prescribe any description of process[5] as a process for the carrying on of which after a prescribed date an authorisation[6] is required under section 6 below[7,8].

(2)  Regulations under subsection (1) above may frame the description of a process by reference to any characteristics of the process or the area or other circumstances in which the process is carried on or the description of person carrying it on.

(3)  Regulations under subsection (1) above may prescribe or provide for the determination under the regulations of different dates for different descriptions of persons and may include such transitional provisions as the Secretary of State considers necessary or expedient as respects the making of applications for authorisations and suspending the application of section 6(1) below until the determination of applications made within the period allowed by the regulations.

(4)  Regulations under subsection (1) above shall, as respects each description of process, designate it as one for central control or one for local control.

(5)  The Secretary of State may, by regulations, prescribe any description of substance[9] as a substance the release[10] of which into the environment[11] is subject to control under sections 6 and 7 below.

(6)  Regulations under subsection (5) above may—

(a)  prescribe separately, for each environmental medium[12], the substances the release of which into that medium is to be subject to control; and

(b)  provide that a description of substance is only prescribed, for any environmental medium, so far as it is released into that medium in such amounts over such periods, in such concentrations or in such other circumstances as may be specified in the regulations;

---

[1] 1968 c.47.

[2] The Environment Agency is established by the Environment Act 1995 (c. 25), s. 1, p. 420 below. SEPA is established by the Environment Act 1995 (c. 25), s. 20, p. 438 below.

[3] SEPA is established by the Environment Act 1995 (c.25), s.20, p.000 below

[4] Paragraph (14) inserted by the Environment Act 1995 (c. 25), s. 120, sch. 22, para. 45(4).

[5] "Process" defined by s. 1(5) above.

[6] "Authorisation" defined by s. 1(9) above.

[7] P. 95 below.

[8] The following regulations have been made under this section: The Environmental Protection (Prescribed Processes and Substances) Regulations 1991, S.I. 1991/472, as amended, p. 566 below. " Substance" defined by s. 1 (13) above.

[9] "Substance" defined by s. 1(13) above.

[10] "Release" defined by s. 1(10) above.

[11] "The Environment" defined by s. 1(2), p. 89 above.

[12] "Environmental medium" defined by s. 1(2), p. 89 above.

and in relation to a substance of a description which is prescribed for releases into the air, the regulations may designate the substance as one for central control or one for local control.

(7)  In this Part "prescribed substance" means any substance of a description prescribed in regulations under subsection (5) above or, in the case of a substance of a description prescribed only for releases in circumstances specified under subsection (6)(b) above, means any substance of that description which is released in those circumstances.

*Emission etc. limits and quality objectives*

3.  (1)  The Secretary of State may make regulations under subsection (2) or (4) below establishing standards, objectives or requirements in relation to particular prescribed processes[1] or particular substances[2].

(2)  Regulations under this subsection may—

(a)  in relation to releases[3] of any substance from prescribed processes into any environmental medium[4], prescribe standard limits for—

(i)  the concentration, the amount or the amount in any period of that substance which may be so released; and

(ii)  any other characteristic of that substance in any circumstances in which it may be so released;

(b)  prescribe standard requirements for the measurement or analysis of, or of releases of, substances for which limits have been set under paragraph (a) above; and

(c)  in relation to any prescribed process, prescribe standards or requirements as to any aspect of the process.

(3)  Regulations under subsection (2) above may make different provision in relation to different cases, including different provision in relation to different processes, descriptions of person, localities or other circumstances.

(4)  Regulations under this subsection may establish for any environmental medium (in all areas or in specified areas) quality objectives or quality standards in relation to any substances which may be released into that or any other medium from any process.

(5)  The Secretary of State may make plans for—

(a)  establishing limits for the total amount, or the total amount in any period, of any substance which may be released into the environment[5] in, or in any area within, the United Kingdom;

(b)  allocating quotas as respects the release of substances to persons carrying on processes in respect of which any such limit is established;

(c)  establishing limits of the descriptions specified in subsection (2)(a) above so as progressively to reduce pollution of the environment[6];

(d)  the progressive improvement in the quality objectives and quality standards established by regulations under subsection (4) above;

and the Secretary of State may, from time to time, revise any plan so made.

(6)  Regulations or plans under this section may be made for any purposes of this Part or for other purposes.

(7)  The Secretary of State shall give notice in the London, Edinburgh and Belfast Gazettes of the making and the revision of any plan under subsection (5) above and shall make the documents containing the plan, or the plan as so revised, available for inspection by members of the public at the places specified in the notice.

[1] "Process" and "prescribed process" defined by s. 1(5), p. 89 above.
[2] "Substance" defined by s. 1(13), p. 91 above.
[3] "Release" defined by s. 1(10), p. 90 above.
[4] "Environmental medium" defined by s. 1(2), p. 89

above.
[5] "The environment" defined by s. 1(2), p. 89 above.
[6] "Pollution of the environment" defined by s. 1(3), p. 89 above.

**(8)** Subject to any Order made after the passing of this Act by virtue of subsection (1)(a) of section 3 of the Northern Ireland Constitution Act 1973[1], the making and revision of plans under subsection (5) above shall not be a transferred matter for the purposes of that Act but shall for the purposes of subsection (2) of that section be treated as specified in Schedule 3 to that Act.

*Discharge and scope of functions*

**4.** **(1)** This section determines the authority by whom the functions conferred or imposed by this Part otherwise than on the Secretary of State are exercisable and the purposes for which they are exercisable.

**(2)** Those functions, in their application to prescribed processes[2] designated for central control, shall be functions of the appropriate Agency[3], and shall be exercisable for the purpose of preventing or minimising pollution of the environment[4] due to the release[4A] of substances[5] into any environmental medium[6].

**(3)** Subject to subsection (4) below, those functions, in their application to prescribed processes designated for local control, shall be functions of—

(*a*) in the case of a prescribed process carried on (or to be carried on ) by means of a mobile plant, where the person carrying on the process has his principal place of business—

(i) in England and Wales, the local authority in whose area that place of business is;

(ii) in Scotland, SEPA[7];

(*b*) in any other cases, where the prescribed processes are (or are to be) carried on—

(i) in England and Wales, the local authority in whose area they are (or are to be) carried on;

(ii) in Scotland, SEPA[8];

and the functions applicable to such processes shall be exercisable for the purpose of preventing or minimising pollution of the environment due to the release of substances into the air[9] (but not into any other environmental medium).

**(4)** The Secretary of State may, as respects the functions under this Part being exercised by a local authority specified in the direction, direct that those functions shall be exercised instead by the Environment Agency[10] while the direction remains in force or during a period specified in the direction.

**(4A)** In England and Wales, a local authority, in exercising the functions conferred or imposed on it under this Part by virtue of subsection (3) above, shall have regard to the strategy for the time being published pursuant to section 80 of the Environment Act 1995[11,12].

**(5)** A transfer of functions under subsection (4) above to the Environment Agency[13] does not make them exercisable by that Agency[14] for the purpose of preventing or minimising pollution of the environment due to releases of substances into any other environmental medium than the air.

**(6)** A direction under subsection (4) above may transfer those functions as exercisable in relation to all or any description of prescribed processes carried on by all or any description of persons (a "general direction") or in relation to a prescribed process carried on by a specified person (a "specific direction").

[1] 1973 c. 36.
[2] "Process" and "prescribed process" defined by s. 1(5), p. 89 above.
[3] "The appropriate Agency" defined by s. 1(14), p. 91 above. Words "the appropriate Agency" inserted by the Environment Act 1995 (c. 25), s. 120, sch. 22, para. 46(2).
[4] "Pollution of the environment" defined by s. 1(3), p. 89 above.
[4A] "Release" defined by s. 1(10), p. 90 above.
[5] "Substance" defined by s .1 (13), p. 91 above.
[6] "Environmental medium" defined by s. 1(2), p. 89 above.
[7] "SEPA" means the Scottish Environment Protection Agency: s. 1(8), p. 90 above.

[8] Paras. (a) and (b) substituted by the Environment Act 1995 (c. 25), s. 120, sch. 22, para. 46 (3).
[9] The medium of air defined by s. 1(2), p. 89 above.
[10] Words "Environment Agency" substituted by the Environment Act 1995 (c. 25), s. 120, sch. 22, para. 46(4).
[11] P. 465 below.
[12] Subsection (4A) inserted by the Environment Act 1995 (c. 25), s. 120, sch. 22, para. 46(5). This amendment is not in force.
[13] Words "Environment Agency" substituted by the Environment Act 1995 (c. 25), s. 120, sch. 22, para. 46(6)(a).
[14] Words "that Agency" substituted by the Environment Act 1995 (c. 25), s. 120, sch. 22, para. 46(6)(b).

(7) A direction under subsection (4) above may include such saving and transitional provisions as the Secretary of State considers necessary or expedient.

(8) The Secretary of State, on giving or withdrawing a direction under subsection (4) above, shall—

(a) in the case of a general direction—

(i) forthwith serve notice of it on the Environment Agency[1] and on the local enforcing authorities affected by the direction; and

(ii) cause notice of it to be published as soon as practicable in the London Gazette[2] and in at least one newspaper circulating in the area of each authority affected by the direction;

(b) in the case of a specific direction—

(i) forthwith serve notice of it on the Environment Agency, the local enforcing authority and the person carrying on or appearing to the Secretary of State to be carrying on the process affected, and

(ii) cause notice of it to be published as soon as practicable in the London Gazette[2] and in at least one newspaper circulating in the authority's area;

and any such notice shall specify the date at which the direction is to take (or took) effect and (where appropriate) its duration.

(8A) The requirements of sub-paragraph (ii) of paragraph (a) or, as the case may be, of paragraph (b) of subsection (8) above shall not apply in any case where, in the opinion of the Secretary of State, the publication of notice in accordance with that sub-paragraph would be contrary to the interests of national security.[3]

(8B) Subsections (4) to (8A) shall not apply to Scotland.[3]

(9) It shall be the duty of local authorities to follow such developments in technology and techniques for preventing or reducing pollution of the environment due to releases of substances from prescribed processes as concern releases into the air of substances from prescribed processes designated for local control.[4]

(10) It shall be the duty of the Environment Agency, SEPA[5] and the local enforcing authorities to give effect to any directions given to them under any provision of this Part.

(11) In this Part "local authority" means, subject to subsection (12) below—

(a) in Greater London, a London borough council, the Common Council of the City of London, the Sub-Treasurer of the Inner Temple and the Under Treasurer of the Middle Temple;

(b) in England[6] outside Greater London, a district council and the Council of the Isles of Scilly;

(bb) in Wales, a county council or county borough council.[7,8]

(12) Where, by an order under section 2 of the Public Health (Control of Disease) Act 1984[1], a port health authority has been constituted for any port health district, the port health authority shall have by virtue of this subsection, as respects its district, the functions conferred or imposed by this Part and no such order shall be made assigning those functions; and "local authority" and "area" shall be construed accordingly.

5. *Repealed by the Environment Act 1995 (c. 25), s. 120, sch. 2 para. 47, sch. 24. This amendment came into force on 1 April 1996: S.I. 1996/186.*

[1] Words "Environment Agency" in this subsection substituted by the Environment Act 1995 (c. 25), s. 120, sch. 22, para. 46 (7)(a).
[2] Former words "or, as the case may be, in the Edinburgh Gazette" repealed by the Environment Act 1995 (c. 25), s. 120, sch. 22, para. 46(7)(b), sch. 24.
[3] Subsections (8A) and (8B) inserted by the Environment Act 1995 (c. 25), s. 120, sch. 22, para. 46 (8).
[4] Subsection (9) substituted by the Environment Act 1995 (c. 25), s. 120, sch. 22, para. 46(9).
[5] Words "the Environment Agency, SEPA" substituted by the Environment Act 1995 (c .25), s .120, sch .22, para .46 (10).
[6] Words "in England" inserted by the Environment Act 1995 (c. 25), s. 120, sch. 22, para. 46(11); words "and Wales" repealed by the Environment Act 1995 (c. 25), s. 120, sch. 24.
[7] Para. (bb) inserted by the Local Government (Wales) Act 1994 (c. 19), s. 22(3), sch. 9, para. 17(1). This amendment came into force on 1 April 1996: S.I. 1996/396.
[8] Former para. (c) repealed by the Environment Act 1995 (c. 25), s. 120, sch. 22, para. 46 (11) (b), sch. 24.

## Authorisations

*Authorisations: general provisions*

**6.** **(1)** No person shall carry on a prescribed process[2] after the date prescribed or determined for that description of process by or under regulations under section 2(1) above[3] (but subject to any transitional provision made by the regulations) except under an authorisation granted by the enforcing authority[4] and in accordance with the conditions to which it is subject.

**(2)** An application for an authorisation shall be made to the enforcing authority in accordance with Part I of Schedule I to this Act[5] and shall be accompanied by

(*a*) in a case where, by virtue of section 41 of the Environment Act 1995[6], a charge prescribed by a charging scheme under that section is required to be paid to the appropriate Agency[7] in respect of the application, the charge so prescribed; or

(*b*) in any other case,[8]

the fee prescribed under section 8(2)(a) below[9].

**(3)** Where an application is duly made to the enforcing authority, the authority shall either grant the authorisation subject to the conditions required or authorised to be imposed by section 7 below or refuse the application .

**(4)** An application shall not be granted unless the enforcing authority considers that the applicant will be able to carry on the process so as to comply with the conditions which would be included in the authorisation.

**(5)** The Secretary of State may, if he thinks fit in relation to any application for an authorisation, give to the enforcing authority directions as to whether or not the authority should grant the authorisation.

**(6)** The enforcing authority shall, as respects each authorisation in respect of which it has functions under this Part, from time to time but not less frequently than once in every period of four years, carry out a review of the conditions of the authorisation.

**(7)** The Secretary of State may, by regulations, substitute for the period for the time being specified in subsection (6) above such other period as he thinks fit.

**(8)** Schedule I to this Act[10] (supplementary provisions) shall have effect in relation to authorisations.

....................................................................................................................................

*Conditions of authorisations*

**7.** **(1)** There shall be included in an authorisation[11]—

(*a*) subject to paragraph (b) below, such specific conditions as the enforcing authority[12] considers appropriate, when taken with the general condition implied by subsection (4) below, for achieving the objectives specified in subsection (2) below;

(*b*) such conditions as are specified in directions given by the Secretary of State under subsection (3) below; and

(*c*) such other conditions (if any) as appear to the enforcing authority to be appropriate;

---

[1] 1984 c. 22.

[2] "Process" and "prescribed process" defined by s. 1(5), p. 89 above.

[3] P. 91 above.

[4] "Enforcing authority" defined by s. 1(7), (8), p. 90 above.

[5] P. 211 below.

[6] P. 452 below.

[7] "The appropriate Agency" defined by s. 1(14), p. 91 above.

[8] Paras. (a) and (b) inserted by the Environment Act 1995 (c. 25), s. 120, sch. 22, para. 48.

[9] P. 97 below.

[10] P. 211 below.

[11] "Authorisation" defined by s. 1(9), p. 90 above.

[12] "Enforcing authority" defined by s. 1(7), (8), p. 90 above.

but no conditions shall be imposed for the purpose only of securing the health of persons at work (within the meaning of Part I of the Health and Safety at Work etc. Act 1974[1]).

(2) Those objectives are—

(a) ensuring that, in carrying on a prescribed process[2], the best available techniques not entailing excessive cost[3] will be used—

    (i) for preventing the release[4] of substances[5] prescribed for any environmental medium[6] into that medium or, where that is not practicable by such means, for reducing the release of such substances to a minimum and for rendering harmless[7] any such substances which are so released; and

    (ii) for rendering harmless any other substances which might cause harm if released into any environmental medium;

(b) compliance with any directions by the Secretary of State given for the implementation of any obligations of the United Kingdom under the Community Treaties or international law relating to environmental protection;

(c) compliance with any limits or requirements and achievement of any quality standards or quality objectives prescribed by the Secretary of State under any of the relevant enactments[8];

(d) compliance with any requirements applicable to the grant of authorisations specified by or under a plan made by the Secretary of State under section 3(5) above[9].

(3) Except as respects the general condition implied by subsection (4) below, the Secretary of State may give directions to the enforcing authorities as to the conditions which are, or are not, to be included in all authorisations, in authorisations of any specified description or in any particular authorisation.

(4) Subject to subsections (5) and (6) below, there is implied in every authorisation a general condition that, in carrying on the process to which the authorisation applies, the person carrying it on must use the best available techniques not entailing excessive cost—

(a) for preventing the release of substances prescribed for any environmental medium into that medium or, where that is not practicable by such means, for reducing the release of such substances to a minimum and for rendering harmless any such substances which are so released; and

(b) for rendering harmless any other substances which might cause harm if released into any environmental medium.

(5) In the application of subsections (1) to (4) above to authorisations granted by a local enforcing authority references to the release of substances into any environmental medium are to be read as references to the release of substances into the air.

(6) The obligation implied by virtue of subsection (4) above shall not apply in relation to any aspect of the process in question which is regulated by a condition imposed under subsection (1) above.

(7) The objectives referred to in subsection (2) above shall, where the process—

(a) is one designated for central control; and

(b) is likely to involve the release of substances into more than one environmental medium;

---

[1] 1974 c. 37.

[2] "Process" and "prescribed process" defined by s. 1(5), p. 89 above.

[3] For "best available techniques not entailing excessive cost", commonly referred to as "BATNEEC", see subsection (10) below. Guidance on BATNEEC is set out in *Integrated Pollution Control: A practical Guide* issued by the Department of the Environment and the Welsh Office (1996, DoE, ISBN 1 85112 003 3).

[4] "Release" defined by s. 1(10), p. 90 above.

[5] "Substance" defined by s. 1(13), p. 91 above.

[6] "Environmental medium" defined by s. 1(2), p. 89 above.

[7] "Harmless" defined by s. 1(4), p. 89 above.

[8] "The relevant enactments" defined by subsection (12) below.

[9] P. 92 above.

include the objective of ensuring that the best available techniques not entailing excessive cost will be used for minimising the pollution which may be caused to the environment[1] taken as a whole by the releases having regard to the best practicable environmental option available as respects the substances which may be released.

(8) An authorisation for carrying on a prescribed process may, without prejudice to the generality of subsection (1) above, include conditions—

(a) imposing limits on the amount or composition of any substance produced by or utilised in the process in any period; and

(b) requiring advance notification of any proposed change in the manner of carrying on the process.

(9) This section has effect subject to section 28 below[2].

(10) References to the best available techniques not entailing excessive cost, in relation to a process, include (in addition to references to any technical means and technology) references to the number, qualifications, training and supervision of persons employed in the process and the design, construction, lay-out and maintenance of the buildings in which it is carried on.

(11) It shall be the duty of enforcing authorities to have regard to any guidance issued to them by the Secretary of State for the purposes of the application of subsections (2) and (7) above as to the techniques and environmental options that are appropriate for any description of prescribed process[3].

(12) In subsection (2) above "the relevant enactments" are any enactments or instruments contained in or made for the time being under—

(a) section 2 of the Clean Air Act 1968[4];

(b) section 2 of the European Communities Act 1972[5];

(c) Part I of the Health and Safety at Work etc. Act 1974[6];

(d) Parts II[7], III or IV[8] of the Control of Pollution Act 1974;

(e) the Water Resources Act 1991[9]; and[10]

(f) section 3 of this Act[11]; and

(g) section 87 of the Environment Act 1995[12,13].

*Fees and charges for authorisations*

8. (1) There shall be charged by and paid to the local enforcing authority[14] such fees and charges as may be prescribed from time to time by a scheme under subsection (2) below (whether by being specified in or made calculable under the scheme).

(2) The Secretary of State may, with the approval of the Treasury, make, and from time to time revise, a scheme prescribing—

(a) fees payable in respect of applications for authorisations[15];

---

[1] "Pollution of the environment" defined by s. 1(3), p. 89 above.

[2] Former words "and, in relation to Scotland, to any regulations made under s. 5(2) above" repealed by the Environment Act 1995 (c. 25), s. 120, sch. 22, para. 49 (1), sch. 24.

[3] A list of guidance issued to enforcing authorities by the Secretary of State is at p. 815 below.

[4] The Clean Air Act 1968 has been repealed and replaced by the Clean Air Act 1993 (c. 11). The corresponding provision in the 1993 Act is s. 5, p. 339 below.

[5] 1972 c. 58.

[6] 1974 c. 37.

[7] P. 16 above.

[8] Part IV has been repealed and replaced by the Clean Air Act 1993 (c. 11). The corresponding provisions in the 1993 Act are ss. 30–40, beginning at p. 352 below.

[9] P. 267 below.

[10] Para. (e) substituted by the Water Consolidation (Consequential Provisions) Act 1991 (c. 60), s. 2(1), sch. 1, para. 56(2). This amendment came into force on 1 December 1991: s. 4(2).

[11] P. 92 above.

[12] P. 471 below.

[13] Para.(g) added by the Environment Act 1995 (c. 25), s. 120, sch. 22, para. 49(2).

[14] "Local enforcing authority" defined by s. 1(7), p. 90 above. Words "local enforcing authority" substituted by the Environment Act 1995 (c. 25), s. 120, sch. 22, para. 50(2).

[15] "Authorisation" defined by s. 1(9), p. 90 above.

(b)  fees payable by persons holding authorisations in respect of, or of applications for, the variation of authorisations; and

(c)  charges payable by such persons in respect of the subsistence of their authorisations.

(3)  The Secretary of State shall, on making or revising a scheme under subsection (2) above, lay a copy of the scheme or of the alterations made in the scheme or, if he considers it more appropriate, the scheme as revised, before each House of Parliament.

(4)  *Repealed by the Environment Act 1995 (c. 25), s. 120, sch. 22, para. 50(3), sch. 24. This amendment came into force on 1 April 1996: S.I. 1996/186.*

(5)  A scheme under subsection (2) above may, in particular—

(a)  make different provision for different cases, including different provision in relation to different persons, circumstances or localities;

(b)  allow for reduced fees or charges to be payable in respect of authorisations for a number of prescribed processes[1] carried on by the same person;

(c)  provide for the times at which and the manner in which the payments required by the scheme are to be made; and

(d)  make such incidental, supplementary and transitional provision as appears to the Secretary of State to be appropriate.

(6)  The Secretary of State, in framing a scheme under subsection (2) above, shall, so far as practicable, secure that the fees and charges payable under the scheme are sufficient, taking one financial year with another, to cover the relevant expenditure attributable to authorisations.

(7)  The "relevant expenditure attributable to authorisations" is the expenditure incurred by the local enforcing authorities[2] in exercising their functions under this Part in relation to authorisations[3].

(8)  If it appears to the local enforcing authority[4] that the holder of an authorisation has failed to pay a charge due in consideration of the subsistence of the authorisation, it may, by notice in writing served on the holder, revoke the authorisation.

(9)  *Repealed by the Environment Act 1995 (c. 25), s. 120, sch. 22, para. 50(6), sch. 24. This amendment came into force on 1 April 1996: S.I. 1996/186.*

(10)  The foregoing provisions of this section shall not apply to Scotland.[5]

*Transfer of authorisations*

**9.** (1)  An authorisation[6] for the carrying on of any prescribed process[7] may be transferred by the holder to a person who proposes to carry on the process in the holder's place.

(2)  Where an authorisation is transferred under this section, the person to whom it is transferred shall notify[8] the enforcing authority[9] in writing of that fact not later than the end of the period of twenty-one days beginning with the date of the transfer.

(3)  An authorisation which is transferred under this section shall have effect on and after the date of the transfer as if it had been granted to that person under section 6 above[10], subject to the same conditions as were attached to it immediately before that date.

---

[1]  "Process" and "prescribed process" defined by s. 1(5), p. 89 above.

[2]  Words "local enforcing authorities" substituted by the Environment Act 1995 (c. 25), s. 120, sch. 22, para. 50(4)(a).

[3]  The remainder of this section, which related to expenditure incurred by the former National Rivers Authority, has been repealed by the Environment Act 1995 (c. 25), s. 120, sch. 22, para. 50(4)(b), sch. 24.

[4]  Words "local enforcing authority" substituted by the Environment Act 1995 (c. 25), s. 120, sch. 22, para. 50(5).

[5]  Subsection (10) substituted, for the earlier subsections (10) and (11), by the Environment Act 1995 (c. 25), s. 120, sch. 22, para. 50(7).

[6]  "Authorisation" defined by s. 1(9), p. 90 above.

[7]  "Process" and "prescribed process" defined by s. 1(5), p. 89 above.

[8]  For provisions relating to notice see s. 160, p. 207 below.

[9]  "Enforcing authority" defined by s. 1(7), (8), p. 90 above.

[10]  P. 95 above.

*Variation of authorisations by enforcing authority*

**10.** **(1)** The enforcing authority[1] may at any time, subject to the requirements of section 7 above[2], and, in cases to which they apply, the requirements of Part II of Schedule 1 to this Act[3], vary[4] an authorisation[5] and shall do so if it appears to the authority at that time that that section requires conditions to be included which are different from the subsisting conditions.

**(2)** Where the enforcing authority has decided to vary an authorisation under subsection (1) above the authority shall notify[6] the holder of the authorisation and serve a variation notice on him.

**(3)** In this Part a "variation notice" is a notice served by the enforcing authority on the holder of an authorisation—

(*a*) specifying variations of the authorisation which the enforcing authority has decided to make; and

(*b*) specifying the date or dates on which the variations are to take effect;

and, unless the notice is withdrawn or is varied under subsection (3A) below[7], the variations specified in a variation notice shall take effect on the date or dates so specified.

**(3A)** An enforcing authority which has served a variation notice may vary that notice by serving on the holder of the authorisation in question a further notice—

(*a*) specifying the variations which the enforcing authority has decided to make to the variation notice; and

(*b*) specifying the date or dates on which the variations specified in the variation notice, as varied by the further notice, are to take effect;

and any reference in this Part to a variation notice, or to a variation notice served under subsection (2) above, includes a reference to such a notice as varied by a further notice served under this subsection[8].

**(4)** A variation notice served under subsection (2) above shall also—

(*a*) require the holder of the authorisation, within such period as may be specified in the notice, to notify the authority what action (if any) he proposes to take to ensure that the process[9] is carried on in accordance with the authorisation as varied by the notice; and

(*b*) require the holder to pay, within such period as may be specified in the notice,—

    (i) in a case where the enforcing authority is the Environment Agency or SEPA[10], the charge (if any) prescribed[11] for the purpose by a charging scheme under section 41 of the Environment Act 1995[12]; or

    (ii) in any other case, the fee (if any) prescribed by a scheme under section 8 above[13,14].

**(5)** Where in the opinion of the enforcing authority any action to be taken by the holder of an authorisation in consequence of a variation notice served under subsection (2) above will involve a substantial change[15] in the manner in which the process is being carried on, the enforcing authority shall notify the holder of its opinion.

**(6)** The Secretary of State may, if he thinks fit in relation to authorisations of any description or particular authorisations, direct the enforcing authorities—

---

[1] "Enforcing authority" defined by s. 1(7), (8), p. 90 above.

[2] P. 95 above.

[3] P. 213 below.

[4] "Vary" defined by subsection (8) below.

[5] "Authorisation" defined by s. 1(9), p. 90 above.

[6] For provisions relating to notice see s. 160, p. 207 below.

[7] Words "or is varied under subsection (3A) below" inserted by the Environment Act 1995 (c. 25), s. 120, sch. 22, para. 51(2) on 12 October 1995: S.I. 1995/2649.

[8] Subsection (3A) inserted by the Environment Act 1995 (c. 25), s. 120, sch. 22, para. 51(3) on 12 October 1995: S.I. 1995/2649. "Process" defined by s. 1(5), p. 89 above. "SEPA" means the Scottish Environment Protection Agency: s. 1(8), p. 90 above.

[9] "Process" defined by s.1(5), p. 89 above.

[10] "SEPA" means the Scottish Environment Protection Agency: s.1(8), p. 90 above.

[11] "Prescribed" defined by subsection (8) below.

[12] P. 452 below.

[13] P. 97 above.

[14] Paragraph (b) substituted by the Environment Act 1995 (c. 25), s. 120, sch. 22, para. 51(4).

[15] "Substantial change" defined by subsection (7) below.

(*a*) to exercise their powers under this section, or to do so in such circumstances as may be specified in the directions, in such manner as may be so specified; or

(*b*) not to exercise those powers, or not to do so in such circumstances or such manner as may be so specified;

and the Secretary of State shall have the corresponding power of direction in respect of the powers of the enforcing authorities to vary authorisations under section 11 below.

(7) In this section and section 11 below a "substantial change", in relation to a prescribed process[1] being carried on under an authorisation, means a substantial change in the substances[2] released[3] from the process or in the amount or any other characteristic of any substance so released; and the Secretary of State may give directions to the enforcing authorities as to what does or does not constitute a substantial change in relation to processes generally, any description of process or any particular process.

(8) In this section and section 11 below—

"prescribed" means prescribed in regulations made by the Secretary of State[4];

"vary",

(*a*) in relation to the subsisting conditions or other provisions of an authorisation, means adding to them or varying or rescinding any of them; and

(*b*) in relation to a variation notice, means adding to, or varying or rescinding the notice or any of its contents[5];

and "variation" shall be construed accordingly.

*Variation of conditions etc: applications by holders of authorisations*

**11.** (1) A person carrying on a prescribed process[6] under an authorisation[7] who wishes to make a relevant change[8] in the process may at any time—

(a) notify[9] the enforcing authority[10] in the prescribed[11] form of that fact, and

(b) request the enforcing authority to make a determination, in relation to the proposed change, of the matters mentioned in subsection (2) below;

and a person making a request under paragraph (b) above shall furnish the enforcing authority with such information as may be prescribed or as the authority may by notice require[12].

(2) On receiving a request under subsection (1) above the enforcing authority shall determine—

(*a*) whether the proposed change would involve a breach of any condition of the authorisation;

(*b*) if it would not involve such a breach, whether the authority would be likely to vary[13] the conditions of the authorisation as a result of the change;

(*c*) if it would involve such a breach, whether the authority would consider varying the conditions of the authorisation so that the change may be made; and

(*d*) whether the change would involve a substantial change[14] in the manner in which the process is being carried on;

and the enforcing authority shall notify the holder of the authorisation of its determination of those matters.

[1] "Prescribed process" defined by s. 1(5), p. 89 above.
[2] "Substance" defined by s. 1(13), p. 91 above.
[3] "Release" defined by s. 1(10), p. 90 above.
[4] The following regulations have been made under this section: The Environmental Protection (Applications, Appeals and Registers) Regulations 1991, S.I. 1991/507, as amended, p. 605 below.
[5] Paragraph (b) inserted by the Environment Act 1995 (c. 25), s. 120, sch. 22, para. 51(5) on 12 October 1995: S.I. 1995/2649.
[6] "Process" and "prescribed process" defined by s. 1(5), p. 89 above.
[7] "Authorisation" defined by s. 1(9), p. 90 above.
[8] "Relevant change" defined by subsection (11) below.
[9] For provisions relating to notice see s. 160, p. 207 below.
[10] "Enforcing authority" defined by s. 1(7), (8), p. 90 above.
[11] "Prescribed" defined by s. 10(8) above.
[12] The following regulations have been made under this section: The Environmental Protection (Applications, Appeals and Registers) Regulations 1991, S.I. 1991/507, as amended, p. 605 below.
[13] "Vary" defined by s. 10(8) above.
[14] "Substantial change" defined by s. 10(7) above.

(3)  Where the enforcing authority has determined that the proposed change would not involve a substantial change, but has also determined under paragraph (b) or (c) of subsection (2) above that the change would lead to or require the variation of the conditions of the authorisation, then—

(a)  the enforcing authority shall (either on notifying its determination under that subsection or on a subsequent occasion) notify the holder of the authorisation of the variations which the authority is likely to consider making; and

(b)  the holder may apply in the prescribed form to the enforcing authority for the variation of the conditions of the authorisation so that he may make the proposed change.

(4)  Where the enforcing authority has determined that a proposed change would involve a substantial change that would lead to or require the variation of the conditions of the authorisation, then—

(a)  the authority shall (either on notifying its determination under subsection (2) above or on a subsequent occasion) notify the holder of the authorisation of the variations which the authority is likely to consider making; and

(b)  the holder of the authorisation shall, if he wishes to proceed with the change, apply in the prescribed form to the enforcing authority for the variation of the conditions of the authorisation.

(5)  The holder of an authorisation may at any time, unless he is carrying on a prescribed process under the authorisation and wishes to make a relevant change in the process, apply to the enforcing authority in the prescribed form for the variation of the conditions of the authorisation.

(6)  A person carrying on a process under an authorisation who wishes to make a relevant change in the process may, where it appears to him that the change will require the variation of the conditions of the authorisation, apply to the enforcing authority in the prescribed form for the variation of the conditions of the authorisation specified in the application.

(7)  A person who makes an application for the variation of the conditions of an authorisation shall furnish the authority with such information as may be prescribed or as the authority may by notice require.

(8)  On an application for variation of the conditions of an authorisation under any provision of this section—

(a)  the enforcing authority may, having fulfilled the requirements of Part II of Schedule 1 to this Act[1] in cases to which they apply, as it thinks fit either refuse the application or, subject to the requirements of section 7 above[2], vary the conditions or, in the case of an application under subsection (6) above, treat the application as a request for a determination under subsection (2) above; and

(b)  if the enforcing authority decides to vary the conditions, it shall serve a variation notice[3] on the holder of the authorisation.

(9)  Any application to the enforcing authority under this section shall be accompanied—

(a)  in a case where the enforcing authority is the Environment Agency or SEPA[4], by the charge (if any) prescribed for the purpose by a charging scheme under section 41 of the Environment Act 1995[5]; or

(b)  in any other case, by the fee (if any) prescribed by a scheme under section 8 above[6,7].

(10)  This section applies to any provision other than a condition which is contained in an authorisation as it applies to a condition with the modification that any reference to the breach of a condition shall be read as a reference to acting outside the scope of the authorisation.

---

[1]  P. 213 below.
[2]  P. 95 above.
[3]  "Variation notice" defined by s. 10(3) above.
[4]  "SEPA" means the Scottish Environment Protection Agency: s. 1(8), p. 90

[5]  P. 452 below.
[6]  P. 97 above.
[7]  Subsection (9) substituted by the Environment Act 1995 (c. 25), s. 120, sch. 22, para. 52.

(11) For the purposes of this section a relevant change in a prescribed process is a change in the manner of carrying on the process which is capable of altering the substances[1] released[2] from the process or of affecting the amount or any other characteristic of any substance so released.

*Revocation of authorisation*

**12.** (1) The enforcing authority[3] may at any time revoke an authorisation[4] by notice[5] in writing to the person holding the authorisation.

(2) Without prejudice to the generality of subsection (1) above, the enforcing authority may revoke an authorisation where it has reason to believe that a prescribed process[6] for which the authorisation is in force has not been carried on or not for a period of twelve months.

(3) The revocation of an authorisation under this section shall have effect from the date specified in the notice; and the period between the date on which the notice is served and the date so specified shall not be less than twenty-eight days.

(4) The enforcing authority may, before the date on which the revocation of an authorisation takes effect, withdraw the notice or vary the date specified in it.

(5) The Secretary of State may, if he thinks fit in relation to an authorisation, give to the enforcing authority directions as to whether the authority should revoke the authorisation under this section.

## Enforcement

*Enforcement notices*

**13.** (1) If the enforcing authority[7] is of the opinion that the person carrying on a prescribed process[8] under an authorisation[9] is contravening any condition of the authorisation, or is likely to contravene any such condition, the authority may serve on him a notice[10] ("an enforcement notice").

(2) An enforcement notice shall—

(a) state that the authority is of the said opinion;

(b) specify the matters constituting the contravention or the matters making it likely that the contravention will arise, as the case may be;

(c) specify the steps that must be taken to remedy the contravention or to remedy the matters making it likely that the contravention will arise, as the case may be; and

(d) specify the period within which those steps must be taken.

(3) The Secretary of State may, if he thinks fit in relation to the carrying on by any person of a prescribed process, give to the enforcing authority directions as to whether the authority should exercise its powers under this section and as to the steps which are to be required to be taken under this section.

(4) The enforcing authority may, as respects any enforcement notice it has issued to any person, by notice in writing served on that person, withdraw the notice[11].

---

[1] "Substance" defined by s. 1(13), p. 91 above.
[2] "Release" defined by s. 1(10), p. 90 above.
[3] "Enforcing authority" defined by s. 1(7), (8), p. 90 above.
[4] "Authorisation" defined by s. 1(9), p. 90 above.
[5] For provisions relating to notice see s. 160, p. 207 below.
[6] "Process" and "prescribed process" defined by s. 1(5), p. 89 above.
[7] "Enforcing authority" defined by s. 1(7), (8), p. 90 above.
[8] "Process" and "prescribed process" defined by s. 1(5), p. 89 above.
[9] "Authorisation" defined by s. 1(9), p. 90 above.
[10] For provisions relating to notice see s. 160, p. 207 below.
[11] Subsection (4) inserted by the Environment Act 1995 (c. 25), s. 120, sch. 22, para. 53 on 12 October 1995: S.I. 1995/2649.

*Prohibition notices*

**14.** **(1)** If the enforcing authority[1] is of the opinion, as respects the carrying on of a prescribed process[2] under an authorisation[3], that the continuing to carry it on, or the continuing to carry it on in a particular manner, involves an imminent risk of serious pollution of the environment[4] the authority shall serve a notice[5] (a "prohibition notice") on the person carrying on the process.

**(2)** A prohibition notice may be served whether or not the manner of carrying on the process in question contravenes a condition of the authorisation and may relate to any aspects of the process, whether regulated by the conditions of the authorisation or not.

**(3)** A prohibition notice shall—

(*a*)  state the authority's opinion;

(*b*)  specify the risk involved in the process;

(*c*)  specify the steps that must be taken to remove it and the period within which they must be taken; and

(*d*)  direct that the authorisation shall, until the notice is withdrawn, wholly or to the extent specified in the notice cease to have effect to authorise the carrying on of the process;

and where the direction applies to part only of the process it may impose conditions to be observed in carrying on the part which is authorised to be carried on.

**(4)** The Secretary of State may, if he thinks fit in relation to the carrying on by any person of a prescribed process, give to the enforcing authority directions as to—

(*a*)  whether the authority should perform its duties under this section; and

(*b*)  the matters to be specified in any prohibition notice in pursuance of subsection (3) above which the authority is directed to issue.

**(5)** The enforcing authority shall, as respects any prohibition notice it has issued to any person, by notice in writing served on that person, withdraw the notice when it is satisfied that the steps required by the notice have been taken.

*Appeals as respects authorisations and against variation, enforcement and prohibition notices*

**15.** **(1)** The following persons, namely—

(*a*)  a person who has been refused the grant of an authorisation[6] under section 6 above[7];

(*b*)  a person who is aggrieved by the conditions attached, under any provision of this Part, to his authorisation;

(*c*)  a person who has been refused a variation of an authorisation on an application under section 11 above[8];

(*d*)  a person whose authorisation has been revoked under section 12 above[9];

may appeal against the decision of the enforcing authority[10] to the Secretary of State (except where the decision implements a direction of his).

**(2)** A person on whom a variation notice[11], an enforcement notice[11] or a prohibition notice[12] is served may appeal against the notice to the Secretary of State (except where the notice implements a direction of his)[13].

[1] "Enforcing authority" defined by s. 1(7), (8), p. 90 above.

[2] "Process" and "prescribed process" defined by s. 1(5), p. 89 above.

[3] "Authorisation" defined by s. 1(9), p. 90 above.

[4] "Pollution of the environment" defined by s. 1(3), p. 89 above.

[5] For provisions relating to notice see s. 160, p. 207 below.

[6] "Authorisation" defined by s. 1(9), p. 90 above.

[7] P. 95 above.

[8] P. 100 above.

[9] P. 102 above.

[10] "Enforcing authority" defined by s. 1(7), (8), p. 90 above.

[11] "Variation notice" defined by s. 10(3), p. 99 above. For "enforcement notice" see s. 13 above.

[12] For "prohibition notice" see s. 14 above.

[13] Words "(except where the notice implements a direction of his)." added by the Environment Act 1995 (c. 25), s. 120, sch. 22, para. 54(2).

(3) This section is subject to section 114 of the Environment Act 1995[1] (delegation or reference of appeals etc)[2].

(4) An appeal under this section shall, if and to the extent required by regulations under subsection (10) below, be advertised in such manner as may be prescribed by regulations under that subsection.

(5) Before determining an appeal under this section, the Secretary of State may, if he thinks fit—

(a) cause the appeal to take or continue in the form of a hearing (which may, if the person hearing the appeal so decides, be held, or held to any extent, in private ); or

(b) cause a local inquiry to be held;

and the Secretary of State shall act as mentioned in paragraph (a) or (b) above if a request is made by either party to the appeal to be heard with respect to the appeal[3].

(6) On determining an appeal against a decision of an enforcing authority under subsection (1) above, the Secretary of State—

(a) may affirm the decision;

(b) where the decision was a refusal to grant an authorisation or a variation of an authorisation, may direct the enforcing authority to grant the authorisation or to vary the authorisation, as the case may be;

(c) where the decision was as to the conditions attached to an authorisation, may quash all or any of the conditions of the authorisation;

(d) where the decision was to revoke an authorisation, may quash the decision;

and where he exercises any of the powers in paragraphs (b), (c) or (d) above, he may give directions as to the conditions to be attached to the authorisation.

(7) On the determination of an appeal under subsection (2) above the Secretary of State may either quash or affirm the notice and, if he affirms it, may do so either in its original form or with such modifications as he may in the circumstances think fit.

(8) Where an appeal is brought under subsection (1) above against the revocation of an authorisation, the revocation shall not take effect pending the final determination or the withdrawal of the appeal.

(9) Where an appeal is brought under subsection (2) above against a notice, the bringing of the appeal shall not have the effect of suspending the operation of the notice.

(10) Provision may be made by the Secretary of State by regulations with respect to appeals under this section and in particular—

(a) as to the period within which and the manner in which appeals are to be brought; and

(b) as to the manner in which appeals are to be considered;

and any such regulations may make different provision for different cases or different circumstances[4,5].

**16–18.** *Repealed by the Environment Act 1995 (c. 25), s. 120, sch. 22, para. 55, sch. 24. This amendment came into force on 1 April 1996: S.I. 1996/186.*

......

*Obtaining of information from persons and authorities*

**19.** (1) For the purposes of the discharge of his functions under this Part, the Secretary of State may, by notice in writing served on an enforcing authority[6], require the authority to furnish such

[1] P. 489 below.
[2] Subsection (3) substituted by the Environment Act 1995 (c. 25), s. 120 sch. 22, para. 54(3).
[3] Subsection (5) substituted by the Environment Act 1995 (c. 25), s. 120, sch. 22, para. 54(4).
[4] The following regulations have been made under this section: The Environmental Protection (Applications, Appeals and Registers) Regulations 1991, S.I. 1991/507, as amended, p. 605 below.
[5] Words "and any such regulations ... circumstances" added by the Environment Act 1995 (c. 25), s. 120, sch. 22, para. 54(5).
[6] "Enforcing authority" defined by s. 1(7), (8), p. 90 above.

information about the discharge of its functions as an enforcing authority under this Part as he may require.

(2) For the purposes of the discharge of their respective functions under this Part, the following authorities, that is to say—

(*a*) the Secretary of State,

(*b*) a local enforcing authority[1],

(*c*) the Environment Agency, and

(*d*) SEPA[2,3]

may, by notice[4] in writing served on any person, require that person to furnish to the authority such information which the authority reasonably considers that it needs as is specified in the notice, in such form and within such period following service of the notice, or at such time[5], as is so specified.

(3) For the purposes of this section the discharge by the Secretary of State of an obligation of the United Kingdom under the Community Treaties or any international agreement relating to environmental protection shall be treated as a function of his under this Part.

## *Publicity*

### *Public registers of information*

**20.** (1) It shall be the duty of each enforcing authority[6], as respects prescribed processes[7] for which it is the enforcing authority, to maintain, in accordance with regulations made by the Secretary of State, a register containing prescribed[8] particulars of or relating to—

(*a*) applications for authorisations[9] made to that authority;

(*b*) the authorisations which have been granted by that authority or in respect of which the authority has functions under this Part;

(*c*) variation notices[10], enforcement notices[11] and prohibition notices[12] issued by that authority;

(*d*) revocations of authorisations effected by that authority;

(*e*) appeals under section 15 above[13];

(*f*) convictions for such offences under section 23(1) below[14] as may be prescribed;

(*g*) information obtained or furnished in pursuance of the conditions of authorisations or under any provision of this Part;

(*h*) directions given to the authority under any provision of this Part by the Secretary of State; and

(*i*) such other matters relating to the carrying on of prescribed processes or any pollution of the environment[15] caused thereby as may be prescribed;

but that duty is subject to sections 21 and 22 below[16].

---

[1] "Local enforcing authority" defined by s. 1(7), (8), p. 90 above.
[2] "SEPA" means the Scottish Environment Protection Agency: s. 1(8), p. 90 above.
[3] Paras. (c) and (d) substituted by the Environment Act 1995 (c. 25), s. 120, sch. 22, para. 56(a).
[4] For provisions relating to notice see s. 160, p. 207 below.
[5] Words ", or at such time," inserted by the Environment Act 1995 (c. 25), s. 120, sch. 22, para. 56(b).
[6] "Enforcing authority" defined by s. 1(7), (8), p. 90 above.
[7] "Process" and "prescribed process" defined by s. 1(5), p. 89 above.

[8] "Prescribed" defined by subsection (10) below.
[9] "Authorisation" defined by s. 1(9), p. 90 above.
[10] "Variation notice" defined by s. 10(3), p. 99 above.
[11] For "enforcement notice" see s. 13, p. 102 above.
[12] For "prohibition notice" see s. 14, p. 103 above.
[13] P. 103 above.
[14] P. 108 below.
[15] "Pollution of the environment" defined by s. 1(3), p. 89 above.
[16] The following regulations have been made under this section: The Environmental Protection (Applications, Appeals and Registers) Regulations 1991, S.I. 1991/507, as amended, p. 605 below.

(2) Subject to subsection (4) below, the register maintained by a local enforcing authority[1] in England and Wales[2] shall also contain prescribed particulars of such information contained in any register maintained by the Environment Agency[3] as relates to the carrying on in the area of the authority of prescribed processes in relation to which the Environment Agency has functions under this Part; and the Environment Agency shall furnish each authority with the particulars which are necessary to enable it to discharge its duty under this subsection.

(3) *Repealed by the Environment Act 1995 (c. 25), s. 120, sch. 22, para. 57(3), sch. 24. This amendment came into force on 1 April 1996: S.I. 1996/186.*

(4) Subsection (2) above does not apply to port health authorities but each local enforcing authority in England and Wales[4] whose area adjoins that of a port health authority shall include corresponding information in the register maintained by it; and the Environment Agency[5] shall furnish each such local enforcing authority with the particulars which are necessary to enable it to discharge its duty under this subsection.

(5) Where information of any description is excluded from any register by virtue of section 22 below[6], a statement shall be entered in the register indicating the existence of information of that description.

(6) The Secretary of State may give to enforcing authorities directions requiring the removal from any register of theirs of any specified information not prescribed for inclusion under subsection (1) or (2) above or which, by virtue of section 21 or 22 below, ought to have been excluded from the register.

(7) It shall be the duty of each enforcing authority—

(a) to secure that the registers maintained by them under this section are available at all reasonable times, for inspection by the public free of charge; and

(b) to afford to members of the public facilities for obtaining copies of entries, on payment of reasonable charges;

and, for the purposes of this subsection, places may be prescribed by the Secretary of State at which any such registers or facilities as are mentioned in paragraph (a) or (b) above are to be available or afforded to the public in pursuance of the paragraph in question[7].

(8) Registers under this section may be kept in any form.

(9) *Repealed by the Environment Act 1995 (c. 25), s. 120, sch. 22, para. 57(6), sch. 24. This amendment came into force on 1 April 1996: S.I. 1996/186.*

(10) In this section "prescribed" means prescribed in regulations under this section.

*Exclusion from registers of information affecting national security*

21. (1) No information shall be included in a register maintained under section 20 above if and so long as, in the opinion of the Secretary of State, the inclusion in the register of that information, or information of that description, would be contrary to the interests of national security.

(2) The Secretary of State may, for the purpose of securing the exclusion from registers of information to which subsection (1) above applies, give to enforcing authorities[8] directions—

(a) specifying information, or descriptions of information, to be excluded from their registers; or

(b) specifying descriptions of information to be referred to the Secretary of State for his determination;

---

[1] "Local enforcing authority" defined by s . 1(7), (8), p. 90 above.
[2] Words "in England and Wales" inserted by the Environment Act 1995 (c. 25), s. 120, sch. 22, para. 57(2).
[3] Words "the Environment Agency" in this subsection substituted by the Environment Act 1995 (c. 25), s. 120, sch. 22, para. 57(2).
[4] Words "in England and Wales" inserted by the

[5] Environment Act 1995 (c. 25), s. 120, sch. 22, para. 57(4).
[5] Words "the Environment Agency" substituted by the Environment Act 1995 (c. 25), s. 120, sch. 22, para. 57(4).
[6] P. 107 below.
[7] Words "and, for the purposes . . . question" added by the Environment Act 1995 (c. 25), s. 120, sch. 22, para. 57(5).
[8] "Enforcing authority" defined by s. 1(7), (8), p. 90 above.

and no information referred to the Secretary of State in pursuance of paragraph (b) above shall be included in any such register until the Secretary of State determines that it should be so included.

(3)  The enforcing authority shall notify the Secretary of State of any information it excludes from the register in pursuance of directions under subsection (2) above.

(4)  A person may, as respects any information which appears to him to be information to which subsection (1) above may apply, give a notice to the Secretary of State specifying the information and indicating its apparent nature; and, if he does so—

(a) he shall notify the enforcing authority that he has done so; and

(b) no information so notified to the Secretary of State shall be included in any such register until the Secretary of State has determined that it should be so included.

*Exclusion from registers of certain confidential information*

**22.** (1)  No information relating to the affairs of any individual or business shall be included in a register maintained under section 20 above[1], without the consent of that individual or the person for the time being carrying on that business, if and so long as the information—

(*a*) is, in relation to him, commercially confidential[2]; and

(*b*) is not required to be included in the register in pursuance of directions under subsection (7) below;

but information is not commercially confidential for the purposes of this section unless it is determined under this section to be so by the enforcing authority[3] or, on appeal, by the Secretary of State.

(2)  Where information is furnished to an enforcing authority for the purpose of—

(*a*) an application for an authorisation[4] or for the variation of an authorisation;

(*b*) complying with any condition of an authorisation; or

(*c*) complying with a notice under section 19(2) above[5];

then, if the person furnishing it applies to the authority to have the information excluded from the register on the ground that it is commercially confidential (as regards himself or another person), the authority shall determine whether the information is or is not commercially confidential.

(3)  A determination under subsection (2) above must be made within the period of fourteen days beginning with the date of the application and if the enforcing authority fails to make a determination within that period it shall be treated as having determined that the information is commercially confidential.

(4)  Where it appears to an enforcing authority that any information (other than information furnished in circumstances within subsection (2) above) which has been obtained by the authority under or by virtue of any provision of this Part might be commercially confidential, the authority shall—

(*a*) give to the person to whom or whose business it relates notice[6] that that information is required to be included in the register unless excluded under this section; and

(*b*) give him a reasonable opportunity—

(i) of objecting to the inclusion of the information on the ground that it is commercially confidential; and

(ii) of making representations to the authority for the purpose of justifying any such objection;

---

[1] P. 105 above.

[2] "Commercially confidential" information defined by subsection (11) below.

[3] "Enforcing authority" defined by s. 1(7), (8), p. 90 above.

[4] "Authorisation" defined by s. 1(9), p. 90 above.

[5] P. 105 above.

[6] For provisions relating to notice see s. 160, p. 207 below.

and, if any representations are made, the enforcing authority shall, having taken the representations into account, determine whether the information is or is not commercially confidential.

(5) Where, under subsection (2) or (4) above, an authority determines that information is not commercially confidential—

(a) the information shall not be entered in the register[1] until the end of the period of twenty-one days beginning with the date on which the determination is notified to the person concerned;

(b) that person may appeal to the Secretary of State against the decision;

and where an appeal is brought in respect of any information, the information shall not be entered in the register until the end of the period of seven days following the day on which the appeal is finally determined or withdrawn[2].

(6) Subsections (5) and (10) of section 15 above[3] shall apply in elation to an appeal under subsection (5) above as they apply in relation to an appeal under that section, but—

(a) subsection (5) of that section shall have effect for the purposes of this subsection with the substitution for the words from "(which may" onwards of the words "(which must be held in private)"; and

(b) subsection (5) above is subject to section 114 of the Environment Act 1995[4] (delegation or reference of appeals etc)[5,6].

(7) The Secretary of State may give to the enforcing authorities directions as to specified information, or descriptions of information, which the public interest requires to be included in registers maintained under section 20 above notwithstanding that the information may be commercially confidential.

(8) Information excluded from a register shall be treated as ceasing to be commercially confidential for the purposes of this section at the expiry of the period of four years beginning with the date of the determination by virtue of which it was excluded; but the person who furnished it may apply to the authority for the information to remain excluded from the register on the ground that it is still commercially confidential and the authority shall determine whether or not that is the case.

(9) Subsections (5) and (6) above shall apply in relation to a determination under subsection (8) above as they apply in relation to a determination under subsection (2) or (4) above.

(10) The Secretary of State may, by order, substitute for the period for the time being specified in subsection (3) above such other period as he considers appropriate.

(11) Information is, for the purposes of any determination under this section, commercially confidential, in relation to any individual or person, if its being contained in the register would prejudice to an unreasonable degree the commercial interests of that individual or person.

*Provisions as to offences*

*Offences*

23. (1) It is an offence for a person—

(a) to contravene section 6(1) above[7];

(b) to fail to give the notice required by section 9(2) above[8];

---

[1] Words "in the register" substituted by the Environment Act 1995 (c. 25), s. 120, sch. 22, para. 58(2)(a).
[2] Words "in the register . . . withdrawn" substituted by the Environment Act 1995 (c. 25), s. 120, sch. 22, para. 58(2)(b).
[3] P. 103 above.
[4] P. 489 below.
[5] Subsection (6) inserted by the Environment Act 1995

(c. 25), s. 120, sch. 22, para. 58(6).
[6] The following regulations have been made under this section:
The Environmental Protection (Applications, Appeals and Registers) Regulations 1991, S.I. 1991/507, as amended, p. 605 below.
[7] P. 95 above.
[8] P. 98 above.

(c) to fail to comply with or contravene any requirement or prohibition imposed by an enforcement notice[1] or a prohibition notice[2];

(d)–(f) *Repealed by the Environment Act 1995 (c. 25), s. 120, sch. 22, para. 59(2), sch. 24. This amendment came into force on 1 April 1996: S.I. 1996/186.*

(g) to fail, without reasonable excuse, to comply with any requirement imposed by a notice under section 19(2) above[3];

(h) to make a statement which he knows to be false or misleading in a material particular, or recklessly to make a statement which is false or misleading in a material particular, where the statement is made—

(i) in purported compliance with a requirement to furnish any information imposed by or under any provision of this Part; or

(ii) for the purpose of obtaining the grant of an authorisation[4] to himself or any other person or the variation of an authorisation;

(i) intentionally to make a false entry in any record required to be kept under section 7 above[5];

(j) with intent to deceive, to forge or use a document issued or authorised to be issued under section 7 above or required for any purpose thereunder or to make or have in his possession a document so closely resembling any such document as to be likely to deceive;

(k) *Repealed by the Environment Act 1995 (c. 25), s. 120, sch. 22, para. 59(2), sch. 24 .*

(l) to fail to comply with an order made by a court under section 26 below[6].

(2) A person guilty of an offence under paragraph (a), (c) or (l) of subsection (1) above shall be liable:

(a) on summary conviction, to a fine not exceeding £20,000 or to imprisonment for a term not exceeding three months, or to both[7];

(b) on conviction on indictment, to a fine or to imprisonment for a term not exceeding two years, or to both.

(3) A person guilty of an offence under paragraph (b), (g), (h), (i) or (j) of subsection (1) above shall be liable—

(a) on summary conviction, to a fine not exceeding the statutory maximum[8];

(b) on conviction on indictment, to a fine or to imprisonment for a term not exceeding two years, or to both.

(4) and (5) *Repealed by the Environment Act 1995 (c. 25), s. 120, sch. 22, para. 59(4), (5), sch. 24. This amendment came into force on 1 April 1996: S.I. 1996/186.*

*Enforcement by High Court*

**24.** If the enforcing authority is of the opinion that proceedings for an offence under section 23(1)(c) above would afford an ineffectual remedy against a person who has failed to comply with the requirements of an enforcement notice[9] or a prohibition notice[10], the authority may take proceedings in the High Court or, in Scotland, in any court of competent jurisdiction for the purpose of securing compliance with the notice.

---

[1] For "enforcement notice" see s. 13, p. 102 above.
[2] For "prohibition notice" see s. 14, p. 103 above.
[3] P. 105 above.
[4] "Authorisation" defined by s. 1(9), p. 90 above.
[5] P. 95 above.
[6] P. 110 below.
[7] Words "or to imprisonment . . . both" inserted by the

Environment Act 1995 (c. 25), s. 120, sch. 22, para. 59(3).
[8] The current statutory maximum is £5,000: Criminal Justice Act 1991 (c. 53), s. 17(2); Criminal Procedure (Scotland) Act 1995 (c. 46), s. 225(8).
[9] For "enforcement notice" see s. 13, p. 102 above.
[10] For "prohibition notice" see s. 14, p. 103 above.

*Onus of proof as regard techniques and evidence*

**25.** (1)  In any proceedings for an offence under section 23(1)(a) above consisting in a failure to comply with the general condition implied in every authorisation[1] by section 7(4) above[2], it shall be for the accused to prove that there was no better available technique not entailing excessive cost[3] than was in fact used to satisfy the condition.

(2)  Where—

(*a*)  an entry is required under section 7 above to be made in any record as to the observance of any condition of an authorisation; and

(*b*)  the entry has not been made;

that fact shall be admissible as evidence that that condition has not been observed.

(3)  Subsection (2) above shall not have effect in relation to any entry required to be made in any record by virtue of a condition of a relevant licence, within the meaning of section 111 of the Environment Act 1995 (which makes corresponding provision in relation to such licences)[3A].

*Power of court to order cause of offence to be remedied*

**26.** (1)  Where a person is convicted of an offence under section 23(1)(a) or (c) above[4] in respect of any matters which appear to the court to be matters which it is in his power to remedy, the court may, in addition to or instead of imposing any punishment, order him, within such time as may be fixed by the order, to take such steps as may be specified in the order for remedying those matters.

(2)  The time fixed by an order under subsection (1) above may be extended or further extended by order of the court on an application made before the end of the time as originally fixed or as extended under this subsection, as the case may be.

(3)  Where a person is ordered under subsection (1) above to remedy any matters, that person shall not be liable under section 23 above in respect of those matters in so far as they continue during the time fixed by the order or any further time allowed under subsection (2) above.

*Power of chief inspector to remedy harm*

**27.** (1)  Where the commission of an offence under section 23(1)(a) or (c) above[5] causes any harm[6] which it is possible to remedy, the appropriate Agency[7] may, subject to subsection (2) below—

(*a*)  arrange for any reasonable steps to be taken towards remedying the harm; and

(*b*)  recover the cost of taking those steps from any person convicted of that offence.

(2)  The Environment Agency or SEPA[8], as the case may be, shall not exercise its[9] powers under this section except with the approval in writing of the Secretary of State and, where any of the steps are to be taken on or will affect land in the occupation of any person other than the person on whose land the prescribed process[10] is being carried on, with the permission of that person.

---

[1] "Authorisation" defined by s. 1(9), p. 90 above.

[2] P. 96 above.

[3] For "best available techniques not entailing excessive cost" see p. 96, n. 3 above.

[3A] P. 487 below. Subsection (3) inserted by the Environment Act 1995, s. 111(6).

[4] P. 108 above.

[5] P. 108 above.

[6] "Harm" defined by s. 1(4), p. 89 above.

[7] "The appropriate Agency" defined by s. 1(14), p. 91 above. Words "the appropriate Agency" substituted by the Environment Act 1995 (c. 25), s. 120 sch. 22, para. 60(1).

[8] "SEPA" means the Scottish Environment Protection Agency: s. 1(8), p. 90 above.

[9] Words "The Environment Agency ... its" inserted by the Environment Act 1995 (c. 25), s. 120, sch. 22, para. 60(2).

[10] "Process" and "prescribed process" defined by s. 1(5), p. 89 above.

*Authorisations and other statutory controls*

*Authorisations and other statutory controls*

**28.** (1) No condition shall at any time be attached to an authorisation[1] so as to regulate the final disposal by deposit in or on land of controlled waste (within the meaning of Part II)[2], nor shall any condition apply to such a disposal[3].

(2) Where any of the activities comprising a prescribed process[4] are regulated both by an authorisation granted by the enforcing authority[5] under this Part and by a registration or authorisation under the Radioactive Substances Act 1993[6], then, if different obligations are imposed as respects the same matter by a condition attached to the authorisation under this Part and a condition attached to the registration or authorisation under that Act, the condition imposed by the authorisation under this Part shall be treated as not binding the person carrying on the process.

(3) and (4) *Repealed by the Environment Act 1995 (c. 25), s. 120, sch. 22, para. 61(2), sch. 24. This amendment came into force on 1 April 1996: S.I. 1996/186.*

# Part II: Waste on Land

## *Preliminary*

*Transfer of functions*

The functions previously conferred on waste regulation authorities under this Part of this Act have been transferred to the Environment Agency, in respect of England and Wales, and the Scottish Environment Protection Agency, SEPA, in respect of Scotland: Environment Act 1995 (c. 25), ss. 2, 21, pp. 421/438 below. The new agencies took over their functions under this Act on the transfer date, 1 April 1996: S.I. 1996/139; S.I. 1996/234.

*Commencement*

The commencement date of the sections in this Part is noted at the end of each section.

Except where otherwise noted the amendments made to this Part by the Environment Act 1995 came into force on 1 April 1996: S.I . 1996/186. To avoid undue repetition this commencement date is not set out in the footnotes which relate to these amendments.

*Modifications*

For modifications to this Part see the Waste Management Licensing Regulations 1994, sch. 4, para. 9, p. 717 below.

*References*

Waste Management: The Duty of Care: A Code of Practice, issued in accordance with s. 34(7) of this Act, is at p. 824 below.

*Additional references to material not set out in this Manual*

Joint Circular: Environmental Protection Act 1990: Part II, Waste Management Licensing, the Framework Directive on Waste. Department of the Environment Circular 11/94, Welsh Office Circular 26/94, Scottish Office Environment Department Circular 10/94 of 19 April 1994.

[1] "Authorisation" defined by s. 1(9), p. 90 above.
[2] "Controlled waste" is defined by s. 75(4), p. 159 below.
[3] The remainder of this subsection, which provided that the enforcing authority notify the waste regulation authority, has been repealed by the Environment Act 1995 (c. 25), s. 120, sch. 22, para. 61(1), sch. 24.
[4] "Process" and "prescribed process" defined by s. 1(5), p. 89 above.
[5] "Enforcing authority" defined by s. 1(7), (8), p. 90 above.
[6] Words "Radioactive Substances Act 1993" substituted by the Radioactive Substances Act 1993 (c. 12), s. 49(1), sch. 4, para. 6. This amendment came into force on 27 August 1993: s. 51(2).

Joint Circular: Environmental Protection Act 1990: Part II, Waste Management Licensing, the Framework Directive on Waste, Department of the Environment Circular 6/95, Welsh Office Circular 25/95, Scottish Office Environment Department Circular 8/95 of 31 March 1995.

Planning Policy Guidance Note 23: Planning and Pollution Control. Department of the Environment, July 1994.

*Note:* the above three documents were published before the enactment of the Environment Act 1995. This Act provided for the transfer of functions to the Environment Agency and SEPA noted above.

*Transitional Provisions*

For transitional and transitory provisions and savings under the Environment Act 1995 see the Environment Act 1995 (c. 25), s. 120 (2), sch. 23, paras. 16–18, p. 533 below.

*Preliminary*

**29.** (1) The following provisions have effect for the interpretation of this Part.

(2) The "environment" consists of all, or any, of the following media, namely land, water and the air.

(3) "Pollution of the environment" means pollution of the environment due to the release or escape (into any environmental medium) from—

(*a*) the land on which controlled waste[1] is treated,

(*b*) the land on which controlled waste is kept,

(*c*) the land in or on which controlled waste is deposited,

(*d*) fixed plant by means of which controlled waste is treated, kept or disposed of,

of substances or articles constituting or resulting from the waste and capable (by reason of the quantity or concentrations involved) of causing harm to man or any other living organisms supported by the environment .

(4) Subsection (3) above applies in relation to mobile plant by means of which controlled waste is treated or disposed of as it applies to plant on land by means of which controlled waste is treated or disposed of.

(5) For the purposes of subsections (3) and (4) above "harm" means harm to the health of living organisms or other interference with the ecological systems of which they form part and in the case of man includes offence to any of his senses or harm to his property; and "harmless" has a corresponding meaning.

(6) The "disposal" of waste[2] includes its disposal by way of deposit in or on land and, subject to subsection (7) below, waste is "treated" when it is subjected to any process, including making it re-usable or reclaiming substances from it and "recycle" (and cognate expressions) shall be construed accordingly.

(7) Regulations made by the Secretary of State may prescribe activities as activities which constitute the treatment of waste for the purposes of this Part or any provision of this Part prescribed in the regulations.

(8) "Land" includes land covered by waters where the land is above the low water mark of ordinary spring tides and references to land on which controlled waste is treated, kept or deposited are references to the surface of the land (including any structure set into the surface).

(9) "Mobile plant" means, subject to subsection (10) below, plant which is designed to move or be moved whether on roads or other land.

(10) Regulations made by the Secretary of State may prescribe descriptions of plant which are to be treated as being, or as not being, mobile plant for the purposes of this Part[3].

---

[1] "Controlled waste" defined by s. 75, p. 159 below.
[2] "Waste" defined by s. 75, p. 159 below.
[3] The following regulations have been made under this

section: The Waste Management Licensing Regulations 1994, S.I. 1994/1056, as amended, p. 675 below.

**(11)** "Substance" means any natural or artificial substance, whether in solid or liquid form or in the form of a gas or vapour[1].

*Authorities for purposes of this Part*

**30. (1)** Any reference in this Part to a waste regulation authority—

(a) in relation to England and Wales, is a reference to the Environment Agency[2]; and

(b) in relation to Scotland, is a reference to the Scottish Environment Protection Agency[3];

and any reference in this Part to the area of a waste regulation authority shall accordingly be taken as a reference to the area over which the Environment Agency or the Scottish Environment Protection Agency, as the case may be, exercises its functions or, in the case of any particular function, the function in question[4].

**(2)** For the purposes of this Part the following authorities are waste disposal authorities, namely—

(a) for any non-metropolitan county in England, the county council;

(b) in Greater London, the following—

(i) for the area of a London waste disposal authority, the authority constituted as the waste disposal authority for that area;

(ii) for the City of London, the Common Council;

(iii) for any other London borough, the council of the borough;

(c) in the metropolitan county of Greater Manchester, the following—

(i) for the metropolitan district of Wigan, the district council;

(ii) for all other areas in the county, the authority constituted as the Greater Manchester Waste Disposal Authority;

(d) for the metropolitan county of Merseyside, the authority constituted as the Merseyside Waste Disposal Authority;

(e) for any district in any other metropolitan county in England, the council of the district;

(f) for any county or county borough in Wales, the council of the county or county borough;[5]

(g) in Scotland, a council constituted under section 2 of the Local Government etc. (Scotland) Act 1994[6].

**(3)** For the purposes of this Part the following authorities are waste collection authorities—

(a) for any district in England[7] not within Greater London, the council of the district;

(b) in Greater London, the following—

(i) for any London borough, the council of the borough;

(ii) for the City of London, the Common Council;

(iii) for the Temples, the Sub-Treasurer of the Inner Temple and the Under Treasurer of the Middle Temple respectively;

(bb) for any county or county borough in Wales, the council of the county or county borough;[8]

(c) in Scotland, a council constituted under section 2 of the Local Government etc. (Scotland) Act 1994[9].

[1] This section came into force on 31 May 1991: S.I. 1991/1319.
[2] The Environment Agency is established by the Environment Act 1995 (c. 25), s. 1, p. 420 below.
[3] The Scottish Environment Protection Agency, also known as SEPA, is established by the Environment Act 1995 (c. 25), s. 20, p. 438 below.
[4] Subsection (1) substituted by the Environment Act 1995 (c. 25), s. 120, sch. 22, para. 62(2).
[5] Para.(f) substituted by the Local Government (Wales) Act 1994 (c. 19), s. 22(3), sch. 9, para. 17(2). This amendment came into force on 1 April 1996: S.I. 1996/396.

[6] 1994 c. 39. Words "a council . . . 1994" substituted by the Local Government etc. (Scotland) Act 1994 (c. 39), s. 180(1), sch. 13, para. 167(3). This amendment came into force on 1 April 1996: S.I. 1996/323.
[7] Former words "and Wales" repealed by the Local Government (Wales) Act 1994 (c. 19), s. 22(3), sch. 9, para. 17(3), s. 66(8), sch. 18.
[8] Para. (bb) inserted by the Local Government (Wales) Act 1994 (c. 19), s. 22(3), sch. 9, para. 17(3).
[9] Words "a council . . . 1994" substituted by the Local Government etc. (Scotland) Act 1994 (c. 39), s. 180(1), sch. 13, para. 167(3).

(4) In this section references to particular authorities having been constituted as waste disposal[1] authorities are references to their having been so constituted by the Waste Regulation and Disposal (Authorities) Order 1985[2] made by the Secretary of State under section 10 of the Local Government Act 1985[3] and the reference to London waste disposal authorities is a reference to the authorities named in Parts I, II, III, IV and V of Schedule 1 to that Order and this section has effect subject to any order made under the said section 10.[4]

(5) In this Part "waste disposal contractors" means a person who in the course of a business collects, keeps, treats[5] or disposes[6] of waste[7], being either—

(a) a company formed for all or any of those purposes by a waste disposal authority whether in pursuance of section 32 below or otherwise; or

(b) either a company formed for all or any of those purposes by other persons or a partnership or an individual;

and "company" has the same meaning as in the Companies Act 1985[8] and "formed", in relation to a company formed by other persons, includes the alteration of the objects of the company[9,10].

(6)–(8) *Repealed by the Environment Act 1995 (c. 25), s. 120, sch. 22, para. 62(4), sch. 24. This amendment came into force on 1 April 1996: S.I. 1996/186.*

**31.** *Repealed by the Environment Act 1995 (c. 25), s. 120, sch. 22, para. 63, sch. 24. This amendment came into force on 1 April 1996: S.I. 1996/186.*

*Transition to waste disposal companies etc.*

**32.** (1) In this section "existing disposal authority" means any authority (including any joint authority) constituted as a waste disposal authority for any area before the day appointed for this section to come into force[11].

(2) The Secretary of State shall, subject to subsection (3) below, give directions to existing disposal authorities or, in the case of joint authorities, to the constituent authorities requiring them, before specified dates, to—

(a) form or participate in forming waste disposal companies; and

(b) transfer to the companies so formed, by and in accordance with a scheme made in accordance with Schedule 2 to this Act[12], the relevant part[13] of their undertakings;

and a waste disposal authority[14] shall accordingly have power to form, and hold securities[15] in, any company so established.

(3) Subject to subsection (4) below, the Secretary of State shall not give any direction under subsection (2) above to an existing disposal authority, or to the constituent authorities of an existing disposal authority, as respects which or each of which he is satisfied that the authority—

(a) has formed or participated in forming a waste disposal company and transferred to it the relevant part of its undertaking;

(b) has, in pursuance of arrangements made with other persons, ceased to carry on itself the relevant part of its undertaking;

[1] Former words "or regulation" repealed by the Environment Act 1995 (c. 25), s. 120, sch. 22, para. 62(3)(a), sch. 24.
[2] S.I. 1985/1884.
[3] 1985 c. 51.
[4] Former words "establishing authorities to discharge any functions to which that section applies" repealed by the Environment Act 1995 (c. 25), s. 120, sch. 22, para. 62(3)(b), sch. 24.
[5] "Treats" defined by s. 29(6), p. 112 above.
[6] "Disposes" defined by s. 29(6), p. 112 above.
[7] "Waste" defined by s. 75, p. 159 below.
[8] 1985 c. 6.
[9] This section came into force on 31 May 1991: S.I. 1991/1319.
[10] Cases: section 30 *R v Avon County Council, ex parte Terry Adams Ltd* [1994] Env LR 442; *Mass Energy Ltd v Birmingham City Council* [1994] Env LR 298.
[11] This section came into force on 31 May 1991: S.I. 1991/1319.
[12] P. 215 below.
[13] "The relevant part" defined by subsection (11) below.
[14] "Waste disposal authority" defined by s. 30(2), p. 113 above.
[15] "Securities" defined by sch. 2, para. 1, p. 215 below: subsection (11) below.

(c) has made arrangements with other persons to cease to carry on itself the relevant part of its undertaking; or

(d) has, in pursuance of arrangements made with other persons, ceased to provide places at which and plant and equipment by means of which controlled waste[1] can be disposed[2] of or deposited for the purposes of disposal.

(4) Subsection (3) above does not apply in a case falling within paragraph (a) unless it appears to the Secretary of State that—

(a) the form of the company and the undertaking transferred are satisfactory; and

(b) the requirements of subsections (8) and (9) below are fulfilled;

and "satisfactory" means satisfactory by reference to the corresponding arrangements to which he would give his approval for the purposes of a transfer scheme under Schedule 2 to this Act.

(5) Where the Secretary of State is precluded from giving a direction under subsection (2) above to any authority by reason of his being satisfied as to the arrangements mentioned in subsection (3)(c) above, then, if those arrangements are not implemented within what appears to him to be a reasonable time, he may exercise his power to give directions under subsection (2) above as respects that authority.

(6) Part I of Schedule 2 to this Act[3] has effect for the purposes of this section and Part II for regulating the functions of waste disposal authorities[4] and the activities of waste disposal contractors[5].

(7) Subject to subsection (8) below, the activities of a company which a waste disposal authority has formed or participated in forming (whether in pursuance of subsection (2)(a) above or otherwise) may include activities which are beyond the powers of the authority to carry on itself, but, in the case of a company formed otherwise than in pursuance of subsection (2)(a) above, only if the Secretary of State has determined under subsection (4)(a) above that the form of the company and the undertaking transferred to it are satisfactory.

(8) A waste disposal authority shall, for so long as it controls[6] a company which it has formed or participated in forming (whether in pursuance of subsection (2)(a) above or otherwise), so exercise its control as to secure that the company does not engage in activities other than the following activities or any activities incidental or conducive to, or calculated to facilitate, them, that is to say, the disposal[7], keeping or treatment[8] of waste[9] and the collection of waste.

(9) Subject to subsection (10) below, a waste disposal authority shall, for so long as it controls a company which it has formed or participated in forming (whether in pursuance of subsection (2)(a) above or otherwise), so exercise its control as to secure that, for the purposes of Part V of the Local Government and Housing Act 1989[10], the company is an arm's length company.

(10) Subsection (9) above shall not apply in the case of a company which a waste disposal authority has formed or participated in forming in pursuance of subsection (2)(a) above until after the vesting date[11] for that company.

(11) In this section and Schedule 2 to this Act—

"control" (and cognate expressions) is to be construed in accordance with section 68 or, as the case requires, section 73 of the Local Government and Housing Act 1989;

"the relevant part" of the undertaking of an existing disposal authority is that part which relates to the disposal, keeping or treatment or the collection of waste;

and in this section "securities" and "vesting date" have the same meaning as in Schedule 2.

(12) This section shall not apply to Scotland[12,13].

[1] "Controlled waste" defined by s. 75, p. 159 below.
[2] "Disposed" defined by s. 29(6), p. 112 above.
[3] P. 215 below.
[4] "Waste disposal authority" defined by s. 30(2), p. 113 above.
[5] "Waste disposal contractor" defined by s. 30(5), p. 114 above.
[6] "Control" defined by subsection (11) below.
[7] "Disposal" defined by s. 29(6), p. 112 above.
[8] "Treatment" defined by s. 29(6), p. 112 above.
[9] "Waste" defined by s. 75, p. 159 below.
[10] 1989 c. 42.
[11] "Vesting date" defined by sch. 2, para. 1, p. 215 below: subsection (11) below.
[12] This section came into force on 31 May 1991: S.I. 1991/1319.
[13] Cases: section 32 *R v Avon County Council, ex parte Terry Adams Ltd* [1994] Env LR 442; *Mass Energy Ltd v Birmingham City Council* [1994] Env LR 298.

*Prohibition on unauthorised or harmful depositing, treatment or disposal of waste*

*Prohibition on unauthorised or harmful deposit, treatment or disposal etc of waste.*

**33.** **(1)** Subject to subsection (2) and (3) below[1] a person shall not—

 (*a*) deposit controlled waste[2], or knowingly cause or knowingly permit controlled waste to be deposited in or on any land[3] unless a waste management licence[4] authorising the deposit is in force and the deposit is in accordance with the licence;

 (*b*) treat[5], keep or dispose[6] of controlled waste, or knowingly cause or knowingly permit controlled waste to be treated, kept or disposed of—

   (i) in or on any land, or

   (ii) by means of any mobile plant[7],

except under and in accordance with a waste management licence;

 (*c*) treat, keep or dispose of controlled waste in a manner likely to cause pollution of the environment[8] or harm[9] to human health.

**(2)** Subsection (1) above does not apply in relation to household waste[10] from a domestic property which is treated, kept or disposed of within the curtilage of the dwelling by or with the permission of the occupier of the dwelling.

**(3)** Subsection (1)(a), (b) or (c) above do not apply in cases prescribed in regulations made by the Secretary of State and the regulations may make different exceptions for different areas[11].

**(4)** The Secretary of State, in exercising his power under subsection (3) above, shall have regard in particular to the expediency of excluding from the controls imposed by waste management licences—

 (*a*) any deposits which are small enough or of such a temporary nature that they may be so excluded;

 (*b*) any means of treatment or disposal which are innocuous enough to be so excluded;

 (*c*) cases for which adequate controls are provided by another enactment than this section.

**(5)** Where controlled waste is carried in and deposited from a motor vehicle, the person who controls or is in a position to control the use of the vehicle shall, for the purposes of subsection (1)(a) above, be treated as knowingly causing the waste to be deposited whether or not he gave any instructions for this to be done.

**(6)** A person who contravenes subsection (1) above or any condition of a waste management licence commits an offence.

**(7)** It shall be a defence for a person charged with an offence under this section to prove—

 (*a*) that he took all reasonable precautions and exercised all due diligence to avoid the commission of the offence; or

 (*b*) that he acted under instructions from his employer and neither knew nor had reason to suppose that the acts done by him constituted a contravention of subsection (1) above; or

 (*c*) that the acts alleged to constitute the contravention were done in an emergency in order to avoid danger to human health in a case where—

---

[1] Former words "and, in relation to Scotland, to section 54 below, " repealed by the Environment Act 1995 (c. 25), s. 120, sch. 24.

[2] "Controlled waste" defined by s. 75, p. 159 below.

[3] "Land" defined by s. 29(8), p. 112 above.

[4] For "waste management licence" see s. 35, p. 119 below.

[5] "Treat" defined by s. 29(6), p. 112 above.

[6] "Dispose" defined by s. 29(6), p. 112 above.

[7] "Mobile plant" defined by s. 29(9),(10), p. 112 above.

[8] "Pollution of the environment" defined by s. 29(3),

p. 112 above; "the environment" defined by s. 29 (2).

[9] "Harm" defined by s. 29(5), p. 112 above, for the purposes of s. 29(3),(4).

[10] " Household waste " from a domestic property defined by s. 75 (2), (5), (8), p. 159 below.

[11] The following regulations have been made under this section:

The Controlled Waste Regulations 1992, S.I. 1992/588, as amended, p. 662 below;

The Waste Management Licensing Regulations 1994, S.I. 1994/1056, as amended, p. 675 below.

(i)  he took all such steps as were reasonably practicable in the circumstances for minimising pollution of the environment and harm to human health; and

(ii)  particulars of the acts were furnished to the waste regulation authority[1] as soon as reasonably practicable after they were done[2].

**(8)**  Except in a case falling within subsection (9) below, a person who commits an offence under this section shall be liable—

(*a*)  on summary conviction, to imprisonment for a term not exceeding six months or a fine not exceeding £20,000 or both; and

(*b*)  on conviction on indictment, to imprisonment for a term not exceeding two years or a fine or both.

**(9)**  A person who commits an offence under this section in relation to special waste[3] shall be liable—

(*a*)  on summary conviction, to imprisonment for a term not exceeding six months or a fine not exceeding £20,000 or both;

(*b*)  on conviction on indictment, to imprisonment for a term not exceeding five years or a fine or both[4].

## Duty of care etc. as respects waste

*Duty of care etc. as respects waste.*

**34**  **(1)**  Subject to subsection (2) below, it shall be the duty of any person who imports, produces, carries, keeps, treats[5] or disposes[6] of controlled waste[7] or, as a broker, has control of such waste to take all such measures applicable to him in that capacity as are reasonable in the circumstances—

(*a*)  to prevent any contravention by any other person of section 33 above;

(*b*)  to prevent the escape of the waste from his control or that of any other person; and

(*c*)  on the transfer of the waste, to secure—

(i)  that the transfer is only to an authorised person or to a person for authorised transport purposes[8]; and

(ii)  that there is transferred such a written description of the waste as will enable other persons to avoid a contravention of that section and to comply with the duty under this subsection as respects the escape of waste[9].

**(2)**  The duty imposed by subsection (1) above does not apply to an occupier of domestic property as respects the household waste[10] produced on the property.

**(3)**  The following are authorised persons for the purpose of subsection (1)(e) above—

(*a*)  any authority which is a waste collection authority[11] for the purposes of this Part;

(*b*)  any person who is the holder of a waste management licence under section 35 below or of a disposal licence under section 5 of the Control of Pollution Act 1974[12];

---

[1] For "waste regulation authority" see s. 30(1), p. 113 above.

[2] Para. (c) substituted by the Environment Act 1995 (c. 25), s. 120, sch. 22, para. 64.

[3] "Special waste" defined by s. 75(9), p. 160 below.

[4] For modifications to this section, see S.I. 1994/1056, sch. 4, para. 9, p. 717 below. S. 33(1)(c), and (2), (6)–(9) insofar as they relate to (1)(c), came into force on 1 April 1992; (3) and (4) came into force on 13 December 1991: S.I. 1991/2829; for the remaining commencement provisions see S.I. 1994/1096, p. 738 below.

[5] "Treats" defined by s. 29(6), p. 112 above.

[6] "Dispose" defined by s. 29(6), p. 112 above.

[7] "Controlled waste" defined by s. 75, p. 159 below.

[8] "Authorised transport purposes" defined by subsection (4) below.

[9] See subsection (4A) below.

[10] "Household waste" defined by s. 75, p. 159 below.

[11] "Waste collection authority" defined by s. 30(3), p. 113 above.

[12] 1974 c. 40. *Prospective repeal*: words "or of a disposal licence under section 5 of the Control of Pollution Act 1974": Environmental Protection Act 1990, s. 162, sch. 16, pt. II.

(c) any person to whom section 33(1) above does not apply by virtue of regulations under subsection (3) of that section;

(d) any person registered as a carrier of controlled waste under section 2 of the Control of Pollution (Amendment) Act 1989[1];

(e) any person who is not required to be so registered by virtue of regulations under section 1(3) of that Act[2]; and

(f) a waste disposal authority[3] in Scotland.

(3A) The Secretary of State may by regulations amend subsection (3) above so as to add, whether generally or in such circumstances as may be prescribed in the regulations, any person specified in the regulations, or any description of person so specified, to the persons who are authorised persons for the purposes of subsection (1)(c) above[4].

(4) The following are authorised transport purposes for the purposes of subsection (1)(c) above—

(a) the transport of controlled waste within the same premises between different places in those premises;

(b) the transport to a place in Great Britain of controlled waste which has been brought from a country or territory outside Great Britain not having been landed in Great Britain until it arrives at that place; and

(c) the transport by air or sea of controlled waste from a place in Great Britain to a place outside Great Britain;

and "transport" has the same meaning in this subsection as in the Control of Pollution (Amendment) Act 1989[5].

(4A) For the purposes of subsection (1)(c)(ii) above—

(a) a transfer of waste in stages shall be treated as taking place when the first stage of the transfer takes place, and

(b) a series of transfers between the same parties of waste of the same description shall be treated as a single transfer taking place when the first of the transfers in the series takes place[6].

(5) The Secretary of State may, by regulations, make provision imposing requirements on any person who is subject to the duty imposed by subsection (1) above as respects the making and retention of documents and the furnishing of documents or copies of documents[7].

(6) Any person who fails to comply with the duty imposed by subsection (1) above or with any requirement imposed under subsection (5) above shall be liable—

(a) on summary conviction, to a fine not exceeding the statutory maximum[8]; and

(b) on conviction on indictment, to a fine.

(7) The Secretary of State shall, after consultation with such persons or bodies as appear to him representative of the interests concerned, prepare and issue a code of practice for the purpose of providing to persons practical guidance on how to discharge the duty imposed on them by subsection (1) above[9].

---

[1] P. 73 above.
[2] P. 72 above.
[3] "Waste disposal authority" defined by s. 30(2), p. 113 above.
[4] Subsection (3A) inserted by the Environment Act 1995 (c. 25), s. 120, sch. 22, para. 65.
[5] See s. 9 of the 1989 Act, p. 80 above.
[6] Subsection (4A) inserted by the Deregulation and Contracting Out Act 1994 (c. 40), s. 33. This amendment came into force on 3 November 1994: s. 82 (3)(b) . For provisions relating to the deemed operation of this subsection before it came into force see s. 33(2) and (3) of the 1994 Act.
[7] The following regulations have been made under this section:
The Environmental Protection (Duty of Care) Regulations 1991, S.I. 1991/2839, p. 650 below.
[8] The current statutory maximum is £5,000: Criminal Justice Act 1991 (c. 53), s. 17 (2); Criminal Procedure (Scotland) Act 1995 (c. 46), s. 225 (8).
[9] The code, Waste Management: The Duty of Care: A Code of Practice, is at p. 824 below.

**(8)** The Secretary of State may from time to time revise a code of practice issued under subsection (7) above by revoking, amending or adding to the provisions of the code.

**(9)** The code of practice prepared in pursuance of subsection (7) above shall be laid before both Houses of Parliament.

**(10)** A code of practice issued under subsection (7) above shall be admissible in evidence and if any provision of such a code appears to the court to be relevant to any question arising in the proceedings it shall be taken into account in determining that question.

**(11)** Different codes of practice may be prepared and issued under subsection (7) above for different areas[1].

*Waste Management Licences*

*Waste management licences: general*

**35. (1)** A waste management licence is a licence granted by a waste regulation authority[2] authorising the treatment[3], keeping or disposal[4] of any specified description of controlled waste[5] in or on specified land[6] or the treatment or disposal of any specified description of controlled waste by means of specified mobile plant[7].

**(2)** A licence[8] shall be granted to the following person, that is to say—

(*a*) in the case of a licence relating to the treatment, keeping or disposal of waste[9] in or on land, to the person who is in occupation of the land; and

(*b*) in the case of a licence relating to the treatment or disposal of waste by means of mobile plant, to the person who operates the plant.

**(3)** A licence shall be granted on such terms and subject to such conditions as appear to the waste regulation authority to be appropriate and the conditions may relate—

(*a*) to the activities which the licence authorises, and

(*b*) to the precautions to be taken and works to be carried out in connection with or in consequence of those activities; and accordingly requirements may be imposed in the licence which are to be complied with before the activities which the licence authorises have begun or after the activities which the licence authorises have ceased.

**(4)** Conditions may require the holder of a licence to carry out works or do other things notwithstanding that he is not entitled to carry out the works or do the thing and any person whose consent would be required shall grant, or join in granting, the holder of the licence such rights in relation to the land as will enable the holder of the licence to comply with any requirements imposed on him by the licence.

**(5)** Conditions may relate, where waste other than controlled waste is to be treated, kept or disposed of, to the treatment, keeping or disposal of that other waste.

**(6)** The Secretary of State may, by regulations, make provision as to the conditions which are, or are not, to be included in a licence; and regulations under this subsection may make different provision for different circumstances[10].

**(7)** The Secretary of State may, as respects any licence for which an application is made to a waste regulation authority, give to the authority directions as to the terms and conditions which

[1] Subsections (1)–(4), (6) and (10) came into force on 1 April 1992; (3A) on 1 April 1996: S.I. 1996/186; (4A) on 3 November 1994: see n. 6 above; and (5), (7)–(9) and (11) on 13 December 1991: S.I. 1991/2829.
[2] For "waste regulation authority" see s. 30(1), p. 113 above.
[3] "Treatment" defined by s. 29(6), p. 112 above.
[4] "Disposal" of waste defined by s. 29(6), p. 112 above.
[5] "Controlled waste" defined by s. 75, p. 159 below.
[6] "Land" defined by s. 29(8), p. 112 above.
[7] "Mobile plant" defined by s. 29(9),(10), p. 112 above.
[8] "Licence" means a waste management licence: subsection (12) below.
[9] "Waste" defined by s. 75, p. 159 below.
[10] The following regulations have been made under this section:
The Waste Management Licensing Regulations 1994, S.I. 1994/1056, as amended, p. 675 below.

are, or are not, to be included in the licence; and it shall be the duty of the authority to give effect to the directions.

**(7A)** In any case where—

(*a*) an entry is required under this section to be made in any record as to the observance of any condition of a licence, and

(*b*) the entry has not been made,

that fact shall be admissible as evidence that that condition has not been observed.

**(7B)** Any person who—

(*a*) intentionally makes a false entry in any record required to be kept under any condition of a licence, or

(*b*) with intent to deceive, forges or uses a licence or makes or has in his possession a document so closely resembling a licence as to be likely to deceive,

shall be guilty of an offence.

**(7C)** A person guilty of an offence under subsection (7B) above shall be liable—

(*a*) on summary conviction, to a fine not exceeding the statutory maximum[1],

(*b*) on conviction on indictment, to a fine or to imprisonment for a term not exceeding two years, or to both[2].

**(8)** It shall be the duty of waste regulation authorities to have regard to any guidance issued to them by the Secretary of State with respect to the discharge of their functions in relation to licences.

**(9)** A licence may not be surrendered by the holder except in accordance with section 39 below[3].

**(10)** A licence is not transferable by the holder but the waste regulation authority may transfer it to another person under section 40 below[4].

**(11)** A licence shall continue in force until it is revoked entirely by the waste regulation authority under section 38 below[5] or it is surrendered or its surrender is accepted under section 39 below.

**(12)** In this Part "licence" means a waste management licence and "site licence" and "mobile plant licence" mean, respectively, a licence authorising the treatment, keeping or disposal of waste in or on land and a licence authorising the treatment or disposal of waste by means of mobile plant[6].

*Compensation where rights granted pursuant to section 35(4) or 38(9A).*

**35A.** **(1)** This section applies in any case where—

(*a*) the holder of a licence[7] is required—

    (i) by the conditions of the licence; or

    (ii) by a requirement imposed under section 38(9) below[8],

    to carry out any works or do any other thing which he is not entitled to carry out or do;

(*b*) a person whose consent would be required has, pursuant to the requirements of section 35(4) above or 38(9A) below, granted, or joined in granting, to the holder of the licence any rights in relation to any land; and

(*c*) those rights, or those rights together with other rights, are such as will enable the holder of the licence to comply with any requirements imposed on him by the licence or, as the case may be, under section 38(9) below.

---

[1] The current statutory maximum is £5,000: Criminal Justice Act 1991 (c. 53), s. 17 (2); Criminal Procedure (Scotland) Act 1995 (c. 46), s. 225 (8).

[2] Subsections (7A)–(7C) inserted by the Environment Act 1995 (c. 25), s. 120, sch. 22, para. 66(2).

[3] P. 129 below.

[4] P. 131 below.

[5] P. 127 below.

[6] For modifications to this section see S.I. 1994/1056, sch. 4, para. 9, p. 000 below. Subsection (6) came into force on 18 February 1993: S.I. 1993/274; (7A)–(7C) on 1 April 1996: S.I. 1996/186; for the remaining commencement provisions see S.I. 1994/1096, p. 738 below.

[7] "Licence" means a waste management licence: s. 35(12) above.

[8] P. 128 below.

(2) In a case where this section applies, any person who has granted, or joined in granting, the rights in question shall be entitled to be paid compensation under this section by the holder of the licence.

(3) The Secretary of State shall by regulations provide for the descriptions of loss and damage for which compensation is payable under this section.

(4) The Secretary of State may by regulations—

(a) provide for the basis on which any amount to be paid by way of compensation under this section is to be assessed;

(b) without prejudice to the generality of subsection (3) and paragraph (a) above, provide for compensation under this section to be payable in respect of—

(i) any effect of any rights being granted, or

(ii) any consequence of the exercise of any rights which have been granted;

(c) provide for the times at which any entitlement to compensation under this section is to arise or at which any such compensation is to become payable;

(d) provide for the persons or bodies by whom, and the manner in which, any dispute—

(i) as to whether any, and (if so) how much and when, compensation under this section is payable; or

(ii) as to the person to or by whom it shall be paid,

is to be determined;

(e) provide for when or how applications may be made for compensation under this section;

(f) without prejudice to the generality of paragraph (d) above, provide for when or how applications may be made for the determination of any such disputes as are mentioned in that paragraph;

(g) without prejudice to the generality of paragraphs (e) and (f) above, prescribe the form in which any such applications as are mentioned in those paragraphs are to be made;

(h) make provision similar to any provision made by paragraph 8 of Schedule 19 to the Water Resources Act 1991[1];

(j) make different provision for different cases, including different provision in relation to different persons or circumstances;

(k) include such incidental, supplemental, consequential or transitional provision as the Secretary of State considers appropriate[2].

## Grant of licences

**36.** (1) An application for a licence[3] shall be made—

(a) in the case of an application for a site licence[4], to the waste regulation authority[5] in whose area the land is situated; and

(b) in the case of an application for a mobile plant licence[6], to the waste regulation authority in whose area the operator of the plant has his principal place of business;

and shall be made on a form provided for the purpose by the waste regulation authority and accompanied by such information as that authority reasonably requires and the charge

[1] 1991 c. 57.

[2] This section inserted by the Environment Act 1995 (c. 25), s. 120, sch. 22, para. 67; this amendment, in so far as it confers power to make regulations or makes provision in relation to the exercise of that power, came into force on 1 February 1996: S.I. 1996/186; otherwise this section is not in force.

[3] "Licence" means a waste management licence: s. 35

(12), p. 120 above.

[4] "Site licence" defined by s. 35(12) above.

[5] For "waste regulation authority", and its area, see s. 30(1), p. 113 above. Mobile plant licence" defined by s. 35(12), p. 120 above.

[6] "Mobile plant licence" defined by s.35(12), p. 120 above.

prescribed for the purpose by a charging scheme under section 41 of the Environment Act 1995[1,2].

(1A)  Where an applicant for a licence fails to provide the waste regulation authority with any information required under subsection (I) above, the authority may refuse to proceed with the application, or refuse to proceed with it until the information is provided[3].

(2)  A licence shall not be issued for a use of land[4] for which planning permission is required in pursuance of the Town and Country Planning Act 1990[5] or the Town and Country Planning (Scotland) Act 1972[6] unless—

(a)  such planning permission is in force in relation to that use of the land[7], or

(b)  an established use certificate is in force under section 192 of the said Act of 1990 or section 90 of the said Act of 1972 in relation to that use of the land[8].

(3)  Subject to subsection (2) above and subsection (4) below, a waste regulation authority to which an application for a licence has been duly made shall not reject the application if it is satisfied that the applicant is a fit and proper person unless it is satisfied that its rejection is necessary for the purpose of preventing—

(a)  pollution of the environment[9];

(b)  harm[10] to human health; or

(c)  serious detriment to the amenities of the locality;

but paragraph (c) above is inapplicable where planning permission is in force in relation to the use to which the land will be put under the licence.

(4)  Where the waste regulation authority proposes to issue a licence, the authority must, before it does so,—

(a)  refer the proposal to the appropriate planning authority[11] and the Health and Safety Executive; and

(b)  consider any representations about the proposal which the authority[12] or the Executive makes to it during the allowed period.

(5) and (6)  *Repealed by the Environment Act 1995 (c. 25), s. 120, sch. 22, para. 68(4), sch. 24. This amendment came into force on 1 April 1996: S.I. 1996/186.*

(7)  Where any part of the land to be used is land which has been notified under section 28(1) of the Wildlife and Countryside Act 1981[13] (protection for certain areas) and the waste regulation authority proposes to issue a licence, the authority must, before it does so—

(a)  refer the proposal to the appropriate nature conservation body; and

(b)  consider any representations about the proposal which the body makes to it during the allowed period;

[1] P. 452 below.

[2] Words "and shall be made . . . 1995" substituted by the Environment Act 1995 (c. 25), s. 120, sch. 22, para. 68(2). This amendment, and that in note 3 below, in so far as it requires an appliction to be accompanied by the prescribed charge, came into force on 1 April 1996: S.I. 1996/186; otherwise it is not in force.

[3] Subsection (1A) substituted by the Environment Act 1995 (c. 25), s. 120, sch. 22, para. 68(2).

[4] "Land" defined by s. 29(8), p. 112 above.

[5] 1990 c. 8.

[6] 1972 c. 54.

[7] For provisions in respect of certificates of lawfulness of existing use or development see the Town and Country Planning Act 1990, s. 191 (7) (c), inserted by the Planning and Compensation Act 1991 (c. 34), s. 10, and the Town and Country Planning (Scotland) Act 1974 (c. 52), s. 90 (7) (c), inserted by s. 42 of the 1991 Act.

[8] These sections have been replaced. For provisions relating to established use certificates under the replacement sections see the Planning and Compensation Act 1991 (c. 34), s. 10(2), in respect of the 1990 Act, and s. 42(2) in respect of the 1972 Act.

[9] "Pollution of the environment" defined by s. 29(3), p. 112 above; "the environment" defined by s. 29(2).

[10] "Harm" defined by s. 29(5), p. 112 above, for the purposes of s. 29(3), (4).

[11] Words "the appropriate planning authority" defined by subsection (11) below. Words "the appropriate planning authority" substituted by the Environment Act 1995 (c. 25), s. 120, sch. 22, para. 68 (3)(a).

[12] Word "authority" substituted by the Environment Act 1995 (c. 25), s. 120, sch. 22, para. 68(3)(b).

[13] 1981 c. 69. S. 28 of the 1981 Act is set out in the companion volume, *A Manual of Nature Conservation Law*, edited by Michael Fry (Oxford, 1995) at p. 168.

and in this section any reference to the appropriate nature conservation body is a reference to the Nature Conservancy Council for England, Scottish Natural Heritage[1] or the Countryside Council for Wales, according as the land is situated in England, Scotland or Wales.

(8)  Until the date appointed under section 131(3) below[2] any reference in subsection (7) above to the appropriate nature conservation body is a reference to the Nature Conservancy Council[3].

(9)  If within the period of four months beginning with the date on which a waste regulation authority received an application for the grant of a licence, or within such longer period as the authority and the applicant may at any time agree in writing, the authority has neither granted the licence in consequence of the application nor given notice to the applicant[4] that the authority has rejected the application, the authority shall be deemed to have rejected the application.

(9A)  Subsection (9) above—

(a)  shall not have effect in any case where, by virtue of subsection (1A) above, the waste regulation authority refuses to proceed with the application in question, and

(b)  shall have effect in any case where, by virtue of subsection (1A) above, the waste regulation authority refuses to proceed with it until the required information is provided, with the substitution for the period of four months there mentioned of the period of four months beginning with the date on which the authority received the information[5].

(10)  The period allowed to the appropriate planning authority, the Health and Safety Executive or the appropriate nature conservancy body for the making of representations under subsection (4) or (7) above about a proposal is the period of twenty-eight days beginning with the day on which the proposal is received by the waste regulation authority or such longer period as the waste regulation authority, the appropriate planning authority, the Executive or the body, as the case may be, agree in writing.

(11)  In this section—

"the appropriate planning authority" means—

(a)  where the relevant land is situated in the area of a London Borough council, that London borough council;

(b)  where the relevant land is situated in the City of London, the Common Council of the City of London;

(c)  where the relevant land is situated in a non-metropolitan county in England, the council of that county;

(d)  where the relevant land is situated in a National Park or the Broads, the National Park authority for that National Park or, as the case may be, the Broads Authority;

(e)  where the relevant land is situated elsewhere in England or Wales, the council of the district or, in Wales, the county or county borough, in which the land is situated;

(f)  where the relevant land is situated in Scotland, the council constituted under section 2 of the Local Government etc. (Scotland) Act 1994[6] for the area in which the land is situated;

"the Broads" has the same meaning as in the Norfolk and Suffolk Broads Act 1988[7];

"National Park authority", subject to subsection (12) below[8], means a National Park authority established under section 63 of the Environment Act 1995[9] which has become the local planning authority for the National Park in question;

[1] Words "Scottish Natural Heritage" substituted by the Natural Heritage (Scotland) Act 1991 (c. 28), s. 4(6), sch. 2, para. 10(2). This amendment came into force on 1 April 1992: S.I. 1991/2633.

[2] The date appointed was 1 April 1991: S.I. 1991/685.

[3] Prospective repeal: subsection (8): Environmental Protection Act 1990, s. 162, sch. 16, pt. II.

[4] For provisions relating to notice see s. 160, p. 207 below.

[5] Subsection (9A) inserted by the Environment Act 1995

(c. 25), s. 120, sch. 22, para. 68(5). This amendment is not in force.

[6] 1994 c. 39.

[7] 1988 c. 4. "The Broads" are defined in s. 2(3) . The 1988 Act is set out in the companion volume, A Manual of Nature Conservation Law, edited by Michael Fry (Oxford, 1995) at p. 220.

[8] Prospective repeal: words "subject to subsection (12) below": Environment Act 1995 (c. 25), s. 120, sch. 24.

[9] 1995 c. 25.

"the relevant land" means—

(a)   in relation to a site licence, the land to which the licence relates; and

(b)   in relation to a mobile plant licence, the principal place of business of the operator of the plant to which the licence relates.

(12)   As respects any period before a National Park authority established under section 63 of the Environment Act 1995 in relation to a National Park becomes the local planning authority for that National Park, any reference in this section to a National Park authority shall be taken as a reference to the National Park Committee or joint or special planning board for that National Park[1].

(13)   The Secretary of State may by regulations amend the definition of "appropriate planning authority" in subsection (11) above.

(14)   This section shall have effect subject to section 36A below[2,3].

*Consultation before the grant of certain licences*

**36A.** (1)   This section applies where an application for a licence[4] has been duly made to a waste regulation authority[5], and the authority proposes to issue a licence subject (by virtue of section 35(4) above) to any condition which might require the holder of the licence to—

(a)   carry out any works, or

(b)   do any other thing,

which he might not be entitled to carry out or do.

(2)   Before issuing the licence, the waste regulation authority shall serve on every person appearing to the authority to be a person falling within subsection (3) below a notice[6] which complies with the requirements set out in subsection (4) below.

(3)   A person falls within this subsection if—

(a)   he is the owner[7], lessee or occupier of any land[8]; and

(b)   that land is land in relation to which it is likely that, as a consequence of the licence being issued subject to the condition in question, rights will have to be granted by virtue of section 35(4) above to the holder of the licence.

(4)   A notice served under subsection (2) above shall—

(a)   set out the condition in question;

(b)   indicate the nature of the works or other things which that condition might require the holder of the licence to carry out or do; and

(c)   specify the date by which, and the manner in which, any representations relating to the condition or its possible effects are to be made to the waste regulation authority by the person on whom the notice is served.

(5)   The date which, pursuant to subsection (4)(c) above, is specified in a notice shall be a date not earlier than the date on which expires the period—

(a)   beginning with the date on which the notice is served, and

(b)   of such length as may be prescribed in regulations made by the Secretary of State.

---

[1] *Prospective repeal*: subsection (12): Environment Act 1995 (c. 25), s. 120, sch. 24.

[2] Subsections (10)–(14) substituted , for the earlier subsection (10), by the Environment Act 1995 (c. 25), s. 120, sch. 22, para. 68(6).

[3] For modifications to this section see S.I. 1994/1056, sch. 4, para. 9, p. 717 below. Subsection (1) came into force on 18 February 1993: S.I. 1993/274; for commencement provisions in respect of (2)–(4), (7)–(9) see S.I. 1994/1096, p. 738 below; (10A)–(14) came into force on 1 April 1996: S.I. 1996/186.

[4] "Licence" means a waste management licence: s. 35 (12), p. 120 above.

[5] For "waste regulation authority" see s. 30(1), p. 113 above.

[6] For provisions relating to notice see s. 160, p. 207 below.

[7] "Owner" defined by subsection (8) below.

[8] "Land" defined by s. 29(8), p. 112 above.

(6) Before the waste regulation authority issues the licence it must, subject to subsection (7) below, consider any representations made in relation to the condition in question, or its possible effects, by any person on whom a notice has been served under subsection (2) above.

(7) Subsection (6) above does not require the waste regulation authority to consider any representations made by a person after the date specified in the notice served on him under subsection (2) above as the date by which his representations in relation to the condition or its possible effects are to be made.

(8) In subsection (3) above—

"owner", in relation to any land in England and Wales, means the person who—

(a) is for the time being receiving the rack-rent of the land, whether on his own account or as agent or trustee for another person; or

(b) would receive the rack-rent if the land were let at a rack-rent,

but does not include a mortgagee not in possession; and

"owner", in relation to any land in Scotland, means a person (other than a creditor in a heritable security not in possession of the security subjects) for the time being entitled to receive or who would, if the land were let, be entitled to receive, the rents of the land in connection with which the word is used and includes a trustee, factor, guardian or curator and in the case of public or municipal land includes the persons to whom the management of the land is entrusted[1].

*Variation of licences.*

37. (1) While a licence[2] issued by a waste regulation authority[3] is in force, the authority may, subject to regulations under section 35(6) above[4] and to subsection (3) below,—

(a) on its own initiative, modify the conditions of the licence to any extent which, in the opinion of the authority, is desirable and is unlikely to require unreasonable expense on the part of the holder; and

(b) on the application of the licence holder accompanied by the charge prescribed for the purpose by a charging scheme under section 41 of the Environment Act 1995[5], modify the conditions of his licence to the extent requested in the application.

(2) While a licence issued by a waste regulation authority is in force, the authority shall, except where it revokes the licence entirely under section 38 below[6], modify the conditions of the licence—

(a) to the extent which in the opinion of the authority is required for the purpose of ensuring that the activities authorised by the licence do not cause pollution of the environment[7] or harm[8] to human health or become seriously detrimental to the amenities of the locality affected by the activities; and

(b) to the extent required by any regulations in force under section 35(6) above.

(3) The Secretary of State may, as respects any licence issued by a waste regulation authority, give to the authority directions as to modifications which are to be made in the conditions of the licence under subsection (1)(a) or (2)(a) above; and it shall be the duty of the authority to give effect to the directions.

(4) Any modification of a licence under this section shall be effected by notice[9] served on the holder of the licence and the notice shall state the time at which the modification is to take effect.

[1] This section inserted by the Environment Act 1995 (c. 25), s. 120, sch. 22, para. 69. This amendment is not in force.

[2] "Licence" means a waste management licence: s. 35(12), p. 120 above.

[3] For "waste regulation authority" see s. 30(1), p. 113 above.

[4] P. 119 above.

[5] P. 452 below. Words "the charge . . . 1995" substituted by the Environment Act 1995 (c. 25), s. 120, sch. 22, para. 70(1).

[6] P. 127 below.

[7] "Pollution of the environment" defined by s. 29(3), p. 112 above; "the environment" defined by s. 29(2).

[8] "Harm" defined by s. 29(5), p. 112 above, for the purposes of s. 29(3), (4).

[9] For provisions relating to notice see s.160, p. 207 below.

**(5)** Section 36(4), (7),[1] and (10) above shall with the necessary modifications apply to a proposal by a waste regulation authority to modify a licence under subsection (1) or (2)(a) above as they apply to a proposal to issue a licence, except that—

(a) the authority may postpone the reference so far as the authority considers that by reason of an emergency it is appropriate to do so; and

(b) the authority need not consider any representations as respects a modification which, in the opinion of the waste regulation authority, will not affect any authority mentioned in the subsection so applied.

**(6)** If within the period of two months beginning with the date on which a waste regulation authority received an application by the holder of a licence for a modification of it, or within such longer period as the authority and the applicant may at any time agree in writing, the authority has neither granted a modification of the licence in consequence of the application nor given notice to the applicant that the authority has rejected the application, the authority shall be deemed to have rejected the application.

**(7)** This section shall have effect subject to section 37A below[2,3].

*Consultation before certain variations*

**37A. (1)** This section applies where—

(a) a waste regulation authority[4] proposes to modify a licence[5] under section 37(1) or (2)(a) above; and

(b) the licence, if modified as proposed, would be subject to a relevant new condition.

**(2)** For the purposes of this section, a "relevant new condition" is any condition by virtue of which the holder of the licence might be required to carry out any works or do any other thing—

(a) which he might not be entitled to carry out or do, and

(b) which he could not be required to carry out or do by virtue of the conditions to which, prior to the modification, the licence is subject.

**(3)** Before modifying the licence, the waste regulation authority shall serve on every person appearing to the authority to be a person falling within subsection (4) below a notice[6] which complies with the requirements set out in subsection (5) below.

**(4)** A person falls within this subsection if—

(a) he is the owner[7], lessee or occupier of any land; and

(b) that land is land in relation to which it is likely that, as a consequence of the licence being modified so as to be subject to the relevant new condition in question, rights will have to be granted by virtue of section 35(4) above[8] to the holder of the licence.

**(5)** A notice served under subsection (3) above shall—

(a) set out the relevant new condition in question;

(b) indicate the nature of the works or other things which that condition might require the holder of the licence to carry out or do but which he could not be required to carry out or do by virtue of the conditions (if any) to which, prior to the modification, the licence is subject; and

[1] Words "(5), (6)" and "(8)" repealed by the Environment Act 1995 (c. 25), s. 120, sch. 22, para. 70 (2), sch. 24.

[2] Subsection (7) added by the Environment Act 1995 (c. 25), s. 120, sch. 22, para. 70(3). This amendment is not in force.

[3] Subsection (3), insofar as it enables the Secretary of State to give directions, came into force on 18 February 1993: S.I. 1973/274; (7) is not in force; for the remaining commencement provisions see S.I. 1994/1096, p. 738 below.

[4] For "waste regulation authority" see s. 30(1), p. 113 above.

[5] "Licence" means a waste management licence: s. 35(12), p. 120 above.

[6] For provisions relating to notice see s. 160, p. 207 below.

[7] "Owner" has the same meaning as in s. 36A, p. 124 above: subsection (10) below.

[8] P. 119 above.

(*c*)  specify the date by which, and the manner in which, any representations relating to the condition or its possible effects are to be made to the waste regulation authority by the person on whom the notice is served.

(6)  The date which, pursuant to subsection (5)(c) above, is specified in a notice shall be a date not earlier than the date on which expires the period—

(*a*)  beginning with the date on which the notice is served, and

(*b*)  of such length as may be prescribed in regulations made by the Secretary of State.

(7)  Before the waste regulation authority issues the licence it must, subject to subsection (8) below, consider any representations made in relation to the condition in question, or its possible effects, by any person on whom a notice has been served under subsection (3) above.

(8)  Subsection (7) above does not require the waste regulation authority to consider any representations made by a person after the date specified in the notice served on him under subsection (3) above as the date by which his representations in relation to the condition or its possible effects are to be made.

(9)  A waste regulation authority may postpone the service of any notice or the consideration of any representations required under the foregoing provisions of this section so far as the authority considers that by reason of an emergency it is appropriate to do so.

(10)  In subsection (3) above, "owner" has the same meaning as it has in subsection (3) of section 36A above[1] by virtue of subsection (8) of that section[2].

*Revocation and suspension of licences*

**38.** (1)  Where a licence[3] granted by a waste regulation authority[4] is in force and it appears to the authority—

(*a*)  that the holder of the licence has ceased to be a fit and proper person[5] by reason of his having been convicted of a relevant offence[6]; or

(*b*)  that the continuation of the activities authorised by the licence would cause pollution of the environment[7] or harm[8] to human health or would be seriously detrimental to the amenities of the locality affected; and

(*c*)  that the pollution, harm or detriment cannot be avoided by modifying the conditions of the licence;

the authority may exercise, as it thinks fit, either of the powers conferred by subsections (3) and (4) below.

(2)  Where a licence granted by a waste regulation authority is in force and it appears to the authority that the holder of the licence has ceased to be a fit and proper person by reason of the management of the activities authorised by the licence having ceased to be in the hands of a technically competent person, the authority may exercise the power conferred by subsection (3) below.

(3)  The authority may, under this subsection, revoke the licence so far as it authorises the carrying on of the activities specified in the licence or such of them as the authority specifies in revoking the licence.

(4)  The authority may, under this subsection, revoke the licence entirely.

---

[1] P. 124 above.
[2] This section inserted by the Environment Act 1995 (c. 25), s. 120, sch. 22, para. 71. This amendment is not in force.
[3] "Licence" means a waste management licence: s. 35(12), p. 120 above.
[4] For "waste regulation authority" see s. 30 (1), p. 113 above.

[5] For meaning of "fit and proper person" see s. 74, p. 158 below.
[6] For "relevant offence" see s. 74(6), p. 158 below.
[7] "Pollution of the environment" defined by s. 29(3), p. 114 above; "the environment" defined by s. 29(2).
[8] "Harm" defined by s. 29(5), p. 114 above, for the purposes of s. 29(3), (4).

**(5)** A licence revoked under subsection (3) above shall cease to have effect to authorise the carrying on of the activities specified in the licence or, as the case may be, the activities specified by the authority in revoking the licence but shall not affect the requirements imposed by the licence which the authority, in revoking the licence, specify as requirements which are to continue to bind the licence holder.

**(6)** Where a licence granted by a waste regulation authority is in force and it appears to the authority—

(a)  that the holder of the licence has ceased to be a fit and proper person by reason of the management of the activities authorised by the licence having ceased to be in the hands of a technically competent person; or

(b)  that serious pollution of the environment or serious harm to human health has resulted from, or is about to be caused by, the activities to which the licence relates or the happening or threatened happening of an event affecting those activities; and

(c)  that the continuing to carry on those activities, or any of those activities, in the circumstances will continue or, as the case may be, cause serious pollution of the environment or serious harm to human health;

the authority may suspend the licence so far as it authorises the carrying on of the activities specified in the licence or such of them as the authority specifies in suspending the licence.

**(7)** The Secretary of State may, if he thinks fit in relation to a licence granted by a waste regulation authority, give to the authority directions as to whether and in what manner the authority should exercise its powers under this section; and it shall be the duty of the authority to give effect to the directions.

**(8)** A licence suspended under subsection (6) above shall, while the suspension has effect, be of no effect to authorise the carrying on of the activities specified in the licence or, as the case may be, the activities specified by the authority in suspending the licence.

**(9)** Where a licence is suspended under subsection (6) above, the authority, in suspending it or at any time while it is suspended, may require the holder of the licence to take such measures to deal with or avert the pollution or harm as the authority considers necessary.

**(9A)** A requirement imposed under subsection (9) above may require the holder of a licence to carry out works or do other things notwithstanding that he is not entitled to carry out the works or do the thing and any person whose consent would be required shall grant, or join in granting, the holder of the licence such rights in relation to the land as will enable the holder of the licence to comply with any requirements imposed on him under that subsection.

**(9B)** Subsections (2) to (8) of section 36A above shall, with the necessary modifications, apply where the authority proposes to impose a requirement under subsection (9) above which may require the holder of a licence to carry out any such works or do any such thing as is mentioned in subsection (9A) above as they apply where the authority proposes to issue a licence subject to any such condition as is mentioned in subsection (1) of that section, but as if—

(a)  the reference in subsection (3) of that section to section 35(4) above were a reference to subsection (9A) above; and

(b)  any reference in those subsections—

(i)  to the condition, or the condition in question, were a reference to the requirement; and

(ii)  to issuing a licence were a reference to serving a notice, under subsection (12) below, effecting the requirement.

**(9C)** The authority may postpone the service of any notice or the consideration of any representations required under section 36A above, as applied by subsection (9B) above, so far as the authority considers that by reason of an emergency it is appropriate to do so[1].

---

[1] Subsections (9A)–(9C) inserted by the Environment Act 1995 (c. 25), s. 120, sch. 22, para. 72(1). This amendment is not in force.

**(10)** A person who, without reasonable excuse, fails to comply with any requirement imposed under subsection (9) above otherwise than in relation to special waste[1] shall be liable—

(*a*)  on summary conviction, to a fine of an amount not exceeding the statutory maximum[2]; and

(*b*)  on conviction on indictment, to imprisonment for a term not exceeding two years or a fine or both.

**(11)** A person who, without reasonable excuse, fails to comply with any requirement imposed under subsection (9) above in relation to special waste shall be liable—

(*a*)  on summary conviction, to imprisonment for a term not exceeding six months or a fine not exceeding the statutory maximum or both; and

(*b*)  on conviction on indictment, to imprisonment for a term not exceeding five years or a fine or both.

**(12)** Any revocation or suspension of a licence or requirement imposed during the suspension of a licence under this section shall be effected by notice[3] served on the holder of the licence and the notice shall state the time at which the revocation or suspension or the requirement is to take effect and, in the case of suspension, the period at the end of which, or the event on the occurrence of which, the suspension is to cease.

**(13)** If a waste regulation authority is of the opinion that proceedings for an offence under subsection (10) or (11) above would afford an ineffectual remedy against a person who has failed to comply with any requirement imposed under subsection (9) above, the authority may take proceedings in the High Court or, in Scotland, in any court of competent jurisdiction for the purpose of securing compliance with the requirement[4,5].

........................................................................................................................................................................

*Surrender of licences*

**39.** **(1)** A licence[6] may be surrendered by its holder to the authority which granted it but, in the case of a site licence[7], only if the authority accepts the surrender.

**(2)** The following provisions apply to the surrender and acceptance of the surrender of a site licence.

**(3)** The holder of a site licence who desires to surrender it shall make an application for that purpose to the authority on a form provided by the authority for the purpose, giving such information and accompanied by such evidence as the authority reasonably requires and accompanied by the charge prescribed for the purpose by a charging scheme under section 41 of the Environment Act 1995[8].

**(4)** An authority which receives an application for the surrender of a site licence—

(*a*)  shall inspect the land[9] to which the licence relates, and

(*b*)  may require the holder of the licence to furnish to it further information or further evidence.

**(5)** The authority shall determine whether it is likely or unlikely that the condition of the land, so far as that condition is the result of the use of the land for the treatment[10], keeping or disposal[11] of waste[12] (whether or not in pursuance of the licence), will cause pollution of the environment[13] or harm[14] to human health.

---

[1] "Special waste" defined by s. 75(9), p. 160 below.

[2] The current statutory maximum is £5,000: Criminal Justice Act 1991 (c. 53), s. 17(2); Criminal Procedure (Scotland) Act 1995 (c. 46), s. 225(8).

[3] For provisions relating to notice see s. 160, p. 207 below.

[4] Subsection (13) added by the Environment Act 1995 (c. 25), s. 120, sch. 22, para. 72(2).

[5] Subsection (7), insofar as it enables the Secretary of State to give directions, came into force on 18 February 1993: S.I. 1973/274; (13) came into force on 1 April 1996: S.I. 1996/186; for the remaining commencement provisions see S.I. 1994/1096, p. 738 below.

[6] "Licence" means a waste management licence: s. 35 (12), p. 120 above.

[7] "Site licence" defined by s. 35(12), p. 120 above.

[8] P. 452 below. Words "on a form . . . 1995" substituted the Environment Act 1995 (c. 25), s. 120, sch. 22, para. 73 (2). This amendment, in so far as it requires an application to be accompanied by the prescribed charge, came into force on 1 April 1996: S.I. 1996/186; otherwise it is not in force.

[9] "Land" defined by s. 29(8), p. 112 above.

[10] "Treatment" defined by s. 29(6), p. 112 above.

[11] "Disposal" of waste defined by s. 29(6), p. 112 above.

[12] "Waste" defined by s. 75, p. 160 below.

[13] "Pollution of the environment" defined by s. 29(3), p. 112 above; "the environment" defined by s. 29(2).

[14] "Harm" defined by s. 29(5), p. 112 above, for the purposes of s. 29(3), (4).

**(6)** If the authority is satisfied that the condition of the land is unlikely to cause the pollution or harm mentioned in subsection (5) above, the authority shall, subject to subsection (7) below, accept the surrender of the licence; but otherwise the authority shall refuse to accept it.

**(7)** Where the authority proposes to accept the surrender of a site licence, the authority must, before it does so,—

(a)  refer the proposal to the appropriate planning authority[1]; and

(b)  consider any representations about the proposal which the appropriate planning authority[2] makes to it during the allowed period.

**(8)** *Repealed by the Environment Act 1995 (c. 25), s. 120, sch. 22, para. 73(4), sch. 24. This amendment came into force on 1 April 1996: S.I. 1996/186.*

**(9)** Where the surrender of a licence is accepted under this section the authority shall issue to the applicant, with the notice of its determination, a certificate (a "certificate of completion") stating that it is satisfied as mentioned in subsection (6) above and, on the issue of that certificate, the licence shall cease to have effect.

**(10)** If within the period of three months beginning with the date on which an authority receives an application to surrender a licence, or within such longer period as the authority and the applicant may at any time agree in writing, the authority has neither issued a certificate of completion nor given notice to the applicant that the authority has rejected the application, the authority shall be deemed to have rejected the application.

**(11)** Section 36(10) above applies for the interpretation of the "allowed period" in subsection (7) above[3].

**(12)** In this section—

"the appropriate planning authority" means—

(a)  where the relevant land is situated in the area of a London borough council, that London borough council;

(b)  where the relevant land is situated in the City of London, the Common Council of the City of London;

(c)  where the relevant land is situated in a non-metropolitan county in England, the council of that county;

(d)  where the relevant land is situated in a National Park or the Broads, the National Park authority for that National Park or, as the case may be, the Broads Authority;

(e)  where the relevant land is situated elsewhere in England or Wales, the council of the district or, in Wales, the county or county borough, in which the land is situated;

(f)  where the relevant land is situated in Scotland, the council constituted under section 2 of the Local Government etc. (Scotland) Act 1994[4] for the area in which the land is situated;

"the Broads" has the same meaning as in the Norfolk and Suffolk Broads Act 1988[5];

"National Park authority", subject to subsection (13) below[6], means a National Park authority established under section 63 of the Environment Act 1995[7] which has become the local planning authority for the National Park in question;

"the relevant land", in the case of any site licence, means the land to which the licence relates.

[1] Words "the appropriate planning authority" defined by subsection (11) below. Words "the appropriate planning authority" in this subsection substituted by the Environment Act 1995 (c. 25), s. 120, sch. 22, para. 73 (3) (a).
[2] Former words following para. (b) repealed by the Environment Act 1995 (c. 25), s. 120, sch. 22, para. 73(3)(b), sch. 24.
[3] Words "subsection (7) above" substituted the Environment Act 1995 (c. 25), s. 120, sch. 22, para. 73 (5).
[4] 1994 c. 39.
[5] 1988 c. 4. "The Broads" are defined in s. 2(3) . The 1988 Act is set out in the companion volume, *A Manual of Nature Conservation Law*, edited by Michael Fry (Oxford, 1995) at p. 220.
[6] *Prospective repeal*: words "subject to subsection (13) below": Environment Act 1995 (c. 25), s. 120, sch. 24.
[7] 1995 c. 25.

**(13)** As respects any period before a National Park authority established under section 63 of the Environment Act 1995 in relation to a National Park becomes the local planning authority for that National Park, any reference in this section to a National Park authority shall be taken as a reference to the National Park Committee or joint or special planning board for that National Park[1].

**(14)** The Secretary of State may by regulations amend the definition of "appropriate planning authority" in subsection (12) above[2,3].

*Transfer of licences.*

**40.** **(1)** A licence[4] may be transferred to another person in accordance with subsections (2) to (6) below and may be so transferred whether or not the licence is partly revoked or suspended under any provision of this Part.

**(2)** Where the holder of a licence desires that the licence be transferred to another person ("the proposed transferee") the licence holder and the proposed transferee shall jointly make an application to the waste regulation authority[5] which granted the licence for a transfer of it.

**(3)** An application under subsection (2) above for the transfer of a licence shall be made on a form provided by the authority for the purpose, accompanied by such information as the authority may reasonably require, the charge prescribed for the purpose by a charging scheme under section 41 of the Environment Act 1995[6] and the licence.

**(4)** If, on such an application, the authority is satisfied that the proposed transferee is a fit and proper person[7] the authority shall effect a transfer of the licence to the proposed transferee.

**(5)** The authority shall effect a transfer of a licence under the foregoing provisions of this section by causing the licence to be endorsed with the name and other particulars of the proposed transferee as the holder of the licence from such date specified in the endorsement as may be agreed with the applicants.

**(6)** If within the period of two months beginning with the date on which the authority receives an application for the transfer of a licence or within such longer period as the authority and the applicants may at any time agree in writing, the authority has neither effected a transfer of the licence nor given notice[8] to the applicants that the authority has rejected the application, the authority shall be deemed to have rejected the application[9].

**41.** *Repealed by the Environment Act 1995 (c. 25), s. 120, sch. 22, para. 75, sch. 24. This amendment came into force on 1 April 1996: S.I. 1996/186.*

*Supervision of licensed activities*

**42.** **(1)** While a licence[10] is in force it shall be the duty of the waste regulation authority[11] which granted the licence to take the steps needed—

  (*a*) for the purpose of ensuring that the activities authorised by the licence do not cause pollution of the environment[12] or harm[13] to human health or become seriously detrimental to the amenities of the locality affected by the activities; and

---

[1] *Prospective repeal*: subsection (13): Environment Act 1995 (c. 25), s. 120, sch. 24.
[2] Subsections (12)–(14) added by the Environment Act 1995 (c. 25), s. 120, sch. 22, para. 73 (6).
[3] Subsection (3) came into force on 18 February 1993: S.I. 1993/274; (12)–(14) came into force on 1 April 1996: S.I. 1996/186; for the remaining commencement provisions see S.I. 1994/1096, p. 738 below.
[4] "Licence" means a waste management licence: s. 35 (12), p. 120 above.
[5] For "waste regulation authority" see s. 30(1), p. 113 above.
[6] P. 452 below. Words "on a form . . . 1995" substituted the Environment Act 1995 (c. 25), s. 120, sch. 22, para. 74. This amendment, in so far as it requires an application to be accompanied by the prescribed charge, came into force on

1 April 1996: S.I. 1996/186; otherwise it is not in force.
[7] For the meaning of "fit and proper person" see s. 74, p. 158 below.
[8] For provisions relating to notice see s. 160, p. 207 below.
[9] Subsection (3) came into force on 18 February 1993: S.I. 1993/274; for the remaining commencement provisions see S.I. 1994/1096, p. 738 below.
[10] "Licence" means a waste management licence: s. 35 (12), p. 120 above.
[11] For "waste regulation authority" see s. 30(1), p. 113 above.
[12] "Pollution of the environment" defined by s. 29(3), p. 112 above; "the environment" defined by s. 29(2).
[13] "Harm" defined by s. 29(5), p. 112 above, for the purposes of s. 29(3), (4).

(*b*)  for the purpose of ensuring that the conditions of the licence are complied with.

(2)  *Repealed by the Environment Act 1995 (c. 25), s. 120, sch. 22, para. 76(2), sch. 24. This amendment came into force on 1 April 1996: S.I. 1996/186.*

(3)  For the purpose of performing the duty imposed on it by subsection (1) above, any officer of the authority authorised in writing for the purpose by the authority may, if it appears to him that by reason of an emergency it is necessary to do so, carry out work on the land[1] or in relation to plant or equipment on the land to which the licence relates or, as the case may be, in relation to the mobile plant[2] to which the licence relates.

(4)  Where a waste regulation authority incurs any expenditure by virtue of subsection (3) above, the authority may recover the amount of the expenditure from the holder, or (as the case may be) the former holder, of the licence [3], except where the holder or former holder of the licence shows that there was no emergency requiring any work or except such of the expenditure as he shows was unnecessary.

(5)  Where it appears to a waste regulation authority that a condition of a licence granted by it is not being complied with or is likely not to be complied with,[4] then, without prejudice to any proceedings under section 33(6) above[5], the authority may—

(*a*)  serve on the holder of the licence a notice[6]—

  (i)  stating that the authority is of the opinion that a condition of the licence is not being complied with or, as the case may be, is likely not to be complied with;

  (ii)  specifying the matters which constitute the non-compliance or, as the case may be, which make the anticipated non-compliance likely;

  (iii)  specifying the steps which must be taken to remedy the non-compliance or, as the case may be, to prevent the anticipated non-compliance from occurring; and

  (iv)  specifying the period within which those steps must be taken[7]; and

(*b*)  if in the opinion of the authority the licence holder has not taken the steps specified in the notice within the period so specified[8], exercise any of the powers specified in subsection (6) below.

(6)  The powers which become exercisable in the event mentioned in subsection (5)(b) above are the following—

(*a*)  to revoke the licence so far as it authorises the carrying on of the activities specified in the licence or such of them as the authority specifies in revoking the licence;

(*b*)  to revoke the licence entirely; and

(*c*)  to suspend the licence so far as it authorises the carrying on of the activities specified in the licence or, as the case may be, the activities specified by the authority in suspending the licence.

(6A)  If a waste regulation authority is of the opinion that revocation or suspension of the licence, whether entirely or to any extent, under subsection (6) above would afford an ineffectual remedy against a person who has failed to comply with any requirement imposed under subsection (5)(a) above, the authority may take proceedings in the High Court or, in Scotland, in any court of competent jurisdiction for the purpose of securing compliance with the requirement[9].

(7)  Where a licence is revoked or suspended under subsection (6) above, subsections (5) and (12) or, as the case may be, subsections (8) to (12) of section 38 [10,11] above shall apply with the

---

[1] "Land" defined by s. 29 (8), p. 112 above.
[2] "Mobile plant" defined by s. 29(9),(10), p. 112 above.
[3] Words "the holder, or (as the case may be) the former holder, of the licence" substituted by the Environment Act 1995 (c. 25), s. 120, sch. 22, para. 76(3) . This amendment came into force on 21 September 1995: S.I. 1995/1983.
[4] Words "or is likely not to be complied with," inserted by the Environment Act 1995 (c. 25), s. 120, sch. 22, para. 76 (4).
[5] P. 116 above.
[6] For provisions relating to notice see s. 160, p. 207 below.
[7] Para.(a) substituted by the Environment Act 1995

(c. 25), s. 120, sch. 22, para. 76(5).
[8] Words "has not taken the steps specified in the notice within the period so specified," substituted by the Environment Act 1995 (c. 25), s. 120, sch. 22, para. 76(6).
[9] Subsection (6A) inserted by the Environment Act 1995 (c. 25), s. 120, sch. 22, para. 76(7).
[10] P. 128 above.
[11] Words "subsections (5) and (12) or, as the case may be, subsections (8) to (12) of section 38" substituted by the Environment Act 1995 (c. 25), s. 120, sch. 22, para. 76(8)(a). This amendment is not in force.

necessary modifications as they respectively apply to revocations or suspensions of licences under that section[1].

**(8)** The Secretary of State may, if he thinks fit in relation to a licence granted by a waste regulation authority, give to the authority directions as to whether and in what manner the authority should exercise its powers under this section; and it shall be the duty of the authority to give effect to the directions[2].

*Appeals to Secretary of State from decisions with respect to licences*

**43.** (1) Where, except in pursuance of a direction given by the Secretary of State,—

(a) an application for a licence[3] or a modification of the conditions of a licence is rejected;

(b) a licence is granted subject to conditions;

(c) the conditions of a licence are modified;

(d) a licence is suspended;

(e) a licence is revoked under section 38[4] or 42 above;

(f) an application to surrender a licence is rejected; or

(g) an application for the transfer of a licence is rejected;

then, except in the case of an application for a transfer, the applicant for the licence or, as the case may be, the holder or former holder of it may appeal from the decision to the Secretary of State and, in the case of an application for a transfer, the proposed transferee may do so.

**(2)** Where an appeal is made to the Secretary of State—

(a) and (b) *Repealed by the Environment Act 1995 (c. 25), s. 120, sch. 22, para. 77, sch. 24 . This amendment came into force on 1 April 1996: S.I. 1996/186.*

(c) if a party to the appeal so requests, or the Secretary of State so decides, the appeal shall be or continue in the form of a hearing (which may, if the person hearing the appeal so decides, be held or held to any extent in private).

**(2A)** This section is subject to section 114 of the Environment Act 1995[5] (delegation or reference of appeals etc)[6].

**(3)** Where, on such an appeal, the Secretary of State or other person determining the appeal determines that the decision of the authority shall be altered it shall be the duty of the authority to give effect to the determination.

**(4)** While an appeal is pending in a case falling within subsection (1)(c) or (e) above, the decision in question shall, subject to subsection (6) below, be ineffective; and if the appeal is dismissed or withdrawn the decision shall become effective from the end of the day on which the appeal is dismissed or withdrawn.

**(5)** Where an appeal is made in a case falling within subsection (1)(d) above, the bringing of the appeal shall have no effect on the decision in question.

**(6)** Subsection (4) above shall not apply to a decision modifying the conditions of a licence under section 37 above[7] or revoking a licence under section 38 or 42 above in the case of which the notice effecting the modification or revocation includes a statement that in the opinion of the authority it is necessary for the purpose of preventing or, where that is not practicable, minimising pollution of the environment[8] or harm[9] to human health that that subsection should not apply.

[1] The remainder of this section, which related to subsection (5)(a), has been repealed by the Environment Act 1995 (c. 25), s. 120, sch. 22, para. 76(8)(b), sch. 24.
[2] Subsection (8), insofar as it enables the Secretary of State to give directions, came into force on 18 February 1993: S.I. 1993/274; for the remaining commencement provisions relating to this section see S.I. 1994/1096, p. 738 below.
[3] "Licence" means a waste management licence: s. 35(12), p. 120 above.
[4] P. 127 above.
[5] P. 489 below.
[6] Subsection (2A) inserted by the Environment Act 1995 (c. 25), s. 120, sch. 22, para. 77.
[7] P. 125 above.
[8] "Pollution of the environment" defined by s. 29(3), p. 112 above; "the environment" defined by s. 29(2).
[9] "Harm" defined by s. 29(5), p. 112 above, for the purposes of s. 29(3),(4).

(7) Where the decision under appeal is one falling within subsection (6) above or is a decision to suspend a licence, if, on the application of the holder or former holder of the licence, the Secretary of State or other person determining the appeal determines that the authority acted unreasonably in excluding the application of subsection (4) above or, as the case may be, in suspending the licence, then—

(a) if the appeal is still pending at the end of the day on which the determination is made subsection (4) above shall apply to the decision from the end of that day; and

(b) the holder or former holder of the licence shall be entitled to recover compensation from the authority in respect of any loss suffered by him in consequence of the exclusion of the application of that subsection or the suspension of the licence;

and any dispute as to a person's entitlement to such compensation or as to the amount of it shall be determined by arbitration or in Scotland by a single arbiter appointed, in default of agreement between the parties concerned, by the Secretary of State on the application of any of the parties.

(8) Provision may be made by the Secretary of State by regulations with respect to appeals under this section and in particular—

(a) as to the period within which and the manner in which appeals are to be brought; and

(b) as to the manner in which appeals are to be considered[1].[2]

*Offences of making false or misleading statements or false entries*

**44.** (1) A person who—

(a) in purported compliance with a requirement to furnish any information imposed by or under any provision of this Part, or

(b) for the purpose of obtaining for himself or another any grant of a licence[3], any modification of the conditions of a licence, an acceptance of the surrender of a licence or any transfer of a licence,

makes a statement which he knows to be false or misleading in a material particular, or recklessly makes any statement which is false or misleading in a material particular, commits an offence.

(2) A person who intentionally makes a false entry in any record required to be kept by virtue of a licence commits an offence.

(3) A person who commits an offence under this section shall be liable—

(a) on summary conviction, to a fine not exceeding the statutory maximum[4];

(b) on conviction on indictment, to a fine or to imprisonment for a term not exceeding two years, or to both[5].

## Collection, disposal or treatment of controlled waste

*National waste strategy: England and Wales*

**44A.** (1) The Secretary of State shall as soon as possible prepare a statement ("the strategy") containing his policies in relation to the recovery and disposal[6] of waste[7] in England and Wales.

(2) The strategy shall consist of or include—

---

[1] The following regulations have been made under this section:

The Waste Management Licensing Regulations 1994, S.I. 1994/1056, as amended, p. 675 below.

[2] Subsection (8) came into force on 18 February 1993: S.I. 1993/274; for the remaining commencement provisions relating to this section see S.I. 1994/1096, p. 738 below.

[3] "Licence" means a waste management licence: s. 35(12), p. 120 above.

[4] The current statutory maximum is £5,000: Criminal Justice Act 1991 (c. 53), s. 17(2); Criminal Procedure (Scotland) Act 1995 (c. 46), s. 225(8).

[5] This section substituted by the Environment Act 1995 (c. 25), s. 112, sch. 19, para. 4(1). This amendment came into force on 1 April 1996: S.I. 1996/186.

[6] "Disposal" defined by s. 29(6), p. 112 above.

[7] "Waste" defined by s. 75, p. 159 below. A White Paper, Making Waste Work, Cm. 3040, was published in Dec. 1995; this is a non-statutory document: see para. 1.113–1.117.

(*a*)  a statement which relates to the whole of England and Wales; or

(*b*)  two or more statements which between them relate to the whole of England and Wales.

(3)  The Secretary of State may from time to time modify the strategy.

(4)  Without prejudice to the generality of what may be included in the strategy, the strategy must include—

(*a*)  a statement of the Secretary of State's policies for attaining the objectives specified in Schedule 2A to this Act[1];

(*b*)  provisions relating to each of the following, that is to say—

    (i)   the type, quantity and origin of waste to be recovered or disposed of;

    (ii)  general technical requirements; and

    (iii) any special requirements for particular wastes.

(5)  In preparing the strategy or any modification of it, the Secretary of State—

(*a*)  shall consult the Environment Agency[2],

(*b*)  shall consult—

    (i)  such bodies or persons appearing to him to be representative of the interests of local government, and

    (ii) such bodies or persons appearing to him to be representative of the interests of industry,

    as he may consider appropriate, and

(*c*)  may consult such other bodies or persons as he considers appropriate.

(6)  Without prejudice to any power to give directions conferred by section 40 of the Environment Act 1995[3], the Secretary of State may give directions to the Environment Agency requiring it—

(*a*)  to advise him on the policies which are to be included in the strategy;

(*b*)  to carry out a survey of or investigation into—

    (i)  the kinds or quantities of waste which it appears to that Agency is likely to be situated in England and Wales,

    (ii) the facilities which are or appear to that Agency likely to be available or needed in England and Wales for recovering or disposing of any such waste,

    (iii) any other matter upon which the Secretary of State wishes to be informed in connection with his preparation of the strategy or any modification of it,

    and to report its findings to him.

(7)  A direction under subsection (6)(b) above—

(*a*)  shall specify or describe the matters or the areas which are to be the subject of the survey or investigation; and

(*b*)  may make provision in relation to the manner in which—

    (i)  the survey or investigation is to be carried out, or

    (ii) the findings are to be reported or made available to other persons.

(8)  Where a direction is given under subsection (6)(b) above, the Environment Agency shall, in accordance with any requirement of the direction,—

(*a*)  before carrying out the survey or investigation, consult—

    (i)  such bodies or persons appearing to it to be representative of local planning authorities, and

---

[1]  P. 222 below.
[2]  The Environment Agency is established by the Environment Act 1995 (c. 25), s. 1, p. 420 below.    [3]  P. 451 above.

(ii)  such bodies or persons appearing to it to be representative of the interests of industry, as it may consider appropriate; and

(b)  make its findings available to those authorities.

**(9)**  In this section—

"local planning authority" has the same meaning as in the Town and Country Planning Act 1990[1];

"strategy" includes the strategy as modified from time to time and "statement" shall be construed accordingly.

**(10)**  This section makes provision for the purpose of implementing Article 7 of the directive of the Council of the European Communities, dated 15th July 1975, on waste[2], as amended by—

(a)  the directive of that Council, dated 18th March 1991, amending directive 75/442/EEC on waste[3]; and

(b)  the directive of that Council, dated 23rd December 1991[4], standardising and rationalising reports on the implementation of certain Directives relating to the environment[5].

## National waste strategy: Scotland

**44B. (1)**  SEPA[6] shall as soon as possible prepare a statement ("the strategy") containing its policies in relation to the recovery and disposal[7] of waste[8] in Scotland.

**(2)**  SEPA may from time to time modify the strategy.

**(3)**  Without prejudice to the generality of what may be included in the strategy, the strategy must include—

(a)  a statement of SEPA's policies for attaining the objectives specified in Schedule 2A to this Act[9];

(b)  provisions relating to each of the following, that is to say—

(i)  the type, quantity and origin of waste to be recovered or disposed of;

(ii)  general technical requirements; and

(iii)  any special requirements for particular wastes.

**(4)**  In preparing the strategy or any modification of it SEPA shall consult—

(a)  such bodies or persons appearing to it to be representative of the interests of industry as it may consider appropriate;

(b)  such local authorities as appear to it to be likely to be affected by the strategy or modification,

and may consult such other bodies or persons as it considers appropriate.

**(5)**  Without prejudice to any power to give directions conferred by section 40 of the Environment Act 1995[10], the Secretary of State may give directions to SEPA—

(a)  as to the policies which are to be included in the strategy;

(b)  requiring it to carry out a survey or investigation into—

(i)  the kinds or quantities of waste which it appears to it is likely to be situated in Scotland,

[1]  1990 c. 8.
[2]  75/442/EEC.
[3]  91/156/EEC.
[4]  91/692/EEC.
[5]  This section inserted by the Environment Act 1995 (c. 25), s. 92 (1). This amendment came into force on 1 April 1996: S.I. 1996/186.

[6]  SEPA, the Scottish Environment Protection Agency, is established by the Environment Act 1995 (c. 25), s. 20, p. 438 below.
[7]  "Disposal" defined by s. 29(6), p. 112 above.
[8]  "Waste" defined by s. 75, p. 159 below.
[9]  P. 222 below.
[10]  P. 451 below.

    (ii)  the facilities which are or appear to it likely to be available or needed in Scotland for recovering or disposing of any such waste,

    (iii)  any other matter which the Secretary of State considers appropriate in connection with its preparation of the strategy or any modifications of it.

**(6)**  A direction under subsection (5)(b) above—

(a)  shall specify or describe the matters or the areas which are to be the subject of the survey or investigation; and

(b)  may make provision in relation to the manner in which—

    (i)  the survey or investigation is to be carried out, or

    (ii)  the findings are to be reported or made available to other persons.

**(7)**  Where a direction is given under subsection (5)(b) above SEPA shall, in accordance with any requirement of the direction—

(a)  before carrying out the survey or investigation, consult—

    (i)  such bodies or persons appearing to it to be representative of planning authorities, and

    (ii)  such bodies or persons appearing to it to be representative of the interests of industry, as it may consider appropriate; and

(b)  make its findings available to those authorities.

**(8)**  In this section—

"planning authority" means an authority within the meaning of section 172 of the Local Government (Scotland) Act 1973[1];

"strategy" includes the strategy as modified from time to time and "statement" shall be construed accordingly.

**(9)**  This section makes provision for the purpose of implementing Article 7 of the directive of the Council of the European Communities dated 15th July 1975 on waste[2], as amended by—

(a)  the directive of that Council dated 18th March 1991 amending directive 75/442/EEC on waste[3]; and

(b)  the directive of that Council dated 23rd December 1991[4] standardising and rationalising reports on the implementation of certain Directives relating to the environment[5].

---

*Collection, disposal or treatment of controlled waste*

*Collection of controlled waste*

**45.**  **(1)**  It shall be the duty of each waste collection authority[6]—

(a)  to arrange for the collection of household waste[7] in its area except waste—

    (i)  which is situated at a place which in the opinion of the authority is so isolated or inaccessible that the cost of collecting it would be unreasonably high, and

    (ii)  as to which the authority is satisfied that adequate arrangements for its disposal[8] have been or can reasonably be expected to be made by a person who controls the waste; and

(b)  if requested by the occupier of premises in its area to collect any commercial waste[9] from the premises, to arrange for the collection of the waste.

[1]  1973 c. 65.
[2]  75/442/EEC.
[3]  91/156/EEC.
[4]  91/692/EEC.
[5]  This section inserted by the Environment Act 1995 (c. 25), s. 92(1). This amendment came into force on 1 April

1996: S.I. 1996/186.
[6]  "Waste collection authority" defined by s. 30(3), p. 113 above.
[7]  "Household waste" defined by s. 75, p. 159 below.
[8]  "Disposal" of waste defined by s. 29(6), p. 112 above.
[9]  "Commercial waste" defined by s. 75, p. 159 below.

**(2)** Each waste collection authority may, if requested by the occupier of premises in its area to collect any industrial waste from the premises, arrange for the collection of the waste; but a collection authority in England and Wales shall not exercise the power except with the consent of the waste disposal authority[1] whose area includes the area of the waste collection authority.

**(3)** No charge shall be made for the collection of household waste except in cases prescribed in regulations made by the Secretary of State; and in any of those cases—

(a)  the duty to arrange for the collection of the waste shall not arise until a person who controls the waste requests the authority to collect it; and

(b)  the authority may recover a reasonable charge for the collection of the waste from the person who made the request[2].

**(4)** A person at whose request waste other than household waste is collected under this section shall be liable to pay a reasonable charge for the collection and disposal of the waste to the authority which arranged for its collection; and it shall be the duty of that authority to recover the charge unless in the case of a charge in respect of commercial waste the authority considers it inappropriate to do so.

**(5)** It shall be the duty of each waste collection authority—

(a)  to make such arrangements for the emptying, without charge, of privies[3] serving one or more private dwellings in its area as the authority considers appropriate;

(b)  if requested by the person who controls a cesspool[4] serving only one or more private dwellings in its area to empty the cesspool, to remove such of the contents of the cesspool as the authority considers appropriate on payment, if the authority so requires, of a reasonable charge.

**(6)** A waste collection authority may, if requested by the person who controls any other privy or cesspool in its area to empty the privy or cesspool, empty the privy or, as the case may be, remove from the cesspool such of its contents as the authority consider appropriate on payment, if the authority so requires, of a reasonable charge.

**(7)** A waste collection authority may—

(a)  construct, lay and maintain, within or outside its area, pipes and associated works for the purpose of collecting waste;

(b)  contribute towards the cost incurred by another person in providing or maintaining pipes or associated works connecting with pipes provided by the authority under paragraph (a) above.

**(8)** A waste collection authority may contribute towards the cost incurred by another person in providing or maintaining plant or equipment intended to deal with commercial or industrial waste before it is collected under arrangements made by the authority under subsection (1)(b) or (2) above.

**(9)** Subject to section 48(1) below[5], anything collected under arrangements made by a waste collection authority under this section shall belong to the authority and may be dealt with accordingly.

**(10)** In relation to Scotland, sections 2, 3, 4 and 41 of the Sewerage (Scotland) Act 1968[6] (maintenance of public sewers etc.) shall apply in relation to pipes and associated works provided or to be provided under subsection (7)(a) above as those sections apply in relation to public sewers but as if—

(a)  the said section 2 conferred a power on a waste collection authority rather than a duty on a sewerage authority;

[1] "Waste disposal authority" defined by s. 30 (2), p. 113 above.
[2] The following regulations have been made under this section:
The Controlled Waste Regulations 1992, S . I. 1992/588, as amended, p. 662 below;
The Waste Management Licensing Regulations 1994, S.I. 1994/1056, as amended, p. 675 below.
[3] "Privy" defined by subsection (12) below.
[4] "Cesspool" defined by subsection (12) below.
[5] P. 141 below.
[6] 1968 c. 47.

(b)   in the said section 3—

(i)   references to a sewerage authority were references to a waste collection authority; and

(ii)  in references to public sewers and public sewage works the word "public" were omitted;

(c)   in the said section 4, the reference to a sewerage authority were a reference to a waste collection authority and the words from "by virtue" to the end were omitted; and

(d)   in the said section 41, the reference to a sewerage authority were a reference to a waste collection authority[1],

and the Pipe-lines Act 1962[2] shall not apply to pipes and associated works provided or to be provided under the said subsection (7)(a).

(11)  In the application of this section to Scotland, subsection (5)(b) and the references to a cesspool occurring in subsection (6) shall be omitted.

(12)  In this section "privy" means a latrine which has a moveable receptacle and "cesspool" includes a settlement tank or other tank for the reception or disposal of foul matter from buildings[3].

*Receptacles for household waste*

**46. (1)**  Where a waste collection authority[4] has a duty by virtue of section 45(1)(a) above to arrange for the collection of household waste[5] from any premises, the authority may, by notice served on him[6], require the occupier to place the waste for collection in receptacles[7] of a kind and number specified.

**(2)**  The kind and number of the receptacles required under subsection (1) above to be used shall be such only as are reasonable but, subject to that, separate receptacles or compartments of receptacles may be required to be used for waste which is to be recycled[8] and waste which is not.

**(3)**  In making requirements under subsection (1) above the authority may, as respects the provision of the receptacles—

(a)   determine that they be provided by the authority free of charge;

(b)   propose that they be provided, if the occupier agrees, by the authority on payment by him of such a single payment or such periodical payments as he agrees with the authority;

(c)   require the occupier to provide them if he does not enter into an agreement under paragraph (b) above within a specified[9] period; or

(d)   require the occupier to provide them.

**(4)**  In making requirements as respects receptacles under subsection (1) above, the authority may, by the notice under that subsection, make provision with respect to—

(a)   the size, construction and maintenance of the receptacles;

(b)   the placing of the receptacles for the purpose of facilitating the emptying of them, and access to the receptacles for that purpose;

(c)   the placing of the receptacles for that purpose on highways or, in Scotland, roads;

(d)   the substances[10] or articles which may or may not be put into the receptacles or compartments of receptacles of any description and the precautions to be taken where particular substances or articles are put into them; and

[1] Para . (a)–(d) substituted for the earlier para. (a) and (b) by the Local Government etc. (Scotland) Act 1994 (c. 39), s. 180(1) sch. 13, para. 167(6) . This amendment came into force on 1 April 1996: S.I. 1996/323.
[2] 1962 c. 58.
[3] This section, insofar as it enables regulations to be made, came into force on 14 February 1992: S.I. 1992/622; otherwise, save for subsection (2) which came into force in Scotland on 1 April 1992 but is not in force in England and Wales, this section came into force on 1 April 1992: S .I. 1992/266.
[4] "Waste collection authority" defined by s. 30(3), p. 113 above.
[5] "Household waste" defined by s. 75, p. 159 below.
[6] For provisions relating to notice see s. 160, p. 207 below.
[7] "Receptacle" defined by subsection (10) below.
[8] "Recycled" defined by s. 29(6), p. 112 above.
[9] "Specified" defined by subsection (10) below.
[10] "Substance" defined by s. 29(11), p. 113 above.

(e) the steps to be taken by occupiers of premises to facilitate the collection of waste from the receptacles.

(5) No requirement shall be made under subsection (1) above for receptacles to be placed on a highway or, as the case may be, road, unless—

(a) the relevant highway authority or roads authority have given their consent to their being so placed; and

(b) arrangements have been made as to the liability for any damage arising out of their being so placed.

(6) A person who fails, without reasonable excuse, to comply with any requirements imposed under subsection (1), (3)(c) or (d) or (4) above shall be liable on summary conviction to a fine not exceeding level 3 on the standard scale[1].

(7) Where an occupier is required under subsection (1) above to provide any receptacles he may, within the period allowed by subsection (8) below, appeal to a magistrates' court or, in Scotland, to the sheriff by way of summary application against any requirement imposed under subsection (1), subsection (3)(c) or (d) or (4) above on the ground that—

(a) the requirement is unreasonable; or

(b) the receptacles in which household waste is placed for collection from the premises are adequate.

(8) The period allowed to the occupier of premises for appealing against such a requirement is the period of twenty-one days beginning—

(a) in a case where a period was specified under subsection (3)(c) above, with the end of that period; and

(b) where no period was specified, with the day on which the notice making the requirement was served on him.

(9) Where an appeal against a requirement is brought under subsection (7) above—

(a) the requirement shall be of no effect pending the determination of the appeal;

(b) the court shall either quash or modify the requirement or dismiss the appeal; and

(c) no question as to whether the requirement is, in any respect, unreasonable shall be entertained in any proceedings for an offence under subsection (6) above.

(10) In this section—

"receptacle" includes a holder for receptacles; and

"specified" means specified in a notice under subsection (1) above[2].

---

*Receptacles for commercial or industrial waste*

**47.** (1) A waste collection authority[3] may, at the request of any person, supply him with receptacles[4] for commercial or industrial waste[5] which he has requested the authority to arrange to collect and shall make a reasonable charge for any receptacle supplied unless in the case of a receptacle for commercial waste the authority considers it appropriate not to make a charge.

(2) If it appears to a waste collection authority that there is likely to be situated, on any premises in its area, commercial waste or industrial waste of a kind which, if the waste is not stored in receptacles of a particular kind, is likely to cause a nuisance or to be detrimental to the amenities of the locality, the authority may, by notice served on him, require the occupier of the premises to provide at the premises receptacles for the storage of such waste of a kind and number specified.

---

[1] The current fine at level 3 on the standard scale is £1,000: Criminal Justice Act 1991 (c. 53), s. 17 (England and Wales); Criminal Procedure (Scotland) Act 1995 (c. 46), s. 225 (Scotland).
[2] This section came into force on 1 April 1992: S.I. 1992/266.

[3] "Waste collection authority" defined by s. 30(3), p. 113 above.
[4] "Receptacle" defined by subsection (10) below.
[5] "Commercial waste" and "industrial waste" defined by s. 75, p. 159 below.

**(3)** The kind and number of the receptacles required under subsection (2) above to be used shall be such only as are reasonable.

**(4)** In making requirements as respects receptacles under subsection (2) above, the authority may, by the notice under that subsection, make provision with respect to—

(a)  the size, construction and maintenance of the receptacles;

(b)  the placing of the receptacles for the purpose of facilitating the emptying of them, and access to the receptacles for that purpose;

(c)  the placing of the receptacles for that purpose on highways or, in Scotland, roads;

(d)  the substances[1] or articles which may or may not be put into the receptacles and the precautions to be taken where particular substances or articles are put into them, and

(e)  the steps to be taken by occupiers of premises to facilitate the collection of waste from the receptacles.

**(5)** No requirement shall be made under subsection (2) above for receptacles to be placed on a highway or, as the case may be, road unless—

(a)  the relevant highway authority or roads authority have given their consent to their being so placed; and

(b)  arrangements have been made as to the liability for any damage arising out of their being so placed.

**(6)** A person who fails, without reasonable excuse, to comply with any requirements imposed under subsection (2) or (4) above shall be liable on summary conviction to a fine not exceeding level 3 on the standard scale[2].

**(7)** Where an occupier is required under subsection (2) above to provide any receptacles he may, within the period allowed by subsection (8) below, appeal to a magistrates' court or, in Scotland, to the sheriff by way of summary application against any requirement imposed under subsection (2) or (4) above on the ground that—

(a)  the requirement is unreasonable; or

(b)  the waste is not likely to cause a nuisance or be detrimental to the amenities of the locality.

**(8)** The period allowed to the occupier of premises for appealing against such a requirement is the period of twenty-one days beginning with the day on which the notice making the requirement was served on him.

**(9)** Where an appeal against a requirement is brought under subsection (7) above—

(a)  the requirement shall be of no effect pending the determination of the appeal;

(b)  the court shall either quash or modify the requirement or dismiss the appeal; and

(c)  no question as to whether the requirement is, in any respect, unreasonable shall be entertained in any proceedings for an offence under subsection (6) above.

**(10)** In this section—

"receptacle" includes a holder for receptacles; and

"specified" means specified in a notice under subsection (2) above[3].

---

*Duties of waste collection authorities as respects disposal of waste collected*

**48. (1)** Subject to subsections (2) and (6) below, it shall be the duty of each waste collection authority[4] to deliver for disposal all waste[5] which is collected by the authority under section 45 above[6] to such places as the waste disposal authority[7] for its area directs.

[1] "Substance" defined by s. 29(11), p. 113 above.
[2] The current fine at level 3 on the standard scale is £1,000: Criminal Justice Act 1991 (c. 53), s. 17 (England and Wales); Criminal Procedure (Scotland) Act 1995 (c. 46), s. 225 (Scotland).
[3] This section came into force on 1 April 1992: S.I. 1992/266.

[4] "Waste collection authority" defined by s. 30(3), p. 113 above.
[5] "Waste" defined by s. 75, p. 159 below.
[6] P. 137 above.
[7] "Waste disposal authority" defined by s. 30(2), p. 113 above.

(2) The duty imposed on a waste collection authority by subsection (1) above does not, except in cases falling within subsection (4) below, apply as respects household waste[1] or commercial waste[2] for which the authority decides to make arrangements for recycling[3] the waste; and the authority shall have regard, in deciding what recycling arrangements to make, to its waste recycling plan under section 49 below.

(3) A waste collection authority which decides to make arrangements under subsection (2) above for recycling waste collected by it shall, as soon as reasonably practicable, by notice in writing, inform the waste disposal authority for the area which includes its area of the arrangements which it proposes to make.

(4) Where a waste disposal authority has made with a waste disposal contractor[4] arrangements, as respects household waste or commercial waste in its area or any part of its area, for the contractor to recycle the waste, or any of it, the waste disposal authority may, by notice served on the waste collection authority, object to the waste collection authority having the waste recycled; and the objection may be made as respects all the waste, part only of the waste or specified descriptions of the waste.

(5) Where an objection is made under subsection (4) above, subsection (2) above shall not be available to the waste collection authority to the extent objected to.

(6) A waste collection authority may, subject to subsection (7) below, provide plant and equipment for the sorting and baling of waste retained by the authority under subsection (2) above.

(7) Subsection (6) above does not apply to an authority which is also a waste disposal authority; but, in such a case, the authority may make arrangements with a waste disposal contractor for the contractor to deal with the waste as mentioned in that subsection.

(8) A waste collection authority may permit another person to use facilities provided by the authority under subsection (6) above and may provide for the use of another person any such facilities as the authority has power to provide under that subsection; and—

(a) subject to paragraph (b) below, it shall be the duty of the authority to make a reasonable charge in respect of the use by another person of the facilities, unless the authority considers it appropriate not to make a charge;

(b) no charge shall be made under this subsection in respect of household waste; and

(c) anything delivered to the authority by another person in the course of using the facilities shall belong to the authority and may be dealt with accordingly.

(9) This section shall not apply to Scotland[5].

*Waste recycling plans by collection authorities*

49. (1) It shall be the duty of each waste collection authority[6], as respects household[7] and commercial waste[8] arising in its area—

(a) to carry out an investigation with a view to deciding what arrangements are appropriate for dealing with the waste by separating, baling or otherwise packaging it for the purpose of recycling[9] it;

(b) to decide what arrangements are in the opinion of the authority needed for that purpose;

(c) to prepare a statement ("the plan") of the arrangements made and proposed to be made by the authority and other persons for dealing with waste in those ways;

(d) to carry out from time to time further investigations with a view to deciding what changes in the plan are needed; and

[1] "Household waste" defined by s. 75, p. 159 below.
[2] "Commercial waste" defined by s. 75, p. 159 below.
[3] "Recycling" defined by s. 29(6), p. 112 above.
[4] "Waste disposal contractor" defined by s. 30(5), p. 114 above.
[5] Subsection (7) is not in force; otherwise this section came into force on 1 April 1992: S.I. 1992/266.
[6] "Waste collection authority" defined by s. 30(3), p. 113 above.
[7] "Household waste" defined by s. 75, p. 159 below.
[8] "Commercial waste" defined by s. 75, p. 159 below.
[9] "Recycling" defined by s. 29(6), p. 112 above.

(*e*)  to make any modification of the plan which the authority thinks appropriate in consequence of any such further investigation.

(2)  In considering any arrangements or modification for the purposes of subsection (1)(c) or (e) above it shall be the duty of the authority to have regard to the effect which the arrangements or modification would be likely to have on the amenities of any locality and the likely cost or saving to the authority attributable to the arrangements or modification.

(3)  It shall be the duty of a waste collection authority to include in the plan information as to—

(*a*)  the kinds and quantities of controlled waste[1] which the authority expects to collect during the period specified in the plan;

(*b*)  the kinds and quantities of controlled waste which the authority expects to purchase during that period;

(*c*)  the kinds and quantities of controlled waste which the authority expects to deal with in the ways specified in subsection (1)(a) above during that period;

(*d*)  the arrangements which the authority expects to make during that period with waste disposal contractors[2] or, in Scotland, waste disposal authorities[3] and waste disposal contractors for them to deal with waste in those ways;

(*e*)  the plant and equipment which the authority expects to provide under section 48(6) above or 53 below[4]; and

(*f*)  the estimated costs or savings attributable to the methods of dealing with the waste in the ways provided for in the plan.

(4)  It shall be the duty of a waste collection authority, before finally determining the content of the plan or a modification, to send a copy of it in draft to the Secretary of State for the purpose of enabling him to determine whether subsection (3) above has been complied with; and, if the Secretary of State gives any directions to the authority for securing compliance with that subsection, it shall be the duty of the authority to comply with the direction.

(5)  When a waste collection authority has determined the content of the plan or a modification it shall be the duty of the authority—

(*a*)  to take such steps as in the opinion of the authority will give adequate publicity in its area to the plan or modification; and

(*b*)  to send to the waste disposal authority and waste regulation authority for the area[5] which includes its area a copy of the plan or, as the case may be, particulars of the modification.

(6)  It shall be the duty of each waste collection authority to keep a copy of the plan and particulars of any modifications to it available at all reasonable times at its principal offices for inspection by members of the public free of charge and to supply a copy of the plan and of the particulars of any modifications to it to any person who requests one, on payment by that person of such reasonable charge as the authority requires.

(7)  The Secretary of State may give to any waste collection authority directions as to the time by which the authority is to perform any duty imposed by this section specified in the direction; and it shall be the duty of the authority to comply with the direction[6].

**50.**  *Repealed by the Environment Act 1995 (c. 25), s. 120, sch. 22, para. 78, sch. 24. This amendment came into force on 1 April 1996: S.I. 1996/186.*

---

[1] "Controlled waste" defined by s. 75, p. 159 below.
[2] "Waste disposal contractor" defined by s. 30(5), p. 114 above.
[3] "Waste disposal authority" defined by s. 30(2), p. 113 above.
[4] P. 146 below.
[5] For "waste regulation authority", and its area, see s. 30(1), p. 113 above.
[6] This section came into force on 1 August 1991: S.I. 1991/1577.

*Functions of waste disposal authorities*

**51.** (1) It shall be the duty of each waste disposal authority[1] to arrange—

   (*a*)  for the disposal[2] of the controlled waste[3] collected in its area by the waste collection authorities[4]; and

   (*b*)  for places to be provided at which persons resident in its area may deposit their household waste[5] and for the disposal of waste so deposited;

in either case by means of arrangements made (in accordance with Part II of Schedule 2 to this Act[6]) with waste disposal contractors[7], but by no other means.

(2)  The arrangements made by a waste disposal authority under subsection (1)(b) above shall be such as to secure that—

   (*a*)  each place is situated either within the area of the authority or so as to be reasonably accessible to persons resident in its area;

   (*b*)  each place is available for the deposit of waste at all reasonable times (including at least one period on the Saturday or following day of each week except a week in which the Saturday is 25th December or 1st January);

   (*c*)  each place is available for the deposit of waste free of charge by persons resident in the area;

but the arrangements may restrict the availability of specified places to specified descriptions of waste.

(3)  A waste disposal authority may include in arrangements made under subsection (1)(b) above arrangements for the places provided for its area for the deposit of household waste free of charge by residents in its area to be available for the deposit of household or other controlled waste by other persons on such terms as to payment (if any) as the authority determines.

(4)  For the purpose of discharging its duty under subsection (1)(a) above as respects controlled waste collected as mentioned in that paragraph a waste disposal authority—

   (*a*)  shall give directions to the waste collection authorities within its area as to the persons to whom and places at which such waste is to be delivered;

   (*b*)  may arrange for the provision, within or outside its area, by waste disposal contractors of places at which such waste may be treated or kept prior to its removal for treatment or disposal;

   (*c*)  may make available to waste disposal contractors (and accordingly own) plant and equipment for the purpose of enabling them to keep such waste prior to its removal for disposal or to treat such waste in connection with so keeping it or for the purpose of facilitating its transportation;

   (*d*)  may make available to waste disposal contractors (and accordingly hold) land[8] for the purpose of enabling them to treat, keep or dispose of such waste in or on the land;

   (*e*)  may contribute towards the cost incurred by persons who produce commercial or industrial waste[9] in providing and maintaining plant or equipment intended to deal with such waste before it is collected; and

   (*f*)  may contribute towards the cost incurred by persons who produce commercial or industrial waste in providing or maintaining pipes or associated works connecting with pipes provided by a waste collection authority within the area of the waste disposal authority.

(5)  For the purpose of discharging its duties under subsection (1)(b) above as respects household waste deposited as mentioned in that paragraph a waste disposal authority—

---

[1] "Waste disposal authority" defined by s. 30(2), p. 113 above.

[2] "Disposal" defined by s. 29(6), p. 112 above.

[3] "Controlled waste" defined by s. 75, p. 159 below.

[4] "Waste collection authority" defined by s. 30(3), p. 113 above.

[5] "Household waste" defined by s. 75, p. 159 below.

[6] P. 221 below.

[7] "Waste disposal contractor" defined by s. 30(5), p. 114 above.

[8] "Land" defined by s. 29(8), p. 112 above.

[9] "Commercial waste" and "industrial waste" defined by s. 75, p. 159 below.

(*a*) may arrange for the provision, within or outside its area, by waste disposal contractors of places at which such waste may be treated or kept prior to its removal for treatment or disposal;

(*b*) may make available to waste disposal contractors (and accordingly own) plant and equipment for the purpose of enabling them to keep such waste prior to its removal for disposal or to treat such waste in connection with so keeping it or for the purpose of facilitating its transportation; and

(*c*) may make available to waste disposal contractors (and accordingly hold) land for the purpose of enabling them to treat, keep or dispose of such waste in or on the land.

(6) Where the arrangements made under subsection (1)(b) include such arrangements as are authorised by subsection (3) above, subsection (5) above applies as respects household or other controlled waste as it applies as respects household waste.

(7) Subsection (1) above is subject to section 77[1].

(8) This section shall not apply to Scotland[2,3].

*Payments for recycling and disposal etc. of waste*

**52.** (1) Where, under section 48(2) above[4], a waste collection authority[5] retains for recycling[6] waste[7] collected by it under section 45 above[8], the waste disposal authority[9] for the area which includes the area of the waste collection authority shall make to that authority payments, in respect of the waste so retained, of such amounts representing its net saving of expenditure on the disposal of the waste as the authority determines.

(2) Where, by reason of the discharge by a waste disposal authority of its functions, waste arising in its area does not fall to be collected by a waste collection authority under section 45 above, the waste collection authority shall make to the waste disposal authority payments, in respect of the waste not falling to be so collected, of such amounts representing its net saving of expenditure on the collection of the waste as the authority determines.

(3) Where a person other than a waste collection authority, for the purpose of recycling it, collects waste arising in the area of a waste disposal authority which would fall to be collected under section 45 above, the waste disposal authority may make to that person payments, in respect of the waste so collected, of such amounts representing its net saving of expenditure on the disposal of the waste as the authority determines.

(4) Where a person other than a waste collection authority, for the purpose of recycling it, collects waste which would fall to be collected under section 45 above, the waste collection authority may make to that person payments, in respect of the waste so collected, of such amounts representing its net saving of expenditure on the collection of the waste as the authority determines.

(5) The Secretary of State may, by regulations, impose on waste disposal authorities a duty to make payments corresponding to the payments which are authorised by subsection (3) above to such persons in such circumstances and in respect of such descriptions or quantities of waste as are specified in the regulations.

(6) For the purposes of subsections (1), (3) and (5) above the net saving of expenditure of a waste disposal authority on the disposal of any waste retained or collected for recycling is the amount of the expenditure which the authority would, but for the retention or collection, have incurred in having it disposed of less any amount payable by the authority to any person in consequence of the retention or collection for recycling (instead of the disposal) of the waste.

[1] P. 161 below.
[2] This section came into force on 31 May 1991: S.I. 1991/1319.
[3] Cases: section 51 *R v Avon County Council, ex parte Terry Adams Ltd* [1994] Env LR 442; *Mass Energy Ltd v Birmingham City Council* [1994] Env LR 298.
[4] P. 142 above.
[5] "Waste collection authority" defined by s. 30(3), p. 113 above.
[6] "Recycling" defined by s. 29(6), p. 112 above.
[7] "Waste" defined by s. 75, p. 159 below.
[8] P. 137 above.
[9] "Waste disposal authority" defined by s. 30 (2), p. 113 above.

(7)  For the purposes of subsections (2) and (4) above the net saving of expenditure of a waste collection authority on the collection of any waste not falling to be collected by it is the amount of the expenditure which the authority would, if it had had to collect the waste, have incurred in collecting it .

(8)  The Secretary of State shall, by regulations, make provision for the determination of the net saving of expenditure for the purposes of subsections (1), (2), (3), (4) and (5) above[1].

(9)  A waste disposal authority shall be entitled to receive from a waste collection authority such sums as are needed to reimburse the waste disposal authority the reasonable cost of making arrangements under section 51(1) above for the disposal of commercial and industrial waste[2] collected in the area of the waste disposal authority.

(10)  A waste disposal authority shall pay to a waste collection authority a reasonable contribution towards expenditure reasonably incurred by the waste collection authority in delivering waste, in pursuance of a direction under section 51(4)(a) above, to a place which is unreasonably far from the waste collection authority's area.

(11)  Any question arising under subsection (9) or (10) above shall, in default of agreement between the two authorities in question, be determined by arbitration[3].

*Duties of authorities as respects disposal of waste collected: Scotland*

**53.**  (1)  It shall be the duty of each waste disposal authority[4] to arrange for the disposal[5] of any waste[6] collected by it, in its capacity as a waste collection authority[7], under section 45 above[8]; and without prejudice to the authority's powers apart from the following provisions of this subsection, the powers exercisable by the authority for the purpose of performing that duty shall include power—

(a)  to provide, within or outside its area, places at which to deposit waste before the authority transfers it to a place or plant or equipment provided under the following paragraph; and

(b)  to provide, within or outside its area, places at which to dispose of or recycle[9] the waste and plant or equipment for processing, recycling or otherwise disposing of it.

(2)  Subsections (7) and (10) of section 45 above shall have effect in relation to a waste disposal authority as if the reference in paragraph (a) of the said subsection (7) to the collection of waste included the disposal of waste under this section and the disposal of anything produced from waste belonging to the authority.

(3)  A waste disposal authority may permit another person to use facilities provided by the authority under the preceding provisions of this section and may provide for the use of another person any such facilities as the authority has power to provide under those provisions, and—

(a)  subject to the following paragraph, it shall be the duty of the authority to make a reasonable charge in respect of the use by another person of the facilities unless the authority considers it appropriate not to make a charge;

(b)  no charge shall be made under this section in respect of household waste[10]; and

(c)  anything delivered to the authority by another person in the course of using the facilities shall belong to the authority and may be dealt with accordingly.

[1] The following regulations have been made under this section:
The Environmental Protection (Waste Recycling Payments) Regulations 1992, S.I. 1992/462, as amended, p. 657 below.
[2] "Commercial waste" and "industrial waste" defined by s. 75, p. 159 below.
[3] Subsections (1), (3)–(7) and (9)–(11) came into force on 1 April 1992: S.I. 1992/266; (8), so far as it relates to (1) and (3) came into force on 13 December 1991: S.I. 1991/2829,

otherwise (8) is not in force; (2) is not in force.
[4] "Waste disposal authority" defined by s. 30(2), p. 113 above.
[5] "Disposal" defined by s. 29(6), p. 112 above.
[6] "Waste" defined by s. 75, p. 159 below.
[7] "Waste collection authority" defined by s. 30(3), p. 113 above.
[8] P. 137 above.
[9] "Recycle" defined by s. 29(6), p. 112 above.
[10] "Household waste" defined by s. 75, p. 159 below.

(4) References to waste in subsection (1) above do not include matter removed from privies under section 45(5)(a) or (6) above, and it shall be the duty of a waste collection authority[1] by which matter is so removed—

(a) to deliver the matter, in accordance with any directions of the sewerage authority[2], at a place specified in the directions (which must be in or within a reasonable distance from the waste collection authority's area), to the sewerage authority or another person so specified;

(b) to give to the sewerage authority from time to time a notice stating the quantity of the matter which the waste collection authority expects to deliver to or as directed by the sewerage authority under the preceding paragraph during a period specified in the notice.

(5) Any question arising under paragraph (a) of the preceding subsection as to whether a place is within a reasonable distance from a waste collection authority's area shall, in default of agreement between the waste collection authority and the sewerage authority[3] in question, be determined by a single arbiter appointed, in default of agreement between the parties concerned, by the Secretary of State on the application of any of the parties; and anything delivered to a sewerage authority under that subsection shall belong to the sewerage authority and may be dealt with accordingly.

(5A) In this section "sewerage authority" shall be construed in accordance with section 62 of the Local Government etc. (Scotland) Act 1994[4,5].

(6) This section applies to Scotland only[6].

..............................................................................................................................................................................

**54.** *This section, which relates to special provisions for land occupied by disposal authorities in Scotland is prospectively repealed by the Environment Act 1995 (c. 25), s. 120, sch. 24.*

..............................................................................................................................................................................

*Powers for recycling waste*

55. (1) This section has effect for conferring on waste disposal authorities[7] and waste collection authorities[8] powers for the purposes of recycling[9] waste.

(2) A waste disposal authority may—

(a) make arrangements with waste disposal contractors[10] for them to recycle waste as respects which the authority has duties under section 51(1) above[11] or agrees with another person for its disposal[12] or treatment[13];

(b) make arrangements with waste disposal contractors for them to use waste for the purpose of producing from it heat or electricity or both;

(c) buy or otherwise acquire waste[14] with a view to its being recycled;

(d) use, sell or otherwise dispose of waste as respects which the authority has duties under section 51(1) above or anything produced from such waste.

(3) A waste collection authority may—

(a) buy or otherwise acquire waste with a view to recycling it;

(b) use, or dispose of by way of sale or otherwise to another person, waste belonging to the authority or anything produced from such waste.

---

[1] Former words "(other than an islands council)" repealed by the Local Government etc. (Scotland) Act 1994 (c. 39), s. 180(1), sch. 13, para. 167(8)(a)(i), sch. 14. This amendment came into force on 1 April 1996: S.I. 1996/323.

[2] "Sewerage authority" defined by subsection (5A) below. Words "sewerage authority" in this section substituted by the Local Government etc. (Scotland) Act 1994 (c. 39), s. 180, sch. 13, para. 167(8)(a)(ii).

[3] Words "sewerage authority" in this section substituted by the Local Government etc. (Scotland) Act 1994 (c. 39), s. 180, sch. 13, para. 167(8)(b).

[4] 1994 c. 39.

[5] Subsection (5A) inserted by the Local Government etc. (Scotland) Act 1994 (c. 39), s. 180, sch. 13, para. 167(8)(c).

[6] This section came into force on 1 April 1992: S.I. 1992/266.

[7] "Waste disposal authority" defined by s. 30(2), p. 113 above.

[8] "Waste collection authority" defined by s. 30(3), p. 113 above.

[9] "Recycling" defined by s. 29(6), p. 112 above.

[10] "Waste disposal contractor" defined by s. 30(5), p. 114 above.

[11] P. 144 above.

[12] "Disposal" defined by s. 29(6), p. 112 above.

[13] "Treatment" defined by s. 29(6), p. 112 above.

[14] "Waste" defined by s. 75, p. 159 below.

(4)   This section shall not apply to Scotland[1].

*Powers for recycling waste: Scotland*

56. (1)   Without prejudice to the powers of waste disposal authorities[2] apart from this section, a waste disposal authority may—

   (a)   do such things as the authority considers appropriate for the purpose of—

      (i)   enabling waste[3] belonging to the authority, or belonging to another person who requests the authority to deal with it under this section, to be recycled[4]; or

      (ii)   enabling waste to be used for the purpose of producing from it heat or electricity or both;

   (b)   buy or otherwise acquire waste with a view to its being recycled;

   (c)   use, sell or otherwise dispose[5] of waste belonging to the authority or anything produced from such waste.

(2)   This section applies to Scotland only[6].

*Power of Secretary of State to require waste to be accepted, treated, disposed of or delivered*

57. (1)   The Secretary of State may, by notice in writing, direct the holder of any waste management licence[7] to accept and keep, or accept and treat or dispose[8] of, controlled waste[9] at specified places on specified terms.

(2)   The Secretary of State may, by notice in writing, direct any person who is keeping controlled waste on any land[10] to deliver the waste to a specified person on specified terms with a view to its being treated or disposed of by that other person.

(3)   A direction under this section may impose a requirement as respects waste of any specified kind or as respects any specified consignment of waste.

(4)   A direction under subsection (2) above may require the person who is directed to deliver the waste to pay to the specified person his reasonable costs of treating or disposing of the waste.

(5)   A person who fails, without reasonable excuse, to comply with a direction under this section shall be liable on summary conviction to a fine not exceeding level 5 on the standard scale[11].

(6)   A person shall not be guilty of an offence under any other enactment prescribed by the Secretary of State by regulations made for the purposes of this subsection by reason only of anything necessarily done or omitted in order to comply with a direction under this section.

(7)   The Secretary of State may, where the costs of the treatment or disposal of waste are not paid or not fully paid in pursuance of subsection (4) above to the person treating or disposing of the waste, pay the costs or the unpaid costs, as the case may be, to that person.

(8)   In this section "specified" means specified in a direction under this section[12].

*Power of Secretary of State to require waste to be accepted, treated, disposed of or delivered: Scotland*

58.   In relation to Scotland, the Secretary of State may give directions to a waste disposal authority[13]

---

[1] This section came into force on 1 April 1992: S.I. 1992/266.

[2] "Waste disposal authority" defined by s. 30(2), p. 113 above.

[3] "Waste" defined by s. 75, p. 159 below.

[4] "Recycled" defined by s. 29(6), p. 112 above.

[5] "Dispose" defined by s. 29(6), p. 112 above.

[6] This section came into force on 1 April 1992: S.I. 1992/266.

[7] "Waste management licence" defined by s. 35(1), p. 119 above.

[8] "Dispose" defined by s. 29(6), p. 112 above.

[9] "Controlled waste" defined by s. 75, p. 159 below.

[10] "Land" defined by s. 29(8), p. 112 above.

[11] The current fine at level 5 on the standard scale is £5,000: Criminal Justice Act 1991 (c. 53), s. 17 (England and Wales); Criminal procedure (Scotland) Act 1995 (c. 46), s. 225 (Scotland).

[12] For commencement provisions relating to this section see S.I. 1994/1096, p. 738 below.

[13] "Waste disposal authority" defined by s. 30(2), p. 113 above.

to accept and keep, or accept and treat[1] or dispose[2] of, controlled waste[3] at specified places on specified terms; and it shall be the duty of the authority to give effect to the directions[4].

*Powers to require removal of waste unlawfully deposited*

59. (1) If any controlled waste[5] is deposited in or on any land[6] in the area of a waste regulation authority[7] or waste collection authority[8] in contravention of section 33(1) above[9], the authority may, by notice[10] served on him, require the occupier to do either or both of the following, that is—

   (*a*)  to remove the waste from the land within a specified period not less than a period of twenty-one days beginning with the service of the notice;

   (*b*)  to take within such a period specified steps with a view to eliminating or reducing the consequences of the deposit of the waste.

(2) A person on whom any requirements are imposed under subsection (1) above may, within the period of twenty-one days mentioned in that subsection, appeal against the requirement to a magistrates' court or, in Scotland, to the sheriff by way of summary application.

(3) On any appeal under subsection (2) above the court shall quash the requirement if it is satisfied that—

   (*a*)  the appellant neither deposited nor knowingly caused nor knowingly permitted the deposit of the waste; or

   (*b*)  there is a material defect in the notice;

and in any other case shall either modify the requirement or dismiss the appeal.

(4) Where a person appeals against any requirement imposed under subsection (1) above, the requirement shall be of no effect pending the determination of the appeal; and where the court modifies the requirement or dismisses the appeal it may extend the period specified in the notice.

(5) If a person on whom a requirement imposed under subsection (1) above fails, without reasonable excuse, to comply with the requirement he shall be liable, on summary conviction, to a fine not exceeding level 5 on the standard scale[11] and to a further fine of an amount equal to one-tenth of level 5 on the standard scale for each day on which the failure continues after conviction of the offence and before the authority has begun to exercise its powers under subsection (6) below.

(6) Where a person on whom a requirement has been imposed under subsection (1) above by an authority fails to comply with the requirement the authority may do what that person was required to do and may recover from him any expenses reasonably incurred by the authority in doing it.

(7) If it appears to a waste regulation authority or waste collection authority that waste has been deposited in or on any land in contravention of section 33(1) above and that—

   (*a*)  in order to remove or prevent pollution of land, water or air or harm[12] to human health it is necessary that the waste be forthwith removed or other steps taken to eliminate or reduce the consequences of the deposit or both; or

   (*b*)  there is no occupier of the land; or

   (*c*)  the occupier neither made nor knowingly permitted the deposit of the waste;

---

[1] "Treat" defined by s. 29(6), p. 112 above.
[2] "Dispose" defined by s. 29(6), p. 112 above.
[3] "Controlled waste" defined by s. 75, p. 159 below.
[4] This section came into force on 1 May 1994: S.I. 1994/1096, p. 738 below.
[5] "Controlled waste" defined by s. 75, p. 159 below.
[6] "Land" defined by s. 29(8), p. 112 above.
[7] For "waste regulation authority" see s. 30(1), p. 113 above.
[8] "Waste collection authority" defined by s. 30(3), p. 113

above.
[9] P. 116 above.
[10] For provisions relating to notice see s. 160, p. 207 below.
[11] The current fine at level 5 on the standard scale is £5,000: Criminal Justice Act 1991 (c. 53), s. 17 (England and Wales); Criminal Procedure (Scotland) Act 1995 (c. 46), s. 225 (Scotland).
[12] "Harm" defined by s. 29(5), p. 112 above, for the purposes of s. 29(3), (4).

the authority may remove the waste from the land or take other steps to eliminate or reduce the consequences of the deposit or, as the case may require, to remove the waste and take those steps.

(8) Where an authority exercises any of the powers conferred on it by subsection (7) above it shall be entitled to recover the cost incurred by it in removing the waste or taking the steps or both and in disposing of the waste—

(a)  in a case falling within subsection (7)(a) above, from the occupier of the land unless he proves that he neither made nor knowingly caused nor knowingly permitted the deposit of the waste;

(b)  in any case, from any person who deposited or knowingly caused or knowingly permitted the deposit of any of the waste;

except such of the cost as the occupier or that person shows was incurred unnecessarily.

(9)  Any waste removed by an authority under subsection (7) above shall belong to that authority and may be dealt with accordingly[1].

*Interference with waste sites and receptacles for waste*

**60.** (1)  No person shall sort over or disturb—

(a)  anything deposited at a place for the deposit of waste[2] provided by a waste collection authority[3], by a waste disposal contractor[4] under arrangements made with a waste disposal authority[5] or by any other local authority or person or, in Scotland, by a waste disposal authority;

(b)  anything deposited in a receptacle for waste, whether for public or private use, provided by a waste collection authority, by a waste disposal contractor under arrangements made with a waste disposal authority, by a parish or community council or by a holder of a waste management licence[6] or, in Scotland, by a waste disposal authority or a roads authority; or

(c)  the contents of any receptacle for waste which, in accordance with a requirement under section 46[7] or 47 above, is placed on any highway or, in Scotland, road or in any other place with a view to its being emptied;

unless he has the relevant consent or right to do so specified in subsection (2) below.

(2)  The consent or right that is relevant for the purposes of subsection (1)(a), (b) or (c) above is—

(a)  in the case of paragraph (a), the consent of the authority, contractor or other person who provides the place for the deposit of the waste;

(b)  in the case of paragraph (b), the consent of the authority, contractor or other person who provides the receptacle for the deposit of the waste;

(c)  in the case of paragraph (c), the right to the custody of the receptacle, the consent of the person having the right to the custody of the receptacle or the right conferred by the function by or under this Part of emptying such receptacles.

(3)  A person who contravenes subsection (1) above shall be liable on summary conviction to a fine of an amount not exceeding level 3 on the standard scale[8].[9]

[1] This section came into force on 1 May 1994: S.I. 1994/1096, p. 738 below.
[2] "Waste" defined by s. 75, p. 159 below.
[3] "Waste collection authority" defined by s. 30(3), p. 113 above.
[4] "Waste disposal contractor" defined by s. 30(5), p. 114 above.
[5] "waste disposal authority" defined by s. 30(2), p. 113 above.
[6] "Waste management licence" defined by s. 35(1), p. 119 above.
[7] P. 139 above.
[8] The current fine at level 3 on the standard scale is £1,000: Criminal Justice Act 1991 (c. 53), s. 17 (England and Wales); Criminal Procedure (Scotland) Act 1995 (c. 46), s. 225 (Scotland).
[9] This section came into force on 31 May 1991 insofar as it relates to anything deposited at a place for the deposit of waste, or in a receptacle for waste, provided by a waste disposal contractor under arrangements made with a waste disposal authority: S.I. 1991/1319; otherwise this section came into force on 1 May 1994: S.I. 1994/1096, p. 738 below.

**61.** *This section, which relates to the duty of waste regulation authorities as respects closed landfills, is prospectively repealed by the Environment Act 1995 (c. 25), s. 120, sch. 22, para. 79, sch. 24.*

## Special waste and non-controlled waste

*Special provision with respect to certain dangerous or intractable waste*

**62.** (1) If the Secretary of State considers that controlled waste[1] of any kind is or may be so dangerous or difficult to treat[2], keep or dispose[3] of that special provision is required for dealing with it he shall make provision by regulations for the treatment, keeping or disposal of waste of that kind ("special waste")[4].

(2) Without prejudice to the generality of subsection (1) above, the regulations may include provision—

(a) for the giving of directions by waste regulation authorities[5] with respect to matters connected with the treatment, keeping or disposal of special waste;

(b) for securing that special waste is not, while awaiting treatment or disposal in pursuance of the regulations, kept at any one place in quantities greater than those which are prescribed and in circumstances which differ from those which are prescribed;

(c) in connection with requirements imposed on consignors or consignees of special waste, imposing, in the event of non-compliance, requirements on any person carrying the consignment to re-deliver it as directed;

(d) for requiring the occupier of premises on which special waste is situated to give notice[6] of that fact and other prescribed information to a prescribed authority;

(e) for the keeping of records by waste regulation authorities and by persons who import, export, produce, keep, treat or dispose of special waste or deliver it to another person for treatment or disposal, for the inspection of the records and for the furnishing by such persons to waste regulation authorities of copies of or information derived from the records;

(f) for the keeping in the register under section 64(1) below[7] of copies of such of those records, or such information derived from those records, as may be prescribed;

(g) providing that a contravention of the regulations shall be an offence and prescribing the maximum penalty for the offence, which shall not exceed, on summary conviction, a fine at level 5 on the standard scale[8] and, on conviction on indictment, imprisonment for a term of two years or a fine or both.

(3) Without prejudice to the generality of subsection (1) above, the regulations may include provision—

(a) for the supervision by waste regulation authorities—

(i) of activities authorised by virtue of the regulations or of activities by virtue of carrying on which persons are subject to provisions of the regulations, or

(ii) of persons who carry on activities authorised by virtue of the regulations or who are subject to provisions of the regulations,

and for the recovery from persons falling within sub-paragraph (ii) above of the costs incurred by waste regulation authorities in performing functions conferred upon those authorities by the regulations[9];

---

[1] "Controlled waste" defined by s. 75, p. 159 below.
[2] "Treat" defined by s. 29(6), p. 112 above.
[3] "Dispose" defined by s. 29(6), p. 112 above.
[4] The following regulations have been made under this section:
The Special Waste Regulations 1996, S.I. 1996/972, p. 763 below.
[5] For "waste regulation authority" see s. 30(1), p. 113 above.
[6] For provisions relating to notice see s. 160, p. 207 below.
[7] P. 152 below.
[8] The current fine at level 5 on the standard scale is £5,000: Criminal Justice Act 1991 (c. 53) s. 17 (England and Wales); Criminal Procedure (Scotland) Act 1995 (c. 46), s. 225 (Scotland).
[9] Para. (a) substituted by the Environment Act 1995 (c. 25), s. 120, sch. 22, para. 80(2). This amendment came into force on 21 September 1995: S.I. 1995/1983.

(b) as to the recovery of expenses or other charges for the treatment, keeping or disposal or the re-delivery of special waste in pursuance of the regulations;

(c) as to appeals to the Secretary of State from decisions of waste regulation authorities under the regulations.

(3A) This section is subject to section 114 of the Environment Act 1995[1] (delegation or reference of appeals etc)[2].

(4) In the application of this section to Northern Ireland "waste regulation authority" means a district council established under the Local Government Act (Northern Ireland) 1972[3].[4]

*Waste other than controlled waste*

63. (1) The Secretary of State may, after consultation with such bodies as he considers appropriate, make regulations providing that prescribed provisions of this Part shall have effect in a prescribed area—

(a) as if references in those provisions to controlled waste[5] or controlled waste of a kind specified in the regulations included references to such waste as is mentioned in section 75(7)(c) below[6] which is of a kind so specified; and

(b) with such modifications as may be prescribed;

and the regulations may make such modifications of other enactments as the Secretary of State considers appropriate.

(2) A person who deposits, or knowingly causes or knowingly permits the deposit of, any waste—

(a) which is not controlled waste, but

(b) which, if it were controlled waste, would be special waste[7],

in a case where he would be guilty of an offence under section 33 above[8] if the waste were special waste and any waste management licence[9] were not in force, shall, subject to subsection (3) below, be guilty of that offence and punishable as if the waste were special waste[10].

(3) No offence is committed by virtue of subsection (2) above if the act charged was done under and in accordance with any consent, licence, approval or authority granted under any enactment (excluding any planning permission under the enactments relating to town and country planning).

(4) Section 45(2)[11] and section 47(1)[12] above shall apply to waste other than controlled waste as they apply to controlled waste[13].

## Publicity

*Public registers*

64. (1) Subject to sections 65 and 66 below, it shall be the duty of each waste regulation authority[14] to maintain a register containing prescribed[15] particulars of or relating to—

(a) current or recently current licences[16] ("licences") granted by the authority;

---

[1] P. 489 below.
[2] Subsection (3A) added by the Environment Act 1995 (c. 25), s. 120, sch. 22, para. 80(3).
[3] 1972 c. 9 (N.I.).
[4] This section came into force on 11 August 1995: S.I. 1995/2152.
[5] "Controlled waste" defined by s. 75, p. 159 below.
[6] P. 160 below.
[7] "Special waste" defined by s. 75(9), p. 160 below.
[8] P. 116 above.
[9] "Waste management licence" defined by s. 35(1), p. 119 above.
[10] Subsection (2) substituted the Environment Act 1995

(c. 25), s. 120, sch. 22, para. 81. This amendment is not in force.
[11] P. 138 above.
[12] P. 140 above.
[13] Subsection (1) came into force on 18 February 1993: S.I. 1993/274; otherwise this section is not in force.
[14] For "waste regulation authority" see s. 30(1), p. 113 above.
[15] "Prescribed" defined by subsection (8) below.
[16] "Licence" means a waste management licence: s. 35(12), p. 120 above; for "recently current" see subsection (3) below.

(b)  current or recently current applications to the authority for licences;

(c)  applications made to the authority under section 37 above[1] for the modification of licences;

(d)  notices issued by the authority under section 37 above effecting the modification of licences;

(e)  notices issued by the authority under section 38 above[2] effecting the revocation or suspension of licences or imposing requirements on the holders of licences;

(f)  appeals under section 43 above[3] relating to decisions of the authority;

(g)  certificates of completion issued by the authority under section 39(9) above[4];

(h)  notices issued by the authority imposing requirements on the holders of licences under section 42(5) above[5];

(i)  convictions of the holders of licences granted by the authority for any offence under this Part (whether in relation to a licence so granted or not);

(j)  the occasions on which the authority has discharged any function under section 42[6] or 61[7] above;

(k)  directions given to the authority under any provision of this Part by the Secretary of State;

(l)  *Repealed by the Environment Act 1995 (c. 25), s. 120, sch. 24. This amendment came into force on 1 April 1996: S.I. 1996/186.*

(m)  such matters relating to the treatment, keeping or disposal[8] of waste[9] in the area of the authority or any pollution of the environment[10] caused thereby as may be prescribed;

and any other document or information required to be kept in the register under any provision of this Act[11].

(2)  Where information of any description is excluded from any register by virtue of section 66 below[12], a statement shall be entered in the register indicating the existence of information of that description.

(2A)  The Secretary of State may give to a waste regulation authority directions requiring the removal from any register of its of any specified information not prescribed for inclusion under subsection (1) above or which, by virtue of section 65 or 66 below, ought to be excluded from the register[13].

(3)  For the purposes of subsection (1) above licences are "recently" current for the period of twelve months after they cease to be in force and applications for licences are "recently" current if they relate to a licence which is current or recently current or, in the case of an application which is rejected, for the period of twelve months beginning with the date on which the waste regulation authority gives notice of rejection or, as the case may be, on which the application is deemed by section 36(9) above[14] to have been rejected.

(4)  It shall be the duty of each waste collection authority[15] in England or Wales[16,17] to maintain a register containing prescribed particulars of such information contained in any register maintained under subsection (1) above as relates to the treatment, keeping or disposal of controlled waste in the area of the authority.

---

[1] P. 125 above.
[2] P. 127 above.
[3] P. 133 above.
[4] P. 130 above.
[5] P. 132 above.
[6] P. 131 above.
[7] P. 151 above.
[8] "Disposal" defined by s. 29(6), p. 112 above.
[9] "Waste" defined by s. 75, p. 159 below.
[10] "Pollution of the environment" defined by s. 29(3), p. 112 above; "the environment" defined by s. 29(2).
[11] The following regulations have been made under this section:

The Waste Management Licensing Regulations 1994, S.I. 1994/1056, as amended, p. 675 below.
[12] P. 154 below.
[13] Subsection (2A) inserted by the Environment Act 1995 (c. 25), s. 120, sch. 22, para. 82(2).
[14] P. 123 above.
[15] "Waste collection authority" defined by s. 30(3), p. 113 above.
[16] Words "or Wales" inserted by the Environment Act 1995 (c. 25), s. 120, sch. 22, para. 82(3)(a).
[17] Former words "which is not a waste regulation authority" repealed by the Environment Act 1995 (c. 25), s. 120, sch. 22, para. 82(3)(b), sch. 24.

(5) The waste regulation authority in relation to England and Wales shall furnish any waste collection authorities in its area with the particulars necessary to enable them to discharge their duty under subsection (4) above[1].

(6) Each waste regulation authority and waste collection authority—

(a) shall secure that any register maintained under this section is open to inspection[1A] by members of the public free of charge at all reasonable hours; and

(b) shall afford to members of the public reasonable facilities for obtaining, on payment of reasonable charges, copies of entries in the register;

and, for the purposes of this subsection, places may be prescribed by the Secretary of State at which any such registers or facilities as are mentioned in paragraph (a) or (b) above are to be available or afforded to the public in pursuance of the paragraph in question[2].

(7) Registers under this section may be kept in any form.

(8) In this section "prescribed" means prescribed in regulations by the Secretary of State[3].

........................................................................................................................................................

*Exclusion from registers of information affecting national security*

65. (1) No information shall be included in a register maintained under section 64 above (a "register") if and so long as, in the opinion of the Secretary of State, the inclusion in the register of that information, or information of that description, would be contrary to the interests of national security.

(2) The Secretary of State may, for the purpose of securing the exclusion from registers of information to which subsection (1) above applies, give to the authorities maintaining registers directions—

(a) specifying information, or descriptions of information, to be excluded from their registers; or

(b) specifying descriptions of information to be referred to the Secretary of State for his determination;

and no information referred to the Secretary of State in pursuance of paragraph (b) above shall be included in any such register until the Secretary of State determines that it should be so included.

(3) An authority maintaining a register shall notify the Secretary of State of any information it excludes from the register in pursuance of directions under subsection (2) above.

(4) A person may, as respects any information which appears to him to be information to which subsection (1) above may apply, give notice to the Secretary of State specifying the information and indicating its apparent nature; and, if he does so—

(a) he shall notify[4] the authority concerned that he has done so; and

(b) no information so notified to the Secretary of State shall be included in the register kept by that authority until the Secretary of State has determined that it should be so included[5].

........................................................................................................................................................

*Exclusion from registers of certain confidential information*

66. (1) No information relating to the affairs of any individual or business shall be included in a register maintained under section 64 above[6] (a "register"), without the consent of that individual or the person for the time being carrying on that business, if and so long as the information—

---

[1] Subsection (5) substituted by the Environment Act 1995 (c. 25), s. 120, sch. 22, para. 82(4).

[1A] Former words "at its principal office" repealed by S.I. 1996/593 on 1 April 1996.

[2] Words "and, for the purposes . . . in question" inserted, and subsection divided into paragraphs, by the Environment Act 1995 (c. 25), s. 120, sch. 22, para. 82(5). This amendment came into force partially on 21 September 1995: S.I. 1995/1983 and completely on 1 April 1996: S.I. 1996/186.

[3] Subsections (1), (4) and (8) came into force on 18 February 1993: S.I. 1993/274; (2), (3), (6) and (7) on 1 May 1994: S.I. 1994/1096; (2A), (5) on 1 April 1996: S.I. 1996/186.

[4] For provisions relating to notice see s. 160, p. 207 below.

[5] Subsection (2), insofar as it enables the Secretary of State to give directions, came into force on 18 February 1993: S.I. 1994/274; otherwise this section came into force on 1 May 1994: S.I. 1994/1096.

[6] P. 152 above.

(a)  is, in relation to him, commercially confidential[1]; and

(b)  is not required to be included in the register in pursuance of directions under subsection (7) below;

but information is not commercially confidential for the purposes of this section unless it is determined under this section to be so by the authority maintaining the register or, on appeal, by the Secretary of State.

(2)  Where information is furnished to an authority maintaining a register for the purpose of—

(a)  an application for, or for the modification of, a licence[2];

(b)  complying with any condition of a licence; or

(c)  complying with a notice under section 71(2) below[3];

then, if the person furnishing it applies to the authority to have the information excluded from the register on the ground that it is commercially confidential (as regards himself or another person), the authority shall determine whether the information is or is not commercially confidential.

(3)  A determination under subsection (2) above must be made within the period of fourteen days beginning with the date of the application and if the authority fails to make a determination within that period it shall be treated as having determined that the information is commercially confidential.

(4)  Where it appears to an authority maintaining a register that any information (other than information furnished in circumstances within subsection (2) above) which has been obtained by the authority under or by virtue of any provision of this Part might be commercially confidential, the authority shall—

(a)  give to the person to whom or whose business it relates notice[4] that that information is required to be included in the register unless excluded under this section; and

(b)  give him a reasonable opportunity—

(i)  of objecting to the inclusion of the information on the grounds that it is commercially confidential; and

(ii) of making representations to the authority for the purpose of justifying any such objection;

and, if any representations are made, the authority shall, having taken the representations into account, determine whether the information is or is not commercially confidential.

(5)  Where, under subsection (2) or (4) above, an authority determines that information is not commercially confidential—

(a)  the information shall not be entered in the register until the end of the period of twenty-one days beginning with the date on which the determination is notified to the person concerned;

(b)  that person may appeal to the Secretary of State against the decision;

and, where an appeal is brought in respect of any information, the information shall not be entered in the register until the end of the period of seven days following the day on which the appeal is finally determined or withdrawn[5].

(6)  Subsections (2) and (8) of section 43 above[6] shall apply in relation to appeals under subsection (5) above as they apply in relation to appeals under that section; but

(a)  subsection (2)(c) of that section shall have effect for the purposes of this subsection with the substitution for the words from "(which may" onwards of the words "(which must be held in private)"; and

---

[1] "Commercially confidential" information defined by subsection (11) below.

[2] "Licence" means a waste management licence: s. 35(12), p. 120 above.

[3] P. 156 below.

[4] For provisions relating to notice see s. 160, p. 207 below.

[5] Words "until the end . . . withdrawn" substituted by the Environment Act 1995 (c. 25), s. 120, sch. 22, para. 83(1).

[6] P. 133 above.

(*b*)  subsection (5) above is subject to section 114 of the Environment Act 1995[1] (delegation of reference of appeals etc)[2].

(7)  The Secretary of State may give to the authorities maintaining registers directions as to specified information, or descriptions of information, which the public interest requires to be included in the registers notwithstanding that the information may be commercially confidential.

(8)  Information excluded from a register shall be treated as ceasing to be commercially confidential for the purposes of this section at the expiry of the period of four years beginning with the date of the determination by virtue of which it was excluded; but the person who furnished it may apply to the authority for the information to remain excluded from the register on the ground that it is still commercially confidential and the authority shall determine whether or not that is the case.

(9)  Subsections (5) and (6) above shall apply in relation to a determination under subsection (8) above as they apply in relation to a determination under subsection (2) or (4) above.

(10)  The Secretary of State may, by order, substitute for the period for the time being specified in subsection (3) above such other period as he considers appropriate.

(11)  Information is, for the purposes of any determination under this section, commercially confidential, in relation to any individual or person, if its being contained in the register would prejudice to an unreasonable degree the commercial interests of that individual or person[3].

**67.**  *Repealed by the Environment Act 1995 (c. 25), s. 120, sch. 22, para. 84, sch. 24. This amendment came into force on 1 April 1996: S.I. 1996/186.*

*Supervision and enforcement*

**68–70.**  *Repealed by the Environment Act 1995 (c. 25), s. 120, sch. 22, para. 85, sch. 24. This amendment came into force on 1 April 1996: S.I. 1996/186.*

*Obtaining of information from persons and authorities*

**71.**  (1)  *Repealed by the Environment Act 1995 (c. 25), s. 120, sch. 22, para. 86(1), sch. 24. This amendment came into force on 1 April 1996: S.I. 1996/186.*

(2)  For the purpose of the discharge of their respective functions under this Part—

(*a*)  the Secretary of State, and

(*b*)  a waste regulation authority[4],

may, by notice[5] in writing served on him, require any person to furnish such information specified in the notice as the Secretary of State or the authority, as the case may be, reasonably considers he or it needs, in such form and within such period following service of the notice, or at such time[6], as is so specified.

(3)  A person who—

(*a*)  fails, without reasonable excuse, to comply with a requirement imposed under subsection (2) above;

(*b*)  *Repealed by the Environment Act 1995 (c. 25), ss. 112, 120, schs. 19, 24. This amendment came into force on 1 April 1996: S.I. 1996/186;*

shall be liable—

[1]  P. 489 below.

[2]  Subsection (6) substituted by the Environment Act 1995 (c. 25), s. 120, sch. 22, para. 83(2).

[3]  Subsection (7), insofar as it enables the Secretary of State to give directions, came into force on 18 February 1993: S.I. 1993/274; (6) on 1 April 1996: S.I. 1996/186; otherwise this section came into force on 1 May 1994: S.I.

1994/1096.

[4]  For "waste regulation authority" see s. 30(1), p. 113 above.

[5]  For provisions relating to notice see s. 160, p. 207 below.

[6]  Words ", or at such time," inserted by the Environment Act 1995 (c. 25), s. 120, sch. 22, para. 86(2).

(i)  on summary conviction, to a fine not exceeding the statutory maximum[1];

(ii)  on conviction on indictment, to a fine or to imprisonment for a term not exceeding two years, or to both[2].

**72.**  *Repealed by the Environment Act 1995 (c. 25), s. 120, sch. 22, para. 87, sch. 24. This amendment came into force on 1 April 1996: S.I. 1996/186.*

## Supplemental

*Appeals and other provisions relating to legal proceedings and civil liability*

**73.**  (1)  An appeal against any decision of a magistrates' court under this Part (other than a decision made in criminal proceedings) shall lie to the Crown Court at the instance of any party to the proceedings in which the decision was given if such an appeal does not lie to the Crown Court by virtue of any other enactment.

(2)  In Scotland an appeal against any decision of the sheriff under this Part (other than a decision made in criminal proceedings) shall lie to the Court of Session at the instance of any party to the proceedings in which the decision was given if such an appeal does not lie to the Court of Session by virtue of any other enactment.

(3)  Where a person appeals to the Crown Court or the Court of Session against a decision of a magistrates' court or the sheriff dismissing an appeal against any requirement imposed under this Part which was suspended pending determination of that appeal, the requirement shall again be suspended pending the determination of the appeal to the Crown Court or Court of Session.

(4)  Where an appeal against a decision of any authority lies to a magistrates' court or to the sheriff by virtue of any provision of this Part, it shall be the duty of the authority to include in any document by which it notifies the decision to the person concerned a statement indicating that such an appeal lies and specifying the time within which it must be brought.

(5)  Where on an appeal to any court against or arising out of a decision of any authority under this Part the court varies or reverses the decision it shall be the duty of the authority to act in accordance with the court's decision.

(6)  Where any damage[3] is caused by waste[4] which has been deposited in or on land[5], any person who deposited it, or knowingly caused or knowingly permitted it to be deposited, in either case so as to commit an offence under section 33(1)[6] or 63(2)[7] above, is liable for the damage except where the damage—

(*a*)  was due wholly to the fault[8] of the person who suffered it; or

(*b*)  was suffered by a person who voluntarily accepted the risk of the damage being caused;

but without prejudice to any liability arising otherwise than under this subsection.

(7)  The matters which may be proved by way of defence under section 33(7) above may be proved also by way of defence to an action brought under subsection (6) above.

(8)  In subsection (6) above—

"damage" includes the death of, or injury to, any person (including any disease and any impairment of physical or mental condition); and

"fault" has the same meaning as in the Law Reform (Contributory Negligence) Act 1945[9].

---

[1] The current statutory maximum is £5,000: Criminal Justice Act 1991 (c. 53), s. 17(2); Criminal Procedure (Scotland) Act 1995 (c. 46), s. 225(8).

[2] This section came into force on 31 May 1991: S.I. 1991/1319.

[3] "Damage" defined by subsection (8) below.

[4] "Waste" defined by s. 75, p. 159 below.

[5] "Land" defined by s. 29(8), p. 112 above.

[6] P. 116 above.

[7] P. 152 above.

[8] "Fault" defined by subsection (8) below.

[9] 1945 c. 28.

(9) For the purposes of the following enactments—

(a) the Fatal Accidents Act 1976[1];

(b) the Law Reform (Contributory Negligence) Act 1945; and

(c) the Limitation Act 1980[2];

and for the purposes of any action of damages in Scotland arising out of the death of, or personal injury to, any person, any damage for which a person is liable under subsection (6) above shall be treated as due to his fault[3].

*Meaning of "fit and proper person"*

**74.** (1) The following provisions apply for the purposes of the discharge by a waste regulation authority[4] of any function under this Part which requires the authority to determine whether a person is or is not a fit and proper person to hold a waste management licence[5].

(2) Whether a person is or is not a fit and proper person to hold a licence[6] is to be determined by reference to the carrying on by him of the activities which are or are to be authorised by the licence and the fulfilment of the requirements of the licence.

(3) Subject to subsection (4) below, a person shall be treated as not being a fit and proper person if it appears to the authority—

(a) that he or another relevant person has been convicted of a relevant offence;

(b) that the management of the activities which are or are to be authorised by the licence are not or will not be in the hands of a technically competent person; or

(c) that the person who holds or is to hold the licence has not made and either has no intention of making or is in no position to make financial provision adequate to discharge the obligations arising from the licence.

(4) The authority may, if it considers it proper to do so in any particular case, treat a person as a fit and proper person notwithstanding that subsection (3)(a) above applies in his case.

(5) It shall be the duty of waste regulation authorities to have regard to any guidance issued to them by the Secretary of State with respect to the discharge of their functions of making the determinations to which this section applies.

(6) The Secretary of State may, by regulations, prescribe the offences that are relevant for the purposes of subsection (3)(a) above and the qualifications and experience required of a person for the purposes of subsection (3)(b) above[7].

(7) For the purposes of subsection (3)(a) above, another relevant person shall be treated, in relation to the licence holder or proposed licence holder, as the case may be, as having been convicted of a relevant offence if—

(a) any person has been convicted of a relevant offence committed by him in the course of his employment by the holder or, as the case may be, the proposed holder of the licence or in the course of the carrying on of any business by a partnership one of the members of which was the holder or, as the case may be, the proposed holder of the licence;

(b) a body corporate has been convicted of a relevant offence committed when the holder or, as the case may be, the proposed holder of the licence was a director, manager, secretary or other similar officer of that body corporate; or

---

[1] 1976 c. 30.

[2] 1980 c. 58.

[3] Subsections (1)–(5) came into force on 1 April 1992: S.I. 1992/266; (6)–(9) on 1 May 1994: S.I. 1994/1096.

[4] For "waste regulation authority" see s. 30(1), p. 113 above.

[5] "Waste management licence" defined by s. 35(1), p. 119 above.

[6] "Licence" means a waste management licence:

s. 35(12), p. 120 above.

[7] The following regulations have been made under this section:

The Waste Management Licensing Regulations 1994, S.I. 1994/1056, as amended, p. 675 below; for relevant offences see reg. 3, p. 678, and for technical competence see reg. 4–5, p. 679.

The Transfrontier Shipment of Waste Regulations 1994, S.I. 1994/1137, p. 741 below.

(*c*) where the holder or, as the case may be, the proposed holder of the licence is a body corporate, a person who is a director, manager, secretary or other similar officer of that body corporate—

    (i)  has been convicted of a relevant offence; or

    (ii)  was a director, manager, secretary or other similar officer of another body corporate at a time when a relevant offence for which that other body corporate has been convicted was committed[1].

*Meaning of "waste" and household, commercial and industrial waste and special waste*

**75.** **(1)** The following provisions apply for the interpretation of this Part.

**(2)** "Waste" means any substance[2] or object in the categories set out in Schedule 2B to this Act[3] which the holder discards or intends or is required to discard; and for the purposes of this definition—

"holder" means the producer of the waste or the person who is in possession of it; and

"producer" means any person whose activities produce waste or any person who carries out pre-processing, mixing or other operations resulting in a change in the nature or composition of this waste[4].

**(3)** *Prospectively repealed by the Environment Act 1995 (c. 25), s. 120, sch. 22, para. 88(3), sch. 24.*

**(4)** "Controlled waste" means household, industrial and commercial waste or any such waste.

**(5)** Subject to subsection (8) below, "household waste" means waste from—

(*a*) domestic property, that is to say, a building or self-contained part of a building which is used wholly for the purposes of living accommodation;

(*b*) a caravan (as defined in section 29(1) of the Caravan Sites and Control of Development Act 1960[5]) which usually and for the time being is situated on a caravan site (within the meaning of that Act);

(*c*) a residential home;

(*d*) premises forming part of a university or school or other educational establishment;

(*e*) premises forming part of a hospital or nursing home.

**(6)** Subject to subsection (8) below, "industrial waste" means waste from any of the following premises—

(*a*) any factory (within the meaning of the Factories Act 1961[6]);

(*b*) any premises used for the purposes of, or in connection with, the provision to the public of transport services by land, water or air;

(*c*) any premises used for the purposes of, or in connection with, the supply to the public of gas, water or electricity or the provision of sewerage services; or

(*d*) any premises used for the purposes of, or in connection with, the provision to the public of postal or telecommunications services.

**(7)** Subject to subsection (8) below, "commercial waste" means waste from premises used wholly or mainly for the purposes of a trade or business or the purposes of sport, recreation or entertainment excluding—

(*a*) household waste;

(*b*) industrial waste;

---

[1] Subsections (1)–(5), (7) came into force on 1 May 1994: S.I. 1994/1096; (6) came into force on 18 February 1993: S.I. 1993/274.

[2] "Substance" defined by s. 29(11), p. 113 above.

[3] P. 223 below.

[4] Subsection (2) substituted by the Environment Act 1995 (c. 25), s. 120, sch. 22, para. 88(2).

[5] 1960 c. 62.

[6] 1961 c. 34.

(c)   waste from any mine or quarry and waste from premises used for agriculture within the meaning of the Agriculture Act 1947[1] or, in Scotland, the Agriculture (Scotland) Act 1948[2]; and

(d)   waste of any other description prescribed by regulations made by the Secretary of State for the purposes of this paragraph[3].

(8)   Regulations made by the Secretary of State may provide that waste of a description prescribed in the regulations shall be treated for the purposes of provisions of this Part prescribed in the regulations as being or not being household waste or industrial waste or commercial waste; but no regulations shall be made in respect of such waste as is mentioned in subsection (7)(c) above and references to waste in subsection (7) above and this subsection do not include sewage (including matter in or from a privy) except so far as the regulations provide otherwise[3].

(9)   "Special waste" means controlled waste as respects which regulations are in force under section 62 above[4].

(10)   Schedule 2B to this Act[5] (which reproduces Annex I to the Waste Directive) shall have effect.

(11)   Subsection (2) above is substituted, and Schedule 2B to this Act is inserted, for the purpose of assigning to "waste" in this Part the meaning which it has in the Waste Directive by virtue of paragraphs (a) to (c) of Article 1 of, and Annex I to, that Directive, and those provisions shall be construed accordingly.

(12)   In this section "the Waste Directive" means the directive of the Council of the European Communities, dated 15th July 1975, on waste[6], as amended by—

(a)   the directive of that Council, dated 18th March 1991, amending directive 75/442/EEC on waste[7]; and

(b)   the directive of that Council, dated 23rd December 1991, standardising and rationalising reports on the implementation of certain Directives relating to the environment[8,9,10].

*Application to the Isles of Scilly*

**76.** (1) Subject to the provisions of any order under this section, this Part shall not apply in relation to the Isles of Scilly.

(2) The Secretary of State may, after consultation with the Council of the Isles of Scilly, by order provide for the application of any provisions of this Part to the Isles of Scilly; and any such order may provide for the application of those provisions to those Isles with such modifications as may be specified in the order.

(3) An order under this section may—

(a)   make different provision for different cases, including different provision in relation to different persons, circumstances or localities; and

(b)   contain such supplemental, consequential and transitional provision as the Secretary of State considers appropriate, including provision saving provision repealed by or under any enactment[11].

---

[1]  1947 c. 48.
[2]  1948 c. 45.
[3]  The following regulations have been made under this section:
The Controlled Waste Regulations 1992, S.I. 1992/588, as amended, p. 662 below;
The Waste Management Licensing Regulations 1994, S.I. 1994/1056, as amended, p. 675 below.
[4]  P. 151 above.
[5]  P. 223 below.

[6]  75/442/EEC.
[7]  91/156/EEC.
[8]  91/692/EEC.
[9]  Subsections (10)–(12) added by the Environment Act 1995 (c. 25), s. 120, sch. 22, para. 88(4).
[10]  Subsections (1), (4)–(9) came into force on 31 May 1991: S.I. 1991/1319; (2), (10)–(12) are not in force.
[11]  S. 76 substituted by the Environment Act 1995 (c. 25), s. 118(3). This amendment came into force on 1 February 1996: S.I. 1996/186.

*Transition from Control of Pollution Act 1974 to this Part*

**77.** **(1)** This section has effect for the purposes of the transition from the provisions of Part I of the Control of Pollution Act 1974[1] ("the 1974 Act") to the corresponding provisions of this Part of this Act and in this section—

"existing disposal authority" has the same meaning as in section 32 above[2];

"existing disposal licence" means a disposal licence under section 5 of the 1974 Act subsisting on the day appointed under section 164(3) below for the repeal of sections 3 to 10 of the 1974 Act and "relevant appointed day for licences" shall be construed accordingly[3];

"existing disposal plant" means a plan under section 2 of the 1974 Act subsisting on the day appointed under section 164(3) below for the repeal of that section and "relevant appointed day for plans" shall be construed accordingly[4];

"relevant part of its undertaking", in relation to an existing disposal authority, has the same meaning as in section 32 above; and

"the vesting date", in relation to an existing disposal authority and its waste disposal contractors, means the vesting date under Schedule 2 to this Act[5].

**(2)** An existing disposal licence shall, on and after the relevant appointed day for licences, be treated as a site licence[6] until it expires or otherwise ceases to have effect; and accordingly it shall be variable and subject to revocation or suspension under this Part of this Act and may not be surrendered or transferred except under this Part of this Act.

**(3)** The restriction imposed by section 33(1) above[7] shall not apply in relation to land[8] occupied by an existing disposal authority for which a resolution of the authority subsists under section 11 of the 1974 Act on the relevant appointed day for licences until the following date, that is to say—

(a) in the case of an authority which transfers the relevant part of its undertaking in accordance with a scheme under Schedule 2 to this Act, the date which is the vesting date for that authority; and

(b) in any other case, the date on which the authority transfers, or ceases itself to carry on, the relevant part of its undertaking or ceases to provide places at which and plant and equipment by means of which controlled waste can be disposed of or deposited for the purposes of disposal.

**(4)** Any existing disposal plan of an existing disposal authority shall, on and after the relevant appointed day for plans, be treated as the plan of that authority under section 50 above and that section shall accordingly have effect as if references in it to "the plan" included the existing disposal plan of that authority.

**(5)** Subsection (4) above applies to Scotland and, for the purposes of that application, "existing disposal authority" means any authority constituted as a disposal authority for any area before the day appointed for this section to come into force and "that authority" means the waste disposal authority for that area under section 30(2) above[9].

**(6)** Subject to subsection (7) below, as respects any existing disposal authority—

(a) the restriction imposed by section 51(1) of this Act[10] on the means whereby the authority arranges for the disposal[11] of controlled waste[12] shall not apply to the authority—

(i) in the case of an authority which transfers the relevant part of its undertaking in accordance with a scheme under Schedule 2 to this Act, until the date which is the vesting date for that authority; and

[1] 1974 c.40.
[2] P. 114 above.
[3] For provisions relating to the repeal of ss.3–10 of the 1974 Act see S.I. 1994/1096, p.000 below.
[4] S.2 of the 1974 Act was repealed on 31 May 1991: S.I. 1991/1319.
[5] P. 215 below.
[6] "Site licence" defined by s.35(12), p. 120 above.
[7] P. 116 above.
[8] "Land" defined by s.29(8), p. 112 above.
[9] P. 113 above.
[10] P. 144 above.
[11] "Disposal" of waste defined by s.29(6), p. 112 above.
[12] "Controlled waste" defined by s.75, p. 159 below.

    (ii) in any other case, until the date on which the authority transfers, or ceases itself to carry on, the relevant part of its undertaking or ceases to provide places at which and plant and equipment by means of which controlled waste can be disposed of or deposited for the purposes of disposal; and

(b) on and after that date, section 14(4) of the 1974 Act shall not authorise the authority to arrange for the disposal of controlled waste except by means of arrangements made (in accordance with Part II of Schedule 2 to this Act) with waste disposal contractors[1].

(7) The Secretary of State may, as respects any existing disposal authority, direct that the restriction imposed by section 51(1) above shall not apply in the case of that authority until such date as he specifies in the direction and where he does so paragraph (a) of subsection (6) above shall not apply and paragraph (b) shall be read as referring to the date so specified.

(8) In section 14(4) of the 1974 Act, after the words "this subsection", there shall be inserted the words "but subject to subsection (6) of section 77 of the Environmental Protection Act 1990 as respects any time after the date applicable to the authority under paragraph (a) or (b) of that subsection".

(9) As respects any existing disposal authority, until the date which is, under subsection (6)(a) above, the date until which the restriction imposed by section 51(1) of this Act is disapplied,—

(a) the powers conferred on a waste disposal authority by section 55(2)(a) and (b) of this Act as respects the recycling[2] of waste[3] and the use of waste to produce heat or electricity shall be treated as powers which the authority may exercise itself; and

(b) the power conferred on a waste disposal authority by section 48(4) of this Act to object to a waste collection authority[4] having waste recycled where the disposal authority has made arrangements with a waste disposal contractor for the contractor to recycle the waste shall be available to the waste disposal authority where it itself has the waste recycled[5].

*This Part and radioactive substances*

78. Except as provided by regulations made by the Secretary of State under this section, nothing in this Part applies to radioactive waste within the meaning of the Radioactive Substances Act 1993[6]; but regulations may—

(a) provide for prescribed provisions of this Part to have effect with such modifications as the Secretary of State considers appropriate for the purposes of dealing with such radioactive waste;

(b) make such modifications of the Radioactive Substances Act 1993 and any other Act as the Secretary of State considers appropriate[7].

# Part IIA[8]: Contaminated Land

*Preliminary*

78A. (1) The following provisions have effect for the interpretation of this Part.

[1] "Waste disposal contractor" defined by s.30(5), p. 114 above.
[2] "Recycling" defined by s.29(6), p. 112 above.
[3] "Waste" defined by s.75, p. 159 below.
[4] "Waste collection authority" defined by s.30(3), p. 113 above.
[5] This section came into force on 31 May 1991: S.I. 1991/1319.
[6] Words "Radioactive Substances Act 1993" in this section substituted by the Radioactive Substances Act 1993 (c.12), s.49(1), sch.4, para.7. This amendment came into force on 27 August 1993: s.52(2).
[7] This section came into force on 13 December 1991: S.I. 1991/2829.
[8] This Part is inserted by the Environment Act 1995 (c. 25), s. 57. S. 57, in so far as the amendments made by the section (a) confer power on the Secretary of State to make regulations or orders, give directions or issue guidance, or (b) make provision with respect to the exercise of any such power, came into force on 21 September 1995: S.I. 1995/1983. Otherwise this Part is not in force.

**(2)** "Contaminated land" is any land which appears to the local authority in whose area it is situated to be in such a condition, by reason of substances in, on or under the land, that—

(a) significant harm is being caused or there is a significant possibility of such harm being caused; or

(b) pollution of controlled waters is being, or is likely to be, caused;

and, in determining whether any land appears to be such land, a local authority shall, subject to subsection (5) below, act in accordance with guidance issued by the Secretary of State in accordance with section 78YA below[1] with respect to the manner in which that determination is to be made.

**(3)** A "special site" is any contaminated land—

(a) which has been designated as such a site by virtue of section 78C(7)[2] or 78D(6)[3] below; and

(b) whose designation as such has not been terminated by the appropriate Agency under section 78Q(4) below[4].

**(4)** "Harm" means harm to the health of living organisms or other interference with the ecological systems of which they form part and, in the case of man, includes harm to his property.

**(5)** The questions—

(a) what harm is to be regarded as "significant",

(b) whether the possibility of significant harm being caused is "significant",

(c) whether pollution of controlled waters is being, or is likely to be, caused,

shall be determined in accordance with guidance issued for the purpose by the Secretary of State in accordance with section 78YA below.

**(6)** Without prejudice to the guidance that may be issued under subsection (5) above, guidance under paragraph (a) of that subsection may make provision for different degrees of importance to be assigned to, or for the disregard of,—

(a) different descriptions of living organisms or ecological systems;

(b) different descriptions of places; or

(c) different descriptions of harm to health or property, or other interference;

and guidance under paragraph (b) of that subsection may make provision for different degrees of possibility to be regarded as "significant" (or as not being "significant") in relation to different descriptions of significant harm.

**(7)** "Remediation" means—

(a) the doing of anything for the purpose of assessing the condition of—

    (i) the contaminated land in question;

    (ii) any controlled waters affected by that land; or

    (iii) any land adjoining or adjacent to that land;

(b) the doing of any works, the carrying out of any operations or the taking of any steps in relation to any such land or waters for the purpose—

    (i) of preventing or minimising, or remedying or mitigating the effects of, any significant harm, or any pollution of controlled waters, by reason of which the contaminated land is such land; or

    (ii) of restoring the land or waters to their former state; or

(c) the making of subsequent inspections from time to time for the purpose of keeping under review the condition of the land or waters;

and cognate expressions shall be construed accordingly.

[1] P. 186 below.
[2] P. 166 below.
[3] P. 168 below.
[4] P. 180 below.

(8) Controlled waters are "affected by" contaminated land if (and only if) it appears to the enforcing authority that the contaminated land in question is, for the purposes of subsection (2) above, in such a condition, by reason of substances in, on or under the land, that pollution of those waters is being, or is likely to be caused.

(9) The following expressions have the meaning respectively assigned to them—

"the appropriate Agency" means—

(a) in relation to England and Wales, the Environment Agency[1];

(b) in relation to Scotland, the Scottish Environment Protection Agency[2];

"appropriate person" means any person who is an appropriate person, determined in accordance with section 78F below[3], to bear responsibility for any thing which is to be done by way of remediation in any particular case;

"charging notice" has the meaning given by section 78P(3)(b) below[4];

"controlled waters"—

(a) in relation to England and Wales, has the same meaning as in Part III of the Water Resources Act 1991[5]; and

(b) in relation to Scotland, has the same meaning as in section 30A of the Control of Pollution Act 1974[6];

"creditor" has the same meaning as in the Conveyancing and Feudal Reform (Scotland) Act 1970[7];

"enforcing authority" means—

(a) in relation to a special site, the appropriate Agency;

(b) in relation to contaminated land other than a special site, the local authority in whose area the land is situated;

"heritable security" has the same meaning as in the Conveyancing and Feudal Reform (Scotland) Act 1970;

"local authority" in relation to England and Wales means—

(a) any unitary authority;

(b) any district council, so far as it is not a unitary authority;

(c) the Common Council of the City of London and, as respects the Temples, the Sub-Treasurer of the Inner Temple and the Under-Treasurer of the Middle Temple respectively;

and in relation to Scotland means a council for an area constituted under section 2 of the Local Government etc. (Scotland) Act 1994[8];

"notice" means notice in writing;

"notification" mans notification in writing;

"owner", in relation to any land in England and Wales, means a person (other than a mortgagee not in possession) who, whether in his own right or as trustee for any other person, is entitled to receive the rack rent of the land, or, where the land is not let at a rack rent, would be so entitled if it were so let;

"owner", in relation to any land in Scotland, means a person (other than a creditor in a heritable security not in possession of the security subjects) for the time being entitled to receive or who would, if the land were let, be entitled to receive, the rents of the land in connection with which the word is used and includes a trustee, factor, guardian or curator and in the case of

---

[1] The Environment Agency is established by the Environment Act 1995 (c. 25), s. 1, p. 420 below.
[2] The Scottish Environment Protection Agency, also known as SEPA, is established by the Environment Act 1995 (c. 25), s. 20, p. 438 below.
[3] P. 169 below.

[4] P. 178 below.
[5] P. 271 below.
[6] P. 18 above.
[7] 1970 c. 35.
[8] 1994 c. 39.

public or municipal land includes the persons to whom the management of the land is entrusted;

"pollution of controlled waters" means the entry into controlled waters of any poisonous, noxious or polluting matter or any solid waste matter;

"prescribed" means prescribed by regulations;

"regulations" means regulations made by the Secretary of State;

"remediation declaration" has the meaning given by section 78H(6) below[1];

"remediation notice" has the meaning given by section 78E(1) below[2];

"remediation statement" has the meaning given by section 78H(7) below[3];

"required to be designated as a special site" shall be construed in accordance with section 78C(8) below[4];

"substance" means any natural or artificial substance, whether in solid or liquid form or in the form of a gas or vapour;

"unitary authority" means—

(a) the council of a county, so far as it is the council of an area for which there are no district councils;

(b) the council of any district comprised in an area for which there is no county council;

(c) the council of a county borough in Wales.

*Identification of contaminated land*

**78B.** (1) Every local authority[5] shall cause its area to be inspected from time to time for the purpose—

(a) of identifying contaminated land[6]; and

(b) of enabling the authority to decide whether any such land is land which is required to be designated as a special site[7].

(2) In performing its functions under subsection (1) above a local authority shall act in accordance with any guidance issued for the purpose by the Secretary of State in accordance with section 78YA below[8].

(3) If a local authority identifies any contaminated land in its area, it shall give notice[9] of that fact to—

(a) the appropriate Agency[10];

(b) the owner[11] of the land;

(c) any person who appears to the authority to be in occupation of the whole or any part of the land; and

(d) each person who appears to the authority to be an appropriate person[12];

and any notice given under this subsection shall state by virtue of which of paragraphs (a) to (d) above it is given.

(4) If, at any time after a local authority has given any person a notice pursuant to subsection (3)(d) above in respect of any land, it appears to the enforcing authority[13] that another person is an appropriate person, the enforcing authority shall give notice to that other person—

[1] P. 172 below.
[2] P. 168 below.
[3] P. 172 below.
[4] P. 167 below.
[5] "Local authority" defined by s. 78A(9) above.
[6] "Contaminated land" defined by s. 78A(2) above.
[7] "Required to be designated as a special site" is construed in accordance with s. 78C(8) below: s. 78A(9) above.
[8] P. 186 below.
[9] "Notice" defined by s. 78A(9) above.
[10] "The appropriate Agency" defined by s. 78A(9) above.
[11] "Owner" defined by s. 78A(9) above.
[12] "Appropriate person" defined by s. 78A(9) above.
[13] "Enforcing authority" defined by s. 78A(9), p. 164 above.

(a) of the fact that the local authority has identified the land in question as contaminated land; and

(b) that he appears to the enforcing authority to be an appropriate person.

*Identification and designation of special sites*

**78C.** (1) If at any time it appears to a local authority[1] that any contaminated land[2] in its area might be land which is required to be designated as a special site[3], the authority

(a) shall decide whether or not the land is land which is required to be so designated; and

(b) if the authority decides that the land is land which is required to be so designated, shall give notice[4] of that decision to the relevant persons.

(2) For the purposes of this section, "the relevant persons" at any time in the case of any land are the persons who at that time fall within paragraphs (a) to (d) below, that is to say—

(a) the appropriate Agency[5];

(b) the owner[6] of the land;

(c) any person who appears to the local authority concerned to be in occupation of the whole or any part of the land; and

(d) each person who appears to that authority to be an appropriate person[7].

(3) Before making a decision under paragraph (a) of subsection (1) above in any particular case, a local authority shall request the advice of the appropriate Agency, and in making its decision shall have regard to any advice given by that Agency in response to the request.

(4) If at any time the appropriate Agency considers that any contaminated land is land which is required to be designated as a special site, that Agency may give notice of that fact to the local authority in whose area the land is situated.

(5) Where notice under subsection (4) above is given to a local authority, the authority shall decide whether the land in question—

(a) is land which is required to be designated as a special site, or

(b) is not land which is required to be so designated,

and shall give notice of that decision to the relevant persons.

(6) Where a local authority makes a decision falling within subsection (1)(b) or (5)(a) above, the decision shall, subject to section 78D below, take effect on the day after whichever of the following events first occurs, that is to say—

(a) the expiration of the period of twenty-one days beginning with the day on which the notice required by virtue of subsection (1)(b) or, as the case may be, (5)(a) above is given to the appropriate Agency; or

(b) if the appropriate Agency gives notification[8] to the local authority in question that it agrees with the decision, the giving of that notification;

and where a decision takes effect by virtue of this subsection, the local authority shall give notice of that fact to the relevant persons.

(7) Where a decision that any land is land which is required to be designated as a special site takes effect in accordance with subsection (6) above, the notice given under subsection (1)(b) or, as the case may be, (5)(a) above shall have effect, as from the time when the decision takes effect, as the designation of that land as such a site.

---

[1] "Local authority" defined by s. 78A(9), p. 164 above.
[2] "Contaminated land" defined by s. 78A(2), p. 163 above.
[3] "Required to be designated as a special site" is construed in accordance with subsection (8) below: s. 78A(9) above.
[4] "Notice" defined by s. 78A(9), p. 164 above.

[5] "The appropriate Agency" defined by s. 78A(9), p. 164 above.
[6] "Owner" defined by s. 78A(9), p. 164 above.
[7] "Appropriate person" defined by s. 78A(9), p. 164 above.
[8] "Notification" defined by s. 78A(9), p. 164 above.

**(8)** For the purposes of this Part, land is required to be designated as a special site if, and only if, it is land of a description prescribed[1] for the purposes of this subsection.

**(9)** Regulations[2] under subsection (8) above may make different provision for different cases or circumstances or different areas or localities and may, in particular, describe land by reference to the area or locality in which it is situated.

**(10)** Without prejudice to the generality of his power to prescribe any description of land for the purposes of subsection (8) above, the Secretary of State, in deciding whether to prescribe a particular description of contaminated land for those purposes, may, in particular, have regard to—

(a) whether land of the description in question appears to him to be land which is likely to be in such a condition, by reason of substances[3] in, on or under the land that—

   (i) serious harm[4] would or might be caused, or

   (ii) serious pollution of controlled waters[5] would be, or would be likely to be, caused[6]; or

(b) whether the appropriate Agency is likely to have expertise in dealing with the kind of significant harm[7], or pollution of controlled waters, by reason of which land of the description in question is contaminated land.

*Referral of special site decisions to the Secretary of State*

**78D.** **(1)** In any case where—

(a) a local authority[8] gives notice[9] of a decision to the appropriate Agency[10] pursuant to subsection (1)(b) or (5)(b) of section 78C above, but

(b) before the expiration of the period of twenty-one days beginning with the day on which that notice is so given, that Agency gives the local authority notice that it disagrees with the decision, together with a statement of its reasons for disagreeing,

the authority shall refer the decision to the Secretary of State and shall send to him a statement of its reasons for reaching the decision.

**(2)** Where the appropriate Agency gives notice to a local authority under paragraph (b) of subsection (1) above, it shall also send to the Secretary of State a copy of the notice and of the statement given under that paragraph.

**(3)** Where a local authority refers a decision to the Secretary of State under subsection (1) above, it shall give notice of that fact to the relevant persons[11].

**(4)** Where a decision of a local authority is referred to the Secretary of State under subsection (1) above, he—

(a) may confirm or reverse the decision with respect to the whole or any part of the land to which it relates; and

(b) shall give notice of his decision on the referral—

   (i) to the relevant persons; and

   (ii) to the local authority.

**(5)** Where a decision of a local authority is referred to the Secretary of State under subsection (1) above, the decision shall not take effect until the day after that on which the Secretary of

1 "Prescribed" defined by s. 78A(9), p. 165 above.
2 "Regulations" defined by s. 78A(9), p. 165 above.
3 "Substance" defined by s. 78A(9), p. 165 above.
4 "Harm" defined by s. 78A(4), p. 163 above.
5 "Controlled waters" and "pollution of controlled waters" defined by s. 78A(9), p. 164 above.
6 For "pollution . . . caused" see s. 78A(5), p. 163 above.
7 For "significant harm" see s. 78A(5), p. 163 above.
8 "Local authority" defined by s. 78A(9), p. 164 above.
9 "Notice" defined by s. 78A(9), p. 164 above.
10 "The appropriate Agency" defined by s. 78A(9), p. 164 above.
11 "The relevant persons" has the same meaning as in s. 78C above: subsection (7) below.

State gives the notice required by subsection (4) above to the persons there mentioned and shall then take effect as confirmed or reversed by him.

(6)  Where a decision which takes effect in accordance with subsection (5) above is to the effect that at least some land is land which is required to be designated as a special site, the notice given under subsection (4)(b) above shall have effect, as from the time when the decision takes effect, as the designation of that land as such a site.

(7)  In this section "the relevant persons" has the same meaning as in section 78C above.

*Duty of enforcing authority to require remediation of contaminated land etc.*

78E.  (1)  In any case where—

    (*a*)  any land has been designated as a special site[1] by virtue of section 78C(7)[2] or 78D(6) above, or

    (*b*)  a local authority has identified any contaminated land[3] (other than a special site) in its area,

the enforcing authority[4] shall, in accordance with such procedure as may be prescribed[5] and subject to the following provisions of this Part, serve on each person who is an appropriate person[6] a notice[7] (in this Part referred to as a "remediation notice") specifying what that person is to do by way of remediation[8] and the periods within which he is required to do each of the things so specified.

(2)  Different remediation notices requiring the doing of different things by way of remediation may be served on different persons in consequence of the presence of different substances[9] in, on or under any land or waters.

(3)  Where two or more persons are appropriate persons in relation to any particular thing which is to be done by way of remediation, the remediation notice served on each of them shall state the proportion, determined under section 78F(7) below, of the cost of doing that thing which each of them respectively is liable to bear.

(4)  The only things by way of remediation which the enforcing authority may do, or require to be done, under or by virtue of this Part are things which it considers reasonable, having regard to—

    (*a*)  the cost which is likely to be involved; and

    (*b*)  the seriousness of the harm[10], or pollution of controlled waters[11], in question.

(5)  In determining for any purpose of this Part—

    (*a*)  what is to be done (whether by an appropriate person, the enforcing authority or any other person) by way of remediation in any particular case,

    (*b*)  the standard to which any land is, or waters are, to be remediated pursuant to the notice, or

    (*c*)  what is, or is not, to be regarded as reasonable for the purposes of subsection (4) above,

the enforcing authority shall have regard to any guidance issued for the purpose by the Secretary of State.

(6)  Regulations[12] may make provision for or in connection with—

    (*a*)  the form or content of remediation notices; or

    (*b*)  any steps of a procedural nature which are to be taken in connection with, or in consequence of, the service of a remediation notice.

[1] "Special site" defined by s. 78A(3), p. 163 above.
[2] P. 166 above.
[3] "Contaminated land" defined by s. 78A(2), p. 163 above.
[4] "Enforcing authority" defined by s. 78A(9), p. 164 above.
[5] "Prescribed" defined by s. 78(9), p. 165 above.
[6] "Appropriate person" defined by s. 78A(9), p. 164 above.
[7] "Notice" defined by s. 78A(9), p. 164 above.
[8] "Remediation" defined by s. 78A(7), p. 163 above.
[9] "Substance" defined by s. 78A(9), p. 165 above.
[10] "Harm" defined by s. 78A(4), p. 163 above.
[11] "Controlled waters" and "pollution of controlled waters" defined by s. 78A(9), p. 164 above.
[12] "Regulations" defined by s. 78A(9), p. 165 above.

*Determination of the appropriate person to bear responsibility for remediation*

**78F.** **(1)** This section has effect for the purpose of determining who is the appropriate person to bear responsibility for any particular thing which the enforcing authority[1] determines is to be done by way of remediation[2] in any particular case.

**(2)** Subject to the following provisions of this section, any person, or any of the persons, who caused or knowingly permitted the substances[3], or any of the substances, by reason of which the contaminated land[4] in question is such land to be in, on or under that land is an appropriate person.

**(3)** A person shall only be an appropriate person by virtue of subsection (2) above in relation to things which are to be done by way of remediation which are to any extent referable to substances which he caused or knowingly permitted to be present in, on or under the contaminated land in question.

**(4)** If no person has, after reasonable inquiry, been found who is by virtue of subsection (2) above an appropriate person to bear responsibility for the things which are to be done by way of remediation, the owner[5] or occupier for the time being of the contaminated land in question is an appropriate person.

**(5)** If, in consequence of subsection (3) above, there are things which are to be done by way of remediation in relation to which no person has, after reasonable inquiry, been found who is an appropriate person by virtue of subsection (2) above, the owner or occupier for the time being of the contaminated land in question is an appropriate person in relation to those things.

**(6)** Where two or more persons would, apart from this subsection, be appropriate persons in relation to any particular thing which is to be done by way of remediation, the enforcing authority shall determine in accordance with guidance issued for the purpose by the Secretary of State whether any, and if so which, of them is to be treated as not being an appropriate person in relation to that thing.

**(7)** Where two or more persons are appropriate persons in relation to any particular thing which is to be done by way of remediation, they shall be liable to bear the cost of doing that thing in proportions determined by the enforcing authority in accordance with guidance issued for the purpose by the Secretary of State.

**(8)** Any guidance issued for the purposes of subsection (6) or (7) above shall be issued in accordance with section 78YA below[6].

**(9)** A person who has caused or knowingly permitted any substance ("substance A") to be in, on or under any land shall also be taken for the purposes of this section to have caused or knowingly permitted there to be in, on or under that land any substance which is there as a result of a chemical reaction or biological process affecting substance A.

**(10)** A thing which is to be done by way of remediation may be regarded for the purposes of this Part as referable to the presence of any substance notwithstanding that the thing in question would not have to be done—

(*a*) in consequence only of the presence of that substance in any quantity; or

(*b*) in consequence only of the quantity of that substance which any particular person caused or knowingly permitted to be present.

---

[1] "Enforcing authority" defined by s. 78A(9), p. 164 above.
[2] "Remediation" defined by s. 78A(7), p. 163 above.
[3] "Substance" defined by s. 78A(9), p. 165 above.
[4] "Contaminated land" defined by s. 78A(2), p. 163 above.
[5] "Owner" defined by s. 78A(9), p. 164 above.
[6] P. 186 below.

*Grant of, and compensation for, rights of entry etc.*

**78G.** **(1)** A remediation notice[1] may require an appropriate person[2] to do things by way of remediation[3], notwithstanding that he is not entitled to do those things.

**(2)** Any person whose consent is required before any thing required by a remediation notice may be done shall grant, or join in granting, such rights in relation to any of the relevant land or waters[4] as will enable the appropriate person to comply with any requirements imposed by the remediation notice.

**(3)** Before serving a remediation notice, the enforcing authority[5] shall reasonably endeavour to consult every person who appears to the authority—

(a)  to be the owner[6] or occupier of any of the relevant land or waters, and

(b)  to be a person who might be required by subsection (2) above to grant, or join in granting, any rights,

concerning the rights which that person may be so required to grant.

**(4)** Subsection (3) above shall not preclude the service of a remediation notice in any case where it appears to the enforcing authority that the contaminated land[7] in question is in such a condition, by reason of substances[8] in, on or under the land, that there is imminent danger of serious harm[9], or serious pollution of controlled waters[10], being caused.

**(5)** A person who grants, or joins in granting, any rights pursuant to subsection (2) above shall be entitled, on making an application within such period as may be prescribed[11] and in such manner as may be prescribed to such person as may be prescribed, to be paid by the appropriate person compensation of such amount as may be determined in such manner as may be prescribed.

**(6)** Without prejudice to the generality of the regulations[12] that may be made by virtue of subsection (5) above, regulations by virtue of that subsection may make such provision in relation to compensation under this section as may be made by regulations by virtue of subsection (4) of section 35A above[13] in relation to compensation under that section.

**(7)** In this section, "relevant land or waters" means—

(a)  the contaminated land in question;

(b)  any controlled waters affected by that land[14]; or

(c)  any land adjoining or adjacent to that land or those waters.

*Restrictions and prohibitions on serving remediation notices*

**78H.** **(1)** Before serving a remediation notice[15], the enforcing authority[16] shall reasonably endeavour to consult—

(a)  the person on whom the notice is to be served,

(b)  the owner[17] of any land to which the notice relates,

[1] "Remediation notice" defined by s. 78A(9), p. 165 above.
[2] "Appropriate person" defined by s. 78A(9), p. 164 above.
[3] "Remediation" defined by s. 78A(7), p. 163 above. For "a thing which is to be done by way of remediation" see s. 78F(10) above.
[4] For "relevant land or waters" see subsection (7) below.
[5] "Enforcing authority" defined by s. 78A(9), p. 164 above.
[6] "Owner" defined by s. 78A(9), p. 164 above.
[7] "Contaminated land" defined by s. 78A(2), p. 163 above.
[8] "Substance" defined by s. 78A(9), p. 165 above.
[9] "Harm" defined by s. 78A(4), p. 163 above.
[10] "Controlled waters" and "pollution of controlled waters" defined by s. 78A(9), p. 164 above.
[11] "Prescribed" defined by s. 78(9), p. 165 above.
[12] "Regulations" defined by s. 78A(9), p. 165 above.
[13] P. 120 above.
[14] For the construction of "controlled waters affected by [contaminated] land" see s. 78A(8), p. 164 above.
[15] "Remediation notice" defined by s. 78A(9), p. 165 above.
[16] "Enforcing authority" defined by s. 78A(9), p. 164 above.
[17] "Owner" defined by s. 78A(9), p. 164 above.

(c)  any person who appears to that authority to be in occupation of the whole or any part of the land, and

(d)  any person of such other description as may be prescribed[1],

concerning what is to be done by way of remediation[2].

(2)  Regulations[3] may make provision for, or in connection with, steps to be taken for the purposes of subsection (1) above.

(3)  No remediation notice shall be served on any person by reference to any contaminated land[4] during any of the following periods, that is to say—

(a)  the period—

(i)  beginning with the identification of the contaminated land in question pursuant to section 78B(1) above[5], and

(ii)  ending with the expiration of the period of three months beginning with the day on which the notice[6] required by subsection (3)(d) or, as the case may be, (4) of section 78B above is given to that person in respect of that land;

(b)  If a decision falling within paragraph (b) of section 78C(1) above[7] is made in relation to the contaminated land in question, the period beginning with the making of the decision and ending with the expiration of the period of three months beginning with—

(i)  in a case where the decision is not referred to the Secretary of State under section 78D above[8], the day on which the notice required by section 78C(6) above is given, or

(ii)  in a case where the decision is referred to the Secretary of State under section 78D above, the day on which he gives notice required by subsection (4)(b) of that section;

(c)  if the appropriate Agency[9] gives a notice under subsection (4) of section 78C above to a local authority[10] in relation to the contaminated land in question, the period beginning with the day on which that notice is given and ending with the expiration of the period of three months beginning with—

(i)  in a case where notice is given under subsection (6) of that section, the day on which that notice is given;

(ii)  in a case where the authority makes a decision falling within subsection (5)(b) of that section and the appropriate Agency fails to give notice under paragraph (b) of section 78D(1) above, the day following the expiration of the period of twenty-one days mentioned in that paragraph; or

(iii)  in a case where the authority makes a decision falling within section 78C(5)(b) above which is referred to the Secretary of State under section 78D above, the day on which the Secretary of State gives the notice required by subsection (4)(b) of that section.

(4)  Neither subsection (1) nor subsection (3) above shall preclude the service of a remediation notice in any case where it appears to the enforcing authority that the land in question is in such a condition, by reason of substances[11] in, on or under the land, that there is imminent danger of serious harm[12], or serious pollution of controlled waters[13], being caused.

(5)  The enforcing authority shall not serve a remediation notice on a person if and so long as any one or more of the following conditions is for the time being satisfied in the particular case, that is to say—

---

[1]  "Prescribed" defined by s. 78(9), p. 165 above.
[2]  "Remediation" defined by s. 78A(7), p. 165 above.
[3]  "Regulations" defined by s. 78A(9), p. 165 above.
[4]  "Contaminated land" defined by s. 78A(2), p. 163 above.
[5]  P. 165 above.
[6]  "Notice" defined by s. 78A(9), p. 164 above.
[7]  P. 166 above.

[8]  P. 167 above.
[9]  "The appropriate Agency" defined by s. 78A(9), p. 164 above.
[10]  "Local authority" defined by s. 78A(9), p. 164 above.
[11]  "Substance' defined by s. 78A(9), p. 165 above.
[12]  "Harm" defined by s. 78A(4), p. 163 above.
[13]  "Controlled waters" and "pollution of controlled waters" defined by s. 78A(9), p. 164 above.

(*a*) the authority is satisfied, in consequence of section 78E(4) and (5) above[1], that there is nothing by way of remediation which could be specified in a remediation notice served on that person;

(*b*) the authority is satisfied that appropriate things are being, or will be, done by way of remediation without the service of a remediation notice on that person;

(*c*) it appears to the authority that the person on whom the notice would be served is the authority itself; or

(*d*) the authority is satisfied that the powers conferred on it by section 78N below[2] to do what is appropriate by way of remediation are exercisable.

(6) Where the enforcing authority is precluded by virtue of section 78E(4) or (5) above from specifying in a remediation notice any particular thing by way of remediation which it would otherwise have specified in such a notice, the authority shall prepare and publish a document (in this Part referred to as a "remediation declaration") which shall record—

(*a*) the reasons why the authority would have specified that thing; and

(*b*) the grounds on which the authority is satisfied that it is precluded from specifying that thing in such a notice.

(7) In any case where the enforcing authority is precluded, by virtue of paragraph (b), (c) or (d) of subsection (5) above, from serving a remediation notice, the responsible person[3] shall prepare and publish a document (in this Part referred to as a "remediation statement") which shall record—

(*a*) the things which are being, have been, or are expected to be, done by way of remediation in the particular case;

(*b*) the name and address of the person who is doing, has done, or is expected to do, each of those things; and

(*c*) the periods within which each of those things is being, or is expected to be, done.

(8) For the purposes of subsection (7) above, the "responsible person" is—

(*a*) in a case where the condition in paragraph (b) of subsection (5) above is satisfied, the person who is doing or has done, or who the enforcing authority is satisfied will do, the things there mentioned; or

(*b*) in a case where the condition in paragraph (c) or (d) of that subsection is satisfied, the enforcing authority.

(9) If a person who is required by virtue of subsection (8)(a) above to prepare and publish a remediation statement fails to do so within a reasonable time after the date on which a remediation notice specifying the things there mentioned could, apart from subsection (5) above, have been served, the enforcing authority may itself prepare and publish the statement and may recover its reasonable costs of doing so from that person.

(10) Where the enforcing authority has been precluded by virtue only of subsection (5) above from serving a remediation notice on an appropriate person but—

(*a*) none of the conditions in that subsection is for the time being satisfied in the particular case, and

(*b*) the authority is not precluded by any other provision of this Part from serving a remediation notice on that appropriate person,

the authority shall serve a remediation notice on that person; and any such notice may be so served without any further endeavours by the authority to consult persons pursuant to subsection (1) above, if and to the extent that that person has been consulted pursuant to that subsection concerning the things which will be specified in the notice.

---

[1] P. 168 above.   [2] P. 176 below.   [3] "Responsible person" defined by subsection (8) below.

*Restrictions on liability relating to the pollution of controlled waters*

**78J.** **(1)** This section applies where any land is contaminated land by virtue of paragraph (b) of sub-section (2) of section 78A above[1] (whether or not the land is also contaminated land by virtue of paragraph (a) of that subsection).

**(2)** Where this section applies, no remediation notice[2] given in consequence of the land in question being contaminated land shall require a person who is an appropriate person by virtue of section 78F(4) or (5) above[3] to do anything by way of remediation[4] to that or any other land, or any waters, which he could not have been required to do by such a notice had paragraph (b) of section 78A(2) above (and all other references to pollution of controlled waters) been omitted from this Part.

**(3)** If, in a case where this section applies, a person permits, has permitted, or might permit, water from an abandoned mine[5] or part of a mine—

(a)  to enter any controlled waters[6], or

(b)  to reach a place from which it is or, as the case may be, was likely, in the opinion of the enforcing authority[7], to enter such waters,

no remediation notice shall require him in consequence to do anything by way of remediation (whether to the contaminated land in question or to any other land or waters) which he could not have been required to do by such a notice had paragraph (b) of section 78A(2) above (and all other references to pollution of controlled waters) been omitted from this Part.

**(4)** Subsection (3) above shall not apply to the owner[8] or former operator of any mine or part of a mine if the mine or part in question became abandoned after 31st December 1999.

**(5)** In determining for the purposes of subsection (4) above whether a mine or part of a mine became abandoned before, on or after 31st December 1999 in a case where the mine or part has become abandoned on two or more occasions, of which—

(a)  at least one falls on or before that date, and

(b)  at least one falls after that date,

the mine or part shall be regarded as becoming abandoned after that date (but without prejudice to the operation of subsection (3) above in relation to that mine or part at, or in relation to, any time before the first of those occasions which falls after that date).

**(6)** Where, immediately before a part of a mine becomes abandoned, that part is the only part of the mine not falling to be regarded as abandoned for the time being, the abandonment of that part shall not be regarded for the purposes of subsection (4) or (5) above as constituting the abandonment of the mine, but only of that part of it.

**(7)** Nothing in subsection (2) or (3) above prevents the enforcing authority from doing anything by way of remediation under section 78N below[9] which it could have done apart from that sub-section, but the authority shall not be entitled under section 78P below[10] to recover from any person any part of the cost incurred by the authority in doing by way of remediation anything which it is precluded by subsection (2) or (3) above from requiring that person to do.

**(8)** In this section "mine" has the same meaning as in the Mines and Quarries Act 1954[11].

*Liability in respect of contaminating substances which escape to other land*

**78K.** **(1)** A person who has caused or knowingly permitted any substances[12] to be in, on or under any land shall also be taken for the purposes of this Part to have caused or, as the case may be,

[1] P. 163 above.
[2] "Remediation notice" defined by s. 78A(9), p. 165 above.
[3] P. 169 above.
[4] "Remediation" defined by s. 78A(7), p. 163 above.
[5] "Mine" defined by subsection (8) below.
[6] "Controlled waters" defined by s. 78A(9), p. 164 above.
[7] "Enforcing authority" defined by s. 78A(9), p. 164 above.
[8] "Owner" in relation to land defined by s. 78A(9), p. 164 above.
[9] P. 176 below.
[10] P. 177 below.
[11] 1954 c. 70.
[12] "Substance" defined by s. 78A(9), p. 165 above.

knowingly permitted those substances to be in, on or under any other land to which they appear[1] to have escaped.

(2) Subsections (3) and (4) below apply in any case where it appears that any substances are or have been in, on or under any land (in this section referred to as "land A") as a result of their escape, whether directly or indirectly, from other land in, on or under which a person caused or knowingly permitted them to be.

(3) Where this subsection applies, no remediation notice[2] shall require a person—

(a) who is the owner[3] or occupier of land A, and

(b) who has not caused or knowingly permitted the substances in question to be in, on or under that land,

to do anything by way of remediation[4] to any land or waters (others than land or waters of which he is the owner or occupier) in consequence of land A appearing to be in such a condition, by reason of the presence of those substances in, on or under it, that significant harm[5] is being caused, or there is a significant possibility of such harm being caused, or that pollution of controlled waters[6] is being, or is likely to be caused[7].

(4) Where this subsection applies, no remediation notice shall require a person—

(a) who is the owner or occupier of land A, and

(b) who has not caused or knowingly permitted the substances in question to be in, on or under that land,

to do anything by way of remediation in consequence of any further land in, on or under which those substances or any of them appear to be or to have been present as a result of their escape from land A ("land B") appearing to be in such a condition, by reason of the presence of those substances in, on or under it, that significant harm is being caused, or there is a significant possibility of such harm being caused, or that pollution of controlled waters is being, or is likely to be caused, unless he is also the owner or occupier of land B.

(5) In any case where—

(a) a person ("person A") has caused or knowingly permitted any substances to be in, on, or under any land,

(b) another person ("person B") who has not caused or knowingly permitted those substances to be in, on or under that land becomes the owner or occupier of that land, and

(c) the substances, or any of the substances, mentioned in paragraph (a) above appear to have escaped to other land,

no remediation notice shall require person B to do anything by way of remediation to that other land in consequence of the apparent acts or omissions of person A, except to the extent that person B caused or knowingly permitted the escape.

(6) Nothing in subsection (3), (4) or (5) above prevents the enforcing authority[8] from doing anything by way of remediation[9] under section 78N below[10] which it could have done apart from that subsection, but the authority shall not be entitled under section 78P below[11] to recover from any person any part of the cost incurred by the authority in doing by way of remediation anything which it is precluded by subsection (3), (4) or (5) above from requiring that person to do.

(7) In this section, "appear" means appear to the enforcing authority, and cognate expressions shall be construed accordingly.

[1] "Appear" defined by subsection (7) below.
[2] "Remediation notice" defined by s. 78A(9), p. 165 above.
[3] "Owner" defined by s. 78A(9), p. 164 above.
[4] "Remediation" defined by s. 78A(7), p. 163 above.
[5] For "significant harm" see s. 78A(5), p. 163 above.
[6] "Controlled waters" and "pollution of controlled waters" defined by s. 78A(9), p. 164 above.
[7] For "pollution . . . caused" see s. 78A(5), p. 163 above.
[8] "Enforcing authority" defined by s. 78A(9), p. 164 above.
[9] "Remediation" defined by s. 78A(7), p. 163 above.
[10] P. 176 below.
[11] P. 177 below.

*Appeals against remediation notices*

**78L.** **(1)** A person on whom a remediation notice[1] is served may, within the period of twenty-one days beginning with the day on which the notice is served, appeal against the notice—

(*a*) if it was served by a local authority[2], to a magistrates' court or, in Scotland, to the sheriff by way of summary application; or

(*b*) if it was served by the appropriate Agency[3], to the Secretary of State;

and in the following provisions of this section "the appellate authority" means the magistrates' court, the sheriff or the Secretary of State, as the case may be.

**(2)** On any appeal under subsection (1) above the appellate authority—

(*a*) shall quash the notice, if it is satisfied that there is a material defect in the notice; but

(*b*) subject to that, may confirm the remediation notice, with or without modification, or quash it.

**(3)** Where an appellate authority confirms a remediation notice, with or without modification, it may extend the period specified in the notice for doing what the notice requires to be done.

**(4)** Regulations[4] may make provision with respect to—

(*a*) the grounds on which appeals under subsection (1) above may be made;

(*b*) the cases in which, grounds on which, court or tribunal to which, or person at whose instance, an appeal against a decision of a magistrates' court or sheriff court in pursuance of an appeal under subsection (1) above shall lie; or

(*c*) the procedure on an appeal under subsection (1) above or on an appeal by virtue of para-graph (b) above.

**(5)** Regulations under subsection (4) above may (among other things)—

(*a*) include provisions comparable to those in section 290 of the Public Health Act 1936[5] (appeals against notices requiring the execution of works);

(*b*) prescribe the cases in which a remediation notice is, or is not, to be suspended until the appeal is decided, or until some other stage in the proceedings;

(*c*) prescribe the cases in which the decision on an appeal may in some respects be less favourable to the appellant than the remediation notice against which he is appealing;

(*d*) prescribe the cases in which the appellant may claim that a remediation notice should have been served on some other person and prescribe the procedure to be followed in those cases;

(*e*) make provision as respect—

(i)  the particulars to be included in the notice of appeal;

(ii)  the persons on whom notice of appeal is to be served and the particulars, if any, which are to accompany the notice; and

(iii)  the abandonment of an appeal;

(*f*) make different provision for different cases or classes of case.

**(6)** This section, so far as relating to appeals to the Secretary of State, is subject to section 114 of the Environment Act 1995[6] (delegation or reference of appeals etc).

........................................................................................................................................................................

[1] "Remediation notice" defined by s. 78A(9), p. 165 above.

[2] "Local authority" defined by s. 78A(9), p. 164 above.

[3] "The appropriate Agency" defined by s. 78A(9), p. 164 above.

[4] "Regulations" defined by s. 78A(9), p. 165 above.

[5] 1936 c. 49.

[6] P. 489 below.

*Offences of not complying with a remediation notice*

**78M.** (1) If a person on whom an enforcing authority[1] serves a remediation notice[2] fails, without reasonable excuse, to comply with any of the requirements of the notice, he shall be guilty of an offence.

(2) Where the remediation notice in question is one which was required by section 78E(3) above[3] to state, in relation to the requirement which has not been complied with, the proportion of the cost involved which the person charged with the offence is liable to bear, it shall be a defence for that person to prove that the only reason why he has not complied with the requirement is that one or more of the other persons who are liable to bear a proportion of that cost refused, or was not able, to comply with the requirement.

(3) Except in a case falling within subsection (4) below, a person who commits an offence under subsection (1) above shall be liable, on summary conviction, to a fine not exceeding level 5 on the standard scale[4] and to a further fine of an amount equal to one-tenth of level 5 on the standard scale for each day on which the failure continues after conviction of the offence and before the enforcing authority has begun to exercise its powers by virtue of section 78N(3)(c) below.

(4) A person who commits an offence under subsection (1) above in a case where the contaminated land[5] to which the remediation notice relates is industrial, trade or business premises[6] shall be liable on summary conviction to a fine not exceeding £20,000 or such greater sum as the Secretary of State may from time to time by order substitute and to a further fine of an amount equal to one-tenth of that sum for each day on which the failure continues after conviction of the offence and before the enforcing authority has begun to exercise its powers by virtue of section 78N(3)(c) below.

(5) If the enforcing authority is of the opinion that proceedings for an offence under this section would afford an ineffectual remedy against a person who has failed to comply with any of the requirements of a remediation notice which that authority has served on him, that authority may take proceedings in the High Court or, in Scotland, in any court of competent jurisdiction, for the purpose of securing compliance with the remediation notice.

(6) In this section, "industrial, trade or business premises" means premises used for any industrial, trade or business purposes or premises not so used on which matter is burnt in connection with any industrial, trade or business process, and premises are used for industrial purposes where they are used for the purposes of any treatment or process as well as where they are used for the purpose of manufacturing.

(7) No order shall be made under subsection (4) above unless a draft of the order has been laid before, and approved by a resolution of, each House of Parliament.

*Powers of the enforcing authority to carry out remediation*

**78N.** (1) Where this section applies, the enforcing authority[7] shall itself have power, in a case falling within paragraph (a) or (b) of section 78E(1) above, to do what is appropriate by way of remediation[8] to the relevant land or waters[9].

(2) Subsection (1) above shall not confer power on the enforcing authority to do anything by way of remediation if the authority would, in the particular case, be precluded by section 78YB below[10] from serving a remediation notice requiring that thing to be done.

---

[1] "Enforcing authority": defined by s. 78A(9), p. 164 above.
[2] "Remediation notice" defined by s. 78A(9), p. 165 above.
[3] P. 168 above.
[4] The current fine at level 5 on the standard scale is £5,000: Criminal Justice Act 1991 (c. 53), s. 17 (England and Wales); Criminal Procedure (Scotland) Act 1995 (c. 46), s. 225 (Scotland).
[5] "Contaminated land" defined by s. 78A(2), p. 163 above.
[6] "Industrial, trade or business premises" defined by subsection (6) below.
[7] "Enforcing authority" defined by s. 78A(9), p. 164 above.
[8] "Remediation" defined by s. 78A(7), p. 163 above.
[9] "Relevant land or waters" defined by subsection (5) below.
[10] P. 186 below.

(3) This section applies in each of the following cases, that is to say—

(*a*) where the enforcing authority considers it necessary to do anything itself by way of remediation for the purpose of preventing the occurrence of any serious harm[1], or serious pollution of controlled waters[2], of which there is imminent danger;

(*b*) where an appropriate person[3] has entered into a written agreement with the enforcing authority for that authority to do, at the cost of that person, that which he would otherwise be required to do under this Part by way of remediation;

(*c*) where a person on whom the enforcing authority serves a remediation notice fails to comply with any of the requirements of the notice;

(*d*) where the enforcing authority is precluded by section 78J[4] or 78K above from including something by way of remediation in a remediation notice;

(*e*) where the enforcing authority considers that, were it to do some particular thing by way of remediation, it would decide, by virtue of subsection (2) of section 78P below[5] or any guidance issued under that subsection—

  (i) not to seek to recover under subsection (1) of that section any of the reasonable cost incurred by it in doing that thing; or

  (ii) to seek so to recover only a portion of that cost;

(*f*) where no person has, after reasonable inquiry, been found who is an appropriate person in relation to any particular thing.

(4) Subject to section 78E(4) and (5) above[6], for the purposes of this section, the things which it is appropriate for the enforcing authority to do by way of remediation are—

(*a*) in a case falling within paragraph (a) of subsection (3) above, anything by way of remediation which the enforcing authority considers necessary for the purpose mentioned in that paragraph;

(*b*) in a case falling within paragraph (b) of that subsection, anything specified in, or determined under, the agreement mentioned in that paragraph;

(*c*) in a case falling within paragraph (c) of that subsection, anything which the person mentioned in that paragraph was required to do by virtue of the remediation notice;

(*d*) in a case falling within paragraph (d) of that subsection, anything by way of remediation which the enforcing authority is precluded by section 78J or 78K above from including in a remediation notice;

(*e*) in a case falling within paragraph (e) or (f) of that subsection, the particular thing mentioned in the paragraph in question.

(5) In this section "the relevant land or waters" means—

(*a*) the contaminated land[7] in question;

(*b*) any controlled waters[8] affected by that land; or

(*c*) any land adjoining or adjacent to that land or those waters.

---

*Recovery of, and security for, the cost of remediation by the enforcing authority*

**78P. (1)** Where, by virtue of section 78N(3)(a), (c), (e) or (f) above, the enforcing authority[9] does any particular thing by way of remediation[10] it shall be entitled, subject to sections 78J(7) and 78K(6)

---

[1] "Harm" defined by s. 78A(4), p. 163 above.

[2] "Controlled waters" and "pollution of controlled waters" defined by s. 78A(9), p. 164 above.

[3] "Appropriate person" defined by s. 78A(9), p. 164 above.

[4] P. 173 above.

[5] P. 178 below.

[6] P. 168 above.

[7] "Contaminated land" defined by s. 78A(2), p. 163 above.

[8] "Controlled waters" defined by s. 78A(9), p. 164 above.

[9] "Enforcing authority" defined by s. 78A(9), p. 164 above.

[10] "Remediation" defined by s. 78A(7), p. 165 above.

above[1,2], to recover the reasonable cost incurred in doing it from the appropriate person[3] or, if there are two or more appropriate persons in relation to the thing in question, from those persons in proportions determined pursuant to section 78F(7) above[4].

(2) In deciding whether to recover the cost, and, if so, how much of the cost, which it is entitled to recover under subsection (1) above, the enforcing authority shall have regard—

(a) to any hardship which the recovery may cause to the person from whom the cost is recoverable; and

(b) to any guidance issued by the Secretary of State for the purposes of this subsection.

(3) Subsection (4) below shall apply in any case where—

(a) any cost is recoverable under subsection (1) above from a person—

(i) who is the owner[5] of any premises which consist of or include the contaminated land[6] in question; and

(ii) who caused or knowingly permitted the substances[7], or any of the substances, by reason of which the land is contaminated land to be in, on or under the land; and

(b) the enforcing authority serves a notice[8] under this subsection (in this Part referred to as a "charging notice") on that person.

(4) Where this subsection applies—

(a) the cost shall carry interest, at such reasonable rate as the enforcing authority may determine, from the date of service of the notice until the whole amount is paid; and

(b) subject to the following provisions of this section, the cost and accrued interest shall be a charge on the premises mentioned in subsection (3)(a)(i) above.

(5) A charging notice shall—

(a) specify the amount of the cost which the enforcing authority claims is recoverable;

(b) state the effect of subsection (4) above and the rate of interest determined by the authority under that subsection; and

(c) state the effect of subsections (7) and (8) below.

(6) On the date on which an enforcing authority serves a charging notice on a person, the authority shall also serve a copy of the notice on every other person who, to the knowledge of the authority, has an interest in the premises capable of being affected by the charge.

(7) Subject to any order under subsection (9)(b) or (c) below, the amount of any cost specified in a charging notice and the accrued interest shall be a charge on the premises—

(a) as from the end of the period of twenty-one days beginning with the service of the charging notice, or

(b) where an appeal is brought under subsection (8) below, as from the final determination or (as the case may be) the withdrawal, of the appeal,

until the cost and interest are recovered.

(8) A person served with a charging notice or a copy of a charging notice may appeal against the notice to a county court within the period of twenty-one days beginning with the date of service.

(9) On an appeal under subsection (8) above, the court may—

(a) confirm the notice without modification;

(b) order that the notice is to have effect with the substitution of a different amount for the amount originally specified in it; or

[1] P. 173 above.
[2] P. 174 above.
[3] "Appropriate person" defined by s. 78A(9), p. 164 above.
[4] P. 169 above.
[5] "Owner" defined by s. 78A(9), p. 164 above.
[6] "Contaminated land" defined by s. 78A(2), p. 163 above.
[7] "Substance" defined by s. 78A(9), p. 165 above.
[8] "Notice" defined by s. 78A(9), p. 164 above.

(*c*)  order that the notice is to be of no effect.

(**10**)  Regulations[1] may make provision with respect to—

(*a*)  the grounds on which appeals under this section may be made; or

(*b*)  the procedure on any such appeal.

(**11**)  An enforcing authority shall, for the purpose of enforcing a charge under this section, have all the same powers and remedies under the Law of Property Act 1925[2], and otherwise, as if it were a mortgagee by deed having powers of sale and lease, of accepting surrenders of leases and of appointing a receiver.

(**12**)  Where any cost is a charge on premises under this section, the enforcing authority may by order declare the cost to be payable with interest by instalments within the specified period until the whole amount is paid.

(**13**)  In subsection (12) above—

"interest" means interest at the rate determined by the enforcing authority under subsection (4) above; and

"the specified period" means such period of thirty years or less from the date of service of the charging notice as is specified in the order.

(**14**)  Subsections (3) to (13) above do not extend to Scotland.

*Special sites*

**78Q.** (**1**)  If, in a case where a local authority[3] has served a remediation notice[4], the contaminated land[5] in question becomes a special site[6], the appropriate Agency[7] may adopt the remediation notice and, if it does so,—

(*a*)  it shall give notice of its decision to adopt the remediation notice to the appropriate person[8] and to the local authority;

(*b*)  the remediation notice shall have effect, as from the time at which the appropriate Agency decides to adopt it, as a remediation notice given by that Agency; and

(*c*)  the validity of the remediation notice shall not be affected by—

(i)  the contaminated land having become a special site;

(ii)  the adoption of the remediation notice by the appropriate Agency; or

(iii)  anything in paragraph (b) above.

(**2**)  Where a local authority has, by virtue of section 78N above[9], begun to do any thing, or any series of things, by way of remediation[10]—

(*a*)  the authority may continue doing that thing, or that series of things, by virtue of that section, notwithstanding that the contaminated land in question becomes a special site; and

(*b*)  section 78P above shall apply in relation to the reasonable cost incurred by the authority in doing that thing or those things as if that authority were the enforcing authority.

(**3**)  If and so long as any land is a special site, the appropriate Agency may from time to time inspect that land for the purpose of keeping its condition under review.

[1]  "Regulations" defined by s. 78A(9), p. 165 above.
[2]  1925 c. 20.
[3]  "Local authority" defined by s. 78A(9), p. 164 above.
[4]  "Remediation notice" defined by s. 78A(9), p. 165 above.
[5]  "Contaminated land" defined by s. 78A(2), p. 163 above.
[6]  "Special site" defined by s. 78A(3), p. 163 above.
[7]  "The appropriate Agency" defined by s. 78A(9), p. 164 above.
[8]  "Appropriate person" defined by s. 78A(9), p. 164 above.
[9]  P. 176 above.
[10]  "Remediation" defined by s. 78A(7), p. 165 above.

(4) If it appears to the appropriate Agency that a special site is no longer land which is required to be designated as such a site, the appropriate Agency may give notice—

(a) to the Secretary of State, and

(b) to the local authority in whose area the site is situated,

terminating the designation of the land in question as a special site as from such date as may be specified in the notice.

(5) A notice under subsection (4) above shall not prevent the land, or any of the land, to which the notice relates being designated as a special site on a subsequent occasion.

(6) In exercising its functions under subsection (3) or (4) above, the appropriate Agency shall act in accordance with any guidance given for the purpose by the Secretary of State.

*Registers*
**78R.** (1) Every enforcing authority[1] shall maintain a register containing prescribed[2] particulars of or relating to—

(a) remediation notices[3] served by that authority;

(b) appeals against any such remediation notices;

(c) remediation statements or remediation declarations prepared and published under section 78H above[4];

(d) in relation to an enforcing authority in England and Wales, appeals against charging notices[5] served by that authority;

(e) notices under subsection (1)(b) or (5)(a) of section 78C above[6] which have effect by virtue of subsection (7) of that section as the designation of any land as a special site;

(f) notices under subsection (4)(b) of section 78D above[7] which have effect by virtue of subsection (6) of that section as the designation of any land as a special site;

(g) notices given by or to the enforcing authority under section 78Q(4) above terminating the designation of any land as a special site;

(h) notifications given to that authority by persons—

    (i) on whom a remediation notice has been served, or

    (ii) who are or were required by virtue of section 78H(8)(a) above to prepare and publish a remediation statement[8],

of what they claim has been done by them by way of remediation[9];

(j) notifications given to that authority by owners[10] or occupiers of land—

    (i) in respect of which a remediation notice has been served, or

    (ii) in respect of which a remediation statement has been prepared and published,

of what they claim has been done on the land in question by way of remediation;

(k) convictions for such offences under section 78M above[11] as may be prescribed;

(l) such other matters relating to contaminated land[12] as may be prescribed;

but that duty is subject to sections 78S and 78T below.

---

[1] "Enforcing authority" defined by s. 78A(9), p. 164 above.
[2] "Prescribed" defined by s. 78(9), p. 165 above.
[3] "Remediation notice" defined by s. 78A(9), p. 165 above.
[4] P. 170 above.
[5] "Charging notice" has the meaning given by s. 78P(3)(b), p. 178 above: s. 78A(9) above.
[6] P. 166 above.
[7] P. 167 above.
[8] "Remediation statement" has the meaning given by s. 78H(7), p. 172 above: s. 78A(9) above.
[9] "Remediation" defined by s. 78A(7), p. 163 above.
[10] "Owner" defined by s. 78A(9), p. 164 above.
[11] P. 176 above.
[12] "Contaminated land" defined by s. 78A(2), p. 164 above.

**(2)** The form of, and the descriptions of information to be contained in, notifications for the purposes of subsection (1)(h) or (j) above may be prescribed by the Secretary of State.

**(3)** No entry made in a register by virtue of subsection (1)(h) or (j) above constitutes a representation by the body maintaining the register or, in a case where the entry is made by virtue of subsection (6) below, the authority which sent the copy of the particulars in question pursuant to subsection (4) or (5) below—

(a) that what is stated in the entry to have been done has in fact been done; or

(b) as to the manner in which it has been done.

**(4)** Where any particulars are entered on a register maintained under this section by the appropriate Agency[1], the appropriate Agency shall send a copy of those particulars to the local authority[2] in whose area is situated the land to which the particulars relate.

**(5)** In any case where—

(a) any land is treated by virtue of section 78X(2) below[3] as situated in the area of a local authority other than the local authority in whose area it is in fact situated, and

(b) any particulars relating to that land are entered on the register maintained under this section by the local authority in whose area the land is so treated as situated,

that authority shall send a copy of those particulars to the local authority in whose area the land is in fact situated.

**(6)** Where a local authority receives a copy of any particulars sent to it pursuant to subsection (4) or (5) above, it shall enter those particulars on the register maintained by it under this section.

**(7)** Where information of any description is excluded by virtue of section 78T below[4] from any register maintained under this section, a statement shall be entered in the register indicating the existence of information of that description.

**(8)** It shall be the duty of each enforcing authority—

(a) to secure that the registers maintained by it under this section are available, at all reasonable times, for inspection by the public free of charge; and

(b) to afford to members of the public facilities for obtaining copies of entries, on payment of reasonable charges;

and, for the purposes of this subsection, places may be prescribed by the Secretary of State at which any such registers or facilities as are mentioned in paragraph (a) or (b) above are to be available or afforded to the public in pursuance of the paragraph in question.

**(9)** Registers under this section may be kept in any form.

*Exclusion from registers of information affecting national security*

**78S.** **(1)** No information shall be included in a register maintained under section 78R above if and so long as, in the opinion of the Secretary of State, the inclusion in the register of that information, or information of that description, would be contrary to the interests of national security.

**(2)** The Secretary of State may, for the purpose of securing the exclusion from registers of information to which subsection (1) above applies, give to enforcing authorities[5] directions—

(a) specifying information, or descriptions of information, to be excluded from their registers; or

(b) specifying descriptions of information to be referred to the Secretary of State for his determination;

---

[1] "The appropriate Agency" defined by s. 78A(9), p. 164 above.
[2] "Local authority" defined by s. 78A(9), p. 164 above.
[3] P. 184 below.

[4] P. 182 below.
[5] "Enforcing authority" defined by s. 78A(9), p. 164 above.

and no information referred to the Secretary of State in pursuance of paragraph (b) above shall be included in any such register until the Secretary of State determines that it should be so included.

(3) The enforcing authority shall notify the Secretary of State of any information which it excludes from the register in pursuance of directions under subsection (2) above.

(4) A person may, as respects any information which appears to him to be information to which subsection (1) above may apply, give a notice[1] to the Secretary of State specifying the information and indicating its apparent nature; and, if he does so—

(a) he shall notify the enforcing authority that he has done so; and

(b) no information so notified to the Secretary of State shall be included in any such register until the Secretary of State has determined that it should be so included.

*Exclusion from registers of certain confidential information*

78T. (1) No information relating to the affairs of any individual or business shall be included in a register maintained under section 78R above[2], without the consent of that individual or the person for the time being carrying on that business, if and so long as the information—

(a) is, in relation to him, commercially confidential[3]; and

(b) is not required to be included in the register in pursuance of directions under subsection (7) below;

but information is not commercially confidential for the purposes of this section unless it is determined under this section to be so by the enforcing authority[4] or, on appeal, by the Secretary of State.

(2) Where it appears to an enforcing authority that any information which has been obtained by the authority under or by virtue of any provision of this Part might be commercially confidential, the authority shall—

(a) give to the person to whom or whose business it relates notice[5] that that information is required to be included in the register unless excluded under this section; and

(b) give him a reasonable opportunity—

(i) of objecting to the inclusion of the information on the ground that it is commercially confidential; and

(ii) of making representations to the authority for the purpose of justifying any such objection;

and, if any representations are made, the enforcing authority shall, having taken the representations into account, determine whether the information is or is not commercially confidential.

(3) Where, under subsection (2) above, an authority determines that information is not commercially confidential—

(a) the information shall not be entered in the register until the end of the period of twenty-one days beginning with the date on which the determination is notified to the person concerned;

(b) that person may appeal to the Secretary of State against the decision;

and, where an appeal is brought in respect of any information, the information shall not be entered in the register until the end of the period of seven days following the day on which the appeal is finally determined or withdrawn.

---

[1] "Notice" defined by s. 78A(9), p. 164 above.
[2] P. 180 above.
[3] For "commercially confidential" information see subsections (10) and (11) below.

[4] "Enforcing authority" defined by s. 78A(9), p. 164 above.
[5] "Notice" defined by s. 78A(9), p. 164 above.

**(4)** An appeal under subsection (3) above shall, if either party to the appeal so requests or the Secretary of State so decides, take or continue in the form of a hearing (which must be held in private).

**(5)** Subsection (10) of section 15 above[1] shall apply in relation to an appeal under subsection (3) above as it applies in relation to an appeal under that section.

**(6)** Subsection (3) above is subject to section 114 of the Environment Act 1995[2] (delegation or reference of appeals etc).

**(7)** The Secretary of State may give to the enforcing authorities directions as to specified information, or descriptions of information, which the public interest requires to be included in registers maintained under section 78R above[3] notwithstanding that the information may be commercially confidential.

**(8)** Information excluded from a register shall be treated as ceasing to be commercially confidential for the purposes of this section at the expiry of the period of four years beginning with the date of the determination by virtue of which it was excluded; but the person who furnished it may apply to the authority for the information to remain excluded from the register on the ground that it is still commercially confidential and the authority shall determine whether or not that is the case.

**(9)** Subsections (3) to (6) above shall apply in relation to a determination under subsection (8) above as they apply in relation to a determination under subsection (2) above.

**(10)** Information is, for the purposes of any determination under this section, commercially confidential, in relation to any individual or person, if its being contained in the register would prejudice to an unreasonable degree the commercial interests of that individual or person.

**(11)** For the purposes of subsection (10) above, there shall be disregarded any prejudice to the commercial interests of any individual or person so far as relating only to the value of the contaminated land[4] in question or otherwise to the ownership or occupation of that land.

*Reports by the appropriate Agency on the state of contaminated land*

**78U.** **(1)** The appropriate Agency[5] shall—

(*a*) from time to time, or

(*b*) if the Secretary of State at any time so requests,

prepare and publish a report on the state of contaminated land[6] in England and Wales or in Scotland, as the case may be.

**(2)** A local authority[7] shall, at the written request of the appropriate Agency, furnish the appropriate Agency with such information to which this subsection applies as the appropriate Agency may require for the purpose of enabling it to perform its functions under subsection (1) above.

**(3)** The information to which subsection (2) above applies is such information as the local authority may have, or may reasonably be expected to obtain, with respect to the condition of contaminated land in its area, being information which the authority has acquired or may acquire in the exercise of its functions under this Part.

*Site-specific guidance by the appropriate Agency concerning contaminated land*

**78V.** **(1)** The appropriate Agency[8] may issue guidance to any local authority[9] with respect to the exercise or performance of the authority's powers or duties under this Part in relation to any

---

[1] P. 103 above.
[2] P. 489 below.
[3] P. 180 above.
[4] "Contaminated land" defined by s. 78A(2), p. 163 above.
[5] "The appropriate Agency" defined by s. 78A(9), p. 164 above.
[6] "Contaminated land" defined by s. 78A(2), p. 163 above.
[7] "Local authority" defined by s. 78A(9), p. 164 above.
[8] "The appropriate Agency" defined by s. 78A(9), p. 164 above.
[9] "Local authority" defined by s. 78A(9), p. 164 above.

particular contaminated land[1]; and in exercising or performing those powers or duties in relation to that land the authority shall have regard to any such guidance so issued.

(2) If and to the extent that any guidance issued under subsection (1) above to a local authority is inconsistent with any guidance issued under this Part by the Secretary of State, the local authority shall disregard the guidance under that subsection.

(3) A local authority shall, at the written request of the appropriate Agency, furnish the appropriate Agency with such information to which this subsection applies as the appropriate Agency may require for the purpose of enabling it to issue guidance for the purposes of subsection (1) above.

(4) The information to which subsection (3) above applies is such information as the local authority may have, or may reasonably be expected to obtain, with respect to any contaminated land in its area, being information which the authority has acquired, or may acquire, in the exercise of its functions under this Part.

*The appropriate Agency to have regard to guidance given by the Secretary of State*

78W. (1) The Secretary of State may issue guidance to the appropriate Agency[2] with respect to the exercise or performance of that Agency's powers or duties under this Part; and in exercising or performing those powers or duties the appropriate Agency shall have regard to any such guidance so issued.

(2) The duty imposed on the appropriate Agency by subsection (1) above is without prejudice to any duty imposed by any other provision of this Part on that Agency to act in accordance with guidance issued by the Secretary of State.

*Supplementary provisions*

78X. (1) Where it appears to a local authority[3] that two or more different sites, when considered together, are in such a condition, by reason of substances[4] in, on or under the land, that—

(*a*) significant harm[5] is being caused or there is a significant possibility of such harm being caused, or

(*b*) pollution of controlled waters[6] is being, or is likely to be, caused[7],

this Part shall apply in relation to each of those sites, whether or not the condition of the land at any of them, when considered alone, appears to the authority to be such that significant harm is being caused, or there is a significant possibility of such harm being caused, or that pollution of controlled waters is being or is likely to be caused.

(2) Where it appears to a local authority that any land outside, but adjoining or adjacent to, its area is in such a condition, by reason of substances in, on or under the land, that significant harm is being caused, or there is a significant possibility of such harm being caused, or that pollution of controlled waters is being, or is likely to be, caused within its area—

(*a*) the authority may, in exercising its functions under this Part, treat that land as if it were land situated within its area; and

(*b*) except in this subsection, any reference—

(i) to land within the area of a local authority, or

(ii) to the local authority in whose area any land is situated,

shall be construed accordingly;

---

[1] "Contaminated land" defined by s. 78A(2), p. 163 above.

[2] "The appropriate Agency" defined by s. 78A(9), p. 164 above.

[3] "Local authority" defined by s. 78A(9), p. 164 above.

[4] "Substance" defined by s. 78A(9), p. 165 above.

[5] For "significant harm" see s. 78A(5), p. 163 above.

[6] "Controlled waters" and "pollution of controlled waters" defined by s. 78A(9), p. 164 above.

[7] For "pollution . . . caused" see s. 78A(5), p. 163 above.

but this subsection is without prejudice to the functions of the local authority in whose area the land is in fact situated.

(3) A person acting in a relevant capacity[1]—

(a) shall not thereby be personally liable, under this Part, to bear the whole or any part of the cost of doing any thing by way of remediation[2], unless that thing is to any extent referable to substances whose presence in, on or under the contaminated land[3] in question is a result of any act done or omission made by him which it was unreasonable for a person acting in that capacity to do or make; and

(b) shall not thereby be guilty of an offence under or by virtue of section 78M above[4] unless the requirement which has not been complied with is a requirement to do some particular thing for which he is personally liable to bear the whole or any part of the cost.

(4) In subsection (3) above, "person acting in a relevant capacity" means—

(a) a person acting as an insolvency practitioner, within the meaning of section 388 of the Insolvency Act 1986[5] (including that section as it applies in relation to an insolvent partnership by virtue of any order made under section 421 of that Act);

(b) the official receiver acting in a capacity in which he would be regarded as acting as an insolvency practitioner within the meaning of section 388 of the Insolvency Act 1986 if subsection (5) of that section were disregarded;

(c) the official receiver acting as receiver or manager;

(d) a person acting as a special manager under section 177 or 370 of the Insolvency Act 1986;

(e) the Accountant in Bankruptcy acting as permanent or interim trustee in a sequestration (within the meaning of the Bankruptcy (Scotland) Act 1985[6]);

(f) a person acting as a receiver or receiver and manager—

(i) under or by virtue of any enactment; or

(ii) by virtue of his appointment as such by an order of a court or by any other instrument.

(5) Regulations[7] may make different provision for different cases or circumstances.

*Application to the Isles of Scilly*

**78Y.** (1) Subject to the provisions of any order under this section, this Part shall not apply in relation to the Isles of Scilly.

(2) The Secretary of State may, after consultation with the Council of the Isles of Scilly, by order provide for the application of any provisions of this Part to the Isles of Scilly; and any such order may provide for the application of those provisions to those Isles with such modifications as may be specified in the order.

(3) An order under this section may—

(a) make different provision for different cases, including different provision in relation to different persons, circumstances or localities; and

(b) contain such supplemental, consequential and transitional provision as the Secretary of State considers appropriate, including provision saving provision repealed by or under any enactment.

---

[1] "Person acting in a relevant capacity" defined by subsection (4) below.

[2] "Remediation" defined by s. 78A(7), p. 163 above.

[3] "Contaminated land" defined by s. 78A(2), p. 163 above.

[4] P. 176 above.

[5] 1986 c. 45.

[6] 1985 c. 66.

[7] "Regulations" defined by s. 78A(9), p. 165 above.

*Supplementary provisions with respect to guidance by the Secretary of State*

**78YA.** (1) Any power of the Secretary of State to issue guidance under this Part shall only be exercisable after consultation with the appropriate Agency[1] and such other bodies or persons as he may consider it appropriate to consult in relation to the guidance in question.

(2) A draft of any guidance proposed to be issued under section 78A(2)[2] or (5), 78B(2)[3] or 78F(6)[4] or (7) above shall be laid before each House of Parliament and the guidance shall not be issued until after the period of 40 days beginning with the day on which the draft was so laid or, if the draft is laid on different days, the later of the two days.

(3) If, within the period mentioned in subsection (2) above, either House resolves that the guidance, the draft of which was laid before it, should not be issued, the Secretary of State shall not issue that guidance.

(4) In reckoning any period of 40 days for the purposes of subsection (2) or (3) above, no account shall be taken of any time during which Parliament is dissolved or prorogued or during which both Houses are adjourned for more than four days.

(5) The Secretary of State shall arrange for any guidance issued by him under this Part to be published in such manner as he considers appropriate.

*Interaction of this Part with other enactments*

**78YB.** (1) A remediation notice[5] shall not be served if and to the extent that it appears to the enforcing authority[6] that the powers of the appropriate Agency[7] under section 27 above[8] may be exercised in relation to—

(a) the significant harm[9] (if any), and

(b) the pollution of controlled waters[10] (if any),

by reason of which the contaminated land[11] in question is such land.

(2) Nothing in this Part shall apply in relation to any land in respect of which there is for the time being in force a site licence under Part II above[12], except to the extent that any significant harm, or pollution of controlled waters, by reason of which that land would otherwise fall to be regarded as contaminated land is attributable to causes other than—

(a) breach of the conditions of the licence; or

(b) the carrying on, in accordance with the conditions of the licence, of any activity authorised by the licence.

(3) If, in a case falling within subsection (1) or (7) of section 59 above[13], the land in question is contaminated land, or becomes such land by reason of the deposit of the controlled waste in question, a remediation notice shall not be served in respect of that land by reason of that waste or any consequences of its deposit, if and to the extent that it appears to the enforcing authority that the powers of a waste regulation authority or waste collection authority under that section may be exercised in relation to that waste or the consequences of its deposit.

(4) No remediation notice shall require a person to do anything the effect of which would be to impede or prevent the making of a discharge in pursuance of a consent given under Chapter

---

[1] "The appropriate Agency" defined by s. 78A(9), p. 164 above.
[2] P. 163 above.
[3] P. 165 above.
[4] P. 169 above.
[5] "Remediation notice" defined by s. 78A(9), p. 165 above.
[6] "Enforcing authority" defined by s. 78A(9), p. 164 above.
[7] "The appropriate Agency" defined by s. 78A(9), p. 164 above.

[8] P. 110 above.
[9] For "significant harm" see s. 78A(5), p. 163 above.
[10] "Controlled waters" and "pollution of controlled waters" defined by s. 78A(9), p. 164 above.
[11] "Contaminated land" defined by s. 78A(2), p. 163 above.
[12] P. 111 above. For the meaning of "site licence" see s. 35(12), p. 120 above.
[13] P. 149 above.

II of Part III of the Water Resources Act 1991[1] (pollution offences) or, in relation to Scotland, in pursuance of a consent given under Part II of the Control of Pollution Act 1974[2].

*This Part and radioactivity*

**78YC.** Except as provided by regulations[3], nothing in this Part applies in relation to harm[4], or pollution of controlled waters[5], so far as attributable to any radioactivity possessed by any substance[6]; but regulations may—

(*a*)  provide for prescribed[7] provisions of this Part to have effect with such modifications as the Secretary of State considers appropriate for the purpose of dealing with harm, or pollution of controlled waters, so far as attributable to any radioactivity possessed by any substances; or

(*b*)  make such modifications of the Radioactive Substances Act 1993[8] or any other Act as the Secretary of State considers appropriate.

# PART III: Statutory Nuisances and Clean Air

## Statutory nuisances[9]

*Statutory nuisances and inspections therefor*

**79.** (**1**)  Subject to subsections (1A) to (6A) below[10], the following matters constitute "statutory nuisances" for the purposes of this Part, that is to say—

(*a*)  any premises in such a state as to be prejudicial to health or a nuisance;

(*b*)  smoke emitted from premises so as to be prejudicial to health or a nuisance;

(*c*)  fumes or gases emitted from premises so as to be prejudicial to health or a nuisance;

(*d*)  any dust, steam, smell or other effluvia arising on industrial, trade or business premises and being prejudicial to health or a nuisance;

(*e*)  any accumulation or deposit which is prejudicial to health or a nuisance;

(*f*)  any animal kept in such a place or manner as to be prejudicial to health or a nuisance;

(*g*)  noise emitted from premises so as to be prejudicial to health or a nuisance;

(*ga*)  noise that is prejudicial to health or a nuisance and is emitted from or caused by a vehicle, machinery or equipment in a street or in Scotland, road[11,12];

(*h*)  any other matter declared by any enactment to be a statutory nuisance;

and it shall be the duty of every local authority to cause its area to be inspected from time to time to detect any statutory nuisances which ought to be dealt with under section 80 below or sections 80 and 80A below[13] and, where a complaint of a statutory nuisance is made to it by a person living within its area, to take such steps as are reasonably practicable to investigate the complaint.

(**1A**)  No matter shall constitute a statutory nuisance to the extent that it consists of, or is caused by, any land being in a contaminated state.

---

[1]  P. 273 below.

[2]  P. 16 above.

[3]  "Regulations" defined by s. 78A(9), p. 165 above.

[4]  "Harm" defined by s. 78A(4), p. 163 above.

[5]  "Controlled waters" and "pollution of controlled waters" defined by s. 78A(9), p. 164 above.

[6]  "Substance" defined by s. 78A(9), p. 165 above.

[7]  "Prescribed" defined by s. 78(9), p. 165 above.

[8]  1993 c. 12, p. 381 below.

[9]  Former words ": England and Wales" in this heading repealed by the Environment Act 1995 (c. 25), s. 120, sch. 24.

[10]  Words "Subject to subsections (1A) to (6A) below" substituted by the Environment Act 1995 (c. 25), s. 120, sch. 22, para. 89(2).

[11]  Words "or in Scotland, road" inserted by the Environment Act 1995 (c. 25), s. 107, sch. 17, para. 2(a).

[12]  Para. (ga) inserted by the Noise and Statutory Nuisance Act 1993 (c. 40), s. 2(2)(b).

[13]  Words "or sections 80 and 80A below" inserted by the Noise and Statutory Nuisance Act 1993 (c. 40), s. 2(2)(c).

**(1B)** Land is in a "contaminated state" for the purposes of subsection (1A) above if, and only if, it is in such a condition, by reason of substances in, on or under the land, that—

(*a*) harm is being caused or there is a possibility of harm being caused; or

(*b*) pollution of controlled waters is being, or is likely to be, caused;

and in this subsection "harm", "pollution of controlled waters" and "substance" have the same meaning as in Part IIA of this Act[1].[2]

**(2)** Subsection (1)(b) and (g) above do not apply in relation to premises—

(*a*) occupied on behalf of the Crown for naval, military or air force purposes or for the purposes of the department of the Secretary of State having responsibility for defence, or

(*b*) occupied by or for the purposes of a visiting force;

and "visiting force" means any such body, contingent or detachment of the forces of any country as is a visiting force for the purposes of any of the provisions of the Visiting Forces Act 1952[3].

**(3)** Subsection (1)(b) above does not apply to—

(i)   smoke emitted from a chimney of a private dwelling within a smoke control area,

(ii)   dark smoke emitted from a chimney of a building or a chimney serving the furnace of a boiler or industrial plant attached to a building or for the time being fixed to or installed on any land,

(iii)   smoke emitted from a railway locomotive steam engine, or

(iv)   dark smoke emitted otherwise than as mentioned above from industrial or trade premises.

**(4)** Subsection (1)(c) above does not apply in relation to premises other than private dwellings.

**(5)** Subsection (1)(d) above does not apply to steam emitted from a railway locomotive engine.

**(6)** Subsection (1)(g) above does not apply to noise caused by aircraft other than model aircraft.

**(6A)** Subsection (1)(ga) above does not apply to noise made—

(*a*)   by traffic,

(*b*)   by any naval, military or air force of the Crown or by a visiting force (as defined in subsection (2) above), or

(*c*)   by a political demonstration or a demonstration supporting or opposing a cause or campaign[4].

**(7)** In this Part—

"chimney" includes structures and openings of any kind from or through which smoke may be emitted;

"dust" does not include dust emitted from a chimney as an ingredient of smoke;

"equipment" includes a musical instrument[5];

"fumes" means any airborne solid matter smaller than dust;

"gas" includes vapour and moisture precipitated from vapour;

"industrial, trade or business premises" means premises used for any industrial, trade or business purposes or premises not so used on which matter is burnt in connection with any industrial, trade or business process, and premises are used for industrial purposes where they are used for the purposes of any treatment or process as well as where they are used for the purposes of manufacturing;

"local authority" means, subject to subsection (8) below,—

[1] These definitions are set out at s. 78A, p. 162 above.
[2] Subsections (1A) and (1B) inserted by the Environment Act 1995 (c. 25), s. 120, sch. 22, para. 89(3).
[3] 1952 c. 67.

[4] Subsection (6A) inserted by the Noise and Statutory Nuisance Act 1993 (c. 40), s. 2(3).
[5] The definition of "equipment" inserted by the Noise and Statutory Nuisance Act 1993 (c. 40), s. 2(4)(a).

(*a*)  in Greater London, a London borough council, the Common Council of the City of London and, as respects the Temples, the Sub-Treasurer of the Inner Temple and the Under-Treasurer of the Middle Temple respectively;

(*b*)  in England and Wales[1] outside Greater London, a district council[2];

(*bb*)  in Wales, a county council or borough council[3];

(*c*)  the Council of the Isles of Scilly; and

(*d*)  in Scotland, a district or islands council or a council constituted under section 2 of the Local Government etc. (Scotland) Act 1994[4,5];

"noise" includes vibration;

"person responsible"—

(*a*)  in relation to a statutory nuisance, means the person to whose act, default or sufferance the nuisance is attributable;

(*b*)  in relation to a vehicle, includes the person in whose name the vehicle is for the time being registered under the Vehicle Excise and Registration Act 1994[6] and any other person who is for the time being the driver of the vehicle;

(*c*)  in relation to machinery or equipment, includes any person who is for the time being the operator of the machinery or equipment[7];

"prejudicial to health" means injurious, or likely to cause injury, to health;

"premises" includes land and, subject to subsection (12) and, in relation to England and Wales[8], section 81A(9)[9] below, any vessel;

"private dwelling" means any building, or part of a building, used or intended to be used, as a dwelling;

"road" has the same meaning as in Part IV of the New Roads and Street Works Act 1991[10];

"smoke" includes soot, ash, grit and gritty particles emitted in smoke;

"street" means a highway and any other road, footway, square or court that is for the time being open to the public[11];

and any expressions used in this section and in the Clean Air Act 1993[12] have the same meaning in this section as in that Act and section 3 of the Clean Air Act 1993[13] shall apply for the interpretation of the expression "dark smoke" and the operation of this Part in relation to it.

**(8)** Where, by an order under section 2 of the Public Health (Control of Disease) Act 1984[14], a port health authority has been constituted for any port health district or in Scotland where by an order under section 172 of the Public Health (Scotland) Act 1897[15] a port local authority or a joint port local authority has been constituted for the whole or part of a port[16], the port health authority, port local authority or joint port local authority, as the case may be[17] shall have by virtue of this

---

[1] Words "in England and Wales" inserted by the Environment Act 1995 (c. 25), s. 107, sch. 17, para. 2(b)(i).

[2] Former word "and" repealed by the Environment Act 1995 (c. 25), s. 107, sch. 17, para. 2(b)(i), sch. 24.

[3] Para. (bb) inserted by the Local Government (Wales) Act 1994 (c. 19), s. 22(3), sch. 9, para. 17(5). This amendment came into force on 1 April 1996: S.I. 1996/396.

[4] 1994 c. 39.

[5] Para. (d) inserted by the Environment Act 1995 (c. 25), s. 107, sch. 17, para. 2(b)(i).

[6] 1994 c. 22. Words "the Vehicle Excise and Registration Act 1994" substituted by the Vehicle Excise and Registration Act 1994 (c. 22), s. 63, sch. 3, para. 27. This amendment came into force on 1 September 1994: s. 66(1).

[7] The definition of "person responsible" substituted by the Noise and Statutory Nuisance Act 1993 (c. 40), s. 2(4)(b).

[8] Words "in relation to England and Wales" inserted by the Environment Act 1995 (c. 25), s. 107, sch. 17, para. 2(b)(ii).

[9] Words "and section 81A(9)" inserted by the Noise and Statutory Nuisance Act 1993 (c. 40), s. 10(1).

[10] 1991 c. 22. The definition of "road" inserted by the Environment Act 1995 (c. 25), s. 107, sch. 17, para. 2(b)(iii).

[11] The definition of "street" inserted by the Noise and Statutory Nuisance Act 1993 (c. 40), s. 2(4)(c).

[12] The Clean Air Act 1993 is at p. 333 below. Words "the Clean Air Act 1993" substituted by the Clean Air Act 1994 (c. 11), s. 67(1), sch. 4, para. 4(a). This amendment came into force on 27 August 1993: s. 68(2).

[13] Words "section 3 of the Clean Air Act 1993" substituted by the Clean Air Act 1993 (c. 11), s. 67(1), sch. 4, para. 4(b).

[14] 1984 c. 22.

[15] 1897 c. 38.

[16] Words "or in Scotland . . . part of a port" inserted by the Environment Act 1995 (c. 25), s. 107, sch. 17, para. 2(c)(i).

[17] Words ", port local authority or joint port local authority, as the case may be" inserted by the Environment Act 1995 (c. 25), s. 107, sch. 17, para. 2(c)(ii).

subsection, as respects its district, the functions conferred or imposed by this Part in relation to statutory nuisances other than a nuisance falling within paragraph (g) or (ga)[1] of subsection (1) above and no such order shall be made assigning those functions; and "local authority" and "area" shall be construed accordingly.

(9) In this Part "best practicable means" is to be interpreted by reference to the following provisions—

(a) "practicable" means reasonably practicable having regard among other things to local conditions and circumstances, to the current state of technical knowledge and to the financial implications;

(b) the means to be employed include the design, installation, maintenance and manner and periods of operation of plant and machinery, and the design, construction and maintenance of buildings and structures;

(c) the test is to apply only so far as compatible with any duty imposed by law;

(d) the test is to apply only so far as compatible with safety and safe working conditions, and with the exigencies of any emergency or unforeseeable circumstances;

and, in circumstances where a code of practice under section 71 of the Control of Pollution Act 1974[2] (noise minimisation) is applicable, regard shall also be had to guidance given in it.

(10) A local authority shall not without the consent of the Secretary of State institute summary proceedings under this Part in respect of a nuisance falling within paragraph (b), (d) or (e) and, in relation to Scotland, paragraph (g) or (ga)[3], of subsection (1) above if proceedings in respect thereof might be instituted under Part I[4] or the Alkali &c. Works Regulation Act 1906[5] or section 5 of the Health and Safety at Work etc. Act 1974[6].

(11) The area of a local authority which includes part of the seashore shall also include for the purposes of this Part the territorial sea lying seawards from that part of the shore; and subject to subsection (12) and, in relation to England and Wales[7], section 81A(9)[8] below, this Part shall have effect, in relation to any area included in the area of a local authority by virtue of this subsection—

(a) as if references to premises and the occupier of premises included respectively a vessel and the master of a vessel; and

(b) with such other modifications, if any, as are prescribed in regulations made by the Secretary of State.

(12) A vessel powered by steam reciprocating machinery is not a vessel to which this Part of this Act applies[9,10].

......................................................................................................................................

*Summary proceedings for statutory nuisances*

80. (1) Where a local authority[11] is satisfied that a statutory nuisance[12] exists, or is likely to occur or recur, in the area[13] of the authority, the local authority shall serve a notice[14] ("an abatement notice") imposing all or any of the following requirements—

---

[1] Words "or (ga)" inserted by the Noise and Statutory Nuisance Act 1993 (c. 40), s. 2(5).

[2] 1974 c. 40.

[3] Words "and, in relation to Scotland, paragraph (g) or (ga)," inserted by the Environment Act 1995 (c. 25), s. 107, sch. 17, para. 2(d).

[4] *Prospective repeal:* words following "Part I" in this subsection: Environmental Protection Act 1990 (c. 43), s. 162, sch. 16, pt. I.

[5] 1906 c. 14.

[6] 1974 c. 37.

[7] Words ", in relation to England and Wales," inserted by the Environment Act 1995 (c. 25), s. 107, sch. 17, para. 2(e).

[8] Words "and section 81A(9)" inserted by the Noise and

Statutory Nuisance Act 1993 (c. 40), s. 10(1).

[9] This section came into force on 1 January 1991: s. 164(2) below. The amendments made to this section by the Noise and Statutory Nuisance Act 1993 (c. 40) came into force on 5 January 1994: s. 12(1). The amendments made by the Environment Act 1995 (c. 25) came into force on 1 April 1996: S.I. 1996/186 save for the amendments made by sch. 22 which are not in force.

[10] **Case: section 79** *Network Housing Association Ltd v. Westminster City Council* [1995] Env LR 176.

[11] Local authority" defined by s. 79(7), (8) above.

[12] "Statutory nuisance" defined by s. 79(1) above.

[13] "Area" of a local authority defined by s. 79(8), (11) above.

[14] For provisions relating to notice see s. 160, p. 207 below.

(*a*) requiring the abatement of the nuisance or prohibiting or restricting its occurrence or recurrence;

(*b*) requiring the execution of such works, and the taking of such other steps, as may be necessary for any of those purposes,

and the notice shall specify the time or times within which the requirements of the notice are to be complied with.

(2) Subject to section 80A(1) below, the abatement notice[1] shall be served—

(*a*) except in a case falling within paragraph (b) or (c) below, on the person responsible[2] for the nuisance;

(*b*) where the nuisance arises from any defect of a structural character, on the owner of the premises[3];

(*c*) where the person responsible for the nuisance cannot be found or the nuisance has not yet occurred, on the owner or occupier of the premises.

(3) A person served with an abatement notice[4] may appeal against the notice to a magistrates' court or in Scotland, the sheriff[5] within the period of twenty-one days beginning with the date on which he was served with the notice.

(4) If a person on whom an abatement notice is served, without reasonable excuse, contravenes or fails to comply with any requirement or prohibition imposed by the notice, he shall be guilty of an offence.

(5) Except in a case falling within subsection (6) below, a person who commits an offence under subsection (4) above shall be liable on summary conviction to a fine not exceeding level 5 on the standard scale[6] together with a further fine of an amount equal to one-tenth of that level for each day on which the offence continues after the conviction.

(6) A person who commits an offence under subsection (4) above on industrial, trade or business premises[7] shall be liable on summary conviction to a fine not exceeding £20,000.

(7) Subject to subsection (8) below, in any proceedings for an offence under subsection (4) above in respect of a statutory nuisance it shall be a defence to prove that the best practicable means[8] were used to prevent, or to counteract the effects of, the nuisance.

(8) The defence under subsection (7) above is not available—

(*a*) in the case of a nuisance falling within paragraph (a), (d), (e), (f) or (g) of section 79(1) above except where the nuisance arises on industrial, trade or business premises;

(*aa*) in the case of a nuisance falling within paragraph (ga) of section 79(1) above except where the noise[9] is emitted from or caused by a vehicle, machinery or equipment[10] being used for industrial, trade or business purposes[11];

(*b*) in the case of a nuisance falling within paragraph (b) of section 79(1) above except where the smoke[12] is emitted from a chimney[13]; and

(*c*) in the case of a nuisance falling within paragraph (c) or (h) of section 79(1) above.

---

[1] Words "Subject to section 80A(1) below, the abatement notice" substituted by the Noise and Statutory Nuisance Act 1993 (c. 40), s. 3(2).

[2] "Person responsible" defined by s. 79(7) above.

[3] "Premises" defined by s. 79(7) above.

[4] Words "A person served with an abatement notice" substituted by the Noise and Statutory Nuisance Act 1993 (c. 40), s. 3(3).

[5] Words "or in Scotland, the sheriff" inserted by the Environment Act 1995 (c. 250), s. 107, sch. 17, para. 3.

[6] The current fine at level 5 on the standard scale is £5,000: Criminal Justice Act 1991 (c. 53), s. 17 (England and Wales); Criminal Procedure (Scotland) Act 1995 (c. 46), s. 225 (Scotland).

[7] "Industrial, trade or business premises" defined by s. 79(7) above.

[8] For the interpretation of "best practicable means" see s. 79(9) above.

[9] "Noise" defined by s. 79(7) above.

[10] "Equipment" defined by s. 79(7) above.

[11] Para. (aa) inserted by the Noise and Statutory Nuisance Act 1993 (c. 40), s. 3(4).

[12] "Smoke" defined by s. 79(7) above.

[13] "Chimney" defined by s. 79(7) above.

(9) In proceedings for an offence under subsection (4) above in respect of a statutory nuisance falling within paragraph (g) or (ga)[1] of section 79(1) above where the offence consists in contravening requirements imposed by virtue of subsection (1)(a) above it shall be a defence to prove—

(a) that the alleged offence was covered by a notice served under section 60 or a consent given under section 61 or 65 of the Control of Pollution Act 1974[2] (construction sites, etc); or

(b) where the alleged offence was committed at a time when the premises were subject to a notice under section 66 of that Act (noise reduction notice), that the level of noise emitted from the premises at that time was not such as to a constitute a contravention of the notice under that section; or

(c) where the alleged offence was committed at a time when the premises were not subject to a notice under section 66 of that Act, and when a level fixed under section 67 of that Act (new buildings liable to abatement order) applied to the premises, that the level of noise emitted from the premises at that time did not exceed that level.

(10) Paragraphs (b) and (c) of subsection (9) above apply whether or not the relevant notice was subject to appeal at the time when the offence was alleged to have been committed[3,4].

*Abatement notice in respect of noise in street*

**80A.** (1) In the case of a statutory nuisance[5] within section 79(1)(ga)[6] above that—

(a) has not yet occurred, or

(b) arises from noise[7] emitted from or caused by an unattended vehicle or unattended machinery or equipment[8],

the abatement notice[9] shall be served in accordance with subsection (2) below.

(2) The notice shall be served—

(a) where the person responsible[10] for the vehicle, machinery or equipment can be found, on that person;

(b) where that person cannot be found or where the local authority[11] determines that this paragraph should apply, by fixing the notice to the vehicle, machinery or equipment.

(3) Where—

(a) an abatement notice is served in accordance with subsection (2)(b) above by virtue of a determination of the local authority, and

(b) the person responsible for the vehicle, machinery or equipment can be found and served with a copy of the notice within an hour of the notice being fixed to the vehicle, machinery or equipment,

a copy of the notice shall be served on that person accordingly.

(4) Where an abatement notice is served in accordance with subsection (2)(b) above by virtue of a determination of the local authority, the notice shall state that, if a copy of the notice is subsequently served under subsection (3) above, the time specified in the notice as the time within which its requirements are to be complied with is extended by such further period as is specified in the notice.

---

[1] Words "or (ga)" inserted by the Noise and Statutory Nuisance Act 1993 (c. 40), s. 3(5).

[2] 1974 c. 40.

[3] This section came into force on 1 January 1991: s. 164(2) below. The amendments made to this section by the Noise and Statutory Nuisance Act 1993 (c. 40) came into force on 5 January 1994: s. 12(1). The amendment made by the Environment Act 1995 (c. 25) came into force on 1 April 1996: S.I. 1996/186.

[4] Cases: section 80 *Aitken v South Hams District Council* [1994] Env LR 373; *East Northamptonshire District Council v*

*Brian Fossett* [1994] Env LR 388. *R v Tunbridge Wells Justices, ex p. Tunbridge Wells BC* [1996] Env LR 88; *Sterling Homes v Birmingham City Council* [1996] Env LR 121; *R v Carrick DC, ex p. Shelley: The Times 15 April 1996.*

[5] "Statutory nuisance" defined by s. 79(1), p. 187 above.

[6] P. 187 above.

[7] "Noise" defined by s. 79(7), p. 189 above.

[8] "Equipment" defined by s. 79(7), p. 188 above.

[9] For "abatement notice" see s. 80 above.

[10] "Person responsible" defined by s. 79(7), p. 189 above.

[11] "Local authority" defined by s. 79(7), (8), p. 188 above.

(5) Where an abatement notice is served in accordance with subsection (2)(b) above, the person responsible for the vehicle, machinery or equipment may appeal against the notice under section 80(3) above as if he had been served with the notice on the date on which it was fixed to the vehicle, machinery or equipment.

(6) Section 80(4) above shall apply in relation to a person on whom a copy of an abatement notice is served under subsection (3) above as if the copy were the notice itself.

(7) A person who removes or interferes with a notice fixed to a vehicle, machinery or equipment in accordance with subsection (2)(b) above shall be guilty of an offence, unless he is the person responsible for the vehicle, machinery or equipment or he does so with the authority of that person.

(8) A person who commits an offence under subsection (7) above shall be liable on summary conviction to a fine not exceeding level 3 on the standard scale[1].[2]

*Supplementary provisions*

81. (1) Subject to subsection (1A) below, where[3] more than one person is responsible[4] for a statutory nuisance[5] section 80 above shall apply to each of those persons whether or not what any one of them is responsible for would by itself amount to a nuisance.

(1A) In relation to a statutory nuisance within section 79(1)(ga) above[6] for which more than one person is responsible (whether or not what any one of those persons is responsible for would by itself amount to such a nuisance), section 80(2)(a) above shall apply with the substitution of "any one of the persons" for "the person".

(1B) In relation to a statutory nuisance within section 79(1)(ga) above caused by noise[7] emitted from or caused by an unattended vehicle or unattended machinery or equipment[8] for which more than one person is responsible, section 80A above shall apply with the substitution—

(a) in subsection (2)(a), of "any of the persons" for "the person" and of "one such person" for "that person",

(b) in subsection (2)(b), of "such a person" for "that person",

(c) in subsection (3), of "any of the persons" for "the person" and of "one such person" for "that person",

(d) in subsection (5), of "any person" for "the person", and

(e) in subsection (7), of "a person" for "the person" and of "such a person" for "that person".[9]

(2) Where a statutory nuisance which exists or has occurred within the area of a local authority[10], or which has affected any part of that area, appears to the local authority to be wholly or partly caused by some act or default committed or taking place outside the area, the local authority may act under section 80 above[11] as if the act or default were wholly within that area, except that any appeal shall be heard by a magistrates' court or in Scotland, the sheriff[12] having jurisdiction where the act or default is alleged to have taken place.

(3) Where an abatement notice[13] has not been complied with the local authority may, whether or not they take proceedings for an offence or, in Scotland, whether or not proceedings have been

[1] The current fine at level 3 on the standard scale is £1,000: Criminal Justice Act 1991 (c. 53), s. 17 (England and Wales); Criminal Procedure (Scotland) Act 1995 (c. 46), s. 225 (Scotland).
[2] This section inserted by the Noise and Statutory Nuisance Act 1993 (c. 40), s. 3(6). This amendment came into force on 5 January 1994: s. 12(1).
[3] Words "Subject to subsection (1A) below, where" substituted by the Noise and Statutory Nuisance Act 1993 (c. 40), s. 4(2).
[4] "Person responsible" defined by s. 79(7), p. 189 above.
[5] "Statutory nuisance" defined by s. 79(1), p. 187 above.
[6] P. 187 above.
[7] "Noise" defined by s. 79(7), p. 189 above.
[8] "Equipment" defined by s. 79(7), p. 188 above.
[9] Subsections (1A) and (1B) inserted by the Noise and Statutory Nuisance Act 1993 (c. 40), s. 4(3).
[10] "Local authority" defined by s. 79(7), (8), p. 188 above; "area" of a local authority defined by s. 79(8), (11), p. 188 above.
[11] P. 190 above.
[12] Words "or in Scotland, the sheriff" inserted by the Environment Act 1995 (c. 25), s. 107, sch. 17, para. 4(a).
[13] For "abatement notice" see s. 80, p. 190 above.

taken for an offence[1], under section 80(4) above, abate the nuisance and do whatever may be necessary in execution of the notice.

(4)  Any expenses reasonably incurred by a local authority in abating, or preventing the recurrence of, a statutory nuisance under subsection (3) above may be recovered by them from the person by whose act or default the nuisance was caused and, if that person is the owner of the premises[2], from any person who is for the time being the owner thereof; and the court or sheriff[3] may apportion the expenses between persons by whose acts or defaults the nuisance is caused in such manner as the court consider or sheriff considers[4] fair and reasonable.

(5)  If a local authority is of opinion that proceedings for an offence under section 80(4) above would afford an inadequate remedy in the case of any statutory nuisance, they may, subject to subsection (6) below, take proceedings in the High Court or, in Scotland, in any court of competent jurisdiction[5], for the purpose of securing the abatement, prohibition or restriction of the nuisance, and the proceedings shall be maintainable notwithstanding the local authority have suffered no damage from the nuisance.

(6)  In any proceedings under subsection (5) above in respect of a nuisance falling within paragraph (g) or (ga)[6] of section 79(1) above, it shall be a defence to prove that the noise was authorised by a notice under section 60 or a consent under section 61 (construction sites) of the Control of Pollution Act 1974[7].

(7)  The further supplementary provisions in Schedule 3 to this Act[8] shall have effect[9].

*Expenses recoverable from owner to be a charge on premises*

81A.  (1)  Where any expenses are recoverable under section 81(4) above from a person who is the owner[10] of the premises[11] there mentioned and the local authority[12] serves a notice on him under this section—

  (a)  the expenses shall carry interest, at such reasonable rate as the local authority may determine, from the date of service of the notice until the whole amount is paid, and

  (b)  subject to the following provisions of this section, the expenses and accrued interest shall be a charge on the premises.

(2)  A notice served under this section shall—

  (a)  specify the amount of the expenses that the local authority claims is recoverable,

  (b)  state the effect of subsection (1) above and the rate of interest determined by the local authority under that subsection, and

  (c)  state the effect of subsections (4) to (6) below.

(3)  On the date on which a local authority serves a notice[13] on a person under this section the authority shall also serve a copy of the notice on every other person who, to the knowledge of the authority, has an interest in the premises capable of being affected by the charge.

(4)  Subject to any order under subsection (7)(b) or (c) below, the amount of any expenses specified in a notice under this section and the accrued interest shall be a charge on the premises—

---

[1] Words "or, in Scotland, whether or not proceedings have been taken for an offence," inserted by the Environment Act 1995 (c. 25), s. 107, sch. 17, para. 4(b).

[2] "Premises" defined by s. 79(7), p. 189 above.

[3] Words "or sheriff" inserted by the Environment Act 1995 (c. 25), s. 107, sch. 17, para. 4(c).

[4] Words "or sheriff considers" inserted by the Environment Act 1995 (c. 25), s. 107, sch. 17, para. 4(c).

[5] Words "or, in Scotland, in any court of competent jurisdiction," inserted by the Environment Act 1995 (c. 25), s. 107, sch. 17, para. 4(d).

[6] Words "or (ga)" inserted by the Noise and Statutory Nuisance Act 1993 (c. 40), s. 4(4).

[7] 1974 c. 40.

[8] P. 224 below.

[9] See also the Noise Act 1996 (c. 37), s. 10. This section came into force on 1 January 1991: s. 164(2) below. The amendments made to this section by the Noise and Statutory Nuisance Act 1993 (c. 40) came into force on 5 January 1994: s. 12(1). The amendments made by the Environment Act 1995 (c. 25) came into force on 1 April 1996: S.I. 1996/186.

[10] "Owner" defined by subsection (9) below.

[11] See subsection (9) below.

[12] "Local authority" defined by s. 79(7), (8), p. 188 above.

[13] For provisions relating to notice see s. 160, p. 207 below.

(*a*)  as from the end of the period of twenty-one days beginning with the date of service of the notice, or

(*b*)  where an appeal is brought under subsection (6) below, as from the final determination of the appeal,

until the expenses and interest are recovered.

(5)  For the purposes of subsection (4) above, the withdrawal of an appeal has the same effect as a final determination of the appeal.

(6)  A person served with a notice or copy of a notice under this section may appeal against the notice to the county court within the period of twenty-one days beginning with the date of service.

(7)  On such an appeal the court may—

(*a*)  confirm the notice without modification,

(*b*)  order that the notice is to have effect with the substitution of a different amount for the amount originally specified in it, or

(*c*)  order that the notice is to be of no effect.

(8)  A local authority shall, for the purpose of enforcing a charge under this section, have all the same powers and remedies under the Law of Property 1925[1], and otherwise, as if it were a mortgagee by deed having powers of sale and lease, of accepting surrenders of leases and of appointing a receiver.

(9)  In this section—

"owner", in relation to any premises, means a person (other than a mortgagee not in possession) who, whether in his own right or as trustee for any other person, is entitled to receive the rack rent of the premises or, where the premises are not let at a rack rent, would be so entitled if they were so let, and

"premises" does not include a vessel.

(10)  This section does not apply to Scotland[2].[3]

........................................................................................................................................................................

*Payment of expenses by instalments*

**81B.**  (1)  Where any expenses are a charge on premises under section 81A above, the local authority[4] may by order declare the expenses to be payable with interest by instalments within the specified period, until the whole amount is paid.

(2)  In subsection (1) above—

"interest" means interest at the rate determined by the authority under section 81A(1) above, and

"the specified period" means such period of thirty years or less from the date of service of the notice under section 81A above as is specified in the order.

(3)  Subject to subsection (5) below, the instalments and interest, or any part of them, may be recovered from the owner or occupier for the time being of the premises.

(4)  Any sums recovered from an occupier may be deducted by him from the rent of the premises.

(5)  An occupier shall not be required to pay at any one time any sum greater than the aggregate of—

(*a*)  the amount that was due from him on account of rent at the date on which he was served with a demand from the local authority together with a notice requiring him not to pay rent to his landlord without deducting the sum demanded, and

---

[1] 1925 c. 20.

[2] Subsection (10) inserted by the Environment Act 1995 (c. 25), s. 107, sch. 17., para. 5 on 1 April 1996: S.I. 1986/186.

[3] This section inserted by the Noise and Statutory Nuisance

Act 1993 (c. 40), s. 10(2). This amendment came into force on 5 January 1994: s. 12(1).

[4] "Local authority" defined by s. 79(7), (8), p. 188 above.

(b)  the amount that has become due from him on account of rent since that date.

(6)  This section does not apply to Scotland[1,2]

---

*Summary proceedings by persons aggrieved by statutory nuisances*

**82.** (1) A magistrates' court may act under this section on a complaint or, in Scotland, the sheriff may act under this section on a summary application,[3] made by any person on the ground that he is aggrieved by the existence of a statutory nuisance[4].

(2) If the magistrates' court or, in Scotland, the sheriff[5] is satisfied that the alleged nuisance exists, or that although abated it is likely to recur on the same premises[6] or, in the case of a nuisance within section 79(1)(ga) above[7], in the same street[8] or, in Scotland, road[9], the court or the sheriff[10] shall make an order for either or both of the following purposes—

(a)  requiring the defendant or, in Scotland, defender[11] to abate the nuisance, within a time specified in the order, and to execute any works necessary for that purpose;

(b)  prohibiting a recurrence of the nuisance, and requiring the defendant or defender[12], within a time specified in the order, to execute any works necessary to prevent the recurrence;

and, in England and Wales,[13] may also impose on the defendant a fine not exceeding level 5 on the standard scale[14].

(3) If the magistrates' court or the sheriff[15] is satisfied that the alleged nuisance exists and is such as, in the opinion of the court or of the sheriff[16], to render premises unfit for human habitation, an order under subsection (2) above may prohibit the use of the premises for human habitation until the premises are, to the satisfaction of the court or of the sheriff, rendered fit for that purpose.

(4) Proceedings for an order under subsection (2) above shall be brought—

(a)  except in a case falling within paragraph (b), (c) or (d) below[17], against the person responsible[18] for the nuisance;

(b)  where the nuisance arises from any defect of a structural character, against the owner of the premises[19];

(c)  where the person responsible for the nuisance cannot be found, against the owner or occupier of the premises;

(d)  in the case of a statutory nuisance within section 79(1)(ga) above caused by noise[20] emitted from or caused by an unattended vehicle or unattended machinery or equipment[21], against the person responsible for the vehicle, machinery or equipment[22].

---

[1] Subsection (6) inserted by the Environment Act 1995 (c. 25), s. 107, sch. 17, para. 5 on 1 April 1996: S.I. 1996/186.

[2] This section inserted by the Noise and Statutory Nuisance Act 1993 (c. 40), s. 10(2). This amendment came into force on 5 January 1994: s. 12(1).

[3] Words "or, in Scotland, the sheriff may act under this section on a summary application," inserted by the Environment Act 1995 (c. 25), s. 107, sch. 17, para. 6(a).

[4] "Statutory nuisance" defined by s. 79(1), p. 187 above.

[5] Words "or, in Scotland, the sheriff" inserted by the Environment Act 1995 (c. 25), s. 107, sch. 17, para. 6(b)(i).

[6] "Premises" defined by s. 79(7), p. 189 above.

[7] P. 187 above.

[8] "Street" defined by s. 79(7), p. 189 above. Words "or, in the case of a nuisance within section 79(1)(ga) above, in the same street" inserted by the Noise and Statutory Nuisance Act 1993 (c. 40), s. 5(2).

[9] "Road" defined by s. 79(7), p. 189 above. Words "or, in Scotland, road" inserted by the Environment Act 1995 (c. 25), s. 107, sch. 17, para. 6(b)(ii).

[10] Words "or the sheriff" inserted by the Environment Act 1995 (c. 25), s. 107, sch. 17, para. 6(b)(iii).

[11] Words "or, in Scotland, defender" inserted by the Environment Act 1995 (c. 25), s. 107, sch. 17, para. 6(b)(iv).

[12] Words "or defender" inserted by the Environment Act 1995 (c. 25), s. 107, sch. 17, para. 6(b)(v).

[13] Words "in England and Wales" inserted by the Environment Act 1995 (c. 25), s. 107, sch. 17, para. 6(b)(vi).

[14] The current fine at level 5 on the standard scale is £5,000: Criminal Justice Act 1991 (c. 53), s. 17 (England and Wales).

[15] Words "or the sheriff" inserted by the Environment Act 1995 (c. 25), s. 107, sch. 17, para. 6(c).

[16] Words "or of the sheriff" in this subsection inserted by the Environment Act 1995 (c. 25), s. 107, sch. 17, para. 6(c).

[17] Words "paragraph (b), (c) or (d) below" substituted by the Noise and Statutory Nuisance Act 1993 (c. 40), s. 5(3)(a).

[18] "Person responsible" defined by s. 79(7), p. 189 above.

[19] "Premises" defined by s. 79(7), p. 189 above.

[20] "Noise" defined by s. 79(7), p. 189 above.

[21] "Equipment" defined by s. 79(7), p. 188 above.

[22] Para. (d) inserted by the Noise and Statutory Nuisance Act 1993 (c. 40), s. 5(3)(b).

**(5)** Subject to subsection (5A) below, where[1] more than one person is responsible for a statutory nuisance, subsections (1) to (4) above shall apply to each of those persons whether or not what any one of them is responsible for would by itself amount to a nuisance.

**(5A)** In relation to a statutory nuisance within section 79(1)(ga) above for which more than one person is responsible (whether or not what any one of those persons is responsible for would by itself amount to such a nuisance), subsection (4)(a) above shall apply with the substitution of "each person responsible for the nuisance who can be found" for "the person responsible for the nuisance".

**(5B)** In relation to a statutory nuisance within section 79(1)(ga) above caused by noise emitted from or caused by an unattended vehicle or unattended machinery or equipment for which more than one person is responsible, subsection (4)(d) above shall apply with the substitution of "any person" for "the person"[2].

**(6)** Before instituting proceedings for an order under subsection (2) above against any person, the person aggrieved by the nuisance shall give to that person such notice in writing of his intention to bring the proceedings as is applicable to proceedings in respect of a nuisance of that description and the notice shall specify the matter complained of.

**(7)** The notice of the bringing of proceedings in respect of a statutory nuisance required by subsection (6) above which is applicable is—

(*a*)  in the case of a nuisance falling within paragraph (g) or (ga)[3] of section 79(1) above, not less than three days' notice; and

(*b*)  in the case of a nuisance of any other description, not less than twenty-one days' notice;

but the Secretary of State may, by order, provide that this subsection shall have effect as if such period as is specified in the order were the minimum period of notice applicable to any description of statutory nuisance specified in the order.

**(8)** A person who, without reasonable excuse, contravenes any requirement or prohibition imposed by an order under subsection (2) above shall be guilty of an offence and liable on summary conviction to a fine not exceeding level 5 on the standard scale together[4] with a further fine of an amount equal to one-tenth of that level for each day on which the offence continues after the conviction.

**(9)** Subject to subsection (10) below, in any proceedings for an offence under subsection (8) above in respect of a statutory nuisance it shall be a defence to prove that the best practicable means[5] were used to prevent, or to counteract the effects of, the nuisance.

**(10)** The defence under subsection (9) above is not available—

(*a*)  in the case of a nuisance falling within paragraph (a), (d), (e), (f) or (g) of section 79(1) above except where the nuisance arises on industrial, trade or business premises[6];

(*aa*)  in the case of a nuisance falling within paragraph (ga) of section 79(1) above except where the noise is emitted from or caused by a vehicle, machinery or equipment being used for industrial, trade or business purposes[7];

(*b*)  in the case of a nuisance falling within paragraph (b) of section 79(1) above except where the smoke[8] is emitted from a chimney[9];

(*c*)  in the case of a nuisance falling within paragraph (c) or (h) of section 79(1) above; and

---

[1] Words "Subject to subsection (5A) below, where" substituted by the Noise and Statutory Nuisance Act 1993 (c. 40), s. 5(4).

[2] Subsections (5A) and (5B) inserted by the Noise and Statutory Nuisance Act 1993 (c. 40), s. 5(5).

[3] Words "or (ga)" inserted by the Noise and Statutory Nuisance Act 1993 (c. 40), s. 5(6).

[4] The current fine at level 5 on the standard scale is £5,000: Criminal Justice Act 1991 (c. 53), s. 17 (England and Wales); Criminal Procedure (Scotland) Act 1995 (c. 46), s. 225

(Scotland).

[5] For the interpretation of "best practicable means" see s. 79(9) above.

[6] "Industrial, trade or business premises" defined by s. 79(7) above.

[7] Para. (aa) inserted by the Noise and Statutory Nuisance Act 1993 (c. 40), s. 5(7).

[8] "Smoke" defined by s. 79(7) above.

[9] "Chimney" defined by s. 79(7) above.

(*d*) in the case of a nuisance which is such as to render the premises unfit for human habitation.

(11) If a person is convicted of an offence under subsection (8) above, a magistrates' court or the sheriff[1] may, after giving the local authority[2] in whose area[3] the nuisance has occurred an opportunity of being heard, direct the authority to do anything which the person convicted was required to do by the order to which the conviction relates.

(12) Where on the hearing of proceedings for an order under subsection (2) above it is proved that the alleged nuisance existed at the date of the making of the complaint or summary application[4], then, whether or not at the date of the hearing it still exists or is likely to recur, the court or the sheriff[5] shall order the defendant or defender (or defendants or defenders[6] in such proportions as appears fair and reasonable) to pay to the person bringing the proceedings such amount as the court or the sheriff considers reasonably sufficient to compensate him for any expenses properly incurred by him in the proceedings.

(13) If it appears to the magistrates' court or to the sheriff[7] that neither the person responsible for the nuisance nor the owner or occupier of the premises or (as the case may be) the person responsible for the vehicle, machinery or equipment[8] can be found the court or the sheriff[9] may, after giving the local authority in whose area the nuisance has occurred an opportunity of being heard, direct the authority to do anything which the court or the sheriff would have ordered that person to do[10,11].

83. *Repealed by the Environment Act 1995 (c. 25), s. 120, sch. 24. This amendment came into force on 1 April 1996: S.I. 1996/186.*

## Termination of existing controls over offensive trades and businesses

*Termination of Public Health Act controls over offensive trades etc.*

84. (1) Where a person carries on, in the area or part of the area of any local authority[12]—

(*a*) in England or Wales, a trade[13] which—

(i) is an offensive trade[14] within the meaning of section 107 of the Public Health Act 1936[15] in that area or part of that area, and

(ii) constitutes a prescribed process[16] designated for local control for the carrying on of which an authorisation is required under section 6 of this Act[17]; or

(*b*) in Scotland, a business which—

(i) is mentioned in section 32(1) of the Public Health (Scotland) Act 1897[18] (or is an offensive business by virtue of that section) in that area or part of that area; and

[1] Words "or the sheriff" inserted by the Environment Act 1995 (c. 25), s. 107, sch. 17, para. 6(d).
[2] "Local authority" defined by s. 79(7), (8), p. 188 above.
[3] "Area" of a local authority defined by s. 79(8), (11), p. 189 above.
[4] Words "or summary application" inserted by the Environment Act 1995 (c. 25), s. 107, sch. 17, para. 6(e).
[5] Words "or the sheriff" in this subsection inserted by the Environment Act 1995 (c. 25), s. 107, sch. 17, para. 6(e).
[6] Words "defendant or defender (or defendants or defenders" substituted by the Environment Act 1995 (c. 25), s. 107, sch. 17, para. 6(e).
[7] Words "or to the sheriff" inserted by the Environment Act 1995 (c. 25), s. 107, sch. 17, para. 6(f).
[8] Words "or (as the case may be) the person responsible for the vehicle, machinery or equipment" inserted by the Noise and Statutory Nuisance Act 1993 (c. 40), s. 5(8).
[9] Words "or the sheriff" in this subsection inserted by the Environment Act 1995 (c. 25), s. 107, sch. 17, para. 6(f).

[10] This section came into force on 1 January 1991: s. 164(2) below. The amendments made to this section by the Noise and Statutory Nuisance Act 1993 (c. 40) came into force on 5 January 1994: s. 12(1). The amendments made by the Environment Act 1995 (c. 25) came into force on 1 April 1996: S.I. 1996/186.
[11] **Cases: section 82** *British Waterways Board v Norman* [1994] COD 262; *Botross v Hammersmith and Fulham London Borough Council*: [1995] Env LR 217; *R v Highbury Corner Magistrates' Court, ex parte Edwards* [1994] Env LR 215; *Carr v Hackney London Borough Council*: [1995] Env LR 372.
[12] "Local authority" defined by s. 79(7), (8), p. 188 above; "area" of a local authority defined by s. 79(8), (11), p. 189 above.
[13] For "trade" see subsection (5) below.
[14] For "offensive trade" see subsection (5) below.
[15] 1936 c. 49.
[16] For "prescribed process" see subsection (5) below.
[17] P. 95 above.
[18] 1897 c. 38.

> (ii) constitutes a prescribed process[1] designated for local control for the carrying on of which an authorisation is required under the said section 6[2],

subsection (2) below shall have effect in relation to that trade or business as from the date on which an authorisation is granted under section 6 of this Act or, if that person has not applied for such an authorisation within the period allowed under section 2(1) above for making applications under that section, as from the end of that period.

(2) Where this subsection applies in relation to the trade or business carried on by any person—

(*a*) nothing in section 107 of the Public Health Act 1936 or in section 32 of the Public Health (Scotland) Act 1897 shall apply in relation to it, and

(*b*) no byelaws or further byelaws made under section 108(2) of the said Act of 1936, or under subsection (2) of the said section 32, with respect to a trade or business of that description shall apply in relation to it;

but without prejudice to the continuance of, and imposition of any penalty in, any proceedings under the said section 107 or the said section 32 which were instituted before the date as from which this subsection has effect in relation to the trade or business.

(3) Subsection (23)(b) above shall apply in relation to the trade of fish frying as it applies in relation to an offensive trade.

(4) When the Secretary of State considers it expedient to do so, having regard to the operation of Part I and the preceding provisions of this Part of this Act in relation to offensive trades or businesses, he may by order repeal—

(*a*) sections 107 and 108 of the Public Health Act 1936; and

(*b*) section 32 of the Public Health (Scotland) Act 1897;

and different days may be so appointed in relation to trades or businesses which constitute prescribed processes and those which do not.

(5) In this section—

"prescribed process" has the same meaning as in Part I of this Act[3]; and

"offensive trade" or "trade" has the same meaning as in section 107 of the Public Health Act 1936[4].

---

**85.** *Repealed by the Clean Air Act 1993 (c. 11), s. 67(3), sch. 6. This amendment came into force on 27 August 1993: s. 68(2).*

---

# PART IV: Litter etc.

*Not Reproduced.*

---

# PART V: Amendment of the Radioactive Substances Act 1960

This Part has been repealed by the Radioactive Substances Act 1993 (c. 12), s. 50, sch. 6, pt. I. The Radioactive Substances Act 1993, which consolidates enactments relating to radioactive substances, including this Part, is at p. 381 below.

---

[1] For "prescribed process" see subsection (5) below.
[2] P. 95 above.
[3] Under s. 1(5), p. 89 above, "prescribed process" means a process prescribed under s. 2(1), p. 91 above.
[4] This section came into force on 1 January 1991: s. 164(2) below.

# PART VI: Genetically Modified Organisms

*Not Reproduced.*

# PART VII: Nature Conservation in Great Britain and Countryside Matters in Wales

This Part, and schedules 6, 7 and 11, are set out in the companion volume, *A Manual of Nature Conservation Law*, edited by Michael Fry (Oxford, 1995) at page 228.

# PART VIII: Miscellaneous

## *Other controls on substances, articles or waste*

*Power to prohibit or restrict the importation, use, supply or storage of injurious substances or articles*

**140.** (1) The Secretary of State may by regulations prohibit or restrict—

(*a*)  the importation into and the landing and unloading in the United Kingdom,

(*b*)  the use for any purpose,

(*c*)  the supply for any purpose, and

(*d*)  the storage,

of any specified[1] substance[2] or article if he considers it appropriate to do so for the purpose of preventing the substance or article from causing pollution of the environment[3] or harm to human health or to the health of animals or plants[4].

(2)  Any such prohibition or restriction may apply—

(*a*)  in all, or only in specified, areas;

(*b*)  in all, or only in specified, circumstances or if conditions imposed by the regulations are not complied with; and

(*c*)  to all, or only to specified descriptions of, persons.

(3)  Regulations under this section may—

(*a*)  confer on the Secretary of State power to direct that any substance or article whose use, supply or storage is prohibited or restricted is to be treated as waste or controlled waste of any description and in relation to any such substance or article—

(i)  to apply, with or without modification, specified provisions of Part II[5]; or

(ii)  to direct that it be disposed of or treated in accordance with the direction;

(*b*)  confer on the Secretary of State power, where a substance or article has been imported, landed or unloaded in contravention of a prohibition or restriction imposed under subsection (1)(a) above, to require that the substance or article be disposed of or treated in or removed from the United Kingdom;

---

[1] "Specified" defined by subsection (11) below.
[2] "Substance" defined by subsection (11) below.
[3] "The environment" defined by subsection (11) below.

[4] A list of the regulations made under this section is at p. 797 below.
[5] P. 111 above.

(c)  confer powers corresponding to those conferred by section 17 above on persons authorised for any purpose of the regulations by the Secretary of State or any local or other authority; and

(d)  include such other incidental and supplemental, and such transitional provisions, as the Secretary of State considers appropriate.

**(4)** The Secretary of State may, by regulations under this section, direct that, for the purposes of any power conferred on him under subsection (3)(b) above, any prohibition or restriction on the importation into or the landing and unloading in the United Kingdom imposed—

(a)  by or under any Community instrument, or

(b)  by or under any enactment,

shall be treated as imposed under subsection (1)(a) above and any power conferred on him under subsection (3)(b) above shall be exercisable accordingly.

**(5)** The Secretary of State may by order establish a committee to give him advice in relation to the exercise of the power to make regulations under this section and Schedule 12 to this Act[1] shall have effect in relation to it[2].

**(6)** Subject to subsection (7) below, it shall be the duty of the Secretary of State before he makes any regulations under this section other than regulations under subsection (4) above—

(a)  to consult the committee constituted under subsection (5) above about the proposed regulations;

(b)  having consulted the committee, to publish in the London Gazette and, if the regulations apply in Scotland or Northern Ireland, the Edinburgh Gazette, or, as the case may be, Belfast Gazette and in any other publication which he considers appropriate, a notice indicating the effect of the proposed regulations and specifying—

  (i)   the date on which it is proposed that the regulations will come into force;

  (ii)  a place where a draft of the proposed regulations may be inspected free of charge by members of the public during office hours; and

  (iii) a period of not less than fourteen days, beginning with the date on which the notice is first published, during which representations in writing may be made to the Secretary of State about the proposed regulations; and

(c)  to consider any representations which are made to him in accordance with the notice.

**(7)** The Secretary of State may make regulations under this section in relation to any substance or article without observing the requirements of subsection (6) above where it appears to him that there is an imminent risk, if those requirements are observed, that serious pollution of the environment will be caused.

**(8)** The Secretary of State may, after performing the duty imposed on him by subsection (6) above with respect to any proposed regulations, make the regulations either—

(a)  in the form of the draft mentioned in subsection (6)(b) above, or

(b)  in that form with such modifications as he considers appropriate;

but the Secretary of State shall not make any regulations incorporating modifications unless he is of opinion that it is appropriate for the requirements of subsection (6) above to be disregarded.

**(9)** Regulations under this section may provide that a person who contravenes or fails to comply with a specified provision of the regulations or causes or permits another person to contravene or fail to comply with a specified provision of the regulations commits an offence and may prescribe the maximum penalty for the offence.

---

[1]  P. 227 below.
[2]  The Advisory Committee on Hazardous Substances Order 1991, S.I. 1991/1487, established the Advisory Committee on Hazardous Substances to give the Secretary of State advice in relation to the exercise of the power to make regulations under this section.

**(10)** No offence under the regulations shall be made punishable with imprisonment for more than two years or punishable on summary conviction with a fine exceeding level 5 on the standard scale[1] (if not calculated on a daily basis) or, in the case of a continuing offence, exceeding one-tenth of the level on the standard scale specified as the maximum penalty for the original offence.

**(11)** In this section—

"the environment" means the air, water and land, or any of those media, and the medium of air includes the air within buildings and the air within other natural or man-made structures above or below ground;

"specified" means specified in the regulations; and

"substance" means any natural or artificial substance, whether in solid or liquid form or in the form of a gas or vapour and it includes mixtures of substances[2].

*Power to prohibit or restrict the importation or exportation of waste*

**141.** **(1)** The Secretary of State may, for the purpose of preventing any risk of pollution of the environment[3] or of harm[4] to human health arising from waste[5] being imported or exported or of conserving the facilities or resources for dealing with waste, make regulations prohibiting or restricting, or providing for the prohibition or restriction of—

(*a*) the importation into and the landing and unloading in the United Kingdom[6], or

(*b*) the exportation, or the loading for exportation, from the United Kingdom,

of waste of any description.

**(2)** Regulations under this section may make different provision for different descriptions of waste or waste of any description in different circumstances.

**(3)** Regulations under this section may, as respects any description of waste, confer or impose on waste regulation authorities[7] or any of them such functions in relation to the importation of waste as appear to be appropriate to the Secretary of State, subject to such limitations and conditions as are specified in the regulations.

**(4)** Regulations under this section may confer or impose on waste regulation authorities or any of them functions of enforcing any of the regulations on behalf of the Secretary of State whether or not the functions fall within subsection (3) above.

**(5)** Regulations under this section may—

(*a*) as respects functions conferred or imposed on waste regulation authorities—

(i) make them exercisable in relation to individual consignments or consignments in a series by the same person but not in relation to consignments or descriptions of consignments generally.

(ii) *Repealed by the Environment Act 1995 (c. 25), s. 120, sch. 22, para. 90, sch. 24. This amendment came into force on 1 April 1996: S.I. 1996/186.*

(*b*) impose or provide for the imposition of prohibitions either absolutely or only if conditions or procedures prescribed in or under the regulations are not complied with;

(*c*) impose duties to be complied with before, on or after any importation or exportation of waste by persons who are, or are to be, consignors, consignees, carriers or holders of the waste or any waste derived from it;

(*d*) confer powers corresponding to those conferred by section 69(3) above;

[1] The current fine at level 5 on the standard scale is £5,000: Criminal Justice Act 1991 (c. 53), s. 17 (England and Wales); Criminal Procedure (Scotland) Act 1995 (c. 46), s. 225 (Scotland).
[2] This section came into force on 1 January 1991: s. 164(2) below.
[3] "The environment" defined by subsection (6) below.
[4] "Harm" defined by subsection (6) below.
[5] For "waste" see subsection (6) below.
[6] "The United Kingdom" defined by subsection (6) below.
[7] For "waste regulation authority" see subsection (6) below.

(e)  provide for appeals to the Secretary of State from determinations made by authorities under the regulations;

(f)  provide for the keeping by the Secretary of State, waste regulation authorities and waste collection authorities[1] of public registers of information relating to the importation and exportation of waste and for the transmission of such information between any of those persons;

(g)  create offences, subject to the limitation that no offence shall be punishable with imprisonment for more than two years or punishable on summary conviction with imprisonment for more than six months or a fine exceeding level 5 on the standard scale[2] (if not calculated on a daily basis) or, in the case of a continuing offence, exceeding one-tenth of the level on the standard scale specified as the maximum penalty for the original offence.

(6)  In this section—

"the environment" means land, water and air or any of them;

"harm" includes offence to any of man's senses;

"waste", "waste collection authority", and "waste regulation authority" have the same meaning as in Part II[3]; and

"the United Kingdom" includes its territorial sea.

(7)  In the application of this section to Northern Ireland and the territorial sea of the United Kingdom adjacent to Northern Ireland "waste regulation authority" means a district council established under the Local Government Act (Northern Ireland) 1972[4].[5]

*Powers to obtain information about potentially hazardous substances*

142.  (1)  The Secretary of State may, for the purpose of assessing their potential for causing pollution of the environment[6] or harm to human health, by regulations make provision for and in connection with the obtaining of relevant information[7] relating to substances[8] which may be specified by him by order for the purposes of this section.

(2)  The Secretary of State shall not make an order under subsection (1) above specifying any substance—

(a)  which was first supplied in any member State on or after 18th September 1981; or

(b)  in so far as it is a regulated substance for the purposes of any relevant enactment[9].

(3)  The Secretary of State shall not make an order under subsection (1) above specifying any substance without consulting the committee established under section 140(5)[10] except where it appears to him that information about the substance needs to be obtained urgently under this section.

(4)  Regulations under this section may—

(a)  prescribe the descriptions of relevant information which are to be furnished under this section in relation to specified substances;

(b)  impose requirements on manufacturers, importers or suppliers generally to furnish information prescribed under paragraph (a) above;

(c)  provide for the imposition of requirements on manufacturers, importers or suppliers generally to furnish relevant information relating to which information has been furnished in pursuance of paragraph (b) above;

[1]  For "waste collection authority" see subsection (6) below.
[2]  The current fine at level 5 on the standard scale is £5,000: Criminal Justice Act 1991 (c. 53), s. 17 (England and Wales); Criminal Procedure (Scotland) Act 1995 (c. 46), s. 225 (Scotland).
[3]  "Waste" is defined by s. 75, p. 159 above; for "waste regulation authority" see s. 30(1), p. 113 above, and subsection (7) below; "waste collection authority" is defined by s. 30(3), p. 113 above.
[4]  1972 c. 9 (N.I.).
[5]  This section came into force on 1 January 1991: s. 164(2) below.
[6]  "The environment" defined by subsection (6) below.
[7]  "Relevant information" defined by subsection (6) below.
[8]  "Substance" defined by subsection (6) below.
[9]  For "regulated substances" and "relevant enactment" see subsection (7) below.
[10]  P. 201 above.

(*d*) provide for the imposition of requirements on particular manufacturers, importers or suppliers to furnish further information relating to specified substances in relation to which information has been furnished in pursuance of paragraph (b) above;

(*e*) provide for the imposition of requirements on particular manufacturers or importers to carry out tests of specified substances and to furnish information of the results of the tests;

(*f*) authorise persons to comply with requirements to furnish information imposed on them by or under the regulations by means of representative persons or bodies;

(*g*) impose restrictions on the disclosure of information obtained under this section and provide for determining what information is, and what information is not, to be treated as furnished in confidence;

(*h*) create offences, subject to the limitation that no offence shall be punishable with imprisonment or punishable on summary conviction with a fine exceeding level 5 on the standard scale[1];

(*i*) make any public authority designated by the regulations responsible for the enforcement of the regulations to such extent as may be specified in the regulations;

(*j*) include such other incidental and supplemental, and such transitional, provisions as the Secretary of State considers appropriate.

(5) The Secretary of State shall have regard, in imposing or providing for the imposition of any requirement under subsection (4)(b), (c), (d) or (e) above, to the cost likely to be involved in complying with the requirement.

(6) In this section—

"the environment" means the air, water and land or any of them;

"relevant information", in relation to substances, products or articles, means information relating to their properties, production, distribution, importation or use or intended use and, in relation to products or articles, to their disposal as waste;

"substance" means any natural or artificial substance, whether in solid or liquid form or in the form of a gas or vapour and it includes mixtures of substances.

(7) The enactments which are relevant for the purposes of subsection (2)(b) above are the following—

the Explosive Substances Act 1875[2];

the Radioactive Substances Act 1993[3];

Parts II, III and VIII of the Medicines Act 1968[4];

Part IV of the Agriculture Act 1970[5];

the Misuse of Drugs Act 1971[6];

Part III of the Food and Environment Protection Act 1985[7]; and

the Food Safety Act 1990[8];

and a substance is a regulated substance for the purposes of any such enactment in so far as any prohibition, restriction or requirement is imposed in relation to it by or under the enactment for the purposes of that enactment[9].

---

[1] The current fine at level 5 on the standard scale is £5,000: Criminal Justice Act 1991 (c. 53), s. 17 (England and Wales); Criminal Procedure (Scotland) Act 1995 (c. 46), s. 225 (Scotland).

[2] 1875 c. 17.

[3] 1993 c. 12. Words "the Radioactive Substances Act 1993" substituted by the Radioactive Substances Act 1993 (c. 12), s. 49(1), sch. 4, para. 8. This amendment came into force on 27 August 1993: s. 51(2).

[4] 1968 c. 67.

[5] 1970 c. 40.

[6] 1971 c. 38.

[7] 1985 c. 48.

[8] 1990 c. 16.

[9] This section came into force on 1 January 1991: s. 164(2) below.

**143.** *This section, relating to public registers of land which may be contaminated, is partially in force in England and Wales. It is prospectively repealed by the Environment Act 1995 (c. 25), s. 120, sch. 22, para. 91, sch. 24.*

*Amendments of hazardous substances legislation*

**144.** Schedule 13 to this Act[1] (which contains miscellaneous amendments to the legislation relating to hazardous substances) shall have effect[2].

*Penalties for offences of polluting controlled waters etc.*

**145.** **(1)** *Repealed by the Water Consolidation (Consequential Provisions) Act 1991 (c. 60), s. 3(1), sch. 3, pt. I. This amendment came into force on 1 December 1991: s. 4(2).*

**(2)** In sections 31(7)(a), 31A(2)(c)(i) and 32(7)(a) of the Control of Pollution Act 1974 (corresponding penalties for Scotland), for the words "the statutory maximum" there shall be substituted "£20,000"[3].

## Pollution at sea

**146–147.** *These sections amend the Food and Environment Protection Act 1985 (c. 48).*

**148.** *Repealed by the Merchant Shipping Act 1995 (c. 21), S. 314, sch. 12. This amendment came into force on 1 January 1996: s. 316(2). The Merchant Shipping Act 1995 consolidates the Merchant Shipping Acts 1894 to 1994 and other enactments relating to merchant shipping.*

## Control of dogs

**149–151.** *Not reproduced.*

## Straw and stubble burning

**152.** *Not reproduced.*

## Environmental expenditure

**153–155.** *Not reproduced.*

# PART IX: General

*Power to give effect to Community and other international obligations etc.*

**156.** **(1)** The Secretary of State may by regulations provide that the provisions to which this section applies shall have effect with such modifications as may be prescribed for the purpose of enabling Her Majesty's Government in the United Kingdom—

(*a*) to give effect to any Community obligation or exercise any related right; or

---

[1] Sch. 13 is not reproduced.
[2] This section, insofar as it relates to sch. 13, came into force on various dates: see S.I. 1991/2829; S.I. 1993/274.

[3] This section came into force on 1 January 1991: s. 164(2) below.

(*b*) to give effect to any obligation or exercise any related right under any international agreement to which the United Kingdom is for the time being a party[1].

(2) This section applies to the following provisions of this Act—

(*a*) Part I;

(*b*) Part II;

(*c*) Part VI; and

(*d*) in Part VIII, sections 140, 141 or 142;

and the provisions of the Radioactive Substances Act 1993[2].

(3) In this section—

"modifications" includes additions, alterations and omissions;

"prescribed" means prescribed in regulations under this section; and

"related right", in relation to an obligation, includes any derogation or other right to make more onerous provisions available in respect of that obligation.

(4) This section, in its application to Northern Ireland, has effect subject to the following modifications, that is to say—

(*a*) in its application in relation to Part VI and sections 140, 141, and 142, the reference to Her Majesty's Government in the United Kingdom includes a reference to Her Majesty's Government in Northern Ireland; and

(*b*) in its application in relation to the Radioactive Substances Act 1993, the reference to the Secretary of State shall be construed as a reference to the Department of the Environment for Northern Ireland and the reference to Her Majesty's Government in the United Kingdom shall be construed as a reference to Her Majesty's Government in Northern Ireland;

and regulations under it made by that Department shall be a statutory rule for the purposes of the Statutory Rules (Northern Ireland) Order 1979[3] and shall be subject to negative resolution within the meaning of section 41(6) of the Interpretation Act (Northern Ireland) 1954[4].[5]

*Offences by bodies corporate*

157. (1) Where an offence under any provision of this Act committed by a body corporate is proved to have been committed with the consent or connivance of, or to have been attributable to any neglect on the part of, any director, manager, secretary or other similar officer of the body corporate or a person who was purporting to act in any such capacity, he as well as the body corporate shall be guilty of that offence and shall be liable to be proceeded against and punished accordingly.

(2) Where the affairs of a body corporate are managed by its members, subsection (1) above shall apply in relation to the acts or defaults of a member in connection with his functions of management as if he were a director of the body corporate[6].

[1] The following regulations have been made under this section:

The Waste Management Licensing Regulations 1994, S.I. 1994/1056, as amended, p. 675 below.

The Environmental Protection Act 1990 (Modification of section 112) Regulations 1992, S.I. 1992/2617. These regulations modify s. 112 of this Act, relating to genetically modified organisms, which is not reproduced in this Manual.

[2] 1993 c. 12. Words "Radioactive Substances Act 1993" in this section substituted by the Radioactive Substances Act 1993 (c. 12), s. 49(1), sch. 4, para. 9. This amendment came into force on 27 August 1993: s. 51(2).

[3] S.I. 1979/1573 (N.I. 12).

[4] 1954 c. 33 (N.I.).

[5] This section came into force on 1 April 1991: S.I. 1991/1042.

[6] This section came into force on 1 January 1991: s. 164(2) below.

*Offences under Parts I, II, IV, VI, etc. due to fault of others*

**158.** Where the commission by any person of an offence under Part I[1], II[2], IV, or VI, or section 140[3], 141[4] or 142[5] above is due to the act or default of some other person, that other person may be charged with and convicted of the offence by virtue of this section whether or not proceedings for the offence are taken against the first-mentioned person[6].

*Application to Crown*

**159.** (1) Subject to the provisions of this section, the provisions of this Act and of regulations and orders made under it shall bind the Crown.

(2) No contravention by the Crown of any provision of this Act or of any regulations or order made under it shall make the Crown criminally liable; but the High Court or, in Scotland, the Court of Session may, on the application of any public or local authority charged with enforcing that provision, declare unlawful any act or omission of the Crown which constitutes such a contravention.

(3) Notwithstanding anything in subsection (2) above, the provisions of this Act and of regulations and orders made under it shall apply to persons in the pubic service of the Crown as they apply to other persons.

(4) If the Secretary of State certifies that it appears to him, as respects any Crown premises and any powers of entry exercisable in relation to them specified in the certificate that it is requisite or expedient that, in the interests of national security, the powers should not be exercisable in relation to the premises, those powers shall not be exercisable in relation to those premises; and in this subsection "Crown premises" means premises held or used by or on behalf of the Crown.

(5) Nothing in this section shall be taken as in any way affecting Her Majesty in her private capacity; and this subsection shall be construed as if section 38(3) of the Crown Proceedings Act 1947[7] (interpretation of references in that Act to Her Majesty in her private capacity) were contained in this Act.

(6) References in this section to regulations or orders are references to regulations or orders made by statutory instrument.

(7) For the purposes of this section in its application to Part II and Part IV the authority charged with enforcing the provisions of those Parts in its area is—

(*a*) in the case of Part II[8], any waste regulation authority[9], and

(*b*) in the case of Part IV, any principal litter authority[10].

*Service of notices*

**160.** (1) Any notice required or authorised by or under this Act to be served on or given to an inspector may be served or given by delivering it to him or by leaving it at, or sending it by post to, his office.

(2) Any such notice required or authorised to be served on or given to a person other than an inspector may be served or given by delivering it to him, or by leaving it at his proper address, or by sending it by post to him at that address.

(3) Any such notice may—

(*a*) in the case of a body corporate, be served on or given to the secretary or clerk of that body;

---

[1] P. 88 above.
[2] P. 111 above.
[3] P. 200 above.
[4] P. 202 above.
[5] P. 203 above.
[6] This section came into force on 1 April 1991: S.I. 1991/1042.
[7] 1947 c. 44.
[8] P. 111 above.
[9] For "waste regulation authority" see s. 30(1), p. 113 above.
[10] This section came into force on 1 January 1991: S.I. 1990/2635.

(b) in the case of a partnership, be served on or given to a partner or a person having the control or management of the partnership business.

(4) For the purposes of this section and of section 7 of the Interpretation Act 1978[1] (service of documents by post) in its application to this section, the proper address of any person on or to whom any such notice is to be served or given shall be his last known address, except that—

(a) in the case of a body corporate or their secretary or clerk, it shall be the address of the registered or principal office of that body;

(b) in the case of a partnership or person having the control or the management of the partnership business, it shall be the principal office of the partnership;

and for the purposes of this subsection the principal office of a company registered outside the United Kingdom or of a partnership carrying on business outside the United Kingdom shall be their principal office within the United Kingdom.

(5) If the person to be served with or given any such notice has specified an address in the United Kingdom other than his proper address within the meaning of subsection (4) above as the one at which he or someone on his behalf will accept notices of the same description as that notice, that address shall also be treated for the purposes of this section and section 7 of the Interpretation Act 1978 as his proper address.

(6) The preceding provisions of this section shall apply to the sending or giving of a document as they apply to the giving of a notice[2].

## Regulations, orders and directions

**161.** (1) Any power of the Secretary of State or the Minister of Agriculture, Fisheries and Food under this Act to make regulations or orders shall be exercisable by statutory instrument; but this subsection does not apply to orders under section 72 above[3] or paragraph 4 of Schedule 3[4].

(2) A statutory instrument containing regulations under this Act shall be subject to annulment in pursuance of a resolution of either House of Parliament.

(3) Except in the cases specified in subsection (4) below, a statutory instrument containing an order under this Act shall be subject to annulment in pursuance of a resolution of either House of Parliament.

(4) Subsection (3) above does not apply to a statutory instrument—

(a) which contains an order under section 78M(4) above[5], or

(b) by reason only that it contains[6] an order under section 130(4), 131(3) or 138(2) above or section 164(3) below.

(5) Any power conferred by this Act to give a direction shall include power to vary or revoke the direction.

(6) Any direction given under this Act shall be in writing[7].

## Consequential and minor amendments and repeals

**162.** (1) The enactments specified in Schedule 15 to this Act[8] shall have effect subject to the amendments specified in that Schedule.

---

[1] 1978 c. 30.
[2] This section came into force on 1 January 1991: s. 164(2) below.
[3] P. 157 above.
[4] P. 226 below.
[5] P. 176 above.

[6] Words "a statutory instrument ... that it contains" inserted by the Environment Act 1995 (c. 25), s. 120, sch. 22, para. 92. This amendment is not in force.
[7] This section came into force on 1 January 1991: s. 164(2) below.
[8] Sch. 15 is not reproduced.

(2)  The enactments specified in Schedule 16 to this Act are hereby repealed subject to section 77 above, Schedule 11 to this Act and any provision made by way of a note in Schedule 16[1].

(3)  The repeal of section 124 of the Civic Government (Scotland) Act 1982[2] shall not affect a compulsory purchase order made for the purposes of that section under the Local Government (Scotland) Act 1973[3] before the coming into force of the repeal and such compulsory purchase order may be proceeded with and shall have effect as if the said section 124 had not been repealed.

(4)  The Secretary of State may by order repeal or amend any provision of any local Act passed before this Act (including an Act confirming a provisional order) or of any order or other instrument made under an Act so passed if it appears to him that the provision is inconsistent with, or has become unnecessary or requires alteration in consequence of, any provision of this Act or corresponds to any provision repealed by this Act.

(5)  Any regulations made under section 100 of the Control of Pollution Act 1974[4] shall have effect after the repeal of that section by subsection (2) above as if made under section 140 of this Act[5].[6]

*Financial provisions*

163.  (1)  There shall be paid out of money provided by Parliament—

(*a*)  any administrative or other expenses incurred by any Minister of the Crown in consequence of the provisions of this Act; and

(*b*)  any increase attributable to this Act in the sums payable out of money so provided under any other Act.

(2)  Any fees or other sums received by any Minister of the Crown by virtue of any provisions of this Act shall be paid into the Consolidated Fund[7].

*Short title, commencement and extent*

164.  (1)  This Act may be cited as the Environmental Protection Act 1990.

(2)  The following provisions of the Act shall come into force at the end of the period of two months beginning with the day on which it is passed, namely—

sections 79 to 85;

section 97;

section 99;

section 105 in so far as it relates to paragraphs 7, 13, 14 and 15 of Schedule 5;

section 140;

section 141;

section 142;

section 145;

section 146;

section 148;

section 153;

section 154;

---

[1]  Schs. 11 and 16 are not reproduced.
[2]  1982 c. 45.
[3]  1973 c. 65.
[4]  1974 c. 40.
[5]  P. 200 above.
[6]  Subsections (1) and (2), insofar as they relate to schs. 15 and 16 have come into force partially on various dates; (3) came into force on 1 April 1992: S.I. 1992/266; (4) is not in force; (5) came into force on 1 January 1991: s. 164(2) below.
[7]  This section came into force on 1 January 1991: s. 164(2) below.

section 155;

section 157;

section 160;

section 161;

section 162(1) in so far as it relates to paragraphs 4, 5, 7, 8, 9, 18, 22, 24 and 31(4)(b) of Schedule 15; but, in the case of paragraph 22, in so far only as that paragraph inserts a paragraph (m) into section 7(4) of the Act of 1984;

section 162(2) in so far as it relates to Part III of Schedule 16 and, in Part IX of that Schedule, the repeal of section 100 of the Control of Pollution Act 1974;

section 162(5);

section 163.

(3) The remainder of this Act (except this section) shall come into force on such day as the Secretary of State may by order appoint and different days may be appointed for different provisions or different purposes[1].

(4) Only the following provisions of this Act (together with this section) extend to Northern Ireland, namely—

section 3(5) to (8);

section 62(2)(e) in so far as it relates to importation;

Part V;

Part VI in so far as it relates to importation and, without that restriction, section 127(2) in so far as it relates to the continental shelf;

section 140 in so far as it relates to importation;

section 141;

section 142 in so far as it relates to importation;

section 146;

section 147;

section 148;

section 153 except subsection (1)(k) and (m);

section 156 in so far as it relates to Part VI and sections 140, 141 and 142 in so far as they extend to Northern Ireland and in so far as it relates to the Radioactive Substances Act 1960[2];

section 158 in so far as it relates to Part VI and sections 140, 141 and 142 in so far as they extend to Northern Ireland.

(5) Where any enactment amended or repealed by this Act extends to any part of the United Kingdom, the amendment or repeal extends to that part, subject, however, to any express provision in Schedule 15 or 16[3].

---

[1] The commencement orders are noted, where appropriate, at the Parts or at the end of sections.

[2] The Radioactive Substances Act 1960 has been repealed and replaced by the Radioactive Substances Act 1993 (c. 12).

[3] This section came into force on 1 November 1990, the date of the Royal Assent: subsection (3) above.

# SCHEDULES

## SCHEDULE 1[1]

(Section 6[2].)

AUTHORISATIONS FOR PROCESSES: SUPPLEMENTARY PROVISIONS

### PART I: GRANT OF AUTHORISATIONS

*Applications for authorisations*

**1.** (1) An application to the enforcing authority[3] for an authorisation must contain such information, and be made in such manner, as may be prescribed in regulations made by the Secretary of State[4].

(2) An application to the enforcing authority for an authorisation must also, unless regulations made by the Secretary of State exempt applications of that class, be advertised in such manner as may be prescribed in regulations so made.

(3) The enforcing authority may, by notice in writing to the applicant, require him to furnish such further information specified in the notice, within the period so specified, as the authority may require for the purpose of determining the application.

(4) If a person fails to furnish any information required under sub-paragraph (3) above within the period specified thereunder the enforcing authority may refuse to proceed with the application.

(5) Regulations under this paragraph may make different provision for different classes of applications.

......................................................................................................................................

*Determination of applications*

**2.** (1) Subject to sub-paragraph (2) below, the enforcing authority shall give notice of any application for an authorisation, enclosing a copy of the application, to the persons who are prescribed or directed to be consulted under this paragraph and shall do so within the specified period for notification.

(2) The Secretary of State may, by regulations, exempt any class of application from the requirements of this paragraph or exclude any class of information contained in applications for authorisations from those requirements, in all cases or as respects specified classes only of persons to be consulted.

(3) Any representations made by the persons so consulted within the period allowed shall be considered by the enforcing authority in determining the application.

(4) For the purposes of sub-paragraph (1) above—

(*a*) persons are prescribed to be consulted on any description of application for an authorisation if they are persons specified for the purposes of applications of that description in regulations made by the Secretary of State;

(*b*) persons are directed to be consulted on any particular application if the Secretary of State specifies them in a direction given to the enforcing authority;

and the "specified period for notification" is the period specified in the regulations or in the direction.

(5) Any representations made by any other persons within the period allowed shall also be considered by the enforcing authority in determining the application.

(6) Subject to sub-paragraph (7) below, the period allowed for making representations is—

(*a*) in the case of persons prescribed or directed to be consulted, the period of twenty-eight days beginning with the date on which notice of the application was given under sub-paragraph (1) above, and

---

[1] This schedule came into force on 1 January 1991: S.I. 1990/2635.

[2] P. 95 above.

[3] "Enforcing authority" defined by s. 1(7), (8), p. 90 above.

[4] The following regulations have been made under this schedule:

The Environmental Protection (Applications, Appeals and Registers) Regulations 1991, S.I. 1991/507, as amended, p. 605 below.

(*b*) in the case of other persons, the period of twenty-eight days beginning with the date on which the making of the application was advertised in pursuance of paragraph 1(2) above.

(7) The Secretary of State may, by order, substitute for the period for the time being specified in sub-paragraph (6)(a) or (b) above, such other period as he considers appropriate.

3. (1) The Secretary of State may give directions to the enforcing authority requiring that any particular application or any class of applications for an authorisation shall be transmitted to him for determination pending a further direction under sub-paragraph (5) below.

(2) The enforcing authority shall inform the applicant of the fact that his application is being transmitted to the Secretary of State.

(3) Where an application for an authorisation is referred to him under sub-paragraph (1) above the Secretary of State may—

(*a*) cause a local inquiry to be held in relation to the application; or

(*b*) afford the applicant and the authority concerned an opportunity of appearing before and being heard by a person appointed by the Secretary of State;

and he shall exercise one of the powers under this sub-paragraph in any case where, in the manner prescribed by regulations made by the Secretary of State, a request is made to be heard with respect to the application by the applicant or the enforcing authority[1] concerned.

(4) Subsections (2) to (5) of section 250 of the Local Government Act 1972[2] (supplementary provisions about local inquiries under that section) or, in relation to Scotland, subsections (2) to (8) of section 210 of the Local Government (Scotland) Act 1973[3] (which make similar provision) shall, without prejudice to the generality of subsection (1) of either of those sections, apply to inquiries in pursuance of sub-paragraph (3) above as they apply to inquiries in pursuance of either of those sections and, in relation to England and Wales, as if the reference to a local authority in subsection (4) of the said section 250 included a reference to the enforcing authority.

(5) The Secretary of State shall, on determining any application transferred to him under this paragraph, give to the enforcing authority such a direction as he thinks fit as to whether it is to grant the application and, if so, as to the conditions that are to be attached to the authorisation.

4. The Secretary of State may give the enforcing authority a direction with respect to any particular application or any class of applications for an authorisation requiring the authority not to determine or not to proceed with the application or applications of that class until the expiry of any such period as may be specified in the direction, or until directed by the Secretary of State that they may do so, as the case may be.

5. (1) Except in a case where an application has been referred to the Secretary of State under paragraph 3 above and subject to sub-paragraph (3) below, the enforcing authority shall determine an application for an authorisation within the period of four months beginning with the day on which it received the application or within such longer period as may be agreed with the applicant.

(2) If the enforcing authority fails to determine an application for an authorisation within the period allowed by or under this paragraph the application shall, if the applicant notifies the authority in writing that he treats the failure as such, be deemed to have been refused at the end of that period.

(3) The Secretary of State may, by order, substitute for the period for the time being specified in sub-paragraph (1) above such other period as he considers appropriate and different periods may be substituted for different classes of application[1].

[1] Words "the enforcing authority" substituted by the Environment Act 1995 (c. 25), s. 120, sch. 22, para. 93(2). This amendment came into force on 1 April 1996: S.I. 1996/186.
[2] 1972 c. 70.
[3] 1973 c. 65.

[4] The following order has been made under this schedule:
The Environmental Protection (Authorisation of Processes) (Determination Periods) Order 1991, S.I. 1991/513, as amended, p. 619 below.

PART II: VARIATION OF AUTHORISATIONS

*Variations by the enforcing authority*

**6.** **(1)** Except as provided by sub-paragraph (1A) below[1], requirements of this paragraph apply where an enforcing authority[2] has decided to vary an authorisation under section 10[3] and is of the opinion that any action to be taken by the holder of the authorisation in consequence of the variation will involve a substantial change[4] in the manner in which the process[5] is being carried on.

**(1A)** The requirements of this paragraph shall not apply in relation to any variations of an authorisation which an enforcing authority has decided to make in consequence of representations made in accordance with this paragraph and which are specified by way of variation of a variation notice by a further notice under section 10(3A) of this Act[6].

**(2)** Subject to sub-paragraph (3) below, the enforcing authority shall give notice of the action to be taken by the holder of the authorisation to the persons who are prescribed or directed to be consulted under this paragraph and shall do so within the specified period for notification; and the holder shall advertise the action in the manner prescribed in regulations made by the Secretary of State.

**(3)** The Secretary of State may, by regulations, exempt any class of variation from all or any of the requirements of this paragraph or exclude any class of information relating to action to be taken by holders of authorisations from all or any of those requirements, in all cases or as respects specified classes only of persons to be consulted[7].

**(4)** Any representations made by the persons so consulted within the period allowed shall be considered by the enforcing authority in taking its decision.

**(5)** For the purposes of sub-paragraph (2) above—

(*a*) persons are prescribed to be consulted on any description of variation if they are persons specified for the purposes of variations of that description in regulations made by the Secretary of State;

(*b*) persons are directed to be consulted on any particular variation if the Secretary of State specifies them in a direction given to the enforcing authority;

and the "specified period for notification" is the period specified in the regulations or in the direction.

**(6)** Any representations made by any other persons within the period allowed shall also be considered by the enforcing authority in taking its decision.

**(7)** Subject to sub-paragraph (8) below, the period allowed for making representations is—

(*a*) in the case of persons prescribed or directed to be consulted, the period of twenty-eight days beginning with the date on which notice was given under sub-paragraph (2) above, and

(*b*) in the case of other persons, the period of twenty-eight days beginning with the date of the advertisement under sub-paragraph (2) above.

**(8)** The Secretary of State may, by order, substitute for the period for the time being specified in sub-paragraph (7)(a) or (b) above, such other period as he considers appropriate.

*Applications for variation*

**7.** **(1)** The requirements of this paragraph apply where an application is made to an enforcing authority under section 11(4)[8] for the variation of an authorisation.

**(2)** Subject to sub-paragraph (3) below, the enforcing authority[9] shall give notice of any such application for a variation of an authorisation, enclosing a copy of the application, to the persons who are prescribed or directed to be consulted under this paragraph and shall do so within the specified period for notification; and the holder of the authorisation shall advertise the application in the manner prescribed in regulations made by the Secretary of State.

[1] Words "Except as provided by sub-paragraph (1A) below" inserted by the Environment Act 1995 (c. 25), s. 120, sch. 22, para. 93(3).
[2] "Enforcing authority" defined by s. 1(7), (8), p. 90 above.
[3] P. 99 above.
[4] "Substantial change" defined by s. 10(7), p. 100 above.
[5] "Process" defined by s. 1(5), p. 89 above.
[6] Para. (1A) inserted by the Environment Act 1995 (c. 25), s. 120, sch. 22, para. 93(4). This amendment came into force on 1 April 1996: S.I. 1996/186.
[7] The following regulations have been made under this schedule:
The Environmental Protection (Applications, Appeals and Registers) Regulations 1991, S.I. 1991/507, as amended, p. 605 below.
[8] P. 101 above.
[9] "Enforcing authority" defined by s. 1(7), (8), p. 90 above.

(3) The Secretary of State may, by regulations, exempt any class of application from all or any of the requirements of this paragraph or exclude any class of information furnished with applications for variations of authorisations from all or any of those requirements, in all cases or as respects specified classes only of persons to be consulted[1].

(4) Any representations made by the persons so consulted within the period allowed shall be considered by the enforcing authority in determining the application.

(5) For the purposes of sub-paragraph (2) above—

(a) persons are prescribed to be consulted on any description of application for a variation if they are persons specified for the purposes of applications of that description in regulations made by the Secretary of State;

(b) persons are directed to be consulted on any particular application if the Secretary of State specifies them in a direction given to the enforcing authority;

and the "specified period for notification" is the period specified in the regulations or in the direction.

(6) Any representation made by any other persons within the period allowed shall also be considered by the enforcing authority in determining the application.

(7) Subject to sub-paragraph (8) below, the period allowed for making representations is—

(a) in the case of persons prescribed or directed to be consulted, the period of twenty-eight days beginning with the date on which notice of the application was given under sub-paragraph (2) above; and

(b) in the case of other persons, the period of twenty-eight days beginning with the date on which the making of the application was advertised in pursuance of sub-paragraph (2) above.

(8) The Secretary of State may, by order, substitute for the period for the time being specified in sub-paragraph (7)(a) or (b) above, such other period as he considers appropriate.

8. (1) The Secretary of State may give directions to the enforcing authority[2] requiring that any particular application or any class of applications for the variation of an authorisation shall be transmitted to him for determination pending a further direction under sub-paragraph (5) below.

(2) The enforcing authority shall inform the applicant of the fact that his application is being transmitted to the Secretary of State.

(3) Where an application for the variation of an authorisation is referred to him under sub-paragraph (1) above the Secretary of State may—

(a) cause a local inquiry to be held in relation to the application; or

(b) afford the applicant and the authority concerned an opportunity of appearing before and being heard by a person appointed by the Secretary of State;

and he shall exercise one of the powers under this sub-paragraph in any case where, in the manner prescribed by regulations made by the Secretary of State, a request is made to be heard with respect to the application by the applicant or the enforcing authority concerned.

(4) Subsections (2) to (5) of section 250 of the Local Government Act 1972[3] (supplementary provisions about local inquiries under that section) or, in relation to Scotland, subsections (2) to (8) of section 210 of the Local Government (Scotland) Act 1973[4] (which make similar provision) shall, without prejudice to the generality of subsection (1) of either of those sections, apply to local inquiries or other hearings in pursuance of sub-paragraph (3) above as they apply to inquiries in pursuance of either of those sections and, in relation to England and Wales, as if the reference to a local authority in subsection (4) of the said section 250 included a reference to the enforcing authority.

(5) The Secretary of State shall, on determining any application transferred to him under this paragraph, give to the enforcing authority such a direction as he thinks fit as to whether it is to grant the application and, if so, as to the conditions that are to be attached to the authorisation by means of the variation notice.

..........

9. The Secretary of State may give the enforcing authority a direction with respect to any particular application or any class of applications for the variation of an authorisation requiring the authority not to determine or not to

[1] The following regulations have been made under this schedule:
The Environmental Protection (Applications, Appeals and Registers) Regulations 1991, S.I. 1991/507, as amended, p. 605 below.
[2] "Enforcing authority" defined by s. 1(7), (8), p. 90 above.
[3] 1972 c. 70.
[4] 1973 c. 65.

proceed with the application or applications of that class until the expiry of any such period as may be specified in the direction, or until directed by the Secretary of State that they may do so, as the case may be.

**10.** (1) Except in a case where an application for the variation of an authorisation has been referred to the Secretary of State under paragraph 8 above and subject to sub-paragraph (3) below, the enforcing authority shall determine an application for the variation of an authorisation within the period of four months beginning with the day on which it received the application or within such longer period as may be agreed with the applicant.

(2) If the enforcing authority fails to determine an application for the variation of an authorisation within the period allowed by or under this paragraph the application shall, if the applicant notifies the authority in writing that he treats the failure as such, be deemed to have been refused at the end of that period.

(3) The Secretary of State may, by order, substitute for the period for the time being specified in sub-paragraph (1) above such other period as he considers appropriate and different periods may be substituted for different classes of application[1].

# SCHEDULE 2[2,3]

(Section 32[4].)

## WASTE DISPOSAL AUTHORITIES AND COMPANIES

### PART I: TRANSITION TO COMPANIES

#### *Preliminary*

**1.** In this Part of this Schedule—

"authority" means an existing disposal authority as defined in section 32(1)[5];

"company" means a waste disposal contractor formed under the Companies Act 1985[6] by a waste disposal authority as mentioned in section 30(5)[7];

"direction" means a direction under section 32(2);

"joint company" means a company in which more than one authority holds securities;

"securities", in relation to a company includes shares, debentures, bonds or other securities of the company, whether or not constituting a charge on the assets of the company; and

"the vesting date" means the date on which property, rights and liabilities vest in a company by virtue of a transfer scheme under paragraph 6 below.

#### *Notice of direction*

**2.** (1) The Secretary of State, before giving any directions to any authority or constituent authority, shall give notice of his intention to do so to that authority.

(2) A notice under this paragraph shall give a general indication of the provisions to be included in the direction, indicating in particular whether the proposed direction will require the formation of one or more than one company and the authority or authorities who are to form or control the company or companies and whether any existing disposal authority will be abolished.

---

[1] Paras. 8–10 inserted by the Environment Act 1995 (c. 25), s. 120, sch. 22, para. 93(5). This amendment came into force on 1 April 1996: S.I. 1996/186.
[2] This schedule came into force on 31 May 1991: S.I. 1991/1319.
[3] **Cases: schedule 2** *R v Avon County Council, ex parte Terry Adams Ltd* [1994] Env LR 442; *Mass Energy Ltd v Birmingham City Council* [1994] Env LR 298.
[4] P. 114 above.
[5] P. 114 above.
[6] 1985 c. 6.
[7] P. 114 above.

(3) A notice under this paragraph shall state that the authority to whom it is given is entitled, within a period specified in the notice, to make to the Secretary of State applications or representations with respect to the proposed direction under paragraph 3 below.

*Applications for exemption from and representations about directions*

3. (1) An authority which has been given notice under paragraph 2 above of a proposed direction may, within the period specified in the notice, make to the Secretary of State either an application under sub-paragraph (2) below or representations under sub-paragraph (3) below.

(2) An authority may, under this sub-paragraph, apply to the Secretary of State requesting him not to make a direction in its case on the ground that the authority falls within any of paragraphs (a), (b), (c) or (d) of section 32(3)[1].

(3) An authority may, under this sub-paragraph, make representations to the Secretary of State requesting him to make, in the direction, other provision than that proposed in the notice.

(4) It shall be the duty of the Secretary of State to consider any application duly made under sub-paragraph (2) above and to notify the authority of his decision.

(5) It shall be the duty of the Secretary of State to consider any representations duly made under sub-paragraph (3) above before he gives a direction.

*Directions*

4. (1) A direction may require the authority or authorities to whom it is given to form or participate in forming one or more than one company or to form or participate in forming one or more than one joint company and it shall specify the date before which the company or companies is or are to be formed.

(2) Where a direction is to require a joint company to be formed the direction may be given to such of the authorities as the Secretary of State considers appropriate (the "representative authority").

(3) Where a direction is given to an authority as the representative authority it shall be the duty of that representative authority to consult the other authorities concerned before forming a company in accordance with the direction.

(4) The Secretary of State may exercise his powers to vary or revoke a direction and give a further direction at any time before the vesting date, whether before or after a company has been formed in accordance with the direction or previous direction, as the case may be.

*Formation and status of companies*

5. (1) An authority which has been directed to form a company shall do so by forming it under the Companies Act 1985 as a company which—

(a) is limited by shares, and

(b) is a wholly-owned subsidiary of the authority or authorities forming it;

and it shall do so before such date as the Secretary of State specifies in the direction.

(2) The authority shall so exercise its control of the company as to secure that, at some time before the vesting date, the conditions specified in section 68(6)(a) to (h) of the Local Government and Housing Act 1989[2] (conditions for "arm's length companies") apply in relation to the company and shall, at some time before the vesting date, resolve that the company shall be an arm's length company for the purposes of Part V of that Act.

(3) In this paragraph "wholly-owned subsidiary", in relation to a company and an authority, is to be construed in accordance with section 736 of the Companies Act 1985.

*Transfer schemes*

6. (1) Where an authority has formed a company or companies in pursuance of a direction, the authority shall, before such date as the Secretary of State may specify in a direction given to the authority under this sub-paragraph, submit to the Secretary of State a scheme providing for the transfer to the company or companies of

---

[1] P. 114 above.   [2] 1989 c. 42.

any property, rights or liabilities of that or that and any other authority, or of any subsidiary of its or theirs, which appear to be appropriate to transfer as representing the relevant part of the undertaking of that authority or of that authority and the other authorities.

(2) In preparing a scheme in pursuance of sub-paragraph (1) above the authority shall take into account any advice given by the Secretary of State as to the provisions he regards as appropriate for inclusion in the scheme (and in particular any advice as to the description of property, rights and liabilities which it is in his view appropriate to transfer to the company).

(3) A scheme under this paragraph shall not come into force until it has been approved by the Secretary of State and the date on which it is to come into force shall be such date as the Secretary of State may, either in giving his approval or subsequently, specify in writing to the authority; and the Secretary of State may approve a scheme either without modifications or with such modifications as he thinks fit after consulting the authority who submitted the scheme.

(4) If it appears to the Secretary of State that a scheme submitted under sub-paragraph (1) above does not accord with any advice given by him, he may do one or other of the following things, as he thinks fit, namely—

(a) approve the scheme under sub-paragraph (3) above with modifications; or

(b) after consulting the authority who submitted the scheme, substitute for it a scheme of his own, to come into force on such date as may be specified in the scheme.

(5) In the case of a scheme for the transfer to a company or joint company of the relevant part of the undertaking of two or more authorities, the representative authority shall consult the other authority or authorities before submitting the scheme under sub-paragraph (1) above; and the Secretary of State shall not approve the scheme (whether with or without modifications), or substitute a scheme of his own unless—

(a) he has given that other authority or (as the case may be) those other authorities an opportunity of making, within such time as he may allow for the purpose, written representations with respect to the scheme; and

(b) he has considered any such representations made to him within that time.

(6) The Secretary of State shall not specify the date on which the scheme is to come into force without consulting the authority which submitted the scheme and, where the scheme was submitted by a representative authority, the other authorities concerned.

(7) On the coming into force of a scheme under this paragraph the property, rights and liabilities affected by the scheme shall be transferred and vest in accordance with the scheme.

(8) As a consequence of the vesting by virtue of the scheme of property, rights and liabilities of an authority in a company, that company shall issue to the authority such securities of the company as are specified in the transfer scheme.

### Transfer schemes: supplementary provisions

7. A scheme under paragraph 6 above may define the property, rights and liabilities to be transferred by the scheme—

(a) by specifying the property, rights and liabilities in question; or

(b) by referring to all the property, rights and liabilities comprised in any specified part of the undertaking or undertakings to be transferred; or

(c) partly in the one way and partly in the other;

and may make such supplemental, incidental and consequential provision as the authority making the scheme considers appropriate.

8. (1) The provisions of this paragraph apply to the transfer to a company of the property, rights and liabilities representing the relevant part of an authority's undertaking.

(2) Any property, rights or liabilities held or subsisting partly for the purpose of the relevant part of the authority's undertaking and partly for the purpose of another part shall, where the nature of the property, rights or liabilities permits, be divided or apportioned between the authority and the company in such proportions as may be appropriate; and where any estate or interest in land falls to be so divided, any rent payable under a lease in respect of that estate or interest, and any rent charged on that estate or interest, shall be correspondingly apportioned or divided so that the one part is payable in respect of, or charged on, only one part of the estate or interest and the other part is payable in respect of, or charged on, only the other part of the estate or interest.

(3) Any property, rights or liabilities held or subsisting as mentioned in sub-paragraph (2) above the nature of which does not permit their division or apportionment as so mentioned shall be transferred to the company or retained by the authority according to which of them appear at the vesting date likely to make use of the property, or, as the case may be, to be affected by the right or liability, to the greater extent, subject to such arrangements for the protection of the other of them as may be agreed between them.

(4) It shall be the duty of the authority and the company, before or after the vesting date, so far as practicable to enter into such written agreements, and to execute such other instruments, as are necessary or expedient to identify or define the property, rights and liabilities transferred to the company or retained by the authority and as will—

(a) afford to the authority and the company as against one another such rights and safeguards as they may require for the proper discharge of the authority's functions and the proper carrying on of the company's undertaking; and

(b) make, as from such date (not being earlier than the vesting date) as may be specified in that agreement or instrument, such clarifications and modifications of the division of the authority's undertaking as will best serve the proper discharge of the authority's functions and the proper carrying on of the company's undertaking.

(5) Any such agreement shall provide so far as it is expedient—

(a) for the granting of leases and for the creation of other liabilities and rights over land whether amounting in law to interests in land or not, and whether involving the surrender of any existing interest or the creation of a new interest or not;

(b) for the granting of indemnities in connection with the severance of leases and other matters;

(c) for responsibility for complying with any statutory requirements as respects matters to be registered and any licences, authorisations or permissions which need to be obtained.

(6) If the authority or the company represents to the Secretary of State, or if it appears to him without such a representation, that it is unlikely in the case of any matter on which agreement is required under sub-paragraph (4) above that such agreement will be reached, the Secretary of State may, whether before or after the vesting date, give a direction determining the manner in which the property, rights or liabilities in question are to be divided between the authority and the company, and may include in the direction any provision which might have been included in an agreement under that sub-paragraph; and any property, rights or liabilities required by the direction to be transferred to the company shall be regarded as having been transferred to, and by virtue of the transfer scheme vested in, the company accordingly.

## Tax and company provisions

9. (1) Any shares in a company which are issued as a consequence of the vesting by a transfer scheme of property, rights and liabilities in the company shall—

(a) be issued as fully paid; and

(b) treated for the purposes of the application of the Companies Act 1985 in relation to that company as if they had been paid up by virtue of the payment to the company of their nominal value in cash.

(2) For the purposes of Chapter I of Part II of the Capital Allowances Act 1990[1] (capital allowance in respect of machinery and plant) property which is vested in a company by virtue of a transfer scheme shall be treated as if—

(a) it had been acquired by the company on the transfer date for the purposes for which it is used by the company on and after that date; and

(b) capital expenditure of an amount equal to the price which the property would have fetched if sold in the open market had been incurred on that date by the company on the acquisition of the property for the purposes mentioned in paragraph (a) above.

## Benefit of certain planning permission

10. (1) This paragraph applies in relation to planning permission deemed to have been granted to the authority under regulation 4 the Town and Country Planning General Regulations 1976[2] (deemed planning permission for development by local authorities) which subsists at the vesting date.

---

[1] 1990 c. 1.     [2] S.I. 1976/1419.

**(2)** Any planning permission to which this paragraph applies which authorises the use of land by the authority for the treatment, keeping or disposal of waste shall, on the transfer of the land to the company by the scheme, enure for the benefit of the land.

### Right to production of documents of title

11. Where on any transfer by virtue of a transfer scheme the authority is entitled to retain possession of any documents relating to the title to, or to the management of, any land or other property transferred to the company, the authority shall be deemed to have given to the company an acknowledgement in writing of the right of the company to production of that document and to delivery of copies thereof; and, in England and Wales, section 64 of the Law of Property Act 1925[1] shall have effect accordingly, and on the basis that the acknowledgement did not contain any such expression of contrary intention as is mentioned in that section.

### Proof of title by certificate

12. **(1)** A joint certificate by or on behalf of the authority and the company that any property specified in the certificate, or any such interest in or right over any such property as may be specified in the certificate, is by virtue of the transfer scheme for the time being vested in the authority or in the company shall be conclusive evidence for all purposes of that fact.

**(2)** If on the expiration of one month after a request from the authority or the company for the preparation of such a joint certificate the authority and the company have failed to agree on the terms of the certificate, they shall refer the matter to the Secretary of State and issue the certificate in such terms as the Secretary of State may direct.

### Construction of agreements

13. Where any of the rights or liabilities transferred by a transfer scheme are rights or liabilities under an agreement to which the authority was a party immediately before the vesting date, whether in writing or not, and whether or not of such a nature that rights and liabilities thereunder could be assigned by the authority, that agreement shall have effect on and after the vesting date as if—

   (a)  the company had been a party to the agreement; and

   (b)  for any reference (however worded and whether express or implied) to the authority there were substituted a reference, as respects anything falling to be done on or after the vesting date, to the company; and

   (c)  any reference (however worded and whether express or implied) to any officer or servant of the authority were, as respects anything falling to be done on or after the vesting date, a reference to such person as the company may appoint or, in default of appointment, to the officer or servant of the company who corresponds as nearly as may be to that officer or servant of the authority; and

   (d)  where the agreement refers to property, rights or liabilities which fall to be apportioned or divided between the authority and the company, as if the agreement constituted two separate agreements separately enforceable by and against the authority and the company respectively as regards the part of the property, rights and liabilities retained by the authority or, as the case may be, the part of the property, rights and liabilities vesting in the company and not as regards the other part;

   and sub-paragraph (d) above shall apply in particular to the covenants, stipulations and conditions of any lease by or to the authority.

14. Without prejudice to the generality of the provisions of paragraph 13 above, the company and any other person shall, as from the vesting date, have the same rights, powers and remedies (and in particular the same rights and powers as to the taking or resisting of legal proceedings or the making or resisting of applications to any authority) for ascertaining, perfecting or enforcing any right or liability transferred to and vested in the company by a transfer scheme as he would have had if that right or liability had at all times been a right or liability of the company, and any legal proceedings or applications to any authority pending on the vesting date by or against the authority, in so far as they relate to any property, right or liability transferred to the company by the scheme, or to any agreement to any such property, right or liability, shall be continued by or against the company to the exclusion of the authority.

---

[1]  1925 c. 20.

### Third parties affected by vesting provisions

**15.** (1) Without prejudice to the provisions of paragraphs 13 and 14 above, any transaction effected between the authority and the company in pursuance of paragraph 8(4) above or of a direction under paragraph 8(6) above shall be binding on all other persons, and notwithstanding that it would, apart from this sub-paragraph, have required the consent or concurrence of any other person.

(2) It shall be the duty of the authority and the company, if they effect any transaction in pursuance of paragraph 8(4) above or of a direction under paragraph 8(6) above, to notify any person who has rights or liabilities which thereby become enforceable as to part by or against the authority and as to part by or against the company; and if such a person applies to the Secretary of State and satisfies him that the transaction operated unfairly against him the Secretary of State may give such directions to the authority and the company as appear to him to be appropriate for varying the transaction.

(3) If in consequence of a transfer by a transfer scheme or of anything done in pursuance of paragraphs 8 to 14 above the rights or liabilities of any person other than the authority which were enforceable against or by the authority become enforceable as to part against or by the authority and as to part against or by the company, and the value of any property or interest of that person is thereby diminished, such compensation as may be just shall be paid to that person by the authority, the company or both, and any dispute as to whether and if so how much compensation is payable, or as to the person by whom it shall be paid, shall be referred to, and determined by, the Lands Tribunal.

### Transfer of staff

**16.** (1) The Transfer of Undertakings (Protection of Employment) Regulations 1981[1] shall apply in relation to the relevant employees of an authority in accordance with sub-paragraph (2) below.

(2) For the purposes of the application of those Regulations in relation to any of the relevant employees of an authority, the relevant part of the undertaking of the authority shall (whether or not it would otherwise be so regarded) be regarded—

(*a*) as a part of an undertaking within the meaning of those Regulations which is transferred from the authority to the company on the vesting date, and

(*b*) as being so transferred by a transfer to which those Regulations apply and which is completed on that date.

(3) Where a person is, in pursuance of section 32, to cease to be employed by an authority and to become employed by a company, none of the agreed redundancy procedures applicable to persons employed by waste disposal authorities shall apply to him.

(4) For the purposes of this paragraph persons are "relevant employees" of an authority if they are to become, in pursuance of section 32, employees of a company to which the relevant part of the undertaking of the authority is to be transferred.

### Information for purposes of transfer scheme

**17.** (1) The Secretary of State may, by directions, prescribe descriptions of information which are to be furnished for purposes connected with the transfer by authorities to companies of the relevant part of the undertakings of authorities.

(2) It shall be the duty of[2] a waste disposal authority, on being requested to do so by a written notice served on it by the Secretary of State, to furnish to the Secretary of State such information of a description prescribed under sub-paragraph (1) above as may be specified in the notice.

---

[1] S.I. 1981/1794.
[2] Former words "a waste regulation authority or" repealed by the Environment Act 1995 (c. 25), s. 120, sch. 22, para. 94, sch. 24. This amendment came into force on 1 April 1996: S.I. 1996/186.

## Part II: Provisions Regulating Waste Disposal Authorities and Companies

### Terms of waste disposal contracts

18. A waste disposal authority[1] shall, in determining the terms and conditions of any contract which the authority proposes to enter into for the keeping, treatment[2] or disposal[3] of waste[4], so frame the terms and conditions as to avoid undue discrimination in favour of one description of waste disposal contractor as against other descriptions of waste disposal contractors.

19. (1) A waste disposal authority shall have regard to the desirability of including in any contract which the authority proposes to enter into for the keeping, treatment or disposal of waste terms or conditions designed to—

   (a) minimize pollution of the environment[5] or harm[6] to human health due to the disposal or treatment of the waste under the contract; and

   (b) maximise the recycling[7] of waste under the contract.

(2) A waste disposal authority shall be entitled—

   (a) to invite tenders for any such contract, and

   (b) to accept or refuse to accept any tender for such a contract and accordingly to enter or not to enter into a contract,

by reference to acceptance or refusal of acceptance by persons tendering for the contract of any terms or conditions included in the draft contract in pursuance of sub-paragraph (1) above.

### Procedure for putting waste disposal contracts out to tender

20. (1) A waste disposal authority which proposes to enter into a contract for the keeping, treatment or disposal of controlled waste[8] shall comply with the following requirements before making the contract and if it does not any contract which is made shall be void.

(2) The authority shall publish, in at least two publications circulating among waste disposal contractors, a notice containing—

   (a) a brief description of the contract work[9];

   (b) a statement that during a specified period any person may inspect a detailed specification of the contract work free of charge at a specified place and time;

   (c) a statement that during that period any person will be supplied with a copy of the detailed specification on request and on payment of the specified charge;

   (d) a statement that any person who wishes to submit a tender for the contract must notify the authority of his wish within a specified period; and

   (e) a statement that the authority intend to invite tenders for the contract, in accordance with sub-paragraph (4) below.

(3) The authority shall—

   (a ensure that the periods, place and time and the charge specified in the notice are such as are reasonable;

   (b) make the detailed specification available for inspection in accordance with the notice; and

   (c) make copies of the detailed specification available for supply in accordance with the notice.

(4) If any persons notified the authority, in accordance with the notice, of their wish to submit tenders for the contract, the authority shall—

   (a) if more than four persons did so, invite at least four of them to tender for the contract;

   (b) if less than four persons did so, invite each of them to tender for the contract.

---

[1] "Waste disposal authority" defined by s. 30(2), p. 113 above.

[2] "Treatment" defined by s. 29(6), p. 112 above.

[3] "Disposal" defined by s. 29(6), p. 112 above.

[4] "Waste" defined by s. 75, p. 159 above.

[5] "Pollution of the environment" defined by s. 29(3), p. 112 above; "the environment" defined by s. 29(2).

[6] "Harm" defined by s. 29(5), p. 112 above, for the purposes of s. 29(3), (4).

[7] "Recycling" defined by s. 29(6), p. 112 above.

[8] "Controlled waste" defined by s. 75, p. 159 above.

[9] "Contract work" defined by sub-paragraph (5) below.

(5) In this paragraph—

"the contract work", in relation to a contract for the keeping, treatment or disposal of waste, means the work comprising the services involved in the keeping, treatment or disposal of the waste under the contract; and

"specified" means specified in the notice under sub-paragraph (2) above.

**21.** A waste disposal authority, in taking any of the following decisions, namely—

(a)  who to invite to tender for the contract under paragraph 20(4)(a) above, and

(b)  who to enter into the contract with,

shall disregard the fact that any waste disposal contractor[1] tendering for the contract is, or is not, controlled by the authority.

### Variation of waste disposal contracts

**22.** Where a waste disposal authority has entered into a contract with a waste disposal contractor under the authority's control, paragraph 18 above shall, with the necessary modifications, apply on any proposed variation of the contract during the subsistence of that control, in relation to the terms and conditions that would result from the variation as it applies to the original contract.

### Avoidance of restrictions on transfer of securities of companies

**23.** (1) Subject to sub-paragraph (3) below, any provision to which this paragraph applies shall be void in so far as it operates—

(a)  to preclude the holder of any securities of a waste disposal contractor from disposing of those securities; or

(b)  to require the holder of any such securities to dispose, or offer to dispose, of those securities to particular persons or to particular classes of persons; or

(c)  to preclude the holder of any securities from disposing of those securities except—

(i)  at a particular time or at particular times; or

(ii)  on the fulfilment of particular conditions or in other particular circumstances.

(2)  This paragraph applies to any provision relating to any securities of a waste disposal contractor which is controlled by a waste disposal authority or to which the authority has transferred the relevant part of its undertaking and contained in—

(a)  the memorandum or articles of association of the company or any other instrument purporting to regulate to any extent the respective rights and liabilities of the members of the company;

(b)  any resolution of the company; or

(c)  any instrument issued by the company and embodying terms and conditions on which any such securities are to be held by persons for the time being holding them.

(3)  No provision shall be void by reason of its operating as mentioned in sub-paragraph (1) above if the Secretary of State has given his approval in writing to that provision.

# SCHEDULE 2A[2]

(Sections 44A[3] and 44B.)

## Objectives for the Purposes of the National Waste Strategy

**1.** Ensuring that waste[4] is recovered or disposed[5] of without endangering human health and without using processes or methods which could harm the environment[6] and, in particular, without—

---

[1] "Waste disposal contractor" defined by s. 30(5), p. 114 above.

[2] Sch. 2A inserted by the Environment Act 1995 (c. 25), s. 92(2), sch. 12. This amendment came into force on 1 April 1996: S.I. 1996/186.

[3] P. 134 above.

[4] "Waste" defined by s. 75, p. 159 above.

[5] "Disposal" defined by s. 29(6), p. 112 above.

[6] "The environment" defined by s. 29(2).

(a) risk to water, air, soil, plants or animals;

(b) causing nuisance through noise or odours; or

(c) adversely affecting the countryside or places of special interest.

2. Establishing an integrated and adequate network of waste disposal installations, taking account of the best available technology not involving excessive costs.

3. Ensuring that the network referred to in paragraph 2 above enables—

(a) the European Community as a whole to become self-sufficient in waste disposal, and the Member States individually to move towards that aim, taking into account geographical circumstances or the need for specialised installations for certain types of waste; and

(b) waste to be disposed of in one of the nearest appropriate installations, by means of the most appropriate methods and technologies in order to ensure a high level of protection for the environment and public health.

4. Encouraging the prevention or reduction of waste production and its harmfulness, in particular by—

(a) the development of clean technologies more sparing in their use of natural resources;

(b) the technical development and marketing of products designed so as to make no contribution or to make the smallest possible contribution, by the nature of their manufacture, use or final disposal, to increasing the amount or harmfulness of waste and pollution hazards; and

(c) the development of appropriate techniques for the final disposal of dangerous substances contained in waste destined for recovery.

5. Encouraging—

(a) the recovery of waste by means of recycling, reuse or reclamation or any other process with a view to extracting secondary raw materials; and

(b) the use of waste as a source of energy.

# SCHEDULE 2B[1]

(Section 75[2].)

## CATEGORIES OF WASTE

1. Production or consumption residues not otherwise specified below.

2. Off-specification products.

3. Products whose date for appropriate use has expired.

4. Materials spilled, lost or having undergone other mishap, including any materials, equipment, etc, contaminated as a result of the mishap.

5. Materials contaminated or soiled as a result of planned actions (e.g. residues from cleaning operations, packing materials, containers, etc.).

6. Unusable parts (e.g. reject batteries, exhausted catalysts, etc.).

7. Substances which no longer perform satisfactorily (e.g. contaminated acids, contaminated solvents, exhausted tempering salts, etc.).

[1] Sch. 2B inserted by the Environment Act 1995 (c. 25), s. 120, sch. 22, para. 95. This amendment is not in force.    [2] P. 159 above.

8. Residues of industrial processes (e.g. slags, still bottoms, etc.).

9. Residues from pollution abatement processes (e.g. scrubber sludges, baghouse dusts, spent filters, etc.).

10. Machining or finishing residues (e.g. lathe turnings, mill scales, etc.).

11. Residues from raw materials extraction and processing (e.g. mining residues, oil field slops, etc.).

12. Adulterated materials (e.g. oils contaminated with PCBs, etc.).

13. Any materials, substances or products whose use has been banned by law.

14. Products for which the holder has no further use (e.g. agricultural, household, office, commercial and shop discards, etc.).

15. Contaminated materials, substances or products resulting from remedial action with respect to land.

16. Any materials, substances or products which are not contained in the above categories.

## SCHEDULE 3[1]

(Section 81[2].)

### STATUTORY NUISANCES: SUPPLEMENTARY PROVISIONS

*Appeals to magistrates' court*

1. (1) This paragraph applies in relation to appeals under section 80(3)[3] against an abatement notice to a magistrates' court.

(2) An appeal to which this paragraph applies shall be by way of complaint for an order and the Magistrates' Courts Act 1980[4] shall apply to the proceedings.

(3) An appeal against any decision of a magistrates' court in pursuance of an appeal to which this paragraph applies shall lie to the Crown Court at the instance of any party to the proceedings in which the decision was given.

(4) The Secretary of State may make regulations as to appeals to which this paragraph applies and the regulations may in particular—

  (a) include provisions comparable to those in section 290 of the Public Health Act 1936[5] (appeals against notices requiring the execution of works);

  (b) prescribe the cases in which an abatement notice is, or is not, to be suspended until the appeal is decided, or until some other stage in the proceedings;

  (c) prescribe the cases in which the decision on appeal may in some respects be less favourable to the appellant than the decision from which he is appealing;

  (d) prescribe the cases in which the appellant may claim that an abatement notice should have been served on some other person and prescribe the procedure to be followed in those cases[6].

---

[1] This schedule came into force on 1 January 1991: s. 164(2) above.
[2] P. 193 above.
[3] P. 191 above.
[4] 1980 c. 43.

[5] 1936 c. 49.
[6] The following regulations have been made under this schedule:
The Statutory Nuisance (Appeals) Regulations 1995, S.I. 1995/2644, p. 753 below.

*Appeals to Sheriff*

**1A.** (1) This paragraph applies in relation to appeals to the sheriff under section 80(3)[1] against an abatement notice.

(2) An appeal to which this paragraph applies shall be by way of a summary application.

(3) The Secretary of State may make regulations as to appeals to which this paragraph applies and the regulations may in particular include or prescribe any of the matters referred to in sub-paragraphs (4)(a) to (d) of paragraph 1 above[2,3].

.................................................................................................................................

*Powers of entry etc*

**2.** (1) Subject to sub-paragraph (2) below, any person authorised by a local authority[4] may, on production (if so required) of his authority, enter any premises[5] at any reasonable time—

(*a*) for the purpose of ascertaining whether or not a statutory nuisance[6] exists; or

(*b*) for the purpose of taking any action, or executing any work, authorised or required by Part III[7].

(2) Admission by virtue of sub-paragraph (1) above to any premises used wholly or mainly for residential purposes shall not except in an emergency be demanded as of right unless twenty-four hours notice of the intended entry has been given to the occupier.

(3) If it is shown to the satisfaction of a justice of the peace[8] on sworn information in writing—

(*a*) that admission to any premises has been refused, or that refusal is apprehended, or that the premises are unoccupied or the occupier is temporarily absent, or that the case is one of emergency[9], or that an application for admission would defeat the object of the entry; and

(*b*) that there is reasonable ground for entry into the premises for the purpose for which entry is required.

the justice may by warrant under his hand authorise the local authority by any authorised person to enter the premises, if need be by force.

(4) An authorised person entering any premises by virtue of sub-paragraph (1) or a warrant under sub-paragraph (3) above may—

(*a*) take with him such other persons and such equipment as may be necessary;

(*b*) carry out such inspections, measurements and tests as he considers necessary for the discharge of any of the local authority's functions under Part III; and

(*c*) take away such samples or articles as he considers necessary for that purpose.

(5) On leaving any unoccupied premises which he has entered by virtue of sub-paragraph (1) above or a warrant under sub-paragraph (3) above the authorised person shall leave them as effectually secured against trespassers as he found them.

(6) A warrant issued in pursuance of sub-paragraph (3) above shall continue in force until the purpose for which the entry is required has been satisfied.

(7) Any reference in this paragraph to an emergency is a reference to a case where the person requiring entry has reasonable cause to believe that circumstances exist which are likely to endanger life or health and that immediate entry is necessary to verify the existence of those circumstances or to ascertain their cause and to effect a remedy.

(8) In the application of this paragraph to Scotland, a reference to a justice of the peace or to a justice includes a reference to the sheriff[10].

.................................................................................................................................

**2A.** (1) Any person authorised by a local authority may on production (if so required) of his authority—

(*a*) enter or open a vehicle, machinery or equipment[11], if necessary by force, or

---

[1] P. 191 above.

[2] The following regulation has been made under this section:

The Statutory Nuisance (Appeals) (Scotland) Regulations, S.I. 1996/1076, p. 793 below.

[3] Para. 1A inserted by the Environment Act 1995 (c. 25), s. 107, sch. 17, para. 7(a). This amendment came into force on 1 April 1996: S.I. 1996/186.

[4] "Local authority" defined by s. 79(7), (8) above.

[5] "Premises" defined by s. 79(7) above.

[6] "Statutory nuisance" defined by s. 79(1) above.

[7] P. 187 above.

[8] For application in Scotland see sub-paragraph (8) below.

[9] "Emergency" defined by sub-paragraph (7) below.

[10] Sub-paragraph (8) inserted by the Environment Act 1995 (c. 25), s. 107, sch. 17, para. 7(b). This amendment came into force on 1 April 1996: S.I. 1996/186.

[11] "Equipment" defined by s. 79(7) above.

(*b*) remove a vehicle, machinery or equipment from a street[1] or, in Scotland, road[2] to a secure place,

for the purpose of taking any action, or executing any work, authorised by or required under Part III in relation to a statutory nuisance within section 79(1)(ga) above[3] caused by noise[4] emitted from or caused by the vehicle, machinery or equipment.

(2) On leaving any unattended vehicle, machinery or equipment that he has entered or opened under sub-paragraph (1) above, the authorised person shall (subject to sub-paragraph (3) below) leave it secured against interference or theft in such manner and as effectually as he found it.

(3) If the authorised person is unable to comply with sub-paragraph (2) above, he shall for the purpose of securing the unattended vehicle, machinery or equipment either—

(*a*) immobilise it by such means as he considers expedient, or

(*b*) remove it from the street to a secure place.

(4) In carrying out any function under sub-paragraph (1), (2) or (3) above, the authorised person shall not cause more damage than is necessary.

(5) Before a vehicle, machinery or equipment is entered, opened or removed under sub-paragraph (1) above, the local authority shall notify the police of the intention to take action under that sub-paragraph.

(6) After a vehicle, machinery or equipment has been removed under sub-paragraph (1) or (3) above, the local authority shall notify the police of its removal and current location.

(7) Notification under sub-paragraph (5) or (6) above may be given to the police at any police station in the local authority's area or, in the case of the Temples, at any police station of the City of London Police.

(8) For the purposes of section 81(4) above, any expenses reasonably incurred by a local authority under sub-paragraph (2) or (3) above shall be treated as incurred by the authority under section 81(3) above in abating or preventing the recurrence of the statutory nuisance in question[5].

## *Offences relating to entry*

**3.** (1) A person who wilfully obstructs any person acting in the exercise of any powers conferred by paragraph 2 or 2A[6] above shall be liable, on summary conviction, to a fine not exceeding level 3 on the standard scale[7].

(2) If a person discloses any information relating to any trade secret obtained in the exercise of any powers conferred by paragraph 2 above he shall, unless the disclosure was made in the performance of his duty or with the consent of the person having the right to disclose the information, be liable, on summary conviction, to a fine not exceeding level 5 on the standard scale[8].

## *Default powers*

**4.** (1) This paragraph applies to the following function of a local authority, that is to say its duty under section 79[9] to cause its area to be inspected to detect any statutory nuisance which ought to be dealt with under section 80 or sections 80 and 80A[10] and its powers under paragraph 2 or 2A[11] above.

(2) If the Secretary of State is satisfied that any local authority has failed, in any respect, to discharge the function to which this paragraph applies which it ought to have discharged, he may make an order declaring the authority to be in default.

(3) An order made under sub-paragraph (2) above which declares an authority to be in default may, for the purpose of remedying the default, direct the authority ("the defaulting authority") to perform the function specified

---

[1] "Street" defined by s. 79(7) above.

[2] "Road" defined by s. 79(7) above. Words "or, in Scotland, road" inserted by the Environment Act 1995 (c. 25), s. 107, sch. 17, para. 7(c). This amendment came into force on 1 April 1996: S.I. 1996/186.

[3] P. 187 above.

[4] "Noise" defined by s. 79(7) above.

[5] Para. 2A inserted by the Noise and Statutory Nuisance Act 1993 (c. 40), s. 4(5). This amendment came into force on 5 January 1994: s. 12(1).

[6] Words "or 2A" inserted by the Noise and Statutory Nuisance Act 1993 (c. 40), s. 4(6).

[7] The current fine at level 3 on the standard scale is £1,000:

Criminal Justice Act 1991 (c. 53), s. 17 (England and Wales); Criminal Procedure (Scotland) Act 1995 (c. 46), s. 225 (Scotland).

[8] The current fine at level 5 on the standard scale is £5,000: Criminal Justice Act 1991 (c. 53), s. 17 (England and Wales); Criminal Procedure (Scotland) Act 1995 (c. 46), s. 225 (Scotland).

[9] P. 187 above.

[10] P. 190 above. Words "or sections 80 and 80A" inserted by the Noise and Statutory Nuisance Act 1993 (c. 40), s. 4(7)(a). This amendment came into force on 5 January 1994: s. 12(1).

[11] Words "or 2A" inserted by the Noise and Statutory Nuisance Act 1993 (c. 40), s. 4(7)(b).

in the order and may specify the manner in which and the time or times within which the function is to be performed by the authority.

(4) If the defaulting authority fails to comply with any direction contained in such an order the Secretary of State may, instead of enforcing the order by mandamus, make an order transferring to himself the function of the authority specified in the order.

(5) Where the function of a defaulting authority is transferred under sub-paragraph (4) above, the amount of any expenses which the Secretary of State certifies were incurred by him in performing the function shall on demand be paid to him by the defaulting authority.

(6) Any expenses required to be paid by a defaulting authority under sub-paragraph (5) above shall be defrayed by the authority in like manner, and shall be debited to the like account, as if the function had not been transferred and the expenses had been incurred by the authority in performing them.

(7) The Secretary of State may by order vary or revoke any order previously made by him under this paragraph.

(8) Any order under this paragraph may include such incidental, supplemental and transitional provisions as the Secretary of State considers appropriate.

(9) This paragraph does not apply to Scotland[1].

*Protection from personal liability*

5. Nothing done by, or by a member of, a local authority or by any officer of or other person authorised by a local authority shall, if done in good faith for the purpose of executing Part III, subject them or any of them personally to any action, liability, claim or demand whatsoever (other than any liability under section 19 or 20 of the Local Government Finance Act 1982[2] (powers of district auditor and court) ).

*Statement of right of appeal in notices*

6. Where an appeal against a notice served by a local authority lies to a magistrates' court or, in Scotland, the sheriff[3] by virtue of section 80[4], it shall be the duty of the authority to include in such a notice a statement indicating that such an appeal lies as aforesaid and specifying the time within which it must be brought.

# SCHEDULE 12[5]

(Sections 140 and 142[6].)

## INJURIOUS OR HAZARDOUS SUBSTANCES: ADVISORY COMMITTEE

1. The Secretary of State shall appoint the members of the committee, and shall appoint one of those members to be chairman.

2. The committee shall include persons who appear to the Secretary of State to be representative of—

    (a) persons engaged in carrying on industrial or commercial undertakings;

    (b) persons having scientific knowledge of matters concerning pollution of the environment;

    (c) bodies concerned with the protection or improvement of the environment; and

    (d) bodies concerned with the protection of persons using substances or articles subject to regulation under section 140[7] or 142 of this Act.

---

[1] Sub-paragraph (9) inserted by the Environment Act 1995 (c. 25), s. 107, sch. 17, para. 7(d). This amendment came into force on 1 April 1996: S.I. 1996/186.

[2] 1982 c. 32.

[3] Words "or, in Scotland, the sheriff" inserted by the Environment Act 1995 (c. 25), s. 107, sch. 17, para. 7(e). This amendment came into force on 1 April 1996: S.I. 1996/186.

[4] P. 190 above.

[5] This schedule came into force on 1 January 1991: s. 164(2) above.

[6] P. 200 above.

[7] P. 200 above.

3. The Secretary of State may make provision by regulations with respect to the terms on which members of the committee are to hold and vacate office, including the terms on which any person appointed as chairman is to hold and vacate office as chairman[1].

.................................................................................................................................................................

4. The Secretary of State shall provide the committee with such services and other facilities as appear to him to be necessary or expedient for the proper performance of the committee's functions.

.................................................................................................................................................................

5. The Secretary of State may pay to the members of the committee such remuneration (if any) and such allowances as may be determined by the Secretary of State with the consent of the Treasury.

[1] The Advisory Committee on Hazardous Substances (Terms of Office) Regulations 1991, S.I. 1991/1488, are made under this schedule.

# Water Industry Act 1991

Chapter 56

*Arrangement of Sections*

*The following sections of this Act are reproduced.*

## Part IV: Sewerage Services

*Chapter III: Trade Effluent*

*Consent for discharge of trade effluent into public sewer*

| | | |
|---|---|---|
| 118. | Consent required for discharge of trade effluent into public sewer | 232 |

*Consents on an application*

| | | |
|---|---|---|
| 119. | Application for consent | 233 |
| 120. | Applications for the discharge of special category effluent | 233 |
| 121. | Conditions of consent | 234 |
| 122. | Appeals to the Director with respect to decisions on applications etc. | 235 |
| 123. | Appeals with respect to the discharge of special category effluent | 236 |
| 124. | Variation of consents | 237 |
| 125. | Variations within time limit | 237 |
| 126. | Appeals with respect to variations of consent | 238 |
| 127. | Review by the Secretary of State of consents relating to special category effluent | 239 |

*Application for variation of time for discharge*

| | | |
|---|---|---|
| 128. | Application for variation of time for discharge | 239 |

*Agreements with respect the disposal etc. of trade effluent*

| | | |
|---|---|---|
| 129. | Agreements with respect to the disposal etc. of trade effluent | 240 |
| 130. | Reference to the Secretary of State of agreements relating to special category effluent | 240 |
| 131. | Review by the Secretary of State of agreements relating to special category effluent | 241 |

*References and reviews relating to special category effluent*

| | | |
|---|---|---|
| 132. | Powers and procedure on references and reviews | 242 |
| 133. | Effect of determination on reference or review | 243 |
| 134. | Compensation in respect of determinations made for the protection of public health etc. | 244 |

*Supplemental provisions of Chapter III*

| | | |
|---|---|---|
| 135. | Restrictions on power to fix charges under Chapter III. | 244 |
| 135A. | Power of the Environment Agency to acquire information for the purpose of its functions in relation to special category effluent | 245 |
| 136. | Evidence from meters etc. | 245 |
| 137. | Statement of case on appeal | 245 |
| 138. | Meaning of "special category effluent" | 246 |
| 139. | Power to apply Chapter III to other effluents | 246 |
| 140. | Pre-1989 Act authority for trade discharges etc. | 247 |

*Interpretation of Chapter III*

| | | |
|---|---|---|
| 141. | Interpretation of Chapter III | 247 |

## Part VII: Information Provisions

*The following sections are reproduced from this Part.*

*Registers, maps etc.*

196.  Trade effluent registers                                                                                       248

*Powers to acquire and duties to provide information*

204.  Provision of information to sewerage undertakers with respect to trade effluent
       discharges                                                                                                    248

*Restriction on disclosure of information*

206.  Restriction on disclosure of information                                                                       249

*Provision of false information*

207.  Provision of false information                                                                                 251

## Part VIII: Miscellaneous and Supplemental

*The following sections are reproduced from this Part.*

*Miscellaneous*

208.  Directions in the interests of national security                                                              251
209.  Civil liability of undertakers for escapes of water etc.                                                       252

*Offences*

210.  Offences by bodies corporate                                                                                   253
211.  Limitation on right to prosecute in respect of sewerage offences                                               253
*Judicial disqualification*
212.  Judicial disqualification                                                                                      253

*Powers to make regulations*

213.  Powers to make regulations                                                                                     254
214.  Power to prescribe forms                                                                                       255

*Local inquiries*

215.  Local inquiries                                                                                                255

*Construction of Act*

216.  Provisions relating to the service of documents                                                               255
217.  Construction of provision conferring powers by reference to undertakers'
       functions                                                                                                     256
218.  Meaning of "domestic purposes" in relation to water supply                                                     257
219.  General interpretation                                                                                         257
220.  Effect of local Acts                                                                                           262

*Other supplemental provisions*

221.  Crown application                                                                                              262
222.  Application to the Isles of Scilly                                                                             263
223.  Short title, commencement and extent                                                                          264

SCHEDULES:

Schedule 8—Pre-1989 Act transitional authority for trade effluent discharges etc.                                    264
Schedule 15—Disclosure of information                                                                                266
Part I—Persons in respect of whose functions disclosure may be made                                                  266
Part II—Enactments etc in respect of which disclosure may be made                                                    266

# Water Industry Act 1991

An Act to consolidate enactments relating to the supply of water and the provision of sewerage services, with amendments to give effect to recommendations of the Law Commission.

[25th July 1991]

## Extracts from this Act and transfer of functions

This Manual sets out Chapter III of Part IV of this Act, relating to trade effluent, and certain additional provisions.

The functions previously conferred on the Secretary of State under Chapter III of Part IV of this Act in relation to special category effluent, other than any function of making regulations or orders under section 139, p.246 below, have been transferred to the Environment Agency: Environment Act 1995 (c.25), s.2, p.421 below. The Environment Agency took over its functions under this Act on the transfer date, 1 April 1996: S.I. 1996/234.

## Commencement

This Act came into force on 1 December 1991: S.223(2), p.264 below.

Except where otherwise noted, the amendments made to the parts of this Act reproduced in this Manual by the Environment Act 1995 came into force on 1 April 1996: S .I. 1996/186. To avoid undue repetition this commencement date is not set out in the footnotes which relate to these amendments.

## Radioactive substances

For the operation of this Act in relation to radioactive substances see the Radioactive Substances Act 1993 (c.12), s.40, p.404 below and sch.3, para.8, p.411 below.

## References to A Manual of Nature Conservation Law

The following provisions of this Act are set out in the companion volume, A Manual of Nature Conservation Law, edited by Michael Fry (Oxford, 1995) commencing at page 273. Note that, in addition to other amendments, by the Environment Act 1995 (c.25), the references in sections 3 and 5 to the NRA (the National Rivers Authority) have been substituted by references to the Environment Agency.

## Part I: Preliminary

### General duties

2.  General duties with respect to water industry
3.  General environmental and recreational duties
4.  Environmental duties with respect to sites of special interest
5.  Codes of practice with respect to environmental and recreational duties

## Part VI: Undertakers' Powers and Works

### *Chapter I: Undertakers' powers*

*Powers in relation to land*

156.   Restriction on disposals of land.

..........................................................................................................................................................................

*References to material not set out in this Manual*

Planning Policy Guidance Note 23: Planning and Pollution Control. Department of the Environment, July 1994.

*Note:* this document was published before the introduction of the Environment Bill into Parliament and the subsequent enactment of the Environment Act 1995. This Act provided for the transfer of functions to the Environment Agency from the Secretary of State noted above.

..........................................................................................................................................................................

## Part IV: Sewerage Services

### *Chapter I: General functions of sewerage undertakers*

*Not reproduced*

### *Chapter II: Provision of sewerage services*

*Not reproduced*

### *Chapter III: Trade Effluent*

#### *Consent for discharge of trade effluent into public sewer*

*Consent required for discharge of trade effluent into public sewer.*

118.   (1) Subject to the following provisions of this Chapter, the occupier of any trade premises[1] in the area of a sewerage undertaker[2] may discharge any trade effluent[3] proceeding from those premises into the undertaker's public sewers[4] if he does so with the undertaker's consent[5].

(2) Nothing in this Chapter shall authorise the discharge of any effluent[6] into a public sewer otherwise than by means of a drain[7] or sewer[8].

(3) The following, that is to say—

(a)   the restrictions imposed by paragraphs (a) and (b) of section 106(2) above[9]; and

(b)   section 111 above[10] so far as it relates to anything falling within paragraph (a) or (b) of subsection (1) of that section,

shall not apply to any discharge of trade effluent which is lawfully made by virtue of this Chapter.

(4) Accordingly, subsections (3) to (8) of section 106 above and sections 108 and 109[11] above shall have effect in relation to communication with a sewer for the purpose of making any

---

[1] "Trade premises" defined by s.141(1),(2), p.247 below.
[2] Part II of this Act relates to the appointment and regulation of sewerage undertakers.
[3] "Trade effluent" defined by s.141(1),(2), p.247 below.
[4] "Public sewer" defined by s.219(1), p.260 below.
[5] Every consent given under this Chapter shall be given in writing: s.141(3) below.
[6] "Effluent" defined by s. 219(1), p.258 below.

[7] "Drain" defined by s.219(1),(2), p.258 below.
[8] "Sewer" defined by s.219(1),(2), p.260 below.
[9] S.106 relates to rights to communicate with public sewers; the restrictions in subsection (2)(a) and (b) relate to discharges into public sewers.
[10] S.111 relates to restrictions on the use of public sewers.
[11] Ss.106–109 relate to the communication of drains and private sewers with public sewers.

discharge which is lawfully made by virtue of this Chapter as they have effect in relation to communication with a sewer for the purpose of making discharges which are authorised by subsection (1) of section 106 above.

(5) If, in the case of any trade premises, any trade effluent is discharged without such consent or other authorisation as is necessary for the purposes of this Chapter, the occupier of the premises shall be guilty of an offence and liable—

(a) on summary conviction, to a fine not exceeding the statutory maximum[1]; and

(b) on conviction on indictment, to a fine.

*Consents on an application*

*Application for consent.*

**119.** (1) An application[2] to a sewerage undertaker for a consent to discharge trade effluent[3] from any trade premises[4] into a public sewer[5] of that undertaker shall be by notice[6] served[7] on the undertaker by the owner[8] or occupier of the premises.

(2) An application under this section with respect to a proposed discharge of any such effluent shall state—

(a) the nature or composition of the trade effluent;

(b) the maximum quantity of the trade effluent which it is proposed to discharge on any one day; and

(c) the highest rate at which it is proposed to discharge the trade effluent.

*Applications for the discharge of special category effluent.*

**120.** (1) Subject to subsection (3) below, where a notice containing an application under section 119 above is served on a sewerage undertaker with respect to discharges of any special category effluent[9], it shall be the duty of the undertaker to refer to the Environment Agency[10] the questions—

(a) whether the discharges to which the notice relates should be prohibited; and

(b) whether, if they are not prohibited, any requirements should be imposed as to the conditions on which they are made.

(2) Subject to subsection (3) below, a reference which is required to be made by a sewerage undertaker by virtue of subsection (1) above shall be made before the end of the period of two months beginning with the day after the notice containing the application is served on the undertaker.

(3) There shall be no obligation on a sewerage undertaker to make a reference under this section in respect of any application if, before the end of the period mentioned in subsection (2) above, there is a refusal by the undertaker to give any consent on the application.

(4) It shall be the duty of a sewerage undertaker where it has made a reference under this section not to give any consent, or enter into any agreement, with respect to the discharges to which the reference relates at any time before the Environment Agency[11] serves notice on the undertaker of his[12] determination on the reference.

(5) Every reference under this section shall be made in writing and shall be accompanied by a copy of the notice containing the application in respect of which it is made.

---

[1] The current statutory maximum is £5,000: Criminal Justice Act 1991 (c.53), s.17(2).
[2] Every application made under this Chapter shall be made in writing: s.141(3) below.
[3] "Trade effluent" defined by s.141(1),(2), p.247 below.
[4] "Trade premises" defined by s.141(1),(2), p.247 below.
[5] "Public sewer" defined by s.219(1), p.260 below.
[6] "Notice" defined by s.219(1), p.259 below.
[7] For provisions relating to service see s.216, p.255 below.
[8] "Owner" defined by s.219(1), p.259 below.
[9] "Special category effluent" has the meaning given by

s.138, p.246 below: s.141(1) below.
[10] The Environment Agency is established by the Environment Act 1995 (c.25), s.1, p.420 below. Words "the Environment Agency" substituted by the Environment Act 1995 (c.25), s.120, sch.22, para.105 (2).
[11] Words "the Environment Agency" substituted by the Environment Act 1995 (c.25), s.120, sch.22, para.105(3).
[12] Following the amendment referred to in n.11 above it appears that for the word "his" there should be substituted a reference to the Agency.

(6)  It shall be the duty of a sewerage undertaker, on making a reference under this section, to serve a copy of the reference on the owner[1] or the occupier of the trade premises[2] in question, according to whether the discharges to which the reference relates are to be by the owner or by the occupier.

(7) and (8)  *Substituted by subsection (9) and (10) below.*

(9)  If a sewerage undertaker fails, within the period provided by subsection (2) above, to refer to the Environment Agency any question which he is required by subsection (1) above to refer to the Agency, the undertaker shall be guilty of an offence and liable—

(*a*)  on summary conviction, to a fine not exceeding the statutory maximum[3];

(*b*)  on conviction on indictment, to a fine.

(10)  If the Environment Agency becomes aware of any such failure as is mentioned in subjection (9) above, the Agency may—

(*a*)  if a consent under this Chapter to make discharges of any special category effluent has been granted on the application in question, exercise its powers of review under section 127[4] or 131[5] below, notwithstanding anything in subsection (2) of the section in question; or

(*b*)  in any other case, proceed as if the reference required by this section had been made.[6]

*Conditions of consent.*

**121.**  (1)  The power of a sewerage undertaker, on an application under section 119 above[7], to give a consent with respect to the discharge of any trade effluent[8] shall be a power to give a consent either unconditionally or subject to such conditions as the sewerage undertaker thinks fit to impose with respect to—

(*a*)  the sewer[9] or sewers into which the trade effluent may be discharged;

(*b*)  the nature or composition of the trade effluent which may be discharged;

(*c*)  the maximum quantity of trade effluent which may be discharged on any one day, either generally or into a particular sewer; and

(*d*)  the highest rate at which trade effluent may be discharged, either generally or into a particular sewer.

(2)  Conditions with respect to all or any of the following matters may also be attached under this section to a consent to the discharge of trade effluent from any trade premises[10]—

(*a*)  the period or periods of the day during which the trade effluent may be discharged from the trade premises into the sewer;

(*b*)  the exclusion from the trade effluent of all condensing water;

(*c*)  the elimination or diminution, in cases falling within subsection (3) below, of any specified constituent of the trade effluent, before it enters the sewer;

(*d*)  the temperature of the trade effluent at the time when it is discharged into the sewer, and its acidity or alkalinity at that time;

(*e*)  the payment by the occupier of the trade premises to the undertaker of charges for the reception of the trade effluent into the sewer and for the disposal[11] of the effluent;

(*f*)  the provision and maintenance of such an inspection chamber or manhole as will enable a person readily to take samples, at any time, of what is passing into the sewer from the trade premises;

[1]  "Owner" defined by s.219(1), p.259 below.
[2]  "Trade premises" defined by s.141(1), (2), p.247 below.
[3]  The current statutory maximum is £5,000: Criminal Justice Act 1991 (c.53), s.17(2).
[4]  P.239 below.
[5]  P.241 below.
[6]  Subsections (9) and (10) substituted by the Environment Act 1995 (c.25), s.120, sch.22, para.105 (4).
[7]  P.233 above.
[8]  "Trade effluent" defined by s.141(1),(2), p.247 below.
[9]  "Sewer" defined by s.219(1),(2), p.260 below.
[10]  "Trade premises" defined by s.141(1),(2), p.247 below.
[11]  "Disposal", in relation to sewage, includes treatment: s.219(1) below.

(g) the provision, testing and maintenance of such meters[1] as may be required to measure the volume and rate of discharge of any trade effluent being discharged from the trade premises into the sewer;

(h) the provision, testing and maintenance of apparatus for determining the nature and composition of any trade effluent being discharged from the premises into the sewer;

(i) the keeping of records of the volume, rate of discharge, nature and composition of any trade effluent being discharged and, in particular, the keeping of records of readings of meters and other recording apparatus provided in compliance with any other condition attached to the consent; and

(j) the making of returns and giving of other information to the sewerage undertaker concerning the volume, rate of discharge, nature and composition of any trade effluent discharged from the trade premises into the sewer.

(3) A case falls within this subsection where the sewerage undertaker is satisfied that the constituent in question, either alone or in combination with any matter with which it is likely to come into contact while passing through any sewers—

(a) would injure or obstruct those sewers, or make the treatment or disposal of the sewage from those sewers especially difficult or expensive; or

(b) in the case of trade effluent which is to be or is discharged—

(i) into a sewer having an outfall in any harbour[2] or tidal water[3]; or

(ii) into a sewer which connects directly or indirectly with a sewer or sewage disposal works having such an outfall,

would cause or tend to cause injury or obstruction to the navigation on, or the use of, the harbour or tidal water.

(4) In the exercise of the power conferred by virtue of subsection (2)(e) above, regard shall be had—

(a) to the nature and composition and to the volume and rate of discharge of the trade effluent discharged;

(b) to any additional expense incurred or likely to be incurred by a sewerage undertaker in connection with the reception or disposal of the trade effluent; and

(c) to any revenue likely to be derived by the undertaker from the trade effluent.

(5) If, in the case of any trade premises, a condition imposed under this section is contravened, the occupier of the premises shall be guilty of an offence and liable—

(a) on summary conviction, to a fine not exceeding the statutory maximum[4]; and

(b) on conviction on indictment, to a fine.

(6) In this section "harbour" and "tidal water" have the same meanings as in the Merchant Shipping Act 1995.[5]

(7) This section has effect subject to the provisions of sections 133[6] and 135(3)[7] below.

*Appeals to the Director with respect to decisions on applications etc.*

**122.** (1) Any person aggrieved by—

(a) the refusal of a sewerage undertaker to give a consent for which application has been duly made to the undertaker under section 119 above[8];

(b) the failure of a sewerage undertaker to give such a consent within the period of two months beginning with the day after service of the notice containing the application; or

---

[1] "Meter" defined by s.219(1), p.259 below.
[2] For "harbour" see subsection (7) below.
[3] For "tidal water" see subsection (7) below.
[4] The current statutory maximum is £5,000: Criminal Justice Act 1991 (c. 53), s.17(2).
[5] 1995 c.21. Words "Merchant Shipping Act 1995" substi-

tuted by the Merchant Shipping Act 1995 (c.21), s.314, sch.13, para.89(a). This amendment came into force on 1 January 1996: s.316(2).
[6] P.243 below.
[7] P.245 below.
[8] P.233 above.

(c)  any condition attached by a sewerage undertaker to such a consent,

may appeal to the Director[1].

(2)  On an appeal under this section in respect of a refusal or failure to give a consent, the Director may give the necessary consent, either unconditionally or subject to such conditions as he thinks fit to impose for determining any of the matters as respects which the undertaker has power to impose conditions under section 121 above[2].

(3)  On an appeal under this section in respect of a condition attached to a consent, the Director may take into review all the conditions attached to the consent, whether appealed against or not, and may—

(a)  substitute for them any other set of conditions, whether more or less favourable to the appellant; or

(b)  annul any of the conditions.

(4)  The Director may, under subsection (3) above, include provision as to the charges to be made in pursuance of any condition attached to a consent for any period before the determination of the appeal.

(5)  On any appeal under this section, the Director may give a direction that the trade effluent[3] in question shall not be discharged until a specified date.

(6)  Any consent given or conditions imposed by the Director under this section in respect of discharges of trade effluent shall have effect for the purposes of this Chapter as if given or imposed by the sewerage undertaker in question.

(7)  The powers of the Director under this section shall be subject to the provisions of sections 123, 128[4], 133[5], 135[6] and 137[7] below.

*Appeals with respect to the discharge of special category effluent.*

**123.**  (1)  Where a reference is made to the Environment Agency[8] under section 120 above[9], the period mentioned in paragraph (b) of subsection (1) of section 122 above shall not begin to run for the purposes of that subsection, in relation to the application to which the reference relates, until the beginning of the day after the Environment Agency serves notice[10] on the sewerage undertaker in question of his determination on the reference.

(2)  If, on an appeal under section 122 above, it appears to the Director[11]—

(a)  that the case is one in which the sewerage undertake in question is required to make a reference under section 120 above before giving a consent; and

(b)  that the undertaker has not made such a reference, whether because the case falls within subsection (3) of that section or otherwise,

the Director shall not be entitled to determine the appeal, otherwise than by upholding a refusal, except where the conditions set out in subsection (3) below are satisfied.

(3)  The conditions mentioned in subsection (2) above are satisfied if the Director—

(a)  has himself referred the questions mentioned in section 120(1) above to the Environment Agency; and

(b)  has been sent a copy of the notice of the Environment Agency's determination on the reference.

(4)  Every reference under this section shall be made in writing and shall be accompanied by a copy of the notice containing the application in respect of which the appeal and reference is made.

---

[1]  "The Director" defined by s.219(1), p.258 below.
[2]  P.234 above.
[3]  "Trade effluent" defined by s.141(1),(2), p.247 below.
[4]  P.239 below.
[5]  P.243 below.
[6]  P.244 below.
[7]  P.245 below.

[8]  Words "the Environment Agency/Agency's" in this subsection substituted by the Environment Act 1995 (c.25), s.120, sch.22, para.106.
[9]  P.233 above.
[10]  "Notice" defined by s.219(1), p.259 below; for provisions relating to service see s.216, p.255 below.
[11]  "The Director" defined by s.219(1), p.258 below.

(5)  It shall be the duty of the Director, on making a reference under this section, to serve a copy of the reference—

(a)  on the owner[1] or the occupier of the trade premises[2] in question, according to whether the discharges to which the reference relates are to be by the owner or by the occupier; and

(b)  on the sewerage undertaker in question.

*Variation of consents.*

**124.**  (1)  Subject to sections 128[3], 133[4] and 135(3)[5] below, a sewerage undertaker may from time to time give a direction varying the conditions[6] which have been attached to any of its consents under this Chapter to the discharge of trade effluent[7] into a public sewer[8].

(2)  Subject to subsections (3) and (4) and section 125 below, no direction shall be given under this section with respect to a consent under this Chapter—

(a)  within two years from the date of the consent; or

(b)  where a previous direction has been given under this section with respect to that consent, within two years from the date on which notice was given of that direction.

(3)  Subsection (2) above shall not prevent a direction being given before the time specified in that subsection if it is given with the consent of the owner[9] and occupier of the trade premises[10] in question.

(4)  A direction given with the consent mentioned in subsection (3) above shall not affect the time at which any subsequent direction may be given.

(5)  The sewerage undertaker shall give to the owner and occupier of the trade premises to which a consent under this Chapter relates notice[11] of any direction under this section with respect to that consent.

(6)  A notice under subsection (5) above shall—

(a)  include information as to the right of appeal conferred by subsection (1) of section 126 below[12]; and

(b)  state the date, being a date not less than two months after the giving of the notice, on which (subject to subsection (2) of that section) the direction is to take effect.

(7)  For the purposes of this section references to the variation of conditions include references to the addition or annulment of a condition and to the attachment of a condition to a consent to which no condition was previously attached.

*Variations within time limit.*

**125.**  (1)  A sewerage undertaker may give a direction under section 124 above before the time specified in subsection (2) of that section and without the consent required by subsection (3) of that section if it considers it necessary to do so in order to provide proper protection for persons likely to be affected by the discharges which could lawfully be made apart from the direction.

(2)  Subject to section 134(3) below[13], where a sewerage undertaker gives a direction by virtue of subsection (1) above, the undertake shall be liable to pay compensation to the owner[14] and occupier of the trade premises[15] to which the direction relates, unless the undertaker is of the opinion that the direction is required—

---

[1]  "Owner" defined by s.219(1), p.259 below.
[2]  "Trade premises" defined by s.141(1),(2), p.247 below.
[3]  P.239 below.
[4]  P.243 below.
[5]  P.245 below.
[6]  For "the variation of conditions" see subsection (7) below.
[7]  "Trade effluent" defined by s.141(1),(2), p.247 below.
[8]  "Public sewer" defined by s.219(1), p.260 below.
[9]  "Owner" defined by s.219(1), p.259 below.
[10]  "Trade premises" defined by s.141(1),(2), p.247 below.
[11]  "Notice" defined by s.219(1), p.259 below.
[12]  P.238 below.
[13]  P.244 below.
[14]  "Owner" defined by s.219(1), p.259 below.
[15]  "Trade premises" defined by s.141(1),(2), p.247 below.

(*a*) in consequence of a change of circumstances which—

(i)  has occurred since the beginning of the period of two years in question; and

(ii)  could not reasonably have been foreseen at the beginning of that period; and

(*b*) otherwise than in consequence of consents for discharges given after the beginning of that period.

(3)  Where a sewerage undertaker gives a direction by virtue of subsection (1) above and is of the opinion mentioned in subsection (2) above, it shall be the duty of the undertaker to give notice[1] of the reasons for its opinion to the owner and occupier of the premises in question.

(4)  For the purposes of this section the circumstances referred to in subsection (2)(*a*) above may include the information available as to the discharges to which the consent in question relates or as to the interaction of those discharges with other discharges or matter.

(5)  The Secretary of State may by regulations make provision as to the manner of determining the amount of any compensation payable under this section, including the factors to be taken into account in determining that amount.

*Appeals with respect to variations of consent.*

**126.**  (1)  The owner[2] or occupier of any trade premises[3] may—

(*a*) within two months of the giving to him under subsection (5) of section 124 above[4] of a notice of a direction under that section; or

(*b*) with the written permission of the Director[5], at any later time,

appeal to the Director against the direction.

(2)  Subject to subsection (3) below, if an appeal against a direction is brought under subsection (1) above before the date specified under section 124(6)(*b*) above in the notice of the direction, the direction shall not take effect until the appeal is withdrawn or finally disposed of.

(3)  In so far as the direction which is the subject of an appeal relates to the making of charges payable by the occupier of any trade premises, it may take effect on any date after the giving of the notice.

(4)  On an appeal under subsection (1) above with respect to a direction, the Director shall have power—

(*a*) to annul the direction given by the sewerage undertaker; and

(*b*) to substitute for it any other direction, whether more or less favourable to the appellant;

and any direction given by the Director may include provision as to the charges to be made for any period between the giving of the notice by the sewerage undertaker and the determination of the appeal.

(5)  A person to whom notice is given in pursuance of section 125(3) above may, in accordance with regulations made by the Secretary of State, appeal to the Director against the notice on the ground that compensation should be paid in consequence of the direction to which the notice relates.

(6)  On an appeal under subsection (5) above the Director may direct that section 125 above shall have effect as if the sewerage undertaker in question were not of the opinion to which the notice relates.

(7)  Any consent given or conditions imposed by the Director under this section in respect of discharges of trade effluent[6] shall have effect for the purposes of this Chapter as if given or imposed by the sewerage undertaker in question.

---

[1] "Notice" defined by s.219(1), p.259 below.
[2] "Owner" defined by s.219(1), p.259 below.
[3] "Trade premises" defined by s.141(1),(2), p.247 below.
[4] P.237 above.
[5] "The Director" defined by s.219(1), p.258 below.
[6] "Trade effluent" defined by s.141 (1), (2), p.247 below.

(8) The powers of the Director under this section shall be subject to the provisions of sections 133[1], 135[2] and 137[3] below.

*Review by the Secretary of State[4] of consents relating to special category effluent.*

**127.** (1) Where any person, as the owner[5] or occupier of any trade premises[6], is (whether or not in accordance with a notice under section 132 below[7]) for the time being authorised by virtue of a consent under this Chapter to make discharges of any special category effluent[8] from those premises into a sewerage undertaker's public sewer[9], the Environment Agency[10] may review the questions—

(*a*) whether the discharges authorised by the consent should be prohibited; and

(*b*) whether, if they are not prohibited, any requirements should be imposed as to the conditions on which they are made.

(2) Subject to subsection (3) below, the Environment Agency shall not review any question under this section unless—

(*a*) the consent or variation by virtue of which the discharges in question are made has not previously been the subject-matter of a review and was given or made—

(i) before 1st September 1989; or

(ii) in contravention of section 133 below[11];

(*b*) a period of more than two years has elapsed since the time, or last time, when notice of the Environment Agency's determination on any reference or review relating to that consent or the consent to which that variation relates was served under section 132 below on the owner or occupier of the trade premises in question; or

(*c*) there has, since the time, or last time, when such a notice was so served, been a contravention of any provision which was included in compliance with a requirement of a notice under section 132 below in the consent or variation by virtue of which the discharges in question are made.

(3) Subsection (2) above shall not apply if the review is carried out—

(*a*) for the purpose of enabling Her Majesty's Government in the United Kingdom to give effect to any Community obligation or to any international agreement to which the United Kingdom is for the time being a party; or

(*b*) for the protection of public health or of flora and fauna dependent on an aquatic environment.

*Application for variation of time for discharge*

*Application for variation of time for discharge.*

**128.** (1) If, after a direction has been given under any of the preceding provisions of this Chapter requiring that trade effluent[12] shall not be discharged until a specified date, it appears to the sewerage undertaker in question that in consequence—

(*a*) of a failure to complete any works required in connection with the reception and disposal[13] of the trade effluent; or

(*b*) of any other exceptional circumstances,

---

[1] P.243 below.
[2] P.244 below.
[3] P.245 below.
[4] This section now relates to the Environment Agency.
[5] "Owner" defined by s.219(1), p.259 below.
[6] "Trade premises" defined by s.141(1), (2), p.247 below.
[7] P.242 below.
[8] "Special category effluent" has the meaning given by s.138, p.246 below: s.141 (1) below.

[9] "Public sewer" defined by s.219(1), p.260 below.
[10] Words "the Environment Agency/Agency's" in this subsection substituted by the Environment Act 1995 (c.25), s.120, sch.22, para.107.
[11] P.243 below.
[12] "Trade effluent" defined by s.141 (1), (2), p.247 below.
[13] "Disposal", in relation to sewage, includes treatment: s.219(1) below.

a later date ought to be substituted for the date so specified in the direction, the undertaker may apply to the Director[1] for such a substitution.

(2) The Director shall have power, on an application under subsection (1) above, to vary the direction so as to extend the period during which the trade effluent may not be discharged until the date specified in the application or, if he thinks fit, any earlier date.

(3) Not less than one month before making an application under subsection (1) above a sewerage undertaker shall give notice[2] of its intention to the owner[3] and occupier of the trade premises[4] from which the trade effluent is to be discharged.

(4) The Director, before varying a direction on an application under subsection (1) above, shall take into account any representations made to him by the owner or occupier of the trade premises in question.

*Agreements with respect the disposal etc. of trade effluent*

*Agreements with respect to the disposal etc of trade effluent.*

**129.** (1) Subject to sections 130 and 133 below[5], a sewerage undertaker may enter into and carry into effect—

(a) an agreement with the owner[6] or occupier of any trade premises[7] within its area for the reception and disposal[8] by the undertaker of any trade effluent[9] produced on those premises;

(b) an agreement with the owner or occupier of any such premises under which it undertakes, on such terms as may be specified in the agreement, to remove and dispose of substances[10] produced in the course of treating any trade effluent on or in connection with those premises.

(2) Without prejudice to the generality of subsection (1) above, an agreement such as is mentioned in paragraph (a) of that subsection may, in particular, provide—

(a) for the construction or extension by the sewerage undertaker of such works as may be required for the reception or disposal of the trade effluent; and

(b) for the repayment by the owner or occupier, as the case may be, of the whole or part of the expenses incurred by the undertaker in carrying out its obligations under the agreement.

(3) It is hereby declared that the power of a sewerage undertaker to enter into an agreement under this section includes a power, by that agreement, to authorise such a discharge as apart from the agreement would require a consent under this Chapter.

*Reference to the Secretary of State[11] of agreements relating to special category effluent.*

**130.** (1) Where a sewerage undertaker and the owner[12] or occupier of any trade premises[13] are proposing to enter into an agreement under section 129 above with respect to, or to any matter connected with, the reception or disposal of any special category effluent[14], it shall be the duty of the undertaker to refer to the Environment Agency[15] the questions—

(a) whether the operations which would, for the purposes of or in connection with the reception or disposal of that effluent, be carried out in pursuance of the proposed agreement should be prohibited; and

---

[1] "The Director" defined by s.219(1), p.258 below.
[2] "Notice" defined by s.219 (1), p.259 below.
[3] "Owner" defined by s.219(1), p.259 below.
[4] "Trade premises" defined by s.141(1),(2), p.247 below.
[5] P.243 below.
[6] "Owner" defined by s.219(1), p.259 below.
[7] "Trade premises" defined by s.141(1),(2), p.247 below.
[8] "Disposal", in relation to sewerage, includes treatment: s.219(1) below.
[9] "Trade effluent" defined by s.141(1),(2), p.247 below.

[10] "Substance" defined by s.219(1), p.261 below.
[11] This section now relates to the Environment Agency.
[12] "Owner" defined by s.219(1), p.259 below.
[13] "Trade premises" defined by s.141(1),(2), p.247 below.
[14] "Special category effluent" has the meaning given by s.138, p.246 below: s.141(1) below.
[15] Words "the Environment Agency" in this subsection substituted by the Environment Act 1995 (c.25), s.120, sch.22, para.108(2).

(b) whether, if they are not prohibited, any requirements should be imposed as to the conditions on which they are carried out.

(2) It shall be the duty of a sewerage undertaker where it has made a reference under this section not to give any consent or enter into any agreement with respect to any such operations as are mentioned in subsection (1)(a) above at any time before the Environment Agency serves notice[1] on the undertaker of his determination on the reference.

(3) Every reference under this section shall be made in writing and shall be accompanied by a copy of the proposed agreement.

(4) It shall be the duty of a sewerage undertaker, on making a reference under this section, to serve a copy of the reference on the owner or the occupier of the trade premises in question, according to whether it is the owner or occupier who is proposing to be a party to the agreement.

(5) and (6) *Substituted by subsection (7)–(9) below.*

(7) If a sewerage undertaker fails, before giving any consent or entering into any agreement with respect to any such operations as are mentioned in paragraph (a) of subsection (1) above, to refer to the Environment Agency any question which he is required by that subsection to refer to the Agency, the undertaker shall be guilty of an offence and liable—

(a) on summary conviction, to a fine not exceeding the statutory maximum[2];

(b) on conviction on indictment, to a fine.

(8) If the Environment Agency becomes aware—

(a) that a sewerage undertaker and the owner or occupier of any trade premises are proposing to enter into any such agreement as is mentioned in subjection (1) above, and

(b) that the sewerage undertaker has not referred to the Agency any question which it is required to refer to the Agency by that subsection,

the Agency may proceed as if the reference required by that subsection had been made.

(9) If the Environment Agency becomes aware that any consent has been given or agreement entered into with respect to any such operations as are mentioned in paragraph (a) of subsection (1) above without the sewerage undertaker in question having referred to the Environment Agency any question which he is required by that subsection to refer to the Agency, the Agency may exercise its powers of review under section 127 above[3], or as the case may be, section 131 below, notwithstanding anything in subsection (2) of the section in question.[4]

*Review by the Secretary of State[5] of agreements relating to special category effluent.*

131. (1) Where any person, as the owner[6] or occupier of any trade premises[7], is (whether or not in accordance with a notice under section 132 below) for the time being a party to any agreement under section 129 above[8] with respect to, or to any matter connected with, the reception or disposal of special category effluent[9], the Environment Agency[10] may review the questions—

(a) whether the operations which, for the purposes of or in connection with the reception or disposal of that effluent, are carried out in pursuance of the agreement should be prohibited; and

(b) whether, if they are not prohibited, any requirements should be imposed as to the conditions on which they are carried out.

---

[1] "Notice" defined by s.219(1), p.259 below; for provisions relating to service see s.216, p.255 below.

[2] The current statutory maximum is £5,000: Criminal Justice Act 1991 (c. 53), s.17(2).

[3] P.239 above.

[4] Subsections (7)–(9) substituted by the Environment Act 1995 (c.25), s.120, sch.22, para.108 (3).

[5] This section now relates to the Environment Agency.

[6] "Owner" defined by s.219(1), p.259 below.

[7] "Trade premises" defined by s.141(1),(2), p.247 below.

[8] P.240 above.

[9] "Special category effluent" has the meaning given by s.138, p.246 below: s.141(1) below.

[10] Words "the Environment Agency/Agency's" in this subsection substituted by the Environment Act 1995 (c.25), s.120, sch.22, para.109.

(2) Subject to subsection (3) below, the Environment Agency shall not review any question under this section unless—

(a) the agreement by virtue of which the operations in question are carried out has not previously been the subject-matter of a review and was entered into—

(i) before 1st September 1989; or

(ii) in contravention of section 133 below[1];

(b) a period of more than two years has elapsed since the time, or last time, when notice of the Environment Agency's determination on any reference or review relating to that agreement was served under section 132 below on the owner or occupier of the trade premises in question; or

(c) there has, since the time, or last time, when such a notice was so served, been a contravention of any provision which was included in compliance with a requirement of a notice under section 132 below in the agreement by virtue of which the operations in question are carried out.

(3) Subsection (2) above shall not apply if the review is carried out—

(a) for the purpose of enabling Her Majesty's Government in the United Kingdom to give effect to any Community obligation or to any international agreement to which the United Kingdom is for the time being a party; or

(b) for the protection of public health or of flora and fauna dependent on an aquatic environment.

(4) References in this section to an agreement include references to an agreement as varied from time to time by a notice under section 132 below.

*References and reviews relating to special category effluent*

*Powers and procedure on references and reviews.*

**132.** (1) This section applies to—

(a) any reference to the Environment Agency[2] under section 120[3], 123[4] or 130 above[5]; and

(b) any review by the Environment Agency under section 127[6] or 131 above.

(2) On a reference or review to which this section applies, it shall be the duty of the Environment Agency, before determining the questions which are the subject-matter of the reference or review—

(a) to give an opportunity of making representations or objections to the Environment Agency—

(i) to the sewerage undertaker in question; and

(ii) to the following person, that is to say, the owner[7] or the occupier of the trade premises[8] in question, according to whether it is the owner or the occupier of those premises who is proposing to be, or is, the person making the discharges or, as the case may be, a party to the agreement;

and

(b) to consider any representations or objections which are duly made to the Agency[9] with respect to those questions by a person to whom the Agency is required to give such an opportunity and which are not withdrawn.

[1] P.243 below.
[2] Words "the Environment Agency" in this subsection substituted by the Environment Act 1995 (c.25), s.120, sch.22, para.110(2).
[3] P.233 above.
[4] P.236 above.
[5] P.240 above.
[6] P.239 above.
[7] "Owner" defined by s.219(1), p.259 below.
[8] "Trade premises" defined by s.141(1),(2), p.247 below.
[9] Words "the Agency" in this paragraph substituted by the Environment Act 1995 (c.25), s.120, sch.22, para.110 (3).

(3) On determining any question on a reference or review to which this section applies, the Environment Agency shall serve notice[1] on the sewerage undertaker in question and on the person specified in subsection (2)(a)(ii) above.

(4) A notice under this section shall state, according to what has been determined—

(a) that the discharges or operations to which, or to the proposals for which, the reference or review relates, or such of them as are specified in the notice, are to be prohibited; or

(b) that those discharges or operations, or such of them as are so specified, are to be prohibited except in so far as they are made or carried out in accordance with conditions which consist in or include conditions so specified; or

(c) that the Environment Agency has no objection to those discharges or operations and does not intend to impose any requirements as to the conditions on which they are made or carried out.

(5) Without prejudice to section 133 below, a notice under this section, in addition to containing such provision as is specified in sub-paragraph (4) above, may do one or both of the following, that is to say—

(a) vary or revoke the provisions of a previous notice with respect to the discharges or operations in question; and

(b) for the purpose of giving effect to any prohibition or other requirement contained in the notice, vary or revoke any consent under this Chapter or any agreement under section 129 above[2].

(6) Nothing in subsection (1) or (2) of section 121 above[3] shall be construed as restricting the power of the Environment Agency, by virtue of subsection (4)(b) above, to specify such conditions as the Agency[4] considers appropriate in a notice under this section.

(7) *Repealed by the Environment Act 1995 (c.25), s.120, sch.22, para.110(5), sch.24. This amendment came into force on 1 April 1996: S.I. 1996/186.*

(8) The Environment Agency shall send a copy of every notice served under this section to the Director[5].

*Effect of determination on reference or review.*

**133.** (1) Where a notice under section 132 above has been served on a sewerage undertaker, it shall be the duty—

(a) of the undertaker; and

(b) in relation to that undertaker, of the Director[6],

so to exercise the powers to which this section applies as to secure compliance with the provisions of the notice.

(2) This paragraph applies to the following powers, that is to say—

(a) in relation to a sewerage undertaker, its power to give a consent under this Chapter, any of its powers under section 121[7] or 124 above[8] and any power to enter into or vary an agreement under section 129 above[9]; and

(b) in relation to the Director, any of his powers under this Chapter.

(3) Nothing in subsection (1) or (2) of section 121 above shall be construed as restricting the power of a sewerage undertaker, for the purpose of complying with this section, to impose any condition specified in a notice under section 132 above.

[1] "Notice" defined by s.219(1), p.259 below; for provisions relating to service see s.216, p.255 below.
[2] P.240 above.
[3] P.234 above.
[4] Words "the Agency" substituted by the Environment Act 1995 (c.25), s.120, sch.22, para.110 (4).
[5] "The Director" defined by s.219(1), p.258 below.
[6] "The Director" defined by s.219(1), p.258 below.
[7] P.234 above.
[8] P.237 above.
[9] P.240 above.

(4) *Substituted by subsections (5) and (6) below.*

(5) A sewerage undertaker which fails to perform its duty under subsection (1) above shall be guilty of an offence and liable—

 (a) on summary conviction, to a fine not exceeding the statutory maximum[1];

 (b) on conviction on indictment, to a fine.

(6) The Environment Agency may, for the purpose of securing compliance with the provisions of a notice under section 132 above, by serving notice[2] on the sewerage undertaker in question and on the person specified in section 132(2)(a)(ii) above, vary or revoke—

 (a) any consent given under this Chapter to make discharges of any special category effluent[3], or

 (b) any agreement under section 129 above.[4]

*Compensation in respect of determinations made for the protection of public health etc.*

**134.** (1) Subject to subsection (2) below, the Environment Agency[5] shall be liable to pay compensation to the relevant person[6] in respect of any loss or damage sustained by that person as a result of any notice under section 132 above[7] containing the Environment Agency's determination on a review which—

 (a) has been carried out for the protection of public health or of flora and fauna dependent on an aquatic environment; and

 (b) but for being so carried out would have been prohibited by virtue of section 127(2)[8] or 131(2)[9] above.

(2) The Environment Agency shall not be required to pay any compensation under this section if the determination in question is shown to have been given in consequence of—

 (a) a change of circumstances which could not reasonably have been foreseen at the time when the period of two years mentioned in section 128(2) or, as the case may be, section 131(2) above began to run; or

 (b) consideration by the Environment Agency of material information which was not reasonably available to the Agency[10] at that time.

(3) No person shall be entitled to any compensation under section 125 above[11] in respect of anything done in pursuance of section 133 above.

(4) In this section "the relevant person", in relation to a review, means the owner[12] or the occupier of the trade premises[13] in question, according to whether it is the owner or the occupier who makes the discharges to which the review relates or, as the case may be, is a party to the agreement to which it relates.

*Supplemental provisions of Chapter III*

*Restrictions on power to fix charges under Chapter III.*

**135.** (1) On any appeal under section 122[14] or 126(1)[15] above conditions providing for the payment of charges to the sewerage undertaker in question shall not be determined by the Director[16]

---

[1] The current statutory maximum is £5,000: Criminal Justice Act 1991 (c.53), s.17(2).

[2] "Notice" defined by s.219(1), p.259 below; for provisions relating to service see s.216, p.255 below.

[3] "Special category effluent" has the meaning given by s.138, p.246 below: s.141(1) below.

[4] Paras. (5) and (6) substituted by the Environment Act 1995 (c.25), s.120, sch.22, para.111.

[5] Words "the Environment Agency/Agency's" in this subsection substituted by the Environment Act 1995 (c.25), s.120, sch.22, para.112(a).

[6] "The relevant person" defined by subsection (4) below.

[7] P.242 above.

[8] P.239 above.

[9] P.241 above.

[10] Words "the Agency" substituted by the Environment Act 1995 (c.25), s.120, sch.22, para.112(b).

[11] P.237 above.

[12] "Owner" defined by s.219(1), p.259 below.

[13] " Trade premises " defined by s.141(1), (2), p.247 below.

[14] P.235 above.

[15] P.238 above.

[16] "The Director" defined by s.219(1), p.258 below.

except in so far as no provision is in force by virtue of a charges scheme under section 143 below in respect of any such receptions, discharges, removals or disposals[1] of effluent[2] or substances[3] as are of the same description as the reception, discharge, removal or disposal which is the subject-matter of the appeal.

(2) In so far as any such conditions as are mentioned in subsection (1) above do fall to be determined by the Director, they shall be determined having regard to the desirability of that undertaker's—

(a)  recovering the expenses of complying with its obligations in consequence of the consent or agreement to which the conditions relate; and

(b)  securing a reasonable return on its capital.

(3) To the extent that subsection (1) above excludes any charges from a determination on an appeal those charges shall be fixed from time to time by a charges scheme under section 143 below but not otherwise.

*Power of the Environment Agency to acquire information for the purpose of its functions in relation to special category effluent.*

135A.  (1) For the purpose of the discharge of its functions under this Chapter, the Environment Agency may, by notice in writing served[4] on any person, require that person to furnish such information specified in the notice as that Agency reasonably considers it needs, in such form and within such period following service of the notice, or at such time, as is so specified.

(2) A person who—

(a)  fails, without reasonable excuse, to comply with a requirement imposed under subsection (1) above, or

(b)  in furnishing any information in compliance with such a requirement, makes any statement which he knows to be false or misleading in a material particular, or recklessly makes a statement which is false or misleading in a material particular,

shall be guilty of an offence.

(3) A person guilty of an offence under subsection (2) above shall be liable—

(a)  on summary conviction, to a fine not exceeding the statutory maximum[5];

(b)  on conviction on indictment, to a fine or to imprisonment for a term not exceeding two years, or to both.[6]

*Evidence from meters etc.*

136.  Any meter[7] or apparatus provided in pursuance of this Chapter in any trade premises[8] for the purpose of measuring, recording or determining the volume, rate of discharge, nature or composition of any trade effluent[9] discharged from those premises shall be presumed in any proceedings to register accurately, unless the contrary is shown.

*Statement of case on appeal.*

137.  (1) At any stage of the proceedings on an appeal under section 122[10] or 126(1) above[11], the Director[12] may, and if so directed by the High Court shall, state in the form of a special case for the decision of the High Court any question of law arising in those proceedings.

---

[1] "Disposal", in relation to sewage, includes treatment: s.219(1) below.

[2] "Effluent" defined by s.219(1), p.258 below.

[3] "Substance" defined by s.219(1), p.261 below.

[4] For provisions relating to service see s.216, p.255 below.

[5] The current statutory maximum is £5,000: Criminal Justice Act 1991 (c.53), s.17(2)

[6] This section inserted by the Environment Act 1995 (c.25), s.120, sch.22, para.113. This amendment came into force on 1 April 1996: S.I. 1996/186.

[7] "Meter" defined by s.219(1), p.259 below.

[8] "Trade premises" defined by s.141(1),(2), p.247 below.

[9] "Trade effluent" defined by s.141(1),(2), p.247 below.

[10] P.235 above.

[11] P.238 above.

[12] "The Director" defined by s.219(1), p.258 below.

(2) The decision of the High Court on a special case under this section shall be deemed to be a judgment of the Court within the meaning of section 16 of the Supreme Court Act 1981[1] (which relates to the jurisdiction to the Court of Appeal); but no appeal to the Court of Appeal shall be brought by virtue of this subsection except with the leave of the High Court or of the Court of Appeal.

*Meaning of "special category effluent".*

**138.**  (1) Subject to subsection (2) below, trade effluent[2] shall be special category effluent for the purposes of this Chapter if—

(*a*)  such substances[3] as may be prescribed[4] under this Act are present in the effluent or are present in the effluent in prescribed concentrations; or

(*b*)  the effluent derives from any such process as may be so prescribed or from a process involving the use of prescribed substances or the use of such substances in quantities which exceed the prescribed amounts[5].

(2) Trade effluent shall not be special category effluent for the purposes of this Chapter if it is produced, or to be produced, in any process which is a prescribed process designated for central control as from the date which is the determination date for that process.

(3) In subsection (2) above "determination date", in relation to a prescribed process, means—

(*a*)  in the case of a process for which authorisation is granted, the date on which the enforcing authority grants it, whether in pursuance of the application or, on an appeal, of a direction to grant it;

(*b*)  in the case of a process for which authorisation is refused, the date of refusal or, on appeal, of the affirmation of the refusal.

(4) In this section—

(*a*)  "authorisation", "enforcing authority" and "prescribed process" have the meanings given by section 1 of the Environmental Protection Act 1990[6]; and

(*b*)  the references to designation for central control and to an appeal are references, respectively, to designation under section 4[7] of that Act and to an appeal under section 15 of that Act[8].

(5) Without prejudice to the power in subsection (3) of section 139 below, nothing in this Chapter shall enable regulations under this section to prescribe as special category effluent any liquid or matter which is not trade effluent but falls to be treated as such for the purposes of this Chapter by virtue of an order under that section.

*Power to apply Chapter III to other effluents.*

**139.**  (1) The Secretary of State may by order provide that, subject to section 138(5) above, this Chapter shall apply in relation to liquid or other matter of any description specified in the order which is discharged into public sewers[9] as it applies in relation to trade effluent[10].

(2) An order applying the provisions of this Chapter in relation to liquid or other matter of any description may provide for it to so apply subject to such modifications[11] (if any) as may be specified in the order and, in particular, subject to any such modification of the meaning for the purposes of this Chapter of the expression "trade premises" as may be so specified.

---

[1]  1981 c.54.
[2]  "Trade effluent" defined by s.141(1),(2), p.247 below.
[3]  "Substance" defined by s.219(1), p.261 below.
[4]  "Prescribed" defined by s.219(1), p.259 below.
[5]  The following regulations are made, or by virtue of the Water Consolidation (Consequential Provisions) Act 1991 (c.60), s.2(2), sch.2, para.1 have effect as if made, under this section:
The Trade Effluents (Prescribed Processes and Substances) Regulations 1989, S.I. 1989/1156, as amended,
p.542 below;
The Trade Effluents (Prescribed Processes and Substances) Regulations 1992, S.I. 1992/339, p.656 below.
[6]  P.89 above.
[7]  P.93 above.
[8]  P.103 above.
[9]  "Public sewer" defined by s.219(1), p.260 below.
[10]  "Trade effluent" defined by s.141(1),(2), p.247 below.
[11]  "Modifications" defined by s.219(1), p.259 below.

(3)  The Secretary of State may include in an order under this section such provisions as appear to him expedient for modifying any enactment[1] relating to sewage as that enactment applies in relation to the discharge into sewers[2] of any liquid or other matter to which any provisions of this Chapter are applied by an order under this section.

(4)  The Secretary of State may include in an order under this section such other supplemental, incidental and transitional provision as appears to him to be expedient.

(5)  The power to make an order under this section shall be exercisable by statutory instrument; and no order shall be made under this section unless a draft of it has been laid before, and approved by a resolution of, each House of Parliament.

*Pre-1989 Act authority for trade effluent discharges etc.*

**140.**  Schedule 8 to this Act[3] shall have effect (without prejudice to the provisions of the Water Consolidation (Consequential Provisions) Act 1991[4] or to sections 16 and 17 of the Interpretation Act 1978[5]) for the purpose of making provision in respect of certain cases where trade effluent[6] was discharged in accordance with provision made before the coming into force of the Water Act 1989[7].

*Interpretation of Chapter III*

*Interpretation of Chapter III.*

**141.**  (1)  In this Chapter, except in so far as the context otherwise requires—

"special category effluent" has the meaning given by section 138 above[8];

"trade effluent"—

(*a*)  means any liquid, either with or without particles of matter in suspension in the liquid, which is wholly or partly produced in the course of any trade or industry carried on at trade premises; and

(*b*)  in relation to any trade premises, means any such liquid which is so produced in the course of any trade or industry carried on at those premises,

but does not include domestic sewage;

"trade premises" means, subject to subsection (2) below, any premises used or intended to be used for carrying on any trade or industry.

(2)  For the purposes of this Chapter any land or premises used or intended for use (in whole or in part and whether or not for profit)—

(*a*)  for agricultural or horticultural purposes or for the purposes of fish farming; or

(*b*)  for scientific research or experiment,

shall be deemed to be premises used for carrying on a trade or industry; and the references to a trade or industry in the definition of "trade effluent" in subsection (1) above shall include references to agriculture, horticulture, fish farming and scientific research or experiment.

(3)  Every application or consent made or given under this Chapter shall be made or given in writing.

(4)  Nothing in this Chapter shall affect any right with respect to water in a river stream or watercourse[9], or authorise any infringement of such a right, except in so far as any such right would dispense with the requirements of this Chapter so far as they have effect by virtue of any regulations under section 138 above[10].

[1]  "Enactment" defined by s.219(1), p.258 below.
[2]  "Sewer" defined by s.219(1),(2), p.260 below.
[3]  P.264 below.
[4]  1991 c.60.
[5]  1978 c.30.
[6]  "Trade effluent" defined by s.141(1),(2), below.
[7]  1989 c.15.
[8]  P.246 above.
[9]  "Watercourse" defined by s.219(1), p.261 below.
[10]  P.246 above.

## Part VII: Information Provisions

*This Manual contains provisions from this Part relating, in respect of trade effluent, to registers, provision of information and restriction on disclosure of information and, in respect of this Act generally, to the provision of false information. Note that the following sections comprise extracts from this Part and that the complete Part is not set out.*

Registers, maps etc.

*Trade effluent registers.*

**196.**   (1)  It shall be the duty of every sewerage undertaker to secure that copies of—

(a)  every consent given or having effect as if given by the undertaker under Chapter III of Part IV of this Act[1];

(b)  every direction given or having effect as if given by the undertaker under that Chapter;

(c)  every agreement entered into or having effect as if entered into by the undertaker under section 129 above[2]; and

(e)  every notice served on the undertaker under section 132 above[3],

are kept available, at all reasonable times, for inspection by the public free of charge at the offices of the undertaker.

(2)  It shall be the duty of every sewerage undertaker, on the payment of such sum as may be reasonable, to furnish a person who requests it with a copy of, or of an extract from, anything kept available for inspection under this section.

(3)  The duties of a sewerage undertaker under this section shall be enforceable under section 18 above[4] by the Director[5].

Powers to acquire and duties to provide information

*Provision of information to sewerage undertakers with respect to trade effluent discharges.*

**204.**   (1)  The owner[6] or occupier of any land on or under which is situated any sewer[7], drain[8], pipe,[9] channel or outlet used or intended to be used for discharging any trade effluent[10] into a sewer of a sewerage undertaker shall, when requested to do so by the undertaker—

(a)  produce to the undertaker all such plans of the sewer, drain, pipe, channel or outlet as the owner or, as the case may be, occupier possesses or is able without expense to obtain;

(b)  allow copies of the plans so produced by him to be made by, or under the directions of, the undertaker; and

(c)  furnish to the undertaker all such information as the owner or, as the case may be, occupier can reasonably be expected to supply with respect to the sewer, drain, pipe, channel or outlet.

(2)  A request by a sewerage undertaker for the purposes of this section shall be made in writing.

(3)  Every person who fails to comply with this section shall be guilty of an offence and liable, on summary conviction to a fine not exceeding level 3 on the standard scale[11].

(4)  Expressions used in this section and in Chapter III of Part IV of this Act have the same meanings in this section as in that Chapter; and, accordingly, section 139 above[12] shall have effect for the purposes of this section as it has effect for the purposes of that Chapter.

[1] Chapter III is set out above.
[2] P.240 above.
[3] P.242 above.
[4] S.18 relates to orders for securing compliance with certain conditions.
[5] "The Director" defined by s.219(1), p.258 below.
[6] "Owner" defined by s.219(1), p.259 below.
[7] "Sewer" defined by s.219(1),(2), p.260 below.
[8] "Drain" defined by s.219(1),(2), p.258 below.
[9] For "pipe" see s. 219(2), p.261 below.
[10] "Trade effluent" defined by s.141(1),(2), p.247 above: subsection (4) below.
[11] The current fine at level 3 on the standard scale is £1,000: Criminal Justice Act 1991 (c.53), s.17.
[12] P.246 above.

*Restriction on disclosure of information*

*Restriction on disclosure of information.*

**206.** (1) Subject to the following provisions of this section, no information with respect to any particular business which—

(a) has been obtained by virtue of any of the provisions of this Act; and

(b) relates to the affairs of any individual or to any particular business,

shall, during the lifetime of that individual or so long as that business continued to be carried on, be disclosed without the consent of that individual or the person for the time being carrying on that business.

(2) No person shall disclose any information furnished to him under section[1] 204 above or under Chapter III of Part IV[2] of this Act except—

(a) with the consent of the person by whom the information was furnished;

(b) in connection with the execution of that Chapter;

(c) for the purposes of any proceedings arising under that Chapter (including any appeal, application to the Secretary of State or the Director[3] or an arbitration);

(d) for the purposes of any criminal proceedings (whether or not so arising); or

(e) for the purposes of any report of any proceedings falling within paragraph (c) or (d) above.

(3) Subsection (1) above does not apply to any disclosure of information which is made—

(a) for the purpose of facilitating the carrying out by the Secretary of State, the Minister, the Environment Agency, the Scottish Environment Protection Agency[4,5], the Director, the Monopolies Commission or a county council or local authority[6] of any of his, its or, as the case may be, their functions by virtue of this Act, any of the other consolidation Acts, the Water Act 1989[8], Part I[9] or IIA[10] of the Environmental Protection Act 1990 or the Environment Act 1995[11,12];

(b) for the purpose of facilitating the performance by a relevant undertaker[13] of any of the duties imposed on it by or under this Act, any of the other consolidation Acts or the Water Act 1989;

(c) in pursuance of any arrangements made by the Director under section 29(6) above or of any duty imposed by section 197(1)(a) or (2) or 203(1) or (2)[14] of the Water Resources Act 1991 (information about water flow and pollution);

(d) for the purpose of facilitating the carrying out by any person mentioned in Part I of Schedule 15 to this Act[15] of any of his functions under any of the enactments or instruments specified in Part II of that Schedule;

(e) for the purpose of enabling or assisting the Secretary of State to exercise any powers conferred on him by the Financial Services Act 1986[16] or by the enactments[17] relating to companies, insurance companies or insolvency or for the purpose of enabling or assisting any inspector appointed by him under the enactments relating to companies to carry out his functions;

[1] Former words "196 or" repealed by the Environment Act 1995 (c.25), s.120, sch.22, para.121 (1), sch.24.

[2] P.232 above.

[3] "The Director" defined by s.219(1), p.258 below.

[4] The Scottish Environment Protection Agency, SEPA, is established under s.20 of the Environment Act 1995 (c.25), p.438 below.

[5] Words "the Environment Agency, the Scottish Environment Agency" substituted by the Environment Act 1995 (c.25), s.120, sch.22, para.121 (2) (a).

[6] "Local Authority" defined by s.219(1), p.259 below.

[7] "The other consolidation Acts" defined by subsection (10) below.

[8] 1989 c.15.

[9] P.88 above.

[10] P.162 above.

[11] P.415 below.

[12] Words ", the Water Act 1989, Part I or IIA of the Environmental Protection Act 1990 or the Environment Act 1995" inserted by the Environment Act 1995 (c.25), s.120, sch.22, para.121(2)(b).

[13] "Relevant undertaker" defined by s.219(1), p.260 below.

[14] P.303 below.

[15] P.266 below.

[16] 1986 c.60.

[17] "Enactment" defined by s.219(1), p.258 below.

(f) for the purpose of enabling an official receiver to carry out his functions under the enactments relating to insolvency or for the purpose of enabling or assisting a recognised professional body for the purposes of section 391 of the Insolvency Act 1986[1] to carry out its functions as such;

(g) for the purpose of facilitating the carrying out by the Health and Safety Commission or the Health and Safety Executive of any of its functions under any enactment or of facilitating the carrying out by any enforcing authority, within the meaning of Part I of the Health and Safety at Work etc. Act 1974[2], of any functions under a relevant statutory provision, within the meaning of that Act;

(h) for the purpose of facilitating the carrying out by the Comptroller and Auditor General of any of his functions under any enactment;

(i) in connection with the investigation of any criminal offence or for the purposes of any criminal proceedings;

(j) for the purposes of any civil proceedings brought under or by virtue of this Act, any of the other consolidation Acts, the Water Act 1989 or any of the enactments or instruments specified in Part II of Schedule 15 to this Act[3], or of any arbitration under this Act, any of the other consolidation Acts or that Act of 1989; or

(k) in pursuance of a Community obligation.

(4) Nothing in subsection (1) above shall be construed—

(a) as limiting the matters which may be published under section 38A, 95A[4] or[5] 201[6] above or may be included in, or made public as part of, a report of the Environment Agency, the Scottish Environment Protection Agency[7], the Director, a customer service committee or the Monopolies Commission under any provision of this Act, Part I or IIA of the Environment Protection Act 1990, the Water Resources Act 1991 or the Environment Act 1995[8]; or

(b) as applying to any information which has been so published or has been made public as part of such a report or to any information exclusively of a statistical nature.

(5) Subject to subsection (6) below, nothing in subsection (1) above shall preclude the disclosure of information—

(a) if the disclosure is of information relating to a matter connected with the carrying out of the functions of a relevant undertaker[9] and is made by one Minister of the Crown or government department to another; or

(b) if the disclosure is for the purpose of enabling or assisting any public or other authority[10] for the time being designated for the purposes of this section by an order made by the Secretary of State to discharge any functions which are specified in the order.

(6) The power to make an order under subsection (5) above shall be exercisable by statutory instrument subject to annulment in pursuance of a resolution of either House of Parliament; and where such an order designates an authority for the purposes of paragraph (b) of that subsection, the order may—

(a) impose conditions subject to which the disclosure of information is permitted by virtue of that paragraph; and

[1] 1986 c.45.
[2] 1974 c.37.
[3] P.266 below.
[4] Ss.38A and 95A relate to information with respect to levels of performance concerning water supply and sewerage services respectively.
[5] Words "38A, 95A or" inserted by the Competition and Service (Utilities) Act 1992(c. 43), s.56 (6), sch.1, para. 27. This amendment came into force on 1 July 1992: Competition and Service (Utilities) Act 1992 (Commencement No.1) Order 1992.

[6] S.201 relates to the publication of certain information and advice.
[7] Words "the Environment Agency, the Scottish Environment Protection Agency" substituted by the Environment Act 1995 (c.25), s.120, sch.22, para.121(3) (a).
[8] Words ", Part I or IIA of the Environment Protection Act 1990, the Water Resources Act 1991 or the Environment Act 1995" substituted by the Environment Act 1995 (c.25), s.120, sch.22, para.121(3)(b).
[9] "Functions" defined by s.219(1), p.259 below.
[10] "Public authority" defined by s.219(1), p.260 below.

(*b*)  otherwise restrict the circumstances in which disclosure is so permitted.

(7)  Any person who discloses any information in contravention of the preceding provisions of this section shall be guilty of an offence.

(8)  A person who is guilty of an offence under this section by virtue of subsection (1) above shall be liable—

(*a*)  on summary conviction, to a fine not exceeding the statutory maximum[1];

(*b*)  on conviction on indictment, to imprisonment for a term not exceeding two years or to a fine or to both.

(9)  A person who is guilty of an offence under this section by virtue of subsection (2) above shall be liable, on summary conviction, to imprisonment for a term not exceeding three months or to a fine not exceeding level 3 on the standard scale[2] or to both.

(10)  In this section "the other consolidation Acts" means the Water Resources Act 1991[3], the Statutory Water Companies Act 1991[4], the Land Drainage Act 1991[5] and the Water Consolidation (Consequential Provisions) Act 1991[6].

*Provision of false information*

*Provision of false information.*

**207.**  (1)  If any person, in furnishing any information or making any application under or for the purposes of any provision of this Act, makes any statement which he knows to be false in a material particular, or recklessly makes any statement which is false in a material particular, he shall be guilty of an offence and liable—

(*a*)  on summary conviction, to a fine not exceeding the statutory maximum[7];

(*b*)  on conviction on indictment, to a fine.

(2)  Proceedings for an offence under subsection (1) above shall not be instituted except by or with the consent of the Secretary of State, the Minister of Agriculture, Fisheries and Food or the Director of Public Prosecutions.

# Part VIII: Miscellaneous and Supplemental

*Miscellaneous*

*Directions in the interests of national security.*

**208.**  (1)  The Secretary of State may, after consultation with a relevant undertaker[8], give to that undertaker such directions of a general character as appear to the Secretary of State to be requisite or expedient in the interests of national security or for the purpose of mitigating the effect of any civil emergency[9] which may occur.

(2)  If it appears to the Secretary of State to be requisite or expedient to do so in the interests of national security or for the purpose of mitigating the effects of any civil emergency which has occurred or may occur, he may, after consultation with a relevant undertaker, give to that undertaker a direction requiring it to do, or not to do, a particular thing specified in the direction.

---

[1] The current statutory maximum is £5,000: Criminal Justice Act 1991 (c.53), s.17(2).

[2] The current fine at level 3 on the standard scale is £1,000: Criminal Justice Act 1991 (c.53), s.17.

[3] 1991 c.57, p.267 below.

[4] 1991 c.58.

[5] 1991 c.59.

[6] 1991 c.60.

[7] The current statutory maximum is £5,000: Criminal Justice Act 1991 (c.53), s.17(2).

[8] "Relevant undertaker" defined by s.219(1), p.000 below.

[9] For "civil emergency" see subsection (7) below.

(3) It shall be the duty of a relevant undertaker, notwithstanding any other duty imposed on it (whether or not by or under this Act), to comply with any direction given to it by the Secretary of State under this section; and the duty of a relevant undertaker to comply with any such direction shall be enforceable under section 18 above[1] by the Secretary of State.

(4) The Secretary of state shall lay before each House of Parliament a copy of every direction given under this section unless he is of the opinion that disclosure of the direction is against the interests of national security.

(5) A person shall not disclose, or be required by virtue of any enactment[2] or otherwise to disclose, anything done by virtue of this section if the Secretary of State has notified him that the Secretary of State is of the opinion that disclosure of that thing is against the interests of national security.

(6) Any person who discloses any matter in contravention of subsection (5) above shall be guilty of an offence and liable, on conviction on indictment, to imprisonment for a term not exceeding two years or to a fine or to both.

(7) Any reference in this section to a civil emergency is a reference to any natural disaster or other emergency which, in the opinion of the Secretary of State, is or may be likely, in relation to any area—

(a) so to disrupt water supplies or sewerage services; or

(b) to involve such destruction of or damage to life or property in that area,

as seriously and adversely to affect all the inhabitants of that area, or a substantial number of them, whether by depriving them of any of the essentials of life or otherwise.

*Civil liability of undertakers for escapes of water etc.*

209.  (1) Where an escape of water, however caused, from a pipe[3] vested in a water undertaker causes loss or damage, the undertaker shall be liable, except as otherwise provided in this section, for the loss or damage.

(2) A water undertaker shall not incur any liability under subsection (1) above if the escape was due wholly to the fault[4] of the person who sustained the loss or damage or of any servant, agent or contractor of his.

(3) A water undertaker shall not incur any liability under subsection (1) above in respect of any loss or damage for which the undertaker would not be liable apart from that subsection and which is sustained—

(a) by the Environment Agency[5], a relevant undertaker[6] or any statutory undertakers, within the meaning of section 336(1) of the Town and Country Planning Act 1990[7];

(b) by any public gas supplier within the meaning of Part I of the Gas Act 1986[8] or the holder of a licence under section 6(1) of the Electricity Act 1989[9];

(c) by any highway authority[10]; or

(d) by any person on whom a right to compensation is conferred by section 82 of the New Roads and Street Works Act 1991[11].

(4) The Law Reform (Contributory Negligence) Act 1945[12], the Fatal Accidents Act 1976[13] and the Limitation Act 1980[14] shall apply in relation to any loss or damage for which a water undertaker is liable under this section, but which is not due to the undertaker's fault, as if it were due to its fault.

[1] S.18 relates to orders for securing compliance with certain conditions.
[2] "Enactment" defined by s.219(1), p.258 below.
[3] For "pipe" see s.219(2), p.261 below.
[4] For "fault" see subsection (7) below.
[5] Words "the Environment Agency" substituted by the Environment Act 1995 (c.25), s.120, sch.22, para.122.
[6] "Relevant undertaker" defined by s.219(1), p.260 below.
[7] 1990 c.8.
[8] 1986 c.44.
[9] 1989 c.29.
[10] "Highway authority" defined by s.219(1), p.259 below.
[11] 1991 c.22.
[12] 1945 c.28.
[13] 1976 c.30.
[14] 1980 c.58.

(5) Nothing in subsection (1) above affects any entitlement which a water undertaker may have to recover contribution under the Civil Liability (Contribution) Act 1978[1]; and for the purposes of that Act, any loss for which a water undertaker is liable under that subsection shall be treated as if it were damage.

(6) Where a water undertaker is liable under any enactment[2] or agreement passed or made before 1st April 1982 to make any payment in respect of any loss or damage the undertaker shall not incur liability under subsection (1) above in respect of the same loss or damage.

(7) In this section "fault" has the same meaning as in the Law Reform (Contributory Negligence) Act 1945.

(8) Until the coming into force of section 82 of the New Roads and Street Works Act 1991[3], subsection (3) above shall have effect as if for paragraph (d) there were substituted the following paragraphs—

"(d) by any bridge authority, bridge managers, street authority or street managers within the meaning of the Public Utilities Street Works Act 1950; or

(e) by any person on whom a right to compensation under section 26 of that Act of 1950 is conferred.";

but nothing in this section shall be taken to prejudice the power of the Secretary of State under that Act of 1991 to make an order bringing section 82 of that Act into force on different days for different purposes (including the purposes of this section).

*Offences*

*Offences by bodies corporate.*

210. (1) Where a body corporate is guilty of an offence under this Act and that offence is proved to have been committed with the consent or connivance of, or to be attributable to any neglect on the part of, any director, manager, secretary or other similar officer of the body corporate or any person who was purporting to act in any such capacity, then he, as well as the body corporate, shall be guilty of that offence and shall be liable to be proceeded against and punished accordingly.

(2) Where the affairs of a body corporate are managed by its members, subsection (1) above shall apply in relation to the acts and defaults of a member in connection with his functions of management as if he were a director of the body corporate.

*Limitation on right to prosecute in respect of sewerage offences.*

211. Proceedings in respect of an offence created by or under any of the relevant sewerage provisions[4] shall not, without the written consent of the Attorney-General, be taken by any person other than—

(a) a party aggrieved;

(b) a sewerage undertaker; or

(c) a body whose function it is to enforce the provisions in question.

*Judicial disqualification*

*Judicial disqualification.*

212. No judge of any court or justice of the peace shall be disqualified from acting in relation to any proceedings to which a relevant undertaker[5] is a party by reason only that he is or may become

---

[1] 1978 c.47.
[2] "Enactment" defined by s.219(1), p.258 below.
[3] S.82 of the New Roads and Street Works Act 1991 (c.22) came into force on 1 January 1993: S.I. 1992/2984.

[4] "The relevant sewerage provisions" defined by s.219(1), p.260 below.
[5] "Relevant undertaker" defined by s.219(1), p.260 below.

liable to pay a charge to that undertaker in respect of any service that is not the subject-matter of the proceedings.

*Powers to make regulations*

*Powers to make regulations.*

**213.** (1) The powers of the Secretary of State to make regulations under this Act shall be exercisable by statutory instrument subject (except in the case of regulations under section 8(1) or (2) above) to annulment in pursuance of a resolution of either House of Parliament.

(2) Subject to subsection (3) below, the provisions of any regulations made by the Secretary of State under this Act may include—

(a)   provision for any duty or other requirement imposed by the regulations on a water undertaker or sewerage undertaker to be enforceable under section 18 above by the Secretary of State, by the Director[1] or by either of them;

(b)   provision, where such a duty or requirement is so enforceable by either of them, for enforcement by the Director to be subject to such consent or authorisation as may be prescribed;

(c)   provision which, in relation to the furnishing of any information or the making of any application under the regulations, makes provision corresponding to section 207 above[2];

(d)   provision for anything that may be prescribed by the regulations to be determined under the regulations and for anything falling to be so determined to be determined by such persons, in accordance with such procedure and by reference to such matters, and to the opinion of such persons, as may be prescribed;

(dd)   as to awarding costs or expenses of proceedings in any determination under the regulations, including the amount of the costs or expenses and the enforcement of the awards;[3]

(e)   different provision for different cases, including different provision in relation to different persons, circumstances or localities; and

(f)   such supplemental, consequential and transitional provision as the Secretary of State considers appropriate.[4]

(2A) Such regulations may include provision—

(a)   for the determination of questions of fact or of law which may arise in giving effect to the regulations;

(b)   for regulating (otherwise than in relation to any court proceedings) any matters relating to the practice and procedure to be followed in connection with the determination of such questions;

(c)   as to the mode of proof of any matter;

(d)   as to parties and their representation; and

(e)   for the right to appear before and be heard by the Secretary of State, the Director and other authorities.

(2B) Any such regulations which prescribe a period within which things are to be done may provide for extending the period so prescribed.[5]

(3) Except to the extent that they would do so apart from this section, the power to make regulations under section 113, 125[6] or 126[7] above or under section 214 below or Schedule 8[8] to this Act—

---

[1] "The Director" defined by s.219(1), p.258 below.
[2] P.251 above.
[3] Para.(dd) inserted by the Competition and Service (Utilities) Act 1992 (c.43), s.56(6), sch.1, para.28. This amendment came into force on 1 July 1992: Competition and Service (Utilities) Act 1992 (Commencement No.1) Order 1992.
[4] The Private Water Supplies Regulations 1991, S.I.

1991/2790, are made under this section.
[5] Paras.(2A)–(2B) inserted by the Competition and Service (Utilities) Act 1992 (c.43), s.52. This amendment came into force on 1 July 1992: Competition and Service (Utilities) Act 1992 (Commencement No.1) Order 1992.
[6] P.237 above.
[7] P.238 above.
[8] P.264 below.

(a)  shall not include the powers conferred by virtue of paragraphs (a) to (d) of subsection (2) above; and

(b)  in the case of the power to make regulations under section 214 below, shall also not include the powers conferred by virtue of paragraphs (e) and (f) of that subsection.

*Power to prescribe forms.*

**214.**  (1)  The Secretary of State may by regulations prescribe the form of any notice or other document to be used for any of the purposes of the relevant sewerage provisions[1].

(2)  If forms are prescribed under this section, those forms or forms to the like effect may be used in all cases to which those forms are applicable.

*Local inquiries*

*Local inquiries.*

**215.**  (1)  The Secretary of State may cause a local inquiry to be held in any case where he is authorised by any of the relevant sewerage provisions[2] to determine any difference, to make any order, to give any consent or otherwise to act under any of those provisions.

(2)  Subject to subsection (3) below, subsections (2) to (5) of section 250 of the Local Government Act 1972[3] (which contain supplementary provisions with respect to local inquiries held in pursuance of that section) shall apply to local inquiries under subsection (1) above or any of the other provisions of this Act as they apply to inquiries under that section.

(3)  Subsection (4) of the said section 250 shall apply in accordance with subsection (2) above in relation to such local inquiries under this Act as are held with respect to any matter affecting the carrying out of any function of the Environment Agency[4] as if the reference to a local authority in that subsection included a reference to the Environment Agency.

*Construction of Act*

*Provisions relating to the service of documents.*

**216.**  (1)  Any document required or authorised by virtue of this Act to be served on any person may be served—

(a)  by delivering it to him or by leaving it at his proper address or by sending it by post to him at that address; or

(b)  if the person is a body corporate, by serving it in accordance with paragraph (a) above on the secretary or clerk of that body; or

(c)  if the person is a partnership, by serving it in accordance with paragraph (a) above on a partner or a person having the control of management of the partnership business.

(2)  For the purposes of this section and section 7 of the Interpretation Act 1978[5] (which relates to the service of documents by post) in its application to this section, the proper address of any person on whom a document is to be served shall be his last known address, except that—

(a)  in the case of service on a body corporate or its secretary or clerk, it shall be the address of the registered or principal office of the body;

(b)  in the case of service on a partnership or a partner or a person having the control or management of a partnership business, it shall be the principal office of the partnership;

and for the purposes of this subsection the principal office of a company registered outside the United Kingdom or of a partnership carrying on business outside the United Kingdom is its principal office within the United Kingdom.

---

[1] "The relevant sewerage provisions" defined by s.219(1), p.260 below.
[2] "The relevant sewerage provisions" defined by s.219(1), p.260 below.
[3] 1972 c.70.
[4] Words "the Environment Agency" in this section substituted by the Environment Act 1995 (c.25), s.120, sch.22, para.123.
[5] 1978 c.30.

(3) If a person to be served by virtue of this Act with any document by another has specified to that other an address within the United Kingdom other than his proper address (as determined in pursuance of subsection (2) above) as the one at which he or someone on his behalf will accept documents of the same description as that document, that address shall also be treated as his proper address for the purposes of this section and for the purposes of the said section 7 in its application to this section.

(4) Where under any provision of this Act any document is required to be served on the owner[1], on a lessee or on the occupier of any premises then—

(a)  if the name or address of the owner, of the lessee or, as the case may be, of the occupier of the premises cannot after reasonable inquiry be ascertained; or

(b)  in the case of service on the occupier, if the premises appear to be or are unoccupied,

that document may be served either by leaving it in the hands of a person who is or appears to be resident or employed on the land or by leaving it conspicuously affixed to some building or object on the land.

(5)  This section shall not apply to any document in relation to the service of which provision is made by rules of court.

*Construction of provision conferring powers by reference to undertakers' functions.*

**217.**  (1)  The purposes to which this section applies shall be the construction of any enactment[2] which, by reference to the functions of a relevant undertaker[3], confers any power on or in relation to that undertaker.

(2)  For the purposes to which this section applies the functions of every relevant undertaker shall be taken to include joining with or acting on behalf of—

(a)  the Environment Agency[4];

(b)  one or more other relevant undertakers; or

(c)  the Environment Agency and one or more other such undertakers,

for the purpose of carrying out any works or acquiring any land which at least one of the bodies with which it joins, or on whose behalf it acts, is authorised to carry out or acquire for the purposes of that body's functions under any enactment or of any function which is taken to be a function of that body for the purposes to which this section or section 3 of the Water Resources Act 1991[5] (functions of Environment Agency for certain purposes) applies.

(3)  For the purposes to which this section applies the functions of every relevant undertaker shall be taken to include the protection against pollution—

(a)  of any waters, whether on the surface or underground, which belong to the Environment Agency or any water undertaker or from which the Environment Agency or any water undertaker is authorised to take water;

(b)  without prejudice to paragraph (a) above, of any reservoir which belongs to or is operated by the Environment Agency or any water undertaker or which the Environment Agency or any water undertaker is proposing to acquire or construct for the purpose of being so operated; and

(c)  of any underground strata[6] from which the Environment Agency or any water undertaker is for the time being authorised to abstract water in pursuance of a licence under Chapter II of Part II of the Water Resources Act 1991.

(4)  For the purposes to which this section applies the functions of every relevant undertaker shall be taken to include the furtherance of research into matters in respect of which functions

[1]  "Owner" defined by s.219(1), p.259 below.
[2]  "Enactment" defined by s.219(1), p.258 below.
[3]  "Relevant undertaker" and "functions" defined by s.219(1), p.260 below.
[4]  Words "Environment Agency" in this section substituted by the Environment Act 1995 (c.25), s.120, sch.22, para.124.
[5]  S.3 has been repealed by the Environment Act 1995 (c.25) and replaced by s.10 of that Act, p.430 below.
[6]  "Underground strata" defined by s.219(1), p.261 below.

are conferred by or under this Act, the other consolidation Acts[1] or the Water Act 1989 on the Environment Agency, on water undertakers or on sewerage undertakers.

(5) For the purposes to which this section applies the functions of every relevant undertaker shall be taken to include the provision of houses[2] and other buildings for the use of persons employed by that undertaker and the provision of recreation grounds for persons so employed.

(6) For the purposes to which this section applies the functions of every water undertaker shall be taken to include the provision of supplies of water in bulk[3], whether or not such supplies are provided for the purposes of, or in connection with, the carrying out of any other function of that undertaker.

(7) For the purposes to which this section applies the function of every water undertaker shall be taken to include the doing of anything in pursuance of any arrangements under section 20 of the Water Resources Act 1991 between that undertaker and the Environment Agency.

(8) In this section "the other consolidation Acts" has the same meaning as in section 206 above[4].

*Meaning of "domestic purposes" in relation to water supply.*

**218.**   (1) Subject to the following provisions of this section, in this Act references to domestic purposes, in relation to a supply of water to any premises or in relation to any cognate expression, are references to the drinking, washing, cooking, central heating and sanitary purposes for which water supplied to those premises may be used.

(2) Where the whole or any part of the premises are or are to be occupied as a house[5], those purposes shall be taken to include—

   (a)   the purposes of a profession carried on in that house or, where—

      (i)   that house and another part of the premises are occupied together; and

      (ii)   the house comprises the greater part of what is so occupied,

      in that other part; and

   (b)   such purposes outside the house (including the washing of vehicles and the watering of gardens) as are connected with the occupation of the house and may be satisfied by a supply of water drawn from a tap inside the house and without the use of a hosepipe or similar apparatus.

(3) No such reference to domestic purposes shall be taken to include a reference—

   (a)   to the use of a bath having a capacity, measured to the centre line of overflow or in such other manner as may be prescribed[6] of more than two hundred and thirty litres;

   (b)   to the purposes of the business of a laundry; or

   (c)   to any purpose of a business of preparing food or drink for consumption otherwise than on the premises.

*General interpretation.*

**219.**   (1) In this Act, except in so far as the context otherwise requires—

"accessories", in relation to a water main, sewer or other pipe, includes any manholes, ventilating shafts, inspection chambers, settling tanks, wash-out pipes, pumps, ferrules or stopcocks for the main, sewer or other pipe, or any machinery or other apparatus which is designed or adapted for use in connection with the use or maintenance of the main, sewer or other pipe

---

[1] "The other consolidation Acts" defined by s.206(10), p.251 above: subsection (8) below.

[2] "House" defined by s.219(1), p.259 below.

[3] "Supply of water in bulk" defined by s.219(1), p.261

below.

[4] P.251 above.

[5] "House" defined by s.219(1), p.259 below.

[6] "Prescribed" defined by s.219(1), p.260 below.

or of another accessory for it, but does not include any telecommunication apparatus (within the meaning of Schedule 2 to the Telecommunications Act 1984[1]) unless it—

(a) is or is to be situated inside or in the close vicinity of the main, sewer or other pipe or inside or in the close vicinity of another accessory for it; and

(b) is intended to be used only in connection with the use or maintenance of the main, sewer or other pipe or of another accessory for it;

"analyse", in relation to any sample of land, water or effluent, includes subjecting the sample to a test of any description, and cognate expressions shall be construed accordingly;

"conservancy authority" means any person who has a duty or power under any enactment to conserve, maintain or improve the navigation of a tidal water, and is not a harbour authority or navigation authority;

"contravention" includes a failure to comply, and cognate expressions shall be construed accordingly;

"customer or potential customer", in relation to a company holding an appointment under Chapter I of Part II of this Act, means—

(a) any person for or to whom that company provides any services in the course of carrying out the functions of a water undertaker or sewerage undertaker; or

(b) any person who might become such a person on making an application for the purpose to the company;

"damage", in relation to individuals, includes death and any personal injury, including any disease or impairment of physical or mental condition;

"the Director" means the Director General of Water Services;

"disposal"—

(a) in relation to land or any interest or right in or over land, includes the creation of such an interest or right and a disposal effected by means of the surrender or other termination of any such interest or right; and

(b) in relation to sewage, includes treatment;

and cognate expressions shall be construed accordingly;

"disposal main" means (subject to subsection (2) below) any outfall pipe or other pipe which—

(a) is a pipe for the conveyance of effluent to or from any sewage disposal works, whether of a sewerage undertaker or of any other person; and

(b) is not a public sewer;

"domestic purposes", except in relation to sewers, shall be construed in accordance with section 218 above;

"drain" means (subject to subsection (2) below) a drain used for the drainage of one building or of any buildings or yards appurtenant to buildings within the same curtilage;

"effluent" means any liquid, including particles of matter and other substances in suspension in the liquid;

"enactment" includes an enactment contained in this Act or in any Act passed after this Act;

"engineering or building operations", without prejudice to the generality of that expression, includes—

(a) the construction, alteration, improvement, maintenance or demolition of any building or structure or of any reservoir, watercourse, dam, weir, well, borehole or other works; and

(b) the installation, modification or removal of any machinery or apparatus;

"financial year" means the twelve months ending with 31st March;

---

[1] 1984 c.12.

"functions", in relation to a relevant undertaker, means the functions of the undertaker under or by virtue of any enactment and shall be construed subject to section 217 above;

"harbour authority" means a person who is a harbour authority within the meaning of Chapter II of Part VI of the Merchant Shipping Act 1995[1] and is not a navigation authority;

"highway" and "highway authority" have the same meanings as in the Highways Act 1980[2];

"house" means any building or part of a building which is occupied as a dwelling-house, whether or not a private dwelling-house, or which, if unoccupied, is likely to be so occupied;

"information" includes anything contained in any records, accounts, estimates or returns;

"inland waters", has the same meaning as in the Water Resources Act 1991[3];

"limited company" means a company within the meaning of the Companies Act 1985[4] which is limited by shares;

"local authority" means the council of a district or of a London borough or the Common Council of the City of London but, in relation to Wales,means the council of a county or county borough[5];

"local statutory provision" means—

(a)  a provision of a local Act (including an Act confirming a provisional order);

(b)  a provision of so much of any public general Act as has effect with respect to a particular area, with respect to particular persons or works or with respect to particular provisions falling within any paragraph of this definition;

(c)  a provision of an instrument made under any provision falling within paragraph (a) or (b) above; or

(d)  a provision of any other instrument which is in the nature of a local enactment;

"meter" means any apparatus for measuring or showing the volume of water supplied to, or of effluent discharged from, any premises;

"micro-organism" includes any microscopic biological entity which is capable of replication;

"modifications" includes additions, alterations and omissions, and cognate expressions shall be construed accordingly;

"the Monopolies Commission" means the Monopolies and Mergers Commission;

the definition of "the NRA" repealed by the Environment Act 1995 (c.25), s.120, sch.22, para.125(a), sch.24.

"navigation authority" means any person who has a duty or power under any enactment to work, maintain, conserve, improve or control any canal or other inland navigation, navigable river, estuary, harbour or dock;

"notice" means notice in writing;

"owner", in relation to any premises, means the person who—

(a)  is for the time being receiving the rack-rent of the premises, whether on his own account or as agent or trustee for another person; or

(b)  would receive the rack-rent if the premises were let at a rack-rent,

and cognate expressions shall be construed accordingly;

"prescribed" means prescribed by regulations made by the Secretary of State;

"protected land", in relation to a company holding an appointment under Chapter I of Part II of this Act, means any land which, or any interest or right in or over which—

[1]  1995 c.21. Words "Chapter II of Part VI of the Merchant Shipping Act 1995" substituted by the Merchant Shipping Act 1995 (c.21), s.314, sch.13, para.89(b). This amendment came into force on 1 January 1996: s.316(2).
[2]  1980 c.66.
[3]  "Inland waters" is defined in s.221(1) of the 1991 Act, p.313 below.
[4]  1985 c.6.
[5]  Words "but . . . county borough" inserted by the Local Government (Wales) Act 1994 (c.19), s.22(5), sch.11, para.2. This amendment came into force on 1 April 1996: S.I. 1996/396.

(a) was transferred to that company in accordance with a scheme under Schedule 2 to the Water Act 1989 or, where that company is a statutory water company, was held by that company at any time during the financial year ending with 31st March 1990;

(b) is or has at any time on or after 1st September 1989 been held by that company for purposes connected with the carrying out of its functions as a water undertaker or sewerage undertaker (including any functions which for the purposes for which section 218[1] above has effect are taken to be such functions by virtue of subsection (6) or (7) of that section); or

(c) has been transferred to that company in accordance with a scheme under Schedule 2 to this Act from another company in relation to which that land was protected land when the other company held an appointment under that Chapter;

"public authority" means any Minister of the Crown or government department, the Environment Agency[2], any local authority or county council or any person certified by the Secretary of state to be a public authority for the purposes of this Act;

"public sewer" means a sewer for the time being vested in a sewerage undertaker in its capacity as such, whether vested in that undertaker by virtue of a scheme under Schedule 2 to the Water Act 1989 or Schedule 2 to this Act or under section 179 above or otherwise, and "private sewer" shall be construed accordingly;

"railway undertakers" means the British Railways Board, London Regional Transport or any other person authorised by any enactment, or by any order, rule or regulation made under any enactment, to construct, work or carry on any railway;

"records" includes computer records and any other records kept otherwise than in a document;

"the relevant sewerage provisions" means the following provisions of this Act, that is to say—

(a) Chapters II and III[3] of Part IV (except sections 98 to 101 and 110 and so much of Chapter III of that Part as provides for regulations under section 138[4] or has effect by virtue of any such regulations);

(b) sections 160, 171, 172(4), 178, 184, 189, 196[5] and 204[6] and paragraph 4 of Schedule 12; and

(c) the other provisions of this Act so far as they have effect for the purposes of any provision falling within paragraph (a) or (b) of this definition;

"relevant undertaker" means a water undertaker or sewerage undertaker;

"resource main" means (subject to subsection (2) below) any pipe, not being a trunk main, which is or is to be used for the purpose of—

(a) conveying water from one source of supply to another, from a source of supply to a regulating reservoir or from a regulating reservoir to a source of supply; or

(b) giving or taking a supply of water in bulk;

"service pipe" means (subject to subsection (2) below) so much of a pipe which is, or is to be, connected with a water main for supplying water from that main to any premises as—

(a) is or is to be subject to water pressure from that main;

or

(b) would be so subject but for the closing of some valve, and includes part of any service pipe;

"service" includes facilities;

"sewer" includes (without prejudice to subsection (2) below) all sewers and drains (not being drains within the meaning given by this subsection) which are used for the drainage of buildings and yards appurtenant to buildings;

---

[1] It appears that the reference to s.218 should be to s.217.
[2] Words "the Environment Agency" substituted by the Environment Act 1995 (c.25), s.120, sch.22, 125(b).
[3] P.232 above.
[4] P.246 above.
[5] P.248 above.
[6] P.248 above.

"sewerage services" includes the disposal of sewage and any other services which are required to be provided by a sewerage undertaker for the purpose of carrying out its functions;

"special administration order" has the meaning given by section 23 above;

"statutory water company" means any company which was a statutory water company for the purposes of the Water Act 1973[1] immediately before 1st September 1989;

"stopcock" includes any box or pit in which a stopcock is enclosed and the cover to any such box or pit;

"street" has, subject to subsection (5) below, the same meaning as in Part III of the New Roads and Street Works 1991[2];

"subordinate legislation" has the same meaning as in the Interpretation Act 1978[3];

"substance" includes micro-organisms and any natural or artificial substance or other matter, whether it is in solid or liquid form or in the form of a gas or vapour;

"supply of water in bulk" means a supply of water for distribution by a water undertaker taking the supply;

"surface water" includes water from roofs;

"trunk main" means a water main which is or is to be used by a water undertaker for the purpose of—

(a) conveying water from a source of supply to a filter or reservoir or from one filter or reservoir to another filter or reservoir; or

(b) conveying water in bulk, whether in the course of taking a supply of water in bulk or otherwise, between different places outside the area of the undertaker, from such a place to any part of that area or from one part of that area to another part of that area;

"underground strata" means strata subjacent to the surface of any land;

"vessel" includes a hovercraft within the meaning of the Hovercraft Act 1968[4];

"water main" means (subject to subsection (2) below) any pipe, not being a pipe for the time being vested in a person other than the undertaker, which is used or to be used by a water undertaker for the purpose of making a general supply of water available to customers or potential customers of the undertaker, as distinct from for the purpose of providing a supply to particular customers;

"watercourse" includes all rivers, streams, ditches, drains, cuts, culverts, dykes, sluices, sewers and passages through which water flows except mains and other pipes which belong to the Environment Agency[5] or a water undertaker or are used by a water undertaker or any other person for the purpose only of providing a supply of water to any premises.

(2) In this Act—

(a) references to a pipe, including references to a main, a drain or a sewer, shall include references to a tunnel or conduit which serves or is to serve as the pipe in question and to any accessories for the pipe; and

(b) references to any sewage disposal works shall include references to the machinery and equipment of those works and any necessary pumping stations and outfall pipes;

and, accordingly, references to the laying of a pipe shall include references to the construction of such a tunnel or conduit, to the construction or installation of any such accessories and to the making of a connection between one pipe and another.

(3) Nothing in Part III or IV of this Act by virtue of which a relevant undertaker owes a duty to any particular person to lay any water main, resource main or service pipe or any sewer, disposal main or discharge pipe shall be construed—

---

[1] 1973 c.37.
[2] 1991 c.22.
[3] 1978 c.30.

[4] 1968 c.59.
[5] Words "the Environment Agency" substituted by the Environment Act 1995.

(a)  as conferring any power in addition to the powers conferred apart from those Parts; or

(b)  as requiring the undertaker to carry out any works which it has no power to carry out.

(4)  References in this Act to the fixing of charges in relation to any premises by reference to volume are references to the fixing of those charges by reference to the volume of water supplied to those premises, to the volume of effluent discharged from those premises, to both of those factors or to one or both of those factors taken together with other factors.

(5)  Until the coming into force of Part III of the New Roads and Street Works Act 1991[1], the definition of "street" in subsection (1) above shall have effect as if the reference to that Part were a reference to the Public Utilities Street Works Act 1950; but nothing in this section shall be taken—

(a)  to prejudice the power of the Secretary of State under that Act of 1991 to make an order bringing Part III of that Act into force on different days for different purposes (including the purposes of this section); or

(b)  in the period before the coming into force of that Part, to prevent references in this Act to a street, where the street is a highway which passes over a bridge or through a tunnel, from including that bridge or tunnel.

(6)  For the purposes of any provision of this Act by or under which power is or may be conferred on any person to recover the expenses incurred by that person in doing anything, those expenses shall be assumed to include such sum as may be reasonable in respect of establishment charges or overheads.

(7)  References in this Act to the later or latest of two or more different times or days are, in a case where those times or days coincide, references to the time at which or, as the case may be, the day on which they coincide.

(8)  Where by virtue of any provision of this Act any function of a Minister of the Crown is exercisable concurrently by different Ministers, that function shall also be exercisable jointly by any two or more of those Ministers.

(9)  Sub-paragraph (1) of paragraph 1 of Schedule 2 to the Water Consolidation (Consequential Provisions) Act 1991[2] has effect (by virtue of sub-paragraph (2)(b) of that paragraph) so that references in this Act to things done under or for the purposes of provisions of this Act or the Water Resources Act 1991 include references to things done, or treated as done, under or for the purposes of the corresponding provisions of the law in force before the commencement of this Act.

*Effect of local Acts.*

**220.**  Subject to any provision to the contrary which is contained in Schedule 26 to the Water Act 1989[3] or in the Water Consolidation (Consequential Provisions) Act 1991[4], nothing in any local statutory provision[5] passed or made before 1st September 1989 shall be construed as relieving any relevant undertaker[6] from any liability arising by virtue of this Act in respect of any act or omission occurring on or after that date.

*Other supplemental provisions*

*Crown application.*

**221.**  (1)  Subject to the provisions of this section, this Act shall bind the Crown.

(2)  No contravention by the Crown of any provision made by or under this Act shall make the Crown criminally liable; but the High Court may, on the application of the Environment

[1]  P.III of the New Roads and Street Works Act 1991 (c.22) came into force on various dates: 14 July 1992: S.I. 1992/1686; 28 November 1992, 1 January 1993, 1 April 1993: S.I. 1992/2984, save for ss.79 and 80 which are not in force.
[2]  1991 c.60.
[3]  1989 c.15.
[4]  1991 c.60.
[5]  "Local statutory provision" defined by s.219(1), p.259 above.
[6]  "Relevant undertaker" defined by s.219(1), p.260 above.

Agency, a water undertaker or a sewerage undertaker, declare unlawful any act or omission of the Crown which constitutes such a contravention.

(3) Notwithstanding anything in subsection (2) above, any provision made by or under this Act shall apply to persons in the public service of the Crown as it applies to other persons.

(4) If the Secretary of State certifies that it appears to him, as respects any Crown premises and any powers of entry exercisable in relation to them specified in the certificate, that it is requisite or expedient that, in the interests of national security, the powers should not be exercisable in relation to those premises, those powers shall not be exercisable in relation to those premises.

(5) Nothing in this section shall be taken as in any way affecting Her Majesty in her private capacity; and this subsection shall be construed as if section 38(3) of the Crown Proceedings Act 1947[1] (interpretation of references to Her Majesty in her private capacity) were contained in this Act.

(6) Subject to subsections (4) and (5) above, the powers conferred by sections 155, 159, 161(2) and 167 above shall be exercisable in relation to land in which there is a Crown or Duchy interest only with the consent of the appropriate authority.

(7) In this section—

"the appropriate authority" has the same meaning as it has in Part XIII of the Town and Country Planning Act 1990[2] by virtue of section 293(2) of that Act;

"Crown or Duchy interest" means an interest which belongs to Her Majesty in right of the Crown or of the Duchy of Lancaster, or to the Duchy of Cornwall, or belonging to a government department or held in trust for Her Majesty for the purposes of a government department;

"Crown premises" means premises held by or on behalf of the Crown.

(8) The provisions of subsection (3) of section 293 of the Town and Country Planning Act 1990 (questions relating to Crown application) as to the determination of questions shall apply for the purposes of this section.[3]

*Application to the Isles of Scilly.*

**222.** (1) Subject to the provisions of any order under this section, this Act shall not apply in relation to the Isles of Scilly.

(2) The Secretary of State may, after consultation with the Council of the Isles of Scilly, by order provide for the application of any provisions of this Act to the Isles of Scilly; and any such order may provide for the application of those provisions to those Isles with such modifications[4] as may be specified in the order.

(3) An order under this section may—

(a) make different provision for different cases, including different provision in relation to different persons, circumstances or localities; and

(b) contain such supplemental, consequential and transitional provision as the Secretary of State considers appropriate, including provision saving provision repealed by or under any enactment.

(4) The power of the Secretary of State to make an order under this section shall be exercisable by statutory instrument subject to annulment in pursuance of a resolution of either House of Parliament.[5]

---

[1] 1947 c.44.
[2] 1990 c.8.
[3] *Prospective amendment:* this section substituted by the Environment Act 1995 (c.25), s.116, sch.21, para.1. This amendment has not come into force.
[4] "Modifications" defined by s.219(1), p.259 above.

[5] This section substituted by the Environment Act 1995 (c.25), s.118(4). This amendment, in so far as it confers power to make an order or make provision in relation to the exercise of that power, came into force on 1 February 1996: S.I. 1996/186; otherwise this amendment has not come into force.

*Short title, commencement and extent.*

**223.** (1) This Act may be cited as the Water Industry Act 1991.

(2) This Act shall come into force on 1st December 1991.

(3) Except for the purpose of giving effect to any scheme under Schedule 2 to this Act, this Act extends to England and Wales only.

# SCHEDULE 8

(Section 140[1].)

PRE-1989 ACT TRANSITIONAL AUTHORITY FOR TRADE EFFLUENT DISCHARGES ETC.

*Trade effluent agreements*

**1.** Nothing in Chapter III of Part IV of this Act[2] (except so far as it relates to special category effluent) or in the repeals made by the Water Consolidation (Consequential Provisions) Act 1991[3] shall affect—

(*a*) any agreement with respect to any trade effluent[4] to which a sewerage undertaker is a party by virtue of its having been duly made before 1st July 1937 between a predecessor of the undertaker and the owner[5] or occupier of any trade premises; or

(*b*) any agreement saved by section 63(8) of the Public Health Act 1961[6] (pre-1961 Act agreements with respect to discharges from premises used for farming or for scientific research or experiment).

*Authorisations having effect as deemed consents under the Control of Pollution Act 1974*

**2.** (1) Where, by virtue of section 43(2) of the Control of Pollution Act 1974[7] there is, immediately before the commencement of this Act, a deemed consent for the purposes of the Public Health (Drainage of Trade Premises) Act 1937[8] which has effect under the Water Act 1989[9] in relation to any sewerage undertaker, that deemed consent shall have effect as a deemed consent for the purposes of Chapter III of Part IV of this Act[10] subject to the following provisions of this paragraph.

(2) The sewerage undertaker—

(*a*) may at any time; and

(*b*) shall if requested to do so by any person entitled to make a discharge in pursuance of the deemed consent,

by notice[11] served on the owner[12] and any occupier of the premises in question cancel the deemed consent and, subject to sub-paragraph (3) below, give its actual consent for such discharges as were authorised by the deemed consent.

(3) An actual consent given under sub-paragraph (2) above shall be so given either conditionally or subject to any conditions which may be attached to consents by virtue of section 121 of this Act[13].

(4) It is hereby declared that the provisions of Chapter III of Part IV of this Act with respect to the variation of conditions of a consent apply in relation to an actual consent under sub-paragraph (2)

---

[1] P.247 above.
[2] P.232 above.
[3] 1991 c.60.
[4] "Trade effluent" defined by s.141(1),(2), p.247 above.
[5] "Owner" defined by s.219(1), p.259 above.
[6] 1961 c.64.
[7] 1974 c.40.

[8] 1937 c.40.
[9] 1989 c.15.
[10] P.232 above.
[11] "Notice" defined by s.219(1), p.259 above.
[12] "Owner" defined by s.219(1), p.259 above.
[13] P.234 above.

above as they apply in relation to any other actual consent under Chapter III of Part IV of this Act.

(5) A notice signifying an actual consent under sub-paragraph (2) above shall indicate that a right of appeal is conferred under the following paragraph in respect of the notice.

### Appeals in respect of consents under paragraph 2

**3.** (1) A person on whom notice is served in pursuance of paragraph 2(2) above may, in accordance with regulations made by the Secretary of State, appeal to the Director[1].

(2) Section 137 of this Act[2] shall apply, with the necessary modifications[3], in relation to appeals under this paragraph as it applies in relation to appeals under section 122 of this Act[4].

(3) On an appeal under this paragraph the Director may give the sewerage undertaker in question any such direction as he thinks fit with respect to the notice and it shall be the duty of the undertaker to comply with the direction.

### Determinations of disputes as to transitional matters

**4.** (1) Any dispute in so far as it—

(a) arises after the commencement of this Act and relates to a deemed consent in respect of discharges previously authorised under section 4 of the Public Health (Drainage of Trade Premises) Act 1937[5]; and

(b) is a dispute as to the nature or composition of any trade effluent[6] discharged from any trade premises[7] into a sewer[8] during any period, as to the quantity of trade effluent so discharged on any one day during any period or as to the rate of trade effluent so discharged during any period,

shall, unless the parties otherwise agree, be referred to the Director[9] for determination.

(2) On a reference under this paragraph the Director may make such order in the matter as he thinks just.

(3) An order on a reference under this paragraph shall be final; but section 137 of this Act[10] shall apply, with the necessary modifications[11], in relation to references under this paragraph as it applies in relation to appeals under section 122 of this Act[12].

### Regulations as to residue of agreements

**5.** The Secretary of State may by regulations make provisions in relation to the provisions of any agreement to which subsection (1) of section 43 of the Control of Pollution Act 1974[13] applied and which apart from that section would be in force after the commencement of this Act—

(a) for determining, by arbitration or otherwise, whether any such agreement continues to have effect as relating to a matter other than the discharge of trade effluent[14] into a sewerage undertaker's sewer;

(b) for determining, by arbitration or otherwise, what modifications[15] (if any) are appropriate in consequence of any prescribed[16] provision of section 43 of that Act or any provision of this Schedule re-enacting any such provision; and

(c) in a case in which the conditions on which any discharges authorised by such an agreement included, immediately before the coming into force of section 43 of that Act, a condition as to charges in respect of the discharges and other matters—

---

[1] "The Director" defined by s.219(1), p.258 above.
[2] P.245 above.
[3] "Modifications" defined by s.219(1), p.259 above.
[4] P.235 above.
[5] 1937 c.40.
[6] "Trade effluent" defined by s.141(1),(2), p.247 above.
[7] "Trade premises" defined by s.141(1),(2), p.247 above.
[8] "Sewer" defined by s.219(1),(2), p.260 above.

[9] "The Director" defined by s.219(1), p.258 above.
[10] P.245 above.
[11] "Modifications" defined by s.219(1), p.259 above.
[12] P.235 above.
[13] 1974 c.40.
[14] "Trade effluent" defined by s.141(1),(2), p.247 above.
[15] "Modifications" defined by s.219(1), p.259 above.
[16] "Prescribed" defined by s.219(1), p.259 above.

(i)  for determining, by arbitration or otherwise, the proportion of the charges attributable to the discharges; and

(ii)  for limiting accordingly the conditions which are to be treated by virtue of section 43 of that Act as included in the deemed consent which has effect by virtue of this Schedule.

## SCHEDULE 15

(Section 206[1].)

### DISCLOSURE OF INFORMATION

### PART I: PERSONS IN RESPECT OF WHOSE FUNCTION DISCLOSURE MAY BE MADE

Any Minister of the Crown.

The Director General of Fair Trading.

The Monopolies Commission.

The Director General of Telecommunications.

The Civil Aviation Authority.

The Director General of Gas Supply.

The Director General of Electricity Supply.

The Rail Regulator.[2]

A local weights and measures authority in England and Wales.

### PART II: ENACTMENTS ETC. IN RESPECT OF WHICH DISCLOSURE MAY BE MADE

The Trade Descriptions Act 1968[3].

The Fair Trading Act 1973[4].

The Consumer Credit Act 1974[5].

The Restrictive Trade Practices Act 1976[6].

The Resale Prices Act 1976[7].

The Estate Agents Act 1979[8].

The Competition Act 1980[9].

The Telecommunications Act 1984[10].

The Airports Act 1986[11].

The Gas Act 1986[12].

The Consumer Protection Act 1987[13].

The Electricity Act 1989[14].

The Railways Act 1993.[15]

Any subordinate legislation made for the purpose of securing compliance with the Directive of the Council of the European Communities dated 10th September 1984 (No. 84/450/EEC) on the approximation of the laws, regulations and administrative provisions of the member States concerning misleading advertising.

---

[1]  P.249 above.

[2]  Words "The Rail Regulator." inserted by the Railways Act 1993 (c.43), s.152(1), sch.12, para.30(a). This amendment came into force on 6 January 1994: S.I. 1993/3237.

[3]  1968 c.29.

[4]  1973 c.41.

[5]  1974 c.39.

[6]  1976 c.34.

[7]  1976 c.53.

[8]  1979 c.38.

[9]  1980 c.21.

[10]  1984 c.12.

[11]  1986 c.31.

[12]  1986 c.44.

[13]  1987 c.43.

[14]  1989 c.29.

[15]  1993 c.43. Words "The Railways Act 1993." inserted by the Railways Act 1993 (c.43), s.152 (1), sch.12, para.30(b). This amendment came into force on 6 January 1994: S.I. 1993/3237.

# Water Resources Act 1991

## Chapter 57

*Arrangement of Sections*

### Part I: Preliminary

1–14.   *Repealed*                                                                 270

*Chapter III: General duties*

15.     General duties with respect to the water industry                          271
16–18.  *Repealed*

### Part II: Water Resources Management

*Not reproduced*

### Part III: Control of Pollution of Water Resources

*Chapter I: Quality objectives*

82.     Classification of quality of waters                                        271
83.     Water quality objectives                                                   272
84.     General duties to achieve and maintain objectives etc                      273

*Chapter II: Pollution offences*

*Principal offences*

85.     Offences of polluting controlled waters                                    273
86.     Prohibition of certain discharges by notice or regulations                 274
87.     Discharges into and from public sewers etc                                 275
88.     Defence to principal offences in respect of authorised discharges          276
89.     Other defences to principal offences                                       277

*Offences in connection with deposits and vegetation in rivers*

90.     Offences in connection with deposits and vegetation in rivers              278

*Consents for the purposes of sections 88 to 90*

90A.    Applications for consent under section 89 or 90                             278
90B.    Enforcement notices                                                        279

*Appeals in respect of consents under Chapter II*

91.     Appeals in respect of consents under Chapter II                            280

*Chapter IIA: Abandoned mines*

91A.    Introductory                                                               282
91B.    Mine operators to give the Agency six months' notice of any proposed abandonment   283

*Chapter III: Powers to prevent and control pollution*

92.     Requirements to take precautions against pollution                         284
93.     Water protection zones                                                     284
94.     Nitrate sensitive areas                                                    285
95.     Agreements in nitrate sensitive areas                                      287

96.    Regulations with respect to consents required by virtue of section 93 or 94    287
97.    Codes of good agricultural practice    288

*Chapter IV: Supplemental provisions with respect to water pollution*

98.    Radioactive substances    289
99.    Consents required by the Agency    289
100.   Civil liability in respect of pollution and savings    289
101.   Limitation for summary offences under Part III    290
102.   Power to give effect to international obligations    290
103.   Transitional pollution provisions    290
104.   Meaning of "controlled waters" etc. in Part III    290

## Part IV: Flood Defence

*Not reproduced*

## Part V: General Control of Fisheries

*Not reproduced*

## Part VI: Financial Provisions in relation to the Agency

*Not reproduced*

## Part VII: Land and Works Powers

*The following sections are reproduced from this Part.*

*Chapter I: Powers of the Agency*

*Anti-pollution works*

161.    Anti-pollution works and operations    292
161A.   Notices requiring persons to carry out anti-pollution works and operations    293
161B.   Grant of, and compensation for, rights of entry etc    294
161C.   Appeals against works notices    295
161D.   Consequences of not complying with a works notice    296
162.    Other powers to deal with foul water and pollution    296

*Interpretation of Part VII*

186.    Interpretation of Part VII    298

## Part VIII: Information provisions

*The following sections are reproduced from this Part.*

*Registers etc. to be kept by the Agency*

190.    Pollution control register    298
191A.   Exclusion from registers of information affecting national security    300
191B.   Exclusion from registers of certain confidential information    300
192.    Maps of freshwater limits    302

*Provision and acquisition of information etc*

202.    Information and assistance required in connection with the control of pollution    303
203.    Exchange of information with respect to pollution incidents etc    303

*Restriction on disclosure of information*

204.    Restriction on disclosure of information    304

*Making of false statements etc*

206.    Making of false statements etc    306

# Part IX: Miscellaneous and Supplemental

*Miscellaneous*

| | | |
|---|---|---|
| 207. | Directions in the interests of national security etc | 306 |
| 208. | Civil liability of the Agency for escapes of *water etc* | 307 |
| 209. | Evidence of samples and abstractions | 308 |

*Byelaws*

210–212.  *Not reproduced*

*Local inquiries*

213–215.  *Repealed*

*Offences etc*

| | | |
|---|---|---|
| 216. | Enforcement: powers and duties | 309 |
| 217. | Criminal liabilities of directors and other third parties | 309 |

*Judicial disqualification*

218.      *Repealed*

*Powers to make regulations*

| | | |
|---|---|---|
| 219. | Powers to make regulations | 310 |

*Construction of Act*

| | | |
|---|---|---|
| 220. | Provisions relating to service of documents | 310 |
| 221. | General interpretation | 311 |

*Other supplemental provisions*

| | | |
|---|---|---|
| 222. | Crown application | 317 |
| 223. | Exemption for visiting forces | 318 |
| 224. | Application to the Isles of Scilly | 318 |
| 225. | Short title, commencement and extent | 318 |

SCHEDULES:

| | |
|---|---|
| Schedule 1—*Repealed* | |
| Schedule 2—*Not reproduced* | |
| Schedules 3–4—*Repealed* | |
| Schedules 5–9—*Not reproduced* | |
| Schedule 10—Discharge consents | 319 |
| Schedule 11—Water protection zone orders | 324 |
| Schedule 12—Nitrate sensitive area orders | 326 |
| Part I—Applications by the Agency for designation orders | 326 |
| Part II—Orders containing mandatory provisions | 326 |
| Schedule 13—Transitional water pollution provisions | 328 |
| Schedules 14–23—*Not reproduced* | |
| Schedule 24—Disclosure of information | 330 |
| Part I—Persons in respect of whose functions disclosure may be made | 330 |
| Part II— Enactments etc in respect of which disclosure may be made | 331 |
| Schedules 25–26—*Not reproduced* | |

# Water Resources Act 1991

An Act to consolidate enactments relating to the National Rivers Authority and the matters in relation to which it exercises functions, with amendments to give effect to recommendations of the Law Commission.

[25th July 1991]

## Transfer of functions

The functions previously conferred on the National Rivers Authority under Parts II, III, IV, V, VII of, and Schedule 2 to, this Act have been transferred to the Environment Agency: Environment Act 1995 (c. 25), s.2, p.421 below . The Environment Agency took over its functions under this Act on the transfer date, 1 April 1996: S.I. 1996/234.

## Commencement

This Act came into force on 1 December 1991: S.225(2), p.318 below.

Except where otherwise noted, the amendments made to the parts of this Act reproduced in this Manual by the Environment Act 1995 came into force on 1 April 1996: S.I. 1996/186. To avoid undue repetition this commencement date is not set out in the footnotes which relate to these amendments.

## Radioactive Substances

For the operation of this Act in relation to radioactive substances see: s.98 of this Act, p.289 below; The Control of Pollution (Radioactive Waste) Regulations 1989, S.I. 1989/1158, p.545 below; and Radioactive Substances Act 1993 (c.12), s.40, p.404 below and sch.3, para.9, p.411 below.

## Amendments to this Act made by the Environment Act 1995

Except where otherwise noted, the words "Agency" and "Agency's" in this Act, referring to the Environment Agency, have been substituted in place of references to the former National Rivers Authority by the Environment Act 1995 (c.25), s.120, sch.22, para.128. The headings of the sections, chapters and parts in this Manual have been amended accordingly.

## References to material not set out in this Manual

Planning Policy Guidance Note 23: Planning and Pollution Control. Department of the Environment, July 1994.

*Note:* this document was published before the introduction of the Environment Bill into Parliament and the subsequent enactment of the Environment Act 1995. This Act provided for the transfer of functions to the Environment Agency from the National Rivers Authority noted above.

# PART I: Preliminary

*Section 15 is set out below. The other sections of this Part, which comprised sections 1–14 and 16–18 have been repealed by the Environment Act 1995 (c.25), s.120, sch.22, paras.129 and 131, sch.24.*

*Chapter III: General Duties*

**15.** (1) It shall be the duty of the Agency, in exercising any of its powers under any enactment[1], to have particular regard to the duties imposed, by virtue of the provisions of Parts II to IV of the Water Industry Act 1991[2], on any water undertaker or sewerage undertaker[3] which appears to the Agency to be or to be likely to be affected by the exercise of the power in question.

(2) It shall be the duty of each of the Ministers[4], in exercising—

(a) any power conferred by virtue of the 1995 Act[5], this Act, the Land Drainage Act 1991[6], the Water Industry Act 1991 or the Water Act 1989[7] in relation to, or to decisions of, the Agency; or

(b) any power which, but for any direction given by one of the Ministers, would fall to be exercised by the Agency,

to take into account the duty imposed on the Agency by subsection (1) above.

# PART II: Water Resources Management

*Not reproduced*

# PART III: Control of Pollution of Water Resources

## Chapter I: Quality Objectives

*Classification of quality of waters.*

**82.** (1) The Secretary of State may, in relation to any description of controlled waters[8] (being a description applying to some or all of the waters of a particular class or of two or more different classes), by regulations prescribe a system of classifying the quality of those waters according to criteria specified in the regulations.

(2) The criteria specified in regulations under this section in relation to any classification shall consist of one or more of the following, that is to say—

(a) general requirements as to the purposes for which the waters to which the classification is applied are to be suitable;

(b) specific requirements as to the substances[9] that are to be present in or absent from the water and as to the concentrations of substances which are or are required to be present in the water;

(c) specific requirements as to other characteristics of those waters;

and for the purposes of any such classification regulations under this section may provide that the question whether prescribed[10] requirements are satisfied may be determined by reference to such samples as may be prescribed[11].

[1] "Enactment" defined by s.221(1), p.212 below.
[2] Part IV, Chapter III of the 1991 Act is at p.232 above.
[3] Part II of the Water Industry Act 1991 (c.56) relates to the appointment and regulation of water and sewerage undertakers.
[4] "The Ministers" defined by s.221(1), p.314 below.
[5] P.415 below. "The 1995 Act" means the Environment Act 1995: s. 221(1), p.311 below. Words "the 1995 Act," inserted by the Environment Act 1995 (c.25), s.120, sch.22, para.130.
[6] 1991 c.59.
[7] 1989 c.15.
[8] "Controlled waters" has the meaning given by s.104(1), p.290 below.
[9] "Substance" defined by s.221(1), p.315 below.
[10] "Prescribed" defined by s.221(1), p.314 below.
[11] The following regulations are made, or by virtue of the Water Consolidation (Consequential Provisions) Act 1991

*Water quality objectives[1].*

**83.** (1)  For the purpose of maintaining and improving the quality of controlled waters[2] the Secretary of State may, by serving[3] a notice[4] on the Agency[5] specifying—

(a)   one or more of the classifications for the time being prescribed[6] under section 82 above; and

(b)   in relation to each specified classification, a date,

establish the water quality objectives for any waters which are, or are included in, waters of a description prescribed for the purposes of that section.

(2)  The water quality objectives for any waters to which a notice under this section relates shall be the satisfaction by those waters, on and at all times after each date specified in the notice, of the requirements which at the time of the notice were the requirements for the classification in relation to which that date is so specified.

(3)  Where the Secretary of State has established water quality objectives under this section for any waters he may review objectives for those waters if—

(a)   five years or more have elapsed since the service of the last notice under subsection (1) or (6) of this section to be served in respect of those waters; or

(b)   the Agency, after consultation with such water undertakers[7] and other persons as it considers appropriate, requests a review;

and the Secretary of State shall not exercise his power to establish objectives for any waters by varying the existing objectives for those waters except in consequence of such a review.

(4)  Where the Secretary of State proposes to exercise his power under this section to establish or vary the objectives for any waters he shall—

(a)   give notice setting out his proposal and specifying the period (not being less than three months from the date of publication of the notice) within which representations or objections with respect to the proposal may be made; and

(b)   consider any representations or objections which are duly made and not withdrawn;

and, if he decides, after considering any such representations or objections, to exercise his power to establish or vary those objectives, he may do so either in accordance with the proposal contained in the notice or in accordance with that proposal as modified in such manner as he considers appropriate.

(5)  A notice under subsection (4) above shall be given—

(a)   by publishing the notice in such manner as the Secretary of State considers appropriate for bringing it to the attention of persons likely to be affected by it; and

(b)   by serving a copy of the notice on the Agency.

(6)  If, on a review under this section or in consequence of any representations or objections made following such a review for the purposes of subsection (4) above, the Secretary of State decides that the water quality objectives for any waters should remain unchanged, he shall serve notice of that decision on the Agency.

---

(c.60), s. 2(2), sch.2, para.1 have effect as if made, under this section:

The Surface Waters (Classification) Regulations 1989, S.I. 1989/1148, p.539 below;

The Surface Waters (Dangerous Substances) (Classification) Regulations 1989, S.I. 1989/2286, p.554 below;

The Bathing Waters (Classification) Regulations 1991, S.I. 1991/1597, p.622 below;

The Surface Waters (Dangerous Substances) (Classification) Regulations 1992, S.I. 1992/337, p.653 below;

The Surface Waters (River Ecosystem) (Classification) Regulations 1994, S.I. 1994/1057, p.735 below.

[1] This section is modified by the following regulations: The Surface Waters (Dangerous Substances) (Classification) Regulations 1989, S.I. 1989/2286, p.554 below;

The Bathing Waters (Classification) Regulations 1991, S.I. 1991/1597, p.622 below;

The Surface Waters (Dangerous Substances) (Classification) Regulations 1992, S.I. 1992/337, p.653 below.

[2] "Controlled waters" has the meaning given by s.104(1), p.290 below.

[3] For provisions relating to service see s.220, p.310 below.

[4] "Notice" defined by s.221(1), p.314 below.

[5] "The Agency" means the Environment Agency: s.221(1) below. The Environment Agency is established by the Environment Act 1995 (c.25), s.1, p.420 below.

[6] "Prescribed" defined by s.221(1), p.314 below.

[7] Part II of the Water Industry Act 1991 (c.56) relates to the appointment and regulation of water undertakers.

*General duties to achieve and maintain objectives etc.*

**84.** (1) It shall be the duty of the Secretary of State and of the Agency[1] to exercise the powers conferred on him or it by or under the water pollution provisions[2] of this Act (other than the preceding provisions of this Chapter and sections 104[3] and 192[4] below) in such manner as ensures, so far as it is practicable by the exercise of those powers to do so, that the water quality objectives specified for any waters in—

(*a*) a notice under section 83 above; or

(*b*) a notice under section 30C of the Control of Pollution Act 1974[5] (which makes corresponding provision for Scotland),

are achieved at all times.

(2) It shall be the duty of the Agency, for the purposes of the carrying out of its functions under the water pollution provisions of this Act—

(*a*) to monitor the extent of pollution in controlled waters[6]; and

(*b*) to consult, in such cases as it may consider appropriate, the Scottish Environment Protection Agency[7].

## Chapter II: Pollution Offences[7A]

### Principal offences

*Offences of polluting controlled waters.*

**85.** (1) A person contravenes[8] this section if he causes or knowingly permits any poisonous, noxious or polluting matter or any solid waste matter to enter any controlled waters[9].

(2) A person contravenes this section if he causes or knowingly permits any matter, other than trade effluent[10] or sewage effluent[11], to enter controlled waters by being discharged from a drain[12] or sewer[13] in contravention of a prohibition imposed under section 86 below.

(3) A person contravenes this section if he causes or knowingly permits any trade effluent or sewage effluent to be discharged—

(*a*) into any controlled waters; or

(*b*) from land in England and Wales, through a pipe[14], into the sea outside the seaward limits of controlled waters.

(4) A person contravenes this section if he causes or knowingly permits any trade effluent or sewage effluent to be discharged, in contravention of any prohibition imposed under section 86 below, from a building or from any fixed plant—

(*a*) on to or into any land; or

(*b*) into any waters of a lake or pond[15] which are not inland freshwaters[16].

(5) A person contravenes this section if he causes or knowingly permits any matter whatever to enter any inland freshwaters so as to tend (either directly or in combination with other matter which he or another person causes or permits to enter those waters) to impede the proper flow of the waters in a manner leading, or likely to lead, to a substantial aggravation of—

[1] "The Agency" means the Environment Agency: s.221(1) below.
[2] "Water pollution provisions" defined by s.221(1), p.315 below.
[3] P.290 below.
[4] P.302 below.
[5] P.20 above.
[6] "'Controlled waters" has the meaning given by s.104(1), p.290 below.
[7] Words "the Scottish Environment Protection Agency" substituted by S.I. 1996/973 on 1 April 1996.
[7A] For references to "waste" in this Chapter, see the Waste Management Licensing Regulations 1994, sch. 4, para. 11, p. 720 below.
[8] "Contravention" defined by s.221(1), p.312 below.
[9] "Controlled waters" has the meaning given by s.104(1), p.290 below.
[10] "Trade effluent" defined by s.221(1), p.315 below.
[11] "Sewage effluent" defined by s.221(1), p.315 below.
[12] "Drain" defined by s.221(1),(2) p.312 below.
[13] "Sewer" defined by s. 221(1),(2) p.315 below.
[14] For "pipe" see s.221(2), p.316 below.
[15] For "waters of a lake or pond" see s.104(2), p.291 below.
[16] "Inland freshwaters" has the meaning given by s.104(1), p.290 below.

(*a*)  pollution due to other causes; or

(*b*)  the consequences of such pollution.

(6)  Subject to the following provisions of this Chapter, a person who contravenes this section or the conditions of any consent given under this Chapter for the purposes of this section shall be guilty of an offence and liable—

(*a*)  on summary conviction, to imprisonment for a term not exceeding three months or to a fine not exceeding £20,000 or to both;

(*b*)  on conviction on indictment, to imprisonment for a term not exceeding two years or to a fine or to both.[1]

*Prohibition of certain discharges by notice or regulations.*

**86.**  (1)  For the purposes of section 85 above a discharge of any effluent[2] or other matter is, in relation to any person, in contravention[3] of a prohibition imposed under this section if, subject to the following provisions of this section—

(*a*)  the Agency[4] has given that person notice[5] prohibiting him from making or, as the case may be, continuing the discharge; or

(*b*)  the Agency has given that person notice prohibiting him from making or, as the case may be, continuing the discharge unless specified conditions are observed, and those conditions are not observed.

(2)  For the purposes of section 85 above a discharge of any effluent or other matter is also in contravention of a prohibition imposed under this section if the effluent or matter discharged—

(*a*)  contains a prescribed[6] substance[7] or a prescribed concentration of such a substance; or

(*b*)  derives from a prescribed process or from a process involving the use of prescribed substances or the use of such substances in quantities which exceed the prescribed amounts.

(3)  Nothing in subsection (1) above shall authorise the giving of a notice for the purposes of that subsection in respect of discharges from a vessel[8]; and nothing in any regulations made by virtue of subsection (2) above shall require any discharge from a vessel to be treated as a discharge in contravention of a prohibition imposed under this section.

(4)  A notice given for the purposes of subsection (1) above shall expire at such time as may be specified in the notice.

(5)  The time specified for the purposes of subsection (4) above shall not be before the end of the period of three months beginning with the day on which the notice is given, except in a case where the Agency is satisfied that there is an emergency which requires the prohibition in question to come into force at such time before the end of that period as may be so specified.

(6)  Where, in the case of such a notice for the purposes of subsection (1) above as (but for this subsection) would expire at a time at or after the end of the said period of three months, an application is made before that time for a consent under this Chapter in respect of the discharge to which the notice relates, that notice shall be deemed not to expire until the result of the application becomes final—

(*a*)  on the grant or withdrawal of the application;

---

[1]  **Cases: section 85** *Wychavon District Council v National Rivers Authority* [1993] Env LR 330; *National Rivers Authority v Welsh Development Agency* [1993] Env LR 407; *National Rivers Authority (Southern Region) v Alfred McAlpine Homes East Ltd* [1994] 4 All ER 286; *Taylor Woodrow Property Management Ltd v National Rivers Authority* [1995] Env LR 52; *R v CPC (UK) Ltd* [1995] Env LR 131; *R v Dovermoss Ltd* [1995] Env LR 258; *National Rivers Authority v Biffa Waste Services Ltd.* The Times 21 November 1995; *National Rivers Authority v Yorkshire Water Services Ltd* [1995] 1 All ER 225; *National Rivers Authority v Wright Engineering* [1994] 4 All ER 281; *R v Yorkshire Water Services Ltd* [1995] Env LR 229; *Attorney General's Ref. (No. 1 of 1994)* [1995] 2 All ER 1007.

[2]  "Effluent" defined by s.221(1), p.312 below.

[3]  "Contravention" defined by s.221(1), p.312 below.

[4]  "The Agency" means the Environment Agency: s.221(1) below.

[5]  "Notice" defined by s.221(1), p.314 below.

[6]  "Prescribed" defined by s.221(1), p.314 below.

[7]  "Substance" defined by s.221(1), p.315 below.

[8]  "Vessel" defined by s.221 (1), p.315 below.

(b)  on the expiration, without the bringing of an appeal with respect to the decision on the application, of any period prescribed as the period within which any such appeal much be brought; or

(c)  on the withdrawal or determination of any such appeal.

..........................................................................................................................................................

*Discharges into and from public sewers etc.*

**87.**  (1)  This section applies for the purpose of determining liability where sewage effluent[1] is discharged as mentioned in subsection (3) or (4) of section 85 above[2] from any sewer[3] or works ("the discharging sewer") vested in a sewerage undertaker[4] ("the discharging undertaker").

(1A)  If the discharging undertaker did not cause, or knowingly permit, the discharge it shall nevertheless be deemed to have caused the discharge if—

(a)  matter included in the discharge was received by it into the discharging sewer or any other sewer or works vested in it;

(b)  it was bound (either unconditionally or subject to conditions which were observed) to receive that matter into that sewer or works; and

(c)  subsection (1B) below does not apply.

(1B)  This subsection applies where the sewage effluent was, before being discharged from the discharging sewer, discharged through a main connection[5] into that sewer or into any other sewer or works vested in the discharging undertaker by another sewerage undertaker ("the sending undertaker") under an agreement having effect between the discharging undertaker and the sending undertaker under section 110A of the Water Industry Act 1991.

(1C)  Where subsection (1B) above applies, the sending undertaker shall be deemed to have caused the discharge if, although it did not cause, or knowingly permit, the sewage effluent to be discharged into the discharging sewer, or into any other sewer or works of the discharging undertaker—

(a)  matter included in the discharge was received by it into a sewer or works vested in it; and

(b)  it was bound (either unconditionally or subject to conditions which were observed) to receive that matter into that sewer or works.[6]

(2)  A sewerage undertaker shall not be guilty of an offence under section 85 above by reason only of the fact that a discharge from a sewer or works vested in the undertaker contravenes[7] conditions of a consent relating to the discharge if—

(a)  the contravention is attributable to a discharge which another person caused or permitted to be made into the sewer or works;

(b)  the undertaker either was not bound to receive the discharge into the sewer or works or was bound to receive it there subject to conditions which were not observed; and

(c)  the undertaker could not reasonably have been expected to prevent the discharge into the sewer or works.

(3)  A person shall not be guilty of an offence under section 85 above in respect of a discharge which he caused or permitted to be made into a sewer or works vested in a sewerage undertaker if the undertaker was bound to receive the discharge there either unconditionally or subject to conditions which were observed.

---

[1] "Sewage effluent" defined by s.221(1), p.315 below.
[2] P.273 above.
[3] "Sewer" defined by s.221(1),(2), p.315 below.
[4] Part II of the Water Industry Act 1991 (c.56) relates to the appointment and regulation of sewerage undertakers.
[5] For "main connection" see subsection (4) below.
[6] Subsections (1)–(1C) substituted by the Competition

and Service (Utilities) Act 1992 (c.43), s.46(1). S.46 of the 1992 Act applies only in relation to discharges occurring after it came into force: s.46(3). S.46 came into force on 1 July 1992: Competition and Service (Utilities) Act 1992 (Commencement No.1) Order 1992.
[7] "Contravention" defined by s.221(1), p.312 below.

(4) In this section "main connection" has the same meaning as in section 110A of the Water Industry Act 1991.[1,2]

..............................................................................................................................................................

*Defence to principal offences in respect of authorised discharges.*

**88.** (1) Subject to the following provisions of this section, a person shall not be guilty of an offence under section 85 above[3] in respect of the entry of any matter into any waters or any discharge if the entry occurs or the discharge is made under and in accordance with, or as a result of any act or omission under and in accordance with—

(a) a consent given under this Chapter or under Part II of the Control of Pollution Act 1974[4] (which makes corresponding provision for Scotland);

(b) an authorisation for a prescribed process designated for central control granted under Part I of the Environmental Protection Act 1990[5];

(c) a waste management or disposal licence[6];

(d) a licence granted under Part II of the Food and Environment Protection Act 1985[7];

(e) section 163 below or section 165 of the Water Industry Act 1991[8] (discharges for works purposes);

(f) any local statutory provision[9] or statutory order[10] which expressly confers powers to discharge effluent[11] into water; or

(g) any prescribed[12] enactment[13].

(2) Schedule 10 to this Act shall have effect[14], subject to section 91 below[15], with respect to the making of applications for consents under this Chapter for the purposes of subsection (1)(a) above and with respect to the giving, revocation and modification of such consents.

(3) Nothing in any disposal licence shall be treated for the purposes of subsection (1) above as authorising—

(a) any such entry or discharge as is mentioned in subsections (2) to (4) of section 85 above; or

(b) any act or omission so far as it results in any such entry or discharge.

(4) In this section—

"disposal licence" means a licence issued in pursuance of section 5 of the Control of Pollution Act 1974[16];

"statutory order" means—

(a) any order under section 168 below or section 167 of the Water Industry Act 1991 (compulsory works orders); or

(b) any order, byelaw, scheme or award made under any other enactment, including an order or scheme confirmed by Parliament or brought into operation in accordance with special parliamentary procedure;

and

---

[1] Subsection (4) inserted by the Competition and Service (Utilities) Act 1992 (c.43), s.46(2). S.46 of the 1992 Act applies only in relation to discharges occurring after it came into force: s.46(3). S.46 came into force on 1 July 1992: Competition and Service (Utilities) Act 1992 (Commencement No.1) Order 1992.

[2] **Case: section 87** *Wychavon District Council v National Rivers Authority* [1993] Env LR 330.

[3] P.273 above.

[4] P.16 above.

[5] P.88 above.

[6] See subsection (4) below.

[7] 1985 c.48.

[8] 1991 c.56.

[9] "Local statutory provision" defined by s.221(1), p.314 below.

[10] "Statutory order" defined by subsection (4) below.

[11] "Effluent" defined by s.221(1), p.312 below.

[12] "Prescribed" defined by s.221(1), p.314 below.

[13] "Enactment" defined by s. 221(1), p.312 below.

[14] P.319 below.

[15] P.280 below.

[16] 1974 c.40.

"waste management licence" means such a licence granted under Part II of the Environmental Protection Act 1990[1].[2]

*Other defences to principal offences.*

89. (1)  A person shall not be guilty of an offence under section 85 above[3] in respect of the entry of any matter into any waters or any discharge if—

(a)  the entry is caused or permitted, or the discharge is made, in an emergency in order to avoid danger to life or health;

(b)  that person takes all such steps as are reasonably practicable in the circumstances for minimising the extent of the entry or discharge and of its polluting effects; and

(c)  particulars of the entry or discharge are furnished to the Agency[4] as soon as reasonably practicable after the entry occurs.

(2)  A person shall not be guilty of an offence under section 85 above by reason of his causing or permitting any discharge of trade or sewage effluent[5] from a vessel[6].

(3)  A person shall not be guilty of an offence under section 85 above by reason only of his permitting water from an abandoned mine[7] or an abandoned part of a mine[8] to enter controlled waters[9].

(3A)  Subsection (3) above shall not apply to the owner[10] or former operator of any mine or part of a mine if the mine or part in question became abandoned after 31st December 1999.

(3B)  In determining for the purposes of subsection (3A) above whether a mine or part of a mine became abandoned before, on or after 31st December 1999 in a case where the mine or part has become abandoned on two or more occasions, of which—

(a)  at least one falls on or before that date, and

(b)  at least one falls after that date,

the mine or part shall be regarded as becoming abandoned after that date (but without prejudice to the operation of subsection (3) above in relation to that mine or part at, or in relation to, any time before the first of those occasions which falls after that date).

(3C)  Where, immediately before a part of a mine becomes abandoned, that part is the only part of the mine not falling to be regarded as abandoned for the time being, the abandonment of that part shall not be regarded for the purposes of subsection (3A) or (3B) above as constituting the abandonment of the mine, but only of that part of it.[11]

(4)  A person shall not, otherwise than in respect of the entry of any poisonous, noxious or polluting matter into any controlled waters, be guilty of an offence under section 85 above by reason of his depositing the solid refuse of a mine or quarry[12] on any land so that it falls or is carried into inland freshwaters[13] if—

(a)  he deposits the refuse on the land with the consent of the Agency;

(b)  no other site for the deposit is reasonably practicable; and

(c)  he takes all reasonably practicable steps to prevent the refuse from entering those inland freshwaters.

[1] For "waste management licence" see s.35 of the 1990 Act, p.119 above.
[2] **Case: section 88** *Taylor Woodrow Property Management Ltd v National Rivers Authority* [1995] Env LR 52.
[3] P.273 above.
[4] "The Agency" means the Environment Agency: s.221(1) below.
[5] "Trade effluent" and "sewage effluent" defined by s.221(1), p.315 below.
[6] "Vessel" defined by s.221(1), p.315 below.
[7] For "mine" see subsection (6) below.
[8] *Prospective amendment:* words "or an abandoned part of a mine" to be inserted by the Environment Act 1995 (c.25), s.60(1).
[9] "Controlled waters" has the meaning given by s.104(1), p.290 below.
[10] "Owner" defined by s.221(1), p.314 below.
[11] *Prospective amendment:* subsections (3A)–(3C) to be inserted by the Environment Act 1995 (c.25), s.60(2).
[12] For "quarry" see subsection (6) below.
[13] "Inland freshwaters" has the meaning given by s.104(1), p.290 below.

(5)  A highway authority or other person entitled to keep open a drain[1] by virtue of section 100 of the Highways Act 1980[2] shall not be guilty of an offence under section 85 above by reason of his causing or permitting any discharge to be made from a drain kept open by virtue of that section unless the discharge is made in contravention of a prohibition imposed under section 86 above.

(6)  In this section "mine" and "quarry" have the same meanings as in the Mines and Quarries Act 1954[3].

*Offences in connection with deposits and vegetation in rivers*

**90.** (1)  A person shall be guilty of an offence under this section if, without the consent of the Agency[4] he—

(*a*)  removes from any part of the bottom, channel or bed of any inland freshwaters[5] a deposit accumulated by reason of any dam, weir or sluice holding back the waters; and

(*b*)  does so by causing the deposit to be carried away in suspension in the waters.

(2)  A person shall be guilty of an offence under this section if, without the consent of the Agency, he—

(*a*)  causes or permits a substantial amount of vegetation to be cut or uprooted in any inland freshwaters, or to be cut or uprooted so near to any such waters that it falls into them; and

(*b*)  fails to take all reasonable steps to remove the vegetation from those waters.

(3)  A person guilty of an offence under this section shall be liable, on summary conviction, to a fine not exceeding level 4 on the standard scale[6].

(4)  Nothing in subsection (1) above applies to anything done in the exercise of any power conferred by or under any enactment[7] relating to land drainage, flood prevention or navigation.

(5)  In giving a consent for the purposes of this section the Agency may make the consent subject to such conditions as it considers appropriate.

(6)  The Secretary of State may by regulations provide that any reference to inland freshwaters in subsection (1) or (2) above shall be construed as including a reference to such coastal waters[8] as may be prescribed[9].

*Consents for the purposes of sections 88 to 90*

*Applications for consent under section 89 or 90.*

90A. (1)  Any application for a consent for the purposes of section 89(4)(a)[10] or 90(1) or (2) above—

(*a*)  must be made on a form provided for the purpose by the Agency[11], and

(*b*)  must be advertised in such manner as may be required by regulations made by the Secretary of State,

except that paragraph (b) above shall not have effect in the case of an application of any class or description specified in the regulations as being exempt from the requirements of that paragraph.

(2)  The applicant for such a consent must, at the time when he makes his application, provide the Agency—

---

[1] "Drain" defined by s.221(1),(2), p.312 below.
[2] 1980 c.66.
[3] 1954 c.70.
[4] "The Agency" means the Environment Agency: s.221(1) below.
[5] "Inland freshwaters" has the meaning given by s.104(1), p.290 below.
[6] The current fine at level 4 on the standard scale is

£2,500: Criminal Justice Act 1991 (c.53), s.17.
[7] "Enactment" defined by s.221 (1), p.312 below.
[8] "Coastal waters" has the meaning given by s.104(1), p.290 below.
[9] "Prescribed" defined by s.221(1), p.314 below.
[10] P.277 above.
[11] "The Agency" means the Environment Agency: s.221(1) below.

(*a*) with all such information as it reasonably requires; and

(*b*) with all such information as may be prescribed[1] for the purpose by the Secretary of State.

(3) The information required by subsection (2) above must be provided either on, or together with, the form mentioned in subsection (1) above.

(4) The Agency may give the applicant notice requiring him to provide it with all such further information of any description specified in the notice as it may require for the purpose of determining the application.

(5) If the applicant fails to provide the Agency with any information required under subsection (4) above, the Agency may refuse to proceed with the application or refuse to proceed with it until the information is provided.[2]

*Enforcement notices.*

**90B.** (1) If the Agency[3] is of the opinion that the holder of a relevant consent[4] is contravening[5] any condition of the consent, or is likely to contravene any such condition, the Agency may serve[6] on him a notice[7] (an "enforcement notice").

(2) An enforcement notice shall—

(*a*) state that the Agency is of the said opinion;

(*b*) specify the matters constituting the contravention or the matters making it likely that the contravention will arise;

(*c*) specify the steps that must be taken to remedy the contravention or, as the case may be, to remedy the matters making it likely that the contravention will arise; and

(*d*) specify the period within which those steps must be taken.

(3) Any person who fails to comply with any requirement imposed by an enforcement notice shall be guilty of an offence and liable—

(*a*) on summary conviction, to imprisonment for a term not exceeding three months or to a fine not exceeding £20,000 or to both;

(*b*) on conviction on indictment, to imprisonment for a term not exceeding two years or to a fine or to both.

(4) If the Agency is of the opinion that proceedings for an offence under subsection (3) above would afford an ineffectual remedy against a person who has failed to comply with the requirements of an enforcement notice, the Agency may take proceedings in the High Court for the purpose of securing compliance with the notice.

(5) The Secretary of State may, if he thinks fit in relation to any person, give to the Agency directions as to whether the Agency should exercise its powers under this section and as to the steps which must be taken.

(6) In this section—

"relevant consent" means—

(*a*) a consent for the purposes of section 89(4)(a)[8] or 90(1) or (2)[9] above; or

(*b*) a discharge consent, within the meaning of section 91 below; and

"the holder", in relation to a relevant consent, is the person who has the consent in question.[10]

---

[1] "Prescribed" defined by s. 221, p.314 below.
[2] *Prospective amendment:* this section inserted by the Environment Act 1995 (c.25), s.120, sch.22, para.142. This amendment has not come into force.
[3] "The Agency" means the Environment Agency: s.221(1) below.
[4] "The holder" and "relevant consent" defined by subsection (6) below.
[5] "Contravention" defined by s.221(1), p.312 below.
[6] For provisions relating to service see s.220, p.310 below.
[7] "Notice" defined by s.221(1), p.314 below.
[8] P.277 above.
[9] P.278 above.
[10] *Prospective amendment:* this section inserted by the Environment Act 1995 (c.25), s.120, sch.22, para.142. This amendment has not come into force.

*Appeals in respect of consents under Chapter II*

**91.** (1) This section applies where the Agency,[1] otherwise than in pursuance of a direction of the Secretary of State—

(a) on an application for a consent under this Chapter for the purposes of section 88(1)(a) above[2], has refused a consent for any discharges;

(b) in giving a discharge consent[3], has made that consent subject to conditions;

(c) has revoked a discharge consent, modified the conditions of any such consent or provided that any such consent which was unconditional shall be subject to conditions;

(d) has, for the purposes of paragraph 8(1)[4] or (2) of Schedule 10[5] to this Act, specified a period in relation to a discharge consent without the agreement of the person who proposes to make, or makes, discharges in pursuance of that consent;

(e) has refused a consent for the purposes of section 89(4)(a) above[6] for any deposit;[7]

(f) has refused a consent for the purposes of section 90 above[8] for the doing of anything by any person or, in giving any such consent, made that consent subject to conditions;

(g) has refused a person a variation of any such consent as is mentioned in paragraphs (a) to (f) above or, in allowing any such variation, has made the consent subject to conditions; or

(h) has served an enforcement notice[9] on any person.[10]

(2) The person, if any, who applied for the consent or variation[11] in question, or any person whose deposits, discharges or other conduct is or would be authorised by the consent, or the person on whom the enforcement notice was served,[12] may appeal against the decision to the Secretary of State.

(2A) This section is subject to section 114 of the 1995 Act[13] (delegation or reference of appeals etc).

(2B) An appeal under this section shall, if and to the extent required by regulations under subsection (2K) below, be advertised in such manner as may be prescribed[14] by regulations under that subsection.

(2C) If either party to the appeal so requests or the Secretary of State so decides, an appeal shall be or continue in the form of a hearing (which may, if the person hearing the appeal so decides, be held, or held to any extent, in private).

(2D) On determining an appeal brought by virtue of any of paragraphs (a) to (g) of subsection (1) above against a decision of the Agency, the Secretary of State—

(a) may affirm the decision;

(b) where the decision was a refusal to grant a consent or a variation of a consent, may direct the Agency to grant the consent or to vary the consent, as the case may be;

(c) where the decision was as to the conditions of a consent, may quash all or any of those conditions;

(d) where the decision was to revoke a consent, may quash the decision;

---

[1] "The Agency" means the Environment Agency: s.221(1) below.

[2] P.276 above.

[3] "Discharge consent" defined by subsection (8) below.

[4] *Prospective amendment:* words "8 (1)" to be substituted by the Environment Act 1995 (c.25), s.120, sch.22, para.143(1)(a).

[5] P.322 below.

[6] P.277 above.

[7] *Prospective amendment:* former word "or" to be repealed by the Environment Act 1995 (c.25), s.120, sch.24.

[8] P.278 above.

[9] "Enforcement notice" has the meaning given by s.90B above: s.221(1) below.

[10] *Prospective amendment:* paras. (g) and (h) to be inserted by the Environment Act 1995 (c.25), s.120, sch.22, para.143 (1)(b).

[11] *Prospective amendment:* words ", or variation" to be inserted by the Environment Act 1995 (c.25), s.120, sch.22, para.143 (2)(a).

[12] *Prospective amendment:* words ", or the person on whom the enforcement notice was served," to be inserted by the Environment Act 1995 (c.25), s.120, sch.22, para.143(2)(b).

[13] P.489 below. "The 1995 Act" means the Environment Act 1995: s.221(1), p.311 below.

[14] "Prescribed" defined by s.221(1), p.314 below.

(e) where the decision relates to a period specified for the purposes of paragraph 8(1) or (2) of Schedule 10 to this Act, may modify[1] any provisions specifying that period;

and where he exercises any of the powers in paragraphs (b), (c) or (d) above, he may give directions as to the conditions to which the consent is to be subject.

(2E) On the determination of an appeal brought by virtue of paragraph (h) of subsection (1) above, the Secretary of State may either quash or affirm the enforcement notice and, if he affirms it, may do so either in its original form or with such modifications as he may in the circumstances think fit.

(2F) Subject to subsection (2G) below, where an appeal is brought by virtue of subsection (1)(c) above against a decision—

(a) to revoke a discharge consent,

(b) to modify the conditions of any such consent, or

(c) to provide that any such consent which was unconditional shall be subject to conditions,

the revocation, modification or provision shall not take effect pending the final determination or the withdrawal of the appeal.

(2G) Subsection (2F) above shall not apply to a decision in the case of which the notice effecting the revocation, modification or provision in question includes a statement that in the opinion of the Agency it is necessary for the purpose of preventing or, where that is not practicable, minimising—

(a) the entry into controlled waters[2] of any poisonous, noxious or polluting matter or any solid waste matter, or

(b) harm to human health,

that that subsection should not apply.

(2H) Where the decision under appeal is one falling within subsection (2G) above, if, on the application of the holder or former holder of the consent, the Secretary of State or other person determining the appeal determines that the Agency acted unreasonably in excluding the application of subsection (2F) above, then—

(a) if the appeal is still pending at the end of the day on which the determination is made, subsection (2F) above shall apply to the decision from the end of that day; and

(b) the holder or former holder of the consent shall be entitled to recover compensation from the Agency in respect of any loss suffered by him in consequence of the exclusion of the application of that subsection;

and any dispute as to a person's entitlement to such compensation or as to the amount of it shall be determined by arbitration.

(2J) Where an appeal is brought under this section against an enforcement notice, the bringing of the appeal shall not have the effect of suspending the operation of the notice.

(2K) Provision may be made by the Secretary of State by regulations with respect to appeals under this section and in particular—

(a) as to the period within which and the manner in which appeals are to be brought; and

(b) as to the manner in which appeals are to be considered.[3]

(3)–(7) *Substituted by subsections (2A)–(2K) above.*

(8) In this section "discharge consent" means such a consent under this Chapter for any discharges or description of discharges as is given for the purposes of section 88(1)(a) above either on an application for a consent or, by virtue of paragraph 6[4] of Schedule 10 to this Act, without such an application having been made.

---

[1] "Modification" defined by s.221(1), p.314 below.
[2] "Controlled waters" has the meaning given by s.104(1), p.290 below.
[3] *Prospective amendment:* subsections (2A)–(2K) to be substituted for subsections (3)–(7) by the Environment Act 1995 (c.25), s.120, sch.22, para.143(3).
[4] *Prospective amendment:* word "6" to be substituted by the Environment Act 1995 (c.25), s.120, sch.22, para.143(4).

## Chapter IIA[1]: Abandoned Mines

*Introductory.*

**91A.** (1) For the purposes of this Chapter, "abandonment", in relation to a mine[2],—

(a) subject to paragraph (b) below, includes—

(i) the discontinuance of any or all of the operations for the removal of water from the mine;

(ii) the cessation of working of any relevant seam, vein or vein-system[3];

(iii) the cessation of use of any shaft or outlet of the mine;

(iv) in the case of a mine in which activities other than mining activities are carried on (whether or not mining activities are also carried on in the mine)—

(A) the discontinuance of some or all of those other activities in the mine; and

(B) any substantial change in the operations for the removal of water from the mine; but

(b) does not include—

(i) any disclaimer under section 178 or 315 of the Insolvency Act 1986[4] (power of liquidator, or trustee of a bankrupt's estate, to disclaim onerous property) by the official receiver acting in a compulsory capacity; or

(ii) the abandonment of any rights, interests or liabilities by the Accountant in Bankruptcy acting as permanent or interim trustee in a sequestration (within the meaning of the Bankruptcy (Scotland) Act 1985[5]);

and cognate expressions shall be construed accordingly.

(2) In this Chapter, except where the context otherwise requires—

"the 1954 Act" means the Mines and Quarries Act 1954[6];

"acting in a compulsory capacity", in the case of the official receiver, means acting as—

(a) liquidator of a company;

(b) receiver or manager of a bankrupt's estate, pursuant to section 287 of the Insolvency Act 1986;

(c) trustee of a bankrupt's estate;

(d) liquidator of an insolvent partnership;

(e) trustee of an insolvent partnership;

(f) trustee, or receiver or manager of the insolvent estate of a deceased person;

"mine" has the same meaning as in the 1954 Act;

"the official receiver" has the same meaning as it has in the Insolvency Act 1986 by virtue of section 399(1) of that Act;

"prescribed" means prescribed in regulations;

"regulations" means regulations made by the Secretary of State;

"relevant seam, vein or vein-system", in the case of any mine, means any seam, vein or vein-system for the purpose of, or in connection with, whose working any excavation constituting or comprised in the mine was made.

---

[1] This Part is inserted by the Environment Act 1995 (c.25), s.58. S.58, in so far as the amendments made by the section (a) confer power on the Secretary of State to make regulations or orders, give directions or issue guidance, or (b) make provision with respect to the exercise of any such power, came into force on 21 September 1995: S.I. 1995/1983. Otherwise this Part has not come into force.

[2] For "mine" see subsection (2) below.
[3] For "relevant seam, vein or vein-system" see subsection (2) below.
[4] 1986 c.45.
[5] 1985 c.66.
[6] 1954 c.70.

*Mine operators to give the Agency six months' notice of any proposed abandonment.*

**91B.** (1) If, in the case of any mine[1], there is to be an abandonment[2] at any time after the expiration of the initial period[3], it shall be the duty of the operator of the mine to give notice[4] of the proposed abandonment to the Agency[5] at least six months before the abandonment takes effect.

(2) A notice under subsection (1) above shall contain such information (if any) as is prescribed[6] for the purpose, which may include information about the operator's opinion as to any consequences of the abandonment.

(3) A person who fails to give the notice required by subsection (1) above shall be guilty of an offence and liable—

(*a*) on summary conviction, to a fine not exceeding the statutory maximum[7];

(*b*) on conviction on indictment, to a fine.

(4) A person shall not be guilty of an offence under subsection (3) above if—

(*a*) the abandonment happens in an emergency in order to avoid danger to life or health; and

(*b*) notice of the abandonment, containing such information as may be prescribed, is given as soon as reasonably practicable after the abandonment has happened.

(5) Where the operator of a mine is—

(*a*) the official receiver acting in a compulsory capacity[8], or

(*b*) the Accountant in Bankruptcy acting as permanent or interim trustee in a sequestration (within the meaning of the Bankruptcy (Scotland) Act 1985[9]),

he shall not be guilty of an offence under subsection (3) above by reason of any failure to give the notice required by subsection (1) above if, as soon as reasonably practicable (whether before or after the abandonment), he gives to the Agency notice of the abandonment or proposed abandonment, containing such information as may be prescribed.

(6) Where a person gives notice under subsection (1), (4)(*b*) or (5) above, he shall publish prescribed particulars of, or relating to, the notice in one or more local newspapers circulating in the locality where the mine is situated.

(7) Where the Agency—

(*a*) receives notice under this section or otherwise learns of an abandonment or proposed abandonment in the case of any mine, and

(*b*) considers that, in consequence of the abandonment or proposed abandonment taking effect, any land has or is likely to become contaminated land, within the meaning of Part IIA of the Environmental Protection Act 1990[10],

it shall be the duty of the Agency to inform the local authority[11] in whose area that land is situated of the abandonment or proposed abandonment.

(8) In this section—

"the initial period" means the period of six months beginning with the day on which subsection (1) above comes into force;

"local authority" means—

(*a*) any unitary authority;

(*b*) any district council, so far as it is not a unitary authority;

---

[1] For "mine" see s.91A (2) above.
[2] "Abandonment" defined by s. 91A(1) above.
[3] "The initial period" defined by subsection (8) below.
[4] "Notice" defined by s.221(1), p.314 below.
[5] "The Agency" means the Environment Agency: s.221(1) below.
[6] "Prescribed" defined by s.91A(2) above.
[7] The current statutory maximum is £5,000: Criminal Justice Act 1991 (c.53), s.17(2).
[8] "Official receiver" and "acting in a compulsory capacity" defined by s.91A(2) above.
[9] 1985 c.66.
[10] "Contaminated land" is defined by s.78A(2) of the 1990 Act, p.163 above.
[11] "Local authority" defined by subsection (8) below.

(c) the Common Council of the City of London and, as respects the Temples, the Sub-Treasurer of the Inner Temple and the Under-Treasurer of the Middle Temple respectively;

"unitary authority" means—

(a) the council of a county, so far as it is the council of an area for which there are no district councils;

(b) the council of any district comprised in an area for which there is no county council;

(c) the council of a London borough;

(d) the council of a county borough in Wales.

## Chapter III: Powers to Prevent and Control Pollution

*Requirements to take precautions against pollution.*

**92.** (1) The Secretary of State may by regulations make provision—

(a) for prohibiting a person from having custody or control of any poisonous, noxious or polluting matter unless prescribed[1] works and prescribed precautions and other steps have been carried out or taken for the purpose of preventing or controlling the entry of the matter into any controlled waters[2];

(b) for requiring a person who already has custody or control of, or makes use of, any such matter to carry out such works for that purpose and to take such precautions and other steps for that purpose as may be prescribed.

(2) Without prejudice to the generality of the power conferred by subsection (1) above, regulations under that subsection may—

(a) confer power on the Agency[3]—

(i) to determine for the purposes of the regulations the circumstances in which a person is required to carry out works or to take any precautions or other steps; and

(ii) by notice to that person, to impose the requirement and to specify or describe the works, precautions or other steps which that person is required to carry out or take;

(b) provide for appeals to the Secretary of State against notices served by the Agency in pursuance of provision made by virtue of paragraph (a) above; and

(c) provide that a contravention of the regulations shall be an offence the maximum penalties for which shall not exceed the penalties specified in subsection (6) of section 85 above[4].

(3) This section is subject to section 114 of the 1995 Act[5] (delegation or reference of appeals etc).[6]

*Water protection zones.*

**93.** (1) Where the secretary of State considers, after consultation (in the case of an area wholly or partly in England) with the Minister[7], that subsection (2) below is satisfied in relation to any area, he may by order make provision—

(a) designating that area as a water protection zone; and

(b) prohibiting or restricting the carrying on in the designated area of such activities as may be specified or described in the order.

---

[1] "Prescribed" defined by s.221(1), p.314 below.
[2] "Controlled waters" has the meaning given by s.104(1), p.290 below.
[3] "The Agency" means the Environment Agency: s.221(1) below.
[4] P.274 above.
[5] P.489 below. "The 1995 Act" means the Environment Act 1995: s.221(1), p.311 below.
[6] Subsection (3) added by the Environment Act 1995 (c.25), s.120, sch.22, para. 144.
[7] "The Minister" defined by s.221(1), p.314 below.

(2) For the purposes of subsection (1) above this subsection is satisfied in relation to any area if (subject to subsection (3) below) it is appropriate, with a view to preventing or controlling the entry of any poisonous, noxious or polluting matter into controlled waters[1], to prohibit or restrict the carrying on in that area of activities which the Secretary of State considers are likely to result in the pollution of any such waters.

(3) The reference in subsection (2) above to the entry of poisonous, noxious or polluting matter into controlled waters shall not include a reference to the entry of nitrate into controlled waters as a result of, or of anything done in connection with, the use of any land for agricultural[2] purposes.

(4) Without prejudice to the generality of the power conferred by virtue of subsection (1) above, an order under this section may—

(a) confer power on the Agency[3] to determine for the purposes of the order the circumstances in which the carrying on of any activities is prohibited or restricted and to determine the activities to which any such prohibition or restriction applies;

(b) apply a prohibition or restriction in respect of any activities to cases where the activities are carried on without the consent of the Agency or in contravention of any conditions subject to which any such consent is given;

(c) provide that a contravention of a prohibition or restriction contained in the order or of a condition of a consent given for the purposes of any such prohibition or restriction shall be an offence the maximum penalties for which shall not exceed the penalties specified in subsection (6) of section 85 above[4];

(d) provide (subject to any regulations under section 96 below[5]) for anything falling to be determined under the order by the Agency to be determined in accordance with such procedure and by reference to such matters and to the opinion of such persons as may be specified in the order;

(e) make different provision for different cases, including different provision in relation to different persons, circumstances or localities; and

(f) contain such supplemental, consequential and transitional provision as the Secretary of State considers appropriate.

(5) The power of the Secretary of State to make an order under this section shall be exercisable by statutory instrument subject to annulment in pursuance of a resolution of either House of Parliament; but the Secretary of State shall not make such an order except on an application made by the Agency in accordance with Schedule 11 to this Act[6] and otherwise in accordance with that Schedule.[7]

*Nitrate sensitive areas.*

**94.** (1) Where the relevant Minister[8] considers that it is appropriate to do so with a view to achieving the purpose specified in subsection (2) below in relation to any land, he may by order make provision designating that land, together with any other land to which he considers it appropriate to apply the designation, as a nitrate sensitive area.

(2) The purpose mentioned in subsection (1) above is preventing or controlling the entry of nitrate into controlled waters[9] as a result of, or of anything done in connection with, the use for agricultural[10] purposes of any land.

[1] "Controlled waters" has the meaning given by s.104(1), p.290 below.
[2] "Agricultural" defined by s.221(1), p.312 below.
[3] "The Agency" means the Environment Agency: s.221(1) below.
[4] P. 274 above.
[5] P.287 below.
[6] P. 324 below.
[7] For transitional provisions and savings in respect of orders relating to byelaws under s.18 of the Water Act 1945 (c.42) see the Water Consolidation (Consequential Provisions) Act 1991 (c.60), s.2(2), sch.2, para.4(3).
[8] "The relevant Minister" defined by subsection (7) below.
[9] "Controlled waters" has the meaning given by s.104(1), p.290 below.
[10] "Agricultural" defined by s.221 (1), p.312 below.

(3) Where it appears to the relevant Minister, in relation to any area which is or is to be designated by an order under this section as a nitrate sensitive area, that it is appropriate for provision
for the imposition of requirements, prohibitions or restrictions to be contained in an order under
this section (as well as for him to be able to enter into such agreements as are mentioned in section 95 below), he may, by a subsequent order under this section or, as the case may be, by the
order designating that area—

(a) with a view to achieving the purpose specified in subsection (2) above, require, prohibit or
restrict the carrying on, either on or in relation to any agricultural land in that area, of such
activities as may be specified or described in the order; and

(b) provide for such amounts (if any) as may be specified in or determined under the order to be
paid by one of the Ministers, to such persons as may be so specified or determined, in respect
of the obligations imposed in relation to that area on those persons by virtue of paragraph (a)
above.

(4) Without prejudice to the generality of subsection (3) above, provision contained in an order
under this section by virtue of that subsection may—

(a) confer power on either of the Ministers to determine for the purposes of the order the circumstances in which the carrying on of any activities is required, prohibited or restricted and
to determine the activities to which any such requirement, prohibition or restriction applies;

(b) provide for any requirement to carry on any activity not to apply in cases where one of the
Ministers has consented to a failure to carry on that activity and any conditions on which the
consent has been given are complied with;

(c) apply a prohibition or restriction in respect of any activities to cases where the activities are
carried on without the consent of one of the Ministers or in contravention of any conditions
subject to which any such consent is given;

(d) provide that a contravention of a requirement, prohibition or restriction contained in the
order or in a condition of a consent given in relation to or for the purposes of any such
requirement, prohibition or restriction shall be an offence the maximum penalties for which
shall not exceed the penalties specified in subsection (6) of section 85 above[1];

(e) provide for amounts paid in pursuance of any provision contained in the order to be repaid
at such times and in such circumstances, and with such interest, as may be specified in or
determined under the order; and

(f) provide (subject to any regulations under section 96 below[2]) for anything falling to be determined under the order by any person to be determined in accordance with such procedure
and by reference to such matters and to the opinion of such persons as may be specified in
the order.

(5) An order under this section may—

(a) make different provision for different cases, including different provision in relation to different persons, circumstances or localities; and

(b) contain such supplemental, consequential and transitional provision as the relevant
Minister considers appropriate.

(6) The power of the relevant Minister to make an order under this section shall be exercisable
by statutory instrument subject to annulment in pursuance of a resolution of either House of
Parliament; but the relevant Minister shall not make such an order except in accordance with any
applicable provisions of Schedule 12 to this Act[3].

(7) In this section and in Schedule 12 to this Act "the relevant Minister"—

(a) in relation to the making of an order in relation to an area which is wholly in England or which
is partly in England and partly in Wales, means the Ministers[4]; and

---

[1] P.274 above.
[2] P.287 below.
[3] P.326 below.
[4] "The Ministers" defined by s.221(1), p.314 below.

(b) in relation to the making of an order in relation to an area which is wholly in Wales, means the Secretary of State.[1]

*Agreements in nitrate sensitive areas.*

**95.** (1) Where—

(a) any area has been designated as a nitrate sensitive area by an order under section 94 above; and

(b) the relevant Minister[2] considers that it is appropriate to do so with a view to achieving the purpose mentioned in subsection (2) of that section,

he may, subject to such restrictions (if any) as may be set out in the order, enter into an agreement falling within subsection (2) below.

(2) An agreement falls within this subsection if it is one under which, in consideration of payments to be made by the relevant Minister—

(a) the owner[3] of the freehold interest in any agricultural[4] land in a nitrate sensitive area; or

(b) where the owner of the freehold interest in any such land has given his written consent to the agreement being entered into by any person having another interest in that land, that other person,

accepts such obligations with respect to the management of that land or otherwise as may be imposed by the agreement.

(3) An agreement such as is mentioned in subsection (2) above between the relevant Minister and a person having an interest in any land shall bind all persons deriving title from or under that person to the extent that the agreement is expressed to bind that land in relation to those persons.

(4) In this section "the relevant Minister"—

(a) in relation to an agreement with respect to land which is wholly in England, means the Minister[5];

(b) in relation to an agreement with respect to land which is wholly in Wales, means the Secretary of State; and

(c) in relation to an agreement with respect to land which is partly in England and partly in Wales, means either of the Ministers[6].

*Regulations with respect to consents required by virtue of section 93 or 94.*

**96.** (1) The Secretary of State may, for the purposes of any orders under section 93 above[7] which require the consent of the Agency[8] to the carrying on of any activities, by regulations make provision with respect to—

(a) applications for any such consent;

(b) the conditions of any such consent;

(c) the revocation or variation of any such consent;

(d) appeals against determinations on any such application;

(e) the exercise by the Secretary of State of any power conferred on the Agency by the orders;

---

[1] The Nitrate Sensitive Areas (Designation) Order 1990, S.I. 1990/1013, as amended, made under this section, is revoked with effect from 1 June 1996: S.I. 1995/1708, reg.3. The Nitrate Sensitive Areas Regulations 1994, S.I. 1994/1729, as amended by S.I. 1995/1708 and S.I. 1995/2095, made under s.2(2) of the European Communities Act 1972 (c.68), allow the Minister to make payments of aid to farmers who give undertakings relating to the management of land in nitrate sensitive areas as defined in reg.2 and sch.1 of the regulations. See also S.I. 1996/888 and S.I. 1996/908.

[2] "The relevant Minister" defined by subsection (4) below.
[3] "Owner" defined by s.221(1), p.314 below.
[4] "Agricultural" defined by s.221(1), p.312 below.
[5] "The Minister" defined by s.221(1), p.314 below.
[6] "The Ministers" defined by s.221(1), p.314 below.
[7] P.284 above.
[8] "The Agency" means the Environment Agency: s.221(1) below.

(*f*) the imposition of charges where such an application has been made, such a consent has been given or anything has been done in pursuance of any such consent; and

(*g*) the registration of any such application or consent.

(2) The Ministers may, for the purposes of any orders under section 94 above[1] which require the consent of either of those Ministers to the carrying on of any activities or to any failure to carry on any activity, by regulations make provision with respect to—

(*a*) applications for any such consent;

(*b*) the conditions of any such consent;

(*c*) the revocation or variation of any such consent;

(*d*) the reference to arbitration of disputes about determinations on any such application;

(*e*) the imposition of charges where such an application has been made, such a consent has been given or there has been any act or omission in pursuance of any such consent; and

(*f*) the registration of any such application or consent.

(3) Without prejudice to the generality of the powers conferred by the preceding provisions of this section, regulations under subsection (1) above may apply (with or without modifications) any enactment[2] having effect in relation to consents under Chapter II of this Part.

(4) This section is subject to section 114 of the 1995 Act[3] (delegation or reference of appeals etc).[4]

*Codes of good agricultural practice.*

97. (1) The Ministers[5] may by order made by statutory instrument approve any code of practice issued (whether by either or both of the Ministers or by another person) for the purpose of—

(*a*) giving practical guidance to persons engaged in agriculture[6] with respect to activities that may affect controlled waters[7]; and

(*b*) promoting what appear to them to be desirable practices by such persons for avoiding or minimising the pollution of any such waters,

and may at any time by such an order approve a modification[8] of such a code or withdraw their approval of such a code or modification[9].

(2) A contravention[10] of a code of practice as for the time being approved under this section shall not of itself give rise to any criminal or civil liability, but the Agency[11] shall take into account whether there has been or is likely to be any such contravention in determining when and how it should exercise—

(*a*) its power, by giving a notice under subsection (1) of section 86 above[12], to impose a prohibition under that section; and

(*b*) any powers conferred on the Agency by regulations under section 92 above[13].

(3) The Ministers shall not make an order under this section unless they have first consulted the Agency.

[1] P.285 above.
[2] "Enactment" defined by s.221(1), p.312 below.
[3] P.489 below. "The 1995 Act" means the Environment Act 1995: s.221(1), p.311 below.
[4] Subsection (4) added by the Environment Act 1995 (c.25), s.120, sch.22, para.145.
[5] "The Ministers" defined by s.221(1), p.314 below.
[6] "Agriculture" defined by s.221(1), p.312 below.
[7] "Controlled waters" has the meaning given by s.104(1), p.290 below.
[8] "Modification" defined by s.221(1), p.314 below.
[9] The Water (Prevention of Pollution) (Code of Practice) Order 1991, S.I. 1991/2285, which by virtue of the Water

Consolidation (Consequential Provisions) Act 1991 (c.60), s.2(2), sch.2, para.1 has effect as if made under this section, approves the Code of Good Agricultural Practice for the Protection of Water issued on 1 July 1991. The explanatory note sets out that the Code may be obtained from MAFF Publications, London, SE99 7TP or Welsh Office Agriculture Department, Crown Offices, Cathays Park, Cardiff, CF1 3NQ.
[10] "Contravention" defined by s.221(1), p.312 below.
[11] "The Agency" means the Environment Agency: s.221(1) below.
[12] P.274 above.
[13] P.284 above.

## Chapter IV: Supplemental Provisions with respect to Water Pollution

*Radioactive substances.*

**98.** (1)  Except as provided by regulations made by the Secretary of State under this section, nothing in this Part shall apply in relation to radioactive waste within the meaning of the Radioactive Substances Act 1993[1].

(2)  The Secretary of State may by regulations—

(a)  provide for prescribed[2] provisions of this Part to have effect with such modifications[3] as he considers appropriate for dealing with such waste;

(b)  make such modifications of the said Act of 1993[4] or, in relation to such waste, of any other enactment as he considers appropriate in consequence of the provisions of this Part and of any regulations made by virtue of paragraph (a) above.[5]

*Consents required by the Agency.*

**99.** (1)  The Secretary of State may by regulations—

(a)  make provision modifying the water pollution provisions[6] of this Act in relation to cases in which consents under Chapter II of this Part[7] are required by the Agency[8]; and

(b)  for the purposes of the application of the provisions of this Part in relation to discharges by the Agency, make such other modifications[9] of those provisions as may be prescribed[10].

(2)  Without prejudice to the generality of subsection (1) above, regulations under this section may provide for such consents as are mentioned in paragraph (a) of that subsection to be required to be given by the Secretary of State (instead of by the Agency) and, in prescribed cases, to be deemed to have been so given.

*Civil liability in respect of pollution and savings.*

**100.**  Except in so far as this Part expressly otherwise provides and subject to the provisions of section 18 of the Interpretation Act 1978[11] (which relates to offences under two or more laws), nothing in this Part—

(a)  confers a right of action in any civil proceedings (other than proceedings for the recovery of a fine) in respect of any contravention of this Part or any subordinate legislation[12], consent or other instrument made, given or issued under this Part;

(b)  derogates from any right of action or other remedy (whether civil or criminal) in proceedings instituted otherwise than under this Part; or

(c)  affects any restriction imposed by or under any other enactment[13], whether public, local or private.

[1] P.381 below. Words "Radioactive Substances Act 1993" substituted by the Radioactive Substances Act 1993 (c.12), s.49(1), sch.4, para.11(a). This amendment came into force on 27 August 1993: s.51(2).
[2] "Prescribed" defined by s.221(1), p.314 below.
[3] "Modifications" defined by s.221(1), p.314 below.
[4] Words "1993" substituted by the Radioactive Substances Act 1993 (c.12), s.49(1), sch.4, para.11(b).
[5] The following regulations, by virtue of the Water Consolidation (Consequential Provisions) Act 1991 (c.60), s.2 (2), sch.2, para.1, have effect as if made under this section:
The Control of Pollution (Radioactive Waste) Regulations 1989, S. I. 1989/1158, p.545 below.
[6] "Water pollution provisions" defined by s.221(1), p.315 below.
[7] P.273 above.
[8] "The Agency" means the Environment Agency: s.221(1) below.
[9] "Modification" defined by s.221(1), p.314 below.
[10] "Prescribed" defined by s.221(1), p.314 below.
[11] 1978 c.30.
[12] "Subordinate legislation" defined by s.221(1), p.315 below.
[13] "Enactment" defined by s.221(1), p.312 below.

*Limitation for summary offences under Part III.*

**101.** Notwithstanding anything in section 127 of the Magistrates' Courts Act 1980[1] (time limit for summary proceedings), a magistrates' court may try any summary offence under this Part, or under any subordinate legislation[2] made under this Part, if the information is laid not more than twelve months after the commission of the offence.

*Power to give effect to international obligations.*

**102.** The Secretary of State shall have power by regulations to provide that the water pollution provisions[3] of this Act shall have effect with such modifications[4] as may be prescribed[5] for the purpose of enabling Her Majesty's Government in the United Kingdom to give effect—

    (*a*) to any Community obligations; or

    (*b*) to any international agreement to which the United Kingdom is for the time being a party.[6]

*Transitional pollution provisions.*

**103.** The provisions of this Part shall have effect subject to the provisions of Schedule 13 to this Act[7] (which reproduce transitional provision originally made in connection with the coming into force of provisions of the Water Act 1989[8]).

*Meaning of "controlled waters" etc. in Part III.*

**104.** (1) References in this Part to controlled waters are references to waters of any of the following classes—

    (*a*) relevant territorial waters, that is to say, subject to subsection (4) below, the waters which extend seaward for three miles[9] from the baselines from which the breadth of the territorial sea adjacent to England and Wales is measured;

    (*b*) coastal waters, that is to say, any waters which are within the area which extends landward from those baselines as far as—

        (*a*) the limit of the highest tide; or

        (*b*) in the case of the waters of any relevant river or watercourse[10], the fresh-water limit[11] of the river or watercourse,

    together with the waters of any enclosed dock which adjoins waters within that area;

    (*c*) inland freshwaters, that is to say, the waters of any relevant lake or pond[12] or of so much of any relevant river or watercourse as is above the fresh-water limit;

    (*d*) ground waters, that is to say, any waters contained in underground strata[13];

    and, accordingly, in this Part "coastal waters", "controlled waters", "ground waters", "inland freshwaters" and "relevant territorial waters" have the meanings given by this subsection.

---

[1] 1980 c.43.
[2] "Subordinate legislation" defined by s.221 (1), p.315 below.
[3] "Water pollution provisions" defined by s.221(1), p.315 below.
[4] "Modifications" defined by s.221(1), p.314 below.
[5] "Prescribed" defined by s.221(1), p.314 below.
[6] The following regulations are made, or by virtue of the Water Consolidation (Consequential Provisions) Act 1991 (c.60), s.2 (2), sch.2, para.1 have effect as if made, under this section:
The Surface Waters (Dangerous Substances) (Classification) Regulations 1989, S.I. 1989/2286, p.554 below;
The Bathing Waters (Classification) Regulations 1991, S.I.

1991/1597, p.622 below.
The Surface Waters (Dangerous Substances) (Classification) Regulations 1992, S.I. 1992/337, p.653 below.
[7] P.328 below.
[8] 1989 c.15.
[9] "Miles" defined by subsection (3) below.
[10] "Relevant river or watercourse" defined by subsection (3) below.
[11] "Fresh-water limit" defined by subsection (3) below.
[12] "Lake or pond" and "relevant lake or pond" defined by subsection (3) below.
[13] "Underground strata" defined by s.221(1), p.315 below. For "water contained in underground strata" see s.221(3), p.316 below.

(2)  In this Part any reference to the waters of any lake or pond or of any river or watercourse[1] includes a reference to the bottom, channel or bed of any lake, pond, river or, as the case may be, watercourse which is for the time being dry.

(3)  In this section—

"fresh-water limit", in relation to any river or watercourse[2], means the place for the time being shown as the fresh-water limit of that river or watercourse in the latest map deposited for that river or watercourse under section 192 below[3];

"miles" means international nautical miles of 1,852 metres;

"lake or pond" includes a reservoir of any description;

"relevant lake or pond" means (subject to subsection (4) below) any lake or pond which (whether it is natural or artificial or above or below ground) discharges into a relevant river or watercourse or into another lake or pond which is itself a relevant lake or pond[4];

"relevant river or watercourse" means (subject to subsection (4) below) any river or watercourse[5] (including an underground river or watercourse and an artificial river or watercourse) which is neither a public sewer[6] nor a sewer[7] or drain[8] which drains into a public sewer.

(4)  The Secretary of State may by order provide—

(a)  that any area of the territorial sea adjacent to England and Wales is to be treated as if it were an area of relevant territorial waters for the purposes of this Part and of any other enactment[9] in which any expression is defined by reference to the meanings given by this section;

(b)  that any lake or pond which does not discharge into a relevant river or watercourse or into a relevant lake or pond is to be treated for those purposes as a relevant lake or pond[10];

(c)  that a lake or pond which does so discharge and is of a description specified in the order is to be treated for those purposes as if it were not a relevant lake or pond;

(d)  that a watercourse of a description so specified is to be treated for those purposes as if it were not a relevant river or watercourse.

(5)  An order under this section may—

(a)  contain such supplemental, consequential and transitional provision as the Secretary of State considers appropriate; and

(b)  make different provision for different cases, including different provision in relation to different persons, circumstances or localities.

(6)  The power of the Secretary of State to make an order under this section shall be exercisable by statutory instrument subject to annulment in pursuance of a resolution of either House of Parliament.

# PART IV: Flood Defence

# PART V: General Control of Fisheries

# PART VI: Financial provisions in relation to the Authority

*Not reproduced.*

[1]  "Watercourse" defined by s.221(1), p.315 below.
[2]  "Watercourse" defined by s.221(1), p.315 below.
[3]  P.302 below.
[4]  See note 10 below.
[5]  "Watercourse" defined by s.221 (1), p.315 below.
[6]  "Public sewer" defined by s.221(1), p.314 below.
[7]  "Sewer" defined by s.221(1),(2), p.315 below.

[8]  "Drain" defined by s.221(1),(2), p.312 below.
[9]  "Enactment" defined by s.221 (1), p.312 below.
[10]  The Controlled Waters (Lakes and Ponds) Order 1989, S.I. 1989/1149, p.541 below, has effect, by virtue of the Water Consolidation (Consequential Provisions) Act 1991 (c.60), s.2(2), sch.2, para.1, as if made under this section.

## PART VII: Land and Works Powers

*This Manual contains provisions from this Part relating to anti-pollution works and interpretation.*

### Chapter I: Powers of the Agency

*Anti-pollution works*

*Anti-pollution works and operations.*

**161.** (1) Subject to subsections (1A) and (2) below[1] where it appears to the Agency[2] that any poisonous, noxious or polluting matter or any solid waste matter is likely to enter, or to be or to have been present in, any controlled waters[3], the Agency shall be entitled to carry out the following works and operations, that is to say—

(a) in a case where the matter appears likely to enter any controlled waters, works and operations for the purpose of preventing it from doing so; or

(b) in a case where the matter appears to be or to have been present in any controlled waters, works and operations for the purpose—

(i) of removing or disposing of the matter;

(ii) of remedying or mitigating any pollution caused by its presence in the waters; or

(iii) so far as it is reasonably practicable to do so, of restoring the waters, including any flora and fauna dependent on the aquatic environment of the waters, to their state immediately before the matter became present in the waters.

and, in either case, the Agency shall be entitled to carry out investigations for the purpose of establishing the source of the matter and the identity of the person who has caused or knowingly permitted it to be present in controlled waters or at a place from which it was likely, in the opinion of the Agency, to enter controlled waters[4].

(1A) Without prejudice to the power of the Agency to carry out investigations under subsection (1) above, the power conferred by that subsection to carry out works and operations shall only be exercisable in a case where—

(a) the Agency considers it necessary to carry out forthwith any works or operations falling within paragraph (a) or (b) of that subsection; or

(b) it appears to the Agency, after reasonable inquiry, that no person can be found on whom to serve a works notice under section 161A below.[5]

(2) Nothing in subsection (1) above shall entitle the Agency to impede or prevent the making of any discharge in pursuance of a consent given under Chapter II of Part III of this Act[6].

(3) Where the Agency carries out any such works operations or investigations[7] as are mentioned in subsection (1) above, it shall, subject to subsection (4) below, be entitled to recover the expenses reasonably incurred in doing so from any person who, as the case may be—

(a) caused or knowingly permitted the matter in question to be present at the place from which it was likely, in the opinion of the Agency, to enter any controlled waters; or

(b) caused or knowingly permitted the matter in question to be present in any controlled waters.

(4) No such expenses shall be recoverable from a person for any works operations or investigations in respect of water from an abandoned mine[8] or an abandoned part of a mine which that person permitted to reach such a place as is mentioned in subsection (3) above or to enter any controlled waters.

---

[1] *Prospective amendment:* words "Subject to subsections (1A) and (2) below," to be substituted by the Environment Act 1995 (c.25), s.120, sch.22, para.161(2).

[2] "The Agency" means the Environment Agency: s.221(1) below.

[3] "Controlled waters" has the meaning given by s.104(1), p.290 above: subsection (6) below.

[4] *Prospective amendment:* words "and, in either case . . . enter controlled waters" to be inserted by the Environment

Act 1995, s.60(3).

[5] *Prospective amendment:* subsection (1A) to be inserted by the Environment Act 1995 (c.25), s.120, sch.22, para.161 (3).

[6] P.273 above.

[7] *Prospective amendment:* words "operations or investigations" to be substituted by the Environment Act 1995, s.60(4).

[8] For "mine" see subsection (6) below. *Prospective*

(4A)  Subsection (4) above shall not apply to the owner or former operator of any mine or part of a mine if the mine or part in question became abandoned after 31st December 1999.

(4B)  Subsections (3B) and (3C) of section 89 above shall apply in relation to subsections (4) and (4A) above as they apply in relation to subsections (3) and (3A) of that section.[1]

(5)  Nothing in this section—

(a)  derogates from any right of action or other remedy (whether civil or criminal) in proceedings instituted otherwise than under this section; or

(b)  affects any restriction imposed by or under any other enactment[2], whether public, local or private.

(6)  In this section—

"controlled waters" has the same meaning as in Part III of this Act[3]; and

"expenses" includes costs;[4]

"mine" has the same meaning as in the Mines and Quarries Act 1954[5].

*Notices requiring persons to carry out anti-pollution works and operations.*

**161A.**  (1)  Subject to the following provisions of this section, where it appears to the Agency[6] that any poisonous, noxious or polluting matter or any solid waste matter is likely to enter, or to be or to have been present in, any controlled waters[7], the Agency shall be entitled to serve[8] a works notice on any person who, as the case may be,—

(a)  caused or knowingly permitted the matter in question to be present at the place from which it is likely, in the opinion of the Agency, to enter any controlled waters; or

(b)  caused or knowingly permitted the matter in question to be present in any controlled waters.

(2)  For the purposes of this section, a "works notice" is a notice requiring the person on whom it is served to carry out such of the following works or operations as may be specified in the notice, that is to say—

(a)  in a case where the matter in question appears likely to enter any controlled waters, works or operations for the purpose of preventing it from doing so; or

(b)  in a case where the matter appears to be or to have been present in any controlled waters, works or operations for the purpose—

(i)  of removing or disposing of the matter;

(ii)  of remedying or mitigating any pollution caused by its presence in the waters; or

(iii)  so far as it is reasonably practicable to do so, of restoring the waters, including any flora and fauna dependent on the aquatic environment of the waters, to their state immediately before the matter became present in the waters.

(3)  A works notice—

(a)  must specify the periods within which the person on whom it is served is required to do each of the things specified in the notice; and

(b)  is without prejudice to the powers of the Agency by virtue of section 161(1A)(a) above.

(4)  Before serving a works notice on any person, the Agency shall reasonably endeavour to consult that person concerning the works or operations which are to be specified in the notice.

*amendment:* Words "operations or investigations" and "or an abandoned part of a mine" to be inserted by the Environment Act 1995, s. 60(5).
[1] *Prospective amendment:* (4A)–(4B) to be inserted by the Environment Act 1995, s.60(6).
[2] "Enactment" defined by s.221(1), p.312 below.
[3] See s.104(1), p.290 above.
[4] *Prospective amendment:* the definition of expenses to be inserted by the Environment Act 1995, s.60(7).
[5] 1954 c. 70.
[6] "The Agency" means the Environment Agency: s.221(1) below.
[7] "Controlled waters" has the meaning given by s.104(1), p.290 above: subsection (13) below.
[8] For provisions relating to service see s.220, p.310 below.

(5)  The Secretary of State may by regulations make provision for or in connection with—

(a)  the form or content of works notices;

(b)  requirements for consultation, before the service of a works notice, with persons other than the person on whom that notice is to be served;

(c)  steps to be taken for the purposes of any consultation required under subsection (4) above or regulations made by virtue of paragraph (b) above; or

(d)  any other steps of a procedural nature which are to be taken in connection with, or in consequence of, the service of a works notice.

(6)  A works notice shall not be regarded as invalid, or as invalidly served, by reason only of any failure to comply with the requirements of subsection (4) above or of regulations made by virtue of paragraph (b) of subsection (5) above.

(7)  Nothing in subsection (1) above shall entitle the Agency to require the carrying out of any works or operations which would impede or prevent the making of any discharge in pursuance of a consent given under Chapter II of Part III of this Act[1].

(8)  No works notice shall be served on any person requiring him to carry out any works or operations in respect of water from an abandoned mine[2] or an abandoned part of a mine which that person permitted to reach such a place as is mentioned in subsection (1)(a) above or to enter any controlled waters.

(9)  Subsection (8) above shall not apply to the owner[3] or former operator of any mine or part of a mine if the mine or part in question became abandoned after 31st December 1999.

(10)  Subsections (3B) and (3C) of section 89 above[4] shall apply in relation to subsections (8) and (9) above as they apply in relation to subsections (3) and (3A) of that section.

(11)  Where the Agency—

(a)  carries out any such investigations as are mentioned in section 161(1) above, and

(b)  serves a works notice on a person in connection with the matter to which the investigations relate,

it shall (unless the notice is quashed or withdrawn) be entitled to recover the costs or expenses reasonably incurred in carrying out those investigations from that person.

(12)  The Secretary of State may, if he thinks fit in relation to any person, give directions to the Agency as to whether or how it should exercise its powers under this section.

(13)  In this section—

"controlled waters" has the same meaning as in Part III of this Act[5];

"mine" has the same meaning as in the Mines and Quarries Act 1954[6,7].

*Grant of, and compensation for, rights of entry etc.*

**161B.**  (1)  A works notice[8] may require a person to carry out works or operations in relation to any land or waters notwithstanding that he is not entitled to carry out those works or operations.

(2)  Any person whose consent is required before any works or operations required by a works notice may be carried out shall grant, or join in granting, such rights in relation to any land or waters as will enable the person on whom the works notice is served to comply with any requirements imposed by the works notice.

[1] P.273 above.
[2] For "mine" see subsection (13) below.
[3] "Owner" defined by s.221(1), p.314 below.
[4] P.277 above.
[5] "Controlled waters" is defined in s.104(1), p.290 above.
[6] 1954 c. 70
[7] This section inserted by the Environment Act 1995 (c.25),
s.120, sch.22, para.162. This amendment, in so far as it (i) confers power on the Secretary of State to make regulations or (ii) makes provision with respect to the exercise of any such power, came into force on 21 September 1995: S.I. 1995/1983; otherwise this amendment has not come into force.
[8] "Works notice" means a notice under s.161A above: subsection (7) below.

(3) Before serving a works notice, the Agency[1] shall reasonably endeavour to consult every person who appears to it—

(*a*) to be the owner[2] or occupier of any relevant land[3], and

(*b*) to be a person who might be required by subsection (2) above to grant, or join in granting, any rights,

concerning the rights which that person may be so required to grant.

(4) A works notice shall not be regarded as invalid, or as invalidly served, by reason only of any failure to comply with the requirements of subsection (3) above.

(5) A person who grants, or joins in granting, any rights pursuant to subsection (2) above shall be entitled, on making an application within such period as may be prescribed[4] and in such manner as may be prescribed to such person as may be prescribed, to be paid by the person on whom the works notice in question is served compensation of such amount as may be determined in such manner as may be prescribed.

(6) Without prejudice to the generality of the regulations that may be made by virtue of subsection (5) above, regulations by virtue of that subsection may make such provision in relation to compensation under this section as may be made by regulations by virtue of subsection (4) of section 35A of the Environmental Protection Act 1990[5] in relation to compensation under that section.

(7) In this section—

"prescribed" means prescribed in regulations made by the Secretary of State;

"relevant land" means—

(*a*) any land or waters in relation to which the works notice in question requires, or may require, works or operations to be carried out; or

(*b*) any land adjoining or adjacent to that land or those waters;

"works notice" means a works notice under section 161A above.[6]

........

*Appeals against works notices.*

**161C.** (1) A person on whom a works notice[7] is served may, within the period of twenty-one days beginning with the day on which the notice is served, appeal against the notice to the Secretary of State.

(2) On any appeal under this section the Secretary of State—

(*a*) shall quash the notice, if he is satisfied that there is a material defect in the notice; but

(*b*) subject to that, may confirm the notice, with or without modification, or quash it.

(3) The Secretary of State may by regulations make provision with respect to—

(*a*) the grounds on which appeals under this section may be made; or

(*b*) the procedure on any such appeal.

(4) Regulations under subsection (3) above may (among other things)—

(*a*) include provisions comparable to those in section 290 of the Public Health Act 1936[1] (appeals against notices requiring the execution of works);

(*b*) prescribe the cases in which a works notice is, or is not, to be suspended until the appeal

[1] "The Agency" means the Environment Agency: s.221(1) below.
[2] "Owner", in relation to premises, defined by s.221(1), p.314 below.
[3] "Relevant land" defined by subsection (7) below.
[4] "Prescribed" defined by subsection (7) below.
[5] P.120 above.
[6] This section inserted by the Environment Act 1995 (c. 25), s.120, sch. 22, para.162. This amendment, in so far as it (i) confers power on the Secretary of State to make regulations or (ii) makes provision with respect to the exercise of any such power, came into force on 21 September 1995: S.I. 1995/1983; otherwise this amendment has not come into force.
[7] "Works notice" means a notice under s.161A, p.293 above: subsection (5) below.

is decided, or until some other stage in the proceedings;

    (c) prescribe the cases in which the decision on an appeal may in some respects be less favourable to the appellant than the works notice against which he is appealing;

    (d) prescribe the cases in which the appellant may claim that a works notice should have been served on some other person and prescribe the procedure to be followed in those cases;

    (e) make provision as respects—

        (i) the particulars to be included in the notice of appeal;

        (ii) the persons on whom notice of appeal is to be served and the particulars, if any, which are to accompany the notice; or

        (iii) the abandonment of an appeal.

    (5) In this section "works notice" means a works notice under section 161A above[2].

    (6) This section is subject to section 114 of the 1995 Act[3] (delegation or reference of appeals).[4]

*Consequences of not complying with a works notice.*

**161D.** (1) If a person on whom the Agency[5] serves a works notice[6] fails to comply with any of the requirements of the notice, he shall be guilty of an offence.

    (2) A person who commits an offence under subsection (1) above shall be liable—

    (a) on summary conviction, to imprisonment for a term not exceeding three months or to a fine not exceeding £20,000 or to both;

    (b) on conviction on indictment to imprisonment for a term not exceeding two years or to a fine or to both.

    (3) If a person on whom a works notice has been served fails to comply with any of the requirements of the notice, the Agency may do what that person was required to do and may recover from him any costs or expenses[7] reasonably incurred by the Agency in doing it.

    (4) If the Agency is of the opinion that proceedings for an offence under subsection (1) above would afford an ineffectual remedy against a person who has failed to comply with the requirements of a works notice, the Agency may take proceedings in the High Court for the purpose of securing compliance with the notice.

    (5) In this section "works notice" means a works notice under section 161A above[8].[9]

*Other powers to deal with foul water and pollution*

**162.** (1) Without prejudice to the powers conferred by sections 161 to 161D[10] above and subsections (2) and (3) below, the Agency[11] shall have power, on any land—

    (a) which belongs to the Agency; or

    (b) over or in which the Agency has acquired the necessary easements or rights,

to construct and maintain drains[1], sewers[2], watercourses[3], catchpits and other works for the

---

[1] 1936 c.49.

[2] P.293 above.

[3] P.489 below. "The 1995 Act" means the Environment Act 1995: s.221(1), p.311 below.

[4] This section inserted by the Environment Act 1995 (c.25), s.120, sch.22, para.162. This amendment, in so far as it (i) confers power on the Secretary of State to make regulations or (ii) makes provision with respect to the exercise of any such power, came into force on 21 September 1995: S. I. 1995/1983, otherwise this amendment has not come into force.

[5] "The Agency" means the Environment Agency: s.221(1) below.

[6] "Works notice" means a notice under s.161A, p.293 above: subsection (5) below.

[7] For "expenses" see s.221 (5), p.316 below.

[8] P.293 above.

[9] This section inserted by the Environment Act 1995 (c.25), s.120, sch.22, para.162. This amendment, in so far as it (i) confers power on the Secretary of State to make regulations or (ii) makes provision with respect to the exercise of any such power, came into force on 21 September 1995: S.I. 1995/1983; otherwise this amendment has not come into force.

[10] *Prospective amendment:* words "sections 161 to 161D" to be substituted by the Environment Act 1995 (c.25), s.120, sch.22, para.163.

[11] "The Agency" means the Environment Agency: s.221(1) below.

purpose of intercepting, treating or disposing of any foul water arising or flowing on that land or of otherwise preventing any such pollution as is mentioned in section 159(5)(*b*) above[4].

(2)  Subject to the following provisions of this Part, the Agency shall, for the purpose of carrying out its functions, have power—

(*a*)  to carry out in a street all such works as are requisite for securing that the water in any relevant waterworks[5] is not polluted or otherwise contaminated; and

(*b*)  to carry out any works requisite for, or incidental to, the purposes of any works falling within paragraph (*a*) above, including for those purposes the following kinds of works, that is to say—

   (i)  breaking up or opening a street[6];

   (ii)  tunnelling or boring under a street;

   (iii)  breaking up or opening a sewer, drain or tunnel;

   (iv)  moving or removing earth and other materials;

and the provisions of section 159 above shall, so far as applicable, have effect in relation to the powers conferred by this subsection as they have effect in relation to the powers conferred by subsection (1) of that section.

(3)  Subject to the following provisions of this Part, the Agency shall, for the purpose of carrying out its functions, have power—

(*a*)  to carry out on any land which is not in, under or over a street all such works as are requisite for securing that the water in any relevant waterworks is not polluted or otherwise contaminated; and

(*b*)  to carry out any works requisite for, or incidental to, the purposes of any works falling within paragraph (*a*) above;

and the provisions of section 160 above[7] shall, so far as applicable, have effect in relation to the powers conferred by this subsection as they have effect in relation to the powers conferred by subsection (1) of that section.

(4)  Without prejudice to the provisions of sections 178 to 184 below[8], nothing in subsection (1) above shall authorise the Agency, without the consent of the navigation authority[9] in question, to intercept or take any water which a navigation authority are authorised to take or use for the purposes of their undertaking.

(5)  Any dispute as to whether any consent for the purposes of subsection (4) above is being unreasonably withheld shall be referred to the arbitration of a single arbitrator to be appointed by agreement between the parties to the dispute or, in default of agreement, by the President of the Institution of Civil Engineers.

(6)  In this section—

"relevant waterworks" means any waterworks which contain water which is or may be used by a water undertaker for providing a supply of water to any premises;

"service pipe" and "water main" have the same meanings as in the Water Industry Act 1991[10];

"waterworks" includes any water main, resource main[11], service pipe or discharge pipe[12] and any spring, well, adit, borehole, service reservoir or tank.

----

[1]  "Drain" defined by s.221(1),(2), p.312 below.
[2]  "Sewer" defined by s.221(1),(2), p.315 below.
[3]  "Watercourse" defined by s.221(1), p.315 below.
[4]  S.159 relates to powers to lay pipes in streets.
[5]  "Relevant waterworks" and "waterworks" defined by subsection (6) below.
[6]  "Street" defined by s.221(1), p.315 below.
[7]  S.160 relates to powers to lay pipes in land which is not in, under or over a street.
[8]  Ss.178–184 relate to protective provisions.
[9]  "Navigation authority" defined by s.221(1), p.314 below.
[10]  "Service pipe" and "water main" are defined by s.219(1),(2) of the 1991 Act at p.260 above.
[11]  "Resource main" defined by s.186(1),(2), p.298 below.
[12]  "Discharge pipe" defined by s.186(1), p.298 below.

*Interpretation of Part VII*

**186.** (1)  In this Part—

"discharge pipe" means a pipe[1] from which discharges are or are to be made under section 163 above[2];

"resource main" means any pipe, not being a trunk main within the meaning of the Water Industry Act 1991[3], which is or is to be used for the purposes of—

(*a*)  conveying water from one source of supply to another, from a source of supply to a regulating reservoir or from a regulating reservoir to a source of supply; or

(*b*)  giving or taking a supply of water in bulk.

(2)  In subsection (1) above—

"source of supply" shall be construed without reference to the definition of that expression in section 221 below; and

"supply of water in bulk" has the same meaning as in section 3[4] above.

(3)  The powers conferred by Chapter I of this Part shall be without prejudice to the powers conferred on the Agency by any other enactment[5] or by any agreement.

# PART VIII: Information Provisions

*This Manual contains provisions from this Part relating, in respect of pollution control, to registers, provision of information and restriction on disclosure of information and, in respect of this Act generally, to the making of false statements.*

## Annual report and publication of information

**187.**  *Repealed by the Environment Act 1995 (c.25), s.120, sch.22, para.168, sch.24.*

**188.**  *This section, which is not reproduced, relates to the duty of the Environment Agency to publish information from which assessments can be made of the demand for water and of water resources.*

## Registers etc. to be kept by the Agency

**189.**  *This section, which is not reproduced, relates to registers of abstraction and impounding licences.*

*Pollution control register.*

**190.** (1)  It shall be the duty of the Agency[6] to maintain, in accordance with regulations made by the Secretary of State, registers containing prescribed[7] particular of or relating to[8]—

(*a*)  any notices of water quality objectives or other notices served under section 83 above[9];

(*b*)  applications made for consents under Chapter II of Part III of this Act[10];

(*c*)  consents given under that Chapter and the conditions to which the consents are subject;

---

[1] For "pipe" see s. 221 (2), p.316 below.
[2] S.163 relates to discharges for works purposes.
[3] "Trunk main" is defined in s.219(1) of the 1991 Act, p.315 below.
[4] S.3 has been repealed by the Environment Act 1995 (c.25) and replaced by s.10 of that Act. S.10(6), p.431 below, defines "supply of water in bulk".
[5] "Enactment" defined by s.221(1), p.312 below.
[6] "The Agency" means the Environment Agency: s.221(1) below.
[7] "Prescribed" defined by s.221(1), p.314 below.
[8] *Prospective amendment:* words "or relating to" to be inserted by the Environment Act 1995 (c.25), s.120, sch.22, para.169(2).
[9] P.272 above.
[10] P.273 above.

(d) *Prospective amendment: to be repealed by the Environment Act 1995 (c.25), s.120, sch.22, para.169(3), sch.24.*

(e) the following, that is to say—

(i) samples of water or effluent[1] taken by the Agency for the purposes of any of the water pollution provisions[2] of this Act;

(ii) information produced by analyses of those samples;

(iii) such information with respect to samples of water or effluent taken by any other person, and the analyses of those samples, as is acquired by the Agency from any person under arrangements made by the Agency for the purposes of any of those provisions; and

(iv) the steps taken in consequence of any such information as is mentioned in any of subparagraphs (i) to (iii) above;

(f) *Prospective amendment: to be repealed by the Environment Act 1995 (c.25), s.120, sch.22, para.169(4), sch.24.*

(g) applications made to the Agency for the variation of discharge consents;

(h) enforcement notices served under section 90B above[3];

(j) revocations, under paragraph 7 of Schedule 10 to this Act[4], of discharge consents[5];

(k) appeals under section 91 above[6];

(l) directions given by the Secretary of State in relation to the Agency's functions under the water pollution provisions of this Act;

(m) convictions, for offences under Part III of this Act[7], of persons who have the benefit of discharge consents;

(n) information obtained or furnished in pursuance of conditions of discharge consents;

(o) works notices under section 161A above[8];

(p) appeals under section 161C above[9];

(q) convictions for offences under section 161D above[10];

(r) such other matters relating to the quality of water or the pollution of water as may be prescribed by the Secretary of State.[11]

(1A) Where information of any description is excluded from any register by virtue of section 191B below[12], a statement shall be entered in the register indicating the existence of information of that description.[13]

(2) It shall be the duty of the Agency—

(a) to secure that the contents of registers maintained by the Agency under this section are available, at all reasonable times, for inspection by the public free of charge; and

(b) to afford members of the public reasonable facilities for obtaining from the Agency, on payment of reasonable charges, copies of entries in any of the registers;

and, for the purposes of this subsection, places may be prescribed by the Secretary of State at which any such registers or facilities as are mentioned in paragraph (a) or (b) above are to be available or afforded to the public in pursuance of the paragraph in question.[14]

---

[1] "Effluent" defined by s.221(1), p.312 below.
[2] "Water pollution provisions" defined by s.221(1), p.315 below.
[3] P.279 above.
[4] P.319 below.
[5] "Discharge consent" has the same meaning as in s.91, p.280 above: subsection (5) below.
[6] P.280 above.
[7] P.271 above.
[8] P.293 above.
[9] P.295 above.

[10] P.296 above.
[11] *Prospective amendment:* subparagraphs (g)–(r) to be added by the Environment Act 1995 (c.25), s.120 sch.22, para.169(4).
[12] P.300 below.
[13] *Prospective amendment:* subsection (1A) to be added by the Environment Act 1995 (c.25), s.120, sch.22, para.169(4).
[14] *Prospective amendment:* words "and, for the purposes of this subsection, . . . in question." to be added by the Environment Act 1995 (c.25), s.120, sch.22, para.169(5).

(3)  Section 101[1] above shall have effect in relation to any regulations under this section as it has effect in relation to any subordinate legislation[2] under Part III of this Act[3].

(4)  The Secretary of State may give to the Agency directions requiring the removal from any register maintained by it under this section of any specified information which is not prescribed for inclusion under subsection (1) above or which, by virtue of section 191A or 191B below, ought to have been excluded from the register.

(5)  In this section "discharge consent" has the same meaning as in section 91 above.[4]

**191.**  *This section, which is not reproduced, relates to the register for the purposes of works discharges.*

*Exclusion from registers of information affecting national security.*

**191A.**  (1)  No information shall be included in a register kept or maintained by the Agency[5] under any provision of this Act if and so long as, in the opinion of the Secretary of State, the inclusion in such a register of that information, or information of that description, would be contrary to the interests of national security.

(2)  The Secretary of State may, for the purpose of securing the exclusion from registers of information to which subsection (1) above applies, give to the Agency directions—

(*a*)  specifying information, or descriptions of information, to be excluded from their registers; or

(*b*)  specifying descriptions of information to be referred to the Secretary of State for his determination;

and no information referred to the Secretary of State in pursuance of paragraph (*b*) above shall be included in any such register until the Secretary of State determines that it should be so included.

(3)  The Agency shall notify the Secretary of State of any information it excludes from a register in pursuance of directions under subsection (2) above.

(4)  A person may, as respects any information which appears to him to be information to which subsection (1) above may apply, give a notice[6] to the Secretary of State specifying the information and indicating its apparent nature; and, if he does so—

(*a*)  he shall notify the Agency that he has done so; and

(*b*)  no information so notified to the Secretary of State shall be included in any such register until the Secretary of State has determined that it should be so included.[7]

*Exclusion from registers of certain confidential information.*

**191B.**  (1)  No information relating to the affairs of any individual or business shall, without the consent of that individual or the person for the time being carrying on that business, be included in a register kept or maintained by the Agency[8] under any provision of this Act, if and so long as the information—

(*a*)  is, in relation to him, commercially confidential[9]; and

(*b*)  is not required to be included in the register in pursuance of directions under subsection (7) below;

[1]  P.290 above.
[2]  "Subordinate legislation" defined by s.221(1), p.315 below.
[3]  P.271 above.
[4]  *Prospective amendment:* subsections (4) and (5) to be added by the Environment Act 1995 (c.25), s.120, sch.22, para.169(6).
[5]  "The Agency" means the Environment Agency: s.221(1) below.
[6]  "Notice" defined by s.221(1), p.314 below.
[7]  *Prospective amendment:* this section inserted by the Environment Act 1995 (c.25), s.120, sch.22, para.170. This amendment has not come into force.
[8]  "The Agency" means the Environment Agency: s.221(1) below.
[9]  "Commercially confidential" information defined by subsection (11) below.

but information is not commercially confidential for the purposes of this section unless it is determined under this section to be so by the Agency or, on appeal, by the Secretary of State.

(2) Where information is furnished to the Agency for the purpose of—

(a) an application for a discharge consent[1] or for the variation of a discharge consent,

(b) complying with any condition of a discharge consent, or

(c) complying with a notice under section 202 below[2],

then, if the person furnishing it applies to the Agency to have the information excluded from any register kept or maintained by the Agency under any provision of this Act, on the ground that it is commercially confidential (as regards himself or another person), the Agency shall determine whether the information is or is not commercially confidential.

(3) A determination under subsection (2) above must be made within the period of fourteen days beginning with the date of the application and if the Agency fails to make a determination within that period it shall be treated as having determined that the information is commercially confidential.

(4) Where it appears to the Agency that any information (other than information furnished in circumstances within subsection (2) above) which has been obtained by the Agency under or by virtue of any provision of any enactment[3] might be commercially confidential, the Agency shall—

(a) give to the person to whom or whose business it relates notice that that information is required to be included in a register kept or maintained by the Agency under any provision of this Act, unless excluded under this section; and

(b) give him a reasonable opportunity—

(i) of objecting to the inclusion of the information on the ground that it is commercially confidential; and

(ii) of making representations to the Agency for the purpose of justifying any such objection;

and, if any representations are made, the Agency shall, having taken the representations into account, determine whether the information is or is not commercially confidential.

(5) Where, under subsection (2) or (4) above, the Agency determines that information is not commercially confidential—

(a) the information shall not be entered on the register until the end of the period of twenty-one days beginning with the date on which the determination is notified to the person concerned; and

(b) that person may appeal to the Secretary of State against the decision;

and, where an appeal is brought in respect of any information, the information shall not be entered on the register until the end of the period of seven days following the day on which the appeal is finally determined or withdrawn.

(6) Subsections (2A), (2C) and (2K) of section 91 above[4] shall apply in relation to appeals under subsection (5) above; but—

(a) subsection (2C) of that section shall have effect for the purposes of this subsection with the substitution for the words from "(which may" onwards of the words "(which must be held in private)"; and

(b) subsection (5) above is subject to section 114 of the 1995 Act[5] (delegation or reference of appeals etc).

[1] "Discharge consent" has the same meaning as in s.91, p.280 above: subsection (12) below.
[2] P.303 below.
[3] "Enactment" defined by s.221(1), p.312 below.
[4] P.280 above.
[5] P.489 below. "The 1995 Act" means the Environment Act 1995: s.221(1), p.311 below.

(7) The Secretary of State may give to the Agency directions as to specified information, or descriptions of information, which the public interest requires to be included in registers kept or maintained by the Agency under any provision of this Act notwithstanding that the information may be commercially confidential.

(8) Information excluded from a register shall be treated as ceasing to be commercially confidential for the purposes of this section at the expiry of the period of four years beginning with the date of the determination by virtue of which it was excluded; but the person who furnished it may apply to the Agency for the information to remain excluded from the register on the ground that it is still commercially confidential and the Agency shall determine whether or not that is the case.

(9) Subsections (5) and (6) above shall apply in relation to a determination under subsection (8) above as they apply in relation to a determination under subsection (2) or (4) above.

(10) The Secretary of State may by regulations substitute (whether in all cases or in such classes or descriptions of case as may be specified in the regulations) for the period for the time being specified in subsection (3) above such other period as he considers appropriate.

(11) Information is, for the purposes of any determination under this section, commercially confidential, in relation to any individual or person, if its being contained in the register would prejudice to an unreasonable degree the commercial interests of that individual or person.

(12) In this section "discharge consent" has the same meaning as in section 91 above[1].[2]

*Maps of fresh-water limits.*

**192.**—(1) The Secretary of State—

    (a) shall deposit maps with the Agency[3] showing what appear to him to be the fresh-water limits of every relevant river or watercourse; and

    (b) may from time to time, if he considers it appropriate to do so by reason of any change of what appears to him to be the fresh-water limit of any river or watercourse, deposit a map showing a revised limit for that river or watercourse.

(2) It shall be the duty of the Agency to keep any maps deposited with it under subsection (1) above available, at all reasonable times, for inspection by the public free of charge.

(3) In this section "relevant river or watercourse" has the same meaning as in section 104 above[4].

*The following sections are not reproduced in this Manual.*

**193.** *Main river maps.*

**194.** *Amendment of main river maps.*

**195.** *Maps of waterworks.*

## Provision and acquisition of information etc.

**196.** *Repealed by the Environment Act 1995 (c.25), s.120, sch.22, para. 171, sch.24.*

*The following sections are not reproduced in this Manual.*

**197.** *Provision of information about water flow etc.*

**198.** *Information about underground water.*

**199.** *Notice etc. of mining operations which may affect water conservation.*

---

[1] P.280 above.
[2] *Prospective amendment:* this section inserted by the Environment Act 1995 (c.25), s.120, sch.22, para.170. This amendment has not come into force.
[3] "The Agency" means the Environment Agency: s.221(1) below.
[4] P.290 above.

**200.** *Gauges and records kept by other persons.*

**201.** *Power to require information with respect to abstraction.*

*Information and assistance required in connection with the control of pollution.*

**202.** (1) It shall be the duty of the Agency,[1] if and so far as it is requested to do so by either of the Ministers[2], to give him all such advice and assistance as appears to it to be appropriate for facilitating the carrying out by him of his functions under the water pollution provisions[3] of this Act.

(2) Subject to subsection (3) below, either of the Ministers or the Agency may serve[4] on any person a notice[5] requiring that person to furnish him or, as the case may be, it, within a period or at times specified in the notice and in a form and manner so specified, with such information as is reasonably required by the Minister in question or by the Agency for the purpose of carrying out any of his or, as the case may be, its functions under the water pollution provisions of this Act.

(3) Each of the Ministers shall have power by regulations to make provision for restricting the information which may be required under subsection (2) above and for determining the form in which the information is to be so required.

(4) A person who fails without reasonable excuse to comply with the requirements of a notice served on him under this section shall be guilty of an offence and liable—

(*a*) on summary conviction, to a fine not exceeding the statutory maximum[6];

(*b*) on conviction on indictment, to a fine or to imprisonment for a term not exceeding two years, or to both.[7]

(5) *Repealed by the Environment Act 1995 (c.25), s.120, sch.22, para. 172(2), sch.24.*

*Exchange of information with respect to pollution incidents etc.*

**203.** (1) It shall be the duty of the Agency[8] to provide a water undertaker with all such information to which this section applies as is in the possession of the Agency and is reasonably requested by the undertaker for purposes connected with the carrying out of its functions.

(2) It shall be the duty of every water undertaker to provide the Agency with all such information to which this section applies as is in the possession of the undertaker and is reasonably requested by the Agency for purposes connected with the carrying out of any of its functions.

(3) Information provided to a water undertaker or to the Agency under subsection (1) or (2) above shall be provided in such form and in such manner and at such times as the undertaker or, as the case may be, the Agency may reasonably require.

(4) Information provided under subsection (1) or (2) above to a water undertaker or to the Agency shall be provided free of charge.

(5) The duties of a water undertaker under subsection (2) above shall be enforceable under section 18 of the Water Industry Act 1991[9] by the Secretary of State.

(6) This section applies to information—

(*a*) about the quality of any controlled waters[10] or of any other waters; or

(*b*) about any incident in which any poisonous, noxious or polluting matter or any solid waste matter has entered any controlled waters or other waters.

[1] "The Agency" means the Environment Agency: s.221(1) below.
[2] "The Ministers" defined by s.221(1), p.314 below.
[3] "Water pollution provisions " defined by s.221(1), p.315 below.
[4] For provisions relating to service see s.220, p.310 below.
[5] "Notice" defined by s.221(1), p.314 below.
[6] The current statutory maximum is £5,000: (Criminal Justice Act 1991 (c.53), s.17(2).

[7] Word "liable-" and paras. (a) and (b) substituted by the Environment Act 1995 (c.25), s.120, sch.22, para.172(1).
[8] "The Agency" means the Environment Agency: s.221(1) below.
[9] S.18 of the 1991 Act relates to orders for securing compliance with certain provisions.
[10] "Controlled waters" has the meaning given by s.104(1), p.290 above: subsection (7) below.

(7) In this section "controlled waters" has the same meaning as in Part III of this Act[1].

*Restriction on disclosure of information*

**204.** (1) Subject to the following provisions of this section, no information with respect to any particular business which—

(a) has been obtained by virtue of any of the provisions of this Act; and

(b) relates to the affairs of any individual or to any particular business,

shall, during the lifetime of that individual or so long as that business continues to be carried on, be disclosed without the consent of that individual or the person for the time being carrying on that business.

(2) Subsection (1) above does not apply to any disclosure of information which is made—

(a) for the purpose of facilitating the carrying out by either of the Ministers[2], the Agency[3], the Scottish Environment Protection Agency[4,5], the Director General of Water Services, the Monopolies Commission or a local authority[6] of any of his, its or, as the case may be, their functions by virtue of this Act, any of the other consolidation Acts[7], the Water Act 1989[8], Part I[9] or IIA[10] of the Environmental Protection Act 1990 or the 1995 Act[11,12];

(b) for the purpose of facilitating the performance by a water undertaker or sewerage undertaker of any of the duties imposed on it by or under this Act, any of the other consolidation Acts or the Water Act 1989;

(c) in pursuance of any duty imposed by section 197(1)(a) or (2)[13] or 203(1) or (2)[14] above or of any arrangements made by the Director General of Water Services under section 29(6) of the Water Industry Act 1991[15];

(d) for the purpose of facilitating the carrying out by any person mentioned in Part I of Schedule 24 to this Act[16] of any of his functions under any of the enactments[17] or instruments specified in Part II of that Schedule;

(e) for the purpose of enabling or assisting the Secretary of State to exercise any powers conferred on him by the Financial Services Act 1986[18] or by the enactments relating to companies, insurance companies or insolvency or for the purpose of enabling or assisting any inspector appointed by him under the enactments relating to companies to carry out his functions;

(f) for the purpose of enabling an official receiver to carry out his functions under the enactments relating to insolvency or for the purpose of enabling or assisting a recognised professional body for the purposes of section 391 of the Insolvency Act 1986[19] to carry out its functions as such;

(g) for the purpose of facilitating the carrying out by the Health and Safety Commission or the Health and Safety Executive of any of its functions under any enactment or of facilitating the carrying out by any enforcing authority, within the meaning of Part I of the Health and

[1] "Controlled waters" is defined in s.104(1), p.290 above.
[2] "The Ministers" defined by s.221(1), p.314 below.
[3] "The Agency" means the Environment Agency: s.221(1) below.
[4] The Scottish Environment Protection Agency, also known as SEPA, is established by the Environment Act 1995 (c.25), s.20, p.438 below.
[5] Words "the Agency, the Scottish Environment Protection Agency" substituted by the Environment Act 1995 (c. 25), s.120, sch.22, para.173 (2)(a).
[6] "Local authority" defined by s.221(1), p.314 below.
[7] "The other consolidation Acts" defined by subsection (7) below.
[8] 1989 c.15.
[9] P.88 above.
[10] P.162 above.

[11] P.415 below. "The 1995 Act" means the Environment Act 1995: s.221(1), p.311 below.
[12] Words ", the Water Act 1989, Part I or IIA of the Environmental Protection Act 1990 or the 1995 Act" substituted by the Environment Act 1995 (c.25), s.120, sch.22, para. 173(2)(b).
[13] S.197 relates to provision of information about water flow etc.
[14] P.303 above.
[15] S.29 of the 1991 Act relates to duties of customer service committees.
[16] P.330 below.
[17] "Enactment" defined by s.221(1), p.312 below.
[18] 1986 c.60.
[19] 1986 c.45.

Safety at Work etc. Act 1974[1], of any functions under a relevant statutory provision, within the meaning of that Act;

(h) for the purpose of facilitating the carrying out by the Comptroller and Auditor General of any of his functions under any enactment;

(i) in connection with the investigation of any criminal offence or for the purposes of any criminal proceedings;

(j) for the purposes of any civil proceedings brought under or by virtue of this Act, any of the other consolidation Acts, the Water Act 1989 or any of the enactments or instruments specified in Part II of Schedule 24 to this Act[2], or of any arbitration under this Act, any of the other consolidation Acts or that Act of 1989; or

(k) in pursuance of a Community obligation.

(3) Nothing in subsection (1) above shall be construed—

(a) as limiting the matters which may be included in, or made public as part of, a report of—

    (i) the Agency;

    (ia) the Scottish Environment Protection Agency;[3]

    (ii) the Director General of Water Services;

    (iii) a customer service committee maintained under the Water Industry Act 1991[4]; or

    (iv) the Monopolies Commission,

under any provision of this Act, Part I or IIA of the Environmental Protection Act 1990, that Act of 1991 or the 1995 Act[5];

(b) as limiting the matters which may be published under section 201 of that Act of 1991[6]; or

(c) as applying to any information which has been made public as part of such a report or has been so published or to any information exclusively of a statistical nature.

(4) Subject to subsection (5) below, nothing in subsection (1) above shall preclude the disclosure of information—

(a) if the disclosure is of information relating to a matter connected with the carrying out of the functions of a water undertaker or sewerage undertaker and is made by one Minister of the Crown or government department to another; or

(b) if the disclosure is for the purpose of enabling or assisting any public or other authority for the time being designated for the purposes of this section by an order made by the Secretary of State to discharge any functions which are specified in the order.

(5) The power to make an order under subsection (4) above shall be exercisable by statutory instrument subject to annulment in pursuance of a resolution of either House of Parliament; and where such an order designates an authority for the purposes of paragraph (b) of that subsection, the order may—

(a) impose conditions subject to which the disclosure of information is permitted by virtue of that paragraph; and

(b) otherwise restrict the circumstances in which disclosure is to permitted.

(6) Any person who discloses any information in contravention of the preceding provisions of this section shall be guilty of an offence and liable—

(a) on summary conviction, to a fine not exceeding the statutory maximum[7];

---

[1] 1974 c.37.
[2] P.331 below.
[3] Sub-paragraph (ia) inserted by the Environment Act 1995 (c.25), s.120, sch.22, para.173(3)(a).
[4] 1991 c.56.
[5] P.415 below. Words "Part I . . . 1995 Act" substituted by the Environment Act 1995 (c.25), s.120, sch.22, para. 173(3)(b).

[6] S.201 of the 1991 Act relates to the publication, arranged by the Secretary of State or the Director General of Water Services, of certain information and advice. Words "of 1991" inserted by the Environment Act 1995 (c.25), s.120, sch.22, 173(4).
[7] The current statutory maximum is £5,000: Criminal Justice Act 1991 (c.53),

(*b*) on conviction on indictment, to imprisonment for a term not exceeding two years or to a fine or to both.

(7) In this section "the other consolidation Acts" means the Water Industry Act 1991[1], the Statutory Water Companies Act 1991[2], the Land Drainage Act 1991[3] and the Water Consolidation (Consequential Provisions) Act 1991[4].

**205.** *This section, which is not reproduced, relates to confidentiality of information relating to underground water etc.*

*Making of false statements etc.*

**206.** (1) If, in furnishing any information or making any application under or for the purposes of any provision of this Act, any person makes a statement which he knows to be false or misleading in a material particular, or recklessly makes any statement which is false or misleading in a material particular, he shall be guilty of an offence under this section.[5]

(2) *Repealed by the Environment Act 1995 (c.25), s.112, sch.19, para.5(3), s.120, sch.24.*

(3) Where—

(*a*) the provisions contained in a licence under Chapter II of Part II of this Act in pursuance of paragraph (*b*) of subsection (2) of section 46 above, or of that paragraph as modified by subsection (6) of that section, require the use of a meter, gauge or other device; and

(*b*) such a device is used for the purposes of those provisions,

any person who wilfully alters or interferes with that device so as to prevent it from measuring correctly shall be guilty of an offence under this section.

(3A) If a person intentionally makes a false entry in any record required to be kept by virtue of a licence under Chapter II of Part II of this Act, or a consent under Chapter II of Part III of this Act[6], he shall be guilty of an offence under this section.[7]

(4) If, in keeping any record or journal or in furnishing any information which he is required to keep or furnish under section 198 or 205 above, any person knowingly or recklessly makes any statement which is false in a material particular, he shall be guilty of an offence under this section.

(5) A person who is guilty of an offence under this section shall be liable—

(*a*) on summary conviction, to a fine not exceeding the statutory maximum[8];

(*b*) on conviction on indictment, to a fine or to imprisonment for a term not exceeding two years, or to both.[9]

# PART IX: Miscellaneous and Supplemental

## *Miscellaneous*

*Directions in the interests of national security etc.*

**207.** (1) The Secretary of State may, after consultation with the Agency[10], give to the Agency such directions of a general character as appear to the Secretary of State to be requisite or expedient

[1] 1991 c.56.
[2] 1991 c.58.
[3] 1991 c.59.
[4] 1991 c.60.
[5] Subsection (1) substituted by the Environment Act 1995 (c.25), s.112, sch.19, para.5(2).
[6] P.273 above.
[7] Subsection (3A) inserted by the Environment Act 1995

(c.25), s.112, sch.19, para.5(4).
[8] The current statutory maximum is £5,000: Criminal Justice Act 1991 (c.53), s.17(2).
[9] Subsection (5) substituted, for the earlier subsections (5)–(7), by the Environment Act 1995 (c.25), s.112, sch.19, para.5(5).
[10] "The Agency" means the Environment Agency: s.221(1) below.

in the interests of national security or for the purpose of mitigating the effects of any civil emergency[1] which may occur.

(2) If it appears to the Secretary of State to be requisite or expedient to do so in the interests of national security or for the purpose of mitigating the effects of any civil emergency which has occurred or may occur, he may, after consultation with the Agency, give to the Agency a direction requiring it to do, or not to do, a particular thing specified in the direction.

(3) The duty of the Agency to comply with a direction under this section is a duty which has effect notwithstanding any other duty imposed on it (whether or not by or under this Act).

(4) The Secretary of State shall lay before each House of Parliament a copy of every direction given under this section unless he is of the opinion that disclosure of the direction is against the interests of national security.

(5) A person shall not disclose, or be required by virtue of any enactment or otherwise to disclose, anything done by virtue of this section if the Secretary of State has notified him that the Secretary of State is of the opinion that disclosure of that thing is against the interests of national security.

(6) Any person who discloses any matter in contravention of subsection (5) above shall be guilty of an offence and liable, on conviction on indictment, to imprisonment for a term not exceeding two years or to a fine or to both.

(7) Any reference in this section to a civil emergency is a reference to any natural disaster or other emergency which, in the opinion of the Secretary of State, is or may be likely, in relation to any area—

(a) so to disrupt water supplies or sewerage services; or

(b) to involve such destruction of or damage to life or property in that area,

as seriously and adversely to affect all the inhabitants of that area, or a substantial number of them, whether by depriving them of any of the essentials of life or otherwise.

(8) In this section "sewerage services" has the same meaning as in the Water Industry Act 1991[2].

*Civil liability of the Authority for escapes of water etc.*

208. (1) Where an escape of water, however caused, from a pipe[3] vested in the Agency[4] causes loss or damage, the Agency shall be liable, except as otherwise provided in this section, for the loss or damage.

(2) The Agency shall not incur any liability under subsection (1) above if the escape was due wholly to the fault[5] of the person who sustained the loss or damage or of any servant, agent or contractor of his.

(3) The Agency shall not incur any liability under subsection (1) above in respect of any loss or damage for which the Agency would not be liable apart from that subsection and which is sustained—

(a) by any water undertaker or sewerage undertaker or by any statutory undertakers, within the meaning of section 336(1) of the Town and Country Planning Act 1990[6];

(b) by any public gas supplier within the meaning of Part I of the Gas Act 1986[7] or the holder of a licence under section 6(1) of the Electricity Act 1989[8];

(c) by any highway authority; or

(d) by any person on whom a right to compensation is conferred by section 82 of the New Roads and Street Works Act 1991[9].

[1] For "civil emergency" see subsection (7) below.
[2] "Sewage services" is defined in s.219(1) of the 1991 Act, p 261 above.
[3] For "pipe" see s.221 (2).
[4] "The Agency" means the Environment Agency: s.221(1) below.
[5] For "fault" see subsection (7) below.
[6] 1990 c.8.
[7] 1986 c.44.
[8] 1989 c.29.
[9] 1991 c.22.

(4)  The Law Reform (Contributory Negligence) Act 1945[1], the Fatal Accidents Act 1976[2] and the Limitation Act 1980[3] shall apply in relation to any loss or damage for which the Agency is liable under this section, but which is not due to the Agency's fault, as if it were due to its fault.

(5)  Nothing in subsection (1) above affects any entitlement which the Authority may have to recover contribution under the Civil Liability (Contribution) Act 1978[4]; and for the purposes of that Act, any loss for which the Agency is liable under that subsection shall be treated as if it were damage.

(6)  Where the Agency is liable under any enactment[5] or agreement passed or made before 1st April 1982 to make any payment in respect of any loss or damage the Agency shall not incur liability under subsection (1) above in respect of the same loss or damage.

(7)  In this section "fault" has the same meaning as in the Law Reform (Contributory Negligence) Act 1945.

(8)  Until the coming into force of section 82 of the New Roads and Street Works Act 1991[6], subsection (3) above shall have effect as if for paragraph (d) there were substituted the following paragraphs—

"(d)  by any bridge authority, bridge managers, street authority or street managers within the meaning of the Public Utilities Street Works Act 1950; or

(e)  by any person on whom a right to compensation under section 26 of that Act of 1950 is conferred.";

but nothing in this section shall be taken to prejudice the power of the Secretary of State under that Act of 1991 to make an order bringing section 82 of that Act into force on different days for different purposes (including the purposes of this section).

*Evidence of samples and abstractions.*

**209.**  (1) and (2)  *Repealed by the Environment Act 1995 (c.25), s.111(1), s.120, sch.24.*

(3)  Where, in accordance with the provisions contained in a licence in pursuance of paragraph (b) of subsection (2) of section 46 above[7], or in pursuance of that paragraph as read with subsection (6) of that section, it has been determined what quantity of water is to be taken—

(a)  to have been abstracted during any period from a source of supply by the holder of the licence; or

(b)  to have been so abstracted at a particular point or by particular means, or for use for particular purposes,

that determination shall, for the purposes of any proceedings under Chapter II of Part II of this Act or any of the related water resources provisions, be conclusive evidence of the matters to which it relates.

(4)  *Repealed by the Environment Act 1995 (c.25), s.111(1), s.120, sch.24.*

## Byelaws

*Sections 210–212 and schedules 25 and 26 relate to the powers of the Environment Agency to make byelaws. Paragraph 4 of schedule 25 makes the following provision.*

*Byelaws for controlling certain forms of pollution*

**4.**  (1)  The Agency[8] may by byelaws make such provision as the Agency considers appropriate—

---

[1] 1945 c.28.
[2] 1976 c.30.
[3] 1980 c.58.
[4] 1978 c.47.
[5] "Enactment" defined by s.221(1), p.000 below.

[6] S.82 came into force on 1 January 1993: S.I. 1992/2984.
[7] S.46 relates to the form and contents of licences concerning abstraction and impounding of water.
[8] "The Agency" means the Environment Agency: s.221(1) below.

(*a*) for prohibiting or regulating the washing or cleaning in any controlled waters of things of a description specified in the byelaws;

(*b*) for prohibiting or regulating the keeping or use on any controlled waters of vessels[1] of a description specified in the byelaws which are provided with water closets or other sanitary appliances.

(2) In this paragraph—

"controlled waters" has the same meaning as in Part III of this Act[2]; and

"sanitary appliance", in relation to a vessel, means any appliance which—

(*a*) not being a sink, bath or shower bath, is designed to permit polluting matter to pass into the water where the vessel is situated; and

(*b*) is prescribed[3] for the purposes of this paragraph.

## Local inquiries

**213–215.** *Repealed by the Environment Act 1995 (c.25), s.120, sch.22, para.174, sch.24.*

### *Offences etc.*

**Enforcement: powers and duties.**

**216.** (1) Without prejudice to its powers of enforcement in relation to the other provisions of this Act, it shall be the duty of the Agency[4] to enforce the provisions to which this section applies.

(2) No proceedings for any offence under any provision to which this section applies shall be instituted except—

(*a*) by the Agency; or

(*b*) by, or with the consent of, the Director of Public Prosecutions.

(3) This section applies to Chapter II of Part II of this Act[5] and the related water resources provisions.

**Criminal liabilities of directors and other third parties.**

**217.** (1) Where a body corporate is guilty of an offence under this Act and that offence is proved to have been committed with the consent or connivance of, or to be attributable to any neglect on the part of, any director, manager, secretary or other similar officer of the body corporate or any person who was purporting to act in any such capacity, then he, as well as the body corporate, shall be guilty of that offence and shall be liable to be proceeded against and punished accordingly.

(2) Where the affairs of a body corporate are managed by its members, subsection (1) above shall apply in relation to the acts and defaults of a member in connection with his functions of management as if he were a director of the body corporate.

(3) Without prejudice to subsections (1) and (2) above, where the commission by any person of an offence under the water pollution provisions[6] of this Act is due to the act or default of some other person, that other person may be charged with and convicted of the offence whether or not proceedings for the offence are taken against the first-mentioned person.

[1] "Vessel" defined by s.221(1), p.315 below.
[2] "Controlled waters" is defined in s.104(1), p.290 above.
[3] "Prescribed" defined by s.221(1), p.314 below.
[4] "The Agency" means the Environment Agency: s.221(1) below.
[5] Chapter II of Part II relates to abstraction and impounding.
[6] "Water pollution provisions" defined by s.221(1), p.315 below.

*Judicial disqualification*

**218.** *Repealed by the Environment Act 1995 (c.25), s.120, sch.22, para.175, sch.24. This amendment came into force on 1 April 1996: S.I. 1996/186.*

*Powers to make regulations*

**219.** (1) Any power of one or both of the Ministers[1] to make regulations under any provision of this Act shall be exercisable by statutory instrument subject (except in the case of regulations made by virtue of paragraph 1(3) of Schedule 15 to this Act[2]) to annulment in pursuance of a resolution of either House of Parliament.

(2)[3] The provisions of any regulations made by one or both the Ministers under this Act may include—

(a) provision for any duty or other requirement imposed by the regulations on a water undertaker or sewerage undertaker to be enforceable under section 18 of the Water Industry Act 1991 by the Secretary of State, by the Director[4] or by either of them;

(b) provision, where such a duty or requirement is so enforceable by either of them, for enforcement by the Director to be subject to such consent or authorisation as may be prescribed[5];

(c) provision which, in relation to the furnishing of any information or the making of any application under the regulations, makes provision corresponding to section 206(1) and (5) above[6];

(d) provision for anything that may be prescribed by the regulations to be determined under the regulations and for anything falling to be so determined to be determined by such persons, in accordance with such procedure and by reference to such matters, and to the opinion of such persons, as may be prescribed;

(e) different provision for different cases, including different provision in relation to different persons, circumstances or localities; and

(f) such supplemental, consequential and transitional provision as the Minister[7] or Ministers exercising the power considers or consider appropriate[8].

(3) *Repealed by the Environment Act 1995 (c.25), s.120, sch.22, para.176(b), sch.24.*

*Construction of Act*

*Provisions relating to service of documents.*

**220.** (1) Any document required or authorised by virtue of this Act to be served on any person may be served—

(a) by delivering it to him or by leaving it at his proper address or by sending it by post to him at that address; or

(b) if the person is a body corporate, by serving it in accordance with paragraph (a) above on the secretary or clerk of that body; or

---

[1] "The Ministers" defined by s.221(1), p.314 below.
[2] Sch.15 relates to drainage charges.
[3] Former words "Subject to subsection (3) below," repealed by the Environment Act 1995 (c.25), s.120, sch.22, para.176(a), sch.24.
[4] S.18 relates to orders for securing compliance with certain provisions. "The Director" means the Director General of Water Services: s.219(1) of the 1991 Act, p.258 above.
[5] "Prescribed" defined by s.221(1), p.314 below.
[6] P.306 above.
[7] "The Minister" defined by s.221(1), p.314 below.

[8] The following regulations are made, or by virtue of the Water Consolidation (Consequential Provisions) Act 1991 (c.60), s.2(2), sch.2, para.1 have effect as if made, under this section:
The Bathing Waters (Classification) Regulations 1991, S.I. 1991/1597, p.622 below;
The Surface Waters (Dangerous Substances) (Classification) Regulations 1992, S.I. 1992/337, p.653 below;
The Surface Waters (River Ecosystem) (Classification) Regulations 1994, S.I. 1994/1057, p.735 below.

(c)  if the person is a partnership, by serving it in accordance with paragraph (a) above on a partner or a person having the control or management of the partnership business.

(2)  For the purposes of this section and section 7 of the Interpretation Act 1978[1] (which relates to the service of documents by post) in its application to this section, the proper address of any person on whom a document is to be served shall be his last known address, except that—

(a)  in the case of service on a body corporate or its secretary or clerk, it shall be the address of the registered or principal office of the body;

(b)  in the case of service on a partnership or a partner or a person having the control or management of a partnership business, it shall be the address of the principal office of the partnership;

and for the purposes of this subsection the principal office of a company registered outside the United Kingdom, or of a partnership carrying on business outside the United Kingdom, is its principal office within the United Kingdom.

(3)  If a person to be served by virtue of this Act with any document by another has specified to that other an address within the United Kingdom other than his proper address (as determined in pursuance of subsection (2) above) as the one at which he or someone on his behalf will accept documents of the same description as that document, that address shall also be treated as his proper address for the purposes of this section and for the purposes of the said section 7 in its application to this section.

(4)  Where under any provision of this Act any document is required to be served on the owner[2], on a lessee or on the occupier of any premises then—

(a)  if the name or address of the owner, of the lessee or, as the case may be, of the occupier of the premises cannot after reasonable inquiry be ascertained; or

(b)  in the case of service on the occupier, if the premises appear to be or are unoccupied,

that document may be served either by leaving it in the hands of a person who is or appears to be resident or employed on the land or by leaving it conspicuously affixed to some building or object on the land.

(5)  This section shall not apply to any document in relation to the service of which provision is made by rules of court.

*General interpretation.*

**221.**  (1)  In this Act, except in so far as the context otherwise requires—

"the 1995 Act" means the Environment Act 1995;[3]

"abstraction", in relation to water contained in any source of supply, means the doing of anything whereby any of that water is removed from that source of supply, whether temporarily or permanently, including anything whereby the water is so removed for the purpose of being transferred to another source of supply; and "abstract" shall be construed accordingly;

"accessories", in relation to a main, sewer or other pipe, includes any manholes, ventilating shafts, inspection chambers, settling tanks, wash-out pipes, pumps, ferrules or stopcocks for the main, sewer or other pipe, or any machinery or other apparatus which is designed or adapted for use in connection with the use or maintenance of the main, sewer or other pipe or of another accessory for it, but does not include any telecommunication apparatus (within the meaning of Schedule 2 to the Telecommunications Act 1984[4]) unless it—

(a)  is or is to be situated inside or in the close vicinity of the main, sewer or other pipe or inside or in the close vicinity of another accessory for it; and

---

[1]  1978 c.30.
[2]  "Owner" defined by s.221(1), p.314 below.
[3]  P.415 below. This definition inserted by the Environ-

ment Act 1995 (c.25), s.120, sch.22, para.177(2).
[4]  1984 c.12.

(b) is intended to be used only in connection with the use or maintenance of the main, sewer or other pipe or of another accessory for it;

and in this definition "stopcock" has the same meaning as in the Water Industry Act 1991[1];

"the Agency" means the Environment Agency;[2]

"agriculture" has the same meaning as in the Agriculture Act 1947[3] and "agricultural" shall be construed accordingly;

"analyse", in relation to any sample of land, water or effluent, includes subjecting the sample to a test of any description, and cognate expressions shall be construed accordingly;

*the definition of "the Authority" repealed by the Environment Act 1995 (c.25), s.120, sch.22, para.177(4), sch.24.*

"conservancy authority" means any person who has a duty or power under any enactment to conserve, maintain or improve the navigation of a tidal water and is not a navigation authority or harbour authority;

*the definition of "constituent council" repealed by the Environment Act 1995 (c.25), s.120, sch.22, para. 177(5), sch.24.*

"contravention" includes a failure to comply, and cognate expressions shall be construed accordingly;

"damage", in relation to individuals, includes death and any personal injury (including any disease or impairment of physical or mental condition);

"discrete waters" means inland waters so far as they comprise—

(a) a lake, pond or reservoir which does not discharge to any other inland waters; or

(b) one of a group of two or more lakes, ponds or reservoirs (whether near to or distant from each other) and of watercourses or mains connecting them, where none of the inland waters in the group discharges to any inland waters outside the group;

"disposal"—

(a) in relation to land or any interest or right in or over land, includes the creation of such an interest or right and a disposal effected by means of the surrender or other termination of any such interest or right; and

(b) in relation to sewage, includes treatment;

and cognate expressions shall be construed accordingly;

"drain" has, subject to subsection (2) below, the same meaning as in the Water Industry Act 1991[4];

"drainage" in the expression "drainage works" has the meaning given by section 113 above for the purposes of Part IV of this Act;

"drought order" means an ordinary drought order under subsection (1) of section 73 above or an emergency drought order under subsection (2) of that section;

"effluent" means any liquid, including particles of matter and other substances in suspension in the liquid;

"enactment" includes an enactment contained in this Act or in any Act passed after this Act;

"enforcement notice" has the meaning given by section 90B above;[5]

"engineering or building operations", without prejudice to the generality of that expression, includes—

---

[1] "Stopcock" is defined by s.219(1) of the 1991 Act at p.261 above.

[2] The Environment Agency is established by the Environment Act 1995 (c.25), s.1, p.000 below. This definition inserted by the Environment Act 1995 (c.25), s.120, sch. 22, para.177(3).

[3] 1947 c.48.

[4] "Drain" is defined by s.219(1) of the 1991 Act at p.258 above.

[5] This definition inserted by the Environment Act 1995 (c.25), s.120, sch.22, para.177(6).

(a) the construction, alteration, improvement, maintenance or demolition of any building or structure or of any reservoir, watercourse, dam, weir, well, borehole or other works; and

(b) the installation, modification or removal of any machinery or apparatus;

"financial year" means the twelve months ending with 31st March;

"flood defence functions", in relation to the Agency, means—

(a) its functions with respect to flood defence and land drainage by virtue of Part IV of this Act, the Land Drainage Act 1991[1] and section 6 of the 1995 Act[2];

(b) those functions transferred to the Agency by section 2(1)(a)(iii) of the 1995 Act[3] which were previously transferred to the Authority by virtue of section 136(8) of the Water Act 1989[4] and paragraph 1(3) of Schedule 15 to that Act (transfer of land drainage functions under local statutory provisions and subordinate legislation); and

(c) any other functions of the Agency under any of the flood defence provisions of this Act;[5]

"flood defence provisions", in relation to this Act, means—

(a) any of the following provisions of this Act, that is to say—

(i) Part IV;

(ii) sections 133 to 141 (including Schedule 15), 143, 147 to 149, 155, 165 to 167, 180, 193, 194 and paragraph 5 of Schedule 25;

(b) any of the following provisions of the 1995 Act, that is to say—

(i) section 6(4)[6] (general supervision of flood defence);

(ii) section 53[7] (inquiries and other hearings); and

(iii) Schedule 5[8] (membership and proceedings of regional and local flood defence committees); and

(c) any other provision of this Act or the 1995 Act so far as it relates to a provision falling within paragraph (a) or (b) above;[9]

"harbour" has the same meaning for the purposes of the flood defence provisions of this Act as in section 313 of the Merchant Shipping Act 1995[10];

"harbour authority" (except in the flood defence provisions of this Act, in which it has the same meaning as in section 313 of the Merchant Shipping Act 1995[11]) means a person who is a harbour authority as defined in section 151 for the purposes of Chapter II of Part VI of that Act[12] and is not a navigation authority.

"highway" has the same meaning as in the Highways Act 1980[13];

"information" includes anything contained in any records, accounts, estimates or returns;

"inland waters" means the whole or any part of—

(a) any river, stream or other watercourse (within the meaning of Chapter II of Part II of this Act), whether natural or artificial and whether tidal or not;

(b) any lake or pond, whether natural or artificial, or any reservoir or dock, in so far as the lake, pond, reservoir or dock does not fall within paragraph (a) of this definition; and

[1] 1991 c.59.
[2] P.425 below.
[3] P.421 below.
[4] 1989 c.15.
[5] This definition inserted by the Environment Act 1995 (c.25), s.120, sch.22, para.177(7).
[6] P.426 below.
[7] P.460 below.
[8] P.511 below.
[9] This definition inserted by the Environment Act 1995 (c.25), s.120, sch.22, para.177(8).
[10] 1995 c.21. Words "s.313 of the Merchant Shipping Act 1995" substituted by the Merchant Shipping Act 1995 (c.21), s.314, sch.13, para.90(a). This amendment came into force on 1 January 1996: s.316(2).
[11] Words "s.313 of the Merchant Shipping Act 1995" substituted by the Merchant Shipping Act 1995 (c.21), s.314, sch.13, para.90(b). This amendment came into force on 1 January 1996: s.316(2).
[12] Words "as defined in s.151 for the purposes of Ch. II of Pt. VI of that Act" substituted by the Merchant Shipping Act 1995 (c.21), s.314, sch.13, para.90(b).
[13] 1980 c.66.

(c) so much of any channel, creek, bay, estuary or arm of the sea as does not fall within paragraph (a) or (b) of this definition;

"joint planning board" has the same meaning as in the Town and Country Planning Act 1990[1];

"local authority" means the council of any county, county borough,[2] district or London borough or the Common Council of the City of London;

"local statutory provision" means—

(a) a provision of a local Act (including an Act confirming a provisional order);

(b) a provision of so much of any public general Act as has effect with respect to a particular area, with respect to particular persons or works or with respect to particular provisions falling within any paragraph of this definition;

(c) a provision of an instrument made under any provision falling within paragraph (a) or (b) above; or

(d) a provision of any other instrument which is in the nature of a local enactment;

"main river" means a main river within the meaning of Part IV of this Act;

"main river map" has, subject to section 194 above, the meaning given by section 193(2) above;

"micro-organism" includes any microscopic, biological entity which is capable of replication;

"minimum acceptable flow", in relation to any inland waters, means (except in sections 21 and 22 above and subject to section 23(3) above) the minimum acceptable flow as for the time being contained in provisions which are in force under section 21(7) above in relation to those waters;

"the Minister" means the Minister of Agriculture, Fisheries and Food;

"the Ministers" means the Secretary of State and the Minister;

"modifications" includes additions, alterations and omissions, and cognate expressions shall be construed accordingly;

"mortgage" includes any charge or lien on any property for securing money or money's worth, and "mortgagee" shall be construed accordingly;

"navigation authority" means any person who has a duty or power under any enactment to work, maintain, conserve, improve or control any canal or other inland navigation, navigable river, estuary, harbour or dock;

"notice" means notice in writing;

"owner", in relation to any premises, means the person who—

(a) is for the time being receiving the rack-rent of the premises, whether on his own account or as agent or trustee for another person; or

(b) would receive the rack-rent if the premises were let at a rack-rent,

but for the purposes of Schedule 2 to this Act, Chapter II of Part II of this Act and the related water resources provisions does not include a mortgagee not in possession, and cognate expressions shall be construed accordingly;

"prescribed" means prescribed by regulations made by the Secretary of State or, in relation to regulations made by the Minister, by those regulations;

"public authority" means any Minister of the Crown or government department, the Agency, any local authority or any person certified by the Secretary of State to be a public authority for the purposes of this Act;

"public sewer" means a sewer for the time being vested in a sewerage undertaker in its capacity as such, whether vested in that undertaker by virtue of a scheme under Schedule 2 to the Water Act 1989[3], section 179 of or Schedule 2 to the Water Industry Act 1991[4] or otherwise;

[1] 1990 c.8.
[2] Words "county borough," inserted by the Local Government (Wales) Act 1994 (c.19), s.22(5), sch.11, para.3(6). This amendment came into force on 1 April 1996:
S.I. 1996/396.
[3] 1989 c.15.
[4] 1991 c.56.

"records" includes computer records and any other records kept otherwise than in a document;

"the related water resources provisions", in relation to Chapter II of Part II of this Act, means—

(a) the following provisions of this Act, that is to say, the provisions—

(i) of sections 21 to 23 (including Schedule 5);

(ii) of sections 120, 125 to 130, 158, 189, 199 to 201, 206(3), 209(3), 211(1) and 216; and

(iii) of paragraph 1 of Schedule 25; and

(b) the following provisions of the 1995 Act, that is to say, the provisions—

(i) of sections 41 and 42 (charging schemes) as they have effect by virtue of subsection (1)(a) of section 41 (licences under Chapter II of Part II of this Act); and

(ii) of subsections (1) and (2) of section 53 (inquiries and other hearings);[1]

"sewage effluent" includes any effluent from the sewage disposal or sewerage works of a sewerage undertaker but does not include surface water;

"sewer" has, subject to subsection (2) below, the same meaning as in the Water Industry Act 1991[2];

"source of supply" means—

(a) any inland waters except, without prejudice to subsection (3) below in its application to paragraph (b) of this definition, any which are discrete waters; or

(b) any underground strata in which water is or at any time may be contained;

"street" has, subject to subsection (4) below, the same meaning as in Part III of the New Roads and Street Works 1991[3];

"subordinate legislation" has the same meaning as in the Interpretation Act 1978[4];

"substance" includes micro-organisms and any natural or artificial substance or other matter, whether it is in solid or liquid form or in the form of a gas or vapour;

"surface water" includes water from roofs;

"trade effluent" includes any effluent which is discharged from premises used for carrying on any trade or industry, other than surface water and domestic sewage, and for the purposes of this definition any premises wholly or mainly used (whether for profit or not) for agricultural purposes or for the purposes of fish farming or for scientific research or experiment shall be deemed to be premises used for carrying on a trade;

"underground strata" means strata subjacent to the surface of any land;

"vessel" includes a hovercraft within the meaning of the Hovercraft Act 1968[5];

"watercourse" includes (subject to sections 72(2) and 113(1) above) all rivers, streams, ditches, drains, cuts, culverts, dykes, sluices, sewers and passages through which water flows, except mains and other pipes which—

(a) belong to the Agency or a water undertaker; or

(b) are used by a water undertaker or any other person for the purpose only of providing a supply of water to any premises;

"water pollution provisions", in relation to this Act, means the following provisions of this Act—

(a) the provisions of Part III of this Act[6];

(b) sections 161 to 161D[7], 190[8], 202[9], and 203[10]; and

---

[1] This definition substituted by the Environment Act 1995 (c.25), s.120, sch.22, para.177(9).

[2] "Sewer" is defined by s.219(1) of the 1991 Act at p.000 above.

[3] 1991 c.22.

[4] 1978 c.30.

[5] 1968 c.59.

[6] P.271 above.

[7] P.292 above. Words "to 161D" inserted by the Environment Act 1995 (c.25), s.120, sch.22, para.177(10)(a)(i).

[8] P.298 above.

[9] P.303 above.

[10] P.303 above. Words "and 203" added by the Environment Act 1995 (c.25), s.120, sch.22, para.177(10)(a)(ii).

(c) paragraph 4 of Schedule 25 to this Act and section 211 above so far as it relates to byelaws made under that paragraph

and the following provisions of the 1995 Act, that is to say, the provisions of subsections (1) and (2) of section 53[1].[2]

(2) References in this Act to a pipe, including references to a main, a drain or a sewer, shall include references to a tunnel or conduit which serves or is to serve as the pipe in question and to any accessories for the pipe; and, accordingly, references to the laying of a pipe shall include references to the construction of such a tunnel or conduit, to the construction or installation of any such accessories and to the making of a connection between one pipe and another.

(3) Any reference in this Act to water contained in underground strata is a reference to water so contained otherwise than in a sewer, pipe, reservoir, tank or other underground works constructed in any such strata; but for the purposes of this Act water for the time being contained in—

(a) a well, borehole or similar work, including any adit or passage constructed in connection with the well, borehole or work for facilitating the collection of water in the well, borehole or work; or

(b) any excavation into underground strata, where the level of water in the excavation depends wholly or mainly on water entering it from those strata,

shall be treated as water contained in the underground strata into which the well, borehole or work was sunk or, as the case may be, the excavation was made.

(4) Until the coming into force of Part III of the New Roads and Street Works Act 1991[3], the definition of "street" in subsection (1) above shall have effect as if the reference to that Part were a reference to the Public Utilities Street Works Act 1950; but nothing in this section shall be taken—

(a) to prejudice the power of the Secretary of State under that Act of 1991 to make an order bringing Part III of that Act into force on different days for different purposes (including the purposes of this section); or

(b) in the period before the coming into force of that Part, to prevent references in this Act to a street, where the street is a highway which passes over a bridge or through a tunnel, from including that bridge or tunnel.

(5) For the purposes of any provision of this Act by or under which power is or may be conferred on any person to recover the expenses incurred by that person in doing anything, those expenses shall be assumed to include such sum as may be reasonable in respect of establishment charges or overheads.

(6) References in this Act to the later or latest of two or more different times or days are, in a case where those times or days coincide, references to the time at which or, as the case may be, the day on which they coincide.

(7) For the purposes of this Act—

(a) references in this Act to more than one Minister of the Crown, in relation to anything falling to be done by those Ministers, are references to those Ministers acting jointly; and

(b) any provision of this Act by virtue of which any function of a Minister of the Crown is exercisable concurrently by different Ministers, shall have effect as providing for that function also to be exercisable jointly by any two or more of those Ministers.

(8) Sub-paragraph (1) of paragraph 1 of Schedule 2 to the Water Consolidation (Consequential Provisions) Act 1991[4] has effect (by virtue of sub-paragraph (2)(b) of that paragraph) so that references in this Act to things done under or for the purposes of provisions of this Act, the Water

---

[1] P.460 below.
[2] Words "and the following . . . section 53." added by the Environment Act 1995 (c.25), s.120, sch.22, para.177(10)(b).
[3] P.III of the New Roads and Street Works Act 1991 (c.22)

came into force on various dates: 14 July 1992: S.I. 1992/1686; 28 November 1992, 1 January 1993, 1 April 1993: S.I. 1992/2984, save for ss.79 and 80 which are not in force.
[4] 1991 c.60.

Industry Act 1991[1] or the Land Drainage Act 1991[2] include references to things done, or treated as done, under or for the purposes of the corresponding provisions of the law in force before the commencement of this Act.

(9) Subject to any provision to the contrary which is contained in Schedule 26 to the Water Act 1989[3] or in the Water Consolidation (Consequential Provisions) Act 1991, nothing in any local statutory provision passed or made before 1st September 1989 shall be construed as relieving any water undertaker or sewerage undertaker from any liability arising by virtue of this Act in respect of any act or omission occurring on or after that date.

*Other supplemental provisions*

*Crown application.*

**222.** (1) Subject to the provisions of this section, this Act binds the Crown.

(2) No contravention by the Crown of any provision made by or under this Act shall make the Crown criminally liable; but the High Court may, on the application of the Agency[4], declare unlawful any act or omission of the Crown which constitutes such a contravention.

(3) Notwithstanding anything in subsection (2) above, the provisions of this Act shall apply to persons in the public service of the Crown as they apply to other persons.

(4) If the Secretary of State certifies that it appears to him, as respects any Crown premises[5] and any powers of entry exercisable in relation to them specified in the certificate, that it is requisite or expedient that, in the interests of national security, the powers should not be exercisable in relation to those premises, those powers shall not be exercisable in relation to those premises.

(5) Subject to subsection (4) above, the powers conferred by sections 154, 156, 160, 162(3)[6] and 168 above shall be exercisable in relation to land in which there is a Crown or Duchy interest[7] only with the consent of the appropriate authority[8].

(6) Nothing in this section shall be taken as in any way affecting Her Majesty in her private capacity; and this subsection shall be construed as if section 38(3) of the Crown Proceedings Act 1947[9] (interpretation of references to Her Majesty in her private capacity) were contained in this Act.

(7) Nothing in this Act, as read with the other provisions of this section, shall be construed as conferring any power of levying drainage charges in respect of lands below the high-water mark of ordinary spring tides.

(8) Section 74 of the Land Drainage Act 1991[10] (Crown application), so far as it relates to land in which there is a Crown or Duchy interest, shall apply in relation to the flood defence provisions of this Act as it applies in relation to that Act; but nothing in this subsection shall affect any power conferred by this Act for the purposes both of the Agency's functions under those provisions and of other functions of the Agency.

(9) In this section—

"the appropriate authority" has the same meaning as it has in Part XIII of the Town and Country Planning Act 1990[11] by virtue of section 293(2) of that Act;

"Crown or Duchy interest" means an interest which belongs to Her Majesty in right of the Crown or of the Duchy of Lancaster, or to the Duchy of Cornwall, or belonging to a government department or held in trust for Her Majesty for the purposes of a government department;

"Crown premises" means premises held by or on behalf of the Crown.

[1] 1991 c.56.
[2] 1991 c.59.
[3] 1989 c.15.
[4] "The Agency" means the Environment Agency: s.221(1) above.
[5] "Crown premises" defined by subsection (9) below.
[6] P.296 above.
[7] "Crown or Duchy interest" defined by subsection (9) below.
[8] "The appropriate authority" defined by subsection (9) below.
[9] 1947 c.44.
[10] 1991 c.59.
[11] 1990 c.8.

(10) The provisions of subsection (3) of section 293 of the Town and Country Planning Act 1990 (questions relating to Crown application) as to the determination of questions shall apply for the purposes of this section.[1]

*Exemption for visiting forces.*

**223.** (1) Chapter II of Part II of this Act and the related water resources provisions shall not apply—

(*a*) to anything done by a member of a visiting force in his capacity as a member of that force; or

(*b*) to any land occupied by or for the purposes of a visiting force.

(2) In this section "visiting force" means any such body, contingent or detachment of the forces of any country as is a visiting force for the purposes of any of the provisions of the Visiting Forces Act 1952[2].

*Application to the Isles of Scilly.*

**224.** (1) Subject to the provisions of any order under this section, this Act shall not apply in relation to the Isles of Scilly.

(2) The Secretary of State may, after consultation with the Council of the Isles of Scilly, by order provide for the application of any provisions of this Act to the Isles of Scilly; and any such order may provide for the application of those provisions to those Isles with such modifications[3] as may be specified in the order.

(3) An order under this section may—

(*a*) make different provision for different cases, including different provision in relation to different persons, circumstances or localities; and

(*b*) contain such supplemental, consequential and transitional provision as the Secretary of State considers appropriate, including provision saving provision repealed by or under any enactment[4].

(4) The power of the Secretary of State to make an order under this section shall be exercisable by statutory instrument subject to annulment in pursuance of a resolution of either House of Parliament.[5]

*Short title, commencement and extent.*

**225.** (1) This Act may be cited as the Water Resources Act 1991.

(2) This Act shall come into force on 1st December 1991.

(3) Subject to subsections (4) to (6) of section 2 and to section 224 above, to the extension of section 166(3) above to Scotland and to the extension, by virtue of any other enactment[6], of any provision of this Act to the territorial sea, this Act extends to England and Wales only.

(4) Nothing in this act, so far as it extends to Scotland, shall authorise the Agency to acquire any land in Scotland compulsorily.

---

[1] *Prospective amendment:* this section substituted by the Environment Act 1995 (c.25), s.116, sch.21, para.2 (4). This amendment has not come into force.
[2] 1952 c.67.
[3] "Modifications" defined by s.221(1), p.314 above.
[4] "Enactment" defined by s.221(1), p.312 above.
[5] This section substituted by the Environment Act 1995 (c.25), s.118(5). This amendment, in so far as it confers power to make an order or make provision in relation to the exercise of that power, came into force on 1 February 1996: S.I. 1996/186; otherwise this amendment has not come into force.
[6] "Enactment" defined by s.221(1), p.312 above.

# SCHEDULE 10[1]

(Section 88[2])

## DISCHARGE CONSENTS

### Application for consent

1. (1) An application for a consent, for the purposes of section 88(1)(a) of this Act, for any discharges—

(a) shall be made to the Agency[3] on a form provided for the purpose by the Agency; and

(b) must be advertised by or on behalf of the applicant in such manner as may be required by regulations made by the Secretary of State.

(2) Regulations made by the Secretary of State may make provision for enabling the Agency to direct or determine that any such advertising of an application as is required under sub-paragraph (1)(b) above may, in any case, be dispensed with if, in that case, it appears to the Agency to be appropriate for that advertising to be dispensed with.

(3) The applicant for such a consent must provide to the Agency, either on, or together with, the form mentioned in sub-paragraph (1) above—

(a) such information as the Agency may reasonably require; and

(b) such information as may be prescribed[4] for the purpose by the Secretary of State;

but, subject to paragraph 3(3) below and without prejudice to the effect (if any) of any other contravention of the requirements of this Schedule in relation to an application under this paragraph, a failure to provide information in pursuance of this sub-paragraph shall not invalidate an application.

(4) The Agency may give the applicant notice[5] requiring him to provide it with such further information of any description specified in the notice as it may require for the purpose of determining the application.

(5) An application made in accordance with this paragraph which relates to proposed discharges at two or more places may be treated by the Agency as separate applications for consents for discharges at each of those places.

### Consultation in connection with applications

2. (1) Subject to sub-paragraph (2) below, the Agency[6] shall give notice[7] of any application under paragraph 1 above, together with a copy of the application, to the persons who are prescribed[8] or directed to be consulted under this paragraph and shall do so within the specified period for notification.

(2) The Secretary of State may, by regulations, exempt any class of application from the requirements of this paragraph or exclude any class of information contained in applications from those requirements, in all cases or as respects specified classes only of persons to be consulted.

(3) Any representations made by the persons so consulted within the period allowed shall be considered by the Agency in determining the application.

(4) For the purposes of sub-paragraph (1) above—

(a) persons are prescribed to be consulted on any description of application if they are persons specified for the purposes of applications of that description in regulations made by the Secretary of State;

(b) persons are directed to be consulted on any particular application if the Secretary of State specifies them in a direction given to the Agency;

and the "specified period for notification" is the period specified in the regulations or in the direction.

(5) Any representations made by any other persons within the period allowed shall also be considered by the Agency in determining the application.

(6) Subject to sub-paragraph (7) below, the period allowed for making representations is—

---

[1] *Prospective amendment:* this schedule to be substituted by the Environment Act 1995 (c.25), s.120, sch.22, para.183. This amendment has not come into force.

[2] P.276 above.

[3] "The Agency" means the Environment Agency: s.221(1) above.

[4] "Prescribed" defined by s.221(1), p.314 above.

[5] "Notice" defined by s.221(1), p.314 above.

[6] "The Agency" means the Environment Agency: s.221(1) above.

[7] "Notice" defined by s.221(1), p.314 above.

[8] "Prescribed" defined by s.221(1), p.314 above.

(*a*) in the case of persons prescribed or directed to be consulted, the period of six weeks beginning with the date on which notice of the application was given under sub-paragraph (1) above, and

(*b*) in the case of other persons, the period of six weeks beginning with the date on which the making of the application was advertised in pursuance of paragraph 1(1)(*b*) above.

(7) The Secretary of State may, by regulations, substitute for any period for the time being specified in sub-paragraph (6)(*a*) or (*b*) above, such other period as he considers appropriate.

......................................................................................................................................

## *Consideration and determination of applications*

3. (1) On an application under paragraph 1 above the Agency[1] shall be under a duty, if the requirements—

(*a*) of that paragraph, and

(*b*) of any regulations made under paragraph 1 or 2 above or of any directions under paragraph 2 above,

are complied with, to consider whether to give the consent applied for, either unconditionally or subject to conditions, or to refuse it.

(2) Subject to the following provisions of this Schedule, on an application made in accordance with paragraph 1 above, the applicant may treat the consent applied for as having been refused if it is not given within the period of four months beginning with the day on which the application is received or within such longer period as may be agreed in writing between the Agency and the applicant.

(3) Where any person, having made an application to the Agency for a consent, has failed to comply with his obligation under paragraph 1(3) or (4) above to provide information to the Agency, the Agency may refuse to proceed with the application, or refuse to proceed with it until the information is provided.

(4) The conditions subject to which a consent may be given under this paragraph shall be such conditions as the Agency may think fit and, in particular, may include conditions—

(*a*) as to the places at which the discharges to which the consent relates may be made and as to the design and construction of any outlets for the discharges;

(*b*) as to the nature, origin, composition, temperature, volume and rate of the discharges and as to the periods during which the discharges may be made;

(*c*) as to the steps to be taken, in relation to the discharges or by way of subjecting any substance likely to affect the description of matter discharged to treatment or any other process, for minimising the polluting effects of the discharges on any controlled waters[2];

(*d*) as to the provision of facilities for taking samples of the matter discharged and, in particular, as to the provision, maintenance and use of manholes, inspection chambers, observation wells and boreholes in connection with the discharges;

(*e*) as to the provision, maintenance and testing of meters for measuring or recording the volume and rate of the discharges and apparatus for determining the nature, composition and temperature of the discharges;

(*f*) as to the keeping of records of the nature, origin, composition, temperature, volume and rate of the discharges and, in particular, of records of readings of meters and other recording apparatus provided in accordance with any other condition attached to the consent; and

(*g*) as to the making of returns and the giving of other information to the Authority[3] about the nature, origin, composition, temperature, volume and rate of the discharges;

and it is hereby declared that a consent may be given under this paragraph subject to different conditions in respect of different periods.

(5) The Secretary of State may, by regulations, substitute for any period for the time being specified in sub-paragraph (2) above, such other period as he considers appropriate.

4. The Secretary of State may give the Agency[4] a direction with respect to any particular application, or any description of applications, for consent under paragraph 1 above requiring the Agency not to determine or not to proceed with the application or applications of that description until the expiry of any such period as may be specified in the direction, or until directed by the Secretary of State that it may do so, as the case may be.

......................................................................................................................................

[1] "The Agency" means the Environment Agency: s.221(1) above.

[2] "Controlled waters" has the meaning given by s.104(1), p.290 above.

[3] It appears that the reference to "the Authority" should be a reference to "the Agency" in accordance with other amendments made to this Act by the Environment Act 1995 which have substituted the word "Agency" for "Authority".

[4] "The Agency" means the Environment Agency: s.221(1) above.

*Reference to Secretary of State of certain applications for consent*

**5.** (1) The Secretary of State may, either in consequence of representations or objections made to him or otherwise, direct the Agency[1] to transmit to him for determination such applications for consent under paragraph 1 above as are specified in the direction or are of a description so specified.

(2) Where a direction is given to the Agency under this paragraph, the Agency shall comply with the direction and inform every applicant to whose application the direction relates of the transmission of his application to the Secretary of State.

(3) Paragraphs 1(1) and 2 above shall have effect in relation to an application transmitted to the Secretary of state under this paragraph with such modifications[2] as may be prescribed[3].

(4) Where an application is transmitted to the Secretary of State under this paragraph, the Secretary of State any at any time after the application is transmitted and before it is granted or refused—

(a) cause a local inquiry to be held with respect to the application; or

(b) afford the applicant and the Agency an opportunity of appearing before, and being heard by, a person appointed by the Secretary of State for the purpose.

(5) The Secretary of State shall exercise his power under sub-paragraph (4) above in any case where a request to be heard with respect to the application is made to him in the prescribed manner by the applicant or by the Agency.

(6) It shall be the duty of the Secretary of State, if the requirements of this paragraph and of any regulations made under it are complied with, to determine an application for consent transmitted to him by the Agency under this paragraph by directing the Agency to refuse its consent or to give its consent under paragraph 3 above (either unconditionally or subject to such conditions as are specified in the direction).

(7) Without prejudice to any of the preceding provisions of this paragraph, the Secretary of State may by regulations make provision for the purposes of, and in connection with, the consideration and disposal by him of applications transmitted to him under this paragraph.

*Consents without applications*

**6.** (1) If it appears to the Agency[4]—

(a) that a person has caused or permitted effluent[5] or other matter to be discharged in contravention—

  (i) of the obligation imposed by virtue of section 85(3)[6] of this Act; or

  (ii) of any prohibition imposed under section 86[7] of this Act; and

(b) that a similar contravention by that person is likely,

the Agency may, if it thinks fit, serve on him an instrument in writing giving its consent, subject to any conditions specified in the instrument, for discharges of a description so specified.

(2) A consent given under this paragraph shall not relate to any discharge which occurred before the instrument containing the consent was served on the recipient of the instrument.

(3) Sub-paragraph (4) of paragraph 3 above shall have effect in relation to a consent given under this paragraph as it has effect in relation to a consent given under that paragraph.

(4) Where a consent has been given under this paragraph, the Agency shall publish notice of the consent in such manner as may be prescribed[8] by the Secretary of State and send copies of the instrument containing the consent to such bodies or persons as may be so prescribed.

(5) It shall be the duty of the Agency to consider any representations or objections with respect to a consent under this paragraph as are made to it in such manner, and within such period, as may be prescribed by the Secretary of State and have not been withdrawn.

(6) Where notice of a consent is published by the Agency under sub-paragraph (4) above, the Agency shall be entitled to recover the expenses of publication from the person on whom the instrument containing the consent was served.

---

[1] "The Agency" means the Environment Agency: s.221(1) above.

[2] "Modification" defined by s.221(1), p.314 above.

[3] "Prescribed" defined by s.221(1), p.314 above.

[4] "The Agency" means the Environment Agency: s.221(1)

above.

[5] "Effluent" defined by s.221(1), p.312 above.

[6] P.273 above.

[7] P.274 above.

[8] "Prescribed" defined by s.221(1), p.314 above.

*Revocation of consents and alteration and imposition of conditions*

7. (1) The Agency[1] may from time to time review any consent given under paragraph 3[2] or 6 above and the conditions (if any) to which the consent is subject.

(2) Subject to such restrictions on the exercise of the power conferred by this sub-paragraph as are imposed under paragraph 8 below, where the Agency has reviewed a consent under this paragraph, it may by a notice[3] served on the person making a discharge in pursuance of the consent—

(a) revoke the consent;

(b) make modifications[4] of the conditions of the consent; or

(c) in the case of an unconditional consent, provide that it shall be subject to such conditions as may be specified in the notice.

(3) If on a review under sub-paragraph (1) above it appears to the Agency that no discharge has been made in pursuance of the consent to which the review relates at any time during the preceding twelve months, the Agency may revoke the consent by a notice served on the holder of the consent.

(4) If it appears to the Secretary of State appropriate to do so—

(a) for the purpose of enabling Her Majesty's Government in the United Kingdom to give effect to any Community obligation or to any international agreement to which the United Kingdom is for the time being a party;

(b) for the protection of public health or of flora and fauna dependent on an aquatic environment; or

(c) in consequence of any representations or objections made to him or otherwise,

he may, subject to such restrictions on the exercise of the power conferred by virtue of paragraph (c) above as are imposed under paragraph 8 below, at any time direct the Agency, in relation to a consent given under paragraph 3 or 6 above, to do anything mentioned in sub-paragraph (2)(a) to (c) above.

(5) The Agency shall be liable to pay compensation to any person in respect of any loss or damage sustained by that person as a result of the Agency's compliance with a direction given in relation to any consent by virtue of sub-paragraph (4)(b) above if—

(a) in complying with that direction the Agency does anything which, apart from that direction, it would be precluded from doing by a restriction imposed under paragraph 8 below; and

(b) the direction is now shown to have been given in consequence of—

(i) a change of circumstances which could not reasonably have been foreseen at the beginning of the period to which the restriction relates; or

(ii) consideration by the Secretary of State of material information which was not reasonably available to the Agency at the beginning of that period.

(6) For the purposes of sub-paragraph (5) above information is material, in relation to a consent, if it relates to any discharge made or to be made by virtue of the consent, to the interaction of any such discharge with any other discharge or to the combined effect of the matter discharged and any other matter.

........................................................................................................................................

*Restriction on variation and revocation of consent and previous variation*

8. (1) Each instrument signifying the consent of the Agency[5] under paragraph 3[6] or 6[7] above shall specify a period during which no notice by virtue of paragraph 7(2) or (4)(c) above shall be served in respect of the consent except, in the case of a notice doing anything mentioned in paragraph 7(2)(b) or (c), with the agreement of the holder of the consent.

(2) Each notice served by the Agency by virtue of paragraph 7(2) or (4)(c) above (except a notice which only revokes a consent) shall specify a period during which a subsequent such notice which alters the effect of the first-mentioned notice shall not be served except, in the case of a notice doing anything mentioned in paragraph 7(2)(b) or (c) above, with the agreement of the holder of the consent.

(3) The period specified under sub-paragraph (1) or (2) above in relation to any consent shall not, unless the person who proposes to make or makes discharges in pursuance of the consent otherwise agrees, be less than the period of four years beginning—

---

[1] "The Agency" means the Environment Agency: s.221(1) above.
[2] P.320 above.
[3] "Notice" defined by s.221(1), p.314 above.
[4] "Modification" defined by s.221(1), p.314 above.

[5] "The Agency" means the Environment Agency: s.221(1) above.
[6] P.320 above.
[7] P.321 above.

(*a*)  in the case of a period specified under sub-paragraph (1) above, with the day on which the consent takes effect; and

(*b*)  in the case of a period specified under sub-paragraph (2) above, with the day on which the notice specifying that period is served.

(4)  A restriction imposed under sub-paragraph (1) or (2) above shall not prevent the service by the Agency of a notice by virtue of paragraph 7(2) or (4)(*c*) above in respect of a consent given under paragraph 6 above if—

(*a*)  the notice is served not more than three months after the beginning of the period prescribed under paragraph 6(5) above for the making of representations and objections with respect to the consent; and

(*b*)  the Agency or, as the case may be, the Secretary of State considers, in consequence of any representations or objections received by it or him within that period, that it is appropriate for the notice to be served.

(5)  A restriction imposed under sub-paragraph (1) or (2) above shall not prevent the service by the Agency of a notice by virtue of paragraph 7(2)(*b*) or (*c*) or (4)(*c*) above in respect of a consent given under paragraph 6 above if the holder has applied for a variation under paragraph 10 below.

### General review of consents

**9.**  (1)  If it appears appropriate to the Secretary of State to do so he may at any time direct the Agency[1] to review—

(*a*)  the consents given under paragraph 3[2] or 6[3] above, or

(*b*)  any description of such consents,

and the conditions (if any) to which those consents are subject.

(2)  A direction given by virtue of sub-paragraph (1) above—

(*a*)  shall specify the purpose for which, and

(*b*)  may specify the manner in which,

the review is to be conducted.

(3)  After carrying out a review pursuant to a direction given by virtue of sub-paragraph (1) above, the Agency shall submit to the Secretary of State its proposals (if any) for—

(*a*)  the modification[4] of the conditions of any consent reviewed pursuant to the direction, or

(*b*)  in the case of any unconditional consent reviewed pursuant to the direction, subjecting the consent to conditions.

(4)  Where the Secretary of State has received any proposals from the Agency under sub-paragraph (3) above in relation to any consent he may, if it appears appropriate to him to do so, direct the Agency to do, in relation to that consent, anything mentioned in paragraph 7(2)(*b*) or (*c*) above[5].

(5)  A direction given by virtue of sub-paragraph (4) above may only direct the Agency to do, in relation to any consent,—

(*a*)  any such thing as the Agency has proposed should be done in relation to that consent, or

(*b*)  any such thing which such modifications as appear to the Secretary of State to be appropriate.

### Applications for variation

**10.**  (1)  The holder of a consent under paragraph 3[6] or 6[7] above may apply to the Agency, on a form provided for the purpose by the Agency[8], for the variation of the consent.

(2)  The provisions of paragraphs 1[9] to 5[10] above shall apply (with the necessary modifications) to applications under sub-paragraph (1) above, and to the variation of consents in pursuance of such applications, as they apply to applications for, and the grant of, consents.

[1]  "The Agency" means the Environment Agency: s.221(1) above.
[2]  P.320 above.
[3]  P.321 above.
[4]  "Modification" defined by s.221(1), p.314 above.
[5]  P.322 above.
[6]  P.320 above.
[7]  P.321 above.
[8]  "The Agency" means the Environment Agency: s.221(1) above.
[9]  P.319 above.
[10]  P.321 above.

*Transfer of consents*

11. (1) A consent under paragraph 3[1] or 6[2] above may be transferred by the holder to a person who proposes to carry on the discharges in place of the holder.

(2) On the death of the holder of a consent under paragraph 3 or 6 above, the consent shall, subject to sub-paragraph (4) below, be regarded as property forming part of the deceased's personal estate, whether or not it would be so regarded apart from this sub-paragraph, and shall accordingly vest in his personal representatives.

(3) If a bankruptcy order is made against the holder of a consent under paragraph 3 or 6 above, the consent shall, subject to sub-paragraph (4) below, be regarded for the purposes of any of the Second Group of Parts of the Insolvency Act 1986[3] (insolvency of individuals; bankruptcy), as property forming part of the bankrupt's estate, whether or not it would be so regarded apart from this sub-paragraph, and shall accordingly vest as such in the trustee in bankruptcy.

(4) Notwithstanding anything in the foregoing provisions of this paragraph, a consent under paragraph 3 or 6 above (and the obligations arising out of, or incidental to, such a consent) shall not be capable of being disclaimed.

(5) A consent under paragraph 3 or 6 above which is transferred to, or which vests in, a person under this section shall have effect on and after the date of the transfer or vesting as if it had been granted to that person under paragraph 3 or 6 above, subject to the same conditions as were attached to it immediately before that date.

(6) Where a consent under paragraph 3 or 6 above is transferred under sub-paragraph (1) above, the person from whom it is transferred shall give notice of that fact to the Agency not later than the end of the period of twenty-one days beginning with the date of the transfer.

(7) Where a consent under paragraph 3 or 6 above vests in any person as mentioned in sub-paragraph (2) or (3) above, that person shall give notice[4] of that fact to the Agency[5] not later than the end of the period of fifteen months beginning with the date of the vesting.

(8) If—

(a) a consent under paragraph 3 or 6 above vests in any person as mentioned in sub-paragraph (2) or (3) above, but

(b) that person fails to give the notice required by sub-paragraph (7) above within the period there mentioned,

the consent, to the extent that it permits the making of any discharges, shall cease to have effect.

(9) A person who fails to give a notice which he is required by sub-paragraph (6) or (7) above to give shall be guilty of an offence and liable—

(a) on summary conviction, to a fine not exceeding the statutory maximum[6];

(b) on conviction on indictment, to a fine or to imprisonment for a term not exceeding two years, or to both.

# SCHEDULE 11

(Section 93[7].)

## Water Protection Zone Orders

*Applications for orders*

1. (1) Where the Agency[8] applies to the Secretary of State for an order under section 93 of this Act, it shall—

(a) submit to the Secretary of State a draft of the order applied for;

(b) publish a notice with respect to the application, at least once in each of two successive weeks, in one or more newspapers circulating in the locality proposed to be designated as a water protection zone by the order;

---

[1] P.320 above.
[2] P.321 above.
[3] 1986 c.45.
[4] "Notice" defined by s.221(1), p.314 above.
[5] "The Agency" means the Environment Agency: s.221(1) above.

[6] The current statutory maximum is £5,000: Criminal Justice Act 1991 (c.53), s.17(2).
[7] P.284 above.
[8] "The Agency" means the Environment Agency: s.221(1) above.

(c) not later than the date on which that notice is first published serve[1] a copy of the notice on every local authority[2] and water undertaker whose area includes the whole or any part of that locality; and

(d) publish a notice in the London Gazette which—

   (i) states that the draft order has been submitted to the Secretary of State;

   (ii) names every local authority on whom a notice is required to be served under this paragraph;

   (iii) specifies a place where a copy of the draft order and of any relevant map or plan may be inspected; and

   (iv) gives the name of every newspaper in which the notice required by virtue of paragraph (b) above was published and the date of an issue containing the notice.

(2) The notice required by virtue of sub-paragraph (1)(b) above to be published with respect to an application for an order shall—

(a) state the general effect of the order applied for;

(b) specify a place where a copy of the draft order and of any relevant map or plan may be inspected by any person free of charge at all reasonable times during the period of twenty-eight days beginning with the date of the first publication of the notice; and

(c) state that any person may, within that period, by notice to the Secretary of State object to the making of the order.

### Supply of copies of draft orders

**2.** Where the Agency has applied for an order under section 93 of this Act[3], it shall, at the request of any person and on payment by that person of such charge (if any) as the Agency may reasonably require, furnish that person with a copy of the draft order submitted to the Secretary of State under paragraph 1 above.

### Modifications of proposals

**3.** (1) On an application for an order under section 93 of this Act[4], the Secretary of State may make the order either in the terms of the draft order submitted to him or, subject to sub-paragraph (2) below, in those terms as modified[5] in such manner as he thinks fit, or may refuse to make an order.

(2) The Secretary of State shall not make such a modification of a draft order submitted to him as he considers is likely adversely to affect any persons unless he is satisfied that the Agency has given and published such additional notices, in such manner, as the Secretary of State may have required.

(3) Subject to sub-paragraph (2) above and to the service of notices of the proposed modification on such local authorities[6] as appear to him to be likely to be interested in it, the modifications that may be made by the Secretary of State of any draft order include any modification of the area designated by the draft order as a water protection zone.

### Consideration of objections etc.

**4.** Without prejudice to section 53 of the 1995 Act[7] (inquiries and other hearings)[8], where an application for an order under section 93 of this Act[9] has been made, the Secretary of State may, if he considers it appropriate to do so, hold a local inquiry before making any order on the application.

---

[1] For provisions relating to service see s.220, p.310 above.
[2] "Local authority" defined by s.221(1), p.314 above.
[3] P.284 above.
[4] P.284 above.
[5] "Modification" defined by s.221(1), p.314 above.
[6] "Local authority" defined by s.221(1), p.314 above.
[7] P.460 below. "The 1995 Act" means the Environment Act 1995: s.221(1), p.311 above.
[8] Words "section 53 . . . hearings)" substituted by the Environment Act 1995 (c.25), s.120, sch.22, para.184.
[9] P.284 above.

# SCHEDULE 12

(Section 94[1].)

## NITRATE SENSITIVE AREA ORDERS

### PART I: APPLICATIONS BY THE AGENCY FOR DESIGNATION ORDERS

#### Orders made only on application

1. (1) Subject to sub-paragraphs (2) and (3) below, the relevant Minister[2] shall not make an order under section 94 of this Act by virtue of which any land is designated as land comprised in a nitrate sensitive area, except with the consent of the Treasury and on an application which—

    (a) has been made by the Agency[3] in accordance with paragraph 2 below; and

    (b) in identifying controlled waters[4] by virtue of sub-paragraph (2)(a) of that paragraph, identified the controlled waters with respect to which that land is so comprised by the order.

    (2) This paragraph shall not apply to an order which reproduces or amends an existing order without adding any land appearing to the relevant Minister to constitute a significant area to the land already comprised in the areas for the time being designated as nitrate sensitive areas.

#### Procedure for applications

2. (1) The Agency shall not for the purposes of paragraph 1 above apply for the making of any order under section 94 of this Act[5] by which any land would be comprised in the areas for the time being designated as nitrate sensitive areas unless it appears to the Agency—

    (a) that pollution is or is likely to be caused by the entry of nitrate into controlled waters[6] as a result of, or of anything done in connection with, the use of particular land in England and Wales for agricultural[7] purposes; and

    (b) that the provisions for the time being in force in relation to those waters and that land are not sufficient, in the opinion of the Agency, for preventing or controlling such an entry of nitrate into those waters.

    (2) An application under this paragraph shall identify—

    (a) the controlled waters appearing to the Agency to be the waters which the nitrate is or is likely to enter; and

    (b) the land appearing to the Agency to be the land the use of which for agricultural purposes, or the doing of anything in connection with whose use for agricultural purposes, is resulting or is likely to result in the entry of nitrate into those waters.

    (3) An application under this paragraph shall be made—

    (a) where the land identified in the application is wholly in Wales, by serving[8] a notice[9] containing the application on the Secretary of State; and

    (b) in any other case, by serving such a notice on each of the Ministers[10].

### PART II: ORDERS CONTAINING MANDATORY PROVISIONS

#### Publication of proposals for order containing mandatory provisions

3. (1) This paragraph applies where the relevant Minister[11] proposes to make an order under section 94 of this Act[12] which—

[1] P.285 above.
[2] For "the relevant Minister" see s.94(7), p.286 above.
[3] "The Agency" means the Environment Agency: s.221(1) above.
[4] "Controlled waters" has the meaning given by s.104(1), p.290 above.
[5] P.285 above.
[6] "Controlled waters" has the meaning given by s.104(1), p.290 above.
[7] "Agricultural" defined by s.221(1), p.312 above.
[8] For provisions relating to service see s.220, p.310 above.
[9] "Notice" defined by s.221(1), p.314 above.
[10] "The Ministers" defined by s.221(1), p.314 above.
[11] For "the relevant Minister" see s.94(7), p.286 above.
[12] P.285 above.

---

(a) makes or modifies[1] any such provision as is authorised by subsection (3)(a) of that section; and

(b) in doing so, contains provision which is not of one of the following descriptions, that is to say—

   (i) provision reproducing existing provisions without modification and in relation to substantially the same area; and

   (ii) provision modifying any existing provisions so as to make them less onerous.

(2) The relevant Minister shall, before making any such order as is mentioned in sub-paragraph (1) above—

(a) publish a notice with respect to the proposed order, at least once in each of two successive weeks, in one or more newspapers circulating in the locality in relation to which the proposed order will have effect;

(b) not later than the date on which that notice is first published, serve[2] a copy of the notice on—

   (i) the Agency[3];

   (ii) every local authority[4] and water undertaker whose area includes the whole or any part of that locality; and

   (iii) in the case of an order containing any such provision as is authorised by section 94(3)(b) of this Act, such owners[5] and occupiers of agricultural[6] land in that locality as appear to the relevant Minister to be likely to be affected by the obligations in respect of which payments are to be made under that provision;

and

(c) publish a notice in the London Gazette which—

   (i) names every local authority on whom a notice is required to be served under this paragraph;

   (ii) specifies a place where a copy of the proposed order and of any relevant map or plan may be inspected; and

   (iii) gives the name of every newspaper in which the notice required by virtue of paragraph (a) above was published and the date of an issue containing the notice.

(3) The notice required by virtue of sub-paragraph (2)(a) above to be published with respect to any proposed order shall—

(a) state the general effect of the proposed order;

(b) specify a place where a copy of the proposed order, and of any relevant map or plan, may be inspected by any person free of charge at all reasonable times during the period of forty-two days beginning with the date of the first publication of the notice; and

(c) state that any person may, within that period, by notice to the Secretary of State or, as the case may be, to one of the Ministers[7] object to the making of the order.

## Supply of copies of proposed orders

**4.** The Secretary of State and, in a case where he is proposing to join in making the order, the Minister[8] shall, at the request of any person and on payment by that person of such charge (if any) as the Secretary of State or the Minister may reasonably require, furnish that person with a copy of any proposed order of which notice has been published under paragraph 3 above.

## Modifications of proposals

**5.** (1) Where notices with respect to any proposed order have been published and served in accordance with paragraph 3 above and the period of forty-two days mentioned in sub-paragraph (3)(b) of that paragraph has expired, the relevant Minister[9] may—

(a) make the order either in the proposed terms or, subject to sub-paragraph (2) below (but without any further compliance with paragraph 3 above), in those terms as modified[10] in such manner as he thinks fit; or

(b) decide not to make any order.

[1] "Modification" defined by s.221(1), p.314 above.
[2] For provisions relating to service see s.220, p.310 above.
[3] "The Agency" means the Environment Agency: s.221(1) above.
[4] "Local authority" defined by s.221(1), p.314 above.
[5] "Owner" defined by s.221(1), p.314 above.
[6] "Agricultural" defined by s.221(1), p.312 above.
[7] "The Ministers" defined by s.221(1), p.314 above.
[8] "The Minister" defined by s.221(1), p.314 above.
[9] For "the relevant Minister" see s.94 (7), p.286 above.
[10] "'Modification" defined by s.221(1), p.314 above.

(2) The relevant Minister shall not make such a modification of a proposed order of which notice has been so published and served as he considers is likely adversely to affect any persons unless he has given such notices[1] as he considers appropriate for enabling those persons to object to the modification.

(3) Subject to sub-paragraph (2) above and to the service[2] of notices of the proposed modification on such local authorities as appear to him to be likely to be interested in it, the modifications that may be made by the relevant Minister include any modification of any area designated by the proposed order as a nitrate sensitive area.

(4) For the purposes of this Schedule it shall be immaterial, in a case in which a modification such as is mentioned in sub-paragraph (3) above incorporates land in England in an area which (but for the modification) would have been wholly in Wales, that any requirements of paragraph 3 above in relation to the proposed order have been complied with by the Secretary of State, rather than by the Ministers[3].

### Consideration of objections etc.

6. Without prejudice to section 53 of the 1995 Act[4] (inquiries and other hearings),[5] where notices with respect to any proposed order have been published and served in accordance with paragraph 3 above[6], the Secretary of State or, as the case may be, the Ministers[7] may, if he or they consider it appropriate to do so, hold a local inquiry before deciding whether or not to make the proposed order or to make it with modifications[8].

### Consent of Treasury for payment provisions

7. The consent of the Treasury shall be required for the making of any order under section 94 of this Act[9] the making of which does not require the consent of the Treasury by virtue of paragraph 2 above but which contains any such provision as is authorised by subsection (3)(b) of that section.

# SCHEDULE 13

(Section 103[10].)

## TRANSITIONAL WATER POLLUTION PROVISIONS

### Transitional power to transfer power of determination with respect to water pollution matters to the Authority

1. Where by virtue of the provisions of Schedule 2 to the Water Consolidation (Consequential Provisions) Act 1991[11] in relation to anything having effect under paragraph 21 of Schedule 26 to the Water Act 1989[12] any matter falls to be determined by the Secretary of State in accordance with any of the provisions of Part III of this Act[13] (other than section 91), that matter shall, if the Secretary of State refers the matter to the Agency[14] for determination, be determined by the Agency instead.

### Order under section 32(3) of the 1974 Act

2. (1) Except in so far as the Secretary of State by order otherwise provides, section 85 of this Act[15] shall not apply to any discharges which are of a kind or in any area specified in an order which was made under subsection (3) of section 32 of the Control of Pollution Act 1974[16] (preservation of existing exemptions) and is in force for the purposes of paragraph 22(1) of Schedule 26 to the Water Act 1989 immediately before the coming into force of this Act[17].

[1] "Notice" defined by s.221(1), p.314 above.
[2] For provisions relating to service see s.220, p.310 above.
[3] "The Ministers" defined by s.221(1), p.314 above.
[4] P.460 below. "The 1995 Act" means the Environment Act 1995: s.221(1), p.311 above.
[5] Words "section 53 . . . hearings)" substituted by the Environment Act 1995 (c.25), s.120, sch.22, para.185.
[6] P.326 above.
[7] "The Ministers" defined by s.221(1), p.314 above.
[8] "Modification" defined by s.221(1), p.314 above.
[9] P.285 above.
[10] P.290 above.
[11] 1991 c.60.
[12] 1989 c.15.
[13] P.271 above.
[14] "The Agency" means the Environment Agency: s.221(1) above.
[15] P.273 above.
[16] 1974 c.20.
[17] See the Control of Pollution (Exemption of Certain Discharges from Control) Order 1983, S.I. 1983/1182, amended by S.I. 1986/1623, and S.I. 1987/1782.

(2) The Secretary of State may by order require the Agency[1] to publish in a manner specified in the order such information about the operation of any provision made by or under this paragraph as may be so specified.

(3) The power to make an order under this paragraph shall be exercisable by statutory instrument subject to annulment in pursuance of a resolution of either House of Parliament.

### Pre-1989 transitional provisions

**3.** (1) A consent which has effect, in accordance with paragraph 24(2) of Schedule 26 to the Water Act 1989 and paragraph 1 of schedule 2 to the Water Consolidation (Consequential Provisions) Act 1991, as a consent given for the purposes of Chapter II of Part III of this Act in respect of an application which itself has effect, by virtue of paragraph 21 of that Schedule 26 and that paragraph 1, as an application made under Schedule 10 to this Act[2] shall cease to have effect on the disposal of that application by—

(a) the giving of an unconditional consent on that application;

(b) the expiration, without an appeal under section 91 of this Act[3] being brought, of the period of three months beginning with the date on which notice is served on the applicant that the consent applied for is refused or is given subject to conditions; or

(c) the withdrawal or determination of any such appeal.

(2) Particulars of consents to which sub-paragraph (1) above applies shall not be required to be contained in any register maintained under section 190 of this Act[4].

### Discharge consents on application of undertakers etc.

**4.** (1) The repeal by the Water Consolidation (Consequential Provisions) Act 1991 of sub-paragraphs (2) and (6) of paragraph 25 of Schedule 26 to the Water Act 1989 shall not affect any provision made under section 113(2) of that Act for the purposes of either of those sub-paragraphs; and, accordingly any such provision shall have effect in accordance with Schedule 2 to that Act of 1991 as if made in exercise of a power conferred by section 99 of this Act[5].

(2) If the Secretary of State determines that this sub-paragraph is to apply in relation to any application which is deemed by virtue of paragraph 25(2)(a) of Schedule 26 to the Water Act 1989 and Schedule 2 to the Water Consolidation (Consequential Provisions) Act 1991 to have been made to the Agency by the successor company[6] of a water authority—

(a) that application shall be treated as having been transmitted to the Secretary of State in accordance with a direction under paragraph 5[7] of Schedule 10 to this Act[8]; but

(b) the Agency shall not be required, by virtue of sub-paragraph (2) of that paragraph 5, to inform that company that the application is to be so treated.

(3) Where an application is deemed to have been so made by the successor company of a water authority, then, whether or not it is treated under sub-paragraph (2) above as having been transmitted to the Secretary of State, the following provisions shall apply in relation to the application and, except in so far as the Secretary of State otherwise directs, shall so apply instead of paragraphs 1(1), apart from paragraph (a), paragraph 2 or, as the case may be paragraph 5(3)[9] of Schedule 10 to this Act[10], that is to say—

(a) the application shall not be considered by the Secretary of State or the Agency unless the company has complied with such directions (if any) as may be given by the Secretary of State with respect to the publicity to be given to the application;

(b) the Secretary of State or, as the case may be, the Agency shall be under a duty to consider only such representations and objections with respect to the application as have been made in writing to the Secretary of State or the Agency before the end of such period as he may determine and as are not withdrawn; and

(c) the Secretary of State shall have power to direct the Agency (pending compliance with any direction under paragraph (a) above or pending his or, as the case may be, its consideration of the application,

---

[1] "The Agency" means the Environment Agency: s.221(1) above.
[2] P.319 above.
[3] P.280 above.
[4] P.298 above.
[5] P.289 above.
[6] "Successor company" defined by para.4(6) below.
[7] *Prospective amendment*: words "5" in sub-paragraphs (a) and (b) to be substituted by the Environment Act 1995 (c.25), s.120, sch.22, para.186(a).
[8] P.321 above.
[9] *Prospective amendment*: words "paragraph 1 . . . paragraph 5(3)" substituted by the Environment Act 1995 (c.25), s.120, sch.22, para.186(b).
[10] P.321 above.

representations and objections) to give such a temporary consent under Chapter II of Part III of this Act[1], or to make such temporary modifications[2] of the conditions of any existing consent, as may be specified in the direction.

(4)  The power of the Secretary of State to make a determination or give a direction under sub-paragraph (2) or (3) above shall be exercisable generally in relation to applications of any such description as he may consider appropriate (as well as in relation to a particular application) and, in the case of a direction to give a temporary consent or to make a temporary modification, shall include—

(a)  power to require a temporary consent to be given either unconditionally or subject to such conditions falling within paragraph 3(4)[3] of Schedule 10 to this Act as may be specified in the direction;

(b)  power, where the direction relates to a description of applications, to require the temporary consent given in pursuance of the direction to be a general consent relating to cases of such a description as may be so specified; and

(c)  power, where the direction is in respect of an application falling to be considered by the Agency, to require the consent or modification to be given or made so as to continue to have effect until the Agency's determination on the application becomes final—

(i)  on the expiration, without the bringing of an appeal against the determination, of the prescribed[4] period for the bringing of such an appeal; or

(ii)  on the withdrawal or determination of any such appeal.

(5)  Without prejudice to the provisions of Schedule 2 to the Water Consolidation (Consequential Provisions) Act 1991, a consent to which sub-paragraph (7) of paragraph 25 of the Water Act 1989 applies immediately before the coming into force of this Act by virtue of its conditions including a condition that is contravened where there is a failure by more than a specified number of samples to satisfy specified requirements, shall continue to have effect as if the only samples falling to be taken into account for the purposes of that condition were samples taken on behalf of the Authority in exercise, at a time after 31st August 1989, of a power conferred by the Water Act 1989 or a corresponding provision of this Act.

(6)  References in this paragraph to the successor company of a water authority shall be construed in accordance with the Water Act 1989.

# SCHEDULE 24

(Section 204[5].)

## DISCLOSURE OF INFORMATION

### PART I: PERSONS IN RESPECT OF WHOSE FUNCTIONS DISCLOSURE MAY BE MADE

Any Minister of the Crown.

The Director General of Fair Trading.

The Monopolies and Mergers Commission.

The Director General of Telecommunications.

The Civil Aviation Authority.

The Director General of Gas Supply.

The Director General of Electricity Supply.

A local weights and measures authority in England and Wales.

The Rail Regulator.[6]

The Coal Authority[7].

---

[1]  P.273 above.
[2]  "Modification" defined by s.221(1), p.314 above.
[3]  *Prospective amendment:* words "3(4)" to be substituted by the Environment Act 1995 (c.25), s.120, sch.22, para.186(c).
[4]  "Prescribed" defined by s.221(1), p.314 above.
[5]  P.304 above.

[6]  Words "The Rail Regulator." inserted by the Railways Act 1993 (c.43), s.152(1), sch.12, para.31(a). This amendment came into force on 6 January 1994: S.I. 1993/3237.
[7]  Words "The Coal Authority." inserted by the Coal Industry Act 1994 (c.21), s.67(1), sch.9, para.43(2)(a). This amendment came into force on 31 October 1994: s.68(2)(d), S.I. 1994/2553.

PART II: ENACTMENTS ETC. IN RESPECT OF WHICH DISCLOSURE MAY BE MADE

The Trade Descriptions Act 1968[1].

The Fair Trading Act 1973[2].

The Consumer Credit Act 1974[3].

The Restrictive Trade Practices Act 1976[4].

The Resale Prices Act 1976[5].

The Estate Agents Act 1979[6].

The Competition Act 1980[7].

The Telecommunications Act 1984[8].

The Airports Act 1986[9].

The Gas Act 1986[10].

The Consumer Protection Act 1987[11].

The Electricity Act 1989[12].

The Railways Act 1993.[13]

The Coal Industry Act 1994.[14]

Any subordinate legislation made for the purpose of securing compliance with the Directive of the Council of the European Communities dated 10th September 1984 (No. 84/450/EEC) on the approximation of the laws, regulations and administrative provisions of the member States concerning misleading advertising.

[1] 1968 c.29.
[2] 1973 c.41.
[3] 1974 c.39.
[4] 1976 c.34.
[5] 1976 c.53.
[6] 1979 c.38.
[7] 1980 c.21.
[8] 1984 c.12.
[9] 1986 c.31.
[10] 1986 c.44.
[11] 1987 c.43.
[12] 1989 c.29.
[13] 1993 c.43. Words "The Railways Act 1993." inserted by the Railways Act 1993 (c.43), s.152(1), sch.12, para.31(b). This amendment came into force on 6 January 1994: S.I. 1993/3237.
[14] 1994 c.21. Words "The Coal Industry Act 1994" inserted by the Coal Industry Act 1994 (c.21), s.67(1), sch.9, para.43(2)(b). This amendment came into force on 31 October 1994: s.68(2)(d), S.I. 1994/2553.

# Clean Air Act 1993

## Chapter 11

*Arrangement of sections*

## Part I: Dark Smoke

1. Prohibition of dark smoke from chimneys.   336
2. Prohibition of dark smoke from industrial or trade premises.   337
3. Meaning of "dark smoke".   338

## Part II: Smoke, Grit, Dust and Fumes

*Installation of furnaces*

4. Requirement that new furnaces shall be so far as practicable smokeless.   338

*Limits on rate of emission of grit and dust*

5. Emission of grit and dust from furnaces.   339

*Arrestment plant for furnaces*

6. Arrestment plant for new non-domestic furnaces.   339
7. Exemptions from section 6.   340
8. Requirement to fit arrestment plant for burning solid fuel in other cases.   341
9. Appeal to Secretary of State against refusal of approval.   341

*Measurement of grit, dust and fumes*

10. Measurement of grit, dust and fumes by occupiers.   341
11. Measurement of grit, dust and fumes by local authorities.   342
12. Information about furnaces and fuel consumed.   343

*Outdoor furnaces*

13. Grit and dust from outdoor furnaces, etc.   343

*Height of chimneys*

14. Height of chimneys for furnaces.   343
15. Applications for approval of height of chimneys of furnaces.   344
16. Height of other chimneys.   345

*Smoke nuisances in Scotland*

17. *Repealed*   346

## Part III: Smoke Control Areas

*Creation of smoke control areas*

18. Declaration of smoke control area by local authority.   346
19. Power of Secretary of State to require creation of smoke control areas.   347

*Prohibition on emission of smoke in smoke control area*

20. Prohibition on emission of smoke in smoke control area.   348
21. Power by order to exempt certain fireplaces.   348
22. Exemptions relating to particular areas.   348

*Dealings with unauthorised fuel*

23. Acquisition and sale of unauthorised fuel in a smoke control area. 348

*Adaptation of fireplaces*

24. Power of local authority to require adaptation of fireplaces in private dwellings. 349
25. Expenditure incurred in relation to adaptations in private dwellings. 350
26. Power of local authority to make grants towards adaptations to fireplaces in churches, chapels, buildings used by charities etc. 350

*Supplementary provisions*

27. References to adaptations for avoiding contraventions of section 20. 351
28. Cases where expenditure is taken to be incurred on execution of works. 351
29. Interpretation of Part III. 352

## Part IV: Control of certain forms of Air Pollution

30. Regulations about motor fuel. 352
31. Regulations about sulphur content of oil fuel for furnaces or engines. 353
32. Provisions supplementary to sections 30 and 31. 354
33. Cable burning. 354

## Part V: Information about Air Pollution

34. Research and publicity. 355
35. Obtaining information. 355
36. Notices requiring information about air pollution. 356
37. Appeals against notices under section 36. 357
38. Regulations about local authority functions under sections 34, 35 and 36. 358
39. Provision by local authorities of information for Secretary of State. 359
40. Interpretation of Part V. 359

## Part VI: Special Cases

41. Relation to Environmental Protection Act 1990. 359
42. Colliery spoilbanks. 359
43. Railway engines. 360
44. Vessels. 360
45. Exemption for purposes of investigations and research. 361
46. Crown premises, etc. 362

## Part VII: Miscellaneous and General

*Power to apply certain provisions to fumes and gases*

47. Application to fumes and gases of certain provisions as to grit dust and smoke. 363

*Power to give effect to international agreements*

48. Power to give effect to international agreements. 363

*Administration and enforcement*

49. Unjustified disclosures of information. 363
50. Cumulative penalties on continuance of certain offences. 364
51. Duty to notify occupiers of offences. 364
52. Offences committed by bodies corporate. 365
53. Offence due to act or default of another. 365
54. Power of county court to authorise works and order payments. 365
55. General provisions as to enforcement. 365
56. Rights of entry and inspection etc. 366

57. Provisions supplementary to section 56. — 367
58. Power of local authorities to obtain information. — 367
59. Local inquiries. — 368
60. Default powers. — 368
61. Joint exercise of local authority functions. — 369
62. Application of certain provisions of Part XII of Public Health Act 1936 and corresponding Scottish legislation. — 370

*General*

63. Regulations and orders. — 371
64. General provisions as to interpretation. — 371
65. Application to Isles of Scilly. — 373
66. Transitory provisions relating to Alkali, &c. Works Regulation Act 1906. — 373
67. Consequential amendments, transitional provisions and repeals. — 373
68. Short title, commencement and extent. — 373

SCHEDULES:

Schedule 1—Coming into operation of smoke control orders. — 374
Schedule 2—Smoke control orders: expenditure on old private dwellings. — 374
Schedule 3—Provisions having effect until repeal of Alkali, &c. Works Regulation Act 1906. — 376
Part I—Relation of this Act to Alkali, &c. Works Regulation Act 1906. — 376
Part II—Modifications of this Act. — 377
Schedule 4—Consequential amendments: *Not reproduced*
Schedule 5—Transitional provisions. — 378
Part I—General transitional provisions and savings. — 378
Part II—Exclusion and modification of certain provisions of this Act. — 378
Part III—Confirmation and coming into operation of certain smoke control orders. — 379
Schedule 6—Repeals: *Not reproduced*

# Clean Air Act 1993

## 1993 Chapter 11

An Act to consolidate the Clean Air Acts 1956 and 1968 and certain related enactments, with amendments to give effect to recommendations of the Law Commission and the Scottish Law Commission.

[27th May 1993[1]]

### Transfer of functions

The functions previously conferred on the Secretary of State under section 19 of this Act, p.347 below, with respect to the creation of smoke control areas by local authorities in Scotland, have been transferred to the Scottish Environment Protection Agency, SEPA: Environment Act 1995(c. 25), s. 21, p. 438 below . SEPA took over its functions under this Act on the transfer date, 1 April 1996: S.I. 1996/139.

### Orders

A list of orders made, or which have effect as if made, under section 21 of this Act is at p.800 below.

### Regulations

A list of regulations made, or which have effect as if made, under this Act is at p.799 below.

## PART I: Dark Smoke

*Prohibition of dark smoke from chimneys.*

1. (1) Dark smoke[2] shall not be emitted from a chimney[3], of any building, and if, on any day, dark smoke is so emitted, the occupier[4] of the building shall be guilty of an offence.

(2) Dark smoke shall not be emitted from a chimney (not being a chimney of a building) which serves the furnace of any fixed boiler or industrial plant[5] and if, on any day[6], dark smoke is so emitted, the person having possession of the boiler or plant shall be guilty of an offence.

(3) This section does not apply to emissions of smoke from any chimney, in such classes of case and subject to such limitations as may be prescribed in regulations made by the Secretary of State, lasting for not longer than such periods as may be so prescribed[7].

(4) In any proceedings for an offence under this section, it shall be a defence to prove—

(a) that the alleged emission was solely due to the lighting up of a furnace which was cold and that all practicable[8] steps had been taken to prevent or minimise the emission of dark smoke;

(b) that the alleged emission was solely due to some failure of a furnace, or of apparatus used in connection with a furnace, and that—

---

[1] This Act came into force on 27 August 1993: s.68(2) below.
[2] "Dark smoke" has the meaning given by s.3(1) below: s.64(1) below.
[3] "Chimney" and "chimney of a building" defined by s.64(1), p.371 below.
[4] For "occupier" see s.64(2), p.372 below.

[5] "Fixed boiler or industrial plant" and "industrial plant" defined by s.64(1), p.371 below.
[6] "Day" defined by s.64(1), p.371 below.
[7] A list of regulations made, or which have effect as if made, under this Act is at p.799 below.
[8] "Practicable" defined by s. 64(1), p.372 below.

(i)  the failure could not reasonably have been foreseen, or, if foreseen, could not reasonably have been provided against; and

(ii)  the alleged emission could not reasonably have been prevented by action taken after the failure occurred; or

(c)  that the alleged emission was solely due to the use of unsuitable fuel and that—

(i)  suitable fuel was unobtainable and the least unsuitable fuel which was available was used; and

(ii)  all practicable steps had been taken to prevent or minimise the emission of dark smoke as the result of the use of that fuel;

or that the alleged emission was due to the combination of two or more of the causes specified in paragraphs (a) to (c) and that the other conditions specified in those paragraphs are satisfied in relation to those causes respectively.

(5)  A person guilty of an offence under this section shall be liable on summary conviction—

(a)  in the case of a contravention of subsection (1) as respects a chimney of a private dwelling[1], to a fine not exceeding level 3 on the standard scale[2]; and

(b)  in any other case, to a fine not exceeding level 5 on the standard scale[3].

(6)  This section has effect subject to section 51[4] (duty to notify offences to occupier or other person liable).

----

*Prohibition of dark smoke from industrial or trade premises.*

**2.**  (1)  Dark smoke[5] shall not be emitted from any industrial or trade premises[6] and if, on any day[7], dark smoke is so emitted the occupier[8] of the premises and any person who causes or permits the emission shall be guilty of an offence.

(2)  This section does not apply—

(a)  to the emission of dark smoke from any chimney to which section 1 above applies; or

(b)  to the emission of dark smoke caused by the burning of any matter prescribed in regulations made by the Secretary of State, subject to compliance with such conditions (if any) as may be so prescribed[9].

(3)  In proceedings for an offence under this section, there shall be taken to have been an emission of dark smoke from industrial or trade premises in any case where—

(a)  material is burned on those premises; and

(b)  the circumstances are such that the burning would be likely to give rise to the emission of dark smoke,

unless the occupier or any person who caused or permitted the burning shows that no dark smoke was emitted.

(4)  In proceedings for an offence under this section, it shall be a defence to prove—

(a)  that the alleged emission was inadvertent; and

(b)  that all practicable[10] steps had been taken to prevent or minimise the emission of dark smoke.

(5)  A person guilty of an offence under this section shall be liable on summary conviction to a fine not exceeding £20,000[11].

----

[1] "Private dwelling" defined by s.64(4), p.372 below.
[2] The current fine at level 3 on the standard scale is £1,000: Criminal Justice Act 1991 (c.53), s.17 (England and Wales); Criminal Procedure (Scotland) Act 1995 (c.46), s. 225 (Scotland).
[3] The current fine at level 5 on the standard scale is £5,000: Criminal Justice Act 1991 (c.53), s.17 (England and Wales); Criminal Procedure (Scotland) Act 1995 (c.46), s.225 (Scotland).
[4] P.364 below.
[5] "Dark smoke" has the meaning given by s.3(1) below:

s.64(1) below.
[6] "Industrial or trade premises" defined by subsection (6) below.
[7] "Day" defined by s.64(1), p.371 below.
[8] For "occupier" see s. 64(2), p.372 below.
[9] A list of regulations made, or which have effect as if made, under this Act is at p.799 below.
[10] "Practicable" defined by s.64(1), p.372 below.
[11] Words "£20,000" substituted by the Environment Act 1995 (c.25), s.120, sch.22, para.195 on 1 April 1996: S.I. 1996/186.

(6  In this section "industrial or trade premises" means—

(a)  premises[1] used for any industrial or trade purposes; or

(b)  premises not so used on which matter is burnt in connection with any industrial or trade process.

(7)  This section has effect subject to section 51[2] (duty to notify offences to occupier or other person liable).[3]

*Meaning of "dark smoke".*

**3.**  (1)  In this Act "dark smoke" means smoke[4] which, if compared in the appropriate manner with a chart of the type known on 5th July 1956 (the date of the passing of the Clean Air Act 1956[5]) as the Ringelmann Chart, would appear to be as dark as or darker than shade 2 on the chart.

(2)  For the avoidance of doubt it is hereby declared that in proceedings—

(a)  for an offence under section 1 or 2 (prohibition of emissions of dark smoke);

(b)  *Repealed by the Environment Act 1995 (c.25), s.120, sch.24. This amendment came into force on 1 April 1996: S.I. 1996/186.*

the court may be satisfied that smoke is or is not dark smoke as defined in subsection (1) notwithstanding that there has been no actual comparison of the smoke with a chart of the type mentioned in that subsection.

(3)  Without prejudice to the generality of subsections (1) and (2), if the Secretary of State by regulations prescribes any method of ascertaining whether smoke is dark smoke as defined in subsection (1), proof in any such proceedings as are mentioned in subsection (2)—

(a)  that that method was properly applied, and

(b)  that the smoke was thereby ascertained to be or not to be dark smoke as so defined,

shall be accepted as sufficient[6].

## PART II: Smoke, Grit, Dust and Fumes

*Installation of furnaces*

*Requirement that new furnaces shall be so far as practicable smokeless.*

**4.**  (1)  No furnace shall be installed in a building or in any fixed boiler or industrial plant[7] unless notice of the proposal to install it has been given to the local authority[8].

(2)  No furnace shall be installed in a building or in any fixed boiler or industrial plant unless the furnace is so far as practicable[9] capable of being operated continuously without emitting smoke[10] when burning fuel of a type for which the furnace was designed.

(3)  Any furnace installed in accordance with plans and specifications submitted to, and approved for the purposes of this section by, the local authority shall be treated as complying with the provisions of subsection (2).

(4)  Any person who installs a furnace in contravention of subsection (1) or (2) or on whose instructions a furnace is so installed shall be guilty of an offence and liable on summary conviction—

---

[1]  "Premises" defined by s.64(1), p.372 below.
[2]  P.364 below.
[3]  **Case: section 2** *O'Fee v Copeland Borough Council* [1996] Env LR 66.
[4]  "Smoke" defined by s.64(1), p.372 below.
[5]  1956 c.52.
[6]  A list of regulations made, or which have effect as if

made, under this Act is at p.799 below.
[7]  "Fixed boiler or industrial plant" and "industrial plant" defined by s. 64(1), p.371 below.
[8]  "Local authority" defined by s.64(1), p.372 below.
[9]  "Practicable" defined by s.64(1), p.372 below.
[10]  "Smoke" defined by s.64(1), p.372 below.

(*a*)  in the case of a contravention of subsection (1), to a fine not exceeding level 3 on the standard scale[1]; and

(*b*)  in the case of a contravention of subsection (2), to a fine not exceeding level 5 on that scale[2].

(5)  This section does not apply to the installation of domestic furnaces[3].

(6)  This section applies in relation to—

(*a*)  the attachment to a building of a boiler or industrial plant which already contains a furnace; or

(*b*)  the fixing to or installation on any land of any such boiler or plant,

as it applies in relation to the installation of a furnace in any fixed boiler or industrial plant.

*Limits on rate of emission of grit and dust*

*Emission of grit and dust from furnaces.*

**5.**  (1)  This section applies to any furnace[4] other than a domestic furnace[5].

(2)  The Secretary of State may by regulations prescribe limits on the rates of emission[6] of grit and dust from the chimneys[7] of furnaces to which this section applies[8].

(3)  If on any day grit or dust is emitted from a chimney serving a furnace to which this section applies at a rate exceeding the relevant limit prescribed under subsection (2), the occupier[9] of any building in which the furnace is situated shall be guilty of an offence.

(4)  In proceedings for an offence under subsection (3) it shall be a defence to prove that the best practicable means[10] had been used for minimising the alleged emission.

(5)  If, in the case of a building containing a furnace to which this section applies and which is served by a chimney to which there is no limit applicable under subsection (2), the occupier fails to use any practicable means there may be for minimising the emission of grit or dust from the chimney, he shall be guilty of an offence.

(6)  A person guilty of an offence under this section shall be liable on summary conviction to a fine not exceeding level 5 on the standard scale[11].

*Arrestment plant for furnaces*

*Arrestment plant for new non-domestic furnaces.*

**6.**  (1)  A furnace[12] other than a domestic furnace[13] shall not be used in a building—

(*a*)  to burn pulverised fuel; or

(*b*)  to burn, at a rate of 45.4 kilograms or more an hour, any other solid matter; or

(*c*)  to burn, at a rate equivalent to 366.4 kilowatts or more, any liquid or gaseous matter,

unless the furnace is provided with plant for arresting grit and dust which has been approved by the local authority[14] or which has been installed in accordance with plans and specifications

---

[1] The current fine at level 3 on the standard scale is £1,000: Criminal Justice Act 1991 (c.53), s.17 (England and Wales); Criminal Procedure (Scotland) Act 1995 (c. 46), s.225 (Scotland).

[2] The current fine at level 5 on the standard scale is £5,000: Criminal Justice Act 1991 (c.53), s.17 (England and Wales); Criminal Procedure (Scotland) Act 1995 (c. 46), s.225 (Scotland).

[3] "Domestic furnace" defined by s.64(1), p.371 below.

[4] For further provisions relating to furnaces see s.13, p.343 below and s.64(6), p.373 below.

[5] "Domestic furnace" defined by s. 64(1), p.371 below.

[6] For "rate of emission" see s.64(3), p.372 below.

[7] "Chimney" defined by s.64(1), p.371 below.

[8] A list of regulations made, or which have effect as if made, under this Act is at p.799 below.

[9] For "occupier" see s.13, p.343 below and s.64(2), p.372 below.

[10] "Practicable" and "practicable means" defined by s.64(1), p.372 below.

[11] The current fine at level 5 on the standard scale is £5,000: Criminal Justice Act 1991 (c.53), s.17 (England and Wales); Criminal Procedure (Scotland) Act 1995 (c.46), s.225 (Scotland).

[12] For further provisions relating to furnaces see s.13, p.343 below and s.64(6), p.373 below.

[13] "Domestic furnace" defined by s.64(1), p.371 below.

[14] "Local authority" defined by s.64(1), p.372 below.

submitted to and approved by the local authority, and that plant is properly maintained and used.[1]

(2) Subsection (1) has effect subject to any exemptions prescribed or granted under section 7.

(3) The Secretary of State may by regulations substitute for any rate mentioned in subsection (1)(b) or (c) such other rate as he thinks fit: but no regulations shall be made so as to reduce any rate unless a draft of the regulations has been laid before and approved by each House of Parliament.[2]

(4) Regulations under subsection (3) reducing any rate shall not apply to a furnace which has been installed, the installation of which has been begun, or an agreement for the purchase or installation of which has been entered into, before the date on which the regulations come into force.

(5) If on any day a furnace is used in contravention of subsection (1), the occupier[3] of the building shall be guilty of an offence and liable on summary conviction to a fine not exceeding level 5 on the standard scale[4].

*Exemptions from section 6.*

7. (1) The Secretary of State may by regulations provide that furnaces of any class prescribed in the regulations shall, while used for a purpose so prescribed, be exempted from the operation of section 6(1)[5].

(2) If on the application of the occupier[6] of a building a local authority[7] are satisfied that the emission of grit and dust from any chimney[8] serving a furnace[9] in the building will not be prejudicial to health or a nuisance if the furnace is used for a particular purpose without compliance with section 6(1), they may exempt the furnace from the operation of that subsection while used for that purpose.

(3) If a local authority to whom an application is duly made for an exemption under subsection (2) fail to determine the application and to give a written notice of their decision to the applicant within—

(a) eight weeks of receiving the application; or

(b) such longer period as may be agreed in writing between the applicant and the authority,

the furnace shall be treated as having been granted an exemption from the operation of section 6(1) while used for the purpose specified in the application.

(4) If a local authority decide not to grant an exemption under subsection (2), they shall give the applicant a written notification of their decision stating their reasons, and the applicant may within twenty-eight days of receiving the notification appeal against the decision to the Secretary of State.

(5) On an appeal under this section the Secretary of State—

(a) may confirm the decision appealed against; or

(b) may grant the exemption applied for or vary the purpose for which the furnace to which the application relates may be used without compliance with section 6(1);

and shall give the appellant a written notification of his decision, stating his reasons for it.

(6) If on any day a furnace which is exempt from the operation of section 6(1) is used for a purpose other than a prescribed purpose or, as the case may be, a purpose for which the furnace may

[1] For transitional provisions see sch.5, para. 6, p.378 below.
[2] A list of regulations made, or which have effect as if made, under this Act is at p.799 below.
[3] For "occupier" see s.13, p.343 below and s.64(2), p.372 below.
[4] The current fine at level 5 on the standard scale is £5,000: Criminal Justice Act 1991 (c.53), s.17 (England and Wales); Criminal Procedure (Scotland) Act 1995 (c.46), s.225 (Scotland).
[5] A list of regulations made, or which have effect as if made, under this Act is at p.799 below.
[6] For "occupier" see s.13, p.343 below and s.64(2), p.372 below.
[7] "Local authority" defined by s.64(1), p.372 below.
[8] "Chimney" defined by s.64(1), p.371 below.
[9] For further provisions relating to furnaces see s.13, p.343 below and s.64(6), p.373 below.

be used by virtue of subsection (2), (3) or (5), the occupier of the building shall be guilty of an offence and liable on summary conviction to a fine not exceeding level 5 on the standard scale[1].

*Requirement to fit arrestment plant for burning solid fuel in other cases.*

8. (1) A domestic furnace[2] shall not be used in a building—

(a) to burn pulverised fuel; or

(b) to burn, at a rate of 1.02 tonnes an hour or more, solid fuel in any other form or solid waste,

unless the furnace is provided with plant for arresting grit and dust which has been approved by the local authority[3] or which has been installed in accordance with plans and specifications submitted to and approved by the local authority, and that plant is properly maintained and used.[4]

(2) If a furnace is used in a building in contravention of subsection (1), the occupier[5] of the building shall be guilty of an offence and liable on summary conviction to a fine not exceeding level 5 on the standard scale[6].

*Appeal to Secretary of State against refusal of approval.*

9. (1) Where a local authority[7] determine an application for approval under section 6[8] or 8, they shall give the applicant a written notification of their decision and, in the case of a decision not to grant approval, shall state their reasons for not doing so.

(2) A person who—

(a) has made such an application to a local authority; or

(b) is interested in a building with respect to which such an application has been made,

may, if he is dissatisfied with the decision of the authority on the application, appeal within twenty-eight days after he is notified of the decision to the Secretary of State; and the Secretary of State may give any approval which the local authority might have given.

(3) An approval given by the Secretary of State under this section shall have the like effect as an approval of the local authority.

### Measurement of grit, dust and fumes

*Measurement of grit, dust and fumes by occupiers.*

10. (1) If a furnace[9] in a building is used—

(a) to burn pulverised fuel;

(b) to burn, at a rate of 45.4 kilograms or more an hour, any other solid matter; or

(c) to burn, at a rate equivalent to 366.4 kilowatts or more, any liquid or gaseous matter,

the local authority[10] may, by notice in writing served on the occupier[11] of the building, direct thàt the provisions of subsection (2) below shall apply to the furnace, and those provisions shall apply accordingly.

[1] The current fine at level 5 on the standard scale is £5,000: Criminal Justice Act 1991 (c.53), s.17 (England and Wales); Criminal Procedure (Scotland) Act 1995 (c.46), s.225 (Scotland).
[2] "Domestic furnace" defined by s.64(1), p.371 below; for further provisions relating to furnaces see s.13, p.343 below and s.64(6), p.373 below.
[3] "Local authority" defined by s.64(1), p.372 below.
[4] For transitional provisions see sch.5, para. 6, p.378 below.
[5] For "occupier" see s.13, p.000 below and s.64(2), p.343 below.
[6] The current fine at level 5 on the standard scale is £5,000: Criminal Justice Act 1991 (c.53), s.17 (England and Wales); Criminal Procedure (Scotland) Act 1995 (c.46), s.225 (Scotland).
[7] "Local authority" defined by s.64(1), p.372 below.
[8] P.339 above.
[9] For further provisions relating to furnaces see s.13, p.343 below and s.64(6), p.373 below.
[10] "Local authority" defined by s.64(1), p.372 below.
[11] For "occupier" see s.13, p.343 below and s. 64(2), p.372 below.

(2) In the case of a furnace to which this subsection for the time being applies, the occupier of the building shall comply with such requirements as may be prescribed as to—

(a) making and recording measurements from time to time of the grit, dust and fumes[1] emitted from the furnace;

(b) making adaptations for that purpose to the chimney[2] serving the furnace;

(c) providing and maintaining apparatus for making and recording the measurements; and

(d) informing the local authority of the results obtained from the measurements or otherwise making those results available to them;

and in this subsection "prescribed" means prescribed (whether generally or for any class of furnace) by regulations made by the Secretary of State[3].

(3) If the occupier of the building fails to comply with those requirements, he shall be guilty of an offence and liable on summary conviction—

(a) to a fine not exceeding level 5 on the standard scale[4]; or

(b) to cumulative penalties on continuance in accordance with section 50[5].

(4) The occupier of a building who by virtue of subsection (2) is under a duty to make and record measurements of grit, dust and fumes emitted from a furnace in the building shall permit the local authority to be represented during the making and recording of those measurements.

(5) The Secretary of State may by regulations substitute for any rate mentioned in subsection (1)(b) or (c) such other rate as he thinks fit; but regulations shall not be made under this subsection so as to reduce any rate unless a draft of the regulations has been laid before and approved by each House of Parliament.

(6) Any direction given by a local authority under subsection (1) with respect to a furnace in a building may be revoked by the local authority by a subsequent notice in writing served on the occupier of the building, without prejudice, however, to their power to give another direction under that subsection.

...........................................................................................................................................................................

*Measurement of grit, dust and fumes by local authorities.*

11. (1) This section applies to any furnace[6] to which section 10(2) (duty to comply with prescribed requirements) for the time being applies and which is used—

(a) to burn, at a rate less than 1.02 tonnes an hour, solid matter other than pulverised fuel; or

(b) to burn, at a rate of less than 8.21 Megawatts, any liquid or gaseous matter.

(2) The occupier[7] of the building in which the furnace is situated may, by notice in writing given to the local authority[8], request that authority to make and record measurements of the grit, dust and fumes[9] emitted from the furnace.

(3) While a notice is in force under subsection (2)—

(a) the local authority shall from time to time make and record measurements of the grit, dust and fumes emitted from the furnace; and

(b) the occupier shall not be under a duty to comply with any requirements of regulations under subsection (2) of section 10 in relation to the furnace, except those imposed by virtue of paragraph (b) of that subsection;

and any such notice given by the occupier of a building may be withdrawn by a subsequent notice in writing given to the local authority by him or any subsequent occupier of that building.

---

[1] "Fumes" defined by s.64(1), p.371 below.

[2] "Chimney" defined by s.64(1), p.371 below.

[3] A list of regulations made, or which have effect as if made, under this Act is at p.799 below.

[4] The current fine at level 5 on the standard scale is £5,000: Criminal Justice Act 1991 (c.53), s.17 (England and Wales); Criminal Procedure (Scotland) Act 1995 (c. 46), s.225 (Scotland).

[5] P.364 below.

[6] For further provisions relating to furnaces see s.13, p.343 below and s.64(6), p.373 below.

[7] For "occupier" see s.13, p.343 below and s.64(2), p.372 below.

[8] "Local authority" defined by s.64(1), p.372 below.

[9] "Fumes" defined by s.64(1), p.371 below.

(4) A direction under section 10(1) applying section 10(2) to a furnace which is used as mentioned in subsection (1)(*a*) or (*b*) of this section shall contain a statement of the effect of subsections (1) to (3) of this section.

*Information about furnaces and fuel consumed.*

**12.** (1) For the purpose of enabling the local authority[1] properly to perform their functions under and in connection with sections 5[2] to 11, the local authority may, by notice in writing served on the occupier[3] of any building, require the occupier to furnish to them, within fourteen days or such longer time as may be limited by the notice, such information as to the furnaces[4] in the building and the fuel or waste burned in those furnaces as they may reasonably require for that purpose.

(2) Any person who, having been duly served with a notice under subsection (1)—

(*a*)  fails to comply with the requirements of the notice within the time limited; or

(*b*)  furnishes any information in reply to the notice which he knows to be false in a material particular,

shall be guilty of an offence and liable on summary conviction to a fine not exceeding level 5 on the standard scale[5].

## Outdoor furnaces

*Grit and dust from outdoor furnaces, etc.*

**13.** (1) Sections 5[6] to 12 shall apply in relation to the furnace of any fixed boiler or industrial plant[7] as they apply in relation to a furnace in a building.

(2) References in those sections to the occupier of the building shall, in relation to a furnace falling within subsection (1), be read as references to the person having possession of the boiler or plant.

(3) The reference in section 6(4)[8] (and the reference in paragraph 6(1) and (3) of Schedule 5[9]) to the installation and to the purchase of a furnace shall, in relation to a furnace which is already contained in any fixed boiler or industrial plant, be read as a reference to attaching the boiler or plant to the building or fixing it to or installing it on any land and to purchasing it respectively.

## Height of chimneys

*Height of chimneys for furnaces.*

**14.** (1) This section applies to any furnace[10] served by a chimney[11].

(2) An occupier[12] of a building shall not knowingly cause or permit a furnace to be used in the building—

(*a*)  to burn pulverised fuel;

(*b*)  to burn, at a rate of 45.4 kilograms or more an hour, any other solid matter; or

(c)  to burn, at a rate equivalent to 366.4 kilowatts or more, any liquid or gaseous matter,

---

[1] "Local authority" defined by s.64(1), p.372 below.
[2] P.339 above.
[3] For "occupier" see s.13, p.343 below and s.64(2), p.372 below.
[4] For further provisions relating to furnaces see s.13, p.343 below and s.64(6), p.373 below.
[5] The current fine at level 5 on the standard scale is £5,000: Criminal Justice Act 1991 (c.53), s.17 (England and Wales); Criminal Procedure (Scotland) Act 1995 (c.46), s.225 (Scotland).

[6] P.339 above.
[7] "Fixed boiler or industrial plant" and "industrial plant" defined by s. 64(1), p.371 below.
[8] P.340 above.
[9] P.378 below.
[10] For further provisions relating to furnaces see s.64(6), p.373 below.
[11] "Chimney" defined by s.64(1), p.371 below.
[12] For "occupier" see s. 64(2), p.372 below.

unless the height of the chimney serving the furnace has been approved for the purposes of this section and any conditions subject to which the approval was granted are complied with.

(3) If on any day[1] the occupier of a building contravenes subsection (2), he shall be guilty of an offence.

(4) A person having possession of any fixed boiler or industrial plant[2], other than an exempted boiler or plant[3], shall not knowingly cause or permit a furnace of that boiler or plant to be used as mentioned in subsection (2), unless the height of the chimney serving the furnace has been approved for the purposes of this section and any conditions subject to which the approval was granted are complied with.

(5) If on any day a person having possession of any boiler or plant contravenes subsection (4), he shall be guilty of an offence.

(6) A person guilty of an offence under this section shall be liable on summary conviction to a fine not exceeding level 5 on the standard scale[4].

(7) In this section "exempted boiler or plant" means a boiler or plant which is used or to be used wholly for any purpose prescribed in regulations made by the Secretary of State[5]; and the height of a chimney is approved for the purposes of this section if approval is granted by the local authority or the Secretary of State under section 15.[6]

*Applications for approval of height of chimneys of furnaces.*

**15.** (1) This section applies to the granting of approval of the height of a chimney[7] for the purposes of section 14.

(2) Approval shall not be granted by a local authority[8] unless they are satisfied that the height of the chimney will be sufficient to prevent, so far as practicable[9], the smoke[10], grit, dust, gases or fumes[11] emitted from the chimney from becoming prejudicial to health or a nuisance having regard to—

(a) the purpose of the chimney;

(b) the position and descriptions of buildings near it;

(c) the levels of the neighbouring ground; and

(d) any other matters requiring consideration in the circumstances.

(3) Approval may be granted without qualification or subject to conditions as to the rate or quality, or the rate and quality, of emissions[12] from the chimney.

(4) If a local authority to whom an application is duly made for approval fail to determine the application and to give a written notification of their decision to the applicant[13] within four weeks of receiving the application or such longer period as may be agreed in writing between the applicant and the authority, the approval applied for shall be treated as having been granted without qualification.

(5) If a local authority decide not to approve the height of a chimney, or to attach conditions to their approval, they shall give the applicant a written notification of their decision which—

(a) states their reasons for that decision; and

(b) in the case of a decision not to approve the height of the chimney, specifies—

---

[1] "Day" defined by s.64(1), p.371 below.
[2] "Fixed boiler or industrial plant" and "industrial plant" defined by s.64(1), p.371 below.
[3] "Exempted boiler or plant" defined by subsection (7) below.
[4] The current fine at level 5 on the standard scale is £5,000: Criminal Justice Act 1991 (c.53), s.17 (England and Wales); Criminal Procedure (Scotland) Act 1995 (c.46), s.225 (Scotland).
[5] A list of regulations made, or which have effect as if

made, under this Act is at p.799 below.
[6] For transitional provisions see sch.5, para.7, p.379 below.
[7] "Chimney" defined by s.64(1), p.371 below.
[8] "Local authority" defined by s. 64(1), p.372 below.
[9] "Practicable" defined by s.64(1), p.372 below.
[10] "Smoke" defined by s.64(1), p.372 below.
[11] "Fumes" defined by s.64(1), p.371 below.
[12] For "rate of emission" see s.64(3), p.372 below.
[13] For "applicant" see subsection (9) below.

    (i)   the lowest height (if any) which they are prepared to approve without qualification; or

    (ii)  the lowest height which they are prepared to approve if approval is granted subject to any specified conditions,

  or (if they think fit) both.

(6)  The applicant may within twenty-eight days of receiving a notification under subsection (5) appeal against the local authority's decision to the Secretary of State.

(7)  On an appeal under this section the Secretary of State may confirm the decision appealed against or he may—

(*a*)  approve the height of the chimney without qualification or subject to conditions as to the rate or quality, or the rate and quality, of emissions from the chimney; or

(*b*)  cancel any conditions imposed by the local authority or substitute for any conditions so imposed any other conditions which the authority had power to impose.

(8)  The Secretary of State shall give the appellant a written notification of his decision on an appeal under this section which—

(*a*)  states his reasons for the decision; and

(*b*)  in the case of a decision not to approve the height of the chimney, specifies—

    (i)   the lowest height (if any) which he is prepared to approve without qualification; or

    (ii)  the lowest height which he is prepared to approve if approval is granted subject to any specified conditions,

  or (if he thinks fit) both.

(9)  References in this section to "the applicant" shall, in a case where the original applicant notifies the local authority that his interest in the application has been transferred to another person, be read as references to that other person.

........................................................................................................................................................

*Height of other chimneys.*

**16.**  (1)  This section applies where plans for the erection or extension of a building outside Greater London or in an outer London borough, other than a building used or to be used wholly for one or more of the following purposes, that is to say—

(*a*)  as a residence or residences;

(*b*)  as a shop or shops; or

(*c*)  as an office or offices,

are in accordance with building regulations[1] deposited with the local authority[2] and the plans show that it is proposed to construct a chimney[3], other than one serving a furnace, for carrying smoke[4], grit, dust or gases from the building.

(2)  The local authority shall reject the plans unless they are satisfied that the height of the chimney as shown on the plans will be sufficient to prevent, so far as practicable[5], the smoke, grit, dust or gases from becoming prejudicial to health or a nuisance having regard to—

(*a*)  the purpose of the chimney;

(*b*)  the position and descriptions of buildings near it;

(*c*)  the levels of the neighbouring ground; and

(*d*)  any other matters requiring consideration in the circumstances.

(3)  If a local authority reject plans under the authority of this section—

(*a*)  the notice given under section 16(6) of the Building Act 1984[6] shall specify that the plans have been so rejected; and

---

[1] "Building regulations" defined by s.64(1), p.371 below.
[2] "Local authority" defined by s.64(1), p.372 below.
[3] "Chimney" defined by s.64(1), p.371 below.
[4] "Smoke" defined by s.64(1), p.372 below.
[5] "Practicable" defined by s.64(1), p.372 below.
[6] 1984 c.55.

(*b*)  any person interested in the building may appeal to the Secretary of State.

(4)  On an appeal under subsection (3) the Secretary of State may confirm or cancel the rejection and, where he cancels the rejection, may, if he thinks it necessary, direct that the time for rejecting the plans otherwise than under the authority of this section shall be extended so as to run from the date on which his decision is notified to the local authority.

(5)  In the application of this section to Scotland—

(*a*)  any reference to plans deposited in accordance with building regulations shall be read as a reference to the plans, specifications and other information submitted with an application for a warrant under section 6 of the Building (Scotland) Act 1959[1];

(*b*)  any reference to a local authority shall be read as a reference to a local authority within the meaning of that Act;

(*c*)  any reference to the rejection of plans shall be read as a reference to the refusal of a warrant under section 6 of that Act;

and subsections (3) and (4) shall be omitted.

*Smoke nuisances in Scotland*

**17.**  *Repealed by the Environment Act 1995 (c.25), s.120, sch.24. This amendment came into force on 1 April 1996: S.I. 1996/186.*

## PART III: Smoke Control Areas

### Creation of smoke control areas

*Declaration of smoke control area by local authority.*

**18.**  (1)  A local authority[2] may by order declare the whole or any part of the district of the authority to be a smoke control area; and any order made under this section is referred to in this Act as a "smoke control order".

(2)  A smoke control order—

(*a*)  may make different provision for different parts of the smoke control area;

(*b*)  may limit the operation of section 20[3] (prohibition of emissions of smoke) to specified classes of building in the area; and

(*c*)  may exempt specified buildings or classes of building or specified fireplaces[4] or classes of fireplace in the area from the operation of that section, upon such conditions as may be specified in the order;

and the reference in paragraph (*c*) to specified buildings or classes of building include a reference to any specified, or to any specified classes of, fixed boiler or industrial plant[5].

(3)  A smoke control order may be revoked or varied by a subsequent order.

(4)  The provisions of Schedule 1[6] apply to the coming into operation of smoke control orders.[7]

---

[1]  1959 c.24.
[2]  "Local authority" defined by s.64(1), p.372 below.
[3]  P.348 below.
[4]  "Fireplace" defined by s.64(1), p.371 below.
[5]  " Fixed boiler or industrial plant" and "industrial plant"
defined by s.64 (1), p.371 below.
[6]  P.374 below.
[7]  For transitional provisions see sch.5, paras.8, 9, p.379 below.

*Power of Secretary of State to require creation of smoke control areas.*

**19.** (1) If, after consultation with a local authority[1], the [*England and Wales*: Secretary of State *Scotland*: Scottish Environment Protection Agency[2] (in this section referred to as "the Agency")[3]] is satisfied—

    (*a*)  that it is expedient to abate the pollution of the air by smoke[4] in the district or part of the district of the authority; and

    (*b*)  that the authority have not exercised, or have not sufficiently exercised, their powers under section 18 (power to declare smoke control area) to abate the pollution,

[*England and Wales*: he *Scotland*: the Agency[5]] may direct the authority to prepare and submit to [*England and Wales*: him *Scotland*: it[6]] for [*England and Wales*: his *Scotland*: its[7]] approval, within such period not being less than six months from the direction as may be specified in the direction, proposals for making and bringing into operation one or more smoke control orders[8] within such period or periods as the authority think fit.

(2)  Any proposals submitted by a local authority in pursuance of a direction under subsection (1) may be varied by further proposals submitted by the authority within the period specified for the making of the original proposals or such longer period as the [*England and Wales*: Secretary of State *Scotland*: Agency[9]] may allow.

(3)  The [*England and Wales*: Secretary of State *Scotland*: Agency[9]] may reject any proposals submitted to [*England and Wales*: him *Scotland*: it[10]] under this section or may approve them in whole or in part, with or without modifications.

(4)  Where a local authority to whom a direction under subsection (1) has been given—

    (*a*)  fail to submit proposals to the [*England and Wales*: Secretary of State *Scotland*: Agency[11]] within the period specified in the direction; or

    (*b*)  submit proposals which are rejected in whole or in part,

[*Scotland*: the Agency, with the consent of[12]] the Secretary of State may make an order declaring them to be in default and directing them for the purposes of removing the default to exercise their powers under section 18 in such manner and within such period as may be specified in the order.

(5)  An order made under subsection (4) may be varied or revoked by a subsequent order so made.

(6)  While proposals submitted by a local authority and approved by the [*England and Wales*: Secretary of State *Scotland*: Agency[13]] under this section are in force, it shall be the duty of the authority to make such order or orders under section 18 as are necessary to carry out the proposals.

---

[1]  "Local authority" defined by s.64(1), p.372 below.

[2]  The Scottish Environment Protection Agency, SEPA, is established by the Environment Act 1995 (c.25), s.20, p.438 below.

[3]  *Scotland:* words "Scottish . . . "the Agency") " substituted by the Environment Act 1995 (c.25), s.120, sch.22, para.196(2)(a). This amendment came into force on 1 April 1996: S.I. 1996/186.

[4]  "Smoke" defined by s.64 (1), p.372 below.

[5]  *Scotland:* words "the Agency" substituted by the Environment Act 1995 (c.25), s.120, sch.22, para.196(2)(b).

[6]  *Scotland:* word "it" substituted by the Environment Act 1995 (c.25), s.120, sch.22, para.196(2)(b).

[7]  *Scotland:* word "its" substituted by the Environment Act 1995 (c.25), s.120, sch.22, para.196(2)(b).

[8]  "Smoke control order" means an order made by a local authority under s.18 above: s.29 below.

[9]  *Scotland:* word "Agency" substituted by the Environment Act 1995 (c.25), s.120, sch.22, para.196(3).

[10]  *Scotland:* word "it" substituted by the Environment Act 1995 (c.25), s.120, sch.22, para.196(4).

[11]  *Scotland:* word "Agency" substituted by the Environment Act 1995 (c.25), s.120, sch.22, para.196(3).

[12]  *Scotland:* words "the Agency, with the consent of" inserted by the Environment Act 1995 (c.25), s.120, sch.22, para.196(5).

[13]  *Scotland:* word "Agency" substituted by the Environment Act 1995 (c.25), s.120, sch.22, para.196(3).

*Prohibition on emission of smoke in smoke control area*

**20.** (1) If, on any day[1], smoke[2] is emitted from a chimney[3] of any building within a smoke control area[4], the occupier[5] of the building shall be guilty of an offence.

(2) If, on any day, smoke is emitted from a chimney (not being a chimney of a building) which serves the furnace of any fixed boiler or industrial plant[6] within a smoke control area, the person having possession of the boiler or plant shall be guilty of an offence.

(3) Subsections (1) and (2) have effect—

    (a)  subject to any exemptions for the time being in force under section 18[7], 21 or 22;

    (b)  subject to section 51[8] (duty to notify offences to occupier or other person liable).

(4) In proceedings for an offence under this section it shall be a defence to prove that the alleged emission was not caused by the use of any fuel other than an authorised fuel[9].

(5) A person guilty of an offence under this section shall be liable on summary conviction to a fine not exceeding level 3 on the standard scale[10].

(6) In this Part "authorised fuel" means a fuel declared by regulations of the Secretary of State to be an authorised fuel for the purposes of this Part[11].

........................................................................................................................................................

*Power by order to exempt certain fireplaces.*

**21.** The Secretary of State may by order exempt any class of fireplace[12], upon such conditions as may be specified in the order, from the provisions of section 20 (prohibition of smoke emissions in smoke control area), if he is satisfied that such fireplaces can be used for burning fuel other than authorised fuels[13] without producing any smoke[14] or a substantial quantity of smoke[15].

........................................................................................................................................................

*Exemptions relating to particular areas.*

**22.** (1) The Secretary of State may, if it appears to him to be necessary or expedient so to do, by order suspend or relax the operation of section 20 (prohibition of smoke emissions in smoke control area) in relation to the whole or any part of a smoke control area.

(2) Before making an order under subsection (1) the Secretary of State shall consult with the local authority[16] unless he is satisfied that, on account of urgency, such consultation is impracticable.

(3) As soon as practicable after the making of such an order the local authority shall take such steps as appear to them suitable for bringing the effect of the order to the notice of persons affected.

........................................................................................................................................................

*Dealings with unauthorised fuel*

*Acquisition and sale of unauthorised fuel in a smoke control area.*

**23.** (1) Any person who—

    (a)  acquires any solid fuel for use in a building in a smoke control area otherwise than in a building or fireplace[17] exempted from the operation of section 20 (prohibition of smoke emissions in smoke control area);

---

[1] "Day" defined by s.64(1), p.371 below.

[2] "Smoke" defined by s.64(1), p.372 below.

[3] "Chimney" and "chimney of a building" defined by s.64(1), p.371 below.

[4] "Smoke control order" means an order made by a local authority under s.18, p.346 above: s.29 below.

[5] For "occupier" see s.64(2), p.372 below.

[6] "Fixed boiler or industrial plant" and "industrial plant" defined by s.64(1), p.371 below.

[7] P.346 above.

[8] P.364 below.

[9] "Authorised fuel" defined by subsection (6) below.

[10] The current fine at level 3 on the standard scale is

£1,000: Criminal Justice Act 1991 (c.53), s.17 (England and Wales); Criminal Procedure (Scotland) Act 1995 (c.46), s.225 (Scotland).

[11] A list of regulations made, or which have effect as if made, under this Act is at p.799 below.

[12] "Fireplace" defined by s.64(1), p.371 below.

[13] "Authorised fuel" has the meaning given by s.20(6) above: s.29 below.

[14] "Smoke" defined by s.64(1), p.372 below.

[15] A list of orders made, or which have effect as if made, under this section is at p.800 below.

[16] "Local authority" defined by s.64(1), p.372 below.

[17] "Fireplace" defined by s.64(1), p.371 below.

(b)  acquires any solid fuel for use in any fixed boiler or industrial plant[1] in a smoke control area, not being a boiler or plant so exempted; or

(c)  sells by retail any solid fuel for delivery by him or on his behalf to—

(i)  a building in a smoke control area; or

(ii)  premises[2] in such an area in which there is any fixed boiler or industrial plant,

shall be guilty of an offence and liable on summary conviction to a fine not exceeding level 3 on the standard scale[3].

(2)  In subsection (1), "solid fuel" means any solid fuel other than an authorised fuel[4].

(3)  Subsection (1) shall, in its application to a smoke control area in which the operation of section 20 is limited by a smoke control order to specified classes of buildings, boilers or plant, have effect as if references to a building, boiler or plant were references to a building, boiler or plant of a class specified in the order.

(4)  The power of the Secretary of State under section 22 (exemptions relating to particular areas) to suspend or relax the operation of section 20 in relation to the whole or any part of a smoke control area includes power to suspend or relax the operation of subsection (1) in relation to the whole or any part of such an area.

(5)  In proceedings for an offence under this section consisting of the sale of fuel for delivery to a building or premises, it shall be a defence for the person accused to prove that he believed and had reasonable grounds for believing—

(a)  that the building was exempted from the operation of section 20 or, in a case where the operation of that section is limited to specified classes of building, was not of a specified class; or

(b)  that the fuel was acquired for use in a fireplace, boiler or plant so exempted or, in a case where the operation of that section is limited to specified classes of boilers or plant, in a boiler or plant not of a specified class.

## Adaptation of fireplaces

*Power of local authority to require adaptation of fireplaces in private dwellings.*

**24.**  (1)  The local authority[5] may, by notice in writing served on the occupier[6] or owner[7] of a private dwelling[8] which is, or when a smoke control order[9] comes into operation will be, within a smoke control area, require the carrying out of adaptations in or in connection with the dwelling to avoid contraventions of section 20[10] (prohibition of smoke emissions in smoke control area).

(2)  The provisions of Part XII of the Public Health Act 1936[11] with respect to appeals against, and the enforcement of, notices requiring the execution of works shall apply in relation to any notice under subsection (1).

(3)  Any reference in those provisions to the expenses reasonably incurred in executing the works[12] shall, in relation to a notice under subsection (1), be read as a reference to three-tenths of those expenses or such smaller fraction of those expenses as the local authority may in any particular case determine.

(4)  In the application of this section to Scotland—

(a)  subsections (2) and (3) shall be omitted;

---

[1] "Fixed boiler or industrial plant" and "industrial plant" defined by s.64(1), p.371 below.

[2] "Premises" defined by s.64(1), p.372 below.

[3] The current fine at level 3 on the standard scale is £1,000: Criminal Justice Act 1991 (c.53), s.17 (England and Wales); Criminal Procedure (Scotland) Act 1995 (c.46), s.225 (Scotland).

[4] "Authorised fuel" has the meaning given by s.20(6), p.348 above: s.29 below.

[5] "Local authority" defined by s.64(1), p.372 below.

[6] For "occupier" see s.64(2), p.372 below.

[7] "Owner" defined by s.64(1), p.372 below.

[8] "Private dwelling" defined by s.64(4), p.372 below.

[9] "Smoke control order" means an order made by a local authority under s.18, p.346 above: s.29 below.

[10] P.348 above. For "adaptations . . . section 20" see s.27, p.351 below.

[11] 1936 c.49.

[12] For "expenses incurred in the execution of works" see s.28, p.351 below.

(b) section 111 of the Housing (Scotland) Act 1987[1] (which provides for an appeal to the sheriff against certain notices, demands and orders under that Act) shall apply in relation to a notice under subsection (1) of this section as it applies in relation to a repair notice under that Act; and

(c) subject to any such right of appeal as is mentioned in paragraph (b), if any person on whom a notice under subsection (1) is served fails to execute the works required by the notice within the time limited by the notice, the local authority may themselves execute the works and may recover from that person three-tenths, or such smaller fraction as the local authority may in any particular case determine, of the expenses reasonably incurred by them in so doing.

*Expenditure incurred in relation to adaptations in private dwellings.*

**25.** (1) Schedule 2 to this Act[2] shall have effect with respect to certain expenditure incurred in adapting old private dwellings in smoke control areas.

(2) In this Part "old private dwelling" means any private dwelling[3] other than one which either—

(a) was erected after 15th August 1964 (which was the date immediately preceding the time when the enactment replaced by this subsection came into force), or

(b) was produced by the conversion, after that date, of other premises, with or without the addition of premises erected after that date;

and for the purposes of this subsection a dwelling or premises shall not be treated as erected or converted after that date unless the erection or conversion was begun after it.

*Power of local authority to make grants towards adaptations to fireplaces in churches, chapels, buildings used by charities etc.*

**26.** (1) If, after the making[4] of a smoke control order[5], the owner[6] or occupier[7] of any premises or part of any premises to which this section applies and which will be within a smoke control area as the result of the order incurs expenditure on adaptations in or in connection with the premises or part to avoid contraventions of section 20[8] (prohibition of smoke emissions in smoke control area), the local authority[9] may, if they think fit, repay to him the whole or any part of that expenditure.

(2) This section applies to any premises or part of any premises which fall within one or more of the following paragraphs, that is to say—

(a) any place of public religious worship, being, in the case of a place in England or Wales, a place which belongs to the Church of England or to the Church in Wales (within the meaning of the Welsh Church Act 1914[10]) or which is for the time being certified as required by law as a place of religious worship;

(b) any church hall, chapel hall or similar premises used in connection with any such place of public religious worship, and so used for the purposes of the organisation responsible for the conduct of public religious worship in that place;

(c) any premises or part of any premises occupied for the purposes of an organisation (whether corporate or unincorporated) which is not established or conducted for profit and whose main objects are charitable or are otherwise concerned with the advancement of religion, education or social welfare.

---

[1] 1987 c.26.
[2] P.374 below.
[3] "Private dwelling" defined by s.64(4), p.372 below.
[4] For transitional provisions see sch.5, para.8(3), p.379 below.
[5] "Smoke control order" means an order made by a local authority under s.18, p.346 above: s.29 below.
[6] "Owner" defined by s.64(1), p.372 below.
[7] For "occupier" see s. 64(2), p.372 below.
[8] P.348 above. For "adaptations . . . section 20" see s.27 below.
[9] "Local authority" defined by s.64(1), p.372 below.
[10] 1914 c.41.

*Supplementary provisions*

*References to adaptations for avoiding contraventions of section 20.*

**27.** (1)  References in this Part to adaptations in or in connection with a dwelling[1] to avoid contraventions of section 20[2] (prohibition of smoke emissions from smoke control area) shall be read as references to the execution of any of the following works (whether in or outside the dwelling), that is to say—

(*a*)  adapting or converting any fireplace[3];

(*b*)  replacing any fireplace by another fireplace or by some other means of heating[4] or cooking;

(*c*)  altering any chimney[5] which serves any fireplace;

(*d*)  providing gas ignition, electric ignition or any other special means of ignition; or

(*e*)  carrying out any operation incidental to any of the operations mentioned in paragraphs (*a*) to (*d*);

being works which are reasonably necessary in order to make what is in all the circumstances suitable provision for heating and cooking[6] without contraventions of section 20.

(2)  For the purposes of this section the provision of any igniting apparatus or appliance (whether fixed or not) operating by means of gas, electricity or other special means shall be treated as the execution of works.

(3)  Except for the purposes of section 24[7] (power of local authority to require certain adaptations), works which make such suitable provision as is mentioned in subsection (1) shall not be treated as not being adaptations to avoid contraventions of section 20 of this Act by reason that they go beyond what is reasonably necessary for that purpose, but any expenditure incurred in executing them in excess of the expenditure which would have been reasonably incurred in doing what was reasonably necessary shall be left out of account.

(4)  References in this section to a dwelling include references to any premises or part of any premises to which section 26 (grants towards certain adaptations in churches and other buildings) applies.

*Cases where expenditure is taken to be incurred on execution of works.*

**28.** (1)  References in this Part to expenses incurred in the execution of works include references to the cost of any fixed cooking or heating[8] appliance installed by means of the execution of the works, notwithstanding that the appliance can be readily removed from the dwelling[9] without injury to itself or the fabric of the dwelling.

(2)  For the purposes of this Part a person who enters into either—

(*a*)  a conditional sale agreement[10] for the sale to him, or

(*b*)  a hire-purchase agreement[11] for the bailment or (in Scotland) hiring to him,

of a cooking or heating appliance shall be treated as having incurred on the date of the agreement expenditure of an amount equal to the price which would have been payable for the appliance if he had purchased it for cash on that date.

(3)  References in this section to a dwelling include references to any premises or part of any premises to which section 26[12] (grants towards certain adaptations in churches and other buildings) applies.

---

[1]  For "dwelling" see subsection (4) below.
[2]  P.348 above.
[3]  "Fireplace" defined by s.64(1), p.371 below.
[4]  "Heating" defined by s.29, p.352 below.
[5]  "Chimney" defined by s.64(1), p.371 below.
[6]  For "works . . . cooking" see s.64(5), p.372 below.
[7]  P.349 above.
[8]  "Heating" defined by s.29 below.
[9]  For "dwelling" see subsection (3) below.
[10]  "Conditional sale agreement" defined by s.29 below.
[11]  "Hire-purchase agreement" defined by s.29 below.
[12]  P.350 above.

*Interpretation of Part III.*

**29.** In this Part, except so far as the context otherwise requires—

"authorised fuel" has the meaning given in section 20(6)[1];

"conditional sale agreement" means an agreement for the sale of goods under which—

(a)   the purchase price or part of it is payable by instalments; and

(b)   the property in the goods is to remain in the seller (notwithstanding that the buyer is to be in possession of the goods) until such conditions as to the payment of instalments or otherwise as may be specified in the agreement are fulfilled;

"heating", in relation to a dwelling, includes the heating of water;

"hire-purchase agreement" means an agreement, other than a conditional sale agreement, under which—

(a)   goods are bailed or (in Scotland) hired in return for periodical payments by the person to whom they are bailed or hired; and

(b)   the property in the goods will pass to that person if the terms of the agreement are complied with and one or more of the following occurs—

(i)    the exercise of an option to purchase by that person;

(ii)   the doing of any other specified act by any party to the agreement; and

(iii)  the happening of any other specified event;

"old private dwelling" has the meaning given in section 25[2]; and

"smoke control order" means an order made by a local authority[3] under section 18[4].

## PART IV: Control of certain forms of Air Pollution

*Regulations about motor fuel.*

**30.** (1) For the purpose of limiting or reducing air pollution, the Secretary of State may by regulations—

(a)   impose requirements as to the composition and contents of any fuel of a kind used in motor vehicles; and

(b)   where such requirements are in force, prevent or restrict the production, treatment, distribution, import, sale or use of any fuel which in any respect fails to comply with the requirements, and which is for use in the United Kingdom[5].

(2) It shall be the duty of the Secretary of State, before he makes any regulations under this section, to consult—

(a)   such persons appearing to him to represent manufacturers and users of motor vehicles;

(b)   such persons appearing to him to represent the producers and users of fuel for motor vehicles; and

(c)   such persons appearing to him to be conversant with problems of air pollution, as he considers appropriate.

(3) Regulations under this section—

(a)   in imposing requirements as to the composition and contents of any fuel, may apply standards, specifications, descriptions or tests laid down in documents not forming part of the regulations; and

---

[1] P.348 above.
[2] P.350 above.
[3] "Local authority" defined by s.64(1), p.372 below.

[4] P.346 above.
[5] A list of regulations made, or which have effect as if made, under this Act is at p.799 below.

(b)  where fuel is subject to such requirements, may, in order that persons to whom the fuel is supplied are afforded information as to its composition or contents, impose requirements for securing that the information is displayed at such places and in such manner as may be prescribed by the regulations.

(4)  It shall be duty of every local weights and measures authority to enforce the provisions of regulations under this section within its area; and subsections (2) and (3) of section 26 of the Trade Descriptions Act 1968[1] (reports and inquiries) shall apply as respects those authorities' functions under this subsection as they apply to their functions under that Act.

(5)  The following provisions of the Trade Descriptions Act 1968 shall apply in relation to the enforcement of regulations under this section as they apply to the enforcement of that Act, that is to say—

section 27 (power to make test purchases);

section 28 (power to enter premises and inspect and seize goods and documents);

section 29 (obstruction of authorised officers);

section 30 (notice of test);

and section 33 of that Act shall apply to the exercise of powers under section 28 as applied by this subsection.

References to an offence under that Act in those provisions as applied by this subsection, except the reference in section 30(2) to an offence under section 28(5) or 29 of that Act, shall be construed as references to an offence under section 32 of this Act[2] (provisions supplementary to this section) relating to regulations under this section.

(6)  In relation to Scotland—

(a)  nothing in subsection (4) authorises a local weights and measures authority to institute proceedings for an offence; and

(b)  regulations under this section may provide that certificates issued by such persons as may be specified by the regulations in relation to such matters as may be so specified shall, subject to the provisions of the regulations, be received in evidence, and be sufficient evidence, of those matters in any proceedings for an offence under regulations made under this section;

and such regulations may apply any of the provisions of subsections (2) to (4) of section 31 of the Trade Descriptions Act 1968 (evidence by certificate).

(7)–(9)  *These subsections relate to Northern Ireland.*

*Regulations about sulphur content of oil fuel for furnaces or engines.*

**31.** (1)  For the purpose of limiting or reducing air pollution, the Secretary of State may by regulations impose limits on the sulphur content of oil fuel[3] which is used in furnaces or engines.[4]

(2)  It shall be the duty of the Secretary of State, before he makes any regulations in pursuance of this section, to consult—

(a)  such persons appearing to him to represent producers and users of oil fuel;

(b)  such persons appearing to him to represent manufacturers and users of plant and equipment for which oil fuel is used; and

(c)  such persons appearing to him to be conversant with problems of air pollution, as he considers appropriate.

(3)  Regulations under this section may—

[1]  1968 c.29.
[2]  P.354 below.
[3]  "Oil fuel" defined by subsection (5) below.
[4]  A list of regulations made, or which have effect as if made, under this Act is at p.799 below.

(a) prescribe the kinds of oil fuel, and the kinds of furnaces and engines, to which the regulations are to apply;

(b) apply standards, specifications, descriptions or tests laid down in documents not forming part of the regulations; and

(c) without prejudice to the generality of section 63(1)(a)[1], make different provision for different areas.

(4) It shall be the duty—

(a) of every local authority[2] to enforce the provisions of regulations under this section within its area, except in relation to a furnace which is part of a process subject to Part I of the Environmental Protection Act 1991[3]; and

(b) of the inspectors appointed under that Part to enforce those provisions in relation to such furnaces;

but nothing in this section shall be taken to authorise a local authority in Scotland to institute proceedings for any offence.

(5) In this section "oil fuel" means any liquid petroleum product produced in a refinery.

*Provisions supplementary to sections 30 and 31.*

**32.** (1) Regulations under section 30 or 31 (regulation of content of motor fuel and fuel oil) may authorise the Secretary of State to confer exemptions from any provision of the regulations.

(2) A person who contravenes or fails to comply with any provision of regulations under section 30 or 31 shall be guilty of an offence and liable—

(a) on conviction on indictment, to a fine; and

(b) on summary conviction, to a fine not exceeding the statutory maximum[4];

but the regulations may in any case exclude liability to conviction on indictment or reduce the maximum fine on summary conviction.

(3) Regulations under section 30 or 31 shall, subject to any provision to the contrary in the regulations, apply to fuel used for, and to persons in, the public service of the Crown as they apply to fuel used for other purposes and to other persons.

(4) A local authority shall not be entitled by virtue of subsection (3) to exercise, in relation to fuel used for and persons in that service, any power conferred on the authority by virtue of sections 56[5] to 58 (rights of entry and inspection and other local authority powers).

*Cable burning.*

**33.** (1) A person who burns insulation from a cable with a view to recovering metal from the cable shall be guilty of an offence unless the burning is part of a process subject to Part I of the Environmental Protection Act 1990[6].

(2) A person guilty of an offence under this section shall be liable on summary conviction to a fine not exceeding level 5 on the standard scale[7].

---

[1] P.371 below.
[2] "Local authority" defined by s.64(1), p.372 below.
[3] P.88 above.
[4] The current statutory maximum is £5,000: Criminal Justice Act 1991 (c.53), s 17(2) (England and Wales); Criminal Procedure (Scotland) Act 1995 (c.46), s.225(8) (Scotland).

[5] P.366 below.
[6] P.88 above.
[7] The current fine at level 5 on the standard scale is £5,000: Criminal Justice Act 1991 (c.53), s.17 (England and Wales); Criminal Procedure (Scotland) Act 1995 (c. 46), s. 225 (Scotland).

# PART V: Information about Air Pollution

*Research and publicity.*

**34.** (1) A local authority[1] may—

   (*a*)  undertake, or contribute towards the cost of, investigation and research relevant to the problem of air pollution;

   (*b*)  arrange for the publication of information on that problem;

   (*c*)  arrange for the delivery of lectures and addresses, and the holding of discussions, on that problem;

   (*d*)  arrange for the display of pictures, cinematograph films or models, or the holding of exhibitions, relating to that problem; and

   (*e*)  prepare, or join in or contribute to the cost of the preparation of, pictures, films, models or exhibitions to be displayed or held as mentioned in paragraph (*d*).

(2) In acting under subsection (l)(*b*), a local authority shall ensure that the material published is presented in such a way that no information relating to a trade secret is disclosed, except with the consent in writing of a person authorised to disclose it.

(3) Breach of a duty imposed by subsection (2) shall be actionable.

(4) In any civil or criminal proceedings (whether or not arising under this Act) brought against a local authority, or any member or officer of a local authority, on the grounds that any information has been published, it shall be a defence to show that it was published in compliance with subsections (1) and (2).

---

*Obtaining information.*

**35.** (1) Without prejudice to the generality of section 34 (research, etc. by local authorities), local authorities[2] may obtain information about the emission of pollutants and other substances into the air[3]—

   (*a*)  by issuing notices under section 36 (information about emissions from premises);

   (*b*)  by measuring[4] land recording the emissions, and for that purpose entering on any premises[5], whether by agreement or in exercise of the power conferred by section 56[6] (rights of entry and inspection); and

   (*c*)  by entering into arrangements with occupiers of premises under which they measure and record emissions on behalf of the local authority;

but references to premises in paragraphs (*b*) and (*c*) do not include private dwellings[7] or caravans[8];

(2) A local authority shall not be entitled to exercise the power of entry mentioned in subsection (1)(*b*) for the purpose of measuring and recording such emissions on any premises unless—

   (*a*)  the authority has given to the occupier of the premises a notice in writing—

      (i)  specifying the kind of emissions in question and the steps it proposes to take on the premises for the purpose of measuring and recording emissions of that kind; and

      (ii)  stating that it proposes to exercise that power for that purpose unless the occupier requests the authority to serve on him a notice under section 36 (information about emissions from premises) with respect to the emissions; and

---

[1] "Local authority" defined by s.64(1), p.372 below.
[2] "Local authority" defined by s.64(1), p.372 below.
[3] For "emission . . . air" see s.40, p.359 below.
[4] For provision relating to measurement see s.40, p.359 below.

[5] "Premises" defined by s.64(1), p.372 below.
[6] P.366 below.
[7] For "private dwelling" see s.64(4), p.372 below.
[8] "Caravan" defined by s.64(1), p.371 below.

(b) the period of twenty-one days beginning with the day on which the notice was given has expired;

and the authority shall not be entitled to exercise that power if, during that period, the occupier gives a notice to the authority requesting it to serve on him a notice under section 36.

(3) Nothing in this section shall authorise a local authority to investigate emissions from any process subject to Part I of the Environmental Protection Act 1990[1] otherwise than—

(a) by issuing notices under section 36; or

(b) by exercising the powers conferred on the authority by section 34(1)(a) (investigation and research etc.) without entering the premises concerned.

(4) So long as a local authority exercises any of its powers under subsection (1), it shall from time to time consult the persons mentioned in subsection (5)—

(a) about the way in which the local authority exercises those powers (under this section and section 36); and

(b) about the extent to which, and the manner in which, any information collected under those powers should be made available to the public.

(5) The consultations required by subsection (4) shall be with—

(a) such persons carrying on any trade or business in the authority's area or such organisations appearing to the authority to be representative of those persons; and

(b) such persons appearing to the authority to be conversant with problems of air pollution or to have an interest in local amenity,

as appear to the authority to be appropriate.

(6) The consultations shall take place as the authority think necessary, but not less than twice in each financial year.

*Notices requiring information about air pollution.*

**36.** (1) A local authority[2] may by notice in writing require the occupier of any premises[3] in its area to furnish, whether by periodical returns or by other means, such estimates or other information as may be specified or described in the notice, concerning the emission of pollutants and other substances into the air[4] from the premises.

(2) This section, does not apply to premises in so far as they consist of a private dwelling[5] or a caravan[6].

(3) If the notice relates to a process subject to Part I of the Environmental Protection Act 1990[7], the person on whom the notice is served shall not be obliged to supply any information which, as certified by an inspector appointed under that Part, is not of a kind which is being supplied to the inspector for the purposes of that Part.

(4) The person on whom a notice is served under this section shall comply with the notice within six weeks of the date of service, or within such longer period as the local authority may by notice allow.

(5) A notice under this section shall not require returns at intervals of less than three months, and no one notice (whether or not requiring periodical returns) shall call for information covering a period of more than twelve months.

(6) Except so far as regulations made by the Secretary of State provide otherwise, this section applies to premises used for, and to persons in, the public service of the Crown as it applies to other premises and persons[8].

---

[1] P.88 above.
[2] "Local authority" defined by s.64(1), p.372 below.
[3] "Premises" defined by s. 64(1), p.372 below.
[4] For "emission . . . air" see s.40, p.359 below.
[5] For "private dwelling" see s.64(4), p.372 below.

[6] "Caravan" defined by s.64(1), p.371 below.
[7] P.88 above.
[8] A list of regulations made, or which have effect as if made, under this Act is at p.799 below.

(7) A local authority shall not be entitled by virtue of subsection (6) to exercise, in relation to premises used for and persons in the public service of the Crown, any power conferred on the authority by virtue of sections 56[1] to 58 (rights of entry and other local authority powers).

(8) A person who—

(a) fails without reasonable excuse to comply with the requirements of a notice served on him in pursuance of this section; or

(b) in furnishing any estimate or other information in compliance with a notice under this section, makes any statement which he knows to be false in a material particular or recklessly makes any statement which is false in a material particular,

shall be guilty of an offence and liable on summary conviction to a fine not exceeding level 5 on the standard scale[2].

(9) Where a person is convicted of an offence under subsection (8) in respect of any premises and information of any kind, nothing in section 35(2) (limits on exercise of power of entry) shall prevent a local authority from exercising the power of entry there mentioned for the purpose of obtaining information of that kind in respect of the premises.

*Appeals against notices under section 36.*

37. (1) A person served with a notice under section 36 (information about air pollution), or any other person having an interest in the premises to which the notice relates, may appeal to the Secretary of State—

(a) on the ground that the giving to the authority or the disclosure to the public of all or part of the information required by the notice would—

(i) prejudice to an unreasonable degree some private interest by disclosing information about a trade secret; or

(ii) be contrary to the public interest; or

(b) on the ground that the information required by the notice is not immediately available and cannot readily be collected or obtained by the recipient of the notice without incurring undue expenditure for the purpose.

(2) If the Secretary of State allows the appeal he may direct the local authority[3] to withdraw or modify the notice, or to take such steps as he may specify to ensure that prejudicial information is not disclosed to the public; and it shall be the duty of the authority to comply with the direction.

(3) The Secretary of State may make regulations as to appeals under this section, including regulations about the time for bringing an appeal and the circumstances in which all or any part of the appellant's case is to be withheld from the respondent[4].

(4) It shall be the duty of the Secretary of State, before he makes any regulations under subsection (3), to consult—

(a) such persons appearing to him to represent local authorities;

(b) such persons appearing to him to represent industrial interests; and

(c) such persons appearing to him to be conversant with problems of air pollution,

as he considers appropriate.

---

[1] P.366 below.
[2] The current fine at level 5 on the standard scale is £5,000: Criminal Justice Act 1991 (c.53), s.17 (England and Wales); Criminal Procedure (Scotland) Act 1995 (c.46), s.225 (Scotland).
[3] "Local authority" defined by s.64(1), p.372 below.
[4] A list of regulations made, or which have effect as if made, under this Act is at p.799 below.

*Regulations about local authority functions under sections 34, 35 and 36.*

**38.** (1) The Secretary of State shall by regulations prescribe the manner in which, and the methods by which, local authorities[1] are to perform their functions under sections 34(1)(*a*) and (*b*)[2], 35[3] and 36 (investigation and research etc. into, and the obtaining of information about, air pollution).[4]

(2) It shall be the duty of the Secretary of State, before he makes regulations under this section, to consult—

(*a*)   such persons appearing to him to represent local authorities;

(*b*)   such persons appearing to him to represent industrial interests; and

(*c*)   such persons appearing to him to be conversant with problems of air pollution,

as he considers appropriate.

(3) Regulations under this section may in particular—

(*a*)   prescribe the kinds of emissions to which notices under section 36[5] (power to require information about air pollution) may relate;

(*b*)   prescribe the kinds of information which may be required by those notices;

(*c*)   prescribe the manner in which any such notice is to be given, and the evidence which is to be sufficient evidence of its having been given, and of its contents and authenticity;

(*d*)   require each local authority to maintain in a prescribed form a register containing—

    (i)   information obtained by the authority by virtue of section 35(1) (powers of local authorities to obtain information), other than information as to which a direction under section 37(2) (appeals against notices under section 36) provides that the information is not to be disclosed to the public; and

    (ii)   such information (if any) as the Secretary of State may determine, or as may be determined by or under regulations, with respect to any appeal under section 37 against a notice served by the authority which the Secretary of State did not dismiss;

(*e*)   specify the circumstances in which local authorities may enter into arrangements with owners[6] or occupiers of premises[7] under which they will record and measure[8] emissions on behalf of the local authorities; and

(*f*)   specify the kinds of apparatus which local authorities are to have power to provide and use for measuring and recording emissions, and for other purposes.

(4) Regulations made by virtue of subsection (3)(*b*) may in particular require returns of—

(*a*)   the total volume of gases, whether pollutant or not, discharged from the premises in question over any period;

(*b*)   the concentration of pollutant in the gases discharged;

(*c*)   the total of the pollutant discharged over any period;

(*d*)   the height or heights at which discharges take place;

(*e*)   the hours during which discharges take place; or

(*f*)   the concentration of pollutants at ground level.

(5) A register maintained by a local authority in pursuance of regulations made by virtue of subsection (3)(*d*) shall be open to public inspection at the principal office of the authority free of charge at all reasonable hours, and the authority shall afford members of the public reasonable facilities for obtaining from the authority, on payment of reasonable charges, copies of entries in the register.

---

[1] "Local authority" defined by s.64(1), p.372 below.
[2] P.355 above.
[3] P.355 above.
[4] A list of regulations made, or which have effect as if made, under this Act is at p.799 below.

[5] P.356 above.
[6] "Owner" defined by s.64(1), p.372 below.
[7] "Premises" defined by s.64(1), p.372 below.
[8] For provision relating to measurement see s.40, p.359 below.

*Provision by local authorities of information for Secretary of State.*

**39.** (1)  The Secretary of State may, for the purpose, of obtaining information about air pollution, direct a local authority[1] to make such arrangements as may be specified in the direction—

    (*a*)  for the provision, installation, operation and maintenance by the local authority of apparatus for measuring[2] and recording air pollution; and

    (*b*)  for transmitting the information so obtained to the Secretary of State;

but before giving the direction under this section the Secretary of State shall consult the local authority.

(2)  Where apparatus is provided in pursuance of a direction under this section, the Secretary of State shall defray the whole of the capital expenditure incurred by the local authority in providing and installing the apparatus.

(3)  It shall be the duty of the local authority to comply with any direction given under this section.

*Interpretation of Part V.*

40. In this Part—

    (*a*)  references to the emission of substances into the atmosphere are to be construed as applying to substances in a gaseous or liquid or solid state, or any combination of those states; and

    (*b*)  any reference to measurement includes a reference to the taking of samples.

## PART VI: Special Cases

*Relation to Environmental Protection Act 1990.*

**41.** (1)  Parts I to III[3] shall not apply to any process which is a prescribed process as from the date which is the determination date for that process.

(2)  The "determination date" for a prescribed process is—

    (*a*)  in the case of a process for which an authorisation is granted, the date on which the enforcing authority grants it, whether in pursuance of the application or, on an appeal, of a direction to grant it, and

    (*b*)  in the case of a process for which an authorisation is refused, the date of the refusal or, on an appeal, of the affirmation of the refusal.

(3)  In this section "authorisation", "enforcing authority" and "prescribed process" have the meaning given in section 1 of the Environmental Protection Act 1990[4] and the reference to an appeal is a reference to an appeal under section 15 of that Act[5].

*Colliery spoilbanks.*

**42.** (1)  This section applies to any mine or quarry[6] from which coal or shale has been, is being or is to be got.

(2)  The owner[7] of a mine or quarry to which this section applies shall employ all practicable[8] means—

    (*a*)  for preventing combustion of refuse deposited from the mine or quarry; and

---

[1] "Local authority" defined by s.64(1), p.372 below.
[2] For provision relating to measurement see s.40, p.359 below.
[3] Pp.336–352 above.
[4] P.88 above.
[5] P.103 above.
[6] "Mine" and "quarry" defined by subsection (6) below.
[7] "Owner" defined by subsection (6) below.
[8] "Practicable" defined by s.64(1), p.372 below.

(*b*)  for preventing or minimising the emission of smoke[1] and fumes[2] from such refuse;

and, if he fails to do so, he shall be guilty of an offence.

(3)  A person guilty of an offence under subsection (2) shall be liable on summary conviction—

(*a*)  to a fine not exceeding level 5 on the standard scale[3]; or

(*b*)  to cumulative penalties on continuance in accordance with section 50[4].

(4)  Neither the provisions of Part III of the Environmental Protection Act 1990[5] nor any provision of Parts I to III of this Act shall apply in relation to smoke, grit or dust from the combustion of refuse deposited from any mine or quarry to which this section applies.

(5)  *Repealed by the Environment Act 1995 (c.25), s.120, sch.24. This amendment came into force on 1 April 1996: S.I. 1996/186.*

(6)  In this section, "mine", "quarry" and "owner" have the same meaning as in the Mines and Quarries Act 1954[6].[7]

*Railway engines*

**43.** (1)  Section 1[8] (prohibition of emissions of dark smoke) shall apply in relation to railway locomotive engines as it applies in relation to buildings.

(2)  In the application of section 1 to such engines, for the reference in subsection (1) of that section to the occupier of the building there shall be substituted a reference to the owner of the engine.

(3)  The owner of any railway locomotive engine shall use any practicable[9] means there may be for minimising the emission of smoke[10] from the chimney[11] on the engine and, if he fails to do so, he shall, if smoke is emitted from that chimney, be guilty of an offence.

(4)  A person guilty of an offence under subsection (3) shall be liable on summary conviction—

(*a*)  to a fine not exceeding level 5 on the standard scale[12]; or

(*b*)  to cumulative penalties on continuance in accordance with section 50[13].

(5)  Except as provided in this section, nothing in Parts I to III applies to smoke, grit or dust from any railway locomotive engine.

*Vessels.*

**44.** (1)  Section 1[14] (prohibition of emissions of dark smoke) shall apply in relation to vessels[15] in waters to which this section applies as it applies in relation to buildings.

(2)  In the application of section 1 to a vessel—

(*a*)  for the reference in subsection (1) of that section to the occupier of the building there shall be substituted a reference to the owner of, and to the master or other officer or person in charge of, the vessel;

(*b*)  references to a furnace shall be read as including references to an engine of the vessel; and

(*c*)  subsection (5) of that section shall be omitted;

---

[1] "Smoke" defined by s.64(1), p.372 below.
[2] "Fumes" defined by s.64 (1), p.371 below.
[3] The current fine at level 5 on the standard scale is £5,000: Criminal Justice Act 1991 (c.53), s.17 (England and Wales); Criminal Procedure (Scotland) Act 1995 (c.46), s.225 (Scotland).
[4] P.364 below.
[5] Part III of the 1990 Act, at p.187 above, relates to statutory nuisances.
[6] 1954 c.70.
[7] For transitional provisions see sch.5, para.10, p.379 below.

[8] P.336 above.
[9] "Practicable" defined by s.64(1), p.372 below.
[10] "Smoke" defined by s.64(1), p.372 below.
[11] "Chimney" defined by s.64(1), p.371 below.
[12] The current fine at level 5 on the standard scale is £5,000: Criminal Justice Act 1991 (c.53), s.17 (England and Wales); Criminal Procedure (Scotland) Act 1995 (c.46), s.225 (Scotland).
[13] P.364 below.
[14] P.336 above.
[15] "Vessel" defined by s.64(1), p.372 below.

and a person guilty of an offence under that section in relation to a vessel shall be liable on summary conviction to a fine not exceeding level 5 on the standard scale[1].

(3)  For the purposes of this Act a vessel in any waters to which this section applies which are not within the district of any local authority[2] shall be deemed to be within the district of the local authority whose district includes that point on land which is nearest to the spot where the vessel is.

(4)  The waters to which this section applies are—

(a)  all waters not navigable by sea-going ships; and

(b)  all waters navigable by sea-going ships which are within the seaward limits of the territorial waters of the United Kingdom and are contained within any port, harbour, river, estuary, haven, dock, canal or other place so long as a person or body of persons is empowered by or under any Act to make charges in respect of vessels entering it or using facilities in it.

(5)  In subsection (4) "charges" means any charges with the exception of light dues, local light dues and any other charges payable in respect of lighthouses, buoys or beacons and of charges in respect of pilotage.

(6)  Except as provided in this section, nothing in Parts I to III applies to smoke, grit or dust from any vessel.

*Exemption for purposes of investigations and research.*

**45.**  (1)  If the local authority[3] are satisfied, on the application of any person interested, that it is expedient to do so for the purpose of enabling investigations or research relevant to the problem of the pollution of the air to be carried out without rendering the applicant liable to proceedings brought under or by virtue of any of the provisions of this Act or the Environmental Protection Act 1990 mentioned below, the local authority may by notice in writing given to the applicant exempt, wholly or to a limited extent,—

(a)  any chimney[4] from the operation of sections 1[5] (dark smoke), 5[6] (grit and dust), 20[7] (smoke in smoke control area) and 43[8] (railway engines) of this Act and Part III of the Environmental Protection Act 1990[9] statutory nuisances);

(b)  any furnace boiler or industrial plant[10] from the operation of section 4 (2)[11] (new furnaces to be as far as practicable smokeless);

(c)  any premises[12] from the operation of section 2[13] (emissions of dark smoke);

(d)  any furnace from the operation of sections 6[14] or 8[15] (arrestment plant) and 10[16] (measurement of grit, dust and fumes by occupier), and

(e)  the acquisition or sale of any fuel specified in the notice from the operation of section 23[17] (acquisition and sale of unauthorised fuel in smoke control area),

in each case subject to such conditions, if any, and for such period as may be specified in the notice.

(2)  Any person who has applied to the local authority for an exemption under this section may, if he is dissatisfied with the decision of the authority on the application, appeal to the Secretary of State; and the Secretary of State may, if he thinks fit, by notice in writing given to the applicant and the local authority, give any exemption which the authority might have given or vary the terms of any exemption which they have given.

---

[1] The current fine at level 5 on the standard scale is £5,000: Criminal Justice Act 1991 (c. 53), s.17 (England and Wales); Criminal Procedure (Scotland) Act 1995 (c.46), s.225 (Scotland).
[2] "Local authority" defined by s.64(1), p.372 below.
[3] "Local authority" defined by s.64(1), p.372 below.
[4] "Chimney" defined by s.64(1), p.371 below.
[5] P.336 above.
[6] P.339 above.
[7] P.350 above.

[8] P.360 above.
[9] P.187 above.
[10] "Industrial plant" defined by s.64(1), p.372 below.
[11] P.338 above.
[12] "Premises" defined by s.64(1), p.372 below.
[13] P.337 above.
[14] P.339 above.
[15] P.341 above.
[16] P.341 above.
[17] P.348 above.

*Crown premises, etc.*

**46.** (1) It shall be part of the functions of the local authority[1], in cases where it seems to them proper to do so, to report to the responsible Minister any cases of—

(a) emissions of dark smoke[2] or of grit or dust, from any premises[3] which are under the control of any Government department and are occupied for the public service of the Crown or for any of the purposes of any Government department;

(b) emissions of smoke[4] whether dark smoke or not, from any such premises which are within a smoke control area;

(c) emissions of smoke, whether dark smoke or not, from any such premises which appear to them to constitute a nuisance to the inhabitants of the neighbourhood; or

(d) emissions of dark smoke from any vessel of Her Majesty's navy, or any Government ship[5] in the service of the Secretary of State while employed for the purposes of Her Majesty's navy, which appear to them to constitute a nuisance to the inhabitants of the neighbourhood,

and on receiving any such report the responsible Minister shall inquire into the circumstances and, if his inquiry reveals that there is cause for complaint, shall employ all practicable[6] means for preventing or minimising the emission of the smoke, grit or dust or for abating the nuisance and preventing a recurrence of it, as the case may be.

(2) Subsection (1) shall apply to premises occupied for the purposes of the Duchy of Lancaster or the Duchy of Cornwall as it applies to premises occupied for the public service of the Crown which are under the control of a Government department, with the substitution, in the case of the Duchy of Cornwall, for references to the responsible Minister of references to such person as the Duke of Cornwall or the possessor for the time being of the Duchy of Cornwall appoints.

(3) The fact that there subsists in any premises an interest belonging to Her Majesty in right of the Crown or of the Duchy of Lancaster, or to the Duchy of Cornwall, or belonging to a Government department or held in trust for Her Majesty for the purposes of a Government department, shall not affect the application of this Act to those premises so long as that interest is not the interest of the occupier of the premises, and this Act shall have effect accordingly in relation to the premises and that and all other interests in the premises.

(4) Section 44[7] (vessels) shall, with the omission of the reference in subsection (2) of that section to the owner, apply to vessels owned by the Crown, except that it shall not apply to vessels of Her Majesty's navy or to Government ships in the service of the Secretary of State while employed for the purposes of Her Majesty's navy.

(5) This Act (except Parts IV[8] and V[9]) shall have effect in relation to premises occupied for the service of a visiting force as if the premises were occupied for the public service of the Crown and were under the control of the Government department by arrangement with whom the premises are occupied.

(6) In this section—

"Government ship" has the same meaning as in the Merchant Shipping Act 1995[10]; and

"visiting force" means any such body, contingent or detachment of the forces of any country as is a visiting force for the purposes of any of the provisions of the Visiting Forces Act 1952[11].

---

[1] "Local authority" defined by s.64(1), p.372 below.
[2] "Dark smoke" has the meaning given by s.3(1), p.338 above: s.64(1) below.
[3] "Premises" defined by s.64(1), p.372 below.
[4] "Smoke" defined by s.64(1), p.372 below.
[5] "Government ship" defined by subsection (6) below.
[6] "Practicable" defined by s.64(1), p.372 below.
[7] P.360 above.

[8] P.352 above.
[9] P.355 above.
[10] 1995 c.21. Words "the Merchant Shipping Act 1995" substituted by the Merchant Shipping Act 1995, s.314, sch.13, para.94(a). This amendment came into force on 1 January 1996: s.316(2).
[11] 1952 c.67.

# PART VII: Miscellaneous and General

*Power to apply certain provisions to fumes and gases*

*Application to fumes and gases of certain provisions as to grit, dust and smoke.*

**47.** (1) The Secretary of State may by regulations—

    (*a*)  apply all or any of the provisions of sections 5[1], 6[2], 7[3], 42(4)[4] 43(5)[5], 44(6)[6] and 46(1) to fumes[7] or prescribed gases[8] or both as they apply to grit and dust;

    (*b*)  apply all or any of the provisions of section 4[9] to fumes or prescribed gases or both as they apply to smoke; and

    (*c*)  apply all or any of the provisions of section 11[10] to prescribed gases as they apply to grit and dust,

subject, in each case, to such exceptions and modifications as he thinks expedient.[11]

(2)  No regulations shall be made under this section unless a draft of the regulations has been laid before and approved by each House of Parliament.

(3)  In the application of any provision of this Act to prescribed gases by virtue of regulations under this section, any reference to the rate of emission of any substance shall be construed as a reference to the percentage by volume or by mass of the gas which may be emitted during a period specified in the regulations.

(4)  In this section—

"gas" includes vapour and moisture precipitated from vapour; and

"prescribed" means prescribed in regulations under this section.

---

*Power to give effect to international agreements*

**48.**  The Secretary of Sate may by regulations provide that any provision of Parts IV[12] and V[13], or of this Part (apart from this section) so far as relating to those Parts, shall have effect with such modifications as are prescribed in the regulations with a view to enabling the Government of the United Kingdom to give effect to any provision made by or under any international agreement to which the Government is for the time being a party.[14]

---

*Administration and enforcement*

*Unjustified disclosures of information.*

**49.** (1)  If a person discloses any information relating to any trade secret used in carrying on any particular undertaking which has been given to him or obtained by him by virtue of this Act, he shall, subject to subsection (2), be guilty of an offence and liable on summary conviction to a fine not exceeding level 5 on the standard scale[15].

(2)  A person shall not be guilty of an offence under subsection (1) by reason of the disclosure of any information if the disclosure is made—

    (*a*)  in the performance of his duty;

---

[1] P.339 above.
[2] P.339 above.
[3] P.340 above.
[4] P.360 above.
[5] P.360 above.
[6] P.361 above.
[7] "Fumes" defined by s.64(1), p.371 below.
[8] "Prescribed" and "gas" defined by subsection (4) below.
[9] P.338 above.
[10] P.342 above.

[11] A list of regulations made, or which have effect as if made, under this Act is at p.799 below.
[12] P.352 above.
[13] P.355 above.
[14] A list of regulations made, or which have effect as if made, under this Act is at p.799 below.
[15] The current fine at level 5 on the standard scale is £5,000: Criminal Justice Act 1991 (c.53), s.17 (England and Wales); Criminal Procedure (Scotland) Act 1995 (c.46), s.225 (Scotland).

(*b*)  in pursuance of section 34(1)(*b*)[1]; or

(*c*)  with the consent of a person having a right to disclose the information.

*Cumulative penalties on continuance of certain offences.*

**50.** (1)  Where

(*a*)  a person is convicted of an offence which is subject to cumulative penalties on continuance in accordance with this section; and

(*b*)  it is shown to the satisfaction of the court that the offence was substantially a repetition or continuation of an earlier offence by him after he had been convicted of the earlier offence,

the penalty provided by subsection (2) shall apply instead of the penalty otherwise specified for the offence.

(2)  Where this subsection applies the person convicted shall be liable on summary conviction to a fine not exceeding—

(*a*)  level 5 on the standard scale[2]; or

(*b*)  £50 for every day on which the earlier offence has been so repeated or continued by him within the three months next following his conviction of that offence,

whichever is the greater.

(3)  Where an offence is subject to cumulative penalties in accordance with this section—

(*a*)  the court by which a person is convicted of the original offence may fix a reasonable period from the date of conviction for compliance by the defendant with any directions given by the court; and

(*b*)  where a court has fixed such a period, the daily penalty referred to in subsection (2) is not recoverable in respect of any day before the end of that period.

*Duty to notify occupiers of offences.*

**51.** (1)  If, in the opinion of an authorised officer[3] of the local authority[4]—

(*a*)  an offence is being or has been committed under section 1[5], 2[6] or 20[7] (prohibition of certain emissions of smoke);

(*b*)  *Repealed by the Environment Act 1995 (c.25), s.120, sch.24. This amendment came into force on 1 April 1996: S.I. 1996/186.*

he shall, unless he has reason to believe that notice of it has already been given by or on behalf of the local authority, as soon as may be notify the appropriate person, and, if his notification is not in writing, shall before the end of the four days next following the day on which he became aware of the offence, confirm the notification in writing.

(2)  For the purposes of subsection (1), the appropriate person to notify is the occupier[8] of the premises[9], the person having possession of the boiler or plant, the owner of the railway locomotive engine or the owner or master or other officer or person in charge of the vessel concerned, as the case may be.

(3)  In any proceedings for an offence under section 1, 2 or 20 it shall be a defence to prove that the provisions of subsection (1) have not been complied with in the case of the offence; and if no such notification as is required by that subsection has been given before the end of the four days next following the day of the offence, that subsection shall be taken not to have been complied with unless the contrary is proved.

---

[1] P.355 above.
[2] The current fine at level 5 on the standard scale is £5,000: Criminal Justice Act 1991 (c.53), s.17 (England and Wales); Criminal Procedure (Scotland) Act 1995 (c.46), s.225 (Scotland).
[3] "Authorised officer" defined by s.64(1), p.371 below.
[4] "Local authority" defined by s.64(1), p.372 below.
[5] P.336 above.
[6] P.337 above.
[7] P.348 above.
[8] For "occupier" see s. 64(2), p.372 below.
[9] "Premises" defined by s.64(1), p.372 below.

*Offences committed by bodies corporate.*

**52.** (1) Where an offence under this Act which has been committed by a body corporate is proved to have been committed with the consent or connivance of, or to be attributable to any neglect on the part of, any director, manager, secretary or other similar officer of the body corporate or any person who was purporting to act in any such capacity, he as well as the body corporate shall be guilty of that offence and be liable to be proceeded against and punished accordingly.

(2) Where the affairs of a body corporate are managed by its members this section shall apply in relation to the acts and defaults of a member in connection with his functions of management as if he were a director of the body corporate.

*Offence due to act or default of another.*

**53.** (1) Where the commission by any person of an offence under this Act is due to the act or default of some other person, that other person shall be guilty of the offence.

(2) A person may be charged with and convicted of an offence by virtue of this section whether or not proceedings for the offence are taken against any other person.

*Power of county court to authorise works and order payments.*

**54.** (1) If works are reasonably necessary in or in connection with a building in order to enable the building to be used for some purpose without contravention of any of the provisions of this Act (apart from Parts IV[1] and V[2]), the occupier[3] of the building—

(a) may, if by reason of a restriction affecting his interest in the building he is unable to carry out the works without the consent of the owner[4] of the building or some other person interested in the building and is unable to obtain that consent, apply to the county court for an order to enable the works to be carried out by him; and

(b) may, if he considers that the whole or any proportion of the cost of carrying out the works should be borne by the owner of the building or some other person interested in the building, apply to the county court for an order directing the owner or other person to indemnify him, either wholly or in part, in respect of that cost;

and on an application under paragraph (a) or (b) the court may make such order as may appear to the court to be just.

(2) In the application of this section to Scotland for any reference to the county court there shall be substituted a reference to the sheriff.

*General provisions as to enforcement.*

**55.** (1) It shall be the duty of the local authority[5] to enforce—

(a) the provisions of Parts I to III[6], section 33[7] and Part VI[8]; and

(b) the provisions of this Part so far as relating to those provisions;

but nothing in this section shall be taken as extending to the enforcement of any building regulations[9].

(2) A local authority in England and Wales may institute proceedings for an offence under section 1[10] or 2[11] (prohibition of emissions of dark smoke) in the case of any smoke[12] which affects any part of their district notwithstanding, in the case of an offence under section 1, that the

[1] P.352 above.
[2] P.355 above.
[3] For "occupier" see s. 64(2), p.372 below.
[4] "Owner" defined by s.64(1), p.372 below.
[5] "Local authority" defined by s.64(1), p.372 below.
[6] Pp.336–352.
[7] P.354 above.
[8] P.359 above.
[9] "Building regulations" defined by s.64(1), p.371 below.
[10] P.336 above.
[11] P.337 above.
[12] "Smoke" defined by s.64(1), p.372 below.

smoke is emitted from a chimney[1] outside their district and, in the case of an offence under section 2, that the smoke is emitted from premises[2] outside their district.

(3) Nothing in this section shall be taken as authorising a local authority in Scotland to institute proceedings for an offence against this Act.

*Rights of entry and inspection etc.*

**56.** (1) Any person authorised in that behalf by a local authority[3] may at any reasonable time—

(a) enter upon any land or vessel[4] for the purpose of—

  (i) performing any function conferred on the authority or that person by virtue of this Act,

  (ii) determining whether, and if so in what manner, such a function should be performed, or

  (iii) determining whether any provision of this Act or of an instrument made under this Act is being complied with; and

(b) carry out such inspections, measurements and tests on the land or vessel or of any articles on it and take away such samples of the land or articles as he considers appropriate for such a purpose.

(2) Subsection (1) above does not, except in relation to work under section 24(1)[5] (adaptations to dwellings in smoke control area), apply in relation to a private dwelling[6].

(3) If it is shown to the satisfaction of a justice of the peace on sworn information in writing—

(a) that admission to any land or vessel which a person is entitled to enter in pursuance of subsection (1) has been refused to that person or that refusal is apprehended or that the land or vessel is unoccupied or that the occupier is temporarily absent or that the case is one of emergency[7] or that an application for admission would defeat the object of the entry; and

(b) that there is reasonable ground for entry upon the land or vessel for the purpose for which entry is required,

then, subject to subsection (4), the justice may by warrant under his hand authorise that person to enter the land or vessel, if need be by force.

(4) A justice of the peace shall not issue a warrant in pursuance of subsection (3) in respect of any land or vessel unless he is satisfied—

(a) that admission to the land or vessel in pursuance of subsection (1) was sought after not less than seven days notice of the intended entry had been served on the occupier[8]; or

(b) that admission to the land or vessel in pursuance of that subsection was sought in an emergency and was refused by or on behalf of the occupier; or

(c) that the land or vessel is unoccupied; or

(d) that an application for admission to the land or vessel would defeat the object of the entry.

(5) A warrant issued in pursuance of this section shall continue in force until the purpose for which the entry is required has been satisfied.

(6) In the application of this section to Scotland—

(a) any reference to a justice of the peace shall be construed as including a reference to the sheriff; and

(b) in subsection (3) for "on sworn information in writing" there is substituted "by evidence on oath".

---

[1] "Chimney" defined by s.64(1), p.371 below.
[2] "Premises" defined by s.64(1), p.372 below.
[3] "Local authority" defined by s.64(1), p.372 below.
[4] "Vessel" defined by s.64(1), p.372 below.
[5] P.349 above.
[6] "Private dwelling" defined by s.64(4), p.372 below.
[7] For "emergency" see s.57(7) below.
[8] For "occupier" see s.64(2), p.372 below.

*Provisions supplementary to section 56.*

**57.** (1) A person authorised to enter upon any land or vessel[1] in pursuance of section 56 shall, if so required, produce evidence of his authority before he enters upon the land or vessel.

(2) A person so authorised may take with him on to the land or vessel in question such other persons and such equipment as may be necessary.

(3) Admission to any land or vessel used for residential purposes and admission with heavy equipment to any other land or vessel shall not, except in an emergency[2] or in a case where the land or vessel is unoccupied, be demanded as of right in pursuance of section 56(1) unless notice of the intended entry has been served on the occupier[3] not less than seven days before the demand.

(4) A person who, in the exercise of powers conferred on him by virtue of section 56 or this section, enters upon any land or vessel which is unoccupied or of which the occupier is temporarily absent shall leave the land or vessel as effectually secured against unauthorised entry as he found it.

(5) It shall be the duty of a local authority[4] to make full compensation to any person who has sustained damage by reason of—

(*a*) the exercise by a person authorised by the authority of any of the powers conferred on the person so authorised by virtue of section 56 or this section; or

(*b*) the failure of a person so authorised to perform the duty imposed on him by subsection (4),

except where the damage is attributable to the default of the person who sustained it; and any dispute as to a person's entitlement to compensation in pursuance of this subsection or as to the amount of the compensation shall be determined by arbitration.

(6) A person who wilfully obstructs another person acting in the exercise of any powers conferred on the other person by virtue of section 56 or this section shall be guilty of an offence and liable on summary conviction to a fine not exceeding level 3 on the standard scale[5].

(7) In section 56 and this section any reference to an emergency is a reference to a case where a person requiring entry to any land or vessel has reasonable cause to believe that circumstances exist which are likely to endanger life or health and that immediate entry to the land or vessel is necessary to verify the existence of those circumstances or to ascertain their cause or to effect a remedy.

*Power of local authorities to obtain information.*

**58.** (1) A local authority[6] may serve on any person a notice requiring him to furnish to the authority, within a period or at times specified in the notice and in a form so specified, any information so specified which the authority reasonably considers that it needs for he purposes of any function conferred on the authority by Part IV[7] or V[8] of this Act (or by this Part of this Act so far as relating to those Parts).

(2) The Secretary of State may by regulations provide for restricting the information which may be required in pursuance of subsection (1) and for determining the form in which the information is to be so required.[9]

(3) Any person who—

(*a*) fails without reasonable excuse to comply with the requirements of a notice served on him in pursuance of this section; or

[1] "Vessel" defined by s.64(1), p.372 below.
[2] For "emergency" see subsection (7) below.
[3] For "occupier" see s. 64(2), p.372 below.
[4] "Local authority" defined by s.64(1), p.372 below.
[5] The current fine at level 3 on the standard scale is £1,000: Criminal Justice Act 1991 (c.53), s.17 (England and Wales); Criminal Procedure (Scotland) Act 1995 (c.46), s.225 (Scotland).
[6] "Local authority" defined by s.64(1), p.372 below.
[7] P.352 above.
[8] P.355 above.
[9] A list of regulations made, or which have effect as if made, under this Act is at p.799 below.

(*b*) in furnishing any information in compliance with such a notice, makes any statement which he knows to be false in a material particular or recklessly makes any statement which is false in a material particular,

shall be guilty of an offence and liable on summary conviction to a fine not exceeding level 5 on the standard scale[1].

*Inquiries[2].*

**59.** (1) The Secretary of State may cause an inquiry[3] to be held in any case in which he considers it appropriate for an inquiry[4] to be held either in connection with a provision of this Act or with a view to preventing or dealing with air pollution at any place.

(2) Subsections (2) to (5) of section 250 of the Local Government Act 1972[5] (which contains supplementary provisions with respect to local issues held in pursuance of that section) shall, without prejudice to the generality of subsection (1) of that section, apply to inquiries in England and Wales in pursuance of subsection (1) as they apply to inquiries in pursuance of that section.

(3) Subsections (2) to (8) of section 210 of the Local Government (Scotland) Act 1973[6] (local inquiries) shall, without prejudice to the generality of subsection (1) of that section, apply to inquiries in Scotland in pursuance of subsection (1) as they apply to inquiries held in pursuance of that section.

*Default powers.*

**60.** (1) If the Secretary of State is satisfied that any local authority[7] (in this section referred to as the "defaulting authority") have failed to perform any functions[8] which they ought to have performed, he may make an order—

(*a*) declaring the authority to be in default; and

(*b*) directing the authority to perform such of their functions as are specified in the order;

and he may specify the manner in which and the time or times within which those functions are to be performed by the authority.

(2) If the defaulting authority fails to comply with any direction contained in such an order, the Secretary of State may, instead of enforcing the order by mandamus, make an order transferring to himself such of the functions of the authority as he thinks fit.

(3) Where any functions of the defaulting authority are transferred in pursuance of subsection (2) above, the amount of any expenses which the Secretary of State certifies were incurred by him in performing those functions shall on demand be paid to him by the defaulting authority.

(4) Where any expenses are in pursuance of subsection (3) required to be paid by the defaulting authority in respect of any functions transferred in pursuance of this section—

(*a*) the expenses shall be defrayed by the authority in the like manner, and shall be debited to the like account, as if the functions had not been transferred and the expenses had been incurred by the authority in performing them; and

(*b*) the authority shall have the like powers for the purpose of raising any money required for the purpose of paragraph (*a*) as the authority would have had for the purpose of raising money required for defraying expenses incurred for the purposes of the functions in question.

(5) An order transferring any functions of the defaulting authority in pursuance of subsection (2) may provide for the transfer to the Secretary of State of such of the property, rights, liabilities and

[1] The current fine at level 5 on the standard scale is £5,000: Criminal Justice Act 1991 (c.53), s.17 (England and Wales); Criminal Procedure (Scotland) Act 1995 (c.46), s.225 (Scotland).

[2] Word "Inquiries" substituted by the Environment Act 1995 (c.25), s.120, sch.22, para.197.

[3] Words "an inquiry" substituted by the Environment Act 1995 (c.25), s.120, sch.22, para.197(a). This amendment

came into force on 1 April 1996: S.I. 1996/186.

[4] Words "an inquiry" substituted by the Environment Act 1995 (c.25), s.120, sch.22, para.197(b).

[5] 1972 c.70.

[6] 1973 c.65.

[7] "Local authority" defined by s.64(1), p.372 below.

[8] "Functions" defined by subsection (8) below.

obligations of the authority as he considers appropriate; and where such an order is revoked the Secretary of State may, by the revoking order or a subsequent order, make such provision as he considers appropriate with respect to any property, rights, liabilities and obligations held by him for the purposes of the transferred functions.

(6)  An order made under this section may be varied or revoked by a subsequent order so made.

(7)  This section does not apply to a failure by a local authority—

(a)  to discharge their functions under section 18[1] (declaration of smoke control areas);

(b)  to submit proposals to [*England and Wales*: the Secretary of State *Scotland*: SEPA[2]] in pursuance of a direction under subsection (1) of section 19[3] ([*England and Wales*: Secretary of State's *Scotland*: SEPA's[4]] power to require creation of smoke control area); or

(c)  to perform a duty imposed on them by or by virtue of subsection (4) or (6) of that section.

(8)  In this section "functions", in relation to an authority, means functions conferred on the authority by virtue of this Act.

........................................................................................................................................................................

*Joint exercise of local authority functions.*

**61.** (1)  Sections 6, 7, 9 and 10 of the Public Health Act 1936[5] (provisions relating to joint boards) shall, so far as applicable, have effect in relation to this Act as if the provisions of this Act were provisions of that Act.

(2)  Section 172 of the Public Health (Scotland) Act 1897[6] (constitution of port health authorities) shall have effect as if the provisions of this Act were provisions of that Act.

(3)  Without prejudice to subsections (1) and (2), any two or more local authorities[7] may combine for the purpose of declaring an area to be a smoke control area and in that event—

(a)  the smoke control area may be the whole of the districts of those authorities or any part of those districts;

(b)  the references in section 18[8], Schedule 1[9] and paragraph 1 of Schedule 2[10] to the local authority shall be read as references to the local authorities acting jointly;

(c)  the reference in paragraph 1 of Schedule 1 to a place in the district of the local authority shall be construed as a reference to a place in each of the districts of the local authorities;

but, except as provided in this subsection, references in this Act to the local authority shall, in relation to a building or dwelling, or to a boiler or industrial plant[11], in the smoke control area, be read as references to that one of the local authorities within whose district the building, dwelling, boiler or plant is situated.

(4)  For the avoidance of doubt it is hereby declared that where a port health authority[12] or joint board has functions, rights or liabilities under this Act—

(a)  any reference in this Act to a local authority or its district includes, in relation to those functions, rights or liabilities, a reference to the port health authority or board or its district;

(b)  for the purposes of this Act, no part of the district of any such port health authority or board is to be treated, in relation to any matter falling within the competence of the authority or board, as forming part of the district of any other authority.

(5)  Any premises[13] which extend into the districts of two or more authorities shall be treated for the purposes of this Act as being wholly within such one of those districts—

---

[1]  P.346 above.
[2]  SEPA, the Scottish Environment Protection Agency, is established by the Environment Act 1995 (c.25), s.20, p.000 below. *Scotland*: word "SEPA" substituted by the Environment Act 1995 (c.25), s.120, sch.22, para.198. This amendment came into force on 1 April 1996: S.I. 1996/186.
[3]  P.347 above.
[4]  *Scotland*: word "SEPA's" substituted by the Environment Act 1995 (c.25), s.120, sch.22, para.198.

[5]  1936 c.49.
[6]  1897 c.38.
[7]  "Local authority" defined by s.64(1), p.372 below.
[8]  P.346 above.
[9]  P.374 below.
[10]  P.374 below.
[11]  "Industrial plant" defined by s.64(1), p.372 below.
[12]  "Port health authority" defined by s.64(1), p.372 below.
[13]  Premises" defined by s.64(1), p.372 below.

(a)  in England and Wales, as may from time to time be agreed by those authorities; or

(b)  in Scotland, as may from time to time be so agreed or, in default of agreement, determined by the Secretary of State.

*Application of certain provisions of Part XII of Public Health Act 1936 and corresponding Scottish legislation.*

62.  (1)  In the application of this Act to England and Wales, the following provisions of Part XII of the Public Health Act 1936[1] shall have effect in relation to the provisions of this Act (apart from Parts IV and V) as if those provisions were provisions of that Act—

section 275 (power of local authority to execute works);

section 276 (power of local authority to sell materials);

section 278 (compensation to individuals for damage resulting from exercise of powers under Act);

section 283 (form of notices);

section 284 (authentication of documents);

section 285 (service of notices);

section 289 (power to require occupier to permit works to be executed by owner);

section 291 (expenses to be a charge on the premises);

section 293 (recovery of expenses);

section 294 (limitation of liability of certain owners);

[2]

section 305 (protection of members and officers of local authorities from personal liability).

(2)  In the application of this Act to Scotland—

(a)  the following enactments shall have effect in relation to the provisions of this Act (apart from Parts IV and V) as if those provisions were provisions of the Act in which that enactment is comprised—

(i)  in the Public Health (Scotland) Act 1897[3], section 161 (joint owners) and section 164 (compensation),and

(ii)  in the Housing (Scotland) Act 1987[4], section 131 and Schedule 9 (charging orders), section 319 (penalty for preventing execution of works), section 325 (furnishing information for service of documents), section 329 (default powers), section 330 (form of notices) and section 336 (limitation on liability of trustee);

(b)  for the purposes of the application of section 329 of the Housing (Scotland) Act 1987 by virtue of paragraph (a) above, subsections (1) and (3) of section 196 of the Housing (Scotland) Act 1966[5] shall apply to section 329 as they originally applied to the provisions which it re-enacted;

(c)  section 109 of the Housing (Scotland) Act 1987 (recovery by local authority of expenses) shall have effect as if the reference to section 108(3) of that Act included a reference to paragraph 1 of Schedule 2 to this Act[6]; and

(d)  section 319 of that Act (penalty for preventing execution of works) shall have effect as if subsection (1) of that section included a reference to this Act (apart from Parts IV and V) and as if sub-paragraphs (b) and (c) were omitted.

[1] 1936 c.49.
[2] Former entry relating to s.299 of the Public Health Act 1936 repealed by the Statute Law (Repeals) Act 1993 (c.50), s.1, sch.1, pt.I, group 4. This amendment came into force on 5 November 1993, the date of the Royal Assent.
[3] 1897 c.38.
[4] 1987 c.26.
[5] 1966 c.49.
[6] P.374 below.

*General*

*Regulations and orders.*

**63.** (1) Any power of the Secretary of State under this Act to make an order or regulations—

(a)  includes power to make different provision in the order or regulations for different circumstances;

(b)  includes power to make such incidental, supplemental and transitional provision as the Secretary of State considers appropriate; and

(c)  is exercisable by statutory instrument except in the case of the powers conferred by [*England and Wales*: sections 19(4)[1] and *Scotland*: section[2]] 60[3] and paragraph 3 of Schedule 3[4].[5]

(2)  Any statutory instrument containing regulations made under this Act, except an instrument containing regulations a draft of which is required by section 6(3)[6], 10(5)[7] or 47(2)[8] to be approved by a resolution of each House of Parliament, shall be subject to annulment in pursuance of a resolution of either House of Parliament.

(3)  Any statutory instrument containing an order under section 21[9] or 22[10] shall be subject to annulment in pursuance of a resolution of either House of Parliament.

*General provisions as to interpretation.*

**64.** (1)  In this Act, except so far as the context otherwise requires,—

"authorised officer" means any officer of a local authority authorised by them in writing, either generally or specially, to act in matters of any specified kind or in any specified matter;

"building regulations" means, as respects Scotland, any statutory enactments, byelaws, rules and regulations or other provisions under whatever authority made, relating to the construction, alteration or extension of buildings;

"caravan" means a caravan within the meaning of Part I of the Caravan Sites and Control of Development Act 1960[11], disregarding the amendment made by section 13(2) of the Caravan Sites Act 1968[12], which usually and for the time being is situated on a caravan site within the meaning of that Act;

"chimney" includes structures and openings of any kind from or through which smoke, grit, dust or fumes may be emitted, and, in particular, includes flues, and references to a chimney of a building include references to a chimney which serves the whole or a part of a building but is structurally separate from the building;

"dark smoke" has the meaning given by section 3(1);

"day" means a period of twenty-four hours beginning at midnight;

"domestic furnace" means any furnace which is—

(a)  designed solely or mainly for domestic purposes, and

(b)  used for heating a boiler with a maximum heating capacity of less than 16.12 kilowatts;

"fireplace" includes any furnace, grate or stove, whether open or closed;

"fixed boiler or industrial plant" means any boiler or industrial plant which is attached to a building or is for the time being fixed to or installed on any land;

"fumes" means any airborne solid matter smaller than dust;

[1] P.347 above.
[2] *Scotland*: word "section" substituted by the Environment Act 1995 (c.25), s.120, sch.22, para.199. This amendment came into force on 1 April 1996: S.I. 1996/186.
[3] P.368 above.
[4] P.377 below.
[5] A list of regulations made, or which have effect as if made, under this Act is at p.799 below; a list of orders made, or which have effect as if made, under section 21 of this Act

is at p.800 below
[6] P.340 above.
[7] P.342 above.
[8] P.363 above.
[9] P.348 above.
[10] P.348 above.
[11] 1960 c.62.
[12] 1968 c.52.

"industrial plant" includes any still, melting pot or other plant used for any industrial or trade purposes, and also any incinerator used for or in connection with any such purposes;

"local authority" means—

(a) in England[1], the council of a district or a London borough, the Common Council of the City of London, the Sub-Treasurer of the Inner Temple and the Under Treasurer of the Middle Temple; and

(aa) in Wales, the council of a county or county borough;[2] and

(b) in Scotland, a council constituted under section 2 of the Local Government etc. (Scotland) Act 1994[3].

"owner", in relation to premises—

(a) as respects England and Wales, means the person for the time being receiving the rackrent of the premises, whether on his own account or as agent or trustee for another person, or who would so receive the rackrent if the premises were let at a rackrent; and

(b) as respects Scotland, means the person for the time being entitled to receive or who would, if the premises were let, be entitled to receive, the rents of the premises and includes a trustee, factor, tutor or curator and, in the case of public or municipal property, includes the persons to whom the management of the property is entrusted;

"port health authority" means, as respects Scotland, a port local authority constituted, under Part X of the Public Health (Scotland) Act 1897[4] and includes a reference to a joint port health authority constituted under that Part;

"practicable" means reasonably practicable having regard, amongst other things, to local conditions and circumstances, to the financial implications and to the current state of technical knowledge, and "practicable means" includes the provision and maintenance of plant and its proper use;

"premises" includes land;

"smoke", includes soot, ash, grit and gritty particles emitted in smoke; and

"vessel" has the same meaning as "ship" in the Merchant Shipping Act 1995[5].

(2) Any reference in this Act to the occupier of a building shall, in relation to any building different parts of which are occupied by different persons, be read as a reference to the occupier or other person in control of the part of the building in which the relevant fireplace is situated.

(3) In this Act any reference to the rate of emission of any substance or any reference which is to be understood as such a reference shall, in relation to any regulations or conditions, be construed as a reference to the quantities of that substance which may be emitted during a period specified in the regulations or conditions.

(4) In this Act, except so far as the context otherwise requires, "private dwelling" means any building or part of a building used or intended to be used as such, and a building or part of a building is not to be taken for the purposes of this Act to be used or intended to be used otherwise than as a private dwelling by reason that a person who resides or is to reside in it is or is to be required or permitted to reside in it in consequence of his employment or of holding an office.

(5) In considering for the purposes of this Act whether any and, if so, what works are reasonably necessary in order to make suitable provision for heating and cooking in the case of a dwelling or are reasonably necessary in order to enable a building to be used for a purpose without contravention of any of the provisions of this Act, regard shall be had to any difficulty there may be in

---

[1] Former words "and Wales" repealed by the Local Government (Wales) Act 1994 (c.19), s.22(3), sch.9, para.18, s.66(8), sch.18. This amendment came into force on 1 April 1996: S.I. 1996/396.

[2] Para.(aa) inserted by the Local Government (Wales) Act 1994 (c.19), s.22(3), sch.9, para.18.

[3] 1994 c.39. Words "a council constituted under section 2 of the Local Government etc. (Scotland) Act 1994" substi-

tuted by the Local Government etc. (Scotland) Act 1994 (c.39), s.180(1), sch.13, para.180. This amendment came into force on 1 April 1996: S.I. 1996/323.

[4] 1897 c.38.

[5] 1995 c.21. Words " 'ship' in the Merchant Shipping Act 1995" substituted by the Merchant Shipping Act 1995 (c.21), s.314, sch.13, para.94(b). This amendment came into force on 1 January 1996: s.316(2).

obtaining, or in obtaining otherwise than at a high price, any fuels which would have to be used but for the execution of the works.

(6) Any furnaces which are in the occupation of the same person and are served by a single chimney shall, for the purposes of sections 5 to 12[1], 14 and 15[2], be taken to be one furnace.

*Application to Isles of Scilly.*

**65.** Parts IV[3] and V[4], and this Part so far as relating to those Parts, shall have effect in their application to the Isles of Scilly with such modifications as the Secretary of State may by order specify.

*Transitory provisions relating to Alkali, &c. Works Regulation Act 1906.*

**66.** (1) Until the coming into force of the repeal by the Environmental Protection Act 1990 of the Alkali, &c. Works Regulation Act 1906[5]—

(a)  Part I of Schedule 3[6] shall have effect;

(b)  this Act shall have effect subject to the modifications in Part II of that Schedule; and

(c)  the Alkali, &c. Works Regulation Act 1906 shall continue to have effect as amended by Schedule 2 to the Clean Air Act 1956[7] notwithstanding the repeal by this Act of the last-mentioned Act.

(2) On the coming into force of the repeal by the Environmental Protection Act 1990 of the Alkali, &c. Works Regulation Act 1906, this section and Schedule 3 shall cease to have effect.[8]

*Consequential amendments, transitional provisions and repeals.*

**67.** (1) The enactments specified in Schedule 4 shall have effect subject to the amendments set out in that Schedule, being amendments consequential on the preceding provisions of this Act.

(2) The transitional provisions and savings contained in Schedule 5[9] (which include provisions preserving the effect of transitional or saving provisions in enactments repealed by this Act) shall have effect.

(3) The enactments specified in Schedule 6 (which include spent enactments) are repealed to the extent specified in the third column of that Schedule.

*Short title, commencement and extent.*

**68.** (1) This Act may be cited as the Clean Air Act 1993.

(2) This Act shall come into force at the end of the period of three months beginning with the day on which it is passed[10].

(3) The following provisions of this Act (apart from this section) extend to Northern Ireland—

(a)  section 30;

(b)  section 32 so far as it relates to regulations under section 30; and

(c)  section 67(3) and Schedule 6, so far as they relate to the repeal of sections 75 and 77 of the Control of Pollution Act 1974;

but otherwise this Act does not extend to Northern Ireland.

[1]  Pp.339–343 above.
[2]  Pp.343–345 above.
[3]  P.352 above.
[4]  P.355 above.
[5]  1906 c.14.
[6]  P.376 below.
[7]  1956 c.52.
[8]  1906 c. 14.
[9]  P.378 below.
[10]  This Act accordingly came into force on 27 August 1993.

# SCHEDULES

# SCHEDULE 1

(Section 18(4)[1].)

## COMING INTO OPERATION OF SMOKE CONTROL ORDERS

1. Before making a smoke control order[2] the local authority[3] shall publish in the London Gazette and once at least in each of two successive weeks in some newspaper circulating in the area to which the order will relate a notice—

    (a) stating that the local authority propose to make the order, and its general effect;

    (b) specifying a place in the district of the local authority where a copy of the order and of any map or plan referred to in it may be inspected by any person free of charge at all reasonable times during a period of not less than six weeks from the date of the last publication of the notice; and

    (c) stating that within that period any person who will be affected by the order may by notice in writing to the local authority object to the making of the order.

2. Besides publishing such a notice, the local authority shall post, and keep posted throughout the period mentioned in paragraph 1(b), copies of the notice in such number of conspicuous places within the area to which the order will relate as appear to them necessary for the purpose of bringing the proposal to make the order to the notice of persons who will be affected.

3. If an objection is duly made to the local authority within the period mentioned in paragraph 1(b), and is not withdrawn, the local authority shall not make the order without first considering the objection.

4. Subject to paragraphs 5 and 6, an order shall come into operation on such date not less than six months after it is made as may be specified in it.

5. An order varying a previous order so as to exempt specified buildings or classes of building or specified fireplaces[4] or classes of fireplace from the operation of section 20[5] ( prohibition of smoke emissions in smoke control area) may come into operation on, or at any time after, the date on which it is made.

6. If, before the date on which the order is to come into operation, the local authority—

    (a) pass a resolution postponing its coming into operation; and

    (b) publish a notice stating the effect of the resolution in the London Gazette and once at least in each of two successive weeks in some newspaper circulating in the area to which the order will relate,

    the order shall, unless its coming into operation is again postponed under this paragraph, come into operation on the date specified in the resolution.

7. In the application of this Schedule to Scotland, for any reference to the London Gazette there shall be substituted a reference to the Edinburgh Gazette.

# SCHEDULE 2

(Section 25(1)[6].)

## SMOKE CONTROL ORDERS: EXPENDITURE ON OLD PRIVATE DWELLINGS

### Grants for expenditure incurred in adaptation of fireplaces

1. (1) This paragraph applies if, after the making[7] of a smoke control order[8] by a local authority[9], the owner[10] or occupier of, or any person interested in, an old private dwelling[11] which is or will be within a smoke control area as a result of the order incurs relevant expenditure.

---

[1] P.346 above.
[2] "Smoke control order" means an order made by a local authority under s.18, p.346 above: s.29 above.
[3] "Local authority" defined by s.64(1), p.372 above.
[4] "Fireplace" defined by s.64(1), p.371 above.
[5] P.348 above.
[6] P.350 above.
[7] For transitional provisions see sch.5, para.8(3), p.379 below.
[8] "Smoke control order" means an order made by a local authority under s.18, p.346 above: s.29 above.
[9] "Local authority" defined by s.64(1), p.372 above.
[10] "Owner" defined by s.64(1), p.372 above.
[11] "Old private dwelling" has the meaning given in s.25, p.350 above: s.29, p.352 above.

(2)  For the purposes of this paragraph "relevant expenditure" is expenditure on adaptations in or in connection with an old private dwelling to avoid contraventions of section 20[1] (prohibition of smoke emissions in smoke control area) which—

(a)  is incurred before the coming into operation of the order and with the approval of the local authority given for the purposes of this paragraph; or

(b)  is reasonably incurred in carrying out adaptations required by a notice given under section 24(1)[2] (power of local authority to require certain adaptations).

(3)  If the adaptations in question are carried out to the satisfaction of the local authority, the local authority—

(a)  shall repay to him seven-tenths of the relevant expenditure; and

(b)  may, if they think fit, also repay to him the whole or any part of the remainder of that expenditure.

(4)  Where relevant expenditure is incurred by the occupier of a private dwelling[3] who is not an owner of the dwelling and the adaptations in question consist of or include the provision of any cooking or heating[4] appliance which can be readily removed from the dwelling without injury to itself or the fabric of the dwelling, the following provisions shall have effect as respects so much of the expenditure as represents the cost of the appliance, that is to say—

(a)  not more than seven-twentieths of that part of that expenditure shall be repaid until two years from the coming into operation of the order; and

(b)  any further repayment of that part of that expenditure shall be made only if the appliance has not by then been removed from the dwelling and, if made, shall be made to the person who is the occupier of the dwelling at the end of the two years.

(5)  The approval of a local authority to the incurring of expenditure may be given for the purposes of this paragraph, if the authority think fit in the circumstances of any particular case, after the expenditure has been incurred.

(6)  This paragraph has effect subject to paragraph 4.

*Exclusion of grants in case of unsuitable appliances*

2.  For the purposes of this Schedule, an appliance is unsuitable for installation in any area or (as the case may be) in any district or part of Great Britain if it tends, by reason of its consumption of fuel (of whatever kind) or its consumption of fuel at times when it is generally used, to impose undue strain on the fuel resources available for that area, district or part.

3.  (1)  Sub-paragraph (2) applies if—

(a)  after a local authority[5] have resolved to make a smoke control order[6] declaring a smoke control area (not being an order varying a previous order so made); and

(b)  before notice of the making of the order is first published in accordance with Schedule 1[7],

the authority pass a resolution designating any class of heating[8] appliance as being, in their opinion, unsuitable for installation in that area.

(2)  No payment shall be made by the authority under paragraph 1 in respect of expenditure incurred in providing, or in executing works for the purpose of the installation of, any heating appliance of the class designated by the resolution in or in connection with a dwelling within the area to which the order relates.

(3)  No payment shall be made under paragraph 1 by a local authority in respect of expenditure incurred in providing, or in executing works for the purpose of the installation of, any heating appliance which, when the expenditure was incurred, fell within any class of appliance for the time being designated for the purposes of this paragraph by the Secretary of State as being in his opinion—

(a)  unsuitable for installation in the district of that authority; or

(b)  generally unsuitable for installation in the part of Great Britain with which the Secretary of State is concerned,

---

[1] P.348 above. For "adaptations . . . section 20" see s.27, p.351 above.
[2] P.349 above.
[3] "Private dwelling" defined by s.64(4), p.372 above.
[4] "Heating" defined by s.29, p.352 above.
[5] "Local authority" defined by s.64(1), p.372 above.
[6] "Smoke control order" means an order made by a local authority under s.18, p.346 above: s.29 above.
[7] P.374 above.
[8] "Heating" defined by s.29, p.352 above.

unless the approval of the local authority in respect of that expenditure was given for the purposes of paragraph 1 at a time when the appliance in question did not fall within any class of appliance so designated.

(4) Retrospective approval of expenditure may only be given by a local authority by virtue of paragraph 1(5) in the case of expenditure incurred in providing, or in executing works[1] for the purpose of the installation of, a heating appliance, if the appliance—

(a) did not at the time when the expenditure was incurred; and

(b) does not when the approval is given,

fall within a class of appliance for the time being designated by the Secretary of State for the purposes of this paragraph as regards the district of that authority or generally.

(5) In accordance with the preceding provisions of this Schedule, expenditure within sub-paragraph (3) or (4) shall be left out of account for the purposes of paragraph 1.

*Exchequer contributions to certain expenditure*

4. (1) The Secretary of State may, out of money provided by Parliament, make a contribution towards the following expenses, of any local authority[2] (if approved by him), that is to say—

(a) any expenses of the local authority in making payments under paragraph 1;

(b) any expenses incurred by them in making, in or in connection with old private dwellings[3] owned by them or under their control, adaptations to avoid contraventions of section 20[4]; and

(c) any expenses incurred by them in carrying out adaptations required by notices under section 24[5] or in connection with old private dwellings.

(2) A contribution under this paragraph in respect of any expenses shall be a single payment equal—

(a) in the case of expenses mentioned in sub-paragraph (1)(a), to four-sevenths of the amount of the expenses;

(b) in the case of expenses mentioned in sub-paragraph (1)(b), to two-fifths of the amount of the expenses; and

(c) in the case of expenses mentioned in sub-paragraph (1)(c), to four-sevenths of the amount arrived at by deducting the recoverable amount from the amount of those expenses.

(3) In sub-paragraph (2)(c), "the recoverable amount" means, in relation to any expenses, the fraction of those expenses (whether three-tenths or some smaller fraction determined by the local authority, in the case of those expenses, under section 24(2) or (3)) which the local authority have power to recover from the occupier or owner by virtue of section 24(2) or (3).

# SCHEDULE 3

(Section 66(1)[6].)

PROVISIONS HAVING EFFECT UNTIL REPEAL OF ALKALI, &C. WORKS REGULATION ACT 1906

PART I: RELATION OF THIS ACT TO ALKALI, &C. WORKS REGULATION ACT 1906

1. (1) In this Part of this Schedule—

"the Alkali Act" means the Alkali, &c. Works Regulation Act 1906[7]; and

"work subject or potentially subject to the Alkali Act" means—

(a) so much of any work registered under section 9 of that Act as is directly concerned in the processes which necessitate its registration under that section; and

(b) so much of any work in the course of erection or alteration as will on completion of the erection or alteration be directly concerned in such processes.

[1] For "expenses incurred in the execution of works" see s.28, p.351 above.
[2] "Local authority" defined by s.64(1), p.372 above.
[3] "Old private dwelling" has the meaning given in s.25, p.350 above: s.29, p.352 above.
[4] P.348 above. For "adaptations . . . section 20" see s.27, p.351 above.
[5] P.349 above.
[6] P.373 above.
[7] 1906 c.14.

(2)  The Secretary of State may from time to time determine how much of any work mentioned in sub-paragraph (1) is or will be directly concerned as there mentioned and his determination shall, until revoked or varied by him, be conclusive.

2.  Subject to paragraphs 3 and 4, Parts I to III[1] of this Act shall not apply to any work subject or potentially subject to the Alkali Act.

3.  If, on the application of the local authority[2], the Secretary of State is satisfied that in all the circumstances it is expedient to do so, he may by order exclude the application of paragraph 2 to the whole or any specified part of any work subject or potentially subject to the Alkali Act.

4.  While, by virtue of an order under paragraph 3 above, paragraph 2 is excluded from applying to any work or to any specified part of any work—

(a)  in any proceedings ,brought under section 1[3], 2[4] or 20[5] in respect of the emission of smoke[6] from the work or (as the case may be) from the specified part of the work it shall be a defence to prove that the best practicable[7] means had been employed to prevent or minimise the alleged emission;

(b)  *Repealed by the Environment Act 1995 (c.25), s.120, sch.24. This amendment came into force on 1 April 1996: S.I. 1996/186.*

5.  Any order made under paragraph 3 may be varied or revoked by a subsequent order of the Secretary of State.

6.  Nothing in section 55[8] shall be taken as extending to the enforcement of any of the provisions of the Alkali Act.

## PART II: MODIFICATIONS OF THIS ACT

7.  In section 31(4)[9]—

(a)  in paragraph (a), after "1990" there is inserted "or a work subject to the Alkali Act"; and

(b)  for paragraph (b) there is substituted—

"(b)  of the inspectors appointed under Part I of the Environmental Protection Act 1990 or, as the case may be, under the Alkali Act, to enforce those provisions in relation to such furnaces;".

8.  In section 35(3)[10], after "1990" there is inserted "or the place at which he does so is a work registered in pursuance of section 9 of the Alkali, &c. Works Regulation Act 1906".

9.  In section 35(3)[11], after "1990" there is inserted "or any work subject to the Alkali Act".

10.  In section 36, after subsection (3) there is inserted—

"(3A)  If the notice relates to a work subject to the Alkali Act, the person on whom the notice is served shall not be obliged to supply any information which, as certified by an inspector appointed under that Act, is not of a kind which is being supplied to the inspector for the purposes of that Act."

11.  At the end of section 40[12] there is inserted—

"and 'the Alkali Act' means the Alkali, &c. Works Regulation Act 1906[13] and 'a work subject to the Alkali Act' means a work registered under section 9 of the Alkali Act, excluding the whole or part of such a work while the work or part is the subject of an order made or treated as made under paragraph 3 of Schedule 3 to this Act."

[1]  Pp.336–352 above.
[2]  "Local authority" defined by s.64(1), p.372 above.
[3]  P.336 above.
[4]  P.337 above.
[5]  P.348 above.
[6]  "Smoke" defined by s.64(1), p.372 above.
[7]  "Practicable" and "practicable means" defined by s.64(1), p.372 above.
[8]  P.365 above.
[9]  P.354 above.
[10]  P.356 above.
[11]  P.356 above.
[12]  P.359 above.
[13]  1906 c.14.

# SCHEDULE 5

(Section 67(2)[1].)

TRANSITIONAL PROVISIONS

## PART I: GENERAL TRANSITIONAL PROVISIONS AND SAVINGS

### Continuity of the law

1. The substitution of this Act for the enactments repealed by this Act does not affect the continuity of the law.

2. Any reference, whether express or implied, in this Act or any other enactment, instrument or document to a provision of this Act shall so far as the context permits, be construed as including, in relation to the times, circumstances and purposes in relation to which the corresponding provision of the enactments repealed by this Act has effect, a reference to that corresponding provision.

3. Any document made, served or issued after the commencement of this Act which contains a reference to any of the enactments repealed by this Act shall be construed, except so far as a contrary intention appears, as referring or, as the case may require, including a reference to the corresponding provision of this Act.

4. Paragraphs 2 and 3 have effect without prejudice to the operation of sections 16 and 17 of the Interpretation Act 1978[2] (which relate to the effect of repeals).

### General saving for old transitional provisions and savings

5. (1) The repeal by this Act of a transitional provision or saving relating to the coming into force of a provision reproduced in this Act does not affect the operation of the transitional provision or saving, in so far as it is not specifically reproduced in this Act but remains capable of having effect in relation to the corresponding provision of this Act.

(2) The repeal by this Act of an enactment previously repealed subject to savings does not affect the continued operation of those savings.

(3) The repeal by this Act of a saving on the previous repeal of an enactment does not affect the operation of the saving in so far as it is not specifically reproduced in this Act but remains capable of having effect.

## PART II: EXCLUSION AND MODIFICATION OF CERTAIN PROVISIONS OF THIS ACT

### Requirements to fit arrestment plan: sections 6 & 8

6. (1) Section 6(1)[3] (arrestment plant for new non-domestic furnaces) does not apply to a furnace which was installed, the installation of which began or an agreement for the purchase or installation of which was entered into before 1st October 1969 (which was the day appointed for the coming into force of the enactments replaced by section 6).

(2) Subject to sub-paragraph (3), section 8(1)[4] (arrestment plant for furnaces burning solid fuel in other cases) applies in relation to a furnace to which, by virtue of sub-paragraph (1), section 6 does not apply as it applies to a domestic furnace.

(3) Section 8(1) does not apply to a furnace which was installed, the installation of which began or an agreement for the purchase or installation of which was entered into—

(a) in relation to a furnace in England and Wales, before 1st June 1958 (which was the day appointed as respects England and Wales for the coming into force of the enactments replaced by section 8); and

(b) in relation to a furnace in Scotland, before 15th November 1958 (which was the day so appointed as respects Scotland).

---

[1] P.373 above.
[2] 1978 c.30.
[3] P.339 above.
[4] P.341 above.

## Height of chimneys for furnaces: section 14

**7.** (1) Subject to sub-paragraph (2) below, section 14[1] (height of chimneys for furnaces) does not apply to any furnace served by a chimney[2] the construction of which was begun or the plans for which were passed before 1st April 1969 (which was the day appointed for the coming into force of the enactments replaced by section 14).

(2) Notwithstanding sub-paragraph (1), section 14 does apply to—

(a) any furnace the combustion space of which has been increased on or after 1st April 1969; or

(b) any furnace the installation of which was begun on or after that day and which replaces a furnace which had a smaller combustion space.

## Smoke control orders

**8.** (1) In relation to any smoke control order made by a local authority under section 18 of this Act[3] which revokes or varies an order made under section 11 of the Clean Air Act 1956[4] before 13th November 1980 (which was the date of the passing of the Local Government, Planning and Land Act 1980[5], which amended section 11 of that Act to omit the requirement that an order made by a local authority should be confirmed by the Secretary of State) the provisions of this Act mentioned in the following provisions of this paragraph shall have effect subject to the modifications there mentioned.

(2) In section 18—

(a) in subsection (1) after the word "order" where it first appears there shall be inserted the words "confirmed by the Secretary of State";

(b) in subsection (3), after the word "order" where it first appears there shall be inserted the words "confirmed by the Secretary of State" and at the end there shall be inserted the words "so confirmed"; and

(c) in subsection (4), after the words "to the" there shall be inserted the words "confirmation and".

(3) In section 26(1)[6] and paragraph 1(1) of Schedule 2[7], for the word "making" there shall be substituted the word "confirmation".

**9.** The provisions of Part III of this Schedule (which are derived from Schedule 1 to the Clean Air Act 1956 as that Schedule had effect immediately before the date mentioned in paragraph 8(1) of this Schedule) shall apply in substitution for Schedule 1 to this Act in relation to any such order; and references in this Act, as it applies in relation to any such order, to Schedule 1 to this Act or to any specified provision of that Schedule shall be read as referring to Part III of this Schedule or the corresponding provision of that Part (as the case may be).

## Colliery spoilbanks: section 42

**10.** Subsections (2) to (4) of section 42[8] (colliery spoilbanks) shall not apply to any deposit of refuse deposited from a mine or quarry before 5th July 1956 (the date of the passing of the Clean Air Act 1956) if at that date the deposit was not longer in use as such and was not under the control of the owner of the mine or quarry.

## PART III: CONFIRMATION AND COMING INTO OPERATION OF CERTAIN SMOKE CONTROL ORDERS

**11.** In this Part of this Schedule "order" means a smoke control order.

**12.** After making an order, the local authority[9] shall publish in the London Gazette and also once at least in each of two successive weeks in some newspaper circulating in the area to which the order relates a notice—

(a) stating that the order has been made and its general effect;

(b) specifying a place in the district of the local authority where a copy of the order and of any map or plan referred to in the order may be inspected by any person free of charge at all reasonable times during a period of not less than six weeks from the date of the last publication of the notice; and

(c) stating that within that period any person who will be affected by the order may by notice in writing to the Secretary of State object to the confirmation of the order.

[1] P.343 above.
[2] "Chimney" defined by s.64(1), p.371 above.
[3] P.346 above.
[4] 1956 c.52.
[5] 1980 c.65.
[6] P.350 above.
[7] P.374 above.
[8] P.359 above.
[9] "Local authority" defined by s.64(1), p.372 above.

13. Besides publishing a notice as required by paragraph 12, the local authority who have made an order shall post, and keep posted throughout the period mentioned in that paragraph, copies of the notice in such number of conspicuous places within the area to which the order relates as appear to them necessary for the purpose of bringing the making of the order to the notice of persons affected.

14. If no objection is duly made to the Secretary of State within the period mentioned in paragraph 12(b), or if every objection so made is withdrawn, the Secretary of State may, if he thinks fit, confirm the order either with or without modifications.

15. In any case other than one within paragraph 14 the Secretary of State shall, before confirming the order, either—

    (a)  cause a local inquiry to be held; or

    (b)  afford to any person by whom an objection has been duly made in accordance with paragraph 12(c) and not withdrawn an opportunity of appearing before and being heard by a person appointed by him for the purpose;

    and, after considering the objection and the report of the person who held the inquiry or the person so appointed, may confirm the order with or without modifications.

16. Section 250(2) to (5) of the Local Government Act 1972[1] (summoning of witnesses and production of documents before, and costs incurred at, local government inquiries held under that section) shall apply to an inquiry held under this Part of this Schedule by the Secretary of State as they apply to inquiries held under that section.

17. Subject to paragraphs 18 and 19, an order when confirmed shall come into operation on such date as may be specified in the order, not being earlier than six months from the date of the confirmation.

18. An order varying a previous order so as to exempt specified buildings or classes of building or specified fireplaces[2] or classes of fireplace from the operation of section 18[3] may come into operation on, or at any time after, the date of its confirmation.

19. (1) If, before the date on which an order is to come into operation, the local authority[4]—

    (a)  pass a resolution postponing its operation; and

    (b)  publish a notice stating the effect of the resolution in the London Gazette and also once at least in each of two successive weeks in some newspaper circulating in the area to which the order relates;

    the order shall, unless its coming into operation is again postponed under this paragraph, come into operation on the date specified in the resolution.

    (2) A local authority shall not without the consent of the Secretary of State exercise their power under sub-paragraph (1) of postponing the coming into operation of an order for a period of more than twelve months or for periods amounting in all to more than twelve months.

20. In the application of this Part of this Schedule to Scotland, for any reference to the London Gazette there shall be substituted a reference to the Edinburgh Gazette.

---

[1] 1972 c.70.
[2] "Fireplace" defined by s.64(1), p.371 above.
[3] P.346 above.
[4] "Local authority" defined by s.64(1), p.372 above.

# Radioactive Substances Act 1993

## Chapter 12

*Arrangement of sections*

*Preliminary*

1. Meaning of "radioactive material".   383
2. Meaning of "radioactive waste".   384
3. Meaning of "mobile radioactive apparatus".   384

*Inspectors and chief inspector*

4. *Repealed.*   384
5. *Repealed.*   384

*Registration relating to use of radioactive material and mobile radioactive apparatus*

6. Prohibition of use of radioactive material without registration.   384
7. Registration of users of radioactive material.   385
8. Exemptions from registration under s. 7.   386
9. Prohibition of use of mobile radioactive apparatus without registration.   387
10. Registration of mobile radioactive apparatus.   387
11. Exemptions from registration under s. 10.   388
12. Cancellation and variation of registration.   388

*Authorisation of disposal and accumulation of radioactive waste*

13. Disposal of radioactive waste.   389
14. Accumulation of radioactive waste.   389
15. Further exemptions from ss. 13 and 14.   390
16. Grant of authorisations.   390
17. Revocation and variation of authorisations.   392
18. Functions of public and local authorities in relation to authorisations under s. 13.   392

*Further obligations relating to registration or authorisation*

19. Duty to display documents.   393
20. Retention and production of site or disposal records.   393

*Enforcement notices and prohibition notices*

21. Enforcement notices.   394
22. Prohibition notices.   395

*Powers of Secretary of State in relation to applications etc.*

23. Power of Secretary of State to give directions to chief inspector.   395
24. Power of Secretary of State to require certain applications to be determined by him.   396
25. Power of Secretary of State to restrict knowledge of applications etc.   397

*Appeals*

26. Registrations, authorisations and notices: appeals from decisions of chief inspector.   398
27. Procedure on appeals under s. 26.   399
28. *Repealed.*   399

*Further powers of Secretary of State in relation to radioactive waste*

29. Provision of facilities for disposal or accumulation of radioactive waste.   400
30. Power of Secretary of State to dispose of radioactive waste.   400

*Rights of entry*

31.   *Repealed.*                                                                                401

*Offences*

32.   Offences relating to registration or authorisation.                                        401
33.   Offences relating to ss. 19 and 20.                                                        401
34.   Disclosure of trade secrets.                                                               402
34A.  Offences of making false or misleading statements or false entries.                        402
35.   *Repealed.*                                                                                403
36.   Offences by bodies corporate.                                                              403
37.   Offence due to another's fault.                                                            403
38.   Restriction on prosecutions.                                                               403

*Public access to documents and records*

39.   Public access to documents and records.                                                    403

*Operation of other statutory provisions*

40.   Radioactivity to be disregarded for purposes of certain statutory provisions.              404

*General*

41.   Service of documents.                                                                      405
42.   Application of Act to Crown.                                                               406
43.   *Repealed.*                                                                                406
44.   Regulations and orders: Great Britain.                                                     407
45.   Regulations and orders: Northern Ireland.                                                  407
46.   Effect of Act on other rights and duties.                                                  407
47.   General interpretation provisions.                                                         407
48.   Index of defined expressions.                                                              409
49.   Consequential amendments and transitional and transitory provisions.                       410
50.   Repeals.                                                                                   410
51.   Short title, commencement and extent.                                                      410

      SCHEDULES:

         Schedule 1—Specified elements.                                                          410
         Schedule 2—*Repealed.*                                                                  411
         Schedule 3—Enactments, other than local enactments, to which s. 40 applies.             411
         Part I—England and Wales.                                                               411
         Part II—Scotland.                                                                       411
         Part III—Northern Ireland.                                                              412
         Schedule 4—Consequential amendments. *Not reproduced.*
         Schedule 5—Transitional and transitory provisions.                                      412
         Part I—General transitional provisions and savings.                                     412
         Part II—Transitory modifications of Schedule 3.                                         412
         Schedule 6—Repeals and revocations. *Not reproduced.*

# Radioactive Substances Act 1993

## 1993 Chapter 12

An Act to consolidate certain enactments relating to radioactive substances with corrections and minor improvements made under the Consolidation of Enactments (Procedure) Act 1949.

[27th May 1993[1]]

### *Transfer of functions*

The functions previously conferred on the chief inspector for England and Wales under this Act, and the functions previously conferred on the Secretary of State under s.30(1) in relation to England and Wales, have been transferred to the Environment Agency: Environment Act 1995 (c.25), s.2, p.421 below. The functions previously conferred on the chief inspector for Scotland under this Act, and the functions previously conferred on the Secretary of State under s.30(1) in relation to Scotland, have been transferred to the Scottish Environment Protection Agency, SEPA: Environment Act 1995 (c.25), s.21, p.438 below. The new agencies took over their functions under this Act on the transfer date, 1 April 1996: S.I. 1996/139; S.I. 1996/234.

### *Amendments to this Act made by the Environment Act 1995*

Except where otherwise noted, the words "appropriate Agency" and "appropriate Agency's" in this Act, referring to the Environment Agency and SEPA, have been substituted in place of references to the chief inspector by the Environment Act 1995 (c .25), s.120, sch.22, para.200.

The amendments made to this Act by the Environment Act 1995, unless otherwise noted, came into force on 1 April 1996: S.I. 1996/186. To avoid undue repetition this commencement date is not set out in the footnotes which relate to these amendments .

### *References to material not set out in this Manual*

*Review of Radioactive Waste Management Policy*, Cm 2919, July 1995: London, HMSO (Government White Paper) .

The earlier publication, *The Radioactive Substances Act 1960, a guide to the administration of the Act*, referred to in Cm 2919, is under revision.

### *Preliminary*

*Meaning of "radioactive material".*

1. (1) In this Act "radioactive material" means anything which, not being waste[2], is either a substance[3] to which this subsection applies or an article[4] made wholly or partly from, or incorporating, such a substance.

   (2) Subsection (1) applies to any substance falling within either or both of the following descriptions, that is to say,—

   (*a*) a substance, containing an element specified in the first column of Schedule 1[5], in such a proportion that the number of becquerels[6] of that element contained in the substance, divided by

---

[1] This Act came into force on 27 August 1993: s.51(2).
[2] "Waste" defined by s.47(1),(4), p.409 below.
[3] "Substance" defined by s.47(1), p.408 below.
[4] "Article" defined by s.47(1), p.407 below.

[5] P.410 below.
[6] Becquerel (Bq) is defined in Cm 2919 as the standard international unit of radioactivity equal to one radioactive transformation per second (Cm 2919, Glossary, p.49).

the number of grams which the substance weighs, is a number greater than that specified in relation to that element in the appropriate column of that Schedule;

(b) a substance possessing radioactivity which is wholly or partly attributable to a process of nuclear fission or other process of subjecting a substance to bombardment by neutrons or to ionising radiations, not being a process occurring in the course of nature, or in consequence of the disposal[1] of radioactive waste, or by way of contamination[2] in the course of the application of a process to some other substance.

(3) In subsection (2)(a) "the appropriate column"—

(a) in relation to a solid substance, means the second column,

(b) in relation to a liquid substance, means the third column, and

(c) in relation to a substance which is a gas or vapour, means the fourth column.

(4) For the purposes of subsection (2)(b), a substance shall not be treated as radioactive material if the level of radioactivity is less than such level as may be prescribed[3] for substances of that description.

(5) The Secretary of State may by order vary the provisions of Schedule 1, either by adding further entries to any column of that Schedule or by altering or deleting any entry for the time being contained in any column.

(6) *This subsection relates to the application of this section to Northern Ireland.*

*Meaning of "radioactive waste".*

**2.** In this Act "radioactive waste" means waste[4] which consists wholly or partly of—

(a) a substance[5] or article[6] which, if it were not waste, would be radioactive material[7], or

(b) a substance or article which has been contaminated[8] in the course of the production, keeping or use of radioactive material, or by contact with or proximity to other waste falling within paragraph (a) or this paragraph.

*Meaning of "mobile radioactive apparatus".*

**3.** In this Act "mobile radioactive apparatus" means any apparatus, equipment, appliance or other thing which is radioactive material[9] and—

(a) is constructed or adapted for being transported from place to place, or

(b) is portable and designed or intended to be used for releasing radioactive material into the environment or introducing it into organisms.

*Inspectors and chief inspector*

**4–5.** *Repealed by the Environment Act 1995 (c.25), s.120, sch.22, para.201, sch.24. This amendment came into force on 1 April 1996: S.I. 1996/186.*

*Registration relating to use of radioactive material and mobile radioactive apparatus*

*Prohibition of use of radioactive material without registration.*

**6.** No person shall, on any premises[10] which are used for the purposes of an undertaking[11] carried on by him keep or use[12], or cause or permit to be kept or used, radioactive material[13] any description,

[1] "Disposal" defined by s.47(1), p.408 below.
[2] For "contamination" see s.47(5), p.409 below.
[3] "Prescribed" defined by s.47(1), p.408 below.
[4] "Waste" defined by s.47(1),(4) p.409 below.
[5] "Substance" defined by s.47(1), p.408 below.
[6] "Article" defined by s.47(1), p.407 below.
[7] "Radioactive material" defined by s.1, p.383 above.

[8] For "contamination" see s.47(5), p.409 below.
[9] "Radioactive material" defined by s.1, p.383 above.
[10] "Premises" defined by s.47(1), p.408 below.
[11] "Undertaking" defined by s.47(1), p.409 below.
[12] For "keep or use" see s.47(3), p.409 below.
[13] "Radioactive material" defined by s.1, p.383 above.

knowing or having reasonable grounds for believing it to be radioactive material, unless either—

(a) he is registered under section 7 in respect of those premises and in respect of the keeping and use on those premises of radioactive material of that description, or

(b) he is exempted from registration under that section in respect of those premises and in respect of the keeping and use on those premises of radioactive material of that description, or

(c) the radioactive material in question consists of mobile radioactive apparatus[1] in respect of which a person is registered under section 10[2] is exempted from registration under that section.

*Registration of users of radioactive material.*

7. (1) Any application for registration under this section shall be made to the appropriate Agency[3] and shall—

(a) specify the particulars mentioned in subsection (2),

(b) contain such other information as may be prescribed[4], and

(c) be accompanied by the charge prescribed for the purpose by a charging scheme under section 41 of the Environment Act 1995[5].

(2) The particulars referred to in subsection (l)(a) are—

(a) the premises[6] to which the application relates,

(b) the undertaking[7] for the purposes of which those premises are used,

(c) the description or descriptions of radioactive material[8] proposed to be kept or used[9] on the premises, and the maximum quantity of radioactive material of each such description likely to be kept or used on the premises at any one time, and

(d) the manner (if any) in which radioactive material is proposed to be used on the premises.

(3) On any application being made under this section, the appropriate Agency shall, subject to directions under section 25[10], send a copy of the application to each local authority[11] in whose area the premises are situated.

(4) Subject to the following provisions of this section, where an application is made to the appropriate Agency for registration under this section in respect of any premises, the appropriate Agency may either—

(a) register the applicant in respect of those premises and in respect of the keeping and use on those premises of radioactive material of the description to which the application relates, or

(b) if the application relates to two or more descriptions of radioactive material, register the applicant in respect of those premises and in respect of the keeping and use on those premises of such one or more of those descriptions of radioactive material as may be specified in the registration, or

(c) refuse the application.

(5) An application for registration under this section which is duly made to the appropriate Agency may be treated by the applicant as having been refused if it is not determined within the prescribed period for determinations[12] or within such longer period as may be agreed with the applicant.

[1] "Mobile radioactive apparatus" defined by s.3, p.384 above.
[2] P.387 below.
[3] "The appropriate Agency" defined by s.47(1), p.407 below.
[4] "Prescribed" defined by s.47(1), p.408 below.
[5] P.452 below. Words "charge ... Environment Act 1995" substituted by the Environment Act 1995 (c.25), s.120, sch.22, para.202(1).
[6] "Premises" defined by s.47(1), p.408 below.
[7] "Undertaking" defined by s.47(1), p.409 below.
[8] "Radioactive material" defined by s.1, p.383 above.
[9] For "keep or use" see s.47(3), p.409 below.
[10] P.397 below.
[11] "Local authority" defined by s.47(1), p.408 below.
[12] "The prescribed period for determinations" defined by s.47(1),(2), p.408 below.

(6) Any registration under this section in respect of any premises may (subject to subsection (7)) be effected subject to such limitations or conditions as the appropriate Agency thinks fit, and in particular (but without prejudice to the generality of this subsection) may be effected subject to conditions of any of the following descriptions—

(a) conditions imposing requirements (including, if the appropriate Agency thinks fit, requirements involving structural or other alterations) in respect of any part of the premises, or in respect of any apparatus, equipment or appliance used or to be used on any part of the premises for the purposes of any use of radioactive material from which radioactive waste[1] is likely to arise,

(b) conditions requiring the person to whom the registration relates, at such times and in such manner as may be specified in the registration, to furnish the appropriate Agency with information as to the removal of radioactive material from those premises to any other premises, and

(c) conditions prohibiting radioactive material from being sold or otherwise supplied from those premises unless it (or the container in which it is supplied) bears a label or other mark—

   (i)   indicating that it is radioactive material, or

   (ii)  if the conditions so require, indicating the description of radioactive material to which it belongs,

and (in either case) complying with any relevant requirements specified in the conditions.

(7) In the exercise of any power conferred on it[2] by subsection (4) or (6), the appropriate Agency, except in determining whether to impose any conditions falling within paragraph (b) or (c) of subsection (6), shall have regard exclusively to the amount and character of the radioactive waste likely to arise from the keeping or use of radioactive material on the premises in question.

(8) On registering a person under this section in respect of any premises, the appropriate Agency—

(a) shall furnish him with a certificate containing all material particulars of the registration, and

(b) subject to directions under section 25[3] shall send a copy of the certificate to each local authority in whose area the premises are situated.

......................................................................................................................................

*Exemptions from registration under s. 7.*

**8.** (1) At any time while a nuclear site licence[4] is in force in respect of a site, and at any time after the revocation or surrender of such a licence but before the period of responsibility of the licensee[5] has come to an end, the licensee (subject to subsection (2)) is exempted from registration under section 7 in respect of any premises[6] situated on that site and in respect of the keeping and use[7] on those premises of radioactive material[8] of every description.

(2) Where, in the case of any such premises as are mentioned in subsection (1), it appears to the appropriate Agency[9] that, if the licensee had been required to apply for registration under section 7 in respect of those premises, the appropriate Agency would have imposed conditions such as are mentioned in paragraph (b) or (c) of subsection (6) of that section, the appropriate Agency may direct that the exemption conferred by subsection (1) of this section shall have effect subject to such conditions (being conditions which in the opinion of the appropriate Agency correspond to those which it[10] would so have imposed) as may be specified in the direction.

(3) On giving a direction under subsection (2) in respect of any premises, the appropriate Agency shall furnish the licensee with a copy of the direction.

---

[1] "Radioactive waste" defined by s.2, p.384 above.
[2] Word "it" substituted by the Environment Act 1995 (c.25), s.120, sch.22, para.202(2).
[3] P.397 below.
[4] "Nuclear site licence" defined by s.47(1), p.408 below.
[5] For "licensee" and "period of responsibility" see definition of "nuclear site licence" at s.47(1), p.408 below.
[6] "Premises" defined by s.47(1), p.408 below.
[7] For "keep or use" see s.47(3), p.409 below.
[8] "Radioactive material" defined by s.1, p.383 above.
[9] "The appropriate Agency" defined by s.47(1), p.407 below.
[10] Word "it" substituted by the Environment Act 1995 (c.25), s.120, sch.22, para.203.

(4) Except as provided by subsection (5), in respect of all premises all persons are exempted from registration under section 7 in respect of the keeping and use on the premises of clocks and watches which are radioactive material.

(5) Subsection (4) does not exempt from registration under section 7 any premises on which clocks or watches are manufactured or repaired by processes involving the use of luminous material.

(6) The Secretary of State may by order grant further exemptions from registration under section 7, by reference to such classes of premises and undertakings[1] and such descriptions of radioactive material, as may be specified in the order.[2]

(7) Any exemption granted by an order under subsection (6) may be granted subject to such limitations or conditions as may be specified in the order.

(8) *This subsection relates to the application of this section to Northern Ireland.*

---

*Prohibition of use of mobile radioactive apparatus without registration.*

**9.** (1) No person shall, for the purpose of any activities to which this section applies—

(a) keep, use, lend or let on hire mobile radioactive apparatus[3] of any description, or

(b) cause or permit mobile radioactive apparatus of any description to be kept, used, lent or let on hire,

unless he is registered under section 10 in respect of that apparatus or is exempted from registration under that section in respect of mobile radioactive apparatus of that description.

(2) This section applies to activities involving the use of the apparatus concerned for—

(a) testing, measuring or otherwise investigating any of the characteristics of substances[4] or articles[5], or

(b) releasing quantities of radioactive material into the environment or introducing such material into organisms.

---

*Registration of mobile radioactive apparatus.*

**10.** (1) Any application for registration under this section shall be made to the appropriate Agency[7] and—

(a) shall specify—

(i) the apparatus to which the application relates, and

(ii) the manner in which it is proposed to use the apparatus,

(b) shall contain such other information as may be prescribed[8] and

(c) shall be accompanied by the charge prescribed for the purpose by a charging scheme under section 41 of the Environment Act 1995[9].

(2) Where an application is made to the appropriate Agency for registration under this section in respect of any apparatus, the appropriate Agency may register the applicant in respect of that apparatus, either unconditionally or subject to such limitations or conditions as the appropriate Agency thinks fit, or may refuse the application.

(3) On any application being made the appropriate Agency shall, subject to directions under section 25[10], send a copy of the application to each local authority[11] in whose area it appears to

---

[1] "Undertaking" defined by s.47(1), p.409 below.
[2] A list of orders made, or which have effect as if made, under this section is at p.803 below.
[3] "Mobile radioactive apparatus" defined by s.3, p.384 above.
[4] "Substance" defined by s.47(1), p.408 below.
[5] "Article" defined by s.47(1), p.407 below.
[6] "Radioactive material" defined by s.1, p.383 above.

[7] "The appropriate Agency" defined by s.47(1), p.407 below.
[8] "Prescribed" defined by s.47(1), p.408 below.
[9] P.452 below. Words "charge . . . Environment Act 1995" substituted by the Environment Act 1995 (c.25), s.120, sch.22, para. 204(1).
[10] P.397 below.
[11] "Local authority" defined by s.47(1), p.408 below.

the appropriate Agency[1] the apparatus will be kept or will be used for releasing radioactive material[2] into the environment.

(4) An application for registration under this section which is duly made to the appropriate Agency may be treated by the applicant as having been refused if it is not determined within the prescribed period for determinations[3] or within such longer period as may be agreed with the applicant.

(5) On registering a person under this section in respect of any mobile radioactive apparatus[4], the appropriate Agency—

(a)  shall furnish him with a certificate containing all material particulars of the registration, and

(b)  shall, subject to directions under section 25, send a copy of the certificate to each local authority in whose area it appears to the appropriate Agency[5] the apparatus will be kept or will be used for releasing radioactive material into the environment.

*Exemptions from registration under s. 10.*

**11.** (1)  The Secretary of State may by order grant exemptions from registration under section 10, by reference to such classes of persons, and such descriptions of mobile radioactive apparatus[6], as may be specified in the order.[7]

(2)  Any exemption granted by an order under subsection (1) may be granted subject to such limitations or conditions as may be specified in the order.

(3)  *This subsection relates to the application of this section to Northern Ireland.*

*Cancellation and variation of registration.*

**12.** (1)  Where any person is for the time being registered under section 7[8] or 10, the appropriate Agency[9] may at any time cancel the registration, or may vary it—

(a)  where the registration has effect without limitations or conditions, by attaching limitations or conditions to it, or

(b)  where the registration has effect subject to limitations or conditions, by revoking or varying any of those limitations or conditions or by attaching further limitations or conditions to the registration.

(2)  On cancelling or varying a registration by virtue of this section, the appropriate Agency shall—

(a)  give notice[10] of the cancellation or variation to the person to whom the registration relates, and

(b)  if a copy of the certificate was sent to a local authority[11] in accordance with section 7(8) or 10(5), send a copy of the notice to that local authority.

---

[1] Words "the appropriate Agency" substituted by the Environment Act 1995 (c.25), s.120, sch.22, para.204(2).

[2] "Radioactive material" defined by s.1, p.383 above.

[3] "The prescribed period for determinations" defined by s.47(1), (2), p.408 below.

[4] "Mobile radioactive apparatus" defined by s.3, p.384 above.

[5] Words "the appropriate Agency" substituted by the Environment Act 1995 (c.25), s.120, sch.22, para.204(2).

[6] "Mobile radioactive apparatus" defined by s.3, p.384

above.

[7] A list of orders made, or which have effect as if made, under this section is at p.803 below.

[8] P.385 above.

[9] "The appropriate Agency" defined by s.47(1), p.407 below.

[10] For provisions relating to service of documents see s.41, p.405 below.

[11] "Local authority" defined by s.47(1), p.408 below.

*Authorisation of disposal and accumulation of radioactive waste*

*Disposal of radioactive waste.*

**13.** (1)  Subject to section 15[1], no person shall, except in accordance with an authorisation granted in that behalf under this subsection, dispose of[2] any radioactive waste[3] on or from any premises[4] which are used for the purposes of any undertaking[5] carried on by him, or cause or permit any radioactive waste to be so disposed of, if (in any such case) he knows or has reasonable grounds for believing it to be radioactive waste.

(2)  Where any person keeps any mobile radioactive apparatus[6] for the purpose of its being used in activities to which section 9 applies[7], he shall not dispose of any radioactive waste arising from any such apparatus so kept by him, or cause or permit any such radioactive waste to be disposed of, except in accordance with an authorisation granted in that behalf under this subsection.

(3)  Subject to subsection (4) and to section 15, where any person, in the course of the carrying on by him of an undertaking, receives any radioactive waste for the purpose of its being disposed of by him, he shall not, except in accordance with an authorisation granted in that behalf under this subsection, dispose of that waste, or cause or permit it to be disposed of, knowing or having reasonable grounds for believing it to be radioactive waste.

(4)  The disposal of any radioactive waste does not require an authorisation under subsection (3) if it is waste which falls within the provisions of an authorisation granted under subsection (1) or (2), and it is disposed of in accordance with the authorisation so granted.

(5)  In relation to any premises which—

(*a*)  are situated on a nuclear site[8], but

(*b*)  have ceased to be used for the purposes of an undertaking carried on by the licensee,

subsection (1) shall apply (subject to section 15) as if the premises were used for the purposes of an undertaking carried on by the licensee.[9]

*Accumulation of radioactive waste.*

**14.** (1)  Subject to the provisions of this section and section 15, no person shall, except in accordance with an authorisation granted in that behalf under this section, accumulate any radioactive waste[10] (with a view to its subsequent disposal[11]) on any premises[12] which are used for the purposes of an undertaking[13] carried on by him, or cause or permit any radioactive waste to be so accumulated, if (in any such case) he knows or has reasonable grounds for believing it to be radioactive waste.

(2)  Where the disposal of any radioactive waste has been authorised under section 13, and in accordance with that authorisation the waste is required or permitted to be accumulated with a view to its subsequent disposal, no further authorisation under this section shall be required to enable the waste to be accumulated in accordance with the authorisation granted under section 13.

(3)  Subsection (1) shall not apply to the accumulation of radioactive waste on any premises situated on a nuclear site[14].

(4)  For the purposes of this section, where radioactive material[15] is produced, kept or used[16] on any premises, and any substance[17] arising from the production, keeping or use of that material

[1] P.390 below.
[2] "Dispose of" defined by s.47(1), p.408 below.
[3] "Radioactive waste" defined by s.2, p.384 above.
[4] "Premises" defined by s.47(1), p.408 below.
[5] "Undertaking" defined by s.47(1), p.409 below.
[6] "Mobile radioactive apparatus" defined by s.3, p.384 above.
[7] P.387 above.
[8] "Nuclear site" defined by s.47(1), p.408 below.
[9] **Cases: section 13** *R v Inspectorate of Pollution and another, ex parte Greenpeace Ltd (No.2)* [1994] 4 All ER 329; *R v Secretary of State for the Environment and others, ex parte Greenpeace Ltd and another* [1994] 4 All ER 352.
[10] "Radioactive waste" defined by s.2, p.384 above.
[11] "Disposal" defined by s.47(1), p.408 below.
[12] "Premises" defined by s.47(1), p.408 below.
[13] "Undertaking" defined by s.47(1), p.409 below.
[14] "Nuclear site" defined by s.47(1), p.408 below.
[15] "Radioactive material" defined by s.1, p.383 above.
[16] For "keep or use" see s.47(3), p.409 below.
[17] "Substance" defined by s.47(1), p.408 below.

is accumulated in a part of the premises appropriated for the purpose, and is retained there for a period of not less than three months, that substance shall, unless the contrary is proved, be presumed—

(a) to be radioactive waste, and

(b) to be accumulated on the premises with a view to the subsequent disposal of the substance.

*Further exemptions from ss.13 and 14.*

15. (1) Sections 13(1)[1] and (3) and 14(1) shall not apply to the disposal[2] or accumulation of any radioactive waste[3] arising from clocks or watches, but this subsection does not affect the operation of section 13(1) or section 14(1) in relation to the disposal or accumulation of radioactive waste arising from clocks or watches on or from premises[4] which, by virtue of subsection (5) of section 8[5], are excluded from the operation of subsection (4) of that section.

(2) Without prejudice to subsection (1), the Secretary of State may by order exclude particular descriptions of radioactive waste from any of the provisions of section 13 or 14, either absolutely or subject to limitations or conditions; and accordingly such of those provisions as may be specified in an order under this subsection shall not apply to a disposal or accumulation of radioactive waste if it is radioactive waste of a description so specified, and (where the exclusion is subject to limitations or conditions) the limitations or conditions specified in the order are complied with.[6]

(3) *This subsection relates to the application of this section to Northern Ireland.*

*Grant of authorisations.*

16. (1) In this section, unless a contrary intention appears, "authorisation" means an authorisation granted under section 13[7] or 14.

(2) [8]The power to grant authorisations shall be exercisable by the appropriate Agency[9].

(3) *Repealed by the Environment Act 1995 (c.25), s.120, sch.22, para.205(3), sch.24.*

(4) Any application for an authorisation shall be accompanied by the charge prescribed for the purpose by a charging scheme under section 41 of the Environment Act 1995[10].

(4A) Without prejudice to subsection (5), on any application for an authorisation under section 13(1) in respect of the disposal[11] of radioactive waste[12] on or from any premises[13] situated on a nuclear site[14] in any part of Great Britain, the appropriate Agency—

(a) shall consult the relevant Minister[15] and the Health and Safety Executive before deciding whether to grant an authorisation on that application and, if so, subject to what limitations or conditions, and

(b) shall consult the relevant Minister concerning the terms of the authorisation, for which purpose that Agency shall, before granting any authorisation on that application, send that Minister a copy of any authorisation which it proposes so to grant.[16]

(5) Before granting an authorisation under section 13(1) in respect of the disposal of radioactive waste on or from premises situated on a nuclear site, the appropriate Agency shall[17] consult with

---

[1] P.389 above.
[2] "Disposal" defined by s.47 (1), p.408 below.
[3] "Radioactive waste" defined by s.2, p.384 above.
[4] "Premises" defined by s.47(1), p.408 below.
[5] P.386 above.
[6] A list of orders made, or which have effect as if made, under this section is at p.803 below.
[7] P.389 above.
[8] Former words "Subject to subsection (3)," repealed by the Environment Act 1995 (c.25), s.120, sch.22, para.205(2), sch.24.
[9] "The appropriate Agency" defined by s.47(1), p.407 below.

[10] P.452 below. Words "charge . . . Environment Act 1995" substituted by the Environment Act 1995 (c.25), s.120, sch.22, para. 205(4).
[11] "Disposal" defined by s.47(1), p.408 below.
[12] "Radioactive waste" defined by s.2, p.384 above.
[13] "Premises" defined by s.47(1), p.408 below.
[14] "Nuclear site" defined by s.47(1), p.408 below.
[15] "Relevant minister" defined by subsection (11) below.
[16] Subsection (4A) inserted by the Environment Act 1995 (c.25), s.120, sch.22, para.205(5).
[17] Word "shall" substituted by the Environment Act 1995 (c.25), s.120, sch.22, para.205(6)(a).

such local authorities[1], relevant water bodies[2] or other public or local authorities[3] as appear to that Agency[4] to be proper to be consulted by that Agency.

(6) On any application being made, the appropriate Agency shall, subject to directions under section 25[5] send a copy of the application to each local authority in whose area, in accordance with the authorisation applied for, radioactive waste is to be disposed of or accumulated.

(7) An application for an authorisation (other than an application for an authorisation under section 13(1) in respect of the disposal of radioactive waste on or from any premises situated on a nuclear site in any part of Great Britain)[6] which is duly made to the appropriate Agency may be treated by the applicant as having been refused if it is not determined within the prescribed period for determinations[7] or such longer period as may be agreed with the applicant.

(8) An authorisation may be granted—

(a) either in respect of radioactive waste generally or in respect of such one or more descriptions of radioactive waste as may be specified in the authorisation, and

(b) subject to such limitations or conditions as the appropriate Agency thinks[8] fit.

(9) Where any authorisation is granted, the appropriate Agency—

(a) shall furnish the person to whom the authorisation is granted with a certificate containing all material particulars of the authorisation, and

(b) shall, subject to directions under section 25, send a copy of the certificate—

(i) to each local authority in whose area, in accordance with the authorisation, radioactive waste is to be disposed of or accumulated, and

(ii) in the case of an authorisation to which subsection (5) applies, to any other public or local authority consulted in relation to the authorisation in accordance with that subsection.

(10) An authorisation shall have effect as from such date as may be specified in it; and in fixing that date, in the case of an authorisation where copies of the certificate are required to be sent as mentioned in subsection (9)(b), the appropriate Agency[9]—

(a) shall have regard to the time at which those copies may be expected to be sent, and

(b) shall fix a date appearing to it[10] to be such as will allow an interval of not less than twenty-eight days after that time before the authorisation has effect,

unless in its[11] opinion it is necessary that the coming into operation of the authorisation should be immediate or should otherwise be expedited.

(11) In this section, "the relevant Minister" means—

(a) in relation to premises in England, the Minister of Agriculture, Fisheries and Food, and

(b) in relation to premises in Wales or Scotland, the Secretary of State.[12,13]

---

[1] "Local authority" defined by s.47(1), p.408 below.
[2] "Relevant water body" defined by s.47(1), p.408 below.
[3] "Public or local authority" defined by s.47(1), p.408 below.
[4] Words "that Agency" in this subsection substituted by the Environment Act 1995 (c.25), s.120, sch.22, para.205(6)(b).
[5] P.397 below.
[6] Words " (other than . . . Great Britain) "substituted by the Environment Act 1995 (c.25), s.120, sch.22, para.205(7).
[7] "The prescribed period for determinations" defined by s.47(1), (2), p.408 below.
[8] Word "thinks" substituted by the Environment Act 1995 (c.25), s.120, sch.22, para.205(8).

[9] Former words "or, as the case may be, the chief inspector and the appropriate Minister" repealed by the Environment Act 1995 (c.25), s.120, sch.22, para.205(9)(a), sch.24.
[10] Word "it" substituted by the Environment Act 1995 (c.25), s.120, sch.22, para.205(9)(b).
[11] Word "its" substituted by the Environment Act 1995 (c.25), s.120, sch.22, para.205(9)(b).
[12] Subsection (11) inserted by the Environment Act 1995 (c.25), s.120, sch.22, para.205(10).
[13] **Cases: section** 16 *R v Inspectorate of Pollution and another, ex parte Greenpeace Ltd (No.2)* [1994] 4 All ER 329; *R v Secretary of State for the Environment and others ex parte Greenpeace Ltd and another* [1994] 4 All ER 352.

*Revocation and variation of authorisations.*

**17.** (1) The appropriate Agency[1] may at any time revoke an authorisation granted under section 13[2] or 14.

(2) The appropriate Agency may at any time vary an authorisation granted under section 13 or 14—

(a) where the authorisation has effect without limitations or conditions, by attaching limitations or conditions to it, or

(b) where the authorisation has effect subject to limitations or conditions, by revoking or varying any of those limitations or conditions or by attaching further limitations or conditions to the authorisation.

(2A) On any proposal to vary an authorisation granted under section 13(1) in respect of the disposal[3] of radioactive waste[4] on or from any premises[5] situated on a nuclear site[6] in any part of Great Britain, the appropriate Agency—

(a) shall consult the relevant Minister[7] and the Health and Safety Executive before deciding whether to vary the authorisation and, if so, whether by attaching, revoking or varying any limitations or conditions or by attaching further limitations or conditions, and

(b) shall consult the relevant Minister concerning the terms of any variation, for which purpose that Agency shall, before varying the authorisation, send that Minister a copy of any variations which it proposes to make.[8]

(3) Where any authorisation granted under section 13 or 14 is revoked or varied, the chief inspector—

(a) shall give notice[9] of the revocation or variation to the person to whom the authorisation was granted, and

(b) if a copy of the certificate of authorisation was sent to a public or local authority in accordance with section 16(9)(b), shall send a copy of the notice to that authority.

(4) *Repealed by the Environment Act 1995 (c.25), s.120, sch.22, para.206(2), sch.24.*

(5) In this section, 'the relevant Minister' has the same meaning as in section 16 above. [10,11]

*Functions of public and local authorities in relation to authorisations under s. 13.*

**18.** (1) If, in considering an application for an authorisation under section 13[12], it appears to the appropriate Agency[13,14] that the disposal[15] of radioactive waste[16] to which the application relates is likely to involve the need for special precautions to be taken by a local authority[17], relevant water body[18] or other public or local authority[19], the appropriate Agency[20] shall consult with that public or local authority before granting the authorisation.

[1] "The appropriate Agency" defined by s.47(1), p.407 below.
[2] P.389 above.
[3] "Disposal" defined by s.47(1), p.408 below.
[4] "Radioactive waste" defined by s.2, p.384 above.
[5] "Premises" defined by s.47(1), p.408 below.
[6] "Nuclear site" defined by s.47(1), p.408 below.
[7] "Relevant Minister" defined by s.16(11) above: subsection (5) below.
[8] Subsection (2A) inserted by the Environment Act 1995 (c.25), s.120, sch.22, para.206(1).
[9] For provisions relating to service of documents see s.41, p.405 below.
[10] Subsection (5) inserted by the Environment Act 1995 (c.25), s.120, sch.22, para.206(3).
[11] **Cases:** section 17 *R v Inspectorate of Pollution and another, ex parte Greenpeace Ltd* [1994] 4 All ER 321; *R v Inspectorate of Pollution and another, ex parte Greenpeace*

*Ltd (No.2)* [1994] 4 All ER 329.
[12] P.389 above.
[13] "The appropriate Agency" defined by s.47(1), p.407 below.
[14] Former words, relating to the power of the appropriate Minister to grant authorisations, repealed by the Environment Act 1995 (c.25), s.120, sch.22, para.207(1)(a), sch.24.
[15] "Disposal" defined by s.47 (1), p.408 below.
[16] "Radioactive waste" defined by s.2, p.384 above.
[17] "Local authority" defined by s.47(1), p.408 below.
[18] "Relevant water body" defined by s.47(1), p.408 below.
[19] "Public or local authority" defined by s.47(1), p.408 below.
[20] Former words "or the appropriate Minister, as the case may be," repealed by the Environment Act 1995 (c.25), s.120, sch.22, para.207(1)(b), sch.24.

(2)  Where a public or local authority take any special precautions in respect of radioactive waste disposed of in accordance with an authorisation granted under section 13, and those precautions are taken—

(*a*)  in compliance with the conditions subject to which the authorisation was granted, or

(*b*)  with the prior approval of the appropriate Agency[1] as being precautions which in the circumstances ought to be taken by that public or local authority,

the public or local authority shall have power to make such charges, in respect of the taking of those precautions, as may be agreed between that authority and the person to whom the authorisation was granted, or as, in default of such agreement, may be determined by the appropriate Agency, and to recover the charges so agreed or determined from that person.

(3)  Where an authorisation granted under section 13 requires or permits radioactive waste to be removed to a place provided by a local authority as a place for the deposit of refuse, it shall be the duty of that local authority to accept any radioactive waste removed to that place in accordance with the authorisation, and, if the authorisation contains any provision as to the manner in which the radioactive waste is to be dealt with after its removal to that place, to deal with it in the manner indicated in the authorisation.

*Further obligations relating to registration or authorisation*

*Duty to display documents.*

**19.**  At all times while—

(*a*)  a person is registered in respect of any premises[2] under section 7[3], or

(*b*)  an authorisation granted in respect of any premises under section 13(1)[4] or 14[5] is for the time being in force,

the person to whom the registration relates, or to whom the authorisation was granted, as the case may be, shall cause copies of the certificate of registration or authorisation issued to him under this Act to be kept posted on the premises, in such characters and in such positions as to be conveniently read by persons having duties on those premises which are or may be affected by the matters set out in the certificate.

*Retention and production of site or disposal records.*

**20.**  (1)  The appropriate Agency[6] may, by notice served[7] on any person to whom a registration under section 7[8] or 10[9] relates or an authorisation under section 13[10] or 14[11] has been granted, impose on him such requirements authorised by this section in relation to site or disposal records kept by that person as the appropriate Agency may specify in the notice.

(2)  The requirements that may be imposed on a person under this section in relation to site or disposal records are—

(*a*)  to retain copies of the records for a specified period after he ceases to carry on the activities regulated by his registration or authorisation, or

(*b*)  to furnish the appropriate Agency with copies of the records in the event of his registration being cancelled or his authorisation being revoked or in the event of his ceasing to carry on the activities regulated by his registration or authorisation.

(3)  *Repealed by the Environment Act 1995 (c.25), s.120, sch.22, para. 208, sch.24.*

---

[1] Former words, relating to the power of the appropriate Minister to grant authorisations, repealed by the Environment Act 1995 (c.25), s.120, sch.22, para.207(2), sch.24.

[2] "Premises" defined by s.47(1), p.408 below.

[3] P.385 above.

[4] P.389 above.

[5] P.389 above.

[6] "The appropriate Agency" defined by s 47(1), p.407 below.

[7] For provisions relating to service of documents see s.41, p.405 below.

[8] P.385 above.

[9] P.387 above.

[10] P.389 above.

[11] P.389 above.

(4) In this section, in relation to a registration and the person registered or an authorisation and the person authorised—

"the activities regulated" by his registration or authorisation means—

(a)  in the case of registration under section 7, the keeping or use of radioactive material[1],

(b)  in the case of registration under section 10, the keeping, using, lending or hiring of the mobile radioactive apparatus[2],

(c)  in the case of an authorisation under section 13, the disposal[3] of radioactive waste[4] and

(d)  in the case of an authorisation under section 14, the accumulation of radioactive waste,

"records" means records required to be kept by virtue of the conditions attached to the registration or authorisation relating to the activities regulated by the registration or authorisation, and "site records" means records relating to the condition of the premises on which those activities are carried on or, in the case of registration in respect of mobile radioactive apparatus, of any place where the apparatus is kept and "disposal records" means records relating to the disposal of radioactive waste on or from the premises on which the activities are carried on, and "specified" means specified in a notice under this section.

*Enforcement notices and prohibition notices*

*Enforcement notices.*

**21.** (1) Subject to the provisions of this section, if the appropriate Agency[5] is of the opinion that a person to whom a registration under section 7[6] or 10[7] relates or to whom an authorisation was granted under section 13[8] or 14[9]—

(a)  is failing to comply with any limitation or condition subject to which the registration or authorisation has effect, or

(b)  is likely to fail to comply with any such limitation or condition,

it[10] may serve[11] a notice under this section on that person.

(2) A notice under this section shall—

(a)  state that the appropriate Agency is of that opinion,

(b)  specify the matters constituting the failure to comply with the limitations or conditions in question or the matters making it likely that such a failure will occur, as the case may be, and

(c)  specify the steps that must be taken to remedy those matters and the period within which those steps must be taken.

(3) *Repealed by the Environment Act 1995 (c.25), s.120, sch.22, para. 209(3), sch.24.*

(4) Where a notice is served under this section the appropriate Agency[12] shall—

(a)  in the case of a registration, if a certificate relating to the registration was sent to a local authority[13] under section 7(8) or 10(5), or

(b)  in the case of an authorisation, if a copy of the authorisation was sent to a public or local authority[14] under section 16(9)(b)[15],

send a copy of the notice to that authority.

---

[1] "Radioactive material" defined by s.1, p.383 above.
[2] "Mobile radioactive apparatus" defined by s.3, p.384 above.
[3] "Disposal" defined by s.47(1), p.408 below.
[4] "Radioactive waste" defined by s.2, p.384 above.
[5] "The appropriate Agency" defined by s.47(1), p.407 below.
[6] P.385 above.
[7] P.387 above.
[8] P.389 above.
[9] P.389 above.
[10] Word "it" substituted by the Environment Act 1995

(c.25), s.120, sch.22, para.209(1).
[11] For provisions relating to service of documents see s.41, p.405 below.
[12] Former words "or, where the notice is served by the appropriate Minister, that Minister" repealed by the Environment Act 1995 (c.25), s.120, sch.22, para.209(3), sch.24.
[13] "Local authority" defined by s.47(1), p.408 below.
[14] "Public or local authority" defined by s.47(1), p.408 below.
[15] P.391 above.

*Prohibition notices.*

**22.** (1) Subject to the provisions of this section, if the appropriate Agency[1] is of the opinion, as respects the keeping or use[2] of radioactive material[3] or of mobile radioactive apparatus[4], or the disposal[5] or accumulation of radioactive waste[6], by a person in pursuance of a registration or authorisation under this Act, that the continuing to carry on that activity (or the continuing to do so in a particular manner) involves an imminent risk of pollution of the environment or of harm to human health, it[7] may serve[8] a notice under this section on that person.

(2) A notice under this section may be served whether or not the manner of carrying on the activity in question complies with any limitations or conditions to which the registration or authorisation in question is subject.

(3) A notice under this section shall—

(*a*) state the appropriate Agency's opinion,

(*b*) specify the matters giving rise to the risk involved in the activity, the steps that must be taken to remove the risk and the period within which those steps must be taken, and

(*c*) direct that the registration or authorisation shall, until the notice is withdrawn, wholly or to the extent specified in the notice cease to have effect.

(4) Where the registration or authorisation is not wholly suspended by the direction given under subsection (3), the direction may specify limitations or conditions to which the registration or authorisation is to be subject until the notice is withdrawn.

(5) *Repealed by the Environment Act 1995 (c.25), s.120, sch.22, para.210(2), sch.24.*

(6) Where a notice is served under this section the appropriate Agency[9] shall—

(*a*) in the case of a registration, if a certificate relating to the registration was sent to a local authority[10] under section 7(8)[11] or 10(5)[12], or

(*b*) in the case of an authorisation, if a copy of the authorisation was sent to a public or local authority[13] under section 16(9)(*b*)[14],

send a copy of the notice to that authority.

(7) The appropriate Agency[15] shall, by notice to the recipient, withdraw a notice under this section when that Agency[16] is satisfied that the risk specified in it has been removed; and on so doing that Agency shall send a copy of the withdrawal notice to any public or local authority to whom a copy of the notice under this section was sent.

*Powers of Secretary of State in relation to applications etc.*

*Power of Secretary of State to give directions to chief inspector.*

**23.** (1) The Secretary of State may, if he thinks fit in relation to—

(*a*) an application for registration under section 7[17] or 10[18],

---

[1] "The appropriate Agency" defined by s.47(1), p.407 below.
[2] For "keep or use" see s.47(3), p.409 below.
[3] "Radioactive material" defined by s.1, p.383 above.
[4] "Mobile radioactive apparatus" defined by s.3, p.384 above.
[5] "Disposal" defined by s.47(1), p.408 below.
[6] "Radioactive waste" defined by s.2, p.384 above.
[7] Word "it" substituted by the Environment Act 1995 (c.25), s.120, sch.22, para.210(1).
[8] For provisions relating to service of documents see s.41, p.405 below.
[9] Former words "or, where the notice is served by the appropriate Minister, that Minister" repealed by the Environment Act 1995 (c.25), s.120, sch.22, para.210(3), sch.24.

[10] "Local authority" defined by s.47(1), p.408 below.
[11] P.386 above.
[12] P.388 above.
[13] "Public or local authority" defined by s.47(1), p.408 below.
[14] P.391 above.
[15] Former words "or, where the notice was served by the appropriate Minister, that Minister" repealed by Environment Act 1995 (c.25), s.120, sch.22, para.210(4)(a), sch.24.
[16] Words "that Agency" in this subsection substituted by the Environment Act 1995 (c.25), s.120, sch.22, para. 210(4)(b).
[17] P.385 above.
[18] P.387 above.

(b)  an application for an authorisation under section 13[1] or 14[2], or

(c)  any such registration or authorisation,

give directions to the appropriate Agency[3] requiring it[4] to take any of the steps mentioned in the following subsections in accordance with the directions.

(2)  A direction under subsection (1) may require the appropriate Agency so to exercise its[5] powers under this Act as—

(a)  to refuse an application for registration or authorisation,

(b)  to effect or grant a registration or authorisation, attaching such limitations or conditions (if any) as may be specified in the direction, or

(c)  to vary a registration or authorisation, as may be so specified, or

(d)  to cancel or revoke (or not to cancel or revoke) a registration or authorisation.

(3)  The Secretary of State may give directions to the appropriate Agency, as respects any registration or authorisation, requiring it[6] to serve[7] a notice under section 21[8] or 22[9] in such terms as may be specified in the directions.

(4)  The Secretary of State may give directions requiring the appropriate Agency to send such written particulars relating to, or to activities carried on in pursuance of, registrations effected or authorisations granted under any provision of this Act as may be specified in the directions to such local authorities[10] as may be so specified.

(4A)  In the application of this section in relation to authorisations, and applications for authorisations, under section 13[11] in respect of premises[12] situated on a nuclear site[13] in England, references to the Secretary of State shall have effect as references to the Secretary of State and the Minister of Agriculture, Fisheries and Food.[14]

(5)  *This subsection relates to the application of this section to Northern Ireland.*

......................................................................................................................................................

*Power of Secretary of State to require certain applications to be determined by him.*

**24.**  (1)  The Secretary of State may—

(a)  give general directions to the appropriate Agency[15] requiring it[16] to refer applications under this Act for registrations or authorisations of any description specified in the directions to the Secretary of State for his determination, and

(b)  give directions to the appropriate Agency in respect of any particular application requiring it to refer the application to the Secretary of State for his determination.

(2)  Where an application is referred to the Secretary of State in pursuance of directions given under this section, the Secretary of State may cause a local inquiry to be held in relation to the application.

(3)  The following provisions shall apply to inquiries in pursuance of subsection (2)—

(a)  in England and Wales, subsections (2) to (5) of section 250 of the Local Government Act 1972[17] (supplementary provisions about local inquiries under that section) but with the omission, in subsection (4) of that section, of the words "such local authority or",

---

[1] P.389 above.
[2] P.389 above.
[3] "The appropriate Agency" defined by s.47(1), p.407 below.
[4] Word "it" substituted by the Environment Act 1995 (c.25), s.120, sch.22, para.211(1)(a).
[5] Word "its" substituted by the Environment Act 1995 (c.25), s.120, sch.22, para.211(1)(b).
[6] Word "it" substituted by the Environment Act 1995 (c.25), s.120, sch.22, para. 211 (1)(a).
[7] For provisions relating to service of documents see s.41, p.405 below.
[8] P.394 above.

[9] P.395 above.
[10] "Local authority" defined by s.47(1), p.408 below.
[11] P.389 above.
[12] "Premises" defined by s.47(1), p.408 below.
[13] "Nuclear site" defined by s.47(1), p.408 below.
[14] Subsection (4A) inserted by the Environment Act 1995 (c.25), s.120, sch.22, para.211(2).
[15] "The appropriate Agency" defined by s.47(1), p.407 below.
[16] Word "it" in this subsection substituted by the Environment Act 1995 (c.25), s.120, sch.22, para.212(1).
[17] 1972 c.70.

(b) in Scotland, subsections (2) to (8) of section 210 of the Local Government (Scotland) Act 1973[1] (power to direct inquiries), and

(c) *This paragraph relates to Northern Ireland.*

(4) After determining any application so referred, the Secretary of State may give the appropriate Agency directions under section 23 as to the steps to be taken by it[2] in respect of the application.

(4A) In the application of this section in relation to authorisations, and applications for authorisations, under section 13[3] in respect of premises[4] situated on a nuclear site[5] in England, references to the Secretary of State shall have effect as references to the Secretary of State and the Minister of Agriculture, Fisheries and Food.[6,7]

......................................................................................................................................................

*Power of Secretary of State to restrict knowledge of applications etc.*

**25.** (1) The Secretary of State may direct the appropriate Agency[8] that in his opinion, on grounds of national security, it is necessary that knowledge of such information as may be specified or described in the directions, being information contained in or relating to—[9]

(a) any particular application for registration under section 7[10] or 10[11] or applications of any description specified in the directions, or

(b) any particular registration or registrations of any description so specified,

should be restricted.

(2) The Secretary of State[12] may direct the appropriate Agency that in his[13] opinion, on grounds of national security, it is necessary that knowledge of such information as may be specified or described in the directions, being information contained in or relating to—[14]

(a) any particular application for authorisation under section 13[15] or 14[16] or applications of any description specified in the directions,

(b) any particular authorisation under either of those sections or authorisations of any description so specified,

should be restricted.

(3) Where it appears to the appropriate Agency that an application, registration or authorisation is the subject of any directions under this section, the appropriate Agency shall not send a copy of so much of[17] the application or the certificate of registration or authorisation, as the case may be as contains the information specified or described in the directions[18]—

(a) to any local authority[19] under any provision of section 7 or 10, or

(b) to any public or local authority[20] under any provision of section 16[21].

[1] 1973 c.65.
[2] Word "it" substituted by the Environment Act 1995 (c.25), s.120, sch.22, para.212 (1).
[3] P.389 above.
[4] "Premises" defined by s.47(1), p.408 below.
[5] "Nuclear site" defined by s.47(1), p.408 below.
[6] Subsection (4A) inserted by the Environment Act 1995 (c.25), s.120, sch.22, para.212(2).
[7] **Case: section 24** *R v Secretary of State for the Environment and others, ex parte Greenpeace Ltd and another* [1994] 4 All ER 352.
[8] "The appropriate Agency" defined by s.47(1), p.407 below.
[9] Words "such information . . . relating to—" inserted by the Environment Act 1995 (c.25), s.120, sch.22, para.213(1). This amendment came into force on 28 July 1995: S.I. 1995/1983.
[10] P.385 above.
[11] P.387 above.
[12] Former words, relating to a power of the Minister of Agriculture, Fisheries and Food, repealed by the Environ-

ment Act 1995 (c.25), s.120, sch.22, para.213(2)(a), sch.24.
[13] Former words "or their" repealed by the Environment Act 1995 (c.25), s.120, sch.22, para.213(2)(a), sch.24.
[14] Words "such information . . . relating to—" inserted by the Environment Act 1995 (c.25), s.120, sch.22, para. 213(2)(b). This amendment came into force on 28 July 1995: S.I. 1995/1983.
[15] P.389 above.
[16] P.389 above.
[17] Words "so much of" inserted by the Environment Act 1995 (c.25), s.120, sch.22, para.213(3)(a). This amendment came into force on 28 July 1995: S.I. 1995/1983.
[18] Words "as contains . . . directions—" inserted by the Environment Act 1995 (c.25), s.120, sch.22, para.213(3) (b). This amendment came into force on 28 July 1995: S.I. 1995/1983.
[19] "Local authority" defined by s.47(1), p.408 below.
[20] "Public or local authority" defined by s.47(1), p.408 below.
[21] P.390 above.

(3A)  No direction under this section shall affect—

(*a*)  any power or duty of the Agency to which it is given to consult the relevant Minister[1]; or

(*b*)  the information which is to be sent by that Agency to that Minister.[2]

(4)  *This subsection relates to the application of this section to Northern Ireland.*

(5)  In this section "the relevant Minister" has the same meaning as in section 16 above[3].[4]

*Appeals*

*Registrations, authorisations and notices: appeals from decisions of chief inspector.*

**26.**  (1)  Where the appropriate Agency[5]—

(*a*)  refuses an application for registration under section 7[6] or 10[7], or refuses an application for an authorisation under section 13[8] or 14[9],

(*b*)  attaches any limitations or conditions to such a registration or to such an authorisation, or

(*c*)  varies such a registration or such an authorisation, otherwise than by revoking a limitation or condition subject to which it has effect, or

(*d*)  cancels such a registration or revokes such an authorisation,

the person directly concerned[10] may, subject to subsection (3), appeal to the Secretary of State.

(2)  A person on whom a notice under section 21[11] or 22[12] is served may, subject to subsections (3) and (4), appeal against the notice to the Secretary of State.

(3)  No appeal shall lie—

(*a*)  *Repealed by the Environment Act 1995 (c.25), s.120, sch.22, para.214(2), sch.24.*

(*b*)  under subsection (1) or (2) in respect of any decision taken by the appropriate Agency in pursuance of a direction of the Secretary of State under section 23[13] or 24[14],

(4)  No appeal shall lie under subsection (2) in respect of any notice served in[15] Northern Ireland by the appropriate Minister in exercise of the power under section 21 or 22.

(5)  In this section "the person directly concerned" means—

(*a*)  in relation to a registration under section 7 or 10, the person applying for the registration or to whom the registration relates;

(*b*)  in relation to an authorisation under section 13 or 14, the person applying for the authorisation or to whom it was granted;

and any reference to attaching limitations or conditions to a registration or authorisation is a reference to attaching limitations or conditions to it either in effecting or granting it or in exercising any power to vary it.

(5A)  In the application of this section in relation to authorisations, and applications for authorisations, under section 13 in respect of premises[16] situated on a nuclear site[17] in England, references in subsection (1) to (3) to the Secretary of State shall have effect as references to the Secretary of State and the Minister of Agriculture, Fisheries and Food.[18]

---

[1] "Relevant Minister" defined by s.16(11), p.391 above: subsection (5) below.

[2] Subsection (3A) inserted by the Environment Act 1995 (c.25), s.120, sch.22, para.213(4).

[3] P.391 above.

[4] Subsection (5) inserted by the Environment Act 1995 (c.25), s.120, sch.22, para.213(5).

[5] "The appropriate Agency" defined by s.47(1), p.407 below.

[6] P.385 above.

[7] P.387 above.

[8] P.389 above.

[9] P.389 above.

[10] "The person directly concerned" defined by subsection (5) below.

[11] P.394 above.

[12] P.395 above.

[13] P.395 above.

[14] P.396 above.

[15] Former words "England, Wales or" repealed by the Environment Act 1995 (c. 25), s.120, sch.22, para. 214(3), sch.24.

[16] "Premises" defined by s.47(1), p.408 below.

[17] "Nuclear site" defined by s.47(1), p.408 below.

[18] Subsection (5A) inserted by the Environment Act 1995 (c.25), s.120, sch.22, para.214(4).

(6) *This subsection relates to the application of this section to Northern Ireland.*

*Procedure on appeals under s. 26.*

**27.** (1) The Secretary of State may refer any matter involved in an appeal under section 26, other than an appeal against any decision of, or notice served by, SEPA[1],[2] to a person appointed by him for the purpose.

(1A) As respects an appeal against any decision of, or notice served by, SEPA, this section is subject to section 114 of the Environment Act 1995[3] (delegation or reference of appeals).[4]

(2) An appeal under section 26 shall, if and to the extent required by regulations under subsection (7) of this section, be advertised in such manner as may be prescribed[5].

(3) If either party to the appeal so requests, an appeal shall be in the form of a hearing (which may, if the person hearing the appeal so decides, be held, or held to any extent, in private).

(4) On determining an appeal from a decision of the appropriate Agency[6] under section 26 the Secretary of State—

(*a*) may affirm the decision,

(*b*) where that decision was the refusal of an application, may direct the appropriate Agency to grant the application,

(*c*) where that decision involved limitations or conditions attached to a registration or authorisation, may quash those limitations or conditions wholly or in part, or

(*d*) where that decision was a cancellation or revocation of a registration or authorisation, may quash the decision,

and where the Secretary of State does any of the things mentioned in paragraph (*b*), (*c*) or (*d*) he may give directions to the appropriate Agency as to the limitations and conditions to be attached to the registration or authorisation in question.

(5) On the determination of an appeal in respect of a notice under section 26(2), the Secretary of State may either cancel or affirm the notice and, if he affirms it, may do so either in its original form or with such modifications as he may think fit.

(6) The bringing of an appeal against a cancellation or revocation of a registration or authorisation shall, unless the Secretary of State otherwise directs, have the effect of suspending the operation of the cancellation or revocation pending the determination of the appeal; but otherwise the bringing of an appeal shall not, unless the Secretary of State so directs, affect the validity of the decision or notice in question during that period.

(7) The Secretary of State may by regulations make provision with respect to appeals under section 26 (including in particular provision as the period within which appeals are to be brought).[7]

(7A) In the application of this section in relation to authorisations, and applications for authorisations, under section 13[8] in respect of premises[9] situated on a nuclear site[10] in England, references in subsections (1) to (6) to the Secretary of State shall have effect as references to the Secretary of State and the Minister of Agriculture, Fisheries and Food.[11]

(8) *This subsection relates to the application of this section to Northern Ireland.*

**28.** *Repealed by the Environment Act 1995 (c.25), s.120, sch.22, para.216, sch.24. This amendment came into force on 1 April 1996: S.I. 1996/186.*

[1] "SEPA" defined by s.47(1), p.408 below.
[2] Words ", other . . . SEPA" inserted by the Environment Act 1995 (c.25), s.120, sch.22, para.215(2).
[3] P.489 below.
[4] Subsection (1A) inserted by the Environment Act 1995 (c.25), s.120, sch.22, para.215(3).
[5] "Prescribed" defined by s.47(1), p.408 below.
[6] "The appropriate Agency" defined by s.47(1), p.407 below.
[7] The following regulations have effect as if made under this section:
The Radioactive Substances (Appeals) Regulations 1990, S.I. 1990/2504, p.563 below.
[8] P.389 above.
[9] "Premises" defined by s.47(1), p.408 below.
[10] "Nuclear site" defined by s.47(1), p.408 below.
[11] Subsection (7A) inserted by the Environment Act 1995 (c.25), s.120, sch.22, para.215(4).

*Further powers of Secretary of State in relation to radioactive waste*

*Provision of facilities for disposal or accumulation of radioactive waste.*

**29.** (1) If it appears to the Secretary of State that adequate facilities are not available for the safe disposal[1] or accumulation of radioactive waste[2], the Secretary of State may provide such facilities, or may arrange for their provision by such persons as the Secretary of State may think fit.

(2) Where, in the exercise of the power conferred by this section, the Secretary of State proposes to provide or to arrange for the provision of, a place for the disposal or accumulation of radioactive waste, the Secretary of State, before carrying out that proposal, shall consult with any local authority[3] in whose area that place would be situated, and with such other public or local authorities[4] (if any) as appear to him to be proper to be consulted by him.

(3) The Secretary of State may make reasonable charges for the use of any facilities provided by him, or in accordance with arrangements made by him, under this section, or, in the case of facilities provided otherwise than by the Secretary of State, may direct that reasonable charges for the use of the facilities may be made by the person providing them in accordance with any such arrangements.

(4) *This subsection relates to the application of this section to Northern Ireland.*

*Power of Secretary of State to dispose of radioactive waste.*

**30.** (1) If there is radioactive waste[5] on any premises[6], and the appropriate Agency[7] is satisfied that—

(*a*) the waste ought to be disposed of[8], but

(*b*) by reason that the premises are unoccupied, or that the occupier is absent, or is insolvent, or for any other reason, it is unlikely that the waste will be lawfully disposed of unless that Agency[9] exercises its[10] powers under this section,

that Agency shall have power to dispose of that radioactive waste as that Agency may think fit, and to recover from the occupier of the premises, or, if the premises are unoccupied, from the owner of the premises, any expenses reasonably incurred by that Agency in disposing of it.

(2) *This subsection relates to the application of this section to Northern Ireland.*

(3) For the purposes of this section in its application to England and Wales and Northern Ireland, the definition of "owner" in section 343 of the Public Health Act 1936[11], and the provisions of section 294 of that Act (which limits the liability of owners who are only agents or trustees), shall apply—

(*a*) with the substitution in section 294 for references to a council of references to the Environment Agency[12] or, in Northern Ireland, the Department of the Environment for Northern Ireland, and

(*b*) in relation to Northern Ireland, as if that Act extended to Northern Ireland.

(4) For the purposes of this section in its application to Scotland, the definition of "owner" in section 3 of the Public Health (Scotland) Act 1897[13] and the provisions of section 336 of the Housing (Scotland) Act 1987[14] shall apply, with the substitution in section 336 of references to SEPA[15] for references to a local authority.

---

[1] "Disposal" defined by s.47(1), p.408 below.
[2] "Radioactive waste" defined by s.2, p.384 above.
[3] "Local authority" defined by s.47(1), p.408 below.
[4] "Public or local authority" defined by s.47(1), p.408 below.
[5] "Radioactive waste" defined by s.2, p.384 above.
[6] "Premises" defined by s.47(1), p.408 below.
[7] "The appropriate Agency" defined by s.47(1), p.407 below. Words "the appropriate Agency" substituted by the Environment Act 1995 (c.25), s.120, sch.22, para.217(2)(a).
[8] "Dispose of" defined by s.47(1), p.408 below.
[9] Words "that Agency" in this subsection substituted by the Environment Act 1995 (c.25), s.120, sch.22, para.2 17(2)(b).
[10] Word "its" substituted by the Environment Act 1995 (c.25), s.120, sch.22, para.217(2)(c).
[11] 1936 c.49.
[12] The Environment Agency is established by the Environment Act 1995 (c.25), s.1, p.420 below. Words "Environment Agency" substituted by the Environment Act 1995 (c.25), s.120, sch.22, para.217(3)
[13] 1897 c.38.
[14] 1987 c.26.
[15] "SEPA" defined by s.47(1), p.408 below. Word "SEPA" substituted by the Environment Act 1995 (c.25), s.120, sch.22, para.217(4).

*Rights of entry*

**31.** *Repealed by the Environment Act 1995 (c.25), s.120, sch.22, para. 218, sch.24. This amendment came into force on 1 Aril 1996: S.I. 1996/186.*

.................................................................

*Offences*

*Offences relating to registration or authorisation.*

**32.** (1) Any person who—

(*a*) contravenes section 6[1], 9[2], 13(1)[3], (2) or (3) or 14(1)[4], or

(*b*) being a person registered under section 7[5] or 10[6] or being (wholly or partly) exempted from registration under either of those sections, does not comply with a limitation or condition subject to which he is so registered or exempted, or

(*c*) being a person to whom an authorisation under section 13[7] or 14[8] has been granted, does not comply with a limitation or condition subject to which that authorisation has effect, or

(*d*) being a person who is registered under section 7 or 10 or to whom an authorisation under section 13 or 14 has been granted, fails to comply, with any requirement of a notice served on him under section 21[9] or 22[10],

shall be guilty of an offence.

(2) A person guilty of an offence under this section shall be liable—

(*a*) on summary conviction, to a fine not exceeding £20,000 or to imprisonment for a term not exceeding six months, or both;

(*b*) on conviction on indictment, to a fine or to imprisonment for a term not exceeding five years, or both.

(3) If the appropriate Agency[11] is of the opinion that proceedings for an offence under subsection (1)(*d*) would afford an ineffectual remedy against a person who has failed to comply with the requirements of a notice served on him under section 21 or 22, that Agency may take proceedings in the High Court or, in Scotland, in any court of competent jurisdiction, for the purpose of securing compliance with the notice.[12]

.................................................................

*Offences relating to ss. 19 and 20.*

**33.** (1) Any person who contravenes section 19[13] shall be guilty of an offence and liable—

(*a*) on summary conviction, to a fine not exceeding the statutory maximum[14];

(*b*) on conviction on indictment, to a fine.

(2) Any person who without reasonable cause pulls down, injures or defaces any document posted in pursuance of section 19 shall be guilty of an offence and liable on summary conviction to a fine not exceeding level 2 on the standard scale[15].

(3) Any person who fails to comply with a requirement imposed on him under section 20[16] shall be guilty of an offence and liable—

(*a*) on summary conviction, to a fine not exceeding the statutory maximum or to imprisonment for a term not exceeding three months, or both;

[1] P.384 above .
[2] P.387 above.
[3] P.389 above.
[4] P.389 above.
[5] P.385 above.
[6] P.387 above.
[7] P.389 above.
[8] P.389 above.
[9] P.394 above.
[10] P.395 above.
[11] "The appropriate Agency" defined by s.47(1), p.407 below.

[12] Subsection (3) inserted by the Environment Act 1995 (c.25), s.120, sch.22, para.219.
[13] P.393 above.
[14] The current statutory maximum is £5,000: Criminal Justice Act 1991 (c.53), s.17(2) (England and Wales); Criminal Procedure (Scotland) Act 1995 (c.46), s.225(8) (Scotland).
[15] The current fine at level 2 on the standard scale is £500: Criminal Justice Act 1991 (c.53), s.17 (England and Wales); Criminal Procedure (Scotland) Act 1995 (c.46), s.225 (Scotland).
[16] P.393 above.

(*b*) on conviction on indictment, to a fine or to imprisonment for a term not exceeding two years, or both.

*Disclosure of trade secrets.*

**34.** (1) If any person discloses any information relating to any relevant process[1] or trade secret used in carrying on any particular undertaking[2] which has been given to or obtained by him under this Act or in connection with the execution of this Act, he shall be guilty of an offence, unless the disclosure is made—

(*a*)  with the consent of the person carrying on that undertaking, or

(*b*)  in accordance with any general or special directions given by the Secretary of State, or

(*bb*) under or by virtue of section 113 of the Environment Act 1995[3], or[4]

(*c*)  in connection with the execution of this Act, or

(*d*)  for the purposes of any legal proceedings arising out of this Act or of any report of any such proceedings.

(2) A person guilty of an offence under this section shall be liable—

(*a*)  on summary conviction, to a fine not exceeding the statutory maximum[5] or to imprisonment for a term not exceeding three months, or both;

(*b*)  on conviction on indictment, to a fine or to imprisonment for a term not exceeding two years, or both.

(3) In this section "relevant process" means any process applied for the purposes of, or in connection with, the production or use of radioactive material[6].

(4) *This subsection relates to the application of this section to Northern Ireland.*

*Offences of making false or misleading statements or false entries.*

**34A.** (1) Any person who—

(*a*)  for the purpose of obtaining for himself or another any registration under section 7[7] or 10[8], any authorisation under section 13[9] or 14[10] or any variation of such an authorisation under section 17[11], or

(*b*)  in purported compliance with a requirement to furnish information imposed under section 31(1)(*d*),

makes a statement which he knows to be false or misleading in a material particular, or recklessly makes a statement which is false or misleading in a material particular, shall be guilty of an offence.

(2) Any person who intentionally makes a false entry in any record—

(*a*)  which is required to be kept by virtue of a registration under section 7 or 10 or an authorisation under section 13 or 14, or

(*b*)  which is kept in purported compliance with a condition which must be complied with if a person is to have the benefit of an exemption under section 8, 11[12] or 15[13].

shall be guilty of an offence.

(3) A person guilty of an offence under this section shall be liable—

[1]  "Relevant process" defined by subsection (3) below.
[2]  "Undertaking" defined by s.47(1), p.409 below.
[3]  P.488 below.
[4]  Para.(bb) inserted by the Environment Act 1995 (c.25), s.120, sch.22, para.220.
[5]  The current statutory maximum is £5,000: Criminal Justice Act 1991 (c.53), s.17(2) (England and Wales); Criminal Procedure (Scotland) Act 1995 (c.46), s.225(8) (Scotland).

[6]  "Radioactive material" defined by s.1, p.383 above.
[7]  P.385 above.
[8]  P.387 above.
[9]  P.389 above.
[10]  P.389 above.
[11]  P.392 above.
[12]  P.388 above.
[13]  P.390 above.

(*a*) on summary conviction, to a fine not exceeding the statutory maximum[1];

(*b*) on conviction on indictment, to a fine or to imprisonment for a term not exceeding two years, or to both.[2]

**35.** *Repealed by the Environment Act 1995 (c.25), s.120, sch.22, para. 221, sch.24. This amendment came into force on 1 April 1996: S.I. 1996/186.*

*Offences by bodies corporate.*

**36.** (1) Where a body corporate is guilty of an offence under this Act, and that offence is proved to have been committed with the consent or connivance of, or to be attributable to any neglect on the part of, any director, manager, secretary or other similar officer of the body corporate, or any person who was purporting to act in any such capacity, he, as well as the body corporate, shall be guilty of that offence, and shall be liable to be proceeded against and punished accordingly.

(2) In this section "director", in relation to a body corporate established by or under any enactment for the purpose of carrying on under national ownership any industry or part of an industry or undertaking, being a body corporate whose affairs are managed by its members, means a member of that body corporate.

*Offence due to another's fault.*

**37.** Where the commission by any person of an offence under this Act is due to the act or default of some other person, that other person may by virtue of this section be charged with and convicted of the offence whether or not proceedings for the offence are taken against the first mentioned person.

*Restriction on prosecutions.*

**38.** (1) Proceedings in respect of any offence under this Act shall not be instituted in England or Wales except—

(*a*) by the Secretary of State,

(*b*) by the Environment Agency[3], or[4]

(*c*) by or with the consent of the Director of Public Prosecutions.

(2)–(3) *These subsections relate to Northern Ireland.*

*Public access to documents and records*

*Public access to documents and records.*

**39.** (1) The appropriate Agency[5] shall keep copies of—

(*a*) all applications made to it[6] under any provision of this Act,

(*b*) all documents issued by it under any provision of this Act,

(*c*) all other documents sent by it to any local authority[7] in pursuance of directions of the Secretary of State, and

---

[1] The current statutory maximum is £5,000: Criminal Justice Act 1991 (c.53), s.17(2) (England and Wales); Criminal Procedure (Scotland) Act 1995 (c.46), s.225(8) (Scotland).

[2] This section inserted by the Environment Act 1995 (c.25), s.112, sch.19, para.6. This amendment came into force on 1 April 1996: S.I. 1996/186.

[3] The Environment Agency is established by the Environment Act 1995 (c.25), s.1, p.420 below.

[4] Para. (b) substituted by the Environment Act 1995 (c.25), s.120, sch.22, para.222.

[5] "The appropriate Agency" defined by s.47(1), p.407 below.

[6] Word "it" in this subsection substituted by the Environment Act 1995 (c.25), s.120, sch.22, para.223(1)(a).

[7] "Local authority" defined by s.47(1), p.408 below.

(d)  such records of convictions under section 32[1], 33[2], 34[3] or 35 as may be prescribed in regulations[4];

and the appropriate Agency[5] shall make copies of those documents available to the public except to the extent that that would involve the disclosure of information relating to any relevant process[6] or trade secret or would involve the disclosure of information[7] as respects which the Secretary of State has directed that knowledge should be restricted on grounds of national security.

(2)  Each local authority shall keep and make available to the public copies of all documents sent to the authority under any provision of this Act unless directed by the appropriate Agency[8] that all or any part of any such document is not to be available for inspection.

(3)  Directions under subsection (2) shall only be given for the purpose of preventing disclosure of relevant processes or trade secrets and may be given generally in respect of all, or any description of, documents or in respect of specific documents.

(4)  The copies of documents required to be made available to the public by this section need not be kept in documentary form.

(5)  The public shall have the right to inspect the copies of documents required to be made available under this section at all reasonable times and, on payment of a reasonable fee, to be provided with a copy of any such document.

(6)  In this section "relevant process" has the same meaning as in section 34[9].

(7)  *This subsection relates to the application of this section to Northern Ireland.*

.....................................................................................................................................................

*Operation of other statutory provisions*
*Radioactivity to be disregarded for purposes of certain statutory provisions.*

**40.**  (1)  For the purposes of the operation of any statutory provision[10] to which this section applies, and for the purposes of the exercise or performance of any power or duty conferred or imposed by, or for the enforcement of, any such statutory provision, no account shall be taken of any radioactivity possessed by any substance[11] or article[12] or by any part of any premises[13].

(2)  This section applies—

(a)  to any statutory provision contained in, or for the time being having effect by virtue of, any of the enactments specified in Schedule 3[14], or any enactment for the time being in force whereby an enactment so specified is amended, extended or superseded, and

(b)  to any statutory provision contained in, or for the time being having effect by virtue of, a local enactment[15] whether passed or made before or after the passing of this Act (in whatever terms the provision is expressed) in so far as—

(i)  the disposal[16] or accumulation of waste[17] or any description of waste, or of any substance which is a nuisance, or so as to be a nuisance, or of any substance which is, or so as to be, prejudicial to health, noxious, polluting or of any similar description, is prohibited or restricted by the statutory provision, or

---

[1] P.401 above.
[2] P.401 above
[3] P.402 above.
[4] See list of instruments, p.803 below.
[5] Words "the appropriate Agency" substituted by the Environment Act 1995 (c.25), s.120, sch.22, para.223(1)(b).
[6] "Relevant process" has the same meaning as in s.34(3), p.402 above: subsection (6) below.
[7] Word "information" substituted by the Environment Act 1995 (c.25), s.120, sch.22, para.223(1)(c). This amendment came into force on 28 July 1995: S.I. 1995/1983.
[8] Former words "or, as the case may be, the appropriate Minister and the chief inspector," repealed by the Environment Act 1995 (c.25), s.120, sch.22, para.223(2), sch.24.
[9] P.402 above.
[10] "Statutory provision" defined by subsection (3) below.
[11] "Substance" defined by s.47(1), p.408 below.
[12] "Article" defined by s. 47(1), p.407 below.
[13] "Premises" defined by s.47(1), p.408 below.
[14] P.411 below.
[15] "Local enactment" defined by subsection (3) below.
[16] For "disposal" see subsection (3) below.
[17] "Waste" defined by s.47(1), (4), p.409 below.

(ii)  a power or duty is conferred or imposed by the statutory provision on the Environment Agency[1] or SEPA[2] or on[3] any local authority[4], relevant water body[5] or other public or local authority[6], or on any officer of a public or local authority, to take any action (whether by way of legal proceedings or otherwise) for preventing, restricting or abating such disposals or accumulations as are mentioned in sub-paragraph (i).

(3)  In this section—

"statutory provision"—

(a)  in relation to Great Britain, means a provision, whether of a general or a special nature, contained in, or in any document made or issued under, any Act, whether of a general or a special nature, and

(b)  in relation to Northern Ireland, has the meaning given by section 1( $f$ ) of the Interpretation Act (Northern Ireland) 1954,

"local enactment" means—

(a)  a local or private Act (including a local or private Act of the Parliament of Northern Ireland or a local or private Measure of the Northern Ireland Assembly), or

(b)  an order confirmed by Parliament (or by the Parliament of Northern Ireland or the Northern Ireland Assembly) or brought into operation in accordance with special parliamentary procedure,

and any reference to disposal, in relation to a statutory provision, is a reference to discharging or depositing a substance or allowing a substance to escape or to enter a stream or other place, as may be mentioned in that provision.

(4)  The references to provisions of the Water Resources Act 1991 in Part I of Schedule 3 shall have effect subject to the power conferred by section 98 of that Act[7].

*General*

*Service of documents.*

**41.**  (1)  Any notice required or authorised by or under this Act to be served on or given to any person may be served or given by delivering it to him, or by leaving it at his proper address, or by sending it by post to him at that address.

(2)  Any such notice may—

(a)  in the case of a body corporate, be served on or given to the secretary or clerk of that body;

(b)  in the case of a partnership, be served on or given to a partner or a person having the control or management of the partnership business.

(3)  For the purposes of this section and of section 7 of the Interpretation Act 1978[8](service of documents by post) in its application to this section, the proper address of any person on or to whom any such notice is to be served or given shall be his last known address, except that—

(a)  in the case of a body corporate or their secretary or clerk, it shall be the address of the registered or principal office of that body;

(b)  in the case of a partnership or person having the control or the management of the partnership business, it shall be the principal office of the partnership;

and for the purposes of this subsection the principal office of a company registered outside the United Kingdom or of a partnership carrying on business outside the United Kingdom shall be their principal office within the United Kingdom.

---

[1] The Environment Agency is established by the Environment Act 1995 (c.25), s.1, p.420 below.

[2] "SEPA" defined by s.47(1), p.408 below.

[3] Words "the Environment Agency or SEPA or on" inserted by the Environment Act 1995 (c.25), s.120, sch.22, para.224.

[4] "Local authority" defined by s.47(1), p.408 below.

[5] "Relevant water body" defined by s 47(1), p.408 below.

[6] "Public or local authority" defined by s.47(1), p.408 below.

[7] P.289 above.

[8] 1978 c.30.

(4) If the person to be served with or given any such notice has specified an address in the United Kingdom other than his proper address within the meaning of subsection (3) as the one at which he or someone on his behalf will accept notices of the same description as that notice, that address shall also be treated for the purposes of this section and section 7 of the Interpretation Act 1978 as his proper address.

(5) The preceding provisions of this section shall apply to the sending or giving of a document as they apply to the giving of a notice.

*Application of Act to Crown.*

**42.** (1) Subject to the following provisions of this section, the provisions of this Act shall bind the Crown.

(2) Subsection (1) does not apply in relation to premises[1]—

(a) occupied on behalf of the Crown for naval, military or air force purposes or for the purposes of the department of the Secretary of State having responsibility for defence, or

(b) occupied by or for the purposes of a visiting force[2].

(3) No contravention by the Crown of any provision of this Act shall make the Crown criminally liable; but the High Court or, in Scotland, the Court of Session may, on the application of any authority charged with enforcing that provision, declare unlawful any act or omission of the Crown which constitutes such a contravention.

(4) Notwithstanding anything in subsection (3), the provisions of this Act shall apply to persons in the public service of the Crown as they apply to other persons.

(5) *Repealed by the Environment Act 1995 (c.25), s.120, sch.22, para.225, sch.24.*

(6) Where, in the case of any such premises as are mentioned in subsection (2)—

(a) arrangements are made whereby radioactive waste[3] is not to be disposed of[4] from those premises except with the approval of the appropriate Agency[5], and

(b) in pursuance of those arrangements the appropriate Agency proposes to approve, or approves, the removal of radioactive waste from those premises to a place provided by a local authority[6] as a place for the deposit of refuse,

the provisions of section 18[7] shall apply as if the proposal to approve the removal of the waste were an application for an authorisation under section 13[8] to remove it, or (as the case may be) the approval were such an authorisation.

(7) Nothing in this section shall be taken as in any way affecting Her Majesty in her private capacity; and this subsection shall be construed as if section 38(3) of the Crown Proceedings Act 1947[9] (interpretation of references in that Act to Her Majesty in her private capacity) were contained in this Act.

(8) In this section "visiting force" means any such body, contingent or detachment of the forces of any country as is a visiting force for the purposes of any of the provisions of the Visiting Forces Act 1952.[10]

(9) *This subsection relates to the application of this section to Northern Ireland.*

**43.** *Repealed by the Environment Act 1995 (c.25), s.120, sch.22, para.226, sch.24. This amendment came into force on 1 April 1996: S.I. 1996/186.*

[1] "Premises" defined by s.47(1), p.408 below.
[2] "Visiting force" defined by subsection (8) below.
[3] "Radioactive waste" defined by s.2, p.384 above.
[4] "Dispose of" defined by s.47(1), p.408 below.
[5] "The appropriate Agency" defined by s.47(1), p.407 below.
[6] "Local authority" defined by s.47(1), p.408 below.
[7] P.392 above.
[8] P.389 above.
[9] 1947 c.44.
[10] 1952 c.67.

*Regulations and orders: Great Britain.*

**44.** (1)  The Secretary of State may make regulations under this Act for any purpose for which regulations are authorised or required to be made under this Act.

(2)  For the purpose of facilitating the exercise of any power under this Act to effect registrations, or grant authorisations, subject to limitations or conditions, the Secretary of State may make regulations setting out general limitations or conditions applicable too such classes of cases as may be specified in the regulations; and any limitations or conditions so specified shall, for the purposes of this Act, be deemed to be attached to any registration or authorisation falling within the class of cases to which those limitations or conditions are expressed to be applicable, subject to such exceptions or modifications (if any) as may be specified in any such registration or authorisation.

(3)  Any power conferred by this Act to make regulations or orders shall be exercisable by statutory instrument.[1]

(4)  Any statutory instrument containing regulations or an order made under this Act, other than an order under Schedule 5[2], shall be subject to annulment in pursuance of a resolution of either House of Parliament.

(5)  This section does not extend to Northern Ireland.

**45.**  *This section extends to Northern Ireland only.*

*Effect of Act on other rights and duties.*

**46.**  Subject to the provisions of section 40 of this Act[3], and of section 18 of the Interpretation Act 1978[4] (which relates to offences under two or more laws), nothing in this Act shall be construed as—

(*a*)  conferring a right of action in any civil proceedings (other than proceedings for the recovery of a fine) in respect of any contravention of this Act, or

(*b*)  affecting any restriction imposed by or under any other enactment, whether contained in a public general Act or in a local or private Act, or

(*c*)  derogating from any right of action or other remedy (whether civil or criminal) in proceedings instituted otherwise than under this Act.

*General interpretation provisions.*

**47.** (1)  In this Act, except in so far as the context otherwise requires—

"the appropriate Agency" means—

(*a*)  in relation to England and Wales, the Environment Agency[5]; and

(*b*)  in relation to Scotland, SEPA[6];[7]

"the appropriate Minister" means—

(*a*)–(*b*)  *Repealed by the Environment Act 1995 (c.25), s.120, sch.22, para.227(3), sch.24.*

(*c*)  in relation to Northern Ireland, the Department of Agriculture for Northern Ireland,

"article" includes a part of an article,

"the chief inspector" means—

(*a*)–(*b*)  *Repealed by the Environment Act 1995 (c.25), s.120, sch.22, para.227(4), sch.24.*

---

[1] A list of orders made, or which have effect as if made, under this Act is at p.803 below.

[2] P.412 below.

[3] P.404 above.

[4] 1978 c.30.

[5] The Environment Agency is established by the Environment Act 1995 (c.25), s.1, p.420 below.

[6] SEPA is established by the Environment Act 1995 (c.25), s.20, p.408 below.

[7] This definition inserted by the Environment Act 1995 (c.25), s.120, sch.22, para.227(2).

(c)  *This paragraph relates to Northern Ireland.*

"disposal", in relation to waste, includes its removal, deposit, destruction, discharge (whether into water or into the air or into a sewer or drain or otherwise) or burial (whether underground or otherwise) and "dispose of" shall be construed accordingly,

"local authority" (except where the reference is to a public or local authority) means—

(a)   in England[1], the council of a county, district or London borough or the Common Council of the City of London or an authority established by the Waste Regulation and Disposal (Authorities) Order 1985[2],

(aa)  in Wales, the council of a county or county borough;[3]

(b)   in Scotland, a council constituted under section 2 of the Local Government etc. (Scotland) Act 1994[4], and

(c)   *this paragraph relates to Northern Ireland.*

"nuclear site" means—

(a)   any site in respect of which a nuclear site licence is for the time being in force, or

(b)   any site in respect of which, after the revocation or surrender of a nuclear site licence, the period of responsibility of the licensee has not yet come to an end,

"nuclear site licence", "licensee" and "period of responsibility" have the same meaning as in the Nuclear Installations Act 1965[5],

"premises" includes any land, whether covered by buildings or not, including any place underground and any land covered by water,

"prescribed" means prescribed by regulations under this Act[6],

"the prescribed period for determinations", in relation to any application under this Act, means, subject to subsection (2), the period of four months beginning with the day on which the application was received,

"public or local authority", in relation to England and Wales, includes a water undertaker or a sewerage undertaker,

"relevant water body" means—

(a)   in England and Wales,[7] a water undertaker, a sewerage undertaker or a local fisheries committee,

(b)   in Scotland,[8] a district salmon fishery board established under section 14 of the Salmon Act 1986[9] or a water and sewerage authority established by section 62 of the Local Government etc. (Scotland) Act 1994[10] and

(c)   *this paragraph relates to Northern Ireland.*

"SEPA" means the Scottish Environment Protection Agency[11];[12]

"substance" means any natural or artificial substance, whether in solid or liquid form or in the form of a gas or vapour,

---

[1] Former words "and Wales" repealed by the Local Government (Wales) Act 1994 (c.19), s.66, sch.16, para. 102(a), sch.18. This amendment came into force on 1 April 1996: S.I. 1996/396.

[2] S.I. 1985/1884.

[3] Para.(aa) inserted by the Local Government (Wales) Act 1994 (c.19), s.66, sch.16, para.102(b). This amendment came into force on 1 April 1996: S.I. 1996/396.

[4] 1994 c.39. Words "council . . . 1994" substituted by the Local Government etc. (Scotland) Act 1994 (c.39), s.180(1), sch.13, para.181(a). This amendment came into force on 1 April 1996: S.I. 1996/323.

[5] 1965 c.57.

[6] Former words, relating to fees and charges, repealed by the Environment Act 1995 (c.25), s.120, sch.22, para.227(5), sch.24.

[7] Former words "the National Rivers Authority" repealed by the Environment Act 1995 (c.25), s.120, sch.22, para. 227(6)(a), sch.24.

[8] Former words " a river purification authority within the meaning of the Rivers (Prevention of Pollution) (Scotland) Act 1951," repealed by the Environment Act 1995 (c.25), s.120, sch.22, para.227(6)(b), sch.24.

[9] 1986 c.62.

[10] 1994 c.39. Words "a water . . . 1994" substituted by the Local Government etc.(Scotland) Act 1994 (c.39), s.180(1), sch.13, para.181(b). This amendment came into force on 1 April 1996: S.I. 1996/323.

[11] SEPA is established by the Environment Act 1995 (c.25), s.20, p.438 below.

[12] This definition inserted by the Environment Act 1995 (c.25), s.120, sch.22, para.227(7).

"undertaking" includes any trade, business or profession and—

(a) in relation to a public or local authority, includes any of the powers or duties of that authority, and

(b) in relation to any other body of persons, whether corporate or unincorporate, includes any of the activities of that body, and

"waste" includes any substance which constitutes scrap material or an effluent or other unwanted surplus substance arising from the application of any process, and also includes any substance or article which requires to be disposed of as being broken, worn out, contaminated or otherwise spoilt[1].

(2) The Secretary of State may by order substitute for the period for the time being specified in subsection (1) as the prescribed period for determinations such other period as he considers appropriate.

(3) In determining, for the purposes of this Act, whether any radioactive material is kept or used on any premises, no account shall be taken of any radioactive material kept or used in or on any railway vehicle, road vehicle, vessel or aircraft if either—

(a) the vehicle, vessel or aircraft is on those premises in the course of a journey, or

(b) in the case of a vessel which is on those premises otherwise than in the course of a journey, the material is used in propelling the vessel or is kept in or on the vessel for use in propelling it.

(4) Any substance or article which, in the course of the carrying on of any undertaking, is discharged, discarded or otherwise dealt with as if it were waste shall, for the purposes of this Act, be presumed to be waste unless the contrary is proved.

(5) Any reference in this Act to the contamination of a substance or article is a reference to its being so affected by either or both of the following, that is to say,—

(a) absorption, admixture or adhesion of radioactive material or radioactive waste, and

(b) the emission of neutrons or ionising radiations,

as to become radioactive or to possess increased radioactivity.

(6) *This subsection relates to the application of this section to Northern Ireland.*

*Index of defined expressions.*

**48.** The following Table shows provisions defining or otherwise explaining expressions for the purposes of this Act—

| | |
|---|---|
| the appropriate Agency[2] | section 47(1) |
| the appropriate Minister | section 47(1) |
| article | section 47(1) |
| [3] | |
| contamination | section 47(5) |
| disposal | section 47(1) |
| licensee (in relation to a nuclear site licence) | section 47(1) |
| local authority | section 47(1) |
| mobile radioactive apparatus | section 3 |
| nuclear site | section 47(1) |
| nuclear site licence | section 47(1) |
| period of responsibility (in relation to a nuclear site licence) | section 47(1) |
| premises | section 47(1) |
| prescribed | section 47(1) |
| the prescribed period for determinations | section 47(1) and (2) |
| public or local authority | section 47(1) |

[1] See also subsection (4) below.
[2] This definition inserted by the Environment Act 1995 (c.25), s.120, sch.22, para.228(a).

[3] The entry relating to the chief inspector repealed by the Environment Act 1995 (c.25), s.120, sch.22, para.228(b), sch.24.

| | |
|---|---|
| radioactive material | section 1 |
| radioactive waste | section 2 |
| relevant water body | section 47(1) |
| SEPA[1] | section 47(1) |
| substance | section 47(1) |
| undertaking | section 47(1) |
| waste | section 47(1) and (4). |

*Consequential amendments and transitional and transitory provisions.*

**49.** (1) The enactments specified in Schedule 4 shall have effect subject to the amendments set out in that Schedule, being amendments consequential on the preceding provisions of this Act.

(2) The transitional and transitory provisions contained in Schedule 5[2] shall have effect.

*Repeals.*

**50.** The enactments and instruments specified in Schedule 6 (which include spent enactments) are repealed or, as the case may be, revoked to the extent specified in the third column of that Schedule, but subject to any provision at the end of any Part of that Schedule.

*Short title, commencement and extent.*

**51.** (1) This Act may be cited as the Radioactive Substances Act 1993.

(2) This Act shall come into force at the end of the period of three months beginning with the day on which it is passed.[3]

(3) This Act extends to Northern Ireland.[4]

# SCHEDULES

## SCHEDULE I

(Section 1[5].)

### SPECIFIED ELEMENTS

| ELEMENT | BECQUERELS PER GRAM (BQ G$^{-1}$) | | |
|---|---|---|---|
| | Solid | Liquid | Gas or Vapour |
| 1. Actinium | 0.37 | $7.40 \times 10^{-2}$ | $2.59 \times 10^{-6}$ |
| 2. Lead | 0.74 | $3.70 \times 10^{-3}$ | $1.11 \times 10^{-4}$ |
| 3. Polonium | 0.37 | $2.59 \times 10^{-2}$ | $2.22 \times 10^{-4}$ |
| 4. Protoactinium | 0.37 | $3.33 \times 10^{-2}$ | $1.11 \times 10^{-6}$ |
| 5. Radium | 0.37 | $3.70 \times 10^{-4}$ | $3.70 \times 10^{-5}$ |
| 6. Radon | — | — | $3.70 \times 10^{-2}$ |
| 7. Thorium | 2.59 | $3.70 \times 10^{-2}$ | $2.22 \times 10^{-5}$ |
| 8. Uranium | 11.1 | 0.74 | $7.40 \times 10^{-5}$ |

[1] This definition inserted by the Environment Act 1995 (c.25), s.120, sch.22, para.228(a).
[2] P.412 below.
[3] This Act accordingly came into force on 27 August 1993.

[4] This Manual does not set out this Act as it applies to Northern Ireland.
[5] P.383 above.

# SCHEDULE 2

*Repealed by the Environment Act 1995 (c.25), s.120, sch.22, para.229, sch.24. This amendment came into force on 1 April 1996: S.I. 1996/186.*

# SCHEDULE 3

(Section 40[1].)

Enactments, other than local enactments, to which s. 40 applies

## Part I: England and Wales

1. Sections 48, 81, 82, 141, 259 and 261 of the Public Health Act 1936[2].

2. Section 16 of the Clean Air Act 1993[3].

3. Section 5 of the Sea Fisheries Regulation Act 1966[4].

4. Section 4 of the Salmon and Freshwater Fisheries Act 1975[5].

5. Section 59 of the Building Act 1984[6].

6. The Planning (Hazardous Substances) Act 1990[7].

7. Part III of the Environmental Protection Act 1990[8].

8. Sections 72, 111 and 113(6) and Chapter III of Part IV[9] of the Water Industry Act 1991 and paragraphs 2 to 4 of Schedule 8[10] to that Act so far as they re-enact provisions of sections 43 and 44 of the Control of Pollution Act 1974.

9. Sections 82[11], 84[12], 85, 86, 87(1), 88(2), 92[13], 93, 99[14], 161[15], 190[16], 202[17], and 203[18] of and paragraph 6 of Schedule 25 to the Water Resources Act 1991.

10. Section 18 of the Water Act 1945[19] so far as it continues to have effect by virtue of Schedule 2 to the Water Consolidation (Consequential Provisions) Act 1991[20] or by virtue of provisions of the Control of Pollution Act 1974[21] not having been brought into force.

## Part II: Scotland

11. Sections[22] 32, 41, 42 and 116 of the Public Health (Scotland) Act 1897[23].

12. Section 16[24] of the Clean Air Act 1993[25].

13. The Sewerage (Scotland) Act 1968[26].

14. Sections 56A to 56N and 97B of the Town and Country Planning (Scotland) Act 1972[27].

---

[1] P.404 above.
[2] 1936 c.49.
[3] P.345 above. Para.2 substituted by the Clean Air Act 1993 (c.11), s.67(1), sch.4, para.6(a). This amendment came into force on 27 August 1993: s.68(2).
[4] 1966 c.38.
[5] P.67 above.
[6] 1984 c.55.
[7] 1990 c.10.
[8] P.187 above.
[9] P.232 above.
[10] P.264 above.
[11] P.271 above.
[12] P.273 above.
[13] P.284 above.
[14] P.289 above.
[15] P.292 above.
[16] P.298 above.
[17] P.303 above.
[18] Words "and 203" substituted by the Environment Act 1995 (c.25), s.120, sch.22, para.230(1).
[19] 1945 c.42.
[20] 1991 c.60.
[21] 1974 c.40.
[22] Former words "16, 17," repealed by the Environment Act 1995 (c.25), s.120, sch.24.
[23] 1897 c.38.
[24] P.345 above. Words "Section 16" substituted for "Sections 10 and 16" by the Environment Act 1995 (c.25), s.107, sch.17, para.8(a).
[25] Para.12 substituted by the Clean Air Act 1993 (c.11), s.67(1), sch.4, para.6(b). This amendment came into force on 27 August 1993: s.68(2).
[26] 1968 c.47.
[27] 1972 c.52.

**15.** Section 201 of the Local Government (Scotland) Act 1973[1].

**16.** Sections 30A[2], 30B, 30D[3], 30F[4], 30G, 30H(1), 31(4), (5), (8) and (9)[5], 31A, 34[6] to 42B, 46[7] to 46D and 56(1) to (3)[8] of the Control of Pollution Act 1974[9].

**17.** Sections 70, 71 and 75 of the Water (Scotland) Act 1980[10].

**17A.** Part III of the Environmental Protection Act 1990.[11]

## PART III: NORTHERN IRELAND

*Not reproduced.*

# SCHEDULE 5

(Section 49(2)[12].)

## TRANSITIONAL AND TRANSITORY PROVISIONS

### PART I: GENERAL TRANSITIONAL PROVISIONS AND SAVINGS

**1.** The substitution of this Act for the enactments repealed by this Act does not affect the continuity of the law.

**2.** Any reference, whether express or implied, in this Act or any other enactment, instrument or document to a provision of this Act shall, so far as the context permits, be construed as including, in relation to the times, circumstances and purposes in relation to which the corresponding provision of the enactments repealed by this Act has effect, a reference to that corresponding provision.

**3.** Any document made, served or issued after the commencement of this Act which contains a reference to any of the enactments repealed by this Act shall be construed, except so far as a contrary intention appears, as referring or, as the case may require, including a reference to the corresponding provision of this Act.

**4.** Paragraphs 2 and 3 have effect without prejudice to the operation of sections 16 and 17 of the Interpretation Act 1978[13] (which relate to the effect of repeals).

**5.** The power to amend or revoke the subordinate legislation reproduced in the definition of "local authority" in section 47(1)[14] shall be exercisable in relation to the provision reproduced to the same extent as it was exercisable in relation to the subordinate legislation.

**6.** Subsection (1) of section 80 of the Health and Safety at Work etc. Act 1974[15] (general power to repeal or modify Acts or instruments) shall apply to provisions of this Act which re-enact provisions previously contained in the Radioactive Substances Act 1960[16] as it applies to provisions contained in Acts passed before the Health and Safety at Work etc. Act 1974.

**7.** *This paragraph relates to Northern Ireland.*

### PART II: TRANSITORY MODIFICATIONS OF SCHEDULE 3

**8.** (1) If—

(a) no date has been appointed before the commencement of this Act as the date on which paragraph 8 of Schedule 15 of the Environmental Protection Act 1990[17] (in this paragraph referred to as "the 1990 provision") is to come into force, or

[1] 1973 c.65.
[2] P.18 above.
[3] P.21 above.
[4] P.21 above.
[5] P.22 above.
[6] P.29 above.
[7] P.41 above.
[8] P.49 above.
[9] Para.16 substituted by the Environment Act 1995 (c.25), s.120, sch.22, para.230(2).
[10] 1980 c.45.
[11] P.187 above. Para.17 inserted by the Environment Act 1995 (c.25), s.107, sch.17, para.8(b).
[12] P.410 above.
[13] 1978 c.30.
[14] P.408 above.
[15] 1974 c.37.
[16] 1960 c.34.
[17] 1990 c.43.

(*b*)  a date has been appointed which is later than that commencement,

paragraph 7 of Schedule 3 to this Act shall be omitted until the appointed day.

(2)  In this paragraph "the appointed day" means—

(*a*)  in the case mentioned in paragraph (*a*) of sub-paragraph (1) above, such day as may be appointed by the Secretary of State by order, and

(*b*)  in the case mentioned in paragraph (*b*) of that sub-paragraph, the date appointed as the day on which the 1990 provision is to come into force.

9.  (1)  If—

(*a*)  no date has been appointed before the commencement of this Act as the date on which the repeal by Schedule 4 to the Control of Pollution Act 1974[1] of the provisions of the Radioactive Substances Act 1960[2] specified in sub-paragraph (2) below (in this paragraph referred to as "the 1974 repeal") is to come into force, or

(*b*)  a date has been appointed which is later than that commencement,

Schedule 3 to this Act shall have effect until the appointed day with the modifications specified in sub-paragraph (3) below.

(2)  The provisions of the Radioactive Substances Act 1960 referred to in sub-paragraph (1)(*a*) above are—

(*a*)  in paragraph 3 of Schedule 1, the words "seventy-nine", and

(*b*)  paragraph 8A of Schedule 1.

(3)  The modifications of Schedule 3 to this Act referred to in sub-paragraph (1) above are as follows—

(*a*)  in paragraph 1 after "48" there shall be inserted "79", and

(*b*)  after paragraph 2 there shall be inserted—

"2A. Sections 2, 5 and 7 of the Rivers (Prevention of Pollution) Act 1961."

(4)  In this paragraph "the appointed day" means—

(*a*)  in the case mentioned in paragraph (*a*) of sub-paragraph (1) above, such day as may be appointed by the Secretary of State by order, and

(*b*)  in the case mentioned in paragraph (*b*) of that sub-paragraph, the date appointed as the day on which the 1974 repeal is to come into force.

10.  (1)  If—

(*a*)  no date has been appointed before the commencement of this Act for the purposes of paragraph 17 of Schedule 4 to the Planning (Consequential Provisions) Act 1990[3], or

(*b*)  a date has been appointed which is later than that commencement,

paragraph 6 of Schedule 3 to this Act shall be omitted until the appointed day.

(2)  In this paragraph "the appointed day" means—

(*a*)  in the case mentioned in paragraph (*a*) of sub-paragraph (1) above, such day as may be appointed by the Secretary of State by order, and

(*b*)  in the case mentioned in paragraph (*b*) of that sub-paragraph, the date appointed for the purposes of paragraph 17 of Schedule 4 to the Planning (Consequential Provisions) Act 1990.

11.  Until the commencement of the repeal by Part II of Schedule 16 to the Environmental Protection Act 1990[4] of subsection (5) of section 30 of the Control of Pollution Act 1974[5] (or, if the repeal of that subsection comes into force on different days, until the last of those days) Schedule 3 to this Act shall have effect—

(*a*)  with the insertion after paragraph 4 of the following paragraph—

"4B. The Control of Pollution (Special Waste) Regulations 1980.", and

(*b*)  with the insertion after paragraph 17 of the following paragraph —

"17A. The Control of Pollution (Special Waste) Regulations 1980."

12.  Until the commencement of the repeal by Part II of Schedule 16 to the Environmental Protection Act 1990[6] of section 124 of the Civic Government (Scotland) Act 1982[7] (or, if the repeal of that section comes into force on

[1]  1974 c.40.
[2]  1960 c.34.
[3]  1990 c. 11.
[4]  1990 c. 43.
[5]  1974 c. 40.
[6]  1990 c.43.
[7]  1982 c.45.

different days, until the last of those days) Schedule 3 to this Act shall have effect with the insertion at the end of Part II of the following paragraph—

"17B. Section 124 of the Civic Government (Scotland) Act 1982."

# Environment Act 1995

## Chapter 25

*Arrangement of sections*

## Part I: The Environment Agency and the Scottish Environment Protection Agency

*Chapter I: The Environment Agency*

*Establishment of the Agency*

|   |   |   |
|---|---|---|
| 1. | The Environment Agency. | 420 |

*Transfer of functions, property etc. to the Agency*

|   |   |   |
|---|---|---|
| 2. | Transfer of functions to the Agency. | 421 |
| 3. | Transfer of property, rights and liabilities to the Agency. | 422 |
| 4. | Principal aim and objectives of the Agency. | 424 |
| 5. | General functions with respect to pollution control. | 424 |
| 6. | General provisions with respect to water. | 425 |
| 7. | General environmental and recreational duties. | 427 |
| 8. | Environmental duties with respect to sites of special interest. | 428 |
| 9. | Codes of practice with respect to environmental and recreational duties. | 429 |
| 10. | Incidental functions of the Agency. | 430 |

*Advisory committees*

|   |   |   |
|---|---|---|
| 11. | Advisory committee for Wales. | 431 |
| 12. | Environment protection advisory committees. | 431 |
| 13. | Regional and local fisheries advisory committees. | 432 |

*Flood defence committees*

|   |   |   |
|---|---|---|
| 14. | Regional flood defence committees. | 433 |
| 15. | Composition of regional flood defence committees. | 434 |
| 16. | Change of composition of regional flood defence committee. | 435 |
| 17. | Local flood defence schemes and local flood defence committees. | 436 |
| 18. | Composition of local flood defence committees. | 437 |
| 19. | Membership and proceedings of flood defence committees. | 438 |

*Chapter II: The Scottish Environment Protection Agency*

*Establishment of SEPA*

|   |   |   |
|---|---|---|
| 20. | The Scottish Environment Protection Agency. | 438 |

*Transfer of functions, property etc. to SEPA*

|   |   |   |
|---|---|---|
| 21. | Transfer of functions to SEPA. | 438 |
| 22. | Transfer of property, rights and liabilities to SEPA. | 440 |
| 23. | Functions of staff commission. | 441 |

*Other functions etc. of SEPA*

|   |   |   |
|---|---|---|
| 24. | Consultation with respect to drainage works. | 442 |

25. Assessing flood risk.   442
26. Power of SEPA to purchase land compulsorily.   442
27. Power of SEPA to obtain information about land.   442
28. Power of SEPA to promote or oppose private legislation.   443
29. Procedure relating to making of byelaws.   443
30. Records held by SEPA.   444

*General powers and duties*

31. Guidance on sustainable development and other aims and objectives.   444
32. General environmental and recreational duties.   445
33. General duties with respect to pollution control.   445
34. General duties with respect to water.   446
35. Environmental duties as respects Natural Heritage Areas and sites of special interest.   447
36. Codes of practice with respect to environmental and recreational duties.   448

## Chapter III: Miscellaneous, general and supplemental provisions relating to the new Agencies

*Additional general powers and duties*

37. Incidental general functions.   448
38. Delegation of functions by Ministers etc. to the new Agencies.   449
39. General duty of the new Agencies to have regard to costs and benefits in exercising powers.   451
40. Ministerial directions to the new Agencies.   451

*Charging schemes*

41. Power to make schemes imposing charges.   452
42. Approval of charging schemes.   454

*Incidental power to impose charges*

43. Incidental power of the new Agencies to impose charges.   455

*General financial provisions*

44. General financial duties.   455
45. Accounts and records.   456
46. Audit.   457
47. Grants to the new Agencies.   458
48. Borrowing powers.   458
49. Government loans to the new Agencies.   458
50. Government guarantees of a new Agency's borrowing.   459

*Information*

51. Provision of information by the new Agencies.   459
52. Annual report.   460

*Supplemental provisions*

53. Inquiries and other hearings.   460
54. Appearance in legal proceedings.   461
55. Continuity of exercise of functions: the new Agencies.   461
56. Interpretation of Part I.   462

## Part II: Contaminated land and abandoned mines

57. Contaminated land. 465
58. Abandoned mines: England and Wales. 465
59. Abandoned mines: Scotland. 465
60. Amendments to sections 89 and 161 of the Water Resources Act 1991. 465

## Part III: National parks

61.–79. *Not reproduced.*

## Part IV: Air quality

80. National air quality strategy. 465
81. Functions of the new Agencies. 466
82. Local authority reviews. 467
83. Designation of air quality management areas. 467
84. Duties of local authorities in relation to designated areas. 467
85. Reserve powers of the Secretary of State or SEPA. 468
86. Functions of county councils for areas for which there are district councils. 469
87. Regulations for the purposes of Part IV. 471
88. Guidance for the purposes of Part IV. 473
89. Application of Part IV to the Isles of Scilly. 474
90. Supplemental provisions. 474
91. Interpretation of Part IV. 474

## Part V: Miscellaneous, general and supplemental provisions

*Waste*

92. National waste strategy. 475
93. Producer responsibility: general. 475
94. Producer responsibility: supplementary provisions. 477
95. Producer responsibility: offences. 480

*Mineral planning permissions*

96. *Not reproduced.*

*Hedgerows etc.*

97.–99. *Not reproduced.*

*Drainage*

100.–101. *Not reproduced.*

*Fisheries*

102.–105. *Not reproduced.*

*New provisions for Scotland*

106. Control of pollution of water in Scotland. 481
107. Statutory nuisances: Scotland. 481

*Powers of entry*

108. Powers of enforcing authorities and persons authorised by them. 481
109. Power to deal with cause of imminent danger of serious pollution etc. 486

110.  Offences.                                                                                    486

*Evidence*

111.  Evidence in connection with certain pollution offences.                                      487

*Offences*

112.  Amendment of certain offences relating to false or misleading statements or false
      entries.                                                                                     488

*Information*

113.  Disclosure of information.                                                                   488

*Appeals*

114.  Power of Secretary of State to delegate his functions of determining, or to refer matters
      involved in, appeals.                                                                        489

*Crown application*

115.  Application of this Act to the Crown.                                                         490
116.  Application of certain other enactments to the Crown.                                         491

*Isles of Scilly*

117.  Application of this Act to the Isles of Scilly.                                               491
118.  Application of certain other enactments to the Isles of Scilly.                               491

*Miscellaneous and supplemental*

119.  Stamp duty.                                                                                  492
120.  Minor and consequential amendments, transitional and transitory provisions, savings
      and repeals.                                                                                 492
121.  Local statutory provisions: consequential amendments etc.                                    493
122.  Directions.                                                                                  494
123.  Service of documents.                                                                        494
124.  General interpretation.                                                                      495
125.  Short title, commencement, extent, etc.                                                      496

SCHEDULES:

    Schedule 1—The Environment Agency.                                          497
    Schedule 2—Transfers of property etc: supplemental provisions.               500
    Part I—Introductory.                                                          500
    Part II—Transfer schemes.                                                     503
    Part III—General provisions with respect to transfers by or under section 3 or 22.   505
    Schedule 3—Environment protection advisory committees.                        506
    Schedule 4—Boundaries of regional flood defence areas.                        508
    Schedule 5—Membership and proceedings of regional and local flood defence
      committees.                                                       511
    Part I—Membership of flood defence committees.                                511
    Part II—Proceedings of flood defence committees.                              514
    Schedule 6—The Scottish Environment Protection Agency.                        516
    Schedules 7–10—*Not reproduced.*
    Schedule 11—Air quality: supplemental provisions.                            520
    Schedule 12—Schedule 2A to the Environmental Protection Act 1990               524
    Schedules 13–15—*Not reproduced.*
    Schedule 16—Pollution of rivers and coastal waters in Scotland: amendment of the
      Control of Pollution Act 1974.                                    524

Schedule 17—Statutory nuisances: Scotland.                                            525
Schedule 18—Supplemental provisions with respect to powers of entry.                  525
Schedule 19—Offences relating to false or misleading statements or false entries.     526
Schedule 20—Delegation of appellate functions of the Secretary of State.              527
Schedule 21—Application of certain enactments to the Crown.                           529
Schedule 22—*Not reproduced.*
Schedule 23—Transitional and transitory provisions and savings.                       529
Part I—General transitional provisions and savings.                                   529
Part II—Transitory provisions in respect of flood defence.                            535
Schedule 24—*Not reproduced.*

# Environment Act 1995

## 1995 Chapter 25

An Act to provide for the establishment of a body corporate to be known as the Environment Agency and a body corporate to be known as the Scottish Environment Protection Agency; to provide for the transfer of functions, property, rights and liabilities to those bodies and for the conferring of other functions on them; to make provision with respect to contaminated land and abandoned mines; to make further provision in relation to National Parks; to make further provision for the control of pollution, the conservation of natural resources and the conservation or enhancement of the environment; to make provision for imposing obligations on certain persons in respect of certain products or materials; to make provision in relation to fisheries; to make provision for certain enactments to bind the Crown; to make provision with respect to the application of certain enactments in relation to the Isles of Scilly; and for connected purposes.

[19th July 1995[1]]

## PART I: The Environment Agency and the Scottish Environment Protection Agency

*Chapter I: The Environment Agency*

*Establishment of the Agency*

*The Environment Agency.*

1. (1) There shall be a body corporate to be known as the Environment Agency or, in Welsh, Asiantaeth yr Amgylchedd (in this Act referred to as "the Agency"), for the purpose of carrying out the functions[2] transferred or assigned to it by or under this Act.

(2) The Agency shall consist of not less than eight nor more than fifteen members of whom—

(a) three shall be appointed by the Minister[3]; and

(b) the others shall be appointed by the Secretary of State.

(3) The Secretary of State shall designate—

(a) one of the members as the chairman of the Agency, and

(b) another of them as the deputy chairman of the Agency.

(4) In appointing a person to be a member of the Agency, the Secretary of State or, as the case may be, the Minister shall have regard to the desirability of appointing a person who has experience of, and has shown capacity in, some matter relevant to the functions of the Agency.

(5) Subject to the provisions of section 38 below[4], the Agency shall not be regarded—

(a) as the servant or agent of the Crown, or as enjoying any status, immunity or privilege of the Crown; or

(b) by virtue of any connection with the Crown, as exempt from any tax, duty, rate, levy or other charge whatsoever, whether general or local;

---

[1] The commencement dates of this Act are noted at the end of each section.
[2] "Functions" includes powers and duties: s.124(1) below.
[3] "The Minister" defined by s.56(1), p.464 below.
[4] P.449 below.

and the Agency's property shall not be regarded as property of, or property held on behalf of, the Crown.

(6) The provisions of Schedule 1 to this Act[1] shall have effect with respect to the Agency.[2]

.......................................................................................................................................................

*Transfer of functions, property etc. to the Agency*

*Transfer of functions to the Agency.*

**2.** (1) On the transfer date[3] there shall by virtue of this section be transferred to the Agency[4]—

(a) the functions[5] of the National Rivers Authority, that is to say—

(i) its functions under or by virtue of Part II (water resources management) of the Water Resources Act 1991 (in this Part referred to as "the 1991 Act");

(ii) its functions under or by virtue of Part III of that Act[6] (control of pollution of water resources);

(iii) its functions under or by virtue of Part IV of that Act (flood defence) and the Land Drainage Act 1991[7] and the functions transferred to the Authority by virtue of section 136(8) of the Water Act 1989[8] and paragraph 1(3) of Schedule 15 to that Act (transfer of land drainage functions under local statutory provisions and subordinate legislation);

(iv) its functions under or by virtue of Part VII of the 1991 Act[9] (land and works powers);

(v) its functions under or by virtue of the Diseases of Fish Act 1937[10], the Sea Fisheries Regulation Act 1966[11], the Salmon and Freshwater Fisheries Act 1975[12], Part V of the 1991 Act or any other enactment relating to fisheries;

(vi) the functions as a navigation authority[13], harbour authority[14] or conservancy authority[15] which were transferred to the Authority by virtue of Chapter V of Part III of the Water Act 1989 or paragraph 23(3) of Schedule 13 to that Act or which have been transferred to the Authority by any order or agreement under Schedule 2 to the 1991 Act;

(vii) its functions under Schedule 2 to the 1991 Act;

(viii) the functions assigned to the Authority by or under any other enactment, apart from this Act;

(b) the functions of waste regulation authorities[16], that is to say, the functions conferred or imposed on them by or under—

(i) the Control of Pollution (Amendment) Act 1989[17], or

(ii) Part II of the Environmental Protection Act 1990[18] (in this Part referred to as "the 1990 Act"),

or assigned to them by or under any other enactment, apart from this Act;

(c) the functions of disposal authorities[19] under or by virtue of the waste regulation provisions of the Control of Pollution Act 1974[20],

---

[1] P.497 below.
[2] This section came into force on 28 July 1995: S.I. 1995/1983.
[3] "The transfer date" defined by s.56(1), p.464 below; the transfer date was 1 April 1996: S.I. 1996/234.
[4] "The Agency" means the Environment Agency: s.124(1) below.
[5] "Functions" includes powers and duties: s.124(1) below.
[6] P.271 above.
[7] 1991 c.59.
[8] 1989 c.15.
[9] P.292 above.

[10] 1937 c.33.
[11] 1966 c.38.
[12] P.67 above.
[13] "Navigation authority" defined by s.56(1), p.464 below.
[14] "Harbour authority" defined by s.56(1), p.464 below.
[15] "Conservancy authority" defined by s.56(1), p.463 below.
[16] "Waste regulation authority" defined by s.56(1), p.464 below.
[17] P.71 above.
[18] P.112 above.
[19] "Disposal authority" defined by s.56(1), p.463 below.
[20] 1974 c.40.

(*d*) the functions of the chief inspector for England and Wales constituted under section 16(3) of the 1990 Act, that is to say, the functions conferred or imposed on him by or under Part I of that Act[1] or assigned to him by or under any other enactment, apart from this Act;

(*e*) the functions of the chief inspector for England and Wales appointed under section 4(2)(*a*) of the Radioactive Substances Act 1993, that is to say, the functions conferred or imposed on him by or under that Act[2] or assigned to him by or under any other enactment, apart from this Act;

(*f*) the functions conferred or imposed by or under the Alkali, &c, Works Regulation Act 1906[3] (in this section referred to as "the 1906 Act") on the chief, or any other, inspector (within the meaning of that Act), so far as exercisable in relation to England and Wales;

(*g*) so far as exercisable in relation to England and Wales, the functions in relation to improvement notices and prohibition notices under Part I of the Health and Safety at Work etc. Act 1974[4] (in this section referred to as "the 1974 Act") of inspectors appointed under section 19 of that Act by the Secretary of State in his capacity as the enforcing authority responsible in relation to England and Wales for the enforcement of the 1906 Act and section 5 of the 1974 Act; and

(*h*) the functions of the Secretary of State specified in subsection (2) below.

(2) The functions of the Secretary of State mentioned in subsection (1)(*h*) above are the following, that is to say—

(*a*) so far as exercisable in relation to England and Wales, his functions under section 30(1) of the Radioactive Substances Act 1993[5] (power to dispose of radioactive waste);

(*b*) his functions under Chapter III of Part IV of the Water Industry Act 1991 in relation to special category effluent[6], within the meaning of that Chapter, other than any function of making regulations or of making orders under section 139 of that Act[7];

(*c*) so far as exercisable in relation to England and Wales, the functions conferred or imposed on him by virtue of his being, for the purposes of Part I of the 1974 Act, the authority which is by any of the relevant statutory provisions made responsible for the enforcement of the 1906 Act and section 5 of the 1974 Act;

(*d*) so far as exercisable in relation to England and Wales, his functions under, or under regulations made by virtue of, section 9 of the 1906 Act (registration of works), other than any functions of his as an appellate authority or any function of making regulations;

(*e*) so far as exercisable in relation to England and Wales, his functions under regulations 7(1) and 8(2) of, and paragraph 2(2)(*c*) of Schedule 2 to, the Sludge (Use in Agriculture) Regulations 1989[8] (which relate to the provision of information and the testing of soil).

(3) The National Rivers Authority and the London Waste Regulation Authority are hereby abolished.[9]

..................................................................................................................................................................

*Transfer of property, rights and liabilities to the Agency.*

**3.** (1) On the transfer date[10]—

(*a*) the property, rights and liabilities—

(i) of the National Rivers Authority, and

(ii) of the London Waste Regulation Authority,

shall, by virtue of this paragraph, be transferred to and vested in the Agency[11];

---

[1] Part I of the 1990 Act is at p.88 above.
[2] The Radioactive Substances Act 1993 is at p.381 above.
[3] 1906 c. 14.
[4] 1974 c. 37.
[5] P.400 above.
[6] P.232 above. "Special category effluent" is defined in s.138 of the 1991 Act at p.246 above.
[7] P.246 above.

[8] P.547 below.
[9] This section came into force on 1 April 1996: S.I. 1996/186.
[10] "The transfer date " defined by s.56(1), p.464 below; the transfer date was 1 April 1996: S.I. 1996/234.
[11] "The Agency" means the Environment.Agency: s.124(1) below.

(b) any property, rights or liabilities which are the subject of—

    (i) a scheme made under the following provisions of this section by the Secretary of State, or

    (ii) a scheme made under those provisions by a body which is a waste regulation authority[1] and approved (with or without modifications) under those provisions by the Secretary of State,

    shall be transferred to and vested in the Agency by and in accordance with the scheme.

(2) The Secretary of State may, before the transfer date, make a scheme for the transfer to the Agency of such of—

(a) his property, rights and liabilities, or

(b) the property, rights and liabilities of any of the inspectors or chief inspectors mentioned in subsection (1) of section 2 above,

as appear to the Secretary of State appropriate to be so transferred in consequence of the transfer of any functions to the Agency by virtue of any of paragraphs (d) to (h) of that subsection.

(3) It shall be the duty of every body which is a waste regulation authority, other than the London Waste Regulation Authority—

(a) to make a scheme, after consultation with the Agency, for the transfer to the Agency of such of the body's property, rights and liabilities as appear to the body appropriate to be so transferred in consequence of the transfer of any functions to the Agency by virtue of section 2(1)(b) or (c) above; and

(b) to submit that scheme to the Secretary of State for his approval before such date as he may direct.

(4) Any body preparing a scheme in pursuance of subsection (3) above shall take into account any guidance given by the Secretary of State as to the provisions which he regards as appropriate for inclusion in the scheme[2].

(5) Where a scheme under subsection (3) above is submitted to the Secretary of State, he may—

(a) approve the scheme;

(b) approve the scheme subject to such modifications[3] as he considers appropriate; or

(c) reject the scheme;

but the power conferred on the Secretary of State by paragraph (b) above shall only be exercisable after consultation with the body which submitted the scheme to him and with the Agency.

(6) The Secretary of State may, in the case of any body which is required to make a scheme under subsection (3) above, himself make a scheme for the transfer to the Agency of such of the body's property, rights or liabilities as appear to him appropriate to be so transferred in consequence of the transfer of any functions to the Agency by virtue of section 2(1)(b) or (c) above, if—

(a) the body fails to submit a scheme under subsection (3) above to him for approval before the due date; or

(b) the Secretary of State rejects a scheme under that subsection submitted to him by that body;

but nothing in this subsection shall prevent the Secretary of State from approving any scheme which may be submitted to him after the due date.

(7) The Secretary of State may, at any time before the transfer date, modify any scheme made or approved by him under this section but only after consultation with the Agency and, in the case of a scheme which was approved by him (with or without modifications), after consultation with the body which submitted the scheme to him for approval.

[1] "Waste regulation authority" defined by s.56(1), p.464 below.
[2] Guidance was published in the Department of the Environment Circular 15/95, *Environment Act 1995: Transfer of property, rights and liabilities from waste regulation authorities to the Environment Agency*, issued on 29 August 1995.
[3] "Modifications" defined by s.124(1), p.495 below.

(8)  Schedule 2 to this Act[1] shall have effect in relation to transfers by or under this section.[2]

*Principal aim and objectives of the Agency.*

**4.**  (1)  It shall be the principal aim of the Agency[3] (subject to and in accordance with the provisions of this Act or any other enactment and taking into account any likely costs[4]) in discharging its functions[5] so to protect or enhance the environment, taken as a whole, as to make the contribution towards attaining the objective of achieving sustainable development mentioned in subsection (3) below.

(2)  The Ministers[6] shall from time to time give guidance to the Agency with respect to objectives which they consider it appropriate for the Agency to pursue in the discharge of its functions.[7]

(3)  The guidance given under subsection (2) above must include guidance with respect to the contribution which, having regard to the Agency's responsibilities and resources, the Ministers consider it appropriate for the Agency to make, by the discharge of its functions, towards attaining the objective of achieving sustainable development.

(4)  In discharging its functions, the Agency shall have regard to guidance given under this section.

(5)  The power to give guidance to the Agency under this section shall only be exercisable after consultation with the Agency and such other bodies or persons as the Ministers consider it appropriate to consult in relation to the guidance in question.

(6)  A draft of any guidance proposed to be given under this section shall be laid before each House of Parliament and the guidance shall not be given until after the period of 40 days beginning with the day on which the draft was so laid or, if the draft is laid on different days, the later of the two days.

(7)  If, within the period mentioned in subsection (6) above, either House resolves that the guidance, the draft of which was laid before it, should not be given, the Ministers shall not give that guidance.

(8)  In reckoning any period of 40 days for the purposes of subsection (6) or (7) above, no account shall be taken of any time during which Parliament is dissolved or prorogued or during which both Houses are adjourned for more than four days.

(9)  The Ministers shall arrange for any guidance given under this section to be published in such manner as they consider appropriate.[8]

*General functions with respect to pollution control.*

**5.**  (1)  The Agency's[9] pollution control powers[10] shall be exercisable for the purpose of preventing or minimising, or remedying or mitigating the effects of, pollution of the environment[11].

(2)  The Agency shall, for the purpose—

(*a*)  of facilitating the carrying out of its pollution control functions[12], or

(*b*)  of enabling it to form an opinion of the general state of pollution of the environment,

compile information relating to such pollution (whether the information is acquired by the Agency carrying out observations or is obtained in any other way).

(3)  If required by either of the Ministers[13] to do so, the Agency shall—

---

[1]  P.500 below.
[2]  Subsection (1) came into force on 1 April 1996: S.I. 1996/186; (2)–(8) came into force on 28 July 1995: S.I. 1995/1983.
[3]  "The Agency" means the Environment Agency: s.124(1) below.
[4]  "Costs" defined by s.56(1), p.463 below.
[5]  "Functions" includes powers and duties: s.124(1) below.
[6]  "The Ministers" defined by s.56(1), p.464 below.
[7]  A note on guidance under this Act is at p.823 below.
[8]  This section came into force on 28 July 1995: S.I.

1995/1983.
[9]  "The Agency" means the Environment Agency: s.124(1) below.
[10]  "Pollution control powers" defined by subsection (5) below.
[11]  "The environment" has the same meaning as in Part I of the Environmental Protection Act 1990: s.56 below; "the environment" is defined in s.1 of the 1990 Act, p.89 above.
[12]  "Pollution control functions" defined by subsection (5) below.
[13]  "The Ministers" defined by s.56(1), p.464 below.

(*a*) carry out assessments (whether generally or for such particular purpose as may be specified in the requirement) of the effect, or likely effect, on the environment of existing or potential levels of pollution of the environment and report its findings to that Minister; or

(*b*) prepare and send to that Minister a report identifying—

    (i) the options which the Agency considers to be available for preventing or minimising, or remedying or mitigating the effects of, pollution of the environment, whether generally or in cases or circumstances specified in the requirement; and

    (ii) the costs[1] and benefits of such options as are identified by the Agency pursuant to sub-paragraph (i) above.

(4) The Agency shall follow developments in technology and techniques for preventing or minimising, or remedying or mitigating the effects of, pollution of the environment.

(5) In this section, "pollution control powers" and "pollution control functions", in relation to the Agency, mean respectively its powers or its functions[2] under or by virtue of the following enactments, that is to say—

(*a*) the Alkali, &c, Works Regulation Act 1906[3];

(*b*) Part I of the Health and Safety at Work etc. Act 1974[4];

(*c*) Part I of the Control of Pollution Act 1974[5];

(*d*) the Control of Pollution (Amendment) Act 1989[6];

(*e*) Parts I[7], II[8] and IIA[9] of the 1990 Act (integrated pollution control etc, waste on land and contaminated land);

(*f*) Chapter III of Part IV of the Water Industry Act 1991[10] (special category effluent);

(*g*) Part III[11] and sections 161[12] to 161D of the 1991 Act (control of pollution of water resources);

(*h*) the Radioactive Substances Act 1993[13];

(*j*) regulations made by virtue of section 2(2) of the European Communities Act 1972[14], to the extent that the regulations relate to pollution.[15]

*General provisions with respect to water.*

**6.** (1) It shall be the duty of the Agency[16], to such extent as it considers desirable, generally to promote—

(*a*) the conservation and enhancement of the natural beauty and amenity of inland and coastal waters and of land associated with such waters;

(*b*) the conservation of flora and fauna which are dependent on an aquatic environment; and

(*c*) the use of such waters and land for recreational purposes;

and it shall be the duty of the Agency, in determining what steps to take in performance of the duty imposed by virtue of paragraph (*c*) above, to take into account the needs of persons who are chronically sick or disabled.

This subsection is without prejudice to the duties of the Agency under section 7 below.

(2) It shall be the duty of the Agency to take all such action as it may from time to time consider, in accordance with any directions given under section 40 below[17], to be necessary or expedient for the purpose—

[1] "Costs" defined by s.56(1), p.463 below.
[2] "Functions" includes powers and duties: s.124(1) below.
[3] 1906 c.14.
[4] 1974 c.37.
[5] 1974 c.40.
[6] P.71 above.
[7] P.89 above.
[8] P.112 above.
[9] P.162 above.
[10] P.232 above.
[11] P.271 above.
[12] P.292 above.
[13] P.381 above.
[14] 1972 c.68.
[15] Subsections (2) and (5) came into force on 1 February 1996; (1), (3) and (4) came into force on 1 April 1996: S.I. 1996/186.
[16] "The Agency" means the Environment Agency: s.124(1) below.
[17] P.451 below.

(*a*) of conserving, redistributing or otherwise augmenting water resources in England and Wales; and

(*b*) of securing the proper use of water resources in England and Wales;

but nothing in this subsection shall be construed as relieving any water undertaker of the obligation to develop water resources for the purpose of performing any duty imposed on it by virtue of section 37 of the Water Industry Act 1991[1] (general duty to maintain water supply system).

(3) The provisions of the 1991 Act[2] relating to the functions[3] of the Agency under Chapter II of Part II of that Act and the related water resources provisions[4] so far as they relate to other functions of the Agency shall not apply to so much of any inland waters as—

(*a*) are part of the River Tweed[5];

(*b*) are part of the River Esk or River Sark at a point where either of the banks of the river is in Scotland; or

(*c*) are part of any tributary stream of the River Esk or the River Sark at a point where either of the banks of the tributary stream is in Scotland.

(4) Subject to section 106 of the 1991 Act (obligation to carry out flood defence functions through committees), the Agency shall in relation to England and Wales exercise a general supervision over all matters relating to flood defence.

(5) The Agency's flood defence functions[6] shall extend to the territorial sea adjacent to England and Wales in so far as—

(*a*) the area of any regional flood defence committee includes any area of that territorial sea; or

(*b*) section 165(2) or (3) of the 1991 Act (drainage works for the purpose of defence against sea water or tidal water, and works etc to secure an adequate outfall for a main river) provides for the exercise of any power in the territorial sea.

(6) It shall be the duty of the Agency to maintain, improve and develop salmon fisheries, trout fisheries, freshwater fisheries and eel fisheries.

(7) The area in respect of which the Agency shall carry out its functions relating to fisheries shall be the whole of England and Wales, together with—

(*a*) such part of the territorial sea adjacent to England and Wales as extends for six miles[7] from the baselines from which the breadth of that sea is measured,

(*b*) in the case of—

   (i)   the Diseases of Fish Act 1937[8],

   (ii)  the Salmon and Freshwater Fisheries Act 1975[9],

   (iii) Part V of the 1991 Act (general control of fisheries), and

   (iv)  subsection (6) above,

so much of the River Esk, with its banks and tributary streams up to their source, as is situated in Scotland, and

(*c*) in the case of sections 31 to 34 and 36(2) of the Salmon and Freshwater Fisheries Act 1975 as applied by section 39(1B) of that Act, so much of the catchment area of the River Esk as is situated in Scotland,

but, in the case of the enactments specified in paragraph (*b*) above, excluding the River Tweed.

(8) In this section—

"miles" means international nautical miles of 1,852 metres;

[1] 1991 c.56.
[2] "The 1991 Act" means the Water Resources Act 1991: s.56(1) below.
[3] "Functions" includes powers and duties: s.124(1) below.
[4] For "the related water resources provisions" see subsection (8) below and p.315 above.
[5] "The River Tweed" defined by subsection (8) below.
[6] "Flood defence functions" defined by s.56(1), p.464 below.
[7] "Miles" defined by subsection (8) below.
[8] 1937 c.33.
[9] P.67 above.

"the related water resources provisions" has the same meaning as it has in the 1991 Act;

"the River Tweed" means "the river" within the meaning of the Tweed Fisheries Amendment Act 1859[1] as amended by byelaws.[2]

........................................................................................................................................................................

*General environmental and recreational duties.*

7. (1) It shall be the duty of each of the Ministers[3] and of the Agency[4], in formulating or considering—

(a) any proposals relating to any functions[5] of the Agency other than its pollution control functions[6], so far as may be consistent—

(i) with the purposes of any enactment relating to the functions of the Agency,

(ii) in the case of each of the Ministers, with the objective of achieving sustainable development,

(iii) in the case of the Agency, with any guidance under section 4 above[7],

(iv) in the case of the Secretary of State, with his duties under section 2 of the Water Industry Act 1991[8],

so to exercise any power conferred on him or it with respect to the proposals as to further the conservation and enhancement of natural beauty and the conservation of flora, fauna and geological or physiographical features of special interest;

(b) any proposals relating to pollution control functions of the Agency, to have regard to the desirability of conserving and enhancing natural beauty and of conserving flora, fauna and geological or physiographical features of special interest;

(c) any proposal relating to any functions of the Agency—

(i) to have regard to the desirability of protecting and conserving buildings[9], sites and objects of archaeological, architectural, engineering or historic interest;

(ii) to take into account any effect which the proposals would have on the beauty or amenity of any rural or urban area or on any such flora, fauna, features, buildings, sites or objects; and

(iii) to have regard to any effect which the proposals would have on the economic and social well-being of local communities in rural areas.

(2) Subject to subsection (1) above, it shall be the duty of each of the Ministers and of the Agency, in formulating or considering any proposals relating to any functions of the Agency—

(a) to have regard to the desirability of preserving for the public any freedom of access to areas of woodland, mountains, moor, heath, down, cliff or foreshore and other places of natural beauty;

(b) to have regard to the desirability of maintaining the availability to the public of any facility for visiting or inspecting any building, site or object of archaeological, architectural, engineering or historic interest; and

(c) to take into account any effect which the proposals would have on any such freedom of access or on the availability of any such facility.

(3) Subsections (1) and (2) above shall apply so as to impose duties on the Agency in relation to—

(a) any proposals relating to the functions of a water undertaker or sewerage undertaker,

---

[1] 1859 c.lxx.

[2] This section came into force on 1 April 1996: S.I. 1996/186.

[3] "The Ministers" defined by s.56(1), p.464 below.

[4] "The Agency" means the Environment Agency: s.124(1) below.

[5] "Functions" includes powers and duties: s.124(1) below.

[6] "Pollution control functions" has the same meaning as in s.5(5) above: subsection (7) below.

[7] P.424 above.

[8] S.2 of the Water Industry Act 1991 is set out in the companion volume: Fry, Michael, *A Manual of Nature Conservation Law*, Oxford, 1995, at p.273.

[9] "Building" includes structure: subsection (7) below.

(*b*) any proposals relating to the management, by the company holding an appointment as such an undertaker, of any land for the time being held by that company for any purpose whatever (whether or not connected with the carrying out of the functions of a water undertaker or sewerage undertaker), and

(*c*) any proposal which by virtue of section 156(7) of the Water Industry Act 1991[1] (disposals of protected land) falls to be treated for the purposes of section 3 of that Act[2] as a proposal relating to the functions of a water undertaker or sewerage undertaker,

as they apply in relation to proposals relating to the Agency's own functions, other than its pollution control functions.

(4) Subject to obtaining the consent of any navigation authority[3], harbour authority[4] or conservancy authority[5] before doing anything which causes obstruction of, or other interference with, navigation which is subject to the control of that authority, it shall be the duty of the Agency to take such steps as are—

(*a*) reasonably practicable, and

(*b*) consistent with the purposes of the enactments relating to the functions of the Agency,

for securing, so long as the Agency has rights to the use of water or land associated with water, that those rights are exercised so as to ensure that the water or land is made available for recreational purposes and is so made available in the best manner.

(5) It shall be the duty of the Agency, in determining what steps to take in performance of any duty imposed by virtue of subsection (4) above, to take into account the needs of persons who are chronically sick or disabled.

(6) Nothing in this section, the following provisions of this Act or the 1991 Act[6] shall require recreational facilities made available by the Agency to be made available free of charge.

(7) In this section—

"building" includes structure;

"pollution control functions" in relation to the Agency, has the same meaning as in section 5 above[7].[8]

---

*Environmental duties with respect to sites of special interest.*

**8.** (1) Where the Nature Conservancy Council for England[9] or the Countryside Council for Wales[10] is of the opinion that any area of land in England or, as the case may be, in Wales—

(*a*) is of special interest by reason of its flora, fauna or geological or physiographical features, and

(*b*) may at any time be affected by schemes, works, operations or activities of the Agency[11] or by an authorisation[12] given by the Agency,

that Council shall notify the fact that the land is of special interest for that reason to the Agency.[13]

[1] S.156 of the Water Industry Act 1991 is set out in the companion volume: Fry, Michael, *A Manual of Nature Conservation Law*, Oxford, 1995, at p.279.
[2] S.3 of the Water Industry Act 1991 is set out in the companion volume: Fry, Michael, *A Manual of Nature Conservation Law*, Oxford, 1995, at p.275.
[3] "Navigation authority" defined by s.56(1), p.464 below.
[4] "Harbour authority" defined by s.56(1), p.464 below.
[5] "Conservancy authority" defined by s.56(1), p.463 below.
[6] "The 1991 Act" means the Water Resources Act 1991: s.56(1) below.
[7] P.424 above.
[8] This section came into force on 28 July 1995: S.I. 1995/1983.
[9] The Nature Conservancy Council for England, also known as English Nature, is established by the Environmental Protection Act 1990, s.128. This section is set out in the companion volume: Fry, Michael, A *Manual of Nature Conservation Law*, Oxford, 1995, at p.229.
[10] The Countryside Council for Wales is established by the Environmental Protection Act 1990, s.128. This section is set out in the companion volume: Fry, Michael, A *Manual of Nature Conservation Law*, Oxford, 1995, at p.229.
[11] "The Agency" means the Environment Agency: s.124(1) below.
[12] "Authorisation" defined by subsection (5) below.
[13] For provisions relating to sites of special scientific interest see the Wildlife and Countryside Act 1981 (c.69), ss.28–33. These sections are set out in the companion volume: Fry, Michael, A *Manual of Nature Conservation Law*, Oxford, 1995, beginning at p.168.

(2)  Where a National Park authority[1] or the Broads Authority[2] is of the opinion that any area of land in a National Park or in the Broads[3]—

(a)  is land in relation to which the matters for the purposes of which sections 6(1)[4] and 7 above (other than section 7(1)(c)(iii) above) have effect are of particular importance, and

(b)  may at any time be affected by schemes, works, operations or activities of the Agency or by an authorisation given by the Agency,

the National Park authority or Broads Authority shall notify the Agency of the fact that the land is such land, and of the reasons why those matters are of particular importance in relation to the land.

(3)  Where the Agency has received a notification under subsection (1) or (2) above with respect to any land, it shall consult the notifying body before carrying out or authorising any works, operations or activities which appear to the Agency to be likely—

(a)  to destroy or damage any of the flora, fauna, or geological or physiographical features by reason of which the land is of special interest; or

(b)  significantly to prejudice anything the importance of which is one of the reasons why the matters mentioned in subsection (2) above are of particular importance in relation to that land.

(4)  Subsection (3) above shall not apply in relation to anything done in an emergency where particulars of what is done and of the emergency are notified to the Nature Conservancy Council for England, the Countryside Council for Wales, the National Park authority in question or, as the case may be, the Broads Authority as soon as practicable after that thing is done.

(5)  In this section—

"authorisation" includes any consent or licence;

"the Broads" has the same meaning as in the Norfolk and Suffolk Broads Act 1988[5]; and

"National Park authority", subject to subsection (6) below, means a National Park authority established under section 63 below which has become the local planning authority for the National Park in question.

(6)  As respects any period before a National Park authority established under section 63 below in relation to a National Park becomes the local planning authority for that National Park, any reference in subsections (1) to (4) above to a National Park authority shall be taken as a reference to the National Park Committee or joint or special planning board for that National Park.[6]

*Codes Or practice with respect to environmental and recreational duties.*

9. (1)  Each of the Ministers[7] shall have power by order to approve any code of practice issued (whether by him or by another person) for the purpose of—

(a)  giving practical guidance to the Agency[8] with respect to any of the matters for the purposes of which sections 6(1)[9], 7 and 8 above have effect, and

(b)  promoting what appear to him to be desirable practices by the Agency with respect to those matters,

and may at any time by such an order approve a modification[10] of such a code or withdraw his approval of such a code or modification.

---

[1]  For "National Park authority" see subsection (5) below.

[2]  The Broads Authority is established by the Norfolk and Suffolk Broads Act 1988 (c.4), s.1. This section is set out in the companion volume: Fry, Michael, *A Manual of Nature Conservation Law*, Oxford, 1995, at p.221.

[3]  For "the Broads" see subsection (5) below.

[4]  P.425 above.

[5]  1988 c.4. "The Broads" are defined in s.2(3) of the 1988 Act. This section is set out in the companion volume: Fry, Michael, *A.Manual of Nature Conservation Law*, Oxford, 1995, at p.222.

[6]  This section came into force on 1 April 1996: S.I. 1996/186.

[7]  "The Ministers" defined by s.56(1), p.464 below.

[8]  "The Agency" means the Environment Agency: s.124(1) below.

[9]  P.425 above.

[10]  "Modification" defined by s.124(1), p.495 below.

(2) In discharging its duties under section 6(1), 7 or 8 above, the Agency shall have regard to any code of practice, and any modifications of a code of practice, for the time being approved under this section.

(3) Neither of the Ministers shall make an order under this section unless he has first consulted—

(a) the Agency;

(b) the Countryside Commission[1], the Nature Conservancy Council for England[2] and the Countryside Council for Wales[3];

(c) the Historic Buildings and Monuments Commission for England;

(d) the Sports Council and the Sports Council for Wales; and

(e) such other persons as he considers it appropriate to consult.

(4) The power of each of the Ministers to make an order under this section shall be exercisable by statutory instrument; and any statutory instrument containing such an order shall be subject to annulment in pursuance of a resolution of either House of Parliament.[4]

*Incidental functions of the Agency*.

**10.** (1) This section has effect—

(a) for the purposes of section 37(1) below[5], as it applies in relation to the Agency[6]; and

(b) for the construction of any other enactment which, by reference to the functions[7] of the Agency, confers any power on or in relation to the Agency;

and any reference in this section to "the relevant purposes" is a reference to the purposes described in paragraphs (a) and (b) above.

(2) For the relevant purposes, the functions of the Agency shall be taken to include the protection against pollution of—

(a) any waters, whether on the surface or underground, which belong to the Agency or any water undertaker or from which the Agency or any water undertaker is authorised to take water;

(b) without prejudice to paragraph (a) above, any reservoir which belongs to or is operated by the Agency or any water undertaker or which the Agency or any water undertaker is proposing to acquire or construct for the purpose of being so operated; and

(c) any underground strata from which the Agency or any water undertaker is for the time being authorised to abstract water in pursuance of a licence under Chapter II of Part II of the 1991 Act[8] (abstraction and impounding).

(3) For the relevant purposes, the functions of the Agency shall be taken to include joining with or acting on behalf of one or more relevant undertakers[9] for the purpose of carrying out any works or acquiring any land which at least one of the undertakers with which it joins, or on whose behalf it acts, is authorised to carry out or acquire for the purposes of—

(a) any function of that undertaker under any enactment; or

(b) any function which is taken to be a function of that undertaker for the purposes to which section 217 of the Water Industry Act 1991[10] applies.

---

[1] For the establishment and functions of the Countryside Commission see the National Parks and Access to the Countryside Act 1949 (c.97), s.1 and the Countryside Act 1968 (c.41), s.1. These sections are set out in the companion volume: Fry, Michael, *A Manual of Nature Conservation Law*, Oxford, 1995, at p.7 and p.114 respectively.

[2] The Nature Conservancy Council for England, also known as English Nature, is established by the Environmental Protection Act 1990, s.128. This section is set out in the companion volume: Fry, Michael, *A.Manual of Nature Conservation Law*, Oxford, 1995, at p.229.

[3] The Countryside Council for Wales is established by the Environmental Protection Act 1990, s.128. This section is set out in the companion volume: Fry, Michael, *A Manual of Nature Conservation Law*, Oxford, 1995, at p.229.

[4] This section came into force on 28 July 1995: S.I. 1995/1983.

[5] P.448 below.

[6] "The Agency" means the Environment Agency: s.124(1) below.

[7] "Functions" includes powers and duties: s.124(1) below.

[8] "The 1991 Act" means the Water Resources Act 1991: s.56(1) below.

[9] "Relevant undertakers" defined by subsection (6) below.

[10] P.256 above.

(4)  For the relevant purposes, the functions of the Agency shall be taken to include the provision of supplies of water in bulk, whether or not such supplies are provided for the purposes of, or in connection with, the carrying out of any other function of the Agency.

(5)  For the relevant purposes, the functions of the Agency shall be taken to include the provision of houses and other buildings for the use of persons employed by the Agency and the provision of recreation grounds for persons so employed.

(6)  In this section—

"relevant undertaker" means a water undertaker or sewerage undertaker; and

"supply of water in bulk" means a supply of water for distribution by a water undertaker taking the supply.[1]

*Advisory committees*

*Advisory committee for Wales.*

**11.**  (1)  The Secretary of State shall establish and maintain a committee for advising him with respect to matters affecting, or otherwise connected with, the carrying out in Wales of the Agency's[2] functions[3].

(2)  The committee shall consist of such persons as may from time to time be appointed by the Secretary of State.

(3)  The committee shall meet at least once a year.

(4)  The Secretary of State may pay to the members of the committee such sums by way of reimbursement (whether in whole or in part) for loss of remuneration, for travelling expenses and for other out-of-pocket expenses as he may determine.[4]

*Environment protection advisory committees.*

**12.**  (1)  It shall be the duty of the Agency[5]—

(a)  to establish and maintain advisory committees, to be known as Environment Protection Advisory Committees, for the different regions of England and Wales;

(b)  to consult the advisory committee for any region as to any proposals of the Agency relating generally to the manner in which the Agency carries out its functions[6] in that region; and

(c)  to consider any representations made to it by the advisory committee for any region (whether in response to consultation under paragraph (b) above or otherwise) as to the manner in which the Agency carries out its functions in that region.

(2)  The advisory committee for any region shall consist of—

(a)  a chairman appointed by the Secretary of State: and

(b)  such other members as the Agency may appoint in accordance with the provisions of the approved membership scheme[7] for that region.

(3)  In appointing the chairman of any advisory committee, the Secretary of State shall have regard to the desirability of appointing a person who has experience of, and has shown capacity in, some matter relevant to the functions of the committee.

(4)  The members of advisory committees appointed by virtue of subsection (2)(b) above—

(a)  must not be members of the Agency; but

[1] This section came into force on 1 April 1996: S.I. 1996/186.
[2] "The Agency" means the Environment Agency: s.124(1) below.
[3] "Functions" includes powers and duties: s.124(1) below.
[4] This section came into force on 1 April 1996: S.I. 1996/186.
[5] "The Agency" means the Environment Agency: s.124(1) below.
[6] "Functions" includes powers and duties: s.124(1) below.
[7] "Approved membership scheme" defined by subsection (9) below.

(*b*) must be persons who appear to the Agency to have a significant interest in matters likely to be affected by the manner in which the Agency carries out any of its functions in the region of the advisory committee in question.

(5) The duty imposed by subsection (1)(*a*) above to establish and maintain advisory committees is a duty to establish and maintain an advisory committee for each area which the Agency considers it appropriate for the time being to regard as a region of England and Wales for the purposes of this section.

(6) It shall be the duty of the Agency, in determining the regions for which advisory committees are established and maintained under this section, to ensure that one of those regions consists wholly or mainly of, or of most of, Wales.

(7) For the purposes of this section, functions of the Agency which are carried out in any area of Scotland, or of the territorial sea, which is adjacent to any region for which an advisory committee is maintained, shall be regarded as carried out in that region.

(8) Schedule 3 to this Act[1] shall have effect with respect to advisory committees.

(9) In this section—

"advisory committee" means an advisory committee under this section;

"approved membership scheme" means a scheme, as in force for the time being, prepared by the Agency and approved (with or without modification) by the Secretary of State under Schedule 3 to this Act[2] which makes provision with respect to the membership of the advisory committee for a region.[3]

*Regional and local fisheries advisory committees.*

**13.**	(1) It shall be the duty of the Agency[4]—

(*a*) to establish and maintain advisory committees of persons who are not members of the Agency but appear to it to be interested in salmon fisheries, trout fisheries, freshwater fisheries or eel fisheries in the different parts of the controlled area[5]; and

(*b*) to consult those committees as to the manner in which the Agency is to perform its duty under section 6(6) above[6].

(2) If the Agency, with the consent of the Ministers[7] so determines, it shall also be under a duty to consult those committees, or such of them as may be specified or described in the determination, as to—

(*a*) the manner in which it is to perform its duties under or by virtue of such of the enactments relating to recreation, conservation or navigation as may be the subject of the determination, or

(*b*) such matters relating to recreation, conservation or navigation as may be the subject of the determination.

(3) Where, by virtue of subsection (2) above, the Agency is under a duty to consult those committees or any of them, there may be included among the members of the committees in question persons who are not members of the Agency but who appear to it to be interested in matters—

(*a*) likely to be affected by the manner in which it performs the duties to which the determination in question relates, or

(*b*) which are the subject of the determination,

---

[1] P.506 below.
[2] P.506 below.
[3] This section came into force on 28 July 1995: S.I. 1995/1983.
[4] "The Agency" means the Environment Agency: s.124(1)

below.
[5] "The controlled area" defined by subsection (8) below.
[6] P.426 above.
[7] "The Ministers" defined by s.56(1), p.464 below.

if the Ministers consent to the inclusion of persons of that description.

(4) The duty to establish and maintain advisory committees imposed by subsection (1) above is a duty to establish and maintain—

(a) a regional advisory committee for each such region of the controlled area as the Agency considers it appropriate for the time being to regard as a region of that area for the purposes of this section; and

(b) such local advisory committees as the Agency considers necessary to represent—

(i) the interests referred to in subsection (1)(a) above, and

(ii) where persons may be appointed members of those committees by virtue of subsection (3) above by reference to any such interests as are mentioned in that subsection, the interests in question,

in the different parts of each such region.

(5) It shall be the duty of the Agency in determining the regions for which regional advisory committees are established and maintained under this section to ensure that one of those regions consists (apart from territorial waters) wholly or mainly of, or of most of, Wales.

(6) In addition to any members appointed under the foregoing provisions of this section, there shall, in the case of each regional advisory committee established and maintained under this section, also be a chairman appointed—

(a) by the Secretary of State, in the case of the committee established and maintained for the region described in subsection (5) above; or

(b) by the Minister[1], in any other case.

(7) There shall be paid by the Agency—

(a) to the chairman of any regional or local advisory committee established and maintained under this section such remuneration and such travelling and other allowances; and

(b) to any other members of that committee such sums by way of reimbursement (whether in whole or in part) for loss of remuneration, for travelling expenses or for any other out-of-pocket expenses,

as may be determined by one of the Ministers.

(8) In this section "the controlled area" means the area specified in section 6(7) above[2] in respect of which the Agency carries out functions under section 6(6) above and Part V of the 1991 Act[3].[4]

---

*Flood defence committees*

*Regional flood defence committees.*

**14.** (1) There shall be committees, known as regional flood defence committees, for the purpose of carrying out the functions which fall to be carried out by such committees by virtue of this Act and the 1991 Act.[5]

(2) Subject to Schedule 4 to this Act[6] (which makes provision for the alteration of the boundaries of and the amalgamation of the areas of regional flood defence committees)—

(a) there shall be a regional flood defence committee for each of the areas for which there was an old committee[7] immediately before the transfer date[8]; but

(b) where under section 165(2) or (3) of the 1991 Act any function[9] of the Agency[10] falls to be

---

[1] "The Minister" defined by s.56(1), p.464 below.

[2] P.426 above.

[3] "The 1991 Act" means the Water Resources Act 1991: s.56(1) below.

[4] This section came into force on 1 April 1996: S.I. 1996/186.

[5] "The 1991 Act" means the Water Resources Act 1991: s.56(1) below.

[6] P.508 below.

[7] "Old committee" defined by subsection (4) below.

[8] "The transfer date" defined by s.56(1), p.464 below; the transfer date was 1 April 1996: S.I. 1996/234.

[9] "Functions" includes powers and duties: s.124(1) below.

[10] "The Agency" means the Environment Agency: s.124(1) below.

carried out at a place beyond the seaward boundaries of the area of any regional flood defence committee, that place shall be assumed for the purposes of this Act and the 1991 Act to be within the area of the regional flood defence committee to whose area the area of sea where that place is situated is adjacent.

(3)  The Agency shall maintain a principal office for the area of each regional flood defence committee.

(4)  In this section "old committee" means a regional flood defence committee for the purposes of section 9 of the 1991 Act.[1]

*Composition of regional flood defence committees.*

**15.**  (1)  Subject to subsection (2) below, a regional flood defence committee shall consist of the following, none of whom shall be a member of the Agency[2], that is to say—

(*a*)  a chairman and a number of other members appointed by the relevant Minister[3];

(*b*)  two members appointed by the Agency;

(*c*)  a number of members appointed by or on behalf of the constituent councils[4].

(2)  Any person who immediately before the transfer date[5] is, by virtue of his appointment—

(*a*)  by a Minister of the Crown,

(*b*)  by or on behalf of any council, or

(*c*)  by the National Rivers Authority,

the chairman or a member of an old committee[6] which, by virtue of section 14 above, is replaced by a new committee[7] shall be treated, on and after that date, for the remainder of the period for which he would, under the terms of his appointment, have held office in relation to the old committee, as if he had been appointed as the chairman or, as the case may be, a member of the new committee, and on the same terms, by that Minister or, as the case may be, by or on behalf of that council or, in the case of a person appointed by the National Rivers Authority, by the Agency.

(3)  Subject to section 16 below and to any order under Schedule 4 to this Act[8] amalgamating the areas of any two or more regional flood defence committees—

(*a*)  the total number of members of a new committee for any area shall be the same as the total number of members of the old committee for that area immediately before the transfer date;

(*b*)  the number of members to be appointed to a new committee for any area by or on behalf of each of the constituent councils or, as the case may be, jointly by or on behalf of more than one of them shall be the same as the number of members of the old committee for that area which fell to be so appointed immediately before the transfer date.

(4)  In any case where—

(*a*)  the appointment of one or more members of a regional flood defence committee is (by virtue of subsection (3) above or an order under section 16(5) below), to be made jointly by more than one constituent council, and

(*b*)  the councils by whom that appointment is to be made are unable to agree on an appointment,

the member or members in question shall be appointed by the relevant Minister on behalf of those councils.

---

[1] This section came into force on 1 April 1996: S.I. 1996/186.

[2] "The Agency" means the Environment Agency: s.124(1) below.

[3] "The relevant Minister" defined by subsection (7) below.

[4] For "constituent council" see subsection (6) below.

[5] "The transfer date" defined by s.56(1), p.464 below; the transfer date was 1 April 1996: S.I. 1996/234.

[6] "Old committee" has the same meaning as in s.14(4) above: subsection (7) below.

[7] "New committee" defined by subsection (7) below.

[8] P.508 below.

(5)  In appointing a person to be the chairman or a member of a regional flood defence committee under subsection (1)(a) or (c) or (4) above the relevant Minister or, as the case may be, a constituent council shall have regard to the desirability of appointing a person who has experience of, and has shown capacity in, some matter relevant to the functions[1] of the committee.

(6)  The councils of every county, county borough, metropolitan district or London borough any part of which is in the area of a regional flood defence committee shall be the constituent councils for the regional flood defence committee for that area, and the Common Council of the City of London shall be a constituent council for the regional flood defence committee for any area which comprises any part of the City.

(7)  In this section—

"old committee" has the same meaning as in section 14 above;

"new committee" means a regional flood defence committee established under section 14 above;

"the relevant Minister"—

(a)  in relation to the regional flood defence committee for an area the whole or the greater part of which is in Wales, means the Secretary of State; and

(b)  in relation to any other regional flood defence committee, means the Minister[2].[3]

*Change of composition of regional flood defence committee.*

**16.**  (1)  The Agency[4] may, in accordance with the following provisions of this section, from time to time make a determination varying the total number of members[5] of a regional flood defence committee.

(2)  The Agency shall submit any determination under subsection (1) above to the relevant Minister[6].

(3)  For the purposes of this section—

(a)  the total number of members of a regional flood defence committee shall not be less than eleven; and

(b)  any determination by the Agency under subsection (1) above that a regional flood defence committee should consist of more than seventeen members shall be provisional and shall take effect only if the relevant Minister makes an order under subsection (4) below.

(4)  If the Agency submits a provisional determination to the relevant Minister with respect to any regional flood defence committee and he considers that the committee should consist of more than seventeen members, he may by order made by statutory instrument—

(a)  confirm it; or

(b)  substitute for the number of members determined by the Agency some other number not less than seventeen.

(5)  Subject to the following provisions of this section, whenever—

(a)  the total number of members of a regional flood defence committee is varied under this section, or

(b)  the relevant Minister considers it necessary or expedient to make an order under this subsection,

the relevant Minister shall by order made by statutory instrument specify the number of members to be appointed to the committee by each of the constituent councils.

(6)  An order under subsection (5) above shall relate—

[1]  "Functions" includes powers and duties: s.124(1) below.
[2]  "The Minister" defined by s.56(1), p.464 below.
[3]  This section came into force on 1 April 1996: S.I. 1996/186.
[4]  "The Agency" means the Environment Agency: s.124(1) below.
[5]  "Member" defined by subsection (9) below.
[6]  "The relevant Minister" has the same meaning as in s.15 (7) above: subsection (9) below.

(a) where paragraph (a) of that subsection applies, to times after the coming into force of the variation; and

(b) where paragraph (b) of that subsection applies, to such times as are specified in the order.

(7) An order under subsection (5) above shall be so framed that the total number of members appointed under section 15(1)(a) and (b) above is one less than the number of those appointed by or on behalf of constituent councils.

(8) For the purpose of determining for the purposes of subsection (5) above the number of persons to be appointed to a regional flood defence committee by or on behalf of each constituent council, the relevant Minister—

(a) if he considers it to be inappropriate that that council should appoint a member of the committee, or

(b) if he considers that one or more members should be appointed jointly by that council and one or more other constituent councils,

may include provision to that effect in the order.

(9) In this section—

"member", in relation to a regional flood defence committee, includes the chairman of the committee;

"the relevant Minister" has the same meaning as in section 15 above.[1]

.........................................................................................................................................................

*Local flood defence schemes and local flood defence committees.*

**17.** (1) A scheme, known as a local flood defence scheme, may be made by the Agency[2], in accordance with the following provisions of this section—

(a) for the creation in the area of a regional flood defence committee of one or more districts, to be known as local flood defence districts; and

(b) for the constitution, membership, functions and procedure of a committee for each such district, to be known as the local flood defence committee for that district.

(2) Any local flood defence scheme which was made under the 1991 Act[3] or continued in force by virtue of paragraph 14(1) of Schedule 2 to the Water Consolidation (Consequential Provisions) Act 1991[4] and which, immediately before the transfer date[5], is in force in relation to the area of a regional flood defence committee, shall on and after that date have effect, and may be amended or revoked, as if it were a local flood defence scheme made under this section in relation to that area; and, accordingly, subject to any such amendment or revocation—

(a) any local flood defence district created by that scheme and in being immediately before that date shall be treated, on and after that date, as a local flood defence district created by a scheme under this section in relation to the area of that regional flood defence committee; and

(b) any local flood defence committee created by that scheme for any such district and in being immediately before that date shall be treated, on and after that date, as the local flood defence committee for that district.

(3) A regional flood defence committee may at any time submit to the Agency—

(a) a local flood defence scheme for any part of their area for which there is then no such scheme in force; or

(b) a scheme varying a local flood defence scheme or revoking such a scheme and, if the committee think fit, replacing it with another such scheme;

and references in the following provisions of this section and in section 18 below to local flood defence schemes are references to schemes under either of paragraphs (*a*) and (*b*) above.

(4) Before submitting a scheme to the Agency under subsection (3) above, a regional flood defence committee shall consult—

(*a*) every local authority any part of whose area will fall within the area to which the scheme is proposed to relate; and

(*b*) such organisations representative of persons interested in flood defence (within the meaning of Part IV of the 1991 Act) or agriculture as the regional flood defence committee consider to be appropriate.

(5) It shall be the duty of the Agency to send any scheme submitted to it under subsection (3) above to one of the Ministers[1].

(6) A local flood defence scheme may define a local flood defence district—

(*a*) by reference to the districts which were local land drainage districts immediately before 1st September 1989;

(*b*) by reference to the area of the regional flood defence committee in which that district is situated;

(*c*) by reference to a map;

or partly by one of those means and partly by another or others.

(7) A local flood defence scheme may contain incidental, consequential and supplementary provisions.

(8) Either of the Ministers may approve a local flood defence scheme with or without modifications[2]; and any scheme approved under this subsection shall come into force on a date fixed by the Minister approving it.[3]

*Composition of local flood defence committees.*

**18.** (1) Subject to subsections (2) and (3) below, a local flood defence scheme shall provide that any local flood defence committee to which it relates shall consist of not less than eleven and not more than fifteen members.

(2) A regional flood defence committee may include in a local flood defence scheme which they submit to the Agency[4] a recommendation that a committee to which the scheme relates should consist of a number of members greater than fifteen; and a scheme so submitted shall be taken to provide for the number of members of a committee if it contains a recommendation under this subsection relating to that committee.

(3) The power conferred on each of the Ministers[5] by section 17(8) above shall include power to direct that a committee to which a recommendation under subsection (2) above relates shall consist either of the recommended number of members or of some other number of members greater than fifteen.

(4) A local flood defence committee shall consist of—

(*a*) a chairman appointed from among their own members by the regional flood defence committee;

(*b*) other members appointed by that committee; and

(*c*) members appointed, in accordance with and subject to the terms of the local flood defence scheme, by or on behalf of constituent councils[6].

[1] "The Ministers" defined by s.56(1), p.464 below.
[2] "Modifications" defined by s.124(1), p.495 below.
[3] This section came into force on 1 April 1996: S.I. 1996/186.
[4] "The Agency" means the Environment Agency: s.124(1) below.
[5] "The Ministers" defined by s.56(1), p.464 below.
[6] For "constituent council" see subsection (8) below.

(5) The number of members appointed to a local flood defence committee by or on behalf of constituent councils shall be one more than the total number of members appointed by the regional flood defence committee.

(6) In appointing a person to be a member of a local flood defence committee, the regional flood defence committee shall have regard to the desirability of appointing a person who has experience of, and has shown capacity in, some matter relevant to the functions[1] of the committee to which he is appointed.

(7) Any person who, immediately before the transfer date[2] is, by virtue of an appointment by an old regional committee[3] or by or on behalf of any council, the chairman or a member of a local flood defence committee which is continued in force by virtue of section 17(2) above shall be treated, on and after that date, for the remainder of the period for which he would, under the terms of his appointment, have held office in relation to the local flood defence committee—

(a) as if he had been appointed as such under this section by the regional flood defence committee or, as the case may be, by or on behalf of that council; and

(b) in the case of the chairman, as if he were a member of the regional flood defence committee.

(8) The councils of every county, county borough, metropolitan district or London borough any part of which is in a local flood defence district shall be the constituent councils for the local flood defence committee for that district, and the Common Council of the City of London shall be a constituent council for the local flood defence committee of any local flood defence district which comprises any part of the City.

(9) In this section "old regional committee" means a regional flood defence committee for the purposes of section 9 of the 1991 Act[4].[5]

*Membership and proceedings of flood defence committees.*

**19.** Schedule 5 to this Act[6] shall have effect in relation to regional flood defence committees and local flood defence committees.[7]

## Chapter II: The Scottish Environment Protection Agency

### Establishment of SEPA

*The Scottish Environment Protection Agency.*

**20.** (1) There shall be a body to be known as the Scottish Environment Protection Agency (in this Act referred to as "SEPA"), for the purpose of carrying out the functions[8] transferred or assigned to it by or under this Act.

(2) Schedule 6 to this Act[9] shall have effect with respect to SEPA.[10]

### Transfer of functions, property etc. to SEPA

*Transfer of functions to SEPA.*

**21.** (1) On the transfer date[11] there shall by virtue of this section be transferred to SEPA[12]—

[1] "Functions" includes powers and duties: s.124(1) below.
[2] "The transfer date" defined by s.56(1), p.464 below; the transfer date was 1 April 1996: S.I. 1996/234.
[3] "Old regional committee" defined by subsection (9) below.
[4] "The 1991 Act" means the Water Resources Act 1991: s.56(1) below.
[5] This section came into force on 1 April 1996: S.I. 1996/186.
[6] P.511 below.
[7] This section came into force on 1 April 1996: S.I. 1996/186.
[8] "Functions" includes powers and duties: s.124(1) below.
[9] P.516 below.
[10] This section came into force on 12 October 1995: S.I. 1995/2649.
[11] "The transfer date" defined by s.56(1), p.464 below; the transfer date was 1 April 1996: S.I. 1996/139.
[12] "SEPA" means the Scottish Environment Protection Agency: s.124(1) below.

(a)  the functions[1] of river purification authorities[2], that is to say—

  (i)  their functions with respect to water resources under or by virtue of Part III of the Rivers (Prevention of Pollution) (Scotland) Act 1951[3] (in this Part referred to as "the 1951 Act") and Part II of the Natural Heritage (Scotland) Act 1991[4];

  (ii)  their functions with respect to water pollution under or by virtue of Part III of the 1951 Act[5], the Rivers (Prevention of Pollution) (Scotland) Act 1965[6] and Part II of the Control of Pollution Act 1974[7];

  (iii)  their functions as enforcing authority, in relation to releases of substances into the environment, under or by virtue of Part I of the 1990 Act[8];

  (iv)  their functions with respect to flood warning systems under or by virtue of Part VI of the Agriculture Act 1970[9]; and

  (v)  the functions assigned to them by or under any other enactment apart from this Act;

(b)  the functions of waste regulation authorities[10], that is to say, the functions conferred or imposed on them by or under—

  (i)  the Control of Pollution (Amendment) Act 1989[11]; or

  (ii)  Part II of the 1990 Act[12],

or assigned to them by or under any other enactment apart from this Act;

(c)  the functions of disposal authorities[13] under or by virtue of sections 3 to 10, 16, 17(1)(a) and 17(2)(b) to (d) of the Control of Pollution Act 1974[14];

(d)  the functions of the chief inspector for Scotland constituted under section 16(3) of the 1990 Act, that is to say, the functions conferred or imposed on him by or under Part I of that Act[15] or assigned to him by or under any other enactment apart from this Act;

(e)  the functions of the chief inspector for Scotland appointed under section 4(2)(b) of the Radioactive Substances Act 1993, that is to say, the functions conferred or imposed on him by or under that Act[16] or assigned to him by or under any other enactment apart from this Act;

(f)  the functions conferred or imposed by or under the Alkali, &c, Works Regulation Act 1906[17] (in this section referred to as "the 1906 Act") on the chief, or any other, inspector (within the meaning of that Act), so far as exercisable in relation to Scotland;

(g)  so far as exercisable in relation to Scotland, the functions in relation to improvement notices and prohibition notices under Part I of the Health and Safety at Work etc. Act 1974[18] (in this section referred to as "the 1974 Act") of inspectors appointed under section 19 of that Act by the Secretary of State in his capacity as enforcing authority responsible in relation to Scotland for the enforcement of the 1906 Act and section 5 of the 1974 Act;

(h)  the functions of local authorities[19] as enforcing authority, in relation to releases of substances into the air, under or by virtue of Part I of the 1990 Act[20]; and

(i)  the functions of the Secretary of State specified in subsection (2) below.

(2)  The functions of the Secretary of State mentioned in subsection (1)(i) above are, so far as exercisable in relation to Scotland—

---

[1] "Functions" includes powers and duties: s.124(1) below.
[2] "River purification authority" defined by s.56(1), p.464 below.
[3] P.4 above.
[4] 1991 c.28.
[5] P.4 above.
[6] P.9 above.
[7] P.18 above.
[8] P.88 above.
[9] 1970 c.40.
[10] "Waste regulation authority" defined by s.56(1), p.464 below.
[11] P.71 above.
[12] P.112 above.
[13] "Disposal authority" defined by s.56(1), p.463 below.
[14] 1974 c.40.
[15] P.88 above.
[16] The Radioactive Substances Act 1993 is at p.381 above.
[17] 1906 c. 14.
[18] 1974 c. 37.
[19] "Local authority" defined by s.56(1), (2), p.464 below.
[20] P.88 above.

(a) the functions conferred or imposed on him by virtue of his being, for the purposes of Part I of the 1974 Act, the authority which is by any of the relevant statutory provisions made responsible for the enforcement of the 1906 Act and section 5 of the 1974 Act;

(b) his functions under, or under regulations made by virtue of, section 9 of the 1906 Act (registration of works), other than any functions of his as an appellate authority or any function of making regulations;

(c) his functions under section 19 of the Clean Air Act 1993[1] with respect to the creation of smoke control areas by local authorities; and

(d) his functions under section 30(1) of the Radioactive Substances Act 1993[2] (power to dispose of radioactive waste).

(3) River purification boards[3] shall be dissolved on the transfer date.[4]

*Transfer of property, rights and liabilities to SEPA.*

**22.** (1) On the transfer date[5]—

(a) the property, rights and liabilities of every river purification board[6] shall, by virtue of this paragraph, be transferred to and vested in SEPA[7];

(b) any property, rights and liabilities which are the subject of a scheme under this section—

    (i) made by the Secretary of State; or

    (ii) made by a local authority[8] and approved by the Secretary of State,

shall be transferred to and vested in SEPA by and in accordance with the scheme.

(2) The Secretary of State may, before the transfer date, make a scheme for the transfer to SEPA of such of—

(a) his property, rights and liabilities; or

(b) the property, rights and liabilities of any of the inspectors or chief inspectors mentioned in subsection (1) of section 21 above,

as appear to the Secretary of State appropriate to be so transferred in consequence of the transfer of any functions to SEPA by virtue of that subsection.

(3) It shall be the duty of every local authority to make a scheme, after consultation with SEPA, for the transfer to SEPA of—

(a) such of the authority's property and rights as are held by it for the purposes of its functions[9] as—

    (i) a waste regulation authority[10];

    (ii) a disposal authority[11] under or by virtue of the provisions mentioned in section 21(1)(c) above;

    (iii) enforcing authority, in relation to releases of substances into the air, by virtue of Part I of the 1990 Act[12]; and

    (iv) in the case of an islands council, a river purification authority[13]; and

(b) such of its liabilities as are liabilities to which it is subject by virtue of its being an authority mentioned in paragraph (a)(i) to (iv) above,

[1] P.347 above.
[2] P.400 above.
[3] "River purification board" defined by s.56(1), p.464 below.
[4] This section came into force on 12 October 1995 S.I. 1995/2649.
[5] "The transfer date" defined by s.56(1), p.464 below; the transfer date was 1 April 1996: S.I. 1996/139.
[6] "River purification board" defined by s.56(1), p.464 below.
[7] "SEPA" means the Scottish Environment Protection Agency: s.124(1) below.
[8] "Local authority" defined by s.56(1),(2), p.464 below.
[9] "Functions" includes powers and duties: s.124(1) below.
[10] "Waste regulation authority" defined by s.56(1), p.464 below.
[11] "Disposal authority" defined by s.56(1), p.463 below.
[12] P.88 above.
[13] "River purification authority" defined by s.56(1), p.464 below.

and to submit that scheme to the Secretary of State for his approval before such date as he may direct.

(4) Any local authority preparing a scheme in pursuance of subsection (3) above shall take into account any guidance given by the Secretary of State as to the provisions which he regards as appropriate for inclusion in the scheme.

(5) Where a scheme under subsection (3) above is submitted to the Secretary of State, he may—

(a) approve the scheme;

(b) approve the scheme subject to such modifications[1] as he considers appropriate; or

(c) reject the scheme;

but the power conferred on the Secretary of State by paragraph (b) above shall be exercisable only after consultation with the local authority which submitted the scheme to him and with SEPA.

(6) The Secretary of State may, in the case of any local authority which is required to make a scheme under subsection (3) above, himself make a scheme for the transfer to SEPA of such of the body's property, rights or liabilities as are mentioned in paragraph (a) or (b) of that subsection, if—

(a) the authority fails to submit a scheme under that subsection to him for his approval before the due date; or

(b) the Secretary of State rejects a scheme under that subsection submitted to him by the authority;

but nothing in this subsection shall prevent the Secretary of State from approving any scheme which may be submitted to him after the due date.

(7) Where the Secretary of State makes a transfer scheme under subsection (6) above, he may recover his reasonable expenses in doing so, or such proportion of those expenses as he thinks fit, from the local authority in question by such means as appear to him to be appropriate including, without prejudice to that generality, setting off the expenses payable by the local authority against revenue support grant or non-domestic rate income payable by the Secretary of State to the local authority under paragraph 3 of Schedule 12 to the Local Government Finance Act 1992[2].

(8) The Secretary of State may, at any time before the transfer date, modify any scheme made or approved by him under this section but only after consultation with SEPA and, in the case of a scheme which was approved by him (with or without modifications), after consultation with the local authority which submitted the scheme to him for approval.

(9) Schedule 2 to this Act[3] shall have effect in relation to transfers by or under this section.[4]

*Functions or staff commission .*

**23.** The functions of the staff commission established under section 12 of the Local Government etc. (Scotland) Act 1994[5] shall include—

(a) considering and keeping under review the arrangements for the transfer to SEPA[6], in consequence of this Act or of any scheme made under it, of staff employed by local authorities[7];

(b) considering such staffing problems arising out of, consequential on or connected with any provision of, or scheme made under, this Act as may be referred to them by the Secretary of State or by any local authority;

(c) advising the Secretary of State as to the steps necessary to safeguard the interests of the staff referred to in paragraph (a) above.[8]

---

[1] "Modifications" defined by s.124(1), p.495 below.
[2] 1992 c.14.
[3] P.500 below.
[4] This section came into force on 12 October 1995: S.I. 1995/2649.
[5] 1994 c.39.

[6] "SEPA" means the Scottish Environment Protection Agency: s.124(1) below.
[7] "Local authority" defined by s.56(1), (2), p.464 below.
[8] This section came into force on 12 October 1995: S.I. 1995/2649.

*Other functions etc. of SEPA*

*Consultation with respect to drainage works.*

**24.** (1)  Subject to subsection (2) below, any person proposing to carry out drainage works[1] shall—

(*a*)  before commencing such works, consult SEPA[2] as to precautions to be taken to prevent pollution to controlled waters[3] as a result of the works; and

(*b*)  in carrying out such works, take account of SEPA's views.

(2)  The Secretary of State may, by regulations made by statutory instrument subject to annulment in pursuance of a resolution of either House of Parliament, prescribe types of drainage works in relation to which subsection (1) above shall not apply.

(3)  In this section, "drainage works" has the same meaning as in the Land Drainage (Scotland) Act 1958[4] and "controlled waters" has the same meaning as in the Control of Pollution Act 1974[5].[6]

..................................................................................................................................................

*Assessing flood risk.*

**25.** (1)  Without prejudice to section 92 of the Agriculture Act 1970[7] (provision of flood warning systems), SEPA[8] shall have the function of assessing, as far as it considers it appropriate, the risk of flooding in any area of Scotland.

(2)  If requested by a planning authority to do so, SEPA shall, on the basis of such information as it holds with respect to the risk of flooding in any part of the authority's area, provide the authority with advice as to such risk.[9]

..................................................................................................................................................

*Power of SEPA to purchase land compulsorily.*

**26.** (1)  The Secretary of State may authorise SEPA[10], for the purpose of any of its functions[11], to purchase land compulsorily.

(2)  The Acquisition of Land (Authorisation Procedure) (Scotland) Act 1947[12] shall apply in relation to the compulsory purchase of land under this section as if this section had been in force immediately before the commencement of that Act and, in relation to such purchase of land, SEPA shall be treated as if it were a local authority within the meaning of that Act.[13]

..................................................................................................................................................

*Power of SEPA to obtain information about land.*

**27.** (1)  Where, with a view to performing a function[14] conferred on it by any enactment, SEPA[15] considers that it ought to have information connected with any land, it may serve[16] on one or more of the persons mentioned in subsection (2) below a notice[17]—

(*a*)  specifying the land, the function and the enactment; and

(*b*)  requiring the recipient of the notice to furnish to SEPA, within such period of not less than 14 days from the date of service of the notice as is specified in the notice—

(i)  the nature of his interest in the land; and

----

[1]  For "drainage works" see subsection (3) below.
[2]  "SEPA" means the Scottish Environment Protection Agency: s.124(1) below.
[3]  For "controlled waters" see subsection (3) below.
[4]  1958 c.24.
[5]  "Controlled waters" is defined in s.30A of the 1974 Act, p.18 above.
[6]  This section has not come into force.
[7]  1970 c.40.
[8]  "SEPA" means the Scottish Environment Protection Agency: s.124(1) below.
[9]  This section came into force on 1 April 1996: S.I. 1996/186.
[10]  "SEPA" means the Scottish Environment Protection

Agency: s.124(1) below.
[11]  "Functions" includes powers and duties: s.124(1) below.
[12]  1947 c.42.
[13]  This section came into force on 1 April 1996: S.I. 1996/186.
[14]  "Functions" includes powers and duties: s.124(1) below.
[15]  "SEPA" means the Scottish Environment Protection Agency: s.124(1) below.
[16]  For provisions relating to the service of documents see s.123, p.494 below.
[17]  "Notice" means notice in writing: s.124(1) below.

(ii)  the name and address of each person whom he believes is, as respects the land, a person mentioned in subsection (2) below.

(2) The persons referred to in subsection (1) above are—

(a) the occupier of the land;

(b) any person—

(i)  who has an interest in the land as owner, creditor in a heritable security or lessee; or

(ii) who directly or indirectly receives rent for the land; and

(c) any person who, in pursuance of an agreement between himself and a person interested in the land, is authorised to manage the land or to arrange for the letting of it.

(3) A person who—

(a) fails to comply with the requirements of a notice served on him in pursuance of subsection (1) above; or

(b) in furnishing any information in compliance with such a notice makes a statement which he knows to be false in a material particular or recklessly makes a statement which is false in a material particular,

shall be guilty of an offence and liable on summary conviction to a fine not exceeding level 5 on the standard scale[1].[2]

*Power of SEPA to promote or oppose private legislation.*

**28.** (1)  SEPA[3] may, where it is satisfied that it is expedient to do so—

(a) with the consent of the Secretary of State, petition for the issue of a provisional order under the Private Legislation Procedure (Scotland) Act 1936[4]; or

(b) oppose any private legislation in Parliament.

(2) An application for the consent mentioned in paragraph (a) of subsection (1) above shall be accompanied by a concise summary of the purposes of the order petitioned for.

(3) In paragraph (b) of subsection (1) above, "private legislation in Parliament" includes—

(a) a provisional order and a Confirmation Bill relating to such an order; and

(b) any local or personal Bill.[5]

*Procedure relating to making of byelaws.*

**29.** The following provisions of the Local Government (Scotland) Act 1973[6]—

(a) section 202 (procedure etc. for byelaws);

(b) section 202C (revocation of byelaws);

(c) section 204 (evidence of byelaws),

shall apply in relation to SEPA[7] as they apply in relation to a local authority, provided that in the application of the said section 202 to SEPA for subsection (13) there shall be substituted—

"(13) The Scottish Environment Protection Agency shall send a copy of any byelaws made by it to the proper officer of the local authority for any area to the whole or any part of which the byelaws will apply.".[8]

---

[1] The current fine at level 5 on the standard scale is £5,000: Criminal Procedure (Scotland) Act 1995 (c.46), s.225.
[2] This section came into force on 1 April 1996: S.I. 1996/186.
[3] "SEPA" means the Scottish Environment Protection Agency: s.124(1) below.
[4] 1936 c.52.
[5] This section came into force on 1 April 1996: S.I. 1996/186.
[6] 1973 c.65.
[7] "SEPA" means the Scottish Environment Protection Agency: s.124(1) below.
[8] This section came into force on 1 April 1996: S.I. 1996/186.

*Records held by SEPA.*

**30.** (1) Subject to subsection (3) below—

    (*a*) this section applies to all records[1] (in whatever form or medium)—

        (i) transferred to and vested in SEPA[2] by or under section 22 above[3];

        (ii) created or acquired by it in the exercise of any of its functions[4]; or

        (iii) otherwise in its keeping;

    (*b*) SEPA shall ensure that the records other than such as are mentioned in paragraph (*c*) below, are preserved and managed in accordance with such arrangements as it, after consulting the Keeper of the Records of Scotland, shall put into effect;

    (*c*) records which in SEPA's opinion are not worthy of preservation may be disposed of by it;

    (*d*) SEPA may from time to time revise the arrangements mentioned in paragraph (*b*) above but before making any material change to those arrangements shall consult the Keeper; and

    (*e*) SEPA—

        (i) shall secure that the Keeper has, at all reasonable hours, unrestricted access to the records preserved by it;

        (ii) may afford members of the public, free of charge or on payment of reasonable charges, facilities for inspecting and for obtaining copies or extracts from those records.

(2) Nothing in subsection (1)(*e*)(ii) above permits infringement of copyright or contravention of conditions subject to which records are in SEPA's keeping.

(3) Insofar as any provision of any enactment, being a provision which relates to records of a specific kind, is (but for this subsection) inconsistent with subsection (1) above, that subsection is subject to the provision in question.[5]

---

*General powers and duties*

*Guidance on sustainable development and other aims and objectives.*

**31.** (1) The Secretary of State shall from time to time give guidance to SEPA[6] with respect to aims and objectives which he considers it appropriate for SEPA to pursue in the performance of its functions[7].[8]

(2) The guidance given under subsection (1) above must include guidance with respect to the contribution which, having regard to SEPA's responsibilities and resources, the Secretary of State considers it appropriate for SEPA to make, by the performance of its functions, towards attaining the objective of achieving sustainable development.

(3) In performing its functions, SEPA shall have regard to guidance given under this section.

(4) The power to give guidance to SEPA under this section shall be exercisable only after consultation with SEPA and such other bodies or persons as the Secretary of State considers it appropriate to consult in relation to the guidance in question.

(5) A draft of any guidance proposed to be given under this section shall be laid before each House of Parliament and the guidance shall not be given until after the period of 40 days beginning with the day on which the draft was so laid or, if the draft is laid on different days, the later of the two days.

---

[1] "Records" defined by s.124(1), p.495 below.
[2] "SEPA" means the Scottish Environment Protection Agency: s.124(1) below.
[3] P.440 above.
[4] "Functions" includes powers and duties: s.124(1) below.
[5] This section came into force on 12 October 1995: S.I. 1995/2649.

[6] "SEPA" means the Scottish Environment Protection Agency: s.124(1) below.
[7] "Functions" includes powers and duties: s.124(1) below.
[8] A note on guidance issued under this Act is at p.823 below.

(6)  If within the period mentioned in subsection (5) above, either House resolves that the guidance, the draft of which was laid before it, should not be given, the Secretary of State shall not give that guidance.

(7)  In reckoning any period of 40 days for the purposes of subsection (5) or (6) above, no account shall be taken of any time during which Parliament is dissolved or prorogued or during which both Houses are adjourned for more than four days.

(8)  The Secretary of State shall arrange for any guidance given under this section to be published in such manner as he considers appropriate.[1]

.........................................................................................................................................................

*General environmental and recreational duties.*

**32.** (1)  It shall be the duty of the Secretary of State and of SEPA[2], in formulating or considering any proposals relating to any functions[3] of SEPA—

(*a*)  to have regard to the desirability of conserving and enhancing the natural heritage of Scotland[4];

(*b*)  to have regard to the desirability of protecting and conserving buildings[5], sites and objects of archaeological, architectural, engineering or historic interest;

(*c*)  to take into account any effect which the proposals would have on the natural heritage of Scotland or on any such buildings, sites or objects; and

(*d*)  to have regard to the social and economic needs of any area or description of area of Scotland and, in particular, to such needs of rural areas.

(2)  Subject to subsection (1) above, it shall be the duty of the Secretary of State and of SEPA, in formulating or considering any proposals relating to any functions of SEPA—

(*a*)  to have regard to the desirability of preserving for the public any freedom of access (including access for recreational purposes) to areas of forest, woodland, mountains, moor, bog, cliff, foreshore, loch or reservoir and other places of natural beauty;

(*b*)  to have regard to the desirability of maintaining the availability to the public of any facility for visiting or inspecting any building, site or object of archaeological, architectural, engineering or historic interest; and

(*c*)  to take into account any effect which the proposals would have on any such freedom of access or on the availability of any such facility.

(3)  In this section—

"building" includes structure; and

"the natural heritage of Scotland" has the same meaning as in section 1(3) of the Natural Heritage (Scotland) Act 1991[6].[7]

.........................................................................................................................................................

*General duties with respect to pollution control.*

**33.** (1)  SEPA's[8] pollution control powers[9] shall be exercisable for the purpose of preventing or minimising, or remedying or mitigating the effects of, pollution of the environment.

(2)  SEPA shall, for the purpose—

(*a*)  of facilitating the carrying out of its pollution control functions[10]; or

---

[1] This section came into force on 12 October 1995: S.I. 1995/2649.

[2] "SEPA" means the Scottish Environment Protection Agency: s.124(1) below.

[3] "Functions" includes powers and duties: s.124(1) below.

[4] For "the natural heritage of Scotland" see subsection (3) below.

[5] "Building" includes structure: subsection (3) below.

[6] 1991 c.28. S.1(3) of the 1991 Act is set out in the companion volume: Fry, Michael, *A Manual of Nature Conservation Law*, Oxford, 1995, at p.245.

[7] This section came into force on 12 October 1995: S.I. 1995/2649.

[8] "SEPA" means the Scottish Environment Protection Agency: s.124(1) below.

[9] "Pollution control powers" defined by subsection (5) below.

[10] "Pollution control functions" defined by subsection (5) below.

(*b*) of enabling it to form an opinion of the general state of pollution of the environment,

compile information relating to such pollution (whether the information is acquired by SEPA carrying out observations or is obtained in any other way).

(3) If required by the Secretary of State to do so, SEPA shall—

(*a*) carry out assessments (whether generally or for such particular purpose as may be specified in the requirement) of the effect, or likely effect, on the environment of existing or potential levels of pollution of the environment and report its findings to the Secretary of State; or

(*b*) prepare and send to the Secretary of State a report identifying—

(i) the options which SEPA considers to be available for preventing or minimising, or remedying or mitigating the effects of, pollution of the environment, whether generally or in cases or circumstances specified in the requirement; and

(ii) the costs[1] and benefits of such options as are identified by SEPA pursuant to sub-paragraph (i) above.

(4) SEPA shall follow developments in technology and techniques for preventing or minimising, or remedying or mitigating the effects of, pollution of the environment.

(5) In this section, "pollution control powers" and "pollution control functions" in relation to SEPA, mean respectively its powers or its functions[2] under or by virtue of—

(*a*) the Alkali, &c. Works Regulation Act 1906[3];

(*b*) Part III of the 1951 Act[4], the Rivers (Prevention of Pollution) (Scotland) Act 1965[5] and Parts I, IA[6] and II[7] of the Control of Pollution Act 1974;

(*c*) Part I of the Health and Safety at Work etc. Act 1974[8];

(*d*) the Control of Pollution (Amendment) Act 1989[9];

(*e*) Parts I[10], II[11] and IIA[12] of the 1990 Act;

(*f*) section 19 of the Clean Air Act 1993[13];

(*g*) the Radioactive Substances Act 1993[14];and

(*h*) regulations made by virtue of section 2(2) of the European Communities Act 1972[15], to the extent that the regulations relate to pollution.[16]

*General duties with respect to water.*

**34.** (1) It shall be the duty of SEPA[17]—

(*a*) to promote the cleanliness of—

(i) rivers, other inland waters and ground waters in Scotland; and

(ii) the tidal waters[18] of Scotland; and

(*b*) to conserve so far as practicable the water resources of Scotland.

(2) Without prejudice to section 32 above[19], it shall be the duty of SEPA, to such extent as it considers desirable, generally to promote—

[1] "Costs" defined by s.56(1), p.463 below.
[2] "Functions" includes powers and duties: s.124(1) below.
[3] 1906 c. 14.
[4] P.4 above. "The 1951 Act" means the Rivers (Prevention of Pollution) (Scotland) Act 1951: s.56(1) below.
[5] P.9 above.
[6] P.15 above.
[7] P.18 above.
[8] 1974 c. 37.
[9] P.71 above.
[10] P.88 above.
[11] P.112 above.
[12] P.162 above.
[13] P.347 above.
[14] P.381 above.
[15] 1972 c.68.
[16] This section came into force on 1 April 1996: S.I. 1996/186.
[17] "SEPA" means the Scottish Environment Protection Agency: s.124(1) below.
[18] "Tidal waters" defined by subsection (4) below.
[19] P.445 above.

(*a*)  the conservation and enhancement of the natural beauty and amenity of inland and coastal waters and of land associated with such waters; and

(*b*)  the conservation of flora and fauna which are dependent on an aquatic environment.

(3)  Subsection (1) above is without prejudice to section 1 of the Water (Scotland) Act 1980[1] (general duties of Secretary of State and water authorities as respects water resources and supplies).

(4)  In subsection (1) above, "tidal waters" means any part of the sea or the tidal part of any river, watercourse or inland water (whether natural or artificial), and includes the waters of any enclosed dock which adjoins tidal waters.[2]

*Environmental duties as respects Natural Heritage Areas and sites of special interest.*

**35.**  (1)  Where an area of land—

(*a*)  has been designated, under section 6(2) of the Natural Heritage (Scotland) Act 1991[3] (in this section referred to as "the 1991 Act") as a Natural Heritage Area; or

(*b*)  is, in the opinion of Scottish Natural Heritage[4] (in this section referred to as "SNH"), of special interest by reason of its flora, fauna or geological or physiographical features[5],

and SNH consider that it may at any time be affected by schemes, works, operations or activities of SEPA[6] or by an authorisation[7] given by SEPA, SNH shall give notice[8] to SEPA in accordance with subsection (2) below.

(2)  A notice under subsection (1) above shall specify—

(*a*)  in the case of an area of land mentioned in paragraph (*a*) of that subsection, SNH's reasons for considering that the area is of outstanding value to the natural heritage of Scotland[9]; and

(*b*)  in the case of an area of land mentioned in paragraph (*b*) of that subsection, SNH's reasons for holding the opinion there mentioned.

(3)  Where SNH has given notice under subsection (1) above in respect of an area of land and—

(*a*)  in the case of an area of land mentioned in paragraph (*a*) of that subsection, the designation is cancelled or varied under section 6(7) of the 1991 Act; or

(*b*)  in the case of an area of land mentioned in paragraph (*b*) of that subsection, SNH ceases to be of the opinion there mentioned,

SNH shall forthwith notify SEPA of that fact.

(4)  Where SEPA has received notice under subsection (1) above with respect to any area of land, it shall (unless SNH has given notice under subsection (3) above with respect to the land) consult SNH before carrying out or authorising any schemes, works, operations or activities which appear to SEPA to be likely—

(*a*)  in the case of an area of land mentioned in subsection (1)(*a*), significantly to prejudice the value of the land, or any part of it, as a Natural Heritage Area; and

(*b*)  in the case of an area of land mentioned in subsection (1)(*b*), to destroy or damage any of the flora or fauna or features by reason of which SNH formed the opinion there mentioned.

[1] 1980 c.45.
[2] This section came into force on 1 April 1996: S.I. 1996/186.
[3] 1991 c.28. S.6 of the 1991 Act is set out in the companion volume: Fry, Michael, *A Manual of Nature Conservation Law*, Oxford, 1995, at p.248.
[4] Scottish Natural Heritage is established by s.1 of the Natural Heritage (Scotland) Act 1991. This section is set out in the companion volume: Fry, Michael, *A Manual of Nature Conservation Law*, Oxford, 1995, at p.245.
[5] For provisions relating to sites of special scientific interest see the Wildlife and Countryside Act 1981 (c.69), ss.28–33. These sections are set out in the companion volume: Fry, Michael, *A Manual of Nature Conservation Law*, Oxford, 1995, beginning at p.168.
[6] "SEPA" means the Scottish Environment Protection Agency: s.124(1) below.
[7] "Authorisation" defined by subsection (6) below.
[8] "Notice" means notice in writing: s.124(1) below; for provisions relating to the service of documents see s.123, p.494 below.
[9] "The natural heritage of Scotland" is defined in s.1 (3) of the Natural Heritage (Scotland) Act 1991 (c.28). This section is set out in the companion volume: Fry, Michael, *A Manual of Nature Conservation Law*, Oxford, 1995, at p.245.

(5) Subsection (4) above shall not apply in relation to anything done in an emergency if particulars of what is done and of the emergency are notified by SEPA to SNH as soon as practicable after the thing is done.

(6) In this section, "authorisation" includes any consent, licence or permission.

(7) Any expression used in this section and in Part I of the 1991 Act and not defined in this Act shall be construed in accordance with that Part.[1]

*Codes of practice with respect to environmental and recreational duties.*

**36.** (1) The Secretary of State shall have power by order to approve any code of practice issued (whether by him or by another person) for the purpose of—

(a) giving practical guidance to SEPA[2] with respect to any of the matters for the purposes of which sections 32[3], 34(2)[4] and 35 above have effect; and

(b) promoting what appear to him to be desirable practices by SEPA with respect to those matters,

and may at any time by such an order approve a modification[5] of such a code or withdraw his approval of such a code or modification.

(2) In discharging its duties under section 32, 34(2) or 35 above, SEPA shall have regard to any code of practice, and any modifications of a code of practice, for the time being approved under this section.

(3) The Secretary of State shall not make an order under this section unless he has first consulted—

(a) SEPA;

(b) Scottish Natural Heritage[6];

(c) Scottish Enterprise;

(d) Highlands and Islands Enterprise;

(e) the East of Scotland Water Authority;

(f) the West of Scotland Water Authority;

(g) the North of Scotland Water Authority; and

(h) such other persons as he considers it appropriate to consult.

(4) The power of the Secretary of State to make an order under this section shall be exercisable by statutory instrument; and any statutory instrument containing such an order shall be subject to annulment in pursuance of a resolution of either House of Parliament.[7]

## Chapter III: Miscellaneous, general and supplemental provisions relating to the new Agencies

### Additional general powers and duties

*Incidental general functions.*

**37.** (1) Each new Agency (that is to say, in this Part, the Agency[8] or SEPA[9])—

---

[1] This section came into force on 1 April 1996: S.I. 1996/186.

[2] "SEPA" means the Scottish Environment Protection Agency: s.124(1) below.

[3] P.445 above.

[4] P.446 above.

[5] "Modification" defined by s.124(1), p.495 below.

[6] Scottish Natural Heritage is established by s.1 of the Natural Heritage (Scotland) Act 1991. This section is set out in the companion volume: Fry, Michael, *A Manual of Nature Conservation Law*, Oxford, 1995, at p.245.

[7] This section came into force on 12 October 1995: S.I. 1995/2649.

[8] "The Agency" means the Environment Agency: s.124(1) below.

[9] "SEPA" means the Scottish Environment Protection Agency: s.124(1) below.

(a) may do anything which, in its opinion, is calculated to facilitate, or is conducive or incidental to, the carrying out of its functions[1]; and

(b) without prejudice to the generality of that power, may, for the purposes of, or in connection
with, the carrying out of those functions, acquire and dispose of land and other property and
carry out such engineering or building operations[2] as it considers appropriate;

and the Agency may institute criminal proceedings in England and Wales.

(2) It shall be the duty of each new Agency to provide the Secretary of State or the Minister[3] with
such advice and assistance as he may request.

(3) Subject to subsection (4) below, each new Agency may provide for any person, whether in or
outside the United Kingdom, advice or assistance, including training facilities, as respects any
matter in which that new Agency has skill or experience.

(4) Without prejudice to any power of either new Agency apart from subsection (3) above to provide advice or assistance of the kind mentioned in that subsection, the power conferred by that
subsection shall not be exercised in a case where the person for whom the advice or assistance is
provided is outside the United Kingdom, except with the consent in writing of the appropriate
Minister[4] which consent may be given subject to such conditions as the Minister giving it thinks
fit.

(5) Each new Agency—

(a) shall make arrangements for the carrying out of research and related activities (whether by
itself or by others) in respect of matters to which its functions relate; and

(b) may make the results of any such research or related activities available to any person in
return for payment of such fee as it considers appropriate.

(6) Subsection (5) above shall not be taken as preventing a new Agency from making the results
of any research available to the public free of charge whenever it considers it appropriate to do
so.

(7) Each new Agency may by agreement with any person charge that person a fee in respect of
work done, or services or facilities provided, as a result of a request made by him for advice or
assistance, whether of a general or specific character, in connection with any matter involving or
relating to environmental licences[5].

(8) Subsection (7) above—

(a) is without prejudice to the generality of the powers of either new Agency to make charges; but

(b) is subject to any such express provision with respect to charging by the new Agency in question as is contained in the other provisions of this Part or in any other enactment.

(9) In this section "engineering or building operations", without prejudice to the generality of
that expression, includes—

(a) the construction, alteration, improvement, maintenance or demolition of any building or
structure or of any reservoir, watercourse, dam, weir, well, borehole or other works; and

(b) the installation, modification or removal of any machinery or apparatus.[6]

*Delegation of functions by Ministers etc. to the new Agencies.*

**38.** (1) Agreements may be made between—

(a) any Minister of the Crown[7], and

---

[1] "Functions" includes powers and duties: s.124(1) below.
[2] "Engineering or building operations" defined by sub-section (9) below.
[3] "The Minister" defined by s.56(1), p.464 below.
[4] "The appropriate Minister" defined by s.56(1), p.463 below.

[5] "Environmental licence" defined by s.56(1), p.463 below.
[6] Subsections(1), (2) and (9) came into force on 28 July 1995: S.I. 1995/1983; the remaining subsections came into force on 1 April 1996: S.I. 1996/186.
[7] "Minister of the Crown" defined by subsection (10) below.

(b) a new Agency[1],

authorising the new Agency (or any of its employees) to exercise on behalf of that Minister, with or without payment, any eligible function[2] of his.

(2) An agreement under subsection (1) above shall not authorise the new Agency (or any of its employees) to exercise on behalf of a Minister of the Crown any function which consists of a power to make regulations or other instruments of a legislative character or a power to fix fees or charges.

(3) An agreement under this section may provide for any eligible function to which it relates to be exercisable by the new Agency in question (or any of its employees)—

(a) either wholly or to such extent as may be specified in the agreement;

(b) either generally or in such cases or areas as may be so specified; or

(c) either unconditionally or subject to the fulfilment of such conditions as may be so specified.

(4) Subsection (5) below applies where, by virtue of an agreement under this section, a new Agency (or any of its employees) is authorised to exercise any function of a Minister of the Crown.

(5) Subject to subsection (6) below, anything done or omitted to be done by the new Agency (or an employee of the new Agency) in, or in connection with, the exercise or purported exercise of the function shall be treated for all purposes as done or omitted to be done by that Minister in his capacity as such.

(6) Subsection (5) above shall not apply—

(a) for the purposes of so much of any agreement made between that Minister and the new Agency as relates to the exercise of the function; or

(b) for the purposes of any criminal proceedings brought in respect of anything done or omitted to be done as mentioned in that subsection .

(7) An agreement under this section shall not prevent a Minister of the Crown exercising any function to which the agreement relates.

(8) Where a Minister of the Crown has power to include, in any arrangements which he makes in relation to the performance by him of an eligible function, provision for the making of payments to him—

(a) by other parties to the arrangements, or

(b) by persons who use any facilities or services provided by him pursuant to the arrangements or in relation to whom the function is otherwise exercisable,

he may include in any such arrangements provision for the making of such payments to him or a new Agency in cases where the new Agency (or any of its employees) acts on his behalf by virtue of an agreement under this section.

(9) The power conferred on a Minister of the Crown by subsection (1) above is in addition to any other power by virtue of which functions of his may be exercised by other persons on his behalf.

(10) In this section—

"eligible function" means any function of a Minister of the Crown which the Secretary of State, having regard to the functions[3] conferred or imposed upon the new Agency in question under or by virtue of this Act or any other enactment, considers can appropriately be exercised by that new Agency (or any of its employees) on behalf of that Minister;

"Minister of the Crown" has the same meaning as in the Ministers of the Crown Act 1975[4].[5]

........................................................................................................................

[1] "New Agency" means the Environment Agency or SEPA, the Scottish Environment Protection Agency: ss.56(1), 124(1) below.

[2] "Eligible function" defined by subsection (10) below.

[3] "Functions" includes powers and duties: s.124(1)

below.

[4] 1975 c.26.

[5] This section came into force on 28 July 1995: S.I. 1995/1983.

*General duty of the new Agencies to have regard to costs and benefits in exercising powers.*

**39.** (1) Each new Agency[1]—

(a) in considering whether or not to exercise any power conferred upon it by or under any enactment, or

(b) in deciding the manner in which to exercise any such power,

shall, unless and to the extent that it is unreasonable for it to do so in view of the nature or purpose of the power or in the circumstances of the particular case, take into account the likely costs[2] and benefits of the exercise or non-exercise of the power or its exercise in the manner in question.

(2) The duty imposed upon a new Agency by subsection (1) above does not affect its obligation, nevertheless, to discharge any duties, comply with any requirements, or pursue any objectives, imposed upon or given to it otherwise than under this section.[3]

*Ministerial directions to the new Agencies.*

**40.** (1) The appropriate Minister[4] may give a new Agency[5] directions[6] of a general or specific character with respect to the carrying out of any of its functions[7].

(2) The appropriate Minister may give a new Agency such directions of a general or specific character as he considers appropriate for the implementation of—

(a) any obligations of the United Kingdom under the Community Treaties, or

(b) any international agreement to which the United Kingdom is for the time being a party.

(3) Any direction under subsection (2) above shall be published in such manner as the Minister giving it considers appropriate for the purpose of bringing the matters to which it relates to the attention of persons likely to be affected by them; and—

(a) copies of the direction shall be made available to the public; and

(b) notice shall be given—

(i) in the case of a direction given to the Agency[8], in the London Gazette, or

(ii) in the case of a direction given to SEPA[9], in the Edinburgh Gazette,

of the giving of the direction and of where a copy of the direction may be obtained.

(4) The provisions of subsection (3) above shall have effect in relation to any direction given to a new Agency under an enactment other than subsection (2) above for the implementation of—

(a) any obligations of the United Kingdom under the Community Treaties, or

(b) any international agreement to which the United Kingdom is for the time being a party,

as those provisions have effect in relation to a direction given under subsection (2) above.

(5) In determining—

(a) any appeal against, or reference or review of, a decision of a new Agency, or

(b) any application transmitted from a new Agency,

the body or person making the determination shall be bound by any direction given under this section or any other enactment by a Minister of the Crown to the new Agency to the same extent as the new Agency.

---

[1] "New Agency" means the Environment Agency or SEPA, the Scottish Environment Protection Agency: ss. 56(1), 124(1) below.
[2] "Costs" defined by s.56(1), p.463 below.
[3] This section came into force on 28 July 1995: S.I. 1995/1983.
[4] "The appropriate Minister" defined by s.56(1), p.463 below.
[5] "New Agency" means the Environment Agency or SEPA, the Scottish Environment Protection Agency: ss. 56(1), 124(1) below.
[6] For provisions relating to directions see s.122, p.494 below.
[7] "Functions" includes powers and duties: s.124(1) below.
[8] "The Agency" means the Environment Agency: s.124(1) below.
[9] "SEPA" means the Scottish Environment Protection Agency: s.124(1) below.

(6) Any power to give a direction under this section shall be exercisable, except in an emergency, only after consultation with the new Agency concerned.

(7) Any power of the appropriate Minister to give directions to a new Agency otherwise than by virtue of this section shall be without prejudice to any power to give directions conferred by this section.

(8) It is the duty of a new Agency to comply with any direction which is given to that new Agency by a Minister of the Crown under this section or any other enactment.[1]

*Charging schemes*

*Power to make schemes imposing charges.*

**41.** (1) Subject to the following provisions of this section and section 42 below—

(a) in the case of any particular licence under Chapter II of Part II of the 1991 Act[2] (abstraction and impounding), the Agency[3] may require the payment to it of such charges as may from time to time be prescribed;

(b) in relation to other environmental licences[4], there shall be charged by and paid to a new Agency[5] such charges as may from time to time be prescribed; and

(c) as a means of recovering costs incurred by it in performing functions conferred by regulations under section 62 of the 1990 Act[6] (dangerous or intractable waste) each of the new Agencies may require the payment to it of such charges as may from time to time be prescribed;

and in this section "prescribed" means specified in, or determined under, a scheme (in this section referred to as a "charging scheme") made under this section by the new Agency in question.

(2) As respects environmental licences, charges may be prescribed in respect of—

(a) the grant or variation of an environmental licence, or any application for, or for a variation of, such a licence

(b) the subsistence of an environmental licence;

(c) the transfer (where permitted) of an environmental licence to another person, or any application for such a transfer;

(d) the renewal (where permitted) of an environmental licence, or any application for such a renewal;

(e) the surrender (where permitted) of an environmental licence, or any application for such a surrender; or

(f) any application for the revocation (where permitted) of an environmental licence.

(3) A charging scheme may, for the purposes of subsection (2)(b) above, impose—

(a) a single charge in respect of the whole of any relevant licensed period;

(b) separate charges in respect of different parts of any such period; or

(c) both such a single charge and such separate charges;

and in this subsection "relevant licensed period" means the period during which an environmental licence is in force or such part of that period as may be prescribed.

(4) Without prejudice to subsection (7)(a) below, a charging scheme may, as respects environmental licences, provide for different charges to be payable according to—

[1] This section came into force on 28 July 1995: S.I. 1995/1983.
[2] "The 1991 Act" means the Water Resources Act 1991: s.56(1) below.
[3] "The Agency" means the Environment Agency: s.124(1) below.
[4] "Environmental licence" defined by s.56(1), p.463 below.
[5] "New Agency" means the Environment Agency or SEPA, the Scottish Environment Protection Agency: ss.56 (1), 124(1) below.
[6] P.151 above. The 1990 Act means the Environmental Protection Act 1990: s.56(1) below.

(a) the description of environmental licence in question;

(b) the description of authorised activity[1] in question;

(c) the scale on which the authorised activity in question is carried on;

(d) the description or amount of the substance to which the authorised activity in question relates;

(e) the number of different authorised activities carried on by the same person.

(5) A charging scheme—

(a) shall specify, in relation to any charge prescribed by the scheme, the description of person who is liable to pay the charge; and

(b) may provide that it shall be a condition of an environmental licence of any particular description that any charge prescribed by a charging scheme in relation to an environmental licence of that description is paid in accordance with the scheme.

(6) Without prejudice to subsection (5)(b) above, if it appears to a new Agency that any charges due and payable to it in respect of the subsistence of an environmental licence have not been paid, it may, in accordance with the appropriate procedure[2], suspend or revoke the environmental licence to the extent that it authorises the carrying on of an authorised activity.

(7) A charging scheme may—

(a) make different provision for different cases, including different provision in relation to different persons, circumstances or localities;

(b) provide for the times at which, and the manner in which, the charges prescribed by the scheme are to be paid;

(c) revoke or amend any previous charging scheme;

(d) contain supplemental, incidental, consequential or transitional provision for the purposes of the scheme.

(8) If and to the extent that a charging scheme relates to licences under Chapter II of Part II of the 1991 Act (abstraction and impounding), the scheme shall have effect subject to any provision made by or under sections 125 to 130 of that Act (exemption from charges, imposition of special charges for spray irrigation and charges in respect of abstraction from waters of the British Waterways Board).

(9) A new Agency shall not make a charging scheme unless the provisions of the scheme have been approved by the Secretary of State under section 42 below.

(10) In this section—

"the appropriate procedure" means such procedure as may be specified or described in regulations made for the purpose by the Secretary of State[3];

"authorised activity" means any activity to which an environmental licence relates.

(11) Any power to make regulations under this section shall be exercisable by statutory instrument; and a statutory instrument containing any such regulations shall be subject to annulment pursuant to a resolution of either House of Parliament.[4]

---

[1] "Authorised activity" defined by subsection (10) below.
[2] "The appropriate procedure" defined by subsection (10) below.
[3] See S.I. 1996/508, p.757 below.
[4] This section, in so far as it confers power to make schemes imposing charges, came into force on 21 September 1995: S.I. 1995/1983; in so far as it confers power on the Secretary of State to make regulations and makes provision in relation to the exercise of that power, this section came into force on 1 February 1996; otherwise this section came into force on 1 April 1996: S.I. 1996/186.

*Approval of charging schemes.*

**42.** (1) Before submitting a proposed charging scheme[1] to the Secretary of State for his approval, a new Agency[2] shall, in such manner as it considers appropriate for bringing it to the attention of persons likely to be affected by the scheme, publish a notice—

(a) setting out its proposals; and

(b) specifying the period within which representations or objections with respect to the proposals may be made to the Secretary of State.

(2) Where any proposed charging scheme has been submitted to the Secretary of State for his approval, he shall, in determining whether or not to approve the scheme or to approve it subject to modifications[3],—

(a) consider any representations or objections duly made to him and not withdrawn; and

(b) have regard to the matter specified in subsection (3) below.

(3) The matter mentioned in subsection (2)(b) above is the desirability of ensuring that, in the case of each of the descriptions of environmental licence specified in the paragraphs of the definition of that expression in section 56 below[4], the amounts recovered by the new Agency in question by way of charges prescribed by charging schemes are the amounts which, taking one year with another, need to be recovered by that new Agency to meet such of the costs and expenses (whether of a revenue or capital nature)—

(a) which it incurs in carrying out its functions[5],

(b) in the case of environmental licences which are authorisations under section 13(1) of the Radioactive Substances Act 1993[6]—

(i) which the Minister[7] incurs in carrying out his functions under or in consequence of that Act and

(ii) which the Secretary of State incurs under that Act in carrying out in relation to Scotland or Wales such of his functions under or in consequence of that Act as are exercised by the Minister in relation to England,

as the Secretary of State may consider it appropriate to attribute to the carrying out of those functions in relation to activities to which environmental licences of the description in question relate.

(4) Without prejudice to the generality of the expression "costs and expenses", in determining for the purposes of subsection (3) above the amounts of the costs and expenses which the Secretary of State considers it appropriate to attribute to the carrying out of a new Agency's or the Minister's or the Secretary of State's functions in relation to the activities to which environmental licences of any particular description relate, the Secretary of State—

(a) shall take into account any determination of the new Agency's financial duties under section 44 below[8]; and

(b) may include amounts in respect of the depreciation of, and the provision of a return on, such assets as are held by the new Agency, the Minister or the Secretary of State, as the case may be, for purposes connected with the carrying out of the functions in question.

(5) If and to the extent that a charging scheme relates to any licence under Chapter II of Part II of the 1991 Act[9] (abstraction and impounding), the Secretary of State may consider it appropriate to attribute to the carrying out of the Agency's functions in relation to activities to which such

---

[1] "Charging scheme" has the same meaning as in s.41 above: subsection (11) below.

[2] "New Agency" means the Environment Agency or SEPA, the Scottish Environment Protection Agency: ss.56(1), 124(1) below.

[3] "Modifications" defined by s.124(1), p.495 below.

[4] P.462 below.

[5] "Functions" includes powers and duties: s.124(1) below.

[6] P.389 above.

[7] "The Minister" defined by s.56(1), p.464 below.

[8] P.455 below.

[9] "The 1991 Act" means the Water Resources Act 1991: s.56(1) below.

a licence relates any costs and expenses incurred by the Agency in carrying out any of its functions under Part II of that Act or under section 6(2) above[1].

(6) Subsection (5) above is without prejudice to what costs and expenses the Secretary of State may consider it appropriate to attribute to the carrying out of any functions of a new Agency, the Minister or the Secretary of State in relation to activities to which environmental licences of any particular description relate.

(7) The consent of the Treasury shall be required for the giving of approval to a charging scheme and, if and to the extent that the scheme relates to authorisations by the Agency under section 13 of the Radioactive Substances Act 1993[2] (disposal of radioactive waste), the consent of the Minister shall also be required.

(8) It shall be the duty of a new Agency to take such steps as it considers appropriate for bringing the provisions of any charging scheme made by it which is for the time being in force to the attention of persons likely to be affected by them.

(9) If and to the extent that any sums recovered by a new Agency by way of charges prescribed by charging schemes may fairly be regarded as so recovered for the purpose of recovering the amount required to meet (whether in whole or in part)—

(a) such of the costs and expenses incurred by the Secretary of State as fall within subsection (3) above, or

(b) such of the costs and expenses incurred by the Minister as fall within that subsection,

those sums shall be paid by that new Agency to the Secretary of State or, as the case may be, to the Minister.

(10) For the purposes of subsection (9) above, any question as to the extent to which any sums may fairly be regarded as recovered for the purpose of recovering the amount required to meet the costs and expenses falling within paragraph (a) or paragraph (b) of that subsection shall be determined—

(a) in the case of costs and expenses falling within paragraph (a) of that subsection, by the Secretary of State; and

(b) in the case of costs and expenses falling within paragraph (b) of that subsection, by the Secretary of State and the Minister.

(11) In this section "charging scheme" has the same meaning as in section 41 above.[3]

*Incidental power to impose charges*

*Incidental power of the new Agencies to impose charges.*

**43.** Without prejudice to the generality of its powers by virtue of section 37(1)(a) above[4] and subject to any such express provision with respect to charging by a new Agency[5] as is contained in the preceding provisions of this Chapter or any other enactment, each new Agency shall have power to fix and recover charges for services and facilities provided in the course of carrying out its functions[6].[7]

*General financial provisions*

*General financial duties.*

**44.** (1) The appropriate Ministers[8] may—

[1] P.425 above.
[2] P.389 above.
[3] This section came into force on 21 September 1995: S.I. 1995/1983.
[4] P.448 above.
[5] "New Agency" means the Environment Agency or SEPA, the Scottish Environment Protection Agency: ss.56(1), 124(1) below.
[6] "Functions" includes powers and duties: s.124(1) below.
[7] This section came into force on 28 July 1995: S.I. 1995/1983.
[8] "The appropriate Ministers" defined by s.56(1), p.463 below.

(*a*) after consultation with a new Agency[1], and

(*b*) with the approval of the Treasury,

determine the financial duties of that new Agency; and different determinations may be made for different functions[2] and activities of the new Agency.

(2) The appropriate Ministers shall give a new Agency notice of every determination of its financial duties under this section, and such a determination may—

(*a*) relate to a period beginning before, on, or after, the date on which it is made;

(*b*) contain supplemental provisions; and

(*c*) be varied by a subsequent determination.

(3) The appropriate Minister may, after consultation with the Treasury and a new Agency, give a direction to that new Agency requiring it to pay to him an amount equal to the whole or such part as may be specified in the direction of any sum, or any sum of a description, so specified which is or has been received by that new Agency.

(4) Where it appears to the appropriate Minister that a new Agency has a surplus, whether on capital or revenue account, he may, after consultation with the Treasury and the new Agency, direct the new Agency to pay to him such amount not exceeding the amount of that surplus as may be specified in the direction.

(5) In the case of the Agency—

(*a*) subsection (1) above is subject to section 118 of the 1991 Act[3] (special duties with respect to flood defence revenue);

(*b*) subsection (3) above is subject to sections 118(1)(*a*) and 119(1) of the 1991 Act (special duties with respect to flood defence revenue and funds raised for fishery purposes under local enactments); and

(*c*) subsection (4) above is subject to sections 118(1)(*b*) and 119(2) of the 1991 Act (which provide for flood defence revenue and certain funds raised under local enactments to be disregarded in determining whether there is a surplus).[4]

*Accounts and records.*

**45.** (1) Each new Agency[5] shall—

(*a*) keep proper accounts and proper accounting records[6]; and

(*b*) prepare in respect of each accounting year[7] a statement of accounts giving a true and fair view of the state of affairs and the income and expenditure of the new Agency.

(2) Every statement of accounts prepared by a new Agency in accordance with this section shall comply with any requirement which the appropriate Ministers[8] have, with the consent of the Treasury, notified in writing to the new Agency and which relates to any of the following matters, namely—

(*a*) the information to be contained in the statement;

(*b*) the manner in which that information is to be presented;

(*c*) the methods and principles according to which the statement is to be prepared.

(3) In this section—

---

[1] "New Agency" means the Environment Agency or SEPA, the Scottish Environment Protection Agency: ss.56(1), 124(1) below.

[2] "Functions" includes powers and duties: s.124(1) below.

[3] "The 1991 Act" means the Water Resources Act 1991: s.56(1) below.

[4] This section came into force on 28 July 1995: S.I. 1995/1983.

[5] "New Agency" means the Environment Agency or SEPA, the Scottish Environment Protection Agency: ss.56(1), 124(1) below.

[6] "Accounting records" defined by subsection (3) below.

[7] "Accounting year" defined by subsection (3) below.

[8] " The appropriate Ministers" defined by s.56(1), p.463 below.

"accounting records", in the case of a new Agency, includes all books, papers and other records[1] of the new Agency relating to, or to matters dealt with in, the accounts required to be kept by virtue of this section;

"accounting year", subject to subsection (4) below, means, in relation to a new Agency, a financial year[2].

(4) If the Secretary of State so directs in relation to any accounting year of either new Agency, that accounting year shall end with such date other than the next 31st March as may be specified in the direction; and, where the Secretary of State has given such a direction, the following accounting year shall begin with the day after the date so specified and, subject to any further direction under this subsection, shall end with the next 31st March[3].[4]

*Audit.*

**46.** (1) The accounts[5] of each new Agency[6] shall be audited by an auditor appointed for each accounting year[7] by the Secretary of State.

(2) A person shall not be qualified for appointment under subsection (1) above unless—

(*a*) he is eligible for appointment as a company auditor under Part II of the Companies Act 1989[8]; and

(*b*) he would not be ineligible for appointment as company auditor of the new Agency in question by virtue of section 27 of that Act (ineligibility on ground of lack of independence), if that new Agency were a body to which section 384 of the Companies Act 1985[9] (duty to appoint auditor) applies.

(3) A copy of—

(*a*) any accounts of a new Agency which are audited under subsection (1) above, and

(*b*) the report made on those accounts by the auditor,

shall be sent to each of the appropriate Ministers[10] as soon as reasonably practicable after the report is received by the new Agency; and the Secretary of State shall lay before each House of Parliament a copy of those accounts and that report.

(4) The Comptroller and Auditor General—

(*a*) shall be entitled to inspect the contents of all accounts and accounting records of a new Agency; and

(*b*) may report to the House of Commons the results of any inspection carried out by him under paragraph (*a*) above;

and section 6 of the National Audit Act 1983[11] (examinations of economy, efficiency and effectiveness) accordingly applies to each new Agency.

(5) In this section—

"accounting records" has the same meaning as in section 45 above;

"accounting year" has the same meaning as in section 45 above;

"accounts", in relation to the Agency, includes any statement under section 45 above.[12]

---

[1] "Records" defined by s.124(1), p.495 below.
[2] "Financial year" defined by s.124(1), p.495 below.
[3] For provisions relating to directions see s.122, p.494 below.
[4] This section came into force on 28 July 1995: S.I. 1995/1983.
[5] "Accounts" defined by subsection (5) below.
[6] "New Agency" means the Environment Agency or SEPA, the Scottish Environment Protection Agency: ss.56(1), 124(1) below.

[7] "Accounting year" has the same meaning as in s.45(3) above: subsection (5) below.
[8] 1989 c.40.
[9] 1985 c.6.
[10] "The appropriate Ministers" defined by s.56(1), p.463 below.
[11] 1983 c.44.
[12] This section came into force on 28 July 1995: S.I. 1995/1983.

*Grants to the new Agencies.*

**47.** The appropriate Minister[1] may, with the approval of the Treasury, make to a new Agency[2] grants of such amounts, and on such terms, as he thinks fit.[3]

*Borrowing powers.*

**48.** (1) Each new Agency[4] shall be entitled to borrow in accordance with the following provisions of this section, but not otherwise.

(2) Subject to subsection (5) below, each new Agency may—

(*a*) with the consent of the appropriate Minister[5], and

(*b*) with the approval of the Treasury,

borrow temporarily in sterling, by way of overdraft or otherwise, from persons other than the appropriate Ministers[6], such sums as it may require for meeting its obligations and carrying out its functions[7].

(3) Subject to subsection (5) below, each new Agency may borrow from the appropriate Minister, by way of temporary loan or otherwise, such sums in sterling as it may require for meeting its obligations and carrying out its functions.

(4) Any consent under subsection (2)(*a*) above may be granted subject to conditions.

(5) The aggregate amount outstanding in respect of the principal of sums borrowed under this section by a new Agency shall not at any time exceed—

(*a*) in the case of the Agency[8], £100 million or such greater sum, not exceeding £160 million, as the Ministers[9] may by order specify; or

(*b*) in the case of SEPA[10], £5 million or such greater sum, not exceeding £10 million as the Secretary of State may by order specify.

(6) The power to make an order under subsection (5) above shall be exercisable by statutory instrument; but no order shall be made under that subsection unless a draft of the order has been laid before, and approved by a resolution of, the House of Commons.[11]

*Government loans to the new Agencies.*

**49.** (1) The appropriate Minister[12] may, with the approval of the Treasury, lend to a new Agency[13] any sums which it has power to borrow under section 48(3) above.

(2) Any loan made under this section by one of the appropriate Ministers[14] shall be repaid to him at such times and by such methods, and interest on the loan shall be paid to him at such rates and at such times, as that Minister may with the approval of the Treasury from time to time determine.

(3) If in any financial year[15] any of the appropriate Ministers lends any sums to a new Agency under this section, he shall—

---

[1] "The appropriate Minister" defined by s.56(1), p.463 below.

[2] "New Agency" means the Environment Agency or SEPA, the Scottish Environment Protection Agency: ss.56(1), 124(1) below.

[3] This section came into force on 28 July 1995: S.I. 1995/1983.

[4] "New Agency" means the Environment Agency or SEPA, the Scottish Environment Protection Agency: ss.56(1), 124(1) below.

[5] "The appropriate Minister" defined by s.56(1), p.463 below.

[6] "The appropriate Ministers" defined by s.56(1), p.463 below.

[7] "Functions" includes powers and duties: s.124(1) below.

[8] "The Agency" means the Environment Agency: s.124(1) below.

[9] "The Ministers" defined by s.56(1), p.464 below.

[10] "SEPA" means the Scottish Environment Protection Agency: s.124(1) below.

[11] This section came into force on 28 July 1995: S.I. 1995/1983.

[12] "The appropriate Minister" defined by s.56(1), p.463 below.

[13] "New Agency" means the Environment Agency or SEPA, the Scottish Environment Protection Agency: ss.56(1), 124(1) below.

[14] "The appropriate Ministers" defined by s.56(1), p.463 below.

[15] "Financial year" defined by s.124(1), p.495 below.

(*a*)  prepare in respect of that financial year an account of the sums so lent by him; and

(*b*)  send that account to the Comptroller and Auditor General before the end of September in the following financial year;

and the form of the account and the manner of preparing it shall be such as the Treasury may direct.

(4)  The Comptroller and Auditor General shall examine, certify and report on each account sent to him under this section and shall lay copies of it and of his report before each House of Parliament.

(5)  The Treasury may issue to any of the appropriate Ministers—

(*a*)  out of the National Loans Fund, or

(*b*)  out of money provided by Parliament,

such sums as are necessary to enable him to make loans to a new Agency under this section; and any sums received by a Minister of the Crown in pursuance of subsection (2) above shall be paid into the National Loans Fund or, as the case may be, the Consolidated Fund.[1]

*Government guarantees of a new Agency's borrowing.*

**50.**  (1)  The appropriate Minister[2] may, with the consent of the Treasury, guarantee, in such manner and on such conditions as he may think fit, the repayment of the principal of, the payment of interest on, and the discharge of any other financial obligation in connection with, any sum which a new Agency[3] borrows from any person.

(2)  A Minister who gives a guarantee under this section shall forthwith lay a statement of the guarantee before each House of Parliament.

(3)  Where any sum is paid out for fulfilling a guarantee under this section the Minister who gave the guarantee shall, as soon as reasonably practicable after the end of each financial year[4] (beginning with that in which the sum is paid out and ending with that in which all liability in respect of the principal of the sum and in respect of interest on it is finally discharged), lay before each House of Parliament a statement relating to that sum.

(4)  If any sums are paid out in fulfilment of a guarantee under this section, the new Agency which borrowed the sum by reference to which the guarantee was given shall make to the Minister who gave the guarantee, at such times and in such manner as he may from time to time direct,—

(*a*)  payments of such amounts as he may so direct in or towards repayment of the sums so paid out; and

(*b*)  payments of interest, at such rate as he may so direct, on what is outstanding for the time being in respect of sums so paid out;

and the consent of the Treasury shall be required for the giving of a direction under this subsection.[5]

### *Information*

*Provision of information by the new Agencies.*

**51.**  (1)  A new Agency[6] shall furnish the appropriate Minister[7] with all such information as he may reasonably require relating to—

(*a*)  the new Agency's property;

[1] This section came into force on 28 July 1995: S I. 1995/1983.

[2] "The appropriate Minister" defined by s.56(1), p.463 below.

[3] "New Agency" means the Environment Agency or SEPA, the Scottish Environment Protection Agency: ss.56(1), 124(1) below.

[4] "Financial year" defined by s.124(1), p.495 below.

[5] This section came into force on 28 July 1995: S.I. 1995/1983.

[6] "New Agency" means the Environment Agency or SEPA, the Scottish Environment Protection Agency: ss.56(1), 124(1) below.

[7] "The appropriate Minister" defined by s.56(1), p.463 below.

(*b*) the carrying out and proposed carrying out of its functions[1]; and

(*c*) its responsibilities generally.

(2) Information required under this section shall be furnished in such form and manner, and be accompanied or supplemented by such explanations, as the appropriate Minister may reasonably require.

(3) The information which a new Agency may be required to furnish to the appropriate Minister under this section shall include information which, although it is not in the possession of the new Agency or would not otherwise come into the possession of the new Agency, is information which it is reasonable to require the new Agency to obtain.

(4) A requirement for the purposes of this section shall be contained in a direction[2] which—

(*a*) may describe the information to be furnished in such manner as the Minister giving the direction considers appropriate; and

(*b*) may require the information to be furnished on a particular occasion, in particular circumstances or from time to time.

(5) For the purposes of this section a new Agency shall—

(*a*) permit any person authorised for the purpose by the appropriate Minister to inspect and make copies of the contents of any accounts or other records[3] of the new Agency; and

(*b*) give such explanation of them as that person or the appropriate Minister may reasonably require.[4]

*Annual report.*

**52.** (1) As soon as reasonably practicable after the end of each financial year[5], each new Agency[6] shall prepare a report on its activities during that year and shall send a copy of that report to each of the appropriate Ministers[7].

(2) Every such report shall set out any directions under section 40 above[8] which have been given to the new Agency in question during the year to which the report relates, other than directions given under subsection (1) of that section which are identified to that new Agency in writing by the appropriate Minister[9] as being directions the disclosure of which would, in his opinion, be contrary to the interests of national security.

(3) The Secretary of State shall lay a copy of every such report before each House of Parliament and shall arrange for copies of every such report to be published in such manner as he considers appropriate.

(4) A new Agency's annual report shall be in such form and contain such information as may be specified in any direction[10] given to the new Agency by the appropriate Ministers.[11]

*Supplemental provisions*

*Inquiries and other hearings.*

**53.** (1) Without prejudice to any other provision of this Act or any other enactment by virtue of which an inquiry or other hearing is authorised or required to be held, the appropriate Minister[12] may cause an inquiry or other hearing to be held if it appears to him expedient to do so—

[1] "Functions" includes powers and duties: s.124(1) below.
[2] For provisions relating to directions see s.122, p.494 below.
[3] "Records" defined by s.124(1), p.495 below.
[4] This section came into force on 28 July 1995: S.I. 1995/1983.
[5] "Financial year" defined by s.124(1), p.495 below.
[6] "New Agency" means the Environment Agency or SEPA, the Scottish Environment Protection Agency: ss.56(1), 124(1) below.
[7] "The appropriate Ministers" defined by s.56(1), p.463 below.
[8] P.451 above.
[9] "The appropriate Minister" defined by s.56(1), p.463 below.
[10] For provisions relating to directions see s.122, p.494 below.
[11] This section came into force on 28 July 1995: S.I. 1995/1983.
[12] "The appropriate Minister" defined by s.56(1), p.463 below.

(a)  in connection with any of the functions[1] of a new Agency[2]; or

(b)  in connection with any of his functions in relation to a new Agency.

(2)  Subsections (2) to (5) of section 250 of the Local Government Act 1972[3] (which contain supplementary provisions with respect to local inquiries held in pursuance of that section) shall apply to inquiries or other hearings under this section or any other enactment—

(a)  in connection with any of the functions of the Agency[4], or

(b)  in connection with any functions of the Secretary of State or the Minister[5] in relation to the Agency,

as they apply to inquiries under that section, but taking the reference in subsection (4) of that section to a local authority as including a reference to the Agency.

(3)  The provisions of subsections (2) to (8) of section 210 of the Local Government (Scotland) Act 1973[6] (which relate to the holding of local inquiries) shall apply to inquiries or other hearings held under this section or any other enactment—

(a)  in connection with any of the functions of SEPA[7], or

(b)  in connection with any functions of the Secretary of State in relation to SEPA,

as they apply to inquiries held under that section.[8]

*Appearance in legal proceedings.*

**54.**  In England and Wales, a person who is authorised by the Agency[9] to prosecute on its behalf in proceedings before a magistrates' court shall be entitled to prosecute in any such proceedings although not of counsel or a solicitor.[10]

*Continuity of exercise of functions: the new Agencies.*

**55.**  (1)  The abolition of—

(a)  the National Rivers Authority,

(b)  the London Waste Regulation Authority, or

(c)  a river purification board[11],

shall not affect the validity of anything done by that Authority or board before the transfer date[12].

(2)  Anything which, at the transfer date, is in the process of being done by or in relation to a transferor[13] in the exercise of, or in connection with, any of the transferred functions[14] may be continued by or in relation to the transferee[15].

(3)  Anything done by or in relation to a transferor before the transfer date in the exercise of, or otherwise in connection with, any of the transferred functions, shall, so far as is required for continuing its effect on and after that date, have effect as if done by or in relation to the transferee.

(4)  Subsection (3) above applies in particular to—

(a)  any decision, determination, declaration, designation, agreement or instrument made by a transferor;

---

[1] "Functions" includes powers and duties: s.124(1) below.

[2] "New Agency" means the Environment Agency or SEPA, the Scottish Environment Protection Agency: ss.56(1), 124(1) below.

[3] 1972 c.70.

[4] "The Agency" means the Environment Agency: s.124(1) below.

[5] "The Minister" defined by s.56(1), p.464 below.

[6] 1973 c.65.

[7] "SEPA" means the Scottish Environment Protection Agency: s.124(1) below.

[8] This section came into force on 1 April 1996: S.I. 1996/186.

[9] "The Agency" means the Environment Agency: s.124(1) below.

[10] This section came into force on 1 April 1996: S.I. 1996/186.

[11] "River purification board" defined by s.56(1), p.464 below.

[12] "The transfer date" defined by s.56(1), p.464 below; the transfer date was 1 April 1996: S.I. 1996/139 (in respect of Chapter II); S.I. 1996/234 (in respect of Chapter I).

[13] "Transferor" defined by subsection (10) below.

[14] "Transferred functions" defined by subsection (10) below.

[15] "Transferee" defined by subsection (10) below.

(b)  any regulations or byelaws made by a transferor;

(c)  any licence, permission, consent, approval, authorisation, exemption, dispensation or relaxation granted by or to a transferor;

(d)  any notice, direction or certificate given by or to a transferor;

(e)  any application, request, proposal or objection made by or to a transferor;

(f)  any condition or requirement imposed by or on a transferor;

(g)  any fee or charge paid by or to a transferor;

(h)  any appeal allowed by or in favour of or against a transferor;

(j)  any proceedings instituted by or against a transferor.

(5)  Any reference in the foregoing provisions of this section to anything done by or in relation to a transferor includes a reference to anything which, by virtue of any enactment, is treated as having been done by or in relation to that transferor.

(6)  Any reference to a transferor in any document constituting or relating to anything to which the foregoing provisions of this section apply shall, so far as is required for giving effect to those provisions, be construed as a reference to the transferee.

(7)  The foregoing provisions of this section—

(a)  are without prejudice to any provision made by this Act in relation to any particular functions[1]; and

(b)  shall not be construed as continuing in force any contract of employment made by a transferor;

and the Secretary of State may, in relation to any particular functions, by order exclude, modify[2] or supplement any of the foregoing provisions of this section or make such other transitional provisions as he thinks necessary or expedient.

(8)  Where, by virtue of any provision of Schedule 15 to this Act[3], the Minister[4] is the transferor in the case of any functions, he shall have the same powers under subsection (7) above in relation to those functions as the Secretary of State.

(9)  The power to make an order under subsection (7) above shall be exercisable by statutory instrument; and any statutory instrument containing such an order shall be subject to annulment pursuant to a resolution of either House of Parliament.

(10)  In this section—

"the transferee", in the case of any transferred functions, means the new Agency[5] whose functions[6] they become by virtue of any provision made by or under this Act;

"transferred functions" means any functions which, by virtue of any provision made by or under this Act, become functions of a new Agency; and

"transferor" means any body or person any or all of whose functions become, by virtue of any provision made by or under this Act, functions of a new Agency.[7]

*Interpretation of Part I.*

**56.**  (1)  In this Part of this Act, except where the context otherwise requires—

"the 1951 Act" means the Rivers (Prevention of Pollution) (Scotland) Act 1951[8];

"the 1990 Act" means the Environmental Protection Act 1990[9];

[1] "Functions" includes powers and duties: s.124(1) below.
[2] "Modification" defined by s.124(1), p.495 below.
[3] Sch.15, which is not reproduced, concerns minor and consequential amendments relating to fisheries.
[4] "The Minister" defined by s.56(1), p.464 below.
[5] "New Agency" means the Environment Agency or SEPA, the Scottish Environment Protection Agency: ss. 56(1),

124(1) below.
[6] "Functions" includes powers and duties: s.124(1) below.
[7] Subsections (1)–(6) came into force on 1 April 1996; (7)–(10) came into force on 1 February 1996: S.I. 1996/186.
[8] P.3 above.
[9] P.83 above.

"the 1991 Act" means the Water Resources Act 1991[1];

"the appropriate Minister"—

(a)  in the case of the Agency[2], means the Secretary of State or the Minister; and

(b)  in the case of SEPA[3], means the Secretary of State;

"the appropriate Ministers"—

(a)  in the case of the Agency[4], means the Secretary of State and the Minister; and

(b)  in the case of SEPA[5], means the Secretary of State;

"conservancy authority" has the meaning given by section 221(1) of the 1991 Act;

"costs" includes—

(a)  costs to any person; and

(b)  costs to the environment;

"disposal authority"—

(a)  in the application of this Part in relation to the Agency, has the same meaning as it has in Part I of the Control of Pollution Act 1974[6] by virtue of section 30(1) of that Act; and

(b)  in the application of this Part in relation to SEPA[7], has the meaning assigned to it by section 30(2) of that Act;

"the environment" has the same meaning as in Part I of the 1990 Act[8];

"environmental licence", in the application of this Part in relation to the Agency[9] means any of the following—

(a)  registration of a person as a carrier of controlled waste under section 2 of the Control of Pollution (Amendment) Act 1989[10],

(b)  an authorisation under Part I of the 1990 Act[11], other than any such authorisation granted by a local enforcing authority,

(c)  a waste management licence under Part II of that Act[12],

(d)  a licence under Chapter II of Part II of the 1991 Act,

(e)  a consent for the purposes of section 88(1)(a)[13], 89(4)(a) or 90 of that Act,

(f)  registration under the Radioactive Substances Act 1993[14],

(g)  an authorisation under that Act,

(h)  registration of a person as a broker of controlled waste under the Waste Management Licensing Regulations 1994[15],

(j)  registration in respect of an activity falling within paragraph 45(1) or (2) of Schedule 3 to those Regulations[16],

so far as having effect in relation to England and Wales;

"environmental licence", in the application of this Part in relation to SEPA[17], means any of the following—

(a)  a consent under Part II of the Control of Pollution Act 1974[18],

---

[1]  P.267 above.
[2]  "The Agency" means the Environment Agency: s.124(1) below.
[3]  "SEPA" means the Scottish Environment Protection Agency: s.124(1) below.
[4]  "The Agency" means the Environment Agency: s.124(1) below.
[5]  "SEPA" means the Scottish Environment Protection Agency: s.124(1) below.
[6]  1974 c.40.
[7]  "SEPA" means the Scottish Environment Protection Agency: s.124(1) below.
[8]  P.88 above.
[9]  "The Agency" means the Environment.Agency: s.124(1) below.
[10]  P.73 above.
[11]  P.88 above.
[12]  P.112 above.
[13]  P.276 above.
[14]  P.381 above.
[15]  P.675 below.
[16]  P.711 below.
[17]  "SEPA" means the Scottish Environment Protection Agency: s.124(1) below.
[18]  P.18 above.

(b) registration of a person as a carrier of controlled waste under section 2 of the Control of Pollution (Amendment) Act 1989[1],

(c) an authorisation under Part I of the 1990 Act[2],

(d) a waste management licence under Part II of that Act[3],

(e) a licence under section 17 of the Natural Heritage (Scotland) Act 1991[4],

(f) registration under the Radioactive Substances Act 1993[5],

(g) an authorisation under that Act,

(h) registration of a person as a broker of controlled waste under the Waste Management Licensing Regulations 1994[6],

(j) registration in respect of an activity falling within paragraph 45(1) or (2) of Schedule 3 to those Regulations[7],

so far as having effect in relation to Scotland;

"flood defence functions", in relation to the Agency[8], has the same meaning as in the 1991 Act;

"harbour authority" has the meaning given by section 221(1) of the 1991 Act;

"local authority", in the application of this Part in relation to SEPA[9], means a district or islands council in Scotland[10];

"the Minister" means the Minister of Agriculture, Fisheries and Food;

"the Ministers" means the Secretary of State and the Minister;

"navigation authority" has the meaning given by section 221(1) of the 1991 Act;

"new Agency" means the Agency[11] or SEPA[12];

"river purification authority" means a river purification authority within the meaning of the 1951 Act;

"river purification board" means a river purification board established by virtue of section 135 of the Local Government (Scotland) Act 1973[13];

"the transfer date" means such date as the Secretary of State may by order made by statutory instrument appoint as the transfer date for the purposes of this Part; and different dates may be appointed for the purposes of this Part—

(i) as it applies for or in connection with transfers under or by virtue of Chapter I above[14], and

(ii) as it applies for or in connection with transfers under or by virtue of Chapter II above[15],

"waste regulation authority"—

(a) in the application of this Part in relation to the Agency[16], means any authority in England or Wales which, by virtue of section 30(1) of the 1990 Act, is a waste regulation authority for the purposes of Part II of that Act; and

(b) in the application of this Part in relation to SEPA[17], means any council which, by virtue of section 30(1)(g) of the 1990 Act, is a waste regulation authority for the purposes of Part II of that Act.

[1] P.73 above.
[2] P.88 above.
[3] P.112 above.
[4] 1991 c.28.
[5] P.381 above.
[6] P.675 below.
[7] P.711 below.
[8] "The Agency" means the Environment Agency: s.124(1) below.
[9] "SEPA" means the Scottish Environment Protection Agency: s.124(1) below.
[10] See subsection (2) below for revision to this definition.
[11] "The Agency" means the Environment Agency: s.124(1) below.
[12] "SEPA" means the Scottish Environment Protection Agency: s.124(1) below.
[13] 1973 c.65.
[14] The transfer date in respect of Chapter I was 1 April 1996: S.I. 1996/234.
[15] The transfer date in respect of Chapter II was 1 April 1996: S.I. 1996/139.
[16] "The Agency" means the Environment Agency: s.124(1) below.
[17] "SEPA" means the Scottish Environment Protection Agency: s.124(1) below.

(2)  In relation to any time on or after 1st April 1996—

(*a*)  subsection (1) above shall have effect as if, in the definition of "local authority", for the words "district or islands council in Scotland" there were substituted the words "council constituted under section 2 of the Local Government etc. (Scotland) Act 1994[1]"; and

(*b*)  in section 22(3)(*a*)(iv) above the reference to an islands council shall be construed as a reference to a council mentioned in section 3(1) of the Local Government etc. (Scotland) Act 1994.

(3)  Where by virtue of any provision of this Part any function of a Minister of the Crown is exercisable concurrently by different Ministers, that function shall also be exercisable jointly by any two or more of those Ministers.[2]

## PART II: Contaminated land and abandoned mines

**57.**  *This section has inserted Part IIA of the Environmental Protection Act 1990. Part IIA relates to contaminated land and is at page 162 above.*

**58.**  *This section has inserted Chapter IIA of the Water Resources Act 1991. Chapter IIA relates to abandoned mines in England and Wales and is at page 282 above.*

**59.**  *This section has inserted Part IA of the Control of Pollution Act 1974. Part IA relates to abandoned mines in Scotland and is at page 15 above.*

**60.**  *This section makes amendments to sections 89 and 161 of the Water Resources Act 1991. These sections are at pages 277 and 292 above respectively.*

## PART III: National Parks

This Part, which comprises sections 61 to 79, is not reproduced.

## PART IV: Air quality[3]

*National air quality strategy.*

**80.**  (1)  The Secretary of State shall as soon as possible prepare and publish a statement (in this Part referred to as "the strategy") containing policies with respect to the assessment or management of the quality of air.

(2)  The strategy may also contain policies for implementing—

(*a*)  obligations of the United Kingdom under the Community Treaties, or

(*b*)  international agreements to which the United Kingdom is for the time being a party,

---

[1]  1994 c.39.
[2]  This section came into force on 28 July 1995: S.I. 1995/1983.
[3]  The background to the provisions in this Part are set out in two papers published by the Department of the Environment:
*Improving Air Quality: A discussion paper on air quality standards and management,* 1994.
*Air Quality: Meeting the Challenge, The Government's strategic policies for air quality management,* January 1995.
A consultation draft of the proposed UK National Air Quality Strategy was published by the DoE on 8 August 1996.

so far as relating to the quality of air.

(3) The strategy shall consist of or include—

(*a*) a statement which relates to the whole of Great Britain; or

(*b*) two or more statements which between them relate to every part of Great Britain.

(4) The Secretary of State—

(*a*) shall keep under review his policies with respect to the quality of air; and

(*b*) may from time to time modify[1] the strategy.

(5) Without prejudice to the generality of what may be included in the strategy, the strategy must include statements with respect to—

(*a*) standards relating to the quality of air;

(*b*) objectives for the restriction of the levels at which particular substances are present in the air; and

(*c*) measures which are to be taken by local authorities[2] and other persons for the purpose of achieving those objectives.

(6) In preparing the strategy or any modification of it, the Secretary of State shall consult—

(*a*) the appropriate new Agency[3];

(*b*) such bodies or persons appearing to him to be representative of the interests of local government as he may consider appropriate;

(*c*) such bodies or persons appearing to him to be representative of the interests of industry as he may consider appropriate; and

(*d*) such other bodies or persons as he may consider appropriate.

(7) Before publishing the strategy or any modification of it, the Secretary of State—

(*a*) shall publish a draft of the proposed strategy or modification together with notice of a date before which, and an address at which, representations may be made to him concerning the draft so published; and

(*b*) shall take into account any such representations which are duly made and not withdrawn. [4]

*Functions of the new Agencies.*

**81.** (1) In discharging its pollution control functions, each new Agency[5] shall have regard to the strategy[6].

(2) In this section "pollution control functions", in relation to a new Agency, means—

(*a*) in the case of the Agency[7], the functions[8] conferred on it by or under the enactments specified in section 5(5) above[9]; or

(*b*) in the case of SEPA[10], the functions conferred on it by or under the enactments specified in section 33(5) above[11].[12]

[1] "Modifications" defined by s.124(1), p.495 below.
[2] "Local authority" defined by s.91(1), p.474 below.
[3] "The appropriate new Agency" defined by s.91(1), p.474 below.
[4] This section came into force on 1 February 1996: S.I. 1996/186.
[5] "New Agency" means the Environment Agency or SEPA, the Scottish Environment Protection Agency: ss.91(1), 124(1) below.
[6] "The strategy" has the meaning given by section 80(1) above: s.91(1) below.
[7] "The Agency" means the Environment Agency: s.124(1) below.
[8] "Functions" includes powers and duties: s.124(1) below.
[9] P.424 above.
[10] "SEPA" means the Scottish Environment Protection Agency: s.124(1) below.
[11] P.116 above.
[12] This section came into force on 1 April 1996: S.I. 1996/186.

*Local authority reviews.*

**82.** (1) Every local authority[1] shall from time to time cause a review to be conducted of the quality for the time being, and the likely future quality within the relevant period[2], of air within the authority's area.

(2) Where a local authority causes a review under subsection (1) above to be conducted, it shall also cause an assessment to be made of whether air quality standards and objectives[3] are being achieved, or are likely to be achieved within the relevant period, within the authority's area.

(3) If, on an assessment under subsection (2) above, it appears that any air quality standards or objectives are not being achieved, or are not likely within the relevant period to be achieved[4], within the local authority's area, the local authority shall identify any parts of its area in which it appears that those standards or objectives are not likely to be achieved within the relevant period.[5]

*Designation of air quality management areas.*

**83.** (1) Where, as a result of an air quality review[6], it appears that any air quality standards or objectives[7] are not being achieved, or are not likely within the relevant period[8] to be achieved[9], within the area of a local authority[10], the local authority shall by order designate as an air quality management area (in this Part referred to as a "designated area") any part of its area in which it appears that those standards or objectives are not being achieved, or are not likely to be achieved within the relevant period.

(2) An order under this section may, as a result of a subsequent air quality review,—

(*a*) be varied by a subsequent order; or

(*b*) be revoked by such an order, if it appears on that subsequent air quality review that the air quality standards and objectives are being achieved, and are likely throughout the relevant period to be achieved, within the designated area.[11]

*Duties of local authorities in relation to designated areas.*

**84.** (1) Where an order under section 83 above comes into operation the local authority[12] which made the order shall, for the purpose of supplementing such information as it has in relation to the designated area[13] in question, cause an assessment to be made of—

(*a*) the quality for the time being, and the likely future quality within the relevant period[14], of air within the designated area to which the order relates; and

(*b*) the respects (if any) in which it appears that air quality standards or objectives[15] are not being achieved, or are not likely within the relevant period to be achieved,[16] within that designated area.

(2) A local authority which is required by subsection (1) above to cause an assessment to be made shall also be under a duty—

(*a*) to prepare, before the expiration of the period of twelve months beginning with the coming into operation of the order mentioned in that subsection, a report of the results of that assessment; and

---

[1] "Local authority" defined by s.91(1), p.474 below.
[2] "The relevant period" defined by s.91(1), p.475 below.
[3] "Air quality standards" and "air quality objectives" defined by s.91(1), p.474 below.
[4] For "appears . . . to be achieved" see s.91 (2), p.475 below.
[5] This section has not come into force.
[6] "Air quality review" defined by s.91(1), p.474 below.
[7] "Air quality standards" and "air quality objectives" defined by s.91(1), p.474 below.
[8] "The relevant period" defined by s.91(1), p.475 below.
[9] For "appears . . . to be achieved" see s.91(2), p.475 below.
[10] "Local authority" defined by s.91(1), p.474 below.
[11] This section has not come into force.
[12] "Local authority" defined by s.91(1), p.474 below.
[13] "Designated area" defined by s.91(1), p.474 below.
[14] "The relevant period" defined by s.91(1), p.475 below.
[15] "Air quality standards" and "air quality objectives" defined by s.91(1), p.474 below.
[16] For "appears . . . to be achieved" see s.91(2), p.475 below.

(b) to prepare, in accordance with the following provisions of this Part, a written plan (in this Part referred to as an "action plan") for the exercise by the authority, in pursuit of the achievement of air quality standards and objectives in the designated area, of any powers exercisable by the authority.

(3) An action plan shall include a statement of the time or times by or within which the local authority in question proposes to implement each of the proposed measures comprised in the plan.

(4) A local authority may from time to time revise an action plan.

(5) This subsection applies in any case where the local authority preparing an action plan or a revision of an action plan is the council of a district in England which is comprised in an area for which there is a county council; and if, in a case where this subsection applies, the county council disagrees with the authority about the contents of the proposed action plan or revision of the action plan—

(a) either of them may refer the matter to the Secretary of State;

(b) on any such reference the Secretary of State may confirm the authority's proposed action plan or revision of the action plan, with or without modifications[1] (whether or not proposed by the county council) or reject it and, if he rejects it, he may also exercise any powers of his under section 85 below; and

(c) the authority shall not finally determine the content of the action plan, or the revision of the action plan, except in accordance with his decision on the reference or in pursuance of directions under section 85 below.[2]

*Reserve powers of the Secretary of State or SEPA.*

**85.** (1) In this section, "the appropriate authority" means—

(a) in relation to England and Wales, the Secretary of State; and

(b) in relation to Scotland, SEPA[3] acting with the approval of the Secretary of State.

(2) The appropriate authority may conduct or make, or cause to be conducted or made,—

(a) a review of the quality for the time being, and the likely future quality within the relevant period[4], of air within the area of any local authority[5];

(b) an assessment of whether air quality standards and objectives[6] are being achieved, or are likely to be achieved within the relevant period, within the area of a local authority;

(c) an identification of any parts of the area of a local authority in which it appears that those standards or objectives are not likely to be achieved within the relevant period; or

(d) an assessment of the respects (if any) in which it appears that air quality standards or objectives are not being achieved, or are not likely within the relevant period to be achieved[7], within the area of a local authority or within a designated area[8].

(3) If it appears to the appropriate authority—

(a) that air quality standards or objectives are not being achieved, or are not likely within the relevant period to be achieved, within the area of a local authority,

(b) that a local authority has failed to discharge any duty imposed on it under or by virtue of this Part,

(c) that the actions, or proposed actions, of a local authority in purported compliance with the provisions of this Part are inappropriate in all the circumstances of the case, or

---

[1] "Modifications" defined by s.124(1), p.495 below.
[2] This section has not come into force.
[3] "SEPA" means the Scottish Environment Protection Agency: s.124(1) below.
[4] "The relevant period" defined by s.91(1), p.475 below.
[5] "Local authority" defined by s.91(1), p.474 below.

[6] "Air quality standards" and "air quality objectives" defined by s.91(1), p.474 below.
[7] For "appears . . . to be achieved" see s.91(2), p.475 below.
[8] "Designated area" defined by s.91(1), p.474 below.

(*d*)  that developments in science or technology, or material changes in circumstances, have rendered inappropriate the actions or proposed actions of a local authority in pursuance of this Part,

the appropriate authority may give directions[1] to the local authority requiring it to take such steps as may be specified in the directions.

(4)  Without prejudice to the generality of subsection (3) above, directions under that subsection may, in particular, require a local authority—

(*a*)  to cause an air quality review to be conducted under section 82 above[2] in accordance with the directions;

(*b*)  to cause an air quality review under section 82 above to be conducted afresh, whether in whole or in part, or to be so conducted with such differences as may be specified or described in the directions;

(*c*)  to make an order under section 83 above[3] designating as an air quality management area an area specified in, or determined in accordance with, the directions;

(*d*)  to revoke, or modify[4] in accordance with the directions, any order under that section;

(*e*)  to prepare in accordance with the directions an action plan for a designated area;

(*f*)  to modify, in accordance with the directions, any action plan prepared by the authority; or

(*g*)  to implement, in accordance with the directions, any measures in an action plan.

(5)  The Secretary of State shall also have power to give directions to local authorities requiring them to take such steps specified in the directions as he considers appropriate for the implementation of—

(*a*)  any obligations of the United Kingdom under the Community Treaties, or

(*b*)  any international agreement to which the United Kingdom is for the time being a party,

so far as relating to the quality of air.

(6)  Any direction given under this section shall be published in such manner as the body or person giving it considers appropriate for the purpose of bringing the matters to which it relates to the attention of persons likely to be affected by them; and—

(*a*)  copies of the direction shall be made available to the public; and

(*b*)  notice shall be given—

(i)  in the case of a direction given to a local authority in England and Wales, in the London Gazette, or

(ii)  in the case of a direction given to a local authority in Scotland, in the Edinburgh Gazette,

of the giving of the direction and of where a copy of the direction may be obtained.

(7)  It is the duty of a local authority to comply with any direction given to it under or by virtue of this Part.[5]

*Functions of county councils for areas for which there are district councils.*

**86.**  (1)  This section applies in any case where a district in England for which there is a district council is comprised in an area for which there is a county council; and in this paragraph—

(*a*)  any reference to the county council is a reference to the council of that area; and

(*b*)  any reference to a district council is a reference to the council of a district comprised in that area.

(2)  The county council may make recommendations to a district council with respect to the carrying out of—

[1] For provisions relating to directions see s.122, p.494 below.
[2] P.467 above.
[3] P.467 above.
[4] "Modifications" defined by s.124(1), p.495 below.
[5] This section has not come into force.

(*a*) any particular air quality review[1],

(*b*) any particular assessment under section 82[2] or 84[3] above, or

(*c*) the preparation of any particular action plan[4] or revision of an action plan,

and the district council shall take into account any such recommendations .

(3) Where a district council is preparing an action plan, the county council shall, within the relevant period[5], submit to the district council proposals for the exercise (so far as relating to the designated area[6]) by the county council, in pursuit of the achievement of air quality standards and objectives[7], of any powers exercisable by the county council.

(4) Where the county council submits proposals to a district council in pursuance of subsection (3) above, it shall also submit a statement of the time or times by or within which it proposes to implement each of the proposals.

(5) An action plan shall include a statement of—

(*a*) any proposals submitted pursuant to subsection (3) above; and

(*b*) any time or times set out in the statement submitted pursuant to subsection (4) above.

(6) If it appears to the Secretary of State—

(*a*) that air quality standards or objectives are not being achieved, or are not likely within the relevant period to be achieved[8], within the area of a district council,

(*b*) that the county council has failed to discharge any duty imposed on it under or by virtue of this Part,

(*c*) that the actions, or proposed actions, of the county council in purported compliance with the provisions of this Part are inappropriate in all the circumstances of the case, or

(*d*) that developments in science or technology, or material changes in circumstances, have rendered inappropriate the actions or proposed actions of the county council in pursuance of this Part,

the Secretary of State may give directions[9] to the county council requiring it to take such steps as may be specified in the directions.

(7) Without prejudice to the generality of subsection (6) above, directions under that subsection may, in particular, require the county council—

(*a*) to submit, in accordance with the directions, proposals pursuant to subsection (3) above or a statement pursuant to subsection (4) above;

(*b*) to modify[10], in accordance with the directions, any proposals or statement submitted by the county council pursuant to subsection (3) or (4) above;

(*c*) to submit any proposals or statement so modified to the district council in question pursuant to subsection (3) or (4) above; or

(*d*) to implement, in accordance with the directions, any measures included in an action plan.

(8) The Secretary of State shall also have power to give directions to county councils for areas for which there are district councils requiring them to take such steps specified in the directions as he considers appropriate for the implementation of—

(*a*) any obligations of the United Kingdom under the Community Treaties, or

(*b*) any international agreement to which the United Kingdom is for the time being a party,

so far as relating to the quality of air.

---

[1] "Air quality review" defined by s.91(1), p.474 below.
[2] P.467 above.
[3] P.467 above.
[4] "Action plan" defined by s.91(1), p.474 below.
[5] "The relevant period" defined by s.91(1), p.464 above.
[6] "Designated area" defined by s.91(1), p.474 below.
[7] "Air quality standards" and "air quality objectives"
defined by s.91(1), p.474 below.
[8] For "appears . . . to be achieved" see s.91(2), p.475 below.
[9] For provisions relating to directions see s.122, p.494 below.
[10] "Modifications" defined by s.124(1), p.495 below.

(9)  Any direction given under this section shall be published in such manner as the Secretary of State considers appropriate for the purpose of bringing the matters to which it relates to the attention of persons likely to be affected by them; and—

(*a*)  copies of the direction shall be made available to the public; and

(*b*)  notice of the giving of the direction, and of where a copy of the direction may be obtained, shall be given in the London Gazette.

(10)  It is the duty of a county council for an area for which there are district councils to comply with any direction given to it under or by virtue of this Part.[1]

*Regulations for the purposes of Part IV.*

**87.**  (1)  Regulations[2] may make provision—

(*a*)  for, or in connection with, implementing the strategy[3];

(*b*)  for, or in connection with, implementing—

(i)  obligations of the United Kingdom under the Community Treaties, or

(ii)  international agreements to which the United Kingdom is for the time being a party,

so far as relating to the quality of air; or

(*c*)  otherwise with respect to the assessment or management of the quality of air.

(2)  Without prejudice to the generality of subsection (1) above, regulations under that subsection may make provision—

(*a*)  prescribing standards relating to the quality of air;

(*b*)  prescribing objectives for the restriction of the levels at which particular substances are present in the air;

(*c*)  conferring powers or imposing duties on local authorities[4];

(*d*)  for or in connection with—

(i)  authorising local authorities (whether by agreements or otherwise) to exercise any functions[5] of a Minister of the Crown on his behalf;

(ii)  directing that functions of a Minister of the Crown shall be exercisable concurrently with local authorities; or

(iii)  transferring functions of a Minister of the Crown to local authorities;

(*e*)  prohibiting or restricting, or for or in connection with prohibiting or restricting,—

(i)  the carrying on of prescribed[6] activities, or

(ii)  the access of prescribed vehicles or mobile equipment to prescribed areas, whether generally or in prescribed circumstances;

(*f*)  for or in connection with the designation of air quality management areas by orders made by local authorities in such cases or circumstances not falling within section 83 above[7] as may be prescribed;

(*g*)  for the application, with or without modifications[8], of any provisions of this Part in relation to areas designated by virtue of paragraph (*f*) above or in relation to orders made by virtue of that paragraph;

(*h*)  with respect to—

(i)  air quality reviews[9];

---

[1]  This section has not come into force.
[2]  "Regulations" defined by s.91(1), p.475 below.
[3]  "The strategy" has the meaning given by section 80(1), p.465 above: s.91(1) below.
[4]  "Local authority" defined by s.91(1), p.474 below.
[5]  "Functions" includes powers and duties: s.124(1) below.
[6]  "Prescribed" defined by s.91(1), p.475 below.
[7]  P.467 above.
[8]  "Modifications" defined by s.124(1), p.495 below.
[9]  "Air quality review" defined by s.91(1), p.474 below.

    (ii)   assessments under this Part;

    (iii)  orders designating air quality management areas[1]; or

    (iv)  action plans[2];

(*j*)  prescribing measures which are to be adopted by local authorities (whether in action plans or otherwise) or other persons in pursuance of the achievement of air quality standards or objectives;

(*k*)  for or in connection with the communication to the public of information relating to quality for the time being, or likely future quality, of the air;

(*l*)  for or in connection with the obtaining by local authorities from any person of information which is reasonably necessary for the discharge of functions conferred or imposed on them under or by virtue of this Part;

(*m*)  for or in connection with the recovery by a local authority from prescribed persons in prescribed circumstances, and in such manner as may be prescribed, of costs incurred by the authority in discharging functions conferred or imposed on the authority under or by virtue of this Part;

(*n*)  for a person who contravenes, or fails to comply with, any prescribed provision of the regulations to be guilty of an offence and liable on summary conviction to a fine not exceeding level 5 on the standard scale[3] or such lower level on that scale as may be prescribed in relation to the offence;

(*o*)  for or in connection with arrangements under which a person may discharge any liability to conviction for a prescribed offence by payment of a penalty of a prescribed amount;

(*p*)  for or in connection with appeals against determinations or decisions made, notices given or served, or other things done under or by virtue of the regulations.

(3) Without prejudice to the generality of paragraph (*h*) of subsection (2) above, the provision that may be made by virtue of that paragraph includes provision for or in connection with any of the following, that is to say—

(*a*)  the scope or form of a review or assessment;

(*b*)  the scope, content or form of an action plan;

(*c*)  the time at which, period within which, or manner in which a review or assessment is to be carried out or an action plan is to be prepared;

(*d*)  the methods to be employed—

    (i)   in carrying out reviews or assessments; or

    (ii)  in monitoring the effectiveness of action plans;

(*e*)  the factors to be taken into account in preparing action plans;

(*f*)  the actions which must be taken by local authorities or other persons in consequence of reviews, assessments or action plans;

(*g*)  requirements for consultation;

(*h*)  the treatment of representations or objections duly made;

(*j*)  the publication of, or the making available to the public of, or of copies of,—

    (i)   the results, or reports of the results, of reviews or assessments; or

    (ii)  orders or action plans;

(*k*)  requirements for—

    (i)   copies of any such reports, orders or action plans, or

---

[1] For designation of air quality management areas see s.83, p.467 above.
[2] "Action plan" defined by s.91(1), p.474 below.
[3] The current fine at level 5 on the standard scale is £5,000: Criminal Justice Act 1991 (c.53), s.17 (England and Wales); Criminal Procedure (Scotland) Act 1995 (c.46), s.225 (Scotland).

    (ii)　prescribed information, in such form as may be prescribed, relating to reviews or assessments,

to be sent to the Secretary of State or to the appropriate new Agency[1].

(4)　In determining—

(a)　any appeal against, or reference or review of, a decision of a local authority under or by virtue of regulations under this Part, or

(b)　any application transmitted from a local authority under or by virtue of any such regulations,

the body or person making the determination shall be bound by any direction given by a Minister of the Crown or SEPA[2] to the local authority to the same extent as the local authority.

(5)　The provisions of any regulations under this Part may include—

(a)　provision for anything that may be prescribed by the regulations to be determined under the regulations and for anything falling to be so determined to be determined by such persons, in accordance with such procedure and by reference to such matters, and to the opinion of such persons, as may be prescribed;

(b)　different provision for different cases, including different provision in relation to different persons, circumstances, areas or localities; and

(c)　such supplemental, consequential, incidental or transitional provision (including provision amending any enactment or any instrument made under any enactment) as the Secretary of State considers appropriate.

(6)　Nothing in regulations under this Part shall authorise any person other than a constable in uniform to stop a vehicle on any road.

(7)　Before making any regulations under this Part, the Secretary of State shall consult—

(a)　the appropriate new Agency;

(b)　such bodies or persons appearing to him to be representative of the interests of local government as he may consider appropriate;

(c)　such bodies or persons appearing to him to be representative of the interests of industry as he may consider appropriate; and

(d)　such other bodies or persons as he may consider appropriate.

(8)　Any power conferred by this Part to make regulations shall be exercisable by statutory instrument; and no statutory instrument containing regulations under this Part shall be made unless a draft of the instrument has been laid before, and approved by a resolution of, each House of Parliament.

(9)　If, apart from this subsection, the draft of an instrument containing regulations under this Part would be treated for the purposes of the Standing Orders of either House of Parliament as a hybrid instrument, it shall proceed in that House as if it were not such an instrument.[3]

---

*Guidance for the purposes of Part IV.*

**88.**　(1)　The Secretary of State may issue guidance to local authorities[4] with respect to, or in connection with, the exercise of any of the powers conferred, or the discharge of any of the duties imposed, on those authorities by or under this Part.

(2)　A local authority, in carrying out any of its functions[5] under or by virtue of this Part, shall have regard to any guidance issued by the Secretary of State under this Part.

---

[1] "The appropriate new Agency" defined by s.91(1), p.474 below.
[2] "SEPA" means the Scottish Environment Protection Agency: s.124(1) below.
[3] This section came into force on 1 February 1996: S.I. 1996/186.
[4] "Local authority" defined by s.91(1), p.474 below.
[5] "Functions" includes powers and duties: s.124(1) below.

(3) This section shall apply in relation to county councils for areas for which there are district councils as it applies in relation to local authorities.[1]

*Application of Part IV to the Isles of Scilly.*

89. (1) Subject to the provisions of any order under this section, this Part, other than section 80[2], shall not apply in relation to the Isles of Scilly.

(2) The Secretary of State may, after consultation with the Council of the Isles of Scilly, by order provide for the application of any provisions of this Part (other than section 80) to the Isles of Scilly; and any such order may provide for the application of those provisions to those Isles with such modifications[3] as may be specified in the order.

(3) An order under this section may—

(a) make different provision for different cases, including different provision in relation to different persons, circumstances or localities; and

(b) contain such supplemental, consequential and transitional provision as the Secretary of State considers appropriate, including provision saving provision repealed by or under any enactment.

(4) The power of the Secretary of State to make an order under this section shall be exercisable by statutory instrument; and a statutory instrument containing such an order shall be subject to annulment in pursuance of a resolution of either House of Parliament.[4]

*Supplemental provisions.*

90. Schedule 11 to this Act[5] shall have effect.[6]

*Interpretation of Part IV*

91. (1) In this Part—

"action plan" shall be construed in accordance with section 84(2)(b) above[7];

"air quality objectives" means objectives prescribed by virtue of section 87(2)(b) above[8];

"air quality review" means a review under section 82[9] or 85[10] above;

"air quality standards" means standards prescribed by virtue of section 87(2)(a) above[11];

"the appropriate new Agency" means—

(a) in relation to England and Wales, the Agency[12];

(b) in relation to Scotland, SEPA[13];

"designated area" has the meaning given by section 83(1) above[14];

"local authority", in relation to England and Wales, means—

(a) any unitary authority,

(b) any district council, so far as it is not a unitary authority,

(c) the Common Council of the City of London and, as respects the Temples, the Sub-Treasurer of the Inner Temple and the Under-Treasurer of the Middle Temple respectively,

[1] This section came into force on 1 February 1996: S.I. 1996/186.
[2] P.465 above.
[3] "Modifications" defined by s.124(1), p.495 below.
[4] This section came into force on 1 February 1996: S.I. 1996/186.
[5] P.520 below.
[6] This section, in so far as it relates to paragraphs 2, 3 and 5 of schedule 11, came into force on 1 February 1996: S.I. 1996/186; otherwise this section is not in force.
[7] P.468 above.
[8] P.471 above.
[9] P.467 above.
[10] P.468 above.
[11] P.471 above.
[12] "The Agency" means the Environment Agency: s.124(1) below.
[13] "SEPA" means the Scottish Environment Protection Agency: s.124(1) below.
[14] P.467 above.

and, in relation to Scotland, means a council for an area constituted under section 2 of the Local Government etc. (Scotland) Act 1994[1];

"new Agency" means the Agency[2] or SEPA[3];

"prescribed" means prescribed, or of a description prescribed, by or under regulations;

"regulations" means regulations made by the Secretary of State;

"the relevant period", in the case of any provision of this Part, means such period as may be prescribed for the purposes of that provision;

"the strategy" has the meaning given by section 80(1) above[4];

"unitary authority" means—

(a)  the council of a county, so far as it is the council of an area for which there are no district councils;

(b)  the council of any district comprised in an area for which there is no county council;

(c)  the council of a London borough;

(d)  the council of a county borough in Wales.

(2)  Any reference in this Part to it appearing that any air quality standards or objectives are not likely within the relevant period to be achieved includes a reference to it appearing that those standards or objectives are likely within that period not to be achieved.[5]

# PART V: Miscellaneous, general and supplemental provisions

## *Waste*

**92.**  *This section has inserted the following provisions of the Environmental Protection Act 1990:*

section 44A, p.134 above, *National waste strategy: England and Wales*

section 44B, p.136 above, *National waste strategy: Scotland*

schedule 2A, p.222 above, *Objectives for the purposes of the national waste strategy.*

## *Producer responsibility: general.*

**93.**  (1)  For the purpose of promoting or securing an increase in the re-use, recovery[6] or recycling of products or materials[7], the Secretary of State may by regulations[8] make provision for imposing producer responsibility obligations[9] on such persons, and in respect of such products or materials, as may be prescribed[10].

(2)  The power of the Secretary of State to make regulations shall be exercisable only after consultation with bodies or persons appearing to him to be representative of bodies or persons whose interests are, or are likely to be, substantially affected by the regulations which he proposes to make.

(3)  Except in the case of regulations for the implementation of—

(a)  any obligations of the United Kingdom under the Community Treaties, or

(b)  any international agreement to which the United Kingdom is for the time being a party,

---

[1]  1994 c.39.

[2]  "The Agency" means the Environment Agency: s.124(1) below.

[3]  "SEPA" means the Scottish Environment Protection Agency: s.124(1) below.

[4]  P.465 above.

[5]  This section came into force on 1 February 1996: S.I. 1996/186.

[6]  "Recovery" defined by subsection (8) below.

[7]  "Product" and "material" defined by subsection (8) below.

[8]  "Regulations" defined by subsection (8) below.

[9]  "Producer responsibility obligation" defined by subsection (8) below.

[10]  "Prescribed" defined by subsection (8) below.

the power to make regulations shall be exercisable only where the Secretary of State, after such consultation as is required by subsection (2) above, is satisfied as to the matters specified in subsection (6) below.

(4) The powers conferred by subsection (1) above shall also be exercisable, in a case falling within paragraph (*a*) or (*b*) of subsection (3) above, for the purpose of sustaining at least a minimum level of (rather than promoting or securing an increase in) re-use, recovery or recycling of products or materials.

(5) In making regulations by virtue of paragraph (*a*) or (*b*) of subsection (3) above, the Secretary of State shall have regard to the matters specified in subsection (6) below; and in its application in relation to the power conferred by virtue of subsection (4) above, subsection (6) below shall have effect as if—

(*a*) any reference to an increase in the re-use, recovery or recycling of products or materials were a reference to the sustaining of at least a minimum level of re-use, recovery or recycling of the products or materials in question, and

(*b*) any reference to the production of environmental or economic benefits included a reference to the sustaining of at least a minimum level of any such existing benefits,

and any reference in this section or section 94 below to securing or achieving any such benefits shall accordingly include a reference to sustaining at least a minimum level of any such existing benefits.

(6) The matters mentioned in subsections (3) and (5) above are—

(*a*) that the proposed exercise of the power would be likely to result in an increase in the re-use, recovery or recycling of the products or materials in question;

(*b*) that any such increase would produce environmental or economic benefits;

(*c*) that those benefits are significant as against the likely costs resulting from the imposition of the proposed producer responsibility obligation;

(*d*) that the burdens imposed on businesses by the regulations are the minimum necessary to secure those benefits; and

(*e*) that those burdens are imposed on persons most able to make a contribution to the achievement of the relevant targets[1]—

   (i) having regard to the desirability of acting fairly between persons who manufacture, process, distribute or supply products or materials; and

   (ii) taking account of the need to ensure that the proposed producer responsibility obligation is so framed as to be effective in achieving the purposes for which it is to be imposed;

but nothing in sub-paragraph (i) of paragraph (*e*) above shall be taken to prevent regulations imposing a producer responsibility obligation on any class or description of person to the exclusion of any others.

(7) The Secretary of State shall have a duty to exercise the power to make regulations in the manner which he considers best calculated to secure that the exercise does not have the effect of restricting, distorting or preventing competition or, if it is likely to have any such effect, that the effect is no greater than is necessary for achieving the environmental or economic benefits mentioned in subsection (6) above.

(8) In this section—

"prescribed" means prescribed in regulations;

"product" and "material" include a reference to any product or material (as the case may be) at a time when it becomes, or has become, waste;

"producer responsibility obligation" means the steps which are required to be taken by relevant persons of the classes or descriptions to which the regulations in question apply in order to secure attainment of the targets specified or described in the regulations;

---

[1] "Relevant targets" defined by subsection (8) below.

"recovery", in relation to products or materials, includes—

(a) composting, or any other form of transformation by biological processes, of products or materials; or

(b) the obtaining, by any means, of energy from products or materials;

"regulations" means regulations under this section;

"relevant persons", in the case of any regulations or any producer responsibility obligation, means persons of the class or description to which the producer responsibility obligation imposed by the regulations applies;

"relevant targets" means the targets specified or described in the regulations imposing the producer responsibility obligation in question;

and regulations may prescribe, in relation to prescribed products or materials, activities, or the activities, which are to be regarded for the purposes of this section and sections 94 and 95 below or any regulations as re-use, recovery or recycling of those products or materials.

(9) The power to make regulations shall be exercisable by statutory instrument.

(10) Subject to the following provisions of this section, a statutory instrument containing regulations shall not be made unless a draft of the instrument has been laid before and approved by a resolution of each House of Parliament.

(11) Subsection (10) above shall not apply to a statutory instrument by reason only that it contains regulations varying any relevant targets.

(12) A statutory instrument which, by virtue of subsection (11) above, is not subject to any requirement that a draft of the instrument be laid before and approved by a resolution of each House of Parliament shall be subject to annulment in pursuance of a resolution of either House of Parliament.[1]

*Producer responsibility: supplementary provisions,*

**94.** (1) Without prejudice to the generality of section 93 above, regulations[2] may, in particular, make provision for or with respect to—

(a) the classes or descriptions of person to whom the producer responsibility obligation[3] imposed by the regulations applies;

(b) the classes or descriptions of products or materials[4] in respect of which the obligation applies;

(c) the targets which are to be achieved with respect to the proportion (whether by weight, volume or otherwise) of the products or materials in question which are to be re-used, recovered[5] or recycled, whether generally or in any prescribed[6] way;

(d) particulars of the obligation imposed by the regulations;

(e) the registration of persons who are subject to a producer responsibility obligation and who are not members of registered exemption schemes[7], the imposition of requirements in connection with such registration, the variation of such requirements, the making of applications for such registration, the period for which any such registration is to remain in force and the cancellation of any such registration;

(f) the approval, or withdrawal of approval, of exemption schemes by the Secretary of State;

---

[1] This section came into force on 21 September 1995: S.I. 1995/1983.
[2] "Regulations" defined by s.93(8) above: subsection (6) below.
[3] "Producer responsibility obligation" defined by s.93(8) above: subsection (6) below.
[4] "Product" and "material" defined by s.93(8) above: subsection (6) below.
[5] "Recovery" defined by s.93(8) above: subsection (6) below.
[6] "Prescribed" defined by s.93(8) above: subsection (6) below.
[7] "Exemption scheme" and "registered exemption scheme" defined by subsection (6) below.

(g)  the imposition of requirements on persons who are not members of registered exemption schemes to furnish certificates of compliance[1] to the appropriate Agency[2];

(h)  the approval of persons by the appropriate Agency for the purpose of issuing certificates of compliance;

(j)  the registration of exemption schemes, the imposition of conditions in connection with such registration, the variation of such conditions, the making of applications for such registration and the period for which any such registration is to remain in force;

(k)  the requirements which must be fulfilled, and the criteria which must be met, before an exemption scheme may be registered;

(l)  the powers of the appropriate Agency in relation to applications received by it for registration of exemption schemes;

(m)  the cancellation of the registration of an exemption scheme;

(n)  competition scrutiny[3] of registered exemption schemes or of exemption schemes in whose case applications for registration have been received by the appropriate Agency;

(o)  the exclusion or modification[4] of any provision of the Restrictive Trade Practices Acts 1976[5] and 1977[6] in relation to exemption schemes or in relation to agreements where at least one of the parties is an operator[7] of an exemption scheme;

(p)  the fees, or the method of determining the fees, which are to be paid to the appropriate Agency—

(i)  in respect of the approval of persons for the purpose of issuing certificates of compliance;

(ii)  on the making of an application for registration of an exemption scheme;

(iii)  in respect of the subsistence of the registration of that scheme;

(iv)  on submission to the appropriate Agency of a certificate of compliance;

(v)  on the making of an application for, or for the renewal of, registration of a person required to register under the regulations;

(vi)  in respect of the renewal of the registration of that person;

(q)  appeals against the refusal of registration, the imposition of conditions in connection with registration, or the cancellation of the registration, of any exemption scheme;

(r)  the procedure on any such appeal;

(s)  cases, or classes of case,—

(i)  in which an exemption scheme is, or is not, to be treated as registered, or

(ii)  in which a person is, or is not, to be treated as a member of a registered exemption scheme, pending the determination or withdrawal of an appeal, and otherwise with respect to the position of persons and exemption schemes pending such determination or withdrawal;

(t)  the imposition on the appropriate Agency of a duty to monitor compliance with any of the obligations imposed by the regulations;

(u)  the imposition on prescribed persons of duties to maintain records[8], and furnish to the Secretary of State or to the appropriate Agency returns, in such form as may be prescribed of such information as may be prescribed for any purposes of, or for any purposes connected with, or related to, sections 93 to 95 of this Act or any regulations;

[1] "Certificate of compliance" defined by subsection (6) below.
[2] "The appropriate Agency" defined by subsection (6) below.
[3] "Competition scrutiny" defined by subsection (6) below.
[4] "Modification" defined by s.124(1), p.495 below.
[5] 1976 c.34.
[6] 1977 c.19.
[7] "Operator" defined by subsection (6) below.
[8] "Records" defined by s.124(1), p.495 below.

(*w*)  the imposition on the appropriate Agency of a duty to maintain, and make available for inspection by the public, a register containing prescribed information relating to registered exemption schemes or persons required to register under the regulations;

(*y*)  the powers of entry and inspection which are exercisable by a new Agency[1] for the purposes of its functions[2] under the regulations;

(*ya*)  the conferring on prescribed persons of power to require, for the purposes of or otherwise in connection with competition scrutiny, the provision by any person of any information which he has, or which he may at any future time acquire, relating to any exemption scheme or to any acts or omissions of an operator of such a scheme or of any person dealing with such an operator.

(2)  If it appears to the Secretary of State—

(*a*)  that any action proposed to be taken by the operator of a registered exemption scheme would be incompatible with—

  (i)  any obligations of the United Kingdom under the Community Treaties, or

  (ii)  any international agreement to which the United Kingdom is for the time being a party, or

(*b*)  that any action which the operator of such a scheme has power to take is required for the purpose of implementing any such obligations or agreement,

he may direct that operator not to take or, as the case may be, to take the action in question.

(3)  Regulations may make provision as to which of the new Agencies is the appropriate Agency for the purposes of any function conferred or imposed by or under this section or section 93 above, or for the purposes of the exercise of that function in relation to the whole or a prescribed part of Great Britain, and may make provision for things done or omitted to be done by either new Agency in relation to any part of Great Britain to be treated for prescribed purposes as done or omitted to be done by the other of them in relation to some other part of Great Britain.

(4)  Persons issuing certificates of compliance shall act in accordance with guidance issued for the purpose by the appropriate Agency, which may include guidance as to matters which are, or are not, to be treated as evidence of compliance or as evidence of non-compliance.

(5)  In making any provision in relation to fees, regard shall be had to the desirability of securing that the fees received by each new Agency under the regulations are sufficient to meet the costs and expenses incurred by that Agency in the performance of its functions under the regulations.

(6)  In this section—

"the appropriate Agency", subject to regulations made by virtue of subsection (3) above, means—

(*a*)  in relation to England and Wales, the Agency[3];

(*b*)  in relation to Scotland, SEPA[4];

"certificate of compliance" means a certificate issued by a person approved for the purpose by the appropriate Agency to the effect that that person is satisfied that the person in respect of whom the certificate is issued is complying with any producer responsibility obligation to which he is subject;

"competition scrutiny", in the case of any scheme, means scrutiny of the scheme for the purpose of enabling the Secretary of State to satisfy himself—

  (i)  whether or not the scheme has or is likely to have the effect of restricting, distorting or preventing competition or, if it appears to him that the scheme has or is likely to have any such effect, that the effect is or is likely to be no greater than is necessary for achieving the environmental or economic benefits mentioned in section 93(6) above; or

---

[1] "New Agency" defined by subsection (6) below.
[2] "Functions" includes powers and duties: s.124(1) below.
[3] "The Agency" means the Environment Agency: s.124(1),

p.495 below.
[4] "SEPA" means the Scottish Environment Protection Agency: s.124(1), p.495 below.

(ii) whether or not the scheme leads or is likely to lead to an abuse of market power;

"exemption scheme" means a scheme which is (or, if it were to be registered in accordance with the regulations, would be) a scheme whose members for the time being are, by virtue of the regulations and their membership of that scheme, exempt from the requirement to comply with the producer responsibility obligation imposed by the regulations;

"new Agency" means the Agency[1] or SEPA[2];

"operator", in relation to an exemption scheme, includes any person responsible for establishing, maintaining or managing the scheme;

"registered exemption scheme" means an exemption scheme which is registered pursuant to regulations;

and expressions used in this section and in section 93 above have the same meaning in this section as they have in that section.

(7) Regulations—

(a) may make different provision for different cases;

(b) without prejudice to the generality of paragraph (a) above, may impose different producer responsibility obligations in respect of different classes or descriptions of products or materials and for different classes or descriptions of person or exemption scheme;

(c) may include incidental, consequential, supplemental or transitional provision.

(8) Any direction under this section—

(a) may include such incidental, consequential, supplemental or transitional provision as the Secretary of State considers necessary or expedient; and

(b) shall, on the application of the Secretary of State, be enforceable by injunction or, in Scotland, by interdict or by an order for specific performance under section 45 of the Court of Session Act 1988[3].[4]

...........................................................................................................................................................................

*Producer responsibility: offences.*

**95.** (1) Regulations[5] may make provision for a person who contravenes a prescribed[6] requirement of the regulations to be guilty of an offence and liable—

(a) on summary conviction, to a fine not exceeding the statutory maximum[7],

(b) on conviction on indictment, to a fine.

(2) Where an offence under any provision of the regulations committed by a body corporate is proved to have been committed with the consent or connivance of, or to have been attributable to any neglect on the part of, any director, manager, secretary or other similar officer of the body corporate or a person who was purporting to act in any such capacity, he as well as the body corporate shall be guilty of that offence and shall be liable to be proceeded against and punished accordingly.

(3) Where the affairs of a body corporate are managed by its members, subsection (2) above shall apply in relation to the acts or defaults of a member in connection with his functions[8] of management as if he were a director of the body corporate.

(4) Where the commission by any person of an offence under the regulations is due to the act or default of some other person, that other person may be charged with and convicted of the

[1] "The Agency" means the Environment Agency: s.124(1), p.000 below.

[2] "SEPA" means the Scottish Environment Protection Agency: s.124(1), p.495 below.

[3] 1988 c.36.

[4] This section came into force on 21 September 1995: S.I. 1995/1983.

[5] "Regulations" defined by s.93(8), p.476 above: subsection (5) below.

[6] "Prescribed" defined by s.93 (8), p.476 above: subsection (5) below.

[7] The current statutory maximum is £5,000: Criminal Justice Act 1991 (c.53), s.17(2) (England and Wales); Criminal Procedure (Scotland) Act 1995 (c.46), s.225 (8) (Scotland).

[8] "Functions" includes powers and duties: s.124(1) below.

offence by virtue of this section whether or not proceedings for the offence are taken against the first-mentioned person.

(5) Expressions used in this section and in section 93 or 94 above have the same meaning in this section as they have in that section.[1]

*Mineral planning permissions*

**96.** *This section, which relates to mineral planning permissions, is not reproduced.*

*Hedgerows etc.*

**97.** *This section, which relates to hedgerows, is not reproduced.*

**98.** *This section, which relates to grants for purposes conducive to conservation, is not reproduced.*

**99.** *This section, which relates to consultation before making or modifying certain subordinate legislation for England, is not reproduced.*

*Drainage*

**100.–101.** *These sections amend enactments relating to drainage in respect of the meaning of "drainage" and grants in connection with drainage works.*

*Fisheries*

**102.–105.** *These sections amend enactments relating to fisheries.*

### New provisions for Scotland

*Control of pollution of water in Scotland.*

**106.** Schedule 16 to this Act (which amends the Control of Pollution Act 1974 as respects the control of pollution of rivers and coastal waters in Scotland) shall have effect[2].

*Statutory nuisances: Scotland.*

**107.** Schedule 17 to this Act (which makes provision with respect to statutory nuisances in Scotland) shall have effect[3].

### Powers of entry

*Powers of enforcing authorities and persons authorised by them.*

**108.** (1) A person who appears suitable to an enforcing authority[4] may be authorised in writing by that authority to exercise, in accordance with the terms of the authorisation, any of the powers specified in subsection (4) below for the purpose—

(*a*) of determining whether any provision of the pollution control enactments[5] in the case of that authority is being, or has been, complied with;

---

[1] This section came into force on 21 September 1995: S.I. 1995/1983.
[2] This Manual sets out the Control of Pollution Act 1974, with the amendments made by sch.16, at p.11 above. This section came into force on 1 April 1996: S.I. 1996/186.
[3] Sch.17 amends the Environmental Protection Act 1990 and the Radioactive Substances Act 1993. This Manual sets out these Acts, with the amendments made by sch.17, at p.83 and p.381 above respectively. This section came into force on 1 April 1996: S.I. 1996/186.
[4] "Enforcing authority" defined by subsection (15) below.
[5] "Pollution control enactments" defined by subsection (15) below.

(b) of exercising or performing one or more of the pollution control functions[1] of that authority; or

(c) of determining whether and, if so, how such a function should be exercised or performed.

(2) A person who appears suitable to the Agency[2] or SEPA[3] may be authorised in writing by the Agency or, as the case may be, SEPA to exercise, in accordance with the terms of the authorisation, any of the powers specified in subsection (4) below for the purpose of enabling the Agency or, as the case may be, SEPA to carry out any assessment or prepare any report which the Agency or, as the case may be, SEPA is required to carry out or prepare under section 5(3)[4] or 33(3)[5] above.

(3) Subsection (2) above only applies where the Minister who required the assessment to be carried out, or the report to be prepared, has, whether at the time of making the requirement or at any later time, notified the Agency or, as the case may be, SEPA that the assessment or report appears to him to relate to an incident or possible incident involving or having the potential to involve—

(a) serious pollution of the environment,

(b) serious harm to human health, or

(c) danger to life or health.

(4) The powers which a person may be authorised to exercise under subsection (1) or (2) above are—

(a) to enter at any reasonable time (or, in an emergency[6], at any time and, if need be, by force) any premises[7] which he has reason to believe it is necessary for him to enter;

(b) on entering any premises by virtue of paragraph (a) above, to take with him—

(i) any other person duly authorised by the enforcing authority and, if the authorised person[8] has reasonable cause to apprehend any serious obstruction in the execution of his duty, a constable; and

(ii) any equipment or materials required for any purpose for which the power of entry is being exercised;

(c) to make such examination and investigation as may in any circumstances be necessary;

(d) as regards any premises which he has power to enter, to direct that those premises or any part of them, or anything in them, shall be left undisturbed (whether generally or in particular respects) for so long as is reasonably necessary for the purpose of any examination or investigation under paragraph (c) above;

(e) to take such measurements and photographs and make such recordings as he considers necessary for the purpose of any examination or investigation under paragraph (c) above;

(f) to take samples, or cause samples to be taken, of any articles or substances found in or on any premises which he has power to enter, and of the air, water or land in, on, or in the vicinity of, the premises;

(g) in the case of any article or substance found in or on any premises which he has power to enter, being an article or substance which appears to him to have caused or to be likely to cause pollution of the environment or harm to human health, to cause it to be dismantled or subjected to any process or test (but not so as to damage or destroy it, unless that is necessary);

(*h*)  in the case of any such article or substance as is mentioned in paragraph (*g*) above, to take possession of it and detain it for so long as is necessary for all or any of the following purposes, namely—

  (i)  to examine it, or cause it to be examined, and to do, or cause to be done, to it anything which he has power to do under that paragraph;

  (ii)  to ensure that it is not tampered with before examination of it is completed;

  (iii)  to ensure that it is available for use as evidence in any proceedings for an offence under the pollution control enactments in the case of the enforcing authority under whose authorisation he acts or in any other proceedings relating to a variation notice, enforcement notice or prohibition notice under those enactments;

(*j*)  to require any person whom he has reasonable cause to believe to be able to give any information relevant to any examination or investigation under paragraph (*c*) above to answer (in the absence of persons other than a person nominated by that person to be present and any persons whom the authorised person may allow to be present) such questions as the authorised person thinks fit to ask and to sign a declaration of the truth of his answers;

(*k*)  to require the production of, or where the information is recorded in computerised form, the furnishing of extracts from, any records[1]—

  (i)  which are required to be kept under the pollution control enactments for the enforcing authority under whose authorisation he acts, or

  (ii)  which it is necessary for him to see for the purposes of an examination or investigation under paragraph (*c*) above,

and to inspect and take copies of, or of any entry in, the records;

(*l*)  to require any person to afford him such facilities and assistance with respect to any matters or things within that person's control or in relation to which that person has responsibilities as are necessary to enable the authorised person to exercise any of the powers conferred on him by this section;

(*m*)  any other power for—

  (i)  a purpose falling within any paragraph of subsection (1) above, or

  (ii)  any such purpose as is mentioned in subsection (2) above,

which is conferred by regulations made by the Secretary of State.

(5)  The powers which by virtue of subsections (1) and (4) above are conferred in relation to any premises for the purpose of enabling an enforcing authority to determine whether any provision of the pollution control enactments in the case of that authority is being, or has been, complied with shall include power, in order to obtain the information on which that determination may be made,—

(*a*)  to carry out experimental borings or other works on those premises; and

(*b*)  to install, keep or maintain monitoring and other apparatus there.

(6)  Except in an emergency, in any case where it is proposed to enter any premises used for residential purposes, or to take heavy equipment on to any premises which are to be entered, any entry by virtue of this section shall only be effected—

(*a*)  after the expiration of at least seven days' notice of the proposed entry given to a person who appears to the authorised person in question to be in occupation of the premises in question, and

(*b*)  either—

  (i)  with the consent of a person who is in occupation of those premises; or

  (ii)  under the authority of a warrant by virtue of Schedule 18 to this Act[2].

---

[1] "Records" defined by s.124(1), p.495 below.      [2] P.525 below.

(7) Except in an emergency, where an authorised person proposes to enter any premises and—

(a) entry has been refused and he apprehends on reasonable grounds that the use of force may be necessary to effect entry, or

(b) he apprehends on reasonable grounds that entry is likely to be refused and that the use of force may be necessary to effect entry,

any entry on to those premises by virtue of this section shall only be effected under the authority of a warrant by virtue of Schedule 18 to this Act.

(8) In relation to any premises belonging to or used for the purposes of the United Kingdom Atomic Energy Authority, subsections (1) to (4) above shall have effect subject to section 6(3) of the Atomic Energy Authority Act 1954[1] (which restricts entry to such premises where they have been declared to be prohibited places for the purposes of the Official Secrets Act 1911[2]).

(9) The Secretary of State may by regulations make provision as to the procedure to be followed in connection with the taking of, and the dealing with, samples under subsection (4)(f) above.

(10) Where an authorised person proposes to exercise the power conferred by subsection (4)(g) above in the case of an article or substance found on any premises, he shall, if so requested by a person who at the time is present on and has responsibilities in relation to those premises, cause anything which is to be done by virtue of that power to be done in the presence of that person.

(11) Before exercising the power conferred by subsection (4)(g) above in the case of any article or substance, an authorised person shall consult—

(a) such persons having duties on the premises where the article or substance is to be dismantled or subjected to the process or test, and

(b) such other persons,

as appear to him appropriate for the purpose of ascertaining what dangers, if any, there may be in doing anything which he proposes to do or cause to be done under the power.

(12) No answer given by a person in pursuance of a requirement imposed under subsection (4)(j) above shall be admissible in evidence in England and Wales against that person in any proceedings, or in Scotland against that person in any criminal proceedings.

(13) Nothing in this section shall be taken to compel the production by any person of a document of which he would on grounds of legal professional privilege be entitled to withhold production on an order for discovery in an action in the High Court or, in relation to Scotland, on an order for the production of documents in an action in the Court of Session.

(14) Schedule 18 to this Act[3] shall have effect with respect to the powers of entry and related powers which are conferred by this section.

(15) In this section—

"authorised person" means a person authorised under subsection (1) or (2) above;

"emergency" means a case in which it appears to the authorised person in question—

(a) that there is an immediate risk of serious pollution of the environment or serious harm to human health, or

(b) that circumstances exist which are likely to endanger life or health,

and that immediate entry to any premises is necessary to verify the existence of that risk or those circumstances or to ascertain the cause of that risk or those circumstances or to effect a remedy;

"enforcing authority" means—

(a) the Secretary of State;

(b) the Agency[4];

(c) SEPA[5]; or

[1] 1954 c.32.
[2] 1911 c.28.
[3] P.525 below.
[4] "The Agency" means the Environment Agency: s.124(1) below.
[5] "SEPA" means the Scottish Environment Protection Agency: s.124(1) below.

(*d*)  a local enforcing authority;

"local enforcing authority" means—

(*a*)  a local enforcing authority, within the meaning of Part I of the Environmental Protection Act 1990[1];

(*b*)  a local authority, within the meaning of Part IIA of that Act[2], in its capacity as an enforcing authority for the purposes of that Part;

(*c*)  a local authority for the purposes of Part IV of this Act[3] or regulations under that Part;

"mobile plant" means plant which is designed to move or to be moved whether on roads or otherwise;

"pollution control enactments", in relation to an enforcing authority, means the enactments and instruments relating to the pollution control functions of that authority;

"pollution control functions", in relation to the Agency or SEPA, means the functions conferred or imposed on it by or under—

(*a*)  the Alkali, &c, Works Regulation Act 1906[4],

(*b*)  Part III of the Rivers (Prevention of Pollution) (Scotland) Act 1951[5];

(*c*)  the Rivers (Prevention of Pollution) (Scotland) Act 1965[6];

(*d*)  Part I of the Health and Safety at Work etc. Act 1974[7];

(*e*)  Parts I, IA[8] and II[9] of the Control of Pollution Act 1974;

(*f*)  the Control of Pollution (Amendment) Act 1989[10];

(*g*)  Parts I[11], II[12] and IIA[13] of the Environmental Protection Act 1990 (integrated pollution control, waste on land and contaminated land);

(*h*)  Chapter III of Part IV of the Water Industry Act 1991 [14] (special category effluent);

(*j*)  Part III[15] and sections 161[16] to 161D of the Water Resources Act 1991;

(*k*)  section 19 of the Clean Air Act 1993[17];

(*l*)  the Radioactive Substances Act 1993[18];

(*m*)  regulations made by virtue of section 2(2) of the European Communities Act 1972[19], to the extent that the regulations relate to pollution;

"pollution control functions", in relation to a local enforcing authority, means the functions conferred or imposed on, or transferred to, that authority—

(*a*)  by or under Part I[20] or IIA[21] of the Environmental Protection Act 1990;

(*b*)  by or under regulations made by virtue of Part IV of this Act[22]; or

(*c*)  by or under regulations made by virtue of section 2(2) of the European Communities Act 1972[23], to the extent that the regulations relate to pollution;

"pollution control functions", in relation to the Secretary of State, means any functions which are conferred or imposed upon him by or under any enactment or instrument and which relate to the control of pollution;

"premises" includes any land, vehicle, vessel or mobile plant.

---

[1]  P.88 above.
[2]  P.162 above.
[3]  P.465 above.
[4]  1906 c. 14.
[5]  P.4 above.
[6]  P.9 above.
[7]  1974 c. 37.
[8]  P.15 above.
[9]  P.18 above.
[10]  P.71 above.
[11]  P.88 above.
[12]  P.112 above.
[13]  P.162 above.
[14]  P.232 above.
[15]  P.271 above.
[16]  P.292 above.
[17]  P.347 above.
[18]  P.381 above.
[19]  1972 c.68.
[20]  P.88 above.
[21]  P.162 above.
[22]  P.465 above.
[23]  1972 c.68.

(16)  Any power to make regulations under this section shall be exercisable by statutory instrument; and a statutory instrument containing any such regulations shall be subject to annulment pursuant to a resolution of either House of Parliament.[1]

*Power to deal with cause of imminent danger of serious pollution etc.*

**109.** (1)  Where, in the case of any article or substance found by him on any premises which he has power to enter, an authorised person[2] has reasonable cause to believe that, in the circumstances in which he finds it, the article or substance is a cause of imminent danger of serious pollution of the environment or serious harm to human health, he may seize it and cause it to be rendered harmless (whether by destruction or otherwise).

(2)  As soon as may be after any article or substance has been seized and rendered harmless under this section, the authorised person shall prepare and sign a written report giving particulars of the circumstances in which the article or substance was seized and so dealt with by him, and shall—

(a)  give a signed copy of the report to a responsible person at the premises where the article or substance was found by him; and

(b)  unless that person is the owner of the article or substance, also serve a signed copy of the report on the owner;

and if, where paragraph (b) above applies, the authorised person cannot after reasonable inquiry ascertain the name or address of the owner, the copy may be served on him by giving it to the person to whom a copy was given under paragraph (a) above.

(3)  In this section, "authorised person" has the same meaning as in section 108 above.[3]

*Offences.*

**110.** (1)  It is an offence for a person intentionally to obstruct an authorised person[4] in the exercise or performance of his powers or duties[5].

(2)  It is an offence for a person, without reasonable excuse,—

(a)  to fail to comply with any requirement imposed under section 108 above[6];

(b)  to fail or refuse to provide facilities or assistance or any information or to permit any inspection reasonably required by an authorised person in the execution of his powers or duties under or by virtue of that section; or

(c)  to prevent any other person from appearing before an authorised person, or answering any question to which an authorised person may require an answer, pursuant to subsection (4) of that section.

(3)  It is an offence for a person falsely to pretend to be an authorised person.

(4)  A person guilty of an offence under subsection (1) above shall be liable—

(a)  in the case of an offence of obstructing an authorised person in the execution of his powers under section 109 above—

(i)  on summary conviction, to a fine not exceeding the statutory maximum[7];

(ii)  on conviction on indictment, to a fine or to imprisonment for a term not exceeding two years, or to both;

---

[1] This section came into force on 1 April 1996: S.I. 1996/186.
[2] "Authorised person" has the same meaning as in s.108 (15) above: subsection (3) below.
[3] This section came into force on 1 April 1996: S.I. 1996/186.
[4] "Authorised person" defined by subsection (6) below.
[5] "Powers and duties" defined by subsection (6) below.
[6] P.481 above.
[7] The current statutory maximum is £5,000: Criminal Justice Act 1991(c.53), s.17 (2) (England and Wales); Criminal Procedure (Scotland) Act 1995 (c.46), s.225(8) (Scotland).

(*b*) in any other case, on summary conviction, to a fine not exceeding level 5 on the standard scale[1].

(5) A person guilty of an offence under subsection (2) or (3) above shall be liable on summary conviction to a fine not exceeding level 5 on the standard scale.

(6) In this section—

"authorised person" means a person authorised under section 108 above[2] and includes a person designated under paragraph 2 of Schedule 18 to this Act[3];

"powers and duties" includes powers or duties exercisable by virtue of a warrant under Schedule 18 to this Act.[4]

..................................................................................................................................................

*Evidence*

*Evidence in connection with certain pollution offences.*

**111.** (1) The following provisions (which restrict the admissibility in evidence of information obtained from samples) shall cease to have effect—

(*a*) section 19(2) to (2B) of the Rivers (Prevention of Pollution) (Scotland) 1951[5];

(*b*) section 49 of the Sewerage (Scotland) Act 1968[6];

(*c*) section 171(4) and (5) of the Water Industry Act 1991[7]; and

(*d*) section 209(1), (2) and (4) of the Water Resources Act 1991[8].

(2) Information provided or obtained pursuant to or by virtue of a condition of a relevant licence[9] (including information so provided or obtained, or recorded, by means of any apparatus[10]) shall be admissible in evidence in any proceedings, whether against the person subject to the condition or any other person.

(3) For the purposes of subsection (2) above, apparatus shall be presumed in any proceedings to register or record accurately, unless the contrary is shown or the relevant licence otherwise provides.

(4) Where—

(*a*) by virtue of a condition of a relevant licence, an entry is required to be made in any record as to the observance of any condition of the relevant licence, and

(*b*) the entry has not been made,

that fact shall be admissible in any proceedings as evidence that that condition has not been observed.

(5) In this section—

"apparatus" includes any meter or other device for measuring, assessing, determining, recording or enabling to be recorded, the volume, temperature, radioactivity, rate, nature, origin, composition or effect of any substance, flow, discharge, emission, deposit or abstraction;

"condition of a relevant licence" includes any requirement to which a person is subject under, by virtue of or in consequence of a relevant licence;

"environmental licence" has the same meaning as it has in Part I above as it applies in relation to the Agency[11] or SEPA[12], as the case may be[13];

---

[1] The current fine at level 5 on the standard scale is £5,000: Criminal Justice Act 1991 (c.53), s.17 (England and Wales); Criminal Procedure (Scotland) Act 1995 (c.46), s.225 (Scotland).
[2] P.481 above.
[3] P.525 below.
[4] This section came into force on 1 April 1996: S.I. 1996/186.
[5] 1951 c.66.
[6] 1968 c.47.
[7] 1991 c.56.
[8] 1991 c.57.
[9] "Condition of a relevant licence" and "relevant licence" defined by subsection (5) below.
[10] "Apparatus" defined by subsection (5) below.
[11] "The Agency" means the Environment Agency: s.124(1) below.
[12] "SEPA" means the Scottish Environment Protection Agency: s.124(1) below.
[13] "Environmental licence" is defined in s.56(1), p.463 above.

"relevant licence" means—

(a)  any environmental licence;

(b)  any consent under Part II of the Sewerage (Scotland) Act 1968 to make discharges of trade effluent;

(c)  any agreement under section 37 of that Act with respect to or to any matter connected with, the reception, treatment or disposal of such effluent;

(d)  any consent under Chapter III of Part IV of the Water Industry Act 1991[1] to make discharges of special category effluent; or

(e)  any agreement under section 129 of that Act with respect to, or to any matter connected with, the reception or disposal of such effluent.

(6)  In section 25 of the Environmental Protection Act, after subsection (2) (which makes similar provision to subsection (4) above) there shall be inserted—

(3)  *This subsection is set out in section 25 of the 1990 Act at p.000 above.*[2]

## Offences

*Amendment of certain offences relating to false or misleading statements or false entries.*

**112.**  Schedule 19 to this Act[3] shall have effect.[4]

## Information

*Disclosure of information.*

**113.**  (1)  Notwithstanding any prohibition or restriction imposed by or under any enactment or rule of law, information of any description may be disclosed—

(a)  by a new Agency[5] to a Minister of the Crown, the other new Agency or a local enforcing authority[6],

(b)  by a Minister of the Crown to a new Agency, another Minister of the Crown or a local enforcing authority, or

(c)  by a local enforcing authority to a Minister of the Crown, a new Agency or another local enforcing authority,

for the purpose of facilitating the carrying out by either of the new Agencies of any of its functions[7], by any such Minister of any of his environmental functions[8] or by any local enforcing authority of any of its relevant functions[9]; and no person shall be subject to any civil or criminal liability in consequence of any disclosure made by virtue of this subsection.

(2)  Nothing in this section shall authorise the disclosure to a local enforcing authority by a new Agency or another local enforcing authority of information—

(a)  disclosure of which would, in the opinion of a Minister of the Crown, be contrary to the interests of national security; or

(b)  which was obtained under or by virtue of the Statistics of Trade Act 1947[10] and which was disclosed to a new Agency or any of its officers by the Secretary of State.

(3)  No information disclosed to any person under or by virtue of this section shall be disclosed by that person to any other person otherwise than in accordance with the provisions of this

---

[1]  P.232 above.

[2]  This section came into force on 1 April 1996: S.I. 1996/186.

[3]  P.526 below.

[4]  This section came into force on 1 April 1996: S.I. 1996/186.

[5]  "New Agency" means the Environment Agency or SEPA, the Scottish Environment Protection Agency: subsection (5) below.

[6]  "Local enforcing authority" defined by subsection (5) below.

[7]  "Functions" includes powers and duties: s.124(1) below.

[8]  "Environmental functions" defined by subsection (5) below.

[9]  For "relevant functions" see definition of local enforcing authority at subsection (5) below.

[10]  1947 c.39.

section, or any provision of any other enactment which authorises or requires the disclosure, if that information is information—

(a)  which relates to a trade secret of any person or which otherwise is or might be commercially confidential in relation to any person; or

(b)  whose disclosure otherwise than under or by virtue of this section would, in the opinion of a Minister of the Crown, be contrary to the interests of national security.

(4)  Any authorisation by or under this section of the disclosure of information by or to any person shall also be taken to authorise the disclosure of that information by or, as the case may be, to any officer of his who is authorised by him to make the disclosure or, as the case may be, to receive the information.

(5)  In this section—

"new Agency" means the Agency[1] or SEPA[2];

"the environment" has the same meaning as in Part I of the Environmental Protection Act 1990[3];

"environmental functions", in relation to a Minister of the Crown, means any function of that Minister, whether conferred or imposed under or by virtue of any enactment or otherwise, relating to the environment; and

"local enforcing authority" means—

(a)  any local authority within the meaning of Part IIA of the Environmental Protection Act 1990[4], and the "relevant functions" of such an authority are its functions under or by virtue of that Part;

(b)  any local authority within the meaning of Part IV of this Act[5], and the "relevant functions" of such an authority are its functions under or by virtue of that Part;

(c)  in relation to England, any county council for an area for which there are district councils, and the "relevant functions" of such a county council are its functions under or by virtue of Part IV of this Act; or

(d)  in relation to England and Wales, any local enforcing authority within the meaning of section 1(7) of the Environmental Protection Act 1990[6], and the "relevant functions" of such an authority are its functions under or by virtue of Part I of that Act.[7]

*Appeals*

*Power of Secretary of State to delegate his functions of determining, or to refer matters involved in, appeals.*

114.  (1)  The Secretary of State may—

(a)  appoint any person to exercise on his behalf, with or without payment, any function[8] to which this paragraph applies; or

(b)  refer any item to which this paragraph applies to such person as the Secretary of State may appoint for the purpose, with or without payment.

(2)  The functions to which paragraph (a) of subsection (1) above applies are any of the Secretary of State's functions of determining—

(a)  an appeal under—

---

[1]  "The Agency" means the Environment Agency: s.124(1) below.
[2]  "SEPA" means the Scottish Environment Protection Agency: s.124(1) below.
[3]  "The environment" is defined in s.1(2) of the 1990 Act at p.89 above.
[4]  "Local authority" is defined in s.78A(9) of Part IIA of the 1990 Act at p.164 above.

[5]  "Local authority" is defined in s.91(1) of Part IV of this Act at p.474 above.
[6]  P.90 above.
[7]  This section came into force on 1 April 1996: S.I. 1996/186.
[8]  "Functions" includes powers and duties: s.124(1) below.

   (i)    section 31A(2)(b)[1], 42B(5)[2], 46C[3] or 49B[4] of the Control of Pollution Act 1974,

   (ii)   section 4 of the Control of Pollution (Amendment) Act 1989[5],

   (iii)  section 15[6], 22(5)[7], 43[8], 62(3)(c)[9], 66(5)[10], 78L[11] or 78T[12] of the Environmental Protection Act 1990,

   (iv)   paragraph 2 or paragraph 3(3) of Schedule 6 to the Natural Heritage (Scotland) Act 1991[13],

   (v)    section 43, 91[14], 92[15], 96[16], 161C[17] or 191B(5)[18] of the Water Resources Act 1991,

   (vi)   section 26 of the Radioactive Substances Act 1993[19] against any decision of, or notice served by, SEPA[20],

   (vii)  paragraph 6 of Schedule 5 to the Waste Management Licensing Regulations 1994[21],

or any matter involved in such an appeal;

   (b)  the questions, or any of the questions, which fall to be determined by the Secretary of State under section 39(1)[22] or section 49(4)[23] of the Control of Pollution Act 1974.

   (3)  The items to which paragraph (b) of subsection (1) above applies are—

   (a)  any matter involved in an appeal falling within subsection (2)(a) above;

   (b)  any of the questions which fall to be determined by the Secretary of State under section 39(1) or section 49(4) of the Control of Pollution Act 1974.

   (4)  Schedule 20 to this Act[24] shall have effect with respect to appointments under subsection (1)(a) above.[25]

*Crown application*

*Application of this Act to the Crown.*

**115.**  (1)  Subject to the provisions of this section, this Act shall bind the Crown.

   (2)  Part III of this Act and any amendments, repeals and revocations made by other provisions of this Act (other than those made by Schedule 21, which shall bind the Crown) bind the Crown to the extent that the enactments to which they relate bind the Crown.

   (3)  No contravention by the Crown of any provision made by or under this Act shall make the Crown criminally liable; but the High Court or, in Scotland, the Court of Session may, on the application of the Agency[26] or, in Scotland, SEPA[27], declare unlawful any act or omission of the Crown which constitutes such a contravention.

   (4)  Notwithstanding anything in subsection (3) above, any provision made by or under this Act shall apply to persons in the public service of the Crown as it applies to other persons.

   (5)  If the Secretary of State certifies that it appears to him, as respects any Crown premises and any powers of entry exercisable in relation to them specified in the certificate, that it is requisite or expedient that, in the interests of national security, the powers should not be exercisable in

[1] P.27 above.
[2] P.40 above.
[3] P.44 above.
[4] P.47 above.
[5] P.75 above.
[6] P.103 above.
[7] P.108 above.
[8] P.133 above.
[9] P.152 above.
[10] P.155 above.
[11] P.175 above.
[12] P.182 above.
[13] 1991 c.28.
[14] P.280 above.
[15] P.284 above.
[16] P.287 above.
[17] P.295 above.
[18] P.301 above.
[19] P.398 above.
[20] "SEPA" means the Scottish Environment Protection Agency: s.124(1) below.
[21] P.727 below.
[22] P.35 above.
[23] P.46 above.
[24] P.527 below.
[25] This section came into force on 1 April 1996: S.I. 1996/186.
[26] "The Agency" means the Environment Agency: s.124(1) below.
[27] "SEPA" means the Scottish Environment Protection Agency: s.124(1) below.

relation to those premises, those powers shall not be exercisable in relation to those premises, and in this subsection "Crown premises" means premises held or used by or on behalf of the Crown.

(6) Nothing in this section shall be taken as in any way affecting Her Majesty in her private capacity; and this subsection shall be construed as if section 38(3) of the Crown Proceedings Act 1947[1] (interpretation of references to Her Majesty in her private capacity) were contained in this Act.[2]

*Application of certain other enactments to the Crown.*

116. Schedule 21 to this Act[3] shall have effect.[4]

### Isles of Scilly

*Application of this Act to the Isles of Scilly.*

117. (1) Subject to sections 77, 80[5] and 89[6] above and the provisions of any order under this section or section 89 above, nothing in this Act shall require or authorise any function, duty or power to be carried out, performed or exercised in relation to the Isles of Scilly by the Agency[7]; and references in the other provisions of this Act (apart from Part III) to England and Wales shall not include references to those Isles.

(2) The Secretary of State may, after consultation with the Council of the Isles of Scilly, by order make provision with respect to the carrying out in those Isles of functions (other than functions under or by virtue of Part III or IV[8] of this Act) falling to be carried out in relation to other parts of England and Wales by the Agency.

(3) Without prejudice to the generality of the power conferred by subsection (2) above, an order under this section may apply any provision of this Act (other than a provision contained in Part III or IV) in relation to the Isles of Scilly with or without modifications[9].

(4) An order under this section may—

(*a*) make different provision for different cases, including different provision in relation to different persons, circumstances or localities; and

(*b*) contain such supplemental, consequential and transitional provision as the Secretary of State considers appropriate, including provision saving provision repealed by or under any enactment.

(5) The power of the Secretary of State to make an order under this section shall be exercisable by statutory instrument; and a statutory instrument containing such an order shall be subject to annulment in pursuance of a resolution of either House of Parliament.[10]

118. *Application of certain other enactments to the Isles of Scilly*

(1) *This subsection inserts section 10A of the Control of Pollution (Amendment) Act 1989, p.81 above.*

(2) *This subsection repeals section 11(3) of the Control of Pollution (Amendment) Act 1989.*

(3) *This subsection substitutes section 76 of the Environmental Protection Act 1990. The substituted section is at p.160 above.*

[1] 1947 c.44.
[2] This section came into force on 1 April 1996: S.I. 1995/2950; S.I. 1996/186.
[3] Sch.21 amends certain enactments in respect of the application of those enactments to the Crown. The Acts so amended in this Manual are the Control of Pollution Act 1974, the Water Industry Act 1991 and the Water Resources Act 1991 which are set out with the amendments.
[4] This section, in so far as it relates to paras.2(1) to (3) of sch.21, which relate to ss.115 and 142 of the Water Resources Act 1991, came into force on 21 September 1995: S.I.
1995/1983; otherwise this section is not in force.
[5] P.465 above.
[6] P.474 above.
[7] "The Agency" means the Environment Agency: s.124(1) below.
[8] P.465 above.
[9] "Modifications" defined by s.124(1), p.495 below. See S.I. 1996/1030, p.792 below.
[10] This section came into force on 1 February 1996: S.I. 1996/186.

(4) *This subsection substitutes section 222 of the Water Industry Act 1991. The substituted section is at p.263 above.*

(5) *This subsection substitutes section 224 of the Water Resources Act 1991. The substituted section is at p.318 above.*

(6) *This subsection substitutes section 75 of the Land Drainage Act 1991 (c.59).*

*Miscellaneous and supplemental*

*Stamp duty.*

**119.** (1) No transfer effected by Part I of this Act[1] shall give rise to any liability to stamp duty.

(2) Stamp duty shall not be chargeable—

(*a*) on any transfer scheme[2]; or

(*b*) on any instrument or agreement which is certified to the Commissioners of Inland Revenue by the Secretary of State as made in pursuance of a transfer scheme.

(3) No transfer scheme, and no instrument which is certified as mentioned in subsection (2)(*b*) above, shall be taken to be duly stamped unless—

(*a*) it has, in accordance with section l 2 of the Stamp Act l 891[3], been stamped with a particular stamp denoting that it is not chargeable with that duty or that it is duly stamped; or

(*b*) it is stamped with the duty to which it would be liable, apart from this section.

(4) In this section "transfer scheme" means a scheme made or approved by the Secretary of State under section 3[4] or 22[5] above for the transfer of property, rights or liabilities to the Agency[6] or to SEPA.[7,8]

*Minor and consequential amendments, transitional and transitory provisions, savings and repeals.*

**120.** (1) The enactments mentioned in Schedule 22 to this Act shall have effect with the amendments there specified (being minor amendments and amendments consequential on provisions of this Act); and, without prejudice to any power conferred by any other provision of this Act, the Secretary of State and the Minister[9] shall each have power by regulations to make such additional consequential amendments—

(*a*) of public general enactments passed before, or in the same Session as, this Act, and

(*b*) of subordinate legislation[10] made before the passing of this Act,

as he considers necessary or expedient by reason of the coming into force of any provision of this Act.

(2) The transitional provisions, transitory provisions and savings contained in Schedule 23 to this Act[11] shall have effect; but those provisions are without prejudice to sections 16 and 17 of the Interpretation Act 1978[12] (effect of repeals).

(3) The enactments mentioned in Schedule 24 to this Act (which include some that are spent or no longer of practical utility) are hereby repealed to the extent specified in the third column of that Schedule.

---

[1] P.420 above.
[2] "Transfer scheme" defined by subsection (4) below.
[3] 1891 c.39.
[4] P.422 above.
[5] P.440 above.
[6] "The Agency" means the Environment Agency: s.124(1) below.
[7] "SEPA" means the Scottish Environment Protection Agency: s.124(1) below.
[8] This section came into force on 1 February 1996: S.I. 1996/186.
[9] "The Minister" defined by subsection (6) below.
[10] "Subordinate legislation" defined by subsection (6) below.
[11] P.529 below.
[12] 1978 c.30.

(4)  The power to make regulations under subsection (1) above shall be exercisable by statutory instrument; and a statutory instrument containing any such regulations shall be subject to annulment in pursuance of a resolution of either House of Parliament.

(5)  The power to make regulations under subsection (1) above includes power to make such incidental, supplemental, consequential and transitional provision as the Secretary of State or the Minister thinks necessary or expedient.

(6)  In this section—

"the Minister" means the Minister of Agriculture, Fisheries and Food;

"subordinate legislation" has the same meaning as in the Interpretation Act 1978.[1]

*Local statutory provisions: consequential amendments etc.*

**121.** (1)  If it appears to the Secretary of State or the Minister[2] to be appropriate to do so—

(*a*)  for the purposes of, or in consequence of, the coming into force of any enactment contained in this Act; or

(*b*)  in consequence of the effect or operation at any time after the transfer date[3] of any such enactment or of anything done under any such enactment,

he may by order repeal, amend or re-enact (with or without modifications[4]) any local statutory provision[5], including, in the case of an order by virtue of paragraph (*b*) above, a provision amended by virtue of paragraph (*a*) above.

(2)  An order made by the Secretary of State or the Minister under subsection (1) above may—

(*a*)  make provision applying generally in relation to local statutory provisions of a description specified in the order;

(*b*)  make different provision for different cases, including different provision in relation to different persons, circumstances or localities;

(*c*)  contain such supplemental, consequential and transitional provision as the Secretary of State or, as the case may be, the Minister considers appropriate; and

(*d*)  in the case of an order made after the transfer date, require provision contained in the order to be treated as if it came into force on that date.

(3)  The power under this section to repeal or amend a local statutory provision shall include power to modify the effect in relation to any local statutory provision of any provision of Schedule 23 to this Act.

(4)  Nothing in any order under this section may abrogate or curtail the effect of so much of any local statutory provision as confers any right of way or confers on or preserves for the public—

(*a*)  any right of enjoyment of air, exercise or recreation on land; or

(*b*)  any right of access to land for the purposes of exercise or recreation.

(5)  The power to make an order under subsection (1) above shall be exercisable by statutory instrument subject to annulment in pursuance of a resolution of either House of Parliament.

(6)  The power to make an order under subsection (1) above shall be without prejudice to any power conferred by any other provision of this Act.

(7)  In this section—

"local statutory provision" means—

---

[1] Subsection (1), in so far as it confers power on the Secretary of State and the Minister to make regulations, and subsections (4) to (6), came into force on 28 July 1995: S.I. 1995/1983; otherwise subsections(1) to (3) have come into force partially on various dates: see S.I. 1995/1983; S.I. 1995/2649; S.I. 1995/2765 and S.I. 1996/186.

[2] "The Minister" defined by subsection (7) below.

[3] "The transfer date" has the same meaning as in s.56(1), p.000 above: subsection (7) below. The transfer date was 1 April 1996: S.I. 1996/139 (in respect of Chapter II); S.I. 1996/234 (in respect of Chapter I).

[4] "Modifications" defined by s.124(1), p.495 below.

[5] "Local statutory provision" defined by subsection (7) below.

(*a*)  a provision of a local Act (including an Act confirming a provisional order);

(*b*)  a provision of so much of any public general Act as has effect with respect to a particular area, with respect to particular persons or works or with respect to particular provisions falling within any paragraph of this definition;

(*c*)  a provision of an instrument made under any provision falling within paragraph (*a*) or (*b*) above; or

(*d*)  a provision of any other instrument which is in the nature of a local enactment;

"the Minister" means the Minister of Agriculture, Fisheries and Food;

"the transfer date" has the same meaning as in Part I of this Act[1].[2]

*Directions.*

**122.**  (1)  Any direction given under this Act shall be in writing.

(2)  Any power conferred by this Act to give a direction shall include power to vary or revoke the direction.

(3)  Subsections (4) and (5) below apply to any direction given—

(*a*)  to the Agency[3] or SEPA[4] under any provision of this Act or any other enactment, or

(*b*)  to any other body or person under any provision of this Act,

being a direction to any extent so given for the purpose of implementing any obligations of the United Kingdom under the Community Treaties.

(4)  A direction to which this subsection applies shall not be varied or revoked unless, notwithstanding the variation or revocation, the obligations mentioned in subsection (3) above, as they have effect for the time being, continue to be implemented, whether by directions or any other instrument or by any enactment.

(5)  Any variation or revocation of a direction to which this subsection applies shall be published in such manner as the Minister giving it considers appropriate for the purpose of bringing the matters to which it relates to the attention of persons likely to be affected by them; and—

(*a*)  copies of the variation or revocation shall be made available to the public; and

(*b*)  notice of the variation or revocation, and of where a copy of the variation or revocation may be obtained, shall be given—

(i)  if the direction has effect in England and Wales, in the London Gazette;

(ii)  if the direction has effect in Scotland, in the Edinburgh Gazette.[5]

*Service of documents.*

**123.**  (1)  Without prejudice to paragraph 17(2)(*d*) of Schedule 7 to this Act[6], any notice required or authorised by or under this Act to be served (whether the expression "serve" or the expression "give" or "send" or any other expression is used) on any person may be served by delivering it to him, or by leaving it at his proper address, or by sending it by post to him at that address.

(2)  Any such notice may—

(*a*)  in the case of a body corporate, be served on the secretary or clerk of that body;

(*b*)  in the case of a partnership, be served on a partner or a person having the control or management of the partnership business.

---

[1] "The transfer date" is defined in s.56(1), p.464 above. The transfer date was 1 April 1996: S.I. 1996/139 (in respect of Chapter II); S.I. 1996/234 (in respect of Chapter I).
[2] This section came into force on 28 July 1995: S.I. 1995/1983.
[3] "The Agency" means the Environment Agency: s.124(1) below.
[4] "SEPA" means the Scottish Environment Protection Agency: s.124(1) below.
[5] This section came into force on 28 July 1995: S.I. 1995/1983.
[6] Sch.7 relates to National Park authorities.

(3) For the purposes of this section and of section 7 of the Interpretation Act 1978[1] (service of documents by post) in its application to this section, the proper address of any person on whom any such notice is to be served shall be his last known address, except that—

(*a*) in the case of a body corporate or their secretary or clerk, it shall be the address of the registered or principal office of that body;

(*b*) in the case of a partnership or person having the control or the management of the partnership business, it shall be the principal office of the partnership;

and for the purposes of this subsection the principal office of a company registered outside the United Kingdom or of a partnership carrying on business outside the United Kingdom shall be their principal office within the United Kingdom.

(4) If the person to be served with any such notice has specified an address in the United Kingdom other than his proper address within the meaning of subsection (3) above as the one at which he or someone on his behalf will accept notices of the same description as that notice, that address shall also be treated for the purposes of this section and section 7 of the Interpretation Act 1978 as his proper address.

(5) Where under any provision of this Act any notice is required to be served on a person who is, or appears to be, in occupation of any premises[2] then—

(*a*) if the name or address of such a person cannot after reasonable inquiry be ascertained, or

(*b*) if the premises appear to be or are unoccupied,

that notice may be served either by leaving it in the hands of a person who is or appears to be resident or employed on the premises or by leaving it conspicuously affixed to some building or object on the premises.

(6) This section shall not apply to any notice in relation to the service of which provision is made by rules of court.

(7) The preceding provisions of this section shall apply to the service of a document as they apply to the service of a notice.

(8) In this section—

"premises" includes any land, vehicle, vessel or mobile plant;

"serve" shall be construed in accordance with subsection (1) above.[3]

---

*General interpretation.*

**124.** (1) In this Act, except in so far as the context otherwise requires—

"the Agency" means the Environment Agency[4];

"financial year" means a period of twelve months ending with 31st March;

"functions" includes powers and duties;

"modifications" includes additions, alterations and omissions and cognate expressions shall be construed accordingly;

"notice" means notice in writing;

"records", without prejudice to the generality of the expression, includes computer records and any other records kept otherwise than in a document;

"SEPA" means the Scottish Environment Protection Agency[5].

(2) The amendment by this Act of any provision contained in subordinate legislation shall not be taken to have prejudiced any power to make further subordinate legislation amending or revoking that provision.

---

[1] 1978 c.30.
[2] "Premises" defined by subsection (8) below.
[3] This section came into force on 28 July 1995: S.I. 1995/1983.

[4] The Environment Agency is established by s.1 of this Act, p.420 above.
[5] SEPA is established by s.20 of this Act, p.438 above.

(3) In subsection (2) above, "subordinate legislation" has the same meaning as in the Interpretation Act 1978[1].[2]

*Short title, commencement, extent, etc.*

**125.** (1) This Act may be cited as the Environment Act 1995.

(2) Part III of this Act, except for section 78, paragraph 7(2) of Schedule 7 and Schedule 10, shall come into force at the end of the period of two months beginning with the day on which this Act is passed.

(3) Except as provided in subsection (2) above and except for this section, section 74 above and paragraphs 76(8)(*a*) and 135 of Schedule 22 to this Act (which come into force on the passing of this Act) and the repeal of sub-paragraph (1) of paragraph 22 of Schedule 10 to this Act (which comes into force in accordance with sub-paragraph (7) of that paragraph) this Act shall come into force on such day as the Secretary of State may specify by order made by statutory instrument; and different days may be so specified for different provisions or for different purposes of the same provision.

(4) Without prejudice to the provisions of Schedule 23 to this Act, an order under subsection (3) above may make such transitional provisions and savings as appear to the Secretary of State necessary or expedient in connection with any provision brought into force by the order.

(5) The power conferred by subsection (4) above includes power to modify any enactment contained in this or any other Act.

(6) An Order in Council under paragraph 1(1)(*b*) of Schedule 1 to the Northern Ireland Act 1974[3] (legislation for Northern Ireland in the interim period) which states that it is made only for purposes corresponding to those of section 98 of this Act—

(*a*) shall not be subject to paragraph 1(4) and (5) of that Schedule (affirmative resolution of both Houses of Parliament); but

(*b*) shall be subject to annulment in pursuance of a resolution of either House of Parliament.

(7) Except for this section and any amendment or repeal by this Act of any provision contained in—

(*a*) the Parliamentary Commissioner Act 1967[4],

(*b*) the Sea Fish (Conservation) Act 1967[5],

(*c*) the House of Commons Disqualification Act 1975[6], or

(*d*) the Northern Ireland Assembly Disqualification Act 1975[7],

this Act shall not extend to Northern Ireland.

(8) Part III of this Act, and Schedule 24 to this Act so far as relating to that Part, extends to England and Wales only.

(9) Section 106[8] of, and Schedule 16 to, this Act extend to Scotland only.

(10) Subject to the foregoing provisions of this section and to any express provision made by this Act to the contrary, any amendment, repeal or revocation made by this Act shall have the same extent as the enactment or instrument to which it relates.[9]

---

[1] 1978 c.30.
[2] This section came into force on 28 July 1995: S.I. 1995/1983.
[3] 1974 c.28.
[4] 1967 c.13.
[5] 1967 c.84.
[6] 1975 c.24.
[7] 1975 c.35.
[8] P.481 above.
[9] This section came into force on 19 July 1995, the date of the Royal Assent: subsection (3) above.

# SCHEDULES

(Section 1[1].)

## SCHEDULE 1: The Environment Agency

### Membership

1. (1) Subject to the following provisions of this paragraph, a member[2] shall hold and vacate office in accordance with the terms of his appointment and shall, on ceasing to be a member, be eligible for re-appointment.

(2) A member may at any time resign his office by giving notice[3] to the appropriate Minister[4].

(3) The appropriate Minister may remove a member from that office if he is satisfied—

(a) that the member has been absent from meetings of the Agency for a period of more than three months without the permission of the Agency;

(b) that the member has been adjudged bankrupt, that his estate has been sequestrated or that he has made a composition or arrangement with, or granted a trust deed for, his creditors; or

(c) that the member is unable or unfit to carry out the functions of a member.

### Chairman and deputy chairman

2. The chairman or deputy chairman of the Agency shall hold office as such unless and until—

(a) he resigns that office by giving notice to the Secretary of State, or

(b) he ceases to be a member,

and shall, on ceasing to be the chairman or deputy chairman, be eligible for further designation as such in accordance with section 1(3) of this Act[5] at any time when he is a member.

### Remuneration, pensions, etc.

3. (1) The Agency shall pay to its members such remuneration, and such travelling and other allowances, as may be determined by the appropriate Minister.

(2) The Agency shall, if so required by the appropriate Minister,—

(a) pay such pension, allowances or gratuities as may be determined by that Minister to or in respect of a person who is or has been a member;

(b) make such payments as may be determined by that Minister towards provision for the payment of a pension, allowances or gratuities to or in respect of a person who is or has been a member; or

(c) provide and maintain such schemes (whether contributory or not) as may be determined by that Minister for the payment of pensions, allowances or gratuities to or in respect of persons who are or have been members.

(3) If, when any member ceases to hold office, the appropriate Minister determines that there are special circumstances which make it right that that member should receive compensation, the Agency shall pay to him a sum by way of compensation of such amount as may be so determined.

### Staff

4. (1) The Agency may appoint such officers and employees as it may determine.

(2) No member or other person shall be appointed by the Agency to act as chief executive of the Agency unless the Secretary of State has consented to the appointment of that person.

(3) The Agency may—

---

[1] P.420 above. S.1 came into force on 28 July 1995: S.I. 1995/1983.
[2] "Member" defined by para.12 below.
[3] "Notice" defined by s.124(1), p.495 above.
[4] "The appropriate Minister" defined by para.12 below.
[5] P.420 above.

(a) pay such pensions, allowances or gratuities to or in respect of any persons who are or have been its officers or employees as it may, with the approval of the Secretary of State, determine;

(b) make such payments as it may so determine towards provision for the payment of pensions, allowances or gratuities to or in respect of any such persons;

(c) provide and maintain such schemes as it may so determine (whether contributory or not) for the payment of pensions, allowances or gratuities to or in respect of any such persons.

(4) Any reference in sub-paragraph (3) above to pensions, allowances or gratuities to or in respect of any such persons as are mentioned in that sub-paragraph includes a reference to pensions, allowances or gratuities by way of compensation to or in respect of any of the Agency's officers or employees who suffer loss of office or employment or loss or diminution of emoluments.

## Proceedings of the Agency

**5.** Subject to the following provisions of this Schedule and to section 106 of the 1991 Act[1] (obligation to carry out flood defence functions through committees) the Agency may regulate its own procedure (including quorum).

## Delegation of powers

**6.** Subject to section 106 of the 1991 Act, anything authorised or required by or under any enactment to be done by the Agency may be done—

(a) by any member, officer or employee of the Agency who has been authorised for the purpose, whether generally or specially, by the Agency; or

(b) by any committee or sub-committee of the Agency which has been so authorised.

## Members' interests

**7.** (1) A member who is in any way directly or indirectly interested in any matter that is brought up for consideration at a meeting of the Agency shall disclose the nature of his interest to the meeting; and, where such a disclosure is made—

(a) the disclosure shall be recorded in the minutes of the meeting; and

(b) the member shall not take any part in any deliberation or decision of the Agency, or of any of its committees or sub-committees, with respect to that matter.

(2) For the purposes of sub-paragraph (1) above, a general notification given at a meeting of the Agency by a member to the effect that he—

(a) is a member of a specified company or firm, and

(b) is to be regarded as interested in any matter involving that company or firm,

shall be regarded as a sufficient disclosure of his interest in relation to any such matter.

(3) A member need not attend in person at a meeting of the Agency in order to make a disclosure which he is required to make under this paragraph if he takes reasonable steps to secure that the disclosure is made by a notice which is read and considered at the meeting.

(4) The Secretary of State may, subject to such conditions as he considers appropriate, remove any disability imposed by virtue of this paragraph in any case where the number of members of the Agency disabled by virtue of this paragraph at any one time would be so great a proportion of the whole as to impede the transaction of business.

(5) The power of the Secretary of State under sub-paragraph (4) above includes power to remove, either indefinitely or for any period, a disability which would otherwise attach to any member, or members of any description, by reason of such interests, and in respect of such matters, as may be specified or described by the Secretary of State.

(6) Nothing in this paragraph precludes any member from taking part in the consideration or discussion of, or voting on, any question whether an application should be made to the Secretary of State for the exercise of the power conferred by sub-paragraph (4) above.

---

[1] "The 1991 Act" means the Water Resources Act 1991: s.56(1) above.

(7) Any reference in this paragraph to a meeting of the Agency includes a reference to a meeting of any committee or sub-committee of the Agency.

## Vacancies and defective appointments

8. The validity of any proceedings of the Agency shall not be affected by a vacancy amongst the members or by a defect in the appointment of a member.

## Minutes

9. (1) Minutes shall be kept of proceedings of the Agency, of its committees and of its sub-committees.

(2) Minutes of any such proceedings shall be evidence of those proceedings if they are signed by a person purporting to have acted as chairman of the proceedings to which the minutes relate or of any subsequent proceedings in the course of which the minutes were approved as a correct record.

(3) Where minutes of any such proceedings have been signed as mentioned in sub-paragraph (2) above, those proceedings shall, unless the contrary is shown, be deemed to have been validly convened and constituted.

## Application of seal and proof of instruments

10. (1) The application of the seal of the Agency shall be authenticated by the signature of any member, officer or employee of the Agency who has been authorised for the purpose, whether generally or specially, by the Agency.

(2) In this paragraph the reference to the signature of a person includes a reference to a facsimile of a signature by whatever process reproduced; and, in paragraph 11 below, the word "signed" shall be construed accordingly.

## Documents served etc. by or on the Agency

11. (1) Any document which the Agency is authorised or required by or under any enactment to serve, make or issue may be signed on behalf of the Agency by any member, officer or employee of the Agency who has been authorised for the purpose, whether generally or specially, by the Agency.

(2) Every document purporting to be an instrument made or issued by or on behalf of the Agency and to be duly executed under the seal of the Agency, or to be signed or executed by a person authorised by the Agency for the purpose, shall be received in evidence and be treated, without further proof, as being so made or issued unless the contrary is shown.

(3) Any notice which is required or authorised, by or under any provision of any other Act, to be given, served or issued by, to or on the Agency shall be in writing.

## Interpretation

12. In this Schedule—

"the appropriate Minister", in relation to any person who is or has been a member, means the Minister[1] or the Secretary of State, according to whether that person was appointed as a member by the Minister or by the Secretary of State; and

"member", except where the context otherwise requires, means any member of the Agency (including the chairman and deputy chairman).

---

[1] "The Minister" means the Minister of Agriculture, Fisheries and Food: s.56(1) above.

# SCHEDULE 2

(Sections 3[1] and 22[2].)

TRANSFERS OF PROPERTY ETC: SUPPLEMENTAL PROVISIONS

## PART I: INTRODUCTORY

### *Interpretation*

1. In this Schedule—

"the chief inspector"—

(a) in the application of this Schedule in relation to transfers by or under section 3 of this Act[3], means any of the inspectors or chief inspectors mentioned in section 2(1) of this Act[4];

(b) in the application of this Schedule in relation to transfers by or under section 22 of this Act[5], means any of the inspectors or chief inspectors mentioned in section 21(1) of this Act[6];

and any reference to the chief inspector for England and Wales or the chief inspector for Scotland shall be construed accordingly;

"the relevant new Agency" means—

(a) in the application of this Schedule in relation to transfers by or under section 3 of this Act, the Agency[7]; and

(b) in the application of this Schedule in relation to transfers by or under section 22 of this Act, SEPA[8];

"transfer scheme" means a scheme under section 3 or 22 of this Act;

"the transferor", in relation to transfers by or under section 3 of this Act, means—

(a) in the case of any transfer by section 3(1)(a) of this Act, the National Rivers Authority or the London Waste Regulation Authority, as the case may be; or

(b) in the case of any transfer scheme, or any transfer by transfer scheme—

    (i) the Secretary of State,

    (ii) the chief inspector, or

    (iii) any waste regulation authority[9],

(as the case may be) from whom any property, rights or liabilities are, or are to be, transferred by that scheme;

"the transferor", in relation to transfers by or under section 22 of this Act, means—

(a) in the case of any transfer by section 22(1)(a) of this Act, the river purification board[10] in question; or

(b) in the case of any transfer scheme, or any transfer by transfer scheme—

    (i) the Secretary of State;

    (ii) the chief inspector; or

    (iii) any local authority[11],

(as the case may be) from whom any property, rights or liabilities are, or are to be, transferred by that scheme; and, as respects any such local authority which is a district or islands council, includes, in relation to any time on or after 1st April 1996, the council for any local government area named in column 1 of Schedule 1 to the Local Government etc. (Scotland) Act 1994[12] which is wholly or partly conterminous with the area of that council.

...................................................................................................................................................................

[1] P.422 above. S.3(8), which gives effect to this schedule in respect of the Environment Agency, came into force on 28 July 1995: S.I. 1995/1983.

[2] P.440 above. S.22, which gives effect to this schedule in respect of SEPA, came into force on 12 October 1995: S.I. 1995/2649.

[3] P.422 above.

[4] P.421 above.

[5] P.440 above.

[6] P.438 above.

[7] "The Agency" means the Environment Agency: s.124(1) above.

[8] "SEPA" means the Scottish Environment Protection Agency: s.124(1) above.

[9] "Waste regulation authority" defined by s.56(1), p.464 above.

[10] "River purification board" defined by s.56(1), p.464 above.

[11] "Local authority" defined by s.S6(1),(2), p.464 above.

[12] 1994 c.39.

## *The property etc. which may be transferred*

2. (1) The property, rights and liabilities which are transferred by, or may be transferred by transfer scheme under, section 3[1] or 22[2] of this Act include—

   (*a*) property, rights and liabilities that would not otherwise be capable of being transferred or assigned by the transferor;

   (*b*) in the case of a transfer scheme, such property, rights and liabilities to which the transferor may become entitled or subject after the making of the scheme and before the transfer date as may be specified in the scheme;

   (*c*) property situated anywhere in the United Kingdom or elsewhere;

   (*d*) rights and liabilities under enactments;

   (*e*) rights and liabilities under the law of any part of the United Kingdom or of any country or territory outside the United Kingdom.

   (2) The transfers authorised by paragraph (*a*) of sub-paragraph (1) above include transfers which, by virtue of that paragraph, are to take effect as if there were no such contravention, liability or interference with any interest or right as there would be, in the case of a transfer or assignment otherwise than by or under section 3 or 22 of this Act, by reason of any provision having effect (whether under any enactment or agreement or otherwise) in relation to the terms on which the transferor is entitled or subject to the property, right or liability in question.

   (3) This paragraph is subject to paragraph 3 below.

......................................................................................................................................................

## *Contracts of employment*

3. (1) The rights and liabilities that may be transferred by and in accordance with a transfer scheme include (subject to the following provisions of this paragraph) any rights or liabilities of the employer under the contract of employment of any person—

   (*a*) who is employed—

      (i)   in the civil service of the State;

      (ii)  by a body which is a waste regulation authority[3] in England or Wales; or

      (iii) by a local authority[4] in Scotland;

   (*b*) who appears to the appropriate authority[5] to be employed for the purposes of, or otherwise in connection with, functions[6] which are by virtue of this Act to become functions of a new Agency[7], and

   (*c*) whom the appropriate authority considers it necessary or expedient to transfer into the employment of that new Agency;

   and in the following provisions of this paragraph any reference to a "qualifying employee" is a reference to such a person.

   (2) A transfer scheme which provides for the transfer of rights or liabilities under the contracts of employment of qualifying employees must identify those employees—

   (*a*) by specifying them;

   (*b*) by referring to persons of a description specified in the scheme (with or without exceptions); or

   (*c*) partly in the one way and partly in the other.

   (3) A transfer scheme shall not operate to transfer rights or liabilities under so much of a contract of employment as relates to an occupational pension scheme[8], other than any provisions of such a pension scheme which do not relate to benefits for old age, invalidity or survivors.

   (4) Where a transfer scheme provides for the transfer of rights or liabilities under the contract of employment of a qualifying employee—

---

[1] P.422 above.
[2] P.440 above.
[3] "Waste regulation authority" defined by s.56(1), p.464 above.
[4] "Local authority" defined by s.56(1), (2), p.464 above.
[5] "The appropriate authority" defined by sub-paragraph (10) below.

[6] "Functions" includes powers and duties: s.124(1) above.
[7] "New Agency" means the Environment Agency or the Scottish Environment Protection Agency, SEPA: ss.56(1), 124(1) above.
[8] "Occupational pension scheme" defined by sub-paragraph (10) below.

(a) all the employer's rights, powers, duties and liabilities under or in connection with the contract of employment shall be transferred to the relevant new Agency on the transfer date[1] by and in accordance with the scheme, and

(b) anything done by or in relation to the employer in respect of the qualifying employee before the transfer date shall be treated on and after that date as done by or in relation to the relevant new Agency,

except in a case where objection is made by the qualifying employee as mentioned in sub-paragraph (8)(b) below.

(5) Sub-paragraphs (6) and (7) below shall have effect in any case where rights or liabilities under the contract of employment of a qualifying employee are transferred by and in accordance with a transfer scheme.

(6) In a case falling within sub-paragraph (5) above—

(a) the transfer shall be regarded for the purposes of section 138 of the Employment Rights Act 1996[2] (renewal of contract or re-engagement) as a renewal of the qualifying employee's contract of employment, or a re-engagement of the qualifying employee, falling within subsection (1) of that section; and

(b) the qualifying employee shall accordingly not be regarded as having been dismissed by virtue of the transfer.

(7) In a case falling within sub-paragraph (5) above, for the purposes of Chapter I of Part XIV of the Employment Rights Act 1996[2A] (ascertainment of the length of an employee's period of employment and whether that employment is continuous)—

(a) so much of the qualifying employee's period of continuous employment as ends with the day preceding the transfer date shall be treated on and after that date as a period of employment with the relevant new Agency; and

(b) the continuity of the period of employment of the qualifying employee shall be treated as not having been broken by the transfer.

(8) Sub-paragraph (9) below shall have effect in any case where—

(a) a transfer scheme contains provision for the transfer of rights or liabilities under the contract of employment of a qualifying employee, but

(b) the qualifying employee informs the appropriate authority or the relevant new Agency that he objects to becoming employed by that new Agency.

(9) In a case falling within sub-paragraph (8) above—

(a) the transfer scheme—

(i) shall not operate to transfer any rights, powers, duties or liabilities under or in connection with the contract of employment; but

(ii) shall operate so as to terminate that contract on the day preceding the transfer date; and

(b) the qualifying employee shall not, by virtue of that termination, be treated for any purpose as having been dismissed.

(10) In this paragraph—

"the appropriate authority" means—

(a) in the case of a person employed in the civil service of the State, the Secretary of State;

(b) in the case of a transfer scheme under section 3 of this Act[3] and a person employed by a body which is a waste regulation authority, that body;

(c) in the case of a transfer scheme under section 22 of this Act[4] and a person employed by a local authority, that authority;

"occupational pension scheme" has the meaning given by section 1 of the Pension Schemes Act 1993[5].

(11) This paragraph shall apply in relation to any qualifying employee as if, as respects any time before the transfer date,—

(a) any reference to a person's contract of employment included a reference to his employment in the civil service of the State or to the terms of that employment, as the case may require; and

[1] "The transfer date" defined by s.56(1), p.464 above. The transfer date was 1 April 1996: S.I. 1996/139 (in respect of Chapter II); S.I. 1996/234 (in respect of Chapter I).
[2] Words "s. 138 of the Employment Rights Act 1996" substituted by the Employment Rights Act 1996 (c. 18), s. 240, sch. 1. This amendment came into force on 22 August 1996: s. 243.

[2A] Words "Chapter I of Part XIV of the Employment Rights Act 1996" substituted by the Employment Rights Act 1996 (c. 18), s. 240, sch. 1.
[3] P.422 above.
[4] P.440 above.
[5] 1993 c.48.

(b)  any reference to the dismissal of a person included a reference to the termination of his employment in that service.

## Part II: Transfer schemes

### *Description of the property etc. to be transferred by scheme*

**4.** A transfer scheme may define the property, rights and liabilities to be transferred by the scheme—

(a)  by specifying or describing the property, rights and liabilities in question;

(b)  by referring to all (or all but so much as may be excepted) of the property, rights and liabilities comprised in a specified part of the undertaking of the transferor; or

(c)  partly in the one way and partly in the other.

### *Division of property etc. to be transferred by scheme: creation of new rights and interests*

**5.** (1)  For the purpose of making any division of property, rights or liabilities which it is considered appropriate to make in connection with the transfer of property, rights and liabilities by and in accordance with a transfer scheme, any such scheme may—

(a)  create in favour of the transferor an interest in, or right over, any property transferred by the scheme;

(b)  create in favour of the relevant new Agency[1] an interest in, or right over, any property retained by the transferor;

(c)  create new rights and liabilities as between the relevant new Agency and the transferor; or

(d)  in connection with any provision made by virtue of paragraph (a), (b) or (c) above, make incidental provision as to the interests, rights and liabilities of persons other than the transferor and the relevant new Agency with respect to the subject-matter of the transfer scheme;

and references in the other provisions of Part I of this Act[2] to the transfer of property, rights or liabilities (so far as relating to transfers by and in accordance with transfer schemes) shall accordingly be construed as including references to the creation of any interest, right or liability by virtue of paragraph (a), (b) or (c) above or the making of provision by virtue of paragraph (d) above.

(2)  The provision that may be made by virtue of paragraph (c) of sub-paragraph (1) above includes—

(a)  provision for treating any person who is entitled by virtue of a transfer scheme to possession of a document as having given another person an acknowledgement in writing of the right of that other person to the production of the document and to delivery of copies of it; and

(b)  in the case of a transfer scheme under section 3 of this Act[3], provision applying section 64 of the Law of Property Act 1925[4] (production and safe custody of documents) in relation to any case in relation to which provision falling within paragraph (a) above has effect.

### *Transfer schemes: incidental, supplemental and consequential provision*

**6.** (1)  A transfer scheme may make such incidental, supplemental and consequential provision—

(a)  as the Secretary of State considers appropriate, in the case of a scheme made by him,

(b)  as a body which is a waste regulation authority[5] considers appropriate in the case of a scheme made by that body under section 3 of this Act[6], or

(c)  as a local authority[7] considers appropriate, in the case of a scheme made by that authority under section 22 of this Act[8].

(2)  Without prejudice to the generality of sub-paragraph (1) above, a transfer scheme may provide—

---

[1]  "New Agency" means the Environment Agency or the Scottish Environment Protection Agency, SEPA: ss.56(1), 124(1) above.

[2]  P.420 above.

[3]  P.422 above.

[4]  1925 c.20.

[5]  "Waste regulation authority" defined by s.56(1), p.464 above.

[6]  P.422 above.

[7]  "Local authority" defined by s.56(1),(2), p.464 above.

[8]  P.440 above.

(a) that disputes as to the effect of the scheme between the transferor and the relevant new Agency are to be referred to such arbitration as may be specified in or determined under the transfer scheme;

(b) that determinations on such arbitrations and certificates given jointly by the transferor and the relevant new Agency as to the effect of the scheme as between them are to be conclusive for all purposes.

## Modification of transfer schemes

7. (1) If at any time after a transfer scheme has come into force the Secretary of State considers it appropriate to do so, he may by order provide that the scheme shall for all purposes be deemed to have come into force with such modifications[1] may be specified in the order.

(2) An order under sub-paragraph (1) above—

(a) may make, with effect from the coming into force of the transfer scheme in question, such provision as could have been made by the scheme; and

(b) in connection with giving effect to that provision from that time, may contain such supplemental, consequential or transitional provision as the Secretary of State considers appropriate.

(3) The Secretary of State shall not make an order under sub-paragraph (1) above except after consultation with—

(a) the relevant new Agency; and

(b) if the transfer scheme in question is—

(i) a scheme under section 3 of this Act[2] which transferred property, rights or liabilities of a waste regulation authority, or

(ii) a scheme under section 22 of this Act[3] which transferred property, rights or liabilities of a local authority,

the body which was the transferor in the case of that scheme.

(4) The power to make an order under sub-paragraph (1) above shall be exercisable by statutory instrument; and a statutory instrument containing any such order shall be subject to annulment in pursuance of a resolution of either House of Parliament.

## Provision of information and assistance to the Secretary of State and the new Agencies in connection with transfer schemes

8. (1) It shall be the duty of each of the following, that is to say—

(a) the chief inspector for England and Wales,

(b) any body which is a waste regulation authority[4] in England or Wales, and

(c) any officer of such a body,

to provide the Secretary of State or the Agency[5] with such information or assistance as the Secretary of State or, as the case may be, the Agency may reasonably require for the purposes of, or in connection with, the exercise of any powers of the Secretary of State or the Agency in relation to transfer schemes.

(2) It shall be the duty of each of the following, that is to say—

(a) the chief inspector for Scotland,

(b) any local authority[6], and

(c) any officer of a local authority,

to provide the Secretary of State or SEPA[7] with such information or assistance as the Secretary of State or, as the case may be, SEPA may reasonably require for the purposes of, or in connection with, the exercise of any powers of the Secretary of State or SEPA in relation to transfer schemes.

---

[1] "Modifications" defined by s.124(1), p.495 above.
[2] P.422 above.
[3] P.440 above.
[4] "Waste regulation authority" defined by s.56(1), p.464 above.

[5] "The Agency" means the Environment Agency: s.124(1) above.
[6] "Local authority" defined by s.56(1),(2), p.464 above.
[7] "SEPA" means the Scottish Environment Protection Agency: s.124(l) above.

PART III: GENERAL PROVISIONS WITH RESPECT TO TRANSFERS BY OR UNDER SECTION 3 OR 22

## Consideration

9. No consideration shall be provided in respect of the transfer of any property, rights or liabilities by or under section 3[1] or 22[2] of this Act; but—

    (a) a transfer scheme may contain provision for consideration to be provided by the relevant new Agency[3] in respect of the creation of interests, rights or liabilities by means of the transfer scheme; and

    (b) any such provision shall be enforceable in the same way as if the interests, rights or liabilities had been created, and (if the case so requires) had been capable of being created, by agreement between the parties.

## Continuity

10. (1) This paragraph applies in relation to—

    (a) any transfer of property, rights or liabilities by section 3[4] or 22[5] of his Act; or

    (b) subject to any provision to the contrary in the transfer scheme in question, any transfer of property, rights or liabilities by a transfer scheme.

(2) Where this paragraph applies in relation to a transfer, then, so far as may be necessary for the purposes of, or in connection with, the transfer—

    (a) any agreements made, transactions effected or other things done by or in relation to the transferor shall be treated as made, effected or done by or in relation to the relevant new Agency[6];

    (b) references (whether express or implied and, if express, however worded) to the transferor in any agreement (whether in writing or not) or in any deed, bond, instrument or other document relating to the property, rights or liabilities transferred shall, as respects anything falling to be done on or after the transfer date[7], have effect as references to the relevant new Agency.

## Remedies

11. (1) Without prejudice to the generality of paragraph 10 above, a new Agency[8] and any other person shall, as from the transfer date, have the same rights, powers and remedies (and, in particular, the same rights and powers as to the taking or resisting of legal proceedings or the making or resisting of applications to any authority) for ascertaining, perfecting or enforcing any right or liability transferred to that new Agency by or under this Act as that new Agency or that person would have had if that right or liability had at all times been a right or liability of that new Agency.

(2) Without prejudice to the generality of paragraph 10 above, any legal proceedings or applications to any authority pending immediately before the transfer date by or against a transferor, in so far as they relate to any property, right or liability transferred to the relevant new Agency by or under this Act or to any agreement relating to any such property, right or liability, shall be continued by or against the relevant new Agency to the exclusion of the transferor.

## Perfection of vesting of foreign property, rights and liabilities

12. (1) This paragraph applies in the case of any transfer by or under section 3[9] or 22[10] of this Act of any foreign property, rights or liabilities.

---

[1] P.422 above.
[2] P.440 above.
[3] "New Agency" means the Environment Agency or the Scottish Environment Protection Agency, SEPA: ss.56(1), 124(1) above.
[4] P.422 above.
[5] P.440 above.
[6] "New Agency" means the Environment Agency or the Scottish Environment Protection Agency, SEPA: ss.56(1),

124(1) above.
[7] "The transfer date" defined by s.56(1), p.464 above. The transfer date was 1 April 1996: S.I. 1996/139 (in respect of Chapter II); S.I. 1996/234 (in respect of Chapter I).
[8] "New Agency" means the Environment Agency or the Scottish Environment Protection Agency, SEPA: ss.56(1), 124(1) above.
[9] P.422 above.
[10] P.440 above.

(2)  It shall be the duty of the transferor and the relevant new Agency[1] to take, as and when that new Agency considers it appropriate, all such steps as may be requisite to secure that the vesting in that new Agency by, or by transfer scheme under, section 3 or 22 of this Act of any foreign property, right or liability is effective under the relevant foreign law.

(3)  Until the vesting in the relevant new Agency by, or by transfer scheme under, section 3 or 22 of this Act of any foreign property, right or liability is effective under the relevant foreign law, it shall be the duty of the transferor to hold that property or right for the benefit of, or to discharge that liability on behalf of, the relevant new Agency.

(4)  Nothing in sub-paragraphs (2) and (3) above shall be taken as prejudicing the effect under the law of any part of the United Kingdom of the vesting in the relevant new Agency by, or by transfer scheme under, section 3 or 22 of this Act of any foreign property, right or liability.

(5)  The transferor shall have all such powers as may be requisite for the performance of his duty under this paragraph, but it shall be the duty of the relevant new Agency to act on behalf of the transferor (so far as possible) in performing the duty imposed on the transferor by this paragraph.

(6)  References in this paragraph to any foreign property, right or liability are references to any property, right or liability as respects which any issue arising in any proceedings would have been determined (in accordance with the rules of private international law) by reference to the law of a country or territory outside the United Kingdom.

(7)  Duties imposed on the transferor or the relevant new Agency by this paragraph shall be enforceable in the same way as if the duties were imposed by a contract between the transferor and that new Agency.

(8)  Any expenses reasonably incurred by the transferor under this paragraph shall be met by the relevant new Agency.

# SCHEDULE 3

(Section 12[2].)

## ENVIRONMENT PROTECTION ADVISORY COMMITTEES

### Introductory

1.  (1)  In this Schedule, "scheme" means a scheme prepared under this Schedule.

(2)  Subject to sub-paragraph (1) above, expressions used in this Schedule and in section 12 of this Act have the same meaning in this Schedule as they have in that section.

### Duty of Agency to prepare and submit schemes for each region

2.  (1)  It shall be the duty of the Agency[3], in accordance with such guidance as may be given for the purpose by the Secretary of State,—

(a)  to prepare, in respect of each region, a scheme with respect to the appointment of persons as members of the advisory committee[4] for that region; and

(b)  to submit that scheme to the Secretary of State for his approval before such date as may be specified in the guidance.

(2)  Every scheme shall—

(a)  specify descriptions of bodies which, or persons who, appear to the Agency likely to have a significant interest in matters likely to be affected by the manner in which it carries out its functions[5] in the region to which the scheme relates;

---

[1]  "New Agency" means the Environment Agency or the Scottish Environment Protection Agency, SEPA: ss.56(1), 124(1) above.
[2]  P.431 above. S.12 came into force on 28 July 1995: S.I. 1995/1983.
[3]  "The Agency" means the Environment Agency: s.124(1) above.
[4]  "Advisory committee" means an advisory committee under s.12, p.431 above: s.12(9).
[5]  "Functions" includes powers and duties: s.124(1) above.

(b) indicate how the membership of the advisory committee is to reflect the different descriptions of bodies or persons so specified;

(c) specify or describe bodies which, and persons whom, the Agency proposes to consult in connection with appointments of persons as members of the advisory committee; and

(d) make provision with respect to such other matters as the Agency considers relevant to the membership of the advisory committee.

## Approval of schemes

3. (1) A scheme shall not come into force unless it has been approved by the Secretary of State or until such date as he may specify for the purpose in giving his approval.

(2) Where the Agency submits a scheme to the Secretary of State for his approval, it shall also submit to him—

(a) a statement of the Agency's reasons for considering that the scheme is one which it is appropriate for him to approve; and

(b) such information in support of those reasons as it considers necessary.

(3) On submitting a scheme to the Secretary of State for his approval, the Agency shall publish the scheme, in such manner as it considers appropriate for bringing it to the attention of persons likely to be interested in it, together with a notice specifying the period within which representations or objections with respect to the scheme may be made to the Secretary of State.

(4) Where a scheme has been submitted to the Secretary of State for his approval, it shall be the duty of the Secretary of State, in determining whether to—

(a) approve the scheme,

(b) reject the scheme, or

(c) approve the scheme subject to modifications[1],

to consider any representations or objections made to him within the period specified pursuant to sub-paragraph (3) above and not withdrawn.

(5) Where the Secretary of State approves a scheme, with or without modifications, it shall be the duty of the Agency to take such steps as it considers appropriate for bringing the scheme as so approved to the attention of persons whom it considers likely to be interested in it.

## Replacement and variation of approved membership schemes

4. (1) The Agency may from time to time, and if required to do so by the Secretary of State shall,—

(a) prepare in accordance with paragraph 2 above a fresh scheme with respect to the appointment of persons as members of the advisory committee for any particular region; and

(b) submit that scheme to the Secretary of State for his approval;

and paragraph 3 above shall have effect accordingly in relation to any such scheme.

(2) An approved membership scheme may from time to time be varied by the Agency with the approval of the Secretary of State.

(3) The provisions of paragraph 3 above shall have effect in relation to any variation of an approved membership scheme as they have effect in relation to a scheme.

## Appointment of members

5. (1) Before appointing a person to be a member of an advisory committee, the Agency—

(a) shall consult such of the associates for that advisory committee as it considers appropriate in the particular case; and

(b) may, if it considers it appropriate to do so, also consult bodies or persons who are not associates for that advisory committee.

---

[1] "Modifications" defined by s.124(1), p.495 above.

(2)  In this paragraph, "associates", in the case of any advisory committee, means those bodies and persons specified or described in the approved membership scheme for that advisory committee pursuant to paragraph 2(2)(c) above.

### *Vacancies, defective appointments etc.*

**6.**  The validity of any proceedings of an advisory committee shall not be affected by—

(*a*)  any vacancy amongst the members;

(*b*)  any defect in the appointment of a member; or

(*c*)  any temporary breach of the terms of the approved membership scheme for the advisory committee.

### *Remuneration and allowances*

**7.** (1)  The Agency shall pay to the chairman of an advisory committee such remuneration, and such travelling and other allowances, as the Secretary of State may determine.

(2)  The Agency shall pay to the members of an advisory committee other than the chairman such sums by way of reimbursement (whether in whole or in part) for loss of remuneration, for travelling expenses and for other out-of-pocket expenses as the Secretary of State may determine.

# SCHEDULE 4

(Section 14[1].)

## BOUNDARIES OF REGIONAL FLOOD DEFENCE AREAS

### *Power to make order*

**1.** (1)  The relevant Minister[2] may by order made by statutory instrument—

(*a*)  alter the boundaries of the area of any regional flood defence committee; or

(*b*)  provide for the amalgamation of any two or more such areas.

(2)  Where an order under this Schedule makes provision by reference to anything shown on a main river map[3], that map shall be conclusive evidence for the purposes of the order of what is shown on the map.

(3)  The power to make an order under this Schedule shall include power to make such supplemental, consequential and transitional provision as the relevant Minister considers appropriate.

(4)  In the case of an order under this Schedule amalgamating the areas of any two or more regional flood defence committees, the provision made by virtue of sub-paragraph (3) above may include provision determining—

(*a*)  the total number of members of the amalgamated committee; and

(*b*)  the total number of such members to be appointed by the constituent councils of that committee;

and subsections (7) and (8) of section 16 of this Act[4] shall apply in relation to so much of an order under this Schedule as is made by virtue of this sub-paragraph as they apply in relation to an order under subsection (5) of that section.

(5)  In this paragraph and the following paragraphs of this Schedule "the relevant Minister"—

(*a*)  in relation to any alteration of the boundaries of an area where the whole or any part of that area is in Wales, means the Ministers[5];

(*b*)  in relation to the amalgamation of any two or more areas where the whole or any part of any one of those areas is in Wales, means the Ministers; and

---

[1] P.433 above. S.14 came into force on 1 April 1996: S.I. 1996/186.

[2] "The relevant Minister" defined by sub-paragraph (5) below.

[3] "Main river map" defined by sub-paragraph (6) below.

[4] P.436 above.

[5] "The Ministers" means the Secretary of State and the Minister of Agriculture, Fisheries and Food: s.56(1) above.

(c) in any other case, means the Minister[1].

(6) In this paragraph—

"main river" means a main river within the meaning of Part IV of the 1991 Act[2]; and

"main river map" has, subject to section 194 of the 1991 Act, the meaning given by section 193(2) of that Act.

## Consultation and notice of intention to make order

2. (1) Before making an order under this Schedule, the relevant Minister shall—

(a) consult such persons or representative bodies as he considers it appropriate to consult at that stage;

(b) prepare a draft order;

(c) publish a notice complying with sub-paragraph (2) below in the London Gazette and in such other manner as he considers appropriate for bringing the draft order to the attention of persons likely to be affected by it if it is made.

(2) A notice for the purposes of sub-paragraph (1)(c) above with respect to a draft order shall—

(a) state the relevant Minister's intention to make the order and its general effect;

(b) specify the places where copies of the draft order and of any map to which it refers may be inspected by any person free of charge at all reasonable times during the period of twenty-eight days beginning with the date on which the notice is first published otherwise than in the London Gazette; and

(c) state that any person may within that period by notice in writing to the relevant Minister object to the making of the order.

(3) The relevant Minister shall also cause copies of the notice and of the draft order to be served[3] on every person carrying out functions under any enactment who appears to him to be concerned.

## Objections to draft order and making of order

3. (1) Before making an order under this Schedule, the relevant Minister—

(a) shall consider any representations or objections which are duly made with respect to the draft order and are not withdrawn; and

(b) may, if he thinks fit, cause a local inquiry to be held with respect to any such representations or objections.

(2) Where notice of a draft order has been published and given in accordance with paragraph 2 above and any representations or objections considered under sub-paragraph (1) above, the relevant Minister may make the order either in the terms of the draft or in those terms as modified[4] in such manner as he thinks fit, or may decide not to make the order.

(3) The relevant Minister shall not make a modification of a draft order in so far as the modification is such as to include in the area of any regional flood defence committee any tidal waters which, if the order had been made in the form of the draft, would have been outside the area of every regional flood defence committee.

## Procedure for making of order

4. (1) Where the relevant Minister makes an order under this Schedule, he shall serve[5] notice[6] of the making of the order on every person (if any) who—

(a) is a person on whom notice is required to have been served under paragraph 2(3) above; and

(b) has duly made an objection to the making of the order that has not been withdrawn.

(2) Where a notice is required to be served under sub-paragraph (1) above with respect to any order, the order shall not have effect before the end of a period of twenty-eight days from the date of service of the last notice served under that sub-paragraph.

(3) If before an order takes effect under sub-paragraph (2) above—

---

[1] "The Minister" means the Minister of Agriculture, Fisheries and Food: s.56(1) above.
[2] "The 1991 Act" means the Water Resources Act 1991: s.56(1) above.

[3] For provisions relating to service see s.123, p.494 above.
[4] "Modifications " defined by s.124(1), p.495 above.
[5] For provisions relating to service see s.123, p.494 above.
[6] "Notice" means notice in writing: s.124(1) above.

(a) any person who has been served with a notice under sub-paragraph (1) above with respect to that order serves notice objecting to the order on the Minister (or, in the case of an order made jointly by the Ministers, on either of them), and

(b) the objection is not withdrawn,

the order shall be subject to special parliamentary procedure.

(4) A statutory instrument containing an order under this Schedule which is not subject to special parliamentary procedure under sub-paragraph (3) above shall be subject to annulment in pursuance of a resolution of either House of Parliament.

## Notice after making of order

5. (1) Subject to sub-paragraph (2) below, after making an order under this Schedule, the relevant Minister shall publish in the London Gazette, and in such other manner as he considers appropriate for bringing the order to the attention of persons likely to be affected by it, a notice—

(a) stating that the order has been made; and

(b) naming the places where a copy of the order may be inspected at all reasonable times.

(2) In the case of an order to which sub-paragraph (2) of paragraph 4 above applies, the notice—

(a) shall not be published until the end of the period of twenty-eight days referred to in that sub-paragraph; and

(b) shall state whether or not the order is to be subject to special parliamentary procedure.

## Questioning of order in courts

6. (1) Subject to sub-paragraph (3) below, if any person desires to question the validity of an order under this Schedule on the ground—

(a) that it is not within the powers of this Schedule, or

(b) that any requirement of this Schedule has not been complied with,

he may, within six weeks after the date of the first publication of the notice required by paragraph 5 above, make an application for the purpose to the High Court.

(2) On an application under this paragraph the High Court, if satisfied—

(a) that the order is not within the powers of this Schedule, or

(b) that the interests of the applicant have been substantially prejudiced by a failure to comply with any of the requirements of this Schedule,

may quash the order either generally or in so far as it affects the applicant.

(3) Sub-paragraph (1) above—

(a) shall not apply to any order which is confirmed by Act of Parliament under section 6 of the Statutory Orders (Special Procedure) Act 1945[1]; and

(b) shall have effect in relation to any other order which is subject to special parliamentary procedure by virtue of the provisions of this Schedule as if the reference to the date of the first publication of the notice required by paragraph 5 above were a reference to the date on which the order becomes operative under that Act of 1945.

(4) Except as provided by this paragraph the validity of an order under this Schedule shall not, either before or after the order has been made, be questioned in any legal proceedings whatsoever.

[1] 1945 c.18.

# SCHEDULE 5

(Section 19[1].)

MEMBERSHIP AND PROCEEDINGS OF REGIONAL AND LOCAL FLOOD DEFENCE COMMITTEES

PART I: MEMBERSHIP OF FLOOD DEFENCE COMMITTEES

*Terms of membership*

1. (1) Members of a flood defence committee (that is to say a regional flood defence committee or a local flood defence committee), other than those appointed by or on behalf of one or more constituent councils[2], shall hold and vacate office in accordance with the terms of their appointment

(2) The first members of a local flood defence committee appointed by or on behalf of any one or more constituent councils—

(*a*) shall come into office on the day on which the committee comes into existence or, in the case of a member who is for any reason appointed after that day, on the day on which the appointment is made; and

(*b*) subject to the following provisions of this Schedule, shall hold office until the end of May in such year as may be specified for the purposes of this paragraph in the scheme establishing the committee.

(3) Any members of a flood defence committee appointed by or on behalf of any one or more constituent councils who are not members to whom sub-paragraph (2) above applies—

(*a*) shall come into office at the beginning of the June next following the day on which they are appointed; and

(*b*) subject to the following provisions of this Schedule, shall hold office for a term of four years.

(4) If for any reason any such member as is mentioned in sub-paragraph (3) above is appointed on or after the day on which he ought to have come into office, he shall—

(*a*) come into office on the day on which he is appointed; and

(*b*) subject to the following provisions of this Schedule, hold office for the remainder of the term.

(5) References in this paragraph and the following provisions of this Schedule to a member of a flood defence committee include references to the chairman of such a committee.

*Membership of constituent council as qualification for membership of committee*

2. (1) Members of a flood defence committee appointed by or on behalf of any one or more constituent councils may be members of that council, or one of those councils, or other persons.

(2) Any member of a flood defence committee appointed by or on behalf of a constituent council who at the time of his appointment was a member of that council shall, if he ceases to be a member of that council, also cease to be a member of the committee with whichever is the earlier of the following—

(*a*) the end of the period of three months beginning with the date when he ceases to be a member of the council; and

(*b*) the appointment of another person in his place.

(3) For the purposes of sub-paragraph (2) above a member of a council shall not be deemed to have ceased to be a member of the council by reason of retirement if he has been re-elected a member of the council not later than the date of his retirement.

*Disqualification for membership of committee*

3. (1) Subject to the following provisions of this paragraph, a person shall be disqualified for appointment as a member of a flood defence committee if he—

(*a*) is a paid officer of the Agency[3]; or

---

[1] P.438 above. S.19 came into force on 1 April 1996: S.I. 1996/186.
[2] For "constituent councils" see s.15(6), p.435 above and s.18(8), p.438 above.
[3] "The Agency" means the Environment Agency: s.124(1) above.

(*b*) is a person who has been adjudged bankrupt, or whose estate has been sequestrated or who has made a composition or arrangement with, or granted a trust deed for, his creditors; or

(*c*) within the period of five years before the day of his appointment, has been convicted, in the United Kingdom, the Channel Islands or the Isle of Man, of any offence and has had passed on him a sentence of imprisonment (whether suspended or not) for a period of not less than three months without the option of a fine; or

(*d*) is disqualified for being elected or for being a member of a local authority under Part III of the Local Government Finance Act 1982[1] (accounts and audit) or Part III of the Representation of the People Act 1983[2] (legal proceedings).

(2) Where a person is disqualified under sub-paragraph (1) above by reason of having been adjudged bankrupt, the disqualification shall cease—

(*a*) unless the bankruptcy order made against that person is previously annulled, on his discharge from bankruptcy; and

(*b*) if the bankruptcy order is so annulled, on the date of the annulment.

(3) Where a person is disqualified under sub-paragraph (1) above by reason of having had his estate sequestrated, the disqualification shall cease—

(*a*) unless the sequestration is recalled or reduced, on the person's discharge under section 54 of the Bankruptcy (Scotland) Act 1985[3]; and

(*b*) if the sequestration is recalled or reduced, on the date of the recall or reduction.

(4) Where a person is disqualified under sub-paragraph (1) above by reason of his having made a composition or arrangement with, or having granted a trust deed for, his creditors, the disqualification shall cease—

(*a*) if he pays his debts in full, on the date on which the payment is completed; and

(*b*) in any other case, at the end of five years from the date on which the terms of the deed of composition or arrangement, or of the trust deed, are fulfilled.

(5) For the purposes of sub-paragraph (1)(*c*) above the date of the conviction shall be taken to be—

(*a*) the ordinary date on which the period allowed for making an appeal or application with respect to the conviction expires; or

(*b*) if such an appeal or application is made, the date on which it is finally disposed of or abandoned or fails by reason of non-prosecution.

(6) Section 92 of the Local Government Act 1972[4] (proceedings for disqualification) shall apply in relation to disqualification under this paragraph for appointment as a member of a flood defence committee as it applies in relation to disqualification for acting as a member of a local authority.

*Vacation of office by disqualifying event*

**4.** (1) The office of a member of a flood defence committee shall become vacant upon the fulfilment of any of the following conditions, that is to say—

(*a*) the person holding that office is adjudged bankrupt, is a person whose estate is sequestrated or makes a composition or arrangement with, or grants a trust deed for, his creditors;

(*b*) that person is convicted, in the United Kingdom, the Channel Islands or the Isle of Man, of any offence and has passed on him a sentence of imprisonment (whether suspended or not) for a period of not less than three months without the option of a fine;

(*c*) that person is disqualified for being elected or for being a member of a local authority under Part III of the Local Government Finance Act 1982[5] (accounts and audit) or Part III of the Representation of the People Act 1983[6] (legal proceedings); or

(*d*) that person has, for a period of six consecutive months been absent from meetings of the committee, otherwise than by reason of illness or some other cause approved during the period by the committee.

(2) For the purposes of sub-paragraph (1)(*d*) above, the attendance of a member of a flood defence committee—

(*a*) at a meeting of any sub-committee of the committee of which he is a member, or

[1] 1982 c.32.
[2] 1983 c.2.
[3] 1985 c.66.

[4] 1972 c.70.
[5] 1982 c.32.
[6] 1983 c.2.

(b) at any joint committee to which he has been appointed by that committee,

shall be treated as attendance at a meeting of the committee.

### Resignation of office by members of regional committee

**5.** (1) The chairman of a regional flood defence committee may resign his office at any time by giving notice to the chairman of the Agency[1] and to one of the Ministers[2].

(2) Any other member of such a committee may resign his office at any time by giving notice to the chairman of the committee and also, if he was appointed by one of the Ministers, to that Minister.

### Resignation of office by members of local committee

**6.** (1) The chairman of a local flood defence committee may resign his office at any time by giving notice to the chairman of the regional flood defence committee.

(2) Any other member of a local flood defence committee may resign his office at any time by giving notice to the chairman of that local flood defence committee.

### Appointments to fill casual vacancies

**7.** (1) Where, for any reason whatsoever, the office of a member of a flood defence committee becomes vacant before the end of his term of office, the vacancy—

(a) shall, if the unexpired portion of the term of office of the vacating member is six months or more, be filled by the appointment of a new member; and

(b) may be so filled in any other case.

(2) A person appointed by virtue of sub-paragraph (1) above to fill a casual vacancy shall hold office for so long only as the former member would have held office.

### Eligibility of previous members for re-appointment

**8.** Subject to the provisions of this Schedule, a member of a flood defence committee shall be eligible for reappointment.

### Appointment of deputies

**9.** (1) Subject to the following provisions of this paragraph, a person nominated by one or more constituent councils may act as deputy for a member of a flood defence committee appointed by or on behalf of that council or those councils and may, accordingly, attend and vote at a meeting of the committee, instead of that member.

(2) A person nominated under sub-paragraph (1) above as deputy for a member of a flood defence committee may, by virtue of that nomination, attend and vote at a meeting of a sub-committee of that committee which—

(a) has been appointed by that committee under Part II of this Schedule; and

(b) is a committee to which the member for whom he is a deputy belongs.

(3) A person acting as deputy for a member of a flood defence committee shall be treated for the purposes for which he is nominated as a member of that committee.

(4) A person shall not act as deputy for a member of a flood defence committee unless his nomination has been notified to such officer of the Agency[3] as is appointed to receive such nominations.

(5) A nomination under this paragraph shall be in writing and may apply either to a particular meeting or to all meetings during a stated period or until the nomination is revoked.

---

[1] "The Agency" means the Environment Agency: s.124(1) above.

[2] "The Ministers" means the Secretary of State and the Minister of Agriculture, Fisheries and Food: s.56(1) above.

[3] "The Agency" means the Environment Agency: s.124(1) above.

(6) A person shall not act as deputy for more than one member of a flood defence committee.

(7) Nothing in this paragraph shall entitle a person to attend and vote at a meeting of a local flood defence committee by reason of his nomination as deputy for a member of a regional flood defence committee.

*Payments to past and present chairmen and to members*

**10.** (1) The Agency[1] shall pay to any person who is a chairman of a flood defence committee such remuneration and allowances as may be determined by the relevant Minister[2].

(2) If the relevant Minister so determines in the case of any person who is or has been chairman of a flood defence committee, the Agency shall pay or make arrangements for the payment of a pension[3] in relation to that person in accordance with the determination.

(3) If a person ceases to be chairman of a flood defence committee and it appears to the relevant Minister that there are special circumstances which make it right that that person should receive compensation in respect of his ceasing to be chairman, the relevant Minister may require the Agency to pay to that person a sum of such amount as that Minister may determine.

(4) The Agency may pay to any person who is a member of a flood defence committee such allowances as may be determined by the relevant Minister.

(5) In this paragraph—

"pension", in relation to any person, means a pension (whether contributory or not) of any kind payable to or in respect of him, and includes an allowance, gratuity or lump sum so payable and a return of contributions with or without interest or any other addition; and

"the relevant Minister"—

(a) in relation to the regional flood defence committee for an area the whole or the greater part of which is in Wales and in relation to any local flood defence committee for any district comprised in the area of such a regional flood defence committee, means the Secretary of State; and

(b) in relation to any other flood defence committee, means the Minister[4]

## PART II: PROCEEDINGS OF FLOOD DEFENCE COMMITTEES

*Appointment of sub-committees, joint sub-committees etc.*

**11.** (1) For the purpose of carrying out any functions in pursuance of arrangements under paragraph 12 below—

(a) a flood defence committee may appoint a sub-committee of the committee;

(b) two or more regional or two or more local flood defence committees may appoint a joint sub-committee of those committees;

(c) any sub-committee may appoint one or more committees of that sub-committee ("under sub-committees").

(2) The number of members of any sub-committee and their terms of office shall be fixed by the appointing committee or committees or, in the case of an under sub-committee, by the appointing sub-committee.

(3) A sub-committee appointed under this paragraph may include persons who are not members of the appointing committee or committees or, in the case of an under sub-committee, the committee or committees of whom they are an under sub-committee; but at least two thirds of the members appointed to any such sub-committee shall be members of that committee or those committees, as the case may be.

(4) A person who is disqualified for being a member of a flood defence committee shall be disqualified also for being a member of a sub-committee or under sub-committee appointed under this paragraph.

---

[1] "The Agency" means the Environment Agency: s.124(1) above.
[2] "The relevant Minister" defined by sub-paragraph (5) below.
[3] "Pension" defined by sub-paragraph (5) below.
[4] "The Minister" means the Minister of Agriculture, Fisheries and Food: s.56(1) above.

*Delegation of functions to sub-committees etc.*

**12.** (1) Subject to section 106 of the 1991 Act[1] and to any other express provision contained in any enactment, a flood defence committee may arrange for the carrying out of any of their functions—

(a)  by a sub-committee, or an under sub-committee of the committee or an officer of the Agency[2]; or

(b)  by any other regional or, as the case may be, local flood defence committee;

and two or more regional or two or more local flood defence committees may arrange to carry out any of their functions[3] jointly or may arrange for the carrying out of any of their functions by a joint sub-committee of theirs.

(2)  Where by virtue of this paragraph any functions of a flood defence committee or of two or more such committees may be carried out by a sub-committee, then, unless the committee or committees otherwise direct, the sub-committee may arrange for the carrying out of any of those functions by an under sub-committee or by an officer of the Agency.

(3)  Where by virtue of this paragraph any functions of a flood defence committee or of two or more such committees may be carried out by an under sub-committee, then, unless the committee or committees or the sub-committee otherwise direct, the under sub-committee may arrange for the carrying out of any of those functions by an officer of the Agency.

(4)  Any arrangements made by a flood defence committee under this paragraph for the carrying out of any function shall not prevent the committee from discharging their functions themselves.

(5)  References in the preceding provisions of this paragraph to the carrying out of any functions of a flood defence committee include references to the doing of anything which is calculated to facilitate, or is conducive or incidental to, the carrying out of any of those functions.

(6)  A regional flood defence committee shall not, under this paragraph, make arrangements for the carrying out in a local flood defence district of any functions which fall to be carried out there by the local flood defence committee.

*Rules of procedure*

**13.** (1)  A flood defence committee may, with the approval of the relevant Minister, make rules for regulating the proceedings of the committee.

(2)  Nothing in section 6(4) of this Act[4] or section 105 or 106 of the 1991 Act[5] shall entitle the Agency[6] to make any arrangements or give any directions for regulating the proceedings of any flood defence committee.

(3)  In this paragraph "the relevant Minister" has the same meaning as in paragraph 10 above.

*Declarations of interest etc.*

**14.** (1)  Subject to the following provisions of this paragraph, the provisions of sections 94 to 98 of the Local Government Act 1972[7] (pecuniary interests of members of local authorities) shall apply in relation of members of a flood defence committee as those provisions apply in relation to members of local authorities.

(2)  In their application by virtue of this paragraph those provisions shall have effect in accordance with the following provisions—

(a)  for references to meetings of the local authority there shall be substituted references to meetings of the committee;

(b)  in section 94(4), for the reference to provision being made by standing orders of a local authority there shall be substituted a reference to provisions being made by directions of the committee;

(c)  in section 96, for references to the proper officer of the local authority there shall be substituted a reference to an officer of the Agency[8] appointed for the purposes of this paragraph; and

[1] "The 1991 Act" means the Water Resources Act 1991: s.56(1) above.
[2] "The Agency" means the Environment Agency: s.124(1) above.
[3] "Functions" includes powers and duties: s.124(1) above.
[4] P.426 above.
[5] "The 1991 Act" means the Water Resources Act 1991: s.56(1) above.
[6] "The Agency" means the Environment Agency: s.124(1) above.
[7] 1972 c.70.
[8] "The Agency" means the Environment Agency: s.124(1) above.

(*d*) section 97 shall apply as it applies to a local authority other than a parish or community council.

(3) Subject to sub-paragraph (4) below, a member of a flood defence committee shall be disqualified, for so long as he remains such a member and for twelve months after he ceases to be such a member, for appointment to any paid office by the Agency or any regional flood defence committee.

(4) Sub-paragraph (3) above shall not disqualify any person for appointment to the office of chairman of a local flood defence committee.

## *Authentication of documents*

**15.** (1) Any notice or other document which a flood defence committee are required or authorised to give, make or issue by or under any enactment may be signed on behalf of the committee by any member of the committee or any officer of the Agency[1] who is generally or specifically authorised for that purpose by a resolution of the committee.

(2) Any document purporting to bear the signature of a person expressed to be authorised as mentioned in sub-paragraph (1) above shall be deemed, unless the contrary is shown, to be duly given, made or issued by authority of the committee.

(3) In this paragraph "signature" includes a facsimile of a signature by whatever process reproduced.

## *Proof and validity of proceedings*

**16.** (1) A minute of the proceedings of a meeting of a flood defence committee, purporting to be signed at that or the next ensuing meeting by—

(*a*) the chairman of the meeting to the proceedings of which the minute relates, or

(*b*) by the chairman of the next ensuing meeting,

shall be evidence of the proceedings and shall be received in evidence without further proof.

(2) Where a minute has been signed as mentioned in sub-paragraph (1) above in respect of a meeting of a committee or sub-committee, then, unless the contrary is shown—

(*a*) the meeting shall be deemed to have been duly convened and held;

(*b*) all the proceedings had at any such meeting shall be deemed to have been duly had; and

(*c*) that committee or sub-committee shall be deemed to have been duly constituted and have had power to deal with the matters referred to in the minute.

(3) The validity of any proceedings of a flood defence committee shall not be affected by any vacancy among the members of the committee or by any defect in the appointment of such a member.

# SCHEDULE 6

(Section 20[2].)

## THE SCOTTISH ENVIRONMENT PROTECTION AGENCY

### *Status*

**1.** SEPA[3] shall be a body corporate with a common seal.

**2.** Subject to section 38 of this Act[4], SEPA shall not—

(*a*) be regarded as a servant or agent of the Crown;

(*b*) have any status, immunity or privilege of the Crown;

---

[1] "The Agency" means the Environment Agency: s.124(1) above.

[2] P.438 above. S.20 came into force on 12 October 1995: S.I. 1995/2649.

[3] "SEPA" means the Scottish Environment Protection Agency: s.124(1) above.

[4] P.449 above.

(c) by virtue of its connection with the Crown, be exempt from any tax, duty, rate, levy or other charge whatsoever whether general or local,

and its property shall not be regarded as property of, or held on behalf of, the Crown.

## Membership

3. SEPA shall consist of not less than eight, nor more than twelve, members appointed by the Secretary of State.

4. In making appointments under paragraph 3 above, the Secretary of State shall have regard to the desirability of appointing persons who have knowledge or experience in some matter relevant to the functions[1] of SEPA.

5. Subject to paragraphs 7 and 8 below, each member—

(a) shall hold and vacate office in accordance with the terms of his appointment;

(b) may, by giving notice to the Secretary of State, resign his office; and

(c) after ceasing to hold office shall be eligible for reappointment as a member.

6. The Secretary of State may, by order made by statutory instrument subject to annulment in pursuance of a resolution of either House of Parliament, amend paragraph 3 above so as to substitute for the numbers for the time being specified as, respectively, the minimum and maximum membership such other numbers as he thinks fit.

7. The Secretary of State may remove a member from office if he is satisfied that the member—

(a) has been absent from meetings of SEPA for a period longer than three months without the permission of SEPA; or

(b) has been adjudged bankrupt, has made an arrangement with his creditors, has had his estate sequestrated or has granted a trust deed for his creditors or a composition contract; or

(c) is unable or unfit to carry out the functions of a member.

## Chairman and deputy chairman

8. (1) The Secretary of State shall appoint one of the members of SEPA to be chairman and another of those members to be deputy chairman.

(2) The chairman and deputy chairman shall hold and vacate office in terms of their appointments.

(3) A member who is chairman or deputy chairman may resign his office by giving notice to the Secretary of State; but if the chairman or deputy chairman ceases to be a member (whether or not on giving notice under paragraph 5(b) above) he shall cease to be chairman or, as the case may be, deputy chairman.

(4) A person who ceases to be chairman or deputy chairman shall be eligible for reappointment as such under sub-paragraph (1) above at any time when he is a member.

## Remuneration, pensions, etc.

9. (1) SEPA shall—

(a) pay to its members such remuneration and such travelling and other allowances (if any); and

(b) as regards any member or former member in whose case the Secretary of State may so determine—

(i) pay such pension, allowance or gratuity to or in respect of him;

(ii) make such payments towards the provision of such pension, allowance or gratuity; or

(iii) provide and maintain such schemes (whether contributory or not) for the payment of pensions, allowances or gratuities,

as the Secretary of State may determine.

(2) If a person ceases to be a member, and it appears to the Secretary of State that there are special circumstances which make it right that he should receive compensation, the Secretary of State may require SEPA to pay to that person a sum of such amount as the Secretary of State may determine.

---

[1] "Functions" includes powers and duties: s.124(1) above.

*Staff*

**10.** (1) There shall be a chief officer of SEPA.

(2) The Secretary of State shall, after consultation with the chairman or person designated to be chairman (if there is a person holding or designated to hold that office), make the first appointment of chief officer on such terms and conditions as he may determine; and thereafter SEPA may, with the approval of the Secretary of State, make subsequent appointments to that office on such terms and conditions as it may with such approval determine.

**11.** SEPA may appoint such other employees as it thinks fit.

**12.** (1) SEPA shall, in the case of such of its employees or former employees as it may, with the approval of the Secretary of State, determine—

(*a*)  pay such pensions, allowances or gratuities to or in respect of those employees;

(*b*)  make such payments towards provision of such pensions, allowances or gratuities; or

(*c*)  provide and maintain such schemes (whether contributory or not) for the payment of such pensions, allowances or gratuities,

as it may, with the approval of the Secretary of State, determine.

(2) References in sub-paragraph (1) above to pensions, allowances or gratuities in respect of employees of SEPA include references to pensions, allowances or gratuities by way of compensation to or in respect of any such employee who suffers loss of office or employment.

*Proceedings*

**13.** (1) SEPA may regulate its own procedure and that of any committee established by it (including making provision in relation to the quorum for its meetings and the meetings of any such committee).

(2) The proceedings of SEPA and of any committee established by it shall not be invalidated by any vacancy amongst its members or the members of such committee or by any defect in the appointment of such member.

*Committees*

**14.** (1) SEPA may appoint persons who are not members of it to be members of any committee established by it, but at least one member of any such committee shall be a member of SEPA.

(2) SEPA shall pay to a person so appointed such remuneration and allowances (if any) as the Secretary of State may determine.

(3) Any committee established by SEPA shall comply with any directions given to them by it.

*Delegation of powers*

**15.** (1) Anything authorised or required by or under any enactment to be done by SEPA may be done by any of its committees which, or by any of its members or employees who, is authorised (generally or specifically) for the purpose by SEPA.

(2) Nothing in sub-paragraph (1) above shall prevent SEPA from doing anything that a committee, member or employee has been authorised or required to do.

*Regional Boards*

**16.** (1) Without prejudice to the generality of its power to establish committees, SEPA shall establish committees (to be known as "Regional Boards") for the purposes of discharging in relation to such areas as it may, with the approval of the Secretary of State, determine, such of its functions[1] as it may, with such approval, determine.

(2) A Regional Board shall have a chairman who shall be a member of SEPA and appointed to that office by SEPA.

---

[1]  "Functions" includes powers and duties: s.124(1) below.

(3)  It shall be the duty of SEPA to comply with such guidance as the Secretary of State may from time to time give as to—

(*a*)  the number of persons to be appointed to a Regional Board;

(*b*)  the qualifications and experience which persons (other than members of SEPA) should have to be eligible for appointment to a Regional Board;

(*c*)  the descriptions of bodies which, or persons who, have a significant interest in matters likely to be affected by the discharge by a Regional Board of its functions; and

(*d*)  how the membership of a Regional Board is to reflect the different descriptions of bodies or persons referred to in paragraph (*c*) above.

(4)  Anything authorised or required to be done by a Regional Board by virtue of sub-paragraph (1) above may be done by any member of the Board, or by any employee of SEPA, who is authorised (generally or specifically) for the purpose by the Board.

(5)  Nothing in sub-paragraph (4) above shall prevent a Regional Board doing anything that a member or employee has been authorised or required to do.

### Members' interests

**17.** (1)  A member who is in any way directly or indirectly interested in any matter that is brought up for consideration at a meeting of SEPA shall disclose the nature of his interest to the meeting; and, where such a disclosure is made—

(*a*)  the disclosure shall be recorded in the minutes of the meeting; and

(*b*)  the member shall not take any part in any deliberation or decision of SEPA or of any of its committees with respect to that matter.

(2)  For the purposes of sub-paragraph (1) above, a general notification given at a meeting of SEPA by a member to the effect that he—

(*a*)  is a member of a specified company or firm, and

(*b*)  is to be regarded as interested in any matter involving that company or firm,

shall be regarded as a sufficient disclosure of his interest in relation to any such matter.

(3)  A member need not attend in person at a meeting of SEPA in order to make a disclosure which he is required to make under this paragraph if he takes reasonable steps to secure that the disclosure is made by a notice which is read and considered at the meeting.

(4)  The Secretary of State may, subject to such conditions as he considers appropriate, remove any disability imposed by virtue of this paragraph in any case where the number of members of SEPA disabled by virtue of this paragraph at any one time would be so great a proportion of the whole as to impede the transaction of business.

(5)  The power of the Secretary of State under sub-paragraph (4) above includes power to remove, either indefinitely or for any period, a disability which would otherwise attach to any member, or members of any description, by reason of such interests, and in respect of such matters, as may be specified or described by the Secretary of State.

(6)  Nothing in this paragraph precludes any member from taking part in the consideration or discussion of, or voting on, any question whether an application should be made to the Secretary of State for the exercise of the power conferred by sub-paragraph (4) above.

(7)  In this paragraph—

(*a*)  any reference to a meeting of SEPA includes a reference to a meeting of any of SEPA's committees; and

(*b*)  any reference to a member includes a reference to a person who is not a member of SEPA but who is a member of any such committee.

### Minutes

**18.** (1)  Minutes shall be kept of proceedings of SEPA and of its committees.

(2)  Minutes of any such proceedings shall be evidence of those proceedings if they are signed by a person purporting to have acted as chairman of the proceedings to which the minutes relate or of any subsequent proceedings in the course of which the minutes were approved as a correct record.

(3)  Where minutes of any such proceedings have been signed as mentioned in sub-paragraph (2) above, those proceedings shall, unless the contrary is shown, be deemed to have been validly convened and constituted.

# SCHEDULE 7

## NATIONAL PARK AUTHORITIES

*Not reproduced*

# SCHEDULE 8

## SUPPLEMENTAL AND INCIDENTAL POWERS OF NATIONAL PARK AUTHORITIES

*Not reproduced*

# SCHEDULE 9

## MISCELLANEOUS STATUTORY FUNCTIONS OF NATIONAL PARK AUTHORITIES

*Not reproduced*

# SCHEDULE 10

## MINOR AND CONSEQUENTIAL AMENDMENTS RELATING TO NATIONAL PARKS

*Not reproduced*

# SCHEDULE 11

(Section 90[1].)

## AIR QUALITY: SUPPLEMENTAL PROVISIONS

### *Consultation requirements*

**1.** (1)  A local authority[2] in carrying out its functions[3] in relation to—

(*a*)  any air quality review[4],

(*b*)  any assessment under section 82[5] or 84[6] of this Act, or

(*c*)  the preparation of an action plan[7] or any revision of an action plan,

shall consult such other persons as fall within sub-paragraph (2) below.

(2)  Those persons are—

(*a*)  the Secretary of State;

(*b*)  the appropriate new Agency[8];

(*c*)  in England and Wales, the highway authority for any highway in the area to which the review or, as the case may be, the action plan or revision relates;

(*d*)  every local authority whose area is contiguous to the authority's area;

---

[1]  P.474 above. S.90, in so far as it relates to paragraphs 2, 3 and 5 of this schedule, came into force on 1 February 1996: S.I. 1996/186; otherwise this schedule is not in force.
[2]  "Local authority" defined by s.91(1), p.474 above.
[3]  "Functions" includes powers and duties: s.124(1) above.

[4]  "Air quality review" defined by s.91(1), p.474 above.
[5]  P.467 above.
[6]  P.467 above.
[7]  "Action plan" defined by s.91(1), p.474 above.
[8]  "Appropriate new Agency" defined by s.91(1), p.474 above.

(e) any county council in England whose area consists of or includes the whole or any part of the authority's area;

(f) any National Park authority for a National Park whose area consists of or includes the whole or any part of the authority's area;

(g) such public authorities exercising functions in, or in the vicinity of, the authority's area as the authority may consider appropriate;

(h) such bodies appearing to the authority to be representative of persons with business interests in the area to which the review or action plan in question relates as the authority may consider appropriate;

(j) such other bodies or persons as the authority considers appropriate.

(3) In this paragraph "National Park authority", subject to sub-paragraph (4) below, means a National Park authority established under section 63 of this Act which has become the local planning authority for the National Park in question.

(4) As respects any period before a National Park authority established under section 63 of this Act in relation to a National Park becomes the local planning authority for that National Park, any reference in sub-paragraph (2) above to a National Park authority shall be taken as a reference to the National Park Committee or joint or special planning board for that National Park.

### Exchange of information with county councils in England

2. (1) This paragraph applies in any case where a district in England for which there is a district council is comprised in an area for which there is a county council; and in this paragraph—

(a) any reference to the county council is a reference to the council of that area; and

(b) any reference to a district council is a reference to the council of a district comprised in that area.

(2) It shall be the duty of the county council to provide a district council with all such information as is reasonably requested by the district council for purposes connected with the carrying out of its functions under or by virtue of this Part.

(3) It shall be the duty of a district council to provide the county council with all such information as is reasonably requested by the county council for purposes connected with the carrying out of any of its functions relating to the assessment or management of the quality of air.

(4) Information provided to a district council or county council under sub paragraph (2) or (3) above shall be provided in such form and in such manner and at such times as the district council or, as the case may be, the county council may reasonably require.

(5) A council which provides information under sub-paragraph (2) or (3) above shall be entitled to recover the reasonable cost of doing so from the council which requested the information.

(6) The information which a council may be required to provide under this paragraph shall include information which, although it is not in the possession of the council or would not otherwise come into the possession of the council, is information which it is reasonable to require the council to obtain.

### Joint exercise of local authority functions

3. (1) The appropriate authority[1] may give directions to any two or more local authorities requiring them to exercise the powers conferred by—

(a) section 101(5) of the Local Government Act 1972[2] (power of two or more local authorities to discharge functions jointly), or

(b) section 56(5) of the Local Government (Scotland) Act 1973[3] (which makes similar provision for Scotland),

in relation to functions under or by virtue of this Part in accordance with the directions.

(2) The appropriate authority may give directions to a local authority requiring it—

(a) not to exercise those powers, or

(b) not to exercise those powers in a manner specified in the directions,

in relation to functions under or by virtue of this Part.

[1] "The appropriate authority" defined by sub-paragraph (4) below.    [2] 1972 c.70.    [3] 1973 c.65.

(3)  Where two or more local authorities have exercised those powers in relation to functions under or by virtue of this Part, the appropriate authority may give them directions requiring them to revoke, or modify in accordance with the directions, the arrangements which they have made.

(4)  In this paragraph, "the appropriate authority" means—

(a)  in relation to England and Wales, the Secretary of State; and

(b)  in relation to Scotland, SEPA[1] acting with the approval of the Secretary of State.

## Public access to information about air quality

**4.** (1)  It shall be the duty of every local authority[2]—

(a)  to secure that there is available at all reasonable times for inspection by the public free of charge a copy of each of the documents specified in sub-paragraph (2) below; and

(b)  to afford to members of the public facilities for obtaining copies of those documents on payment of a reasonable charge.

(2)  The documents mentioned in sub-paragraph (1)(a) above are—

(a)  a report of the results of any air quality review[3] which the authority has caused to be conducted;

(b)  a report of the results of any assessment which the authority has caused to be made under section 82[4] or 84[5] of this Act;

(c)  any order made by the authority under section 83 of this Act[6];

(d)  any action plan[7] prepared by the authority;

(e)  any proposals or statements submitted to the authority pursuant to subsection (3) or (4) of section 86 of this Act[8];

(f)  any directions given to the authority under this Part;

(g)  in a case where section 86 of this Act applies, any directions given to the county council under this Part.

## Fixed penalty offences

**5.** (1)  Without prejudice to the generality of paragraph (o) of subsection (2) of section 87 of this Act[9], regulations[10] may, in particular, make provision—

(a)  for the qualifications, appointment or authorisation of persons who are to issue fixed penalty notices[11];

(b)  for the offences in connection with which, the cases or circumstances in which, the time or period at or within which, or the manner in which fixed penalty notices may be issued;

(c)  prohibiting the institution, before the expiration of the period for paying[12] the fixed penalty, of proceedings against a person for an offence in connection with which a fixed penalty notice has been issued;

(d)  prohibiting the conviction of a person for an offence in connection with which a fixed penalty notice has been issued if the fixed penalty is paid before the expiration of the period for paying it;

(e)  entitling, in prescribed cases, a person to whom a fixed penalty notice is issued to give, within a prescribed period, notice requesting a hearing in respect of the offence to which the fixed penalty notice relates;

(f)  for the amount of the fixed penalty to be increased by a prescribed amount in any case where the person liable to pay the fixed penalty fails to pay it before the expiration of the period for paying it, without having given notice requesting a hearing in respect of the offence to which the fixed penalty notice relates;

(g)  for or in connection with the recovery of an unpaid fixed penalty as a fine or as a civil debt or as if it were a sum payable under a county court order;

(h)  for or in connection with execution or other enforcement in respect of an unpaid fixed penalty by prescribed persons;

[1] "SEPA" means the Scottish Environment Protection Agency: s.124(1) above.
[2] "Local authority" defined by s.91(1), p.474 above.
[3] "Air quality review" defined by s.91(1), p.474 above.
[4] P.467 above.
[5] P.467 above.
[6] P.467 above.
[7] "Action plan" defined by s.91(1), p.474 above.
[8] P.470 above.
[9] P.472 above.
[10] "Regulations" defined by sub-paragraph (6) below.
[11] "Fixed penalty" and "fixed penalty notice" defined by sub-paragraph (6) below.
[12] "The period for paying" defined by sub-paragraph (6) below.

(*j*)  for a fixed penalty notice, and any prescribed proceedings or other prescribed steps taken by reference to the notice, to be rendered void in prescribed cases where a person makes a prescribed statutory declaration, and for the consequences of any notice, proceedings or other steps being so rendered void (including extension of any time limit for instituting criminal proceedings);

(*k*)  for or in connection with the extension, in prescribed cases or circumstances, by a prescribed person of the period for paying a fixed penalty;

(*l*)  for or in connection with the withdrawal, in prescribed circumstances, of a fixed penalty notice, including—

(i)  repayment of any amount paid by way of fixed penalty in pursuance of a fixed penalty notice which is withdrawn; and

(ii)  prohibition of the institution or continuation of proceedings for the offence in connection with which the withdrawn notice was issued;

(*m*)  for or in connection with the disposition of sums received by way of fixed penalty;

(*n*)  for a certificate purporting to be signed by or on behalf of a prescribed person and stating either—

(i)  that payment of a fixed penalty was, or (as the case may be) was not, received on or before a date specified in the certificate, or

(ii)  that an envelope containing an amount sent by post in payment of a fixed penalty was marked as posted on a date specified in the certificate, to be received as evidence of the matters so stated and to be treated, without further proof, as being so signed unless the contrary is shown;

(*o*)  requiring a fixed penalty notice to give such reasonable particulars of the circumstances alleged to constitute the fixed penalty offence to which the notice relates as are necessary for giving reasonable information of the offence and to state—

(i)  the monetary amount of the fixed penalty which may be paid;

(ii)  the person to whom, and the address at which, the fixed penalty may be paid and any correspondence relating to the fixed penalty notice may be sent;

(iii)  the method or methods by which payment of the fixed penalty may be made;

(iv)  the period for paying the fixed penalty;

(v)  the consequences of the fixed penalty not being paid before the expiration of that period;

(*p*)  similar to any provision made by section 79 of the Road Traffic Offenders Act 1988[1] (statements by constables in fixed penalty cases);

(*q*)  for presuming, in any proceedings, that any document of a prescribed description purporting to have been signed by a person to whom a fixed penalty notice has been issued has been signed by that person;

(*r*)  requiring or authorising a fixed penalty notice to contain prescribed information relating to, or for the purpose of facilitating, the administration of the fixed penalty system[2];

(*s*)  with respect to the giving of fixed penalty notices, including, in particular, provision with respect to—

(i)  the methods by which,

(ii)  the officers, servants or agents by, to or on whom, and

(iii)  the places at which,

fixed penalty notices may be given by, or served on behalf of, a prescribed person;

(*t*)  prescribing the method or methods by which fixed penalties may be paid;

(*u*)  for or with respect to the issue of prescribed documents to persons to whom fixed penalty notices are or have been given;

(*w*)  for a fixed penalty notice to be treated for prescribed purposes as if it were an information or summons or any other document of a prescribed description.

(2)  The provision that may be made by regulations prescribing fixed penalty offences[3] includes provision for an offence to be a fixed penalty offence—

(*a*)  only if it is committed in such circumstances or manner as may be prescribed; or

(*b*)  except if it is committed in such circumstances or manner as may be prescribed.

(3)  Regulations may provide for any offence which is a fixed penalty offence to cease to be such an offence.

---

[1]  1988 c.53.
[2]  "Fixed penalty system" defined by sub-paragraph (6) below.

[3]  "Fixed penalty offence" defined by sub-paragraph (6) below.

(4)  An offence which, in consequence of regulations made by virtue of sub paragraph (3) above, has ceased to be a fixed penalty offence shall be eligible to be prescribed as such an offence again.

(5)  Regulations may make provision for such exceptions, limitations and conditions as the Secretary of State considers necessary or expedient.

(6)  In this paragraph—

"fixed penalty" means a penalty of such amount as may be prescribed (whether by being specified in, or made calculable under, regulations);

"fixed penalty notice" means a notice offering a person an opportunity to discharge any liability to conviction for a fixed penalty offence by payment of a penalty of a prescribed amount;

"fixed penalty offence" means, subject to sub-paragraph (2) above, any offence (whether under or by virtue of this Part or any other enactment) which is for the time being prescribed as a fixed penalty offence;

"the fixed penalty system" means the system implementing regulations made under or by virtue of paragraph (o) of subsection (2) of section 87 of this Act[1];

"the period for paying", in relation to any fixed penalty, means such period as may be prescribed for the purpose;

"regulations" means regulations under or by virtue of paragraph (o) of subsection (2) of section 87 of this Act.

# SCHEDULE 12

## SCHEDULE 2A TO THE ENVIRONMENTAL PROTECTION ACT 1990

This schedule inserts schedule 2A to the Environmental Protection Act 1990. Schedule 2A of the 1990 Act is at p.222 above.

# SCHEDULE 13

## REVIEW OF OLD MINERAL PLANNING PERMISSIONS

*Not reproduced*

# SCHEDULE 14

## PERIODIC REVIEW OF MINERAL PLANNING PERMISSIONS

*Not reproduced*

# SCHEDULE 15

## MINOR AND CONSEQUENTIAL AMENDMENTS RELATING TO FISHERIES

*Not reproduced*

# SCHEDULE 16

## POLLUTION OF RIVERS AND COASTAL WATERS IN SCOTLAND: AMENDMENT OF THE CONTROL OF POLLUTION ACT 1974.

This schedule amends the Control of Pollution Act 1974. This Manual sets out the 1974 Act, with the amendments made by this schedule, at p.11 above.

[1]  P.471 above.

## SCHEDULE 17

### Statutory Nuisances: Scotland

This schedule amends the Environmental Protection Act 1990 and the Radioactive Substances Act 1993. This Manual sets out these Acts, with the amendments made by this schedule, at p.000 and p.000 above respectively.

## SCHEDULE 18

(Section 108[1].)

### Supplemental provisions with respect to powers of entry

#### Interpretation

1. (1) In this Schedule—

"designated person" means an authorised person, within the meaning of section 108 of this Act[2] and includes a person designated by virtue of paragraph 2 below;

"relevant power" means a power conferred by section 108 of this Act including a power exercisable by virtue of a warrant under this Schedule.

(2) Expressions used in this Schedule and in section 108 of this Act have the same meaning in this Schedule as they have in that section.

#### Issue of warrants

2. (1) If it is shown to the satisfaction of a justice of the peace or, in Scotland, the sheriff or a justice of the peace, on sworn information in writing—

(a) that there are reasonable grounds for the exercise in relation to any premises[3] of a relevant power; and

(b) that one or more of the conditions specified in sub-paragraph (2) below is fulfilled in relation to those premises,

the justice or sheriff may by warrant authorise an enforcing authority[4] to designate a person who shall be authorised to exercise the power in relation to those premises, in accordance with the warrant and, if need be, by force.

(2) The conditions mentioned in sub-paragraph (1)(b) above are—

(a) that the exercise of the power in relation to the premises has been refused;

(b) that such a refusal is reasonably apprehended;

(c) that the premises are unoccupied;

(d) that the occupier is temporarily absent from the premises and the case is one of urgency; or

(e) that an application for admission to the premises would defeat the object of the proposed entry.

(3) In a case where subsection (6) of section 108 of this Act applies, a justice of the peace or sheriff shall not issue a warrant under this Schedule by virtue only of being satisfied that the exercise of a power in relation to any premises has been refused, or that a refusal is reasonably apprehended, unless he is also satisfied that the notice required by that subsection has been given and that the period of that notice has expired.

(4) Every warrant under this Schedule shall continue in force until the purposes for which the warrant was issued have been fulfilled.

#### Manner of exercise of powers

3. A person designated as the person who may exercise a relevant power shall produce evidence of his designation and other authority before he exercises the power.

---

[1] P.481 above. S.108 came into force on 1 April 1996: S.I. 1996/186.
[2] P.481 above.
[3] "Premises" defined by s.108(15), p.485 above.
[4] "Enforcing authority" defined by s.108(15), p.484 above.

*Information obtained to be admissible in evidence*

**4.** (1) Subject to section 108(12) of this Act, information obtained in consequence of the exercise of a relevant power, with or without the consent of any person, shall be admissible in evidence against that or any other person.

(2) Without prejudice to the generality of sub-paragraph (1) above, information obtained by means of monitoring or other apparatus installed on any premises in the exercise of a relevant power, with or without the consent of any person in occupation of the premises, shall be admissible in evidence in any proceedings against that or any other person.

*Duty to secure premises*

**5.** A person who, in the exercise of a relevant power enters on any premises which are unoccupied or whose occupier is temporarily absent shall leave the premises as effectually secured against trespassers as he found them.

*Compensation*

**6.** (1) Where any person exercises any power conferred by section 108(4)(*a*) or (*b*) or (5) of this Act, it shall be the duty of the enforcing authority under whose authorisation he acts to make full compensation to any person who has sustained loss or damage by reason of—

(*a*)  the exercise by the designated person of that power; or

(*b*)  the performance of, or failure of the designated person to perform, the duty imposed by paragraph 5 above.

(2) Compensation shall not be payable by virtue of subparagraph (1) above in respect of any loss or damage if the loss or damage—

(*a*)  is attributable to the default of the person who sustained it; or

(*b*)  is loss or damage in respect of which compensation is payable by virtue of any other provision of the pollution control enactments[1].

(3) Any dispute as to a person's entitlement to compensation under this paragraph, or as to the amount of any such compensation, shall be referred to the arbitration of a single arbitrator or, in Scotland, arbiter appointed by agreement between the enforcing authority in question and the person who claims to have sustained the loss or damage or, in default of agreement, by the Secretary of State.

(4) A designated person shall not be liable in any civil or criminal proceedings for anything done in the purported exercise of any relevant power if the court is satisfied that the act was done in good faith and that there were reasonable grounds for doing it.

# SCHEDULE 19

### OFFENCES RELATING TO FALSE OR MISLEADING STATEMENTS OR FALSE ENTRIES

This schedule amends certain enactments. The enactments amended by this schedule which are in this Manual are the Control of Pollution Act 1974, p.11 above, the Control of Pollution ( Amendment ) Act 1989, p.71 above, the Environmental Protection Act 1990, p.83 above, the Water Resources Act 1991, p.267 above, and the Radioactive Substances Act 1993, p.381 above.

[1]  "Pollution control enactments" defined by s.108(15), p.485 above.

# SCHEDULE 20

(Section 114[1].)

## DELEGATION OF APPELLATE FUNCTIONS OF THE SECRETARY OF STATE

*Interpretation*

**1.** In this Schedule—

"appointed person" means a person appointed under section 114(1)(*a*) of this Act[2]; and

"appointment", in the case of any appointed person, means appointment under section 114(1)(*a*) of this Act.

*Appointments*

**2.** An appointment under section 114(1)(*a*) of this Act must be in writing and—

(*a*) may relate to any particular appeal, matters or questions specified in the appointment or to appeals, matters or questions of a description so specified;

(*b*) may provide for any function to which it relates to be exercisable by the appointed person either unconditionally or subject to the fulfilment of such conditions as may be specified in the appointment; and

(*c*) may, by notice in writing given to the appointed person, be revoked at any time by the Secretary of State in respect of any appeal, matter or question which has not been determined by the appointed person before that time.

*Powers of appointed person*

**3.** Subject to the provisions of this Schedule, an appointed person shall, in relation to any appeal, matter or question to which his appointment relates, have the same powers and duties as the Secretary of State, other than—

(*a*) any function of making regulations;

(*b*) any function of holding an inquiry or other hearing or of causing an inquiry or other hearing to be held; or

(*c*) any function of appointing a person for the purpose—

(i) of enabling persons to appear before and be heard by the person so appointed; or

(ii) of referring any question or matter to that person.

*Holding of local inquiries and other hearings by appointed persons*

**4.** (1) If either of the parties to an appeal, matter or question expresses a wish to appear before and be heard by the appointed person, the appointed person shall give both of them an opportunity of appearing and being heard.

(2) Whether or not a party to an appeal, matter or question has asked for an opportunity to appear and be heard, the appointed person—

(*a*) may hold a local inquiry or other hearing in connection with the appeal, matter or question, and

(*b*) shall, if the Secretary of State so directs, hold a local inquiry in connection with the appeal, matter or question,

but this sub-paragraph is subject to sub-paragraph (3) below.

(3) No local inquiry shall be held by virtue of this Schedule in connection with an appeal under—

(*a*) section 42B(5) of the Control of Pollution Act 1974[3],

(*b*) section 22(5)[4], 66(5)[5] or 78T(3)[6] of the Environmental Protection Act 1990, or

(*c*) section 191B(5) of the Water Resources Act 1991[7],

---

[1] P.489 above. S.114 came into force on 1 April 1996: S.I. 1996/186.
[2] P.489 above.
[3] P.40 above.
[4] P.108 above.
[5] P.155 above.
[6] P.182 above.
[7] P.301 above.

(appeals against decisions that information is not commercially confidential), or any matter involved in such an appeal, and any hearing held by virtue of this Schedule in connection with any such appeal or matter must be held in private.

(4)  Where an appointed person holds a local inquiry or other hearing by virtue of this Schedule, an assessor may be appointed by the Secretary of State to sit with the appointed person at the inquiry or hearing and advise him on any matters arising, notwithstanding that the appointed person is to determine the appeal, matter or question.

(5)  Subject to paragraph 5 below, the costs of a local inquiry held under this Schedule shall be defrayed by the Secretary of State.

### *Local inquiries under this Schedule: evidence and costs*

**5.** (1)  In relation to England and Wales, subsections (2) to (5) of section 250 of the Local Government Act 1972[1] (local inquiries: evidence and costs) shall apply to local inquiries or other hearings held under this Schedule by an appointed person as they apply to inquiries caused to be held under that section by a Minister, but with the following modifications, that is to say—

(a)  with the substitution in subsection (2) (evidence) for the reference to the person appointed to hold the inquiry of a reference to the appointed person;

(b)  with the substitution in subsection (4) (recovery of costs of holding the inquiry) for the references to the Minister causing the inquiry to be held of references to the Secretary of State;

(c)  taking the reference in that subsection to a local authority as including the Agency[2]; and

(d)  with the substitution in subsection (5) (orders as to the costs of the parties) for the reference to the Minister causing the inquiry to be held of a reference to the appointed person or the Secretary of State.

(2)  In relation to Scotland, subsections (3) to (8) of section 210 of the Local Government (Scotland) Act 1973[3] (which relate to the costs of and holding of local inquiries) shall apply to local inquiries or other hearings held under this Schedule as they apply to inquiries held under that section, but with the following modifications, that is to say—

(a)  with the substitution in subsection (3) (notice of inquiry) for the reference to the person appointed to hold the inquiry of a reference to the appointed person;

(b)  with the substitution in subsection (4) (evidence) for the reference to the person appointed to hold the inquiry and, in paragraph (b), the reference to the person holding the inquiry of references to the appointed person;

(c)  with the substitution in subsection (6) (expenses of witnesses etc.) for the references to the Minister causing the inquiry to be held of a reference to the appointed person or the Secretary of State;

(d)  with the substitution in subsection (7) (expenses) for the references to the Minister of references to the appointed person or the Secretary of State;

(e)  with the substitution in subsection (7A) (recovery of entire administrative expense)—

(i)  for the first reference to the Minister of a reference to the appointed person or the Secretary of State;

(ii)  in paragraph (a), for the reference to the Minister of a reference to the Secretary of State; and

(iii)  in paragraph (b), for the reference to the Minister holding the inquiry of a reference to the Secretary of State;

(f)  with the substitution in subsection (7B) (power to prescribe daily amount)—

(i)  for the first reference to the Minister of a reference to the Secretary of State;

(ii)  in paragraphs (a) and (c), for the references to the person appointed to hold the inquiry of references to the appointed person; and

(iii)  in paragraph (d), for the reference to the Minister of a reference to the appointed person or the Secretary of State; and

(g)  with the substitution in subsection (8) (certification of expenses) for the reference to the Minister, the reference to him and the reference to the Crown of references to the appointed person or the Secretary of State.

[1]  1972 c.70.      [2]  "The Agency" means the Environment Agency: s.124(1) above.      [3]  1973 c.65.

*Revocation of appointments and making of new appointments*

**6.** (1)  Where under paragraph 2(*c*) above the appointment of the appointed person is revoked in respect of any appeal, matter or question, the Secretary of State shall, unless he proposes to determine the appeal, matter or question himself, appoint another person under section 114(1)(*a*) of this Act[1] to determine the appeal, matter or question instead.

(2)  Where such a new appointment is made, the consideration of the appeal, matter or question. or any hearing in connection with it, shall be begun afresh.

(3)  Nothing in sub-paragraph (2) above shall require any person to be given an opportunity of making fresh representations or modifying or withdrawing any representations already made.

*Certain acts and omissions of appointed person to be treated as those of the Secretary of State*

**7.** (1)  Anything done or omitted to be done by an appointed person in, or in connection with, the exercise or purported exercise of any function to which the appointment relates shall be treated for all purposes as done or omitted to be done by the Secretary of State in his capacity as such.

(2)  Sub-paragraph (1) above shall not apply—

(*a*)  for the purposes of so much of any contract made between the Secretary of State and the appointed person as relates to the exercise of the function; or

(*b*)  for the purposes of any criminal proceedings brought in respect of anything done or omitted to be done as mentioned in that sub paragraph.

# SCHEDULE 21

## Application of certain enactments to the Crown

This schedule amends certain enactments. The enactments amended by this schedule which are in this Manual are the Control of Pollution Act 1974, p.11 above, the Water Industry Act 1991, p.229 above, and the Water Resources Act 1991, p.267 above.

# SCHEDULE 22

## Minor and consequential amendments

The legislation in this Manual is set out with the amendments made by this schedule.

# SCHEDULE 23

(Section 120[2].)

## Transitional and transitory provisions and savings

## Part I: General transitional provisions and savings

### *Interpretation of Part I*

**1.**  In this Part of this Schedule, the "transfer date" has the same meaning as in Part I of this Act[3].

---

[1]  P.489 above.
[2]  P.492 above. S.120, in so far as it relates to paragraphs 1 to 6, 8 to 10, 12, 13, 14(1) to (4), (7) and (8) (in so far as that sub-paragraph relates to the definitions of "approval" and "the transfer date") and 16 to 24 of this schedule, came into force on 1 April 1996: S.I. 1996/186; in so far at it relates to paragraphs 14(5), (6) and to the definition of "grating" and "the substitution date" in 14(8) of this schedule, this section will come into force on 1 January 1999: S.I. 1995/1983.
[3]  "The transfer date" is defined in s.56(1), p.464 above. The transfer date was 1 April 1996: S.I. 1996/139 (in respect of Chapter II); S.I. 1996/234 (in respect of Chapter I).

## *Directions*

2. Any directions given to the National Rivers Authority for the purposes of section 19 of the Water Resources Act 1991[1] shall have effect on and after the transfer date as directions given to the Agency[2] or the purposes of section 6(2) of this Act[3].

## *Regional and local fisheries advisory committees*

3. If and so long as the Agency requires, on and after the transfer date any advisory committee established and maintained before the transfer date by the National Rivers Authority under section 8(1) of the Water Resources Act 1991 shall be treated as if—

(*a*) it had been established by the Agency,

(*b*) the area by reference to which that committee was established had been determined by the Agency, and

(*c*) in the case of a regional advisory committee, the chairman of that committee had been appointed,

in accordance with section 13 of this Act[4].

## *Charging schemes*

4. (1) Without prejudice to section 55 of this Act[5], any charging scheme—

(*a*) which relates to any transferred functions,

(*b*) which was made before the transfer date, and

(*c*) which is in force immediately before that date or would (apart from this Act) have come into force at any time after that date,

shall, subject to the provisions of section 41 of this Act[6], have effect on and after the transfer date, with any necessary modifications[7], and for the remainder of the period for which the charging scheme would have been in force apart from any repeal made by this Act, as a scheme made under that section by the transferee in accordance with section 42 of this Act[8].

(2) Any costs or expenses incurred before the transfer date by any person in carrying out functions transferred to a new Agency by or under this Act may be treated for the purposes of subsections (3) and (4) of section 42 of this Act as costs or expenses incurred by that new Agency in carrying out those functions.

(3) In this paragraph—

"charging scheme" means a scheme specifying, or providing for the determination of, any fees or charges;

"new Agency" means the Agency or SEPA[9];

"transferred functions" means any functions which, by virtue of any provision made by or under this Act, become functions of a new Agency and "the transferee" means the new Agency whose functions they so become.

## *Preparation of reports*

5. (1) The first report prepared by the Agency[10] under section 52 of this Act[11] may, to the extent that it relates to functions transferred to the Agency from any other body or person include a report on the exercise and performance of those functions by the transferor during the period between the end of the last year in respect of which the transferor prepared a report and the transfer date.

(2) SEPA[12] shall, as soon as reasonably practicable after the transfer date, prepare a report on—

(*a*) the exercise and performance of the functions of each river purification board[13] during the period between

---

[1] 1991 c.57.

[2] "The Agency" means the Environment Agency: s.124(1) above.

[3] P.425 above.

[4] P.432 above.

[5] P.461 above.

[6] P.452 above.

[7] "Modifications" defined by s.124(1), p.495 above.

[8] P.454 above.

[9] "SEPA" means the Scottish Environment Protection Agency: s.124(1) above.

[10] "The Agency" means the Environment Agency: s.124(1) below.

[11] P.460 above.

[12] "SEPA" means the Scottish Environment Protection Agency: s.124(1) below.

[13] "River purification board" defined by s.56(1), p.464 above.

the end of the last year in respect of which the board sent a report to the Secretary of State under section 16 of the Rivers (Prevention of Pollution) (Scotland) Act 1951[1] and the transfer date; and

(b) the exercise and performance of the functions of each waste regulation authority[2] during the period between the end of the last financial year in respect of which the authority prepared and published a report under section 67 of the Environmental Protection Act 1990[3] and the transfer date.

(3) Subsections (3) and (4) of section 52 of this Act shall apply to a report prepared under sub-paragraph (2) above as they apply to a report prepared under that section.

## Preparation of accounts

6. Notwithstanding the repeal by this Act of subsection (9) of section 135 of the Local Government (Scotland) Act 1973[4] (application to river purification board of certain provisions of that Act), the provisions applied to a river purification board by virtue of that section shall, as respects the period between the end of the last financial year in respect of which accounts have been made up by the board and the transfer date, continue to apply in relation to the board; but anything which shall or may be done or enjoyed, or any access, inspection or copying which shall or may be allowed, under or by virtue of any of those provisions or of section 118 of that Act (financial returns) by, or by an officer of, the board shall, or as the case may be may, after the transfer date, be done, enjoyed or allowed by, or by an officer of, SEPA in place of the board or of an officer of the board.

## Membership of Welsh National Park authorities

7. *Not reproduced.*

## The Alkali, &c., Works Regulation Act 1906

8. Any dispensation which was granted under the proviso to subsection (5) of section 9 of the Alkali, &c, Works Regulation Act 1906[5] before the transfer date and which would, apart from this Act, have been in force on that date shall have effect on and after that date notwithstanding the repeal of that proviso by this Act.

## The Public Records Act 1958

9. (1) Such of the administrative and departmental records (in whatever form or medium) of a transferor as are transferred to and vested in the Agency by or under section 3 of this Act shall be treated for the purposes of the Public Records Act 1958[6] as administrative or departmental records of the Agency.

(2) In this paragraph, "transferor" means any body or person any or all of whose administrative and departmental records are transferred to and vested in the Agency by or under section 3 of this Act.

## The Parliamentary Commissioner Act 1967

10. (1) Nothing in this Act shall prevent the completion on or after the transfer date of any investigation begun before that date under the Parliamentary Commissioner Act 1967[7] in pursuance of a complaint made in relation to the National Rivers Authority.

(2) Nothing in this Act shall prevent the making on or after the transfer date of a complaint under that Act in respect of any action which was taken by or on behalf of the National Rivers Authority before that date.

(3) Notwithstanding the amendment of that Act by paragraph 11 of Schedule 22 to this Act, the provisions of that Act shall have effect on and after the transfer date in relation to any complaint to which sub-paragraph (1) or (2) above applies and to its investigation as they would have had effect before that date; but, in relation to any such complaint, the Agency shall on and after that date stand in the place of the National Rivers Authority for the purposes of this paragraph.

---

[1] 1951 c.66.
[2] "Waste regulation authority" defined by s.56(1), p.464 above.
[3] 1990 c.43.

[4] 1973 c.65.
[5] 1906 c. 14.
[6] 1958 c.51.
[7] 1967 c.13.

## The Local Government Act 1974

11. *This paragraph, which relates to National Park planning boards and National Park authorities, is not reproduced.*

12. (1) Nothing in this Act shall prevent the completion on or after the transfer date by a Local Commissioner of any investigation which he began to conduct before that date and which is an investigation under Part III of the Local Government Act 1974[1] in pursuance of a complaint made in relation to the National Rivers Authority.

(2) Nothing in this Act shall prevent the making on or after the transfer date of a complaint under Part III of that Act in respect of any action which was taken by or on behalf of the National Rivers Authority before that date.

(3) Notwithstanding the amendment of Part III of that Act by paragraph 18 of Schedule 22 to this Act, the provisions of that Part shall have effect on and after the transfer date in relation to any complaint to which sub-paragraph (1) or (2) above applies and to its investigation as they would have had effect before that date; but, in relation to any such complaint, the Agency shall on and after that date stand in the place of the National Rivers Authority for the purposes of this paragraph.

## The Control of Pollution Act 1974

13. As respects England and Wales, any resolution passed in pursuance of section 11 of the Control of Pollution Act 1974[2] (special provision for land occupied by disposal authorities: resolutions etc) which is in force immediately before the day on which the repeals in that section made by this Act come into force shall have effect on and after that day as if it were a waste management licence granted by the Environment Agency under Part II of the Environmental Protection Act 1990[3] subject to the conditions specified in the resolution pursuant to subsection (3)(e) of that section.

## The Salmon and Freshwater Fisheries Act 1975

14. (1) Any approval or certificate given under or by virtue of section 8(2), 9(1) or 11(4) of the Salmon and Freshwater Fisheries Act 1975[4] by a Minister of the Crown before the transfer date shall, so far as is required for continuing its effect on and after that date, have effect as if given by the Agency.

(2) Any application for the grant of an approval or certificate by a Minister of the Crown under or by virtue of any of the provisions specified in sub paragraph (1) above which, at the transfer date, is in the process of being determined shall on and after that date be treated as having been made to the Agency.

(3) Any notice given by a Minister of the Crown under section 11(2) of that Act before the transfer date shall, so far as is required for continuing its effect on and after that date, have effect as if given by the Agency.

(4) Any extension of a period granted by a Minister of the Crown under section 11(3) of that Act before the transfer date shall, so far as is required for continuing its effect on and after that date, have effect as if granted by the Agency .

(5) Without prejudice to section 16 or 17 of the Interpretation Act 1978[5], any exemption granted under subsection (1) or (2) of section 14 of the Salmon and Freshwater Fisheries Act 1975 which is in force immediately before the substitution date shall have effect on and after that date as an exemption granted by the Agency under subsection (2) or, as the case may be, subsection (3) of section 14 of that Act as substituted by paragraph 13 of Schedule 15 to this Act.

(6) Any grating constructed and placed in a manner and position approved under section 14(3) of that Act as it had effect before the substitution date (including a grating so constructed and placed at any time as a replacement for a grating so constructed and placed) shall, if—

(a) the approval was in force immediately before the substitution date, and

(b) the grating is maintained in accordance with the approval,

be taken for the purposes of section 14 of that Act, as substituted by paragraph 13 of Schedule 15 to this Act, to be a screen which complies with the requirements of subsection (2)(a) or (3)(a) of that section, according to the location of the grating, and with the requirements of subsections (4) to (6) of that section.

(7) Any notice given, or objection made, under subsection (2) of section 18 of that Act before the transfer date shall, so far as is required for continuing its effect on and after that date, have effect as a notice given under that subsection as it has effect on and after that date.

---

[1] 1974 c.7.
[2] 1974 c.40.
[3] P.112 above.

[4] 1975 c.51.
[5] 1978 c.30.

(8) In this paragraph—

"approval" includes a provisional approval;

"grating" means a device in respect of which there is in force, immediately before the substitution date, an approval given for the purposes of the definition of "grating" in section 41(1) of the Salmon and Freshwater Fisheries Act 1975 as it had effect before that date;

"the substitution date" means the date on which paragraph 13 of Schedule 15 to this Act comes into force;

"the transfer date" means the date which, by virtue of section 56(1) of this Act, is the transfer date for the purposes of Part I of this Act as it applies in relation to the Agency.

## The Local Government Finance Act 1988

15. *This paragraph, which relates to Welsh National Park planning boards and National Park authorities, is not reproduced.*

## The Environmental Protection Act 1990

16. (1) Subject to sub-paragraph (2) below, if, at the transfer date, the content of the strategy required by section 44A of the Environmental Protection Act 1990[1] has not been finally determined, any plan or modification under section 50 of that Act, in its application to England and Wales, whose content has been finally determined before that date shall continue in force until the contents of the strategy are finally determined, notwithstanding the repeal by this Act of that section.

(2) If the strategy required by section 44A of that Act consists, or is to consist, of more than one statement sub-paragraph (1) above shall apply as if—

(*a*) references to the strategy were references to any such statement; and

(*b*) references to a plan or modification under section 50 of that Act were references to such plans or modifications as relate to the area covered, or to be covered, by that statement.

17. If, at the transfer date, the content of the strategy required by section 44B of that Act[2] has not been finally determined, any plan or modification under section 50 of that Act, in its application to Scotland, whose content has been finally determined before that date shall continue in force until the contents of the strategy are finally determined, notwithstanding the repeal by this Act of that section.

18. (1) This paragraph applies to—

(*a*) any resolution of a waste regulation authority under section 54 of that Act (special provision for land occupied by disposal authorities in Scotland);

(*b*) any resolution of a waste disposal authority having effect by virtue of subsection (16) of that section as if it were a resolution of a waste regulation authority under that section,

which is in force on the transfer date.

(2) A resolution to which this paragraph applies shall continue in force—

(*a*) where no application is made under section 36(1) of that Act for a waste management licence in respect of the site or mobile plant covered by the resolution, until the end of the period of 6 months commencing with the transfer date;

(*b*) where an application as mentioned in sub-paragraph (*a*) above is made, until—

(i)   the application is withdrawn;

(ii)  the application is rejected and no appeal against the rejection is timeously lodged under section 43 of that Act;

(iii) any appeal against a rejection of the application is withdrawn or rejected; or

(iv)  the application is granted.

(3) In relation to a resolution continued in force by sub-paragraph (2) above, the said section 54 shall have effect subject to the amendments set out in the following provisions of this paragraph.

(4) In subsection (2), for paragraph (*b*) there shall be substituted—

[1] P.134 above.    [2] P.136 above.

"(b) specified in a resolution passed by a waste regulation authority, or by a waste disposal authority under Part I of the Control of Pollution Act 1974, before the transfer date within the meaning of section 56(1) of the Environment Act 1995".

(5) In subsection (3) for paragraph (b) there shall be substituted—

"(b) by another person, that it is on land which is the subject of a resolution, that it is with the consent of the waste disposal authority and that any conditions to which such consent is subject are within the terms of the resolution."

(6) Subsections (4) to (7) shall cease to have effect.

(7) For subsections (8) and (9) there shall be substituted—

"(8) Subject to subsection (9) below, a resolution continued in force by paragraph 18 of Schedule 23 to the Environment Act 1995 may be varied or rescinded by SEPA by a resolution passed by it.

(9) Before passing a resolution under subsection (8) above varying a resolution, SEPA shall—

(a) prepare a statement of the variation which it proposes to make;

(b) refer that statement to the Health and Safety Executive and to the waste disposal authority in whose area the site is situated or, as the case may be, which is operating the plant; and

(c) consider any representations about the variation which the Health and Safety Executive or the waste disposal authority makes to it during the allowed period.

(9A) The period allowed to the Health and Safety Executive and the waste disposal authority for the making of representations under subsection (9)(c) above is the period of 28 days beginning with that on which the statement is received by that body, or such longer period as SEPA and that body agree in writing.

(9B) SEPA may—

(a) postpone the reference under subsection (9)(b) above so far as it considers that by reason of an emergency it is appropriate to do so;

(b) disregard the Health and Safety Executive in relation to a resolution which in SEPA's opinion will not affect the Health and Safety Executive."

(8) In subsection (10)—

(a) for the words "the authority which passed the resolution" and "the waste regulation authority" there shall be substituted the words "SEPA";

(b) the words "the waste disposal authority to discontinue the activities and of" shall cease to have effect.

(9) Subsections (11) to (15) shall cease to have effect.

## The Water Industry Act 1991

19. (1) Where, before the coming into force of the repeal by this Act of section 151 of the Water Industry Act 1991[1] (financial contributions to rural services), the Secretary of State has received an application from a relevant undertaker for a contribution under that section, he may, notwithstanding the coming into force of that repeal—

(a) give any such undertaking for any contribution sought by that application as he could have given under that section prior to the coming into force of that repeal;

(b) make any payments provided for in an undertaking given by virtue of this sub-paragraph.

(2) Notwithstanding the coming into force of the repeal by this Act of that section—

(a) the Secretary of State may make any payments provided for in an undertaking given by him under that section prior to the coming into force of that repeal;

(b) subsection (4) of that section (withholding and reduction of contributions) shall—

(i) continue to have effect in relation to contributions which the Secretary of State, before that repeal of that section, gave an undertaking under that section to make; and

(ii) have effect in relation to contributions which the Secretary of State has, by virtue of sub-paragraph (1) above, undertaken to make.

---

[1] 1991 c.56.

*The Water Resources Act 1991*

20. Notwithstanding any provision restricting the power of the Agency to grant a licence under Chapter II of Part II of the Water Resources Act 1991[1] (abstracting or impounding of water), or the power of the Secretary of State to direct the Agency to grant such a licence, the Agency may grant, and the Secretary of State may direct it to grant, such licences as are necessary to ensure that water may continue to be abstracted or impounded by or on behalf of the Crown in the manner in which, and to the extent to which,—

    (*a*) it may be so abstracted or impounded immediately before the coming into force of sub-paragraph (4) of paragraph 2 of Schedule 21 to this Act in relation to that Chapter, or

    (*b*) it has been so abstracted or impounded at any time in the period of five years immediately preceding the coming into force of that sub-paragraph in relation to that Chapter.

21. (1) This paragraph applies to any consent—

    (*a*) which was given under paragraph 2 of Schedule 10 to the Water Resources Act 1991 (discharge consents), as in force before the transfer date; and

    (*b*) which is in force immediately before that date.

    (2) On and after the transfer date, a consent to which this paragraph applies—

    (*a*) shall, for so long as it would have continued in force apart from this Act, have effect as a consent given under paragraph 3 of Schedule 10 to that Act, as substituted by this Act, subject to the same conditions as were attached to the consent immediately before the transfer date; and

    (*b*) shall—

        (i) during the period of six months beginning with the transfer date, not be limited to discharges by any particular person but extend to discharges made by any person; and

        (ii) after that period, extend, but be limited, to discharges made by any person who before the end of that period gives notice to the Agency that he proposes to rely on the consent after that period.

PART II: TRANSITORY PROVISIONS IN RESPECT OF FLOOD DEFENCE

**22.–24.** *Not reproduced.*

# SCHEDULE 24

## REPEALS AND REVOCATIONS

This schedule is not reproduced.

[1]  1991 c.57.

Part II

# Secondary Legislation

# The Surface Waters (Classification) Regulations 1989

S.I. 1989 No. 1148

The Secretary of State for the Environment and the Secretary of State for Wales, acting jointly in exercise of the powers conferred on them by section 104(1) of the Water Act 1989[1] hereby make the following Regulations:—

*Citation and commencement*

1. These Regulations may be cited as the Surface Waters (Classification) Regulations 1989 and shall come into force on 1st September 1989.

*Classification of waters*

2. The classifications prescribed by these Regulations apply only in relation to inland waters (including any lake or pond which, by virtue of an order made under section 103(5) of the Water Act 1989,[2] is to be treated as a relevant lake or pond).

..............................................................................................................................

3. The classifications DW1, DW2 and DW3 and the criteria for those classifications set out in the Schedule to these Regulations shall apply for classifying waters by reference to their suitability for abstraction by water undertakers for supply (after treatment) as drinking water.

## SCHEDULE

(Regulation 3)

*Criteria for the classification of waters*

The limits set out below are maxima

| (1)<br>No.<br>in Annex<br>II to<br>75/440/EEC | (2)<br>Parameters | | (3)<br>DW1 | (4)<br>DW2 | (5)<br>DW3 |
|---|---|---|---|---|---|
| 2 | Coloration (after simple filtration) | mg/1 Pt Scale | 20 | 100 | 200 |
| 4 | Temperature | °C | 25 | 25 | 25 |
| 7 | Nitrates | mg/1 $NO_3$ | 50 | 50 | 50 |
| 8(1) | Fluorides | mg/1 F | 1.5 | | |
| 10 | Dissolved iron | mg/1 Fe | 0.3 | 2 | |
| 12 | Copper | mg/1 Cu | 0.05 | | |

[1] This reference has effect as a reference to s.82(1) of the Water Resources Act 1991, p.271 above: Water Consolidation (Consequential Provisions) Act 1991 (c.60), s.2, sch.2, para.1.

[2] See the Controlled Waters (Lakes and Ponds) Order 1989, S.I. 1989/1149, below. This reference has effect as a reference to s.104(4) of the Water Resources Act 1991, p.291 above: Water Consolidation (Consequential Provisions) Act 1991 (c.60), s.2, sch.2, para.1.

| (1) | (2) | | (3) | (4) | (5) |
|---|---|---|---|---|---|
| 13 | Zinc | mg/1 Zn | 3 | 5 | 5 |
| 19 | Arsenic | mg/1 As | 0.05 | 0.05 | 0.1 |
| 20 | Cadmium | mg/1 Cd | 0.005 | 0.005 | 0.005 |
| 21 | Total chromium | mg/1 Cr | 0.05 | 0.05 | 0.05 |
| 22 | Lead | mg/1 Pb | 0.05 | 0.05 | 0.05 |
| 23 | Selenium | mg/1 Se | 0.01 | 0.01 | 0.01 |
| 24 | Mercury | mg/1 Hg | 0.001 | 0.001 | 0.001 |
| 25 | Barium | mg/1 Ba | 0.1 | 1 | 1 |
| 26 | Cyanide | mg/1 Cn | 0.05 | 0.05 | 0.05 |
| 27 | Sulphates | mg/1 $SO_4$ | 250 | 250 | 250 |
| 31 | Phenols (phenol index) paranitraniline 4 aminoantipyrine | mg/1 $C_6H_5OH$ | 0.001 | 0.005 | 0.1 |
| 32 | Dissolved or emulsified hydrocarbons (after extraction by petroleum ether) | mg/1 | 0.05 | 0.2 | 1 |
| 33 | Polycyclic aromatic hydrocarbons | mg/1 | 0.0002 | 0.0002 | 0.001 |
| 34 | Total pesticides (parathion, BHC, dieldrin) | mg/1 | 0.001 | 0.0025 | 0.005 |
| 39 | Ammonia | mg/1 $NH_4$ | | 1.5 | 4 |

*Note*
(1) The value given is an upper limit set in relation to the mean annual temperature (high and low).

## Explanatory Note

### (This note is not part of the Regulations)

These Regulations prescribe the system of classifying the quality of inland waters (as defined in section 103(1)(c) of the Water Act 1989[1]) according to their suitability for abstraction by water undertakers for supply (after treatment) as drinking water.

The classifications DW1, DW2 and DW3 reflect the mandatory values assigned by Annex II to Council Directive 75/440/EEC, (OJ No. L 194, 25.7.75, p.26) (concerning the quality required of surface water intended for the abstraction of drinking water) to the parameters listed in the Schedule to the Regulations.

The classifications are relevant for the purposes of setting water quality objectives for rivers, lakes and other inland waters under section 105 of the Act[2] and for ascertaining the treatment to which the water is to be subjected before it is supplied for public use, in accordance with Part VI of the Water Supply (Water Quality) Regulations 1989 (S.I. 1989/1147).

[1] This reference has effect as a reference to s.104(1)(c) of the Water Resources Act 1991, p.290 above: Water Consolidation (Consequential Provisions) Act 1991 (c.60), s.2, sch.2, para.1.

[2] This reference has effect as a reference to s.83 of the Water Resources Act 1991, p.272 above: Water Consolidation (Consequential Provisions) Act 1991 (c.60), s.2, sch.2, para.1.

# The Controlled Waters (Lakes and Ponds) Order 1989

S.I. 1989 No. 1149

---

The Secretary of State for the Environment, as respects England, and the Secretary of State for Wales, as respects Wales, in exercise of the powers conferred on them by section 103(5)(b) of the Water Act 1989[1] hereby make the following Order:

*Citation and commencement*

1. This Order may be cited as the Controlled Waters (Lakes and Ponds) Order 1989 and shall come into force on 1st September 1989.

*Reservoirs to be treated as relevant lakes or ponds*

2. (1) A reservoir to which this article applies shall be treated for the purposes of Chapter I of Part III of the Water Act 1989,[2] (control of pollution) as a relevant lake or pond.

   (2) This article applies to a reservoir–

   (a) which does not discharge into a relevant river or watercourse or into a relevant lake or pond;[3] and

   (b) which does not contain water treated with a view to complying with regulation 23 of the Water Supply (Water Quality) Regulations 1989.[4]

## Explanatory Note

### (This note is not part of the Regulations)

Chapter I of Part III of the Water Act 1989[5] (control of pollution) applies to waters of various classes including waters of certain reservoirs. This Order defines as waters to which Chapter I[5] applies other reservoirs except those which contain water that has been treated with a view to complying with regulation 23 of the Water Supply (Water Quality) Regulations 1989 (S.I. 1989/1147).

---

[1] This reference has effect as a reference to s.104(4)(b) of the Water Resources Act 1991, p.291 above: Water Consolidation (Consequential Provisions) Act 1991 (c.60), s.2, sch.2, para.1.

[2] This reference has effect as a reference to Part III of the Water Resources Act 1991, p.271 above: Water Consolidation (Consequential Provisions) Act 1991 s.2, sch.2, para.1.

[3] "Relevant river or watercourse" and "relevant lake or pond" defined by the Water Resources Act 1991, s.104(3), p.291 above.

[4] S.I. 1989/1147.

[5] This reference has effect as a reference to Part III of the Water Resources Act 1991, p.271 above: Water Consolidation (Consequential Provisions) Act 1991 (c.60), s.2, sch.2, para.1.

# The Trade Effluents (Prescribed Processes and Substances) Regulations 1989

S.I. 1989 No. 1156

*Note:* The legislation referred to in this instrument has been consolidated in the Water Industry Act 1991. For provisions relating to trade effluent, including special category effluent, see Part IV, Chapter III of the 1991 Act, p.247 above.

Under the Environment Act 1995 (c.25), s.2(2)(b), p.422 above, the functions of the Secretary of State in relation to special category effluent under that Chapter, other than any function of making regulations or orders under s.139 of the Water Industry Act 1991, were transferred to the Environment Agency on the transfer date, 1 April 1996.

The Secretary of State for the Environment, and the Secretary of State for Wales, acting jointly in exercise of the powers conferred on them by sections 74[1] and 185(2)[2] of the Water Act 1989, and of all other powers enabling them in that behalf, hereby make the following Regulations:–

*Citation and commencement*

1. These Regulations may be cited as the Trade Effluents (Prescribed Processes and Substances) Regulations 1989 and shall come into force on 1st September 1989.

*Interpretation*

2. In these Regulations–

"the 1989 Act" means the Water Act 1989;

"asbestos" means any of the fibrous silicates, namely, crocidolite, actinolite, anthophyllite, chrysotile, amosite and tremolite; and

"background concentration", in relation to any substance, means such concentration of the substance as would, but for anything done on the premises in question, be present in the effluent discharged from those premises; and without prejudice to the generality of the foregoing, includes such concentrations of the substance as are present–

(a) in water supplied to the premises;

(b) in water abstracted for use in the premises; and

(c) in precipitation onto the site within which the premises are situated.

*Trade effluent containing prescribed substances*

3. Section 74 of the 1989 Act[3] (control of exercise of trade effluent functions in certain cases) shall apply to trade effluent in which any of the substances listed in Schedule 1 to these Regulations is present in a concentration greater than the background concentration.

---

[1] The corresponding provision in the water consolidation legislation is s.138(1) of the Water Industry Act 1991, p.246 above.

[2] The corresponding provision in the water consolidation legislation is s.213(2) of the Water Industry Act 1991, p.254 above.

[3] The corresponding provision in the water consolidation legislation is s.138(1) of the Water Industry Act 1991, p.246 above.

*Trade effluent derived from prescribed processes*

**4.** Section 74 of the 1989 Act[1] shall apply to trade effluent deriving from a process of a description mentioned in Schedule 2 to these Regulations if either asbestos[2] or chloroform is present in that effluent in a concentration greater than the background concentration.[3]

*Variation of existing consents*

**5.** (1) A sewerage undertaker shall, in the circumstances referred to in paragraph (2), notify the Secretary of State of its proposal to vary, by direction under section 60(1) of the Public Health Act 1961, the conditions attached to a consent having effect as if given by the undertaker under the Public Health (Drainage of Trade Premises) Act 1937 (consent to the discharge of trade effluent into a public sewer) or to vary any agreement having effect as if entered into by the undertaker under section 7 of that Act (agreements for the reception and disposal of trade effluent).[4]

(2) The circumstances mentioned in paragraph (1) are that—

(a) the consent or agreement[5] has not been reviewed by the Secretary of State in accordance with paragraph 2 of Schedule 9 to the 1989 Act; and

(b) if the proposed variation were made, the consent or agreement would authorise the discharge of effluent containing a concentration of a substance referred to in Schedule 1 to these Regulations in excess of the background concentration[6] or deriving from a process of a description mentioned in Schedule 2 to these Regulations where either asbestos[7] or chloroform would be present in the effluent in a concentration greater than the background concentration.[8]

(3) A notification under paragraph (1) shall be treated as a reference to the Secretary of State under paragraph 1 of the said Schedule 9 of the question whether the relevant operations should be prohibited; and paragraphs 3 and 4 of that Schedule shall have effect accordingly.

(4) Where the undertaker has notified the Secretary of State in accordance with paragraph (1)—

(a) it shall inform the owner[9] or occupier of the trade premises[10] in question of that notification; and

(b) it shall not vary the consent or agreement before[11] the Secretary of State has given such a notice as is described in paragraph 3[12] of the said Schedule 9.

(5) The requirements imposed on a sewerage undertaker by this regulation shall be enforceable under section 20 of the 1989 Act[13] by the Secretary of State.

## SCHEDULE 1

(Regulation 3)

### PRESCRIBED SUBSTANCES

Mercury and its compounds
Cadmium and its compounds
gamma-Hexachlorocyclohexane
DDT

---

[1] The corresponding provision in the water consolidation legislation is s.138(1) of the Water Industry Act 1991, p.246 above.

[2] "Asbestos" defined by reg.2 above.

[3] "Background concentration" defined by reg.2 above.

[4] Words "or to vary ... effluent)" inserted by S.I. 1990/1629, reg.2(2). This amendment came into force on 31 August 1990: reg.1.

[5] Words "or agreement" in this paragraph inserted by S.I. 1990/1629, reg.2(3).

[6] "Background concentration" defined by reg.2 above.

[7] "Asbestos" defined by reg.2 above.

[8] Words "or deriving ... concentration" inserted by S.I.

1990/1629, reg.2(3).

[9] For the definition of "owner" in the Water Industry Act 1991 see s.219(1), p.259 above.

[10] For the definition of "trade premises" in the Water Industry Act 1991 see s.141(1), p.247 above.

[11] Words "or agreement before" substituted by S.I. 1990/1629, reg.2(4).

[12] Words "paragraph 3" substituted by S.I. 1990/1629, reg.2(4)

[13] The corresponding provision in the water consolidation legislation is at ss.18 and 19 of the Water Industry Act 1991.

Pentachlorophenol and its compounds[1]
Hexachlorobenzene
Hexachlorobutadiene
Aldrin
Dieldrin
Endrin
Carbon Tetrachloride
Polychlorinated Biphenyls
Dichlorvos
1, 2-Dichloroethane
Trichlorobenzene
Atrazine
Simazine
Tributyltin compounds
Triphenyltin compounds
Trifluralin
Fenitrothion
Azinphos-methyl
Malathion
Endosulfan

# SCHEDULE 2

(Regulation 4)

## PRESCRIBED PROCESSES

### *Description of process*

Any process for the production of chlorinated organic chemicals

Any process for the manufacture of paper pulp

[2]

Any process for the manufacture of asbestos cement

Any process for the manufacture of asbestos paper or board

Any industrial process involving the use in any 12 month period of more than 100 kilograms of the product resulting from the crushing of asbestos ore.[3]

*The explanatory note is not reproduced.*

---

[1] Words "and its compounds" inserted by S.I. 1990/1629, reg.2(5).
[2] Former words "Any industrial process in which cooling waters or effluents are chlorinated" revoked by S.I. 1990/1629, reg.2(6)(a).
[3] Words "Any industrial process . . . asbestos ore" added by S.I. 1990/1629, reg.2(6)(b).

# The Control of Pollution (Radioactive Waste) Regulations 1989

## S.I. 1989 No. 1158

The Secretary of State for the Environment, as respects England, and the Secretary of State for Wales, in exercise of the powers conferred on them by section 123 of the Water Act 1989[1] and of all other powers enabling them in that behalf, hereby make the following Regulations:–

*Citation and commencement*

1. These Regulations may be cited as the Control of Pollution (Radioactive Waste) Regulations 1989 and shall come into force on 1st September 1989.

*Interpretation*

2. In these Regulations–

"the 1989 Act" means the Radioactive Substances Act 1960;[2]

"the 1989 Act" means the Water Act 1989;[3] and

"radioactive waste" has the same meaning as in the 1960 Act.[4]

*Certain provisions of the 1989 Act to apply to radioactive waste*

3. The provisions of Chapter I of Part III of the 1989 Act specified in the Schedule to these Regulations[5] shall have effect, without modification, in relation to any radioactive waste as they have effect in relation to any effluent or other matter or substance which is not radioactive waste.

*Modification of the 1960 Act*

4. Section 9(1) of the 1960 Act[6] (no account to be taken of radioactivity for the purposes of powers, duties and enforcement of other enactments) shall apply in relation to the provisions specified in the Schedule to these Regulations.[7]

---

[1] This reference has effect as a reference to s.98 of the Water Resources Act 1991, p.289 above: Water Consolidation (Consequential Provisions) Act 1991 (c.60), s.2, sch.2, para.1. See also the definition of "prescribed" in s.221(1) of the Water Resources Act 1991, p.314 above.

[2] The Radioactive Substances Act 1993 consolidates the 1960 Act and other enactments.

[3] The 1989 Act has largely been consolidated in the water consolidation legislation of 1991; the provisions of the 1989 Act referred to in this instrument are consolidated in Part III of the Water Resources Act 1991.

[4] "Radioactive waste" is defined by s.2 of the Radioactive Substances Act 1993, p.384 above.

[5] The annotations in the schedule refer to the main corresponding provisions in the Water Resources Act 1991; see note 1, page 546 below.

[6] The corresponding provision in the Radioactive Substances Act 1993 is s.40(1), p.404 above.

[7] The remainder of this regulation, which amended the 1960 Act, was revoked, subject to savings, by the Water Consolidation (Consequential Provisions) Act 1991 (c.60), s.3, sch.3, part II. This amendment came into force on 1 December 1991: s.4(2).

# SCHEDULE

(Regulation 3)

| Provisions of Chapter I of Part III of the 1989 Act applied[1] | Subject matter of provisions |
|---|---|
| Section 104[2] | Classification of quality of waters |
| Section 106[3] | General duties to achieve and maintain objectives etc. |
| Section 107[4] | Offences of polluting controlled waters etc. |
| Section 110[5] | Requirements to take precautions against pollution |
| Section 113[6] | Consents under Chapter I and application to the Authority |
| Section 115[7] | Anti-pollution works and operations |
| Section 117[8] | Registers for the purposes of Chapter I |
| Section 118[9] | Information and assistance |
| Section 119[10] | Exchange of information with respect to pollution incidents etc. |
| Section 120[11] | Local inquiries for the purposes of Chapter I |

*Explanatory note*
*(This note is not part of the Regulations)*

The provisions of Chapter I of Part III of the Water Act 1989[12] (which relate to the pollution of water) do not apply in relation to radioactive waste within the meaning of the Radioactive Substances Act 1960;[13] but the Secretary of State may by regulations provide for any of those provisions to apply and may make consequential modifications of the 1960 Act.

These Regulations bring radioactive waste within the scope of those provisions of Chapter I of Part III of the 1989 Act which are specified in the Schedule to the Regulations, but in such a manner that no account will be taken of the radioactive properties of such waste, which will remain subject to control under the 1960 Act.[14]

[1] The annotations in this schedule set out the main corresponding provisions in the Water Resources Act 1991. Note that certain sections do not correspond exactly and for the complete references to the provisions in the consolidation legislation reference should be made to the legislation.

[2] See s.82 of the Water Resources Act 1991, p.271 above.

[3] See s. 84 of the Water Resources Act 1991, p.273 above.

[4] See ss.85, 86, 87(1) of the Water Resources Act 1991, p.273 above.

[5] See s. 92 of the Water Resources Act 1991, p.284 above.

[6] See ss.88(2) and 99 of the Water Resources Act 1991, p.276 and 289 above.

[7] See s.161 of the Water Resources Act 1991, p.292 above.

[8] See s.190 of the Water Resources Act 1991, p.298 above.

[9] See s.202 of the Water Resources Act 1991, p.303 above.

[10] See s.203 of the Water Resources Act 1991, p.303 above.

[11] See s.213(2), (3) of the Water Resources Act 1991, relating to local inquiries is repealed by the Environment Act 1995. For provisions relating to inquiries in the 1995 Act see s.53, p.460 above.

[12] The corresponding provisions in the Water Resources Act 1991 are in Part III, p.271 above.

[13] The Radioactive Substances Act 1993 consolidates the 1960 Act and other enactments.

[14] The final paragraph of this note relates mainly to the revoked part of reg.4 and is not reproduced.

# The Sludge (Use in Agriculture) Regulations 1989

## S.I. 1989 No. 1263

The Secretary of State for the Environment, as respects England, and the Secretary of State for Wales as respects Wales and the Secretary of State for Scotland as respects Scotland, in exercise of the powers conferred on them by section 2(2) of the European Communities Act 1972,[1] and being the Ministers designated[2] for the purposes of that subsection in relation to the regulation and control of the use of sludge in agriculture, hereby make the following Regulations:

*Citation, commencement and application*

1. (1) These Regulations may be cited as the Sludge (Use in Agriculture) Regulations 1989, and shall come into force on 1st September 1989.

   (2) *Omitted by S.I. 1990/880, reg.2(2). This amendment came into force on 8 May 1990: reg.1.*

*Interpretation*

2. (1) In these Regulations–

   "agriculture" means the growing of all types of commercial food crops, including for stock-rearing purposes, and cognate words shall be construed accordingly;

   "agricultural unit" means an area of agricultural land used for a single agricultural purpose, not exceeding 5 hectares;

   "dedicated site" means an area of agricultural land which on 17th June 1986 was dedicated to the disposal of sludge but on which commercial food crops were being grown exclusively for animal consumption;

   "the operative date" means 1st September 1989;

   "sludge" means residual sludge from sewage plants treating domestic or urban waste waters and from other sewage plants treating waste waters of a composition similar to domestic and urban waste waters;

   "septic tank sludge" means residual sludge from septic tanks and other similar installations for the treatment of sewage;

   "sludge producer" means any person who manages a plant at which sludge is produced for disposal;

   "the sludge table" means the table set out in Schedule 1;

   "the soil table" means the table set out in Schedule 2;

   "treated sludge" means sludge or septic tank sludge which has undergone biological, chemical or heat treatment, long-term storage or any other appropriate process so as significantly to reduce its fermentability and the health hazards resulting from its use, and "untreated sludge" shall be construed accordingly; and

   "use" means spreading on the soil or any other application on or in the soil, and "used" shall be construed accordingly.

   (2) In these Regulations, references to a numbered regulation or Schedule are references to the regulation or Schedule bearing that number in these Regulations.

*Prohibition on use or supply of sludge*

3. (1) No person shall cause or knowingly permit sludge[3] to be used[4] on agricultural land unless the following requirements are fulfilled; and no person shall supply sludge for use on agricultural[5]

---

[1] 1972 c.68.
[2] S.I. 1988/785.
[3] "Sludge" defined by reg.2(1) above.

[4] "Used" defined by reg.2(1) above.
[5] "Agricultural" defined by reg.2(1) above.

land if he knows or has reason to believe that the requirements of paragraph (6) below will not be fulfilled when the sludge is so used, or that the precautions set out in regulation 4 will not be observed after such use.

(2)  The sludge shall be tested in accordance with Schedule 1.[1]

(3)  The soil on the land shall be tested or assessed in accordance with Schedule 2.[2]

(4)  Unless the land is a dedicated site:[3]

(a)  the average annual rate of addition to the land by means of the sludge of any of the elements listed in column (1) of the sludge table[4] shall not exceed the limit (in kilograms per hectare per year) specified in column (2) thereof; and

(b)  the concentration in the soil of any of the elements listed in column (1) of the soil table[5] shall not exceed the limit specified in column (2) thereof; and where that limit is not exceeded at the time of the use, it shall not be exceeded by reason of the use.

(5)  The pH value of the soil shall not be less than 5.

(6)  No fruit or vegetable crops, other than fruit trees, shall be growing or being harvested in the soil at the time of the use.

(7)  The sludge shall be used in such a way that account is taken of the nutrient needs of the plants and that the quality of the soil and of the surface and ground water is not impaired.

*Precautions to be taken after sludge is used*

**4.** (1)  Where any sludge[6] or septic tank sludge[7] has been used on agricultural[8] land, no person shall cause or knowingly permit the activities specified in column (1) of the Table below to be carried out on that land before the expiry of the period specified in column (2) thereof.

TABLE

| (1) Activity | (2) Period |
| --- | --- |
| Grazing animals or harvesting forage crops | Three weeks commencing on the date of the use |
| Harvesting fruit and vegetable crops which are grown in direct contact with the soil and normally eaten raw | Ten months commencing on the date of the use |

(2)  Where any untreated sludge[9] has been used on agricultural land[10] without being injected into the soil, the occupier of the land affected shall, as soon as reasonably practicable thereafter, cause such sludge to be worked into the soil of the land affected.

*Information to be supplied to sludge producer*

**5.**  Where sludge[11] has been used on any agricultural land,[12] other than by or on behalf of the sludge producer,[13] the occupier of that land shall forthwith provide the following information to the sludge producer:–

(a)  the address and area of the agricultural unit[14] concerned;

---

[1] P.550 below.
[2] P.551 below.
[3] "Dedicated site" defined by reg.2(1) above.
[4] "The sludge table" means the table set out in sch.1, p.551 below: reg.2(1) above.
[5] "The soil table" means the table set out in sch.2, p.552 below: reg.2(1) above.
[6] "Sludge" defined by reg.2(1) above.
[7] "Septic tank sludge" defined by reg.2(1) above.
[8] "Agricultural" defined by reg.2(1) above.
[9] For "untreated sludge" see definition of "treated

sludge" in reg.2(1) above.
[10] Words "on agricultural land" substituted by S.I. 1990/880, reg.2(3). This amendment came into force on 8 May 1990: reg.1.
[11] "Sludge" defined by reg.2(1), p.547 above.
[12] "Agricultural" defined by reg.2(1) above; words "on agricultural land" substituted by S.I. 1990/880, reg.2(4). This amendment came into force on 8 May 1990: reg.1.
[13] "Sludge producer" defined by reg.2(1), p.547 above.
[14] "Agricultural unit" defined by reg.2(1), p.547 above.

(b) the date on which the sludge was used;

(c) the quantity of sludge so used; and

(d) where the occupier has used sludge not supplied by the sludge producer, the name and address of the person who supplied that sludge, and the quantity of sludge so used which was supplied by that person.

### Register to be kept by sludge producer

**6.** (1) Every sludge producer[1] shall prepare and maintain a register containing the following particulars:–

(a) the total quantity of sludge[2] produced in any year;

(b) in relation to sludge supplied for the purpose of use in agriculture[3] in any year:–

(i) the total quantity of sludge supplied;

(ii) the composition and properties of that sludge as determined in accordance with Schedule 1;[4]

(iii) the quantities of treated sludge[5] supplied, and the type of treatment;

(iv) the names and addresses of the persons to whom the sludge was supplied; and

(v) the address and area of each agricultural unit[6] on which sludge has been used, the quantity of sludge used thereon, and the amount of each of the elements listed in the sludge table[7] which have been added thereto;

(c) a copy of every analysis or assessment made under Schedule 2,[8] or in accordance with advice given for the purposes of regulation 8(4),[9] relating to the soil of an agricultural unit on which sludge has been used; and

(d) a copy of any advice issued for the purposes of regulation 8(3)(a).[10]

(2) In this regulation "year" means the period from the operative date to December 31st 1989, and thereafter the period of twelve months commencing on January 1st.

### Supply of information about sludge

**7.** (1) A sludge producer[11] shall make the register maintained under regulation 6 available for inspection by the Environment Agency[12] or, in Scotland, the Scottish Environment Protection Agency[13] at all reasonable times; and shall furnish the Environment Agency or, in Scotland, the Scottish Environment Protection Agency with such information or facilities as it[14] may reasonably require relating to (or to verifying the information contained in) the register or otherwise relating to sludge[15] supplied by the sludge producer, including facilities for analysis of representative samples of sludge or soil.

(2) As soon as reasonably practicable after testing sludge in accordance with Schedule 1,[16] the sludge producer shall provide details of the analysis made under that Schedule to all persons to whom the sludge producer supplies sludge.

[1] "Sludge producer" defined by reg.2(1), p.547 above.
[2] "Sludge" defined by reg.2(1), p.547 above.
[3] "Agriculture" defined by reg.2(1), p.547 above.
[4] P.550 below.
[5] "Treated sludge" defined by reg.2(1), p.547 above.
[6] "Agricultural unit" defined by reg.2(1), p.547 above.
[7] "The sludge table" means the table set out in sch.1, p.551 below: reg.2(1) above.
[8] P.551 below.
[9] Words "regulation 8(4)" substituted by S.I. 1990/880, reg.2(5)(a). This amendment came into force on 8 May 1990: reg.1.
[10] Words "regulation 8(3)(a)" substituted by S.I. 1990/880, reg.2(5)(b).
[11] "Sludge producer" defined by reg.2(1), p.547 above.

[12] The Environment Agency is established by s.1 of the Environment Act 1995, p.420 above. Words "the Environment Agency" in this regulation substituted by S.I. 1996/593, reg.3, sch.2, para.5(2)(a). This amendment came into force on 1 April 1996: reg.1.
[13] The Scottish Environment Protection Agency, SEPA, is established by s.20 of the Environment Act 1995, p.438 above. Words "or, in Scotland, the Scottish Environment Protection Agency" in this regulation substituted by S.I. 1996/973, reg.2, sch., para.9(2). This amendment came into force on 1 April 1996: reg.1.
[14] Word "it" substituted by S.I. 1996/593, reg.3, sch.2, para.5(2)(b).
[15] "Sludge" defined by reg.2(1), p.547 above.
[16] P.550 below.

*Dedicated sites*

**8.** (1) In this regulation–

"occupier" means the occupier of a dedicated site;[1]

"the actual concentration" means the concentration of any of the substances listed in column (1) of the soil table[2] in the soil of an agricultural unit[3] forming part of a dedicated site; and

"the permitted concentration" means the concentration in milligrams per kilogram of dry matter specified for that substance in column (2) of that Table.[4]

(2) Every sludge producer[5] shall notify the Environment Agency[6] or, in Scotland, the Scottish Environment Protection Agency[7] in writing as soon as may be after the operative date[8] of the address and area of every dedicated site to which he supplies sludge.[9]

(3) Where the actual concentration exceeds the permitted concentration, the occupier shall not:–

(a) sell or offer for sale any crop grown on the agricultural unit affected except in accordance with the advice referred to in paragraph (4) below; or

(b) grow any commercial food crops on that unit other than crops intended for animal consumption.[10]

(4) Where the actual concentration exceeds (or if sludge were used would exceed) the permitted concentration, the occupier shall not use sludge on the agricultural unit;[11]

except in accordance with advice in writing from:–

(i) in England, the Minister of Agriculture Fisheries and Food;

(ii) in Wales, the Secretary of State for Wales; or

(iii) in Scotland, the Secretary of State for Scotland.

*Penalties*

**9.** Any person who contravenes any of the foregoing regulations shall be guilty of an offence, and liable on summary conviction to a fine not exceeding level 5 on the standard scale.[12]

# SCHEDULE 1

(Regulation 3)

## TESTING OF SLUDGE

**1.** Every sludge producer[13] shall ensure that sludge[14] produced by him and supplied for the purpose of use in agriculture[15] is tested in accordance with this Schedule as soon as reasonably practicable after the operative date,[16] and thereafter at intervals of not more than

[1] "Dedicated site" defined by reg.2(1) above.
[2] "The soil table" means the table set out in sch.2, p.552 below: reg.2(1) above.
[3] "Agricultural unit" defined by reg.2(1), p.547 above.
[4] Para.1 substituted by S.I. 1990/880, reg.2(6)(a). This amendment came into force on 8 May 1990: reg.1.
[5] "Sludge producer" defined by reg.2(1), p.547 above.
[6] The Environment Agency is established by s.1 of the Environment Act 1995, p.420 above. Words "the Environment Agency" substituted by S.I. 1996/593, reg.3, sch.2, para.5(3). This amendment came into force on 1 April 1996: reg.1.
[7] The Scottish Environment Protection Agency, SEPA, is established by s.20 of the Environment Act 1995, p.438 above. Words "or, in Scotland, the Scottish Environment Protection Agency" substituted by S.I. 1996/973, reg.2, sch., para.9(3). This amendment came into force on 1 April 1996:

reg.1.
[8] "The operative date" means 1st September 1989: reg.2(1) above.
[9] "Sludge" defined by reg.2(1), p.547 above.
[10] Para.3 substituted by S.I. 1990/880, reg.2(6)(b). This amendment came into force on 8 May 1990: reg.1.
[11] Words "Where the actual concentration . . . the agricultural unit" substituted by S.I. 1990/880, reg.2(6)(c).
[12] The current fine at level 5 on the standard scale is £5,000: Criminal Justice Act 1991 (c.53), s.17 (England and Wales); Criminal Procedure (Scotland) Act 1995 (c.46), s.225 (Scotland).
[13] "Sludge producer" defined by reg.2(1), p.547 above.
[14] "Sludge" defined by reg.2(1), p.547 above.
[15] "Agriculture" defined by reg.2(1), p.547 above.
[16] "The operative date" means 1st September 1989: reg.2(1) above.

six months, and in any event where changes occur in the characteristics of the waste water being treated.

2. Representative samples of sludge intended to be used on agricultural[1] land shall be taken after processing, but before delivery to the user.

3. Each sample shall be analysed so as to determine–

(a) the pH value thereof;

(b) the percentage content of dry matter, organic matter, nitrogen and phosphorus; and

(c) the concentration in milligrams per kilogram of dry matter of:

(i) chromium;

(ii) the elements listed in column 1 of the sludge table below.

4. The average annual rate of addition referred to in regulation 3(4)[2] shall be ascertained for each of the elements in the sludge table by taking the average amount of that element in the sludge used on that land in the period of ten years ending on the date of such use.

SLUDGE TABLE

| (1) Element | (2) Kilograms per hectare per year | (3) Limit of detection (mg/kg of dry matter) |
| --- | --- | --- |
| Zinc | 15 | 50 |
| Copper | 7.5 | 25 |
| Nickel | 3 | 10 |
| Cadmium | 0.15 | 1 |
| Lead | 15 | 25 |
| Mercury | 0.1 | 0.1 |

5. The analysis requisite to ascertain the concentration of metals referred to in paragraph 3(c) above shall be carried out following strong acid digestion; the reference method of analysis shall be that of atomic absorption spectrometry, and the limit of detection for each metal shall not exceed the appropriate limit value specified in column (3) of the sludge table or, in the case of chromium, 25 milligrams per kilogram of dry matter.

# SCHEDULE 2

(Regulation 3)

## TESTING OF AGRICULTURAL SOIL

1. The sludge producer[3] shall ensure that agricultural[4] soil is tested or assessed in accordance with this Schedule.

2. (1) Where–

(a) sludge[5] has been used on an agricultural unit[6] before the operative date;[7] and

(b) adequate scientific evidence is available as to the characteristics of the soil thereof, and the sludge used thereon, before that date;

an assessment shall be made as soon as possible after the operative date of the pH value of the soil as at that date, and the probable concentrations in the soil as at that date of–

[1] "Agricultural" defined by reg.2(1), p.547 above.
[2] P.548 above.
[3] "Sludge producer" defined by reg.2(1), p.547 above.
[4] "Agricultural" defined by reg.2(1), p.547 above.

[5] "Sludge" defined by reg.2(1), p.547 above.
[6] "Agricultural unit" defined by reg.2(1), p.547 above.
[7] "The operative date" means 1st September 1989: reg.2(1) above.

(i) chromium;

(ii) the elements listed in column 1 of the soil table;

and the soil shall be tested not later than 31st December 1991.

(2) Subject to paragraph (1) above, the soil of agricultural land shall be tested–

(a) where sludge is to be used on that land for the first time after the operative date;

(b) as soon as may be after the twentieth anniversary of the date when the soil was last tested in accordance with this Schedule; or

(c) where the sludge producer is so requested in writing by the occupier of the land or by the Environment Agency[1] or, in Scotland, the Scottish Environment Protection Agency,[2] and not less than five years have elapsed since the soil was last tested in accordance with this Schedule.

3. For each agricultural unit on which sludge is to be used, a representative sample of soil shall be obtained by mixing together 25 separate core samples, each taken to the depth of the soil or 25 centimetres, whichever is the lesser depth.

4. Each representative sample shall be analysed so as to ascertain–

(a) the pH value of the sample;

(b) the concentration in that sample of the following metals–

(i) chromium;

(ii) the elements set out in the soil table below.

5. For the purposes of regulation 3(4),[3] the specified limit of concentration of elements in any representative sample, expressed in milligrams per kilogram of dry matter, is set out in the soil table below.

SOIL TABLE

| (1) Element | (2) Limit According to pH of soil | | | |
|---|---|---|---|---|
| | 5.0 < 5.5 | 5.5 < 6.0 | 6.0–7.0 | > 7.0 |
| Zinc | 200 | 250 | 300 | 450 |
| Copper | 80 | 100 | 135 | 200 |
| Nickel | 50 | 60 | 75 | 110 |
| | For pH 5.0 and above | | | |
| Lead | 300 | | | |
| Cadmium | 3 | | | |
| Mercury | 1 | | | |

6. The analysis requisite to ascertain the concentration of metals referred to in paragraph 4(b) above shall be carried out following strong acid digestion; the reference method of analysis shall be that of atomic absorption spectrometry, and the limit of detection for each metal shall not exceed 10% of the appropriate limit value specified in the soil table or, in the case of chromium, 25 milligrams per kilogram of dry matter.

### Explanatory Note
### (This note is not part of the Regulations)

These Regulations implement Council Directive No. 86/278/EEC (OJ No. L181/6) on the protection of the environment, and in particular of the soil, when sewage sludge is used in agriculture.

[1] The Environment Agency is established by s.1 of the Environment Act 1995, p.420 above. Words "the Environment Agency" substituted by S.I. 1996/593, reg.3, sch.2, para.5(4). This amendment came into force on 1 April 1996: reg.1.
[2] The Scottish Environment Protection Agency, SEPA, is established by s.20 of the Environment Act 1995, p.438 above. Words "or, in Scotland, the Scottish Environment Protection Agency" substituted by S.I. 1996/973, reg.2, sch., para.9(4). This amendment came into force on 1 April 1996: reg.1.
[3] P.548 above.

Regulation 3 prohibits sludge from sewage plants from being used in agriculture unless specified requirements are fulfilled. They include the testing of the sludge and the soil (Schedules 1 and 2).

Regulation 4 specifies precautions which must be taken after sludge from sewage plants or septic tanks is used on agricultural land.

Regulation 5 requires the occupier of land on which sludge has been used to provide the sludge producer with information about the land and the sludge used.

Regulations 6 and 7 require every sludge producer to maintain a register of the quantities of sludge produced and supplied for use in agriculture, including details of the amount of sludge used on each agricultural unit and the results of analysis of the sludge and the soil. The register is to be available to the Secretary of State[1] for inspection, together with such information or facilities as he may reasonably require, including facilities for analysing the sludge or soil. The sludge producer is required to provide persons he supplies with the results of analysis of the sludge.

Regulation 8 makes special provision for dedicated sites, which on 17th June 1986 (the date of notification of the Directive) were dedicated to the disposal of sludge but on which commercial food crops were being grown exclusively for animal consumption.

Regulation 9 provides an offence of contravening the Regulations, which carries a maximum fine on summary conviction of level 5 on the standard scale.

---

[1] This function of the Secretary of State has been transferred to the Environment Agency or, in Scotland, the Scottish Environment Protection Agency.

# The Surface Waters (Dangerous Substances) (Classification) Regulations 1989

S.I. 1989 No. 2286

The Secretary of State for the Environment and the Secretary of State for Wales, acting jointly in exercise of the powers conferred on them by sections 104[1] and 171[2] of the Water Act 1989 hereby make the following Regulations:

*Citation, commencement and interpretation*

1. (1) These Regulations may be cited as the Surface Waters (Dangerous Substances) (Classification) Regulations 1989 and shall come into force on 1st January 1990.

(2) In these Regulations "the Act" means the Water Act 1989,[3] and references to inland waters and relevant territorial waters include, respectively, references to waters which are, by virtue of an order under section 103(5) of the Act,[4] to be treated as a relevant lake or pond and to waters which are, by virtue of such an order, to be treated as relevant territorial waters.[5]

*Classification of waters*

2. (1) A system employing the classification DS1 is prescribed as a system of classification applying to inland waters additional to the system prescribed by the Surface Waters (Classification) Regulations 1989.[6]

(2) A system employing the classification DS2 is prescribed as a system of classification applying to coastal waters[7] and relevant territorial waters.

3. (1) The criterion for classification DS1 is that the annual mean concentrations of the substances listed in column (1) of Schedule 1 hereto do not exceed the concentrations specified in column (2) of that Schedule.

(2) The criterion for classification DS2 is that the annual mean concentrations of the substances listed in column (1) of Schedule 2 hereto do not exceed the concentrations specified in column (2) of that Schedule.

*Modification of section 105 of the Water Act 1989*

4. For the purpose of complying with Community obligations, section 105(4) and (5) of the Act[8] shall not apply to the initial establishment of water quality objectives so far as they involve the specification of a classification prescribed by these Regulations.

---

[1] This reference has effect as a reference to s.82 of the Water Resources Act 1991, p.271 above: Water Consolidation (Consequential Provisions) Act 1991 (c.60), s.2, sch.2, para.1.

[2] This reference has effect as a reference to s.102 of the Water Resources Act 1991, p.290 above: Water Consolidation (Consequential Provisions) Act 1991 (c.60), s.2, sch.2, para.1.

[3] This reference has effect as a reference to the Water Resources Act 1991: Water Consolidation (Consequential Provisions) Act 1991 (c.60), s.2, sch.2, para.1.

[4] This reference has effect as a reference to s.104(4) of the Water Resources Act 1991: Water Consolidation (Consequential Provisions) Act 1991 (c.60), s.2, sch.2, para.1; see the Controlled Waters (Lakes and Ponds) Order 1989, S.I. 1989/1149, p.541 above.

[5] "Inland freshwaters", "relevant territorial waters" and "relevant lake or pond" are defined in s.104, p.290 above.

[6] S.I. 1989/1148, p.539 above.

[7] "Coastal waters" defined in s.104(1), p.290 above.

[8] This reference has effect as a reference to ss.83(4) and (5) of the Water Resources Act 1991, p.272 above: Water Consolidation (Consequential Provisions) Act 1991 (c.60), s.2, sch.2, para.1.

# SCHEDULE 1

(Regulation 3(1))

## CLASSIFICATION OF INLAND WATERS (DS1)

| (1)<br>Substance | (2)<br>Concentration in<br>microgrammes per litre<br>(annual mean) |
|---|---|
| Aldrin, Dieldrin, Endrin and<br>  Isodrin | (i) 0.03 for the four substances in total;<br>(ii) 0.005 for endrin |
| Cadmium and its compounds | 5 (total cadmium: both soluble and insoluble forms) |
| Carbon tetrachloride | 12 |
| Chloroform | 12 |
| DDT (all isomers) | 0.025 |
| para-para-DDT | 0.01 |
| Hexachlorobenzene | 0.03 |
| Hexachlorobutadiene | 0.1 |
| Hexachlorocyclohexane<br>(all isomers) | 0.1 |
| Mercury and its compounds | 1 (total mercury: both soluble and insoluble forms) |
| Pentachlorophenol and its<br>  compounds | 2 |

# SCHEDULE 2

(Regulation 3(2))

## CLASSIFICATION OF COASTAL WATERS AND RELEVANT TERRITORIAL WATERS (DS2)

| (1)<br>Substance | (2)<br>Concentration in<br>microgrammes per litre<br>(annual mean) |
|---|---|
| Aldrin, Dieldrin, Endrin and<br>  Isodrin | (i) 0.03 for the four substances in total;<br>(ii) 0.005 for endrin |
| Cadmium and its compounds | 2.5 (dissolved cadmium) |
| Carbon tetrachloride | 12 |
| Chloroform | 12 |
| DDT (all isomers) | 0.025 |
| para-para-DDT | 0.01 |
| Hexachlorobenzene | 0.03 |
| Hexachlorobutadiene | 0.1 |
| Hexachlorocyclohexane<br>(all isomers) | 0.02 |
| Mercury and its compounds | 0.3 (dissolved mercury) |
| Pentachlorophenol and its<br>  compounds | 2 |

*Explanatory Note*
*(This note is not part of the Regulations)*

These Regulations prescribe the system of classifying the quality of inland waters, coastal waters and relevant terri-torial waters (as defined in section 103(1)(c) of the Water Act 1989[1]) according to the presence in them of concen-trations of the dangerous substances listed in the Schedules to the Regulations.

With two exceptions, the classifications DS1 (in relation to inland waters) and DS2 (in relation to coastal waters and relevant territorial waters) reflect the quality objectives specified in Annex II to Council Directive 82/176/EEC (OJ NO. L81, 27.3.82, p.29) (mercury and its compounds), Annex II to Council Directive 83/513/EEC (OJ No. L291, 24.10.83, p.1) (cadmium and its compounds), Annex II to Council Directive 84/156/EEC (OJ No. L74, 17.3.84, p.49) (mercury and its compounds), Annex II to Council Directive 84/491/EEC (OJ No. L274, 17.10.84, p.11) (hexachloro-cyclohexane), Annex II to Council Directive 86/280/EEC (OJ No. L181, 4.7.85, p.16) (carbon tetrachloride, DDT and pentachlorophenol) and Council Directive 88/347/EEC (OJ No. L158, 25.6.88, p.35) which amends the 1986 Directive by adding quality objectives for aldrin, dieldrin, endrin and isodrin, hexachlorobenzene, hexachlorobuta-diene and chloroform. The exceptions relate to the quality objectives for concentrations of cadmium and mercury in classification DS2. The Directive specifies an annual mean of not more than 5 and 0.5 microgrammes per litre for cadmium and mercury respectively in esturial waters but the classification DS2 (which applies to esturial waters) specifies a more stringent annual mean of not more than 2.5 and 0.3 microgrammes per litre.

The classifications are relevant for the purposes of setting water quality objectives for inland waters, coastal waters and relevant territorial waters under section 105 of the Water Act 1989.[2] Regulation 4 modifies that section for the purpose of complying with Community obligations arising by virtue of Council Directive 76/464/EEC by relieving the Secretary of State of the requirements to give at least three months' notice before establishing initial water qual-ity objectives giving effect to that and other Directives relating to discharges of dangerous substances, and to con-sider representations or objections to his proposals to establish those objectives.

---

[1] This reference has effect as a reference to s.104(1)(c) of the Water Resources Act 1991, p.290 above: Water Con-solidation (Consequential Provisions) Act 1991 (c.60), s.2, sch.2, para.1.

[2] This reference has effect as a reference to s.83 of the Water Resources Act 1991, p.272 above: Water Consolida-tion (Consequential Provisions) Act 1991 (c.60), s.2, sch.2, para.1.

# The Controlled Waters (Lochs and Ponds (Scotland) Order 1990

S.I. 1990 No. 120 (S.12)

The Secretary of State, in exercise of the powers conferred on him by section 30A(5)(b) and (6)(b) of the Control of Pollution Act 1974,[1] hereby makes the following Order:

*Citation and commencement*

1. This Order may be cited as the Controlled Waters (Lochs and Ponds) (Scotland) Order 1990 and shall come into force on 1st May 1990.

*Reservoirs to be treated as relevant lochs or ponds*

2. (1) A reservoir to which this article applies shall be treated for the purposes of Part II of the Control of Pollution Act 1974[2] as a relevant loch or pond.

(2) This article applies to a reservoir–

(a) which does not discharge into a relevant river or watercourse or into a relevant loch or pond;[3] and

(b) which does not contain water treated with a view to complying with regulation 23 of the Water Supply (Water Quality) (Scotland) Regulations 1990.[4]

## *Explanatory Note*
### *(This note is not part of the Regulations)*

Part II of the Control of Pollution Act 1974, which makes provision on water quality and control of discharges to water, applies to waters of various classes including waters of certain reservoirs. This Order defines as waters to which Part II applies other reservoirs except those which contain water that has been treated with a view to complying with regulation 23 of the Water Supply (Water Quality) (Scotland) Regulations 1990 (S.I. 1990/119).

[1] P.19 above.
[2] P.18 above.

[3] "Relevant river or watercourse" and "relevant loch or pond" are defined in s.30A(4), p.19 above.
[4] S.I. 1990/119.

# The Surface Waters (Classification) (Scotland) Regulations 1990

S.I. 1990 No. 121 (S.13)

The Secretary of State, in exercise of the powers conferred on him by section 30B of the Control of Pollution Act 1974,[1] hereby makes the following Regulations:

*Citation and commencement*

1. These Regulations may be cited as the Surface Waters (Classification) (Scotland) Regulations 1990 and shall come into force on 1st May 1990.

*Classification of waters*

2. These Regulations, and the system of classification prescribed by these Regulations, apply in relation to inland waters[2] (including any loch or pond which, by virtue of an order made under section 30A(5)(b) of the Control of Pollution Act 1974, is to be treated as a relevant loch or pond[3]).

3. The waters to which these Regulations apply shall be classified DW1, DW2 or DW3, as the case may be, according to the criteria set out in the Schedule to these Regulations, which criteria shall determine their suitability for abstraction by water authorities within the meaning of the Water (Scotland) Act 1980[4] for supply (after treatment) as drinking water.

## SCHEDULE

*Criteria for the classification of waters*

The limits set out below are maxima

| (1) No. in Annex II to 75/440/EEC | (2) Parameters | | (3) DW1 | (4) DW2 | (5) DW3 |
|---|---|---|---|---|---|
| 2 | Coloration (after simple filtration) | mg/1 Pt Scale | 20 | 100 | 200 |
| 4 | Temperature | °C | 25 | 25 | 25 |
| 7 | Nitrates | mg/1 NO³ | 50 | 50 | 50 |
| 8(1) | Fluorides | mg/1 F | 1.5 | | |
| 10 | Dissolved iron | mg/1 Fe | 0.3 | 2 | |
| 12 | Copper | mg/1 Cu | 0.05 | | |
| 13 | Zinc | mg/1 Zn | 3 | 5 | 5 |
| 19 | Arsenic | mg/1 As | 0.05 | 0.05 | 0.1 |
| 20 | Cadmium | mg/1 Cd | 0.005 | 0.005 | 0.005 |
| 21 | Total chromium | mg/1 Cr | 0.05 | 0.05 | 0.05 |
| 22 | Lead | mg/1 Pb | 0.05 | 0.05 | 0.05 |
| 23 | Selenium | mg/1 Se | 0.01 | 0.01 | 0.01 |

[1] P.19 above.
[2] "Inland Waters" defined in s.30A(1), p.18 above.
[3] See the Controlled Waters (Lochs and Ponds) (Scotland) Order 1990, S.I. 1990/120, above. "Loch or pond" includes a reservoir of any description: s.30A(4) above.
[4] 1980 c.45. New water authorities have been established under s.62 of the Local Government etc. (Scotland) Act 1994 (c.39).

| (1)<br>No. in<br>Annex II<br>to 75/440/EEC | (2)<br>Parameters | | (3)<br>DW1 | (4)<br>DW2 | (5)<br>DW3 |
|---|---|---|---|---|---|
| 24 | Mercury | mg/1 Hg | 0.001 | 0.001 | 0.001 |
| 25 | Barium | mg/1 Ba | 0.1 | 1 | 1 |
| 26 | Cyanide | mg/1 Cn | 0.05 | 0.05 | 0.05 |
| 27 | Sulphates | mg/1 SO$^4$ | 250 | 250 | 250 |
| 31 | Phenols (phenol index)<br>paranitraniline 4<br>aminoantipyrine | mg/1 C$^6$H$^5$OH | 0.001 | 0.005 | 0.1 |
| 32 | Dissolved or emulsified<br>hydrocarbons (after extraction<br>by petroleum ether) | mg/1 | 0.05 | 0.2 | 1 |
| 33 | Polycyclic aromatic<br>hydrocarbons | mg/1 | 0.0002 | 0.0002 | 0.001 |
| 34 | Total pesticides (parathion,<br>BHC, dieldrin) | mg/1 | 0.001 | 0.0025 | 0.005 |
| 39 | Ammonia | mg/1 NH$^4$ | | 1.5 | 4 |

*Note*
(1) The value is an upper limit set in relation to the mean annual temperature (high and low).

*Explanatory Note*
*(This note is not part of the Regulations)*

These Regulations prescribe the system of classifying the quality of inland waters (as defined in section 30A(5)(b) of the Control of Pollution Act 1974) according to their suitability for abstraction by water authorities for supply (after treatment) as drinking water.

The classifications DW1, DW2 and DW3 reflect the mandatory values assigned by Annex II to Council Directive 75/440/EEC, (OJ No. L194, 25.7.75, p.26) (concerning the quality required of surface water intended for the abstraction of drinking water) to the parameters listed in the Schedule to the Regulations.

The classifications are relevant for the purposes of setting water quality objectives for rivers, lochs and other inland waters under section 30C of the Act[1] and for ascertaining the treatment to which the water is to be subjected before it is supplied for public use, in accordance with Part VI of the Water Supply (Water Quality) (Scotland) Regulations 1990 (S.I. 1990/119).

---

[1] P.20 above.

# The Surface Waters (Dangerous Substances) (Classification) (Scotland) Regulations 1990

S.I. 1990 No. 126 (S.15)

---

The Secretary of State, in exercise of the powers conferred on him by section 30B of the Control of Pollution Act 1974[1] and by section 2(2) of the European Communities Act 1972,[2] being the Minister designated[3] for the purposes of that subsection in relation to the prevention, reduction and elimination of pollution of water, and of all other powers enabling him in that behalf, hereby makes the following Regulations:

*Citation, commencement, extent and interpretation*

1. (1) These Regulations may be cited as the Surface Waters (Dangerous Substances) (Classification) (Scotland) Regulations 1990, shall come into force on 27th February 1990 and shall extend to Scotland only.

(2) In these Regulations "the Act" means the Control of Pollution Act 1974 and references to inland waters and relevant territorial waters include, respectively, references to waters which are, by virtue of an order made under section 30A(5) of the Act,[4] to be treated as a relevant loch or pond and to waters which are, by virtue of such an order, to be treated as relevant territorial waters.[5]

*Classification of waters*

2. (1) A system employing the classification DS1 is prescribed as a system of classification applying to inland waters.

(2) A system employing the classification DS2 is prescribed as a system of classification applying to coastal waters[6] and relevant territorial waters.

..................................................................................................................

3. (1) The criterion for classification DS1 is that the annual mean concentrations of the substances listed in column (1) of Schedule 1 hereto do not exceed the concentrations specified in column (2) of that Schedule.

(2) The criterion for classification DS2 is that the annual mean concentrations of the substances listed in column (1) of Schedule 2 hereto do not exceed the concentrations specified in column (2) of that Schedule.

*Modification of section 30C of the Control of Pollution Act 1974*

4. Section 30C(4) and (5) of the Act[7] shall not apply to the initial establishment of water quality objectives so far as they involve the specification of a classification prescribed by these Regulations.

---

[1] P.19 above.
[2] 1972 c.68.
[3] S.I. 1989/2393.
[4] P.19 above; see the Controlled Waters (Lochs and Ponds) (Scotland) Order 1990, S.I. 1990/120, p.557 above.

[5] "Inland waters", "relevant territorial waters" and "relevant loch or pond" are defined in s.30A, p.18 above.
[6] "Coastal waters" defined in s.30A(1)(b), p.18 above.
[7] P.20 above.

# SCHEDULE 1

(Regulation 3(1))

## CRITERIA FOR THE CLASSIFICATION OF INLAND WATERS (DS1)

| (1)<br>Substance | (2)<br>Concentration in microgrammes per litre<br>(annual mean) |
|---|---|
| Aldrin, Dieldrin, Endrin and Isodrin | (i) 0.03 for the four substances in total;<br>(ii) 0.005 for endrin |
| Cadmium and its compounds | 5 (total cadmium: both soluble and insoluble forms) |
| Carbon tetrachloride | 12 |
| Chloroform | 12 |
| DDT (all isomers) | 0.025 |
| para-para-DDT | 0.01 |
| Hexachlorobenzene | 0.03 |
| Hexachlorobutadiene | 0.1 |
| Hexachlorocyclohexane (all isomers) | 0.1 |
| Mercury and its compounds | 1 (total mercury: both soluble and insoluble forms) |
| Pentachlorophenol and its compounds | 2 |

# SCHEDULE 2

(Regulation 3(2))

## CRITERIA FOR THE CLASSIFICATION OF COASTAL WATERS AND RELEVANT TERRITORIAL WATERS (DS2)

| (1)<br>Substance | (2)<br>Concentration in microgrammes per litre<br>(annual mean) |
|---|---|
| Aldrin, Dieldrin, Endrin and Isodrin | (i) 0.03 for the four substances in total;<br>(ii) 0.005 for endrin |
| Cadmium and its compounds | 2.5 (dissolved cadmium) |
| Carbon tetrachloride | 12 |
| Chloroform | 12 |
| DDT (all isomers) | 0.025 |
| para-para-DDT | 0.01 |
| Hexachlorobenzene | 0.03 |
| Hexachlorobutadiene | 0.1 |
| Hexachlorocyclohexane (all isomers) | 0.02 |
| Mercury and its compounds | 0.3 (dissolved mercury) |
| Pentachlorophenol and its compounds | 2 |

*Explanatory Note*
*(This note is not part of the Regulations)*

These Regulations prescribe the system of classifying the quality of inland waters, coastal waters and relevant territorial waters (as defined in section 30A(1) of the Control of Pollution Act 1974) according to the presence in them of concentrations of the dangerous substances listed in the Schedules to the Regulations.

With two exceptions, the classifications DS1 (in relation to inland waters) and DS2 (in relation to coastal waters and relevant territorial waters) reflect the quality objectives specified in Annex II to Council Directive 82/176/EEC (OJ

No. L81, 27.3.82, p. 29) (mercury and its compounds), Annex II to Council Directive 83/513/EEC (OJ No. L291, 24.10.83, p. 1) (cadmium and its compounds), Annex II to Council Directive 84/156/EEC (OJ No. L74, 17.3.84, p. 49) (mercury and its compounds), Annex II to Council Directive 84/491/EEC (OJ No. L274, 17.10.84, p. 11) (hexachlorocyclohexane), Annex II to Council Directive 86/280/EEC (OJ No. L181, 4.7.86, p.16) (carbon tetrachloride, DDT and pentachlorophenol) and Council Directive 88/347/EEC (OJ No. L158, 25.6.88, p. 35) which amends the 1986 Directive by adding quality objectives for aldrin, dieldrin, endrin and isodrin, hexachlorobenzene, hexachlorobutadiene and chloroform. The exceptions relate to the quality objectives for concentrations of cadmium and mercury in classification DS2. The Directive specifies an annual mean of not more than 5 and 0.5 microgrammes per litre for cadmium and mercury respectively in estuarial waters but the classification DS2 (which applies to estuarial waters) specifies a more stringent annual mean of not more than 2.5 and 0.3 microgrammes per litre.

The classifications are relevant for the purposes of setting water quality objectives for inland waters, coastal waters and relevant territorial waters under section 30C of the Control of Pollution Act 1974.[1] Regulation 4 modifies that section for the purpose of complying with Community obligations arising by virtue of Council Directive 76/474/EEC by relieving the Secretary of State of the requirements to give at least three months' notice before establishing initial water quality objectives giving effect to that and other Directives relating to discharges of dangerous substances, and to consider representations or objections to his proposals to establish those objectives.

[1] P.20 above.

# The Radioactive Substances (Appeals) Regulations 1990

S.I. 1990 No. 2504

*Note:* This instrument was made under the Radioactive Substances Act 1960. The 1960 Act was repealed by, and provisions within it re-enacted in, the Radioactive Substances Act 1993, p.381 above. Where this instrument refers to the 1960 Act, the annotations provide the corresponding reference to the 1993 Act.

The Secretary of State for the Environment as respects England, the Secretary of State for Wales as respects Wales and the Secretary of State for Scotland as respects Scotland, in exercise of their powers under sections 11D(6) and (11) of the Radioactive Substances Act 1960[1] and of all other powers enabling them in that behalf, hereby make the following Regulations:

*Citation, commencement and interpretation*

1. (1) These Regulations may be cited as the Radioactive Substances (Appeals) Regulations 1990 and shall come into force on 1st January 1991.

    (2) In these Regulations "the 1960 Act" means the Radioactive Substances Act 1960.

*Notice of appeal*

2. (1) A person who wishes to appeal to the Secretary of State under section 11D of the 1960 Act[2] shall give written notice of the appeal to the Secretary of State.

    (2) The notice of appeal shall be accompanied by the following—

    (a) a full statement of the appellant's case;

    (b) a copy of any relevant application;

    (c) a copy of any relevant certificate of registration or authorisation;

    (d) a copy of any relevant correspondence between the appellant and the appropriate Agency;[3]

    (e) a copy of any decision or notice which is the subject-matter of the appeal;

    (f) a statement indicating whether the appellant wishes the appeal to be in the form of a hearing or to be disposed of on the basis of written representations.

    (3) Any request by the appellant that an appeal be withdrawn shall be made to the Secretary of State in writing.

*Time limit for bringing appeal*

3. (1) Subject to paragraph (2) below, notice of appeal pursuant to regulation 2(1) above is to be given before the expiry of the period of two months beginning with the date on which—

    (a) a copy of the decision or notice which is the subject-matter of the appeal is sent to the appellant; or

---

[1] The corresponding provision in the Radioactive Substances Act 1993 is at s.27(2) and (7), p.399 above. See the definition of "prescribed" in s.47(1), p.408 above.

[2] The corresponding provision in the Radioactive Substances Act 1993 is at s.26, p.398 above. See also s.27.

[3] "The appropriate Agency" means, in relation to England and Wales, the Environment Agency, and, in relation to Scotland, the Scottish Environment Protection Agency, SEPA; words "the appropriate Agency" substituted by the Environment Act 1995 (c.25): s.120, sch.22, para.233. This amendment came into force on 1 April 1996: S.I. 1996/186.

(b) the relevant application is treated as having been refused pursuant to section 1(3A), 3(4B) or 8(3B) of the 1960 Act,[1]

or before the expiry of such longer period as may be allowed by the Secretary of State.

(2) Where the appeal is against the decision of the appropriate Agency[2] to cancel a registration or to revoke an authorisation, notice of appeal shall be given before the expiry of the period of 28 days beginning with the date on which notice of the decision is given to the appellant under section 5(2) or 8(8) of the 1960 Act[3] or before the expiry of such longer period as may be allowed by the Secretary of State.

*Action upon receipt of notice of appeal*

**4.** (1) Upon receipt of a notice of appeal accompanied by the documents specified in regulation 2(2) above, the Secretary of State shall send to the appropriate Agency[4] a copy of the notice of appeal, the statement of the appellant's case and the appellant's statement indicating whether he wishes the appeal to be in the form of a hearing or to be disposed of on the basis of written representations.

(2) Where the appeal is against a decision in respect of an application for an authorisation under section 6 of the 1960 Act[5] on which the appropriate Agency consulted any local authority, local fisheries committee,[6] statutory water undertakers or other public or local authority under section 9(3) of the 1960 Act,[7] the appropriate Agency shall notify the Secretary of State of the names of the authorities consulted.

(3) The Secretary of State shall send to any authority whose name is notified to him under paragraph (2) above a notice stating that an appeal has been lodged and that within a period of 21 days beginning with the date of service of that notice the authority may make representations to the Secretary of State with respect to the subject-matter of the appeal.

*Written representations*

**5.** (1) Where the appellant informs the Secretary of State that he wishes the appeal to be disposed of on the basis of written representations, the appropriate Agency[8] may submit written representations to the Secretary of State not later than 28 days after receiving a copy of the appellant's statements.

(2) The appellant may make further representations by way of reply to any representations from the appropriate Agency not later than 17 days after the date of submission of those representations by the chief inspector.

(3) Any representations made by the appropriate Agency or the appellant shall be dated and submitted to the Secretary of State on the date they bear.

(4) When the appellant or the appropriate Agency submits any representations to the Secretary of State under paragraph (3) above he shall at the same time send a copy to the other party.

[1] The corresponding provision in the Radioactive Substances Act 1993 is at s.7(5), p.385 above, s.10(4), p.388 above, and s.16(7), p.391 above, respectively.
[2] "The appropriate Agency" means, in relation to England and Wales, the Environment Agency, and, in relation to Scotland, the Scottish Environment Protection Agency, SEPA; words "the appropriate Agency" substituted by the Environment Act 1995 (c.25):s.120, sch.22, para.233. This amendment came into force on 1 April 1996: S.I. 1996/186.
[3] The corresponding provisions in the Radioactive Substances Act 1993 are at s.12(2), p.388 above, and s.17(3), p.392 above, respectively.
[4] "The appropriate Agency" means, in relation to England and Wales, the Environment Agency, and, in relation to Scotland, the Scottish Environment Protection Agency, SEPA; words "the appropriate Agency" substituted by the Environment Act 1995 (c.25):s.120, sch.22, para.233.

This amendment came into force on 1 April 1996: S.I. 1996/186.
[5] The corresponding provision in the Radioactive Substances Act 1993 is at s.13, p.389 above. See also s.15.
[6] Former words "river purification authority," revoked by S.I. 1996/973, reg.2, sch., para.10. This amendment came into force on 1 April 1996: reg.1.
[7] The corresponding provision in the Radioactive Substances Act 1993 is at s.18(1), p.392 above. "Local authority" and "public or local authority" are defined by s.47(1) of the 1993 Act, p.408 above.
[8] "The appropriate Agency" means, in relation to England and Wales, the Environment Agency, and, in relation to Scotland, the Scottish Environment Protection Agency, SEPA; words "the appropriate Agency" substituted by the Environment Act 1995 (c.25):s.120, sch.22, para.233. This amendment came into force on 1 April 1996: S.I. 1996/186.

(5)  The Secretary of State shall send to the appellant and the appropriate Agency a copy of any representations made to him by the authorities mentioned in regulation 4(2) above and shall allow the appellant and the appropriate Agency a period of not less than 14 days in which to make representations thereon.

(6)  The Secretary of State may in a particular case set later time limits than those mentioned in this regulation.

## Hearings

6.  (1)  The Secretary of State shall give the appellant and the appropriate Agency[1] at least 28 days written notice of the date, time and place for the holding of any hearing unless they agree to a shorter period of notice.

(2)  Subject to paragraph (3) below, in the case of a hearing which is to be held wholly or partly in public, the Secretary of State shall, at least 21 days before the date fixed for the hearing—

(a)  publish a copy of the notice mentioned in paragraph (1) above in at least one newspaper circulating in the locality in which the activity which is the subject-matter of the appeal is or would be carried on; and

(b)  in a case where the Secretary of State is informed under regulation 4(2) above that the appropriate Agency has consulted any authority, serve a copy of that notice on every authority which was consulted.

(3)  The Secretary of State may vary the date fixed for the holding of any hearing and paragraphs (1) and (2) above shall apply to the variation of a date as they applied to the date originally fixed.

(4)  The Secretary of State may also vary the time or place for the holding of a hearing but shall give such notice of any such variation as appears to him to be reasonable.

(5)  After the conclusion of the hearing the person appointed to conduct the hearing shall make a report in writing to the Secretary of State which shall include his conclusions together with his recommendations or his reasons for not making any recommendations.

## Notification of determination

7.  (1)  The Secretary of State shall notify the appellant in writing of his determination of the appeal and of his reasons for it and, if a hearing is held, shall at the same time provide him with a copy of the report of the person who conducted the hearing.

(2)  The Secretary of State shall at the same time send a copy of those documents to the appropriate Agency and to any authority to which he was required to give notice of the appeal under regulation 4(3) above.

### Explanatory Note

*The explanatory note refers to the provisions of the Radioactive Substances Act 1960. It sets out that these regulations make procedural provision with respect to appeals to the Secretary of State. The 1960 Act has been superseded by the Radioactive Substances Act 1993 and, accordingly, the explanatory note is not reproduced.*

---

[1] "The appropriate Agency" means, in relation to England and Wales, the Environment Agency, and, in relation to Scotland, the Scottish Environment Protection Agency, SEPA; words "the appropriate Agency" substituted by the Environment Act 1995 (c.25):s.120, sch.22, para.233. This amendment came into force on 1 April 1996: S.I. 1996/186.

# The Environmental Protection (Prescribed Processes and Substances) Regulations 1991

S.I. 1991 No. 472

*Note:* This instrument has been amended on seven occasions. Three of the amending instruments incorporate transitional provisions which relate to the date from which an authorisation is required under Part I of the Environmental Protection Act 1990.

Schedule 3 to these Regulations, relating to the date from which an authorisation is required under section 6 of the 1990 Act, and the three transitionals, are set out at the end of these Regulations. The schedules to these Regulations and the transitionals are accordingly in the following order.

| Schedule | Page |
|---|---|
| 1 | 569 |
| 2 | 590 |
| 4 | 592 |
| 5 | 593 |
| 6 | 593 |
| 3 | 594 |
| S.I. 1992/614, sch.2, Transitionals | 598 |
| S.I. 1994/1271, sch.6, Transitionals | |
| (as substituted by S.I. 1994/1329) | 599 |
| S.I. 1995/3247, sch.2, Transitionals | 602 |

The Secretary of State for the Environment as respects England, the Secretary of State for Wales as respects Wales and the Secretary of State for Scotland as respects Scotland, in exercise of their powers under section 2 of the Environmental Protection Act 1990[1] and of all other powers enabling them in that behalf hereby make the following Regulations:

*Citation, application and commencement*

**1.** (1) These Regulations may be cited as the Environmental Protection (Prescribed Processes and Substances) Regulations 1991.

(2) These Regulations shall come into force in England and Wales on 1st April 1991 and in Scotland on 1st April 1992.

*Interpretation*

**2.** In these Regulations–.

"the Act" means the Environmental Protection Act 1990;

"background concentration" has the meaning given to that term in regulation 4(7);

"Part A process" means a process falling within a description set out in Schedule 1 hereto[2] under the heading "Part A" and "Part B process" means a process falling within a description so set out under the heading "Part B"; and

"particulate matter" means grit, dust or fumes.

---

[1] P.91 above.     [2] P.569 below.

*Prescribed Provisions*

**3.** (1) Subject to the following provisions of these Regulations, the descriptions of processes set out in Schedule 1 hereto[1] are hereby prescribed pursuant to section 2(1) of the Act[2] as processes for the carrying on of which after the prescribed date an authorisation is required under section 6.[3]

(2) Schedule 2[4] has effect for the interpretation of Schedule 1.

(3) In paragraph (1), the prescribed date means the appropriate date set out or determined in accordance with Schedule 3.[5]

*Exceptions*

**4.** (1) Subject to paragraph (6), a process shall not be taken to be a Part A process[6] if it has the following characteristics, namely—

(i) that it cannot result in the release[7] into the air of any substance prescribed by regulation 6(1) or there is no likelihood that it will result in the release into the air of any such substance except in a quantity which is so trivial that it is incapable of causing harm[8] or its capacity to cause harm is insignificant; and

(ii) that it cannot result in the release into water of any substance prescribed by regulation 6(2) except—

(a) in a concentration which is no greater than the background concentration;[9] or

(b) in a quantity which does not, in any 12 month period, exceed the background quantity[10] by more than the amount specified in relation to the description of substance in column 2 of Schedule 5;[11, 12]

(iii) that it cannot result in the release into land of any substance prescribed by regulation 6(3) or there is no likelihood that it will result in the release into land of any such substance except in a quantity which is so trivial that it is incapable of causing harm or its capacity to cause harm is insignificant.

(2) Subject to paragraph (6), a process shall not be taken to be a Part B process[13] unless it will, or there is a likelihood that it will, result in the release into the air of one or more substances prescribed by regulation 6(1) in a quantity greater than that mentioned in paragraph (1)(i) above.

(3) A process shall not be taken to fall within a description of Schedule 1 if it is carried on in a working museum to demonstrate an industrial process of historic interest or if it is carried on for educational purposes in a school as defined in section 114 of the Education Act 1944[14] or, in Scotland, section 135(1) of the Education (Scotland) Act 1980.[15]

(4) The running on or within an aircraft, hovercraft, mechanically propelled road vehicle, railway locomotive or ship or other vessel of an engine which propels or provides electricity for[16] it shall not be taken to fall within a description of Schedule 1.

(4A) The running of an engine[17] in order to test it before installation or in the course of its development shall not be taken to fall within a description in Schedule 1.[18]

---

[1] P.569 below.
[2] P.91 above.
[3] P.95 above.
[4] P.590 below.
[5] P.594 below.
[6] "Part A process" defined by reg.2 above.
[7] For the definition of "release" in Part I of the 1990 Act, see s.1(10), p.90 above.
[8] For the definition of "harm" in Part I of the 1990 Act, see s.1(4), p.89 above.
[9] "Background concentration" defined by para. (7) and (8) below.
[10] "Background quantity" defined by para. (7) and (8) below.
[11] P.593 below.

[12] Sub-paragraph (ii) substituted by S.I. 1994/1271, reg.4(1), sch.2, para.1. This amendment came into force on 1 December 1994: reg.1(2).
[13] "Part B process" defined by reg.2 above.
[14] 1944 c.31 which is replaced by the Education Act 1996 (c.56).
[15] 1980 c.44.
[16] Words "or provides electricity for" inserted by S.I. 1994/1271, reg.4(1), sch.2, para.2.
[17] Former words "which is designed to propel an aircraft, hovercraft, mechanically propelled road vehicle, railway locomotive or ship or other vessel" omitted by S.I. 1994/1271, reg.4(1), sch.2, para.3.
[18] Para.4(A) inserted by S.I. 1992/614, reg.2, sch.1, para.2. This amendment came into force on 1 April 1992: reg.1(1).

(4B)　The use of a fume cupboard shall not be taken to fall within a description in Schedule 1 if it is used as a fume cupboard in a laboratory for research or testing, and it is not—

(a)　a fume cupboard which is an industrial and continuous production process enclosure; or

(b)　a fume cupboard in which substances or materials are manufactured.

In this paragraph, "fume cupboard" has the meaning given by the British Standard "Laboratory fume cupboards" published by the British Standards Institution numbered BS 7258: Part 1: 1990.[1,2]

(5)　A process shall not be taken to tall within a description of Schedule 1 if it is carried on as a domestic activity in connection with a private dwelling.

(5A)　*This paragraph, inserted by S.I. 1992/614, was omitted by S.I. 1994/1271, reg.4(1), sch.2, para.4. The amendment made by S.I. 1994/1271 came into force on 1 December 1994: reg.1(2).*

(6)　Paragraphs (1) and (2) do not exempt any process described in Schedule 1 from the requirement for authorisation if the process may give rise to an offensive smell noticeable outside the premises where the process is carried on.

(7)　In these Regulations—

"background concentration" means any concentration of the relevant substance which would be present in the release irrespective of any effect the process may have had on the composition of the release and, without prejudice to the generality of the foregoing, includes such concentration of the substance as is referred to in paragraph (8) below; and

"background quantity" means such quantity of the relevant substance as is referred to in paragraph (8) below.

(8)　The concentration or, as the case may be, quantity mentioned in paragraph (7) above is such concentration or quantity as is present in—

(a)　water supplied to the premises where the process is carried on;

(b)　water abstracted for use in the process; and

(c)　precipitation onto the premises on which the process is carried on.[3]

*Enforcement*

**5.** (1)　The descriptions of processes set out in Schedule 1 under the heading "Part A" are designated pursuant to section 2(4) of the Act[4] for central control.

(2)　The descriptions of processes set out in Schedule 1 under the heading "Part B" are so designated for local control.

*Prescribed substances: release into the air, water or land*

**6.** (1)　The description of substances set out in Schedule 4[5] are prescribed pursuant to section 2(5) of the Act[6] as substances the release of which into the air is subject to control under sections 6 and 7 of the Act.[7]

(2)　The descriptions of substances set out in column 1 of Schedule 5[8] are so prescribed as substances the release of which into water is subject to control under those sections.

(3)　The descriptions of substances set out in Schedule 6[9] are so prescribed as substances the release of which into land is subject to control under those sections.

---

[1] The International Standard Book Number (ISBN) in respect of BS 7258: Part 1: 1990 is 0 580 17977 X.

[2] Para.4(B) inserted by S.I. 1994/1271, reg.3, sch.1, para.1. This amendment came into force on 1 June 1994: reg.1(1).

[3] Para. (7) and (8) substituted for the earlier para. (7) by S.I. 1994/1271, reg.4(1), sch.2, para.5. This amendment came into force on 1 December 1994: reg.1(2).

[4] P.91 above.

[5] P.592 below.

[6] P.91 above.

[7] P.95 above.

[8] P.593 below; words "column 1 of Schedule 5" substituted by S.I. 1994/1271, reg.4(2). This amendment came into force on 1 December 1994: reg.1(2).

[9] P.593 below.

# SCHEDULE 1

(Regulation 3(1))

DESCRIPTIONS OF PROCESSES

CHAPTER 1: FUEL PRODUCTION PROCESSES, COMBUSTION PROCESSES (INCLUDING POWER GENERATION)[1] AND ASSOCIATED PROCESSES

*Section 1.1 Gasification and associated processes*

## PART A

(a)  Reforming natural gas.

(aa)  Refining natural gas if that process is related to another Part A process or is likely to involve the use in any 12 month period of 1000 tonnes or more of natural gas.[2]

(b)  Odorising natural gas or liquified petroleum gas if that process is related to another Part A process.[3]

(c)  Producing gas from coal, lignite, oil or other carbonaceous material or from mixtures thereof other than from sewage or the biological degradation of waste, unless carried on as part of a process which is a combustion process (whether or not that process falls within Section 1.3 of this Schedule).[4]

(d)  Purifying or refining any product of any of the processes described in paragraphs (a), (b) or (c) or converting it into a different product.

In this Section, "carbonaceous material" includes such materials as charcoal, coke, peat and rubber.

## PART B

(a)  Odorising natural gas or liquified petroleum gas, except where that process is related to a Part A process.

(b)  Blending odorant for use with natural gas or liquified petroleum gas.

(c)  Any process for refining natural gas not falling within paragraph (aa) of Part A of this Section.[5]

In paragraph (c) of Part B of this Section, "refining natural gas"[6] does not include refining mains gas.[7]

*Section 1.2 Carbonisation and associated processes*

## PART A

(a)  The pyrolysis, carbonisation, distillation, liquefaction, partial oxidation or other heat treatment of coal (other than the drying of coal),[8] lignite, oil, other carbonaceous material (as defined in Section 1.1) or mixtures thereof otherwise than with a view to gasification or making of charcoal.

(b)  The purification or refining of any of the products of a process mentioned in paragraph (a) or its conversion into a different product.

Nothing in paragraph (a) or (b) refers to the use of any substance as a fuel or its incineration as a waste or to any process for the treatment of sewage.

[1] These words in this heading substituted by S.I. 1992/614, reg.2, sch.1, para.4. This amendment came into force on 1 April 1992: reg.1.

[2] Para. (a) and (aa) substituted, for the former para. (a) by S.I. 1994/1271, reg.4(3), sch.3, para.1(a). This amendment came into force on 1 December 1994: reg.1(2).

[3] Words "if that process is related to another Part A process" added by S.I. 1994/1271, reg.4(3), sch.3, para.1(b).

[4] Words ", unless carried on . . . within Section 1.3 of this Schedule)" added by S.I. 1994/1271, reg.4(3), sch.3, para.1(c).

[5] Part B substituted by S.I. 1994/1271, reg.4(3), sch.3, para.2.

[6] Words "In paragraph (c) . . . "refining natural gas" substituted by S.I. 1995/3247, reg.2, sch.1, para.1. This amendment came into force on 8 January 1996: reg.1(1).

[7] This sentence added by S.I. 1994/1271, reg.4(3), sch.3, para.3. This amendment came into force on 1 December 1994: reg.1(2).

[8] Words "(other than the drying of coal)" inserted by S.I. 1994/1271, reg.4(3), sch.3, para.4.

In paragraph (a), the heat treatment of oil does not include heat treatment of waste oil or waste emulsions containing oil in order to recover the oil.[1]

## PART B

Nil

### *Section 1.3  combustion processes*

## PART A

The following processes, if carried on primarily for the purpose of producing energy, namely—

(a) Burning any fuel in a combustion appliance with a net rated thermal input of 50 megawatts or more;[2]

(b) *Omitted by S.I. 1995/3247, reg.2, sch.1, para.2(b). This amendment came into force on 8 January 1996: reg.1(1).*

(c) burning any of the following in an appliance with a net rated thermal input of 3 megawatts or more otherwise than as a processes which is related to a Part B process—

  (i)   waste oil;

  (ii)  recovered oil;

  (iii) any fuel manufactured from, or comprising, any other waste.

For the purposes of paragraph (a) above, where—

  (i)  two or more boilers or furnaces with an aggregate net rated thermal input of 50 megawatts or more (disregarding any boiler or furnace with a net rated thermal input of less than 3 megawatts); or

  (ii) two or more gas turbines or compression ignition engines with an aggregate net rated thermal input of 50 megawatts or more (disregarding any such turbine or engine with a net rated thermal input of less than 3 megawatts),

are operated by the same person at the same location those boilers or furnaces or, as the case may be, those turbines or engines, shall be treated as a single combustion appliance with a net rated thermal input of 50 megawatts or more.[3]

Nothing in this Part of this Section applies to the burning of any fuel in a boiler, furnace or other appliance with a net rated thermal input of less than 3 megawatts.[4]

## PART B

The following processes unless[5] carried on in relation to and as part of[6] any Part A process—

(a) burning any fuel in a boiler or furnace with a net rated thermal input of not less than 20 megawatts (but less than 50 megawatts);

(b) burning any fuel in a gas turbine or compression ignition engine with a net rated thermal input of not less than 20 megawatts (but less than 50 megawatts);

(c) burning as fuel, in an appliance with a net rated thermal input of less than 3 megawatts, waste oil or recovered oil;

(d) burning in an appliance with a net rated thermal input of less than 3 megawatts solid fuel which has been manufactured from waste by a process involving the application of heat;

(e) burning, in any appliance, fuel manufactured from, or including, waste (other than waste oil or recovered oil or such fuel as is mentioned in paragraph (d)) if the appliance has a net rated thermal input of less than 3 megawatts but at least 0.4 megawatts or is used together with (whether or not it is operated simultaneously

---

[1] Words "In paragraph (a), . . . recover the oil." inserted by S.I. 1992/614, reg.2, sch.1, para.5. This amendment came into force on 1 April 1992: reg.1.
[2] This paragraph substituted by S.I. 1995/3247, reg.2, sch.1, para.2(a). This amendment came into force on 8 January 1996: reg.1(1).
[3] Words "For the purposes of . . . single combustion appliance with a net rated thermal input of 50 megawatts or more." inserted by 1995/3247, reg.2, sch.1, para.2(c).

[4] This sentence added by S.I. 1994/1271, reg.4(3), sch.3, para.5. This amendment came into force on 1 December 1994: reg.1(2).
[5] Word "unless" substituted by S.I. 1992/614, reg.2, sch.1, para.7. This amendment came into force on 1 April 1992: reg.1(1).
[6] Words "and as part of" inserted by S.I. 1994/1271, reg.4(3), sch.3, para.6. This amendment came into force on 1 December 1994: reg.1(2).

with)[1] other appliances which each have a net rated thermal input of less than 3 megawatts and the aggregate net rated thermal input of all the appliances is at least 0.4 megawatts.[2]

In paragraph (c) of Part A and paragraph (e) of Part B, "fuel" does not include gas produced by biological degradation of waste; and for the purposes of this Section—

"net rated thermal input" is the rate at which fuel can be burned at the maximum continuous rating of the appliance multiplied by the net calorific value of the fuel and expressed as megawatts thermal; and

"waste oil" means any mineral based lubricating or industrial oil which has become unfit for the use for which it was intended and, in particular, used combustion engine oil, gearbox oil, mineral lubricating oil, oil for turbines and hydraulic oil; and

"recovered oil" means waste oil which has been processed before being used.

### Section 1.4 Petroleum processes

## PART A

(a) The loading, unloading or other handling of, the storage of, or the physical, chemical or thermal treatment of—

 (i) crude oil;

 (ii) stabilised crude petroleum;

 (iii) crude shale oil;

 (iv) if related to another process described in this paragraph, any associated gas or condensate.[3]

(b) *Omitted by S.I. 1994/1271, reg.4(3), sch.3, para.7(b). This amendment came into force on 1 December 1994: reg.1(2).*

(c) Any process not falling within any other description in this Schedule by which the product of any process described in paragraph (a)[4] above is subject to further refining or conversion or is used (otherwise than as a fuel or solvent) in the manufacture of a chemical.

## PART B

Nil

## CHAPTER 2: METAL PRODUCTION AND PROCESSING

### Section 2.1 Iron and Steel

## PART A

(a) Loading, unloading or otherwise handling or storing iron ore except in the course of mining operations.

(b) Loading, unloading or otherwise handling or storing burnt pyrites.

(c) Crushing, grading, grinding, screening, washing or drying iron ore or any mixture of iron ore and other materials.

(d) Blending or mechanically mixing rades or iron ore with other materials.

(e) Pelletising, calcining, roasting or sintering iron ore or any mixture of iron ore and other materials.[5]

(f) Making, melting or refining iron, steel or any ferrous alloy[6] in any furnace other than a furnace described in Part B of this Section.

(g) Any process for the refining or making of iron, steel or any ferrous alloy[6] in which air or oxygen or both are used unless related to a process described in Part B of this Section.

[1] Words "used together . . . simultaneously with)" substituted by S.I. 1994/1271, reg.3, sch.1, para.2. This amendment came into force on 1 June 1994: reg.1(1).
[2] Words "which each have . . . least 0.4 megawatts" substituted by S.I. 1992/614, reg.2, sch.1, para.7. This amendment came into force on 1 April 1992: reg.1(1).
[3] This sub-paragraph substituted by S.I. 1994/1271, reg.4(3), sch.3, para.7(a). This amendment came into force on 1 December 1994: reg.1(2).
[4] Former words "or (b)" omitted by S.I. 1994/1271, reg.4(3), sch.3, para.7(c).
[5] This paragraph inserted by S.I. 1994/1271, reg.4(3), sch.3, para.8(a). This amendment came into force on 1 December 1994: reg.1(2).
[6] Words "ferrous alloy" substituted by S.I. 1994/1271, reg.4(3), sch.3, para.8(b).

(h) The desulphurisation of iron, steel or any ferrous alloy[1] made by a process described in this Part of this Section.

(i) Heating iron, steel or any ferrous alloy[2] (whether in a furnace or other appliance) to remove grease, oil or any other non-metallic contaminant (including such operations as the removal by heat of plastic or rubber covering from scrap cable), if related to another process described in this Part of this Section.

(j) Any foundry process (including ancillary foundry operations such as the manufacture and recovery of moulds, the reclamation of sand, fettling, grinding and shot-blasting) if related to another process described in this Part of this Section.

(k) *Omitted by S.I. 1994/1271, reg.4(3), sch.3, para.8(c). This amendment came into force on 1 December 1994: reg.1(4).*

(l) Handling slag in conjunction with a process described in paragraph (f) or (g).

(m) Any process for rolling iron, steel or any ferrous alloy carried on in relation to any process described in paragraph (f) or (g), and any process carried on in conjunction with such rolling involving the scarfing or cutting with oxygen of iron, steel or any ferrous alloy.[3]

Nothing in paragraph (a) or (b) of this Part of this Section applies to the handling or storing of other minerals in association with the handling or storing of iron ore or burnt pyrites.

A process does not fall within paragraph (a), (b), (c) or (d) of this Part of this Section unless—

(i) it is carried on as part of or is related to a process falling within a paragraph of this Part of this Section other than paragraph (a), (b), (c) or (d); or

(ii) it consists of, forms part of or is related to a process which is likely to involve the unloading in any 12 month period of more than 500,000 tonnes of iron ore or burnt pyrites or, in aggregate, both.[4]

## PART B

(a) Making, melting or refining iron, steel or any ferrous alloy[5] in—

(i) an electric arc furnace with a designed holding capacity of less than 7 tonnes; or

(ii) a cupola, crucible furnace, reverberatory furnace,[6] rotary furnace, induction furnace or resistance furnace.

(b) Any process for the refining or making of iron, steel or any ferrous alloy in which air or oxygen or both are used, if related to a process described in this Part of this Section.[7]

(c) The desulphurisation of iron, steel or any ferrous alloy,[8] if the process does not fall within paragraph (h) of Part A of this Section.

(d) Any such process as is described in paragraph (i) of Part A above, if not falling within that paragraph; but a process does not fall within this paragraph if—

(i) it is a process for heating iron, steel or any ferrous alloy[8] in one or more furnaces or other appliances the primary combustion chambers of which have in aggregate a net rated thermal input of less than 0.2 megawatts;

(ii) it does not involve the removal by heat of plastic or rubber covering from scrap cable or of any asbestos contaminant; and

(iii) it is not related to any other process described in this Part of this Section.[9]

(e) Any foundry process (including ancillary foundry operations such as the manufacture and recovery of moulds, the reclamation of sand, fettling, grinding and shot-blasting) if related to another process described in this Part of this Section.

(f) Any other process involving the casting of iron, steel or any ferrous alloy from deliveries of 50 tonnes or more at one time of molten metal.[10]

---

[1] Words "ferrous alloy" substituted by S.I. 1994/1271, reg.4(3), sch.3, para.8(b).

[2] Former words "or (b)" omitted by S.I. 1994/1271, reg.4(3), sch.3, para.7(c).

[3] This paragraph inserted by S.I. 1994/1271, sch.3, para.8(d).

[4] Words "A process does not fall ... or, in aggregate, both." added by S.I. 1994/1271, reg.4(3), sch.3, para.8(e).

[5] Words "ferrous alloy" substituted by S.I. 1994/1271, reg.4(3), sch.3, para.8(b).

[6] Words ", crucible furnace, reverberatory furnace" inserted by S.I. 1994/1271, reg.4(3), sch.3, para.9(a).

[7] This paragraph substituted by S.I. 1994/1271, reg.4(3), sch.3, para.9(c).

[8] Words "ferrous alloy" substituted by S.I. 1994/1271, reg.4(3), sch.3, para.9(b).

[9] Words ", but a process ... this Part of this Section." added by S.I. 1994/1271, reg.3, sch.1, para.3. This amendment came into force on 1 June 1994: reg.1(1).

[10] This paragraph inserted by S.I. 1994/1271, reg.4(3), sch.3, para.9(d). This amendment came into force on 1 December 1994: reg.1(2).

Any description of a process in this Section includes, where the process produces slag, the crushing, screening or grading or other treatment of the slag if that process is related to the process in question.

In this Section "net rated thermal input" has the same meaning as in Section 1.3.[1]

In this Section and Section 2.2, "ferrous alloy" means an alloy of which iron is the largest constituent, or equal to the largest constituent, by weight, whether or not that alloy has also a non-ferrous metal content greater than any percentage specified in Section 2.2 below, and "non-ferrous metal alloy" shall be construed accordingly.[2]

*Section 2.2 Non-ferrous metals*

## PART A

(a)   The extraction or recovery from any material—

   (i)   by chemical means or the use of heat of any non-ferrous metal or alloy of non-ferrous metal[3] or any compound of a non-ferrous metal; or

   (ii)   by electrolytic means, of aluminium,

   if the process may result in the release into the air of particulate matter[4] or any metal, metalloid or any metalloid compound or in the release into water of a substance described in Schedule 5 and does not fall[5] within paragraph (b) of Part B of this Section.

   In this paragraph "material" includes ores, scrap and other waste.

(b)   The mining of zinc or tin where the process may result in the release into water of cadmium or any compound of cadmium.

(c)   The refining of any non-ferrous metal (other than the electrolytic refining of copper)[6] or non-ferrous metal alloy except where the process is related to a process falling within a description in paragraphs (a), (c) or (d)[7] of Part B of this Section.

(d)   Any process other than a process described in paragraphs (b), (c) or (d) of Part B[8] of this Section for making or melting any non-ferrous metal or non-ferrous metal alloy in a furnace, bath or other holding vessel if the furnace, bath or vessel employed has a designed holding capacity of 5 tonnes or more.

(e)   Any process for producing, melting or recovering by chemical means or by the use of heat lead or any lead alloy, if—

   (i)   the process may result in the release into the air of particulate matter[9] or smoke which contains lead; and

   (ii)   in the case of lead alloy, the percentage by weight of lead in the alloy in molten form exceeds 23% if the alloy contains copper and 2% in other cases.[10]

(ee)   Any process for[11] recovering any of the elements listed below if the process may result in the release into the air of particulate matter or smoke which contains any of those elements—

   gallium
   indium
   palladium
   tellurium
   thallium.[12]

(f)   Any process for producing, melting or recovering (whether by chemical means or by electrolysis or by the use of heat) cadmium or mercury or any alloy containing more than 0.05 per cent by weight of either of those metals or of both of those metals in aggregate.[13]

[1] This sentence added by S.I. 1994/1271, reg.3, sch.1, para. 4. This amendment came into force on 1 June 1994: reg.1(1).

[2] This sentence added by S.I. 1994/1271, reg.4(3), sch.3, para. 10. This amendment came into force on 1 December 1994: reg.1(2).

[3] For "alloy of non-ferrous metal" see the definition at the end of Secton 2.1 above.

[4] "Particulate matter" defined by reg.2, p.566 above.

[5] Words "and does not fall" substituted by S.I. 1995/3247, reg.2, sch.1, para.3(a). This amendment came into force on 8 January 1996: reg.1(1).

[6] Words "(other than the electrolytic refining of copper)" inserted by S.I. 1994/1271, reg.4(3), sch.3, para.11(a)(i). This amendment came into force on 1 December 1994: reg.1(2).

[7] Words "paragraph (a), (c) or (d)" substituted by S.I. 1995/3247, reg.2, sch.1, para.3(b).

[8] Words "paragraph (b), (c) or (d) of Part B" substituted by S.I. 1995/3247, reg.2, sch.1, para.3(c).

[9] "Particulate matter" defined by reg.2, p.566 above.

[10] This paragraph substituted by S.I. 1994/1271, reg.4(3), sch.3, para.11(c). This amendment came into force on 1 December 1994: reg.1(2).

[11] Former words "producing or" omitted by S.I. 1994/1271, reg.4(3), sch.3, para.11(d).

[12] This paragraph inserted by S.I. 1993/2405, reg.2(1)(a). This amendment came into force on 26 October 1993: reg.1(1).

[13] This paragraph substituted by S.I. 1994/1271, reg.4(3), sch.3, para.11(e). This amendment came into force on 1 December 1994: reg.1(2).

(g) Any manufacturing or repairing process involving the manufacture or[1] use of beryllium or selenium or an alloy of one or both of those metals if the process may occasion the release into the air of any substance described in Schedule 4;[2] but a process does not fall within this paragraph by reason solely of its involving the melting of an alloy of beryllium if that alloy contains less than 0.1 per cent by weight of beryllium in molten form and the process falls within a description in paragraph (a) or (d)[3] of Part B of this Section.[4]

(h) The heating in a furnace or other appliance of any non-ferrous metal or non-ferrous metal alloy for the purpose of removing grease, oil or any other non-metallic contaminant (including such operations as the removal by heat of plastic or rubber covering from scrap cable[5]), if related to another process described in this Part of this Section.

(i) Any foundry process (including ancillary foundry operations such as the manufacture and recovery of moulds, the reclamation of sand, fettling, grinding and shot-blasting) if related to another process described in this Part of this Section.

(j) *Omitted by S.I. 1994/1271, reg.4(3), sch.3, para.11(h). This amendment came into force on 1 December 1994: reg.1(2).*

(k) Pelletising, calcining, roasting or sintering any non-ferrous metal ore or any mixture of such ore and other materials.[6]

## PART B

(a) The making or melting of any non-ferrous metal or non-ferrous metal alloy (other than tin or any alloy which, in molten form, contains 50% or more by weight of tin)[7] in any furnace, bath or other holding vessel with a designed holding capacity of less than 5 tonnes (together with any incidental refining).

(b) The separation of copper, aluminium, magnesium or zinc from mixed scrap by differential melting.[8]

(bb) The fusion of calcined bauxite for the production of artificial corundum.[9]

(c) Melting zinc or a zinc alloy in conjunction with a galvanising process.

(d) Melting zinc, aluminium or magnesium or an alloy of one or more of these metals in conjunction with a die-casting process.[10]

(e) Any such process as is described in paragraph (h) of Part A above, if not related to another process described in that Part; but a process does not fall within this paragraph if—

  (i) it involves the use of one or more furnaces or other appliances the primary combustion chambers of which have in aggregate a net rated thermal input of less than 0.2 megawatts; and

  (ii) it does not involve the removal by heat of plastic or rubber covering from scrap cable or of any asbestos contaminant.[11]

(f) Any foundry process (including ancillary foundry operations such as the manufacture and recovery of moulds, the reclamation of sand, fettling, grinding and shot-blasting) if related to another process described in this Part of this Section.

(g) *Omitted by S.I. 1995/3247, reg.2, sch.1, para.3(g). This amendment came into force on 8 January 1996: reg.1(1).*

The processes described in paragraphs (a), (c) and (d)[12] above include any related process for the refining of any non-ferrous metal or non-ferrous metal alloy.[13]

In this section "net rated thermal input" has the same meaning as in Section 1.3.[14]

[1] Words "manufacture or" inserted by S.I. 1994/1271, reg.4(3), sch.3, para.11(f)(i).

[2] P.592 below.

[3] Words "paragraph (a) or (d)" substituted by S.I. 1995/3247, reg.2, sch.1, para.3(d). This amendment came into force on 8 January 1996: reg.1(1).

[4] Words "; but a process . . . Part B of this Section." inserted by S.I. 1994/1271, reg.4(3), sch.3, para.11(f)(ii). This amendment came into force on 1 December 1994: reg.1(2).

[5] Words "scrap cable" substituted by S./I. 1994/1271, reg.4(3), sch.3, para.11(g).

[6] This paragraph added by S.I. 1994/1271, reg.4(3), sch.3, para.11(i).

[7] Words "(other than tin or . . . weight of tin)" inserted by S.I. 1994/1271, reg.3, sch.1, para.5(a). This amendment came into force on 1 June 1994: reg.1(1).

[8] This paragraph substituted by S.I. 1995/3247, reg.2, sch.1, para.3(e). This amendment came into force on 8 January 1996: reg.1(1).

[9] This paragraph inserted by S.I. 1994/1271, reg.4(3), sch.3, para.12(a). This amendment came into force on 1 December 1994: reg. 1(3).

[10] This paragraph substituted by S.I. 1995/3247, reg.2, sch.1, para.3(f). This amendment came into force on 8 January 1996: reg.1(1).

[11] Words "; but a process does not fall within . . . asbestos contaminant" added by S.I. 1994/1271, reg.3, sch.1, para.5(b). This amendment came into force on 1 June 1994: reg.1(1).

[12] Words "paragraphs (a), (c) and (d)" substituted by S.I. 1995/3247, reg.2, sch.1, para.3(h).

[13] This sentence added by S.I. 1994/1271, reg.4(3), sch.3, para.12(b). This amendment came into force on 1 December 1994: reg.1(2).

[14] This sentence added by S.I. 1994/1271, reg.3, sch.1, para.6. This amendment came into force on 1 June 1994: reg.1(1).

Nothing in this Section shall be taken to prescribe the processes of hand soldering or flow soldering.[1]

### Section 2.3 Smelting processes

*Omitted by S.I. 1994/1271, reg.4(3), sch.3, para.14. This amendment came into force on 1 December 1994: reg.1(2).*

## CHAPTER 3: MINERAL INDUSTRIES

### Section 3.1 Cement and lime manufacture and associated processes

## PART A

(a)  Making cement clinker.

(b)  Grinding cement clinker.

(c)  Any of the following processes, where the process is related to a process described in paragraph (a) or (b), namely, blending cement; putting cement into silos for bulk storage; removing cement from silos in which it has been stored in bulk; and any process involving the use of cement in bulk, including the bagging of cement and cement mixtures, the batching of ready-mixed concrete and the manufacture of concrete blocks and other cement products.

(d)  The heating of calcium carbonate or calcium magnesium carbonate for the purpose of making lime where the process is likely to involve the heating in any 12 month period of 5,000 tonnes or more of either substance or, in aggregate, of both.[2]

(e)  The slaking of lime for the purpose of making calcium hydroxide or calcium magnesium hydroxide where the process is related to a process described in paragraph (d) above.

## PART B

(a)  Any of the following processes, if not related to a process falling within a description in Part A of this Section—

   (i)  storing, loading or unloading cement or cement clinker in bulk prior to further transportation in bulk;

   (ii)  blending cement in bulk or using cement in bulk other than at a construction site, including the bagging of cement and cement mixtures, the batching of ready-mixed concrete and the manufacture of concrete blocks and other cement products.

(b)  The slaking of lime for the purpose of making calcium hydroxide or calcium magnesium hydroxide unless related to and carried on as part of[3] a process falling within another description in this Schedule.

(c)  The heating of calcium carbonate or calcium magnesium carbonate for the purpose of making lime where the process is not likely to involve the heating in any 12 month period of 5,000 tonnes or more of either substance or, in aggregate, of both.[4]

### Section 3.2 Processes involving asbestos

## PART A

(a)  Producing raw asbestos by extraction from the ore except where the process is directly associated with the mining of the ore.

(b)  The manufacture and, where related to the manufacture, the industrial finishing of the following products where the use of asbestos is involved—

asbestos cement
asbestos cement products
asbestos fillers
asbestos filters
asbestos floor coverings
asbestos friction products
asbestos insulating board
asbestos jointing, packaging and reinforcement material

---

[1] This sentence added by S.I. 1994/1271, reg.4(3), sch.3, para.13. This amendment came into force on 1 December 1994: reg.1(2).

[2] Words "where the process . . . of both." added by S.I. 1994/1271, reg.4(3), sch.3, para. 15. This amendment came into force on 1 December 1994: reg.1(2).

[3] Words "and carried on as part of" inserted by S.I. 1994/1271, reg.4(3), sch.3, para.16(a).

[4] This paragraph added by S.I. 1994/1271, reg.4(3), sch.3, para.16(b).

asbestos packing
asbestos paper or card
asbestos textiles.

(c) The stripping of asbestos from railway vehicles except—

   (i) in the course of the repair or maintenance of the vehicle;

   (ii) in the course of recovery operations following an accident; or

   (iii) where the asbestos is permanently bonded in cement or in any other material (including plastic, rubber or a resin).[1]

(d) The destruction by burning of a railway vehicle if asbestos has been incorporated in, or sprayed on to, its structure.

## Part B

The industrial finishing of any product mentioned in paragraph (b) of Part A of this Section if the process does not fall within that paragraph.

In this Section, "asbestos" means any of the following fibrous silicates—

actinolite, amosite, anthophyllite, chrysotile, crocidolite and tremolite.

### Section 3.3 Other mineral fibres

## Part A

Manufacturing—

   (i) glass fibre;

   (ii) any fibre from any mineral other than asbestos.

## Part B

Nil

### Section 3.4 Other mineral processes

## Part A

Nil

## Part B

(a) The crushing, grinding or other size reduction (other than the cutting of stone)[2] or the grading, screening or heating of any designated mineral or mineral product except where—

   (i) the process falls within a description in another Section of this Schedule;

   (ii) the process is related to and carried on as part of[3] another process falling within such a description; or

   (iii) the operation of the process is unlikely to result in the release into the air of particulate matter.

(b) Any of the following processes unless carried on at an exempt location or as part of a process falling within another description in this Schedule—

   (i) crushing, grinding or otherwise breaking up coal or coke or any other coal product;

   (ii) screening, grading or mixing coal, or coke or any other coal product;

   (iii) loading or unloading petroleum coke,[4] coal, coke or any other coal product except unloading on retail sale.

---

[1] Words "cement ... resin)" substituted by S.I. 1994/1271, reg.4(3), sch.3, para.17.

[2] Words "(other than the cutting of stone)" inserted by S.I. 1994/1271, reg.3, sch.1, para.7. This amendment came into force on 1 June 1994: reg.1(1).

[3] Words "and carried on as part of" inserted by S.I. 1994/1271, reg.4(3), sch.3, para.18(a). This amendment came into force on 1 December 1994: reg.1(2).

[4] Words "petroleum coke" inserted by S.I. 1994/1271, reg.4(3), sch.3, para.18(b).

(c) The crushing, grinding or other size reduction, with machinery designed for that purpose, of bricks, tiles or concrete.

(d) Screening the product of any such process as is described in paragraph (c).

(e) Coating roadstone with tar or bitumen.

(f) Loading, unloading, or storing pulverised fuel ash in bulk prior to further transportation in bulk, unless carried on as part of or in relation to a process falling within another description in this Schedule.[1]

In this section—

"coal" includes lignite;

"designated mineral or mineral product" means—

(i)   clay, sand and any other naturally occurring mineral other than coal or lignite;

(ii)  metallurgical slag;

(iii) boiler or furnace ash produced from the burning of coal, coke or any other coal product;

(iv) gypsum which is a by-product of any process; and

"exempt location" means—

(i)   any premises used for the sale of petroleum coke, coal, coke, or any coal product where the throughput of such substances at those premises in any 12 month period is in aggregate likely to be less than 10,000 tonnes; or

(ii)  any premises to which petroleum coke, coal, coke, or any coal product is supplied only for use there;[2]

"retail sale" means sale to the final consumer.[3]

Nothing in this Section applies to any process carried on underground.

## Section 3.5 Glass manufacture and production

### PART A

The manufacture of glass frit or enamel frit and its use in any process where that process is related to its manufacture and the aggregate quantity of such substances manufactured in any 12 month period is likely to be 100 tonnes or more.[4]

### PART B

(a) The manufacture of glass at any location where the person concerned has the capacity to make 5,000 tonnes or more of glass in any 12 month period, and any process involving the use of glass which is carried on at any such location in conjunction with its manufacture.

(b) The manufacture of glass where the use of lead or any lead compound is involved.

(c) The making of any glass product where lead or any lead compound has been used in the manufacture of the glass except—

(i)  the making of products from lead glass blanks;

(ii) the melting, or mixing with another substance, of glass manufactured elsewhere to produce articles such as ornaments or road paint;

(d) Polishing or etching glass or glass products in the course of any manufacturing process if—

(i)  hydrofluoric acid is used; or

(ii) hydrogen fluoride may be released into the air.

(e) The manufacture of glass frit or enamel frit and its use in any process where that process is related to its manufacture if not falling within Part A of this Section.[5]

---

[1] This paragraphs inserted by S.I. 1994/1271, reg.4(3), sch.3, para.18(c).

[2] This definition substituted by S.I. 1994/1271, reg.4(3), sch.3, para.19(a).

[3] This definition inserted by S.I. 1994/1271, reg.4(3), sch.3, para.19(b).

[4] Words "and the aggregate quantity . . . 100 tonnes or more" inserted by S.I. 1994/1271, reg.4(3), sch.3, para.20.

[5] This paragraph added by S.I. 1994/1271, reg.4(3), sch.3, para.21. This amendment came into force on 1 December 1994: reg.1(2).

*Section 3.6 Ceramic production*[1]

## PART A

Firsing heavy clay goods or refractory material in a kiln where a reducing atmosphere is used for a purpose other than coloration.

## PART B

(a) Firing heavy clay goods or refractory material (other than heavy clay goods) in a kiln where the process does not fall within a description in part A of this Section.

(b) Vapour glazing earthenware or clay with sales.

In this Section—

"clay" includes a blend of clay with ash, sand or other materials;

"refractory material" means material (such as fireclay, silica, magnesite, chrome-magnesite, sillimanite, sintered alumina, beryllia and boron nitride) which is able to withstand high temperatures and to function as a furnace lining or in other similar high temperature applications.

## CHAPTER 4: THE CHEMICAL INDUSTRY

(See paragraph 4 of Schedule 2 as to cases where processes described in this chapter of the Schedule fall within two or more descriptions).

Except where paragraph 2 or 8 of Schedule 2 applies, nothing in this chapter of this Schedule applies to the operation of waste treatment plant.[2]

*Section 4.1 Petrochemical processes*

## PART A

(a) Any process for the manufacture of unsaturated hydrocarbons.[3]

(b) Any process for the manufacture of any chemical which involves the use of a product of a process described in paragraph (a).

(c) Any process for the manufacture of any chemical which involves the use of a product of a process described in paragraph (b) otherwise than as a fuel or solvent.

(d) Any process for the polymerisation or co-polymerisation of any unsaturated hydrocarbons (other than the polymerisation or co-polymerisation of a pre-formulated resin or pre-formulated gel coat which contains any unsaturated hydrocarbons, or which contains any product of a process mentioned in paragraph (b) or (c) of Part A of this Section) which is likely to involve, in any 12 month period, the polymerisation or co-polymerisation of 50 tonnes or more of unsaturated hydrocarbons or of any such products or, in aggregate, of any combination of those materials and products.[4]

(e) Any process, if related to and carried on as part of a process falling within another paragraph of this Part of this Section, for the polymerisation or co-polymerisation of any pre-formulated resin or pre-formulated gel coat which contains any unsaturated hydrocarbons, or which contains any product of a process mentioned in paragraph (b) or (c) of Part A of this Section, which is likely to involve, in any 12 month period, the polymerisation or co-polymerisation of 100 tonnes or more of unsaturated hydrocarbons or of any such products or, in aggregate, of any combination of those materials and products.[5]

## PART B[6]

Any process, unless related to and carried on as part of a process falling within Part A of this Section, for the polymerisation or co-polymerisation of any pre-formulated resin or pre-formulated gel coat which contains any unsat-

---

[1] This section substituted by S.I. 1994/1271, reg.4(3), sch.3, para.22.

[2] This sentence inserted by S.I. 1994/1271, reg.4(3), sch.3, para.23. This amendment came into force on 1 December 1994: reg.1(2).

[3] Words "unsaturated hydrocarbons" substituted by S.I. 1994/1271, reg.4(3), sch.3, para.24(a).

[4] This paragraph substituted by S.I. 1995/3247, reg.2, sch.1, para.4(a). This amendment came into force on 8 January 1996: reg.1(1).

[5] This paragraph inserted by S.I. 1995/3247, reg.2, sch.1, para.4(b).

[6] This Part substituted by S.I. 1995/3247, reg.2, sch.1, para.4(c).

urated hydrocarbons, or which contains any product of a process mentioned in paragraph (b) or (c) of Part A of this Section, which is likely to involve, in any 12 month period, the polymerisation or co-polymerisation of 100 tonnes or more of unsaturated hydrocarbons or of any such products or, in aggregate, of any combination of those materials and products.

In this Section and in Section 4.2, "pre-formulated resin or pre-formulated gel coat" means any resin or gel coat which has been formulated before being introduced into the polymerisation or co-polymerisation process (whether or not the resin or gel coat contains a colour pigment, activator or catalyst).[1]

## *Section 4.2 The manufacture and use of organic chemicals*

### PART A

Any of the following processes unless falling within a description set out in Section 6.8—

(a)   the manufacture of styrene or vinyl chloride;[2]

(aa)  the polymerisation or co-polymerisation of styrene or vinyl chloride (other than the polymerisation or co-polymerisation of a pre-formulated resin or pre-formulated gel coat[3] which contains any styrene) where the process is likely to involve, in any 12 month period, the polymerisation or co-polymerisation of 50 tonnes or more of either of those materials or, in aggregate, of both;[4]

(ab)  any process, if related to and carried on as part of a process falling within another paragraph of this Part of this Section, for the polymerisation or co-polymerisation of any pre-formulated resin or pre-formulated gel coat which contains any styrene, which is likely to involve, in any 12 month period, the polymerisation or co-polymerisation of 100 tonnes or more of styrene;[5]

(b)   any process of manufacture involving the use of vinyl chloride;

(c)   the manufacture of acetylene, any aldehyde, amine, isocyanate, nitrile, any carboxylic acid or any anhydride of carboxylic acid,[6] any organic sulphur compound or any phenol, if the process may result in the release of any of those substances into the air;

(d)   any process for the manufacture of a chemical involving the use of any substance mentioned in paragraph (c) if the process may result in the release of any such substance into the air;[7]

(e)   the manufacture or recovery of carbon disulphide;

(f)   any manufacturing process which may result in the release of carbon disulphide into the air;

(g)   the manufacture or recovery of pyridine, or of any substituted pyridines;[8]

(h)   the manufacture of any organo-metallic compound;

(i)   the manufacture, purification or recovery of any designated acrylate;[9]

(j)   any process for the manufacture of a chemical which is likely to involve the use in any 12 month period of 1 tonne or more of any designated acrylate or, in aggregate, of more than one such designated acrylate.[10]

In this Part of this Section, "designated acrylate" means any of the following, namely, acrylic acid, substituted acrylic acids, the esters of acrylic acid and the esters of substituted acrylic acids.[11]

### PART B[12]

Any process, unless related to and carried on as part of a process falling within Part A of this Section, for the polymerisation or co-polymerisation of any pre-formulated resin or pre-formulated gel coat which contains any

---

[1] This sentence added by S.I. 1995/3247, reg.2, sch.1, para.4(d).

[2] This paragraph substituted by S.I. 1994/1271, reg.4(3), sch.3, para.25(a). This amendment came into force on 1 December 1994: reg.1(2).

[3] For "pre-formulated resin or pre-formulated gel coat" see the definition at the end of Section 4.1 above.

[4] This paragraph substituted by S.I. 1995/3247, reg.2, sch.1, para.5(a). This amendment came into force on 8 January 1996: reg.1(1).

[5] This paragraph inserted by S.I. 1995/3247, reg.2, sch.1, para.5(b).

[6] Words "any carboxylic acid or any anhydride of carboxylic acid" substituted by S.I. 1994/1271, reg.4(3), sch.3, para.25(b). This amendment came into force on 1 December 1994: reg.1(2).

[7] This paragraph substituted by S.I. 1994/1271, reg.4(3), sch.3, para.25(c).

[8] This paragraph substituted by S.I. 1994/1271, reg.4(3), sch.3, para.25(d). This amendment came into force on 1 December 1994: reg.1(2).

[9] Words "any designated acrylate" substituted by S.I. 1994/1271, reg.4(3), sch.3, para.25(e).

[10] Words "which is likely to involve ... one such designated acrylate." substituted by S.I. 1994/1271, reg.4(3), sch.3, para.25(f).

[11] This sentence added by S.I. 1994/1271, reg.4(3), sch.3, para.25(g).

[12] This Part substituted by S.I. 1995/3247, reg.2, sch.1, para.5(c). This amendment came into force on 8 January 1996: reg.1(1).

styrene, which is likely to involve, in any 12 month period, the polymerisation or co-polymerisation of 100 tonnes or more of styrene.

*Section 4.3 Acid processes*

## PART A

(a) Any process for the manufacture, recovery, concentration or distillation of sulphuric acid or oleum.

(b) Any process for the manufacture of any oxide of sulphur but excluding any combustion or incineration process other than the burning of sulphur.

(c) Any process for the manufacture of a chemical which uses, or may result in the release into the air of, any oxide of sulphur but excluding any combustion or incineration process other than the burning of sulphur and excluding also any process where such a release could only occur as a result of the storage and use of $SO_2$ in cylinders.[1]

(d) Any process for the manufacture or recovery of nitric acid.

(e) Any process for the manufacture of any acid-forming oxide of nitrogen.

(f) Any other process (except the combustion or incineration of carbonaceous material as defined in Section 1.1 of this Schedule) which is not described in Part B of this Section, does not fall within a description in Section 2.1 or 2.2 of this Schedule and is not treated as so falling by virtue of the rules in Schedule 2, and[2] which is likely to result in the release into the air of any acid-forming oxide of nitrogen.

(g) Any process for the manufacture or purification[3] of phosphoric acid.

## PART B[4]

Any process for the surface treatment of metal which is likely to result in the release into the air of any acid-forming oxide of nitrogen and which does not fall within a description in Section 2.1 or 2.2 of this Schedule and is not treated as so falling by virtue of the rules in Schedule 2.

*Section 4.4 Processes involving halogens*

## PART A

The following processes if not falling within a description in any other Section of this Schedule—

(a) any process for the manufacture of fluorine, chlorine, bromine or iodine or of any compound comprising only—

(i) two or more of those halogens; or

(ii) any one or more of those halogens and oxygen;

(b) any process of manufacture which involves the use of, or which is likely to result in the release into the air or into water of, any of those four halogens or any of the compounds mentioned in paragraph (a) other than the use of any of them as a pesticide (as defined in Schedule 6) in water;

(c) any process for the manufacture of hydrogen fluoride, hydrogen chloride, hydrogen bromide or hydrogen iodide or any of their acids;

(d) any process for the manufacture of chemicals which may result in the release into the air of any of the four compounds mentioned in paragraph (c);

(e) any process of manufacture (other than the manufacture of chemicals) involving the use of any of the four compounds mentioned in paragraph (c) or any of their acids[5] which may result in the release of any of those compounds into the air, other than the coating, plating or surface treatment[6] of metal.

---

[1] Words "and excluding also . . . $SO_2$ in cylinders" added by S.I. 1994/1271, reg.4(3), shc.3, para.26(a). This amendment came into force on 1 December 1994: reg.1(2).

[2] Words "which is not described in Part B of this Section, . . . the rules in Schedule 2, and" inserted by S.I. 1994/1271, reg.4(3), sch.3, para.26(b).

[3] Words "or purification" inserted by S.I. 1994/1271,

reg.4(3), sch.3, para.26(c).

[4] This Part substituted by S.I. 1994/1271, reg.4(3), sch.3, para.27.

[5] Words "or any of their acids" inserted by S.I. 1994/1271, reg.4(3), sch.3, para.28(a).

[6] Words "surface treatment" substituted by S.I. 1994/1271, reg.4(3), sch.3, para.28(b).

PART B

Nil

*Section 4.5 Inorganic chemical processes*

## PART A

(a)   The manufacture of hydrogen cyanide or hydrogen sulphide other than in the course of fumigation.

(b)   Any manufacturing process involving the use of hydrogen cyanide or hydrogen sulphide.

(c)   Any process for the manufacture of a chemical which may result in the release into the air of hydrogen cyanide or hydrogen sulphide.

(d)   The production of any of the following or of any compound containing any of the following[1]—

antimony
arsenic
beryllium
gallium
indium
lead
palladium
platinum
selenium
tellurium
thallium,

where the process may result in the release into the air of any of those elements or compounds or the release into water of any substance described in Schedule 5 in a quantity which, in any 12 month period, exceeds the background quantity[2] by more than the amount specified in relation to the description of substance in column 2 of that Schedule.[3]

(e)   The recovery of any[4] compound referred to in paragraph (d) where the process may result in any such release as is mentioned in that paragraph.

(f)   The use in any process of manufacture, other than the application of a glaze or vitreous enamel, of any element or compound referred to in paragraph (d) where the process may result in such a release as is mentioned in that paragraph.

(g)   The production or recovery of any compound of cadmium or mercury.[5]

(h)   Any process of manufacture which involves the use of cadmium or mercury or of any compound of either of those elements or which may result in the release into the air of either of those elements or any of their compounds.

(i)   The production of any compound of—

chromium
[6]
manganese
nickel
zinc.

(j)   The manufacture of any metal carbonyl.

(k)   Any process for the manufacture of a chemical involving the use of a metal carbonyl.[7]

(l)   The manufacture or recovery of ammonia.

---

[1] Words "any compound containing any of the following" substituted by S.I. 1993/2405, reg.2(2)(a). This amendment came into force on 26 October 1993: reg.1(1).

[2] "Background quantity" defined by reg.4(7), (8), p.568 above.

[3] Words "in a quantity which, ... column 2 of that Schedule" added by S.I. 1995/3247, reg.2, sch.1, para.6(a). This amendment came into force on 8 January 1995: reg.1(1).

[4] Former words "element or" omitted by S.I. 1993/2405, reg.2(2)(b). This amendment came into force on 26 October 1993: reg.1(1).

[5] This paragraph substituted by S.I. 1993/2405, reg.2(2)(c).

[6] Former word "magnesium" omitted by S.I. 1933/2405, reg.2(2)(d).

[7] This paragraph substituted by S.I. 1993/2405, reg.2(2)(e).

(m) Any process for the manufacture of a chemical which involves the use of ammonia or may result in the release of ammonia into the air other than a process in which ammonia is used only as a refrigerant.

(n) The production of phosphorus or of any oxide, hydride or halide of phosphorus.

(o) Any process for the manufacture of a chemical which involves the use of phosphorus or any oxide, hydride or halide of phosphorus or which may result in the release into the air of phosphorus or of any such oxide, hydride or halide.

(p) The extraction of any magnesium compound from sea water.[1]

## PART B

Nil

### Section 4.6 Chemical Fertiliser Production

## PART A

(a) The manufacture of chemical fertilisers.

(b) The conversion of chemical fertilisers into granules.

In this Section, "chemical fertilisers" means any inorganic chemical to be applied to the soil to promote plant growth; and "inorganic chemical" includes urea; and "manufacture of chemical fertilisers" shall be taken to include any process for blending chemical fertilisers which is related to a process for their manufacture.[2]

## PART B

Nil

### Section 4.7 Pesticide production

## PART A[3]

The manufacture or the formulation of chemical pesticides if the process may result in the release into water of any substance described in Schedule 5 in a quantity which, in any 12 month period, exceeds the background quantity[4] by more than the amount specified in relation to the description of substance in column 2 of that Schedule.[5]

## PART B

Nil

In this Section "pesticide" has the same meaning as in Schedule 6.[6]

### Section 4.8 Pharmaceutical production

## PART A[7]

The manufacture or the formulation of a medicinal product if the process may result in the release into water of any substance described in Schedule 5 in a quantity which, in any 12 month period, exceeds the background quantity by more than the amount specified in relation to the description of substance in column 2 of that Schedule.[8]

---

[1] This paragraph added by S.I. 1993/2405, reg.2(2)(f).

[2] Words "; and 'manufacture of chemical fertilisers' ... process for their manufacture." added by S.I. 1994/1271, reg.4(3), sch.3, para.29. This amendment came into force on 1 December 1994: reg.1(2).

[3] This Part substituted by S.I. 1994/1271, reg.4(3), sch.3, para.30. This amendment came into force on 1 December 1994: reg.1(2).

[4] "Background quantity" defined by reg.4(7), (8), p.568 above.

[5] Words "in a quantity which, ... column 2 of that

Schedule" added by S.I. 1995/3247, reg.2, sch.1, para.6(b). This amendment came into force on 8 January 1996: reg.1(1).

[6] P.593 below.

[7] This Part substituted by S.I. 1994/1271, reg.4(3), sch.3, para.31. This amendment came into force on 1 December 1994: reg.1(2).

[8] Words "in a quantity which, ... column 2 of that Schdule" added by S.I. 1995/3247, reg.2, sch.1, para.6(c). This amendment came into force on 8 January 1996: reg.1(1).

## PART B

Nil

In this Section, "medicinal product" means any substance or article (not being an instrument, apparatus or appliance) manufactured for use in one of the ways specified in section 130(1) of the Medicines Act 1968.[1]

### Section 4.9 The storage of chemicals in bulk[2]

## PART A

Nil

## PART B

The storage in a rank or tanks, other than as part of a Part A process, and other than in a tank for the time being forming part of a powered vehicle, of any of the substances listed below except where the total capacity of the tanks installed at the location in question in which the relevant substance may be stored is less than the figure specified below in relation to that substance;

| any one or more designated acrylates | 20 | tonnes |
| acrylonitrile | 20 | tonnes |
| anhydrous ammonia | 100 | tonnes |
| anhydrous hydrogen fluoride | 1 | tonne |
| toluene di-isocyanate | 20 | tonnes |
| vinyl chloride monomer | 20 | tonnes |
| ethylene | 8,000 | tonnes |

In this Section, "designated acrylate" has the same meaning as in Part A of Section 4.2.

## CHAPTER 5: WASTE DISPOSAL AND RECYCLING

### Section 5.1 Incineration

## PART A

(a) The destruction by burning in an incinerator of any waste chemicals or waste plastic arising from the manufacture of a chemical or the manufacture of a plastic.

(b) The destruction by burning in an incinerator, other than incidentally in the course of burning other waste, of any waste chemicals being, or comprising in elemental or compound form, any of the following—

bromine
cadmium
chlorine
fluorine
iodine
lead
mercury
nitrogen
phosphorus
sulphur
zinc

(c) The destruction by burning of any other waste, including animal remains, otherwise than by a process related to and carried on as part of[3] a Part B process, on premises where there is plant designed to incinerate such waste at a rate of 1 tonne or more per hour.

(d) The cleaning for reuse of metal containers used for the transport or storage of a chemical by burning out their residual content.

---

[1] 1968 c.67.
[2] This Section substituted by S.I. 1994/1271, reg.4(3), sch.3, para.32. This amendment came into force on 1 December 1994: reg.1(2).

[3] Words "and carried on as part of" inserted by S.I. 1994/1271, reg.4(3), sch.3, para. 33. This amendment came into force on 1 December 1994: reg.1(2).

## PART B

(a) The destruction by burning in an incinerator other than an exempt incinerator of any waste, including animal remains, except where related to a Part A process.

(b) The cremation of human remains.

In this section—

"exempt incinerator" means any incinerator on premises where there is plant designed to incinerate waste, including animal remains[1] at a rate of not more than 50 kgs per hour, not being an incinerator employed to incinerate clinical waste, sewage sludge, sewage screenings or municipal waste (as defined in Article 1 of EC Directive 89/369/EEC[2]); and for the purposes of this section, the weight of waste shall be determined by reference to its weight as fed into the incinerator;

"waste" means solid or liquid wastes or gaseous wastes (other than gas produced by biological degradation of waste); and[3]

"clinical waste" means waste (other than waste consisting wholly of animal remains) which falls within sub-paragraph (a) or (b) of the definition of such waste in paragraph (2) of regulation 1 of the Controlled Waste Regulations 1992[4] (or would fall within one of those sub-paragraphs but for paragraph (4) of that regulation).[5]

### Section 5.2 Recovery processes

## PART A[6]

(a) The recovery by distillation of any oil or organic solvent.

(b) The cleaning or regeneration of carbon, charcoal or ion exchange resins by removing matter which is, or includes, any substance described in Schedule 4, 5 or 6.

Nothing in this Part of this Section applies to—

(i) the distillation of oil for the production or cleaning of vacuum pump oil; or

(ii) a process which is ancillary and related to another process which involves the production or use of the substance which is recovered, cleaned or regenerated.

## PART B

Nil

### Section 5.3 The production of fuel from waste

## PART A

Making solid fuel from waste by any process involving the use of heat other than making charcoal.

## PART B

Nil

## CHAPTER 6: OTHER INDUSTRIES

### Section 6.1 Paper and pulp manufacturing processes

## PART A

(a) The making of paper pulp by a chemical method if the person concerned has the capacity at the location in question to produce more than 25,000 tonnes of paper pulp in any 12 month period.

---

[1] Words "incinerate waste, including animal remains substituted by S.I. 1992/614, reg.2, sch.1, para.9(a). This amendment came into force on 1 April 1992: reg.1(1).

[2] OJ No. L163, 14.6.89, p. 32.

[3] This definition substituted by S.i. 1992/614, reg.2, sch.1, para.9(b).

[4] P.662 below.

[5] This definition substituted by S.I. 1994/1271, reg.4(3), sch.3, para. 34. This amendment came into force on 1 June 1994: reg.1(1).

[6] This Part substituted by S.I. 1994/1271, reg.4(3), sch.3, para. 34. This amendment came into force on 1 December 1994: reg.1(2).

(b)  Any process associated with[1] making paper pulp or paper (including processes connected with the recycling of paper such as de-inking) if the process may result in the release into water of any substance described in Schedule 5 in a quantity which, in any 12 month period, exceeds the background quantity[2] by more than the amount specified in relation to the description of substance in column 2 of that Schedule.[3]

In this paragraph, "paper pulp" includes pulp made from wood, grass, straw and similar materials and references to the making of paper are to the making of any product using paper pulp.

## Part B

Nil

### Section 6.2 Di-isocyanate processes

## Part A

(a)  Any process for the manufacture of any di-isocyanate or a partly polymerised di-isocyanate.

(b)  Any manufacturing process involving the use of toluene di-isocyanate or partly polymerised toluene di-isocynate if—

    (i)  1 tonne or more of toluene di-isocyanate monomer is likely to be used in any 12 month period; and

    (ii)  the process may result in a release into the air which contains toluene di-isocyanate.[4]

(c)  *Omitted by S.I. 1994/1271. reg.4(3), sch.3, para.36(b). This amendment came into force on 1 December 1994: reg.1(2).*

(d)  The flame bonding of polyurethane foams or polyurethane elastomers, and the hot wire cutting of such substances where such cutting is related to any other Part A process.[5]

## Part B[6]

(a)  Any process not falling within any other description in this Schedule where the carrying on of the process by the person concerned at the location in question is likely to involve the use in any 12 month period of 5 tonnes or more of any di-isocyanate or of any partly polymerised di-isocyanate or, in aggregate, of both.

(b)  Any process not falling within any other description in this Schedule involving the use toluene di-isocyanate or partly polymerised toluene di-isocyanate if—

    (i)  less than 1 tonne of toluene di-isocyanate monomer is likely to be used in any 12 month period; and

    (ii)  the process may result in a release into the air which contains toluene di-isocyanate.

(c)  The hot wire cutting of polyurethane foams or polyurethane elastomers, except where this process is related to any other Part A process.

### Section 6.3 Tar and bitumen processes[7]

## Part A

Any process not falling within any other description in this Schedule involving—

    (a)  the distillation of tar or bitumen in connection with any process of manufacture; or

    (b)  the heating of tar or bitumen for the manufacture of electrodes or carbon-based refractory materials,

where the carrying on of the process by the person concerned at the location in question is likely to involve the use in any 12 month period of 5 tonnes or more of tar or of bitumen or, in aggregate, of both.

---

[1]  Words "associated with" substituted by S.I. 1994/1271, reg.4(3), sch.3, para.35. This amendment came into force on 1 December 1994: reg.1(2).

[2]  "Background quantity" defined by reg.4(7), (8), p.568 above.

[3]  Words "in a quantity which, . . . column 2 of that Schedule" added by S.I. 1995/3247, reg.2, sch.1, para.6(d). This amendment came into force on 8 January 1996: reg.1(1).

[4]  Paragraph (b) substituted by S.I. 1994/1271, reg.4(3), sch.3, para.36(a).This amendment came into force on 1 December 1994: reg.1(2).

[5]  This paragraph substituted by S.I. 1994/1271, reg.4(3), sch.3, para.36(c).

[6]  This Part substituted by S.I. 1994/1271, reg.4(3), sch.3, para. 37. This amendment came into force on 1 December 1994: reg.1(2).

[7]  This Section substituted by S.I. 1994/1271, reg.4(3), sch.3, para. 38. This amendment came into force on 1 December 1994: reg.1(2).

## Part B

Any process not falling within Part A of this Section or within any other description in this Schedule involving—

(a)  the heating, but not the distillation, of tar or bitumen in connection with any process of manufacture; or

(b)  (unless the process is related to and carried on as part of a process falling within Part A of Section 1.4 of this Schedule) the oxidation of bitumen by blowing air through it,

where the carrying on of the process by the person concerned at the location in question is likely to involve the use in any 12 month period of 5 tonnes or more of tar or bitumen or, in aggregate, of both.

In this Section the expressions "tar" and "bitumen" include pitch.

### Section 6.4 Processes involving uranium

*This section omitted by S.I. 1994/1271, reg.493), sch.3, para.39. This amendment came into force on 1 December 1994: reg.1(2).*

### Section 6.5 Coating Processes and Printing

## Part A

(a)  The application or removal of a coating material containing one or more tributyltin compounds or triphenyltin compounds, if carried out at a shipyard or boatyard where vessels of a length of 25 metres or more can be built or maintained or repaired.

(b)  The treatment of textiles if the process may result in the release into water of any substance described in Schedule 5 in a quantity which, in any 12 month period, exceeds the background quantity[1] by more than the amount specified in relation to the description of substance in column 2 of that Schedule.[2]

(c)  *Omitted by S.I. 1994/1271, reg.4(3), sch.3, para.40. This amendment came into force on 1 December 1994: reg.1(2).*

## Part B[3]

(a)  Any process (other than for the repainting or respraying of or of parts of aircraft or road or railway vehicles) for the application to a substrate of, or the drying or curing after such application of, printing ink or paint or any other coating material as, or in the course of, a manufacturing process where—

(i)  the process may result in the release into the air of particulate matter[4] or of any volatile organic compound; and

(ii)  the carrying on of the process by the person concerned at the location in question is likely to involve the use in any 12 month period of—

(aa)  20 tonnes or more applied in solid form of any printing ink, paint or other coating material; or

(bb)  20 tonnes or more of any metal coatings which are sprayed on in molten form; or

(cc)  25 tonnes or more of organic solvents in respect of any cold set web offset printing process or any sheet fed offset litho printing process or, in respect of any other process, 5 tonnes or more of organic solvents.

(b)  Any process for the repainting or respraying of or of parts of road vehicles if the process may result in the release into the air of particulate matter or of any volatile organic compound and the carrying on of the process by the person concerned at the location in question is likely to involve the use of 1 tonne or more of organic solvents in any 12 month period.

(c)  Any process for the repainting or respraying of or of parts of aircraft or railway vehicles if the process may result in the release into the air of particulate matter or of any volatile organic compound and the carrying on of the process by the person concerned at the location in question is likely to involve the use in any 12 month period of—

---

[1]  "Background quantity" defined by reg.4(7), (8), p.568 above.

[2]  Words "in a quantity which, ... column 2 of that Schedule" added by S.I. 1995/3247, reg.2, sch.1, para.6(e). This amendment came into force on 8 January 1996: reg.1(1).

[3]  This Part substituted by S.I. 1994/1271, reg.4(3), sch.3, para.41. This amendment came into force on 1 December 1994: reg.1(2).

[4]  "Particulate matter" defined by reg.2, p.566 above.

(i)   20 tonnes or more applied in solid form of any paint or other coating material; or

(ii)  20 tonnes or more of any metal coatings which are sprayed on in molten form; or

(iii) 5 tonnes or more of organic solvents.

In this Section—

"aircraft" includes gliders and missiles;

"coating material" means paint, printing ink, varnish, lacquer, dye, any metal oxide coating, any adhesive coating, any elastomer coating, any metal or plastic coating and any other coating material;[1] and

the amount of organic solvents used in a process shall be calculated as—

(a)  the total input of organic solvents into the process, including both solvents contained in coating materials and solvents used for cleaning or other purposes; less

(b)  any organic solvents that are removed from the process for re-use or for recovery for re-use.[2]

*Section 6.6 The manufacture of dyestuffs, printing ink and coating materials*

## PART A[3]

Any process for the manufacture of dyestuffs if the process involves the use of hexachlorobenzene.

## PART B

Any process–[4]

(a)  for the manufacture or formulation of printing ink or any other coating material containing, or involving the use of, an organic solvent, where the carrying on of the process by the person concerned at the location in question is likely to involve the use of 100 tonnes or more of organic solvents in any 12 month period;

(b)  for the manufacture of any powder for use as a coating material[5] where there is the capacity to produce 200 tonnes or more of such powder in any 12 month period.

In this Section, "coating material" has the same meaning as in Section 6.5, and the amount of organic solvents used in a process shall be calculated as—

(a)  the total input of organic solvents into the process, including both solvents contained in coating materials and solvents used for cleaning or other purposes; less

(b)  any organic solvents (not contained in coating materials) that are removed from the process for re-use or for recovery for re-use.[6]

*Section 6.7 Timber processes*

## PART A

(a)  The curing or chemical treatment as part of a manufacturing process of timber or of products wholly or mainly made of wood if any substance described in Schedule 5 is used.

(b)  *Omitted by S.I. 1994/1271, reg.4(3), sch.3, para.45. This amendment came into force on 1 December 1994: reg.1(2).*

---

[1] Words "In this Section– . . . and any other coating material" substituted by S.I. 1994/1271, reg.4(3), sch.3, para.42.

[2] Words "the amount of organic solvents . . . for re-use or for recovery for re-use": substituted by S.I. 1994/1271, reg.3, sch.1, para.10. This amendment came into force on 1 June 1994: reg.1(1).

[3] This Part substituted by S.I. 1994/1271, reg.4(3), sch.3, para. 43. This amendment came into force on 1 December 1994: reg.1(2).

[4] Former words "not falling within a description in any other Section in this Schedule" omitted by S.I. 1994/1271, reg.4(3), sch.3, para.44(a).

[5] Words "use as a coating material" substituted by S.I. 1994/1271, reg.4(3), sch.3, para.44(b).

[6] Words ", and the amount of organic solvents used in a process . . . for recovery for re-use." substituted by S.I. 1994/1271, reg.3, sch.1, para.11. This amendment came into force on 1 June 1994: reg.1(1).

## Part B

The manufacture of products wholly or mainly of wood at any works if the process involves the sawing, drilling, sanding, shaping, turning, planing, curing or chemical treatment of wood ("relevant processes")[1] and the throughput of the works in any 12 month period is likely to exceed—

(i)   10,000 cubic metres, in the case of works at which wood is sawed but at which wood is not subjected to any other relevant processes or is subjected only to relevant processes which are exempt processes; or

(ii)  1,000 cubic metres in any other case.[2]

For the purposes of this paragraph—

relevant processes other than sawing are "exempt processes" where, if no sawing were carried on at the works, the activities carried on there would be treated as not falling within this Part of this Section by virtue of regulation 4(2);[3,4]

   "throughput" shall be calculated by reference to the amount of wood which is subjected to any of the relevant processes:[5] but where, at the same works, wood is subject to two or more relevant processes,[6] no account shall be taken of the second or any subsequent process;

   "wood" includes any product consisting wholly or mainly of wood;[7] and

   "works" includes a sawmill or any other premises on which relevant processes are carried out on wood.

### Section 6.8 Processes involving rubber

#### Part A

Nil

#### Part B

(a)  The mixing, milling or blending of—

(i)   natural rubber; or

(ii)  synthetic organic[8] elastomers,

if carbon black is used.

(b)  Any process which converts the product of a process falling within paragraph (a) into a finished product if related to a process falling within that paragraph.

### Section 6.9 The treatment and processing of animal or vegetable matter

#### Part A

Any of the following processes, unless falling within a description in another Section of the Schedule or an exempt process, namely, the processing in any way whatsoever, storing or drying by the application of heat of any dead animal (or part thereof) or any vegetable matter[9] if the process may result in the release into water of any substance described in Schedule 5 in a quantity which, in any 12 month period, exceeds the background quantity[10] by more than the amount specified in relation to the description of substance in column 2 of that Schedule:[11] but excluding any process for the treatment of effluent so as to permit its discharge into controlled waters or into a sewer unless the treatment process involves the drying of any material with a view to its use as an animal feedstuff.

---

[1] Words "('relevant processes')" inserted by S.I. 1992/614, reg.2, sch.1, para.11(a). This amendment came into force on 1 April 1992: reg.1(1).

[2] Words "12 month period . . . in any other case." substituted by S.I. 1994/1271, reg.3, sch.1, para.12(a). This amendment came into force on 1 June 1994: reg.1(1).

[3] P.567 above.

[4] Words "relevant processes other than sawing are 'exempt processes' 'where . . . by virtue of rergulation 4(2);" inserted by S.I. 1994/1271, reg.3, sch.1, para.12(b).

[5] Words "of the relevant processes" substituted by S.I. 1992/614, reg.2, sch.1, para.11(c). This amendment came into force on 1 April 1992: reg.1(1).

[6] Words "relevant processes" substituted by S.I. 1992/614, reg.2, sch.1, para.11(c).

[7] This definition substituted by S.I. 1994/1271, reg.4(3), sch.3, para.46. This amendment came into force on 1 December 1994: reg.1(2).

[8] Word "organic" inserted by S.I. 1994/1271, reg.3, sch.1, para.13. This amendment came into force on 1 June 1994: reg.1(1).

[9] Words "vegetable matter" substituted by S.I. 1992/614, reg.2, sch.1, para.12. This amendment came into force on 1 April 1992: reg.1(1).

[10] "Background quantity" defined by reg.4(7), (8), p.568 above.

[11] Words "if the process . . . of that Schedule" substituted by S.I. 1995/3247, reg.2, sch.1, para.7. This amendment came into force on 8 January 1996: reg.1(1).

## PART B

(a) Any process mentioned in Part A, of this Section unless an exempt process—

    (i) where the process has the characteristics described in regulation 4(1)(ii) above; but[1]

    (ii) may release into the air a substance described in Schedule 4[2] or any offensive smell noticeable outside the premises on which the process is carried on.

(b) Breeding maggots in any case where 5 kg or more of animal or of vegetable matter or, in aggregate, of both are introduced into the process in any week.

In this Section—

"animal" includes a bird or a fish; and

"exempt process" means—

(i)     any process carried on on a farm or agricultural holding other than the manufacture of goods for sale;

(ii)    the manufacture or preparation of food or drink for human consumption but excluding—

    (a) the extraction, distillation or purification of animal or vegetable oil or fat otherwise than as a process incidental to the cooking of food for human consumption;

    (b) any process involving the use of green offal or the boiling of blood except the cooking of food (other than tripe) for human consumption;

    (c) the cooking of tripe for human consumption elsewhere than on premises on which it is to be consumed;

(iii)   the fleshing, cleaning and drying of pelts of fur-bearing mammals;[3]

(iv)   any process carried on in connection with the operation of a knacker's yard, as defined in article 3(1) of the Animal By-Products Order 1992;[4]

(v)    any process for the manufacture of soap not falling within a description in Part A of Section 4.2 of this Schedule;

(vi)   the storage of vegetable matter otherwise than as part of any prescribed process;

(vii)  the cleaning of shellfish shells;

(viii) the manufacture of starch;

(ix)   the processing of animal or vegetable matter at premises for feeding a recognised pack of hounds registered under article 10 of the Animal By-Products Order 1992;

(x)    the salting of hides or skins, unless related to any other prescribed process;

(xi)   any process for composting animal or vegetable matter or a combination of both, except where that process is carried on for the purposes of cultivating mushrooms;

(xii)  any process for cleaning, and any related process for drying or dressing, seeds, bulbs, corms or tubers;

(xiii) the drying of grain or pulses;

(xiv) any process for the production of cotton yarn from raw cotton or for the conversion of cotton yarn into cloth;[5]

"food" includes drink, articles and substances of no nutritional value which are used for human consumption, and articles and substances used as ingredients in the preparation of food;[6] and

"green offal" means the stomach and intestines of any animal, other than poultry or fish, and their contents.

---

[1] Sub-paragraph (i) substituted by S.I. 1994/1271, reg.4(3), sch.3, para.47. This amendment came into force on 1 December 1994: reg.1(2).

[2] P.592 below.

[3] Sub-paragraph (iii) added by S.I. 1993/1749, reg.2(2). This amendment came into force on 30 July 1993: reg.1.

[4] S.I. 1993/3303.

[5] Sub-paragraphs (iv) to (xiv) added by S.I. 1994/1271, reg.3, sch.1, para.14(a). This amendment came into force on 1 June 1994: reg.1(1).

[6] This definition inserted by S.I. 1994/1271, reg.3, sch.1, para.14(b).

# SCHEDULE 2

(Regulation 3(2))

## RULES FOR THE INTERPRETATION OF SCHEDULE 1

1. These rules apply for the interpretation of Schedule 1 subject to any specific provision to the contrary in that Schedule.

..........

2. (1) Any description of a process includes any other process carried on at the same location by the same person as part of that process; but this rule does not apply in relation to any two or more processes described in different Sections of Schedule 1 which, accordingly, require distinct authorisation.

(2) For the purposes of this paragraph, two or more processes which are described in Part A of different Sections of Chapter 4 of Schedule 1 shall be treated as if they were described in the same Section.

..........

2A. Notwithstanding the rule set out in paragraph 2, where a combustion process described in Part A of Section 1.3 of Schedule 1 is operated, or where one or more boilers, furnaces or other combustion appliances which are operated as part of a process so described are operated, as an inherent part of and primarily for the purpose of a process described in Part A of Section 1.1, Part A of Section 1.4, Part A of Section 2.1,[1] Part A of Section 6.3[2] or Part A of any Section of Chapter 4 of that Schedule ("the other process"), that combustion process or, as the case may be, the operation of those boilers, furnaces or appliances shall be treated as part of the other process and not as, or as part of, a separate combustion process.[3]

..........

2B. Notwithstanding the rule set out in paragraph 2, where a process of reforming natural gas described in paragraph (a) of Part A of Section 1.1 of Schedule 1 is carried on as an inherent part of and primarily for the purpose of producing a feedstock for a process described in Part A of any Section of Chapter 4 of that Schedule ("the other process"), that reforming process shall be treated as part of the other process and not as a separate process.

..........

2C. Notwithstanding the rule set out in paragraph 2, where the same person carries on at the same location two or more Part B processes described in the provisions of Schedule 1 mentioned in any one of the following sub-paragraphs, those processes shall be treated as requiring authorisation as a single process falling within part B of the Section first mentioned in the relevant sub-paragraph—

(a) Section 2.1 and Section 2.2;

(b) Section 3.1 and Section 3.4;

(c) Section 3.6 and Section 3.4;

(d) Section 6.5 and Section 6.6;

(e) Section 6.7 and paragraph (e) of Part B of Section 1.3 insofar as it relates to any process for the burning of waste wood.[4]

..........

3. Where a person carries on a process which includes two or more processes described in the same Section of Schedule 1 those processes shall be treated as requiring authorisation as a single process; and if the processes involved are described in both Part A and Part B of the same Section, they shall all be regarded as part of a Part A process and so subject to central control.

..........

3A. Where a person carries on a process which includes two or more processes described in Part A of different Sections of Chapter 4 of Schedule 1, those processes shall be treated as a single process falling within a description determined in accordance with the rule set out in paragraph 4.

..........

[1] Words "Part A of Section 2.1," inserted by S.I. 1995/3247, reg.2, sch.1, para.8. This amendment came into force on 8 January 1996: reg.1(1).
[2] Words ", Part A of Section 6.3" inserted by S.I. 1994/1271, reg.4(4), sch.4, para.1. This amendment came into force on 1 December 1994: reg.1(2).

[3] Para.2 and 2A substituted, for the earlier para.2, by S.I. 1993/2405, reg.3. This amendment came into force on 26 October 1993.
[4] Para. 2B and 2C inserted by S.I. 1994/1271, reg.3, sch.1, para.15. This amendment came into force on 1 June 1994: reg.1(1).

**3B.** (1) Where paragraph 3A does not apply, but—

(a) two or more processes falling within descriptions in Part A of any Sections of Chapter 4 of Schedule 1 are carried on at the same location by the same person; and

(b) the carrying on of both or all of those processes at that location by that person is not likely to produce more than 250 tonnes of relevant products in any 12 month period,

those processes shall be treated as a single process falling within the description in whichever relevant Section is first mentioned in the sequence set out in paragraph 4.

(2) In sub-paragraph (1), "relevant products" means any products of the processes in question, other than—

(a) solid, liquid, or gaseous waste;

(b) by-products, if the total value of all such by-products is insignificant in comparison to the total value of the output of the processes; or

(c) any substance or material retained in or added to the final product formulation, not as an active ingredient, but as a dilutent, stabiliser or preservative or for a similar purpose.[1]

..................................................................................................................

**4.** Where a process falls within two or more descriptions in Schedule 1, that process shall be regarded as falling only within that description which fits it most aptly: but where two or more descriptions are equally apt and a process[2] falls within descriptions in different Sections of Chapter 4, it shall be taken to fall within the description in whichever relevant Section is first mentioned in the sequence, 4.5; 4.2; 4.1; 4.4; 4.3; 4.6; 4.7; 4.8; 4.9.

..................................................................................................................

**5.** Notwithstanding the rules set out in paragraphs 2 and 3—

(a) the processes described in Part B of section 1.3 do not include the incidental storage, handling or shredding of tyres which are to be burned;

(b) the process described in paragraph (b) of Part B of Section 2.2 does not include the incidental storage or handling of scrap which is to be heated other than its loading into a furnace;

(c) the process described in paragraph (a) of Part B of Section 5.1 does not involve the incidental storage or handling of wastes and residues other than animal remains intended for burning in an incinerator used wholly or mainly for the incineration of such remains or residues from the burning of such remains in such an incinerator;

(d) the process described in Part B of Section 6.5 does not include the cleaning of used storage drums prior to painting and their incidental handling in connection with such cleaning.

(e) any description of a Part B process includes any related process which would fall within paragraph (c) of Part A of Section 1.3 if it were not so related.[3]

..................................................................................................................

**6.** The following activities, that is to say—

(a) the unloading, screening, trading, mixing or otherwise handling of petroleum coke, coal, lignite, coke or any other coal product;

(b) the unloading of iron ore or burnt pyrites,

for use in a prescribed process by a person other than the person carrying on the process at the place where the process is carried on shall be treated as part of that process.[4]

..................................................................................................................

**7.** (1) Where by reason of the use at different times of different fuels or different materials or the disposal at different times of different wastes, processes of different descriptions are carried out with the same plant or machinery and those processes include one or more Part A processes and one or more other processes, the other processes shall be regarded as within the descriptions of the Part A processes.

(2) Where by reason of such use or disposal as is mentioned in paragraph (1), processes of different descriptions are carried out with the same plant or machinery and those processes include one or more Part B processes and

---

[1] Para.3, 3A and 3B substituted, for the earlier para.3, by S.I. 1993/2405, reg.3. This amendment came into force on 26 October 1993.

[2] Words "but where two or more . . . and a process" substituted by S.I. 1992/614, reg.2, sch.1, para.13(a). This amendment came into force on 1 April 1992: reg.1(1).

[3] This sub-paragraph added by S.I. 1994/1271, reg.4(4), sch.4, para.2. This amendment came into force on 1 December 1994: reg.1(2).

[4] This paragraph substituted by S.I. 1995/3247, reg.2, sch.1, para.9. This amendment came into force on 8 January 1996: reg.1(1).

one or more other processes (but no Part A processes), all those processes shall be regarded as within the descriptions of the Part B processes.

(3)  where by reason of such use or disposal as is mentioned in sub-paragraph (1), processes of different descriptions are carried out with the same plant and machinery and those processes include Part B processes falling within different Sections of Schedule 1 (but no Part A processes), those processes shall, notwithstanding the rule set out in paragraph 2, be treated as a single Part B process falling within the description in whichever of those Sections first appears in that Schedule.[1]

.........

**7A.**  The reference to "any other process" in paragraph 2 and the references to "other processes" in paragraph 7 do not include references to a process (other than one described in Schedule 1) of loading or unloading any ship or other vessel.[2]

.........

**8.**  Where in the course of, or as a process ancillary to, any prescribed process the person carrying on that process uses, treats or disposes of waste at the same location (whether as fuel or otherwise), the use, treatment or disposal of that waste shall, not withstanding the rule set out in paragraph 2, be regarded as falling within the description of that process, whether the waste was produced by the person carrying on the process or acquired by him for such use, treatment or disposal.[3]

.........

**9.**  References in Schedule 1 and this Schedule to related processes are references to separate processes carried on by the same person at the same location.

.........

**10.**  *Omitted by S.I. 1994/1271, reg.4(4), sch.4, para.5. This amendment came into force on 1 December 1994: reg.1(2).*

.........

**11.**  References to a process involving the release of a substance falling within a description in Schedule 4 or 5 hereto do not affect the application of paragraphs (1) and (2) of regulation 4.

.........

Schedule 3 is at p.594 below.

# SCHEDULE 4

(Regulation 6(1)[4])

## RELEASE INTO THE AIR: PRESCRIBED SUBSTANCES

Oxides of sulphur and other sulphur compounds
Oxides of nitrogen and other nitrogen compounds
Oxides of carbon
Organic compounds and partial oxidation products
Metals, metalloids and their compounds
Asbestos (suspended particulate matter and fibres), glass fibres and mineral fibres
Halogens and their compounds
Phosphorus and its compounds
Particulate matter.

[1] Sub-paragraph (3) added by S.I. 1994/1271, reg.4(4), sch.4, para.3. This amendment came into force on 1 December 1994: reg.1(2).
[2] This paragraph inserted by S.I. 1992/614, reg.2, sch.1, para.13(c). This amendment came into force on 1 April 1992: reg.1(1).
[3] This paragraph substituted by S.I. 1994/1271, reg.4(4), sch.4, para.4. This amendment came into force on 1 December 1994: reg.1(2).
[4] P.568 above.

# SCHEDULE 5[2]

(Regulations 4(1)[3] and 6(2)[4])

## RELEASE INTO WATER: PRESCRIBED SUBSTANCES

| (1)<br>Substance | (2)<br>Amount in excess of background quantity<br>released in any 12 month period<br>(Grammes) | |
| --- | --- | --- |
| Mercury and its compounds | 200 | (expressed as metal) |
| Cadmium and its compounds | 1000 | (expressed as metal) |
| All isomers of hexachlorocyclohexane | 20 | |
| All isomers of DDT | 5 | |
| Pentachlorophenol and its compounds | 350 | (expressed as PCP)[5] |
| Hexachlorobenzene | 5 | |
| Hexachlorobutadiene | 20 | |
| Aldrin | 2 | |
| Dieldrin | 2 | |
| Endrin | 1 | |
| Polychlorinated Biphenyls | 1 | |
| Dichlorvos | 0.2 | |
| 1,2-Dichloroethane | 2000 | |
| All isomers of trichlorobenzene | 75 | |
| Atrazine | 350* | |
| Simazine | 350* | |
| Tributyltin compounds | 4 | (expressed as TBT)[6] |
| Triphenyltin compounds | 4 | (expressed as TPT)[7] |
| Trifluralin | 20 | |
| Fenitrothion | 2 | |
| Azinphos-methyl | 2 | |
| Malathion | 2 | |
| Endosulfan | 0.5 | |

* Where both Atrazine and Simazine are released, the figure in aggregate is 350 grammes.

# SCHEDULE 6

(Regulation 6(3)[8])

## RELEASE INTO LAND: PRESCRIBED SUBSTANCES

Organic solvents
Azides
Halogens and their covalent compounds
Metal carbonyls
Organo-metallic compounds
Oxidising agents
Polychlorinated dibenzofuran and any congener thereof
Polychlorinated dibenzo-p-dioxin and any congener thereof
Polyhalogenated biphenyls, terphenyls and naphthalenes
Phosphorus

[2] This Schedule substituted by S.I. 1994/1271, reg.4(5), sch.5. This amendment came into force on 1 December 1994: reg.1(2).
[3] P.567 above.
[4] P.568 above.
[5] Words "(expressed as TBT)" inserted by S.I. 1995/3247, reg.2, sch.1, para.10(a). This amendment came into force on 8 January 1996: reg.1(1).
[6] Words "(expressed as TBT)" inserted by S.I. 1995/3247, reg.2, sch.1, para.10(b).
[7] Words "(expressed as TPT)" inserted by S.I. 1995/3247, reg.2, sch.1, para.10(c).
[8] P.568 above.

Pesticides, that is to say, any chemical substance or preparation prepared or used for destroying any pest, including those used for protecting plants or wood or other plant products from harmful organisms; regulating the growth of plants; giving protection against harmful creatures; rendering such creatures harmless; controlling organisms with harmful or unwanted effects on water systems, buildings or other structures, or on manufactured products; or protecting animals against ectoparasites.

Alkali metals and their oxides and alkaline earth metals and their oxides.

# SCHEDULE 3

(Regulation 3(1) and (3)[1])

## DATE FROM WHICH AUTHORISATION IS REQUIRED UNDER SECTION 6 OF THE ACT

### PART I

1. This Part of this Schedule applies in the case of a Part A process[2] carried on in England or Wales.

..............

2. The prescribed date in the case of a Part A process is, except in the case of an existing process,[3] 1st April 1991.

..............

3. (1) In the case of an existing process, the prescribed date is—

(i) in a case falling within paragraph (2), the date at which the change mentioned in that paragraph is made unless later than the date applicable in accordance with sub-paragraph (ii);

(ii) where sub-paragraph (i) does not apply and subject to paragraph 5, the day after that on which the period for applying for authorisation in accordance with the Table in paragraph 4 expires.

(2) A case falls within this paragraph if the person carrying on the process makes a substantial change[4] in the process on or after 1 April 1991 and that change—

(i) has not occasioned construction work which is in progress on that date; or

(ii) is not the subject of a contract for construction work entered into before that date.

..............

4. Application for authorisation to carry on an existing process shall be made in the relevant period specified in the following Table—

TABLE

| Any process falling within a description set out in– | Application to be made | |
|---|---|---|
| | Not earlier than | Not later than |
| Paragraph (a) of Section 1.3 | 1st April 1991 | 30th April 1991 |
| Any other paragraph of Chapter 1 | 1st April 1992 | 30th June 1992 |
| Section 2.1 or 2.3 | 1st January 1995 | 31st March 1995 |
| Section 2.2 | 1st May 1995 | 31st July 1995 |
| Chapter 3 | 1st December 1992 | 28th February 1993 |
| Section 4.1, 4.2, 4.7 or 4.8 | 1st May 1993 | 31st October 1993[5] |
| Section 4.3, 4.4 or paragraph (a) of Section 4.6[6] | 1st November 1993 | 31st January 1994 |

[1] P.567 above.
[2] "Part A process" defined by reg.2, p.566 above.
[3] For "existing process" see para.6 and 7 below.
[4] "Substantial change" has the same meaning as in s.10 of the 1990 Act, p.99 above: para.8 below.
[5] Words "31st October 1993" substituted by S.I. 1993/1749, reg.2(3). This amendment came into force on 30 July 1993: reg.1.
[6] Words "Section 4.3, . . . Section 4.6" substituted by S.I. 1993/2405, reg.4(a). This amendment came into force on 26 October 1993: reg.1(1).

| Any process falling within a description set out in– | Application to be made | |
|---|---|---|
| | *Not earlier than* | *Not later than* |
| Section 4.5, paragraph (b) of Section 4.6, or Section 4.9[1] | 1st May 1994 | 31st July 1994 |
| Chapter 5 | 1st August 1992 | 31st October 1992 |
| Chapter 6 | 1st November 1995 | 31st January 1996 |

5.  Where paragraph 3(1)(ii) would otherwise apply and application is duly made in accordance with section 6 of the Act within the appropriate period specified in paragraph 4 for authorisation to carry on a process, the prescribed date as respects the carrying on by the applicant (or other person in his place) of the process to which the application relates is the determination date for that process.[2]

6.  Subject to paragraph 7 below, references in this Part to an existing process are to a process—
   (i)  which was being carried on at some time in the 12 months immediately preceding 1st April 1991; or
   (ii)  which is to be carried on at a works, plant or factory or by means of mobile plant which was under construction or in course of manufacture or in the course of commission at that date, or the construction or supply of which was the subject of a contract entered into before that date.

7.  A process shall cease to be an existing process for the purposes of this Part if at any time between 1st April 1990 and the last day by which an application is otherwise required to be made for authorisation for the carrying on of that process, the process ceases to be carried on and is not carried on again at the same location (or with the same mobile plant) within the following 12 months.

8.  In this Part and subsequent provisions of this Schedule—
   "the determination date" for a prescribed process is—
   (a)  in the case of a process for which an authorisation is granted, the date on which the enforcing authority grants it, whether in pursuance of the application or, on an appeal, of a direction to grant it;
   (b)  in the case of a process for which an authorisation is refused, the date of the refusal or, on an appeal, of the affirmation of the refusal;
   "substantial change" has the same meaning as in section 10 of the Act.[3],[4]

## PART II

9.  This Part of this Schedule applies in the case of a Part B process[5] carried on in England or Wales.

10.  The prescribed date in the case of a Part B process is, except in the case of an existing process,[6] the date specified in paragraph 12 below as the date from which application may be made for authorisation to carry on an existing process of the same description.

11.  (1)  In the case of an existing process, the prescribed date is, subject to paragraph 13,—
   (i)  in a case falling within paragraph (2), the date at which the change mentioned in that paragraph is made;
   (ii)  where sub-paragraph (i) does not apply, the day after that on which the period for applying for authorisation in accordance with the Table in paragraph 12 expires.

   (2)  A case falls within this paragraph if the person carrying on the process makes a substantial change[7] in the process in the period specified in paragraph 12 in relation to the description of processes which comprise that process (when changed) and that change—
   (i)  has not occasioned construction work which is in progress at the beginning of that period; or

---

[1]  Words "Section 4.5, . . . Section 4.9" substituted by S.I. 1993/2405. reg.4(b).
[2]  "The determination date" defined by para.8 below; words "the determination date for that process" substituted by S.I. 1991/836, reg.2(2). This amendment came into force on the same dates as these Regulations: reg.1(2).

[3]  P.99 above.
[4]  This paragraph substituted by S.I. 1991/836, reg.2(3).
[5]  "Part B process" defined by reg.2, p.566 above.
[6]  For "existing process" see para.14 below.
[7]  "Substantial change" has the same meaning as in s.10 of the 1990 Act, p.99 above: para.8 above.

(ii)  is not the subject of a contract for construction work entered into before the beginning of that period.

**12.** Application for authorisation for an existing process shall be made in the relevant period determined in accordance with the following Table—

TABLE

|  | Application to be made | |
| --- | --- | --- |
| Any process falling within a description set out in– | Not earlier than | Not later than |
| Paragraph (a), (b), (c) or (e) of Section 1.3, Section 3.5, 3.6, 5.1 or 6.7 or paragraph (b) of Section 6.9 | 1st April 1991 | 30th September 1991 |
| Section 2.1, 2.2, 3.1, 3.2 or 3.4 | 1st October 1991 | 31st March 1992 |
| Paragraph (d) of Section 1.3, Section 6.2, 6.5, 6.6 or 6.8 or paragraph (a) of Section 6.9 | 1st April 1992 | 30th September 1992 |

**13.** Where application is duly made in accordance with section 6 of the Act for authorisation for the carrying on of an existing Part B process, the prescribed date as respects the carrying on by the applicant (or another person in his place) of the process to which the application relates is the determination date for that process.[1]

**14.** References in this Part to an existing process are to a process—

(i)  which was being carried on at some time in the 12 months immediately preceding the earlier date mentioned in paragraph 12 in relation to the description of processes within which the process falls; or

(ii)  which is to be carried on at a works, plant or factory or by means of mobile plant which was under construction or in course of manufacture or in the course of commission at that earlier date, or the construction or supply of which was the subject of a contract entered into before that date.

## PART III

**15.** This Part of this Schedule applies in the case of a Part A process[2] carried on in Scotland.

**16.** The prescribed date in the case of a Part A process is, except in the case of an existing process,[3] 1st April 1992.

**17.** (1)  In the case of an existing process, the prescribed date is—

(i)  in a case falling within paragraph (2), the date at which the change mentioned in that paragraph is made unless later than the date applicable in accordance with sub-paragraph (ii);

(ii)  where sub-paragraph (i) does not apply and subject to paragraph 19, the day after that on which the period for applying for authorisation in accordance with the Table in paragraph 18 expires.

(2)  A case falls within this paragraph if the person carrying on the process makes a substantial change[4] in the process on or after 1 April 1992 and that change—

(i)  has not occasioned construction work which is in progress on that date; or

(ii)  is not the subject of a contract for construction work entered into before that date.

**18.** Application for authorisation to carry on an existing process shall be made in the relevant period specified in the following Table—

TABLE

| Any process falling within a description set out in– | Application to be made | |
| --- | --- | --- |
| | Not earlier than | Not later than |
| Chapter 1 | 1st April 1992 | 30th June 1992 |
| Section 2.1 or 2.3 | 1st January 1995 | 31st March 1995 |
| Section 2.2 | 1st May 1995 | 31st July 1995 |
| Chapter 3 | 1st December 1992 | 28th February 1993 |
| Section 4.1, 4.2, 4.7 or 4.8 | 1st May 1993 | 31st October 1993[1] |
| Section 4.3, 4.4 or paragraph (a) of Section 4.6[2] | 1st November 1993 | 31st January 1994 |
| Section 4.5, paragraph (b) of Section 4.6, or Section 4.9[3] | 1st May 1994 | 31st July 1994 |
| Chapter 5 | 1st August 1992 | 31st October 1992 |
| Chapter 6 | 1st November 1995 | 31st January 1996 |

19. Where paragraph 17(1)(ii) would otherwise apply and application is duly made in accordance with Section 6 of the Act within the period specified in paragraph 18 for authorisation to carry on a process, the prescribed date as respects the carrying on by the applicant (or another person in his place) of the process to which the application relates is the determination date for that process.[4]

20. Subject to paragraph 21 below, references in this Part to an existing process are to a process—

   (i)  which was being carried on at some time in the 12 months immediately preceding 1st April 1992; or

  (ii)  which is to be carried on at a works, plant or factory or by means of mobile plant which was under construction or in course of manufacture or in the course of commission at that date, or, where construction or manufacture had not been begun before that date, the construction or supply of which was the subject of a contract entered into before that date.

21. A process shall cease to be an existing process for the purposes of this Part if at any time between 1st April 1992 and the last date by which an application is otherwise required to be made for authorisation for the carrying on of that process, the process ceases to be carried on and is not carried on again at the same location (or with the same mobile plant) within the following 12 months.

## Part IV

22. This Part of this Schedule applies in the case of a Part B process[5] carried on in Scotland.

23. The prescribed date in the case of a Part B process is, except in the case of an existing process,[2] the date specified in paragraph 25 below as the date from which application may be made for authorisation to carry on an existing process of the same description.

24. (1) In the case of an existing process the prescribed date is, subject to paragraph 26,—

   (i)  in a case falling within paragraph (2), the date at which the change mentioned in that paragraph is made;

  (ii)  where sub-paragraph (i) does not apply, the day after that on which the period for applying for authorisation in accordance with the Table in paragraph 25 expires.

[1] Words "31st October 1993" substituted by S.I. 1993/1749, reg.2(3). This amendment came into force on 30 July 1993: reg.1.

[2] Words "Section 4.3, . . . Section 4.6" substituted by S.I. 1993/2405, reg.4(a). This amendment came into force on 26 October 1993: reg.1(1).

[3] Words "Section 4.5, . . . Section 4.9" substituted by S.I. 1993/2405, reg.4(b).

[4] "The determination date" defined by para.8 above; words "the determination date for that process" substituted by S.I. 1991/836, reg.2(2). This amendment came into force on the same dates as these Regulations: reg.1(2).

[5] "Part B process" defined by reg.2, p.566 above.

[6] For "existing process" see para.27 below.

(2) A case falls within this paragraph if the person carrying on the process makes a substantial change[1] in the process in the period specified in paragraph 25 in relation to the description of processes which comprise that process (when changed) and that change—

(i) has not occasioned construction work which is in progress at the beginning of that period; or

(ii) is not the subject of a contract for construction work entered into before the beginning of that period.

25. Application for authorisation for an existing process shall be made in the relevant period specified in the following Table—

TABLE

| | Application to be made | |
|---|---|---|
| Any process falling within a description set out in– | Not earlier than | Not later than |
| Paragraph (a), (b), (d) or (e) of Section 1.3, Section 3.2, 3.5, 3.6, 5.1 or 6.7 or paragraph (b) of Section 6.9 | 1st April 1992 | 31st July 1992 |
| Paragraph (c) of Section 1.3 | 1st April 1992 | 30th September 1992 |
| Section 2.1, 2.2, 3.1 or 3.4 | 1st August 1992 | 30th November 1992 |
| Section 6.2, 6.5, 6.6 or 6.8 or paragraph (a) of Section 6.9 | 1st December 1992 | 31st March 1993 |

26. Where application is duly made in accordance with section 6 of the Act for authorisation for the carrying on of an existing Part B process, the prescribed date as respects the carrying on by the applicant (or another person in his place) of the process to which the application relates is the determination date for that process.[2]

27. References in this Part to an existing process are to a process—

(i) which was being carried on at some time in the 12 months immediately preceding the earlier date mentioned in paragraph 25 in relation to the description of processes within which the process falls; or

(ii) which is to be carried on at a works, plant or factory or by means of mobile plant which was under construction or in course of manufacture or in the course of commission at that earlier date, or the construction or supply of which was the subject of a contract entered into before that date.

## SCHEDULE 2 TO S.I. 1992/614

### TRANSITIONALS

Note: The references in this schedule to "these Regulations" are references to the regulations of S.I. 1992/614; the references to "the 1991 Regulations" are references to the Environmental Protection (Prescribed Processes and Substances) Regulations, S.I. 1991/472, set out above.

The annotations to the text of S.I. 1991/472 indicate the amendments made by S.I. 1992/614. Note that amendments which have been superseded by later amendments are not indicated in the text.

1. Part I of Schedule 3 to the 1991 Regulations shall apply to a process which by virtue of these Regulations becomes a process to which paragraph (a) of Part A of Section 1.3 of Schedule 1 to the 1991 Regulations applies as if—

(a) in paragraph 2, for "1st April 1991" there were substituted "1st April 1992";

(b) in paragraph 3(1)(ii), for the words from "the day after" to the end of the sub-paragraph there were substituted "1st July 1992";

(c) in paragraph 3(2), for "1 April 1991" there were substituted "1st April 1992";

(d) paragraph 4 were omitted;

[1] "Substantial change" has the same meaning as in s.10 of the 1990 Act, p.99 above: para.8 above.
[2] "The determination date" defined by para.8 above; words "the determination date for that process" substituted by S.I. 1991/836, reg.2(2). This amendment came into force on the same dates as these Regulations: reg.1(2).

(e) in paragraph 5, for the words "within the appropriate period specified in paragraph 4" there were substituted "by not later than 30th June 1992";

(f) in paragraph 6, for "1st April 1991" there were substituted "1st April 1992"; and

(g) in paragraph 7, for the words from "1st April 1990" to "of that process" there were substituted "1st April 1991 and 30th June 1992".

2. Part II of Schedule 3 to the 1991 Regulations shall apply to a process which by virtue of these Regulations becomes a process to which Part B of Section 1.3, 2.2 or 5.1 of Schedule 1 to the 1991 Regulations applies as if—

(a) in paragraph 10, for the words from "the date specified" to the end of the paragraph there were substituted "1st April 1992";

(b) in paragraph 11(1)(ii), for the words from "the day after" to the end of the sub-paragraph there were substituted "1st July 1992";

(c) in paragraph 11(2), for the words from "in the period" to "(when changed)" there were substituted "on or after 1st April 1992 and before 1st July 1992";

(d) paragraph 12 were omitted;

(e) in paragraph 14(i), for the words from "the earlier date" to "falls" there were substituted "1st April 1992"; and

(f) in paragraph 14(ii), for "that earlier date" there were substituted "1st April 1992".

## SCHEDULE 6 TO S.I. 1994/1271

### TRANSITIONALS

Note: This is schedule 6 as substituted by S.I. 1994/1329, reg.2, sch.

The references in this schedule to regulations are references to the regulations of S.I. 1994/1271; the references to "the principal Regulations" are references to the Environmental Protection (Prescribed Processes and Substances) Regulations, S.I. 1991/472, set out above.

The annotations to the text of S.I. 1991/472 indicate the amendments made by S.I. 1994/1271. Note that amendments which have been superseded by later amendments are not indicated in the text.

Interpretation

1. In this Schedule—

"the central enforcing authority" means the chief inspector or, in the case of a process carried on in Scotland, the chief inspector or the river purification authority as determined under the Environmental Protection (Determination of Enforcing Authority Etc) (Scotland) Regulations 1992;[1]

"existing process" means a process—

(a) which was being carried on at some time in the 12 months immediately preceding 1st December 1994; or

(b) which is to be carried on at a works, plant or factory or by means of mobile plant which was under construction or in the course of manufacture or in the course of commission at that date, or the construction or supply of which was the subject of a contract entered into before that date;

"the determination date" for a prescribed process means—

(a) in the case of a process for which an authorisation is granted by the enforcing authority, whether in pursuance of the application or of a direction under section 6(5) of or paragraph 3(5) of Schedule 1 to the Act, the date on which the authorisation is granted;

(b) in the case of a process for which an authorisation is refused by the enforcing authority in pursuance of a direction under section 6(5) of or paragraph 3(5) of Schedule 1 to the Act, the date on which the authorisation is refused;

(c) in the case of a process for which authorisation is refused by the enforcing authority other than as described in (b) above—

(i) if the applicant appeals against the refusal and the enforcing authority is directed to grant an authorisation, the date on which the authorisation is granted in pursuance of the direction;

[1] S.I. 1992/530.

(ii) if the applicant appeals against the refusal and the refusal is affirmed, the date of the affirmation of the refusal;

(iii) if no appeal is made against the refusal, the date immediately following the last day, determined in accordance with regulation 10(1) of the Environmental Protection (Applications, Appeals and Registers) Regulations 1991,[2] on which notice of appeal might have been given;

"Part A process" and "Part B process" have the same meaning as in the principal Regulations.[3]

### Processes which cease to be prescribed processes

**2.** (1) This paragraph applies to a prescribed process—

(a) which, by virtue of regulation 4 above, will cease to be a prescribed process on 1st December 1994; and

(b) in respect of which no authorisation under section 6 of the Act is in force on 1st June 1994.

(2) Regulation 3(3) of the principal Regulations (the prescribed date) shall not apply to a prescribed process to which this paragraph applies.

(3) For the purposes of regulation 3(1) of the principal Regulations, the prescribed date in the case of a prescribed process to which this paragraph applies shall be 30th November 1994.

### Processes which become Part A prescribed processes

**3.** (1) Where, by virtue of regulation 4 above, an existing process which is not a prescribed process before 1st December 1994 becomes a Part A process on that date, then, with effect from that date—

(a) regulation 3(3) of the principal Regulations (the prescribed date) shall not apply in respect of that process;

(b) for the purposes of regulation 3(1) of the principal Regulations, the prescribed date in respect of that process shall, subject to paragraph 8 below, be whichever is the latest of the following—

(i) 30th November 1994; or

(ii) where application is duly made to the central enforcing authority in accordance with section 6 of the Act before 1st November 1994 for authorisation to carry on the process, the determination date for that process; or

(iii) the date which would be determined in accordance with Schedule 3 to the principal Regulations if that Schedule applied with the modifications set out in sub-paragraph (2) below.

(2) The modifications of Schedule 3 to the principal Regulations referred to in sub-paragraph (1) above are—

(a) in paragraph 2, for "1st April 1991" substitute "30th November 1994";

(b) in paragraphs 3(2) and 6, for "1st April 1991" substitute "1st December 1994";

(c) in paragraph 7, for "1st April 1990" substitute "1st December 1993";

(d) in paragraph 16, for "1st April 1992" substitute "30 November 1994";

(e) in paragraphs 17(2) and 20, for "1st April 1992" substitute "1st December 1994";

(f) in paragraph 21, for "1st April 1992" substitute "1st December 1993".

### Processes which transfer from Part B to Part A

**4.** Where, by virtue of regulation 4 above, an existing Part B process becomes a Part A process on 1st December 1994, then, with effect from that date—

(a) regulation 3(3) of the principal Regulations (the prescribed date) shall not apply in respect of that process;

(b) for the purposes of regulation 3(1) of the principal Regulations, the prescribed date in respect of that process shall, subject to paragraph 8 below, be whichever is the later of the following—

(i) 31st December 1994; or

(ii) where application is duly made to the central enforcing authority in accordance with section 6 of the Act before 1st January 1995 for authorisation to carry on the process, the determination date for that process.

---

[2] P.612 below.    [3] See reg.2 of S.I. 1991/472, p.566 above.

## Processes which become Part B prescribed processes

**5.** Where, by virtue of regulation 4 above, an existing process which is not a prescribed process before 1st December 1994 becomes a Part B process on that date, then, with effect from that date—

(a) regulation 3(3) of the principal Regulations (the prescribed date) shall not apply in respect of that process;

(b) for the purposes of regulation 3(1) of the principal Regulations, the prescribed date in respect of that process shall, subject to paragraph 8 below, be whichever is the later of the following—

    (i) 31st May 1995; or

    (ii) where application is duly made to the local enforcing authority in accordance with section 6 of the Act before 1st June 1995 for authorisation to carry on the process, the determination date for that process.

## Processes which transfer from Part A to Part B

**6.** Where, by virtue of regulation 4 above, an existing Part A process becomes a Part B process on 1st December 1994 and, immediately before that date, that Part A process is one for the carrying on of which an application for an authorisation under section 6 of the Act is not yet required to be made, then, with effect from that date—

(a) regulation 3(3) of the principal Regulations (the prescribed date) shall not apply in respect of that process;

(b) for the purposes of regulation 3(1) of the principal Regulations, the prescribed date in respect of that process shall, subject to paragraph 8 below, be whichever is the later of the following—

    (i) 31st May 1995; or

    (ii) where application is duly made to the local enforcing authority in accordance with section 6 of the Act before 1st June 1995 for authorisation to carry on the process, the determination date for that process.

**7.** (1) Where, by virtue of regulation 4 above, an existing Part A process becomes a Part B process on 1st December 1994 but paragraph 6 above does not apply, then, with effect from that date—

(a) regulation 3(3) of the principal Regulations (the prescribed date) shall not apply in respect of that process;

(b) for the purposes of regulation 3(1) of the principal Regulations, the prescribed date in respect of that process shall, subject to paragraph 8 below, be whichever is the later of the following—

    (i) 31st December 1994; or

    (ii) where application is duly made to the local enforcing authority in accordance with section 6 of the Act before 1st January 1995 for authorisation to carry on the process, the determination date for that process.

(2) The requirements of paragraphs 1(2) and 2 of Schedule 1 to the Act (advertisement and consultation) shall not apply in relation to an application made as described in sub-paragraph (1)(b)(ii) above if, in respect of the process to which that application relates—

(a) an authorisation under section 6 of the Act granted by the central enforcing authority is in force on 30th November 1994; or

(b) an application for an authorisation under section 6 of the Act has been made to the central enforcing authority and the requirements of those paragraphs have been fulfilled in relation to that application after 31st May 1993.

## Substantial changes

**8.** (1) This paragraph applies where the person carrying on an existing process described in any of paragraphs 3 to 7 above makes a substantial change in the process on or after 1st December 1994 and that change—

    (i) has not occasioned construction work which is in progress on that date; and

    (ii) is not the subject of a contract for construction work entered into before that date.

(2) Where this paragraph applies, the prescribed date in respect of that process shall be the date at which the change mentioned in sub-paragraph (1) above is made unless later than the date applicable in accordance with paragraphs 3 to 7 above.

(3) In this paragraph "substantial change" has the same meaning as in section 10 of the Act.[1]

---

[1] P.99 above.

SCHEDULE 2 TO S.I. 1995/3247

TRANSITIONALS

Note: The references in this schedule to regulations are references to the regulations of S.I. 1995/3247; the references to "the principal Regulations" are references to the Environmental Protection (Prescribed Processes and Substances) Regulations, S.I. 1991/472, set out above.

The annotations to the text of S.I. 1991/472 indicate the amendments made by S.I. 1995/3247. Note that amendments which have been superseded by later amendments are not indicated in the text.

*Interpretation*

1. In this Schedule—

"the central enforcing authority" means the chief inspector or, in the case of a process carried on in Scotland, the chief inspector or the river purification authority as determined under the Environmental Protection (Determination of Enforcing Authority Etc) (Scotland) Regulations 1992;[1]

"existing process" means a process—

(a) which was being carried on some at some time in the 12 months immediately preceding 8th January 1996; or

(b) which is to be carried on at a works, plant or factory or by means of mobile plant which was under construction or in the course of manufacture or in the course of commission at that date, or the construction or supply of which was the subject of a contract entered into before that date;

"the determination date" for a prescribed process means—

(a) in the case of a process for which an authorisation is granted by the enforcing authority, whether in pursuance of the application or of a direction under section 6(5) of or paragraph 3(5) of Schedule 1 to the Act, the date on which the authorisation is granted;

(b) in the case of a process for which an authorisation is refused by the enforcing authority in pursuance of a direction under section 6(5) of or paragraph 3(5) of Schedule 1 to the Act, the date on which the authorisation is refused;

(c) in the case of a process for which an authorisation is refused by the enforcing authority other than as described in (b) above—

(i) if the applicant appeals against the refusal and the enforcing authority is directed to grant an authorisation, the date on which the authorisation is granted in pursuance of the direction;

(ii) if the applicant appeals against the refusal and the refusal is affirmed, the date of the affirmation of the refusal;

(iii) if no appeal is made against the refusal, the date immediately following the last day, determined in accordance with regulation 10(1) of the Environmental Protection (Applications, Appeals and Registers) Regulations 1991,[2] on which notice of appeal might have been given;

"Part A process" and "Part B process" have the same meaning as in the principal Regulations.[3]

*Processes, other than existing processes, which became Part A or Part B prescribed processes*

2. Regulation 3(3) of the principal Regulations (the prescribed date) shall not apply in respect of a process which is not an existing process and which falls within a description of process which, by virtue of regulation 2 above—

(a) becomes a prescribed process on 8th January 1996 but immediately before that date was not a prescribed process;

(b) becomes a Part A process on 8th January 1996 but immediately before that date was a Part B process; or

(c) becomes a Part B process on 8th January 1996 but immediately before that date was a Part A process,

and for the purposes of regulation 3(1) of the principal Regulations the prescribed date in respect of any such process shall be 7th January 1996.

---

[1] S.I. 1992/530 amended by S.I. 1995/2742.    [2] P.612 below.    [3] See reg.2 of S.I. 1991/472, p.566 above.

*Existing processes which become Part A prescribed processes*

3. (1)  Where, by virtue of regulation 2 above, an existing process which immediately before 8th January 1996 is not a prescribed process or is a Part B Process becomes a Part A process on that date, then, with effect from that date—

(a)  regulation 3(3) of the principal Regulations (the prescribed date) shall not apply in respect of that process;

(b)  for the purposes of regulation 3(1) of the principal Regulations, the prescribed date in respect of that process shall, subject to paragraph 5 below, be whichever is the later of the following—

(i)  7th May 1996; or

(ii)  where application is duly made to the central enforcing authority in accordance with section 6 of the Act before 8th May 1996 for authorisation to carry on the process, the determination date for that process.

*Existing processes which become Part B prescribed processes*

4. (1)  Where, by virtue of regulation 2 above, an existing process which immediately before 8th January 1996 is not a prescribed process or is a Part A process becomes a Part B process on that date, then, with effect from that date—

(a)  regulation 3(3) of the principal Regulations (the prescribed date) shall not apply in respect of that process;

(b)  for the purposes of regulation 3(1) of the principal Regulations, the prescribed date in respect of that process shall, subject to paragraph 5 below, be whichever is the later of the following—

(i)  7th January 1997; or

(ii)  where application is duly made to the local enforcing authority in accordance with section 6 of the Act after 7th July 1996 and before 8th January 1997 for authorisation to carry on the process, the determination date for that process.

(2)  The requirements of paragraphs 1(2) and 2 of Schedule 1 to the Act (advertisement and consultation) shall not apply in relation to an application made as described in sub-paragraph (1)(b)(ii) above if, in respect of the process to which that application relates—

(a)  an authorisation under section 6 of the Act granted by the central enforcing authority is in force on 7th January 1996; or

(b)  an application for an authorisation under section 6 of the Act has been made to the central enforcing authority and the requirements of those paragraphs have been fulfilled in relation to that application after 8th July 1994.

*Substantial changes*

5. (1)  This paragraph applies where the person carrying on an existing process described in paragraph 3 or 4 above makes a substantial change in the process on or after 8th January 1996 and that change—

(i)  has not occasioned construction work which is in progress on that date; and

(ii)  is not the subject of a contract for construction work entered into before that date.

(2)  Where this paragraph applies, the prescribed date in respect of that process shall be the date at which the change mentioned in sub-paragraph (1) above is made unless later than the date applicable in accordance with paragraphs 3 and 4 above.

(3)  In this paragraph "substantial change" has the same meaning as in section 10 of the Act.[1]

........................................................................................................................................................................

*Explanatory Note*
*(This note is not part of the Regulations)*

Part I of the Environmental Protection Act 1990 makes provision for integrated pollution control. It also makes provision for the control of air pollution by local authorities.

Under Part I prescribed processes require authorisation. In granting authorisation the enforcing authority must seek to ensure that the best available techniques not entailing excessive cost are employed to prevent or minimise the release of any substance prescribed for any environmental medium.

---

[1]  P.99 above.

These regulations—

(i) specify the processes which are prescribed for the purposes of Part I of the 1990 Act;

(ii) prescribe the substances the release of which into a particular medium is controlled;

(iii) designate the prescribed processes either for central integrated pollution control by Her Majesty's Inspectorate of Pollution in England and Wales or by Her Majesty's Industrial Pollution Inspectorate or river purification authorities in Scotland[1] or for local authority air pollution control.[2]

The regulations provide a framework for the implementation of a substantial number of EC Directives relating to the control of pollution such as 84/360/EEC on the combating of air pollution from industrial plants (OJ L188/20: 16.7.1984).

## The listed processes and control

The processes for which authorisation is required are listed in Schedule 1 to the regulations. Schedule 1 is to be read in conjunction with Schedule 2 which sets out rules for the interpretation of Schedule 1 and regulation 4 which sets out general exceptions.

Processes described in Schedule 1 under the heading "Part A" are subject to integrated pollution control; those listed under the heading "Part B" to local air pollution control (regulation 5).

The main exceptions (set out in regulation 4) are for Part A processes which have no (or a minimal) capacity to result in the release into the air, or on or into land or into water of substances prescribed for those media; and for Part B processes which have no (or minimal) capacity to result in the release into the air of substances prescribed for air. There are also exceptions for domestic activities; vehicle engines; and processes carried on for educational purposes. Schedule 2 deals with such matters as the position of processes falling within 2 or more descriptions; and processes forming part of larger processes.

## The prescribed substances

The prescribed substances the release of which must be prevented or restricted are listed in Schedules 4 to 6. Schedule 4 relates to release into the air; Schedule 5 to release into water; Schedule 6 to release into land.

## Commencement and transitional provision

Part I of the 1990 Act also provides that the Secretary of State shall specify the date from which authorisation is to be required to carry on particular processes. Regulation 3(1) and (3) and Schedule 3 are concerned with this matter. Processes are brought within control over extended periods and special provision is made as respects existing processes which are defined very widely to include processes to be carried on at plants under construction (or the subject of construction contracts) when the regulations come into force. Different dates are prescribed for Part A and Part B processes and for England and Wales and for Scotland.

---

[1] The functions of these bodies have been transferred to the Environment Agency in England and Wales and the Scottish Environment Protection Agency, SEPA, in Scotland: see s.2 of the Environment Act 1995, p.421 above, and s.21, p.438 above.

[2] In Scotland this function has been transferred to the Scottish Environment Protection Agency, SEPA; see s.21 of the Environment Act 1995, p.438 above.

# The Environmental Protection (Applications, Appeals and Registers) Regulations 1991

S.I. No. 507

The Secretary of State for the Environment as respects England, the Secretary of State for Wales as respects Wales and the Secretary of State for Scotland as respects Scotland, in exercise of the powers conferred on them by sections 10(8), 11(1), (3) to (7), 15(10), 20(1) to (3), (10) and 22(6) of and paragraphs 1 to 3, 6 and 7 of Schedule 1 to the Environmental Protection Act 1990[1] and of all other powers enabling them in that behalf, hereby make the following Regulations:

*Citation, commencement and interpretation*

1. (1) These Regulations may be cited as the Environmental Protection (Applications, Appeals and Registers) Regulations 1991 and shall come into force in England and Wales on 1st April 1991 and in Scotland on 1st April 1992.

   (2) In these Regulations, "the 1990 Act" means the Environmental Protection Act.

*Applications for an authorisation*

2. (1) An application to an enforcing authority for an authorisation under section 6 of the 1990 Act[2] shall be in writing and, subject to paragraphs (2) and (3) below, shall contain the following information—

   (a) the name of the applicant, his telephone number and address and, if different, any address to which correspondence relating to the application should be sent and, if the applicant is a body corporate, the address of its registered or principal office and, if that body corporate is a subsidiary of a holding company (within the meaning of section 736 of the Companies Act 1985,[3] the name of the ultimate holding company and the address of its registered or principal office;[4]

   (b) in a case where the prescribed process will not be carried on by means of mobile plant[5]—

      (i) the name of any local authority in whose area the prescribed process will be carried on;

      (ii) the address of the premises where the prescribed process will be carried on;

      (iii) a map or plan showing the location of those premises; and

      (iv) if only part of those premises will be used for carrying on the process, a plan or other means of identifying that part;

   (c) in a case where the prescribed process will be carried on by means of mobile plant—

      (i) the name of the local authority in whose area the applicant has his principal place of business; and

      (ii) the address of that place of business;

---

[1] Part I of the Environmental Protection Act 1990 begins at p.88 above; sch.1 begins at p.211 above.

[2] P.95 above; "enforcing authority", "local enforcing authority" and "prescribed process" are defined in s.1 of the 1990 Act, p.90 above.

[3] 1985 c.6; a new s.736 was substituted by s.144(1) of the Companies Act 1989 (c.40).

[4] Words "and, if that body corporate is a subsidiary . . . or principal office" added by S.I. 1996/667, reg.2, sch., para.1. This amendment came into force on 1 April 1996: reg.1(1).

[5] "Mobile plant" defined by s.1(6) of the 1990 Act, p.90 above.

(d) a description of the prescribed process;

(e) a list of prescribed substances[1] (and any other substances which might cause harm[2] if released into any environmental medium[3]) which will be used in connection with, or which will result from, the carrying on of that process;

(f) a description of the techniques to be used for preventing the release into any environmental medium of such substances, for reducing the release of such substances to a minimum and for rendering harmless any such substances which are released;

(g) details of any proposed release of such substances into any environmental medium and an assessment of the environmental consequences;

(h) proposals for monitoring any release of such substances, the environmental consequences of any such release and the use of any techniques described in accordance with sub-paragraph (f) above;

(i) the matters on which the applicant relies to establish that the objectives mentioned in section 7(2) of the 1990 Act[4] (including the objective referred to in section 7(7)) will be achieved and that he will be able to comply with the general condition implied by section 7(4);

(j) any additional information which he wishes the enforcing authority to take into account in considering his application.

(2) Paragraph (1) above shall apply in relation to an application to a local enforcing authority for an authorisation in respect of a prescribed process designated for local control[5] (other than that mentioned in paragraph (3) below) as if the words in brackets in sub-paragraph (i) were omitted and references to the release of substances into any environmental medium were references to the release of substances into the air.

(3) Paragraph (1) above shall apply in relation to an application to a local enforcing authority for an authorisation to carry on any prescribed process involving only the burning of waste oil in an appliance with a net rated thermal input of less than 0.4 megawatts as if the following sub-paragraphs were substituted for sub-paragraphs (d) to (i)—

"(d) the name and number of the appliance (if any) and the name of its manufacturer;

(e) the net rated thermal input of the appliance and whether or not it is constructed or adapted so as to comply with the specification for fixed, flued fan-assisted heaters in Part 2 of the specification for oil-burning air heaters published by the British Standards Institution and numbered BS 4256 1972;

(f) details of the type of fuel to be used and its source;

(g) details of the height and location of any chimney through which waste gases produced by the appliance would be carried away;

(h) details of the efflux velocity of the waste gases leaving such a chimney produced by the appliance in normal operation;

(i) details of the location of the fuel storage tanks of the appliance;".

(4) In this regulation—

"net rated thermal input" is the rate at which fuel can be burned at the maximum continuous rating of the appliance multiplied by the net calorific value of the fuel and expressed as megawatts thermal;

"waste oil" means any mineral based lubricating or industrial oil which—

(a) has become unfit for the use for which it was intended and, in particular, used combustion engine oil, gearbox oil, mineral lubricating oil, oil for turbines and hydraulic oil; and

---

[1] For "prescribed substance" see s.2(7) of the 1990 Act, p.92 above and S.I. 1991/472, p.566 above.
[2] For the definition of "harm" in Part I of the 1990 Act, see s.1(4), p.89 above.
[3] For "released into any environmental medium" see s.1(10) of the 1990 Act, p.90 above; for environmental media see s.1(2).
[4] P.96 above.
[5] For "designated for local control" see s.2 of the 1990 Act, p.91 above.

(b) is generated only as a result of activities carried out by the applicant on the premises where the process is to be carried on.

*Variation of conditions of an authorisation*

**3.** (1) Any notice given to an enforcing authority under section 11(1)(a) of the 1990 Act[1] of a proposed relevant change in a prescribed process shall be in writing.

(2) An application to an enforcing authority under any provision of section 11 of the 1990 Act for the variation of the conditions of a authorisation shall be in writing.

(3) A person making—

(a) a request to an enforcing authority under section 11(1)(b) of the 1990 Act for a determination of the matters mentioned in section 11(2); or

(b) an application to such an authority under any provision of section 11 for the variation of the conditions of an authorisation,

shall furnish the authority with his name, address and telephone number and shall also furnish the authority—

(i) in a case where the prescribed process will not be carried on by means of mobile plant,[2] with the address of the premises where the prescribed process will be carried on;

(ii) in a case where the process will be carried on by means of mobile plant, with the address of his principal place of business;

(iii) in all cases, with a statement of any changes as respects any information supplied under regulation 2(1)(a) to (c) above.

(iv) in a case where the holder of the authorisation is a body corporate which is a subsidiary of a holding company (within the meaning of section 736 of the Companies Act 1985[3]) and the information has not already been supplied under regulation 2(1)(a) above, with the name of the ultimate holding company and the address of its registered or principal office.[4]

(4) Subject to paragraph (5) below, a person making—

(a) a request to an enforcing authority under section 11(1)(b) of the 1990 Act for a determination of the matters mentioned in section 11(2); or

(b) an application to such an authority under section 11(5) for the variation of the conditions of an authorisation,

shall also furnish the authority with—

(i) a description of any proposed change in the manner in which the prescribed process will be carried on;

(ii) a statement of any changes as respects the matters dealt with in regulation 2(1)(e) to (i) above which would result if any proposed change in the manner of carrying on the prescribed process were made;

(iii) any additional information which he wishes the authority to take into account in considering his application; and

(iv) in the case of an application under section 11(5) of the 1990 Act, an indication of the variations which he wishes the authority to make.

(5) Paragraph (4) above shall apply in relation to a process mentioned in regulation 2(3) above as if sub-paragraph (ii) were omitted.

---

[1] P.100 above.
[2] "Mobile plant" defined by s.1(6) of the 1990 Act, p.90 above.
[3] 1985 c.6; a new s.736 was substituted by s.144(1) of the

Companies Act 1989 (c.40).
[4] Sub-paragraph (iv) added by S.I. 1996/667, reg.2, sch., para.2. This amendment came into force on 1 April 1996: reg.1(1).

(6) A person making an application to an enforcing authority under section 11(3)(b) or (4)(b) of the 1990 Act[1] for the variation of the conditions of an authorisation shall also furnish the authority with—

(a) an indication of the variations which he wishes the authority to make;

(b) a statement of any changes in any information supplied to the authority under paragraph (3) above; and

(c) any additional information which he wishes the authority to take into account in considering his application.

(7) A person making an application to an enforcing authority for the variation of the conditions of an authorisation under section 11(6) of the 1990 Act shall also furnish the authority with—

(a) an indication of the variations which he wishes the authority to make; and

(b) any additional information which he wishes the authority to take into account in considering his application.

*Consultation*

**4.** (1) Subject to regulations 6 and 7(2) below, the persons to be consulted under paragraph 2, 6 or 7 of Schedule 1 to the 1990 Act[2] are—

(a) the Health and Safety Executive, in all cases except, in the case of a prescribed process designated for local control,[3] where the enforcing authority has, within the period specified in paragraph (2) below, notified the Health and Safety Executive that the application has been made or, as the case may be, that notification has been given pursuant to section 10(5) of the 1990 Act;[4]

(b) the Minister of Agriculture, Fisheries and Food, in the case of all prescribed processes designated for central control[5] which will be carried on in England;

(c) the Secretary of State for Wales, in the case of all prescribed processes designated for central control which will be carried on in Wales;

(d) the Secretary of State for Scotland, in the case of all prescribed processes designated for central control which will be carried on in Scotland;

(e) *Omitted by S.I. 1996/667, reg.2, sch., para.3(1)(b). This amendment came into force on 1 April 1996: reg.1(1).*

(f) the sewerage undertaker or, in relation to Scotland, the sewerage authority,[6] in the case of all prescribed processes designed for central control which may involve the release of any substance into a sewer vested in the undertaker or the authority;[7]

(g) the Nature Conservancy Council for England,[8] Scottish Natural Heritage[9] or the Countryside Council for Wales[10]—

---

[1] Former words "to an enforcing authority" omitted by S.I. 1991/836, reg.3(a). This amendment came into force on the same dates as these regulations.

[2] P.211 above.

[3] For "designated for local control" see s.2 of the 1990 Act, p.91 above.

[4] P.99 above; words "except, in the case of a prescribed process . . . the 1990 Act" inserted by S.I. 1996/667, reg.2, sch., para.3(1)(a). This amendment came into force on 1 April 1996: reg.1(1). The amendments made by S.I. 1996/667, sch., para.3(1) do not apply in cases where the relevant day referred to in sub-paragraph (a), (b) or, as the case may be, (c) of regulation 4(2) of these Regulations falls before 1 April 1996: para.3(2).

[5] For the designation of processes for central control or local control see s.2 of the 1990 Act, p.91 above.

[6] Words "sewerage authority" substituted by S.I. 1996/667, reg.2, sch., para.3(1)(c)(i).

[7] Words "the authority" substituted by S.I. 1996/667, reg.2, sch., para.3(l)(ii).

[8] The Nature Conservancy Council for England, also known as English Nature, is established by s.128 of the Environmental Protection Act 1990 (c.43). This section is set out in the companion volume: Fry, Michael, *A Manual of Nature Conservation Law*, Oxford, 1995, at p.229.

[9] Scottish Natural Heritage is established by s.1 of the Natural Heritage (Scotland) Act 1991 (c.28). This section is set out in the companion volume: Fry, Michael, *A Manual of Nature Conservation Law*, Oxford, 1995, at p.245. Words "Scottish Natural Heritage" substituted by S.I. 1996/667, reg.2, sch., para. 3(1)(d)(i).

[10] The Countryside Council for Wales is established by s.128 of the Environmental Protection Act 1990 (c.43). This section is set out in the companion volume: Fry, Michael, *A Manual of Nature Conservation Law*, Oxford, 1995, at p.229.

(i) in the case of all prescribed processes designated for central control which may involve a release of any substance;

(ii) in the case of all prescribed processes designated for local control which may involve a release of any substance into the air,

which may affect a site of special scientific interest[1] within the body's[2] area;

(h) the harbour authority, in the case of all prescribed processes designated for central control which may involve a release of any substance into a harbour managed by the harbour authority.

(i) *This sub-paragraph, which was inserted by S.I. 1994/1271, is omitted by S.I. 1996/667, reg.2, sch., para.3(1)(e). This amendment came into force on 1 April 1996: reg.1(1).*

(j) the local authority in whose area the process will be carried on, in the case of all prescribed processes (other than those which will be carried on by means of mobile plant[3]) designated for central control, or in respect of which a direction under section 4(4) of the 1990 Act[4] is in force, which will be carried on in England and Wales;

(k) the local authority in whose area the process will be carried on, in the case of all prescribed processes (other than those which will be carried on by means of mobile plant) which will be carried on in Scotland;

(l) the local fisheries committee, in the case of all prescribed processes designated for central control which may involve a release of any substance directly into relevant territorial waters or coastal waters within the sea fisheries district of that committee.[5]

(2) Subject to regulation 7(5)(a) below, the period for notification under paragraph 2(1), 6(2) or 7(2) of Schedule 1 to the 1990 Act[6] shall be the period of 14 days beginning with—

(a) in the case of a notification under paragraph 2(1), the day on which the enforcing authority receives the application for an authorisation;

(b) in the case of a notification under paragraph 6(2), the day on which the authority notifies the holder of an authorisation in accordance with section 10(5) of that Act;[7] and

(c) in the case of a notification under paragraph 7(2), the day on which the authority receives the application for a variation of an authorisation.

(3) In paragraph (1)(h) above and regulation 7(3)(c) below, "harbour authority" has the same meaning as in section 57(1) of the Harbours Act 1964.[8]

(4) In paragraph (1)(f) above "sewerage authority" shall be construed in accordance with section 62 of the Local Government etc. (Scotland) Act 1994.[9]

(5) In paragraph (1)(j) above "local authority" means—

(a) in England—

(i) the council of a county, so far as it is the council of an area for which there are no district councils;

(ii) a district council;

(iii) the council of a London borough;

(iv) the Council of the Isles of Scilly;

(v) the Common Council of the City of London and, as respects the Temples, the Sub-Treasurer of the Inner Temple and the Under-Treasurer of the Middle Temple respectively;

[1] For provisions relating to sites of special scientific interest see ss.28–33 of the Wildlife and Countryside Act 1981 (c.69). These sections are set out in the companion volume: Fry, Michael, *A Manual of Nature Conservation Law*, Oxford, 1995, beginning at p.168.
[2] Words "the body's" substituted by S.I. 1996/667, reg.2, sch., para.3(1)(d)(ii).
[3] "Mobile plant" defined by s.1(6) of the 1990 Act, p.90 above.
[4] P.93 above.
[5] Paras. (j)–(l) added by S.I. 1996/667, reg.2, sch., para.3(1)(f).
[6] P.211 above.
[7] P.99 above.
[8] 1964 c.40.
[9] 1994 c.39.

(b) in Wales, the council of a county or county borough.

(6) In paragraph (1)(k) above "local authority" means a council for an area constituted under section 2 of the Local Government etc. (Scotland) Act 1994.

(7) In paragraph (1)(l) above "relevant territorial waters" and "coastal waters" have the same meaning as in Part III of the Water Resources Act 1991.[1],[2]

*Advertisements*

5. (1) Subject to paragraph (4) and regulation 6 below, an advertisement—

(a) by an applicant under paragraph 1(2) of Schedule 1 to the 1990 Act;[3] or

(b) by the holder of an authorisation under paragraph 6(2) or 7(2) of that Schedule, shall be published in one or more newspapers circulating in the locality in which the prescribed process will be carried on and also, in the case of a prescribed process designated for central control—

  (i) if the process will be carried on in England and Wales otherwise than by means of mobile plant,[4] or will be carried on by means of mobile plant by a person whose principal place of business in Great Britain is in England and Wales, in the London Gazette;

  (ii) if the process will be carried on in Scotland otherwise than by means of mobile plant, or will be carried on by means of mobile plant by a person whose principal place of business in Great Britain is in Scotland, in the Edinburgh Gazette.[5]

(2) Subject to regulation 7(5)(b) below, any such advertisement as is mentioned in paragraph (1) above shall be published within a period of 28 days beginning 14 days after—

(a) in the case of an advertisement under paragraph 1(2) of Schedule 1 to the 1990 Act, the day on which the application for an authorisation is made;

(b) in the case of an advertisement under paragraph 6(2) of that Schedule, the day on which the holder of the authorisation is notified in accordance with section 10(5) of that Act;[6]

(c) in the case of an advertisement under paragraph 7(2) of that Schedule, the day on which the application for a variation is made.

(3) Subject to regulation 7(4) below, any such advertisement as is mentioned in paragraph (1) above shall—

(a) state the name of the applicant or, as the case may be, of the holder of the authorisation;

(b) except in the case of a prescribed process which will be carried on by means of mobile plant[7] give the address of the premises on which the prescribed process will be carried on;

(c) describe briefly the prescribed process;

(d) state where any register which contains particulars of the application or of the action to be taken may be inspected and that it may be inspected free of charge;

(e) explain that any person may make representations in writing to the enforcing authority within the period of 28 days beginning with the date of the advertisement and give the authority's address; and

(f) explain that any such representations made by any person will be entered in a public register unless that person requests in writing that they should not be so placed, and that where such a request is made there will be included in the register a statement indicating only that representations have been made which have been the subject of such a request.[8]

---

[1] See s.104(1) of the 1991 Act, p.290 above.
[2] Paras.(4)–(7) added by S.I. 1996/667, reg.2, sch., para.3(1)(g).
[3] P.211 above.
[4] "Mobile plant" defined by s.1(6) of the 1990 Act, p.90 above.
[5] Words "and also, . . . Edinburgh Gazette" added by S.I. 1996/667, reg.2, sch., para.4(1)(a). This amendment came into force on 1 April 1996: reg.1(1). The amendments made

by S.I. 1996/667, sch., para.4(1) do not apply in cases where the relevant day referred to in sub-paragraph (a), (b) or, as the case may be, (c) of regulation 5(2) of these Regulations falls before 1 April 1996: para.4(2).
[6] P.99 above.
[7] Words "except in the case of . . . mobile plant" inserted by S.I. 1996/667, reg.2, sch., para.4(1)(b).
[8] This sub-paragraph added by S.I. 1996/667, reg.2, sch., para.4(1)(c).

(4)  The requirement in paragraph (1) of this regulation to publish an advertisement in one or more newspapers circulating in the locality in which the prescribed process will be carried on does not apply[1] in relation to any prescribed process which will be carried on by means of mobile plant.

*Exemption for waste oil burners*

**6.**  (1)  The requirements of paragraph 1(2), 2, 6 or 7 of Schedule 1 to the 1990 Act[2] shall not apply in relation to any process involving only the burning of waste oil in an appliance with a net rated thermal input of less than 0.4 megawatts.

(2)  In this regulation—

"net rated thermal input" has the same meaning as in regulation 2(4) above;[3] and

"waste oil" means any mineral based lubricating or industrial oil which has become unfit for the use for which it was intended and, in particular, used combustion engine oil, gearbox oil, mineral lubricating oil, oil for turbines and hydraulic oil.

*National security and confidential information*

**7.**  (1)  This regulation applies where in relation to an application or an authorisation—

(a)  a direction given by the Secretary of State under section 21(2) of the 1990 Act[4] applies;

(b)  notice is given to the Secretary of State under section 21(4) of that Act;

(c)  an application is made to an enforcing authority under section 22(2) of that Act; or

(d)  an objection is made to such an authority under section 22(4) of that Act.

(2)  Subject to paragraph (3) below, the requirements of paragraph 2(1), 6(2) or 7(2) of Schedule 1 to the 1990 Act shall not apply in so far as they would require a person mentioned in regulation 4(1)(f), (g), or (h) above to be consulted on information which is not to be included in the register by virtue of section 21 or 22 of that Act.

(3)  Information which is not to be included in the register by virtue of section 22 of the 1990 Act shall not be excluded by paragraph (2) above if—

(a)  in the case of any person mentioned in regulation 4(1)(f) above, it is information about the release of any substance into a sewer vested in that person;

(b)  in the case of any person mentioned in regulation 4(1)(g) above, it is information about the release of any substance—

(i)   designated for central control;[5]

(ii)  designated for local control which may involve a release of any substance into the air,

which may affect a site of special interest in that person's area; or

(c)  in the case of any person mentioned in regulation 4(1)(h) above, it is information about the release of any substance into a harbour managed by a harbour authority.

(4)  The requirements of paragraph 1(2), 6(2) or 7(2) of Schedule 1 to the 1990 Act shall not apply in so far as they would require the advertisement of information mentioned in regulation 5(3) above which is not to be included in the register by virtue of section 21 or 22 of that Act.

(5)  Where a matter falls to be determined under section 21 or 22 of the 1990 Act—

(a)  the period for notification under paragraph 2(1), 6(2) or 7(2) of Schedule 1 to that Act shall be the period of 14 days beginning 14 days after the day on which the matters to be determined under section 21 or 22 of that Act are finally disposed of;

(b)  the period within which an advertisement is to be published in the manner specified in regulation 5(1) above shall be the period of 28 days beginning 14 days after the day on which the matters to be determined under section 21 or 22 of the 1990 Act are finally disposed of.

---

[1] Words "The requirement ... does not apply" substituted by S.I. 1996/667, reg.2, sch., para.4(1)(d).
[2] P.211 above.
[3] P.606 above.

[4] P.106 above.
[5] For the designation of processes for central control or local control see s.2 of the 1990 Act, p.91 above.

(6) For the purposes of paragraph (5) above, the matters to be determined under section 21 or 22 of the 1990 Act are finally disposed of—

(a) on the date on which the Secretary of State determines under section 21 of that Act whether or not information is to be included in the register;

(b) on the date on which the enforcing authority is treated under section 22(3) of that Act as having made a determination;

(c) in a case where the enforcing authority determines under section 22(2) or (4) of that Act that the information in question is commercially confidential, on the date of the authority's determination;

(d) in a case where the enforcing authority determines under section 22(2) or (4) of that Act that the information in question is not commercially confidential, on the date on which the period for bringing an appeal expires without an appeal being brought or, if such an appeal is brought within that period, on the date of the Secretary of State's final determination of the appeal or, as the case may be, the date on which the appellant withdraws his appeal.

*Transmitted applications*

**8.** Where an application for an authorisation is transmitted under paragraph 3(1) of Schedule 1 to the 1990 Act[1] to the Secretary of State for determination, a request by the applicant or the enforcing authority concerned that the Secretary of State exercise one of the powers under paragraph 3(3) of that Schedule shall be made to him in writing within the period of 21 days beginning with the day on which the applicant is informed that the application is being transmitted to the Secretary of State.

*Notice of appeal*

**9.** (1) A person who wishes to appeal to the Secretary of State under section 15[2] or 22(5)[3] of the 1990 Act shall give to the Secretary of State written notice of the appeal together with the documents specified in paragraph (2) below and shall at the same time send to the enforcing authority a copy of that notice together with the documents specified in paragraph (2)(a) and (f) below.

(2) The documents mentioned in paragraph (1) above are—

(a) a statement of the grounds of appeal;

(b) a copy of any relevant application;

(c) a copy of any relevant authorisation;

(d) a copy of any relevant correspondence between the appellant and the enforcing authority;

(e) a copy of any decision or notice which is the subject-matter of the appeal;

(f) a statement indicating whether the appellant wishes the appeal to be in the form of a hearing or to be disposed of on the basis of written representations.

(3) If the appellant wishes to withdraw an appeal he shall do so by notifying the Secretary of State in writing and shall send a copy of that notification to the enforcing authority.

*Time limit for bringing appeal*

**10.** (1) Subject to paragraph (2) below, notice of appeal in accordance with regulation 9(1) above is to be given—

(a) in the case of an appeal by a person who has been refused the grant of an authorisation under section 6 of the 1990 Act,[4] before the expiry of the period of six months beginning with—

(i)   the date of the decision which is the subject-matter of the appeal; or

(ii)  in the case of an appeal against a deemed refusal of an application for an authorisation, the date on which the application is deemed under the provisions of paragraph 5(2) of Schedule 1 to the 1990 Act[1] to have been refused;

(b)  in the case of an appeal by a person who is aggrieved by the conditions attached to his authorisation or who has been refused a variation of an authorisation on an application under section 11 of the 1990 Act,[2] before the expiry of the period of six months beginning with the date of the decision which is the subject-matter of the appeal;

(c)  in the case of an appeal in respect of a decision of an enforcing authority to revoke an authorisation, before the date on which the revocation of the authorisation takes effect;

(d)  in the case of an appeal by a person on whom a variation notice, an enforcement notice or a prohibition notice is served, before the expiry of the period of two months beginning with the date of the notice which is the subject-matter of the appeal;

(e)  in the case of an appeal in respect of a decision of an enforcing authority that information is not commercially confidential, before the expiry of the period of 21 days beginning with the date of the notice of determination.

(2)  The Secretary of State may in a particular case allow notice of appeal to be given after the expiry of the periods mentioned in paragraph (1)(a), (b) or (d) above.

*Action upon receipt of notice of appeal*

**11.**  (1)  Subject to paragraph (4) below, the enforcing authority shall, within 14 days of receipt of the copy of the notice of appeal in accordance with regulation 9(1) above—

(a)  in the case of an appeal by a person in respect of a decision of an enforcing authority to revoke an authorisation or on whom a variation notice, an enforcement notice or a prohibition notice is served, give written notice of it to any person who appears to the enforcing authority likely to have a particular interest in the subject-matter of the appeal; and

(b)  in any other case give written notice of it—

(i)   to any person who made representations to the authority with respect to the grant or variation of the authorisation; and

(ii)  to any person who was required to be consulted on the application under paragraph 2 or 7[3] of Schedule 1 to the 1990 Act pursuant to regulation 4(1) above.

(2)  A notice under paragraph (1) above shall—

(a)  state that an appeal has been lodged;

(b)  give the name of the appellant and—

(i)   where the prescribed process will not be carried on by means of mobile plant,[4] the address of the premises where the prescribed process will be carried on;

(ii)  where the prescribed process will be carried on by means of mobile plant, the address of this principal place of business;

(c)  describe the application or authorisation to which the appeal relates;

(d)  *Omitted by S.I. 1996/667, reg.2, sch., para.5(1)(b). This amendment came into force on 1 April 1996: reg.1(1).*

(e)  state that representations with respect to the appeal may be made to the Secretary of State in writing by any recipient of the notice within a period of 21 days beginning with the date

---

[1] P.212 above.
[2] P.100 above.
[3] Words "2 or 7" substituted by S.I. 1996/667, reg.2, sch., para.5(1)(a). This amendment came into force on 1 April 1996: reg.1(1). The amendments made by S.I. 1996/667, sch., para.5(1) do not apply in cases where the enforcing authority receives the copy of the notice of appeal in accordance with regulation 9(1) of these Regulations before 1 April 1996: para.5(2).

[4] "Mobile plant" defined by s.1(6) of the 1990 Act, p.90 above.

of the notice, and that copies of any representations so made will be furnished to the appellant and to the enforcing authority;[1]

(ea) explain that any such representations made by any person will be entered in a public register unless that person requests in writing that they should not be so placed, and that where such a request is made there will be included in the register a statement indicating only that representations have been made which have been the subject of such a request;[2] and

(f) state that if a hearing is to be held wholly or partly in public, a person mentioned in paragraph (1)(a) or b(i) above who makes representations with respect to the appeal and any person mentioned in paragraph (1)(b)(ii) above will be notified of the date of the hearing.

(3) The enforcing authority shall, within 14 days of sending a notice under paragraph (1) above,[3] notify the Secretary of State of the persons to whom and the date on which the notice was sent.

(3A) In the event of an appeal being withdrawn, the enforcing authority shall give written notice of the withdrawal to every person to whom notice was given under paragraph (1) above.[4]

(4) The preceding provisions of this regulation do not apply in the case of an appeal brought under section 22(5) of the 1990 Act.

*Written representations*

**12.** (1) Where the appellant informs the Secretary of State that he wishes the appeal to be disposed of on the basis of written representations, the enforcing authority shall submit any written representations to the Secretary of State not later than 28 days after receiving a copy of the documents mentioned in regulation 9(2)(a) and (f) above.[5]

(2) The appellant shall make any further representations by way of reply to any representations from the enforcing authority not later than 17 days after the date of submission of those representations by the enforcing authority.

(3) Any representations made by the appellant or the enforcing authority shall be dated and submitted to the Secretary of State on the date they bear.

(4) When the enforcing authority or the appellant submits any representations to the Secretary of State they shall at the same time send a copy of them to the other party.

(5) The Secretary of State shall send to the appellant and the enforcing authority a copy of any representations made to him by the persons mentioned in regulation 11(1) above and shall allow the appellant and the enforcing authority a period of not less than 14 days in which to make representations thereon.

(6) The Secretary of State may in a particular case—

(a) set later time limits than those mentioned in this regulation;

(b) require exchanges of representations between the parties in addition to those mentioned in paragraphs (1) and (2) above.

*Hearings*

**13.** (1) The Secretary of State shall give the appellant and the enforcing authority at least 28 days written notice (or such shorter period of notice as they may agree) of the date, time and place fixed for the holding of any hearing in respect of an appeal under section 15[6] or 22(5)[7] of the 1990 Act.

(2) Subject to paragraph (4) and (5) below, in the case of a hearing which is to be held wholly or partly in public, the Secretary of State shall, at least 21 days before the date fixed for the holding of the hearing, publish a copy of the notice mentioned in paragraph (1) above—

[1] Words ", and that copies . . . the enforcing authority" added by S.I. 1996/667, reg.2, sch., para.5(1)(c).

[2] This sub-paragraph inserted by S.I. 996/667, reg.2, sch., para.5(1)(d).

[3] Former words "send to the Secretary of State a copy of any representations made to that authority by any person mentioned in paragraph (1)(b) above and shall" omitted by

S.I. 1996/667, reg.2, sch., para.5(1)(e).

[4] This paragraph inserted by S.I. 1996/667, reg.2, sch., para.5(1)(f).

[5] P.612 above.

[6] P.103 above.

[7] P.108 above.

(a) in a case where the prescribed process will not be carried on by means of mobile plant,[1] in a newspaper circulating in the locality in which the prescribed process which is the subject of the appeal will be carried on; and

(b) in a case where the appeal is in respect of a decision of an enforcement authority to revoke an authorisation or against a variation notice, an enforcement notice or a prohibition notice in respect of a prescribed process carried on by means of mobile plant, in a newspaper circulating in the locality in which the prescribed process was carried on at the time when the notice of revocation, variation notice, enforcement notice or prohibition notice was served,

and shall serve a copy of the notice mentioned in paragraph (1) above on every person mentioned in regulation 11(1)(a) and (b)(i) above who has made representations in writing to the Secretary of State and on any person who was required under regulation 11(1)(b)(ii) above to be notified of the appeal.

(3) The Secretary of State may vary the date fixed for the holding of any hearing and paragraphs (1) and (2) above shall apply to the variation of a date as they applied to the date originally fixed.

(4) The Secretary of State may also vary the time or place for the holding of a hearing but shall give such notice of any such variation as appears to him to be reasonable.

(5) Paragraph (2) above shall not apply in the case of a hearing in respect of an appeal brought under section 22(5) of the 1990 Act.[2]

(6) The persons entitled to be heard at a hearing are—

(a) the appellant;

(b) the enforcing authority; and

(c) any person required under regulation 11(1)(b)(ii) above to be notified of the appeal.

(7) Nothing in paragraph (6) above shall prevent the person appointed to conduct the hearing of the appeal from permitting any other person to be heard at the hearing and such permission shall not be unreasonably withheld.

(8) After the conclusion of a hearing, the person appointed to conduct the haring shall, unless he has been appointed under section 114(1)(a) of the Environment Act 1995[3] to determine the appeal,[4] make a report in writing to the Secretary of State which shall include his conclusions and his recommendations or his reasons for not making any recommendations.

*Notification of determination*

**14.** (1) The Secretary of State shall notify the appellant in writing of his determination of the appeal and shall provide him with a copy of any report mentioned in regulation 13(8) above.

(2) The Secretary of State shall at the same time send—

(a) a copy of the documents mentioned in paragraph (1) above to the enforcing authority and to any persons required under regulation 11(1)(b)(ii) above[5] to be notified of the appeal; and

(b) a copy of his determination of the appeal to a person mentioned in regulation 11(1)(a) and (b)(i) above who made representations to the Secretary of State and, if a hearing was held, to any other person who made representations in relation to the appeal at the hearing.

*Registers*

**15.** Subject to sections 21 and 22 of the 1990 Act, a register maintained by an enforcing authority under section 20 of that Act[6] shall be maintained in accordance with regulation 15A below and shall contain—

(a) all particulars of any application for an authorisation, or for a variation of the conditions of an authorisation, made to the authority;

---

[1] "Mobile plant" defined by s.1(6) of the 1990 Act, p.90 above.

[2] P.108 above.

[3] P.489 above.

[4] Words ", unless he has been appointed under section 114(1)(a) of the Environment Act 1995 to determine the appeal," inserted by S.I. 1996/667, reg.2, sch., para.6. This amendment came into force on 1 April 1996: reg.1(1).

[5] P.613 above.

[6] P.105 above.

(b) all particulars of any advertisement published pursuant to regulation 5 above;[1]

(c) all particulars of any notice to the applicant by the authority under paragraph 1(3) of Schedule 1 to that Act[2] and of any information furnished in response to such a notice;

(ca) all particulars of any representations made by any person required to be consulted under paragraph 2, 6 or 7 of Schedule 1 to the 1990 Act pursuant to regulation 4(1) above;[3]

(d) all particulars of any representations made by any person in response to an advertisement published pursuant to regulation 5 above which contains the explanation required by paragraph (3)(f) of that regulation, or a notice given pursuant to regulation 11(1) above[4] which contains the explanation required by paragraph (2)(ea) of that regulation, other than representations which the person who made them requested should not be placed in the register;

(e) in a case where any such representations are omitted from the register at the request of the person who made them, a statement by the authority that such representations have been made which have been the subject of such a request (but such statement shall not identify the person who made the representations in question);

(f) all particulars of any authorisation granted by the authority;

(g) all particulars of any written notice of the transfer of an authorisation given to the authority pursuant to section 9(2) of that Act;[5]

(h) all particulars of any notification given to the holder of an authorisation by the authority under section 10(5) of that Act;

(i) all particulars of any revocation of an authorisation effected by the authority;

(j) all particulars of any variation notice, enforcement notice or prohibition notice issued by the authority;

(k) all particulars of any notice issued by the authority withdrawing an enforcement notice or a prohibition notice;

(l) all particulars of any notice of appeal under section 15 of that Act[6] against a decision by the authority, the documents relating to the appeal mentioned in regulation 9(2)(a), (d) and (e) above,[7] any written notification of the Secretary of State's determination of such an appeal and any report accompanying any such written notification;

(m) details of any conviction of any person for any offence under section 23(1) of that Act[8] which relates to the carrying on of a prescribed process under an authorisation granted by the authority, or without such an authorisation in circumstances where one is required by section 6(1) of the 1990 Act,[9] including the name of the offender, the date of conviction, the penalty imposed and the name of the Court;

(n) all particulars of any monitoring information relating to the carrying on of a prescribed process under an authorisation granted by the authority obtained by the authority as a result of its own monitoring or furnished to the authority in writing by virtue of a condition of the authorisation or section 19(2) of that Act;[10]

(o) in a case where any such monitoring information is omitted from the register by virtue of section 22 of that Act,[11] a statement by the authority, based on the monitoring information from time to time obtained by or furnished to them, indicating whether or not there has been compliance with any relevant condition of the authorisation;

(p) all particulars of any other information furnished to the authority on or after 1st April 1996 in compliance with a condition of the authorisation, a variation notice, enforcement notice or prohibition notice, or section 19(2) of that Act;

---

[1] P.610 above.
[2] P.211 above.
[3] This paragraph inserted by S.I. 1996/979, reg.2. This amendment came into force on 24 April 1996: reg.1(1).
[4] P.613 above.
[5] P.98 above.

[6] P.103 above.
[7] P.612 above.
[8] P.108 above.
[9] P.95 above.
[10] P.104 above.
[11] P.107 above.

(q) all particulars of any report published by an enforcing authority relating to an assessment of the environmental consequences of the carrying on of a prescribed process in the locality of premises where the prescribed process is carried on under an authorisation granted by the authority; and

(r) all particulars of any direction (other than a direction under section 21(2) of that Act) given to the authority by the Secretary of State under any provision of Part I of that Act.[1]

**15A.** (1) Where an advertisement is required to be published in accordance with regulation 5 above—

(a) in the case of an advertisement under paragraph 1(2)[2] or 7(2)[3] of Schedule 1 to the 1990 Act, the particulars referred to in paragraph (a) of regulation 15 above shall be entered in the register not later than 14 days after the receipt by the enforcing authority of the application to which the advertisement relates;

(b) in the case of an advertisement under paragraph 6(2) of the Schedule, the particulars referred to in paragraph (h) of regulation 15 above shall be entered in the register not later than 14 days after the giving of the notification under section 10(5) of the 1990 Act.[4]

(2) Where an application for an authorisation is withdrawn by the applicant at any time before it is determined, all particulars relating to that application which are already in the register shall be removed from that register not less than two months and not more than three months after the date of withdrawal of the application, and no further particulars relating to that application shall be entered in the register.

(3) Where, by virtue of any regulations made under section 2(1) of the 1990 Act[5] a description of process ceases to be a prescribed process, all particulars relating to processes of that description shall be removed from the register not less than two months and not more than three months after the date on which that description of process ceases to be prescribed.[6]

**16.** A register maintained by a local enforcing authority[7] in England and Wales which is not a port health authority shall (in addition to the particulars required by regulation 15 above) contain all particulars of such information contained in any register maintained by the Environment Agency as relates to the carrying on in the area of the local enforcing authority of prescribed processes in relation to which that Agency has functions under Part I of the 1990 Act.[8]

**17.** Nothing in regulation 15 or 16 above shall require an enforcing authority to keep in a register maintained by them—

(a) monitoring information relating to a particular process four years after that information was entered in the register; or

(b) information relating to a particular process which has been superseded by later information relating to that process four years after that later information was entered in the register,

but nothing in this regulation shall apply to any aggregated monitoring data relating to overall emissions of any substance or class of substances from prescribed processes generally or from any class of prescribed process.[9]

[1] This regulation substituted by S.I. 1996/667, reg.2, sch., para.7. This amendment came into force on 1 April 1996: reg.1(1).

[2] P.211 above.

[3] P.213 above.

[4] P.99 above.

[5] P.91 above.

[6] This regulation inserted by S.I. 1996/667, reg.2, para. 8. This amendment came into force on 1 April 1996: reg.1(1).

[7] "Local enforcing authority" defined by s.1(7) of the 1990 Act, p.90 above.

[8] This regulation substituted by S.I. 1996/667, reg.2, sch., para.9. This amendment came into force on 1 April 1996: reg.1(1).

[9] This regulation substituted by S.I. 1996/667, reg.2, sch., para.10. This amendment came into force on 1 April 1996: reg.1(1).

*Explanatory Note*
*(This note is not part of the Regulations)*

These Regulations regulate the procedures to be followed in connection with applications for authorisation to carry on a prescribed process made under section 6 of the Environmental Protection Act 1990 and with the variation of such authorisations under sections 10 and 11 of that Act. The Regulations provide exemptions from the procedure for certain waste oil producers and in cases involving information affecting national security or which is commercially confidential.

The Regulations also regulate the procedures and time limits in connection with appeals made to the Secretary of State under section 15 or 22(5) of the Environmental Protection Act 1990.

The Regulations also prescribe the particulars of the matters required by section 20 of the Environmental Protection Act 1990 to be included in registers to be maintained by enforcing authorities.

Copies of the document published by the British Standards Institution referred to in regulation 2(3) may be obtained from any of the sales outlets of the British Standards Institution, Linford Wood, Milton Keynes MK14 6LE (Telephone number: Milton Keynes (STD 01908) 220022).

# The Environmental Protection (Authorisation of Processes) (Determination Periods) Order 1991

S.I. 1991 No. 513

The Secretary of State for the Environment, as respects England, the Secretary of State for Wales, as respects Wales, and the Secretary of State for Scotland, as respects Scotland, in exercise of the powers conferred upon them by paragraph 5(3) of Schedule 1 to the Environmental Protection Act 1990[1] and of all other powers enabling them in that behalf, hereby make the following Order:

*Citation, commencement and interpretation*

1. (1) This Order may be cited as the Environmental Protection (Authorisation of Processes) (Determination Periods) Order 1991 and shall come into force in England and Wales on 1st April 1991 and in Scotland on 1st April 1992.

(2) In this Order "the 1990 Act" means the Environmental Protection Act.

2. (1) Subject to article 3(6) below, in the case of an application to which paragraph (2) below applies, for the period mentioned in paragraph 5(1) of Schedule 1 to the 1990 Act[2] there shall be substituted the period mentioned in paragraph (3) below.

(2) This paragraph applies to an application for an authorisation to carry on a process in relation to which—

(a) a matter falls to be determined by the Secretary of State under section 21(2) or (4) of the 1990 Act;[3]

(b) an application is made to an enforcing authority under section 22(2) of that Act;[4] or

(c) an objection is made to such an authority under section 22(4) of that Act.

(3) The period to be substituted in paragraph 5(1) of Schedule 1 to the 1990 Act is the period of four months beginning with the day on which the matters to be determined under section 21 or 22 of that Act are finally disposed of or such longer period as the enforcing authority may agree with the applicant.

(4) For the purposes of paragraph (3) above and article 3(6) below, the matters to be determined under section 21 or 22 of the 1990 Act are finally disposed of—

(a) on the date on which the Secretary of State determines under section 21 whether or not the information in question is to be included in the register;

(b) on the date on which the enforcing authority is treated under section 22(3) as having made a determination;

(c) in a case where the enforcing authority determines under section 22(2) that the information in question is commercially confidential, on the date of the authority's determination;

(d) in a case where the enforcing authority determines under section 22(2) or (4) that the information in question is not commercially confidential, on the date on which the period for bringing an appeal expires without an appeal being brought or, if such an appeal is brought

---

[1] P.212 above.
[2] P.212 above.
[3] P.106 above.
[4] P.107 above.

within that period, on the date of the Secretary of State's final determination of the appeal or, as the case may be, the date on which the appellant withdraws his appeal.

*Extension of period for consideration of applications by local authorities*

3. (1) Subject to paragraph (6) below, in the case of an application to which paragraph (2) below applies, for the period mentioned in paragraph 5(1) of Schedule 1 to the 1990 Act[1] there shall be substituted—

(a) in England and Wales, the period of eighteen months;

(b) in Scotland, the period of fifteen months,

beginning with the day on which the enforcing authority received the application or within such longer period as it may agree with the applicant.

(2) This paragraph applies to an application for an authorisation to carry on a process which—

(a) falls within the description set out in paragraph (c) of Part B of section 1.3 in Schedule 1 to the Environmental Protection (Prescribed Processes and Substances) Regulations 1991[2] (burning waste oil to produce energy);

(b) involves only the use of one or more appliances having a net rated thermal input, or aggregate net rated thermal input, not exceeding 0.4 megawatts; and

(c) is an existing process[3] for which the prescribed date is, in the case of a process carried on in England or Wales, that referred to in paragraph 11(1)(ii) of Schedule 3 to those Regulations[4] and, in the case of a process carried on in Scotland, that referred to in paragraph 24(1)(ii) of that Schedule.[5]

(3) Subject to paragraph (6) below, in the case of an application to which paragraph (4) below applies, for the period mentioned in paragraph 5(1) of Schedule 1 to the 1990 Act[6] there shall be substituted, the period of fourteen days beginning with the day on which the enforcing authority received the application or within such longer period as it may agree with the applicant.

(4) This paragraph applies to an application for an authorisation to carry on any process which—

(a) is not an existing process;

(b) falls within paragraph (2)(a) and (b) above; and

(c) does not involve the burning of waste oil generated otherwise than as a result of activities carried on by the applicant on the premises where the process is to be carried on.

(5) Subject to paragraph (6) below, in the case of an application for an authorisation to carry on any existing process subject to local control which is described in paragraph (2)(c) above but does not fall within paragraph (2)(a) and (b) above or paragraph (5A) below,[7] for the period mentioned in paragraph 5(1) of Schedule 1 to the 1990 Act there shall be substituted—

(a) in England and Wales, the period of twelve months;

(b) in Scotland, the period of nine months,

beginning with the day on which the enforcing authority received the application or within such longer period as it may agree with the applicant.

(5A) Subject to paragraph (6) below, in the case of an application for an authorisation to carry on a process subject to local control in respect of which paragraph 5, 6 or 7 of Schedule 6 to the Environmental Protection (Prescribed Processes and Substances Etc.) (Amendment) Regulations 1994[8] applies but which does not fall within paragraph (2)(a) and (b) above, for the period mentioned in paragraph 5(1) of Schedule 1 to the 1990 Act there shall be substituted the period of nine months beginning with the day on which the enforcing authority received the application or such longer period as it may agree with the applicant.[9]

---

[1] P.212 above.
[2] P.570 above.
[3] For "existing process" see para.(7) below.
[4] P.595 above.
[5] P.597 above.
[6] P.212 above.

[7] Words "or paragraph 5(A) below" inserted by S.I. 1994/2347, art.2(1). This amendment came into force on 1 December 1994: art.1.
[8] S.I. 1994/1271; sch.6, as substituted by S.I. 1994/1329, is at p.599 above.
[9] This paragraph inserted by S.I. 1994/2847, art.2(3).

(6) In the case of an application to which paragraph (2), (4), (5) or (5A)[1] above applies and to which article 2(2) above also applies, the period mentioned in paragraph (1), (3), (5) and (5A)[2] above shall begin with the day on which the matters to be determined under section 21 or 22 of the 1990 Act[3] are finally disposed of.

(7) In this article, "existing process" has the same meaning as in the Environmental Protection (Prescribed Processes and Substances) Regulations 1991.[4]

*Explanatory Note*
*(This note is not part of the Order)*

This Order varies the period available to enforcing authorities to consider applications under Part I of the Environmental Protection Act 1990 for authorisation to carry on prescribed processes.

Where the exclusion from public registers of information affecting national security or certain confidential information is to be considered, article 2 of the Order provides for the period laid down in the Act (4 months beginning with the day the enforcing authority receives the application) to begin when that consideration is completed.

Article 3 of the Order makes provision in relation to processes for which local authority authorisation is required in accordance with the Environmental Protection (Prescribed Processes and Substances) Regulations 1991.

Article 3[5] generally extends the period laid down in the Act (4 months) to 12 months in England and Wales and 9 months in Scotland for processes which are existing processes when those Regulations come into force: but

(i) a period of 14 days is specified for new small heating installations using waste or recovered oil generated on the same premises such as heaters in commercial garages using oil drained from vehicles there;

(ii) a period of 18 months or, in Scotland, 15 months is specified for other existing small heating installations using waste or recovered oil.

---

[1] Words "paragraph (2), (4), (5) or (5A)" substituted by S.I. 1994/2847, art.2(4)(a).
[2] Words "paragraph (1), (3), (5) and (5A)" substituted by S.I. 1994/2847, art.2(4)(b).
[3] P.106 above.

[4] S.I. 1991/472; for "existing process" in the case of a Part B process carried on in England or Wales see sch.3, para.14, p.596 above; in the case of a Part B process carried on in Scotland see sch.3, para.27, p.598 above.
[5] Note the amendment made to art.3 by S.I. 1994/2847.

# The Bathing Waters (Classification) Regulations 1991

S.I. 1991 No. 1597

The Secretary of State for the Environment and the Secretary of State for Wales, acting jointly in exercise of the powers conferred on them by sections 104,[1] 171[2] and 185(2)[3] of the Water Act 1989,[4] hereby make the following Regulations:

*Citation and commencement*

1. (1)  These Regulations may be cited as the Bathing Waters (Classification) Regulations 1991 and shall come into force on 9th August 1991.

*Classification of waters*

2. (1)  A system employing the classification BW1 is prescribed as a system of classification applying to relevant territorial waters, coastal waters and inland waters[5] which are bathing waters.

(2)  For the purposes of paragraph (1) above "bathing waters" are waters which are bathing water within the meaning of Article 1.2 of Council Directive 76/160/EEC[6] and other waters which are used for bathing.

(3)  Schedules 1, 2 and 3 (which specify criteria for classification BW1, impose sampling requirements and set out quality standards) shall have effect.

*Modification of section 105 of the Water Act 1989*

3. Section 105 of the Water Act 1989[7] shall have effect as if—

(a)  it imposed a duty on the Secretary of State to exercise his powers under that section to apply the classification BW1 to relevant territorial waters, coastal waters and inland waters which are bathing water within the meaning of Article 1.2 of Council Directive 76/160/EEC; and

(b)  in relation to the establishment of water quality objectives in pursuance of that duty, subsections (4) and (5) of that section were omitted.

## SCHEDULE 1

(Regulation 2(3))

### CRITERIA FOR CLASSIFICATION BW1

1.  Subject to the following provisions of this Schedule, the criteria for the classification BW1 are that—

(a)  at least 95 per cent of samples of the waters taken and tested in accordance with Schedule 2 must conform to the parametric values specified in Schedule 3;

---

[1] This reference has effect as a reference to s.82 of the Water Resources Act 1991, p.271 above: Water Consolidation (Consequential Provisions) Act 1991 (c.60), s.2, sch.2, para.1.

[2] This reference has effect as a reference to s.102 of the Water Resources Act 1991, p.290 above: Water Consolidation (Consequential Provisions) Act 1991 (c.60), s.2, sch.2, para.1.

[3] This reference has effect as a reference to s.219(2) of the Water Resources Act 1991, p.310 above: Water Consolidation (Consequential Provisions) Act 1991 (c.60), s.2, sch.2, para.1.

[4] See the definition of "prescribed" in s.221(1) of the 1991 Act, p.314 above.

[5] "Relevant territorial waters", "coastal waters" and "inland freshwaters" are defined in s.104, p.290 above.

[6] OJ No. L 31/1, 5.2.76, p.1.

[7] This reference has effect as a reference to s.83 of the Water Resources Act 1991, p.272 above: Water Consolidation (Consequential Provisions) Act 1991 (c.60), s.2, sch.2, para.1.

(b) no sample of the waters taken in accordance with Schedule 2 which when tested for compliance with the phenols parameter by the absorption method or with the transparency parameter fails to comply shall have a value which deviates from the relevant parametric value for that parameter specified in Schedule 3 by more than 50 per cent;

(c) consecutive samples of the waters taken in accordance with Schedule 2 at statistically suitable intervals shall not when tested deviate from the relevant parametric values specified in Schedule 3.

2. For the purposes of paragraph 1 above samples shall be disregarded if they deviate from the parametric values specified in Schedule 3 as a result of abnormal weather conditions, floods or other natural disasters.

3. (1) Subject to sub-paragraph (2), where in the case of particular waters to which the classification BW1 applies—

   (a) any requirement relating to the parameter for pH, colour or transparency cannot be complied with as a result of exceptional weather or geographical conditions; or

   (b) any requirement relating to any parameter cannot be complied with as a result of the waters having undergone a process of natural enrichment from the soil without human intervention,

   the Secretary of State may by notice served on the Environment Agency[1] modify or disapply that requirement in relation to those waters.

   (2) The Secretary of State shall not exercise his powers under this paragraph so as to permit a risk to public health.

# SCHEDULE 2

(Regulation 2(3))

## Sampling Requirements

1. Samples must be taken in accordance with the requirements of Schedule 3 in any year throughout the period beginning on 1st May and ending on 30th September.

2. Additional samples must be taken during that period if there are grounds to suspect that the quality of the waters is deteriorating for any reason or is likely to deteriorate as a result of any discharge.

3. All samples must be taken at the same point at the place in the particular waters where the daily average density of bathers is at its highest, and preferably 30 centimetres below the surface, except in the case of samples for testing for mineral oils, which must be taken at surface level.

4. The methods of analysis and inspection specified in Schedule 3, or methods which are at least as reliable, must be used for determining whether the parametric values specified in that Schedule are met.

[1] Words "the Environment Agency" substituted by the Environment Act 1995 (c.25), s.120, sch.22, para.233(1). This amendment came into force on 1 April 1996: S.I. 1996/186.

The Environment Agency is established by s.1 of the Environment Act 1995, p.420 above.

# SCHEDULE 3

(Regulation 2(3))

## QUALITY AND ADDITIONAL SAMPLING REQUIREMENTS

| Parameter | Parametric value | Minimum sampling frequency | Methods of analysis and inspection |
|---|---|---|---|
| **Micro-biological:** | | | |
| Total coliforms | 10,000/ 100ml | Fortnightly (see Note 1) | Fermentation in multiple tubes. Sub-culturing of the positive tubes on a confirmation medium. Either counting according to MPN (most probable number) or membrane filtration, culturing on an appropriate medium, subculturing and identification of the suspect colonies. |
| Faecal coliforms | 2,000/ 100ml | Fortnightly (see Note 1) | |
| | | | The incubation temperature is variable according to whether total or faecal coliforms are being investigated. |
| Salmonella | Absent in 1 litre | (see Note 2) | Membrane filtration, culturing on an appropriate medium, sub-culturing and identification of the suspect colonies. |
| Entero viruses | No plaque forming units in 10 litres | (see Note 2) | Concentration (by filtration, flocculation or centrifuging) and confirmation. |
| **Physico-chemical:** | | | |
| pH | 6 to 9 | (see Note 2) | Electrometry with calibration at pH 7 and 9. |
| Colour | No abnormal change in colour | Fortnightly (see Note 1) | Visual inspection or photometry with standards on the platinum cobalt scale. |
| Mineral oils | No film visible on the surface of the water and no odour | Fortnightly (see Note 1) | Visual and olfactory inspection. |
| Surface-active substances reacting with methylene blue | No lasting foam | Fortnightly (see Note 1) | Visual inspection. |
| Phenols (phenol indices) | No specific odour | Fortnightly (see Note 1) | Olfactory inspection. |
| | $\leq 0.05$ mg/litre ($C_6H_5OH$) | (see Note 2) | Absorption spectrophotometry 4-aminoantipyrine (4 AAP) method. |
| Transparency | 1 metre | Fortnightly (see Note 1) | Secchi's disc. |

**Notes**
1. Samples may be taken at intervals of four weeks where samples taken in previous years show that the waters are of an appreciably higher standard than that required for the classification in question and the quality of the waters has not subsequently deteriorated and is unlikely to do so.
2. Samples must be taken in relation to this parameter when there are grounds for suspecting that there has been a deterioration in the quality of the waters or the substance is likely to be present in the waters.

*Explanatory Note*
*(This note is not part of the Regulations)*

These Regulations prescribe a system of classifying the quality of relevant territorial waters, coastal waters and inland waters which are bathing waters. The classification BW1 prescribed by the Regulations reflects the mandatory standards laid down in the Annex to Council directive 76/160/EEC concerning the quality of bathing water.

The system of classification prescribed by the Regulations will be used for establishing quality objectives under section 105 of the Water Act 1989[1] for bathing waters (regulation 2 and Schedules 1 to 3). Paragraph 3 of Schedule 1 gives the Secretary of State power to grant derogations from certain requirements of the objectives in circumstances permitted by Article 8 of Council Directive 76/160/EEC. There are sampling requirements in Schedules 2 and 3 and the Secretary of State will use his powers under section 146 of the Water Act 1989[2] to direct the Environment Agency[3] to sample and test waters to which classification BW1 applies in accordance with those requirements.

Regulation 3 imposes a duty on the Secretary of State to use his powers under section 105 of the Water Act 1989[4] to apply the classification BW1 to waters which are "bathing water" within the meaning of Council Directive 76/160/EEC. It also dispenses with the requirements of section 105(4) and (5)[4] (representations and objections) in cases where the Secretary of State is performing that duty.

---

[1] This reference has effect as a reference to s.83 of the Water Resources Act 1991, p.272 above: Water Consolidation (Consequential Provisions) Act 1991 (c.60), s.2, sch.2, para.1.
[2] This provision has been replaced by s.40 of the Environment Act 1995, p.451 above.

[3] Words "the Environment Agency" substituted by the Environment Act 1995 (c.25), s.120, sch.22, para.233(1).
[4] The references to s.105 have effect as references to s.83 of the Water Resources Act 1991, p.272 above: Water Consolidation (Consequential Provisions) Act 1991 (c.60), s.2, sch.2, para.1.

# The Bathing Waters (Classification) (Scotland) Regulations 1991

## 1991 No. 1609 (S.144)

The Secretary of State, in exercise of the powers conferred on him by sections 30B,[1] 102(1),[2] 104(1)[3] and 105(1)[4] of the Control of Pollution Act 1974 and by section 2(2) of the European Communities Act 1972,[5] being the Minister designated[6] for the purposes of that subsection in relation to the prevention, reduction and elimination of pollution of water, and of all other powers enabling him in that behalf, hereby makes the following Regulations:

*Citation, commencement and extent*

1. These Regulations may be cited as the Bathing Waters (Classification) (Scotland) Regulations 1991, shall come into force on 9th August 1991 and shall extend to Scotland only.

*Classification of waters*

2. (1) A system employing the classification BW1 is prescribed as a system of classification applying to relevant territorial waters, coastal waters and inland waters[7] which are bathing waters.

(2) For the purposes of paragraph (1) above "bathing waters" are waters which are bathing water within the meaning of Article 1.2 of Council Directive 76/160/EEC[8] and other waters which are used for bathing.

(3) Schedules 1, 2 and 3 to these Regulations (which specify criteria for classification BW1, impose sampling requirements and set out quality standards) shall have effect.

*Modification of section 30C of the Control of Pollution Act 1974*

3. Section 30C of the Control of Pollution Act 1974[9] shall have effect as if—

(a) it imposed a duty on the Secretary of State to exercise his powers under that section to apply the classification BW1 to relevant territorial waters, coastal waters and inland waters which are bathing water within the meaning of Article 1.2 of Council Directive 76/160/EEC; and

(b) in relation to the establishment of water quality objectives in pursuance of that duty, subsections (4) and (5) of that section were omitted.

## SCHEDULE 1

(Regulation 2(3))

### CRITERIA FOR CLASSIFICATION BW1

1. Subject to the following provisions of this Schedule, the criteria for the classification BW1 are that—

(a) at least 95 per cent of samples of the waters taken and tested in accordance with Schedule 2 must conform to the parametric values specified in Schedule 3;

---

[1] P.19 above.
[2] P.60 above.
[3] P.60 above.
[4] P.61 above; s.105(1) contains a definition of "prescribed" relevant to the exercise of the statutory powers under which these Regulations are made.
[5] 1972 c.68.
[6] S.I. 1989/2393.
[7] "Relevant territorial waters", "coastal waters" and "inland waters" are defined in s.30A, p.18 above.
[8] OJ No. L 31, 5.2.76, p.1.
[9] P.20 above.

(b) no sample of the waters taken in accordance with Schedule 2 which, when tested for compliance with the phenols parameter by the absorption method or with the transparency parameter fails to comply, shall have a value which deviates from the relevant parametric value for that parameter specified in Schedule 3 by more than 50 per cent; and

(c) consecutive samples of the waters taken in accordance with Schedule 2 at statistically suitable intervals shall not when tested deviate from the relevant parametric values specified in Schedule 3.

2. For the purposes of paragraph 1 above samples shall be disregarded if they deviate from the parametric values specified in Schedule 3 as a result of abnormal weather conditions, floods or other natural disasters.

3. (1) Subject to sub-paragraph (2) below, where in the case of particular waters to which the classification BW1 applies—

(a) any requirement relating to the parameter for pH, colour or transparency cannot be complied with as a result of exceptional weather or geographical conditions; or

(b) any requirement relating to any parameter cannot be complied with as a result of the waters having undergone a process of natural enrichment from the soil without human intervention,

the Secretary of State may by notice served on the Scottish Environment Protection Agency[1] modify or disapply that requirement in relation to those waters.

(2) The Secretary of State shall not exercise his powers under this paragraph so as to permit a public health risk.

# SCHEDULE 2

(Regulation 2(3))

## SAMPLING REQUIREMENTS

1. Samples must be taken in accordance with the requirements of Schedule 3 in any year throughout the period beginning on 1st May and ending on 30th September.

2. Additional samples must be taken during that period if there are grounds to suspect that the quality of the waters is deteriorating for any reason or is likely to deteriorate as a result of any discharge.

3. All samples must be taken at the same point at the place in the particular waters where the daily average density of bathers is at its highest, and preferably 30 centimetres below the surface, except in the case of samples for testing for mineral oils, which must be taken at surface level.

4. The methods of analysis and inspection specified in Schedule 3, or methods which are at least as reliable, must be used for determining whether the parametric values specified in that Schedule are met.

[1] Words "the Scottish Environment Protection Agency" substituted by S.I. 1996/973, reg.2, sch., para.13. This amendment came into force on 1 April 1996: reg.1. The Scottish Environment Protection Agency, SEPA, is established by s.20 of the Environment Act 1995, p.438 above.

# SCHEDULE 3

(Regulation 2(3))

## QUALITY AND ADDITIONAL SAMPLING REQUIREMENTS

| Parameter | Parametric value | Minimum sampling frequency | Methods of analysis and inspection |
|---|---|---|---|
| Micro-biological: | | | |
| Total coliforms | 10,000/100ml | Fortnightly (*see Note 1*) | Fermentation in multiple tubes. Sub-culturing of the positive tubes on a confirmation medium. Either counting according to MPN (most probable number) or membrane filtration, culturing on an appropriate medium, subculturing and identification of the suspect colonies. |
| Faecal coliforms | 2,000/100ml | Fortnightly (*see Note 1*) | The incubation temperature is variable according to whether total or faecal coliforms are being investigated. |
| Faecal coliforms | 2,000/100ml | Fortnightly (*see Note 1*) | |
| Salmonella | Absent in 1 litre | (*see Note 2*) | Membrane filtration, culturing on an appropriate medium, sub-culturing and identification of the suspect colonies. |
| Entero viruses | No plaque forming units in 10 litres | (*see Note 2*) | Concentration (by filtration, flocculation or centrifuging) and confirmation. |
| Physico-chemical: | | | |
| pH | 6 to 9 | (*see Note 2*) | Electrometry with calibration at pH 7 and 9. |
| Colour | No abnormal change in colour | Fortnightly (*see Note 1*) | Visual inspection or photometry with standards on the platinum cobalt scale. |
| Mineral oils | No film visible on the surface of the water and no odour | Fortnightly (*see Note 1*) | Visual and olfactory inspection. |
| Surface-active substances reacting with methylene blue | No lasting foam | Fortnightly (*see Note 1*) | Visual inspection. |
| Phenols (phenol indices) | No specific odour | Fortnightly (*see Note 1*) | Olfactory inspection. |
| | $\leq 0.05$ mg/litre ($C_6H_5OH$) | (*see Note 2*) | Absorption spectrophotometry 4-aminoantipyrine (4 AAP) method. |
| Transparency | 1 metre | Fortnightly (*see Note 1*) | Secchi's disc. |

Notes
1. Samples may be taken at intervals of four weeks where samples taken in previous years show that the waters are of an appreciably higher standard than that required for classification BW1 and the quality of the waters has not subsequently deteriorated and is unlikely to do so.
2. Samples must be taken in relation to this parameter when there are grounds for suspecting that there has been a deterioration in the quality of the waters or the substance is likely to be present in the waters.

*Explanatory Note*
*(This note is not part of the Regulations)*

These Regulations, which extend to Scotland only, prescribe a system of classification for determining the quality of relevant territorial waters, coastal waters and inland waters which are bathing waters. The classification BW1 prescribed by the Regulations reflects the mandatory standards laid down in the Annex to Council Directive 76/160/EEC (OJ No. L31, 5.2.76, p.1) concerning the quality of bathing water.

The system of classification prescribed by the Regulations will be used for establishing quality objectives under section 30C of the Control of Pollution Act 1974 ("the 1974 Act") for bathing waters (regulation 2 and Schedules 1 to 3).

Paragraph 3 of Schedule 1 gives the Secretary of State power to grant derogations from certain requirements of the objectives in circumstances permitted by Article 8 of Council Directive 76/160/EEC. There are sampling requirements in Schedules 2 and 3 and the Secretary of State will use his powers under section 54 of the 1974 Act to direct the Scottish Environment Protection Agency[1] to sample and test waters within their areas to which classification BW1 applies in accordance with those requirements.

Regulation 3 imposes a duty on the Secretary of State to use his powers under section 30C of the 1974 Act to apply the classification BW1 to waters which are "bathing water" within the meaning of Council Directive 76/160/EEC. It also dispenses with the requirements of section 30C(4) and (5) (representations and objections) in cases where the Secretary of State is performing that duty.

---

[1] Words "the Scottish Environment Protection Agency" substituted by the Editor. S.54 of the 1974 Act has been replaced by s.40 of the Environment Act 1995, p.451 above.

# The Controlled Waste (Registration of Carriers and Seizure of Vehicles) Regulations 1991

S.I. 1991 No. 1624

*Arrangement of regulations*

| | | |
|---|---|---|
| 1. | Citation, commencement and interpretation | 631 |
| 2. | Exemption from registration | 631 |
| 3. | Registers | 632 |
| 4. | Applications for registration | 633 |
| 5. | Refusal of applications | 633 |
| 6. | Registration as a carrier | 634 |
| 7. | Amendment of entries | 635 |
| 8. | Change of circumstances and registration of additional partners | 635 |
| 9. | Copies of certificates of registration | 636 |
| 10. | Revocation of registration | 636 |
| 11. | Duration of registration | 636 |
| 12. | Alteration of register to reflect cessation of registration | 637 |
| 13. | Duty to return certificates etc | 637 |
| 14. | Production of authority | 637 |
| 15. | Appeals | 638 |
| 16. | Time limit for bringing an appeal | 638 |
| 17. | Hearings | 638 |
| 18. | Notification of determination | 638 |
| 19. | Prescribed information | 639 |
| 20. | Prescribed steps to be taken before applying for a warrant to seize property | 639 |
| 21. | Removal of vehicles seized | 639 |
| 22. | Return of property seized | 640 |
| 23. | Disposal of property seized | 640 |
| 24. | Notice of disposal of a vehicle | 641 |
| 25. | Application of proceeds of sale | 641 |
| 26. | Service of notices | 641 |

SCHEDULES

| | |
|---|---|
| Schedule 1—Prescribed offences: relevant enactments | 641 |
| Schedule 2—Application forms | 642 |
| Schedule 3—Certificate of registration under the Control of Pollution (Amendment) Act 1989 | 646 |

The Secretary of State for the Environment as respects England, the Secretary of State for Wales as respects Wales and the Secretary of State for Scotland as respects Scotland, in exercise of the powers conferred on them by sections 1(3)(a), 2, 3, 4(6), 5(3) and (6)(a), 6(1)(c) and (5) to (7), 8(2) and 9(1) of the Control of Pollution (Amendment) Act 1989[1] and of all other powers enabling them in that behalf, hereby make the following Regulations:

---

[1] The Control of Pollution (Amendment) Act 1989 is at p.71 above. See the definition of "prescribed" in s.9(1), p.80 above.

*Citation, commencement and interpretation*

**1.** These Regulations may be cited as the Controlled Waste (Registration of Carriers and Seizure of Vehicles) Regulations 1991 and shall come into force on 14th October 1991.

(2) In these Regulations—

"the 1989 Act" means the Control of Pollution (Amendment) Act 1989;[1]

"another relevant person" has the meaning given by section 3(5) of the 1989 Act;[2]

"date of expiry" means, in relation to a carrier's registration, the date on which the period of three years mentioned in regulation 11(2)[3] expires;

"disposed of", in relation to an appeal, has the meaning given by section 4(8) of the 1989 Act;[4]

"notice" means notice in writing;

"prescribed offence" means an offence under an enactment listed in Schedule 1;[5]

"relevant period" has the meaning given by section 4(1) of the 1989 Act.[6]

(3) For the purposes of these Regulations, an application for registration or for the renewal of a registration as a carrier of controlled waste shall be treated as pending—

(a) whilst it is being considered by the regulation authority;[7] or

(b) if it has been refused or the relevant period from the making of the application has expired without the applicant having been registered, whilst either—

    (i) the period for appealing in relation to that application has not expired; or

    (ii) the application is the subject of an appeal which has not been disposed of.

*Exemption from registration*

**2.** (1) The following persons shall not be required for the purposes of section 1 of the 1989 Act[8] to be registered carriers of controlled waste—

(a) an authority which is a waste collection authority, waste disposal authority or waster regulation authority for the purposes of Part II of the Environmental Protection Act 1990;[9]

(b) the producer of the controlled waste in question except where it is building or demolition waste;

(c) any wholly owned subsidiary of the British Railways Board which has applied in accordance with these Regulations for registration as a carrier of controlled waste but only—

    (i) if it is registered under paragraph 12 of Schedule 4 to the Waste Management Licensing Regulations 1994;[10] and

    (ii) whilst its application is pending;[11],[12]

(d) a ferry operator in relation to the carriage on the ferry of any vehicle carrying controlled waste;

(e) the operator of a vessel, aircraft, hovercraft, floating container or vehicle in relation to its use, after it has been loaded with waste in circumstances in which a licence under Part II of the Food and Environment Protection Act 1985[13] is needed or would be needed but for an order under section 7 of that Act, for transporting the waste in order to carry out any operation mentioned in section 5 or 6 of that Act;

(f) a charity;

---

[1] P.71 above.
[2] P.75 above.
[3] P.636 below.
[4] P.74 above.
[5] P.641 below.
[6] P.75 above.
[7] "Regulation authority" defined by s.9(1) of the 1989 Act, p.80 above.

[8] P.72 above.
[9] See definitions in s.30 of the 1990 Act, p.113 above.
[10] P.720 below.
[11] For "application is pending" see reg.1(3) above.
[12] Sub-paragraph (c) substituted by S.I. 1994/1056, reg.23(2). This amendment came into force on 1 May 1994: reg.1(1).
[13] 1985 c.48.

(g) a voluntary organisation within the meaning of section 48(11) of the Local Government Act 1985[1] or section 83(2D) of the Local Government (Scotland) Act 1973;[2]

(h) a person who before 1st April 1992 applies in accordance with these Regulations for registration as a carrier of controlled waste but only whilst his application is pending.

(i) a person who—

(i) is the holder of a knacker's yard licence or a licence under article 5(2)(c) or 6(2)(d) of the Animal By-Products Order 1992;[3] or

(ii) has obtained an approval under article 8 of that Order; or

(iii) is registered under article 9 or 10 of that Order,

in relation to the transport of animal by-products in accordance with Schedule 2 to that Order in connection with the activity to which the licence, approval or registration relates.[4]

(2) In this regulation—

"animal by-products" has the same meaning as in article 3(1) of the Animal By-Products Order 1992;[5]

"building or demolition waste" means waste arising from works of construction or demolition, including waste arising from work preparatory thereto;

"construction" includes improvement, repair or alteration;[6]

"knacker's yard licence"—

(a) in relation to England and Wales, has the same meaning as in section 34 of the Slaughterhouses Act 1974;[7]

(b) in relation to Scotland, means a licence under section 6 of the Slaughter of Animals (Scotland) Act 1980;[8],[9]

"registered broker of controlled waste" has the same meaning as in regulation 20 of,[10] and Schedule 5 to,[11] the Waste Management Licensing Regulations 1994;[12]

"vessel" has the same meaning as in section 742 of the Merchant Shipping Act 1894;[13]

"wholly owned subsidiary" has the same meaning as in section 736 of the Companies Act 1985.[14]

*Registers*

**3.** (1) It shall be the duty of each regulation authority[15] to establish and maintain a register of carriers of controlled waste and—

(a) to secure that the register is open for inspection[16] by members of the public free of charge at all reasonable hours; and

(b) to afford to members of the public reasonable facilities for obtaining copies of entries in the register on payment of reasonable charges.

(2) A register under this regulation may be kept in any form but shall be indexed and arranged so that members of the public can readily trace information contained in it.

---

[1] 1985 c.51.
[2] 1973 c.65; s.83(2D) was added by s.3(3) of the Local Government Act 1986 (c.10).
[3] S.I. 1992/3303.
[4] Sub-paragraph (i) added by S.I. 1994/1056, reg.23(3). This amendment came into force on 1 May 1994: reg.1(1).
[5] This definition inserted by S.I. 1994/1056, reg.23(4). This amendment came into force on 1 May 1994: reg.1(1).
[6] This definition inserted by S.I. 1992/588, reg.10. This amendment came into force on 1 June 1992: reg.1(1).
[7] 1974 c.3.
[8] 1980 c.13.
[9] This definition inserted by S.I. 1994/1056, reg.23(4).

This amendment came into force on 1 May 1994: reg.1(1).
[10] P.694 below.
[11] P.725 below.
[12] This definition inserted by S.I. 1994/1056, reg.23(4).
[13] 1894 c.60.
[14] This definition inserted by S.I. 1994/1056, reg.23(4).
[15] "Regulation authority" defined by s.9(1) of the 1989 Act, p.80 above.
[16] Former words "at their principal office" omitted by the Environment Act 1995 (Consequential Amendments) Regulations 1996, S.I. 1996/593, reg.9(2). This amendment came into force on 1 April 1996: reg.1.

*Applications for registration*

**4.** (1) An application for registration or for the renewal of a registration as a carrier of controlled waste shall be made to the regulation authority[1] for the area in which the applicant has or proposes to have his principal place of business in Great Britain; but if the applicant does not have or propose to have a place of business in Great Britain, the applicant may apply to any regulation authority.

(2) Subject to paragraphs (3) to (5), a person shall not make an application for registration or for the renewal of a registration whilst—

(a) a previous application of his is pending;[2] or

(b) he is registered.

(3) Paragraph (2) shall not prevent a person from applying for the renewal of a registration where his application is made within the period of six months mentioned in regulation 11(4).[3]

(4) An application for registration or for the renewal of a registration in respect of a business which is or is to be carried on by a partnership shall be made by all of the partners or prospective partners.

(5) A prospective partner in a business carried on by a partnership whose members are already registered may make an application for registration as a partner in that business to the regulation authority with whom the business is registered.

(6) An application for registration shall be made on a form corresponding to the form in Part I of Schedule 2,[4] or on a form substantially to the like effect, and shall contain the information required by that form.

(7) An application for the renewal of a registration shall be made on a form corresponding to the form in Part II of Schedule 2,[5] or on a form substantially to the like effect, and shall contain the information required by that form.

(8) A regulation authority shall provide a copy of the appropriate application form free of charge to any person requesting one.

(9) Subject to paragraph 3(11)(a) and (b) of Schedule 5 to the Waste Management Licensing Regulations 1994,[6,7] a regulation authority shall charge an applicant in respect of their consideration of his application—

(a) in the case of an application for registration, £95;

(b) in the case of an application for the renewal of a registration, £65,

(c) in the case of an application by a registered broker of controlled waste for registration as a carrier of controlled waste, £25,[8]

and the applicant shall pay the charge when he makes his application.

(10) A regulation authority shall, on receipt of an application for registration or for the renewal of a registration, ensure that the register contains a copy of the application.

(11) A regulation authority may remove from their register a copy of an application included under paragraph (10) at any time more than six years after the application was made.

*Refusal of applications*

**5.** (1) Subject to section 3(6) of the 1989 Act,[9] a regulation authority[10] may refuse an application for registration or for the renewal of a registration if, and only if—

---

[1] "Regulation authority", and its area, defined by s.9(1) of the 1989 Act, p.80 above.
[2] For "application is pending" see reg.1(3) above.
[3] P.636 below.
[4] P.642 below.
[5] P.645 below.
[6] P.725 below.

[7] Words "Subject . . . 1994" inserted by S.I. 194/1056, reg.23(5). This amendment came into force on 1 May 1994: reg.1(1).
[8] Sub-paragraph (c) inserted by S.I. 1994/1056, reg.23(6).
[9] P.75 above.
[10] "Regulation authority" defined by s.9(1) of the 1989 Act, p.80 above.

(a) there has, in relation to that application, been a contravention of any of the requirements of regulation 4; or

(b) the applicant or another relevant person[1] has been convicted of a prescribed offence[2] and, in the opinion of the authority, it is undesirable for the applicant to be authorised to transport controlled waste.

(2) Where a regulation authority decide to refuse an application for registration or for the renewal of a registration, the authority shall give notice[3] to the applicant informing him that his application is refused and of the reasons for their decision.

(3) If an appeal is made under section 4(1) of the 1989 Act[4] in accordance with these Regulations, the regulation authority shall, as soon as reasonably practicable, make appropriate entries in their register indicating when the appeal was made and the result of the appeal.

(4) If no such appeal is made, the regulation authority shall, as soon as reasonably practicable make an appropriate entry in their register indicating that the application has not been accepted and that no appeal has been made.

(5) A regulation authority may remove an entry made under paragraph (3) or (4) at any time more than six years after the application in question was made.

*Registration as a carrier*

**6.** (1) On accepting a person's application for registration or on being directed under section 4(3) of the 1989 Act[5] to register a person following an appeal in respect of such an application, the regulation authority[6] shall make an entry in their register—

(a) showing that person as a registered carrier of controlled waste and allocating him a registration number (which may include any letter);

(b) specifying the date on which the registration takes effect and its date of expiry;[7]

(c) stating any business name of his and the address of his principal place of business (together with any telephone, telex or fax number of his) and, in the case of an individual, his date of birth;

(d) in the case of a body corporate, listing the names of each director, manager, secretary or other similar officer of that body and their respective dates of birth;

(e) in the case of a company registered under the Companies Acts, specifying its registered number and, in the case of a company incorporated outside Great Britain, the country in which it was incorporated;

(f) in a case where the person who is registered or another relevant person[8] has been convicted of a prescribed offence,[9] giving the person's name, details of the offence, the date of conviction, the penalty imposed, the name of the Court and, in the case of an individual, his date of birth; and

(g) in a case where the person who is registered or any company in the same group of companies as that person is the holder of a waste management licence or a disposal licence, stating the name of the holder of the licence and the name of the authority which granted it.

(2) In the case of a business which is or is to be carried on by a partnership, all the partners shall be registered under one entry and only one registration number shall be allocated to the partnership.

(3) On making an entry in their register under paragraph (1) the regulation authority shall—

---

[1] "Another relevant person" has the meaning given by s.3(5) of the 1989 Act, p.75 above: reg.1(2) above.
[2] "Prescribed offence" means an offence under an enactment listed in sch.1, p.641 below: reg.1(2) above.
[3] "Notice" means notice in writing: reg.1(2) above; for service of notices see reg.26, p.641 below.
[4] P.75 above.
[5] P.75 above.

[6] "Regulation authority" defined by s.9(1) of the 1989 Act, p.80 above.
[7] "Date of expiry" defined by reg.1(2), p.631 above.
[8] "Another relevant person" has the meaning given by s.3(5) of the 1989 Act, p.75: reg.1(2) above.
[9] "Prescribed offence" means an offence under an enactment listed in sch.1, p.641 below: reg.1(2) above.

(a) issue to the registered person or partnership a certificate of registration free of charge which shall be in the form set out in Schedule 3,[1] or in a form substantially to the like effect, and shall contain the information required by that form; and

(b) provide him or them free of charge with a copy of the entry in the register.

(4) In this regulation—

"Companies Acts" has the same meaning as in section 744 of the Companies Act 1985;[2]

"business name" means a name under which a person carries on business and by virtue of which the Business Names Act 1985[3] applies;

"disposal licence" has the same meaning as in section 30(1) of the Control of Pollution Act 1974;[4]

"group" has the same meaning as in section 53(1) of the Companies Act 1989;[5] and

"waste management licence" has the same meaning as in section 35 of the Environmental Protection Act 1990.[6]

### Amendment of entries

7. (1) On accepting a person's application for the renewal of a registration or on being directed under section 4(3) of the 1989 Act[7] to register a person following an appeal in respect of such an application, the regulation authority[8] shall amend the relevant entry in the register—

(a) to show the date on which the renewal takes effect and the revised date of expiry[9] of the registration;

(b) to record any other change disclosed as a result of the application; and

(c) to note in the register the date on which the amendments are made.

(2) The regulation authority shall at the same time as amending the register—

(a) issue to the registered person or partnership an amended certificate of registration free of charge which shall be in the form set out in Schedule 3,[10] or in a form substantially to the like effect, and shall contain the information required by that form;

(b) provide him or them free of charge with a copy of the amended entry in the register.

### Change of circumstances and registration of additional partners

8. (1) A person who is registered shall notify the regulation authority[11] which maintain the relevant register of any change of circumstances affecting information in the entry relating to him.

(2) On—

(a) being notified of any change of circumstances in accordance with paragraph (1);

(b) accepting a prospective partner's application for registration in relation to a business carried on by a partnership whose members are already registered; or

(c) being directed under section 4(3) of the 1989 Act[12] to register a prospective partner,

the regulation authority shall—

(i) amend the relevant entry to reflect the change of circumstances or the registration of the prospective partner;

(ii) note in the register the date on which the amendment is made;

(iii) if the amendment of the register affects information contained in the certificate of registration, issue to the registered person or partnership free of charge an amended

---

[1] P.646 below.
[2] 1985 c.6.
[3] 1985 c.7.
[4] 1974 c.40.
[5] 1989 c.40.
[6] P.119 above.
[7] P.75 above.

[8] "Regulation authority" defined by s.9(1) of the 1989 Act, p.80 above.
[9] "Date of expiry" defined by reg.1(2), p.631 above.
[10] P.646 below.
[11] "Regulation authority" defined by s.9(1) of the 1989 Act, p.80 above.
[12] P.75 above.

certificate of registration which shall be in the form set out in Schedule 3,[1] or in a form substantially to the like effect, and shall contain the information required by that form;

(iv) provide him or them free of charge with a copy of the amended entry in the register.

*Copies of certificates of registration*

**9.** (1) The regulation authority[2] shall, on payment of their reasonable charges, provide a person who is registered with such copies of his certificate of registration as he may request.

(2) The regulation authority shall ensure that the copies of the certificate are numbered and marked so as to show that they are copies and that they have been provided by the authority under this regulation.

*Revocation of registration*

**10.** (1) Subject to section 3(6) of the 1989 Act,[3] a regulation authority[4] may revoke a person's registration as a carrier of controlled waste if, and only if—

(a) that person or another relevant person[5] has been convicted of a prescribed offence;[6] and

(b) in the opinion of the authority, it is undesirable for the registered carrier to continue to be authorised to transport controlled waste.

(2) Where a regulation authority decide to revoke a person's registration as a carrier of controlled waste, they shall give notice[7] to the carrier informing him of the revocation and of the reasons for their decision.

*Duration of registration*

**11.** (1) This regulation is subject to—

(a) section 3(2) of the 1989 Act[8] (which ensures that a registration ceases to have effect if the registered carrier gives written notice requiring the removal of his name from the register); and

(b) section 4(7)[9] and (8) of the 1989 Act (which extend the period during which the registration has effect where an appeal under that section is made).

(2) Subject to paragraphs (4) to (6), a person's registration as a carrier of controlled waste shall cease to have effect on the expiry of the period of three years beginning with the date of the registration or, if it has been renewed, beginning with the date on which it was renewed or, as the case may be, last renewed.

(3) The regulation authority[10] shall, no later than six months before the expiry of the period of three years mentioned in paragraph (2), serve on a registered person—

(a) a notice[11] informing him of the date on which that period expires and of the effect of paragraph (4); and

(b) an application form for the renewal of his registration and a copy of his current entry in the register.

(4) Where an application for the renewal of a registration is made within the last six months of the period of three years mentioned in paragraph (2), the registration shall, notwithstanding the expiry of that period, continue in force—

(a) until the application is withdrawn or accepted; or

[1] P.646 below.
[2] "Regulation authority" defined by s.9(1) of the 1989 Act, p.80 above.
[3] P.75 above.
[4] "Regulation authority" defined by s.9(1) of the 1989 Act, p.80 above.
[5] "Another relevant person" has the meaning given by s.3(5) of the 1989 Act, p.75 above: reg.1(2) above.
[6] "Prescribed offence" means an offence under an enactment listed in sch.1, p.641 below: reg.1(2) above.
[7] "Notice" means notice in writing: reg.1(2) above; for service of notices see reg.26, p.641 below.
[8] P.74 above.
[9] P.74 above.
[10] "Regulation authority" defined by s.9(1) of the 1989 Act, p.80 above.
[11] "Notice" means notice in writing: reg.1(2) above; for service of notices see reg.26, p.641 below.

(b)  if the regulation authority[1] refuse the application or the relevant period[2] from the making of the application has expired without the applicant having been registered, until,—

  (i)  the expiry of the period for appealing; or

  (ii)  where the applicant indicates within that period that he does not intend to make or continue with an appeal, the date on which such an indication is given.

(5)  Where a regulation authority revoke a person's registration, the registration shall, notwithstanding the revocation, continue in force until—

(a)  the expiry of the period for appealing against the revocation; or

(b)  where that person indicates within that period that he does not intend to make or continue with an appeal, the date on which such an indication is given.

(6)  A registration in respect of a business which is carried on by a partnership shall cease to have effect if any of the partners ceases to be registered or if any person who is not registered becomes a partner.

(7)  The duration of a registration in respect of a business which is carried on by a partnership shall not be affected if a person ceases to be a partner or if a prospective partner is registered under regulation 8(2) in relation to the partnership.

(8)  Where a regulation authority accept an application for the renewal of a registration within the period of three years mentioned in paragraph (2), the renewal shall for the purposes of these Regulations take effect at the expiry of that period.

*Alteration of register to reflect cessation of registration*

**12.**  (1)  Where by virtue of regulation 11 or section 3(2)[3] or 4(7)[4] and (8) of the 1989 Act a registration ceases to have effect, the regulation authority[5] shall record this fact in the appropriate entry in the register and the date on which it occurred.

(2)  The regulation authority may remove the appropriate entry from their register at any time more than six years after the registration ceases to have effect.

*Duty to return certificates etc*

**13.**  Where—

(a)  a person's registration as a carrier of controlled waste ceases to have effect by virtue of regulation 11 or section 3(2)[6] or 4(7)[7] and (8) of the 1989 Act; or

(b)  a person is issued with an amended certificate under regulation 7(2) or 8(2),

he shall immediately return to the regulation authority[8] his certificate of registration, or, as the case may be, his previous certificate of registration, together with any copies of it issued by that authority.

*Production of authority*

**14.**  (1)  Where a person is required by virtue of section 5 of the 1989 Act[9] to produce an authority for transporting controlled waste and does not do so by producing it forthwith to the person requiring its production, he shall produce it at or send it to an office[10] of the regulation authority for the area[11] in which he is stopped no later than 7 days after the day on which he was required to produce it.

[1]  "Regulation authority" defined by s.9(1) of the 1989 Act, p.80 above.
[2]  "Relevant period" has the meaning given by s.4(1) of the 1989 Act, p.75 above: reg.1(2) above.
[3]  P.74 above.
[4]  P.76 above.
[5]  "Regulation authority" defined by s.9(1) of the 1989 Act, p.80 above.
[6]  P.74 above.
[7]  P.76 above.
[8]  "Regulation authority" defined by s.9(1) of the 1989 Act, p.80 above.
[9]  P.76 above.
[10]  Words "an office" substituted by the Environment Act 1995 (Consequential Amendments) Regulations 1996, S.I. 1996/593, reg.9(3). This amendment came into force on 1 April 1996: reg.1.
[11]  "Regulation authority" and its area, defined by s.9(1) of the 1989 Act, p.80 above.

(2) A copy of a person's certificate of registration as a carrier of controlled waste shall for the purposes of section 5 of the 1989 Act be authority for transporting controlled waste if it was provided by the regulation authority under regulation 9.

*Appeals*

**15.** (1) Notice of an appeal to the Secretary of State under section 4(1)[1] or (2) of the 1989 Act shall be given in writing by the appellant to the Secretary of State.

(2) The notice of appeal shall be accompanied by the following—

(a) a statement of the grounds of appeal;

(b) in the case of an appeal under section 4(1) of the 1989 Act, a copy of the relevant application;

(c) in the case of an appeal under section 4(2) of the 1989 Act, a copy of the appellant's entry in the register;

(d) a copy of any relevant correspondence between the appellant and the regulation authority;

(e) a copy of any notice given to the appellant under regulation 5(2)[2] or 10(2);[3]

(f) a statement indicating whether the appellant wishes the appeal to be conducted by written representations or by a hearing.

(3) The appellant shall at the same time as giving notice of appeal to the Secretary of State serve on the regulation authority a copy of the notice and a copy of the documents mentioned in paragraph (2)(a) and (f).

*Time limit for bringing an appeal*

**16.** Notice of appeal is to be given before the expiry of the period of 28 days beginning with—

(a) in the case of an appeal under section 4(1)(a) of the 1989 Act,[4] the date on which the appellant is given notice[5] by the regulation authority[6] that his application has been refused; or

(b) in the case of an appeal under section 4(1)(b) of the 1989 Act, the date on which the relevant period from the making of the application expired without the appellant having been registered; or

(c) in the case of an appeal under section 4(2) of the 1989 Act, the date on which the appellant is given notice by the regulation authority that his registration as a carrier of controlled waste has been revoked,

or before such later date as the Secretary of State may allow.

*Hearings*

**17.** (1) If either party to an appeal requests a hearing or the Secretary of State so decides, the appeal shall be or continue in the form of a hearing before a person appointed for the purpose by the Secretary of State.

(2) The person holding the hearing shall after its conclusion make a written report to the Secretary of State which shall include his conclusions and recommendations or his reasons for not making any recommendations.

*Notification of determination*

**18.** (1) The Secretary of State shall notify the appellant in writing of his determination of the appeal and of his reasons for it and, if a hearing is held, shall also provide him with a copy of the report of the person who conducted the hearing.

(2) The Secretary of State shall at the same time send a copy of those documents to the regulation authority.

---

[1] P.75 above.
[2] P.634 above.
[3] P.636 above.
[4] P.75 above.

[5] "Notice" means notice in writing: reg.1(2) above; for service of notices see reg.26, p.641 below.
[6] "Regulation authority" defined by s.9(1) of the 1989 Act, p.80 above.

*Prescribed information*

**19.** The prescribed information for the purposes of section 6(1)(c) of the 1989 Act[1] is the name and address of the person who was using the vehicle at the time when the offence was committed.

*Prescribed steps to be taken before applying for a warrant to seize property*

**20.** (1) The prescribed steps for the purposes of section 6(1)(c) of the 1989 Act[2] are as follows.

(2) The regulation authority[3] shall—

(a) in the case of a vehicle with a G.B. registration mark, obtain from the Secretary of State the name and address of the person shown in his records, at the time when the offence was committed, as the keeper and user of the vehicle;

(b) in the case of a vehicle with a Northern Ireland registration mark, provide the Secretary of State for Transport with details of the registration mark and of the time when the offence was committed and a brief description of the vehicle, request his help in finding the person who was the owner of the vehicle at that time and explain the reason for making the request; and

(c) in any other case, provide the chief officer of the police force in whose area the offence was committed with details of the foreign registration mark (if any) and of the time when the offence was committed and a brief description of the vehicle, request his help in finding the person who was the owner of the vehicle at that time and explain the reason for making the request.

(3) The regulation authority shall serve notice under section 71(2) of the Environmental Protection Act 1990[4] on any person who they consider (whether as a result of action taken under paragraph (2) or otherwise) may be able to provide them with the name and address of the person who was using the vehicle at the time when the offence was committed, requiring him, if he is able to do so, to provide them with the name and address of that person.

(4) In this regulation—

"G.B. registration mark" means a registration mark issued in relation to a vehicle under the Vehicles (Excise) Act 1971;[5]

"Northern Ireland registration mark" means a mark indicating registration in Northern Ireland;

"foreign registration mark" means a mark indicating registration in some country other than Great Britain or Northern Ireland;

"owner" includes a person entitled to possession of a vehicle under a hiring agreement or hire purchase agreement.

*Removal of vehicles seized*

**21.** (1) A vehicle seized under section 6 of the 1989 Act[6] on behalf of a regulation authority[7] may be removed under subsection (5) of that section in the following manner.

(2) The vehicle may be driven, towed or removed by such other means as are reasonable in the circumstances and any necessary steps may be taken in relation to the vehicle in order to facilitate its removal.

(3) Contents of the vehicle may be removed separately in cases where—

(a) it is reasonable to do so to facilitate removal of the vehicle;

(b) there is good reason for storing them at a different place from the vehicle; or

(c) their condition requires them to be disposed of without delay.

[1] P.77 above.
[2] P.77 above.
[3] "Regulation authority" defined by s.9(1) of the 1989 Act, p.80 above.
[4] P.156 above.
[5] 1971 c.10 which has been replaced by the Vehicle Excise and Registration Act 1994 (c.22).
[6] P.77 above.
[7] "Regulation authority" defined by s.9(1) of the 1989 Act, p.80 above.

*Return of property seized*

**22.** (1) Unless the relevant property has already been disposed of under regulation 23, a regulation authority[1] shall return any property seized under section 6 of the 1989 Act[2] to a person who—

(a) produces satisfactory evidence of his entitlement to it and of his identity and address; or

(b) where he seeks to recover the property as the agent of another person, produces satisfactory evidence of his identity, his address and his authority to act on behalf of his principal and of his principal's identity, address and entitlement to the property; and

(c) where the property is a vehicle and the person seeking its return (or in a case falling within sub-paragraph (b), his principal) purports to be the keeper or the user of the vehicle, produces the registration book for the vehicle.

(2) Where the person claiming to be entitled to a vehicle establishes is entitlement, he shall be treated for the purposes of this regulation as also entitled to its contents unless and to the extent that another person has claimed them or part of them.

(3) Where there is more than one claim to the property, the regulation authority shall determine which person is entitled to it on the basis of the evidence provided to them.

*Disposal of property seized*

**23.** (1) The regulation authority[3] may sell, destroy or deposit at any place property seized under section 6 of the 1989 Act[4] if—

(a) the authority have published a notice in a newspaper circulating in the area in which the property was seized—

    (i) giving the authority's name, a brief description of the property seized and the vehicle's registration mark (if any);

    (ii) indicating the time and place at which, and the powers under which, it was seized on behalf of the authority;

    (iii) stating that it may be claimed at the place and at the time specified in the notice and that, if no-one establishes within the period specified in the notice that he is entitled to the return of the property, the authority intend to dispose of it after the expiry of that period unless its condition requires its earlier disposal;

(b) the authority have served a copy of the notice on—

    (i) any person on whom a notice under section 71(2) of the Environmental Protection Act 1990[5] has been served by virtue of regulation 20(3) in relation to the relevant vehicle;

    (ii) the chief officer of the police force in whose area the property was seized;

    (iii) the Secretary of State for Transport;

    (iv) H.P. Information plc; and

(c) either—

    (i) the period of 28 days, beginning with the date on which notice is published under sub-paragraph (a) or, if later, a copy of that notice is served under sub-paragraph (b), has expired without any obligation arising under regulation 22 for the regulation authority to return the property to any person; or

    (ii) the condition of the property requires it to be disposed of without delay.

(2) The period specified in a notice under paragraph (1)(a)(iii) shall be the period mentioned in paragraph (1)(c)(i).

---

[1] "Regulation authority" defined by s.9(1) of the 1989 Act, p.80 above.
[2] P.77 above.
[3] "Regulation authority" defined by s.9(1) of the 1989 Act,
[4] P.77 above.
[5] P.156 above.

*Notice of disposal of a vehicle*

**24.** After disposing of any vehicle under regulation 23, the regulation authority[1] shall serve notice of the disposal on the following persons—

(a)  the chief officer of the police force in whose area it was seized;

(b)  the Secretary of State for Transport; and

(c)  H.P. Information plc.

*Application of proceeds of sale*

**25.** (1)  The proceeds of sale of any property sold by a regulation authority[2] under regulation 23 shall be applied towards meeting expenses incurred by the authority in exercising their functions by virtue of section 6 of the 1989 Act[3] and, in so far as they are not so applied, in meeting any claim to the proceeds of sale made and established in accordance with paragraph (2).

(2)  A claim to the proceeds of sale of any property shall be established if the claimant provides the regulation authority with satisfactory evidence that he would have been entitled to the return of the property under regulation 22 if the property had not been sold.

*Service of notices*

**26.** Any notice or other document required by these Regulations to be served on or given to a person may be served or given in accordance with section 160 of the Environmental Protection Act 1990.[4]

# SCHEDULE 1

(Regulation 1(2)[5])

## PRESCRIBED OFFENCES: RELEVANT ENACTMENTS

Section 22 of the Public Health (Scotland) Act 1897.[6]

Section 95(1) of the Public Health Act 1936.[7]

Section 60 of the Transport Act 1968.[8]

Sections 3, 5(6), 16(4), 18(2), 31(1), 32(1), 34(5),[9] 78, 92(6)[10] and 93(3)[11] of the Control of Pollution Act 1974.

Section 2 of the Refuse Disposal (Amenity) Act 1978.[12]

The Control of Pollution (Special Waste) Regulations 1980.[13]

Section 9(1) of the Food and Environment Protection Act 1985.[14]

The Transfrontier Shipment of Hazardous Waste Regulations 1988.[15]

The Merchant Shipping (Prevention of Pollution by Garbage) Regulations 1988.[16]

Sections 1,[17] 5,[18] 6(9)[19] and 7(3)[20] of the Control of Pollution (Amendment) Act 1989.

Sections 107,[21] 118(4)[22] and 175(1)[23] of the Water Act 1989.

---

[1] "Regulation authority" defined by s.9(1) of the 1989 Act, p.80 above.

[2] "Regulation authority" defined by s.9(1) of the 1989 Act, p.80 above.

[3] P.77 above.

[4] P.207 above.

[5] P.631 above.

[6] 1897 c.38.

[7] 1936 c.49.

[8] 1968 c.73.

[9] P.30 above.

[10] P.55 above.

[11] P.56 above.

[12] 1978 c.3.

[13] S.I. 1980/1709; these regulations were revoked, subject to a saving, by S.I. 1996/972, reg.26, which came into force on 1 September 1996: reg.1(1).

[14] 1985 c.48.

[15] S.I. 1988/1562; these regulations were revoked, subject to a saving, by S.I. 1994/1137, reg.21, which came into force on 6 May 1994: reg.1.

[16] S.I. 1988/2292.

[17] P.72 above.

[18] P.76 above.

[19] P.78 above.

[20] P.79 above.

[21] S.107 of the 1989 Act has been replaced by ss.85–87 of the Water Resources Act 1991, p.273 above.

[22] S.118(4) of the 1989 Act has been replaced by s.202(4) of the Water Resources Act 1991, p.303 above.

[23] S.175 of the 1989 Act has been replaced by s.206 of the Water Resources Act 1991, p.306 above.

Sections 23(1),[1] 33,[2] 34(6),[3] 44,[4] 47(6),[5] 57(5),[6] 59(5),[7] 63(2)[8] 69(9), 70(4), 71(3)[9] and 80(4)[10] of the Environmental Protection Act 1990.

The Transfrontier Shipment of Waste Regulations 1994.[11]

The Special Waste Regulations 1996.[12]

## SCHEDULE 2

(Regulation 4(6) and (7)[13])

### APPLICATION FORMS

### PART I

### APPLICATION FOR REGISTRATION AS A CARRIER OF CONTROLLED WASTE

*Please read the guidance notes before completing this form*

1. Full name of applicant (*note 1*)

   Former name (if applicable)

   Date of birth (if applicable)

2. Name under which applicant carries on business
   (if different from 1)

3. Address for correspondence

   Post Code

4. Address of principal place of business
   (if different from 3)

   Post Code

5. Telephone/Telex/Fax number

   Tel.        Telex        Fax

6. If applicant has previously been
   a registered carrier, give:

   (a) registration number or numbers

   (b) name of regulation authority
       or authorities

7. If applicant is a company registered
   under the Companies Acts, give:

   (a) company's registered number

   (b) address of registered office

   Post Code

   (c) in the case of a company incorporated
       outside Great Britain, the country in which
       it was incorporated

---

[1] P.108 above.
[2] P.116 above.
[3] P.118 above.
[4] P.134 above.
[5] P.141 above.
[6] P.148 above.
[7] P.149 above.
[8] P.152 above.
[9] P.156 above.

[10] P.191 above.
[11] S.I. 1994/1137, p.741 below. These Regulations are added by S.I. 1994/1137, reg.19(1). This amendment came into force on 6 May 1994: reg.1.
[12] S.I. 1996/972, p.763 below. These Regulations are added by S.I. 1996/972, reg.22. This amendment came into force on 1 September 1996: reg.1(1).
[13] P.633 above.

8. If applicant is a registered company or other body corporate, for each director, manager, secretary or other similar officer, give:

| Full name | Position held | Address | Date of birth |
|---|---|---|---|
| | | | |
| | | | |
| | | | |
| | | | |
| | | | |

9. If applicant is a prospective partner in a business carried on by a partnership whose members are already registered carriers, give:

   (a) full name of partnership

   (b) registration number of partnership

10. Has the applicant or another relevant person (*note 2*) been convicted of any offence listed in the Controlled Waste (Registration of Carriers and Seizure of Vehicles) Regulations 1991 (*notes 3 and 4*)?      Yes ☐      No ☐

If **Yes**, give full details of each offence—

| Full name of person convicted | Position held | Name of Court | Date of conviction | Offence and penalty imposed |
|---|---|---|---|---|
| | | | | |

If details of any conviction have been given, use the following space to provide the regulation authority with any additional information which you wish the authority to take into account in determining whether or not it is undesirable for the applicant to be authorised to transport controlled waste—

11. Is the applicant or another company in the same group (within the meaning of section 53(1) of the Companies Act 1989) the holder of a disposal licence or a waste management licence?      Yes ☐      No ☐

If **Yes**, give details of licence:

| Full name of holder of licence | Date of birth (if applicable) | Date of issue of licence | Name of authority which issued the licence |
|---|---|---|---|
| | | | |

**Declaration**

I declare that I have personally checked the information given in this application form and that it is true to the best of my knowledge, information and belief. I understand that registration may be refused if false or incomplete information is given and that untrue statements may result in prosecution and could lead to revocation of registration.

Signature:                                            Date:

Position held:

Have you enclosed the fee of £95? (*note 5*)        Yes ☐

**GUIDANCE NOTES**

1. In the case of a partnership or proposed partnership, each partner must apply for registration and his details must be included in this application form.

2. Details of an offence listed in the Controlled Waste (Registration of Carriers and Seizure of Vehicles) Regulations 1991 must be given if the applicant was convicted of the offence or if the person convicted of the offence ("the relevant person")—

   (a) committed it in the course of his employment by the applicant;

   (b) committed it in the course of the carrying on of any business by a partnership one of the members of which was the applicant;

   (c) was a body corporate and at the time when the offence was committed the applicant was a director, manager, secretary or other similar officer of that body;

   (d) was a director, manager, secretary or other similar officer of the applicant (where the applicant is a body corporate);

   (e) was a body corporate and at the time when the offence was committed a director, manager, secretary or other similar officer of the applicant held such an office in the body corporate which committed the offence.

3. The offences listed in the Controlled Waste (Registration of Carriers and Seizure of Vehicles) Regulations 1991 are offences under any of the following provisions[1]—

   section 22 of the Public Health (Scotland) Act 1897;

   section 95(1) of the Public Health Act 1936;

   section 60 of the Transport Act 1968;

   sections 3, 5(6), 16(4), 18(2), 31(1), 32(1), 34(5), 78, 92(6) and 93(3) of the Control of Pollution Act 1974;

   section 2 of the Refuse Disposal (Amenity) Act 1978;

   the Control of Pollution (Special Waste) Regulations 1980;

   section 9(1) of the Food and Environment Protection Act 1985;

   the Transfrontier Shipment of Hazardous Waste Regulations 1988;

   the Merchant Shipping (Prevention of Pollution by Garbage) Regulations 1988;

   sections 1, 5, 6(9) and 7(3) of the Control of Pollution (Amendment) Act 1989;

   sections 107, 118(4) and 175(1) of the Water Act 1989;

   sections 23(1), 33, 34(6), 44, 47(6), 57(5), 59(5), 63(2), 69(9), 70(4), 71(3) and 80(4) of the Environmental Protection Act 1990.

   the Transfrontier Shipment of Waste Regulations 1994.[2]

4. Details of a conviction need not be given where under the terms of the Rehabilitation of Offenders Act 1974 the conviction is spent.

5. The fee of £95 must be sent with the application. The regulation authority may refuse the application if the fee is not enclosed.

---

[1] See sch.1, p.641 above, for annotations.
[2] S.I. 1994/1137, p.741 below. These Regulations added by S.I. 1994/1137, reg.19(2). This amendment came into force on 6 May 1994: reg.1.

PART II

APPLICATION FOR RENEWAL OF REGISTRATION AS A CARRIER OF CONTROLLED WASTE
*Please read the guidance notes before completing this form*

1. Full name of applicant (*note 1*)

   Former name (if applicable)

   Date of birth (if applicable)

2. Address for correspondence

   Post Code

3. Telephone/Telex/Fax number

   Tel.　　Telex　　Fax

4. Registration number as a carrier

5. Has the applicant or another relevant person (*note 2*) been convicted of any offence listed in the Controlled Waste (Registration of Carriers and Seizure of Vehicles) Regulations 1991 (*notes 3 and 4*)?　　Yes ☐　　No ☐

   If **Yes**, give full details of each offence—

| Full name of person convicted | Position held | Name of Court | Date of conviction | Offence and penalty imposed |
|---|---|---|---|---|
| | | | | |

   If details of any conviction have been given, use the following space to provide the regulation authority with any additional information which you wish the authority to take into account in determining whether or not it is undesirable for the applicant to be authorised to transport controlled waste—

6. Give details of any changes in any other information in the applicant's existing entry in the register (*note 5*)—

**Declaration**

I declare that I have personally checked the information given in this application form and that it is true to the best of my knowledge, information and belief. I understand that registration may be refused if false or incomplete information is given and that untrue statements may result in prosecution and could lead to revocation of registration.

Signature:　　　　　　　　Date:

Position held:

Have you enclosed the fee of £65? (*note 6*)　　Yes ☐

**Guidance Notes**

1. In the case of a partnership, each partner must apply for registration and his details must be included in this application form.

2. Details of an offence listed in the Controlled Waste (Registration of Carriers and Seizure of Vehicles) Regulations 1991 must be given if the applicant was convicted of the offence or if the person convicted of the offence ("the relevant person")—

   (a) committed it in the course of his employment by the applicant;

   (b) committed it in the course of the carrying on of any business by a partnership one of the members of which was the applicant;

   (c) was a body corporate and at the time when the offence was committed the applicant was a director, manager, secretary or other similar officer of that body;

   (d) was a director, manager, secretary or other similar officer of the applicant (where the applicant is a body corporate);

   (e) was a body corporate and at the time when the offence was committed a director, manager, secretary or other similar officer of the applicant held such an office in the body corporate which committed the offence.

3. The offences listed in the Controlled Waste (Registration of Carriers and Seizure of Vehicles) Regulations 1991 are offences under any of the following provisions[1]—

   section 22 of the Public Health (Scotland) Act 1897;

   section 95(1) of the Public Health Act 1936;

   section 60 of the Transport Act 1968;

   sections 3, 5(6), 16(4), 18(2), 31(1), 32(1), 34(5), 78, 92(6) and 93(3) of the Control of Pollution Act 1974;

   section 2 of the Refuse Disposal (Amenity) Act 1978;

   the Control of Pollution (Special Waste) Regulations 1980;

   section 9(1) of the Food and Environment Protection Act 1985;

   the Transfrontier Shipment of Hazardous Waste Regulations 1988;

   the Merchant Shipping (Prevention of Pollution by Garbage) Regulations 1988;

   sections 1, 5, 6(9) and 7(3) of the Control of Pollution (Amendment) Act 1989;

   sections 107, 118(4) and 175(1) of the Water Act 1989;

   sections 23(1), 33, 34(6), 44, 47(6), 57(5), 59(5), 63(2), 69(9), 70(4), 71(3) and 80(4) of the Environmental Protection Act 1990.

   the Transfrontier Shipment of Waste Regulations 1994.[2]

4. Details of a conviction need not be given where under the terms of the Rehabilitation of Offenders Act 1974 the conviction is spent.

5. Check the information in the copy of the current entry in the register sent with the regulation authority's reminder that registration needs to be renewed or, if no such copy has been received, ask the authority for one.

6. The fee of £65 must be sent with the application. The regulation authority may refuse the application if the fee is not enclosed.

## SCHEDULE 3

(Regulations 6(3),[3] 7(2) and 8(2))

### CERTIFICATE OF REGISTRATION UNDER THE CONTROL OF POLLUTION (AMENDMENT) ACT 1989

| Regulation Authority |
| --- |
| Name: |
| Address: |
| Post Code: |
| Tel:          Telex:          Fax: |

[1] See sch.1, p.641 above, for annotations.
[2] S.I. 1994/1137, p.741 below. These Regulations added by S.I. 1994/1137, reg.19(2). This amendment came into force on 6 May 1994: reg.1.
[3] P.634 above.

---

The following information is hereby certified by the above-mentioned authority to be information which at the date of this certificate† is entered in the register which they maintain under regulation 3 of the Controlled Waste (Registration of Carriers and Seizure of Vehicles) Regulations 1991—

Name(s) of registered carrier:

Registration number:

Business name (if any):

Address of registered carrier's
principal place of business:

Tel:                                          Telex:                                          Fax:

Date of registration:

Date of expiry of registration*:

Date on which last amendment (if any) was made to the carrier's
entry in the register:

---

Signature of authorised officer

of the regulation authority:                              Date:

†You can check whether there has been any change in the information contained in this certificate by contacting the regulation authority named above.

*Registration will expire on this date unless—

(a) it is revoked before expiry;

(b) the carrier requests the removal of his name from the register at an earlier time;

(c) an application for renewal is made within the six months ending on the expiry date and the application is still outstanding, or is the subject of an appeal, on that date;

(d) in the case of a registered partnership, if any of the partners ceases to be registered or if anyone who is not registered becomes a partner.

### Explanatory Note
### (This note is not part of the Regulations)

The Control of Pollution (Amendment) Act 1989 makes it a criminal offence for a person who is not a registered carrier to transport controlled waste to or from any place in Great Britain. It also provides for the seizure and disposal of vehicles used for illegal waste disposal.

These Regulations establish a system for registration of carriers of controlled waste and supplement the provisions of the Act dealing with the seizure and disposal of vehicles used for illegal waste disposal.

Regulation 2 exempts certain persons from registration either completely or in defined circumstances.

Regulation 3 requires each waste regulation authority to establish and maintain a register for the registration of carriers of controlled waste and to make it accessible to members of the public free of charge.

Regulations 4 to 14 contain provisions dealing with applications for registration, the circumstances in which registration may be refused, the information to be included in the register, the provision of certificates of registration and copies of entries, amendment of the register, revocation of registration, the duration of registration and the production of a person's authority to transport controlled waste.

Regulations 15 to 18 deal with the procedure for appeals against refusal of registration, failure to deal with an application for registration and the revocation of registration.

Regulations 19 to 25 prescribe steps to be taken before applying for a warrant to seize vehicles used for illegal waste disposal, deal with the manner in which vehicles may be removed, specify the circumstances in which property seized must be returned and the steps which must be taken before and after selling or otherwise disposing of such property and provide for the application of the proceeds of any sale.

Regulation 26 deals with the service of notices and other documents under the Regulations.

# The Control of Pollution (Radioactive Waste) (Scotland) Regulations 1991

S.I. 1991 No. 2539 (S.200)

The Secretary of State, in exercise of the powers conferred on him by section 30(5) of the Control of Pollution Act 1974, as applied by section 56(6) of that Act,[1] and of all other powers enabling him in that behalf, hereby make the following Regulations:

*Citation, commencement and extent*

1. These Regulations may be cited as the Control of Pollution (Radioactive Waste) (Scotland) Regulations 1991, shall come into force on 2nd December 1991 and shall extend to Scotland only.

*Interpretation*

2. In these Regulations—

   "the 1960 Act" means the Radioactive Substances Act 1960;

   "the 1974 Act" means the Control of Pollution Act 1974; and

   "radioactive waste" has the same meaning as in the 1960 Act.[2]

*Certain provisions of Part II of the 1974 Act to apply to radioactive waste*

3. The provisions of the 1974 Act specified in the Schedule to these Regulations shall have effect, without modification, in relation to any radioactive waste as they have effect in relation to effluent or other matter or substance which is not radioactive waste.

*Modification of the 1960 Act*

4. *Revoked by the Radioactive Substances Act 1993 (c.12), s.50, sch.6, pt.IV. This amendment came into force on 27 August 1993: s.51(2).*

*Revocations*

5. The Control of Pollution (Radioactive Waste) Regulations 1984,[3] so far as still in force, and the Control of Pollution (Radioactive Waste) Regulations 1985[4] are hereby revoked.

## SCHEDULE

(Regulation 3)

| *Provisions of Part II of the 1974 Act applied*[5] | *Subject matter of provisions* |
| --- | --- |
| Section 30A | Waters to which Part II applies |
| Section 30B | Classification of quality of waters |

---

[1] S.30(5), which is prospectively repealed by the Environmental Protection Act 1990, s.162, sch.16, part II, contains similar wording to the prospective amendment of s.56(6) set out at p.50 above. The present wording of s.56(6) is set out at p.50 above, note 5. See also the definitions of "prescribed" and "regulations" in section 105(1) of the 1974 Act, p.61 above.

[2] "Radioactive waste" is defined by s.2 of the Radioactive Substances Act 1993, p.384 above. The 1993 Act consolidates the 1960 Act and other enactments.
[3] S.I. 1984/863.
[4] S.I. 1985/708.
[5] Part II of the 1974 Act begins at p.18 above.

| Provisions of Part II of the 1974 Act applied | Subject matter of provisions |
| --- | --- |
| Section 30D | General duties to achieve and maintain objectives etc. |
| Sections 30F to J, 31(4), (5), (8) and (9)[1] | Control of pollution of rivers and coastal waters etc. |
| Section 31A | Requirements to take precautions against pollution |
| [2] | |
| Section 34 | Consents for discharges of trade and sewage effluent etc. |
| Section 35 | Reference to Secretary of State of certain applications for consent |
| Section 36 | Provisions supplementary to sections 34 and 35 |
| Section 37 | Revocation of consents and alteration and imposition of conditions |
| Section 38 | Restriction on variation and revocation of consent and of previous variation |
| Section 39 | Appeals to Secretary of State |
| Section 40 | Transitional provisions relating to consents |
| Section 41 | Registers |
| Sections 42A and 42B | Exclusion from registers of certain information.[3] |
| Section 46 | Operations by the Scottish Environment Protection Agency[4] to remedy or forestall pollution of water |
| [5] | |
| Section 56(1) to (3)[6] | Interpretation etc. of Part II |

## *Explanatory Note*
### *(This note is not part of the Regulations)*

These Regulations revoke and re-enact for Scotland the substance of the Control of Pollution (Radioactive Waste) Regulations 1984 and 1985, taking into account changes made to Part II of the Control of Pollution Act 1974 by the Water Act 1989, Schedule 23.[7]

The provisions of Part II of the 1974 Act (which relate to the control of water pollution) do not apply in relation to radioactive waste within the meaning of the Radioactive Substances Act 1960[8] but the Secretary of State may by regulations provide for any of these provisions to apply and may make consequential modifications of the 1960 Act.

These Regulations bring radioactive waste within the scope of those provisions of Part II of the 1974 Act which are specified in the Schedule to the Regulations, but in such a manner that no account will be taken of the radioactive properties of such waste, which will remain subject to control under the 1960 Act.[9]

[1] Words "Sections 30F to J, 31(4), (5), (8) and (9)" inserted by S.I. 1996/973, reg.2, sch., para.14(2)(a). This amendment came into force on 1 April 1996: reg.1.

[2] The former entry relating to s.32 was revoked by S.I. 1996/973, reg.2, sch., para.14(2)(b).

[3] This entry substituted by S.I. 1996/973, reg.2, sch., para.14(2)(c).

[4] The Scottish Environment Protection Agency, SEPA, is established by the Environment Act 1995 (c.25), s.20, p.438 above. Words "the Scottish Environment Protection Agency" substituted by S.I. 1996/973, reg.2, sch., para.14(2)(d).

[5] The entries relating to ss.53 and 55 were revoked by S.I. 1996/973, reg.2, sch., para.14(2)(e).

[6] Words "Section 56(1) to (3)" substituted by S.I. 1996/973, reg.2, sch., para.14(2)(f).

[7] Further changes have since been made to Part II of the 1974 Act by the Environment Act 1995 (c.25).

[8] The Radioactive Substances Act 1993 consolidates the 1960 Act and other enactments.

[9] The final paragraph of this note relates to reg.4, which has been revoked, and is accordingly not reproduced.

# The Environmental Protection (Duty of Care) Regulations 1991

S.I. 1991 No. 2839

The Secretary of State for the Environment as respects England, the Secretary of State for Wales as respect Wales and the Secretary of State for Scotland as respects Scotland, in exercise of the powers conferred on them by section 34(5) of the Environmental Protection Act 1990,[1] and of all other powers enabling them in that behalf, hereby make the following Regulations:

*Citation, commencement and interpretation*

1. (1) These Regulations may be cited as the Environmental Protection (Duty of Care) Regulations 1991 and shall come into force on 1st April 1992.

   (2) In these Regulations—

   "the 1990 Act" means the Environmental Protection Act 1990;

   "transferor" and "transferee" mean respectively, in relation to a transfer of controlled waste by a person who is subject to the duty imposed by section 34(1) of the 1990 Act,[2] the person who in compliance with that section transfers a written description of the waste and the person who receives that description.

*Transfer notes*

2. (1) Subject to paragraph (3),[3] the transferor and the transferee shall, at the same time as the written description of the waste is transferred, ensure that such a document as is described in paragraph (2) ("a transfer note") is completed and signed on their behalf.

   (2) A transfer note shall—

   (a) identify the waste to which it relates and state—

       (i) its quantity and whether on transfer it is loose or in a container;

       (ii) if in a container, the kind of container; and

       (iii) the time and place of transfer;

   (b) give the name and address of the transferor and the transferee;

   (c) state whether or not the transferor is the producer or importer of the waste and, if so, which;

   (d) if the transfer is to a person for authorised transport purposes, specify which of those purposes; and

   (e) state as respects the transferor and the transferee which, if any, of the categories of person shown in column 1 of the following Table describes him and provide any relevant additional information specified in column 2 of the Table.

---

[1] P.118 above.
[2] P.117 above.
[3] Words "Subject to paragraph (3)," added by S.I.

1996/972, reg.23(a). This amendment came into force on 1 September 1996: reg.1(1).

TABLE

| Category of person | Additional information |
| --- | --- |
| An authority which is a waste collection authority for the purposes of Part II of the 1990 Act.[1] | |
| A person who is the holder of a waste management licence under section 35 of the 1990 Act[2] or of a disposal licence under section 5 of the Control of Pollution Act 1974.[3] | If the waste is to be kept, treated or disposed of by that person, the relevant licence number and the name of the licensing authority. |
| A person to whom section 33(1) of the 1990 Act[4] does not apply by virtue of regulations under subsection (3) of that section.[5] | |
| A person registered as a carrier of controlled waste under section 2 of the Control of Pollution (Amendment) Act 1989.[6] | The name of the waste regulation authority with whom he is registered and his registration number. |
| A person who is not required to be so registered by virtue of regulations under section 1(3) of that Act.[7] | |
| A waste disposal authority in Scotland. | |

(3)  Paragraph (1) shall not apply where the waste transferred is special waste within the meaning of the Special Waste Regulations 1996[8] and the consignment note and, where appropriate, schedule required by those Regulations are completed and dealt with in accordance with those Regulations.[9]

*Duty to keep copies of written descriptions of waste and transfer notes*

3.  The transferor and the transferee[10] shall each keep the written description of the waste and the transfer note or copies thereof for a period of two years from the transfer of the controlled waste.

*Duty to furnish documents*

4.  A person who has been served by a waste regulation authority[11] with a notice in writing specifying or describing any document and requiring its production shall if the document is one which at that time he is under a duty to keep under regulation 3, furnish the authority with a copy of it at the authority's office specified in the notice and within the period (not being less than 7 days) so specified.

*Explanatory Note*
*(This note is not part of the Regulations)*

Section 34(1) of the Environmental Protection Act 1990 imposes a duty of care on any person who imports, produces, carries, keeps, treats or disposes of controlled waste or, as a broker, has control of such waste. The duty requires such persons to ensure that there is no unauthorised or harmful deposit, treatment or disposal of the waste, to prevent the escape of the waste from their control or that of any other person, and on the transfer of the waste to

[1] "Waste collection authority" is defined in s.30 of the 1990 Act, p.113 above.
[2] P.119 above.
[3] 1974 c.40.
[4] P.116 above.
[5] See S.I. 1992/588, p.662 below, and S.I. 1994/1056, p.675 below.
[6] P.73 above.
[7] P.72 above; see S.I. 1991/1624, p.630 above.
[8] P.763 below; see reg.2 for the meaning of "special waste".
[9] This paragraph inserted by S.I. 1996/972, reg.23(b). This amendment came into force on 1 September 1996: reg.1(1).
[10] "Transferor" and "transferee" defined by reg.1(2) above.
[11] "Waste regulation authority" defined by s.30(1) of the 1990 Act, p.113 above.

ensure that the transfer is only to an authorised person or to a person for authorised transport purposes and that a written description of the waste is also transferred.

These Regulations impose requirements under section 34(5) of the 1990 Act on any person who is subject to the duty of care as respects the making and retention of documents and the furnishing of copies of them.

Breach of the duty of care or of these Regulations is a criminal offence. The duty of care and these Regulations do not apply to an occupier of domestic property as respects the household waste produced on the property.

Regulation 2 requires the transferor and the transferee to complete and sign a transfer note at the same time as the written description of the waste is transferred. The transfer note must identify the waste in question and state its quantity, how it is stored, the time and place of transfer, the name and address of the transferor and the transferee, whether the transferor is the producer or importer of the waste, which (if any) authorised transport purpose applies, in which category of person the transferor and the transferee are and certain additional information.

Regulation 3 requires the transferor and the transferee to keep the written description of the waste and the transfer note or copies of them for two years from the transfer.

Regulation 4 imposes a duty on a person who is under a duty to keep any document by virtue of regulation 3 to furnish a copy of that document to a waste regulation authority if he is required to do so by the authority.

# The Surface Waters (Dangerous Substances) (Classification) Regulations 1992

## S.I. 1992 No. 337

The Secretary of State for the Environment and the Secretary of State for Wales, acting jointly in exercise of the powers conferred on them by sections 82,[1] 102[2] and 219(2)[3] of the Water Resources Act 1991 and of all other powers enabling them in that behalf, hereby make the following Regulations:

### Citation and commencement

1. These Regulations may be cited as the Surface Waters (Dangerous Substances) (Classification) Regulations 1992 and shall come into force on 20th March 1992.

### Classification of waters

2. (1) A system employing the classification DS3 is prescribed as a system of classification applying to relevant territorial waters, coastal waters and inland freshwaters.[4]

(2) The criterion for the classification DS3 is that the annual mean concentration of each substance listed in column (1) of the Schedule in samples taken and tested in accordance with these Regulations must not exceed the relevant concentration specified in column (2) of the Schedule.

### Sampling and analysis

3. (1) The provisions of this regulation apply as respect the taking and testing of samples of any waters to which the classification DS3 is for the time being applied.

(2) Samples must be taken in relation to such waters at a frequency sufficient to show any changes in the aquatic environment, having regard in particular to natural variations in hydrological conditions.

(3) Where a discharge containing any substance listed in column (1) of the Schedule is made to such waters, samples must be taken at a point sufficiently close to the discharge point to be representative of the quality of the aquatic environment in the area affected by the discharge.

(4) Samples taken in relation to such waters shall be analysed using the relevant reference methods of measurement specified in column (3) of the Schedule or other methods which have limits of detection, precision and accuracy at least as good.

### Modification of section 83 of the Water Resources Act 1991

4. Section 83 of the Water Resources Act 1991[5] shall have effect as if—

(a) it imposed a duty on the Secretary of State to exercise his powers under that section to apply the classification DS3 to all relevant territorial waters, coastal waters and inland freshwaters; and

(b) in relation to the establishment of water quality objectives in pursuance of that duty, subsections (4) and (5) of that section were omitted.

---

[1] P.271 above.
[2] P.290 above.
[3] P.310 above.

[4] "Relevant territorial waters", "coastal waters" and "inland freshwaters" are defined in s.104, p.290 above.
[5] P.272 above.

# THE SCHEDULE

(Regulations 2(2), 3(2) and (3))

CLASSIFICATION OF RELEVANT TERRITORIAL WATERS, COASTAL WATERS AND INLAND
FRESHWATERS (DS3)

| (1)<br>Substance | (2)<br>Concentration in<br>microgrammes per<br>litre (annual mean) | (3)<br>Reference method of<br>measurement |
| --- | --- | --- |
| 1,2-Dichloroethane | 10 | Gas chromatography with electron capture detection after extraction by means of an appropriate solvent or gas chromatography following isolation by means of the "purge and trap" process and trapping by using a cryogenically cooled capillary trap. The limit of determination is 1µg/l. (*see Note*) |
| Trichloroethylene | 10 | Gas chromatography with electron capture detection after extraction by means of an appropriate solvent. The limit of determination is 0.1µg/l. (*see Note*) |
| Perchloroethylene | 10 | |
| Trichlorobenzene | 0.4 (but there must be no significant increase over time in the concentration of trichlorobenzene in sediments and/or molluscs and/or shellfish and/or fish). | Gas chromatography with electron capture detection after extraction by means of an appropriate solvent or, when used to determine the concentration in sediments and organisms, after appropriate preparation of the sample. The limit of determination for each isomer separately is 10 ng/l for the water environment and 1 µg/kg of dry matter for sediments and organisms. (*see Note*) |

*Note*

The accuracy and precision of the method must be plus or minus 50% at a concentration which represents twice the value of the limit of determination.

*Explanatory Note*
*(This note is not part of the Regulations)*

These Regulations prescribe a system of classifying the quality of relevant territorial waters, coastal waters and inland freshwaters.

The classification DS3 prescribed by the Regulations reflects the quality objectives specified in the Annex to Council Directive 90/415/EEC[1] which amends Annex II to Council Directive 86/280/EEC[2] on limit values and quality objectives for discharges of certain dangerous substances included in List I of the Annex to Council directive 76/464/EEC.[3]

The system of classification prescribed by the Regulations will be used for establishing quality objectives under section 83 of the Water Resources Act 1991.[4] Sampling requirements are specified in regulation 3 and the Secretary of

[1] OJ No. L 219, 14.8.90, p.49.
[2] OJ No. L 181, 4.7.86, p.16.
[3] OJ No. L 129, 18.5.76, p.23.
[4] P.272 above.

State will use his powers under section 5 of the Water Resources Act 1991[1] to direct the Environment Agency[2] to sample and test waters to which classification DS3 applies in accordance with those requirements.

Regulation 4 modifies section 83 of the Water Resources Act 1991 for the purpose of complying with Community obligations arising under Council Directive 90/415/EEC. It imposes a duty on the Secretary of State to use his powers under section 83 to apply the classification DS3 to territorial waters up to three miles out, coastal waters and inland freshwaters. It also dispenses with the requirements of section 83(4) and (5) (representations and objections) in cases where the Secretary of State is performing that duty.

---

[1] This provision has been replaced by s.40 of the Environment Act 1995, p.451 above.

[2] Words "the Environment Agency" substituted by the Environment Act 1995 (c.25), s.120, sch.22, para.233(1).

# The Trade Effluents (Prescribed Processes and Substances) Regulations 1992

S.I. 1992 No. 339

The Secretary of State for the Environment and the Secretary of State for Wales, acting jointly in exercise of the powers conferred on them by section 138(1) of the Water Industry Act 1991[1] and of all other powers enabling them in that behalf, hereby make the following Regulations:

*Citation and commencement*

1. These Regulations may be cited as the Trade Effluents (Prescribed Processes and Substances) Regulations 1992 and shall come into force on 20th March 1992.

*Trade effluent derived from prescribed processes*

2. Trade effluent which derives from any process which occasions liquid discharges containing trichloroethylene or perchloroethylene in quantities of thirty kilogrammes per year or more shall be special category effluent for the purposes of Chapter III of Part IV of the Water Industry Act 1991.[2]

*Explanatory Note*
*(This note is not part of the Regulations)*

This discharge of special category effluent is subject to control by the Secretary of State under the provisions of Chapter III of Part IV of the Water Industry Act 1991.

These Regulations provide that trade effluent derived from any process which occasions liquid discharges of trichloroethylene or perchloroethylene in quantities of thirty kilogrammes or more per year shall be special category effluent for the purposes of that Chapter.

The Regulations are made in order to implement Council Directive 90/415/EEC[3] in relation to the discharge to sewer of trichloroethylene or perchlorethylene.

Council Directive 90/415/EEC amends Annex II to Council Directive 86/280/EEC[4] on limit values and quality objectives for discharges of certain dangerous substances included in List I of the Annex to Council Directive 76/464/EEC.[5]

---

[1] P.246 above. See the definition of "prescribed" in s.219(1), p.259 above.
[2] P.232 above.

[3] OJ No. L 219, 14.8.90, p.49.
[4] OJ No. L 181, 4.7.86, p.16.
[5] OJ No. L 129, 18.5.76, p.23.

# The Environmental Protection (Waste Recycling Payments) Regulations 1992

S.I. 1992 No. 462

The Secretary of State for the Environment as respects England, the Secretary of State for Wales as respects Wales and the Secretary of State for Scotland as respects Scotland, in exercise of the powers conferred on them by section 52(8) of the Environmental Protection Act 1990[1] and of all other powers enabling them in that behalf, hereby make the following Regulations:

*Citation, commencement and interpretation*

1. (1) These Regulations may be cited as the Environmental Protection (Waste Recycling Payments) Regulations 1992 and shall come into force on 1st April 1992.

    (2) In these Regulations—

    "the 1990 Act" means the Environmental Protection Act 1990; and

    "transport costs" includes any contribution made by a waste disposal authority to a collection authority under section 52(1) of the 1990 Act.[2]

*Determination of a waste disposal authority's net saving of expenditure where waste is to be recycled*

2. (1) A waste disposal authority's net saving of expenditure for the purposes of section 52(1) or (3) of the 1990 Act[3] in relation to waste which is retained or collected for recycling shall be determined in accordance with the following provisions of this regulation.

    (2) The authority's net saving of expenditure shall be an amount equal to the expenditure which it would have incurred in disposing of the waste at a cost per tonne equal to its average cost per tonne at the relevant time of disposing of similar waste using its most expensive disposal method for waste collected in the relevant area.

    (2A) In paragraph (2) above, "the relevant area" means the waste collection authority area in which the waste in question is collected or, where the waste in question is collected by a person other than a waste collection authority in the area of more than one waste collection authority and it is not reasonably practicable for that person to determine how much of that waste was collected in each such area, the area consisting of the areas of all those waste collection authorities.[4]

    (3) In determining its average cost per tonne of disposing of similar waste, the authority shall take into account—

    (a) the market value at the relevant time of any of its assets (including land) used in connection with disposal of that waste;

    (b) any expenditure incurred by the authority in operating any site or transfer station used in connection with the disposal of that waste;

    (c) any transport costs[5] incurred by the authority in relation to that waste;

    (d) any expenditure which will be incurred in closing, restoring and subsequently maintaining any site belonging to the authority which is used for the disposal of that waste; and

    (e) any other expenditure incurred by the authority in relation to that waste.

---

[1] P.146 above.
[2] P.145 above.
[3] P.145 above.
[4] Para. (2) and (2A) substituted, for the earlier para. (2), by

S.I. 1994/522, reg.2(2). This amendment came into force on 1 April 1994: reg.1.
[5] "Transport costs" defined by reg.1(2) above.

(4)  No account shall be taken of expenditure incurred by the authority in determining the amount of, or in making, any payment under section 52(1) or (3) of the 1990 Act.

(5)  If a determination cannot be made under paragraph (2) because sufficient accurate information is not available or could only be obtained at a disproportionate cost, the authority's net saving of expenditure shall be determined by reference to the relevant figure shown in the Schedule hereto.

## THE SCHEDULE[1]

(Regulation 2(5))

### REPRESENTATIVE SAVINGS IN WASTE DISPOSAL COSTS

| Type of waste disposal authority | Saving in waste disposal costs per tonne |
| --- | --- |
| A London waste disposal authority for an area which includes an inner London borough. The council of an inner London borough. The Common Council of the City of London. | £36.66 |
| A London waste disposal authority which comprises outer London boroughs. The council of an outer London borough. | £31.09 |
| The Greater Manchester Waste Disposal Authority. The Merseyside Waste Disposal Authority. The council of a metropolitan district. | £24.45 |
| Any other waste disposal authority. | £17.78 where the authority incurs any transport costs in disposing of similar waste and £10.00 in other cases. |

### Explanatory Note
*(This note is not part of the Regulations)*

Section 52(1) of the Environmental Protection Act 1990 requires waste disposal authorities to pay waste collection authorities amounts representing their net savings on the disposal of waste retained by the collection authorities for recycling.

Section 52(3) of that Act confers a power on waste disposal authorities to pay persons other than waste collection authorities equivalent amounts for waste collected by them for recycling.

These Regulations discharge the Secretary of State's duty to make provision for the determination of a waste disposal authority's net saving of expenditure for the purposes of section 52(1) or (3) of that Act in relation to such waste (the corresponding duty in relation to section 52(2), (4) and (5) has not yet been commenced).

[2]  This schedule substituted by S.I. 1996/634, reg.6. This amendment came into force on 1 April 1996: reg.1(1).

# The Surface Waters (Dangerous Substances) (Classification) (Scotland) Regulations 1992

S.I. 1992 No. 574 (S.63)

The Secretary of State, in exercise of the powers conferred on him by sections 30B,[1] 55A,[2] 104(1)[3] and 105(1)[4] of the Control of Pollution Act 1974(a) and of all other powers enabling him in that behalf, hereby make the following Regulations:

*Citation, commencement and extent*

1. These Regulations may be cited as the Surface Waters (Dangerous Substances) (Classification) (Scotland) Regulations 1992, shall come into force on 1st April 1992 and shall extend to Scotland only.

*Classification of waters*

2. (1) A system employing the classification DS3 is prescribed as a system of classification applying to relevant territorial waters, coastal waters and inland waters.[5]

(2) The criterion for the classification DS3 is that the annual mean concentration of each substance listed in column (1) of the Schedule hereto in samples taken and tested in accordance with these Regulations must not exceed the relevant concentration specified in column (2) of that Schedule.

*Sampling and analysis*

3. (1) Samples must be taken in relation to the waters at a frequency sufficient to show any changes in the aquatic environment, having regard in particular, to natural variations in hydrological conditions.

(2) Where a discharge containing any substance listed in column (1) of the Schedule is made to the waters, samples must be taken at a point sufficiently close to the discharge point to be representative of the quality of the aquatic environment in the area affected by the discharge.

(3) Samples taken in relation to the waters shall be analysed using the relevant reference methods of measurement specified in column (3) of the Schedule or other methods which have limits of detection, precision and accuracy at least as good.

*Modification of section 30C of the Control of Pollution Act 1974*

4. Section 30C of the Control of Pollution Act 1974[6] shall have effect as if—

(a) it imposed a duty on the Secretary of State to exercise his powers under that section to apply the classification DS3 to all relevant territorial waters, coastal waters and inland waters; and

(b) in relation to the establishment of water quality objectives in pursuance of that duty, subsections (4) and (5) of that section were omitted.

---

[1] P.19 above.
[2] P.49 above.
[3] P.60 above.
[4] P.61 above; s.105(1) contains a definition of "prescribed" relevant to the exercise of the statutory powers under which these Regulations are made.
[5] "Relevant territorial waters", "coastal waters" and "inland waters" are defined in s.30A, p.18 above.
[6] P.20 above.

# SCHEDULE

(Regulations 2(2), 3(2) and (3))

CLASSIFICATION OF RELEVANT TERRITORIAL WATERS, COASTAL WATERS AND INLAND WATERS (DS3)

| (1) Substance | (2) Concentration in microgrammes per litre (annual mean) | (3) Reference method of measurement |
|---|---|---|
| 1,2-Dichloroethane | 10 | Gas chromatography with electron capture detection after extraction by means of an appropriate solvent or gas chromatography following isolation by means of the "purge and trap" process and trapping by using a cryogenically cooled capillary trap. The limit of determination is 1µg/l. (*see Note 1*) |
| Trichloroethylene<br>Perchloroethylene } | 10 | Gas chromatography with electron capture detection after extraction by means of an appropriate solvent. The limit of determination is 0.1µg/l. (*see Note 1*) |
| Trichlorobenzene | 0.4 | Gas chromatography with electron capture detection after extraction by means of an appropriate solvent or, when used to determine the concentration in sediments and organisms, after appropriate preparation of the sample. The limit of determination for each isomer separately is 10ng/l for the water environment and 1µg/kg of dry matter for sediments and organisms. (*See Notes 1 and 2*) |

*Notes*

1. The accuracy and precision of the method must be plus or minus 50% at a concentration which represents twice the value of the limit of determination.

2. There must be no significant increase over time in the concentration of trichlorobenzene in sediments and/or molluscs and/or shellfish and/or fish.

*Explanatory Note*
*(This note is not part of the Regulations)*

These Regulations, which extend to Scotland only, prescribe a system of classifying the quality of relevant territorial waters, coastal waters and inland water.

The classification DS3 prescribed by the Regulations reflects the quality objectives specified in the Annex to Council Directive 90/415/EEC (OJ No. L219, 14.8.90, p.49) which amends Annex II to Council Directive 86/280/EEC (OJ No. L181, 4.7.86, p.16) on limit values and quality objectives for discharges of certain dangerous substances included in List I of the Annex to Council Directive 76/464/EEC (OJ No. L129, 18.5.76, p.23).

The system of classification prescribed by the Regulations will be used for establishing quality objectives under section 30C of the Control of Pollution Act 1974. Sampling requirements are specified in regulation 3 and the Secretary of State will use his powers under section 54 of the Control of Pollution Act 1974[1] to direct the river purification authorities[2] to sample and test waters to which classification DS3 applies in accordance with those requirements.

---

[1] This provision has been replaced by s.40 of the Environment Act 1995, p.451 above.
[2] The functions of river purification authorities have been transferred to the Scottish Environment Protection Agency: Environment Act 1995, s.21, p.438 above. This transfer took place on 1 April 1996: S.I. 1996/139.

Regulation 4 modifies section 30C of the Control of Pollution Act 1974 for the purpose of complying with Community obligations arising under Council Directive 90/415/EEC. It imposes a duty on the Secretary of State to use his powers under section 30C to apply the classification DS3 to relevant territorial waters, coastal waters and inland waters. It also dispenses with the requirements of section 30C(4) and (5) (representations and objections) in cases where the Secretary of State is performing that duty.

# The Controlled Waste Regulations 1992

## S.I. 1992 No. 588

The Secretary of State for the Environment as respects England, the Secretary of State for Wales as respects Wales and the Secretary of State for Scotland as respects Scotland, in exercise of the powers conferred on them by sections 1(3)(a),[1] 8(2)[2] and 9(1)[3] of the Control of Pollution (Amendment) Act 1989 and sections 33(3),[4] 45(3),[5] 75(7)(d)[6] and (8) and 96 of the Environmental Protection Act 1990, and of all other powers enabling them in that behalf, hereby make the following Regulations:

*Citation, commencement and interpretation*

1. These Regulations may be cited as the Controlled Waste Regulations 1992 shall come into force on 1st April 1992 save for regulation 10, which shall come into force on 1st June 1992.

   (2) In these Regulations—

   "the Act" means the Environmental Protection Act 1990;

   "the 1989 Regulations" means the Sludge (Use in Agriculture) Regulations 1989;[7]

   "camp site" means land on which tents are pitched for the purposes of human habitation and land the use of which is incidental to land on which tents are so pitched;

   "charity" means any body of persons or trust established for charitable purposes only;

   "clinical waste" means—

   (a) any waste which consists wholly or partly of human or animal tissue, blood or other body fluids, excretions, drugs or other pharmaceutical products, swabs or dressings, or syringes, needles or other sharp instruments, being waste which unless rendered safe may prove hazardous to any person coming into contact with it; and

   (b) any other waste arising from medical, nursing, dental, veterinary, pharmaceutical or similar practice, investigation, treatment, care, teaching or research, or the collection of blood for transfusion, being waste which may cause infection to any person coming into contact with it;

   "composite hereditament" has the same meaning as in section 64(9) of the Local Government Finance Act 1988;[8]

   "construction" includes improvement, repair or alteration;

   "Directive waste" has the meaning given by regulation 1(3) of the Waste Management Licensing Regulations 1994;[9],[10]

   "part residential subjects" has the same meaning as in section 99(1) of the Local Government Finance Act 1992;[11]

   "scrap metal" has the same meaning as in section 9(2) of the Scrap Metal Dealers Act 1964;[12]

   "septic tank sludge" and "sludge" have the same meaning as in regulation 2(1) of the 1989 Regulations;[13] and

   "vessel" includes a hovercraft within the meaning of section 4(1) of the Hovercraft Act 1968.[14]

---

[1] P.72 above.
[2] P.80 above.
[3] P.80 above. See the definition of "prescribed" in s.9(1) of the 1989 Act.
[4] P.116 above.
[5] P.138 above.
[6] P.160 above.
[7] P.547 above.
[8] 1988 c.41.

[9] P.678 below.
[10] This definition inserted by S.I. 1994/1056, reg.24(2)(a). This amendment came into force on 1 May 1994: reg.1(1).
[11] 1992 c.15. Words "section 99(1) of the Local Government Finance Act 1992" substituted by S.I. 1994/1056, reg.24(2)(b).
[12] 1964 c.69.
[13] P.547 above.
[14] 1968 c.59.

(3) Any reference in these Regulations to a section is, except where the context otherwise requires, a reference to a section of the Act.

(4) References in these Regulations to waste—

(a) do not include waste from any mine or quarry or waste from premises used for agriculture within the meaning of the Agriculture Act 1947[1] or, in Scotland, the Agriculture (Scotland) Act 1948;[2]

(b) except so far as otherwise provided, do not include sewage (including matter in or from a privy).

*Waste to be treated as household waste*

2. (1) Subject to paragraph (2) and regulations 3 and 7A,[3] waste of the descriptions set out in Schedule 1[4] shall be treated as household waste for the purposes of Part II of the Act.[5]

(2) Waste of the following descriptions shall be treated as household waste for the purposes only of section 34(2) (household waste produced on domestic property)[6]—

(a) waste arising from works of construction[7] or demolition, including waste arising from work preparatory thereto; and

(b) septic tank sludge.[8]

*Waste not to be treated as household waste*

3. (1) Waste of the following descriptions shall not be treated as household waste for the purposes of section 33(2)[9] (treatment, keeping or disposal of household waste within the curtilage of a dwelling)—

(a) any mineral or synthetic oil or grease;

(b) asbestos; and

(c) clinical waste.[10]

(2) Scrap metal[11] shall not be treated as household waste for the purposes of section 34[12] at any time before 1st October 1995.[13]

*Charges for the collection of household waste*

4. The collection of any of the types of household waste set out in Schedule 2[14] is prescribed for the purposes of section 45(3)[15] as a case in respect of which a charge for collection may be made.

*Waste to be treated as industrial waste*

5. (1) Subject to paragraph (2) and regulations 7 and 7A,[16] waste of the descriptions set out in Schedule 3[17] shall be treated as industrial waste for the purposes of Part II of the Act.[18]

(2) Waste of the following descriptions shall be treated as industrial waste for the purposes of Part II of the Act (except section 34(2)[19])—

[1] 1947 c.48.
[2] 1948 c.45.
[3] Words "Subject to paragraph (2) and regulations 3 and 7A," substituted by S.I. 1994/1056, reg.24(3). This amendment came into force on 1 May 1994: reg.1(1).
[4] P.665 below.
[5] "Household waste" is defined in s.75 of the 1990 Act, p.159 above.
[6] P.117 above.
[7] "Construction" defined by reg.1(2) above.
[8] "Septic tank sludge" defined in reg.2(1) of the 1989 Regulations, p.547 above: reg.1(2) above.
[9] P.116 above.
[10] "Clinical waste" defined by reg.1(2) above.
[11] "Scrap metal" defined by reg.1(2) above.
[12] P.117 above.
[13] Words "1st October 1995" substituted by S.I. 1995/288, reg.2(1). This amendment came into force on 1 April 1995: reg.1(1).
[14] P.666 below.
[15] P.138 above.
[16] Words "regulations 7 and 7A" substituted by S.I. 1994/1056, reg.24(4). This amendment came into force on 1 May 1994: reg.1(1).
[17] P.667 below.
[18] "Industrial waste" is defined in s.75 of the 1990 Act, p.159 above.
[19] P.117 above.

(a) waste arising from works of construction[1] or demolition, including waste arising from work preparatory thereto;

(b) septic tank sludge[2] not falling within regulation 7(1)(c) or (c).[3]

*Waste to be treated as commercial waste*

**6.** Subject to regulations 7 and 7A,[4] waste of the descriptions set out in Schedule 4[5] shall be treated as commercial waste for the purposes of Part II of the Act.[6]

*Waste not to be treated as industrial or commercial waste*

**7.** (1) Waste of the following descriptions shall not be treated as industrial waste or commercial waste[7] for the purposes of Part II of the Act—

(a) sewage, sludge or septic tank sludge[8] which is treated, kept or disposed of (otherwise than by means of mobile plant) within the curtilage of a sewage treatment works as an integral part of the operation of those works;

(b) sludge which is supplied or used in accordance with the 1989 Regulations;[9]

(c) septic tank sludge which is used on agricultural land within the meaning of[10] the 1989 Regulations.[11]

(2) Scrap metal[12] shall not be treated as industrial waste or commercial waste for the purposes of section 34[13] at any time before 1st October 1995.[14]

(3) Animal by-products which are collected and transported in accordance with Schedule 2 to the Animal By-Products Order 1992[15] shall not be treated as industrial waste or commercial waste for the purposes of section 34 (duty of care etc. as respects waste).

(4) In this regulation, "animal by-products" has the same meaning as in article 3(1) of the Animal By-Products Order 1992.[16]

*Waste not to be treated as household, industrial or commercial waste*

**7A.** For the purposes of Part II of the Act, waste which is not Directive waste[17] shall not be treated as household waste, industrial waste or commercial waste.[18,19]

*Application of Part II of the Act to litter and refuse*

**8.** Part II of the Act shall have effect as if—

(a) references to controlled waste included references to litter and refuse to which section 96 applies;

(b) references to controlled waste of a description set out in the first column of Table A below included references to litter and refuse of a description set out in the second column thereof;

(c) references to controlled waste collected under section 45[20] included references to litter and refuse collected under sections 89(1)(a) and (c) and 92(9); and

---

[1] "Construction" defined by reg.1(2) above.

[2] "Septic tank sludge" defined in reg.2(1) of the 1989 Regulations, p.547 above: reg.1(2) above.

[3] Words "regulation 7(1)(a) or (c)" substituted by S.I. 1994/1056, reg.24(5).

[4] Words "regulations 7 and 7A" substituted by S.I. 1994/1056, rg.24(6). This amendment came into force on 1 May 1994: reg.1(1).

[5] P.669 below.

[6] "Commercial waste" is defined in s.75 of the 1990 Act, p.159 above.

[7] "Industrial waste" and "commercial waste" are defined in s.75 of the 1990 Act, p.159 above.

[8] "Sludge" and "septic tank sludge" are defined in reg.2(1) of the 1989 Regulations, p.547 above: reg.1(2) above.

[9] P.547 above.

[10] Words "on agricultural land within the meaning of" substituted by S.I. 1995/288, reg.2(2). This amendment

came into force on 1 April 1995: reg.1(1).

[11] "Agricultural land" defined in reg.2(1) of the 1989 Regulations, p.547 above.

[12] "Scrap metal" defined in reg.1(2) above.

[13] P.117 above.

[14] Words "1st October 1995" substituted by S.I. 1995/288, reg.2(1). This amendment came into force on 1 April 1995: reg.1(1).

[15] S.I. 1992/3303.

[16] Paragraphs (3) and (4) added by S.I. 1994/1056, reg.24(7). This amendment came into force on 1 May 1994: reg.1(1).

[17] "Directive waste" defined by reg.1(2) above.

[18] See definitions in s.75 of the 1990 Act, p.159 above.

[19] This regulation inserted by S.I. 1994/1056, reg.24(8). This amendment came into force on 1 May 1994: reg.1(1).

[20] P.137 above.

(d) references to controlled waste collected under section 45 which is waste of a description set out in the first column of Table B below included references to litter and refuse of a description set out in the second column thereof.

### TABLE A

| Description of waste | Description of litter and refuse |
| --- | --- |
| Household waste. | Litter and refuse collected under section 89(1)(a), (c) and (f). |
| Industrial waste. | Litter and refuse collected under section 89(1)(b) and (e). |
| Commercial waste. | Litter and refuse collected under sections 89(1)(d) and (g), 92(9) and 93. |

### TABLE B

| Description of waste | Description of litter and refuse |
| --- | --- |
| Household waste. | Litter and refuse collected under section 89(1)(a) and (c). |
| Commercial waste. | Litter and refuse collected under section 92(9). |

*Exceptions from section 33(1) of the Act*

**9.** (1) Subject to the following provisions of this regulation, section 33(1)[1] shall not apply—

(a) *This sub-paragraph revoked by S.I. 1995/288, reg.2(3). This amendment came into force on 1 April 1995: reg.1(1).*

(b) as respects the use of land by a waste disposal authority in accordance with a resolution under section 11 of that Act.[2]

(2) Paragraph (1)(b) shall cease to apply in relation to a waste disposal authority in England and Wales as from the date on which the restriction imposed by section 51(1)[3] applies to that authority in accordance with section 77(6) and (7).[4]

*Amendment of the Controlled Waste (Registration of Carriers and Seizure of Vehicles) Regulations 1991*

**10.** *The amendment made by this regulation is included in the Controlled Waste (Registration of Carriers and Seizure of Vehicles) Regulations 1991, p.630 above.*

## SCHEDULE 1

(Regulation 2(1)[5])

### WASTE TO BE TREATED AS HOUSEHOLD WASTE

1. Waste from a hereditament or premises exempted from local non-domestic rating by virtue of—

(a) in England and Wales, paragraph 11[6] of Schedule 5 to the Local Government Finance Act 1988[7] (places of religious worship etc.);

(b) in Scotland, section 22[8] of the Valuation and Rating (Scotland) Act 1956[9] (churches etc).

---

[1] P.116 above.
[2] The Control of Pollution Act 1974 (c.40).
[3] P.144 above.
[4] P.161 above.
[5] P.663 above.
[6] Amended by para.3 of sch.10 to the Local Government

Finance Act 1992 (c.14).
[7] 1988 c.41.
[8] Amended by para.10 of sch.13 to the Local Government Finance Act 1992 (c.14).
[9] 1956 c.60.

2. Waste from premises occupied by a charity[1] and wholly or mainly used for charitable purposes.

3. Waste from any land belonging to or used in connection with domestic property, a caravan or a residential home.

4. Waste from a private garage which either has a floor area of 25 square metres or less or is used wholly or mainly for the accommodation of a private motor vehicle.

5. Waste from private storage premises used wholly or mainly for the storage of articles of domestic use.

6. Waste from a moored vessel[2] used wholly for the purposes of living accommodation.

7. Waste from a camp site.[3]

8. Waste from a prison or other penal institution.

9. Waste from a hall or other premises used wholly or mainly for public meetings.

10. Waste from a royal palace.

11. Waste arising from the discharge by a local authority of its duty under section 89(2).

# SCHEDULE 2

(Regulation 4[4])

## Types of Household Waste for which a Charge for Collection may be Made

1. Any article of waste which exceeds 25 kilograms in weight.

2. Any article of waste which does not fit, or cannot be fitted into—
   (a) a receptacle for household waste provided in accordance with section 46;[5] or
   (b) where no such receptacle is provided, a cylindrical container 750 millimetres in diameter and 1 metre in length.

3. Garden waste.

4. Clinical waste[6] from a domestic property, a caravan or from a moored vessel[7] used wholly for the purposes of living accommodation.

5. Waste from a residential hostel, a residential home or from premises forming part of a university, school or other educational establishment or forming part of a hospital or nursing home.

6. Waste from domestic property or a caravan used in the course of a business for the provision of self-catering holiday accommodation.

---

[1] "Charity" defined by reg.1(2), p.662 above.
[2] "Vessel" defined by reg.1(2), p.662 above.
[3] "Camp site" defined by reg.1(2), p.662 above.
[4] P.663 above.
[5] P.139 above.
[6] "Clinical waste" defined by reg.1(2), p.662 above.
[7] "Vessel" defined by reg.1(2), p.662 above.

7.  Dead domestic pets.

........................................................................................................

8.  Any substances or articles which, by virtue of a notice served by a collection authority under section 46,[1] the occupier of the premises may not put into a receptacle for household waste provided in accordance with that section.

........................................................................................................

9.  Litter and refuse collected under section 89(1)(f).

........................................................................................................

10. Waste from—

    (a)  in England and Wales, domestic property forming part of a composite hereditament;[2]

    (b)  in Scotland, the residential part of part residential subjects.[3]

........................................................................................................

11. Any mineral or synthetic oil or grease.

........................................................................................................

12. Asbestos.

........................................................................................................

13. Waste from a caravan which in accordance with any licence or planning permission regulating the use of the caravan site on which the caravan is stationed is not allowed to be used for human habitation throughout the year.

........................................................................................................

14. Waste from a camp site,[4] other than from any domestic property on that site.

........................................................................................................

15. Waste from premises occupied by a charity[5] and wholly or mainly used for charitable purposes, unless it is waste falling within paragraph 1 of Schedule 1.

........................................................................................................

16. Waste from a prison or other penal institution.

........................................................................................................

17. Waste from a hall or other premises used wholly or mainly for public meetings.

........................................................................................................

18. Waste from a royal palace.

# SCHEDULE 3

(Regulation 5(1)[6])

## Waste to be Treated as Industrial Waste

1.  Waste from premises used for maintaining vehicles, vessels[7] or aircraft, not being waste from a private garage to which paragraph 4 of Schedule 1 applies.

........................................................................................................

2.  Waste from a laboratory.

........................................................................................................

3.  (1) Waste from workshop or similar premises not being a factory within the meaning of section 175 of the Factories Act 1961[8] because the people working there are not employees or because the work there is not carried on by way of trade or for purposes of gain.

---

[1] P.139 above.
[2] "Composite hereditament" defined by reg.1(2), p.662 above.
[3] "Part residential subjects" defined by reg.1(2), p.662 above.

[4] "Camp site" defined by reg.1(2), p.662 above.
[5] "Charity" defined by reg.1(2), p.662 above.
[6] P.663 above.
[7] "Vessel" defined by reg.1(2), p.662 above.
[8] 1961 c.34.

(2) In this paragraph, "workshop" does not include premises at which the principal activities are computer operations or the copying of documents by photographic or lithographic means.

4. Waste from premises occupied by a scientific research association approved by the Secretary of State under section 508 of the Income and Corporation Taxes Act 1988.[1]

5. Waste from dredging operations.

6. Waste arising from tunnelling or from any other excavation.

7. Sewage not falling within a description in regulation 7[2] which—

    (a) is treated, kept or disposed of in or on land, other than by means of a privy, cesspool or septic tank;

    (b) is treated, kept or disposed of by means of mobile plant; or

    (c) has been removed from a privy or cesspool.

8. Clinical waste[3] other than—

    (a) clinical waste from a domestic property, caravan, residential home or from a moored vessel used wholly for the purposes of living accommodation;

    (b) waste collected under section 22(3) of the Control of Pollution Act 1974[4] or section 25(2) of the Local Government and Planning (Scotland) Act 1982;[5] or

    (c) waste collected under sections 89, 92(9) or 93.

9. Waste arising from any aircraft, vehicle or vessel[6] which is not occupied for domestic purposes.

10. Waste which has previously formed part of any aircraft, vehicle or vessel and which is not household waste.

11. Waste removed from land on which it has previously been deposited and any soil with which such waste has been in contact, other than—

    (a) waste collected under section 22(3) of the Control of Pollution Act 1974 or section 25(2) of the Local Government and Planning (Scotland) Act 1982;[7] or

    (b) waste collected under sections 89, 92(9) or 93.

12. Leachate from a deposit of waste.

13. Poisonous or noxious waste arising from any of the following processes undertaken on premises used for the purposes of a trade or business—

    (a) mixing or selling paints;

    (b) sign writing;

    (c) laundering or dry cleaning;

    (d) developing photographic film or making photographic prints;

    (e) selling petrol, diesel fuel, paraffin, kerosene, heating oil or similar substances; or

    (f) selling pesticides, herbicides or fungicides.

[1] 1988 c.1.
[2] P.664 above.
[3] "Clinical waste" defined by reg.1(2), p.662 above.
[4] 1974 c.40.
[5] 1982 c.43. Words "or section 25(2) . . . 1982" inserted by S.I. 1994/1056, reg.24(9). This amendment came into force on 1 May 1994: reg.1(1).
[6] "Vessel" defined by reg.1(2), p.662 above.
[7] 1982 c.43. Words "or section 25(2) . . . 1982" inserted by S.I. 1994/1056, reg.24(9). This amendment came into force on 1 May 1994: reg.1(1).

**14.** Waste from premises used for the purposes of breeding, boarding, stabling or exhibiting animals.

........................................................................................................................................

**15.** (1)  Waste oil, waste solvent or (subject to regulation 7(2)[1]) scrap metal,[2] other than—

(a)  waste from a domestic property, caravan or residential home;

(b)  waste falling within paragraphs 3 to 6 of Schedule 1.

(2)  In this paragraph—

"waste oil" means mineral or synthetic oil which is contaminated, spoiled or otherwise unfit for its original purpose; and

"waste solvent" means solvent which is contaminated, spoiled or otherwise unfit for its original purpose.

........................................................................................................................................

**16.** Waste arising from the discharge by the Secretary of State of his duty under section 89(2).

........................................................................................................................................

**17.** Waste imported into Great Britain.

........................................................................................................................................

**18.** (1)  Tank washings or garbage landed in Great Britain.

(2)  In this paragraph—

"tank washings" has the same meaning as in paragraph 36 of Schedule 3 to the Waste Management Licensing Regulations 1994;[3] and

"garbage" has the same meaning as in regulation 1(2) of the Merchant Shipping (Reception Facilities for Garbage) Regulations 1988.[4]

# SCHEDULE 4

(Regulation 6[5])

## WASTE TO BE TREATED AS COMMERCIAL WASTE

**1.** Waste from an office or showroom.

........................................................................................................................................

**2.** Waste from a hotel within the meaning of—

(a)  in England and Wales, section 1(3) of the Hotel Proprietors Act 1956;[6] and

(b)  in Scotland, section 139(1) of the Licensing (Scotland) Act 1976.[7]

........................................................................................................................................

**3.** Waste from any part of a composite hereditament,[8] or, in Scotland, of part residential subjects,[9] which is used for the purposes of a trade or business.

........................................................................................................................................

**4.** Waste from a private garage which either has a floor area exceeding 25 square metres or is not used wholly or mainly for the accommodation of a private motor vehicle.

........................................................................................................................................

**5.** Waste from premises occupied by a club, society or any association of persons (whether incorporated or not) in which activities are conducted for the benefit of the members.

........................................................................................................................................

**6.** Waste from premises (not being premises from which waste is by virtue of the Act[10] or of any other provision of these Regulations to be treated as household waste or industrial waste) occupied by—

---

[1]  P.664 above.

[2]  "Scrap metal" defined by reg.1(2), p.662 above.

[3]  P.706 below; this definition substituted by S.I. 1996/972, reg.24. This amendment came into force on 1 September 1996: reg.1(1).

[4]  S.I. 1988/2293.

[5]  P.664 above.

[6]  1956 c.52.

[7]  1976 c.66.

[8]  "Composite hereditament" defined by reg.1(2), p.662 above.

[9]  "Part residential subjects" defined by reg.1(2), p.662 above.

[10]  "The Act" means the Environmental Protection Act 1990: reg.1(2) above.

(a) a court;

(b) a government department;

(c) a local authority;

(d) a body corporate or an individual appointed by or under any enactment to discharge any public functions; or

(e) a body incorporated by a Royal Charter.

7. Waste from a tent pitched on land other than a camp site.[1]

8. Waste from a market or fair.

9. Waste collected under section 22(3) of the Control of Pollution Act 1974[2] or section 25(2) of the Local Government and Planning (Scotland) Act 1982.[3]

## Explanatory Note
### (This note is not part of the Regulations)

Part II of the Environmental Protection Act 1990 ("the 1990 Act") defines three sorts of controlled waste: household, industrial and commercial waste. The 1990 Act enables regulations to be made whereby waste of any description, including litter and refuse, is to be treated for the purposes of the provisions of Part II as being of one or other of those categories.

Regulation 2(1) provides for certain descriptions of waste to be treated as household waste for the purposes of Part II. Regulation 2(2) provides for two types of waste to be treated as household waste only for the purposes of section 34(2) of the 1990 Act, which relieves the occupier of domestic property of the duty of care under section 34(1) in relation to his household waste.

Regulation 3 prescribes certain types of waste which are not to be treated as household waste.

Regulation 4 prescribes a number of cases where a charge may be made for the collection of household waste.

Regulation 5(1) prescribed certain types of waste which are to be treated as industrial waste. Regulation 5(2) provides for two types of waste to be treated as industrial waste except for the purposes of section 34(2) of the 1990 Act.

Regulation 6 prescribes certain types of waste which are to be treated as commercial waste.

Regulation 7 prescribes certain types of waste which are not to be treated as industrial or commercial waste.

Regulation 8 provides for certain types of litter and refuse to be treated as controlled waste, for the purposes of Part II.

Regulation 9 exempts from the duty under section 33(1) of the Act (prohibition on unauthorised or harmful deposit, treatment or disposal etc. of controlled waste) cases where a disposal licence is not required under Part I of the Control of Pollution Act 1974, and certain land used by existing disposal authorities.

Regulation 10 amends the definition of "building and demolition waste" in the Controlled Waste (Registration of Carriers and Seizure of Vehicles) Regulations 1991.

[1] "Camp site" defined by reg.1(2), p.662 above.
[2] 1974 c.40.
[3] 1982 c.43. Words "or section 25(2) . . . 1982" inserted by S.I. 1994/1056, reg.24(9). This amendment came into force on 1 May 1994: reg.1(1).

# The Environmental Information Regulations 1992

S.I. 1992 No. 3240

Whereas a draft of these Regulations has been approved by resolution of each House of Parliament in pursuance of paragraph 2(2) of Schedule 2 to the European Communities Act 1972;[1]

Now, therefore, the Secretary of State, being a Minister designated[2] for the purposes of subsection (2) of section 2 of that Act in relation to freedom of access to, and the dissemination of, information on the environment held by public authorities or bodies with public responsibilities for the environment and which are under the control of a public authority, in exercise of the powers conferred on him by that subsection and of all other powers enabling him in that behalf, hereby makes the following Regulations:

*Citation, commencement and extent*

1. (1) These Regulations may be cited as the Environmental Information Regulations 1992.

   (2) These Regulations shall come into force on 31st December 1992.

   (3) These Regulations shall extend to Great Britain only.

*Construction of Regulations*

2. (1) These Regulations apply to any information which—

   (a) relates to the environment;[3]

   (b) is held by a relevant person in an accessible form and otherwise than for the purposes of any judicial or legislative functions; and

   (c) is not (apart from these Regulations) either—

      (i) information which is required, in accordance with any statutory provision, to be provided on request to every person who makes a request; or

      (ii) information contained in records which are required, in accordance with any statutory provision, to be made available for inspection by every person who wishes to inspect them.

   (2) For the purposes of these Regulations information relates to the environment if, and only if, it relates to any of the following, that is to say—

   (a) the state of any water or air, the state of any flora or fauna, the state of any soil or the state of any natural site or other land;

   (b) any activities or measures (including activities giving rise to noise or any other nuisance) which adversely affect anything mentioned in sub-paragraph (a) above or are likely adversely to affect anything so mentioned;

   (c) any activities or administrative or other measures (including any environmental management programmes) which are designed to protect anything so mentioned.

   (3) For the purposes of these Regulations the following are relevant persons, that is to say—

---

[1] 1972 c.68.
[2] The European Communities (Designation) (No. 2) Order 1992 (S.I. 1992/1711).

[3] **Case:** *R v British Coal Corporation ex p. Ibstock Building Products Ltd* [1995] JEL 297.

(a) all such Ministers of the Crown, Government departments, local authorities and other persons carrying out functions of public administration at a national, regional or local level as, for the purposes of or in connection with their functions, have responsibilities in relation to the environment; and

(b) any body with public responsibilities for the environment which does not fall within sub-paragraph (a) above but is under the control of a person falling within that sub-paragraph.

(4) In these Regulations—

"information" includes anything contained in any records;

"records" includes registers, reports and returns, as well as computer records and other records kept otherwise than in a document; and

"statutory provision" means any provision made by or under any enactment.

*Obligation to make environmental information available*

3. (1) Subject to the following provisions of these Regulations, a relevant person[1] who holds any information[2] to which these Regulations apply[3] shall make that information available to every person who requests it.

(2) It shall be the duty of every relevant person who holds information to which these Regulations apply to make such arrangements for giving effect to paragraph (1) above as secure—

(a) that every request made for the purposes of that paragraph is responded to as soon as possible;

(b) that no such request is responded to more than two months after it is made; and

(c) that, where the response to such a request contains a refusal to make information available, the refusal is in writing and specifies the reasons for the refusal.

(3) Arrangements made by a relevant person for giving effect to paragraph (1) above may include provision entitling that person to refuse a request for information in cases where a request is manifestly unreasonable or is formulated in too general a manner.

(4) The arrangements made by a relevant person for giving effect to paragraph (1) above may—

(a) include provision for the imposition of a charge on any person in respect of the costs reasonably attributable to the supply of information to that person in pursuance of that paragraph; and

(b) make the supply of any information in pursuance of that paragraph conditional on the payment of such a charge.

(5) The obligation of a relevant person to make information available in pursuance of paragraph (1) above shall not require him to make it available except in such form, and at such times and places, as may be reasonable.

(6) Without prejudice to any remedies available apart from by virtue of this paragraph in respect of any failure by a relevant person to comply with the requirements of these Regulations, the obligation of such a person to make information available in pursuance of paragraph (1) above shall be a duty owed to the person who has requested the information.

(7) Subject to regulation 4 below, where any statutory provision[4] or rule of law imposes any restriction or prohibition on the disclosure of information by any person, that restriction or prohibition shall not apply to any disclosure of information in pursuance of these Regulations.

*Exceptions to right to information*

4. (1) Nothing in these Regulations shall—

(a) require the disclosure of any information[5] which is capable of being treated as confidential; or

---

[1] "Relevant person" defined by reg.2(3) above.
[2] "Information" defined by reg.2(4) above.
[3] For "information to which these Regulations apply" see

reg.2(1) and (2) above.
[4] "Statutory provision" defined by reg.2(4) above.
[5] "Information" defined by reg.2(4), above.

(b) authorise or require the disclosure of any information which must be so treated.

(2) For the purposes of these Regulations information is to be capable of being treated as confidential if, and only if, it is—

(a) information relating to matters affecting international relations, national defence or public security;

(b) information relating to, or to anything which is or has been the subject-matter of, any legal or other proceedings[1] (whether actual or prospective);

(c) information relating to the confidential deliberations of any relevant person[2] or to the contents of any internal communications of a body corporate or other undertaking or organisation;

(d) information contained in a document or other record which is still in the course of completion; or

(e) information relating to matters to which any commercial or industrial confidentiality attaches or affecting any intellectual property.

(3) For the purposes of these Regulations information must be treated as confidential if, and only if, in the case of any request made to a relevant person under regulation 3 above—

(a) it is capable of being so treated and its disclosure in response to that request would (apart from regulation 3(7) above) contravene any statutory provision[3] or rule of law or would involve a breach of any agreement;

(b) the information is personal information contained in records held in relation to an individual who has not given his consent to its disclosure;

(c) the information is held by the relevant person in consequence of having been supplied by a person who—

    (i) was not under, and could not have been put under, any legal obligation to supply it to the relevant person;

    (ii) did not supply it in circumstances such that the relevant person is entitled apart from these Regulations to disclose it; and

    (iii) has not consented to its disclosure;

    or

(d) the disclosure of the information in response to that request would, in the circumstances, increase the likelihood of damage to the environment affecting anything to which the information relates.

(4) Nothing in this regulation shall authorise a refusal to make available any information contained in the same record as, or otherwise held with, other information which is withheld by virtue of this regulation unless it is incapable of being separated from the other information for the purpose of making it available.

(5) In this regulation "legal or other proceedings" includes any disciplinary proceedings, the proceedings at any local or other public inquiry and the proceedings at any hearing conducted by a person appointed under any enactment for the purpose of affording an opportunity to persons to make representations or objections with respect to any matter.

*Existing rights to information*

5. Where any information[4] which is not information to which these Regulations apply[5] is required under any statutory provision[6] to be made available to any person, the arrangements made by any relevant person for giving effect to the requirements of that provision shall be such as to secure—

---

[1] "Legal or other proceedings" defined by para. (5) below.
[2] "Relevant person" defined by reg.2(3), p.671 above.
[3] "Statutory provision" defined by reg.2(4), p.672 above.
[4] For "information to which these Regulations apply" see

reg.2(1) and (2), p.671 above.
[5] "Information" defined by reg.2(4), p.672 above.
[6] "Statutory provision" defined by reg.2(4), p.672 above.

(a) that every request for information relating to the environment which is made for the purposes of that provision is responded to as soon as possible;

(b) that no such request is responded to more than two months after it is made;

(c) that, where the response to such a request contains a refusal to make information available, the refusal is in writing and specifies the reasons for the refusal; and

(d) that no charge that exceeds a reasonable amount is made for making information relating to the environment available in accordance with that provision.

*Explanatory Note*
*(This note is not part of the Regulations)*

These Regulations implement Council Directive 90/313/EEC on the freedom of access to information on the environment (OJ No. L158, 23.6.90, p.56).

Regulation 2(1) provides that the Regulations apply where the information requested is not the subject of other statutory obligations of disclosure. Paragraph (2) of regulation 2 provides a definition for the purposes of the Regulations of information which relates to the environment and paragraph (3) indicates the public authorities and other persons who are subject to the obligation to make such information available under the Regulations. These paragraphs are based on Articles 2 and 6 of the Directive.

Regulation 3(1) contains the primary obligation for environmental information to be made available on request. Paragraphs (2) to (6) of regulation 3 give effect to the provisions of the Directive relating to procedural arrangements and make clear that failure to comply with the requirements of the Regulations will be a breach of the duty owed to the person making the request. Paragraph (7) of regulation 3 disapplies any statutory provision or rule of law restricting or prohibiting disclosure of information inconsistently with the requirements of the Regulations.

Regulation 4 provides for the categories of information to which the obligation of disclosure does not apply: paragraph (2) provides for those cases where the information is not required to be disclosed and paragraph (3) provides for those cases where the Regulations neither authorise nor require the disclosure of the information.

Regulation 5 provides that where any environmental information not covered by the Regulations is required by any statutory provision to be made available to any person, arrangements for doing so must be sufficient to satisfy the requirements imposed by the Directive and set out in the regulation.

# The Waste Management Licensing Regulations 1994

## S.I. 1994 No. 1056

*Arrangement of Regulations*
1. Citation, commencement, interpretation and extent    676
2. Application for a waste management licence or for the surrender or transfer of a waste management licence    678
3. Relevant offences    678
4. Technical competence    679
5. Technical competence—transitional provisions    680
6. Notice of appeal    681
7. Time limit for making an appeal    682
8. Reports of hearings    682
9. Notification of determination    683
10. Particulars to be entered in public registers    683
11. Information to be excluded or removed from register    685
12. Mobile plant    685
13. Health at work    686
14. Waste oils    686
15. Groundwater    687
16. Exclusion of activities under other control regimes from waste management licensing    688
17. Exemptions from waste management licensing    689
18. Registration in connection with except activities    690
19. Waste Framework Directive    692
20. Registration of brokers    692
21. Amendment of the Deposits in the Sea (Exemptions) Order 1985    693
22. Amendment of the Collection and Disposal of Waste Regulations 1988    694
23. Amendment of the Controlled Waste (Registration of Carriers and Seizure of Vehicles) Regulations 1991    694
24. Amendment of the Controlled Waste Regulations 1992    695

## SCHEDULES

Schedule 1—Information and evidence required in relation to an application for the surrender of a site licence    695
Schedule 2—Information required in relation to an application for the transfer of a waste management licence    696
Schedule 3—Activities exempt from waste management licensing    697
Schedule 4—Waste Framework Directive etc.    712
Schedule 5—Registration of brokers of controlled waste    723

The Secretary of State for the Environment as respects England, the Secretary of State for Wales as respects Wales and the Secretary of State for Scotland as respects Scotland, being Ministers designated[1] for the purposes of section 2(2) of the European Communities Act 1972[2] in relation to

---

[1] S.I. 1989/2393 and S.I. 1992/2870.    [2] 1972 c.68.

measures relating to the prevention, reduction and elimination of pollution of water and the prevention, reduction and elimination of pollution caused by waste, in exercise of the powers conferred on them by section 2(2) of that Act, sections 30(4) and 104(1)[1] of the Control of Pollution Act 1974, sections 1(3)(a), 2, 8(2) and 9(1) of the Control of Pollution (Amendment) Act 1989,[2] sections 29(10), 33(3), 35(6), 36(1), 39(3), 40(3), 43(8), 45(3), 50(3), 54(14), 64(1), (4) and (8), 74(6), 75(8) and 156 of the Environmental Protection Act 1990[3] (having in particular had regard in exercising their powers under section 33(3) of that Act[4] to the matters specified in section 33(4) of that Act) and of all other powers enabling them in that behalf hereby make the following Regulations:

*Citation, commencement, interpretation and extent*

1. (1) These Regulations may be cited as the Waste Management Licensing Regulations 1994 and, except for regulations 4 and 5, shall come into force on 1st May 1994.

(2) Regulations 4 and 5 shall come into force on 10th August 1994.

(3) In these Regulations, unless the context otherwise requires—

"the 1990 Act" means the Environmental Protection Act 1990;[5]

"the 1991 Regulations" means the Environmental Protection (Prescribed Processes and Substances) Regulations 1991;[6]

"construction work" includes the repair, alteration or improvement of existing works;

"the Directive" means Council Directive 75/442/EEC on waste[7] as amended by Council Directives 91/156/EEC[8] and 91/692/EEC;[9]

"Directive waste" means any substance or object in the categories set out in Part II of Schedule 4[10] which the producer or the person in possession of it discards or intends or is required to discard but with the exception of anything excluded from the scope of the Directive by Article 2 of the Directive, "discard" has the same meaning as in the Directive, and "producer" means anyone whose activities produce Directive waste or who carries out preprocessing, mixing or other operations resulting in a change in its nature or composition;[11]

"disposal" means any of the operations listed in Part III of Schedule 4,[12] and any reference to waste being disposed of is a reference to its being submitted to any of those operations;

"disposal licence" and "disposal authority" have the meaning given by sections 3(1) and 30(2) to (2D) respectively of the Control of Pollution Act 1974;[13]

"enforcing authority" and "local enforcing authority" have the meaning given by section 1(7) and (8) of the 1990 Act;[14]

"exempt activity" means any of the activities set out in Schedule 3;[15]

"inland waters"—

(a) in England and Wales, has the meaning given by section 221(1) of the Water Resources Act 1991;[16]

(b) in Scotland, has the meaning given by section 30A of the Control of Pollution Act 1974[17] except that it includes any loch or pond whether or not it discharges into a river or watercourse;

---

[1] P.60 above.
[2] The Control of Pollution (Amendment) Act 1989 is at p.71 above; see the definition of "prescribed" in s.9(1), p.80 above.
[3] The Environmental Protection Act 1990 is at p.83 above.
[4] P.116 above.
[5] P.83 above.
[6] P.542 above.
[7] OJ No. L 194, 25.7.1975, p.39.
[8] OJ No. L 078, 26.3.1991, p.32.
[9] OJ No. L 377, 31.12.1991, p.48.
[10] P.721 below.
[11] Annex I and II of the following joint circular sets out guidance on the definition of Directive waste:

Joint Circular: Environmental Protection Act 1990: Part II, Waste Management Licensing, the Framework Directive on Waste. Department of the Environment Circular 11/94, Welsh Office Circular 26/94, Scottish Office Environment Department Circular 10/94 of 19 April 1994.
[12] P.721 below.
[13] 1974 c.40; s.30(2A) to (2D) is inserted by para. 11(b) of sch.2 to the Waste Regulation and Disposal (Authorities) Order 1985, S.I. 1985/1884.
[14] P.90 above.
[15] P.697 below.
[16] P.313 above.
[17] P.18 above.

"operational land" has the meaning given by sections 263 and 264 of the Town and Country Planning Act 1990[1] or, in Scotland, section 211 and 212 of the Town and Country Planning (Scotland) Act 1972;[2]

"recovery" means any of the operations listed in Part IV of Schedule 4,[3] and any reference to waste being recovered is a reference to its being submitted to any of those operations;

"scrap metal" has the meaning given by section 9(2) of the Scrap Metal Dealers Act 1964;[4]

"special waste" has the meaning given in regulation 2 of the Special Waste Regulations 1966,[5] except that it does not include radioactive waste within the meaning of the Radioactive Substances Act 1993;[6,7]

"waste" means Directive waste;

"waste management licence" has the meaning given by section 35(1) of the 1990 Act,[8] and "site licence" has the meaning given by section 35(12) of the 1990 Act;

"waste oil" means any mineral-based lubricating or industrial oil which has become unfit for the use for which it was originally intended and, in particular, used combustion engine oil, gearbox oil, mineral lubricating oil, oil for turbines and hydraulic oil;

"waste regulation authority", "waste disposal authority" and "waste collection authority" have the meaning given by section 30 of the 1990 Act;[9] and

"work" includes preparatory work.

(4) Any reference in these Regulations to carrying on business as a scrap metal dealer has the meaning given by section 9(1) of the Scrap Metal Dealers Act 1964, and any reference, in relation to Scotland, to carrying on business as a metal dealer has the meaning given by section 37(2) of the Civic Government (Scotland) Act 1982.[10]

(5) Regulations 13, 14 and 15, and Schedule 4, shall apply in relation to land in the area of a waste disposal authority in Scotland which is occupied by the authority as if—

(a) references to a waste management licence were references to a resolution under section 54 of the 1990 Act;

(b) references to an application being made for a waste management licence were references to consideration being given to passing such a resolution;

(c) references to granting or issuing a waste management licence were references to passing, and references to rejecting an application were references to not passing, such a resolution;

(d) references to the terms or conditions of a waste management licence were references to the terms or conditions specified in such a resolution; and

(e) references to varying or revoking a waste management licence under section 37 or 38 of the 1990 Act were references to varying or rescinding such a resolution under section 54(8) of that Act.

(6) These Regulations do not extend to Northern Ireland.

(7) The provisions of section 160 of the 1990 Act[11] shall apply to—

(a) the service or giving of any notice required or authorised by these Regulations to be served on or given to a person; or

(b) the sending or giving of any document required or authorised by these Regulations to be sent or given to a person,

[1] 1990 c.8.
[2] 1972 c.52.
[3] P.722 below.
[4] 1964 c.69.
[5] P.766 below.
[6] "Radioactive waste" is defined in s.2 of the 1993 Act, p.384 above.

[7] This definition substituted by S.I. 1996/972, reg.25, sch.3. This amendment came into force on 1 September 1996: reg.1(1).
[8] P.119 above.
[9] P.113 above.
[10] 1982 c.45.
[11] P.207 above.

as if the service or giving of any such notice or, as the case may be, the sending or giving of any such document, was required or authorised by or under that Act.[1]

*Application for a waste management licence or for the surrender or transfer to a waste management licence*

**2.** (1) An application for a waste management licence[2] shall be made in writing.

(2) An application for the surrender of a site licence[3] shall be made in writing and shall, subject to paragraphs (3) and (4) below, include the information and be accompanied by the evidence prescribed by Schedule 1.[4]

(3) Nothing in paragraph (2) above shall require the information prescribed by paragraphs 3 to 6 of Schedule 1 to be provided to the waste regulation authority[5] if the information has previously been provided by the applicant to the authority or a predecessor of the authority in connection with a waste management licence, or a disposal licence[6] under section 5 of the Control of Pollution Act 1974, in respect of the site in question or any part of it.

(4) Insofar as the information prescribed by paragraphs 4, 5(a) and 6(a) of Schedule 1 relates to activities carried on, or works carried out, at the site at a time prior to the applicant's first involvement with the site, paragraph (2) above only requires that information to be included in the application so far as it is known to either the applicant or, where the applicant is a partnership or body corporate, to any of the partners or, as the case may be, to any director, manager, secretary or other similar officer of the body corporate.

(5) An application for the transfer of a waste management licence shall be made in writing and shall include the information prescribed by Schedule 2.[7]

*Relevant offences*

**3.** An offence is relevant for the purposes of section 74(3)(a) of the 1990 Act[8] if it is an offence under any of the following enactments—

(a)  section 22 of the Public Health (Scotland) Act 1897;[9]

(b)  section 95(1) of the Public Health Act 1936;[10]

(c)  section 3, 5(6), 16(4), 18(2), 31(1), 32(1), 34(5),[11] 78, 92(6)[12] or 93(3)[13] of the Control of Pollution Act 1974;

(d)  section 2 of the Refuse Disposal (Amenity) Act 1978;[14]

(e)  the Control of Pollution (Special Waste) Regulations 1980;[15]

(f)  section 9(1) of the Food and Environment Protection Act 1985;[16]

(g)  the Transfrontier Shipment of Hazardous Waste Regulations 1988;[17]

(h)  the Merchant Shipping (Prevention of Pollution by Garbage) Regulations 1988;[18]

(i)  section 1,[19] 5,[20] 6(9)[21] or 7(3)[22] of the Control of Pollution (Amendment) Act 1989;

---

[1] Para.7 added by S.I. 1995/288, reg.3(2). This amendment came into force on 1 April 1995: reg.1(1).

[2] "Waste management licence" has the meaning given by s.35(1) of the 1990 Act, p.119 above: reg.1(3) above.

[3] "Site licence" has the meaning given by s.35(12) of the 1990 Act, p.120 above: reg.1(3) above.

[4] P.695 below.

[5] "Waste regulation authority" has the meaning given by s.30 of the 1990 Act, p.113 above: reg.1(3) above.

[6] "Disposal licence" defined by reg.1(3) above.

[7] P.696 below.

[8] P.158 above.

[9] 1897 c.38.

[10] 1936 c.49.

[11] P.30 above.

[12] P.55 above.

[13] P.56 above.

[14] 1978 c.3.

[15] S.I. 1980/1709; these regulations were revoked, subject to a saving, by S.I. 1996/972, reg.26, which came into force on 1 September 1996: reg.1(1).

[16] 1985 c.48.

[17] S.I. 1988/1562; these regulations were revoked, subject to a saving, by S.I. 1994/1137, reg.21, which came into force on 6 May 1994: reg.1.

[18] S.I. 1988/2292.

[19] P.72 above.

[20] P.76 above.

[21] P.78 above.

[22] P.79 above.

(j)   section 107,[1] 118(4)[2] or 175(1)[3] of the Water Act 1989;

(k)   section 23(1),[4] 33,[5] 34(6),[6] 44,[7] 47(6),[8] 57(5),[9] 59(5),[10] 63(2),[11] 69(9), 70(4), 71(3) or 80(4)[12] of the 1990 Act;

(l)   section 85,[13] 202[14] or 206[15] of the Water Resources Act 1991;

(m)   section 33 of the Clean Air Act 1993;[16]

(n)   the Transfrontier Shipment of Waste Regulations 1994;[17]

(o)   the Special Waste Regulations 1996.[18]

### Technical competence

**4.** (1)  Subject to paragraph (2) and regulation 5 below, a person is technically competent for the purposes of section 74(3)(b) of the 1990 Act[19] in relation to a facility of a type listed in Table 1 below if, and only if, he is the holder of one of the certificates awarded by the Waste Management Industry Training and Advisory Board specified in that Table as being a relevant certificate of technical competence for that type of facility.

**Table 1**

| Type of facility | Relevant certificate of technical competence |
| --- | --- |
| A landfill site[20] which receives special waste.[21] | Managing landfill operations: special waste (level 4). |
| A landfill site which receives biodegradable waste or which for some other reason requires substantial engineering works to protect the environment but which in either case does not receive any special waste. | 1. Managing landfill operations: biodegradable waste (level 4); or<br><br>2. Managing landfill operations: special waste (level 4). |
| Any other type of landfill site with a total capacity exceeding 50,000 cubic metres. | 1. Landfill operations: inert waste (level 3); or<br><br>2. Managing landfill operations: biodegradable waste (level 4); or<br>3. Managing landfill operations: special waste (level 4). |
| A site on which waste is burned in an incinerator designed to incinerate waste at a rate of more than 50 kilograms per hour but less than 1 tonne per hour. | Managing incinerator operations: special waste (level 4). |

[1] S.107 of the 1989 Act has been replaced by ss.85–87 of the Water Resources Act 1991, p.273 above.
[2] S.118(4) of the 1989 Act has been replaced by s.202(4) of the Water Resources Act 1991, p.303 above.
[3] S.175 of the 1989 Act has been replaced by s.206 of the Water Resources Act 1991, p.306 above.
[4] P.108 above.
[5] P.116 above.
[6] P.118 above.
[7] P.134 above.
[8] P.141 above.
[9] P.148 above.
[10] P.149 above.
[11] P.152 above.
[12] P.191 above.
[13] P.273 above.
[14] P.303 above.
[15] P.306 above.
[16] P.354 above.
[17] P.741 below; this paragraph added by S.I. 1994/1137, reg.19(3). This amendment came into force on 6 May 1994: reg.1.
[18] P.763 below; this paragraph added by S.I. 1996/972, reg.25, sch.3. This amendment came into force on 1 September 1996: reg.1(1).
[19] P.158 above. See also:

The Waste Management Licensing (Amendment etc.) Regulations 1995, reg.4, p.751 below;
The Waste Management Regulations 1996, reg.4, p.759 below;
The Waste Management Licensing (Scotland) Regulations 1996, reg.2, p.761 below.
[20] "Landfill site" defined by paragraph (3) below.
[21] "Special waste" defined by reg.1(3), p.677 above.

| Type of facility | Relevant certificate of technical competence |
|---|---|
| A waste treatment plant where biodegradable, clinical[1] or special waste is subjected to a chemical or physical process.[2] | Managing treatment operations: special waste (level 4). |
| A waste treatment plant where waste other than biodegradable, clinical or special waste is subjected to a chemical or physical process.[2] | 1. Treatment operations: inert waste (level 3); or 2. Managing treatment operations: special waste (level 4). |
| A transfer station[3] where— (a) biodegradable, clinical or special waste is dealt with; and (b) the total quantity of waste at the station at any time exceeds 5 cubic metres. | Managing transfer operations: special waste (level 4). |
| A transfer station where— (a) no biodegradable, clinical or special waste is dealt with; and (b) the total quantity of waste at the station at any time exceeds 50 cubic metres. | 1. Transfer operations: inert waste (level 3); or 2. Managing transfer operations: special waste (level 4). |
| A civic amenity site.[4] | Civic amenity site operations (level 3). |

(2) Paragraph (1) above does not apply in relation to a facility which is used exclusively for the purposes of—

(a) carrying on business as a scrap metal dealer[5] or, in Scotland, as a metal dealer; or

(b) dismantling motor vehicles.

(3) In this regulation—

"civic amenity site" means a place provided under section 1 of the Refuse Disposal (Amenity) Act 1978[6] or by virtue of section 51(1)(b) of the 1990 Act;[7]

"clinical waste" has the meaning given by regulation 1(2) of the Controlled Waste Regulations 1992;[8] and

"landfill site" does not include a site used only for the burial of dead domestic pets;[9]

"transfer station" means a facility where waste is unloaded in order to permit its preparation for further transport for treatment, keeping or disposal elsewhere.

*Technical competence—transitional provisions*

**5.** (1) Subject to paragraph (4),[10] where before 10th August 1994 a person has applied to the Waste Management Industry Training and Advisory Board for a certificate of technical competence and at any time in the 12 months ending on that date he acted as the manager of a facility of a type

[1] "Clinical waste" has the meaning given by S.I. 1992/588, reg.1(2), p.676 above: paragraph (3) below.
[2] This description substituted by S.I. 1996/634, reg.2(2)(a). This amendment came into force on 1 April 1996: reg.1(1).
[3] "Transfer station" defined by paragraph (3) below.
[4] "Civil amenity site" defined by paragraph (3) below.
[5] "Scrap metal" defined by reg.1(3), p.677 above; for "scrap metal dealer" see reg.1(4) above.
[6] 1978 c.3; s.1(1) is prospectively repealed by s.1(8), S.1(3) and (4) is modified for certain purposes by para.14(1), and s.1(7) is amended by para.14(4), of sch.2 to the Waste

Regulation and Disposal (Authorities) Order 1985, S.I. 1985/1884, (paragraph 14(1) of that Order is amended by article 5 of the Local Government Reorganisation (Miscellaneous Provision) (No.5) Order 1986, S.I. 1986/564).
[7] P.144 above.
[8] P.662 above.
[9] This definition added by S.I. 1996/634, reg.2(3)(b). This amendment came into force on 1 April 1996: reg.1(1).
[10] Words "Subject to paragraph (4)," added by S.I. 1996/634, reg.2(3)(a). This amendment came into force on 1 April 1996: reg.1(1).

listed in Table 1 above for which the certificate is a relevant certificate, then, until 10th August 1999, regulation 4 shall not apply to him in relation to either—

(a) any facility of that type; or

(b) a facility of any other type if—

    (i) the certificate is a relevant certificate for that other type of facility; and

    (ii) the entry for that other type of facility appears, in Table 1 above, after the entry in that Table for the type of facility in respect of which he acted as the manager,

and he shall be treated as technically competent for the purposes of section 74(3)(b) of the 1990 Act[1] in relation to any such facility.

(2) Subject to paragraph (4),[2] where a person is 55 or over on 10th August 1994 and in the 10 years ending on that date he has had at least 5 years experience as the manager of a facility of a type listed in table 1 above, then, until 10th August 2004, regulation 4 shall not apply to him in relation to either—

(a) any facility of that type; or

(b) a facility of any other type if each certificate which is a relevant certificate for the type of facility in relation to which he has had such experience as manager is also a relevant certificate for that other type of facility,

and he shall be treated as technically competent for the purposes of section 74(3)(b) of the 1990 Act in relation to any such facility.

(3) A person shall be treated as the manager of a facility for the purposes of paragraph (1) or (2) above if at the relevant time he was the manager of activities which were carried on at that facility and which were authorised by a disposal licence[3] under section 5 of the Control of Pollution Act 1974,[4] a resolution under section 11 of that Act or under section 54 of the 1990 Act, or a waste management licence.[5]

(4) Subject to paragraphs (6) and (7), in their application in relation to a person mentioned in paragraph (5), paragraphs (1) and (2) shall apply as if the following dates were substituted for the dates in those paragraphs which are specified—

(a) in paragraph (1)

    (i) for "10th August 1994", "1st October 1996";

    (ii) for "10th August 1999", "1st October 2001"; and

(b) in paragraph (2),

    (i) for "10th August 1994", "1st October 1996";

    (ii) for "10th August 2004", "1st October 2006".

(5) The person mentioned in paragraph (4) is the manager of a facility at which activities were authorised by a resolution under section 11 of the Control of Pollution Act 1974.

(6) Paragraph (4) does not apply to a person who is to be treated as technically competent by virtue of other provisions than those in that paragraph.

(7) Paragraph (4) does not apply in Scotland.[6]

*Notice of appeal*

**6.** (1) A person who wishes to appeal to the Secretary of State under section 43[7] or 66(5)[8] of the 1990 Act (appeals to the Secretary of State from decisions with respect to waste management licences

---

[1] P.158 above. See also the Waste Management Regulations 1996, reg.5, p.760 below.
[2] Words "Subject to paragraph (4)," added by S.I. 1996/634, reg.2(3)(b). This amendment came into force on 1 April 1996: reg.1(1).
[3] "Disposal licence" defined by reg.1(3), p.676 above.
[4] 1974 c.40.

[5] "Waste management licence" has the meaning given by s.35(1) of the 1990 Act, p.119 above.
[6] Paragraphs (4)–(7) added by S.I. 1996/634, reg.2(3)(c). This amendment came into force on 1 April 1996: reg.1(1).
[7] P.133 above.
[8] P.155 above.

or from determinations that information is not commercially confidential) shall do so by notice in writing.

(2) The notice shall be accompanied by—

(a) a statement of the grounds of appeal;

(b) where the appeal relates to an application for a waste management licence or for the modification, surrender or transfer of a waste management licence, a copy of the appellant's application and any supporting documents;

(c) where the appeal relates to a determination under section 66(2) or (4) of the 1990 Act that information is not commercially confidential, the information in question;

(d) where the appeal relates to an existing waste management licence (including a waste management licence which has been suspended or revoked), a copy of that waste management licence;

(e) a copy of any correspondence relevant to the appeal;

(f) a copy of any other document relevant to the appeal including, in particular, any relevant consent, determination, notice, planning permission, established use certificate or certificate of lawful use or development; and

(g) a statement indicating whether the appellant wishes the appeal to be in the form of a hearing or to be determined on the basis of written representations.

(3) The appellant shall serve a copy of his notice of appeal on the waste regulation authority[1] together with copies of the documents mentioned in paragraph (2) above.

(4) If the appellant wishes to withdraw an appeal, he shall do so by notifying the Secretary of State in writing and shall send a copy of that notification to the waste regulation authority.

*Time limit for making an appeal*

7. (1) Subject to paragraph (2) below, notice of appeal shall be given—

(a) in the case of an appeal under section 43 of the 1990 Act,[2] before the expiry of the period of 6 months beginning with—

(i) the date of the decision which is the subject of the appeal; or

(ii) the date on which the waste regulation authority is deemed by section 36(9),[3] 37(6),[4] 39(10)[5] or 40(6)[6] of the 1990 Act to have rejected the application;

(b) in the case of an appeal under section 66(5) of the 1990 Act,[7] before the expiry of the period of 21 days beginning with the date on which the determination which is the subject of the appeal is notified to the person concerned.

(2) The Secretary of State may in relation to an appeal under section 43 of the 1990 Act at any time allow notice of appeal to be given after the expiry of the period mentioned in paragraph (1)(a) above.

*Reports of hearings*

8. The person hearing an appeal under section 43(2)(c) of the 1990 Act[8] shall, unless he has been appointed to determine the appeal under section 114(1)(a) of the Environment Act 1995,[9] make a written report to the Secretary of State which shall include his conclusions and recommendations or his reasons for not making any recommendations.

---

[1] "Waste regulation authority" has the meaning given by s.30 of the 1990 Act, p.113 above.
[2] P.133 above.
[3] P.123 above.
[4] P.126 above.
[5] P.130 above.
[6] P.131 above.
[7] P.155 above.
[8] P.133 above; s.43(2) is applied by s.66(6) to appeals under s.66(5).
[9] P.489 above; words "section 114(1)(a) of the Environment Act 1995" substituted by S.I. 1996/593, reg.3, sch.2, para.10(2). This amendment came into force on 1 April 1996: reg.1.

*Notification of determination*

**9.** (1) The Secretary of State or other person determining an appeal shall notify the appellant in writing of his decision and of his reasons.

(2) If the Secretary of State determines an appeal after a hearing under section 43(2)(c) of the 1990 Act,[1] he shall provide the appellant with a copy of any report made to him under regulation 8.

(3) The Secretary of State or other person determining an appeal shall, at the same time as notifying the appellant of his decision, send the waste regulation authority[2] a copy of any document sent to the appellant under this regulation.

*Particulars to be entered in public registers*

**10.** (1) Subject to sections 65 and 66 of the 1990 Act[3] and regulation 11, a register maintained by a waste regulation authority[4] under section 64(1) of the 1990 Act shall contain full particulars of—

(a) current or recently current waste management licences[5] ("licences") granted by the authority and any associated working plans;

(b) current or recently current applications to the authority for licences, or for the transfer or modification of licences, including details of—

    (i) documents submitted by applicants containing supporting information;

    (ii) written representations considered by the authority under section 36(4)(b),[6] (6)(b) or 7(b) or 37(5)[7] of the 1990 Act;

    (iii) decisions of the Secretary of State under section 36(5), or, in Scotland, section 36(6), of the 1990 Act;

    (iv) notices by the authority rejecting applications;

    (v) emergencies resulting in the postponement of references under section 37(5)(a) of the 1990 Act;

(c) notices issued by the authority under section 37 of the 1990 Act[8] effecting the modification of licences;

(d) notices issued by the authority under section 38 of the 1990 Act[9] effecting the revocation or suspension of licences or imposing requirements on the holders of licences;

(e) notices of appeal under section 43 of the 1990 Act[10] relating to decisions of the authority and other documents relating to such appeals served on or sent to the authority under regulation 6(3) or (4) or 9(3);

(f) convictions of holders of licences granted by the authority for any offence under Part II of the 1990 Act (whether or not in relation to a licence) including the name of the offender, the date of conviction, the penalty imposed and the name of the Court;

(g) reports produced by the authority in discharge of any functions under section 42 of the 1990 Act,[11] including details of—

    (i) *This sub-paragraph repealed, in respect of Scotland only, by S.I. 1996/973, reg.2, sch., para.17(2). This amendment came into force on 1 April 1996: reg.1. In respect of England and Wales, this sub-paragraph relates to s.42(2) of the Environmental Protection Act 1990 which was repealed on 1 April 1996: S.I. 1996/186.*

    (ii) remedial or preventive action taken by the authority under section 42(3) of the 1990 Act;

    (iii) notices issued by the authority under section 42(5) of the 1990 Act;

---

[1] P.133 above.
[2] "Waste regulation authority" has the meaning given by s.30 of the 1990 Act, p.113 above.
[3] P.154 above.
[4] "Waste regulation authority" has the meaning given by s.30 of the 1990 Act, p.113 above.
[5] "Waste management licence" has the meaning given by

s.35(1) of the 1990 Act, p.119 above.
[6] P.122 above.
[7] P.126 above.
[8] P.125 above.
[9] P.127 above.
[10] P.133 above.
[11] P.131 above.

(h) any monitoring information relating to the carrying on of any activity under a licence granted by the authority which was obtained by the authority as a result of its own monitoring or was furnished to the authority in writing by virtue of any condition of the licence or section 71(2) of the 1990 Act;[1]

(i) directions given by the Secretary of State to the authority under section 35(7),[2] 37(3),[3] 38(7),[4] 42(8),[5] 50(9), 54(11) or (15), 58[6] or 66(7)[7] of the 1990 Act;

(j) any summary prepared by the authority of the amount of special waste[8] produced or disposed of in their area;

(k) registers and records provided to the authority under regulation 13(5) or 14(1) of the Control of Pollution (Special Waste) Regulations 1980 or regulation 15(5) or 16(1) of the Special Waste Regulations 1996;[9]

(l) applications to the authority under section 39 of the 1990 Act[10] for the surrender of licences, including details of—

  (i) documents submitted by applicants containing supporting information and evidence;

  (ii) information and evidence obtained under section 39(4) of the 1990 Act;

  (iii) written representations considered by the authority under section 39(7)(b) or (8)(b) of the 1990 Act;

  (iv) decisions by the Secretary of State under section 39(7) or (8) of the 1990 Act; and

  (v) notices of determination and certificates of completion issued under section 39(9) of the 1990 Act;

(m) written reports under section 70(3) of the 1990 Act by inspectors appointed by the authority or written reports under section 109(2) of the Environment Act 1995[11] by persons authorised by the authority under section 108(1) or (2) of that Act where the articles or substances seized and rendered harmless are waste;[12]

(n) in Scotland, resolutions made by the authority under section 54 of the 1990 Act, including details of—

  (i) proposals made in relation to land in the area of the authority by a waste disposal authority under section 54(4) of the 1990 Act;

  (ii) statements made and written representations considered by the authority under section 54(4) of the 1990 Act;

  (iii) requests made to, and disagreements with, the authority which are referred to the Secretary of State under section 54(7) of the 1990 Act and his decisions on such references;

  (iv) emergencies resulting in the postponement of references under section 54(4) of the 1990 Act.

(2) The register shall also contain the following—

(a) where an inspector appointed by the authority exercises any power under section 69(3) of the 1990 Act, a record showing when the power was exercised and indicating what information was obtained, and what action was taken, on that occasion;

(aa) where a person authorised by the authority exercises any power under section 108(4) of the Environment Act 1995[13] in connection with the authority's functions under Part II of the

[1] P.156 above.
[2] P.119 above.
[3] P.125 above.
[4] P.128 above.
[5] P.133 above.
[6] P.148 above.
[7] P.156 above.
[8] "Special waste" defined by reg.1(3), p.677 above.
[9] P.774 below; words "or regulation 15(5) or 16(1) of the Special Waste Regulations 1996" added by S.I. 1996/972, reg.25, sch.3. This amendment came into force on 1 September 1996: reg.1(1).
[10] P.129 above.
[11] P.486 above.
[12] Words "or written reports ... waste" added by S.I. 1996/593, reg.3, sch.2, para.10(3)(a). This amendment came into force on 1 April 1996: reg.1.
[13] P.480 above.

Environmental Protection Act 1990, a record showing when the power was exercised and indicating what information was obtained, and what action was taken, on that occasion;[1]

(b) where any information is excluded from the register by virtue of section 66 of the 1990 Act[2] and the information shows whether or not there is compliance with any condition of a waster management licence, a statement based on that information indicating whether or not there is compliance with that condition.

(3) A register maintained under section 64(4) of the 1990 Act[3] by a waste collection authority[4] in England or Wales[5] shall contain full particulars of the following information contained in any register maintained under section 64(1) of the 1990 Act, to the extent that it relates to the treatment, keeping or disposal[6] of controlled waste in the area of the authority—

(a) current or recently current waste management licences;[7]

(b) notices issued under section 37 of the 1990 Act[8] effecting the modification of waste management licences;

(c) notices issued under section 38 of the 1990 Act[9] effecting the revocation or suspension of waste management licences;

(d) certificates of completion issued under section 39(9) of the 1990 Act.[10]

(4) For the purposes of this regulation, waste management licences are "recently" current for the period of twelve months after they cease to be in force, and applications for waste management licences, or for the transfer or modification of such licences, are "recently" current if they relate to a waste management licence which is current or recently current or, in the case of an application which is rejected, for the period of twelve months beginning with the date on which the waste regulation authority gives notice of rejection or, as the case may be, on which the application is deemed by section 36(9),[11] 37(6)[12] or 40(6)[13] of the 1990 Act to have been rejected.

*Information to be excluded or removed from a register*

**11.** (1) Nothing in regulation 10(1)(g) or (m) or (2) shall require a register maintained by a waste regulation authority[14] under section 64(1) of the 1990 Act[15] to contain information relating to, or to anything which is the subject-matter of, any criminal proceedings (including prospective proceedings) at any time before those proceedings are finally disposed of.

(2) Nothing in regulation 10 shall require a register maintained by a waste regulation authority or waste collection authority[16] under section 64 of the 1990 Act to contain—

(a) any such monitoring information as is mentioned in regulation 10(1)(h) after 4 years have elapsed from that information being entered in the register; or

(b) any information which has been superseded by later information after 4 years have elapsed from that later information being entered in the register.

*Mobile plant*

**12.** (1) Plant of the following descriptions, if it is designed to move or be moved by any means from place to place with a view to being used at each such place or, if not so designed, is readily capable of so moving or being so moved, but no other plant, shall be treated as being mobile plant for the purposes of Part II of the 1990 Act—

---

[1] Sub-paragraph (aa) added by S.I. 1996/593, rg.3, sch.2, para.10(3)(b). This amendment came into force on 1 April 1996: reg.1.

[2] P.154 above.

[3] P.153 above.

[4] "Waste collection authority" has the meaning given by s.30 of the 1990 Act, p.113 above.

[5] Words "or Wales" inserted, and former words "which is not a waste regulation authority" omitted by S.I. 1996/593, reg.3, sch.2, para.10(3)(c).

[6] "Disposal" defined by reg.1(3), p.676 above.

[7] "Waste management licence" has the meaning given by

s.35(1) of the 1990 Act, p.119 above.

[8] P.125 above.

[9] P.127 above.

[10] P.130 above.

[11] P.123 above.

[12] P.126 above.

[13] P.131 above.

[14] "Waste regulation authority" has the meaning given by s.30 of the 1990 Act, p.113 above.

[15] P.152 above.

[16] "Waste collection authority" has the meaning given by s.30 of the 1990 Act, p.113 above.

(a) an incinerator which is an exempt incinerator for the purposes of Section 5.1 of Schedule 1 to the 1991 Regulations;[1]

(b) plant for—

    (i) the recovery, by filtration or heat treatment, of waste oil[2] from electrical equipment; or

    (ii) the destruction by dechlorination of waste polychlorinated biphenyls or terphenyls (PCBs or PCTs);

(c) plant for the vitrification of waste;

(d) plant for the treatment of microwave of clinical waste;

(e) plant for the treatment of waste soil.[3]

(2) For the purposes of paragraph (1)(d) above, "clinical waste" has the meaning given by regulation 1(2) of the Controlled Waste Regulations 1992.[4,5]

*Health at work*

**13.** No conditions shall be imposed in any waste management licence[6] for the purpose only of securing the health of persons at work (within the meaning of Part I of the Health and Safety at Work etc. Act 1974[7]).

*Waste oils*

**14.** (1) Where a waste management licence[8] or disposal licence[9] authorises the regeneration of waste oil,[10] it shall include conditions which ensure that base oils derived from regeneration do not constitute a toxic and dangerous waste and do not contain PCBs or PCTs at all or do not contain them in concentrations beyond a specified maximum limit which is no case is to exceed 50 parts per million.

(2) Where a waste management licence or disposal licence authorises the keeping of waste oil, it shall include conditions which ensure that it is not mixed with toxic and dangerous waste or PCBs or PCTs.

(3) In this regulation—

"PCBs or PCTs" means polychlorinated biphenyls, polychlorinated terphenyls and mixtures containing one or both of such substances; and

"toxic and dangerous waste" has the meaning given by Article 1(b) of Council Directive 78/319/EEC.[11]

*Groundwater*

*Note:* This regulation transposes certain provisions of Council Directive 80/68/EEC, on the protection of groundwater against pollution caused by certain dangerous substances, into British law. Annex 7 of the following joint circular sets out guidance on this directive:

Joint Circular: Environmental Protection Act 1990: Part II, Waste Management Licensing, the Framework Directive on Waste. Department of the Environment Circular 11/94, Welsh Office Circular 26/94, Scottish Office Environment Department Circular 10/94 of 19 April 1994.

Regulation 15(12) provides that expressions which are used both in this regulation and the directive have the same meaning as in the directive. Annex 7 of the joint circular refers to the definitions of "groundwater", "pollution", "direct discharge" and "indirect discharge". The annex to the directive

---

[1] P.583 above.
[2] "Waste oil" defined by reg.1(3), p.677 above.
[3] Sub-paragraph (e) addd by S.I. 1996/634, reg.2(4). This amendment came into force on 1 April 1996: reg.1(1).
[4] P.662 above.
[5] This regulation substituted by S.I. 1995/288, reg.3(3). This amendment came into force on 1 April 1995: reg.1(1).
[6] "Waste management licence" has the meaning given by

s.35(1) of the 1990 Act, p.119 above.
[7] 1974 c.37; see s.52(1) for the meaning of "at work".
[8] "Waste management licence" has the meaning given by s.35(1) of the 1990 Act, p.119 above.
[9] "Disposal licence" defined by reg.1(3), p.676 above.
[10] "Waste oil" defined by reg.1(3), p.677 above.
[11] OJ No. L 084, 31.3.1978, p.43, as amended by Council Directive 91/692/EEC (OJ No. L 377, 31.12.1991, p.48).

sets out the families and groups of substances in list I and list II. Annex 7 of the joint circular includes reference to the annex of the directive.

**15.** (1) Where a waste regulation authority[1] proposes to issue a waste management licence[2] authorising—

(a) any disposal[3] or tipping for the purpose of disposal of a substance in list I which might lead to an indirect discharge into groundwater of such a substance;

(b) any disposal or tipping for the purpose of disposal of a substance in list II which might lead to an indirect discharge into groundwater of such a substance;

(c) a direct discharge into groundwater of a substance in list I; or

(d) a direct discharge into groundwater of a substance in list II,

the authority shall ensure that the proposed activities are subjected to prior investigation.

(2) The prior investigation referred to in paragraph (1) above shall include examination of the hydrogeological conditions of the area concerned, the possible purifying powers of the soil and sub-soil and the risk of pollution and alteration of the quality of the groundwater from the discharge and shall establish whether the discharge of substances into groundwater is a satisfactory solution from the point of view of the environment.

(3) A waste management licence shall not be issued in any case within paragraph (1) above until the waste regulation authority has checked that the groundwater, and in particular its quality, will undergo the requisite surveillance.

(4) In a case within paragraph (1)(a) or (c) above—

(a) where the waste regulation authority is satisfied, in the light of the investigation, that the groundwater which may be affected by a direct or indirect discharge of a substance in list I is permanently unsuitable for other uses, especially domestic and agricultural, the waste management licence may only be issued if the authority is also satisfied that—

(i) the presence of that substance once discharged into groundwater will not impede exploitation of ground resources; and

(ii) all technical precautions will be taken to ensure that no substance in list I can reach other aquatic systems or harm other ecosystems; and

(b) where the waste regulation authority is not satisfied, in the light of the investigation, that the groundwater which may be affected by such a discharge is permanently unsuitable for other uses, especially domestic and agricultural, a waste management licence may only be issued if it is made subject to such conditions as the authority, in the light of the investigations, is satisfied will ensure the observance of all technical precautions necessary to prevent any discharges into groundwater of substances in list I.

(5) In a case within paragraph (1)(b) or (d) above, if a waste management licence is issued, it shall be issued subject to such conditions as the waste regulation authority, in the light of the investigation, is satisfied will ensure the observance of all technical precautions for preventing groundwater pollution by substances in list II.

(6) Where a waste management licence is granted in any case within paragraph (1)(a) or (b) above, the licence shall be granted on such terms and subject to such conditions as specify—

(a) the place where any disposal or tipping which might lead to a discharge into groundwater of any substances in list I or II is to be done;

(b) the methods of disposal or tipping which may be used;

(c) the essential precautions which must be taken, paying particular attention to the nature and concentration of the substances present in the matter to be disposed of or tipped, the

[1] "Waste regulation authority" has the meaning given by s.30 of the 1990 Act, p.113 above.
[2] "Waste management licence" has the meaning given by
s.35(1) of the 1990 Act, p.119 above.
[3] "Disposal" defined by reg.1(3), p.676 above.

characteristics of the receiving environment and the proximity of the water catchment areas, in particular those for drinking, thermal and mineral water;

(d) the maximum quantity permissible, during one or more specified periods of time, of matter containing substances in list I or II and, where possible, of those substances themselves, to be disposed of or tipped and the appropriate requirements as to the concentration of those substances;

(e) the technical precautions required by paragraph (4)(b) or (5) above;

(f) if necessary, the measures for monitoring the groundwater, and in particular its quality.

(7) Where a waste management licence is granted in any case within paragraph (1)(c) or (d) above, the licence shall be granted on such terms and subject to such conditions as specify—

(a) the place where any substances in list I or II are to be discharged into groundwater;

(b) the method of discharge which may be used;

(c) the essential precautions which must be taken, paying particular attention to the nature and concentration of the substances present in the effluents, the characteristics of the receiving environment and the proximity of the water catchment areas, in particular those for drinking, thermal and mineral water;

(d) the maximum quantity of a substance in list I or II permissible in an effluent during one or more specified periods of time and the appropriate requirements as to the concentration of those substances;

(e) the arrangements enabling effluents discharged into groundwater to be monitored;

(f) if necessary, the measures for monitoring the groundwater, and in particular its quality.

(8) Any authorisation granted by a waste management licence for an activity within paragraph (1) above shall be granted for a limited period only.

(9) Any authorisation granted by a waste management licence for an activity within paragraph (1) above shall be reviewed at least every 4 years.

(10) Waste regulation authorities shall review all waste management licences current on 1st May 1994 which authorise any activity within paragraph (1) above and shall, so far as may be necessary to give effect to Council Directive 80/68/EEC,[1] exercise their powers under sections 37 and 38 of the 1990 Act[2] (variation and revocation etc. of waste management licences) in relation to any such authorisation.

(11) The foregoing provisions of this regulation apply, with any necessary modifications, to the granting or review by disposal authorities of disposal licences under Part I of the Control of Pollution Act 1974[3] as they apply to the granting or review by waste regulation authorities of waste management licences.

(12) Expressions used both in this regulation and in Council Directive 80/68/EEC have for the purposes of this regulation the same meaning as in that Directive.

*Exclusion of activities under other control regimes from waste management licensing*

16. (1) Subject to paragraph (2) below, section 33(1)(a), (b) and (c) of the 1990 Act[4] shall not apply in relation to the carrying on of any of the following activities—

(a) the deposit in or on land,[5] recovery[6] or disposal[7] of waste[8] under an authorisation granted under Part I of the 1990 Act where the activity is or forms part of a process designated for central control under section 2(4) of the 1990 Act;[9]

---

[1] OJ No. L 020, 26.1.80, p.43.
[2] P.125 above.
[3] 1974 c.40.
[4] P.116 above.
[5] Words "deposit in or on land," inserted by S.I. 1995/288, reg.3(4). This amendment came into force on 1 April 1995:

reg.1(1).
[6] "Recovery" defined by reg.1(3), p.677 above.
[7] "Disposal" defined by reg.1(3), p.676 above.
[8] "Waste" defined by reg.1(3), p.677 above.
[9] P.91 above.

(b) the disposal of waste under an authorisation granted under Part I of the 1990 Act where the activity is or forms part of a process within paragraph (a) of Part B of Section 5.1 (incineration) of Schedule 1 to the 1991 Regulations[1] insofar as the activity results in releases of substances into the air;

(c) the disposal of liquid waste under a consent under Chapter II of Part III of the Water Resources Act 1991[2] or under Part II of the Control of Pollution Act 1974;[3] and

(d) the recovery or disposal of waste where the activity is or forms part of an operation which is for the time being either—

(i) the subject of a licence under Part II of the Food and Environment Protection Act 1985;[4] or

(ii) carried on in circumstances where such a licence would be required but for an order under section 7 of that Act.

(2) Paragraph (1)(a) and (b) above does not apply insofar as the activity involves the final disposal of waste by deposit in or on land.

*Exemptions from waste management licensing*

**17.** (1) Subject to the following provisions of this regulation and to any conditions or limitations in Schedule 3,[5] section 33(1)(a) and (b) of the 1990 Act[6] shall not apply in relation to the carrying on of any exempt activity set out in that Schedule.

(1A) Paragraph (1) above does not apply to the carrying on of an exempt activity falling within paragraph 45(1), (2) or (5) of Schedule 3[7] where the carrying on of that activity is authorised by a waste management licence[8] granted upon an application made after 31st March 1995 under section 36 of the 1990 Act.[9,10]

(2) In the case of an exempt activity set out in paragraph 4, 7, 9, 11, 13, 14, 15, 17, 18, 19, 25, 37, 40, 41 or 45[11] of Schedule 3,[12] paragraph (1) above only applies if—

(a) the exempt activity is carried on by or with the consent of the occupier of the land where the activity is carried on; or

(b) the person carrying on the exempt activity is otherwise entitled to do so on that land.

(3) Unless otherwise indicated in Schedule 3, paragraph (1) above does not apply to the carrying on of an exempt activity insofar as it involves special waste.[13]

(3A) Paragraph (1) does not apply to the carrying on of an exempt activity insofar as it involves the carrying out, by an establishment or undertaking, of their own waste disposal at the place of production if the waste being disposed of is special waste.[14]

(4) Paragraph (1) above only applies in relation to an exempt activity involving the disposal[15] or recovery[16] of waste by an establishment or undertaking if the type and quantity of waste submitted to the activity, and the method of disposal or recovery, are consistent with the need to attain the objectives mentioned in paragraph 4(1)(a) of Part I of Schedule 4.[17]

(5) For the purposes of Schedule 3, a container, lagoon or place is secure in relation to waste kept in it if all reasonable precautions are taken to ensure that the waste cannot escape from it and members of the public are unable to gain access to the waste, and any reference to secure storage means storage in a secure container, lagoon or place.

---

[1] P.584 above.
[2] P.273 above.
[3] P.18 above.
[4] 1985 c.48; Part II is amended by ss.146 and 147 of, and Part VIII of sch.16 to, the 1990 Act.
[5] P.697 below.
[6] P.116 above.
[7] P.709 below.
[8] "Waste management licence" has the meaning given by s.35(1) of the 1990 Act, p.119 above.
[9] P.121 above.
[10] Paragraph (1A) inserted by S.I. 1995/288, reg.3(5). This

amendment came into force on 1 April 1995: reg.1(1).
[11] Words "40, 41 or 45" substituted by S.I. 1995/288, reg.3(6).
[12] Sch.3 is at p.697 below.
[13] "Special waste" defined by reg.1(3), p.677 above.
[14] This paragraph inserted by S.I. 1996/972, reg.25, sch.3. This amendment came into force on 1 September 1996: reg.1(1).
[15] "Disposal" defined by reg.1(3), p.676 above.
[16] "Recovery" defined by reg.1(3), p.677 above.
[17] P.715 below.

*Registration in connection with exempt activities*

**18.** (1) Subject to paragraphs (1A), (1B) and (7)[1] below, it shall be an offence for an establishment or undertaking to carry on, after 31st December 1994, an exempt activity[2] involving the recovery[3] or disposal[4] of waste[5] without being registered with the appropriate registration authority.[6]

(1A) In the case of an exempt activity falling within paragraph 45(1) or (2) of Schedule 3,[7] paragraph (1) above shall have effect as if "30th September 1995" were substituted for "31st December 1994".

(1B) Paragraph (1) above shall not apply in the case of an exempt activity to which a resolution under section 54 of the 1990 Act relates and which is carried on in accordance with the conditions, specified in the resolution, which relate to it.[8]

(2) It shall be the duty of each appropriate registration authority to establish and maintain a register for the purposes of paragraph (1) above of establishments and undertakings carrying on exempt activities involving the recovery or disposal of waste in respect of which it is the appropriate registration authority.

(3) Subject to paragraph (4) below, the register shall contain the following particulars in relation to each such establishment or undertaking—

(a) the name and address of the establishment or undertaking;

(b) the activity which constitutes the exempt activity; and

(c) the place where the activity is carried on.

(4) Subject to paragraphs (4A) and (4B) below,[9] the appropriate registration authority shall enter the relevant particulars in the register in relation to an establishment or undertaking if it receives notice of them in writing or otherwise becomes aware of those particulars.

(4A) Paragraph (4) above shall not apply in the case of an exempt activity falling within paragraph 45(1) or (2) of Schedule 3[10] and, in such a case, the appropriate registration authority shall enter the relevant particulars in the register in relation to an establishment or undertaking only if—

(a) it receives notice of them in writing;

(b) that notice is provided to it by that establishment or undertaking;

(c) that notice is accompanied by a plan of each place at which any such exempt activity is carried on showing—

(i) the boundaries of that place;

(ii) the locations within that place at which the exempt activity is to be carried on;

(iii) the location and specifications of any such impermeable pavements, drainage systems or hardstandings as are mentioned in paragraph 45(1)(c) or (2)(f) or (g) of Schedule 3; and

(iv) the location of any such secure containers as are mentioned in paragraph 45(2)(e) of Schedule 3;

and

(d) that notice is also accompanied by payment of a fee of £400[11] in respect of each place where any such exempt activity is carried on.

---

[1] Words "paragraphs (1A), (1B) and (7)" inserted by S.I. 1995/288, reg.3(7). This amendment came into force on 1 April 1995: reg.1(1).
[2] "Exempt activity" defined by reg.1(3), p.676 above.
[3] "Recovery" defined by reg.1(3), p.677 above.
[4] "Disposal" defined by reg.1(3), p.676 above.
[5] "Waste" defined by reg.1(3), p.677 above.
[6] "Appropriate regulation authority" defined by para.10 below.
[7] P.709 below.
[8] Para.(1A) and (1B) inserted by S.I. 1995/288, reg.3(8). This amendment came into force on 1 April 1995: reg.1(1).
[9] Words "Subject to paragraphs (4A) and (4B) below," inserted by S.I. 1995/288, reg.3(9).
[10] P.709 below.
[11] Words "£400" substituted by S.I. 1996/634, reg.2(5). This amendment came into force on 1 April 1996: reg.1(1).

(4B)  Where any fee payable under paragraph 45(3)(d) of Schedule 3 is not received by the appropriate registration authority within 2 months of the due date for its payment as ascertained in accordance with paragraph 45(4) of Schedule 3—

(a)  in a case where the establishment or undertaking is registered for exempt activities falling within paragraph 45(1) or (2) in respect of only one place, or where it is so registered in respect of more than one place and the fee in respect of each such place is then unpaid, the registration of the establishment or undertaking shall be cancelled and the authority shall remove from its register the relevant entry in respect of the establishment or undertaking;

(b)  in any other case, the registration of the establishment or undertaking in respect of those activities shall be cancelled insofar as it relates to any place in respect of which the fee is then unpaid and the authority shall amend the relevant entry in its register accordingly,

and where the authority removes or amends an entry from or in its register by virtue of this paragraph it shall notify the establishment or undertaking in writing of the removal or amendment.[1]

(5)  For the purposes of paragraph (4) above, the appropriate registration authority shall be taken to be aware of the relevant particulars in relation to an exempt activity mentioned in paragraph (10)(a), (b) or (c) below.

(6)  A person guilty of an offence under paragraph (1) above shall be liable on summary conviction to a fine not exceeding—

(a)  in the case of an exempt activity falling within paragraph 45(1) or (2) of Schedule 3, level 2 on the standard scale;[2] and

(b)  in any other case, £10.[3]

(7)  The preceding provisions of this regulation shall not apply in the case of an exempt activity to which paragraph 7(3)(c) of Schedule 3 applies,[4] but the appropriate registration authority shall enter in its register the particulars furnished to it pursuant to that provision.

(8)  Each appropriate registration authority shall secure that any register maintained by it under this regulation is open to inspection[5] by members of the public free of charge at all reasonable hours and shall afford to members of the public reasonable facilities for obtaining, on payment of reasonable charges, copies of entries in the register.

(9)  Registers under this regulation may be kept in any form.

(10)  For the purposes of this regulation, the appropriate registration authority is—

(a)  in the case of an exempt activity falling within—

    (i)  paragraph 1, 2, 3 or 24 of Schedule 3;[6] or

    (ii)  paragraph 4 of Schedule 3 if it involves the coating or spaying of metal containers as or as part of a process within Part B of Section 6.5 (coating processes and printing) of Schedule 1 to the 1991 Regulations[7] and the process is for the time being the subject of an authorisation granted under Part I of the 1990 Act, or if it involves storage related to that process; or

    (iii)  paragraph 12 of Schedule 3 if it involves the composting of biodegradable waste as or as part of a process within paragraph (a) of Part B of Section 6.9 (treatment or processing of animal or vegetable matter) of Schedule 1 to the 1991 Regulations,[8] the compost is to be used for the purpose of cultivating mushrooms and the process is for the time being the subject of an authorisation granted under Part I of the 1990 Act, or if it involves storage related to that process,

[1] Para. (4A) and (4B) inserted by S.I. 1995/288, reg.3(10). This amendment came into force on 1 April 1995: reg.1(1).

[2] The current fine at level 2 on the standard scale is £500: Criminal Justice Act 1991 (c.53), s.17 (England and Wales); Criminal Procedure (Scotland) Act 1995 (c.46), s.225 (Scotland).

[3] Words "not exceeding—" and para.(a) and (b) added by S.I. 1995/288, reg.3(11).

[4] P.699 below.

[5] Former words "at its principal office" omitted by S.I. 1996/593, rerg.3, sch.2, para.10(4). This amendment came into force on 1 April 1996: reg.1.

[6] Sch.3 is at p.697 below.

[7] P.586 above.

[8] P.589 above.

the local enforcing authority[1] responsible for granting the authorisation under Part I of the 1990 Act for the prescribed process involving the exempt activity, or to which the exempt activity relates;

(b) in a case falling within paragraph 16 of Schedule 3,[2] the issuing authority responsible for granting the licence under article 7 or 8 of the Diseases of Animals (Waste Food) Order 1973[3] under which the exempt activity is carried on;

(c) in a case falling within paragraph 23 of Schedule 3[4]—

    (i) where the exempt activity is carried on by virtue of a licence under article 5(2)(c) or 6(2)(d), or an approval under article 8, of the Animal By-Products Order 1992,[5] the Minister;

    (ii) where the exempt activity is carried on by virtue of a registration under article 9 or 10 of that Order, the appropriate Minister;

    (iii) where the exempt activity is carried on at a knacker's yard in respect of which the occupier holds a licence under section 1 of the Slaughterhouses Act 1974[6] authorising the use of that yard as a knacker's yard or, in Scotland, in respect of which a licence has been granted under section 6 of the Slaughter of Animals (Scotland) Act 1980,[7] the local authority;

and in this sub-paragraph "the Minister" and "the appropriate Minister" have the meaning given by section 86(1) of the Animal Health Act 1981,[8] and "knacker's yard" and "local authority" have the meaning given by section 34 of the Slaughterhouses Act 1974 or, in Scotland, have the meaning given by section 22 of the Slaughter of Animals (Scotland) Act 1980;

(d) in any other case, the waste regulation authority[9] for the area in which the exempt activity is carried on.

## Waste Framework Directive

**19.** Schedule 4[10] (which implements certain provisions of Council Directive 75/442/EEC on waste[11]) shall have effect.

## Registration of brokers

**20.** (1) Subject to paragraphs (2) to (4) below, it shall be an offence for an establishment or undertaking after 31st December 1994 to arrange (as dealer or broker) for the disposal[12] or recovery[13] of controlled waste[14] on behalf of another person unless it is a registered broker of controlled waste.

(2) Paragraph (1) above shall not apply in relation to an arrangement under which an establishment or undertaking will itself carry out the disposal or recovery of the waste and either—

(a) it is authorised to carry out the disposal or recovery of the waste by a waste management licence,[15] an authorisation under Part I of the 1990 Act,[16] a consent under Chapter II of Part III of the Water Resources Act 1991[17] or under Part II of the Control of Pollution Act 1974[18] or a licence under Part II of the Food and Environment Protection Act 1985;[19] or

---

[1] For "local enforcing authority" see the definition of "enforcing authority" in reg.1(3) above.

[2] P.702 below.

[3] S.I. 1973/1936; see article 2(1) for the definition of "issuing authority".

[4] P.704 below.

[5] S.I. 1992/3303.

[6] 1974 c.3.

[7] 1980 c.13.

[8] 1981 c.22.

[9] "Waste regulation authority" has the meaning given by s.30 of the 1990 Act, p.113 above.

[10] P.712 below.

[11] OJ No. L 194, 25.7.1975, p.39; as amended by Council Directives 91/156/EEC (OJ No. L 078, 26.3.1991, p.32) and 91/692/EEC (OJ No. L 377, 31.12.1991, p.48).

[12] "Disposal" defined by reg.1(3), p.676 above.

[13] "Recovery" defined by reg.1(3), p.677 above.

[14] For the definition of "controlled waste" in Part II of the Environmental Protection Act 1990, see s.75, p.159 above, and the Controlled Waste Regulations 1992, p.662 above.

[15] "Waste management licence" has the meaning given by s.35(1) of the 1990 Act, p.119 above.

[16] P.88 above.

[17] P.273 above.

[18] P.18 above.

[19] 1985 c.48.

   (b)  the recovery of the waste is covered by an exemption conferred by—

       (i)  regulation 17(1) of,[1] and Schedule 3 to,[2] these Regulations; or

      (ii)  article 3 of the Deposits in the Sea (Exemptions) Order 1985.[3]

(3)  Paragraph (1) above shall not apply in relation to an arrangement for the disposal or recovery of controlled waste made by a person who is registered as a carrier of controlled waste, or who is registered for the purposes of paragraph 12(1) of Part I of Schedule 4,[4] if as part of the arrangement he transports the waste to or from any place in Great Britain.

(4)  Paragraph (1) above shall not apply to an establishment or undertaking which—

   (a)  is a charity;

   (b)  is a voluntary organisation within the meaning of section 48(11) of the Local Government Act 1985[5] or section 83(2D) of the Local Government (Scotland) Act 1973;[6]

   (c)  is an authority which is a waste collection authority, waste disposal authority or waste regulation authority;[7] or

   (d)  applies before 1st January 1995 in accordance with Schedule 5[8] for registration as a broker of controlled waste but only whilst its application is pending (and paragraph 1(4) and (5) of Part I of Schedule 5 shall apply for the purpose of determining whether an application is pending).

(5)  A person guilty of an offence under this section shall be liable on summary conviction to a fine not exceeding level 5 on the standard scale.[9]

(6)  Section 157 of the 1990 Act[10] shall apply in relation to an offence under this section as it applies in relation to an offence under that Act.

(7)  Schedule 5 (which makes provision for the registration of brokers of controlled waste) shall have effect.

(8)  Sections 68(3) to (5), 69 and 71(2)[11] and (3) of the 1990 Act (power to appoint inspectors, powers of entry and power to obtain information) shall have effect as if the provisions of this regulation and Schedule 5 were provisions of Part II of that Act.

*Amendment of the Deposits in the Sea (Exemptions) Order 1985*

**21.**  (1)  The Deposits in the Sea (Exemptions) order 1985[12] shall be amended as follows.

   (2)  In article 3, before "A licence is not needed", there shall be inserted "Subject to article 4,".

   (3)  After article 3, there shall be added the following articles—

*"Provisions relating to exemptions involving waste*

   **4.**  (1)  Article 3 only applies to an establishment or undertaking in relation to an operation specified in the Schedule to this Order involving the recovery or disposal of waste if—

     (a)  it is carrying out—

        (i)  its own waste disposal at the place of production; or

       (ii)  waste recovery; and

     (b)  the type and quantity of waste involved, and the method of disposal or recovery, are consistent with the need to attain the objective of ensuring that waste is recovered or disposed of without endangering human health and without using processes or methods which could harm the environment and in particular without—

---

[1] P.689 above.
[2] P.697 below.
[3] S.I. 1985/1699.
[4] P.718 below.
[5] 1985 c.51.
[6] 1973 c.65; s.83(2D) is added by s.3(3) of the Local Government Act 1986 (c.10).
[7] See definitions in s.30 of the 1990 Act, p.113 above: reg.1(3) above.

[8] P.723 below.
[9] The current fine at level 5 on the standard scale is £5,000: Criminal Justice Act 1991 (c.53), s.17 (England and Wales); Criminal Procedure (Scotland) Act 1995 (c.46), s.225 (Scotland).
[10] P.206 above.
[11] P.156 above.
[12] S.I. 1985/1699.

    (i)   risk to water, air, soil, plants or animals; or

    (ii)  causing nuisance through noise or odours; or

    (iii) adversely affecting the countryside or places of special interest.

(2) In this article and in article 5 below, "disposal", "recovery" and "waste" have the meaning given by regulation 1(3) of the Waste Management Licensing Regulations 1994.

*Registration of establishments and undertakings carrying on exempt operations*

**5.** (1) It shall be an offence for an establishment or undertaking to carry on, after 31st December 1994, an exempt activity without being registered with the licensing authority.

(2) It shall be the duty of each licensing authority to establish and maintain a register for the purposes of paragraph (1) above of establishments and undertakings carrying on exempt activities in the area for which it is the licensing authority.

(3) The register shall contain the following particulars in relation to each such establishment or undertaking—

(a) the name and address of the establishment or undertaking;

(b) the activity which constitutes the exempt activity; and

(c) the place where the activity is carried on.

(4) The licensing authority shall enter those particulars in the register in relation to an establishment or undertaking if it receives notice of them in writing or otherwise becomes aware of those particulars.

(5) A person guilty of an offence under paragraph (1) above shall be liable on summary conviction to a fine not exceeding level 2 on the standard scale.

(6) Each licensing authority shall secure that any register maintained by the authority under this article is available, at all reasonable times, for inspection by the public free of charge and shall afford to members of the public facilities for obtaining copies of entries, on payment of reasonable charges.

(7) Registers under this article may be kept in any form.

(8) In this article, "exempt activity" means any operation specified in the Schedule to this Order involving the disposal or recovery of waste to which article 3 applies.".

*Amendment of the Collection and Disposal of Waste Regulations 1988*

**22.** (1) The Collection and Disposal of Waste Regulations 1988[1] shall be amended as follows.

(2) At the beginning of regulation 3, there shall be inserted "Subject to regulations 4 and 7A,".

(3) At the beginning of each of regulations 6 and 7, there shall be inserted "Subject to regulation 7A,".

(4) After regulation 7, the following shall be inserted—

"*Waste not to be treated as household, industrial or commercial waste*

**7A.** (1) For the purposes of all the provisions of Part I of the Act, waste which is not Directive waste shall not be treated as household waste, industrial waste or commercial waste.

(2) In this regulation, "Directive waste" has the meaning given by regulation 1(3) of the Waste Management Licensing Regulations 1994.".

*Amendment of the Controlled Waste (Registration of Carriers and Seizure of Vehicles) Regulations 1991*

**23.** *The amendments made by this regulation are included in the Controlled Waste (Registration of Carriers and Seizure of Vehicles) Regulations 1991, p.630 above.*

---

[1] S.I. 1988/819, amended by S.I. 1989/1968.

*Amendment of the Controlled Waste Regulations 1992*

**24.** *The amendments made by this regulation are included in the Controlled Waste Regulations 1992, p.662 above.*

# SCHEDULE 1

(Regulation 2(2), (3) and (4)[1])

## INFORMATION AND EVIDENCE REQUIRED IN RELATION TO AN APPLICATION FOR THE SURRENDER OF A SITE LICENCE

1. The full name, address and daytime telephone, fax and telex number (if any) of the holder of the site licence and, where the holder employs an agent in relation to the application, of that agent.

2. The number (if any) of the site licence, and the address or a description of the location of the site.

3. A map or plan—

    (a) showing the location of the site;

    (b) indicating whereabouts on the site the different activities mentioned in paragraph 4 were carried on; and

    (c) indicating relevant National Grid references.

4. A description of the different activities involving the treatment, keeping or disposal[2] of controlled waste which were carried on at the site (whether or not in pursuance of the licence), an indication of when those activities were carried on and an estimate of the total quantities of the different types of waste which were dealt with at the site.

5. Where the site is a landfill or lagoon—

    (a) particulars of all significant engineering works carried out for the purpose of preventing or minimising pollution of the environment or harm to human health as a result of activities carried on at the site, including—

        (i) an indication of when those works were carried out and a copy of all relevant plans or specifications; and

        (ii) details of works of restoration carried out after completion of operations at the site;

    (b) geological, hydrological and hydrogeological information relating to the site and its surrounds, including information about the flows of groundwater;

    (c) monitoring data on the quality of surface water or groundwater which could be affected by the site and on the production of any landfill gas or leachate at the site and information about the physical stability of the site; and

    (d) where special waste[3] has been deposited at the site, a copy of the records and plans relating to the deposits kept under regulation 14 of the Control of Pollution (Special Waste) Regulations 1980;[4]

and any estimate under paragraph 4 of the total quantities of the different types of waste dealt with at the site shall, in particular, differentiate between biodegradable waste, non-biodegradable waste and special waste.

6. Where the site is not a landfill or lagoon—

    (a) details of the contaminants likely to be present at the site having regard to—

        (i) the different activities involving the treatment, keeping or disposal of controlled waste carried on at the site (whether or not in pursuance of the licence); and

        (ii) the nature of the different types of waste dealt with at the site; and

    (b) a report which—

---

[1] P.678 above.
[2] "Disposal" defined by reg.1(3), p.676 above.
[3] "Special waste" defined by reg.1(3), p.677 above.

[4] See reg.16 of the Special Waste Regulations 1996, p.774 below.

(i) records the results of the analysis of samples taken in such numbers, and at such locations at the site, that they provide a reliable indication of the locations where contaminants are likely to be present in high concentrations; and

(ii) shows how many (and from where) samples were taken.

7. Any other information which the applicant wishes the waste regulation authority to take into account.

# SCHEDULE 2

(Regulation 2(5)[1])

## INFORMATION REQUIRED IN RELATION TO AN APPLICATION FOR THE TRANSFER OF A WASTE MANAGEMENT LICENCE

1. The full name, address and daytime telephone, fax and telex number (if any) of the holder of the waste management licence and, where the application is made by an agent of the holder, of the agent.

2. The number (if any) of the waste management licence and, except in the case of mobile plant, the address or a description of the location of the licensed premises.

3. In the case of mobile plant, sufficient information to identify the plant.

4. Where the proposed transferee is an individual, his full name, date of birth, address and daytime telephone, fax and telex number (if any).

5. Where the proposed transferee is a registered company or other body corporate—

   (a) its name and, in the case of a registered company, its registered number;

   (b) the address, telephone, fax and telex number (if any) of its registered or principal office;

   (c) the full name, position, address and date of birth of each director, manager, secretary or other similar officer of the proposed transferee.

6. Where the proposed transferee is a partnership—

   (a) the name of the partnership;

   (b) its address, telephone, fax and telex number (if any);

   (c) the full name, address and date of birth of each partner.

7. If the proposed transferee has a business name different from any name of the transferee mentioned above, the transferee's business name.

8. Where the proposed transferee has appointed an agent to deal with the transfer, the agent's full name, address and daytime telephone, fax and telex number (if any).

9. Details of any conviction of the proposed transferee or of another relevant person[2] for any offence which is relevant for the purposes of section 74(3)(a) of the 1990 Act, including the date of conviction, the penalty imposed and the name of the Court.

10. The full name of the person who is to manage the activities which are authorised by the waste management licence and information to establish that he is technically competent for the purposes of section 74(3)(b) of the 1990 Act, including—

---

[1] P.680 above.    [2] See the definition of "relevant person" in s.74(7) of the 1990 Act, p.158 above.

    (a) details of any relevant certificate of technical competence (within the meaning of regulation 4[1]) he holds; or

    (b) in a case where the transferee relies on regulation 5(1)[2] or (2), sufficient information to establish that that provision applies.

11. Details of the financial provision which the proposed transferee has made or proposes to make to discharge the obligations arising from the waste management licence.

12. Any other information which the applicant wishes the waste regulation authority to take into account.

# SCHEDULE 3

(Regulations 1(3)[3] and 17[4])

## ACTIVITIES EXEMPT FROM WASTE MANAGEMENT LICENSING

1. (1) The use, under an authorisation granted under Part I of the 1990 Act,[5] of waste glass as part of a process within Part B of Section 3.5 (glass manufacture and production) of Schedule 1 to the 1991 Regulations[6] if the total quantity of waste glass so used in that process does not exceed 600,000 tonnes in any period of twelve months.

    (2) The storage, at the place where the process is carried on, of any such waste which is intended to be so used.

2. (1) The operation, under an authorisation granted under Part I of the 1990 Act,[7] of a scrap metal furnace with a designed holding capacity of less than 25 tonnes to the extent that it is or forms part of a process within paragraph (a), (b) or (d) of Part B of Section 2.1[8] (iron and steel), or paragraph (a), (b) or (e) of Part B of Section 2.2[9] (non-ferrous metals), of Schedule 1 to the 1991 Regulations.

    (2) The loading or unloading of such a furnace in connection with its operation in a manner covered by the exemption conferred by sub-paragraph (1) above.

    (3) The storage, at the place where such a furnace is located (but not in cases where that place is used for carrying on business as a scrap metal dealer[10] or, in Scotland, as a metal dealer), of scrap metal intended to be submitted to an operation covered by the exemption conferred by sub-paragraph (1) above.

3. The carrying on of any of the following operations—

    (a) burning as a fuel, under an authorisation granted under Part I of the 1990 Act,[11] of—

        (i) straw, poultry litter or wood;

        (ii) waste oil[12] (including waste oil which is special waste[13]);[14] or

        (iii) solid fuel which has been manufactured from waste[15] by a process involving the application of heat,

    to the extent that it is or forms part of a process within Part B of any Section of Schedule 1[16] to the 1991 Regulations;

    (b) the secure storage on any premises of any wastes mentioned in sub-paragraph (a) above, other than waste oil, which are intended to be burned as mentioned in that sub-paragraph, and the feeding of such wastes into an appliance in which they are to be so burned;

    (c) the secure storage of waste oil (including waste oil which is special waste)[17] at the place where it is produced for a period not exceeding twelve months if the waste oil is intended to be submitted to an operation covered by the exemption conferred by sub-paragraph (a) above;

---

[1] P.679 above.
[2] P.680 above.
[3] P.676 above.
[4] P.689 above.
[5] P.88 above.
[6] P.577 above.
[7] P.88 above.
[8] P.572 above.
[9] P.574 above.
[10] "Scrap metal" defined by reg.1(3), p.677 above; for "scrap metal dealer" see reg.1(4) above.

[11] P.88 above.
[12] "Waste oil" defined by reg.1(3), p.677 above.
[13] "Special waste" defined by reg.1(3), p.677 above.
[14] Words "(including waste oil which is special waste)" inserted by S.I. 1996/972, reg.25, sch.3. This amendment came into force on 1 September 1996: reg.1(1).
[15] "Waste" defined by reg.1(3), p.677 above.
[16] P.569 above.
[17] Words "(including waste oil which is special waste)" inserted by S.I. 1996/972, reg.25, sch.3. This amendment came into force on 1 September 1996: reg.1(1).

(d) burning as a fuel, under an authorisation granted under Part I of the 1990 Act, of tyres to the extent that it is or forms part of a process within Part B of Section 1.3 of Schedule 1[1] to the 1991 Regulations, and the shredding and feeding of tyres into an appliance in which they are to be so burned;

(e) the storage in a secure place[2] on any premises of tyres where—

    (i) the tyres are intended to be submitted to an operation covered by the exemption conferred by sub-paragraph (d) above;

    (ii) the tyres are stored separately;

    (iii) none of the tyres is stored on the premises for longer than twelve months; and

    (iv) the number of the tyres stored on the premises at any one time does not exceed 1,000.

4. (1) The cleaning, washing, spraying or coating of waste consisting of packaging or containers so that it or they can be reused if the total quantity of such waste so dealt with at any place does not exceed 1,000 tonnes in any period of seven days.

(2) The storage of waste in connection with the carrying on of any activities described in sub-paragraph (1) above if that storage is at the place where the activity is carried on unless—

(a) the total quantity of such waste stored in that place exceeds 1,000 tonnes; or

(b) more than 1 tonne of metal containers used for the transport or storage of any chemical are dealt with in any period of seven days.

5. (1) Burning waste[3] as a fuel in an appliance if the appliance has a net rated thermal input of less than 0.4 megawatts or, where the appliance is used together with (whether or not it is operated simultaneously with)[4] other appliances, the aggregate net rated thermal input of all the appliances is less than 0.4 megawatts.

(2) The secure storage of waste intended to be submitted to such burning.

(3) In this paragraph, "net rated thermal input" means the rate at which fuel can be burned at the maximum continuous rating of the appliance multiplied by the net calorific value of the fuel and expressed as megawatts thermal.

6. (1) Burning waste oil[5] as a fuel in an engine of an aircraft, hovercraft, mechanically propelled vehicle, railway locomotive, ship or other vessel if the total amount burned of such waste does not exceed 2,500 litres an hour in any one engine.

(2) The storage, in a secure container,[6] of waste oil intended to be so burned.

7. (1) The spreading of any of the wastes listed in Table 2 on land which is used for agriculture.[7]

(2) The spreading of any of the wastes listed in Part I of Table 2 on—

(a) operational land[8] of a railway, light railway, internal drainage board[9] or the Environment Agency;[10] or

(b) land which is a forest, woodland, park, garden, verge, landscaped area, sports ground, recreation ground, churchyard or cemetery.

Table 2

PART I

Waste soil or compost.
Waste wood, bark or other plant matter.

[1] P.570 above.
[2] See reg.17(5), p.689 above.
[3] "Waste" defined by reg.1(3), p.677 above.
[4] Words "(whether or not it is operated simultaneously with)" inserted by S.I. 1995/288, reg.3(12). This amendment came into force on 1 April 1995: reg.1(1).
[5] "Waste oil" defined by reg.1(3), p.677 above.
[6] See reg.17(5), p.689 above.
[7] "Agriculture" defined by para.(8) below.
[8] "Operational land" defined by reg.1(3), p.677 above; see also para.(9) below.
[9] "Internal drainage board" defined by para.(9) below.
[10] Words "the Environment Agency" substituted by the Environment Act 1995 (c.25), s.120, sch.22, para.233. This amendment came into force on 1 April 1996: S.I. 1996/186.

PART II

Waste food, drink or materials used in or resulting from the preparation of food or drink.
Blood and gut contents from abattoirs.
Waste lime.
Lime sludge from cement manufacture or gas processing.
Waste gypsum.
Paper waste sludge, waste paper and de-inked paper pulp.
Dredgings from any inland waters.
Textile waste.
Septic tank sludge.[1]
Sludge from biological treatment plants.
Waste hair and effluent treatment sludge from a tannery.

---

(3) Sub-paragraphs (1) and (2) above only apply if—

(a) no more than 250 tonnes or, in the case of dredgings from inland waters, 5,000 tonnes of waste per hectare are spread on the land in any period of twelve months;

(b) the activity in question results in benefit to agriculture or ecological improvement; and

(c) where the waste is to be spread by an establishment or undertaking on land used for agriculture, it furnishes to the waste regulation authority[2] in whose area the spreading is to take place the particulars listed in sub-paragraph (4) below—

(i) in a case where there is to be a single spreading, in advance of carrying out the spreading; or

(ii) in a case where there is to be regular or frequent spreading of waste of a similar composition, every six months or, where the waste to be spread is of a description different from that last notified, in advance of carrying out the spreading.

(4) The particulars referred to in sub-paragraph (3)(c) above are—

(a) the establishment or undertaking's name and address, and telephone or fax number (if any);

(b) a description of the waste, including the process from which it arises;

(c) where the waste is being or will be stored pending spreading;

(d) an estimate of the quantity of the waste or, in such a case as is mentioned in sub-paragraph (3)(c)(ii) above, an estimate of the total quantity of waste to be spread during the next six months; and

(e) the location, and intended date or, in such a case as is mentioned in sub-paragraph (3)(c)(ii) above, the frequency, of the spreading of the waste.

(5) Subject to sub-paragraph (6) below, the storage, at the place where it is to be spread, of any waste (other than septic tank sludge) intended to be spread in reliance upon the exemption conferred by sub-paragraph (1) or (2) above.

(6) Sub-paragraph (5) above does not apply to the storage of waste in liquid form unless it is stored in a secure container or lagoon[3] and no more than 500 tonnes is stored in any one container or lagoon.

(7) The storage, in a secure container or lagoon (or, in the case of dewatered sludge, in a secure place), of septic tank sludge intended to be spread in reliance upon the exemption conferred by sub-paragraph (1) above.

(8) In this paragraph and paragraph 8, "agriculture" has the same meaning as in the Agriculture Act 1947[4] or, in Scotland, the Agriculture (Scotland) Act 1948.[5]

(9) In this paragraph and paragraph 30, "internal drainage board" has the meaning given by section 1(1) of the Land Drainage Act 1991[6] and, for the purposes of the definition of operational land, an internal drainage board shall be deemed to be a statutory undertaker.

(10) In this paragraph and paragraphs 8 and 10, "septic tank sludge" has the meaning given by regulation 2(1) of the Sludge (Use in Agriculture) Regulations 1989.[7]

..................................................................................................................................................................

---

[1] "Septic tank sludge" defined by para.10 below.
[2] "Waste regulation authority" has the meaning given by s.30 of the 1990 Act, p.113 above: reg.1(3) above.
[3] See reg.17(5), p.689 above.

[4] 1947 c.48; see s.109(3).
[5] 1948 c.45; see s.86(3).
[6] 1991 c.59.
[7] P.547 above.

**8.** (1) The storage, in a secure container or lagoon[1] (or, in the case of dewatered sludge, in a secure place) on land used for agriculture,[2] of sludge which is to be used in accordance with the 1989 Regulations.[3]

(2) The spreading of sludge on land which is not agricultural land within the meaning of the 1989 Regulations[4] if—

(a) it results in ecological improvement; and

(b) it does not cause the concentration in the soil of any of the elements listed in column 1 of the soil table set out in Schedule 2 to the 1989 Regulations[5] to exceed the limit specified in column 2 of the table.

(3) The storage, in a secure container or lagoon (or, in the case of dewatered sludge, in a secure place), of sludge intended to be spread in reliance upon the exemption conferred by sub-paragraph (2) above.

(4) In this paragraph, "the 1989 Regulations" means the Sludge (Use in Agriculture) Regulations 1989 and "used", in relation to sludge, has the meaning given by regulation 2(1) of the 1989 Regulations.[6]

(5) In this paragraph, and in paragraphs 9 and 10, "sludge" has the meaning given by regulation 2(1) of the 1989 Regulations.

..............................................................................................................................................................

**9.** (1) Subject to sub-paragraph (3) below, the spreading of waste consisting of soil, rock, ash or sludge,[7] or of waste[8] from dredging any inland waters[9] or arising from construction[10] or demolition work, on any land in connection with the reclamation or improvement of that land if—

(a) by reason of industrial or other development the land is incapable of beneficial use without treatment;

(b) the spreading is carried out in accordance with a planning permission for the reclamation or improvement of the land and results in benefit to agriculture or ecological improvement; and

(c) no more than 20,000 cubic metres per hectare of such waste is spread on the land.

(2) The storage, at the place where it is to be spread, of any such waste which is intended to be spread in reliance upon the exemption conferred by sub-paragraph (1) above.

(3) Sub-paragraph (1) above does not apply to the disposal[11] of waste at a site designed or adapted for the final disposal of waste by landfill.

..............................................................................................................................................................

**10.** (1) Any recovery[12] operation carried on within the curtilage of a sewage treatment works in relation to sludge[13] or septic tank sludge[14] brought from another sewage treatment works if the total quantity of such waste brought to the works in any period of twelve months does not exceed 10,000 cubic metres.

(2) The treatment within the curtilage of a water treatment works of waste arising at the works from water treatment if the total quantity of such waste which is treated at the works in any period of twelve months does not exceed 10,000 cubic metres.

(3) The storage of waste intended to be submitted to the activities mentioned in sub-paragraph (1) or (2) above if that storage is at the place where those activities are to be carried on.

..............................................................................................................................................................

**11.** Carrying on at any place, in respect of a kind of waste listed in Table 3, any of the activities specified in that Table in relation to that kind of waste where—

(a) the activity is carried on with a view to the recovery[15] or reuse of the waste (whether or not by the person carrying on the activity listed in that Table); and

(b) the total quantity of any particular kind of waste dealt with at that place does not in any period of seven days exceed the limit specified in relation to that kind of waste in that Table.

---

[1] See reg.17(5), p.689 above.
[2] "Agriculture" defined by para.7(8) above.
[3] P.547 above; see para.(4) and (5) below.
[4] See reg.2(1) of the 1989 Regulations, p.547 above.
[5] P.552 above.
[6] P.547 above.
[7] "Sludge" has the meaning given by s.2(1) of the 1989 regulations, p.547 above; reg.8(5) above.
[8] "Waste" defined by reg.1(3), p.677 above.

[9] "Inland waters" defined by reg.1(3), p.676 above.
[10] "Construction work" defined by reg.1(3), p.676 above.
[11] "Disposal" defined by reg.1(3), p.676 above.
[12] "Recovery" defined by reg.1(3), p.677 above.
[13] "Sludge" has the meaning given by s.2(1) of the 1989 regulations, p.547 above; reg.8(5) above.
[14] "Septic tank sludge" has the meaning given by s.2(1) of the 1989 regulations, p.547 above; reg.7(10) above.
[15] "Recovery" defined by reg.1(3), p.677 above.

**Table 3**

| Kind of waste | Activities | Limit (tonnes per week) |
|---|---|---|
| Waste paper or cardboard | Baling, sorting or shredding | 3,000 |
| Waste textiles | Baling, sorting or shredding | 100 |
| Waste plastic | Baling, sorting, shredding, densifying or washing | 100 |
| Waste glass | Sorting, crushing or washing | 1,000 |
| Waste steel cans, aluminium cans or aluminium foil | Sorting, crushing, pulverising, shredding, compacting or baling | 100 |
| Waste food or drink cartons | Sorting, crushing, pulverising, shredding, compacting or baling | 100 |

**12.** (1) Composting biodegradable waste at the place where the waste is produced or where the compost is to be used, or at any other place occupied by the person producing the waste or using the compost, if the total quantity of waste being composted at that place at any time does not exceed—

(a) in the case of waste composted or to be composted for the purposes of cultivating mushrooms, 10,000 cubic metres; and

(b) in any other case, 1,000 cubic metres.

(2) The storage of biodegradable waste which is to be composted if that storage is at the place where the waste is produced or is to be composted.

(3) In this paragraph, "composting" includes any other biological transformation process that results in materials which may be spread on land for the benefit of agriculture or ecological improvement.

..............................................................................................................................................................

**13.** (1) The manufacture from—

(a) waste which arises from demolition or construction work[1] or tunnelling or other excavations; or

(b) waste which consists of ash, slag, clinker, rock, wood, bark, paper, straw or gypsum, of timber products, straw board, plasterboard, bricks, blocks, roadstone or aggregate.

(2) The manufacture of soil or soil substitutes from any of the wastes listed in sub-paragraph (1) above if—

(a) the manufacture is carried out at the place where either the waste is produced or the manufactured product is to be applied to land; and

(b) the total amount manufactured at that place on any day does not exceed 500 tonnes.

(3) The treatment of waste soil or rock which, when treated, is to be spread on land under paragraph 7 or 9, if—

(a) it is carried out at the place where the waste is produced or the treated product is to be spread; and

(b) the total amount treated at that place in any day does not exceed 100 tonnes.

(4) The storage of waste which is to be submitted to any of the activities mentioned in sub-paragraphs (1) to (3) above if—

(a) the waste is stored at the place where the activity is to be carried on; and

(b) the total quantity of waste stored at that place does not exceed—

(i) in the case of the manufacture of roadstone from road planings, 50,000 tonnes; and

(ii) in any other case, 20,000 tonnes.

..............................................................................................................................................................

**14.** (1) The manufacture of finished goods from any of the following kinds of waste, namely waste metal, plastic, glass, ceramics, rubber, textiles, wood, paper or cardboard.

(2) The storage of any such waste intended to be used in reliance upon the exemption conferred by sub-paragraph (1) above if—

(a) the waste is stored at the place of manufacture; and

(b) the total amount of any particular kind of waste stored at that place at any time does not exceed 15,000 tonnes.

..............................................................................................................................................................

[1] "Construction work" defined by reg.1(3), p.676 above.

**15.** (1) The beneficial use of waste[1] if—

(a) it is put to that use without further treatment; and

(b) that use of the waste does not involve its disposal.[2]

(2) The storage of waste intended to be used in reliance upon the exemption conferred by sub-paragraph (1) above insofar as that storage does not amount to disposal of the waste.

(3) This paragraph does not apply to the use or storage of waste if that activity is covered by an exemption conferred by paragraph 7,[3] 8, 9, 19[4] or 25,[5] or would be so covered but for any condition or limitation to which that exemption is subject by virtue of any provision contained in the paragraph by which that exemption is conferred.

**16.** The carrying on, in accordance with the conditions and requirements of a licence granted under article 7 or 8 of the Diseases of Animals (Waste Food) Order 1973,[6] of any activity authorised by the licence.

**17.** (1) The storage in a secure place[7] on any premises of waste of a kind described in Table 4 below if—

(a) the total quantity of that kind of waste stored on those premises at any time does not exceed the quantity specified in that Table;

(b) the waste is to be reused, or used for the purposes of—

(i) an activity described in paragraph 11;[8] or

(ii) any other recovery[9] operation;

(c) each kind of waste listed in the Table stored on the premises is kept separately; and

(d) no waste is stored on the premises for longer than twelve months.

Table 4

| Kind of waste | Maximum total quantity |
| --- | --- |
| Waste paper or cardboard | 15,000 tonnes |
| Waste textiles | 1,000 tonnes |
| Waste plastics | 500 tonnes |
| Waste glass | 5,000 tonnes |
| Waste steel cans, aluminium cans or aluminium foil | 500 tonnes |
| Waste food or drink cartons | 500 tonnes |
| Waste articles which are to be used for construction work[10] which are capable of being so used in their existing state | 100 tonnes |
| Solvents (including solvents which are special waste[11]) | 5 cubic metres |
| Refrigerants and halons (including refrigerants and halons which are special waste) | 18 tonnes |
| Tyres | 1,000 tyres |
| waste mammalian protein[12] | 60,000 tonnes |
| waste mammalian tallow[12] | 45,000 tonnes |

(2) In this paragraph, "refrigerants" means dichlorodifluoromethane, chlorotrifluoromethane, dichlorotetrafluoroethane, chloropentafluoroethane, bromotrifluoromethane, chlorodifluoromethane, chlorotetrafluoroethane, trifluoromethane, difluoromethane, pentafluoroethane, tetrafluoroethane, chlorodifluoroethane, difluoroethane, trichlorofluoromethane, trichlorotrifluoroethane, dichlorotrinifluoroethane, dichlorofluoroethane and mixtures containing any of those substances.

---

[1] "Waste" defined by reg.1(3), p.677 above.
[2] "Disposal" defined by reg.1(3), p.676 above.
[3] P.698 above.
[4] P.703 below.
[5] P.704 below.
[6] S.I. 1973/1936.
[7] See reg.17(5), p.689 above.

[8] P.700 above.
[9] "Recovery" defined by reg.1(3), p.677 above.
[10] "Construction work" defined by reg.1(3), p.676 above.
[11] "Special waste" defined by reg.1(3), p.677 above.
[12] This kind of waste added by S.I. 1996/1279, reg.2(1)(a). This amendment came into force on 14 May 1996: reg.1. See sub-paragraph (3) below.

(3) In this paragraph—

"mammalian protein" means proteinaceous material and "mammalian tallow" means fat, which in each case is derived from the whole or part of any dead mammal by a process of crushing, cooking or grinding.[1]

18. (1) The storage on any premises in a secure container[2] or containers of waste of a kind described in sub-paragraph (2) below if—

(a) the storage capacity of the container or containers does not exceed 400 cubic metres in total;

(b) in the case of waste oil,[3] the storage capacity of any container or containers used for its storage does not exceed 3 cubic metres in total, and provision is made to prevent oil escaping into the ground or a drain;

(c) there are no more than 20 containers on those premises;

(d) the waste will be reused, or used for the purposes of—

(i) any activity described in paragraph 11[4] carried on at those premises; or

(ii) any other recovery[5] activity;

(e) each kind of waste described in sub-paragraph (2) below stored on the premises is kept separately;

(f) no waste is stored on the premises for longer than twelve months; and

(g) the person storing the waste is the owner of the container or has the consent of the owner.

(2) Sub-paragraph (1) above applies to the following kinds of waste—

(a) any waste described in paragraph 17 other than waste solvents, refrigerants or halons;

(b) waste oil (including waste oil which is special waste[6])[7]

19. (1) The storage on a site of waste[8] which arises from demolition or construction work[9] or tunnelling or other excavations or which consists of ash, slag, clinker, rock, wood or gypsum, if—

(a) the waste in question is suitable for use for the purposes of relevant work which will be carried on at the site; and

(b) in the case of waste which is not produced on the site, it is not stored there for longer than three months before relevant work starts.

(2) The use of waste of a kind mentioned in sub-paragraph (1) above for the purposes of relevant work if the waste is suitable for use for those purposes.

(3) The storage on a site of waste consisting of road planings which are to be used for the purposes of relevant work carried on elsewhere if—

(a) no more than 50,000 tonnes of such waste are stored at the site; and

(b) the waste is stored there for no longer than 3 months.

(4) In this paragraph, "relevant work" means construction work, including the deposit of waste on land in connection with—

(a) the provision of recreational facilities on that land; or

(b) the construction, maintenance or improvement of a building, highway, railway, airport, dock or other transport facility on that land,

but not including either any deposit of waste in any other circumstances or any work involving land reclamation.

20. (1) Laundering or otherwise cleaning textiles with a view to their recovery[10] or reuse.

(2) The storage of waste textiles at the place where they are to be so laundered or cleaned.

---

[1] This sub-paragraph added by S.I. 1996/1279, reg.2(1)(b).
[2] See reg.17(5), p.689 above.
[3] "Waste oil" defined by reg.1(3), p.677 above.
[4] P.700 above.
[5] "Recovery" defined by reg.1(3), p.677 above.
[6] "Special waste" defined by reg.1(3), p.677 above.

[7] Words "(including waste oil which is special waste)" inserted by S.I. 1996/972, reg.25, sch.3. This amendment came into force on 1 September 1996: reg.1(1).
[8] "Waste" defined by reg.1(3), p.677 above.
[9] "Construction work" defined by reg.1(3), p.676 above.
[10] "Recovery" defined by reg.1(3), p.677 above.

21. (1) Chipping, shredding, cutting or pulverising waste plant matter (including wood or bark), or sorting and baling sawdust or wood shavings, on any premises if—

(a) those activities are carried on for the purposes of recovery[1] or reuse; and

(b) no more than 1,000 tonnes of such waste are dealt with on those premises in any period of seven days.

(2) The storage of waste in connection with any activity mentioned in sub-paragraph (1) above at the premises where it is carried on if the total amount of waste stored at those premises does not at any time exceed 1,000 tonnes.

22. (1) The recovery,[2] at any premises, of silver from waste produced in connection with printing or photographic processing if no more than 50,000 litres of such waste are dealt with on those premises in any day.

(2) The storage, at those premises, of waste which is to be submitted to such a recovery operation as is mentioned in sub-paragraph (1) above.

23. (1) The keeping or treatment of animal by-products in accordance with the Animal By-Products Order 1992.[3]

(2) In this paragraph, "animal by-products" has the same meaning as in article 3(1) of the Animal By-Products Order 1992.

24. (1) Crushing, grinding or other size reduction of waste bricks, tiles or concrete, under an authorisation granted in Part I of the 1990 Act,[4] to the extent that it is or forms part of a process within paragraph (c) of Part B of Section 3.4 (other mineral processes) of Schedule 1[5] to the 1991 Regulations.

(2) Where any such crushing, grinding or other size reduction is carried on otherwise than at the place where the waste is produced, the exemption conferred by sub-paragraph (1) above only applies if those activities are carried on with a view to recovery[6] or reuse of the waste.

(3) The storage, at the place where the process is carried on, of any such waste which is intended to be so crushed, ground or otherwise reduced in size, if the total quantity of such waste so stored at that place at any one time does not exceed 20,000 tonnes.

25. (1) Subject to sub-paragraphs (2) to (4) below, the deposit of waste[7] arising from dredging inland waters,[8] or from clearing plant matter from inland waters, if either—

(a) the waste is deposited along the bank or towpath of the waters where the dredging or clearing takes place; or

(b) the waste is deposited along the bank or towpath of any inland waters so as to result in benefit to agriculture or ecological improvement.

(2) The total amount of waste deposited along the bank or towpath under sub-paragraph (1) above on any day must not exceed 50 tonnes for each metre of the bank of towpath along which it is deposited.

(3) Sub-paragraph (1) above does not apply to waste deposited in a container or lagoon.

(4) Sub-paragraph (1)(a) above only applies to an establishment or undertaking where the waste deposited is the establishment or undertaking's own waste.

(5) The treatment by screening or dewatering of such waste as is mentioned in sub-paragraph (1) above—

(a) on the bank or towpath of the waters where either the dredging or clearing takes place or the waste is to be deposited, prior to its being deposited in reliance upon the exemption conferred by the foregoing provisions of this paragraph;

(b) on the bank or towpath of the waters where the dredging or clearing takes place, or at a place where the waste is to be spread, prior to its being spread in reliance upon the exemption conferred by paragraph 7(1)[9] or (2); or

(c) in the case of waste from dredging, on the bank or towpath of the waters where the dredging takes place, or at a place where the waste is to be spread, prior to its being spread in reliance upon the exemption conferred by paragraph 9(1).[10]

---

[1] "Recovery" defined by reg.1(3), p.677 above.
[2] "Recovery" defined by reg.1(3), p.677 above.
[3] S.I. 1992/3303.
[4] P.88 above.
[5] P.576 above.
[6] "Recovery" defined by reg.1(3), p.677 above.
[7] "Waste" defined by reg.1(3), p.677 above.
[8] "Inland waters" defined by reg.1(3), p.676 above.
[9] P.698 above.
[10] P.700 above.

**26.** (1) The recovery[1] or disposal[2] of waste,[3] at the place where it is produced, as an integral part of the process that produces it.

(2) The storage, at the place where it is produced, of waste which is intended to be so recovered or disposed of.

(3) Sub-paragraph (1) above does not apply to the final disposal of waste by deposit in or on land.

..................

**27.** (1) Baling, compacting, crushing, shredding or pulverising waste[4] at the place where it is produced.

(2) The storage, at the place where it is produced, of waste which is to be submitted to any of those operations.

..................

**28.** The storage of returned goods that are waste,[5] and the secure storage[6] of returned goods that are special waste,[7] pending recovery[8] or disposal,[9] for a period not exceeding one month, by their manufacturer, distributor or retailer.[10]

..................

**29.** (1) The disposal[11] of waste[12] at the place where it is produced, by the person producing it, by burning it in an incinerator which is an exempt incinerator for the purposes of Section 5.1 (incineration) of Schedule 1[13] to the 1991 Regulations.

(2) The secure storage[14] at that place of any such waste intended to be submitted to such burning.

..................

**30.** (1) Subject to sub-paragraph (2) below, burning waste[15] on land in the open if—

(a) the waste consists of wood, bark or other plant matter;

(b) it is produced on land which is operational land[16] of a railway, light railway, tramway, internal drainage board[17] or the Environment Agency,[18] or which is a forest, woodland, park, garden, verge, landscaped area, sports ground, recreation ground, churchyard or cemetery, or it is produced on other land as a result of demolition work;

(c) it is burned on the land where it is produced; and

(d) the total quantity burned in any period of 24 hours does not exceed 10 tonnes.

(2) Sub-paragraph (1) above only applies to the burning of waste by an establishment or undertaking where the waste burned is the establishment or undertaking's own waste.

(3) The storage pending its burning, on the land where it is to be burned, of waste which is to be burned in reliance upon the exemption conferred by sub-paragraph (1) above.

..................

**31.** The discharge of waste[19] onto the track of a railway from a sanitary convenience or sink forming part of a vehicle used for the carriage of passengers on the railway if the discharge in question does not exceed 25 litres.

..................

**32.** The burial on premises of waste[20] arising from the use on those premises of a sanitary convenience which is equipped with a removable receptacle if the total amount buried in any period of twelve months does not exceed 5 cubic metres.

..................

**33.** (1) The keeping or deposit of waste[21] consisting of excavated materials arising from peatworking at the place where that activity takes place.

---

[1] "Recovery" defined by reg.1(3), p.677 above.
[2] "Disposal" defined by reg.1(3), p.676 above.
[3] "Waste" defined by reg.1(3), p.677 above.
[4] "Waste" defined by reg.1(3), p.677 above.
[5] "Waste" defined by reg.1(3), p.677 above.
[6] See reg.17(5), p.689 above.
[7] "Special waste" defined by reg.1(3), p.677 above.
[8] "Recovery" defined by reg.1(3), p.677 above.
[9] "Disposal" defined by reg.1(3), p.676 above.
[10] This paragraph substituted by S.I. 1996/972, reg.25, sch.3. This amendment came into force on 1 September 1996: reg.1(1).
[11] "Disposal" defined by reg.1(3), p.676 above.
[12] "Waste" defined by reg.1(3), p.677 above.

[13] P.583 above.
[14] See reg.17(5), p.689 above.
[15] "Waste" defined by reg.1(3), p.677 above.
[16] "Operational land" defined by reg.1(3), p.676 above; see also para.7(9), p.699 above.
[17] For the definition of "internal drainage board" see para.7(9), p.699 above.
[18] Words "the Environment Agency" substituted by the Environment Act 1995 (c.25), s.120, sch.22, para.233. This amendment came into force on 1 April 1996: S.I. 1996/186.
[19] "Waste" defined by reg.1(3), p.677 above.
[20] "Waste" defined by reg.1(3), p.677 above.
[21] "Waste" defined by reg.1(3), p.677 above.

(2) Sub-paragraph (1) above only applies to the keeping or deposit of waste by an establishment or undertaking where the waste kept or deposited is the establishment or undertaking's own waste.

34. (1) The keeping or deposit on land at the place where it is produced of spent ballast if the land is operational land[1] of a railway, light railway or tramway and the total amount kept or deposited at that place does not exceed 10 tonnes for each metre of track from which the ballast derives.

(2) Sub-paragraph (1) above only applies to the keeping or deposit of waste by an establishment or undertaking where the waste kept or deposited is the establishment or undertaking's own waste.

35. (1) The deposit of waste[2] consisting of excavated material from a borehole or other excavation made for the purpose of mineral exploration if—

(a) it is deposited in or on land at the place where it is excavated; and

(b) the total quantity of waste so deposited over any period of 24 months does not exceed 45,000 cubic metres per hectare.

(2) Sub-paragraph (1) above only applies if—

(a) the drilling of the borehole or the making of any other excavation is development for which planning permission is granted by article 3 of, and Class A or B of Part 22 of Schedule 2 to, the Town and Country Planning General Development Order 1988[3] or, in Scotland, which is permitted by Class 53, 54 or 61 of Schedule 1 to the Town and Country Planning (General Permitted Development) (Scotland) Order 1992;[4] and

(b) the conditions subject to which the development is permitted are observed.

(3) Expressions used in this paragraph which are also used in the Town and Country Planning General Development Order 1988 or, in Scotland, the Town and Country Planning (General Permitted Development) (Scotland) Order 1992, shall have the same meaning as in the relevant Order.

36. (1) The temporary storage of waste consisting of garbage, including any such waste which is special waste,[5] at reception facilities provided within a harbour area in accordance with the Merchant Shipping (Reception Facilities for Garbage) Regulations 1988,[6] where such storage is incidental to the collection or transport of the waste and so long as—

(a) the amount of garbage so stored within a harbour area at any time does not exceed 20 cubic metres for each ship from which garbage has been landed; and

(b) no garbage is so stored for more than seven days.

(2) The temporary storage of waste consisting of tank washings, including any such waste which is special waste, at reception facilities provided within a harbour area in accordance with the Prevention of Pollution (Reception Facilities) Order 1984,[7] where such storage is incidental to the collection or transport of the waste and so long as—

(a) the amount of tank washings consisting of dirty ballast so stored within a harbour area at any time does not exceed 30% of the total deadweight of the ships from which such washings have been landed;

(b) the amount of tank washings consisting of waste mixtures containing oil so stored within a harbour area at any time does not exceed 1% of the total deadweight of the ships from which such washings have been landed.

(3) In this paragraph—

"garbage" has the same meaning as in the Merchant Shipping (Reception Facilities for Garbage) Regulations 1988;

"harbour area" has the same meaning as in the Dangerous Substances in Harbour Areas Regulations 1987;[8]

"ship" means a vessel of any type whatsoever operating in the marine environment including submersible craft, floating craft and any structure which is a fixed or floating platform; and

---

[1] "Operational land" defined by reg.1(3), p.676 above.
[2] "Waste" defined by reg.1(3), p.677 above.
[3] S.I. 1988/1813 which has been revoked and replaced by S.I. 1995/418 and 1995/419..
[4] S.I. 1992/223; to which there are amendments not relevant to these regulations.
[5] "Special waste" defined by reg.1(3), p.677 above.
[6] S.I. 1988/2293.
[7] S.I. 1984/862.
[8] S.I. 1987/37.

"tank washings" means waste residues from the tanks (other than the fuel tanks) or holds of a ship or waste arising from the cleaning of such tanks or holds.

37. (1) Subject to sub-paragraph (2) below, the burial of a dead domestic pet in the garden of a domestic property where the pet lived.

(2) This paragraph does not apply if—

(a) the dead domestic pet may prove hazardous to anyone who may come into contact with it; or

(b) the burial is carried out by an establishment or undertaking and the pet did not die at the property.

38. The deposit or storage of samples of waste,[1] including samples of waste which is special waste,[2] which are being or are to be subjected to testing and analysis, at any place where they are being or are to be tested or analysed, if the samples are taken—

(a) in the exercise of any power under the Radioactive Substances Act 1993,[3] the Sewerage (Scotland) Act 1968,[4] the Control of Pollution Act 1974,[5] the 1990 Act,[6] the Water Industry Act 1991[7] or the Water Resources Act 1991;[8]

(b) by or on behalf of the holder of a waste management licence[9] in pursuance of the conditions of that licence;

(c) by or on behalf of a person carrying on in relation to the waste an activity described in this Schedule or in regulation 16(1);[10]

(d) by or on behalf of the owner or occupier of the land from which the samples are taken;

(e) by or on behalf of any person to whom section 34 of the 1990 Act[11] applies in connection with his duties under that section; or

(f) for the purposes of research.

39. (1) The secure storage[12] at a pharmacy, pending their disposal there or elsewhere, of waste medicines (including those which are special waste[13]) which have been returned to the pharmacy from households or by individuals if—

(a) the total quantity of such returned waste medicines at the pharmacy does not exceed 5 cubic metres at any time; and

(b) any waste medicine so returned to the pharmacy is not stored there for longer than six months.

(2) The storage at the premises of a medical, nursing or veterinary practice of waste (including special waste) produced in carrying on that practice if—

(a) the total quantity of that waste at the premises does not at any time exceed 5 cubic metres; ;and

(b) no such waste is stored at those premises for longer than three months.

40. (1) The storage of non-liquid waste[14] at any place other than the premises where it is produced if—

(a) it is stored in a secure container or containers, does not at any time exceed 50 cubic metres in total and is not kept for a period longer than 3 months;

(b) the person storing the waste is the owner of the container or has the consent of the owner;

(c) the place where it is stored is not a site designed or adapted for the reception of waste with a view to its being disposed[15] of or recovered[16] elsewhere; and

(d) such storage is incidental to the collection or transport of the waste.

---

[1] "Waste" defined by reg.1(3), p.677 above.
[2] "Special waste" defined by reg.1(3), p.677 above.
[3] P.381 above.
[4] 1968 c.47.
[5] P.11 above.
[6] P.83 above.
[7] P.229 above.
[8] P.267 above.
[9] "Waste management licence" has the meaning given by

s.35(1) of the 1990 Act, p.119 above.
[10] P.688 above.
[11] P.117 above.
[12] See reg.17(5), p.689 above.
[13] "Special waste" defined by reg.1(3), p.677 above.
[14] "Waste" defined by reg.1(3), p.677 above.
[15] "Disposal" defined by reg.1(3), p.676 above.
[16] "Recovery" defined by reg.1(3), p.677 above.

(1A)  Sub-paragraph (1) above does not apply to the storage of waste at a place designed or adapted for the recovery of scrap metal[1] or the dismantling of waste motor vehicles.[2]

(2)  The temporary storage of scrap rails on operational land[3] of a railway, light railway or tramway if the total quantity of that waste in any one place does not at any time exceed 10 tonnes and the storage is incidental to the collection or transport of the scrap rails.

**41.**  (1)  The temporary storage of waste,[4] pending its collection, on the site where it is produced.

(1A)  Sub-paragraph (1) above does not apply to the storage of waste at a place designed or adapted for the recovery[5] of scrap metal[6] or the dismantling of waste motor vehicles.[7]

(2)  Sub-paragraph (1) above shall apply to special waste[8] if—

(a)  it is stored on the site for no more than twelve months;

(b)  in the case of liquid waste, it is stored in a secure container[9] and the total volume of that waste does not at any time exceed 23,000 litres; and

(c)  in any other case, either—

(i)  it is stored in a secure container and the total volume of that waste does not at any time exceed 80 cubic metres; or

(ii)  it is stored in a secure place and the total volume of that waste does not at any time exceed 50 cubic metres.

**42.**  (1)  The treatment, keeping or disposal[10] by any person at any premises of waste[11] (including special waste[12]) consisting of scrap metal[13] or waste motor vehicles which are to be dismantled if—

(a)  he was carrying on the activity in question at those premises before 1st April 1995;[14] and

(b)  he has applied, before that date, for a disposal licence under Part I of the Control of Pollution Act 1974[15] authorising that activity and that application is pending on that date.

(2)  The exemption conferred by sub-paragraph (1) above, in relation to the carrying on of an activity at any premises, shall cease to have effect in relation to the carrying on of that activity at those premises on the date on which the licence applied for is granted or, if the application is (or is deemed to be) rejected, on the date on which—

(a)  the period for appealing expires without an appeal being made; or

(b)  any appeal is withdrawn or finally determined.

**43.**  (1)  The treatment, keeping or disposal[16] by any person at any premises of waste[17] (including special waste[18]) if—

(a)  he was carrying on the activity in question at those premises before 1st May 1994; and

(b)  before that date no disposal licence was required under Part I of the Control of Pollution Act 1974[19] for that activity.

(2)  Subject to sub-paragraph (3) below, the exemption conferred by sub-paragraph (1) above, in relation to an activity carried on by a person at any premises, shall—

(a)  after 30th September 1996,[20] in the case of an activity falling within paragraph 8 or 9 of Part III of Schedule 4;[21]

---

[1] "Scrap metal" defined by reg.1(3), p.677 above.
[2] Paragraph (1A) inserted by S.I. 1995/288, reg.3(13). This amendment came into force on 1 April 1995: reg.1(1).
[3] "Operational land" defined by reg.1(3), p.677 above.
[4] "Waste" defined by reg.1(3), p.677 above.
[5] "Recovery" defined by reg.1(3), p.677 above.
[6] "Scrap metal" defined by reg.1(3), p.677 above.
[7] Paragraph (1A) inserted by S.I. 1995/288, reg.3(13). This amendment came into force on 1 April 1995: reg.1(1).
[8] "Special waste" defined by reg.1(3), p.677 above.
[9] See reg.17(5), p.689 above.
[10] "Disposal" defined by reg.1(3), p.676 above.
[11] "Waste" defined by reg.1(3), p.677 above.
[12] "Special waste" defined by reg.1(3), p.677 above.
[13] "Scrap metal" defined by reg.1(3), p.677 above.

[14] Words "1st April 1995" substituted by S.I. 1995/288, reg.3(14). This amendment came into force on 1 April 1995: reg.1(1).
[15] 1974 c.40; "disposal licence" has the meaning given by s.3(1).
[16] "Disposal" defined by reg.1(3), p.676 above.
[17] "Waste" defined by reg.1(3), p.677 above.
[18] "Special waste" defined by reg.1(3), p.677 above.
[19] 1974 c.40; "disposal licence" has the meaning given by s.3(1).
[20] Words "30th September 1996" substituted by S.I. 1996/634, reg.2(6). This amendment came into force on 30 March 1996: reg.1(2).
[21] P.721 below.

(b)  after 31st July 1995, in any other case,

cease to have effect[1] in relation to the carrying on of that activity at those premises unless on or before that date he applies for a waste management licence[2] in relation to the activity in question.

(3)  Where a person makes such an application as is mentioned in sub-paragraph (2) above, the exemption conferred by sub-paragraph (1) above shall continue to have effect in relation to the activity in question until the date on which the licence applied for is granted or, if the application is (or is deemed to be) rejected, until the date on which—

(a)  the period for appealing expires without an appeal being made; or

(b)  any appeal is withdrawn or finally determined.

44.  (1)  Heating iron, steel or any ferrous-alloy, non-ferrous metal or non-ferrous metal alloy, in one or more furnaces or other appliances the primary combustion chambers of which have in aggregate a net rated thermal input of less than 0.2 megawatts, for the purpose of removing grease, oil or any other non-metallic contaminant.

(2)  Sub-paragraph (1) does not apply to the removal by heat of plastic or rubber covering from scrap cable or of any asbestos contaminant.

(3)  In the case of a process involving the heating of iron, steel or any ferrous-alloy, sub-paragraph (1) does not apply if that process is related to a process described in any of paragraphs (a) to (h), or (j) to (m), of Part A or paragraphs (a) to (c), or (e) or (f), of Part B of Section 2.1 of Schedule 1[3] to the 1991 Regulations.

(4)  In the case of a process involving the heating of any non-ferrous metal or non-ferrous metal alloy, sub-paragraph (1) does not apply if that process is related to a process described in any of paragraphs (a) to (g), or (i) to (k), of Part A of Section 2.2 of Schedule 1[4] to the 1991 Regulations.

(5)  The secure storage[5] of waste intended to be submitted to heating to which sub-paragraph (1) applies if the waste or, as the case may be, any container in which the waste is stored, is stored on an impermeable pavement which is provided with a sealed drainage system.[6]

(6)  In this paragraph, "net rated thermal input" means the rate at which fuel can be burned at the maximum continuous rating of the appliance multiplied by the net calorific value of the fuel and expressed as megawatts thermal.

(7)  In this paragraph, "ferrous alloy" means an alloy of which iron is the largest constituent, or equal to the largest constituent, by weight, whether or not that alloy also has a non-ferrous metal content greater than any percentage specified in Section 2.2 of Schedule 1 to the 1991 Regulations, and "non-ferrous metal alloy" shall be construed accordingly.[7]

45.  (1)  Subject to sub-paragraph (3) below, the carrying on, at any secure place[8] designed or adapted for the recovery[9] of scrap metal[10] or the dismantling of waste motor vehicles, in respect of a kind of waste described in Table 4A, of any of the activities specified in that Table in relation to that kind of waste if—

(a)  the total quantity of any particular kind of waste so dealt with at that place does not in any period of seven days exceed the limit specified in relation to that kind of waste in that Table;

(b)  the activity is carried on with a view to the recovery of the waste (whether or not by the person carrying on the activity listed in that Table);

(c)  every part of that place upon which the activity is carried out is surfaced with an impermeable pavement provided with a sealed drainage system;[11] and

(d)  the plant or equipment used in carrying on the activity is maintained in reasonable working order.

[1]  Words "shall— . . . cease to have effect" substituted by S.I. 1995/1950, reg.2. This amendment came into force on 29 July 1995: reg.1.
[2]  "Waste management licence" has the meaning given by s.35(1) of the 1990 Act, p.119 above.
[3]  P.572 above.
[4]  P.573 above.
[5]  See reg.17(5), p.689 above.
[6]  For "sealed drainage system" see para.45(7) below.
[7]  Reg.44 inserted by S.I. 1995/288, reg.3(16). This amendment came into force on 1 April 1995: reg.1(1).
[8]  See reg.17(5), p.689 above.
[9]  "Recovery" defined by reg.1(3), p.677 above.
[10]  "Scrap metal" defined by reg.1(3), p.677 above.
[11]  For "sealed drainage system" see para.(7) below.

Table 4A

| Kind of Waste | Activities | Seven day limit |
|---|---|---|
| Ferrous metal or ferrous alloys in metallic non-dispersible form (but not turnings, shavings or chippings of those metals or alloys) | Sorting; grading; baling; shearing[1] by manual feed; compacting; crushing; cutting by hand-held equipment | 8,000 tonnes |
| The following non-ferrous metals, namely copper, aluminium, nickel, lead, tin, tungsten, cobalt, molybdenum, vanadium, chromium, titanium, zirconium, manganese or zinc, or non-ferrous alloys, in metallic non-dispersible form, of any of those metals (but not turnings, shavings or chippings of those metals or alloys) | Sorting; grading; baling; shearing by manual feed; compacting; crushing; cutting by hand-held equipment | 400 tonnes |
| Turnings, shavings or chippings of any of the metals or alloys listed in either of the above categories | Sorting; grading; baling; shearing by manual feed; compacting; crushing; cutting by hand-held equipment | 300 tonnes |
| Motor vehicles (including any substance which is special waste[2] and which forms part of, or is contained in, a vehicle and was necessary for the normal operation of the vehicle) | Dismantling, rebuilding, restoring or reconditioning, but, in relation to lead acid batteries, only their removal from motor vehicles | 40 vehicles |
| Lead acid motor vehicle batteries (including those whose contents are special waste), whether or not forming part of, or contained in, a motor vehicle | Sorting (including removal from motor vehicles) | 20 tonnes |

(2) Subject to sub-paragraph (3) below, the storage, at any secure place designed or adapted for the recovery of scrap metal or the dismantling of waste motor vehicles, of waste of a kind listed in Table 4B if—

(a) the waste is to be submitted to any of the activities specified in Table 4A in relation to that kind of waste, or to a recycling or reclamation operation authorised by a waste management licence[3] or an authorisation under Part I of the 1990 Act;[4]

(b) the total quantity of waste of that kind stored at that place does not exceed the maximum total quantity specified in Table 4B in relation to that kind of waste;

(c) no waste is stored at that place for a period exceeding 12 months;

(d) each kind of waste is either stored separately or is kept in separate containers, but in a case where a consignment consisting of more than one kind of waste is delivered to that place it may be stored unseparated at that place pending sorting for a period not exceeding 2 months;

(e) in the case of waste which is liquid or consists of motor vehicle batteries, it is stored in a secure container;

(f) in the case of waste motor vehicles from which all fluids have been drained, they are, unless stored on a hardstanding, stored on an impermeable pavement;

(g) subject to paragraph (f) above, the waste or, as the case may be, any container in which it is stored, is stored on an impermeable pavement which is provided with a sealed drainage system; and

(h) the height of any pile or stack of waste does not exceed 5 metres.

[1] "Shearing" defined by para.(6) below.
[2] Special waste" defined by reg.1(3), p.677 above.
[3] "Waste management licence" has the meaning given by s.35(1) of the 1990 Act, p.119 above.
[4] P.88 above.

Table 4B

| Kind of waste | Maximum total quantity |
| --- | --- |
| Ferrous metals or ferrous alloys in metallic non-dispersible form (but not turnings, shavings or chippings of those metals or alloys) | 50,000 tonnes |
| The following non-ferrous metals, namely copper, aluminium, nickel, lead, tin, tungsten, cobalt, molybdenum, vanadium, chromium, titanium, zirconium, manganese or zinc, or non-ferrous alloys, in metallic non-dispersible form, of any of those metals (but not turnings, shavings or chippings of those metals or alloys) | 1,500 tonnes |
| Turnings, shavings or chippings of any of the metals or alloys listed in either of the above categories | 1,000 tonnes |
| Motor vehicles (including any substance which is special waste and which forms part of, or is contained in, a vehicle and was necessary for the normal operation of the vehicle): | |
| —where any such vehicle is stored on a hardstanding which is not an impermeable pavement: | 100 vehicles |
| —where all such vehicles are stored on an impermeable pavement: | 1,000 vehicles |
| Lead acid motor vehicle batteries (including those whose contents are special waste) whether or not forming part of, or contained in, a motor vehicle | 40 tonnes |

(3) Sub-paragraph (1) or (2) above only applies to the carrying on of an activity at a place if—

(a) the person responsible for the management of that place—

   (i) has established administrative arrangements to ensure that—

      (A) waste accepted at that place is of a kind listed in Table 4A or, as the case may be, Table 4B; and

      (B) no waste is accepted at that place in such a quantity as would cause there to be a breach of any of the terms and conditions of the exemption;

   and

   (ii) carries out a monthly audit to confirm compliance with the terms and conditions of the exemption;

(b) the records required by paragraph 4 of Part I of Schedule 4[1] are kept in such a form as to show, for each month, the total quantity of each kind of waste recovered during that month at that place, and details of the total quantity of each kind of waste recovered at that place during the preceding 12 months are sent annually to the appropriate registration authority with the annual fee referred to in paragraph (d) below;

(c) an up to date plan of that place containing the details referred to in regulation 18(4A)(c)(i) to (iv)[2] is sent annually to the appropriate registration authority with the annual fee referred to in paragraph (d) below; and

(d) a fee of £150[3] is paid annually in respect of that place to the appropriate registration authority by the due date which shall be ascertained in accordance with sub-paragraph (4) below.

(4) For the purposes of ascertaining the due date in any year for payment of the fee referred in sub-paragraph (3)(d) above in respect of any place—

(a) the appropriate registration authority shall serve notice in accordance with the following provisions of this sub-paragraph on the establishment or undertaking from which notice has been received by the authority under regulation 18(4A) in respect of that place;

(b) a notice required by paragraph (a) above shall be served not later than one month before the anniversary of the date when the notice, plan and fee referred to in regulation 18(4A) were received by the authority in respect of that place and shall specify—

   (i) the amount of the payment due,

   (ii) the method of payment,

   (iii) the date of such anniversary,

   (iv) that payment is due on that date or, later, upon the day falling one month after the date of the notice, and

---

[1] P.715 below.
[2] P.690 above.

[3] Words "£150" substituted by S.I. 1996/634, reg.2(7). This amendment came into force on 1 April 1996: reg.1(1).

(v)  the effect of payment not being made by the date on which it is due,

and the due date for payment of the annual fee for that year by that establishment or undertaking in respect of that place shall be the date specified for payment in the notice.

(5)  The temporary storage of waste (in this sub-paragraph referred to as "the non-scrap waste"), pending its collection, at a secure place designed or adapted for the recovery of scrap metal or the dismantling of waste motor vehicles if—

(a)  the non-scrap waste is not of a kind described in Table 4B;

(b)  the non-scrap waste was delivered to that place as part of a consignment of waste of which—

(i)  at least 70 per cent by weight was waste consisting of waste motor vehicles; or

(ii)  at least 95 per cent by weight was waste of any kind described in Table 4B other than waste motor vehicles,

and is capable of being separated from that waste by sorting or hand dismantling;

(c)  the non-scrap waste is stored at that place for no more than 3 months;

(d)  in a case where the non-scrap waste is liquid, it is stored in a secure container; and

(e)  the non-scrap waste or, as the case may be, the container in which the non-scrap waste is stored, is stored on an impermeable pavement which is provided with a sealed drainage system.

(6)  In Table 4A, "shearing" means the cold cutting of metal by purpose-made shears.

(7)  For the purposes of this paragraph and paragraph 44 above, "sealed drainage system", in relation to an impermeable pavement, means a drainage system with impermeable components which does not leak and which will ensure that—

(a)  no liquid will run off the pavement otherwise than via the system; and

(b)  except where they may be lawfully discharged, all liquids entering the system are collected in a sealed sump.[1]

# SCHEDULE 4

(Regulations 1(3)[2] and 19[3])

## WASTE FRAMEWORK DIRECTIVE ETC.

## PART I

## GENERAL

### *Interpretation of Schedule 4*

**1.**  In this Schedule, unless the context otherwise requires—

"competent authority" has the meaning given by paragraph 3;

"development", "development plan", "government department" and "planning permission" have the same meaning as in the Town and Country Planning Act 1990[4] or, in Scotland, as in the Town and Country Planning (Scotland) Act 1972;[5]

"licensing authority" and "the Ministers" have the meaning given by section 24(1) of the Food and Environment Protection Act 1985;[6]

"local planning authority" and "the planning Acts" have the same meaning as in the Town and Country Planning Act 1990;[7]

---

[1]  Reg.44 inserted by S.I. 1995/288, reg.3(16). This amendment came into force on 1 April 1995: reg.1(1).
[2]  P.676 above.
[3]  P.692 above.

[4]  1990 c.8; see s.336(1).
[5]  1972 c.52; see s.275(1).
[6]  1985 c.48.
[7]  1990 c.8; see s.336(1).

"permit" means a waste management licence,[1] a disposal licence,[2] an authorisation under Part I of the 1990 Act,[3] a resolution under section 54 of the 1990 Act, a licence under Part II of the Food and Environment Protection Act 1985 or a consent under Chapter II of Part III of the Water Resources Act 1991[4] or under Part II of the Control of Pollution Act 1974[5] (and, in relation to a permit, "grant" includes give, issue or pass, "modify" includes vary, and cognate expressions shall be construed accordingly);

"plan-making provisions" means paragraph 5 below, section 50 of the 1990 Act,[6] Part II of the Town and Country Planning Act 1990 or, in Scotland, Part II of the Town and Country Planning (Scotland) Act 1972 and section 44A of the Environmental Protection Act 1990[7] or in Scotland, section 44B of that Act;[8]

"planning authority" means the local planning authority, the person appointed under paragraph 1 of Schedule 6 to the Town and Country Planning Act 1990 or, as the case may be, the government department responsible for discharging a function under the planning Acts or, in Scotland, the planning authority (as defined in section 172 of the Local Government (Scotland) Act 1973,[9]), the person appointed under paragraph 1 of Schedule 7 to the Town and Country Planning (Scotland) Act 1972, or, as the case may be, the government department responsible for discharging a function under the Town and Country Planning (Scotland) Act 1972, and the Secretary of State shall be treated as a planning authority in respect of his functions under the planning Acts or, in Scotland, the Town and Country Planning (Scotland) Act 1972;

"pollution control authority" means any competent authority other than a planning authority;

10

"specified action" means any of the following—

(a) determining—

    (i) an application for planning permission; or

    (ii) an appeal made under section 78 of the Town and Country Planning Act 1990[11] or, in Scotland, under section 33 of the Town and Country Planning (Scotland) Act 1972,[12] in respect of such an application;

(b) deciding whether to take any action under section 141(2) or (3) or 177(1)(a) or (b)[13] of the Town and Country Planning Act 1990, or under section 196(5) of that Act[14] as originally enacted, or under section 35(5) of the Planning (Listed Buildings and Conservation Areas) Act 1990[15] or, in Scotland, under section 85(5)(a), (b) or (c),[16] 91(3) (as enacted prior to its repeal)[17] or 172(2) or (3) of, or paragraph 2(6) of Schedule 17 to, the Town and Country Planning (Scotland) Act 1972;

(c) deciding whether to direct under section 90(1), (2) or (2A) of the Town and Country Planning Act 1990[18] or, in Scotland, section 37(1) of the Town and Country Planning (Scotland) Act 1972[19] or paragraph 7(1) of Schedule 8 to the Electricity Act 1989,[20] that planning permission shall be deemed to be granted;

(d) deciding whether—

---

[1] "Waste management licence" has the meaning given by s.35(1) of the 1990 Act, p.119 above.

[2] "Disposal licence" defined by reg.1(3), p.676 above.

[3] P.88 above.

[4] P.273 above

[5] P.18 above.

[6] Former word "and" omitted by S.I. 1996/593, reg.3, sch.2, para.10(5)(a)(i).

[7] P.134 above.

[8] P.136 above. Words "and section 44A ... that Act" inserted by S.I. 1996/593, reg.3, sch.2, para.10(5)(a)(ii). This amendment came into force on 1 April 1996: reg.1.

[9] 1973 c.65; s.172(4) is amended by para.22 of sch.3 to the Local Government and Planning (Scotland) Act 1982 (c.43).

[10] The definition of "river purification authority" omitted by S.I. 1996/973, reg.2, sch., para.17(3)(a).

[11] 1990 c.8; s.78 is amended by s.17(2) of the Planning and Compensation Act 1991 (c.34).

[12] S.33 is amended by s.172(2) of the Local Government (Scotland) Act 1973 (c.65), by para.11 of sch.2 to the Local Government and Planning (Scotland) Act 1982 (c.43), by paras.55 and 56 of sch.11 to the Housing and Planning Act 1986 (c.673) and by para.11 of sch.13 to the Planning and Compensation Act 1991 (c.34).

[13] S.177(1)(a) is substituted by para.24(1)(a) of sch.7 to the Planning and Compensation Act 1991 (c.34).

[14] S.196(5) is repealed by para.33(e) of sch.7 to the Planning and Compensation Act 1991 (c.34), but that repeal does not apply to appeals arising out of applications made under s.192(1) (as originally enacted) before 27 July 1992.

[15] 1990 c.9.

[16] S.85(5) is amended by para.20(c) of sch.2 to the Local Government and Planning (Scotland) Act 1982 (c.43); extended by s.3(9) of the Town and Country Planning Act 1984 (c.10); and amended by para.20(c) of sch.13, and part IV of sch.19, to the Planning and Compensation Act 1991 (c.34).

[17] S.91(3) is amended by s.172(2) of the Local Government (Scotland) Act 1973 (c.65) and by sch.4 to the Local Government (Miscellaneous Provisions) (Scotland) Act 1981 (c.23); s.91(3) is repealed by para.26 of sch.13, and part IV of sch.19, to the Planning and Compensation Act 1991 (c.34), but that repeal does not apply to appeals arising out of applications made under s.90(2) before 25 September 1992.

[18] S.90(2A) is inserted by s.16(1) of the Transport and Works Act 1992 (c.42).

[19] S.37(1) is amended by part I of sch.4 to the Local Government and Planning (Scotland) Act 1982 (c.43) and extended by para.2(1)(xxv) of sch.7 to the Gas Act 1986 (c.44).

[20] 1989 c.29; para.7 of sch.8 is repealed in England and Wales by part II of sch.1 to the Planning (Consequential Provisions) Act 1990 (c.11), and repealed (in part) in Scotland by Part III of that sch.

(i) in making or confirming a discontinuance order, to include in the order any grant of planning permission; or

(ii) to confirm (with or without modifications) a discontinuance order insofar as it grants planning permission,

and, for the purposes of this sub-paragraph, "discontinuance order" means an order under section 102 of the Town and Country Planning Act 1990[1] (including an order made under that section by virtue of section 104 of that Act), or under paragraph 1 of Schedule 9 to that Act[2] (including an order made under that paragraph by virtue of paragraph 11 of that Schedule), or, in Scotland, an order under section 49 of the Town and Country Planning (Scotland) Act 1972[3] (including an order made under that section by virtue of section 260 of that Act[4]);

(e) discharging functions under Part II of the Town and Country Planning Act 1990 or, in Scotland, Part II of the Town and Country Planning (Scotland) Act 1972.

## Duties of competent authorities

2. (1) Subject to the following provisions of this paragraph, the competent authorities[5] shall discharge their specified functions, insofar as they relate to the recovery[6] or disposal[7] of waste,[8] with the relevant objectives.[9]

(2) Nothing in sub-paragraph (1) above requires a planning authority[10] to deal with any matter which the relevant pollution control authority[11] has the power to deal with.

(3) In a case where the recovery or disposal of waste is or forms part of a prescribed process designated for local control under Part I of the 1990 Act,[12] and either requires a waste management licence[13] or is covered by an exemption conferred by regulation 17(1)[14] of, and Schedule 3[15] to, these Regulations, nothing in sub-paragraph (1) above shall require a competent authority to discharge its functions under—

(a) Part I of the 1990 Act in order to control pollution of the environment due to the release of substances into any environmental medium other than the air; or

(b) Part II of the 1990 Act in order to control pollution of the environment due to the release of substances into the air resulting from the carrying on of the prescribed process.

(4) In sub-paragraph (3) above, "prescribed process", "designated for local control", "pollution of the environment due to the release of substances into the air" and "pollution of the environment due to the release of substances into any environmental medium other than the air" have the meaning which they have in Part I of the 1990 Act.[16]

## Meaning of "competent authority" etc.

3. (1) For the purposes of this Schedule, "competent authority" means any of the persons or bodies listed in column (1) of Table 5 below and, subject to sub-paragraph (2) below, in relation to a competent authority "specified function" means any function of that authority listed in column (2) of that Table opposite the entry for that authority.

---

[1] S.102 is amended by para.6 of sch.1, and para.21 of sch.7, to the Planning and Compensation Act 1991 (c.34).

[2] Para.1 of sch.9 is amended by para.15 of sch.1 to the Planning and Compensation Act 1991 (c.34).

[3] S.49 is amended by s.172(2) of the Local Government (Scotland) Act 1973 (c.65), s.26 of the Town and Country Planning (Minerals) Act 1981 (c.36), and para.5 of sch.8, and para.16 of sch.13, to the Planning and Compensation Act 1991 (c.34).

[4] S.260 is amended by s.172(2) of, para.31 of sch.23, para.48 of sch.25 and sch.29 to the Local Government (Scotland) Act 1973 (c.65), by sch.4 of the Local Government (Miscellaneous Provisions) (Scotland) Act 1981 (c.23), by para.10 of sch.2 to the Town and Country Planning (Minerals) Act 1981 (c.36) and by para.51 of sch.11 to the Housing and Planning Act 1986 (c.63).

[5] "Competent authority" has the meaning given by para.3 below: para.1 above.

[6] "Recovery" defined by reg.1(3), p.677 above.

[7] "Disposal" defined by reg.1(3), p.676 above.

[8] "Waste" defined by reg.1(3), p.677 above.

[9] For "relevant objectives" see para.4 below.

[10] "Planning authority" defined by reg.1(3), p.677 above.

[11] "Pollution control authority" defined by para.1 above.

[12] P.88 above.

[13] "Waste management licence" has the meaning given by s.35(1) of the 1990 Act, p.119 above.

[14] P.687 above.

[15] P.697 above.

[16] See s.2(4), p.91 above, for the meaning of "designated for local control", and s.1, p.89 above, for the meaning of the other phrases.

**Table 5**

| Competent authorities (1) | Specified functions (2) |
|---|---|
| Any planning authority.[1] | The taking of any specified action. |
| A waste regulation authority,[2] the Secretary of State or a person appointed under section 114(1)(a) of the Environment Act 1995.[3] | Their respective functions under Part II of the 1990 Act[4] in relation to waste management licences,[5] including preparing plans or modifications of them under section 50 of the 1990 Act and preparing the strategy, or any modification of it, under section 44A or 44B of that Act.[6] |
| A disposal authority[7] or the Secretary of State. | Their respective functions under Part I of the Control of Pollution Act 1974 in relation to disposal licences[8] and resolutions under section 11 of that Act. |
| A licensing authority or the Ministers.[9] | Their respective functions under Part II of the Food and Environment Protection Act 1985, or under paragraph 5 below. |
| An enforcing authority,[10] the Secretary of State or a person appointed under section 114(1)(a) of the Environment Act 1995.[11] | Their respective functions under Part I of the 1990 Act[12] in relation to prescribed processes except when— (a) the process is designated for local control; and (b) it is an exempt activity[13] carried out subject to the conditions and limitations specified in Schedule 3.[14] |
| The Environment Agency[15] or the Secretary of State. | Their respective functions in relation to the giving of consents under Chapter II of Part III of the Water Resources Act 1991[16] (offences in relation to pollution of water resources) for any discharge of waste in liquid form other than waste waters. |
| In Scotland, the Scottish Environment Protection Agency[17] or the Secretary of State. | Their respective functions in relation to the giving of consents under Part II of the Control of Pollution Act 1974[18] (pollution of water) for any discharge of waste in liquid form other than waste waters. |

(2) In Table 5 above, references to functions do not include functions of making, revoking, amending, revising or re-enacting orders, regulations or schemes where those functions are required to be discharged by statutory instrument.

### Relevant objectives

**4.** (1) For the purposes of this Schedule, the following objectives are relevant objectives in relation to the disposal[19] or recovery[20] of waste[21]—

[1] "Planning authority" defined by reg.1(3), p.677 above.
[2] "Waste regulation authority" has the meaning given by s.30 of the 1990 Act, p.113 above.
[3] P.489 above. Words "section 114(1)(a) of the Environment Act 1995" substituted by S.I. 1996/593, reg.3, sch.2, para.10(5)(b)(i). This amendment came into force on 1 April 1996: reg.1.
[4] P.88 above.
[5] "Waste management licence" has the meaning given by s.35(1) of the 1990 Act, p.119 above.
[6] Words "and . . . that Act" added by S.I. 1996/593, reg.3, sch.2, para.10(5)(b)(ii).
[7] "Disposal authority" defined by reg.1(3), p.676 above.
[8] "Disposal licence" defined by reg.1(3), p.676 above.
[9] "Licensing authority" and "the Ministers" defined by para.1, p.712 above.
[10] "Enforcing authority" defined by reg.1(3), p.676 above.

[11] P.489 above. Words "section 114(1)(a) of the Environment Act 1995" substituted by S.I. 1996/593, reg.3, sch.2, para.10(5)(b)(iii).
[12] P.88 above.
[13] "Exempt authority" defined by reg.1(3), p.676 above.
[14] P.697 above.
[15] Words "the Environment Agency" substituted by the Environment Act 1995 (c.25), s.120, sch.22, para.233. This amendment came into force on 1 April 1996: S.I. 1996/186.
[16] P.273 above.
[17] Words "the Scottish Environment Protection Agency" substituted by S.I. 1996/973, reg.2, sch., para.17(3)(b). This amendment came into force on 1 April 1996: reg.1.
[18] P.18 above.
[19] "Disposal" defined by reg.1(3), p.676 above.
[20] "Recovery" defined by reg.1(3), p.677 above.
[21] "Waste" defined by reg.1(3), p.677 above.

(a) ensuring that waste is recovered or disposed of without endangering human health and without using processes or methods which could harm the environment and in particular without—

    (i)    risk to water, air, soil, plants or animals; or

    (ii)   causing nuisance through noise or odours; or

    (iii)  adversely affecting the countryside or places of special interest;

(b) implementing, so far as material, any plan made under the plan-making provisions.[1]

(2) The following additional objectives are relevant objectives in relation to the disposal of waste—

(a) establishing an integrated and adequate network of waste disposal installations, taking account of the best available technology not involving excessive costs; and

(b) ensuring that the network referred to at paragraph (a) above enables—

    (i)    the European Community as a whole to become self-sufficient in waste disposal, and the Member States individually to move towards that aim, taking into account geographical circumstances or the need for specialized installations for certain types of waste; and

    (ii)   waste to be disposed of in one of the nearest appropriate installations, by means of the most appropriate methods and technologies in order to ensure a high level of protection for the environment and public health.

(3) The following further objectives are relevant objectives in relation to functions under the plan-making provisions—

(a) encouraging the prevention or reduction of waste production and its harmfulness, in particular by—

    (i)    the development of clean technologies more sparing in their use of natural resources;

    (ii)   the technical development and marketing of products designed so as to make no contribution or to make the smallest possible contribution, by the nature of their manufacture, use or final disposal, to increasing the amount of harmfulness of waste and pollution hazards; and

    (iii)  the development of appropriate techniques for the final disposal of dangerous substances contained in waste destined for recovery; and

(b) encouraging—

    (i)    the recovery of waste by means of recycling, reuse or reclamation or any other process with a view to extracting secondary raw materials; and

    (ii)   the use of waste as a source of energy.

### Preparation of offshore waste management plan

**5.** (1) Subject to sub-paragraph (2) below, it shall be the duty of a licensing authority[2] to prepare a statement ("the plan") containing the authority's policies in relation to the recovery[3] or disposal[4] of waste[5] for attaining the relevant objectives in those parts of United Kingdom waters and United Kingdom controlled waters for which the authority is the licensing authority.

(2) Two or more licensing authorities may join together to prepare a single statement covering the several parts of United Kingdom waters and United Kingdom controlled waters for which they are the licensing authorities.

(3) The plan shall relate in particular to—

(a) the type, quantity and origin of waste to be recovered or disposed of;

(b) general technical requirements;

(c) any special arrangements for particular wastes; and

(d) suitable disposal sites or installations.

(4) The licensing authority shall make copies of the plan available to the public on payment of reasonable charges.

(5) In this paragraph, "United Kingdom waters" and "United Kingdom controlled waters" have the meaning given by section 24(1) of the Food and Environment Protection Act 1985.[6]

[1] "Plan-making provisions" defined by para.1, p.713 above. See S.I. 1994/1137, reg. 11(6), p.745 below.

[2] "Licensing authority" defined by para.1, p.712 above.

[3] "Recovery" defined by reg.1(3), p.677 above.

[4] "Disposal" defined by reg.1(3), p.676 above.

[5] "Waste" defined by reg.1(3), p.677 above.

[6] 1985 c.48; the definition of "United Kingdom controlled waters" is inserted by s.146(7) of the Environmental Protection Act 1990.

*Matters to be covered by permits*

6. When a pollution control authority[1] grants or modifies a permit,[2] and the activities authorised by the permit include the disposal[3] of waste,[4] the pollution control authority shall ensure that the permit covers—

    (a)  the types and quantities of waste,

    (b)  the technical requirements,

    (c)  the security precautions to be taken,

    (d)  the disposal site, and

    (e)  the treatment method.

*Modifications of provisions relating to development plans*

7. (1) Subject to sub-paragraph (2) below, sections 12(3A), 31(3) and 36(3) of the Town and Country Planning Act 1990[5] or, in Scotland, sections 5(3)(a) and 9(3)(a) of the Town and Country Planning (Scotland) Act 1972,[6] shall have effect as if the policies referred to in those sections also included policies in respect of suitable waste disposal sites or installations.

    (2) In the case of the policies referred to in section 36(3) of the Town and Country Planning Act 1990, sub-paragraph (1) above shall have effect subject to the provisions of section 36(5) of that Act.[7]

    (3) Section 38(1) of the Town and Country Planning Act 1990[8] shall have effect as if the definition of waste policies included detailed policies in respect of suitable disposal sites or installations for the carrying on of such development as is referred to in that definition.

*Modifications of Part I of the Environmental Protection Act 1990*

8. (1) Subject to section 28(1) of the 1990 Act,[9] Part I of the 1990 Act shall have effect in relation to prescribed processes involving the disposal[10] or recovery[11] of waste[12] with such modifications as are needed to allow an enforcing authority[13] to exercise its functions under that Part for the purpose of achieving the relevant objectives.[14]

    (2) Nothing in sub-paragraph (1) above requires an enforcing authority granting an authorisation in relation to such a process to take account of the relevant objectives insofar as they relate to the prevention of detriment to the amenities of the locality in which the process is (or is to be) carried on if planning permission,[15] resulting from the taking of a specified action by a planning authority[16] after 30th April 1994, is or, before the process is carried on, will be in force.

*Modifications of Part II of the Environmental Protection Act 1990*

9. (1) Part II of the 1990 Act[17] shall have effect subject to the following modifications.

    (2) Any reference to waste shall include a reference to Directive waste.[18]

    (3) In sections 33(1)(a)[19] and (5), 54(1)(a), (2), (3) and (4)(d) and 69(2), any reference to the deposit of waste in or on land shall include a reference to any operation listed in Part III[20] or IV of this Schedule involving such a deposit.

    (4) In sections 33(1)(b), 54(1)(b), (2), (3) and (4)(d) and 69(2), any reference to the treatment or disposal, or to the treatment, keeping or disposal, of controlled waste shall be taken to be a reference to submitting controlled

---

[1] "Pollution control authority" defined by para.1, p.713 above.

[2] "Permit" defined by para.1, p.712 above.

[3] "Disposal" defined by reg.1(3), p.676 above.

[4] "Waste" defined by reg.1(3), p.677 above.

[5] 1990 c.8; ss.12(3A), 31(3) and 36(3) are substituted by paras.2(1), 16 and 17 respectively of sch.4 to the Planning and Compensation Act 1991 (c.34).

[6] 1972 c.52; ss.5(3)(a) and 9(3)(a) are amended by paras.3 and 4 of sch. 13 to the Planning and Compensation Act 1991 (c.34).

[7] S.36(5) is inserted by para.17 of sch.4 to the Planning and Compensation Act 1991 (c.34).

[8] S.38 is inserted by para.17 of sch.4 to the Planning and Compensation Act 1991 (c.34).

[9] P.111 above.

[10] "Disposal" defined by reg.1(3), p.676 above.

[11] "Recovery" defined by reg.1(3), p.677 above.

[12] "Waste" defined by reg.1(3), p.677 above.

[13] "Enforcing authority" defined by reg.1(3), p.676 above.

[14] For "relevant objectives" see para.4 above.

[15] "Planning permission" defined by para.1, p.712 above.

[16] "Planning authority" defined by para.1, p.713 above.

[17] P.88 above.

[18] "Directive waste" defined by reg.1(3), p.676 above.

[19] P.116 above.

[20] P.721 below.

waste to any of the operations listed in Part III or IV of this Schedule other than an operation mentioned in sub-paragraph (3) above.

(5) In sections 33(1)(c) and 35,[1] any reference to the treatment or disposal, or to the treatment, keeping or disposal, of controlled waste shall include a reference to submitting controlled waste to any of the operations listed in Part III or Part IV of this Schedule.

(6) Section 33(2) shall not apply to the treatment, keeping or disposal[2] of household waste[3] by an establishment or undertaking.

(7) In section 36(3),[4] the reference to planning permission shall be taken to be a reference to planning permission[5] resulting from the taking of a specified action by a planning authority[6] after 30th April 1994.

(8) In section 50(3), any reference to the disposal of waste shall include a reference to the recovery of waste.

(9) In subsection (1) of section 62,[7] any reference to the treatment, keeping or disposal of such waste as is referred to in that subsection shall include a reference to submitting such waste to any of the operations listed in Part III or IV of this Schedule.[8]

(10) In subsection (2) of section 62, any reference to the treatment, keeping or disposal of special waste[9] shall include a reference to submitting special waste to any of the operations listed in Part III or IV of this Schedule.[10]

## Modifications of Part I of the Control of Pollution Act 1974

10. (1) Part I of the Control of Pollution Act 1974[11] shall have effect, in a case where the planning permission referred to in section 5(3) of that Act does not result from the taking of a specified action by a planning authority after 30th April 1994, as if the duty imposed upon the disposal authority by that subsection was a duty not to reject the application unless the authority is satisfied that its rejection is necessary for the purpose of preventing—

(a) pollution of the environment;

(b) danger to public health; or

(c) serious detriment to the amenities of the locality.

(2) In sub-paragraph (1) above, "pollution of the environment" has the same meaning as in Part II of the 1990 Act.[12]

(3) Part I of the Control of Pollution Act 1974 shall have effect as if any reference in that Part to waste included a reference to Directive waste.[13]

## References to "waste" in Planning and Water legislation

11. In the Town and Country Planning Act 1990, the Town and Country Planning (Scotland) Act 1972, Part II of the Control of Pollution Act 1974[14] and Chapter II of Part III of the Water Resources Act 1991,[15] any reference to "waste" shall include a reference to Directive waste.

## Registration by professional collectors and transporters of waste, and by dealers and brokers

12. (1) Subject to sub-paragraph (3) below, it shall be an offence for an establishment or undertaking falling within sub-paragraph (a), (c), (f) or (g) of regulation 2(1) of the Controlled Waste (Registration of Carriers and Seizure of Vehicles) Regulations 1991[16] after 31st December 1994 to collect or transport waste[17] on a professional basis unless it is registered in accordance with the provisions of this regulation.

(2) Subject to sub-paragraph (3) below, it shall be an offence for an establishment or undertaking falling within sub-paragraph (a), (b) or (c) of regulation 20(4)[18] after 31st December 1994 to arrange for the recovery[19] or

---

[1] P.119 above.
[2] "Disposal" defined by reg.1(3), p.676 above.
[3] "Household waste" defined by s.75 of the 1990 Act, p.159 above.
[4] P.122 above.
[5] "Planning permission" defined by para.1, p.712 above.
[6] "Planning authority" defined by para.1, p.713 above.
[7] P.151 above.
[8] P.721 below.
[9] "Special waste" defined by reg.1(3), p.677 above.
[10] Sub-paragraphs (9) and (10) added by S.I. 1996/972,

reg.25, sch.3. This amendment came into force on 1 September 1996: reg.1(1).
[11] 1974 c.40.
[12] See s.29 of the 1990 Act, p.112 above.
[13] "Directive waste" defined by reg.1(3), p.676 above.
[14] P.18 above.
[15] P.273 above.
[16] P.630 above.
[17] "Waste" defined by reg.1(3), p.677 above.
[18] P.692 above.
[19] "Recovery" defined by reg.1(3), p.677 above.

disposal[1] of waste on behalf of another person unless it is registered in accordance with the provisions of this paragraph.

(3)  Sub-paragraphs (1) and (2) above do not apply in cases where the establishment or undertaking is carrying on the activities therein mentioned pursuant to, and in accordance with the terms and conditions of, a permit.

(4)  An establishment or undertaking shall register with the waste regulation authority[2] in whose area its principal place of business in Great Britain is located or, where it has no place of business in Great Britain, with any waste regulation authority.

(5)  Each waste regulation authority shall establish and maintain a register of establishments and undertakings registering with it under the provisions of this paragraph.

(6)  The register shall contain the following particulars in relation to each such establishment or undertaking—

(a)  the name of the establishment or undertaking;

(b)  the address of its principal place of business; and

(c)  the address of any place at or from which it carries on its business.

(7)  The waste regulation authority shall enter the relevant particulars in the register in relation to an establishment or undertaking if it receives notice of them in writing or otherwise becomes aware of those particulars.

(8)  A person guilty of an offence under sub-paragraph (1) or (2) above shall be liable on summary conviction to a fine not exceeding level 2 on the standard scale.[3]

(9)  Each waste regulation authority shall secure that any register maintained by it under this paragraph is open to inspection[4] by members of the public free of charge at all reasonable hours and shall afford to members of the public reasonable facilities for obtaining, on payment of reasonable charges, copies of entries in the register.

(10)  Registers under this paragraph may be kept in any form.

(11)  In this paragraph, "registered carrier" and "controlled waste" have the same meaning as they have in the Control of Pollution (Amendment) Act 1989,[5] "registered broker" has the same meaning as in regulation 20[6] and Schedule 5,[7] and "collect" and "transport" have the same meaning as they have in Article 12 of the Directive.

### *Duty to carry out appropriate periodic inspections*

**13.**  (1)  Subject to sub-paragraphs (3) to (5) below,[8] any establishment or undertaking which carries out the recovery[9] or disposal[10] of controlled waste,[11] or which collects or transports controlled waste on a professional basis, or which arranges for the recovery or disposal of controlled waste on behalf of others (dealers or brokers), and producers of special waste,[12] shall be subject to appropriate periodic inspections by the competent authorities.[13]

(2)  Section[14] 71(2) and (3) of the 1990 Act[15] ([16] power to obtain information) shall have effect as if the provisions of this paragraph were provisions of Part II of that Act and as if, in those sections, references to a waste regulation authority[17] were references to a competent authority.[18]

(2A)  Section 108 of the Environment Act 1995[19] (powers of entry) shall apply as if the competent authority was an enforcing authority[20] and its functions under this paragraph were pollution control functions.[21]

---

[1]  "Disposal" defined by reg.1(3), p.676 above.

[2]  "Waste regulation authority" has the meaning given by s.30 of the 1990 Act, p.113 above.

[3]  The current fine at level 2 on the standard scale is £500: Criminal Justice Act 1991 (c.53), s.17 (England and Wales); Criminal Procedure (Scotland) Act 1995 (c.46), s.225 (Scotland).

[4]  Former words "at its principal office" omitted by S.I. 1996/593, reg.3, sch.2, para.10(5)(c). This amendment came into force on 1 April 1996: reg.1.

[5]  P.71 above.

[6]  P.692 above.

[7]  P.723 below.

[8]  Words "Subject to sub-paragraphs (3) to (5) below," inserted by S.I. 1995/288, reg.3(17). This amendment came into force on 1 April 1995: reg.1(1).

[9]  "Recovery" defined by reg.1(3), p.677 above.

[10]  "Disposal" defined by reg.1(3), p.676 above.

[11]  For the definition of "controlled waste" in Part II of the Environmental Protection Act 1990, see s.75, p.159 above,

and the Controlled Waste Regulations 1992, p.662 above.

[12]  "Special waste" defined by reg.1(3), p.677 above; words "and producers of special waste," inserted by S.I. 1996/972, reg.25, sch.3. This amendment came into force on 1 September 1996: reg.1(1).

[13]  "Competent authority" defined by para.1, p.712 above.

[14]  Word "Section" substituted by S.I. 1996/593, reg.3, sch.2, para.10(5)(d)(i). This amendment came into force on 1 April 1996: reg.1.

[15]  P.156 above.

[16]  Former words "power to appoint inspectors, powers of entry and" omitted by S.I. 1996/593, reg.3, sch.2, para.10(5)(d)(i).

[17]  "Waste regulation authority" has the meaning given by s.30 of the 1990 Act, p.113 above.

[18]  "Competent authority" defined by para.1, p.712 above.

[19]  P.481 above.

[20]  "Enforcing authority" defined by reg.1(3), p.676 above.

[21]  Para.(2A) added by S.I. 1996/593, reg.3, sch.2, para.10(5)(d)(ii).

(3) Subject to sub-paragraph (4) below, in a case where an establishment or undertaking is carrying on an exempt activity[1] in reliance upon an exemption conferred by regulation 17(1)[2] of, and paragraph 45(1) or (2) of Schedule 3 to,[3] these Regulations, a competent authority which is a waste regulation authority shall discharge its duty under sub-paragraph (1) in respect of any place where such an activity is so carried on by—

(a) carrying out an initial inspection of that place within two months of having received in respect of that place the notice, plan and fee referred to in regulation 18(4A); and

(b) thereafter carrying out periodic inspections of that place at intervals not exceeding 12 months.

(4) Where the notice, plan and fee referred to in paragraph (a) of sub-paragraph (3) above are received by the authority before 1st October 1995, that paragraph shall have effect as if for the reference to carrying out an initial inspection within two months of the receipt of such notice, plan and fee there were substituted a reference to carrying out such an inspection within nine months of their receipt.

(5) In the case of any such place as is mentioned in sub-paragraph (3) above, but without prejudice to any duties of waste regulation authorities imposed otherwise than by this paragraph, sub-paragraph (1) above does not require (but does permit) a competent authority which is a waste regulation authority to carry out the periodic inspections referred to in sub-paragraph (3)(b) above at intervals of less than 10 months.[4]

*Record keeping*

**14.** (1) Subject to paragraph 45(3)(b) of Schedule 3[5] and [6] sub-paragraph (2) below, an establishment or undertaking which carries out the disposal[7] or recovery[8] of controlled waste[9] shall—

(a) keep a record of the quantity, nature, origin and, where relevant, the destination, frequency of collection, mode of transport and treatment method of any waste which is disposed of or recovered; and

(b) make that information available, on request, to the competent authorities[10] or, in the case of special waste,[11] to a previous holder; and for this purpose "holder", in respect of any such waste, means the producer or the person in possession of it.[12]

(1A) Where special waste is recovered or disposed of by an establishment or undertaking, it shall keep a record of the carrying out and supervision of the operation and, in the case of a disposal operation, of the after-care of the disposal site.[13]

(2) Subject to sub-paragraph (3) below,[14] sub-paragraph (1) above does not apply where the disposal or recovery of the waste is covered by an exemption conferred by—

(a) regulation 17(1)[15] of, and Schedule 3[16] to, these Regulations; or

(b) article 3 of the Deposits in the Sea (Exemptions) Order 1985.[17]

(3) Sub-paragraph (1) above does apply to an activity subject to an exemption conferred by regulation 17(1) of, and paragraph 45(1) or (2) of Schedule 3[18] to, these Regulations.[19]

(4) Subject to sub-paragraph (5) below, it shall be an offence for an establishment or undertaking to fail to comply with any of the foregoing provisions of this paragraph insofar as that provision imposes any requirement or obligation upon it.

(5) Paragraph (2) of regulation 18 of the Special Waste Regulations 1996[20] (defence in cases of emergency etc.) shall apply to a person charged with an offence under sub-paragraph (4) above as it applies to a person charged with an offence under paragraph (1) of that regulation.

(6) A person who, in purported compliance with a requirement to furnish any information imposed by or under any of the provisions of this paragraph, makes a statement which he knows to be false or misleading in a

---

[1] "Exempt activity" defined by reg.1(3), p.676 above.
[2] P.689 above.
[3] P.697 above.
[4] Paras. (3)–(5) added by S.I. 1995/288, reg.3(18). This amendment came into force on 1 April 1995, reg.1.
[5] P.711 above.
[6] Words "Paragraph 45(3)(b) of Schedule 3 and" inserted by S.I. 1995/288, reg.3(19). This amendment came into force on 1 April 1995, reg.1.
[7] "Disposal" defined by reg.1(3), p.676 above.
[8] "Recovery" defined by reg.1(3), p.677 above.
[9] For the definition of "controlled waste" in Part II of the Environmental Protection Act 1990, see s.75, p.159 above, and the Controlled Waste Regulations 1992, p.662 above.
[10] "Competent authority" defined by para.1, p.712 above.

[11] "Special waste" defined by reg.1(3), p.677 above.
[12] Words "or, in the case of special waste . . . in possession of it" added by S.I. 1996/972, reg.25, sch.3. This amendment came into force on 1 September 1996: reg.1(1).
[13] Sub-paragraph (1A) added by S.I. 1996/972, reg.25, sch.3.
[14] Words "Subject to sub-paragraph (3) below," inserted by S.I. 1995/288, reg.3(20).
[15] P.689 above.
[16] P.697 above.
[17] S.I. 1985/1699.
[18] P.709 above.
[19] Sub-paragraph (3) added by S.I. 1995/288, reg.3(21).
[20] P.775 below.

material particular, or recklessly makes any statement which is false or misleading in a material particular, commits an offence.

(7) A person who intentionally makes a false entry in any record required to be kept by virtue of any of the provisions of this paragraph commits an offence.

(8) Paragraphs (5) to (9) of regulation 18 of the Special Waste Regulations 1996 (offence where act or default causes offence by another, offences by bodies corporate and penalties) shall apply to an offence under this paragraph as they apply to an offence under that regulation.[1]

## Part II

### Substances or Objects which are Waste when Discarded etc.

1. Production or consumption residues not otherwise specified in this Part of this Schedule (Q1).
2. Off-specification products (Q2).
3. Products whose date for appropriate use has expired (Q3).
4. Materials spilled, lost or having undergone other mishap, including any materials, equipment, etc., contaminated as a result of the mishap (Q4).
5. Materials contaminated or soiled as a result of planned actions (e.g. residues from cleaning operations, packing materials, containers, etc.) (Q5).
6. Unusable parts (e.g. reject batteries, exhausted catalysts, etc.) (Q6).
7. Substances which no longer perform satisfactorily (e.g. contaminated acids, contaminated solvents, exhausted tempering salts, etc.) (Q7).
8. Residues of industrial processes (e.g. slags, still bottoms, etc.) (Q8).
9. Residues from pollution abatement processes (e.g. scrubber sludges, baghouse dusts, spent filters, etc.) (Q9).
10. Machining or finishing residues (e.g. lathe turnings, mill scales, etc.) (Q10).
11. Residues from raw materials extraction and processing (e.g. mining residues, oil field slops, etc.) (Q11).
12. Adulterated materials (e.g. oils contaminated with PCBs, etc.) (Q12).
13. Any materials, substances or products whose use has been banned by law (Q13).
14. Products for which the holder has no further use (e.g. agricultural, household, office, commercial and shop discards, etc.) (Q14).
15. Contaminated materials, substances or products resulting from remedial action with respect to land (Q15).
16. Any materials, substances or products which are not contained in the above categories (Q16).

(Note: the reference in brackets at the end of each paragraph of this Part of this Schedule is the number of the corresponding paragraph in Annex I to the Directive.)

## Part III

### Waste Disposal Operations

1. Tipping of waste above or underground (e.g. landfill, etc.) (D1).
2. Land treatment of waste (e.g. biodegradation of liquid or sludge discards in soils, etc.) (D2).
3. Deep injection of waste (e.g. injection of pumpable discards into wells, salt domes or naturally occurring repositories, etc.) (D3).
4. Surface impoundment of waste (e.g. placement of liquid or sludge discards into pits, ponds or lagoons, etc.) (D4).
5. Specially engineered landfill of waste (e.g. placement of waste into lined discrete cells which are capped and isolated from one another and the environment, etc.) (D5).
6. Release of solid waste into a water body except seas or oceans (D6).
7. Release of waste into seas or oceans including seabed insertion (D7).

[29] Sub-paragraphs (4)–(8) added by S.I. 1996/972, reg.25, sch.3.

8. Biological treatment of waste not listed elsewhere in this Part of this Schedule which results in final compounds or mixtures which are disposed of by means of any of the operations listed in this Part of this Schedule (D8).

9. Physico-chemical treatment of waste not listed elsewhere in this Part of this Schedule which results in final compounds or mixtures which are disposed of by means of any of the operations listed in this Part of this Schedule (e.g. evaporation, drying, calcination, etc.) (D9).

10. Incineration of waste on land (D10).

11. Incineration of waste at sea (D11).

12. Permanent storage of waste (e.g. emplacement of containers in a mine, etc.) (D12).

13. Blending or mixture of waste prior to the waste being submitted to any of the operations listed in this Part of this Schedule (D13).

14. Repackaging of waste prior to the waste being submitted to any of the operations listed in this Part of this Schedule (D14).

15. Storage of waste pending any of the operations listed in this Part of this Schedule, but excluding temporary storage, pending collection, on the site where the waste is produced (D15).

(Note: the reference in brackets at the end of each paragraph of this Part of this Schedule is the number of the corresponding paragraph in Annex IIA to the Directive.)

## Part IV

### Waste Recovery Operations

1. Reclamation or regeneration of solvents (R1).

2. Recycling or reclamation of organic substances which are not used as solvents (R2).

3. Recycling or reclamation of metals and metal compounds (R3).

4. Recycling or reclamation of other inorganic materials (R4).

5. Regeneration of acids or bases (R5).

6. Recovery of components used for pollution abatement (R6).

7. Recovery of components from catalysts (R7).

8. Re-refining, or other reuses, of oil which is waste (R8).

9. Use of waste principally as a fuel or for other means of generating energy (R9).

10. Spreading of waste on land resulting in benefit to agriculture or ecological improvement, including composting and other biological transformation processes, except in the case of waste excluded under Article 2(1)(b)(iii) of the Directive (R10).

11. Use of wastes obtained from any of the operations listed in paragraphs 1 to 10 of this Part of this Schedule (R11).

12. Exchange of wastes for submission to any of the operations listed in paragraphs 1 to 11 of this Part of this Schedule (R12).

13. Storage of waste consisting of materials intended for submission to any operation listed in this Part of this Schedule, but excluding temporary storage, pending collection, on the site where it is produced (R13).

(Note: the reference in brackets at the end of each paragraph of this Part of this Schedule is the number of the corresponding paragraph in Annex IIB to the Directive.)

# SCHEDULE 5

(Regulation 20(7)[1])

## REGISTRATION OF BROKERS OF CONTROLLED WASTE

## PART I

## GENERAL

### *Interpretation*

**1.** (1)  In this Schedule—

"the Carriers Regulations" means the Controlled Waste (Registration of Carriers and Seizure of Vehicles) Regulations 1991;[2]

"date of expiry", in relation to a broker's registration, in a case to which sub-paragraph (2) or (3) of paragraph 7 applies, has the meaning given by that sub-paragraph, and in any other case means the date on which the period of three years mentioned in paragraph 7(1) expires;

"notice" means notice in writing;

"relevant offence" means an offence under any of the enactments listed in regulation 3;[3] and

"relevant period" means two months or, except in the case of an application for the renewal of his registration by a person who is already registered, such longer period as may be agreed between the applicant and the waste regulation authority.[4]

(2)  In determining for the purposes of paragraph 3(13) or 5(1) whether it is desirable for any individual to be or to continue to be authorised to arrange (as dealer or broker) for the disposal or recovery of controlled waste on behalf of other persons, a waste regulation authority shall have regard, in a case in which a person other than the individual has been convicted of a relevant offence, to whether that individual has been a party to the carrying on of a business in a manner involving the commission of relevant offences.

(3)  In relation to any applicant for registration or registered broker, another relevant person shall be treated for the purposes of paragraph 3(13) or 5(1) as having been convicted of a relevant offence if—

(a)  any person has been convicted of a relevant offence committed by him in the course of his employment by the applicant or registered broker or in the course of the carrying on of any business by a partnership one of the members of which was the applicant or registered broker;

(b)  a body corporate has been convicted of a relevant offence committed at a time when the applicant or registered broker was a director, manager, secretary or other similar officer of that body corporate; or

(c)  where the applicant or registered broker is a body corporate, a person who is a director, manager, secretary or other similar officer of that body corporate—

 (i)  has been convicted of a relevant offence; or

 (ii)  was a director, manager, secretary or other similar officer of another body corporate at a time when a relevant offence for which that other body corporate has been convicted was committed.

(4)  For the purposes of this Schedule, an application for registration or for the renewal of a registration as a broker of controlled waste shall be treated as pending—

(a)  whilst it is being considered by the waste regulation authority; or

(b)  if it has been refused or the relevant period from the making of the application has expired without the applicant having been registered, whilst either—

 (i)  the period for appealing in relation to that application has not expired; or

 (ii)  the application is the subject of an appeal which has not been disposed of.

(5)  For the purposes of this Schedule, an appeal is disposed of when any of the following occurs—

---

[1]  P.693 above.
[2]  P.630 above.
[3]  P.678 above.

[4]  "Waste regulation authority" has the meaning given by s.30 of the 1990 Act, p.113 above.

(a) the appeal is withdrawn;

(b) the appellant is notified by the Secretary of State or the waste regulation authority in question that his appeal has been dismissed; or

(c) the waste regulation authority complies with any direction of the Secretary of State to renew the appellant's registration or to cancel the revocation.

(6) *Revoked by S.I. 1995/288, reg.3(22). This amendment came into force on 1 April 1995: reg.1(1).*

## Registers

**2.** (1) It shall be the duty of each waste regulation authority[1] to establish and maintain a register of brokers of controlled waste and—

(a) to secure that the register is open for inspection[2] by members of the public free of charge at all reasonable hours; and

(b) to afford to members of the public reasonable facilities for obtaining copies of entries in the register on payment of reasonable charges.

(2) A register under this paragraph may be kept in any form.

## Applications for registration

**3.** (1) An application for registration or for the renewal of a registration as a broker of controlled waste shall be made to the waste regulation authority[3] for the area in which the applicant has or proposes to have his principal place of business in Great Britain; but if the applicant does not have or propose to have a place of business in Great Britain, the applicant may apply to any waste regulation authority.

(2) Subject to sub-paragraphs (3) to (5) below, a person shall not make an application for registration or for the renewal of a registration whilst—

(a) a previous application of his is pending;[4] or

(b) he is registered.

(3) Sub-paragraph (2) above shall not prevent a person from applying for the renewal of a registration where his application is made within the period of six months mentioned in paragraph 7(5).

(4) An application for registration or for the renewal of a registration in respect of a business which is or is to be carried on by a partnership shall be made by all of the partners or prospective partners.

(5) A prospective partner in a business carried on by a partnership whose members are already registered may make an application for registration as a partner in that business to the waste regulation authority with whom the business is registered.

(6) An application for registration shall be made on a form corresponding to the form in Part II of this Schdule,[5] or on a form substantially to the like effect, and shall contain the information required by that form.

(7) An application for the renewal of a registration shall be made on a form corresponding to the form in Part III of this Schedule,[6] or on a form substantially to the like effect, and shall contain the information required by that form.

(8) Where an applicant wishes to apply to be registered both as a carrier and as a broker of controlled waste, he may, instead of making the application on the forms provided for by regulation 4(6) of the Carriers Regulations[7] and sub-paragraph (6) above, make a combined application on a form containing the information required by those forms.

(9) Where an applicant wishes to apply both for the renewal of his registration as a carrier of controlled waste and for the renewal of his registration as a broker of controlled waste, he may, instead of making an application on the forms provided for by regulation 4(7) of the Carriers Regulations and sub-paragraph (7) above, make a combined application on a form containing the information required by those forms.

(10) A waste regulation authority shall provide a copy of the appropriate application form free of charge to any person requesting one.

---

[1] "Waste regulation authority" has the meaning given by s.30 of the 1990 Act, p.113 above.

[2] Former words "at its principal office" omitted by S.I. 1996/593, reg.3, sch.2, para.10(6)(a). This amendment came into force on 1 April 1996: reg.1.

[3] "Waste regulation authority" has the meaning given by s.30 of the 1990 Act, p.113 above.

[4] See para.1(4) above.

[5] P.729 below.

[6] P.732 below.

[7] P.633 above.

(11)  A waste regulation authority shall charge an applicant in respect of its consideration of his application—

(a)  subject to paragraph (c) below, in the case of either an application for registration as a broker of controlled waste or a combined application for registration as both a carrier and broker of controlled waste, £95;

(b)  in the case of either an application for the renewal of a registration as a broker of controlled waste or a combined application for renewal of registration both as a carrier and as a broker of controlled waste, £65;

(c)  in the case of an application by a registered carrier of controlled waste for registration as a broker of controlled waste, £25,

and the applicant shall pay the charge when he makes his application.

(12)  A waste regulation authority shall, on receipt of an application for registration or for the renewal of a registration, ensure that the register contains a copy of the application.

(13)  A waste regulation authority may refuse an application for registration or for the renewal of a registration if, and only if—

(a)  there has, in relation to that application, been a contravention of any of the requirements of the preceding provisions of this paragraph; or

(b)  the applicant or another relevant person has been convicted of a relevant offence[1] and, in the opinion of the authority, it is undesirable for the applicant to be authorised to arrange (as dealer or broker) for the disposal[2] or recovery[3] of controlled waste[4] on behalf of other persons.

(14)  Where a waste regulation authority decides to refuse an application for registration or for the renewal of a registration, the authority shall give notice[5] to the applicant informing him that his application is refused and of the reasons for its decision.

(15)  If an appeal is made under and in accordance with paragraph 6, the waste regulation authority shall, as soon as reasonably practicable, make appropriate entries in its register indicating when the appeal was made and the result of the appeal.

(16)  If no such appeal is made, the waste regulation authority shall, as soon as reasonably practicable, make an appropriate entry in its register indicating that the application has not been accepted and that no appeal has been made.

(17)  A waste regulation authority may remove from its register—

(a)  a copy of an application included under sub-paragraph (12) above; or

(b)  an entry made under sub-paragraph (15) or (16) above,

at any time more than six years after the application in question was made.

### Registration as a broker and amendment of entries

4.  (1)  On accepting a person's application for registration or on being directed under paragraph 6(9) to register a person following an appeal in respect of such an application, the waste regulation authority[6] shall make an entry in its register—

(a)  showing that person as a registered broker of controlled waste and allocating him a registration number (which may include any letter);

(b)  specifying the date on which the registration takes effect and its date of expiry;[7]

(c)  stating any business name of his and the address of his principal place of business (together with any telephone, telex or fax number of his) and, in the case of an individual, his date of birth;

(d)  in the case of a body corporate, listing the names of each director, manager, secretary or other similar officer of that body and their respective dates of birth;

(e)  in the case of a company registered under the Companies Acts, specifying its registered number and, in the case of a company incorporated outside Great Britain, the country in which it was incorporated;

---

[1] "Relevant offence" defined by para.1(1) above, see also para.1(2) and (3) above.

[2] "Disposal" defined by reg.1(3), p.676 above.

[3] "Recovery" defined by reg.1(3), p.677 above.

[4] For the definition of "controlled waste" in Part II of the Environmental Protection Act 1990, see s.75, p.159 above,

and the Controlled Waste Regulations 1992, p.662 above.

[5] "Notice" means notice in writing: para.1(1) above; see also reg.1(7), p.677 above.

[6] "Waste regulation authority" has the meaning given by s.30 of the 1990 Act, p.113 above.

[7] "Date of expiry" defined by para.1(1), p.723 above.

(f) in a case where the person who is registered or another relevant person has been convicted of a relevant offence,[1] giving the person's name, details of the offence, the date of conviction, the penalty imposed, the name of the Court and, in the case of an individual, his date of birth; and

(g) in a case where the person who is registered or any company in the same group of companies as that person is the holder of a waste management licence,[2] stating the name of the holder of the licence and the name of the authority which granted it.

(2) In the case of a business which is, or is to be, carried on by a partnership, all the partners shall be registered under one entry and only one registration number shall be allocated to the partnership.

(3) On making an entry in its register under sub-paragraph (1) above the waste regulation authority shall provide the registered person or partnership free of charge with a copy of the entry in the register.

(4) On accepting a person's application for the renewal of a registration or on being directed under paragraph 6(9) to register a person following an appeal in respect of such an application, the waste regulation authority shall amend the relevant entry in the register—

(a) to show the date on which the renewal takes effect and the revised date of expiry of the registration;

(b) to record any other change disclosed as a result of the application; and

(c) to note in the register the date on which the amendments are made.

(5) The waste regulation authority shall at the same time as amending the register under sub-paragraph (4) above provide the registered person or partnership free of charge with a copy of the amended entry in the register.

(6) A person who is registered shall notify the waste regulation authority which maintains the relevant register of any change of circumstances affecting information in the register relating to him.

(7) On—

(a) being notified of any change of circumstances in accordance with sub-paragraph (6) above;

(b) accepting a prospective partner's application for registration in relation to a business carried on by a partnership whose members are already registered; or

(c) being directed under paragraph 6(9) to register a prospective partner,

the waste regulation authority shall—

(i) amend the relevant entry to reflect the change of circumstances or the registration of the prospective partner;

(ii) note in the register the date on which the amendment is made;

(iii) provide the registered person or partnership free of charge with a copy of the amended entry in the register.

(8) In this regulation—

"Companies Acts" has the meaning given by section 744 of the Companies Act 1985;[3]

"business name" means a name under which a person carries on business and by virtue of which the Business Names Act 1985[4] applies; and

"group" has the meaning given by section 53(1) of the Companies Act 1989.[5]

### Revocation of registration

5. (1) A waste regulation authority[6] may revoke a person's registration as a broker of controlled waste if, and only if—

(a) that person or another relevant person has been convicted of a relevant offence;[7] and

(b) in the opinion of the authority, it is undesirable for the registered broker to continue to be authorised to arrange (as dealer or broker) for the disposal[8] or recovery[9] of controlled waste[10] on behalf of other persons.

[1] "Relevant offence" defined by para.1(1), p.723 above.
[2] "Waste management licence" has the meaning given by s.35(1) of the 1990 Act, p.119 above.
[3] 1985 c.6.
[4] 1985 c.7.
[5] 1989 c.40.
[6] "Waste regulation authority" has the meaning given by s.30 of the 1990 Act, p.113 above.

[7] "Relevant offence" defined by para.1(1), p.723 above; see also para.1(2) and (3) above.
[8] "Disposal" defined by reg.1(3), p.676 above.
[9] "Recovery" defined by reg.1(3), p.677 above.
[10] For the definition of "controlled waste" in Part II of the Environmental Protection Act 1990, see s.75, p.159 above, and the Controlled Waste Regulations 1992, p.662 above.

(2) Where a waste regulation authority decides to revoke a person's registration as a broker of controlled waste, it shall give notice to the broker informing him of the revocation and the reasons for its decision.

## Appeals

**6.** (1) Where a person has applied to a waste regulation authority[1] to be registered as a broker of controlled waste in accordance with paragraph 3, he may appeal to the Secretary of State if—

(a) his application is refused; or

(b) the relevant period[2] from the making of the application has expired without his having been registered.

(2) A person whose registration as a broker of controlled waste has been revoked may appeal against the revocation to the Secretary of State.

(3) Notice of an appeal to the Secretary of State under sub-paragraph (1) or (2) above shall be given by the appellant to the Secretary of State.

(4) The notice of appeal shall be accompanied by the following—

(a) a statement of the grounds of appeal;

(b) in the case of an appeal under sub-paragraph (1) above, a copy of the relevant application;

(c) in the case of an appeal under sub-paragraph (2) above, a copy of the appellant's entry in the register;

(d) a copy of any relevant correspondence between the appellant and the waste regulation authority;

(e) a copy of any notice given to the appellant under paragraph 3(14) or 5(2);

(f) a statement indicating whether the appellant wishes the appeal to be in the form of a hearing or to be determined on the basis of written representations.

(5) The appellant shall at the same time as giving notice of appeal to the Secretary of State serve on the waste regulation authority[3] a copy of the notice and a copy of the documents referred to in sub-paragraph (4)(a) and (f) above.

(6) Notice of appeal is to be given before the expiry of the period of 28 days beginning with—

(a) in the case of an appeal under sub-paragraph (1)(a) above, the date on which the appellant is given notice by the waste regulation authority that his application has been refused;

(b) in the case of an appeal under sub-paragraph (1)(b) above, the date on which the relevant period from the making of the application expired without the appellant having been registered; or

(c) in the case of an appeal under sub-paragraph (2) above, the date on which the appellant is given notice by the waste regulation authority that his registration as a broker of controlled waste has been revoked.

or before such later date as the Secretary of State may at any time allow.

(7) If either party to an appeal requests a hearing or the Secretary of State so decides, the appeal shall be or continue in the form of a hearing before a person appointed for the purpose by the Secretary of State.

(8) The person holding such a hearing shall after its conclusion make a written report to the Secretary of State which shall include his conclusions and recommendations or his reasons for not making any recommendations.

(9) On an appeal under this paragraph the Secretary of State may, as he thinks fit, either dismiss the appeal or give the waste regulation authority in question a direction to register the appellant or, as the case may be, to cancel the revocation.

(10) The Secretary of State shall—

(a) notify the appellant in writing of his determination of the appeal and of his reasons for it and, if a hearing is held, shall also provide him with a copy of the report of the person who conducted the hearing; and

(b) at the same time send a copy of those documents to the waste regulation authority.

(11) Where on an appeal made by virtue of sub-paragraph (1)(b) above the Secretary of State dismisses an appeal, he shall direct the waste regulation authority in question not to register the appellant.

(12) It shall be the duty of a waste regulation authority to comply with any direction under this paragraph.

(13) This paragraph is subject to section 114 of the Environment Act 1995[4] (delegation or reference of appeals).[5]

---

[1] "Waste regulation authority" has the meaning given by s.30 of the 1990 Act, p.113 above.

[2] "Relevant period" defined by para.1(1), p.723 above.

[3] For provisions relating to the service of documents see reg.1(7), p.677 above.

[4] P.489 above.

[5] Para.(13) added by S.I. 1996/593, reg.3, sch.2, para.10(6)(b). This amendment came into force on 1 April 1996: reg.1.

*Duration of registration*

7. (1) Subject to the following provisions of this paragraph, a person's registration as a broker of controlled waste shall cease to have effect on the expiry of the period of three years beginning with the date of the registration or, if it has been renewed, beginning with the date on which it was renewed or, as the case may be, last renewed.

(2) Where a registered carrier of controlled waste is registered as a broker of controlled waste otherwise than by way of renewal of an existing registration as a broker, and his registration as a carrier will expire within three years of the date of his registration as a broker, if at the time of making his application for registration as a broker he so requests, his registration as a broker shall expire on the same date as his registration as a carrier.

(3) Where a registered broker of controlled waste is registered as a carrier of controlled waste otherwise than by way of renewal of an existing registration as a carrier, and his registration as a broker will expire within three years of the date of his registration as a carrier, if on the next application for renewal of his registration as a broker which he makes after having been registered as a carrier he so requests, his renewed registration as a broker shall expire on the same date as his registration as a carrier.

(4) Registration as a registered broker shall cease to have effect if the registered broker gives notice[1] requiring the removal of his name from the register.

(5) The waste regulation authority[2] shall, no later than six months before the date of expiry[3] of a broker's registration, serve on a registered broker—

(a) a notice informing him of the date of expiry and of the effect of sub-paragraph (6) below; and

(b) an application form for the renewal of his registration and a copy of his current entry in the register.

(6) Where an application for the renewal of a registration is made within the last six months prior to its date of expiry, the registration shall, notwithstanding the passing of the expiry date, continue in force—

(a) until the application is withdrawn or accepted; or

(b) if the waste regulation authority refuse the application or the relevant period[4] from the making of the application has expired without the applicant having been registered, until—

   (i) the expiry of the period for appealing; or

   (ii) where the applicant indicates within that period that he does not intend to make or continue with an appeal, the date on which such an indication is given.

(7) Where a waste regulation authority revokes a broker's registration, the registration shall, notwithstanding the revocation, continue in force until—

(a) the expiry of the period for appealing against the revocation; or

(b) where that person indicates within that period that he does not intend to make or continue with an appeal, the date on which such an indication is given.

(8) Where an appeal is made under and in accordance with the provisions of paragraph 6—

(a) by a person whose appeal is in respect of such an application for the renewal of his registration as was made, in accordance with paragraph 3, at a time when he was already registered; or

(b) by a person whose registration has been revoked,

that registration shall continue in force after its date of expiry or, as the case may be, notwithstanding the revocation, until the appeal is disposed of.[5]

(9) A registration in respect of a business which is carried on by a partnership shall cease to have effect if any of the partners ceases to be registered or if any person who is not registered becomes a partner.

(10) The duration of a registration in respect of a business which is carried on by a partnership shall not be affected if a person ceases to be a partner or if a prospective partner is registered under paragraph 4(7) in relation to the partnership.

(11) Where a waste regulation authority accepts an application for the renewal of a broker's registration before the expiry date, the renewal shall for the purposes of this Schedule take effect from the expiry date.

---

[1] "Notice" means notice in writing: para.1(1), p.723 above.
[2] "Waste regulation authority" has the meaning given by s.30 of the 1990 Act, p.113 above.
[3] "Date of expiry" defined by para.1(1), p.723 above.
[4] "Relevant period" defined by para.1(1), p.723 above.
[5] See para.1(5), p.723 above.

*Cessation of registration*

8. Where by virtue of paragraph 6(11) or 7 a registration ceases to have effect, the waste regulation authority[1]—

    (a)  shall record this fact in the appropriate entry in its register and the date on which it occurred;

    (b)  may remove the appropriate entry from its register at any time more than six years after the registration ceases to have effect.

## PART II

## FORM OF APPLICATION FOR REGISTRATION AS A BROKER OF CONTROLLED WASTE
*Please read the guidance notes before completing this form*

1. Full name of applicant (*note 1*)
   Former name (if applicable)
   Date of birth (if applicable)

2. Name under which applicant
   carries on business (if different from 1)

3. Address for correspondence

                              Post Code

4. Address of principal place of
   business (if different from 3)
                              Post Code

5. Telephone/Telex/Fax number     Tel.     Telex     Fax

6. If applicant has previously been
   a registered broker give:

    (a)  registration number or numbers

    (b)  name of waste regulation authority
         or authorities

7. If applicant is a company
   registered under the Companies Act,
   give:

    (a)  company's registered number

    (b)  address of registered office

    (c)  in the case of a company                           Post Code
       incorporated outside Great
       Britain, the country in which
       it was incorporated

---

[1] "Waste regulation authority" has the meaning given by s.30 of the 1990 Act, p.113 above.

**8.** If applicant is a registered company or other body corporate, for each director, manager, secretary or other similar officer, give:

| Full name | Position held | Address | Date of birth |
|---|---|---|---|
| | | | |
| | | | |
| | | | |
| | | | |
| | | | |

**9.** If applicant is a prospective partner in a business carried on by a partnership whose members are already registered brokers, give:

(a) full name of partnership

(b) registration of partnership

**10.** Has the applicant or another relevant person (*note 2*) been convicted of any offence listed in regulation 3 of the Waste Management Licensing Regulations 1994 (*notes 3 and 4*)?

Yes ☐ No ☐

If **Yes**, give full details of each offence—

| Full name of person convicted | Position held | Name of Court | Date of conviction | Offence and penalty imposed |
|---|---|---|---|---|
| | | | | |

If details of any conviction have been given, use the following space to provide the waste regulation authority with any additional information which you wish the authority to take into account in determining whether or not it is undesirable for the applicant to be authorised to arrange (as dealer or broker) for the disposal or recovery of controlled waste on behalf of other persons—

**11.** If the applicant is already a registered carrier of controlled waste, does he want his registration as a broker to expire on the same date as that on which his registration as a carrier expires (instead of lasting for 3 years)?

Yes ☐ No ☐

**12.** Is the applicant or another company in the same group (within the meaning of section 53(1) of the Companies Act 1989) the holder of a waste management licence?

Yes ☐ No ☐

If **Yes**, give details of licence:

| Full name of holder of licence | Date of birth (if applicable) | Date of issue of licence | Name of authority which issued the licence |
|---|---|---|---|
|  |  |  |  |

**Declaration**

I declare that I have personally checked the information given in this application form and that it is true to the best of my knowledge, information and belief. I understand that registration may be refused if false or incomplete information is given and that untrue statements may result in prosecution and could lead to revocation of registration.

Signature:                                   Date:

Position held:

Have you enclosed the fee of £95 (or where you are already a registered carrier of controlled waste, £25)? (*note 5*)
Yes ☐

**GUIDANCE NOTES**

1. In the case of a partnership or proposed partnership, each partner must apply for registration and his details must be included in this application form.

2. Details of an offence listed in regulation 3 of the Waste Management Licensing Regulations 1994 must be given if the applicant was convicted of the offence or if the person convicted of the offence ("the relevant person")—

   (a) committed it in the course of his employment by the applicant;

   (b) committed it in the course of the carrying on of any business by a partnership one of the members of which was the applicant;

   (c) was a body corporate and at the time when the offence was committed the applicant was a director, manager, secretary or other similar officer of that body;

   (d) was a director, manager, secretary or other similar officer of the applicant (where the applicant is a body corporate);

   (e) was a body corporate and at the time when the offence was committed a director, manager, secretary or other similar officer of the applicant held such an office in the body corporate which committed the offence.

3. The offences listed in regulation 3 of the Waste Management Licensing Regulations 1994 are offences under any of the following provisions[1]—

   section 22 of the Public Health (Scotland) Act 1897;

   section 95(1) of the Public Health Act 1936;

   section 3, 5(6), 16(4), 18(2), 31(1), 32(1), 34(5), 78, 92(6) or 93(3) of the Control of Pollution Act 1974;

   section 2 of the Refuse Disposal (Amenity) Act 1978;

   the Control of Pollution (Special Waste) Regulations 1980;

   section 9(1) of the Food and Environment Protection Act 1985;

   the Transfrontier Shipment of Hazardous Waste Regulations 1988;

   the Merchant Shipping (Prevention of Pollution by Garbage) Regulations 1988;

   section 1, 5, 6(9) or 7(3) of the Control of Pollution (Amendment) Act 1989;

   section 107, 118(4) or 175(1) of the Water Act 1989;

   section 23(1), 33, 34(6), 44, 47(6), 57(5), 59(5), 63(2), 69(9), 70(4), 71(3) or 80(4) of the Environmental Protection Act 1990;

   section 85, 202 or 206 of the Water Resources Act 1991;

   section 33 of the Clean Air Act 1993;

---

[1] See reg.3, p.678 above, for annotations.

the Transfrontier Shipment of Waste Regulations 1994;[1]

the Special Waste Regulations 1996.[2]

4. Details of a conviction need not be given where under the terms of the Rehabilitation of Offenders Act 1974 the conviction is spent.

5. The fee of £95 (or, if you are already a registered carrier of controlled waste, £25) must be sent with the application. The regulation authority may refuse the application if the fee is not enclosed.

## PART III

### FORM OF APPLICATION FOR RENEWAL OF REGISTRATION AS A BROKER OF CONTROLLED WASTE
*Please read the guidance notes before completing this form*

1. Full name of applicant (*note 1*)
   Former name (if applicable)
   Date of birth (if applicable)

2. Address for correspondence

   Post Code

3. Telephone/Telex/Fax number    Tel.    Telex    Fax

4. Registration number as broker

5. Has the applicant or another relevant person (*note 2*) been convicted of any offence listed in regulation 3 of the Waste Management Licensing Regulations 1994 (*notes 3 and 4*)?

   Yes ☐ No ☐

   If **Yes**, give full details of each offence—

| *Full name of person convicted* | *Position held* | *Name of Court* | *Date of conviction* | *Offence and penalty imposed* |
|---|---|---|---|---|
|  |  |  |  |  |

If details of any convictions have been given, use the following space to provide the waste regulation authority with any additional information which you wish the authority to take into account in determining whether or not it is undesirable for the applicant to be authorised to arrange (as dealer or broker) for the disposal or recovery of controlled waste on behalf of others—

6. Give details of any changes in any other information in the applicant's existing entry in the register (*note 5*)—

7. If the applicant has been registered as a carrier of controlled waste since the commencement of his current registration as a broker, does he want his renewed registration as a broker to expire when his registration as a carrier expires (instead of it lasting for 3 years)?

   Yes ☐ No ☐

---

[1] P.741 below. Words "the Transfrontier Shipment of Waste Regulations 1994" added by S.I. 1994/1137, reg.19(4). This amendment came into force on 6 May 1994, reg.1.

[2] P.763 below. Words "the Special Waste Regulations 1996" added by S.I. 1996/972, reg.25, sch.3. This amendment came into force on 1 September 1996: reg.1(1).

**Declaration**

I declare that I have personally checked the information given in this application form and that it is true to the best of my knowledge, information and belief. I understand that registration may be refused if false or incomplete information is given and that untrue statements may result in prosecution and could lead to revocation of registration.

Signature:                                    Date:

Position held:

Have you enclosed the fee of £65 (*note 6*) Yes ☐

**GUIDANCE NOTES**

1. In the case of a partnership, each partner must apply for registration and his details must be included in this application form.

2. Details of an offence listed in regulation 3 of the Waste Management Licensing Regulations 1994 must be given if the applicant was convicted of the offence or if the person convicted of the offence ("the relevant person")—

    (a) committed it in the course of his employment by the applicant;

    (b) committed it in the course of the carrying on of any business by a partnership one of the members of which was the applicant;

    (c) was a body corporate and at the time when the offence was committed the applicant was a director, manager, secretary or other similar officer of that body;

    (d) was a director, manager, secretary or other similar officer of the applicant (where the applicant is a body corporate);

    (e) was a body corporate and at the time when the offence was committed a director, manager, secretary or other similar officer of the applicant held such an office in the body corporate which committed the offence.

3. The offences listed in regulation 3 of the Waste Management Licensing Regulations 1994 are offences under any of the following provisions[1]—

    section 22 of the Public Health (Scotland) Act 1897;

    section 95(1) of the Public Health Act 1936;

    section 3, 5(6), 16(4), 18(2), 31(1), 32(1), 34(5), 78, 92(6) or 93(3) of the Control of Pollution Act 1974;

    section 2 of the Refuse Disposal (Amenity) Act 1978;

    the Control of Pollution (Special Waste) Regulations 1980;

    section 9(1) of the Food and Environment Protection Act 1985;

    the Transfrontier Shipment of Hazardous Waste Regulations 1988;

    the Merchant Shipping (Prevention of Pollution by Garbage) Regulations 1988;

    section 1, 5, 6(9) or 7(3) of the Control of Pollution (Amendment) Act 1989;

    section 107, 118(4) or 175(1) of the Water Act 1989;

    section 23(1), 33, 34(6), 44, 47(6), 57(5), 59(5), 63(2), 69(9), 70(4), 71(3) or 80(4) of the Environmental Protection Act 1990;

    section 85, 202 or 206 of the Water Resources Act 1991;

    section 33 of the Clean Air Act 1993;

    the Transfrontier Shipment of Waste Regulations 1994;[2]

    the Special Waste Regulations 1996.[3]

4. Details of a conviction need not be given where under the terms of the Rehabilitation of Offenders Act 1974 the conviction is spent.

5. Check the information in the copy of the current entry in the register sent with the regulation authority's reminder that registration needs to be renewed or, if no such copy has been received, ask the authority for one.

6. The fee of £65 must be sent with the application. The regulation authority may refuse the application if the fee is not enclosed.

---

[1] See reg.3, p.678 above, for annotations.
[2] P.741 below. Words "the Transfrontier Shipment of Waste Regulations 1994" added by S.I. 1994/1137, reg.19(4). This amendment came into force on 6 May 1994, reg.1.

[3] P.763 below. Words "the Special Waste Regulations 1996" added by S.I. 1996/972, reg. 25, sch.3. This amendment came into force on 1 September 1996: reg.1(1).

*Explanatory Note*
*(This note is not part of the Regulations)*

These Regulations make provision related to the bringing into force of the waste management licensing system under Part II of the Environmental Protection Act 1990 ("the 1990 Act") and for the purpose of implementing certain Council Directives relating to waste.

Regulation 2, and Schedules 1 and 2, provide for the form and contents of applications both for waste management licences and for their surrender or transfer. Regulations 3 to 5 make provision in connection with determining whether an applicant for a licence is a fit and proper person. Regulations 6 to 9 contain procedural provisions in relation to appeals under sections 43 and 66 of the 1990 Act.

Regulations 10 and 11 make provision in relation to the contents of public registers maintained under section 64 for the 1990 Act. Regulation 12 prescribes what is to be treated as mobile plant for the purposes of Part II of the 1990 Act.

Regulation 13 prohibits the imposition of conditions in waste management licences for the purpose of securing the health of persons at work. Regulation 14 makes provision, pursuant to Council Directive 75/439/EEC on the disposal of waste oils (OJ No. L 194, 25.7.1975, p.23, as amended by Council Directive 87/101/EEC, OJ No. L 42, 12.2.1987, p.43) as to conditions which are to be included in a licence which relates to waste oil. Regulation 15, for the purpose of implementing Council Directive 80/68/EEC on the protection of groundwater against pollution caused by certain dangerous substances, makes provision for the method of dealing with applications for licences in respect of waste activities which could lead to the discharge into groundwater of the substances in lists I and II of that Directive.

Regulations 16 and 17 exempt certain activities from the need to have a waste management licence. Regulation 16 disapplies section 33(1) of the 1990 Act in the case of certain waste activities controlled by other systems. Regulation 17 disapplies section 33(1)(a) and (b) of the 1990 Act in the case of the activities set out in Schedule 3. Regulation 18 provides a system of registration for the activities exempted by regulation 17.

Regulation 19 and Schedule 4 contain provisions which implement Council Directive 75/442/EEC on waste (as amended) ("the Waste Framework Directive"). Part I of Schedule 4 modifies Parts I and II of the 1990 Act, Parts I and II of the Control of Pollution Act 1974, Part II of the Food and Environment Protection Act 1985, Chapter II of Part III of the Water Resources Act 1991 and the Town and Country Planning legislation, and requires certain functions under those enactments to be discharged with the objectives set out in the Waste Framework Directive. Part I of that Schedule also provides for the preparation of offshore waste management plans, registration of waste collectors, transporters, brokers and dealers who would otherwise not be subject to registration, and the inspection of, and record keeping by, establishments or undertakings carrying out waste disposal or recovery. Part II of Schedule 4 lists objects or substances which are waste when discarded, and Parts III and IV of that Schedule list waste disposal and recovery operations.

Regulation 20 and Schedule 5 provide for the registration of waste brokers and dealers in respect of their activities on or after 1st January 1995. Schedule 5 makes provision as to the keeping of registers, and in respect of applications for registration, the duration and revocation of registration, and related appeals.

Regulations 21 to 24 amend the Deposits in the Sea (Exemptions) Order 1985, the Collection and Disposal of Waste Regulations 1988, the Controlled Waste (Registration of Carriers and Seizure of Vehicles) Regulations 1991 and the Controlled Waste Regulations 1992.

An assessment of the cost to business of complying with these Regulations has been prepared and copies may be obtained from the Department of the Environment, Room A2.22, Romney House, 43 Marsham Street, London SW1P 3PY. A copy has been placed in the library of each of the Houses of Parliament.

# The Surface Waters (River Ecosystem) (Classification) Regulations 1994

S.I. 1994 No. 1057

The Secretary of State for the Environment and the Secretary of State for Wales, acting jointly in exercise of the powers conferred on them by sections 82[1] and 219(2)[2] of the Water Resources Act 1991[3] and of all other powers enabling them in that behalf, hereby make the following Regulations:

*Citation, commencement and extent*

1. (1) These Regulations may be cited as the Surface Waters (River Ecosystem) (Classification) Regulations 1994 and shall come into force on 10th May 1994.

(2) In these Regulations references to a numbered column are references to the column so numbered in the Schedule to these Regulations.

*Classification of waters*

2. (1) A system employing the classifications RE1, RE2, RE3, RE4 and RE5 is prescribed as a system of classification applying to inland freshwaters which are relevant rivers or watercourses.[4]

(2) The criteria for each of the classifications RE1 to RE5 are that the following requirements are satisfied by a series of samples of water taken and analysed in accordance with regulation 3, that is to say—

(a) the 10 percentile of the saturation of dissolved oxygen shall not be less than the value specified in respect of that classification in column (2);

(b) the 90 percentile of the biochemical oxygen demand shall not exceed the value specified in respect of that classification in column (3);

(c) the 90 percentile of the concentration of total ammonia shall not exceed the value specified in respect of that classification in column (4);

(d) the 95 percentile of the concentration of un-ionised ammonia shall not exceed the value, if any, specified in respect of that classification in column (5);

(e) the 5 percentile of the pH value shall not be less than the lower value, if any, specified in respect of that classification in column (6), and the 95 percentile of the pH value shall not exceed the higher value, if any, so specified;

(f) the 95 percentile of the concentration of dissolved copper shall not exceed the value, if any, which is specified in respect of that classification in column (8) by reference to the hardness of the water as described in column (7); and

(g) the 95 percentile of the concentration of total zinc shall not exceed the value, if any, which is specified in respect of that classification in column (9) by reference to the hardness of the water as described in column (7).

*Sampling, analysis and compliance*

3. The following matters, that is to say—

(a) the frequency, location and methods of sampling;

---

[1] P.271 above.
[2] P.310 above.
[3] See s.221(7), p.316 above, as to the joint exercise of functions exercisable concurrently.
[4] "Inland freshwaters" and "relevant river or watercourse" are defined in s.104, p.290 above.

# SCHEDULE

(Regulation 2(2))

## RIVER ECOSYSTEM CLASSIFICATIONS

| (1) Class | (2) Dissolved Oxygen % saturation 10 percentile | (3) BOD (ATU) mg/l 90 percentile | (4) Total Ammonia mg N/l 90 percentile | (5) un-ionised Ammonia mg N/l 95 percentile | (6) pH lower limit as 5 percentile; upper limit as 95 percentile | (7) Hardness mg/l $CaCO_3$ | (8) Dissolved Copper µg/l 95 percentile | (9) Total Zinc µg/l 95 percentile |
|---|---|---|---|---|---|---|---|---|
| RE1 | 80 | 2.5 | 0.25 | 0.021 | 6.0–9.0 | ≤10<br>>10 and ≤50<br>>50 and ≤100<br>>100 | 5<br>22<br>40<br>112 | 30<br>200<br>300<br>500 |
| RE2 | 70 | 4.0 | 0.6 | 0.021 | 6.0–9.0 | ≤10<br>>10 and ≤50<br>>50 and ≤100<br>>100 | 5<br>22<br>40<br>112 | 30<br>200<br>300<br>500 |
| RE3 | 60 | 6.0 | 1.3 | 0.021 | 6.0–9.0 | ≤10<br>>10 and ≤50<br>>50 and ≤100<br>>100 | 5<br>22<br>40<br>112 | 300<br>700<br>1000<br>2000 |
| RE4 | 50 | 8.0 | 2.5 | — | 6.0–9.0 | ≤10<br>>10 and ≤50<br>>50 and ≤100<br>>100 | 5<br>22<br>40<br>112 | 300<br>700<br>1000<br>2000 |
| RE5 | 20 | 15.0 | 9.0 | — | — | — | — | — |

(b)  the samples to be used, or to be disregarded, for the purpose of assessing whether any requirement specified in regulation 2(2) is satisfied;

(c)  the requirements for analysis of samples; and

(d)  the methods of determining percentile values,

shall be determined by the Environment Agency[1] in accordance with the procedures, and by ref-
erence to the principles, set out in the document dated 30th March 1994 and entitled "Water
Quality Objectives: Procedures used by the National Rivers Authority for the purpose of the
Surface Waters (River Ecosystem) (Classification) Regulations 1994".

### Explanatory Note
#### (This note is not part of the Regulations)

These Regulations prescribe a system of classifying the general quality of inland freshwaters which are relevant
rivers or watercourses (as defined in section 104 of the Water Resources Act 1991 ("the Act")). The system, which
consists of five classes ranging in order of decreasing quality from RE1 to RE5, will be used for establishing quality
objectives under section 83 of the Act.[2]

Compliance with the requirements prescribed for each classification is determined in accordance with procedures
and by reference to principles set out in a document dated 30th March 1994 and entitled "Water Quality Objectives:
Procedures used by the National Rivers Authority for the purpose of the Surface Waters (River Ecosystem)
(Classification) Regulations 1994". Copies of the document may be inspected free of charge at, and obtained from,
the regional offices of the Environment Agency.[1]

A compliance cost assessment in respect of these Regulations may be obtained from Water Quality Division,
Department of the Environment, Room A412, Romney House, 43 Marsham Street, London SW1P 3PY, or
Environment Division, Welsh Office, Cathays Park, Cardiff CF1 3NQ.

---

[1] Words "the Environment Agency" substituted by the
Environment Act 1995 (c.25), s.120, sch.22, para.233(1). This
amendment came into force on 1 April 1996: S.I. 1996/186.

The Environment Agency is established by s.1 of the
Environment Act 1995, p.420 above.
[2] P.272 above.

# The Environmental Protection Act 1990 (Commencement No. 15) Order 1994

## S.I. 1994 No. 1096 (C.18)

The Secretary of State, in exercise of his powers under section 164(3) of the Environmental Protection Act 1990,[1] hereby makes the following Order:

*Citation and interpretation*

**1.** (1) This Order may be cited as the Environmental Protection Act 1990 (Commencement No. 15) Order 1994.

(2) In this Order—

"appropriate date", in relation to an appeal, means the date on which—

(a) the period for appealing expires without an appeal being made; or

(b) any appeal is withdrawn or finally determined;

"authorisation" has the meaning given in section 1(9) of the Environmental Protection Act 1990;[2]

"existing process" and "prescribed date" have the same meaning as in Schedule 3 to the Environmental Protection (Prescribed Processes and Substances) Regulations 1991;[3]

"relevant date", in relation to an application for a licence, means the date on which the licence applied for is granted or, if the application is (or is deemed to be) rejected, the date on which—

(a) the period for appealing expires without an appeal being made; or

(b) any appeal is withdrawn or finally determined;

and

"scrap metal" has the same meaning as in the Scrap Metal Dealers Act 1964.[4]

*Provisions coming into force on 1st May 1994*

**2.** (1) The following provisions of the Environmental Protection Act 1990 shall come into force on 1st May 1994—

section 54[5] (insofar as not already in force);

sections 58[6] and 59;

section 60 (insofar as not already in force);

sections 64[7] to 67 (insofar as not already in force);

sections 73[8] and 74 (insofar as not already in force);

section 162(1) insofar as it relates to paragraph 27 of Schedule 15;[9]

section 162(2) insofar as it relates to the following repeals in Part II of Schedule 16—

the repeal of section 1 of the Control of Pollution Act 1974;[10]

in relation to Scotland only, the repeal of section 11 of the Control of Pollution Act 1974.

---

[1] P.210 above.
[2] P.90 above.
[3] P.594 above.
[4] 1964 c.69; see s.9(2).
[5] P.147 above.
[6] P.148 above.

[7] P.152 above.
[8] P.157 above.
[9] Para.27 relates to an amendment to the Local Government Act 1988 (c.9).
[10] 1974 c.40.

(2)  The provisions of the Environmental Protection Act 1990 set out in paragraph (3) below shall come into force on 1st May 1994, save for the purposes of their application to the following activities—

(a)  an activity which on that date is the subject of a pending application for a disposal licence under Part I of the Control of Pollution Act 1974;

(b)  an activity in respect of which on that date an appeal in pursuance of section 10(1)(d) of the Control of Pollution Act 1974 (appeals to Secretary of State where a disposal licence is revoked) is pending or where the period for making such an appeal has not expired;

(c)  an activity which involves treating, keeping or disposing of scrap metal[1] or motor vehicles which are to be dismantled;

(d)  an activity—

   (i)  which on that date is the subject of a disposal licence under Part I of the Control of Pollution Act 1974;

   (ii)  which is or forms part of an existing process for which no authorisation[2] has been granted; and

   (iii)  to which, if an authorisation were granted, section 33(1)(a) and (b) of the Environmental Protection Act 1990[3] would not apply by virtue of the Waste Management Licensing Regulations 1994.[4]

(3)  The provisions referred to in paragraph (2) are—

section 33 (insofar as not already in force);

sections 35[5] to 40 (insofar as not already in force);

sections 42[6] and 43 (insofar as not already in force);

section 44;

section 57;[7]

section 162(1) insofar as it relates to paragraph 26 of Schedule 15;[8]

section 162(2) insofar as it relates to the following repeals in Part II of Schedule 16—

   the repeal of sections 3 to 10, 18 and 27 of the Control of Pollution Act 1974.

*Provisions coming into force after 1st May 1994*

3.  (1)  Subject to paragraphs (2) and (3) below, the provisions of the Environmental Protection Act 1990 set out in article 2(3) ("the relevant provisions") shall come into force—

(a)  for the purposes of their application to an activity falling within article 2(2)(a), on the day immediately following the relevant date[9] in relation to the application in question;

(b)  for the purposes of their application to an activity falling within article 2(2)(b), on the day immediately following the appropriate date[10] in relation to the appeal in question.

(2)  Subject to paragraph (3) below, where an activity falls within article 2(2)(c) (whether or not it also falls within article 2(2)(a) or (b)), the relevant provisions shall come into force for the purposes of their application to that activity—

(a)  if on 1st April 1995[11] that activity is the subject of a pending application for a disposal licence under Part I of the Control of Pollution Act 1974, on the day immediately following the relevant date in relation to the application in question;

---

[1] "Scrap metal" defined by art.1(2) above.
[2] "Existing process" and "Authorisation" defined by art.1(2) above.
[3] P.116 above.
[4] P.675 above; see regs.16 and 17, p.688 above, and sch.3, p.697 above.
[5] P.119 above.
[6] P.131 above.
[7] P.148 above.
[8] Para.26 relates to an amendment to the Local Government Act 1985 (c.51).
[9] "Relevant date" defined by art.1(2) above.
[10] "Appropriate date" defined by art.1(2) above.
[11] Words "1st April 1995" substituted by S.I. 1994/3234.

(b)  if on 1st April 1995[1] an appeal in pursuance of section 10(1)(d) of the Control of Pollution Act 1974 (appeals to Secretary of State where a disposal licence is revoked) is pending in respect of that activity or the period for making such an appeal has not expired, on the day immediately following the appropriate date in relation to that appeal;

(c)  in any other case, on 1st April 1995.[2]

(3)  Where an activity falls within article 2(2)(d) (whether or not it also falls within any other sub-paragraph of article 2(2)), the relevant provisions shall come into force for the purposes of their application to that activity on the day immediately following the prescribed date[3] in relation to the process in question.

*Explanatory Note*
*(This note is not part of the Order)*

This Order brings into force on 1st May 1994 the provisions of Part II of the Environmental Protection Act 1990 ("the 1990 Act)" relating to waste management licensing, with exceptions for the following four cases for which a later date is specified in article 3:—

(a)  activities which may be the subject of pending applications for disposal licences under Part I of the Control of Pollution Act 1974 ("the 1974 Act");

(b)  activities which may be the subject of appeals to the Secretary of State against the revocation of disposal licences under Part I of the 1974 Act;

(c)  activities which involve treating, keeping or disposing of scrap metal or motor vehicles which are to be dismantled; and

(d)  activities which are the subject of existing disposal licences under Part I of the 1974 Act and which consist of or include an existing process falling within Schedule 1 to the Environmental Protection (Prescribed Processes and Substances) Regulations 1991, but which would be excluded or exempted from waste management licensing under Part II of the 1990 Act if an authorisation were granted under Part I of that Act.

[1]  Words "1st April 1995" substituted by S.I. 1994/3234.   [2]  Words "1st April 1995" substituted by S.I. 1994/3234.
[3]  "Prescribed date" defined by art.1(2) above.

# The Transfrontier Shipment of Waste Regulations 1994

## S.I. 1994 No. 1137

*Reference to material not set out in this Manual*

Joint Circular:

European Communities Act 1972,

Council Regulation (EEC) No. 259/93 on the supervision and control of shipments of waste within, into and out of the European Community,

The Transfrontier Shipment of Waste Regulations 1994.

Department of the Environment Circular 13/94, Welsh Office Circular 44/94, Scottish Office Environment Department Circular 21/94, 1994, HMSO.

*Note:* A letter of 26 January 1995 from the Head of the Waste Management Division of the Department of the Environment to waste regulation authorities supplements or replaces some of the advice contained in this circular.

Basel Convention on the Control of Transboundary Movements of Hazardous Wastes and their Disposal, Presented to Parliament December 1995, HMSO, Treaty Series No.100 (1995), Cm 3108, ISBN 0 10 131082 X.

United Kingdom Management Plan for Exports and Imports of Waste, 1996, HMSO, ISBN 0 11 7531812.

The Secretary of State, being the Minister designated[1] for the purposes of section 2(2) of the European Communities Act 1972[2] in relation to measures relating to the regulation and control of the transit, import and export of waste (including recyclable materials) and the prevention, reduction and elimination of pollution caused by waste, in exercise of the powers conferred on him by section 2(2) of that Act, sections 2, 3 and 9(1) of the Control of Pollution (Amendment) Act 1989,[3] section 74(6) of the Environmental Protection Act 1990[4] and of all other powers enabling him in that behalf, hereby makes the following Regulations:

*Citation and commencement*

1. (1) These Regulations may be cited as the Transfrontier Shipment of Waste Regulations 1994 and shall come into force on 6th May 1994.

*Interpretation*

2. (1) In these Regulations "the principal Regulation" means Council Regulation (EEC) No. 259/93 on the supervision and control of shipments of waste within, into and out of the European Community.[5]

    (2) Unless the context otherwise requires—

    (a) expressions used in these Regulations shall have the meaning they bear in the principal Regulation;[6] and

---

[1] S.I. 1993/2661 and S.I. 1992/2870.

[2] 1972 c.68.

[3] The Control of Pollution (Amendment) Act 1989 is at p.71 above. See the definition of "prescribed" in s.9(1), p.80 above.

[4] P.158 above.

[5] OJ No. L 30, 6.2.1993, p.1.

[6] DOE Circular 13/94, referred to in the list of references at the beginning of these Regulations, includes reference to the interpretation of, and definitions in, the principal Regulation.

(b) any reference in these Regulations to an Article is to an Article of the principal Regulation, including that Article as applied by any other provision of the principal Regulation.

*Competent authorities of dispatch and destination*

3. The following authorities shall be the competent authorities of dispatch and destination in relation to their areas for the purpose of the principal Regulation[1]—

(a) in Great Britain, waste regulation authorities within the meaning of section 30 of the Environmental Protection Act 1990;[2]

(b) in Northern Ireland, district councils within the meaning of section 1 of the Local Government Act (Northern Ireland) 1972.[3]

*Competent authority of transit*

4. The Secretary of State shall be the competent authority of transit for the purpose of the principal Regulation.[4]

*Correspondent*

5. The Secretary of State shall be the correspondent for the purpose of the principal Regulation.[5]

*Transmission of notification by competent authority of dispatch*

6. (1) If a competent authority of dispatch[6] decides, in relation to the notifications referred to in Article 3(1), 6(1) or 15(1)[7] relating to shipments of waste dispatched from its area, or in relation to any class of such notifications, to transmit the notification itself to the competent authority of destination, with copies to the consignee and to any competent authority of transit, it shall give notice by advertisement[8] of that decision.

(2) A notice of a decision under paragraph (1) above shall describe the notifications to which the competent authority's decision applies and the decision which is the subject of the notice shall take effect 2 weeks after the publication of the last of the notices required to be published.

(3) Where a decision under paragraph (1) above takes effect, a notifier who intends to make a shipment of waste which requires a notification to which the competent authority's decision applies shall send the required notification to the authority which published the notice and shall not send copies of that notification to any other competent authority or to the consignee.

(4) Subject to paragraph (5) below, a competent authority which receives a notification in accordance with paragraph (3) above shall, within 3 working days of receiving the notification, transmit it to the competent authority of destination, with copies to the consignee and any competent authority of transit.

(5) Where the notification relates to the shipment of waste for disposal, paragraph (4) above shall not apply if the competent authority of dispatch has immediate objections to raise against the shipment in accordance with Article 4(3).

(6) A competent authority which has published notice of a decision in accordance with this regulation may withdraw it at any time by giving notice by advertisement of the withdrawal and the withdrawal shall take effect 2 weeks after the publication of the last of the notices required to be published.

(7) In this regulation "notice by advertisement" means—

(a) in relation to notice by a competent authority in England or Wales, a notice published in the London Gazette and in such other manner as the authority consider appropriate for bringing the matters to which it relates to the attention of persons likely to be affected by them;[9]

---

[1] "The principal regulation" defined by reg.2(1) above.
[2] P.113 above.
[3] 1972 c.9. (N.I.).
[4] "The principal regulation" defined by reg.2(1) above.
[5] "The principal regulation" defined by reg.2(1) above.
[6] See reg.3 above.
[7] For "Article" see reg.2(2)(b) above.
[8] "Notice by advertisement" defined by para.(7) below.
[9] Words "in such other manner ... affected by them" substituted by S.I. 1996/593, reg.3, sch.2, para.11(2). This amendment came into force on 1 April 1996: reg.1.

(b) in relation to notice by a competent authority in Scotland, a notice published in the Edinburgh Gazette and in such other manner as the authority consider appropriate for bringing the matters to which it relates to the attention of persons likely to be affected by them;[1] and

(c) in relation to notice by a competent authority in Northern Ireland, a notice published in the Belfast Gazette and in at least 3 local newspapers circulating in the area of that authority.

*Financial guarantees or equivalent insurance*

7. (1) No person shall ship waste into or out of the United Kingdom unless a certificate has been issued in relation to the shipment under this regulation.

(2) An application for a certificate under this regulation shall be made to the authority which is the competent authority of dispatch, destination[2] or transit[3] in the United Kingdom (as the case may be) in relation to the shipment.

(3) A competent authority which receives an application under paragraph (2) above shall issue the certificate requested if it is satisfied that there is in force in respect of the shipment, or will be at the time the waste is shipped into or out of the United Kingdom (as the case may be), a financial guarantee or equivalent insurance satisfying the requirements of Article 27.[4]

(4) A competent authority shall make its decision on an application under paragraph (2) above—

(a) in respect of a shipment to which Article 3 applies, within 20 days following receipt of the application if it is a competent authority of dispatch or transit or within 30 days if it is a competent authority of destination;

(b) in respect of a shipment to which Article 6 applies, within 30 days following receipt of the application;

(c) in respect of a shipment to which Article 15 applies, within 70 days following receipt of the application;

(d) in respect of a shipment to which Article 20 applies, within 60 days following receipt of the application if it is a competent authority of transit or 70 days if it is a competent authority of destination;

(e) in respect of a shipment to which Article 23 applies, within 60 days following receipt of the application if it is the last competent authority of transit within the Community or otherwise within 20 days.

(5) A certificate issued under this regulation shall certify that the competent authority is satisfied as mentioned in paragraph (3) above.

*Power of competent authority of dispatch to ensure return of waste*

8. (1) Where a competent authority of dispatch[5] is required by Article 25(1) or 26(2)[6] to ensure that waste is returned to the United Kingdom it may serve a notice on the notifier concerned under paragraph (2) below.

(2) A notice served under this paragraph shall require the notifier to return the waste to an area within the United Kingdom specified in the notice by a date so specified.

(3) The date specified in a notice under paragraph (2) above shall allow the notifier a reasonable time to comply with the notice, having regard, in particular, to the location of the waste at the time the notice is served.

(4) Where a notifier fails to comply with a notice served on him under paragraph (2) above, the competent authority may serve a further notice on the notifier stating that the authority intends to act as the agent of the notifier to effect the return of the waste to the United Kingdom in order to fulfil the obligations of the authority under Article 25(1) or 26(2), as the case may be.

---

[1] Words "in such other manner ... affected by them" substituted by S.I. 1996/593, reg.3, sch.2, para.11(2). This amendment came into force on 1 April 1996: reg.1.
[2] See reg.3, p.742 above.
[3] See reg.4, p.742 above.
[4] For "Article" see reg.2(2)(b), p.741 above.
[5] See reg.3, p.742 above.
[6] For "Article" see reg.2(2)(b), p.741 above.

(5) Where a competent authority serves a notice under paragraph (4) above it may act as the agent of the notifier so far as is necessary to effect the return of the waste as mentioned in that paragraph and the notifier shall provide the competent authority with such information and assistance as the authority may reasonably request in writing to enable it to effect the return of the waste.

(6) Where a competent authority acts under paragraph (5) above it shall be deemed to be the duly authorised agent of the notifier acting within the scope of its authority.

*Power of competent authority of destination to ensure disposal of waste*

**9.** (1) Where a competent authority of destination[1] is required by Article 26(3)[2] to ensure the disposal or recovery of waste in an environmentally sound manner it may serve a notice on the consignee concerned under paragraph (2) below.

(2) A notice served under this paragraph shall require the consignee to ensure the disposal or recovery of waste in an environmentally sound manner in accordance with the notice and by a date specified in the notice.

(3) The date specified in a notice under paragraph (2) above shall allow the consignee a reasonable time to comply with the notice.

(4) Where a consignee fails to comply with a notice served on him under paragraph (2) above the competent authority may serve a further notice on the consignee stating that the powers set out in paragraph (6) below will be exercised on behalf of the authority so far as is necessary to enable it to effect the disposal or recovery of the waste in order to fulfil its obligations under Article 26(3).

(5) The powers referred to in paragraph (4) above shall be exercised on behalf of the competent authority,[3] by a person authorised in writing by the authority to exercise those powers ("authorised person").

(6) Pursuant to a notice served under paragraph (4) above, an[4] authorised person may, on production of his authority—

(a) enter any land which he has reason to believe it is necessary for him to enter and on entering any land take with him—

    (i) any person duly authorised by the competent authority and, if he has reasonable cause to apprehend any serious obstruction in the execution of the powers conferred by this regulation, a constable; and

    (ii) any equipment or materials required for any purpose for which the power of entry is being exercised;

(b) make such examination and investigation as may in any circumstances be necessary;

(c) remove any waste from the land, or arrange for its removal, for the purpose of its disposal or recovery;

(d) dispose of or recover waste, or arrange for its disposal or recovery.

(7) An[5] authorised person may exercise any of the powers set out in paragraph (6) above so far as is necessary to enable him to effect the disposal or recovery of the waste in order to fulfil the obligations of the competent authority under Article 26(3) and the consignee shall provide the[5] authorised person and the competent authority with such information and assistance as the[5] authorised person or the authority may reasonably request in writing to enable the competent authority to fulfil those obligations.

---

[1] See reg.3, p.742 above.
[2] For "Article" see reg.2(2)(b), p.741 above.
[3] Former words "in Great Britain, by an inspector appointed under section 68(3) of the Environmental Protection Act 1990 and, in Northern Ireland," omitted by S.I. 1996/593, reg.3, sch.2, para.11(3)(a). This amendment came into force on 1 April 1996: reg.1.
[4] Former words "inspector or" omitted by S.I. 1996/593, reg.3, sch.2, para.11(3)(b).
[5] Former words "inspector or" omitted by S.I. 1996/593, reg.3, sch.2, para.11(3)(c).

*Power of customs officer to detain shipment*

**10.** (1) On a request made upon him by a competent authority of dispatch or destination[1] in the United Kingdom for the purpose of facilitating the exercise of any functions conferred on it by the principal Regulation[2] or these Regulations, a customs officer may detain, for not more than 3 working days, waste specified in that request which has been imported into the United Kingdom or brought to a place for the purpose of being exported from the United Kingdom.

(2) Anything detained under this regulation shall be dealt with during the period of its detention in such manner as the Commissioners of Customs and Excise may direct.

(3) In this regulation and in regulation 12 below "customs officer" means any officer within the meaning of the Customs and Excise Management Act 1979.[3]

*Objections to shipments of waste in accordance with a waste management plan made by the Secretary of State*

**11.** (1) The Secretary of State shall prepare a waste management plan ("the plan")[4] in accordance with Article 7 of Council Directive 75/442/EEC[5] which shall contain his policies in relation to the import and export of waste for recovery or disposal into and out of the United Kingdom.

(2) Any provision in the plan relating to the prevention of imports or exports of waste for disposal shall be in accordance with the principles referred to in Article 4(3)(a)(i), but shall be subject to Article 4(3)(a)(ii) and (iii).[6]

(3) For the purpose of preventing movements of waste which are not in accordance with the plan—

(a) a competent authority of destination[7] shall, within the applicable time limit, object to any shipment of waste notified under Article 3(1) or 20(1), which the plan indicates should not be imported into the United Kingdom;

(b) a competent authority of dispatch[8] shall, within the applicable time limit, object to any shipment of waste notified under Article 3(1) or 15(1), which the plan indicates should not be exported from the United Kingdom.

(4) In the case of shipments of waste to which Article 7(4) applies, competent authorities of destination and dispatch shall, within the applicable time limit, raise reasoned objections under the first indent of Article 7(4)(a) to prevent movements of waste which are not in accordance with the plan.

(5) It shall be the duty of the Secretary of State—

(a) to send a copy of the plan to each competent authority of dispatch and destination; and

(b) to make copies of the plan available to the public on payment of such reasonable charges as he thinks fit.

(6) Paragraph 4(1)(b) of Schedule 4 to the Waste Management Licensing Regulations 1994[9] shall have effect as if the reference to any plan made under the plan-making provisions included a reference to a plan made under this regulation.

*Offences*

**12.** (1) Any person who contravenes a provision of the principal Regulation[10] in the United Kingdom so that waste is shipped in circumstances which are deemed to be illegal traffic under Article 26[11] commits an offence.

---

[1] See reg.3, p.742 above.
[2] "The principal regulation" defined by reg.2(1), p.741 above.
[3] 1979 c.2.
[4] The United Kingdom Management Plan for Exports and Imports of Waste, 1996, HMSO, ISBN 011 7531812, has been prepared to fulfil reg.11(1). The Plan came into force on 1 June 1996.
[5] OJ No. L 194, 25.7.1975, p.47; the Directive was amended by Council Directive 91/156/EEC, OJ No. L 78,

26.3.91, p.32 and by Council Directive 91/692/EEC, OJ No. L 377, 31.12.91, p.48.
[6] For "Article" see reg.2(2)(b), p.741 above.
[7] See reg.3, p.742 above.
[8] See reg.3, p.742 above
[9] P.716 above.
[10] "The principal regulation" defined by reg.2(1), p.741 above.
[11] For "Article" see reg.2(2)(b), p.741 above.

(2) Any person who transports, recovers, disposes of, or otherwise handles waste in the United Kingdom in contravention of a condition imposed under the principal Regulation on the shipment of waste commits an offence.

(3) Any consignee who, in relation to waste shipped to the United Kingdom, fails to send a certificate of disposal or recovery pursuant to Article 5(6), 8(6) or 20(9) (as the case may be) within the time limit set out in the applicable Article, or sends a certificate which is false in a material particular, commits an offence.

(4) Any person who contravenes regulation 7 of these Regulations[1] commits an offence.

(5) Any person who supplies information which is false in a material particular to a competent authority in the United Kingdom for the purpose of obtaining a certificate under regulation 7 of these Regulations commits an offence.

(6) Any person who, in the United Kingdom, mixes wastes which are the subject of different notifications during shipment contrary to Article 29 commits an offence.

(7) Any notifier who ships waste from the United Kingdom without having entered into a contract with the consignee in accordance with Article 3(6), 6(6) or 15(4) where required to do so by the principal Regulation commits an offence.

(8) Any notifier who ships waste from the United Kingdom which is required to be accompanied by the information set out in Article 11, signed as required by that Article, and which is not so accompanied whilst in the United Kingdom, commits an offence.

(9) Any person who fails to comply with a notice served on him under regulation 8(2) or 9(2) of these Regulations commits an offence.

(10) Any person who intentionally obstructs an inspector or authorised person in the exercise of his powers under regulation 9 of these Regulations or a customs officer in the exercise of his powers under regulation 10 of these Regulations commits an offence.

(11) Where the commission by any person of an offence under this regulation is due to the act or default of some other person, that other person shall be guilty of the offence, and a person may be charged with and convicted of an offence by virtue of this paragraph whether or not proceedings are taken against the first-mentioned person.

*Offences by corporations etc.*

**13.** (1) Where an offence under regulation 12 above which has been committed by a body corporate is proved to have been committed with the consent or connivance of, or to have been attributable to any neglect on the part of, a director, manager, secretary or other similar officer of the body corporate, or any other person purporting to act in any such capacity, he, as well as the body corporate, shall be guilty of that offence and shall be liable to be proceeded against and punished accordingly.

(2) Where the affairs of a body corporate are managed by its members, paragraph (1) above shall apply in relation to the acts or defaults of a member in connection with his functions of management as if he were a director of the body corporate.

(3) Where, in Scotland, an offence under regulation 12 above which has been committed by a Scottish partnership or an unincorporated association (other than a partnership) is proved to have been committed with the consent or connivance of, or to have been attributable to any neglect on the part of, a partner in the partnership or, as the case may be, a person concerned in the management or control of the association, he, as well as the partnership or association, shall be guilty of that offence and shall be liable to be proceeded against and punished accordingly.

*Defences*

**14.** (1) In any proceedings for an offence under regulation 12 above it shall be a defence for the person charged to prove that he took all reasonable steps and exercised all due diligence to avoid the commission of the offence.

[1] P.743 above.

(2)  In any proceedings for an offence under regulation 12(2) above, it shall be a defence for the person charged to prove that he was not reasonably able to comply with the condition concerned by reason of an emergency.

(3)  In any proceedings for an offence under regulation 12(3) above on the grounds that the consignee has not sent a certificate of disposal or recovery (as the case may be) within the applicable time limit, it shall be a defence for the consignee to prove—

(a)  that he was not able to send the certificate within that time limit because he had not been able to dispose of or recover the waste in time as a result of an emergency; and

(b)  that he disposed of or recovered the waste as soon as was reasonably practicable or that he is taking all reasonable steps to ensure that the waste is disposed of or recovered as soon as is reasonably practicable.

*Penalties*

**15.** (1)  Subject to paragraph (2) below, a person who commits an offence under regulation 12 above shall be liable on summary conviction to a fine not exceeding—

(a)  in Great Britain, the statutory maximum;[1]

(b)  in Northern Ireland, £2,000;

or on conviction on indictment to imprisonment for a term not exceeding two years, or a fine, or both.

(2)  A person who commits an offence under paragraph (8) of regulation 12 above shall be liable on summary conviction to a fine not exceeding—

(a)  in Great Britain, level 3 on the standard scale;[2]

(b)  in Northern Ireland, £400.

*Provision of information etc.*

**16.**  For the purpose of performing any of his functions under the principal Regulation[3] the Secretary of State may, by notice in writing, require any competent authority in the United Kingdom to furnish such information and documents as may be specified in the notice.[4]

*Notices*

**17.** (1)  Any notice which is authorised to be served on a notifier under regulation 8 above[5] or on a consignee under regulation 9 above may be served on the person in question either by delivering it to him, or by leaving it at his proper address, or by sending it by post to him at that address.

(2)  Any such notice may—

(a)  in the case of a body corporate, be served on the secretary or clerk of that body; and

(b)  in the case of a partnership, be served on a partner or a person having the control or management of that partnership business.

(3)  For the purpose of this regulation and section 7 of the Interpretation Act 1978 (service of documents by post)[6] in its application to this regulation, the proper address of any person on whom a notice is to be served shall be the address given for him on the consignment note relating to the shipment of waste in connection with which the notice is to be served.

---

[1] The current statutory maximum is £5,000: Criminal Justice Act 1991 (c.53), s.17 (England and Wales); Criminal Procedure (Scotland) Act 1995 (c.46), s.225 (Scotland).

[2] The current fine at level 3 on the standard scale is £1,000: Criminal Justice Act 1991 (c.53), s.17 (England and Wales); Criminal Procedure (Scotland) Act 1995 (c.46), s.225 (Scotland).

[3] "The principal regulation" defined by reg.2(1), p.741 above.

[4] See DOE Circular 13/94, para.3, Annex 3. This circular is referred to in the list of references at the beginning of these Regulations, p.741 above.

[5] P.743 above.

[6] 1978 c.30.

*Amendment of the Control of Pollution (Special Waste) Regulations 1980 and the Pollution Control (Special Waste) Regulations (Northern Ireland) 1981*

**18.** (1) and (2)   *These paragraphs are revoked, subject to savings, by S.I. 1996/972, reg.26, p.777 below.*

(3) and (4)   These paragraphs relate to Northern Ireland.

*Amendment of the Controlled Waste (Registration of Carriers and Seizure of Vehicles) Regulations 1991 and the Waste Management Licensing Regulations 1994*

**19.** *The amendments made by this regulation are included in the Controlled Waste (Registration of Carriers and Seizure of Vehicles) Regulations 1991, p.630 above, and the Waste Management Licensing Regulations 1994, p.675 above.*

*Registration of dealers and brokers*

**20.** (1)   The register established and maintained by a waste regulation authority[1] pursuant to paragraph 12(5) of Part I of Schedule 4 to the Waste Management Licensing Regulation 1994[2] shall also be a register of establishments or undertakings registering with the authority under this regulation.

(2)   The register shall contain the following particulars in relation to each such establishment or undertaking—

(a)   the name of the establishment or undertaking;

(b)   the address of its principal place of business; and

(c)   the address of any place at or from which it carries on business.

(3)   The waste regulation authority shall enter the relevant particulars in the register in relation to an establishment or undertaking which arranges (as dealer or broker) for the disposal or the recovery of waste if it becomes aware of them as a result of either—

(a)   that establishment or undertaking applying, before 1st January 1995, to the authority under paragraph 3 of Part I of Schedule 5 to the Waste Management Licensing Regulations 1994[3] to be registered as a broker of controlled waste; or

(b)   the authority being otherwise notified in writing before 1st January 1995 of those particulars.

(4)   An establishment or undertaking registering under paragraph (3)(b) above shall register with the waste regulation authority in whose area its principal place of business in Great Britain is located or, where it has no place of business in Great Britain, with any waste regulation authority.

(5)   In the case of an establishment or undertaking registered by virtue of paragraph (3)(a) above, its registration under this regulation shall have effect only for so long as its application to be registered as a broker of controlled waste is pending.

(6)   In the case of an establishment or undertaking registered by virtue of paragraph (3)(b) above, its registration under this regulation shall cease to have effect on 1st January 1995 unless—

(a)   it has before that date applied to be registered as a broker of controlled waste; and

(b)   immediately before that date that application is pending,

in which event its registration under this regulation shall continue to have effect for so long as its application to be registered as a broker of controlled waste is pending.

(7)   For the purposes of this regulation, paragraph 1(4) and (5) of Part I of Schedule 5 to the Waste Management Licensing Regulations 1994[4] shall apply for the purpose of determining whether an application to be registered as a broker of controlled waste is pending.

(8)   Where a registration under this regulation ceases to have effect, the waste regulation authority—

---

[1]   "Waste regulation authority" has the meaning given by s.30 of the 1990 Act, p.113 above: paragraph (9) below.
[2]   P.719 above.
[3]   P.724 above.
[4]   P.723 above.

(a) shall record this fact in the appropriate entry in its register and the date on which it occurred; and

(b) may remove the appropriate entry from its register at any time more than three years after the registration ceases to have effect.

(9) In this regulation, "waste regulation authority" has the meaning given by section 30 of the Environmental Protection Act 1990.[1]

*Revocations*

**21.** (1) Subject to paragraph (2) below, the Transfrontier Shipment of Hazardous Waste Regulations 1998,[2] the Control of Pollution (Special Waste) (Amendment) Regulations 1988[3] and the Transfrontier Shipment of Hazardous Waste Regulations (Northern Ireland) 1989[4] are hereby revoked.

(2) The Transfrontier Shipment of Hazardous Waste Regulations 1988 and the Transfrontier Shipment of Hazardous Waste Regulations (Northern Ireland) 1989 shall continue to apply in relation to shipments of waste effected before 6th November 1994 under an acknowledgement of receipt issued under Articles 4 and 5 of Council Directive 84/631/EEC on the supervision and control within the European Community of the transfrontier shipment of hazardous waste[5] before these Regulations come into force.

## Explanatory Note
### (This note is not part of the Regulations)

These Regulations make provision in relation to Council Regulation (EEC) No. 259/93 on the supervision and control of shipments of waste within, into and out of the European Community and for the purpose of implementing Council Directive 75/442/EEC (as amended) ("the Waste Framework Directive") in respect of imports and exports of waste.

The Council Regulation provides for a system of prior notification and authorization where a person intends to ship waste within, into or out of the Community. The Council Regulation requires member States to deal with a number of matters by means of their domestic legislation in relation to the operation of the new system. These Regulations deal with those matters in the United Kingdom; in particular—

(a) designate the authorities which are to be the competent authorities and the correspondent in the United Kingdom under the new system (regulations 3, 4 and 5);

(b) enable a competent authority of dispatch to require notifications of shipments of waste from their area to be routed through the authority rather than being sent to competent authorities by the notifier (regulation 6);

(c) require a certificate relating to financial guarantees and insurance to be obtained prior to shipments of waste entering or leaving the United Kingdom (regulation 7);

(d) confer powers on competent authorities to ensure that waste is returned to the United Kingdom or is recovered or disposed of where the authority is under an obligation to secure the return, recovery or disposal of the waste in accordance with the Council Regulation (regulations 8 and 9);

(e) confer powers on customs officers to detain shipments of waste to facilitate the exercise by the competent authorities of their functions under the Council Regulation (regulation 10);

(f) provide for the preparation of a waste management plan by the Secretary of State in accordance with the Waste Framework Directive and require competent authorities of dispatch and destination to object to shipments of waste in accordance with the plan (regulation 11);

(g) set out offences and penalties in relation to non-compliance with the Council Regulation or United Kingdom Regulations (regulations 12 to 15);

(h) confer power on the Secretary of State to require competent authorities to provide information to enable him to fulfil his functions under the Council Regulation (regulation 16);

(i) set out how certain notices given under the United Kingdom Regulations may be served (regulation 17);

---

[1] P.113 above.
[2] S.I. 1988/1562.
[3] S.I. 1988/1790.

[4] S.R. 1989/115.
[5] OJ No. L 326, 13.12.1984, p.31.

(j)  amend the Control of Pollution (Special Waste) Regulations 1980 and the Pollution Control (Special Waste) Regulations (Northern Ireland) 1981 to avoid an overlap between the control system under those Regulations and the new system under the Council Regulation (regulation 18);

(k)  amend the Controlled Waste (Registration of Carriers and Seizure of Vehicles) Regulations 1991 and the Waste Management Licensing Regulations 1994 to make the offences under regulation 12 prescribed offences under the 1991 Regulations and relevant offences under the 1994 Regulations (regulation 19);

(l)  provide a transitional registration system for dealers and brokers to enable them to act as notifiers under the Council Regulation (regulation 20);

(m)  revoke certain provisions which will be superseded on the coming into force of the new system (regulation 21).

# The Waste Management Licensing (Amendment etc.) Regulations 1995

S.I. 1995 No. 288

The Secretary of State for the Environment as respects England, the Secretary of State for Wales as respects Wales and the Secretary of State for Scotland as respects Scotland, being Ministers designated[1] for the purposes of section 2(2) of the European Communities Act 1972[2] in relation to measures relating to the prevention, reduction and elimination of pollution caused by waste, in exercise of the powers conferred on them by section 2(2) of that Act, sections 29(10), 33(3), 74(6) and 75(8) of the Environmental Protection Act 1990[3] (having in particular had regard in exercising their powers under section 33(3) of that Act to the matters specified in section 33(4) of that Act), and of all other powers enabling them in that behalf, hereby make the following Regulations:

*Citation, commencement and interpretation*

1. (1) These Regulations may be cited as the Waste Management Licensing (Amendment etc.) Regulations 1995 and shall come into force on 1st April 1995.

   (2) In these Regulations, unless the context otherwise requires—

   "the 1990 Act" means the Environmental Protection Act 1990;

   "the 1991 Regulations" means the Environmental Protection (Prescribed Processes and Substances) Regulations 1991;[4] and

   "the Principal Regulations" means the Waste Management Licensing Regulations 1994.[5]

*Amendment of the Controlled Waste Regulations 1992*

2. *The amendments made by this regulation are included in the Controlled Waste Regulations 1992, p.662 above.*

*Amendment of the Waste Management Licensing Regulations 1994*

3. *The amendments made by this regulation are included in the Waste Management Licensing Regulations 1994, p.675 above.*

*Technical competence—transitional provisions*

4. (1) Where before 10th July 1995 a person has applied to the Waste Management Industry Training and Advisory Board for a certificate of technical competence and at any time in the 23 months ending on that date he acted as the manager of a facility of a type listed in Table 1 in the Principal Regulations[6] for which the certificate is a relevant certificate, then, until 10th August 1999, regulation 4 of the Principal Regulations shall not apply to him in relation to either—

   (a) any facility of that type; or

   (b) a facility of any other type if—

   (i) the certificate is a relevant certificate for that other type of facility; and

---

[1] S.I. 1992/2870.
[2] 1972 c.68.
[3] Part II of the 1990 Act is at p.112 above.
[4] P.566 above.
[5] P.675 above.
[6] P.679 above.

(ii) the entry for that other type of facility appears, in Table 1 in the Principal Regulations, after the entry in that Table for the type of facility in respect of which he acted as the manager,

and he shall be treated as technically competent for the purposes of section 74(3)(b) of the 1990 Act[1] in relation to any such facility.

(2) A person shall be treated as the manager of a facility for the purposes of paragraph (1) above if at the relevant time he was the manager of activities which were carried on at that facility and either—

(a) those activities involved the recovery or disposal of waste as or as part of a process designated for central control under section 2(4) of the 1990 Act[2] and were authorised by an authorisation granted under Part I of that Act; or

(b) those activities involved the disposal of waste as or as part of a process designated for local control under section 2(4) of the 1990 Act and falling within paragraph (a) of Part B of Section 5.1 (incineration) of Schedule 1 to the 1991 Regulations[3] and were authorised by an authorisation granted under Part I of that Act.

(3) Where at any time in the 15 months ending on 31st July 1995 a person has acted as the manager of a facility the operation of which at that time was not in breach of section 33(1)(a) or (b) of the 1990 Act[4] solely by virtue of the exemption provided by regulation 17[5] of, and paragraph 43[6] of Schedule 3 to, the Principal Regulations, then, until the date specified in paragraph (4) below, regulation 4 of the Principal Regulations shall not apply to him in relation to that facility and he shall be treated as technically competent for the purposes of section 74(3)(b) of the 1990 Act in relation to that facility.

(4) The date referred to in paragraph (3) above as being specified in this paragraph is 31st July 1995 except in the following cases—

(a) where the facility is of a type listed in Table 1 in the Principal Regulations, and the person has applied on or before 31st July 1995 to the Waste Management Industry Training and Advisory Board for a certificate of technical competence which is a relevant certificate, then the specified date is 10th August 1999;

(b) where the facility is not of a type listed in Table 1 in the Principal Regulations, and an application is made on or before 31st July 1995 for a waste management licence which, if granted, would authorise the operation of the facility, then the specified date is the day after the day upon which the licence is granted or, if the application is (or is deemed to be) rejected, the day after—

(i) the day on which the period for appealing expires without any appeal having been made; or

(ii) the day on which any appeal is withdrawn or finally determined.

(5) In their application in relation to the manager of a facility at which activities falling within paragraph 8 or 9 of Part III of Schedule 4 to the Principal Regulations[7] are carried on, paragraphs (3) and (4) above shall have effect as if—

(a) in paragraph (3), for the words "the 15 months ending on 31st July 1995" there were substituted the words "the 29 months ending on 30th September 1996";[8]

(b) in paragraph (4), for the words "31st July 1995" in each place where they occur there were substituted the words "30th September 1996".[9,10]

## Explanatory Note

*This is not reproduced. The explanatory note relates mainly to the amendments made by this instrument.*

[1] P.158 above.
[2] P.91 above.
[3] P.584 above.
[4] P.116 above.
[5] P.702 above.
[6] P.708 above.
[7] P.722 above.

[8] Words "the 29 months ending on 30th September 1996" substituted by S.I. 1996/634, reg.3(a). This amendment came into force on 30 March 1996: reg.1(2).
[9] Words "30th September 1996" substituted by S.I. 1996/634, reg.3(b).
[10] Para.(5) added by S.I. 1995/1950, reg.3. This amendment came into force on 29 July 1995: reg.1.

# The Statutory Nuisance (Appeals) Regulations 1995

## S.I. 1995 No. 2644

The Secretary of State for the Environment, as respects England, and the Secretary of State for Wales, as respects Wales, in exercise of the powers conferred on them by paragraph 1(4) of Schedule 3 to the Environmental Protection Act 1990[1] and of all other powers enabling them in that behalf, hereby make the following Regulations:

### Citation, commencement and interpretation

1. (1) These Regulations may be cited as the Statutory Nuisance (Appeals) Regulations 1995 and shall come into force on 8th November 1995.

    (2) In these Regulations—

    "the 1974 Act" means the Control of Pollution Act 1974;[2]

    "the 1990 Act" means the Environmental Protection Act 1990; and

    "the 1993 Act" means the Noise and Statutory Nuisance Act 1993.[3]

### Appeals under section 80(3) of the 1990 Act

2. (1) The provisions of this regulation apply in relation to an appeal brought by any person under section 80(3) of the 1990 Act[4] (appeals to magistrates) against an abatement notice served upon him by a local authority.[5]

    (2) The grounds on which a person served with such a notice may appeal under section 80(3) are any one or more of the following grounds that are appropriate in the circumstances of the particular case—

    (a) that the abatement notice is not justified by section 80 of the 1990 Act (summary proceedings for statutory nuisances);

    (b) that there has been some informality, defect or error in, or in connection with, the abatement notice, or in, or in connection with, any copy of the abatement notice served under section 80A(3)[6] (certain notices in respect of vehicles, machinery or equipment);

    (c) that the authority have refused unreasonably to accept compliance with alternative requirements, or that the requirements of the abatement notice are otherwise unreasonable in character or extent, or are unnecessary;

    (d) that the time, or where more than one time is specified, any of the times, within which the requirements of the abatement notice are to be complied with is not reasonably sufficient for the purpose;

    (e) where the nuisance to which the notice relates—

      (i) is a nuisance falling within section 79(1)(a), (d), (e), (f) or (g) of the 1990 Act[1] and arises on industrial, trade, or business premises, or

---

[1] P.224 above.
[2] 1974 c.40.
[3] 1993 c.40.
[4] P.191 above.

[5] "Local authority" defined by s.79(7), (8) of the 1990 Act, p.188 above.
[6] P.192 above.

    (ii)  is a nuisance falling within section 79(1)(b) of the 1990 Act and the smoke is emitted from a chimney, or

    (iii)  is a nuisance falling within section 79(1) (ga) of the 1990 Act and is noise emitted from or caused by a vehicle, machinery or equipment being used for industrial, trade or business purposes.

that the best practicable means[2] were used to prevent, or to counteract the effects of, the nuisance;

  (f)  that, in the case of a nuisance under section 79(1)(g) or (ga) of the 1990 Act (noise emitted from premises), the requirements imposed by the abatement notice by virtue of section 80(1)(a) of the Act are more onerous than the requirements for the time being in force, in relation to the noise to which the notice relates, of—

    (i)  any notice served under section 60 or 66 of the 1974 Act[3] (control of noise on construction sites and from certain premises), or

    (ii)  any consent given under section 61 or 65 of the 1974 Act (consent for work on construction sites and consent for noise to exceed registered level in a noise abatement zone), or

    (iii)  any determination made under section 67 of the 1974 Act (noise control of new buildings);

  (g)  that, in the case of a nuisance under section 79(1)(ga) of the 1990 Act (noise emitted from or caused by vehicles, machinery or equipment), the requirements imposed by the abatement notice by virtue of section 80(1)(a) of the Act are more onerous than the requirements for the time being in force, in relation to the noise to which the notice relates, of any condition of a consent given under paragraph 1 of Schedule 2 to the 1993 Act[4] (loudspeakers in streets or roads);

  (h)  that the abatement notice should have been served on some person instead of the appellant, being—

    (i)  the person responsible[5] for the nuisance, or

    (ii)  the person responsible for the vehicle, machinery or equipment, or

    (iii)  in the case of a nuisance arising from any defect of a structural character, the owner of the premises, or

    (iv)  in the case where the person responsible for the nuisance cannot be found or the nuisance has not yet occurred, the owner or occupier of the premises;

  (i)  that the abatement notice might lawfully have been served on some person instead of the appellant being—

    (i)  in the case where the appellant is the owner of the premises, the occupier of the premises, or

    (ii)  in the case where the appellant is the occupier of the premises, the owner of the premises,

and that it would have been equitable for it to have been so served;

  (j)  that the abatement notice might lawfully have been served on some person in addition to the appellant, being—

    (i)  a person also responsible for the nuisance, or

    (ii)  a person who is also owner of the premises, or

    (iii)  a person who is also an occupier of the premises, or

    (iv)  a person who is also the person responsible for the vehicle, machinery or equipment,

and that it would have been equitable for it to have been so served.

---

[1] P.187 above; s.79(7) defines terms used in this paragraph.
[2] "Best practicable means" defined by s.79(9) of the 1990 Act, p.190 above.
[3] "The 1974 Act" means the Control of Pollution Act 1974 (c.40): reg.1(2) above.
[4] "The 1993 Act" means the Noise and Statutory Nuisance Act 1993 (c.40): reg.1(2) above.
[5] "Person responsible" defined by s. 79(7) of the 1990 Act, p.189 above.

(3) If and so far as an appeal is based on the ground of some informality, defect or error in, or in connection with, the abatement notice, or in, or in connection with, any copy of the notice served under section 80A(3), the court shall dismiss the appeal if it is satisfied that the informality, defect or error was not a material one.

(4) Where the grounds upon which an appeal is brought include a ground specified in paragraph (2)(i) or (j) above, the appellant shall serve a copy of his notice of appeal on any other person referred to, and in the case of any appeal to which these regulations apply he may serve a copy of his notice of appeal on any other person having an estate or interest in the premises, vehicle, machinery or equipment in question.

(5) On the hearing of the appeal the court may—

(a) quash the abatement notice to which the appeal relates, or

(b) vary the abatement notice in favour of the appellant in such manner as it thinks fit, or

(c) dismiss the appeal;

and an abatement notice that is varied under sub-paragraph (b) above shall be final and shall otherwise have effect, as so varied, as if it had been so made by the local authority.

(6) Subject to paragraph (7) below, on the hearing of an appeal the court may make such order as it thinks fit—

(a) with respect to the person by whom any work is to be executed and the contribution to be made by any person towards the cost of the work, or

(b) as to the proportions in which any expenses which may become recoverable by the authority under Part III of the 1990 Act[1] are to be borne by the appellant and by any other person.

(7) In exercising its powers under paragraph (6) above the court—

(a) shall have regard, as between an owner and an occupier, to the terms and conditions, whether contractual or statutory, of any relevant tenancy and to the nature of the works required, and

(b) shall be satisfied before it imposes any requirement thereunder on any person other than the appellant, that that person has received a copy of the notice of appeal in pursuance of paragraph (4) above.

*Suspension of notice*

**3.** (1) Where—

(a) an appeal is brought against an abatement notice served under section 80 or section 80A of the 1990 Act,[2] and—

(b) either—

    (i) compliance with the abatement notice would involve any person in expenditure on the carrying out of works before the hearing of the appeal, or

    (ii) in the case of a nuisance under section 79(1)(g) or (ga) of the 1990 Act,[3] the noise to which the abatement notice relates is noise necessarily caused in the course of the performance of some duty imposed by law on the appellant, and

(c) either paragraph (2) does not apply, or it does apply but the requirements of paragraph (3) have not been met,

the abatement notice shall be suspended until the appeal has been abandoned or decided by the court.

(2) This paragraph applies where—

(a) the nuisance to which the abatement notice relates—

    (i) is injurious to health, or

    (ii) is likely to be of a limited duration such that suspension of the notice would render it of no practical effect, or

---

[1] P.187 above.  [2] P.190 above.  [3] P.187 above.

(b) the expenditure which would be incurred by any person in the carrying out of works in compliance with the abatement notice before any appeal has been decided would not be disproportionate to the public benefit to be expected in that period from such compliance.

(3) Where paragraph (2) applies the abatement notice—

(a) shall include a statement that paragraph (2) applies, and that as a consequence it shall have effect notwithstanding any appeal to a magistrates' court which has not been decided by the court, and

(b) shall include a statement as to which of the grounds set out in paragraph (2) apply.

*Revocations*

**4.** The Statutory Nuisance (Appeals) Regulations 1990[1] and the Statutory Nuisance (Appeals) (Amendment) Regulations 1990[2] are hereby revoked.

*Explanatory Note*
*(This note is not part of the Regulations)*

These Regulations make provision with respect to appeals to magistrates' courts against abatement notices served under section 80 of the Environmental Protection Act 1990 (as amended by the Noise and Statutory Nuisance Act 1993) and those served under section 80A of the 1990 Act (as added by the 1993 Act). Regulation 2 sets out grounds on which such appeals may be made, prescribes the procedure to be followed in certain cases in which the appellant claims that a notice should have been served on some other person, and the action which the court may take to give effect to its decision on an appeal. Regulation 3 prescribes the cases in which an abatement notice is to be suspended pending the abandonment of, or a decision by a magistrates' court on, an appeal. Regulation 4 revokes the Statutory Nuisance (Appeals) Regulations 1990 and the Statutory Nuisance (Appeals) (Amendment) Regulations 1990.

---

[1] S.I. 1990/2276.    [2] S.I. 1990/2483.

# The Environmental Licences (Suspension and Revocation) Regulations 1996

## S.I. 1996 No. 508

The Secretary of State, in exercise of powers conferred on him by section 41(6) and (10) of the Environment Act 1995[1] and of all other powers enabling him in that behalf, hereby makes the following Regulations:

*Citation and commencement*

**1.** (1) These Regulations may be cited as the Environment Licences (Suspension and Revocation) Regulations 1996 and shall come into force on 1st April 1996.

*Interpretation*

**2.** In these Regulations—

"holder" in relation to an environmental licence means the person liable to pay any charges due and payable in respect of the subsistence of that licence.

*Notice demanding payment*

**3.** The appropriate procedure, where a new Agency[2] proposes to suspend or revoke an environmental licence[3] under section 41(6) of the Environment Act 1995,[4] is as follows—

(a) before taking any action under regulation 5 below to suspend or revoke an environmental licence, the new Agency shall first serve on the holder of the environmental licence a notice demanding payment within twenty-eight days after the service of the notice of any charges due and payable in respect of the subsistence of the licence; and

(b) the new Agency shall allow the period of twenty-eight days to expire before taking further action to suspend or revoke the environmental licence.

*Contents of notice demanding payment*

**4.** A notice demanding the payment of any charges which is served for the purposes of regulation 3 shall state—

(a) that the environmental licence may be suspended or revoked if the charges are not paid within twenty-eight days after the service of the notice; and

(b) the effect of suspension or revocation.

*Notice of suspension or revocation*

**5.** (1) Suspension or revocation of a licence under section 41(6) of the Environment Act 1995[5] shall be effected by the service of a notice of suspension or revocation on the holder of the environmental licence.

---

[1] P.453 above.
[2] "New Agency" means the Environment Agency or the Scottish Environment Protection Agency, SEPA: Environment Act 1995, ss.56(1), 124(1).
[3] "Environmental licence" defined in s.56(1) of the 1995 Act, p.463 above.
[4] P.453 above.
[5] P.453 above.

(2) A notice of suspension or revocation shall—

(a) set out the reason for the suspension or revocation and the date and time at which it will take effect; and

(b) in the case of a suspension of an environmental licence, set out the circumstances in which the suspension may be lifted.

*Explanatory Note*
*(This note is not part of the Regulations)*

These Regulations set out the procedure whereby new Agencies, that is, the Environment Agency and the Scottish Environment Protection Agency, "SEPA", can seek the suspension or revocation of environmental licences where charges due and payable in respect of the subsistence of such licences remain unpaid.

Environmental licences are defined in section 56(1) of the Environment Act 1995, by reference to the environmental legislation applicable to the Environment Agency and to SEPA.

# The Waste Management Regulations 1996

S.I. 1996 No. 634

The Secretary of State for the Environment as respects England, the Secretary of State for Wales as respects Wales and the Secretary of State for Scotland as respects Scotland, being Ministers designated[1] for the purposes of section 2(2) of the European Communities Act 1972[2] in relation to measures relating to the prevention, reduction and elimination of pollution caused by waste, in exercise of powers conferred on them by section 2(2) of that Act, sections 29(10), 33(3), 52(8) and 74(6) of the Environment Act 1990[3] (having in particular had regard in exercising their powers under section 33(3) to the matters specified in section 33(4) of that Act), and of all other powers enabling them in that behalf, hereby make the following Regulations:

*Citation, commencement and extent*

1. (1) These Regulations may be cited as the Waste Management Regulations 1996 and, except for regulations 2(6) and 3, shall come into force on 1st April 1996.

   (2) Regulations 2(6) and 3 shall come into force on 30th March 1996.

   (3) Regulation 2(3) does not extend to Scotland.

*Amendment of the Waste Management Licensing Regulations 1994*

2. *The amendments made by this regulation are included in the Waste Management Licensing Regulations 1994, p.675 above.*

*Amendment of the Waste Management Licensing (Amendment etc.) Regulations 1995*

3. *The amendments made by this regulation are included in the Waste Management Licensing (Amendment etc.) Regulations 1995, p.751 above.*

*Pre-qualification technical competence*

4. (1) Where—

   (a) a person has applied to the Waste Management Industry Training and Advisory Board for a certificate of technical competence in relation to one of the types of facility mentioned in paragraph (2);

   (b) an application has been made for a waste management licence to authorise activities whose management is intended to be in that person's hands;

   (c) the activities mentioned in sub-paragraph (b) are to be carried on at a facility of the same type as that in relation to which the application mentioned in sub-paragraph (a) was made; and

   (d) the relevant Agency as defined in paragraph (3) is satisfied that, but for regulation 4 of the Waste Management Licensing Regulations 1994,[4] he would be a technically competent person;[5]

---

[1] S.I. 1992/2870.
[2] 1972 c.68.
[3] Part II of the 1990 Act is at p.112 above.
[4] P.679 above.
[5] S.74(5) of the 1990 Act, p.158 above, provides that it shall be the duty of the Agencies to have regard to any guidance issued to them by the Secretary of State with respect to the discharge of their functions of making determinations to which s.74 applies.

then, in relation to the facility in respect of which the application mentioned in sub-paragraph (b) was made and until the expiry of two years from the grant of a licence pursuant to that application, regulation 4 of those Regulations shall not apply to that person and he shall be treated as technically competent for the purposes of section 74(3)(b) of the Environmental Protection Act 1990.[1]

(2) The types of facility mentioned in paragraph (1)(a) are all those listed in Table 1 of regulation 4(1) of the Waste Management Licensing Regulations 1994[2] other than any type of landfill site.

(3) The relevant Agency mentioned in paragraph (1)(d) is:

(a) in relation to England and Wales, the Environment Agency established by section 1 of the Environment Act 1995;[3] and

(b) in relation to Scotland, the Scottish Environment Protection Agency established by section 20 of that Act.[4]

*Transitional provision for certificates of technical competence: waste treatment plants*

5. (1) Paragraph (2) of this regulation applies to a person who has made an application to the Waste Management Industry Training and Advisory Board for a "Treatment operations: inert waste (level 3)" certificate of technical competence before 10th August 1994, in a case where that application has not been determined.

(2) Unless he notifies the Board in writing that he does not wish this regulation to apply to him, the person mentioned in paragraph (1) shall be treated for the purposes of regulation 5 of the Waste Management Licensing Regulations 1994[5] as if the certificate for which he applied was a "Managing treatment operations: special waste (level 4)" certificate of technical competence.

(3) Paragraph (4) of this regulation applies to a person who has made an application to the Waste Management Industry Training and Advisory Board for a "Treatment operations: inert waste (level 3)" certificate of technical competence before 1st April 1996, in a case where that application has not been determined.

(4) Unless he notifies the Board in writing that he does not wish this regulation to apply to him, the person mentioned in paragraph (3) shall be treated for the purposes of regulation 4 of the Waste Management Licensing (Amendment etc.) Regulations 1995[6] as if the certificate for which he applied was a "Managing treatment operations: special waste (level 4)" certificate of technical competence.

*Amendment to the Environmental Protection (Waste Recycling Payments) Regulations 1992*

**6.** *The amendment made by this regulation is included in the Environmental Protection (Waste Recycling Payments) Regulations 1992, p.657 above.*

*Explanatory Note*

*This is not reproduced. The explanatory note relates mainly to the amendments made by this instrument.*

---

[1] P.158 above.
[2] P.679 above.
[3] P.420 above.

[4] P.438 above.
[5] P.680 above.
[6] P.751 above.

# The Waste Management Licensing (Scotland) Regulations 1996

## S.I. 1996 No. 916 (S.100)

The Secretary of State, in exercise of powers conferred on him by section 74(6) of the Environment Act 1990[1] and of all other powers enabling him in that behalf, hereby makes the following Regulations:

### Citation, commencement, application and interpretation

1. (1) These Regulations may be cited as the Waste Management Licensing (Scotland) Regulations 1996, shall extend to Scotland only and shall come into force on 1st May 1996.

   "the 1990 Act" means the Environment Protection Act 1990;

   "the principal Regulations" means the Waste Management Licensing Regulations 1994;[2] and

   "Table 1" means Table 1 in regulation 4(1) of the principal Regulations.[3]

### Technical competence—transitional provisions

2. (1) Where before 1st October 1996 a person has applied to the Waste Management Industry Training and Advisory Board for a certificate of technical competence and at any time in the 15 months ending on that date he acted as the manager of a facility of a type listed in Table 1 for which the certificate is a relevant certificate, then, until 1st October 2001, regulation 4 of the principal Regulations[4] shall not apply to him in relation to either—

   (a) any facility of that type; or

   (b) a facility of any other type if—

   (i) the certificate is a relevant certificate for that other type of facility; and

   (ii) the entry for that other type of facility appears, in Table 1, after the entry in that Table for the type of facility in respect of which he acted as the manager,

   and he shall be treated as technically competent for the purposes of section 74(3)(b) of the 1990 Act[5] in relation to any such facility.

   (2) Where a person is aged 55 or over on 1st October 1996 and in the 10 years ending on that date he has had at least 5 years experience as the manager of a facility of a type listed in Table 1, then, until 1st October 2006, regulation 4 of the principal Regulations shall not apply to him in relation to either—

   (a) any facility of that type; or

   (b) a facility of any other type if each certificate which is a relevant certificate for the type of facility in relation to which he has had such experience as manager is also a relevant certificate for that other type of facility,

   and he shall be treated as technically competent for the purposes of section 74(3)(b) of the 1990 Act in relation to any such facility.

   (3) Where at any time in the 12 months ending on 1st October 1996 a person has acted as the manager of a facility, regulation 4 of the principal Regulations shall not apply to him in relation to that

[1] P.158 above.
[2] P.675 above.
[3] P.679 above.
[4] P.679 above.
[5] P.158 above.

facility and he shall be treated as technically competent for the purposes of section 74(3)(b) of the 1990 Act in relation to that facility.

(4) A person shall be treated as the manager of a facility for the purposes of paragraph (1), (2) or (3) above if and only if at the relevant time he was the manager of activities which were carried on at that facility and which were authorised by a resolution under section 54 of the 1990 Act.[1]

### Explanatory Note
#### (This note is not part of the Regulations)

These Regulations disapply regulation 4 of the Waste Management Licensing Regulations 1994 (qualifications required for a person to be technically competent) to managers of specified waste facilities operated by local authorities, who meet certain criteria as to age and experience. Such managers will be treated as technically competent for the purposes of section 74(3)(b) of the Environmental Protection Act 1990.

[1] S.54 was amended by the Environment Act 1995 (c.25), sch.23, para.18, p.533 above.

# The Special Waste Regulations 1996

S.I. 1996 No. 972

---

*Amendment*

As noted in the text these regulations have been amended by the Special Waste (Amendment) Regulations 1996, S.I. 1996/2019, reg.2, sch. These amending regulations came into force on 31 August 1996: reg.1.

*References to material not set out in this Manual*

Joint Circular: Environmental Protection Act 1990: Part II, Special Waste Regulations 1996. Department of the Environment Circular 6/96, Welsh Office Circular WO 21/96, Scottish Office Agriculture Environment and Fisheries Department Circular SOAEFD 13/96 of 13 June 1996. This circular is amended and updated by the following circular.

Joint Circular: Environmental Protection Act 1990: Part II, Special Waste (Amendment) Regulations 1996. Department of the Environment Circular 14/96, Welsh Office Circular WO 39/96, Scottish Office Agriculture Environment and Fisheries Department Circular SOAEFD 26/96 of 23 August 1996.

*Arrangement of regulations*

1. Citation, commencement, extent, application and interpretation   764
2. Meaning of special waste   766
3. Certain radioactive waste to be special waste   766
4. Coding of consignments   766
5. Consignment notes: standard procedure   767
6. Consignment notes: cases in which pre-notification is not required   767
7. Consignment notes: procedure where pre-notification is not required   768
8. Consignment notes: carrier's rounds   769
9. Consignment notes: removal of ships' waste to reception facilities   770
10. Consignment notes etc.: duty of consignee not accepting delivery of a consignment   771
11. Consignment notes: duties of the Agencies   771
12. Consignment notes: provisions as to furnishing   772
13. Consignment notes: importers and exporters   772
14. Fees   773
15. Registers   774
16. Site records   774
17. Restrictions on mixing special waste   775
18. Offences   775
19. Responsibilities of the Agencies   776
20. Transitional provisions for certificates of technical competence   776
21. Amendment of regulations relating to the assessment of environmental effects   777
22. Amendment of the Controlled Waste (Registration of Carriers and Seizure of Vehicles) Regulations 1991   777
23. Amendment of the Environmental Protection (Duty of Care) Regulations 1991   777
24. Amendment of the Controlled Waste Regulations 1992   777
25. Amendment of the Waste Management Licensing Regulations 1994   777
26. Revocations and savings   777

# SCHEDULES

Schedule 1—Forms of consignment note and schedule    778
Schedule 2—Special waste    781
Schedule 3—Amendments to the Waste Management Licensing Regulations 1994    790

The Secretary of State for the Environment, as respects England, the Secretary of State for Wales, as respects Wales, and the Secretary of State for Scotland, as respects Scotland, being Ministers designated[1] for the purposes of section 2(2) of the European Communities Act 1972[2] in relation to measures relating to the regulation and control of the transit, import and export of waste (including recyclable materials), the prevention, reduction and elimination of pollution caused by waste and the requirement for an assessment of the impact on the environment of projects likely to have significant effects on the environment, in exercise of the powers conferred upon them by section 2(2) of that Act, sections 3(1), 17, 30(4) and (5) and 104(1) of the Control of Pollution Act 1974,[3] sections 33(3), 34(5), 62(1) to (3), 74(6), 75(8) and 78 of the Environmental Protection Act 1990[4] (having, in particular, had regard in exercising their powers under section 33(3) of that Act to the matters specified in section 33(4) of that Act) and of all other powers enabling them in that behalf, hereby make the following Regulations:

*Citation, commencement, extent, application and interpretation*

1. (1) These Regulations may be cited as the Special Waste Regulations 1996, and shall come into force on 1st September 1996.

(2) These Regulations do not extend to Northern Ireland.

(3) These Regulations do not apply in relation to any special waste in respect of which, in accordance with regulation 26 below, the Control of Pollution (Special Waste) Regulations 1980[5] continue to have effect.

(4) In these Regulations, unless the context otherwise requires—

"the 1990 Act" means the Environmental Protection Act 1990;

"the 1994 Regulations" means the Waste Management Licensing Regulations 1994;[6]

"Agency" means

(a) in relation to places, premises and sites in England and Wales, the Environment Agency established by section 1 of the Environment Act 1995;[7] and

(b) in relation to places, premises and sites in Scotland, the Scottish Environment Protection Agency established by section 20 of that Act;[8]

"the approved classification and labelling guide" means the document entitled "Approved guide to the classification and labelling of substances and preparations dangerous for supply (Second edition)"[9] approved by the Health and Safety Commission on 18th October 1994 for the purposes of the Chemicals (Hazard Information and Packaging for Supply) Regulations 1994;[10]

"the approved supply list" means the document entitled "Approved Supply List (3rd Edition)— Information approved for the classification and labelling of substances and preparations danger-

---

[1] S.I. 1993/2661, 1992/2870 and 1988/785.
[2] 1972 c.68.
[3] 1774 c.40; s.3(1) is repealed, and s.17 is prospectively repealed, by Part II of sch.16 to the Environmental Protection Act 1990 (c.43); the repeal of s.3(1) came into force on 1 May 1994 (save for certain purposes, in respect of which other dates are appointed) by virtue of S.I. 1994/1096, p.738 above.
[4] Part II of the 1990 Act is at p.84 above.
[5] S.I. 1980/1709, amended by S.I. 1988/1562, 1988/1790

and 1994/1137 and by Part IV of sch.6 to the Radioactive Substances Act 1993 (c.12).
[6] P.675 above.
[7] P.420 above.
[8] P.438 above.
[9] The approved classification and labelling guide is available from HSE Books, PO Box 1999, Sudbury, Suffolk, CO10 6FS.
[10] S.I. 1994/3247.

ous for supply" approved by the Health and Safety Commission on 24th January 1996 for the purposes of the Chemicals (Hazard Information and Packaging for Supply) Regulations 1994;[1]

"carrier", in relation to a consignment of special waste, means the person who collects that waste from the premises at which it is being held and transports it to another place;

"carrier's round" in relation to consignments of special waste, means a journey made by a carrier during which he collects more than one consignment of special waste and transports all consignments collected to the same consignee who is specified in the consignment note;

"carrier's schedule" means a schedule prepared in accordance with regulation 8;[2]

"consignee", in relation to a consignment of special waste, means the person to whom that waste is to be transported;

"consignment note", in relation to a consignment of special waste, means a note in a form corresponding to the form set out in Schedule 1 to these Regulations,[3] or in a form substantially to the like effect, and giving at any time the details required by these Regulations to be shown in respect of that consignment (including, where the consignment is one in a succession of consignments, any details required to be shown in respect of other consignments in the succession);

"consignor", in relation to a consignment of special waste, means the person who causes that waste to be removed from the premises at which it is being held;

"controlled waste" has the same meaning as in Part II of the 1990 Act;[4]

"conveyance" includes a vehicle designed to carry goods by road or rail and a vessel designed to carry goods by water;

"harbour area" has the same meaning as in the Dangerous Substances in Harbour Areas Regulations 1987;[5]

"the Hazardous Waste Directive" means Council Directive 91/689/EEC on hazardous waste, as amended by Council Directive 94/31/EC;[6]

"household waste" means waste which is household waste for the purposes of Part II of the 1990 Act[7] or which is treated as household waste for those purposes by virtue of regulation 2(1) of the Controlled Waste Regulations 1992[8], other than—

(a) asbestos;

(b) waste from a laboratory;

(c) waste from a hospital, other than waste from a self-contained part of a hospital which is used wholly for the purposes of living accommodation;[9]

"premises" includes any ship;

"relevant code", in relation to a consignment note or carrier's schedule, means the code assigned in accordance with regulation 4[10] to the consignment of special waste to which the consignment note or carrier's schedule relates or, where the consignment is one in a carrier's round, to the consignments in that round;

"risk phrase" means the risk phrase shown under Part III of the approved supply list;

"ship" means a vessel of any type whatsoever operating in the marine environment including submersible craft, floating craft and any structure which is a fixed or floating platform;

"special waste" has the meaning given by regulation 2 of these Regulations; and

[1] The approved supply list is available from HSE Books, PO Box 1999, Sudbury, Suffolk, CO10 6FS. Words "3rd edition" and "24th January 1996" substituted by S.I. 1996/2019, sch., para.2(a).

[2] P.769 below.

[3] P.778 below.

[4] See s.75 of the 1990 Act, p.159 above, and the Controlled Waste Regulations 1992, p.662 above.

[5] S.I. 1987/37.

[6] Council Directive 91/689/EEC is to be found at OJ No. L 377, 31.12.1991, p.20; Council Directive 94/31/EC at OJ No. L 168, 2.7.1994, p.28. See also Council Decision 94/904/EC (OJ No. L 356, 31.12.94, p.14).

[7] See s.75(5) of 1990 Act, p.159 above.

[8] P.663 above.

[9] This definition substituted by S.I. 1996/2019, sch., para.2(b).

[10] P.766 below.

"waste management licence" has the meaning given by section 35(1) of the 1990 Act.[1]

*Meaning of special waste*

2. (1) Any controlled waste[2], other than household waste[3],

(a) to which a six-digit code is assigned in the list set out in Part I of Schedule 2 to these Regulations[4] (which reproduces the list of hazardous waste annexed to Council Decision 94/904/EC[5] establishing a list of hazardous waste pursuant to Article 1(4) of the Hazardous Waste Directive[6]); and

(b) which displays any of the properties specified in Part II of that Schedule[7] (which reproduces Annex III to the Hazardous Waste Directive),

is special waste.

(2) Any other controlled waste, other than household waste which—

(a) displays the property H3A (first indent), H4, H5, H6, H7 or H8 specified in Part II of Schedule 2 to these Regulations, or

(b) is a medicinal product, as defined in section 130 of the Medicines Act 1968[8] (meaning of "medicinal product" etc.), of a description, or falling within a class, specified in an order under section 58 of that Act[9] (medicinal products on prescription only),

is special waste.

(3) For the purposes of paragraphs (1) and (2), waste shall be treated as displaying none of the properties H4 to H8 specified in Part II of Schedule 2 to these Regulations if it satisfies none of the criteria set out in Part III of that Schedule.[10]

(4) Part IV of Schedule 2 to these Regulations[11] (which contains rules for the interpretation of that Schedule) shall have effect.[12]

*Certain radioactive waste to be special waste*

3. Section 62 (special provision with respect to certain dangerous and intractable waste) of the 1990 Act[13] shall have effect, without modification, so as to empower the Secretary of State to make provision for waste which would be controlled waste[14] but for the fact that it is radioactive waste within the meaning of the Radioactive Substances Act 1993;[15] and paragraphs (1) and (2) of regulation 2 shall apply to any such waste as if it were controlled waste.

*Coding of consignments*

4. (1) Subject to paragraph (3),[16] an Agency[17] shall assign or supply forthwith to any person, on request, for the purpose of assigning to a consignment of special waste[18] or, where the consignment is one in a carrier's round,[19] to the consignments in that round, a code unique to that consignment or round, as the case may be.

(2) A code assigned or supplied in accordance with paragraph (1) may consist of letters, numbers or symbols, or any combination of letters, numbers and symbols, or a bar code which enables the consignment or carrier's round, as the case may be, to be identified electronically.

---

[1] P.119 above.
[2] "Controlled waste" defined by reg.1(4) above.
[3] "Household waste" defined by reg.1(4) above.
[4] P.781 below.
[5] OJ No. L 356, 31.12.1994, p.14.
[6] "The Hazardous Waste Directive" defined by reg.1(4) above.
[7] P.789 below.
[8] 1968 c.67; s.130 is amended by para.3(7) to (10) of sch.1, and sch.2, to the Animal Health and Welfare Act 1984 (c.40).
[9] S.58 is amended by s.1 of the Medicinal Products: Prescription by Nurses etc. Act 1992 (c.28).
[10] P.790 below.
[11] P.790 below.

[12] This regulation substituted by S.I. 1996/2019, sch., para.3.
[13] P.151 above.
[14] "Controlled waste" defined by reg.1(4), p.765 above.
[15] "Radioactive waste" defined by s.2 of the 1993 Act, p.384 above; s.78 of the 1990 Act, p.162 above, provides that Part II of the 1990 Act does not apply to radioactive waste as defined in the 1993 Act save to the extent that the Secretary of State so provides in regulations.
[16] Words "Subject to paragraph (3)," inserted by S.I. 1996/2019, sch., para.4(a).
[17] "Agency" defined by reg.1(4), p.764 above.
[18] "Special waste" has the meaning given by reg.2 above: reg.1(4) above.
[19] "Carrier's round" defined by reg.1(4), p.765 above.

(3) The Agency need not assign or supply a code for a consignment or round until any fee required in respect of it under regulation 14(1)[1] has been paid.[2]

*Consignment notes: standard procedure*

5. (1) Except in a case to which regulation 6, 8 or 9 applies, this regulation applies where a consignment of special waste[3] is to be removed from the premises[4] at which it is being held.

(2) Before the consignment is removed—

(a) five copies of the consignment note[5] shall be prepared, and, on each copy, Parts A and B shall be completed and the relevant code[6] entered;

(b) the consignor[7] shall ensure that one of those copies (on which Parts A and B have been completed and the relevant code entered) is furnished to the Agency[8] for the place to which the consignment is to be transported;

(c) the carrier[9] shall complete Part C on each of the four remaining copies; and

(d) the consignor—

(i) shall complete Part D on each of those copies;

(ii) shall retain one copy (on which Parts A to D have been completed and the relevant code entered); and

(iii) shall give the three remaining copies (on which Parts A to D have been completed and the relevant code entered) to the carrier.

(3) The carrier shall ensure that the copies which he has received—

(a) travel with the consignment; and

(b) are given to the consignee[10] on delivery of the consignment.

(4) Subject to regulation 10,[11] on receiving the consignment the consignee shall—

(a) complete Part E on the three copies of the consignment note given to him;

(b) retain one copy;

(c) give one copy to the carrier; and

(d) forthwith furnish one copy to the Agency for the place to which the consignment has been transported.

(5) The carrier shall retain the copy of the consignment note given to him by the consignee.

*Consignment notes: cases in which pre-notification is not required*

6. (1) For the purposes of regulation 7, except in a case to which regulation 8 applies, this regulation applies—

(a) subject to paragraph (2)(a), to the removal, from the premises[12] at which it is being held, of each of the second and any subsequent consignment of special waste[13] in a succession of consignments of special waste,

(b) subject to paragraph (2)(b), to the removal as a consignment of special waste of a product or material for the purposes of the return by the person to whom the product or material had been supplied to the person who supplied it to him or who manufactured it,

[1] P.773 below.
[2] Para.3 inserted by S.I. 1996/2019, sch., para.4(b).
[3] "Special waste" has the meaning given by reg.2, p.766 above: reg.1(4) above.
[4] "Premises" defined by reg.1(4), p.765 above.
[5] "Consignment note" defined by reg.1(4), p.765 above.
[6] "Relevant code" defined by reg.1(4), p.765 above.
[7] "Consignor" defined by reg.1(4), p.765 above.
[8] "Agency" defined by reg.1(4), p.764 above.
[9] "Carrier" defined by reg.1(4), p.765 above.
[10] "Consignee" defined by reg.1(4), p.765 above.
[11] P.771 below.
[12] "Premises" defined by reg.1(4), p.765 above.
[13] "Special waste" has the meaning given by reg.2, p.766 above: reg.1(4) above.

(c) subject to paragraph (2)(c), to the removal of a consignment of special waste where the consignor[1] and the consignee[2] are bodies corporate belonging to the same group,[3]

(d) to the removal from a ship[4] in a harbour area[5] of a consignment of special waste to a conveyance[6] for transportation to a place outside that area, and

(e) to the removal of a consignment of special waste which consists entirely of lead acid motor vehicle batteries.

(2) This regulation does not apply unless—

(a) in the case mentioned in paragraph (1)(a), in respect of each consignment—

   (i) the waste is of the same description as the waste in the first of the consignments in the succession;

   (ii) the consignor is the same person;

   (iii) the consignee is the same person;

   (iv) the premises from which the consignment is removed are the same;

   (v) the place to which the consignment is transported is the same; and

   (vi) the removal of the consignment takes place within one year of the removal of the first consignment in the succession;

(b) in the case mentioned in paragraph (1)(b), the person to whom the product or material was supplied is satisfied that, as supplied, the product or material fails to meet any specification which he expected it to meet;

(c) in the case mentioned in paragraph (1)(c), the removal is for the purposes of an operation within either paragraph 15 of Part III,[7] or paragraph 13 of Part IV,[8] of Schedule 4 to the 1994 Regulations, and the consignee either—

   (i) is the holder of a waste management licence[9] which authorises the relevant operation; or

   (ii) carries on any activity to which section 33(1)(a) and (b) of the 1990 Act[10] does not apply by virtue of regulation 16 or 17 of the 1994 Regulations.[11]

(3) In paragraph (1)(c) "group", in relation to a body corporate, means that body corporate, any other body corporate which is its holding company or subsidiary and any other body corporate which is a subsidiary of that holding company; and for these purposes—

"body corporate" does not include a corporation sole or a Scottish partnership, but includes a company incorporated elsewhere than in Great Britain; and

"holding company" and "subsidiary" have the meaning given by section 736 of the Companies Act 1985.[12]

*Consignment notes: procedure where pre-notification is not required*

7. Paragraph (2), with the exception of sub-paragraph (b), and paragraphs (3) to (5) of regulation 5 shall apply in cases to which regulation 6 applies as if—

(a) "four" were substituted for "five" in sub-paragraph (a) of paragraph (2);

(b) references to the consignor were references—

   (i) in relation to the case mentioned in regulation 6(1)(b), to the person to whom the product or material was supplied; and

   (ii) in relation to the case mentioned in regulation 6(1)(d), to the master of the ship; and

---

[1] "Consignor" defined by reg.1(4), p.765 above.
[2] "Consignee" defined by reg.1(4), p.765 above.
[3] "Group" defined by para.(3) below.
[4] "Ship" defined by reg.1(4), p.765 above.
[5] "Harbour area" defined by reg.1(4), p.765 above.
[6] "Conveyance" defined by reg.1(4), p.765 above.
[7] P.722 above.

[8] P.722 above.
[9] "Waste management licence" has the meaning given by s.35(1) of the 1990 Act, p.119 above.
[10] P.116 above.
[11] P.688 above.
[12] 1985 c.6; s.736 is substituted by s.144(1) of the Companies Act 1989 (c.40).

(c) references to the consignee were references, in relation to the case mentioned in regulation 6(1)(b), to the person to whom the product or material is to be returned.

*Consignment notes: carrier's rounds*

**8.** (1) This regulation applies to a carrier's round[1] or to a succession of such rounds by the same carrier[2] starting and ending within a twelve month period in respect of which:

(a) every consignor[3] is a person specified in the consignment note[4] or in the schedule prepared in accordance with paragraph (2)(b)(iii) or whose particulars are notified in writing to the Agency[5] not less than 72 hours before the removal of the first waste on the carrier's round;

(b) the premises[6] from which the special waste[7] is removed are:

   (i) specified in the consignment note or in the schedule prepared in accordance with paragraph (2)(b)(iii) or notified in writing to the Agency not less than 72 hours before the removal of the first waste on the carrier's round; and

   (ii) so located that the Agency for each of those premises is the same;

(c) the special waste is of a description specified in the consignment note; and

(d) in the case of a single round other than a round that satisfies the requirements of regulation 14(2)(a),[8] the time between the collection of the first consignment and delivery to the consignee[9] is no more than 24 hours.

(2) Before the first removal of waste, the carrier shall,

(a) on any carrier's round which is not in a succession or on the first round in such a succession, ensure that

   (i) Parts A and B of the consignment note are completed and that the relevant code[10] is entered;

   (ii) except where the special waste to be collected on the carrier's round consists entirely of lead acid motor vehicle batteries,[11] one copy of the consignment note is furnished to the Agency for the place to which the special waste is to be transported;

(b) on every round—

   (i) prepare three[12] copies of the consignment note in addition to one copy for each consignor from whom waste is to be collected during the round;

   (ii) complete on those copies Parts A and B, the carrier's particulars and particulars of transport in Part C, the code assigned or supplied under regulation 4[13] in respect of the round and, if it is a second or subsequent round, the code in respect of the first round; and

   (iii) ensure that four copies of a schedule are prepared in the form set out in Part II of Schedule 1 to these Regulations,[14] or in a form substantially to the like effect, in addition to one consignor's copy for each site from which waste is to be collected during that round.

(2A) In a case where waste of more than one description is specified in the consignment note, either—

(a) the schedule referred to in paragraph (2)(b)(iii) shall contain a separate entry for each description of waste to be collected from each consignor showing the description of waste to which that entry relates; or

(b) each entry in the schedule shall show the different descriptions of the waste to be collected and, for each such description, the quantity of the waste to be collected.[15]

[1] "Carrier's round" defined by reg.1(4), p.765 above.
[2] "Carrier" defined by reg.1(4), p.765 above.
[3] "Consignor" defined by reg.1(4), p.765 above.
[4] "Consignee note" defined by reg.1(4), p.765 above.
[5] "Agency" defined by reg.1(4), p.764 above.
[6] "Premises" defined by reg.1(4), p.765 above.
[7] "Special waste" has the meaning given by reg.2, p.766 above: reg.1(4) above.
[8] P.773 below.
[9] "Consignee" defined by reg.1(4), p.765 above.
[10] "Relevant code" defined by reg.1(4), p.765 above.
[11] Words "except . . . batteries," inserted by S.I. 1996/2019, sch., para.5(a).
[12] Word "three" substituted by S.I. 1996/2019, sch., para.5(b).
[13] P.766 above.
[14] P.779 below.
[15] Para.(2A) inserted by S.I. 1996/2019, sch., para.5(c).

(3) The consignor shall, before the removal of waste from a site, complete on all the copies that part of the schedule indicated on it as for completion by him.

(4) The carrier shall ensure, before the removal of the waste, that—

(a) the part of the schedule indicated on it as for completion by him is completed on all the copies and includes a record of the time at which it is completed[1]; and

(b) he has all copies of the schedule (on which the part to be completed by the consignor has been completed) except the copy to be retained by the consignor under paragraph (5).

(5) The consignor shall retain in respect of each site one copy of the consignment note and of that part of the schedule on which the parts to be completed by him and by the carrier have been completed.

(5A)  Before the removal of the last consignment of waste on the carrier's round, the carrier shall complete Part C on the three copies of the consignment note retained by him.[2]

(6) The carrier shall ensure that the copies of the consignment note and of the schedule which he has received—

(a) *omitted by S.I. 1996/2019, sch., para.5(f)*;

(b) travel with the waste to which they refer;

(c) are given to the consignee on delivery of the waste.

(7) Subject to regulation 10, on receiving the waste collected on each round, the consignee shall—

(a) complete Part E on the three copies of the consignment note given to him;

(b) retain one copy of the consignment note and one copy of the schedule;

(c) give to the carrier a copy of the consignment note and a copy of the schedule; and

(d) forthwith furnish to the Agency for the place to which the consignment has been transported one copy of the consignment note and one copy of the schedule.

(8) The carrier shall retain the copies given to him in accordance with paragraph (7)(c).

*Consignment notes: removal of ships' waste to reception facilities*

**9.** (1) This regulation applies where special waste[3] is removed from a ship[4] in a harbour area[5] to—

(a) reception facilities provided within that harbour area; or

(b) by pipeline to any such facilities provided outside a harbour area.

(2) Before the waste is removed from the ship—

(a) three copies of the consignment note[6] shall be prepared and Parts A and B shall be completed and the relevant code[7] entered on each of those copies;

(b) the operator of the facilities shall complete Part C on each of those copies; and

(c) the master of the ship—

(i) shall ensure that Part D is completed on each of those copies;

(ii) shall retain one copy (on which Parts A to D have been completed); and

(iii) shall give the two remaining copies (on which Parts A to D have been completed) to the operator of the facilities.

(3) On receiving a consignment of special waste the operator of the facilities shall—

(a) complete Part E on the copies of the consignment note which he has received;

(b) retain one copy; and

(c) forthwith furnish the other copy to the Agency[8] for the place where the facilities are situated.

[1] Words "and includes . . . completed" inserted by S.I. 1996/2019, sch., para.5(d).
[2] Para.(5A) inserted by S.I. 1996/2019, sch., para.5(e).
[3] "Special waste" has the meaning given by reg.2, p.766 above: reg.1(4) above.
[4] "Ship" defined by reg.1(4), p.765 above.
[5] "Harbour area" defined by reg.1(4), p.765 above.
[6] "Consignment note" defined by reg.1(4), p.765 above.
[7] "Relevant code" defined by reg.1(4), p.765 above.
[8] "Agency" defined by reg.1(4), p.764 above.

*Consignment notes etc.: duty of consignee not accepting delivery of a consignment*

**10.** (1) This regulation applies where the consignee[1] does not accept delivery of a consignment of special waste.[2]

(2) In a case to which this regulation applies the requirements of regulation 5(4)[3] (including that paragraph as applied in cases to which regulation 6 applies) or 8(7),[4] as the case may be, shall not apply to the consignee.

(3) If, in a case to which this regulation applies, copies of the consignment note[5] have been given to the consignee he shall—

(a) indicate on Part E of each copy that he does not accept the consignment and the reasons why he does not accept the consignment;

(b) retain one copy;

(c) ensure that one copy, accompanied by one copy of any carrier's schedule[6] given to him in accordance with regulation 8, are furnished forthwith to the Agency[7] for the place to which the special waste has been transported; and

(d) ensure that the other copy is returned to the carrier[8] forthwith.

(4) If, in a case to which this regulation applies, no copies of the consignment note have been given to the consignee he shall ensure that a written explanation of his reasons for not accepting delivery, including such details of the consignment and of the carrier as are known to him, is furnished forthwith to the Agency for the place to which the special waste has been transported.

(5) In a case to which this regulation applies—

(a) on being informed that the consignee will not accept delivery of the consignment, the carrier shall inform the Agency and seek instructions from the consignor;[9]

(b) the consignor shall forthwith inform the carrier and the Agency of his intentions as regards the consignment; and

(c) the carrier shall take all reasonable steps to ensure that the consignor's intentions are fulfilled.

(6) For the purposes of paragraph (5), the consignor may propose one of the following, namely—

(a) the delivery of the consignment to the premises[10] from which it had been collected;

(b) the delivery of the consignment to the premises at which it had been produced;

(c) the delivery of the consignment to other specified premises in respect of which there is held any waste management licence[11] necessary to authorise the receipt of the waste.

*Consignment notes: duties of the Agencies*

**11.** (1) Subject to paragraph (2), where—

(a) an Agency[12] ("the receiving Agency") has been furnished with a copy of a consignment note[13] under regulation 5,[14] 7, 8, 9 or 10 or with a copy of the explanation under regulation 10(4); and

(b) the other Agency is the Agency for the premises[15] from which the special waste[16] was removed,

the receiving Agency shall, within two weeks of receipt, send to the other Agency one copy of the consignment note or explanation as the case may be.

---

[1] "Consignee" defined by reg.1(4), p.765 above.
[2] "Special waste" has the meaning given by reg.2, p.766 above: reg.1(4) above.
[3] P.767 above.
[4] P.770 above.
[5] "Consignment note" defined by reg.1(4), p.765 above.
[6] "Carrier's schedule" defined by reg.1(4), p.765 above.
[7] "Agency" defined by reg.1(4), p.764 above.
[8] "Carrier" defined by reg.1(4), p.765 above.
[9] "Consignor" defined by reg.1(4), p.765 above.

[10] "Premises" defined by reg.1(4), p.765 above.
[11] "Waste management licence" has the meaning given by s.35(1) of the 1990 Act, p.119 above: reg.1(4) above.
[12] "Agency" defined by reg.1(4), p.764 above.
[13] "Consignment note" defined by reg.1(4), p.765 above.
[14] P.767 above.
[15] "Premises" defined by reg.1(4), p.765 above.
[16] "Special waste" has the meaning given by reg.2, p.766 above: reg.1(4) above.

(2) Where copies have been furnished—

(a) under regulation 7[1] in a case to which regulation 6 applies by virtue of paragraph (1)(d) of that regulation, or

(b) under regulation 9(3)(c),

paragraph (1) shall have effect as if the reference to the premises from which the special waste was removed were a reference to the harbour area[2] in which the special waste was removed from the ship.[3]

*Consignment notes: provisions as to furnishing*

12. (1) Subject to paragraphs (2), (3) and (6), a copy of a consignment note[4] required by regulation 5[5] or 8[6] to be furnished to an Agency[7] must be furnished not more than one month and not less than 72 hours before the removal of the consignment.

(2) Subject to paragraphs (3) and (6), a copy of a consignment note required to be furnished by regulation 8(2)(a)(ii) shall be furnished not less than 72 hours before the removal of the first consignment to which the consignment note relates.

(3) The copy of the consignment note mentioned in paragraphs (1) and (2) may be furnished to the Agency within 72 hours before the removal where—

(a) the consignment is to be delivered to other specified premises pursuant to a proposal under regulation 10(6)(c);

(b) the consignment cannot lawfully remain where it is for 72 hours.

(4) The requirements of paragraphs (1) and (2) shall be treated as satisfied if—

(a) a facsimile of the copy is furnished to the Agency by telephonic, electronic or other similar means of transmission in compliance with the time limits set out in those paragraphs, and

(b) the copy is furnished to the Agency before or, in accordance with paragraph (5) below, forthwith upon removal of the consignment.

(5) A copy of a consignment note or a written explanation of reasons for refusing to accept delivery of any special waste[8] is furnished to an Agency in accordance with this paragraph if it, and any document required to be furnished with it, is—

(a) delivered to the Agency, or

(b) posted to the Agency by pre-paid first class post,

within one day of the receipt, removal or refusal to accept delivery of the special waste in question, as the case may be.

(6) In reckoning any period of hours for the purposes of paragraphs (1), (2) and (3), the hours of any Saturday, Sunday, Good Friday, Christmas Day, bank holiday or other public holiday shall be disregarded.

*Consignment notes: importers and exporters*

13. (1) Subject to paragraphs (3) and (4), regulations 5[9] to 12 shall apply to special waste[10] imported into Great Britain from Northern Ireland or Gibraltar as if—

(a) any reference to the consignor were a reference to the person importing the special waste;

(b) any reference to the premises at which the special waste is being held and from which it is removed were a reference to the place where it first enters Great Britain; and

(c) the special waste is removed from that place at the time when it first enters Great Britain.

---

[1] P.768 above.
[2] "Harbour area" defined by reg.1(4), p.765 above.
[3] "Ship" defined by reg.1(4), p.765 above.
[4] "Consignment note" defined by reg.1(4), p.765 above.
[5] P.767 above.
[6] P.769 above.
[7] "Agency" defined by reg.1(4), p.764 above.
[8] "Special waste" has the meaning given by reg.2, p.766 above: reg.1(4) above.
[9] P.767 above.
[10] "Special waste" has the meaning given by reg.2, p.766 above: reg.1(4) above.

(2) Subject to paragraph (4), these Regulations shall apply to special waste exported from Great Britain to Northern Ireland or Gibraltar as if—

(a) any reference to the consignee were a reference to the person exporting the waste; and

(b) the consignment of special waste is received by that person at the place where and the time when it leaves Great Britain.

(3) Paragraph (1) does not apply in a case to which either regulation 6(1)(d)[1] or regulation 9[2] applies.

(4) Nothing in regulations 5 to 12 shall apply in relation to shipments of waste to which the provisions of Council Regulation (EEC) No. 259/93,[3] other than Title III of that Regulation, apply.

*Fees*

**14.** (1) Subject to paragraph (2), in connection with the assignment or supply of[4] a code for a consignment or a carrier's round[5] in accordance with regulation 4(1),[6] an Agency[7] shall require payment of a fee of—

(a) £10 in respect of a code relating to a consignment, or a round, which consists entirely of lead acid motor vehicle batteries;

(b) £15 in other cases.

(2) An Agency shall not require payment of a fee where the code is assigned or supplied in connection with:

(a) a second or subsequent carrier's round in a succession of such rounds in which a single vehicle is used and in respect of which[8]—

   (i) the carrier is also the consignee[9] in relation to every consignment in all the rounds;

   (ii) no more than one consignment is collected from any consignor[10] during the succession;

   (iii) the total weight of special waste[11] collected in each round does not exceed 400 kg; and

   (iv) the time between the collection of the first consignment on the first round in the succession and the delivery of the last consignment to the place to which it is to be transported is no more than one week.

(b) the removal of a single consignment of special waste for the purposes set out in regulation 6(1)(b)[12] provided that the person to whom the product or material was supplied is satisfied that it fails to meet any specification which he expected it to meet; or

(c) the removal of special waste from a ship[13] in a harbour area[14]—

   (i) to a conveyance[15] for transportation to a place outside that area;

   (ii) to reception facilities provided within the same harbour area; or

   (iii) by pipeline to reception facilities provided outside the harbour area.

(3) Where an Agency assigns or suppies a code under regulation 4(1) without the fee required under this regulation having been paid to it, the person who requested the assignment or supply shall be required to pay the fee to that Agency within the period of two months beginning with the date on which the request was made.[16]

---

[1] P.768 above.
[2] P.770 above.
[3] OJ No. L 30, 6.2.1993, p.1.
[4] Words "in connection with the assignment of supply of" substituted by S.I. 1996/2019, sch., para.6(a).
[5] "Carrier" and "Carrier's round" defined by reg.1(4), p.765 above.
[6] P.766 above.
[7] "Agency" defined by reg.1(4), p.764 above.
[8] Words "such rounds . . . which" substituted by S.I. 1996/2019, sch., para.6(b).

[9] "Consignee" defined by reg.1(4), p.765 above.
[10] "Consignor" defined by reg.1(4), p.765 above.
[11] "Special waste" has the meaning given by reg.2, p.766 above: reg.1(4) above.
[12] P.767 above.
[13] "Ship" defined by reg.1(4), p.765 above.
[14] "Harbour area" defined by reg.1(4), p.765 above.
[15] "Conveyance" defined by reg.1(4), p.765 above.
[16] "Special waste" has the meaning given by reg.2, p.766 above: reg.1(4) above.

*Registers*

**15.** (1) At each site from which any consignment of special waste[1] has been removed, the consignor[2] shall keep a register containing—

(a) a copy of the consignment note;[3] and

(b) where the consignment is one to which regulation 8[4] applies, a copy of that part of the carrier's schedule[5] retained under regulation 8(5),

applicable to each consignment removed from that site.

(2) Every carrier[6] shall keep a register containing—

(a) a copy of the consignment note; and

(b) where the consignment is one to which regulation 8 applies, a copy of the carrier's schedule,

applicable to each consignment which he has transported.

(3) At each site at which any consignment of special waste has been received, the consignee[7] shall keep a register containing—

(a) a copy of the consignment note; and

(b) where the consignment is one to which regulation 8 applies, a copy of the carrier's schedule,

applicable to each consignment, other than a consignment to which regulation 10[8] applies, received at that site.

(4) A consignment note or carrier's schedule required by paragraph (1) or (2) to be kept in a register shall be retained in the register for not less than three years from the date on which the waste to which it relates was removed from the premises[9] at which it was being held.

(5) Subject to paragraphs (6) and (7), consignment notes and carrier's schedules required by paragraph (3) to be kept by a person shall be retained until his waste management licence[10] for the site in question is surrendered or revoked entirely, at which time he shall send the register to the Agency[11] for the site; and that Agency shall retain the register for not less than three years after its receipt.

(6) Where, by virtue of regulation 16(1)(a) or (b) of the 1994 Regulations,[12] section 33(1)(a), (b) and (c) of the 1990 Act[13] does not apply to any of the activities carried on at a site at which special waste is received, paragraph (5) shall have effect as if any reference to the surrender or revocation of a person's waste management licence were a reference to the surrender or revocation of his authorisation under Part I of the 1990 Act[14] for the site in question.

(7) Where, in circumstances other than those mentioned in paragraph (6), section 33(1)(a) and (b) of the 1990 Act does not apply to any of the activities carried on at a site at which special waste is received, each consignment note and carrier's schedule required to be kept in a register shall be kept in that register for not less than three years from the date on which the consignment of special waste to which it relates was received at the site to which it was transported.

(8) Insofar as is consistent with the foregoing provisions of this regulation, registers under this regulation may be kept in any form.

*Site records*

**16.** (1) Any person who makes a deposit of special waste[15] in or on any land shall record the location of each such deposit, shall keep such records until his waste management licence[16] is surrendered or revoked and shall then send the records to the Agency[17] for the site.

---

[1] "Special waste" has the meaning given by reg.2, p.766 above: reg.1(4) above.

[2] "Consignor" defined by reg.1(4), p.765 above.

[3] "Consignment note" defined by reg.1(4), p.765 above.

[4] P.769 above.

[5] "Carrier's schedule" defined by reg.1(4), p.765 above.

[6] "Carrier" defined by reg.1(4), p.765 above.

[7] "Consignee" defined by reg.1(4), p.765 above.

[8] P.771 above.

[9] "Premises" defined by reg.1(4), p.765 above.

[10] "Waste management licence" has the meaning given

by s.35(1) of the 1990 Act, p.119 above: reg.1(4) above.

[11] "Agency" defined by reg.1(4), p.764 above.

[12] P.688 above.

[13] P.116 above.

[14] P.88 above.

[15] "Special waste" has the meaning given by reg.2, p.766 above: reg.1(4) above.

[16] "Waste management licence" has the meaning given by s.35(1) of the 1990 Act, p.119 above.

[17] "Agency" defined by reg.1(4), p.764 above.

(2)  Such records shall comprise either—

(a)  a site plan marked with a grid, or

(b)  a site plan with overlays on which deposits are shown in relation to the contours of the site.

(3)  Deposits shall be described in such records by reference to the register of consignment notes kept under regulation 15, save that where waste is disposed of—

(a)  by pipeline, or

(b)  within the curtilage of the premises at which it is produced,

the deposits shall be described by reference to a record of the quantity and composition of the waste and the date of its disposal.

(4)  In the case of liquid wastes discharged without containers into underground strata or disused workings the record shall comprise only a written statement of the quantity and composition of special waste so discharged and the date of its disposal.

(5)  Every record made pursuant to regulation 14 of the Control of Pollution (Special Waste) Regulations 1980[1] shall—

(a)  be kept with the records referred to in paragraph (1) above for so long as is mentioned in that paragraph, and

(b)  shall accompany those records when they are sent to the Agency in accordance with that paragraph.

*Restrictions on mixing special waste*

17.  (1)  Subject to paragraph (2), an establishment or undertaking which carries out the disposal or recovery of special waste,[2] or which collects or transports special waste, shall not—

(a)  mix different categories of special waste; or

(b)  mix special waste with waste which is not special waste.

(2)  Paragraph (1) above shall not apply if the mixing—

(a)  is authorised by a waste management licence[3] or under an authorisation granted under Part I of the 1990 Act;[4] or

(b)  is an activity to which, by virtue of regulation 17 of the 1994 Regulations,[5] section 33(1)(a) and (b) of the 1990 Act[6] does not apply.

*Offences*

18.  (1)  Subject to paragraph (2) below, it shall be an offence for a person (other than a member, officer or employee of an Agency[7] who is acting as authorised by that Agency), to fail to comply with any of the foregoing provisions of these Regulations insofar as that provision imposes any obligation or requirement upon him.

(2)  It shall be a defence for a person charged with an offence under paragraph (1) to prove that he was not reasonably able to comply with the provision in question by reason of an emergency or grave danger and that he took all steps as were reasonably practicable in the circumstances for—

(a)  minimising any threat to the public or the environment; and

(b)  ensuring that the provision in question was complied with as soon as reasonably practicable after the event.

[1]  S.I. 1980/1709, as amended by S.I. 1988/1562, 1988/1790, 1994/1137 and by Part IV of sch.6 to the Radioactive Substances Act 1993 (c.12).
[2]  "Special waste" has the meaning given by reg.2, p.766 above: reg.1(4) above.
[3]  "Waste management licence" has the meaning given by s.35(1) of the 1990 Act, p.119 above.
[4]  P.88 above.
[5]  P.689 above.
[6]  P.116 above.
[7]  "Agency" defined by reg.1(4), p.764 above.

(3)  A person who, in purported compliance with a requirement imposed by or under any of the foregoing provisions of these Regulations to furnish any information, makes a statement which he knows to be false or misleading in a material particular, or recklessly makes any statement which is false or misleading in a material particular, commits an offence.

(4)  A person who intentionally makes a false entry in any record or register required to be kept by virtue of any of the foregoing provisions of these Regulations commits an offence.

(5)  Where the commission by any person of an offence under this regulation is due to the act or default of some other person, that other person may be charged with and convicted of an offence by virtue of this paragraph whether or not proceedings are taken against the first-mentioned person.

(6)  Where an offence under this regulation which has been committed by a body corporate is proved to have been committed with the consent or connivance of, or to have been attributable to, any neglect on the part of a director, manager, secretary or other similar officer of the body corporate, or any person who was purporting to act in any such capacity, he, as well as the body corporate, shall be liable to be proceeded against and punished accordingly.

(7)  Where the affairs of a body corporate are managed by its members, paragraph (6) shall apply in relation to the acts or defaults of a member in connection with his functions of management as if he were a director of the body corporate.

(8)  Where, in Scotland, an offence under this regulation which has been committed by a partnership or an unincorporated association (other than a partnership) is proved to have been committed with the consent or connivance of, or to have been attributable to any neglect on the part of, a partner in the partnership or, as the case may be, a person concerned in the management or control of the association, he, as well as the partnership or association, shall be liable to be proceeded against and punished accordingly.

(9)  A person who commits an offence under this regulation shall be liable—

(a)  on summary conviction, to a fine not exceeding level 5 on the standard scale;[1]

(b)  on conviction on indictment, to a fine or to imprisonment for a term not exceeding two years, or to both.

*Responsibilities of the Agencies*

**19.**  The Agencies[2] shall be responsible for supervising the persons and activities subject to any provision of these Regulations.

*Transitional provisions for certificates of technical competence*

**20.**  (1)  This regulation applies in relation to—

(a)  waste defined as special waste under regulation 2 of these Regulations[3] which was not so defined under regulation 2 of the Control of Pollution (Special Waste) Regulations 1980[4] ("waste now defined as special waste"); and

(b)  persons to be treated as technically competent for the purposes of section 74(3)(b) of the 1990 Act[5]—

(i)  pursuant to regulation 4 of the 1994 Regulations;[6] or

(ii)  pursuant to regulation 5 of the 1994 Regulations,[7] or to regulation 4(1) or (3) of the Waste Management Licensing (Amendment etc.) Regulations 1995.[8]

(2)  For the purposes only of operations concerning waste now defined as special waste and provided that both the conditions set out in paragraph (3) are satisfied, the persons referred to in paragraph (1)(b) shall continue to be treated as technically competent—

[1] The current fine at level 5 on the standard scale is £5,000: Criminal Justice Act 1991 (c.53), s.17 (England and Wales); Criminal Procedure (Scotland) Act 1995 (c.46), s.225 (Scotland).
[2] "Agency" defined by reg.1(4), p.764 above.
[3] P.766 above.
[4] S.I. 1980/1709, amended by S.I. 1988/1790.
[5] P.158 above.
[6] P.679 above.
[7] P.680 above.
[8] P.751 above.

(a) in the case of those referred to in paragraph (1)(b)(i), until 10th August 2000; and

(b) in the case of those referred to in paragraph (1)(b)(ii), in accordance with the Regulations mentioned there, except that paragraph (1) of regulation 5 of the 1994 Regulations and paragraphs (1) and (4) of regulation 4 of the Waste Management Licensing (Amendment etc.) Regulations 1995 shall have effect as if for the date "10th August 1999" there were substituted the date "10th August 2000".

(3) The conditions referred to in paragraph (2) are that:

(a) before 1st March 1997, the person applies to the Waste Management Industry Training and Advisory Board for a certificate of technical competence at Level 4 in respect of special waste; and

(b) before 1st September 1996, the person was entitled to act as the manager of a facility in respect of which there was in force a waste management licence[1] authorising activities concerning waste now defined as special waste.

*Amendment of regulations relating to the assessment of environmental effects*

**21.** (1) In regulation 2(1) of the Town and Country Planning (Assessment of Environmental Effects) Regulations 1988,[2] for the definition of "special waste" there shall be substituted—

" 'special waste' means waste which is special waste for the purposes of the Special Waste Regulations 1996;".

(2) In regulation 4(1) of the Environmental Assessment (Scotland) Regulations 1988,[3] for the definition of "special waste" there shall be substituted—

" 'special waste' means waste which is special waste for the purposes of the Special Waste Regulations 1996;".

*Amendment of the Controlled Waste (Registration of Carriers and Seizure of Vehicles) Regulations 1991*

**22.** *The amendments made by this regulation are included in the Controlled Waste (Registration of Carriers and Seizure of Vehicles) Regulations 1991, p.630 above.*

*Amendment of the Environmental Protection (Duty of Care) Regulations 1991*

**23.** *The amendments made by this regulation are included in the Environmental Protection (Duty of Care) Regulations 1991, p.650 above.*

*Amendment of the Controlled Waste Regulations 1992*

**24.** *The amendment made by this regulation is included in the Controlled Waste Regulations 1992, p.662 above.*

*Amendment of the Waste Management Licensing Regulations 1994*

**25.** *The amendments made by this regulation and Schedule 3 to these Regulations are included in the Waste Management Licensing Regulations 1994, p.675 above.*

*Revocations and savings*

**26.** (1) Subject to paragraph (2), the following are hereby revoked—

(a) the Control of Pollution (Special Waste) Regulations 1980[4] ("the 1980 Regulations");

(b) the Control of Pollution (Landed Ships' Waste) Regulations 1987;[5]

---

[1] "Waste management licence" has the meaning given by s.35(1) of the 1990 Act, p.119 above.

[2] S.I. 1988/1199, to which there are amendments not relevant to these Regulations.

[3] S.I. 1988/1221.

[4] S.I. 1980/1709, as amended by S.I. 1988/1562, 1988/1790 and 1994/1137 and by Part IV of sch.6 to the Radioactive Substances Act 1993 (c.12).

[5] S.I. 1987/402.

(c)  the Control of Pollution (Landed Ships' Waste) (Amendment) Regulations 1989;[3] and

(d)  paragraphs (1) and (2) of regulation 18 of the Transfrontier Shipment of Waste Regulations 1994.[4]

(2)  Subject to paragraph (3) of this regulation, the 1980 Regulations shall continue to have effect in relation to any special waste in respect of which the consignment note (within the meaning of those Regulations) was furnished or is treated as having been furnished to the Agency,[5] in accordance with regulation 4 of those Regulations, before the coming into force of these Regulations.

(3)  Paragraph (2) of this regulation shall not apply in relation to any special waste in respect of which consignment notes or copies of consignment notes are furnished pursuant to regulation 9 of the 1980 Regulations and after 31st August 1996 any direction made under regulation 9 of the 1980 Regulations shall have no effect.

## SCHEDULE 1

(Regulation 1(4))

### PART I

### FORM OF CONSIGNMENT NOTE

SPECIAL WASTE REGULATIONS 1996
Nᵒ of prenotice (*if different*) _____

Consignment Note Nᵒ _____
Sheet    of

A  CONSIGNMENT DETAILS                                   PLEASE TICK IF YOU ARE A TRANSFER STATION ☐
1. The waste described below is to be removed
   from (name, address and postcode)
2. The waste will be taken to (address & postcode)
3. The consignment(s) will be:        one single ☐   a succession ☐   carrier's round ☐   other ☐
4. Expected removal date of first consignment:          last consignment:
5. Name                                                 On behalf of (company)
   Signature                                            Date
6. ☎                              7. The waste producer was (if different from 1)

B  DESCRIPTION OF THE WASTE        Nᵒ of additional sheet(s) ☐
1. The waste is
3. Physical Form: Liquid ☐   Powder ☐   Sludge ☐   Solid ☐   Mixed ☐     2. Classification
5. Total quantity for removal   quantity   units (e.g. kg/ltrs/tonnes)     4. Colour
6. The chemical/biological components that make the waste special are:      Container type, number and size:

| Component | Concentration (% or mg/kg) | Component | Concentration (% or mg/kg) |
|---|---|---|---|
|  |  |  |  |

7. The hazards are:
8. The process giving rise to waste is:

C  CARRIER'S CERTIFICATE   I certify that I today collected the consignment and that the details in A1, A2 and B1 above
                           are correct. The Quantity collected in the load is:
   Name                                          On behalf of (company) (name & address)

   Signature                                     Date              at        hrs.
1. Carrier registration nᵒ/reason for exemption  2. Vehicle registration nᵒ (or mode of transport, if not
                                                    road)

---

[3]  S.I. 1989/65.    [4]  S.I. 1994/1137; these Regulations are at p.741 above.
[5]  "Agency" defined by reg.1(4), p.764 above.

D CONSIGNOR'S CERTIFICATE
I certify that the information in B and C above are correct, that the carrier is registered or exempt and was advised of the appropriate precautionary measures.

Name                                  On behalf of (company)
Signature                             Date

---

E CONSIGNEE'S CERTIFICATE
1. I received this waste on    at            hrs.      2. Quantity received   quantity        units (e.g.
                                                          kg/ltrs/tonnes)
3. Vehicle registration nº                             4. Management Operation
I certify that waste management licence/authorisation/
exemption nº                                           authorises the management of the waste described in
                                                       B.
Name                                                   On behalf of (company)
Signature                                              Date

FED 1041 (03/96 DDP)

# SCHEDULE 1

(Regulation 8(2))

## PART II

## FORM OF SCHEDULE

SPECIAL WASTE REGULATIONS 1996: CARRIER SCHEDULE        Consignment Note Nº _____
                                                        Sheet       of

---

Name and address of premises from which waste was removed

Consignment Note Nº

I certify that today I collected the quantity of waste shown from the address given here and will take it to the address given in A2 on the consignment note

| Quantity of waste removed | Carrier's signature and Date |

I certify that the waste collected is as detailed above and conforms with the description given in B on the relevant consignment note

| Name of Consignor | Signature and Date |

---

Name and address of premises from which waste was removed

Consignment Note Nº

I certify that today I collected the quantity of waste shown from the address given here and will take it to the address given in A2 on the consignment note

| Quantity of waste removed | Carrier's signature and Date |

I certify that the waste collected is as detailed above and conforms with the description given in B on the relevant consignment note

| Name of Consignor | Signature and Date |

| Name and address of premises from which waste was removed | I certify that today I collected the quantity of waste shown from the address given here and will take it to the address given in A2 on the consignment note | |
| --- | --- | --- |
| | Quantity of waste removed | Carrier's signature and Date |
| | I certify that the waste collected is as detailed above and conforms with the description given in B on the relevant consignment note | |
| Consignment Note N° | Name of Consignor | Signature and Date |

| Name and address of premises from which waste was removed | I certify that today I collected the quantity of waste shown from the address given here and will take it to the address given in A2 on the consignment note | |
| --- | --- | --- |
| | Quantity of waste removed | Carrier's signature and Date |
| | I certify that the waste collected is as detailed above and conforms with the description given in B on the relevant consignment note | |
| Consignment Note N° | Name of Consignor | Signature and Date |

| Name and address of premises from which waste was removed | I certify that today I collected the quantity of waste shown from the address given here and will take it to the address given in A2 on the consignment note | |
| --- | --- | --- |
| | Quantity of waste removed | Carrier's signature and Date |
| | I certify that the waste collected is as detailed above and conforms with the description given in B on the relevant consignment note | |
| Consignment Note N° | Name of Consignor | Signature and Date |

| Name and address of premises from which waste was removed | I certify that today I collected the quantity of waste shown from the address given here and will take it to the address given in A2 on the consignment note | |
| --- | --- | --- |
| | Quantity of waste removed | Carrier's signature and Date |
| | I certify that the waste collected is as detailed above and conforms with the description given in B on the relevant consignment note | |
| Consignment Note N° | Name of Consignor | Signature and Date |

# SCHEDULE 2

(Regulation 2)

## SPECIAL WASTE

## PART I

## HAZARDOUS WASTE LIST

| Waste code (6 digits)/ Chapter Heading (2 and 4 digits) | Description |
|---|---|
| 02 | WASTE FROM AGRICULTURAL, HORTICULTURAL, HUNTING, FISHING AND AQUA-CULTURE PRIMARY PRODUCTION, FOOD PREPARATION AND PROCESSING |
| 0201 | PRIMARY PRODUCTION WASTE |
| 020105 | agrochemical wastes |
| 03 | WASTES FROM WOOD PROCESSING AND THE PRODUCTION OF PAPER, CARDBOARD, PULP, PANELS AND FURNITURE |
| 0302 | WOOD PRESERVATION WASTE |
| 030201 | non-halogenated organic wood preservatives |
| 030202 | organochlorinated wood preservatives |
| 030203 | organometallic wood preservatives |
| 030204 | inorganic wood preservatives |
| 04 | WASTES FROM THE LEATHER AND TEXTILE INDUSTRIES |
| 0401 | WASTES FROM THE LEATHER INDUSTRY |
| 040103 | degreasing wastes containing solvents without a liquid phase |
| 0402 | WASTES FROM TEXTILE INDUSTRY |
| 040211 | halogenated wastes from dressing and finishing |
| 05 | WASTES FROM PETROLEUM REFINING, NATURAL GAS PURIFICATION AND PYROLYTIC TREATMENT OF COAL |
| 0501 | OILY SLUDGES AND SOLID WASTES |
| 050103 | tank bottom sludges |
| 050104 | acid alkyl sludges |
| 050105 | oil spills |
| 050107 | acid tars |
| 050108 | other tars |
| 0504 | SPENT FILTER CLAYS |
| 050401 | spent filter clays |
| 0506 | WASTE FROM THE PYROLYTIC TREATMENT OF COAL |
| 050601 | acid tars |
| 050603 | other tars |
| 0507 | WASTE FROM NATURAL GAS PURIFICATION |
| 050701 | sludges containing mercury |
| 0508 | WASTES FROM OIL REGENERATION |
| 050801 | spent filter clays |
| 050802 | acid tars |

| Waste code (6 digits)/ Chapter Heading (2 and 4 digits) | Description |
| --- | --- |
| 050803 | other tars |
| 050804 | aqueous liquid waste from oil regeneration |
| 06 | WASTES FROM INORGANIC CHEMICAL PROCESSES |
| 0601 | WASTE ACIDIC SOLUTIONS |
| 060101 | sulphuric acid and sulphurous acid |
| 060102 | hydrochloric acid |
| 060103 | hydrofluoric acid |
| 060104 | phosphoric and phosphorous acid |
| 060105 | nitric acid and nitrous acid |
| 060199 | waste not otherwise specified |
| 0602 | ALKALINE SOLUTIONS |
| 060201 | calcium hydroxide |
| 060202 | soda |
| 060203 | ammonia |
| 060299 | wastes not otherwise specified |
| 0603 | WASTE SALTS AND THEIR SOLUTIONS |
| 060311 | salts and solutions containing cyanides |
| 0604 | METAL-CONTAINING WASTES |
| 060402 | metallic salts (except 0603) |
| 060403 | wastes containing arsenic |
| 060404 | wastes containing mercury |
| 060405 | wastes containing heavy metals |
| 0607 | WASTES FROM HALOGEN CHEMICAL PROCESSES |
| 060701 | wastes containing asbestos from electrolysis |
| 060702 | activated carbon from chlorine production |
| 0613 | WASTES FROM OTHER INORGANIC CHEMICAL PROCESSES |
| 061301 | inorganic pesticides, biocides and wood preserving agents |
| 061302 | spent activated carbon (except 060702) |
| 07 | WASTES FROM ORGANIC CHEMICAL PROCESSES |
| 0701 | WASTE FROM THE MANUFACTURE, FORMULATION, SUPPLY AND USE (MFSU) OF BASIC ORGANIC CHEMICALS |
| 070101 | aqueous washing liquids and mother liquors |
| 070103 | organic halogenated solvents, washing liquids and mother liquors |
| 070104 | other organic solvents, washing liquids and mother liquors |
| 070107 | halogenated still bottoms and reaction residues |
| 070108 | other still bottoms and reaction residues |
| 070109 | halogenated filter cakes, spent absorbents |
| 070110 | other filter cakes, spent absorbents |
| 0702 | WASTE FROM THE MFSU OF PLASTICS, SYNTHETIC RUBBER AND MAN-MADE FIBRES |
| 070201 | aqueous washing liquids and mother liquors |
| 070203 | organic halogenated solvents, washing liquids and mother liquors |
| 070204 | other organic solvents, washing liquids and mother liquors |
| 070207 | halogenated still bottoms and reaction residues |

| Waste code (6 digits)/ Chapter Heading (2 and 4 digits) | Description |
|---|---|
| 070208 | other still bottoms and reaction residues |
| 070209 | halogenated filter cakes, spent absorbents |
| 070210 | other filter cakes, spent absorbents |
| 0703 | WASTE FROM THE MFSU FOR ORGANIC DYES AND PIGMENTS (EXCLUDING 0611) |
| 070301 | aqueous washing liquids and mother liquors |
| 070303 | organic halogenated solvents, washing liquids and mother liquors |
| 070304 | other organic solvents, washing liquids and mother liquors |
| 070307 | halogenated still bottoms and reaction residues |
| 070308 | other still bottoms and reaction residues |
| 070309 | halogenated filter cakes, spent absorbents |
| 070310 | other filter cakes, spent absorbents |
| 0704 | WASTE FROM THE MFSU FOR ORGANIC PESTICIDES (EXCEPT 020105) |
| 070401 | aqueous washing liquids and mother liquors |
| 070403 | organic halogenated solvents, washing liquid and mother liquors |
| 070404 | other organic solvents, washing liquids and mother liquors |
| 070407 | halogenated still bottoms and reaction residues |
| 070408 | other still bottoms and reaction residues |
| 070409 | halogenated filter cakes, spent absorbents |
| 070410 | other filter cakes, spent absorbents |
| 0705 | WASTE FROM THE MFSU OF PHARMACEUTICALS |
| 070501 | aqueous washing liquids and mother liquors |
| 070503 | organic halogenated solvents, washing liquid and mother liquors |
| 070504 | other organic solvents, washing liquids and mother liquors |
| 070507 | halogenated still bottoms and reaction residues |
| 070508 | other still bottoms and reaction residues |
| 070509 | halogenated filter cakes, spent absorbents |
| 070510 | other filter cakes, spent absorbents |
| 0706 | WASTE FROM THE MFSU OF FATS, GREASE, SOAPS, DETERGENTS, DISINFECTANTS AND COSMETICS |
| 070601 | aqueous washing liquids and mother liquors |
| 070603 | organic halogenated solvents, washing liquid and mother liquors |
| 070604 | other organic solvents, washing liquids and mother liquors |
| 070607 | halogenated still bottoms and reaction residues |
| 070608 | other still bottoms and reaction residues |
| 070609 | halogenated filter cakes, spent absorbents |
| 070610 | other filter cakes, spent absorbents |
| 0707 | WASTE FROM THE MFSU OF FINE CHEMICALS AND CHEMICAL PRODUCTS NOT OTHERWISE SPECIFIED |
| 070701 | aqueous washing liquids and mother liquors |
| 070703 | organic halogenated solvents, washing liquid and mother liquors |
| 070704 | other organic solvents, washing liquids and mother liquors |
| 070707 | halogenated still bottoms and reaction residues |
| 070708 | other still bottoms and reaction residues |

| Waste code (6 digits)/ Chapter Heading (2 and 4 digits) | Description |
| --- | --- |
| 070709 | halogenated filter cakes, spent absorbents |
| 070710 | other filter cakes, spent absorbents |
| 08 | WASTES FROM THE MANUFACTURE, FORMULATION, SUPPLY AND USE (MFSU) OF COATINGS (PAINTS, VARNISHES AND VITREOUS ENAMELS), ADHESIVE, SEALANTS AND PRINTING INKS |
| 0801 | WASTES FROM MFSU OF PAINT AND VARNISH |
| 080101 | waste paints and varnish containing halogenated solvents |
| 080102 | waste paints and varnish free of halogenated solvents |
| 080106 | sludges from paint or varnish removal containing halogenated solvents |
| 080107 | sludges from paint or varnish removal free of halogenated solvents |
| 0803 | WASTES FROM MFSU OF PRINTING INKS |
| 080301 | waste ink containing halogenated solvents |
| 080302 | waste ink free of halogenated solvents |
| 080305 | ink sludges containing halogenated solvents |
| 080306 | ink sludges free of halogenated solvents |
| 0804 | WASTES FROM MFSU OF ADHESIVE AND SEALANTS (INCLUDING WATER-PROOFING PRODUCTS) |
| 080401 | waste adhesives and sealants containing halogenated solvents |
| 080402 | waste adhesives and sealants free of halogenated solvents |
| 080405 | adhesive and sealants sludges containing halogenated solvents |
| 080406 | adhesives and sealants sludges free of halogenated solvents |
| 09 | WASTES FROM THE PHOTOGRAPHIC INDUSTRY |
| 0901 | WASTES FROM PHOTOGRAPHIC INDUSTRY |
| 090101 | water based developer and activator solutions |
| 090102 | water based offset plate developer solutions |
| 090103 | solvent based developer solutions |
| 090104 | fixer solutions |
| 090105 | bleach solutions and bleach fixer solutions |
| 090106 | waste containing silver from on-site treatment of photographic waste |
| 10 | INORGANIC WASTES FROM THERMAL PROCESSES |
| 1001 | WASTES FROM POWER STATION AND OTHER COMBUSTION PLANTS (EXCEPT 1900) |
| 100104 | oil fly ash |
| 100109 | sulphuric acid |
| 1003 | WASTES FROM ALUMINIUM THERMAL METALLURGY |
| 100301 | tars and other carbon-containing wastes from anode manufacture |
| 100303 | skimmings |
| 100304 | primary smelting slags/white drosses |
| 100307 | spent pot lining |
| 100308 | salt slags from secondary smelting |
| 100309 | black drosses from secondary smelting |
| 100310 | waste from treatment of salt slags and black drosses treatment |
| 1004 | WASTES FROM LEAD THERMAL METALLURGY |
| 100401 | slags (1st and 2nd smelting) |

| Waste code (6 digits)/ Chapter Heading (2 and 4 digits) | Description |
|---|---|
| 100402 | dross and skimmings (1st and 2nd smelting) |
| 100403 | calcium arsenate |
| 100404 | flue gas dust |
| 100405 | other particulates and dust |
| 100406 | solid waste from gas treatment |
| 100407 | sludges from gas treatment |
| 1005 | WASTES FROM ZINC THERMAL METALLURGY |
| 100501 | slags (1st and 2nd smelting) |
| 100502 | dross and skimmings (1st and 2nd smelting) |
| 100503 | flue gas dust |
| 100505 | solid waste from gas treatment |
| 100506 | sludges from gas treatment |
| 1006 | WASTES FROM COPPER THERMAL METALLURGY |
| 100603 | flue gas dust |
| 100605 | waste from electrolytic refining |
| 100606 | solid waste from gas treatment |
| 100607 | sludges from gas treatment |
| 11 | INORGANIC WASTE WITH METALS FROM METAL TREATMENT AND THE COATING OF METALS; NON-FERROUS HYDRO-METALLURGY |
| 1101 | LIQUID WASTES AND SLUDGES FROM METAL TREATMENT AND COATING OF METALS (e.g. GALVANIC PROCESSES, ZINC COATING PROCESSES, PICKLING PROCESSES, ETCHING, PHOSPHATIZING, ALKALINE DE-GREASING) |
| 110101 | cyanidic (alkaline) wastes containing heavy metals other than chromium |
| 110102 | cyanidic (alkaline) wastes which do not contain heavy metals |
| 110103 | cyanide-free wastes containing chromium |
| 110105 | acidic pickling solutions |
| 110106 | acids not otherwise specified |
| 110107 | alkalis not otherwise specified |
| 110108 | phosphatizing sludges |
| 1102 | WASTES AND SLUDGES FROM NON-FERROUS HYDROMETALLURGICAL PROCESSES |
| 110202 | sludges from zinc hydrometallurgy (including jarosite, geothite) |
| 1103 | SLUDGES AND SOLIDS FROM TEMPERING PROCESSES |
| 110301 | wastes containing cyanide |
| 110302 | other wastes |
| 12 | WASTES FROM SHAPING AND SURFACE TREATMENT OF METALS AND PLASTICS |
| 1201 | WASTES FROM SHAPING (INCLUDING FORGING, WELDING, PRESSING, DRAWING, TURNING, CUTTING AND FILING) |
| 120106 | waste machining oils containing halogens (not emulsioned) |
| 120107 | waste machining oils free of halogens (not emulsioned) |
| 120108 | waste machining emulsions containing halogens |
| 120109 | waste machining emulsions free of halogens |
| 120110 | synthetic machining oils |
| 120111 | machining sludges |

| Waste code (6 digits)/ Chapter Heading (2 and 4 digits) | Description |
|---|---|
| 120112 | spent waxes and fats |
| 1203 | WASTES FROM WATER AND STEAM DEGREASING PROCESSES (EXCEPT 1100) |
| 120301 | aqueous washing liquids |
| 120302 | steam degreasing wastes |
| 13 | OIL WASTES (EXCEPT EDIBLE OILS, 0500 AND 1200) |
| 1301 | WASTE HYDRAULIC OILS AND BRAKE FLUIDS |
| 130101 | hydraulic oils, containing PCBs or PCTs |
| 130102 | other chlorinated hydraulic oils (not emulsions) |
| 130103 | non-chlorinated hydraulic oils (not emulsions) |
| 130104 | chlorinated emulsions |
| 130105 | non-chlorinated emulsions |
| 130106 | hydraulic oils containing only mineral oil |
| 130107 | other hydraulic oils |
| 130108 | brake fluids |
| 1302 | WASTE ENGINE, GEAR AND LUBRICATING OILS |
| 130201 | chlorinated engine, gear and lubricating oils |
| 130202 | non-chlorinated engine, gear and lubricating oils |
| 130203 | other machine, gear and lubricating oils |
| 1303 | WASTE INSULATING AND HEAT TRANSMISSION OILS AND OTHER LIQUIDS |
| 130301 | insulating or heat transmission oils and other liquids containing PCBs or PCTs |
| 130302 | other chlorinated insulating and heat transmission oils and other liquids |
| 130303 | non-chlorinated insulating and heat transmission oils and other liquids |
| 130304 | synthetic insulating and heat transmission oils and other liquids |
| 130305 | mineral insulating and heat transmission oils |
| 1304 | BILGE OILS |
| 130401 | bilge oils from inland navigation |
| 130402 | bilge oils from jetty sewers |
| 130403 | bilge oils from other navigation |
| 1305 | OIL/WATER SEPARATOR CONTENTS |
| 130501 | oil/water separator solids |
| 130502 | oil/water separator sludges |
| 130503 | interceptor sludges |
| 130504 | desalter sludges or emulsions |
| 130505 | other emulsions |
| 1306 | OIL WASTE NOT OTHERWISE SPECIFIED |
| 130601 | oil waste not otherwise specified |
| 14 | WASTES FROM ORGANIC SUBSTANCES EMPLOYED AS SOLVENTS (EXCEPT 0700 AND 0800) |
| 1401 | WASTES FROM METAL DEGREASING AND MACHINERY MAINTENANCE |
| 140101 | chlorofluorocarbons |
| 140102 | other halogenated solvents and solvent mixes |
| 140103 | other solvents and solvent mixes |

| Waste code (6 digits)/ Chapter Heading (2 and 4 digits) | Description |
|---|---|
| 140104 | aqueous solvent mixes containing halogens |
| 140105 | aqueous solvent mixes free of halogens |
| 140106 | sludges or solid wastes containing halogenated solvents |
| 140107 | sludges or solid wastes free of halogenated solvents |
| 1402 | WASTES FROM TEXTILE CLEANING AND DEGREASING OF NATURAL PRODUCTS |
| 140201 | halogenated solvents and solvent mixes |
| 140202 | solvent mixes or organic liquids free of halogenated solvents |
| 140203 | sludges or solid wastes containing halogenated solvents |
| 140204 | sludges or solid wastes containing other solvents |
| 1403 | WASTES FROM THE ELECTRONIC INDUSTRY |
| 140301 | chlorofluorocarbons |
| 140302 | other halogenated solvents |
| 140303 | solvents and solvent mixes free of halogenated solvents |
| 140304 | sludges or solid wastes containing halogenated solvents |
| 140305 | sludges or solid wastes containing other solvents |
| 1404 | WASTES FROM COOLANTS, FOAM/AEROSOL PROPELLANTS |
| 140401 | chlorofluorocarbons |
| 140402 | other halogenated solvents and solvent mixes |
| 140403 | other solvents and solvent mixes |
| 140404 | sludges or solid wastes containing halogenated solvents |
| 140405 | sludges or solid wastes containing other solvents |
| 1405 | WASTES FROM SOLVENT AND COOLANT RECOVERY (STILL BOTTOMS) |
| 140501 | chlorofluorocarbons |
| 140502 | halogenated solvents and solvent mixes |
| 140503 | other solvents and solvent mixes |
| 140504 | sludges containing halogenated solvents |
| 140505 | sludges containing other solvents |
| 16 | WASTES NOT OTHERWISE SPECIFIED IN THE CATALOGUE |
| 1602 | DISCARDED EQUIPMENT AND SHREDDER RESIDUES |
| 160201 | transformers and capacitors containing PCBs or PCTs |
| 1604 | WASTE EXPLOSIVES |
| 160401 | waste ammunition |
| 160402 | fireworks waste |
| 160403 | other waste explosives |
| 1606 | BATTERIES AND ACCUMULATORS |
| 160601 | lead batteries |
| 160602 | Ni-Cd batteries |
| 160603 | mercury dry cells |
| 160606 | electrolyte from batteries and accumulators |
| 1607 | WASTE FROM TRANSPORT AND STORAGE TANK CLEANING (EXCEPT 0500 AND 1200) |
| 160701 | waste from marine transport tank cleaning, containing chemicals |
| 160702 | waste from marine transport tank cleaning, containing oil |

| Waste code (6 digits)/ Chapter Heading (2 and 4 digits) | Description |
|---|---|
| 160703 | waste from railway and road transport tank cleaning, containing oil |
| 160704 | waste from railway and road transport tank cleaning, containing chemicals |
| 160705 | waste from storage tank cleaning, containing chemicals |
| 160706 | waste from storage tank cleaning, containing oil |
| 17 | CONSTRUCTION AND DEMOLITION WASTE (INCLUDING ROAD CONSTRUCTION) |
| 1706 | INSULATION MATERIALS |
| 170601 | insulation materials containing asbestos |
| 18 | WASTE FROM HUMAN OR ANIMAL HEALTH CARE AND/OR RELATED RESEARCH (EXCLUDING KITCHEN AND RESTAURANT WASTES WHICH DO NOT ARISE FROM IMMEDIATE HEALTH CARE) |
| 1801 | WASTE FROM NATAL CARE, DIAGNOSIS, TREATMENT OR PREVENTION OF DISEASE IN HUMANS |
| 180103 | other wastes whose collection and disposal is subject to special requirements in view of the prevention of infection |
| 1802 | WASTE FROM RESEARCH, DIAGNOSIS, TREATMENT OR PREVENTION OF DISEASE INVOLVING ANIMALS |
| 180202 | other wastes whose collection and disposal is subject to special requirements in view of the prevention of infection |
| 180204 | discarded chemicals |
| 19 | WASTES FROM WASTE TREATMENT FACILITIES, OFF-SITE WASTE WATER TREATMENT PLANTS AND THE WATER INDUSTRY |
| 1901 | WASTES FROM INCINERATION OR PYROLYSIS OF MUNICIPAL AND SIMILAR COMMERCIAL, INDUSTRIAL AND INSTITUTIONAL WASTES |
| 190103 | fly ash |
| 190104 | boiler dust |
| 190105 | filter cake from gas treatment |
| 190106 | aqueous liquid waste from gas treatment and other aqueous liquid wastes |
| 190107 | solid waste from gas treatment |
| 190110 | spent activated carbon from flue gas treatment |
| 1902 | WASTES FROM SPECIFIC PHYSICO/CHEMICAL TREATMENTS OF INDUSTRIAL WASTES (e.g. DECHROMATATION, DECYANIDATION, NEUTRALIZATION) |
| 190201 | metal hydroxide sludges and other sludges from metal insolubilization treatment |
| 1904 | VITRIFIED WASTES AND WASTES FROM VITRIFICATION |
| 190402 | fly ash and other flue gas treatment wastes |
| 190403 | non-vitrified solid phase |
| 1908 | WASTES FROM WASTE WATER TREATMENT PLANTS NOT OTHERWISE SPECIFIED |
| 190803 | grease and oil mixture from oil/waste water separation |
| 190806 | saturated or spent ion exchange resins |
| 190807 | solutions and sludges from regeneration of ion exchangers |
| 20 | MUNICIPAL WASTES AND SIMILAR COMMERCIAL INDUSTRIAL AND INSTITUTIONAL WASTES INCLUDING SEPARATELY COLLECTED FRACTIONS |
| 2001 | SEPARATELY COLLECTED FRACTIONS |
| 200112 | paint, inks, adhesives and resins |
| 200113 | solvents |

| Waste code (6 digits)/ Chapter Heading (2 and 4 digits) | Description |
|---|---|
| 200117 | photo chemicals |
| 200119 | pesticides |
| 200121 | fluorescent tubes and other mercury containing waste |

## PART II

### HAZARDOUS PROPERTIES

H1   "Explosive": substances and preparations which may explode under the effect of flame or which are more sensitive to shocks or friction than dinitrobenzene.

H2   "Oxidizing": substances and preparations which exhibit highly exothermic reactions when in contact with other substances, particularly flammable substances.

H3-A   "Highly flammable":

—liquid substances and preparations having a flash point below 21°C (including extremely flammable liquids), or

—substances and preparations which may become hot and finally catch fire in contact with air at ambient temperature without any application of energy, or

—solid substances and preparations which may readily catch fire after brief contact with a source of ignition and which continue to burn or to be consumed after removal of the source of ignition, or

—gaseous substances and preparations which are flammable in air at normal pressure, or

—substances and preparations which, in contact with water or damp air, evolve highly flammable gases in dangerous quantities.

H3-B   "Flammable": liquid substances and preparations having a flash point equal to or greater than 21°C and less than or equal to 55°C.

H4   "Irritant": non-corrosive substances and preparations which, through immediate, prolonged or repeated contact with the skin or mucous membrane, can cause inflammation.

H5   "Harmful": substances and preparations which, if they are inhaled or ingested or if they penetrate the skin, may involve limited health risks.

H6   "Toxic": substances and preparations (including very toxic substances and preparations) which, if they are inhaled or ingested or if they penetrate the skin, may involve serious, acute or chronic health risks and even death.

H7   "Carcinogenic": substances and preparations which, if they are inhaled or ingested or if they penetrate the skin, may induce cancer or increase its incidence.

H8   "Corrosive": substances and preparations which may destroy living tissue on contact.

H9   "Infectious": substances containing viable micro-organisms, or their toxins which are known or reliably believed to cause disease in man or other living organisms.

H10   "Teratogenic": substances and preparations which, if they are inhaled or ingested or if they penetrate the skin, may induce non-hereditary congenital malformations or increase their incidence.

H11   "Mutagenic": substances and preparations which, if they are inhaled or ingested or if they penetrate the skin, may induce hereditary genetic defects or increase their incidence.

H12   Substances and preparations which release toxic or very toxic gases in contact with water, air or an acid.

H13   Substances and preparations capable by any means, after disposal, of yielding another substance, e.g. a leachate, which possesses any of the characteristics listed above.

H14   "Ecotoxic": substances and preparations which present or may present immediate or delayed risks for one or more sectors of the environment.

## PART III

### THRESHOLDS FOR CERTAIN HAZARDOUS PROPERTIES

In the waste:

—the total concentration of substances classified as irritant and having assigned to them any of the risk phrases R36 ("irritating to the eyes"), R37 ("irritating to the respiratory system") or R38 ("irritating to the skin") is equal to or greater than 20%;

—the total concentration of substances classified as irritant and having assigned to them the risk phrase R41 ("risk of serious damage to eyes") is equal to or greater than 10%;

—the total concentration of substances classified as harmful is equal to or greater than 25%;

—the total concentration of substances classified as very toxic is equal to or greater than 0.1%;

—the total concentration of substances classified as toxic is equal to or greater than 3%;

—the total concentration of substances classified as carcinogenic and placed by the approved classification and labelling guide in category 1 or 2 of that classification is equal to or greater than 0.1%;

—the total concentration of substances classified as corrosive and having assigned to them the risk phrase R34 ("causes burns") is equal to or greater than 5%; and

—the total concentration of substances classified as corrosive and having assigned to them the risk phrase R35 ("causes severe burns") is equal to or greater than 1%.

## PART IV[1]

### RULES FOR THE INTERPRETATION OF THIS SCHEDULE

1. Except in the case of a substance listed in the approved supply list,[2] the test methods to be used for the purposes of deciding which (if any) of the properties mentioned in Part II of this Schedule are to be assigned to a substance are those described in Annex V to Council Directive 67/548/EEC,[3] as amended by Commission Directive 92/69/EEC.[4]

2. Any reference in Part III of this Schedule to a substance being classified as having a hazardous property, having assigned to it a particular risk phrase,[5] or being placed within a particular category of a classification is a reference to that substance being so classified, having that risk phrase assigned to it or being placed in that category—

   (i) in the case of a substance listed in the approved supply list, on the basis of Part V of that list;

   (ii) in the case of any other substance, on the basis of the criteria laid down in the approved classification and labelling guide.[6]

3. Any reference in Part III of this Schedule to the total concentration of any substances being equal to or greater than a given percentage is a reference to the proportion by weight of those substances in any waste being equal to or, as the case may be, greater than that percentage.

## SCHEDULE 3

(Regulation 25)

### AMENDMENTS TO THE WASTE MANAGEMENT LICENSING REGULATIONS 1994

*The amendments made by this Schedule are included in the Waste Management Licensing Regulations 1994, **p.000** above.*

[1] This Part added by S.I. 1996/1019, sch., para.7.
[2] "The approved supply list" defined by reg.1(4) above.
[3] OJ No. L 196, 16.8.1967, p.1.
[4] OJ No. L 383, 29.12.1992, p.1.
[5] "Risk phrase" defined by reg.1(4) above.
[6] "The approved classification and labelling guide" defined by reg.1(4) above.

*Explanatory Note*
*(This note is not part of the Regulations)*

These Regulations provide a new definition of special waste. They make provision for handling such waste and for implementing Council Directive 91/689/EEC on hazardous waste (OJ No. L 377, 31.12.1991, p.20), ("the Directive").

Regulation 2 defines special waste, making reference to Parts I, II and III of Schedule 2. This is to implement the definition of hazardous waste in the Directive and in particular in the List annexed to Council Decision 94/904/EC (OJ No. L 356, 31.12.94, p.14). The definition extends, in accordance with Article 4 of the Directive, to certain other waste considered by the United Kingdom to display particular hazardous properties. Household waste is excluded from the definition.

Regulation 4 requires the Environment Agency (in relation to England and Wales) and the Scottish Environment Protection Agency (in relation to Scotland) ("the Agencies"), to give unique codes to be applied to consignments of waste or to carrier's rounds. Carrier's rounds consist of several consignments collected on the same journey and delivered to one place. The codes are to be shown, together with other required information, on consignment notes which are to accompany the waste when transported. Regulations 5 to 10 and 12 and 13 and Schedule 1 provide for the completion and handling of these notes and for pre-notification to the Agency of the consignment or round. Completion of such identification forms and their transport with waste are required by Article 5 of the Directive. The pre-notification provisions (regulations 5(2)(b), 8(2)(a)(ii) and 12) are not implementing specific Community obligations.

Regulation 11 requires the Agencies to provide certain information to one another, following notification, where waste is to be transported from England and Wales to Scotland or vice versa. Regulation 14 requires the Agencies to charge fees on supplying a code under regulation 4. The amount is generally £15 per consignment or round and £10 where the waste consists entirely of lead acid batteries. Rounds of low quantity fulfilling certain conditions attract no fees. Regulations 11 and 14 do not implement Community obligations.

Regulation 15 implements Article 4.3 of the Directive on the keeping of records by those consigning and carrying hazardous waste. They are both required to keep the documents for three years, although the Directive only requires carriers to keep records for at least twelve months. Together with regulation 16, it also implements the requirements of Article 2.1 of the Directive on the keeping of records for sites where hazardous waste is deposited.

Regulation 17 prohibits the mixing of special waste with other waste or other categories of special waste except where this is authorised under, or exempted from the effect of, certain other waste management legislation. This regulation is to implement Articles 2.2 and 2.3 of the Directive.

Regulation 18 makes failure to comply with the Regulations a criminal offence except for an Agency member, officer or employee. There is a defence for those who take certain steps in cases of emergency or grave danger. The Agencies are made responsible by regulation 19 for supervising activities and persons subject to the Regulations. Insofar as they relate to provisions which implement Community obligations (as stated in this Note), these provisions are part of that implementation because their purpose is to make the implementation effective.

Regulation 20 makes transitional provision for applications for certificates of technical competence under the Waste Management Licensing Regulations 1994 (S.I. 1994/1056 as amended) where such applications were made before 1st March 1997 where the applicant was licensed to deal with special waste before the change in definition made by these Regulations. This provision does not implement a Community obligation.

Regulations 21 to 26 and Schedule 3 make consequential amendments to, and revocations and saving in respect of, other legislation. Regulation 21 makes consequential amendment to regulations implementing Directive 85/337/EEC. Regulation 25 makes consequential amendment to the Waste Management Licensing Regulations 1994. Parts of those Regulations, in particular Schedule 4, implement Community obligations. Regulations 22, 23, 24 and 26 do not implement Community obligations.

A compliance cost assessment in respect of these Regulations may be obtained from Waste Policy Division (Branch 3), Department of the Environment, Room A 231, Romney House, 43 Marsham Street, London SW1P 3PY. A copy has been placed in the library of each of the Houses of Parliament.

# The Environment Act 1995 (Isles of Scilly) Order 1996

S.I. 1996 No. 1030

The Secretary of State, after consultation with the Council of the Isles of Scilly, in exercise of the powers conferred on him by sections 117(2) and (3) of the Environment Act 1995,[1] hereby makes the following Order:

*Citation and commencement*

1. This Order may be cited as the Environment Act 1995 (Isles of Scilly) Order 1996 and shall come into force on 1st May 1996.

*Functions of the Environment Agency to be carried out in the Isles of Scilly*

2. (1) The Environment Agency shall carry out in the Isles of Scilly the functions falling to be carried out in relation to other parts of England and Wales by that Agency by virtue of section 2(1)(d), (e), (f), (g) and (h) and (2) of the Environment Act 1995[2] (transfer of functions to the Agency), with the exception of the functions specified in section 2(2)(b) and (e) of that Act.

(2) Chapters I[3] and III of Part I, sections 108[4] to 115 and 119[5] to 125, of the Environment Act 1995 shall apply in relation to the Isles of Scilly in so far as they relate to the functions conferred on the Environment Agency by virtue of paragraph (1) above.

*Grants for purposes conducive to conservation etc*

3. Sections 98 and 99 of the Environment Act 1995 (grants for purposes conducive to conservation etc) shall apply in relation to the Isles of Scilly.

*Explanatory Note*
*(This note is not part of the Order)*

Article 2 of this Order gives the Environment Agency, with effect from 1st May 1996, certain functions in the Isles of Scilly which it has in other parts of England and Wales. The functions specified in Article 2 are those discharged before that date by Her Majesty's Inspectorate of Pollution. They concern integrated pollution control, radioactive substances and related matters, and include related functions of the Secretary of State.

Article 3 applies in the Isles of Scilly from the same date sections 98 and 99 of that Act. This gives the Minister of Agriculture, Fisheries and Food powers in the Isles of Scilly to make provision by regulations for grants for purposes conducive to conservation, and extends to the Isles of Scilly the Minister's powers, following consultation, to make and modify subordinate legislation specified in section 99.

[1] P.491 above.
[2] P.422 above.
[3] P.420 above.

[4] P.481 above.
[5] P.492 above.

# The Statutory Nuisance (Appeals) (Scotland) Regulations 1996

S.I. 1996 No. 1076 (S.116)

---

The Secretary of State, in exercise of the powers conferred on him by paragraph 1A(3) of Schedule 3 to the Environmental Protection Act 1990,[1] sections 70(2) and (3) and 104(1) of the Control of Pollution Act 1974[2] and of all other powers enabling him in that behalf, hereby makes the following Regulations:

*Citation, commencement, interpretation and extent*

**1.** (1) These Regulations may be cited as the Statutory Nuisance (Appeals) (Scotland) Regulations 1996, shall come into force on 2nd May 1996 and shall extend to Scotland only.

(2) In these Regulations—

"the 1974 Act" means the Control of Pollution Act 1974;[3]

"the 1990 Act" means the Environmental Protection Act 1990; and

"the 1993 Act" means the Noise and Statutory Nuisance Act 1993.[4]

*Appeals under section 80(3) of the 1990 Act*

**2.** (1) The provisions of this regulation apply in relation to an appeal brought by any person under section 80(3) of the 1990 Act[5] (appeals to the sheriff) against an abatement notice served upon him by a local authority.[6]

(2) The grounds on which a person served with such notice may appeal under section 80(3) of the 1990 Act are such one or more of the following grounds as are appropriate in the circumstances of the particular case:—

(a) that the abatement notice is not justified by section 80 of the 1990 Act (summary proceedings for statutory nuisances);

(b) that there has been some informality, defect or error in, or in connection with, the abatement notice, or in, or in connection with, any copy of the abatement notice served under section 80A(3) of the 1990 Act[7] (certain notices in respect of vehicles, machinery or equipment);

(c) that the authority have refused unreasonably to accept compliance with alternative requirements, or that the requirements of the abatement notice are otherwise unreasonable in character or extent, or are unnecessary;

(d) that the time or, where more than one time is specified, any of the times, within which the requirements of the abatement notice are to be complied with is not reasonably sufficient for the purpose;

(e) where the nuisance to which the notice relates—

(i) is a nuisance falling within section 79(1)(a), (d), (e), (f) or (g) of the 1990 Act[8] and arises on industrial, trade, or business premises; or

---

[1] P.225 above.
[2] P.60 above.
[3] 1974 c.40.
[4] 1993 c.40.
[5] P.191 above.

[6] "Local authority" defined by s.79(7), (8) of the 1990 Act, p.188 above.
[7] P.192 above.
[8] P.187 above; s.79(7) defined terms used in this paragraph.

    (ii)  is a nuisance falling within section 79(1)(b) of the 1990 Act and the smoke is emitted from a chimney; or

    (iii)  is a nuisance falling within section 79(1)(ga) of the 1990 Act and is noise emitted from or caused by a vehicle, machinery or equipment being used for industrial, trade or business purposes,

    that the best practicable[1] means were used to prevent, or to counteract the effects of, the nuisance;

(f)  that, in the case of a nuisance under section 79(1)(g) or (ga) of the 1990 Act, the requirements imposed by the abatement notice by virtue of section 80(1)(a) of the 1990 Act are more onerous than the requirements for the time being in force, in relation to the noise to which the notice relates, of—

    (i)  any notice served under section 60 or 66 of the 1974 Act[2] (control of noise on construction sites and from certain premises); or

    (ii)  any consent given under section 61 or 65 of the 1974 Act (consent for work on construction sites and consent for noise to exceed registered level in a noise abatement zone); or

    (iii)  any determination made under section 67 of the 1974 Act (noise control of new buildings);

(g)  that, in the case of a nuisance under section 79(1)(ga) of the 1990 Act, the requirements imposed by the abatement notice by virtue of section 80(1)(a) of the 1990 Act are more onerous than the requirements for the time being in force, in relation to the noise to which the notice relates, of any condition of a consent given under paragraph 1 of Schedule 2 to the 1993 Act[3] (loudspeakers in streets or roads);

(h)  that the abatement notice should have been served on some person instead of the appellant, being—

    (i)  the person responsible[4] for the nuisance; or

    (ii)  the person responsible for the vehicle, machinery or equipment; or

    (iii)  in the case of a nuisance arising from any defect of a structural character, the owner of the premises; or

    (iv)  in the case where the person responsible for the nuisance cannot be found or the nuisance has not yet occurred, the owner or occupier of the premises;

(i)  that the abatement notice might lawfully have been served on some person instead of the appellant being—

    (i)  in the case where the appellant is the owner of the premises, the occupier of the premises; or

    (ii)  in the case where the appellant is the occupier of the premises, the owner of the premises,

    and that it would have been equitable for it to have been so served;

(j)  that the abatement notice might lawfully have been served on some person in addition to the appellant, being—

    (i)  a person also responsible for the nuisance; or

    (ii)  a person who is also owner of the premises; or

    (iii)  a person who is also an occupier of the premises; or

    (iv)  a person who is also the person responsible for the vehicle, machinery or equipment,

    and that it would have been equitable for it to have been so served.

---

[1] "Best practicable means" defined by s.79(9) of the 1990 Act, p.190 above.
[2] "The 1974 Act" means the Control of Pollution Act 1974 (c.40): reg.1(2) above.

[3] "The 1993 Act" means the Noise and Statutory Nuisance Act 1993 (c.40): reg.1(2) above.
[4] "Person responsible" defined by s.79(7) of the 1990 Act, p.189 above.

(3) If and so far as an appeal is based on the ground of some informality, defect or error in, or in connection with, the abatement notice, or in, or in connection with any copy of the notice served under section 80A(3) of the 1990 Act, the court shall dismiss the appeal if it is satisfied that the informality, defect or error was not a material one.

(4) Where the grounds upon which an appeal is brought include a ground specified in paragraph (2)(i) or (j) above, the appellant shall serve a copy of his notice of appeal on any other person referred to, and in the case of any appeal to which this regulation applies he may serve a copy of his notice of appeal on any other person having an interest in the premises, vehicle, machinery or equipment in question.

(5) On the hearing of the appeal the court may—

(a) quash the abatement notice to which the appeal relates; or

(b) vary the abatement notice in favour of the appellant in such manner as it thinks fit; or

(c) dismiss the appeal,

and an abatement notice that is varied under sub-paragraph (b) above shall be final and shall otherwise have effect, as so varied, as if it had been so made by the local authority.

(6) Subject to paragraph (7) below, on the hearing of an appeal the court may make such order as it thinks fit—

(a) with respect to the person by whom any work is to be executed and the contribution to be made by any person towards the cost of the work, or

(b) as to the proportions in which any expenses which may become recoverable by the authority under Part III of the 1990 Act[1] are to be borne by the appellant and by any other person.

(7) In exercising its powers under paragraph (6) above the court—

(a) shall have regard, as between an owner and an occupier, to the terms and conditions, whether contractual or statutory, of any relevant tenancy and to the nature of the works required; and

(b) shall be satisfied before it imposes any requirement thereunder on any person other than the appellant, that that person has received a copy of the notice of appeal in pursuance of paragraph (4) above.

*Suspension of notice*

3. (1) Where—

(a) an appeal is brought against an abatement notice served under section 80 or section 80A of the 1990 Act;[2] and

(b) either—

    (i) compliance with the abatement notice would involve any person in expenditure on the carrying out of works before the hearing of the appeal; or

    (ii) in the case of a nuisance under section 79(1)(g) or (ga) of the 1990 Act,[3] the noise to which the abatement notice relates is noise necessarily caused in the course of the performance of some duty imposed by law on the appellant; and

(c) either paragraph (2) below does not apply, or it does apply but the requirements of paragraph (3) below have not been met,

the abatement notice shall be suspended until the appeal has been abandoned or determined by the court.

(2) This paragraph applies where—

(a) the nuisance to which the abatement notice relates—

    (i) is injurious to health; or

---

[1] P.187 above.     [2] P.190 above.     [3] P.187 above.

(ii) is likely to be of a limited duration such that suspension of the notice would render it of no practical effect; or

(b) the expenditure which would be incurred by any person in the carrying out of works in compliance with the abatement notice before any appeal has been decided would not be disproportionate to the public benefit to be expected in that period from such compliance.

(3) Where paragraph (2) above applies the abatement notice—

(a) shall include a statement that paragraph (2) above applies, and that as a consequence it shall have effect notwithstanding any appeal to the sheriff which has not been determined by the sheriff; and

(b) shall include a statement as to which of the grounds set out in paragraph (2) above apply.

*Amendment of the Control of Noise (Appeals) (Scotland) Regulations 1983*

**4.** In the Control of Noise (Appeals) (Scotland) Regulations 1983[1]—

(a) in regulation 2(1) (interpretation), in the definition of "local authority", for the words "an islands or district council", substitute the words "a council constituted under section 2 of the Local Government etc. (Scotland) Act 1994";[2]

(b) regulation 4 (appeals under section 58(3) of the 1974 Act) shall be omitted; and

(c) in regulation 10(1) (suspension of notices), the word "58", shall be omitted.

*Explanatory Note*
*(This note is not part of the Regulations)*

These Regulations make provision as regards Scotland with respect to appeals to the sheriff against abatement notices served under section 80 of the Environmental Protection Act 1990 (as amended by the Noise and Statutory Nuisance Act 1993) and those served under section 80A of the 1990 Act (as inserted by the 1993 Act).

Regulation 2 sets out grounds on which such appeals may be made, prescribes the procedure to be followed in certain cases in which the appellant claims that a notice should have been served on some other person, and the action which the court may take to give effect to its decision on an appeal.

Regulation 3 prescribes the cases in which an abatement notice is to be suspended pending the decision of a sheriff on an appeal or until the abandonment of such an appeal.

Regulation 4 amends the Control of Noise (Appeals) (Scotland) Regulations 1983 firstly to refer to new unitary local authorities and secondly to revoke references to appeals under section 58 of the Control of Pollution Act 1974 which section has now been repealed.

[1] S.I. 1983/1455.    [2] 1994 c.39.

# List of regulations relating to the control of injurious substances
# Environmental Protection Act 1990, s.140

This list contains regulations made under s.100 of the Control of Pollution Act 1974 and s.140 of the Environmental Protection Act 1990, p.200 above. S.100 of the 1974 Act has been repealed; by s.162(5) of the 1990 Act, p.209 above, regulations made under s.100 of the 1974 Act have effect as if made under s.140 of the 1990 Act.

The list refers to the substance or article which is the subject of the regulations. For the full description of the substance or article and for provisions relating to prohibitions, restrictions, offences and other matters reference should be made to the regulations.

### The Control of Pollution (Supply and Use of Injurious Substances) Regulations 1986, S.I. 1986/902

These regulations have been amended by S.I. 1992/31. The penalty in reg. 6 has been revised by the Criminal Justice Act 1988 (c.51).

*Substance/article:*
(i) a PCB: this is defined in reg.2 as any polychlorinated biphenyl other than a dichlorinated biphenyl;
(ii) a PCT: this is defined in reg.2 as any polychlorinated terphenyl;
(iii) a preparation or a waste oil with a PCB or PCT content higher than 0.005 per cent by weight.

### The Control of Pollution (Anglers' Lead Weights) Regulations 1986, S.I. 1986/1992

These regulations have been amended by S.I. 1993/49. The penalty in reg.6 has been revised by the Criminal Justice Act 1988 (c.51).

*Substance/article:*
lead weight as defined in reg.2.

### The Control of Pollution (Anti-Fouling Paints and Treatments) Regulations 1987, S.I. 1987/783

The penalty in reg.5 has been revised by the Criminal Justice Act 1988 (c.51).

*Substance/article:*
anti-fouling paint or treatment containing a tri-organotin compound: see definitions in reg.2.

### The Environmental Protection (Controls on Injurious Substances) Regulations 1992, S.I. 1992/31

*Substance/article:*
(i) lead paint as specified in reg.3;
(ii) mercury compounds intended for use in the impregnation of heavy-duty industrial textiles, or of yarn intended for the manufacture of such textiles: see reg.4;
(iii) mercury, arsenic or organostannic compounds intended for use in the treatment of industrial waters: see reg.5.
(iv) DBB, defined in reg.2, as specified in reg.6.

### The Environmental Protection (Controls on Injurious Substances) (No.2) Regulations 1992, S.I. 1992/1583

*Substance/article:*
(i) Ugilec 141: see reg.2;
(ii) Ugilec 121 or Ugilec 21: see reg.3;

(iii)   DBBT: see reg.4:

see reg.1 for definitions.

*The Environmental Protection (Controls on Injurious Substances) Regulations 1993, S.I. 1993/1*

*Substance/article:*

PCP, defined in reg.2 as Pentachlorophenol CAS Number 87-86-5 and its salts and esters

*The Environmental Protection (Controls on Injurious Substances) (No.2) Regulations 1993, S.I. 1993/1643*

*Substance/article:*

The use of cadmium, defined in reg.2:

(i)     to give colour to finished products made from certain plastics: see reg.2;

(ii)    in certain paints: see reg.3;

(iii)   to stabilise certain finished products made from PVC: see reg.4;

(iv)    in the metallic plating of certain products: see reg.5.

*The Environmental Protection (Non-Refillable Refrigerant Containers) Regulations 1994, S.I. 1994/199*

These regulations have been amended by S.I. 1996/506.

*Substance/article:*

Non-refillable containers containing certain chlorofluorocarbons (CFCs) and hydrochlorofluorocarbons (HCFCs).

*The Environmental Protection (Controls on Substances that Deplete the Ozone Layer) Regulations 1996, S.I. 1996/506*

These Regulations make provision in relation to Council Regulation (EC) No. 3093/94, OJ No. L 333, 22.12.1994, p.1, on substances that deplete the ozone layer.

# List of statutory instruments made, or having effect as if made, under the Clean Air Act 1993

This list contains regulations made under the Clean Air Act 1993 and earlier legislation relating to clean air consolidated in the 1993 Act. The list also contains orders made under s.21 of the 1993 Act and its predecessor, s.11(4) of the Clean Air Act 1956. The instruments made under the earlier legislation have effect as if made under the Clean Air Act 1993 by virtue of s.17(2) of the Interpretation Act 1978.

The Clean Air Act 1993 is at p.333 above.

From 1961, Statutory Instruments appear in numerical order in the blue bound volumes published annually by HMSO. Prior to that date the instruments were grouped under particular subjects. The volumes are arranged into parts and sections. In this list, following the S.I. number, the part, section and page number of the bound volume is given.

*Section 1(3)*

The Dark Smoke (Permitted Periods) Regulations 1958, S.I. 1958/498. Part I, page 312.

The Dark Smoke (Permitted Periods) (Scotland) Regulations 1958, S.I. 1958/1933 (S.106) . Part I, page 313.

The Dark Smoke (Permitted Periods) (Vessels) Regulations 1958, S.I. 1958/878. Part I, page 314.

The Dark Smoke (Permitted Periods) (Vessels) (Scotland) Regulations 1958, S.I. 1958/1934 (S.107). Part I, page 316.

*Section 2(2)*

The Clean Air (Emission of Dark Smoke) (Exemption) Regulations 1969, S.I. 1969/1263. Part III, section 1, page 3781.

The Clean Air (Emission of Dark Smoke) (Exemption) (Scotland) Regulations 1969, S.I. 1969/1389 (S.109) . Part III, section 1, page 4119.

*Section 5(3)*

The Clean Air (Emission of Grit and Dust from Furnaces) Regulations 1971, S.I. 1971/162. Part I, section 1, page 500.

The Clean Air (Emission of Grit and Dust from Furnaces) (Scotland) Regulations 1971, S.I. 1971/625 (S.88). Part I, section 2, page 1644.

*Section 7(1)*

The Clean Air (Arrestment Plant) (Exemption) Regulations 1969, S.I. 1969/1262. Part III, section 1, page 3777.

The Clean Air (Arrestment Plant) (Exemption) (Scotland) Regulations 1969, S.I. 1969/1388 (S.108). Part III, section 1, page 4115.

*Section 10(2)*

The Clean Air (Measurement of Grit and Dust from Furnaces) Regulations 1971, S.I. 1971/161. Part I, section 1, page 497.

The Clean Air (Measurement of Grit and Dust from Furnaces) (Scotland) Regulations 1971, S.I. 1971/626 (S.89).

Part I, section 2, page 1650.

*Section 14(7)*

The Clean Air (Height of Chimneys) (Exemption) Regulations 1969, S.I. 1969/411. Part I, section 2, page 1155.

The Clean Air (Height of Chimneys) (Exemption) (Scotland) Regulations 1969, S.I. 1969/465 (S.38) . Part I, section 2, page 1333.

*Section 20(6)*

The Smoke Control Areas (Authorised Fuels) Regulations 1991, S.I. 1991/1282. Part II, section 1, page 3270. These Regulations have been amended by:

S.I. 1992/72      :   Part I, section 1, page 271

S.I. 1992/3148    :   Part III, section 3, page 8103

S.I. 1993/2499    :   Part III, section 1, page 5823

S.I. 1996/1145.

*Section 21*

The following Smoke Control Areas (Exempted Fireplaces) Orders have been made, or have effect as if made, under this section.

S.I. 1970/615    : Part I, section 2, page 1948,
amended by S.I. 1974/855: Part II, section 1, page 3312.

S.I. 1970/1667   : Part III, section 1, page 5438,
amended by S.I. 1974/762: Part I, section 3, page 2922.

S.I. 1971/1265   : Part II, section 2, page 3630,
amended by S.I. 1974/762: Part I, section 3, page 2922.

S.I. 1972/438    : Part I, section 2, page 1640,
amended by S.I. 1974/762: Part I, section 3, page 2922.

S.I. 1972/955    : Part II, section 1, page 2980,
amended by S.I. 1974/762: Part I, section 3, page 2922.

S.I. 1973/2166   : Part III, section 4, page 7568,
amended by S.I. 1974/762: Part I, section 3, page 2922.

S.I. 1975/1001   : Part II, section 2, page 3457.

S.I. 1975/1111   : Part II, section 2, page 3901.

S.I. 1978/1609   : Part III, section 1, page 4844.

S.I. 1982/448 (S.55)  : Part l, section 2, page 1198.
amended by S.I. 1983/1573: Part III, section 1, page 5081.

S.I. 1982/1615  : Part III, section 1, page 4818.

S.I. 1983/277    : Part I, section 1, page 815.

S.I. 1983/426    : Part I, section 2, page 1265.

S.I. 1983/1018  : Part II, section 2, page 3177.

S.I. 1983/1573 (S.147) : Part III, section 1, page 5081.

S.I. 1984/1649   : Part III, section 1, page 4822,
amended by S.I. 1985/864: Part II, section 2, page 2757.

S.I. 1984/1805 (S.142) : Part III, section 1, page 5124.
amended by S.I. 1985/315: Part I, section 1, page 845.

S.I. 1985/315 (S.32)  : Part I, section 1, page 845.

S.I. 1986/638    : Part I, section 3, page 2252.

S.I. 1987/383 (S.33) : Part I, section 2, page 1151.

S.I. 1988/2282  : Part III, section 3, page 6234.

S.I. 1989/888 (S.89)  : Part II, section 1, page 2490.

S.I. 1989/1769  : Part III, section 1, page 4358.

S.I. 1990/345  :Part I, section 1, page 906.

S.I. 1990/2457  : Part III, section 2, page 5846.

S.I. 1991/2892  : Part III, section 3, page 7496,

amended by S.I. 1996/1108.

S.I. 1992/2811  : Part III, section 2, page 6835.

S.I. 1993/2277  : Part III, section 1, page 5586.

S.I. 1996/1108.

*Section 30(1), (3)*

The Motor Fuel (Composition and Content) Regulations 1994, S.I. 1994/2295.

*Section 31*

*See:* The Marketing of Gas Oil (Sulphur Content) Regulations 1994, S.I. 1994/2249.

These regulations are made under s.2(2) of the European Communities Act 1972 and not under the Clean Air Act 1993. The regulations are made to implement provisions of Council Directive 93/12/EEC in relation to gas oils to which Article 2 (2) applies .

Reg.3(4) provides that ss.56–58 of the Clean Air Act 1993 shall apply for the purposes of that regulation as if it were a provision of Part IV of that Act.

*Section 36(6)*

The Control of Atmospheric Pollution (Exempted Premises) Regulations 1977, S.I. 1977/18. Part I, section 1, page 36.

*Section 37(3)*

The Control of Atmospheric Pollution (Appeals) Regulations 1977, S.I. 1977/17. Part 1, section 1, page 33.

*Section 38(1)*

The Control of Atmospheric Pollution (Research and Publicity) Regulations 1977, S.I. 1977/19. Part I, section 1, page 40.

# Regulations relating to clean air made under the European Communities Act 1972

The following regulations are made under powers conferred by s.2(2) of the European Communities Act 1972. The explanatory notes to the instruments are set out.

## *The Air Quality Standards Regulations 1989, S.I. 1989/317*

These regulations have been amended by S.I. 1995/3146.

*Explanatory note (reference to a revoked provision has been omitted):*

These Regulations, which extend throughout Great Britain, implement Council Directives No. 80/779/EEC on air quality limit values and guide values for sulphur dioxide and suspended particulates, No. 82/884/EEC on a limit value for lead in air and No. 85/203/EEC on air quality standards for nitrogen dioxide. They require the Secretary of State to ensure that the amounts in the air of suspended particulates and sulphur dioxide (considered both separately and in association), lead, and nitrogen dioxide are measured and reduced below specified limit values. They do not apply to exposure to lead in the air as a result of a person's occupation, nor to nitrogen dioxide in the atmosphere at work or within buildings.

## *The Ozone Monitoring and Information Regulations 1994, S.I. 1994/440.*

*Explanatory note:*

These Regulations implement, in the United Kingdom, Council Directive 92/72/EEC on air pollution by ozone. Reg.2 requires the Secretary of State to designate or establish measuring stations for monitoring ozone concentrations and reg.3 provides for the method to be used for measuring those concentrations. Reg.4 requires the Secretary of State to take the necessary steps to inform the public in the event of certain ozone concentration thresholds being exceeded.

## *The Marketing of Gas Oil (Sulphur Content) Regulations 1994, S.I. 1994/2249*

See reference at p.801 above under s.31 of the Clean Air Act 1993.

# List of statutory instruments made, or having effect as if made, under the Radioactive Substances Act 1993

This list contains orders and regulations made under the Radioactive Substances Act 1993 and earlier legislation relating to radioactive substances consolidated in the 1993 Act. The instruments made under the earlier legislation have effect as if made under the Radioactive Substances Act 1993 by virtue of s.17(2) of the Interpretation Act 1978.

The Radioactive Substances Act 1993 is at p.381 above.

From 1961, Statutory Instruments appear in numerical order in the blue bound volumes published annually by HMSO. The volumes are arranged into parts and sections. In this list, following the S.I. number, the part, section and page number of the bound volume is given.

*Section 8(6)*

The Radioactive Substances (Exhibitions) Exemption Order 1962, S.I. 1962/2645: Part III, page 3590.

The Radioactive Substances (Exhibitions) Exemption (Scotland) Order 1962, S.I. 1962/2768 (S.128): Part III, page 3911.

The Radioactive Substances (Storage in Transit) Exemption Order 1962, S.I. 1962/2646: Part III, page 3595.

The Radioactive Substances (Storage in Transit) Exemption (Scotland) Order 1962, S.I. 1962/2765 (S.125): Part III, page 3898.

The Radioactive Substances (Phosphatic Substances, Rare Earths etc.) Exemption Order 1962, S.I. 1962/2648: Part III, page 3601.

The Radioactive Substances (Phosphatic Substances, Rare Earths etc.) Exemption (Scotland) Order 1962, S.I. 1962/2769 (S.129): Part III, page 3917.

The Radioactive Substances (Lead) Exemption Order 1962, S.I. 1962/2649: Part III, page 3604.

The Radioactive Substances (Lead) Exemption (Scotland) Order 1962, S.I. 1962/2762 (S.122): Part III, page 3888.

The Radioactive Substances (Uranium and Thorium) Exemption Order 1962, S.I. 1962/2710: Part III, page 3672.

The Radioactive Substances (Uranium and Thorium) Exemption (Scotland) Order 1962, S.I. 1962/2766 (S.126): Part III, page 3902.

The Radioactive Substances (Prepared Uranium and Thorium Compounds) Exemption Order 1962, S.I. 1962/2711: Part III, page 3677.

The Radioactive Substances (Prepared Uranium and Thorium Compounds) Exemption (Scotland) Order 1962, S.I. 1962/2772 (S.132): Part III, page 3927.

The Radioactive Substances (Geological Specimens) Exemption Order 1962, S.I. 1962/2712: Part III, page 3682.

The Radioactive Substances (Geological Specimens) Exemption (Scotland) Order 1962, S.I. 1962/2771 (S.131): Part III, page 3923.

The Radioactive Substances (Schools etc.) Exemption Order 1963, S.I. 1963/1832: Part III, page 3426.

The Radioactive Substances (Schools etc.) Exemption (Scotland) Order 1963, S.I. 1963/1878 (S.95): Part III, page 3468.

The Radioactive Substances (Precipitated Phosphate) Exemption Order 1963, S.I. 1963/1836: Part III, page 3447.

The Radioactive Substances (Precipitated Phosphate) Exemption (Scotland) Order 1963, S.I. 1963/1882 (S.99): Part III, page 3489.

The Radioactive Substances (Electronic Valves) Exemption Order 1967, S.I. 1967/1797: Part III, section 2, page 4801.

The Radioactive Substances (Electronic Valves) Exemption (Scotland) Order 1967, S.I. 1967/1803 (S.166): Part III, section 2, page 4807.

The Radioactive Substances (Smoke Detectors) Exemption Order 1980, S.I. 1980/953: Part II, section 1, page 3149; amended by S.I. 1991/477: Part I, section 2, page 957.

The Radioactive Substances (Smoke Detectors) Exemption (Scotland) Order 1980, S.I. 1980/1599 (S.126): Part III, section 1, page 5290; amended by S.I. 1991/563 (S.48): Part I, section 2, page 1245.

The Radioactive Substances (Gaseous Tritium Light Devices) Exemption Order 1985, S.I. 1985/1047: Part II, section 2, page 3343.

The Radioactive Substances (Luminous Articles) Exemption Order 1985, S.I. 1985/1048: Part II, section 2, page 3349.

The Radioactive Substances (Testing Instruments) Exemption Order 1985, S.I. 1985/1049: Part II, section 2, page 3354.

The Radioactive Substances (Substances of Low Activity) Exemption Order 1986, S.I. 1986/1002: Part II, section 1, page 2979; amended by S.I. 1992/647: Part I, section 3, page 2290.

The Radioactive Substances (Hospitals) Exemption Order 1990, S.I. 1990/2512: Part III, section 2, page 6089; amended by S.I. 1995/2395.

*Section 11(1)*

The Radioactive Substances (Electronic Valves) Exemption Order 1967, S.I. 1967/1797: Part III, section 2, page 4801.

The Radioactive Substances (Electronic Valves) Exemption (Scotland) Order 1967, S.I. 1967/1803 (S.166): Part III, section 2, page 4807.

The Radioactive Substances (Testing Instruments) Exemption Order 1985, S.I. 1985/1049: Part II, section 2, page 3354.

*Section 15(2)*

The Radioactive Substances (Storage in Transit) Exemption Order 1962, S.I. 1962/2646: Part III, page 3595.

The Radioactive Substances (Storage in Transit) Exemption (Scotland) Order 1962, S.I. 1962/2765 (S.125): Part III, page 3898.

The Radioactive Substances (Phosphatic Substances, Rare Earths etc.) Exemption Order 1962, S.I. 1962/2648: Part III, page 3601.

The Radioactive Substances (Phosphatic Substances, Rare Earths etc.) Exemption (Scotland) Order 1962, S.I. 1962/2769 (S.129): Part III, page 3917.

The Radioactive Substances (Lead) Exemption Order 1962, S.I. 1962/2649: Part III, page 3604.

The Radioactive Substances (Lead) Exemption (Scotland) Order 1962, S.I. 1962/2762 (S.122): Part III, page 3888.

The Radioactive Substances (Uranium and Thorium) Exemption Order 1962, S.I. 1962/2710: Part III, page 3672.

The Radioactive Substances (Uranium and Thorium) Exemption (Scotland) Order 1962, S.I. 1962/2766 (S.126): Part III, page 3902.

The Radioactive Substances (Prepared Uranium and Thorium Compounds) Exemption Order 1962, S.I. 1962/2711: Part III, page 3677.

The Radioactive Substances (Prepared Uranium and Thorium Compounds) Exemption (Scotland) Order 1962, S.I. 1962/2772 (S.132): Part III, page 3927.

The Radioactive Substances (Geological Specimens) Exemption Order 1962, S.I. 1962/2712: Part III, page 3682.

The Radioactive Substances (Geological Specimens) Exemption (Scotland) Order 1962, S.I. 1962/2771 (S.131): Part III, page 3923.

The Radioactive Substances (Waste Closed Sources) Exemption Order 1963, S.I. 1963/1831: Part III, page 3422.

The Radioactive Substances (Waste Closed Sources) Exemption (Scotland) Order 1963, S.I. 1963/1877 (S.94): Part III, page 3464.

The Radioactive Substances (Schools etc.) Exemption Order 1963, S.I. 1963/1832: Part III, page 3426.

The Radioactive Substances (Schools etc.) Exemption (Scotland) Order 1963, S.I. 1963/1878 (S.95): Part III, page 3468.

The Radioactive Substances (Electronic Valves) Exemption Order 1967, S.I. 1967/1797: Part III, section 2, page 4803.

The Radioactive Substances (Electronic Valves) Exemption (Scotland) Order 1967, S.I. 1967/1803 (S.166): Part III, section 2, page 4807.

The Radioactive Substances (Smoke Detectors) Exemption Order 1980, S.I. 1980/953: Part I, section 2, page 957; amended by S.I. 1991/477: Part II, section 1, page 3149.

The Radioactive Substances (Smoke Detectors) Exemption (Scotland) Order 1980, S.I. 1980/1599 (S.126): Part I, section 2, page 1245; amended by S.I. 1991/563 (S.48): Part III, section 1, page 5290.

The Radioactive Substances (Gaseous Tritium Light Devices) Exemption Order 1985, S.I. 1985/1047: Part II, section 2, page 3343.

The Radioactive Substances (Luminous Articles) Exemption Order 1985, S.I. 1985/1048: Part II, section 2, page 3349.

The Radioactive Substances (Testing Instruments) Exemption Order 1985, S.I. 1985/1049: Part II, section 2, page 3354.

The Radioactive Substances (Substances of Low Activity) Exemption Order 1986, S.I. 1986/1002: Part II, section 1, page 2979; amended by S.I. 1992/647: Part I, section 3, page 2290.

The Radioactive Substances (Hospitals) Exemption Order 1990, S.I. 1990/2512: Part III, section 2, page 6089; amended by S.I. 1995/2395.

*Section 27(7)*

The Radioactive Substances (Appeals) Regulations 1990, S.I. 1990/2504, p.563 above .

*Section 39(1)*

The Radioactive Substances (Records of Convictions) Regulations 1992, S.I. 1992/1685: Part II, section 2, page 4366.

# Regulations under revision

At the time of preparing this Manual, revisions have been proposed to certain regulations in England and Wales. These regulations are accordingly not included in this edition of the Manual.

The references to the regulations at present in force are set out below together with references to similar regulations in Scotland.

*Water: Control of Pollution Regulations*

*England and Wales*

Following the amendments made to the Water Resources Act 1991 by the Environment Act 1995, the Department of the Environment and the Welsh Office are revising the regulations which have effect under that Act.

In a consultation paper issued on 15 February 1996, the Department of the Environment proposed that existing regulations be replaced by a single comprehensive set which would include regulations made under the amended provisions of the 1991 Act.

The following regulations would be revoked and replaced by new regulations:

The Control of Pollution (Consents for Discharges etc.) (Secretary of State Functions) Regulations 1989, S.I. 1989/1151;

The Control of Pollution (Discharges by the National Rivers Authority) Regulations 1989, S.I. 1989/1157; and

The Control of Pollution (Registers) Regulations 1989, S.I. 1989/1160.

A further consultation paper was issued by the Department on 22 August 1996 which includes draft regulations relating to discharge consents, appeals, enforcement notices and pollution control registers. The Department is to issue a separate paper in relation to anti-pollution works notices.

*Scotland*

The following regulations, relating to water pollution, have been made under Part II of the Control of Pollution Act 1974:

The Control of Pollution (Consents for Discharges) (Notices) Regulations 1984, S.I. 1984/864;

The Control of Pollution (Consents for Discharges) (Secretary of State Functions) Regulations 1984, S.I. 1984/865;

The Control of Pollution (Registers) (Scotland) Regulations 1993, S.I. 1993/1155 (S.172) .

The above three regulations have been amended by S.I. 1996/973 (S.104).

*Control of Pollution (Silage, Slurry and Agricultural Fuel Oil) Regulations 1991*

*England and Wales*

The Control of Pollution (Silage, Slurry and Agricultural Fuel Oil) Regulations 1991, S.I. 1991/324, have effect as if made under s.92 of the Water Resources Act 1991.

The Department of the Environment and the Ministry of Agriculture, Fisheries and Food reviewed these regulations to address the expiry, at the end of August 1996, of the transitional arrangements established by the regulations and other matters. Following a consultation paper issued on 20 September 1995, a further consultation paper, including a draft of amending regulations, was issued on 7 June 1996.

The Control of Pollution (Silage, Slurry and Agricultural Fuel Oil) (Amendment) Regulations 1996, S.I. 1996/2044, which amend S.I. 1991/324, came into force on 31 August 1996.

At the time of writing the Departments plan to issue a consultation paper relating to the outstanding proposed amendments to S.I. 1991/324.

*Scotland*

The Control of Pollution (Silage, Slurry and Agricultural Fuel Oil) (Scotland) Regulations 1991, S.I. 1991/346, are made under section 31A of the Control of Pollution Act 1974. Note that these regulations have been amended by S.I. 1996/973 (S.104).

Part III

# Associated Material

# Addresses

*Environment Agency*

The 24-hour emergency hotline number for reporting all environmental incidents relating to air, land and water is 0800 80 70 60.

The general enquiry line is 0645 333 111.

*Head Office*

The Head Office is responsible for overall policy and relationships with national bodies including Government. The address is:

Rivers House
Waterside Drive
Aztec West
Almondsbury
Bristol BS12 4UD
Tel: 01454 624 400
Fax: 01454 624 409.

There are eight Environment Agency regions sub-divided into areas as set out below. These provide the point of contact for local issues.

*Anglian Region*

*Regional Office*

Kingfisher House
Goldhay Way
Orton Goldhay
Peterborough PE2 5ZR
Tel: 01733 371811
Fax: 01733 231840.

*Northern Area*

Harvey Street
Lincoln LN1 lTF
Tel: 01522 513 100
Fax: 01522 512 927.

*Central Region*

Bromholme Lane
Brampton
Huntingdon PE18 8NE
Tel: 01480 414 581
Fax: 01480 413 381.

*Eastern Area*

Cobham Road
Ipswich
Suffolk IP3 9JE
Tel: 01473 727 712
Fax: 01473 724 205.

*North East Region*

*Regional Office*

Rivers House
21 Park Square South
Leeds LS1 2QG
Tel: 0113 244 0191
Fax: 0113 246 1889.

*Northumbria Area*

Tyneside House
Skinnerburn Road
Newcastle Upon Tyne NE4 7AR
Tel: 0191 203 4000
Fax: 0191 203 4004.

*Dales Area*

Coverdale House
Amy Johnson Way
Clifton Moor
York YO3 4UZ
Tel: 01904 692296
Fax: 01904 693748.

*Ridings Area*

Olympia House
Gelderd Lane
Gelderd Road
Leeds LS12 6DD
Tel: 0113 244 0191
Fax: 0113 231 2116.

*North West Region*

*Regional Office*

PO Box 12
Richard Fairclough House
Knutsford Road
Warrington WA4 1HG
Tel: 01925 653 999
Fax: 01925 415 961.

*South Area*

Mirwell
Carrington Lane
Sale M33 5NL
Tel: 0161 973 2237
Fax: 0161 973 4601.

*Central Area*

Lutra House
Dodd Way
Walton Summit
Bamber Bridge
Preston PR5 8BX
Tel: 01772 39882
Fax: 01772 627 730.

*North Area*

Chertsey Hill
London Road
Carlisle CA1 2QX
Tel: 01228 25151
Fax: 01228 49734.

*Midlands Region*

*Regional Office*

Sapphire East
550 Streetsbrook Road
Solihull
West Midlands B91 1QT
Tel: 0121 711 2324
Fax: 0121 711 5824.

*Upper Severn Area*

Hafren House
Welshpool Road
Shelton
Shrewsbury SY3 8BB
Tel: 01743 272828
Fax: 01743 272138.

*Lower Severn Area*

Riversmeet House
Newtown Industrial Estate
Northway Lane
Tewkesbury GL20 8JG
Tel: 01684 850951
Fax: 01684 293599.

*Upper Trent Area*

Sentinel House
Wellington Crescent
Fradley Park
Lichfield WS13 8RR
Tel: 01543 444141
Fax: 01543 444161.

*Lower Trent Area*

Trentside Offices
Scarrington Road
West Bridgford
Nottingham NG2 5FA
Tel: 0115 9455722
Fax: 0115 9817743.

*Southern Region*

*Regional Office*

Guildbourne House
Chatsworth Road
Worthing
Sussex BN11 1LD
Tel: 01903 832000
Fax: 01903 821832.

*Hampshire & Isle of Wight Area*

Sarum Court
Sarum Road
Winchester
Hampshire SO22 5DP
Tel: 01962 713267
Fax: 01962 841573.

*Kent Area*

Millbrook House
114 Mill Street
East Malling
Kent ME19 6BU
Tel: 01732 875587
Fax: 01732 875057.

*Sussex Area*

Rivers House
3 Liverpool Gardens
Worthing
West Sussex BN11 1TF
Tel: 01903 215835
Fax: 01903 215884.

*South West*

*Regional Office*

Manley House
Kestrel Way
Exeter EX2 7LQ
Tel: 01392 444 000
Fax: 01392 444 238.

*Cornwall Area*

Sir John Moore House
Victoria Square
Bodmin PL31 1EB
Tel: 01208 78301
Fax: 01208 78321.

*Devon Area*

Manley House
Kestrel Way
Exeter EX2 7LQ
Tel: 01392 444 000
Fax: 01392 444 238.

*North Wessex Area*

Rivers House
East Quay
Bridgwater TA6 4YS
Tel: 01278 457 333
Fax: 01278 452 985.

*South Wessex Area*

Rivers House
Sunrise Business Park
Higher Shaftesbury Road
Blandford DT11 8ST
Tel: 01258 456 080
Fax: 01258 455 998.

*Thames*

*Regional Office*

Kings Meadow House
Kings Meadow Road
Reading
Berkshire RG1 8DQ
Tel: 0118 953 5000
Fax: 0118 950 0388.

*North East Area*

Gade House
London Road
Rickmansworth
Hertfordshire WD3 1RS
Tel: 01992 635 566
Fax: 01992 645 468.

*South East Area*

Riverside Works
Fordbridge Road
Sunbury on Thames
Middlesex TW16 6AP
Tel: 01932 789 833
Fax: 01932 786 463.

*West Area*

Isis House
Howbery Park
Wallingford
Oxfordshire OX10 8BD
Tel: 01491 832 801
Fax: 0118 953 3302.

*Welsh*

Asiantaeth yr Amgylchedd/Environment Agency

*Regional & South East Area Office*

Plas yr Afon/Rivers House
St Mellons Business Park
Fortran Road
Llaneirwg/St Mellons
Caerdydd/Cardiff CF3 0LT
Ffôn/Tel: 01222 770 088
Ffacs/Fax: 01222 798 555.

*South West Area*

Llys Afon
Hawthorn Rise
Hwlffordd/Haverfordwest
Dyfed SA61 2BQ
Ffôn/Tel: 01437 760 081
Ffacs/Fax: 01437 760 881.

*Northern Area*

Ffordd Penlan
Parc Menai
Bangor
Gwynedd LL57 4BP
Ffôn/Tel: 01248 670 770
Ffacs/Fax: 01248 670 561.

*Scottish Environment Protection Agency*

The head office of SEPA is in Stirling. SEPA has three regional offices and local offices in each region.

*Head Offiee*

Erskine Court
The Castle Business Park
Stirling FK9 4TR
Tel: 01786 457700
Fax: 01786 446885.

*East Region HQ*

Clearwater House
Heriot-Watt Research Park
Avenue North
Riccarton
Edinburgh EH14 4AP
Tel: 0131 449 7296
Fax: 0131 449 7277.

*Local offices*

Arbroath
Tel: 01241 874370
Fax: 01241 430695.

Riccarton, Edinburgh
Tel: 0131 449 7296
Fax: 0131 449 7277.

Galashiels
Tel: 01896 754797
Fax: 01896 754412.

Glenrothes
Tel: 01592 759361
Fax: 01592 759446.

Perth
Tel: 01738 627989
Fax: 01738 630997

Stirling
Tel: 01786 461407
Fax: 01786 461425

*North Region HQ*

Graesser House
Fodderty Way
Dingwall IV15 9XB
Tel: 01349 862021
Fax: 01349 863987

*Local offices*

Aberdeen
Tel: 01224 248338
Fax: 01224 248591

Dingwall
Tel: 01349 862021
Fax: 01349 863987

Elgin
Tel: 01343 547663
Fax: 01343 540884

Fort William
Tel: 01397 704426
Fax: 01397 705404

Fraserburgh
Tel: 01346 510502
Fax: 01346 515444

Kirkwall
Tel: 01856 871080
Fax: 01856 871090

Lerwick
Tel: 01595 696926
Fax: 01595 696946

Stornoway
Tel: 01851 706477
Fax: 01851 703510.

Thurso
Tel: 01847 894422
Fax: 01847 893365.

*West Region HQ*

Rivers House
Murray Road
East Kilbride G75 0LA
Tel: 01355 238181
Fax: 01355 264323.

*Local offices*

Ayr
Tel: 01292 264047
Fax: 01292 611130.

Dumfries
Tel: 01387 720502
Fax: 01387 721154.

East Kilbride
Tel: 01355 238181
Fax: 01355 264323.

Lochgilphead
Tel: 01546 602876
Fax: 01546 602337.

Newton Stewart
Tel: 01671 402618
Fax: 01671 404121.

# Guidance Notes: Part I of the Environmental Protection Act 1990

*Integrated Pollution Control*

*Note:* These guidance notes are not issued under s.7(11) of the Environmental Protection Act 1990. A reference is made to the status of the process-specific guidance notes in *Integrated Pollution Control: A practical Guide* issued by the Department of the Environment and the Welsh Office (1996, DoE, ISBN 1 85112 003 3), paragraphs 7.14 to 7.20.

The following is the Environment Agency list of guidance notes. This list is current at July 1996.

The following are available from HMSO bookshops, their accredited agents, and some larger bookshops.

**Series 2**

**Chief Inspector's Guidance Notes (prepared by Her Majesty's Inspectorate of Pollution)**

**Fuel Production Processes, Combustion Processes (including Power Generation)**

S2 1.01 *Combustion processes: large boilers and furnaces 50MW(th) and over*
November 1995, £9.95 ISBN 0–11–753206–1
**Supersedes IPR 1/1**

IPR 1/2 *Combustion processes: gas turbines*
September 1994, £4.00 ISBN 0–11–752954–0

S2 1.03 *Combustion processes: compression ignition engine 50 MW(th) and over*
September 1995, £7.95 ISBN 0–11–753166–9
**Supersedes IPR 1/3**

S2 1.04 *Combustion processes: waste and recovered oil burners 3MW(th) and over*
September 1995, £7.95 ISBN 0–11–753167–7
**Supersedes IPR 1/4**

S2 1.05 *Combustion processes: combustion of fuel manufactured from or comprised of solid waste in appliances 3MW(th) and over*
September 1995, £9.95 ISBN 0–11–753168–5
**Supersedes IPR 1/5–1/8**

S2 1.06 *Carbonisation processes: coke manufacture*
September 1995, £9.95 ISBN 0–11–753176–6
**Supersedes IPR 1/9**

S2 1.07 *Carbonisation and associated processes: smokeless fuel, activated carbon and carbon black manufacture*
September 1995, £9.95 ISBN 0–11–753177–4
**Supersedes IPR 1/10**

S2 1.08 *Gasification processes: gasification of solid and liquid feedstocks*
November 1995, £9.95 ISBN 0–11–753202–9
**Supersedes IPR 1/11**

S2 1.09 *Gasification processes: refining of natural gas*
November 1995, £9.95 ISBN 0–11–753202–7
**Supersedes IPR 1/12 and 1/13**

S2 1.10 *Petroleum processes: oil refining and associated processes*
November 1995, £14.00 ISBN 0–11–753204–5
**Supersedes IPR 1/14 and 1/15**

S2 1.11 *Petroleum processes: on-shore oil production*
November 1995, £8.25 ISBN 0–11–753205–3
**Supersedes IPR 1/16**

S2 1.12 *Combustion processes: reheat and heat treatment furnaces 50MW(th) and over*
September 1995, £8.50 ISBN 0–11–753178–2
**Supersedes IPR 1/17**

**IPC Guidance Notes (prepared by the Environment Agency)**

**Mineral Industry Sector**

S2 3.01 *Cement manufacture, lime manufacture and associated processes*
August 1996
**Supersedes IPR 3/1 and IPR 3/2**

S2 3.02 *Asbestos processes*
August 1996
**Supersedes IPR 3/3**

S2 3.03 *Manufacture of glass fibres, other non-asbestos mineral fibres, glass frit, enamel frit and associated processes*
August 1996
**Supersedes IPR 3/4 and IPR 3/5**

S2 3.04 *Ceramic processes*
August 1996
**Supersedes IPR 3/6**

**Waste Disposal and Recycling Sector**

S2 5.01 *Waste incineration*
August 1996
**Supersedes IPR 5/1, 5/2, 5/3, 5/4, 5/5 and 5/11**

S2 5.02 *Making solid fuel from waste*
July 1996, £12.50 ISBN 0–11–310114–7
**Supersedes IPR 5/6**

S2 5.03 *Cleaning and regeneration of carbon*
July 1996, £12.50 ISBN 0–11–310115–5
**Supersedes IPR 5/7**

S2 5.04 *Recovery of organic solvents and oil by distillation*
July 1996, £12.50 ISBN 0–11–310116–3
**Supersedes IPR 5/8 and IPR 5/10**

**Series 1**

**Chief Inspector's Guidance Notes (prepared by Her Majesty's Inspectorate of Pollution)**

**Metals Production and Processing**

IPR2/1 *Iron and steel making processes: integrated iron and steel works*
October 1994, £13.00 ISBN 0–11–752961–3

IPR2/2 *Ferrous foundry processes*
October 1994, £10.00 ISBN 0–11–752962–1

IPR2/3 *Processes for electric arc steelmaking, secondary steelmaking and special alloy production*
October 1994, £10.00 ISBN 0–11–752963–X

IPR2/4 *Processes for the production of zinc and zinc alloys*
November 1994, £7.50 ISBN 0–11–753024–7

IPR2/5 *Processes for the production of lead and lead alloys*
November 1994, £7.50 ISBN 0–11–753025–5

IPR2/6 *Processes for the production of refractory metals*
November 1994, £6.50 ISBN 0–11–753026–3

IPR2/7 *Processes for the production, melting and recovery of cadmium, mercury and their alloys*
November 1994, £7.00 ISBN 0–11–753027–1

IPR2/8 *Processes for the production of aluminium*
November 1994, £8.50 ISBN 0–11–753028–X

IPR2/9 *Processes for the production of copper and copper alloys*
November 1994, £7.00 ISBN 0–11–753029–8

IPR2/10 *Processes for the production of precious metals and platinum group metals*
November 1994, £8.00 ISBN 0–11–753030–1

IPR2/11 *The extraction of nickel by the carbonyl process and the production of cobalt and nickel alloys*
November 1994, £7.50 ISBN 0–11–753031–X

IPR2/12 *Tin and bismuth processes*
November 1994, £7.50 ISBN 0–11–753032–8

**Chemical Industry Sector**

IPR4/1 *Petrochemical processes*
January 1993, £8.50 ISBN 0–11–752738–6

IPR4/2 *Processes for the production and use of amines, nitrile, isocyanates and pyridines*
January 1993, £9.00 ISBN 0–11–752739–4

IPR4/3 *Processes for the production or use of acetylene, aldehydes etc.*
January 1993, £8.50 ISBN 0–11–752740–8

IPR4/4 *Processes for the production or use of organic sulphur compounds, and production, use or recovery of carbon disulphide*
January 1993, £8.65 ISBN 0–11–752741–6

IPR4/5 *Batch manufacture of organic chemicals in multipurpose plant*
January 1993, £8.00 ISBN 0–11–752742–4

IPR4/6 *Production and Polymerisation of organic monomer*
January 1993, £10.00 ISBN 0–11–752743–2

IPR4/7 *Processes for the manufacture of organometallic compounds*
January 1993, £7.70 ISBN 0–11–752744–0

IPR4/8 *Pesticide processes*
January 1993, £7.50 ISBN 0–11–752745–9

IPR4/9 *Pharmaceutical processes*
January 1993, £8.50 ISBN 0–11–752746–7

IPR4/10 *Processes for the manufacture, use or release of oxides of sulphur and the manufacture, recovery, condensation or distillation of sulphuric acid or oleum*
August 1993, £12.50 ISBN 0–11–752833–1

IPR4/11 *Processes for the manufacture or recovery of nitric acid and processes involving the manufacture or release of acid-forming oxides of nitrogen*
August 1993, £9.90 ISBN 0–11–752834–X

IPR4/12 *Processes for the sulphonation or nitration of organic chemicals*
August 1993, £10.70 ISBN 0–11–752835–8

IPR4/13 *Processes for the manufacture of, or which use or release halogens, mixed halogen compounds or oxo-halocompounds*
August 1993, £11.70 ISBN 0–11–752836–6

IPR4/14 *Processes for the manufacture of, or which use or release hydrogen halides or any of their acids*
August 1993, £11.00 ISBN 0–11–752837–4

IPR4/15 *Processes for the halogenation of organic chemicals*
August 1993, £10.70 ISBN 0–11–752838–2

IPR4/16 *The manufacture of chemical fertilizers or their conversion into granules*
August 1993, £9.80 ISBN 0–11–752839–0

IPR4/17 *Bulk storage installations*
August 1993, £9.80 ISBN 0–11–752840–4

IPR4/18 *Processes for the manufacture of ammonia*
December 1993, £9.75 ISBN 0–11–752904–4

IPR4/19 *Processes involving the use, release or recovery of ammonia*
December 1993, £11.00 ISBN 0–11–752905–2

IPR4/20 *The production, and the use of, in any process for the manufacture of a chemical, phosphorus and any oxide, hydride, or halide of phosphorus*
December 1993, £12.00 ISBN 0–11–752906–0

IPR4/21 *Processes involving the manufacture, use or release of hydrogen cyanide or hydrogen sulphide*
December 1993, £7.00 ISBN 0–11–752907–9

IPR4/22 *Processes involving the use or release of antimony, arsenic, beryllium, gallium, indium,*

*lead, palladium, platinum, selenium, tellurium, thallium or their compounds*
December 1993, £12.00 ISBN 0–11–752908–7

IPR4/23 *Processes involving the use or release of cadmium or any compounds of cadmium*
December 1993, £9.50 ISBN 0–11–752909–5

IPR4/24 *Processes involving the use or release of mercury or any compounds of mercury*
December 1993, £10.50 ISBN 0–11–752910–9

IPR4/25 *Processes for the production of compounds of chromium, magnesium, manganese, nickel, and zinc*
December 1993, £11.00 ISBN 0–11–752911–7

**Waste Disposal and Recycling Sector**

IPR5/9 *Regeneration of ion exchange resins*
May 1992, £4.30 ISBN 0–11–752650–9

**Other Industries**

IPR6/1 *Application or removal of tributyltin or triphenyltin coatings at shipyards or boatyards*
March 1995, £6.00 ISBN 0–11–753079–4

IPR6/2 *Tar and bitumen processes*
March 1995, £7.00 ISBN 0–11–753080–8

IPR6/3 *Timber preservation processes*
March 1995, £6.00 ISBN 0–11–753081–6

IPR6/4 *Di-isocyanate manufacture*
March 1995, £8.00 ISBN 0–11–753082–4

IPR6/5 *Toluene di-isocyanate use and flame bonding of polyurethanes*
March 1995, £7.00 ISBN 0–11–753083–2

IPR6/6 *Textile treatment processes*
March 1995, £7.00 ISBN 0–11–753084–0

IPR6/7 *Processing of animal hides and skins*
March 1995, £7.00 ISBN 0–11–753085–9

IPR6/8 *The making of paper pulp by chemical methods*
May 1995, £8.50 ISBN 0–11–753105–7

IPR6/9 *Paper making and related processes, including mechanical pulping, re-cycled fibres and de-inking*
May 1995, £10.00 ISBN 0–11–753106–5

## Technical Guidance Notes

### Monitoring

M1 *Sampling facility requirements for the monitoring of particulates in gaseous releases to atmosphere*
March 1993, £5.00 ISBN 0–11–752777–7

M2 *Monitoring emissions of pollutants at source*
January 1994, £10.00 ISBN 0–11–752922–2

M3 *Standards for IPC Monitoring · Part 1: Standards, organisations and the measurement infrastructure*
August 1995, £11.00 ISBN 0–11–753133–2

M4 *Standards for IPC Monitoring Part 2: Standards in support of IPC Monitoring*
August 1995, £11.00 ISBN 0–11–753134–0

M5 *Routine Measurement of gamma ray air kerma rate in the environment*
September 1995, £11.00 ISBN 0–11–753132–4

### Dispersion

D1 *Guidelines on discharge stack heights for polluting emissions*
July 1993, £8.00 ISBN 0–11–752794–7

### Abatement

A1 *Guidance on effective flaring in the gas, petroleum, petrochemical and associated industries*
December 1993, £4.25 ISBN 0–11–752916–8

A2 *Pollution abatement technology for the reduction of solvent vapour emissions*
October 1994, £5.00 ISBN 0–11–752925–7

A3 *Pollution abatement technology for particulate and trace gas removal*
April 1994, £15.00 ISBN 0–11–752983–4

### Environmental

E1 *Environmental, economic and BPEO assessment principles of Integrated Pollution Control*
(To be published 1996)

### *Local Air Pollution Control System*

This note relates to the air pollution control system enforced by local authorities in England and Wales and SEPA in Scotland: see section 4 of the Environmental Protection Act 1990.

The list below sets out general guidance notes and process guidance notes. Not all of these notes constitute statutory guidance issued under s.7(11) of the Environmental Protection Act 1990.

This list is reproduced from the briefing note of the Department of the Environment entitled *Environmental Protection Act 1990, Part I: Local Air Pollution Control System* of July 1996. This note also contains additional information including reference to developments in the previous six months, which is updated every 2–3 months and sets out references to additional guidance notes to local authorities, appeal decisions and progress with the four year review of process guidance notes.

The briefing note can be obtained from the Air & Environmental Quality Division of the Department of the Environment at Room B350, Romney House, 43 Marsham Street, London SW1P 3PY.

### General guidance notes

Five general guidance notes, which explain the main controls and procedures, have been issued by the Department of the Environment. One "upgrading guidance" (UG) note has also been issued. They are as follows:

*GG1—introduction to Part I of the Act* This includes a general explanation of BATNEEC, guidance on interpreting "substantial" change, an explanation of what is meant by *existing* process, a copy of the charging scheme, and the variation notice procedures. (HMSO, £5.00, ISBN 0–11–752423–9)

*GG2—authorisations.* This contains advice for local authorities on drawing up authorisations, and includes an outline authorisation and a range of specimen conditions. (HMSO, £3.75, ISBN 0–11–752424–7)

*GG3—applications and registers.* This explains the procedures for making an application and the public register requirements. It includes a suggested application form, flow chart of the main stages in the application procedures, and a list of the names and addresses of the statutory consultees (HMSO, £4.00, ISBN 0–11–752425-5)

*GG4—interpretation of terms used in process guidance notes.* As its title suggests, this provides additional guidance on some of the terminology commonly found in the process guidance notes (HMSO, £1.90, ISBN 0–11–752426–3)

*GG5—appeals.* This summarises the procedures for making appeals and for the handling of appeals at a hearing or by exchange of written representations (HMSO, £1.90, ISBN 0–11–752427–l)

*UG-1 revisions/additions to existing process and general guidance notes: No 1.* This note contains amendments to PGs 1/1, 1/3, 1/5, 1/10, 3/2, 5/1, 5/2, 5/4, 5/5, and minor corrections to 6/3, 6/21, 6/22, 6/23, +6/26, as well as additional general guidance (HMSO, £4.35, ISBN 0–11–752661–4)

Process guidance notes

All Notes are headed "Environmental Protection Act 1990, Part I; Processes Prescribed for Air Pollution Control by Local Authorities; Secretary of State's Guidance". The heading then specifies the name of the individual process, as listed below.

Some notes have been amended by guidance note UG-1 (see previous page). The notes marked with an asterisk (*) have also been amended and copies of these amendments are available from the DoE at the address referred to in the introductory note above.

*NB.* All the notes will be subject to a 4-year review conducted by the Departments, with appropriate consultation, between mid-1994 and mid-1996. The broad aim is to issue any amendments that arise out of the review at around the fourth anniversary of the publication date of the original note. Where revised notes have been published following review, they are identified by an "#". Notes that have been cancelled as a result of the review or otherwise are marked "+". New notes are marked ○

PG1/1(95)# — waste oil burners, less than 0.4MW net rated thermal input (ISBN 0–11–753194–4, £5.25)

PG1/2(95)# — waste oil or recovered oil burners, less than 3MW net rated thermal input (ISBN 0–11–753195–2, £4.50)

PG1/3(95)# — boilers and furnaces, 20–50MW net rated thermal input (ISBN 0–11–753146–4, £4.50)

PG1/4(95)# — gas turbines, 20–50MW net rated thermal input (ISBN 0–11–753147–2, £4.50)

PG1/5(95)# — compression ignition engines, 20–50MW net rated thermal input (ISBN 0–11–753220–7. £5.25)

PG1/6(91)+ — tyre and rubber combustion processes between 0.4 and 3MW net rated thermal input (ISBN 0–11–752404–2, £2.70) [superseded by PG1/12(95)]

PG1/7(91)+ — straw combustion processes between 0.4 and 3MW net rated thermal input (ISBN 0–11–752401–8, £2.70) [superseded by PG1/12(95)]

PG1/8(91)+ — wood combustion processes between 0.4 and 3MW net rated thermal input (ISBN 0–11–752406–9, £2 70) [superseded by PG1/12(95)]

PG1/9(91)+ — poultry litter combustion processes between 0.4 and 3MW net rated thermal input (ISBN 0–11–752399–2, £2.70) [superseded by PG1/12(95)]

PG1/10(92) — waste derived fuel combustion processes less than 3MW (ISBN 0–11–752594–4. £3.45)

PG1/11(92) — reheat and heat treatment furnaces, 20–50MW net rated thermal input (ISBN 0–11–752670–3, £2.75)

PG1/12(95)○ — combustion of fuel manufactured from or comprised of solid waste in appliances between 0.4 and 3MW net rated thermal input (ISBN 0–11–753196–0, £5.25)

PG2/1(96)# — furnaces for the extraction of non-ferrous metal from scrap (ISBN 0–11–753247–9, £5.25)

| | |
|---|---|
| PG2/2(96)# | — hot dip galvanising processes (ISBN 0–11–753248–7, £5.25) |
| PG2/3(96)# | — electrical and rotary furnaces (ISBN 0–11–753249–5, £5.25) |
| PG2/4(96)# | — Iron, steel and non-ferrous metal foundry processes (ISBN 0–11–753250–9, £7.00) |
| PG2/5(96)# | — hot and cold blast cupolas (ISBN 0–11-753251–7, £5.25) |
| PG2/6(96)# | — aluminium and aluminium alloy processes (ISBN 0–11–753252–5, £5.25) |
| PG2/7(96)# | — zinc and zinc alloy processes (ISBN 0–11–753253–3, £5.25) |
| PG2/8(96)# | — copper and copper alloy processes (ISBN 0–11–753254–1, £5.25) |
| PG2/9(96)# | — metal decontamination processes (ISBN 0–11–753255–X, £5.25) |
| PG3/1(95)# | — blending, packing, loading and use of bulk cement (ISBN 0–11–753148–0, £4.50) |
| PG3/2(95)# | — manufacture of heavy clay goods and refractory goods (ISBN 0–11–753197-9, £4.50) |
| PG3/3(95)# | — glass (excluding lead glass) manufacturing processes (ISBN 0–11–753149-9, £4.50) |
| PG3/4(95)# | — lead glass manufacturing processes (ISBN 0–11–753150–2, £4.50) |
| PG3/5(95)# | — coal, coke, coal product and petroleum coke processes (ISBN 0–11–753221-5, £4.50) |
| PG3/6(95)# | — processes for the polishing or etching of glass or glass products using hydrofluoric acid (ISBN 0–11–753151–0, £4.00) |
| PG3/7(95)# | — exfoliation of vermiculite and expansion of perlite (ISBN 0–11–753222–3, £4.50) |
| PG3/8(96)# | — quarry processes (ISBN 0–11–753279–7, £4.75) |
| PG3/9(91) | — sand drying and cooling (ISBN 0–11–752464–6, £2.70) |
| PG3/10(91)+ | — china and ball clay (ISBN 0–11–752470–0, £2.70) [superseded by PG3/17(95)] |
| PG3/11(91)+ | — spray drying of ceramic materials (ISBN 0–11–752468–9, £2.70) [superseded by PG3/17(95)] |
| PG3/12(95)# | — plaster processes (ISBN 0–11–753223–1, £4.50) |
| PG3/13(95)# | — asbestos processes (ISBN 0–11–753224–X, £5.25) |
| PG3/14(95)# | — lime processes (ISBN 0–11–753225–8, £4.50) |
| PG3/15(96)○ | — mineral drying and roadstone coating processes (ISBN 0–11–753278–9, £5.75) |
| PG3/16(96)○ | — mobile crushing and screening processes (ISBN 0–11–753277–0, £5.25) |
| PG3/17(95)○– | — china and ball clay processes including the spray drying of ceramics (ISBN 0–11–753226–6, £5.00) |
| PG4/1(94) | — processes for the surface treatment of metals (ISBN 0–11–753072–7, £4.50) |
| PG5/1(95)# | — clinical waste incineration processes under 1 tonne an hour (ISBN 0–11–753152–9, £6.25) |
| PG5/2(95)# | — crematoria (ISBN 0–11–753153–7, £5.75) |
| PG5/3(95)# | — animal carcase incineration processes under 1 tonne an hour (ISBN 0–11–753154–5, £5.25) |
| PG5/4(95)# | — general waste incineration processes under 1 tonne an hour (ISBN 0–11–753155–3, £5.25) |
| PG5/5(91) | — sewage sludge incineration processes under 1 tonne an hour (ISBN 0–11–752400–X, £2.70) [no revision of 1991 note planned; no plant under 1 te/hr currently known to exist] |
| PG6/1(91) | — animal by product rendering (ISBN 0–11–752461–1, £2.70) |
| PG6/2(95)# | — manufacture of timber and wood-based products (ISBN 0–11–753198–7, £4.00) |
| PG6/3(91)* | — chemical treatment of timber and wood-based products (ISBN 0–11–752402–6, £2.70) |

PG6/4(95)#    — processes for the manufacture of particleboard and fibreboard (ISBN 0–11–753156–1, £4.50)

PG6/5(91)#    — maggot breeding processes (ISBN 0–11–753227–4, £6.00)

PG6/6(91)+    — fur breeding processes (ISBN 0–11–752391–7 £2.70) [fur processes exempted from EPA Part I by SI 1993/1749]

PG6/7(91)     — printing and coating of metal packaging (ISBN 0–11–752462–X, £3.75)

PG6/8(91)     — textile and fabric coating and finishing processes (ISBN 0–11–752466–2, £3.40)

PG6/9(96)#    — manufacture of coating powder (ISBN 0–11–753280–0, £4.50)

PG6/10(92)    — coating manufacturing (ISBN 0–11–752595–2, £3.45)

PG6/11(92)    — manufacture of printing ink (ISBN 0–11–752596–0, £2.75)

PG6/12(91)    — production of natural sausage casings, tripe, chitterlings and other boiled green offal products (ISBN 0–11–752465–4, £1.90)

PG6/13(91)*   — coil coating processes (ISBN 0–11–752472–7, £3.40)

PG6/14(91)    — film coating processes (ISBN 0–11–752477–8, £3.40)

PG6/15(91)*   — coating in drum manufacturing and reconditioning processes (ISBN 0–11–752475–1, £3.75)

PG6/16(92)*   — printworks (ISBN 0–11–752597–9, £1.75)

PG6/17(92)    — printing of flexible packaging (ISBN 0–11–752598–7, £2.75)

PG6/18(92)    — paper coating (ISBN 0–11–752599–5, £2.75)

PG6/19(92)    — fish meal and fish oil (ISBN 0–11–752600–2 £2.75)

PG6/20(92)    — paint application in vehicle manufacturing (ISBN 0–11–752601–0, £3.90)

PG6/21(92)    — hide and skin processes (ISBN 0–11–752602–9, £2.75)

PG6/22(92)    — leather finishing (ISBN 0–11–752603–7, £2.75)

PG6/23(94)    — coating of metal and plastic (second *revised* edition—ISBN 0–11–752604–5, £4.50)

PG6/24(92)    — pet food manufacturing (ISBN 0–11–752605–3, £2.75)

PG6/25(92)    — vegetable oil extraction and fat and oil refining (ISBN 0–11–752606–1, £2.75)

PG6/26(92)    — animal feed compounding (ISBN 0–11–752607–X, £2.75)

PG6/27(92)    — vegetable matter drying (ISBN 0–11–752608–8, £2.75)

PG6/28(92)    — rubber processes (ISBN 0–11–752609–6, £3.85)

PG6/29(92)*   — di-isocyanate processes (ISBN 0–11–752610–X, £1.95)

PG6/30(92)    — production of compost for mushrooms (ISBN 0–11–752611–8, £2.75)

PG6/31(96)#   — powder coating (including sheradizing) (ISBN 0–11–753282–7, £5.25)

PG6/32(92)    — adhesive coating (ISBN 0–11–752613–4, £4.35)

PG6/33(92)*   — wood coating (ISBN 0–11–752614–2, £3.90)

PG6/34(92)*   — respraying of road vehicles (ISBN 0–11–752615–0, £3.45)

PG6/35(92)#   — metal and other thermal spraying processes (ISBN 0–11–753281–9, £5.25)

PG6/36(92)    — tobacco processing (ISBN 0–11–752617–7, £2.75)

PG6/37(92)    — knackers yards (ISBN 0–11–752618–5, £1.95) [knackers yards were exempted from EPA Part I by SI 1994/1271]

PG6/38(92)    — blood processing (ISBN 0–11–752619–3, £1.95)

PG6/39(92)    — animal by-product dealers (ISBN 0–11–752620–7, £1.95)

PG6/40(94)    — coating and recoating of aircraft and aircraft components (ISBN 0–11–753040–9, £4.50)

PG6/41 (94)   — coating and recoating of rail vehicles (ISBN 0–11–753041–7, £4.50)

PG6/42(94)    — bitumen and tar processes (ISBN 0–11–753042–5, £3.60)

# Waste Management Papers

A list of new series waste management papers is set out below. This list is not definitive and other waste management papers which have been published in the first series and new series may also be available. All waste management papers are published by HMSO.

This list is compiled from information provided by the Wastes Regulatory Policy Group, Wastes Technical Division of the Environment Agency.

*New Series*

| No. | Subject | Publication date | ISBN |
|-----|---------|------------------|------|
| 1 | A review of options | 2nd edition, 1992 | 0 11 752644 4 |
| 2/3 | *See no. 29* | | |
| 4 | Licensing of waste management facilities | March 1994 | 0 11 752727 0 |
| 4A | Licensing of metal recycling sites | September 1995 | 0 11 753064 6 |
| 6 | Polychlorinated biphenyl (PCB) waste— a technical memorandum on reclamation, treatment and disposal | December 1994 | 0 11 752952 4 |
| 26A | Landfill completion | March 1994 | 0 11 752807 2 |
| 26B | Landfill design, construction and operational practice | November 1995 | 0 11 753185 5 |
| 26C | *Now part of 26B* | | |
| 27 | Landfill gas—a technical memorandum on the monitoring and control of landfill gas | 2nd edition, 1991 | 0 11 752488 3 |
| 28 | Recycling—a memorandum providing guidance to local authorities on recycling | 1991 | 0 11 752445 X |
| 29 | Waste management planning—principles and practice. *Note*: This paper began as a waste management paper but was published free-standing, rather than in the WMP series. | December 1995 | 0 11 753209 6 |

*Provisional list of forthcoming waste management papers*

| No | Subject | Draft publication timetable |
|----|---------|------------------------------|
| 7 | Oily wastes | *Not known* |
| 11 | Metal-finishing waste | *Not known* |
| 16 | Wood preservatives | 1996 |
| 23 | Special waste | 1996 |
| 25 | Clinical waste | 1996 |
| 26D | Landfill monitoring | 1996 |
| 26E | Landfill restoration | 1996 |
| 26F | Landfill co-disposal | 1996 |
| 27X | Landfill gas [supplementary note] | 1996 |
| 30 | CFCs | 1996 |
| 31 | Landspreading wastes | *Not known* |
| 32 | Composting | *Not known* |

# Statutory Guidance

*Section 4 of the Environment Act 1995*

This section provides that the Ministers shall give guidance to the Environment Agency with respect to objectives for the Agency including guidance on the contribution of the Agency towards attaining the objective of sustainable development.

A draft of proposed guidance under this section was laid before Parliament by the Government on 19 June 1996. In accordance with the requirements of section 4 guidance cannot be given until after 40 sitting days have elapsed. This period will not expire until after the commencement of the 1996–7 session.

In a letter of 19 June 1996, the Department of the Environment set out that, subject to Parliamentary approval, it is proposed to issue the guidance to the Environment Agency with an explanatory document which restates the principles of sustainable development, provides non-statutory guidance on particular functions and offers a commentary on the Agency's duty to take account of likely costs and benefits.

*Section 31 of the Environment Act 1995*

This section provides that the Secretary of State shall give guidance to SEPA with respect to objectives for the Agency including guidance on the contribution of the Agency towards attaining the objective of sustainable development.

A draft of proposed guidance under this section was laid before Parliament by the Government on 12 July 1996. In accordance with the requirements of section 31 guidance cannot be given until after 40 sitting days have elapsed. This period will not expire until after the commencement of the 1996–7 session.

*Part IIA of the Environmental Protection Act 1990 (inserted by section 57 of the Environment Act 1995)*

A final working draft of statutory guidance under the contaminated land provisions of Part IIA of the Environmental Protection Act 1990 was issued by the Department of the Environment on 26 June 1996. The draft relates to guidance in respect of England, Scotland and Wales under sections 78A(2), (5) and (6), 78B(2), 78E(5), 78F(6) and (7), 78P(2)(b) and in accordance with section 78YA of the 1990 Act.

Following a round of informal consultations on the final working draft, the Department of the Environment intend to issue a package for consultation, allowing 3 months for consultation.

At the time of writing, it is planned to present draft guidance to Parliament for approval in the 1996–7 session with a view to implementing section 57 of the Environment Act 1995 early in 1997.

The Department of the Environment
The Scottish Office
Welsh Office/Y Swyddfa Gymreig

# Waste Management: The Duty of Care: A Code of Practice

## ENVIRONMENTAL PROTECTION ACT 1990 SECTION 34

**CONTENTS**

| | Page |
|---|---|
| **Introduction** | 825 |
| *THE CODE OF PRACTICE* | |
| **STEP BY STEP GUIDANCE** | |
| Identify and describe the waste | 826 |
| Keep the waste safely | 829 |
| Transfer to the right person | 830 |
| Receiving waste | 833 |
| Checking up | 835 |
| Expert help and advice | 837 |
| The duty of care and scrap metal | 838 |
| **SUMMARY CHECKLIST** | 842 |
| **ANNEXES** | |
| A. The law on the duty of care | 843 |
| B. Responsibilities under the duty of care | 845 |
| C. Regulations on keeping records | 847 |
| D. Other legal controls | 850 |
|    i. Waste management licensing | 850 |
|    ii. The registration of waste carriers | 850 |
|    iii. The registration of brokers | 851 |
|    iv. Special waste | 852 |
|    v. Road transport of dangerous substances | 852 |
|    vi. International waste transfers | 852 |
|    vii. Health and safety | 853 |
| E. Glossary of terms used in this code of practice | 853 |
| **Appendix:** The definition of waste | 855 |

# INTRODUCTION

i. This code of practice consists of the guidance in Sections 1–7 together with their related Annexes. It is issued by the Secretary of State for the Environment, the Secretary of State for Scotland and the Secretary of State for Wales in accordance with section 34(7) and (8) of the Environmental Protection Act 1990[1] ("the 1990 Act"). This code supersedes that issued in December 1991 which is hereby revoked. This introduction is not part of the code of practice.

ii. Section 34 of the 1990 Act imposes a duty of care on persons concerned with **controlled waste.** The duty applies to any person who produces, imports, carries, keeps, treats or disposes of controlled waste, or as a broker has control of such waste. Breach of the duty of care is an offence, with a penalty of an unlimited fine if convicted on indictment.

iii. Waste poses a threat to the environment and to human health if it is not managed properly and recovered or disposed of safely. The duty of care is designed to be an essentially self regulating system which is based on good business practice. It places a duty on anyone who in any way has a responsibility for controlled waste to ensure that it is managed properly and recovered or disposed of safely. The purpose of this code is to provide practical guidance for waste holders and brokers subject to the duty of care. It has been revised to take account of changes in waste management law since the code was first issued in December 1991. These changes include the application of the duty of care to the scrap metal industry from 1 October 1995.

iv. The code recommends a series of steps which should normally be enough to meet the duty. The code cannot cover every contingency. The legal obligation is to comply with the duty of care itself rather than with the code. Annex A[2] gives a detailed explanation of the law.

v. The Code makes reference to the Environment Agency and to the Scottish Environment Protection Agency. In England and Wales, local authorities' waste regulation functions are transferred to the Environment Agency by section 2 of the Environment Act 1995 with effect from I April 1996. Until that date, waste regulation is a function of the local authorities designated in section 30(1) of the Environmental Protection Act 1990.

vi. In Scotland, local authorities' waste regulation functions are transferred to the Scottish Environment Protection Agency by section 21 of the Environment Act 1995 with effect from 1 April 1996.

vii The code is divided into:

—Sections 1-7: Step by step guidance on following the duty;

—A summary check list; and

Annexes A:  the law on the duty of care;

B:  responsibilities under the duty;

C:  Regulations on keeping records;

D:  an outline of some other legal requirements; and

E:  a glossary of terms used in the code.

viii. Guidance on the definition of waste, which does not form part of the code of practice, is contained in the Appendix.

*Is it "waste"?*

ix. The duty of care applies to waste which is controlled waste (see paragraphs 1.1–1.2 below). The first question, therefore, is whether any particular substance is "waste". Since 1 May 1994 the common European definition of waste in the Framework Directive[1] on waste has been in force. The legal definition of waste is:

"any substance or object . . . which the producer[2] or the person in possession of it discards or intends or is required to discard."

---

[1] P.118 above.      [2] P.843 below.

x. Whether or not a substance is waste must be determined on the facts of the case; and interpretation of the law is a matter for the Courts. The Departments[3] have provided guidance on the interpretation of the definition of waste in DOE Circular 11/94.[4] In the Departments' view the purpose of the Framework Directive is to treat as waste, and accordingly to supervise the collection, transport, storage, recovery and disposal of, those substances or objects which fall out of the commercial cycle or out of the chain of utility. The Departments have suggested, therefore, that to determine whether a substance or object has been discarded the following question may be asked:—

Has the substance or object been discarded so that it is no longer part of the normal commercial cycle or chain of utility?

xi. An answer of "no" to this question should provide a reasonable indication that the substance or object concerned is not waste. As indicated, however, the purpose of the Framework Directive is to supervise the collection, transport, storage, recovery and disposal of waste; and these are activities which themselves may be of a commercial nature. A distinction must be drawn, therefore, between the normal commercial cycle and the commercial cycle which exists for the purpose of collecting, transporting, storing, recovering and disposing of waste. It is also essential to bear in mind that a substance or object does not cease to be waste as soon as it is transferred for collection, transport, storage, recovery or disposal. A substance or object which is waste at the point of its original production should be regarded as waste until it is recovered or disposed of. **The Appendix**[4A] provides a summary of the main questions which need to be addressed in reaching a view on whether a particular substance or object is waste; and when it may cease to be waste.

STEP BY STEP GUIDANCE

SECTION 1

IDENTIFY AND DESCRIBE THE CONTROLLED WASTE

**1.1.** The duty of care applies to anyone who is the holder[5] of controlled waste.[6] The only exception to this is for the occupiers of domestic property for the household waste which comes from their home. Anyone subject to the duty of care who has some "controlled waste" must identify and describe the kind of waste it is.

*Is it "controlled waste"?*

**1.2.** "Controlled waste" means waste from households,[7] commerce or industry. At present, the main kinds of waste that are not "controlled waste" are waste from agricultural premises, waste from mines and quarries, explosives and most radioactive waste. However, the Departments intend to issue a consultation paper containing proposals for the extension of the definition of controlled waste to include certain categories of agricultural waste and of mines and quarries waste. Unless the context indicates otherwise, subsequent references in the code to "waste" should be read as references to "controlled waste".

*What are the problems of the waste?*

**1.3.** Waste cannot be simply divided between the safe and the hazardous. There are safe ways of dealing with any waste. Equally, any waste can be hazardous to human health or the environment if it is wrongly managed. Deciding whether any waste poses a problem requires consideration not

---

[1] Council Directive 75/442/EEC as amended by Directives 91/156/EEC and 91/692/EEC.

[2] "Producer" means anyone whose activities produce waste or who carries out pre-processing, mixing or other operations resulting in a change in its nature or composition.

[3] The Department of the Environment, the Welsh Office and The Scottish Office Agriculture, Environment and Fisheries Department.

[4] Welsh Office Circular 26/94 and The Scottish Office Environment Department Circular 10/94.

[4A] P.855 below.

[5] "Holder" means a person who imports, produces, carries, keeps, treats, or disposes of controlled waste or, as a broker, has control of it.

[6] Only waste which is "Directive waste" is treated as controlled waste - see the glossary of terms at Annex E, p.853 below.

[7] Householders are exempt from the duty of care for their own household waste (Annex A paragraph A.9).

only of its composition but of what will happen to it. For most waste it is not necessary to know more than what it is in very general terms. But subsequent holders must be provided with a description of the waste that is full enough to enable them to manage the waste properly. Even everyday items may cause problems in handling or treatment.

**1.4.** In looking for waste problems it may help to ask such questions as:

(a) does the waste need a special container to prevent its escape or to protect it from the elements;

(b) what type of container suits it and what material can the container be made of;

(c) can it safely be mixed with any other waste or are there wastes with which it should not be mixed;

(d) can it safely be crushed and transferred from one vehicle to another;

(e) can it safely be incinerated or are there special requirements for its incineration, such as minimum temperature and combustion time;

(f) can it be disposed of safely in a landfill site with other waste; and

(g) is it likely to change its physical state during storage or transport?

**1.5.** Anything unusual in waste can pose a problem. So can anything which is out of proportion. Ordinary household waste, and waste from shops or offices, often contains small amounts of potentially hazardous substances. This may not matter if they are mixed in a large quantity of other waste. What should be identified as potential problems in a consignment of waste, are significant quantities of an unexpected substance, or unusual amounts of an expected substance.

**1.6.** Note that certain particularly dangerous or difficult wastes are subject to strict legal controls quite apart from and additional to the requirements of the duty of care. These wastes are known as "special wastes" (see **Annex D** paragraphs D.16-D.18[1]).

*What goes in a description?*

**1.7.** A transfer note must be completed, signed and kept by the parties involved if waste is transferred. This is a requirement of the Environmental Protection (Duty of Care) Regulations 1991[2]("the 1991 Regulations"). Any breach of the 1991 Regulations is an offence (see **Annex C**[3] on keeping records). Amongst other things, the transfer note must state:

(a) the quantity of waste transferred—most waste management companies, in particular landfill operators, receive quantities of waste by weight. Wherever possible, therefore, a transfer note should record the weight of waste transferred;

(b) how it is packed—whether loose or in a container; and

(c) if in a container, the kind of container.

**1.8.** There must also be a description of the waste. This may be provided separately or combined as a single document with the transfer note. At the time of the publication of this code, a national waste classification scheme is the subject of consultation. One of the aims of the scheme is to provide a comprehensive list of waste types which may be generally accepted as the reference point for describing waste. The description of waste should, therefore, wherever possible refer to the appropriate entry in the national waste classification scheme when, subject to consultation, it is introduced. It is good practice to label drums or similar closed containers with a description of the waste. Under the 1991 Regulations the parties must keep the transfer note and the description for two years. The description should always mention any **special problems**, requirements or knowledge. In addition it should include some combination of:

(a) the type of premises or business from which the waste comes;

(b) the name of the substance or substances;

(c) the process that produced the waste; and

---

[1] P.852 below.  [2] P.650 above.  [3] P.847 below.

(d) a chemical and physical analysis.

1.9. The description must provide enough information to enable subsequent holders to avoid mismanaging the waste. When writing a description it is open to the holder to ask the manager who will handle the waste what he needs to know. For most wastes, those that need only a simple description, either 1.8(a) or (b) above will do. However, in some cases it may not be enough simply to describe the waste as "household", "commercial" or "industrial" waste without providing a clearer idea of what the substance is or providing details about the premises from which it originated. Each element of the description is dealt with in paragraphs 1.11–1.17 below.

**Special problems**

1.10. The description should always contain any information which might affect the handling of the waste. This should include:

(a) special problems identified under paragraphs 1.3 to 1.6 above;

(b) any information, advice or instructions about the handling, recovery or disposal of the waste given to the holder by the Environment Agency or by the Scottish Environment Protection Agency[1] or the suppliers of material or equipment;

(c) details of problems previously encountered with the waste;

(d) changes to the description since a previous load.

*A) Source of the waste: type of premises or business*

1.11. It may sometimes be enough to describe the source of the waste by referring either to the use of the premises where the waste is produced or to the occupation of the waste producer.

1.12. Such a "source of waste" description is recommended as the commonsense simple description where businesses produce a mixture of wastes none of which has special handling or disposal requirements; or where there are no special handling or disposal requirements which cannot be identified from such a simple description. Such a description must make it clear what type of wastes are produced and the contents of the wastes; and their proportions must be only such as might be expected.

*B) Name of the substance*

1.13. The waste may be described by saying what it is made of. This may be in physical and chemical terms or by the common name of the waste where this is equally helpful. Such a description by name is recommended for waste composed of a single simple material or a simple mixture.

*C) Process producing the waste*

1.14. The waste may be described by saying how it was produced. Such a description would include details of materials used or processed, the equipment used and the treatment and changes that produced the waste. If necessary this would include information obtained from the supplier of the materials and equipment.

1.15. This should form part of the description for most industrial wastes and some commercial wastes.

*D) Chemical and physical analysis*

1.16. A description based on the process producing the waste (C) will not go far enough where the holder does not know enough about the source of the waste. It will often not be adequate where:

[1] In the case of processes regulated under Integrated Pollution Control in England and Wales, the Environment Agency may give advice to the producer of waste that is relevant to its subsequent management prior to its final disposal or treatment. In Scotland the Integrated Pollution control authority is the Scottish Environment Protection Agency. This advice should also be included in the description.

(a) wastes, especially industrial wastes, from different activities or processes are mixed; or

(b) the activity or process alters the properties or composition of the materials put in.

**1.17.** For such wastes an analysis will usually be needed. In cases of doubt, the holder may find it helpful to consult the intended waste manager as to whether he needs an analysis to manage the waste properly. Where it is necessary the holder should detail the physical and chemical composition of the waste itself including, where different substances are mixed, their dilutions or proportions. The holder might either provide this information himself or obtain a physical or chemical analysis from a laboratory or from a waste management contractor.

SECTION 2

## KEEP THE WASTE SAFELY

*The problem*

**2.1.** All waste holders must act to keep waste safe against:

(a) corrosion or wear of waste containers;

(b) accidental spilling or leaking or inadvertent leaching from waste unprotected from rainfall;

(c) accident or weather breaking contained waste open and allowing it to escape;

(d) waste blowing away or falling while stored or transported;

(e) scavenging of waste by vandals, thieves, children, trespassers or animals.

**2.2.** Holders should protect waste against these risks while it is in their possession. They should also protect it for its future handling requirements. Waste should reach not only its next holder but a licensed facility or other appropriate destination without escape. Where waste is to be mixed immediately, for example in a transfer station, a civic amenity site or a municipal collection vehicle, it only needs to be packed well enough to reach that immediate destination. Preventing its escape after that stage is up to the next holder. However, there are wastes that may need to reach a disposal or treatment site in their original containers. For example, drummed waste. In such cases, holders will need to know through how many subsequent hands; under what conditions; for how long; and to what ultimate treatment their waste will go in order to satisfy themselves that it is packed securely enough to reach its final destination intact. If an intermediate holder alters waste in any way, by mixing, treating or repacking it, then he will be responsible for observing all this guidance on keeping waste safe.

*Storing waste securely*

**2.3.** Security precautions at sites where waste is stored should prevent theft, vandalism or scavenging of waste. Holders should take particular care to secure waste material attractive to scavengers, for example, building and demolition materials and scrap metal. Special care should also be taken to secure waste which has a serious risk attached to it, for example certain types of clinical waste. Waste holders should undertake regular reviews of the waste in their possession to ensure that it has not been disturbed or tampered with.

**2.4.** Segregation of different categories of waste where they are produced may be necessary to prevent the mixing of incompatible wastes. For example, avoiding reactions in mixtures. Segregation may assist the disposal of waste to specialist outlets. Where segregation is practised on sites, the waste holder should ensure that his employees and anyone else handling waste there are aware of the locations and uses of each segregated waste container.

*Containers*

**2.5.** Waste handed over to another person should be in some sort of container, which might include a skip. The only reasonable exception would be loose material loaded into a vehicle and then covered sufficiently to prevent escape before being moved. Waste containers should suit the material put in them.

**2.6.** It is good practice to label drums or similar closed containers with a note of the contents when stored or handed over. This could be a copy of the waste description. To avoid confusion, old labels should be removed from drums which are reused.

*Waste left for collection*

**2.7.** Waste left for collection outside premises should be in containers that are strong and secure enough to resist not only wind and rain but also animal disturbance, especially for food waste. All containers left outside for collection will therefore need to be secured or sealed. For example, drums with lids, bags tied up, skips covered. To minimise the risks, waste should not be left outside for collection longer than is necessary. Waste should only be put out for collection on or near the advertised collection times.

SECTION 3

TRANSFER TO THE RIGHT PERSON

**3.1.** Waste may be handed on only to authorised persons or to persons for authorised transport purposes. This **Section** of the code advises on who these persons are; and what checks to carry out *before* making an arrangement or contract for transferring waste.

**3.2.** Section 34(3) of the 1990 Act[1] sets out those who are authorised persons. The list of authorised persons is:

(a) any authority which is a waste collection authority for the purposes of Part II of the 1990 Act;

(b) any person who is the holder of a waste management licence under section 35 of the 1990 Act;

(c) any person who does not need a waste management licence because the activity he carries out is exempt from licensing by virtue of regulation 16 or 17 of[2] and Schedule 3 to[3] the Waste Management Licensing Regulations 1994 ("the 1994 Regulations");

(d) any person who is registered as a carrier of controlled waste under section 2 of the Control of Pollution (Amendment) Act 1989[4] ("the 1989 Act");

(e) any person exempt from registration as a carrier of controlled waste under regulation 2 of the Controlled Waste (Registration of Carriers and Seizure of Vehicles) Regulations 1991;[5] and

(f) In Scotland, a waste disposal authority acting in accordance with a resolution made under section 54 of the Environmental Protection Act 1990 (see paragraphs 3.20–3.21).

**3.3.** The list of authorised transport purposes is set out in section 34(4) of the 1990 Act which is reproduced at the end of **Annex A**.[6]

**3.4.** It should be noted that it is an offence under Regulation 20 of the 1994 Regulations[7] (subject to various provisions) for anyone to arrange on behalf of another person for the disposal or recovery of controlled waste if he is not a registered broker. Anyone subject to the duty of care must ensure that insofar as they use a broker when transferring waste, they use a registered broker (that is any person registered as a waste broker in accordance with regulation 20 of the 1994 Regulations) or one exempt from the registration requirements (in accordance with regulation 20 of the 1994 Regulations) (see Annex paragraphs D. 11–D.15[8]).

*Public waste collection*

**3.5.** Local authorities collect waste from households and from some commercial premises. They do this either with their own labour or using private contractors who will be registered carriers (**Annex D** paragraphs D.7–D.10). Private persons are exempt from the duty in connection with their own household waste produced on their premises (**Annex A** paragraph A.9[9]). If there is any

---

[1] P.119 above.
[2] P.688 above.
[3] P.697 above.
[4] P.73 above.
[5] P.630 above.

[6] S.34 is at p.117 above.
[7] P.692 above.
[8] P.851 below.
[9] P.844 below.

doubt about whether or not a particular waste can go in the normal collection, the producer should ask the local authority (the borough or district council or in Scotland on 1 April 1996, the council, or in Wales on 1 April 1996, the county or county borough council).

## Using a waste carrier

**3.6.** A waste holder or broker may transfer waste to someone who transports it—a waste carrier who may or may not also be a waste manager (**Annex D** paragraphs D.7–D.10). Subject to certain exemptions, anyone carrying waste in the course of their business, or in any other way for profit, must be registered with the Environment Agency or with the Scottish Environment Protection Agency. The Agencies' register of carriers is open to public inspection. For the purpose of the duty of care, holders may use these registers as a reference list of carriers who are authorised to transport waste. However, inclusion on the Agencies' register is *not* a recommendation or guarantee of a carrier's suitability to accept any particular type of waste. The holder or broker should remain alert to any sign that the waste may not be legally dealt with by a carrier.

**3.7.** Anyone intending to transfer waste to a carrier will need to check that the carrier is registered or is exempt from registration. A registered carrier's authority for transporting waste is either his certificate of registration or a copy of his certificate of registration *if it was provided by the Agencies (or before 1 April 1996 by the relevant waste regulation authority)*. The certificate or copy certificate will show the date on which the carrier's registration expires. All copy certificates must be numbered and marked to show that they are copies and have been provided by the Agencies (or before 1 April 1996 by the relevant waste regulation authority). Photocopies are not valid and **do not** provide evidence of the carrier's registration.

**3.8.** In all cases other than those involving repeated transfers of waste, the holder should ask to see, and should check the details of, the carrier's certificate or copy certificate of registration. In addition, before using any carrier for the first time, the holder should check with the Environment Agency or the Scottish Environment Protection Agency that the carrier's registration is still valid, even if his certificate appears to be current. The holder should provide the appropriate Agency with the carrier's name and registration number as shown on the certificate.

**3.9.** In practice, the only exempt carriers who might take waste from a holder are:

(a) charities and voluntary organisations;

(b) waste collection authorities (local authorities) collecting any waste themselves (though an authority's contractors are not exempt); waste disposal authorities and the Agencies;

(c) wholly owned subsidiaries of British Rail when carrying waste by rail;[1]

(d) ship operators where waste is to be disposed of under licence at sea;

(e) persons who are authorised under the Animal By-Products Order 1992 to hold or deal with animal waste or the holder of a knackers yard licence.[2]

**3.10.** It should be noted that animal waste which is collected and transported in accordance with Schedule 2 to the Animal By-Products Order 1992 is not controlled waste for the purposes of the duty of care (see **Annex A** paragraph A. 10[3]).

**3.11.** Charities and voluntary organisations, waste collection, disposal authorities and the Agencies and British Rail subsidiaries need to be registered as exempt carriers in the Agencies' register of professional collectors and transporters of waste.[4]

---

[1] Regulation 23(2) of the 1994 Regulations amends the controlled Waste (Registration of Carriers and Seizure of Vehicles) Regulations 1991 to provide an exemption from carrier registration for any wholly owned subsidiary of the British Railways Board which has applied for registration as a carrier of controlled waste. The exemption applies only where the subsidiary of the British Railways Board is registered under the provisions of paragraph 12 of Schedule 4 to the 1994 Regulations, and for the period whilst its application for registration under the Controlled Waste Regulations

1991 is pending.

[2] That is, a knackers yard licence which in England and Wales has the same meaning as in Section 34 of the Slaughterhouses Act 1974 and in Scotland means a licence under Section 6 of the Slaughter of Animals (Scotland) Act 1980.

[3] P.844 below.

[4] See paragraphs 1.70–1.84 of DOE Circular 11/94 (Welsh Office Circular 26/94 and The Scottish Office Environment Department Circular 10/94).

**3.12.** In all cases other than those involving repeated transfers of waste, the holder should ask the carrier to confirm the type of exemption under which he transports waste. In addition, before using for the first time a carrier who claims to be exempt, the holder should ask the carrier to provide evidence that the exemption which he claims is valid.

*Sending waste for disposal, treatment or recovery*

**3.13.** A "waste manager" is anyone:

(a) who stores waste or who processes it in some intermediate way short of final disposal;[1]

(b) who carries out a waste recovery operation;[2] or

(c) who carries out a waste disposal operation.[3]

**3.14.** All of these activities are subject to the waste management licensing requirements of Part II of the 1990 Act. Where a licence is necessary it is issued by the Agencies (and before 1 April 1996 by the relevant waste regulation authority). The licence will usually set out the types and quantities of waste that the operator may deal with and the way in which the waste is managed. It may also cover such matters as operating hours and pollution control on site.

**3.15.** *Before* choosing a waste manager as the next person to take waste, a holder will need to:

(a) check that the manager has a licence; and

(b) establish that the licence permits the manager to take the type and quantity of waste involved.

**3.16.** A waste holder should check this not merely by asking the waste manager but by examining his licence. The holder in turn should show the manager the description of the waste involved. If the holder doubts whether the licence covers his particular waste he can ask the waste manager or, if he is still not satisfied, the Agency which issued the licence.

**3.17.** Some forms of waste disposal, treatment or recovery do not require a licence because the activity concerned has been exempted from licensing.[4] If a selected waste manager is not licensed because what he is doing is exempt then he should say so and state which type of exemption he comes under. It is not taking enough care for a holder to consign waste to a contractor who states that he is exempt but does not give the grounds. The holder delivering waste to an exempt waste manager should check that the waste is within the scope of the exemption. The exemptions are limited to specific circumstances and types of waste. If in doubt about the exemption of a particular activity the holder may seek advice from the Agencies. (For more information on licensing and exemptions see Annex D paragraphs D.2–D.4[5]).

**3.18.** A holder of waste should make these same checks on licences and exemptions wherever he delivers waste even if he is not the producer. A carrier should always check that the next holder he delivers to is an authorised person and that the description of the waste he carries is within the licence or exemption of any waste manager to whom he delivers, unless he is only providing the transport to a contract directly between the producer and the waste manager. In that case the producer should make all the checks on the waste manager.

*Responsibility of brokers*

**3.19.** A broker, by arranging for the transfer of waste, shares responsibility for its proper transfer with the two holders directly involved. He should follow the relevant part of the guidance in paragraphs 3.6–3.18 above when undertaking checks in connection with arrangements he intends to make, or has made, for waste.

---

[1] These activities may involve the deposit of waste under section 33(1)(a) of the 1990 Act or they may be a recovery or disposal operation—see the two following footnotes.
[2] Waste recovery operations are listed in Part IV of Schedule 4 to the 1994 Regulations, p.722 above.
[3] Waste disposal operations are listed in Part III of Schedule 4 to the 1994 Regulations, p.721 above.
[4] By virtue of regulations 16 and 17 of and Schedule 3 to the 1994 Regulations as amended by the Waste Management Licensing (Amendment Etc.) Regulations 1995, p.688 and p.697 above.
[5] P.850 below.

*Waste disposal authorities in Scotland, England and Wales*

**3.20.** *In Scotland,* local authorities may operate their own disposal sites for publicly collected waste. In some cases, such sites may also take waste directly from commerce or industry. Sites of this kind are not licensed but are operated subject to the terms and conditions of resolutions passed by the authorities which are broadly similar to those in waste management licences. In relation to these sites, it is necessary to:—

    (a) check that they are operated by the local waste disposal authority; and

    (b) establish that the resolution permits the authority to take the type and quantity of waste involved.

**3.21.** The Environment Act 1995 transfers waste regulation functions to the Scottish Environment Protection Agency on 1 April 1996. A period of six months will be allowed from this date for an authority operating a site under a resolution to apply for a waste management licence under Part II of the 1990 Act. Thereafter, the resolution will continue to operate only for so long as it takes to deal with the licence application including the time taken to settle any appeal.

**3.22.** *In England and Wales,* waste disposal authorities will not normally be responsible for the operation of waste facilities. The Environment Act 1995 nevertheless provides that, from the transfer on 1 April 1996 of waste regulation functions to the Environment Agency, any waste facilities still operated by waste disposal authorities are to be subject to the waste management licensing system under Part II of the 1990 Act.

*Checks on repetitive transfers*

**3.23.** Full checks on carriers and waste managers do not need to be repeated if transfers of waste are repetitive—the same type of waste from the same origin to the same destination. The obvious example is waste collection from commercial premises. However, it would be advisable to make occasional checks to ensure that the contents or composition of the waste which is being transferred under cover of a season ticket remains consistent with the waste description.

**3.24.** For a series of identical loads making up one transaction there is no need to see every time a load of waste is transferred the licence of a waste manager or, in Scotland, the local authority's resolution (see paragraphs 3.20–3.21 above); or the registration certificate of a waste carrier. However, licences, resolutions, registration or evidence of exemption *should* be examined afresh in the following cases:—

    (a) whenever a new transaction is involved, that is if the description or destination of the waste has changed;

    (b) where several different carriers or disposers are collecting waste at one place and there might be a danger of an unauthorised carrier collecting a load. For example, a construction or demolition site from which several hauliers are taking waste away;

    (c) as a minimum precaution, the licence, resolution, registration or evidence of exemption should be seen and checked at least once a year even if nothing has changed in a series of transfers;

    (d) where there has been a change in the licence or resolution conditions of the destination; or

    (e) where there has been a change in the waste carrier transporting the waste.

SECTION 4

RECEIVING WASTE

**4.1.** The previous three Sections of this code look at transfers from the point of view of the person transferring the waste to someone else. This **Section** offers guidance to persons receiving waste, whether at its ultimate destination or as an intermediate holder.

*Checking on the source of waste*

**4.2.** Checking is not only in one direction. No-one should accept waste from a source that seems to be in breach of the duty of care. Waste may only come *either* from the person who first produces or imports it *or* from someone who has received it. The person who receives it must be one of the persons entitled to receive waste—that is an authorised person or a person for authorised transport purposes (**Section 3**). On the handover of waste, the previous holder and the recipient will complete a transfer note in which the previous holder will declare which category of person entitled to hold waste he is. The recipient should ensure that this is properly completed before accepting waste. Checking back in this way need not be as thorough as checking forward.

**4.3.** Recipients should not normally need to see any waste management licence of the previous holder; and there is no explicit requirement for a person receiving waste from a waste carrier to check on whether or not the carrier is registered. In the Departments' view, it is not an offence under section 34(1) of the 1990 Act for a recipient to accept waste from an unregistered carrier. However, an offence might have been committed earlier in the chain. For example, a waste producer who transfers waste to someone who is not authorised to accept it. This may be a carrier who was required to be registered but was not. The carrier himself would also be in breach of the carrier registration legislation if he was required to be registered but was not. Paragraphs 5.10–5.12 below[1] provide guidance on reporting to the Agencies.

**4.4.** However, the first time a carrier delivers waste, the recipient should satisfy himself that he is dealing with someone who is properly registered to transport the waste. In this case, it would be reasonable to ask to see either the carrier's registration certificate or official copy certificate, or to request confirmation of the type of exemption under which the carrier is transporting the waste.

**4.5.** Before receiving any waste, a holder should establish that it is contained in a manner suitable for its subsequent handling and final disposal or recovery. Where the recipient provides containers he should advise what waste may be placed in them.

**4.6.** The recipient should also look at the description and seek more information from the previous holder if this is necessary to manage the waste.

*Co-operation with the previous holder*

**4.7.** Anyone receiving waste should co-operate with the previous holder in any steps they are taking to comply with the duty. That means in particular supplying correct and adequate information that the previous holder may *need*.

**4.8.** The previous holder needs to know enough about the later handling of his waste—how it is likely to be carried, stored and treated—to pack and describe it properly. The recipient should give such information.

**4.9.** Under the 1991 Regulations[2] (**Annex C**[3]) anyone receiving waste must receive a description and complete a transfer note. The recipient must declare on the transfer note which category of authorised person he is, with details. Before making any arrangement to receive waste, a waste manager should show to the previous holder his waste management licence or a statement of the type of exemption from licensing under which he is operating; and a carrier should show his certificate of registration, an official copy of his certificate of registration or evidence of the type of exemption from registration under which he transports waste. It would be sensible for every waste management site office to hold a copy of the waste management licence or a statement of the type of exemption; and for every vehicle used by a carrier to carry an official copy of the carrier's certificate of registration or evidence of the type of exemption under which he transports waste. Where an establishment or undertaking is carrying out an exempt activity, the statement of the type of exemption may take the form of a copy of its entry in the Agencies' register of exempt activities.[4]

**4.10.** A broker, by arranging for the transfer of waste, shares responsibility for its proper transfer with the two holders directly involved. To enable the broker and the other parties to the transfer to

---

[1] P.836 below.
[2] P.650 above.
[3] P.847 below.

[4] Regulation 18(8) of the 1994 Regulations, p.690 above, requires the Agencies to provide reasonable facilities for obtaining, on payment of reasonable charges, copies of entries in their register of exempt activities.

discharge their duty of care, information may need to be exchanged between the broker and the previous holder or recipient of the waste, in line with the guidance in this **Section**.

SECTION 5

## CHECKING UP

**5.1.** The previous **Sections** describe normal procedures for transferring waste from the producer to its final destination. Most of the checking that is reasonable is already built into these procedures and the transfer note system (**Annex C**[1]). This **Section** gives guidance on what further checks are advisable and the action to take when checks show that something is wrong.

### Checks after transfer

**5.2.** Most waste transfers require no further action from the person transferring waste after the waste has been transferred. A producer is under no specific duty to audit his waste's final destination. However, undertaking such an audit and subsequent periodic site visits would be a prudent means of protecting his position by being able to demonstrate the steps he had taken to prevent illegal treatment of his waste.

**5.3.** One exception is where a holder makes arrangements with more than one party. For example, a producer arranges two contracts, one for disposal and another for transport to the disposal site. In that case the producer should establish that he not only handed the waste to the carrier but that it reached the disposer. Similar considerations apply to a broker who may make arrangements on behalf of a waste producer with several parties (carrier, disposer etc).

### Checks after receipt

**5.4.** Any waste holder, but especially a waste manager receiving waste, has a strong practical interest in the description being correct and containing adequate information. A waste management licence will control the quantities and types of waste that may be accepted and how they may be managed. It is within his capacity as a waste manager to ensure that descriptions of waste received are indeed correct. Anyone receiving waste should make at least a quick visual check that it appears to match the description. For a waste manager it would be good practice to go beyond this by fully checking the composition of samples of waste received.

### Causes for concern

**5.5.** Every waste holder should be alert for any evidence that suggests that the duty of care is not being observed or that illegal waste handling is taking place. Obvious causes for concern that any holder should notice when he accepts or transfers waste include:

(a) waste that is wrongly or inadequately described being delivered to a waste management site;

(b) waste being delivered or taken away without proper packing so that it is likely to escape;

(c) failure of the person delivering or taking waste to complete a transfer note properly, or an apparent falsehood on the transfer note;

(d) an unsupported claim of exemption from licensing or registration as a carrier; and

(e) failure of waste consigned via a carrier to arrive at a destination with whom the transferring holder has an arrangement; or

(f) damage to, or interference with containers.

**5.6.** Other causes of concern may come to light. Waste holders do not *have* to check up after waste is handed on, but they may become aware of where it is going, and should act on such information if it suggests illegal or careless waste management. Similarly, a broker who suspects misman-agement of waste for which he has made arrangements should take appropriate action. For instance, he may need to make further checks to establish the facts, or use different waste carriers and managers unless and until problems are remedied. Paragraphs 5.10–5.12 give guidance on informing the Environment Agency or the Scottish Environment Protection Agency.

*Action to take with other holders*

**5.7.** A holder who only suspects that his waste is not being dealt with properly should first of all check his facts, in the first place with the next (or sometimes the previous) holder. This may involve asking that further details should be added to a waste description, for more information about the exact status of the holder for the purposes of waste management licensing or carrier registration, why they may be entitled to an exemption, or simply where waste went to or came from.

**5.8.** If a holder is not satisfied with the information or is certain that waste he handles is being wrongly managed by another person then his first action should normally be to refuse to transfer or accept further consignments of the waste in question to or from that person, unless and until the problem is remedied. Such a step may not be practicable in all cases. For example, to avoid breach of a contract to deliver or accept waste or because there is no other outlet immediately available for the waste. Steps should be taken to minimise such inflexibility. One possible measure would be for new waste contracts to provide for termination if a breach of the duty occurs and a notice to rectify is not complied with.

**5.9.** If an arrangement that has proved wrong in some respect has to continue temporarily then the holder should take stringent precautions. For example, where waste has been misdescribed he should analyse further consignments; where waste has been collected or delivered without being properly packed he should inspect each further load; and where it has not reached its legitimate destination he should check that each subsequent load arrives at the appointed place. He should also, if appropriate, bring the situation to the attention of the Agencies, which may be able to offer guidance.

*Reporting to the Environment Agency or to the Scottish Environment Protection Agency*

**5.10.** The Environment Agency and the Scottish Environment Protection Agency are responsible for the licensing of waste management facilities; the registration of establishments or undertakings carrying out activities exempt from licensing; the registration of waste carriers; and the registration of waste brokers.

**5.11.** The Agencies do not have a specific duty to enforce the duty of care. However, they have a major interest in breaches of the duty which might contribute to illegal waste management. They are also equipped with the powers and expertise to prevent or pursue offences and to advise on the legal and environmentally sound management of waste. Fly tipping (ie disposing of waste without a waste management licence or an exemption from licensing) is one such offence. Fly tipping is a serious offence, and the Courts may impose fines and/or imprison those responsible. The Government is keen to ensure that fly-tipping does not increase following the introduction of the landfill tax in October 1996. The Departments therefore expect the Agencies to give a high priority to the prevention of fly-tipping and to draw the financial gains made by perpetrators to the attention of the Courts.

**5.12.** Any person who imports, produces, carries, keeps, treats or disposes of waste or who has control of it as a broker is required to take all reasonable measures to prevent the unlawful deposit, recovery or disposal of the waste by themselves or another person. Holders should tell the Agencies where they know or suspect that:

(a) there is a breach of the duty of care; or

(b) waste is carried by an unregistered carrier not entitled to exemption; or

(c) waste is stored, disposed of, treated or recovered:

　　(i)　without a licence or in a way not permitted by the licence;

　　(ii)　contrary to the terms or conditions of a licence exemption; or

　　(iii)　in Scotland, contrary to the terms and conditions of an authority's resolution.

EXPERT HELP AND GUIDANCE

**6.1.** A waste holder may not always have the knowledge or expertise to discharge his duty of care. He should then seek expert help and guidance. The holder is still the person responsible for discharging his own duty of care, a responsibility that cannot be transferred to an expert adviser.

*Help with analysing, describing and handling waste*

**6.2.** Waste consultants and waste managers offer services to examine waste problems, identify wastes and recommend storage and handling methods. A waste holder may also use an analytical laboratory to establish the nature of unknown waste that he needs to describe. A consultant or laboratory acting in this way can only advise, and cannot take over the duty of care from the holder. However reliable the expert, the holder himself needs to ask the right questions. Where he is faced with an unknown substance or a known waste but no disposal outlet, he needs to establish not only what it is but what special needs it has for storage, transport or treatment, and what the possible outlets for it may be, whether disposal or reclamation.

*Help with choosing a destination*

**6.3.** A consultant may put a waste holder in touch with a legitimate outlet for his waste. Alternatively, waste managers or carriers themselves may offer expert advice on a destination for a waste. A large waste management organisation with a variety of disposal or recovery methods under its control may be able to provide all the waste management services a holder needs. Otherwise it may be necessary to ask several firms for advice on whether or not they would accept a waste. If a consultant arranges a waste transfer to such an extent that he controls what happens to the waste, he is a broker, and shares responsibility with the two holders directly involved for the proper transfer of the waste (**Section 3** paragraph 3.19[1] and **Annex B** paragraph B.12[2]).

**6.4.** If the next holder is himself a source of advice he may sometimes undertake the analysis and write the waste description on behalf of the previous holder. What he may not do is to undertake the checks or complete a transfer note for which the previous holder is responsible.

*Help from relevant authorities*

**6.5.** *A waste collection authority will* be able to tell a waste holder whether a particular waste may or will be collected by the authority as part of its normal public waste collection.

**6.6.** *The Environment Agency and the Scottish Environment Protection Agency* have expertise in the management of all types of controlled waste. Although the Agencies will help as far as possible, they are not in a position to offer advice to every waste holder on how he should deal with his waste. Information that *is* held by the Agencies and is available for any enquirer to examine on request is:—

   (a) the register which the Agencies[3] are required to maintain under section 64 of the 1990 Act as amended by the 1995 Act.[4] The information on the register includes details of current or recently current waste management licences;[5]

   (b) the register which the Agencies are required to maintain under regulation 18 of the 1994 Regulations[6] of establishments or undertakings carrying on exempt activities involving the recovery or disposal of waste;

   (c) the register of waste carriers which the Agencies are required to maintain under regulation 3 of the Controlled Waste (Registration of Carriers and Seizure of Vehicles) Regulations 1991;[7]

---

[1] P.832 above.
[2] P.847 below.
[3] And waste collection authorities in England and, from 1 April 1996, waste collection authorities in Wales.
[4] P.152 above.

[5] Regulation 10 of the 1994 Regulations, p.683 above, sets out the information which the register must contain.
[6] P.690 above.
[7] P.632 above.

(d) the register of waste brokers which the Agencies are required to maintain under regulation 20 of[1] and Schedule 5 to[2] the 1994 Regulations; and

(e) the register of professional collectors, transporters, dealers and brokers of waste which the Agencies are required to maintain under paragraph 12 of Part I of Schedule 4 to the 1994 Regulations.[3]

*Waste Management Papers*

**6.7.** Detailed advice on good practice is given in the series of Waste Management Papers[4] issued by the Departments and published by HMSO. These cover subjects including the handling, disposal, treatment and recovery of particular wastes and waste management licensing.

SECTION 7

THE DUTY OF CARE AND SCRAP METAL

**7.1.** Scrap metal became a controlled waste for the purposes of the duty of care from 1 October 1995.[5] The duty of care and the guidance in the previous **Sections** of this code therefore apply to holders of scrap metal as they do to holders of other types of controlled waste. The purpose of this **Section** is to supplement that guidance and, in so doing, to take account of the distinctive features of scrap metal and the circumstances in which it is recovered.

**7.2.** Metal recycling sites (MRSs) are classified as recovery operations for the purposes of waste management licensing. In this context, the Secretary of State has advised in DOE Circular 6/95[6] that waste regulation authorities (which from 1 April 1996 should be taken to mean the Environment Agency or the Scottish Environment Protection Agency):—

"(a) should have regard to the fact that scrap metal recovery and waste motor vehicle dismantling are a source of benefit to the environment and sustainable development;

(b) should strike an appropriate balance between advice and encouragement and regulation and legal enforcement; and

(c) should distinguish between and act proportionately in relation to 'technical' breaches of the Regulations,[7] the 1994 Regulations[8] or Part II of the 1990 Act where there is no threat of pollution to the environment or harm to human health; and breaches which do give rise to such a threat. In the former case waste regulation authorities' main aim should be to ensure that the person responsible is made aware of his legal responsibilities and that steps are taken by the authority or the person concerned to prevent the commission of any further 'technical' offences."

**7.3.** The Secretary of State has also recognised the distinctive nature of MRSs in the guidance on the licensing of these facilities which he has issued in Waste Management Paper No.4A (see paragraph 6.7 above). For example, the operator of a MRS is likely to have a sound knowledge of the materials he receives; and unlike many other types of controlled waste, a significant proportion of the scrap metal which he receives will have a positive value both to the person transferring it and the person to whom it is transferred. A consequence of this is that the operator of a MRS is likely to have a direct interest in taking measures "to prevent the escape of waste from his control".[9] Many MRSs operate under the terms of exemptions from waste management licensing. The terms of these exemptions require that the activity concerned is carried on at a "*secure place* designed or adapted for the recovery of scrap metal or the dismantling of waste motor vehicles. . . ."[10]

[1] P.692 above.
[2] P.723 above.
[3] P.718 above.
[4] A list is at p.822 above.
[5] Regulations 3(2) and 7(2) of the Controlled Waste Regulation 1992 (S.I. 1992 No.588), p.662 above.
[6] Welsh Office Circular 25/95 and The Scottish Office Environment Department Circular 8/95.
[7] The Waste Management Licensing (Amendment etc.) Regulations 1995, p.751 above.
[8] The Waste Management Licensing Regulations 1994, p.675 above.
[9] Section 34(1)(b) of the 1990 Act, p.117 above.
[10] Paragraph 45(1) and (2) of Schedule 3 to the Waste Management Licensing Regulations 1994, p.709 above.

*The transfer note system*

**7.4.** As explained in paragraphs 1.7–1.9 above,[1] if waste is transferred from one person to another a transfer note must be completed, signed and kept by the parties to the transfer. The format of the transfer note is not prescriptive. However, the transfer note must include the information shown on the suggested standard form for voluntary use at **Annex C**.[2]

**7.5.** Operators of MRSs are well placed to meet the requirements of the 1991 Regulations because of the records which they are required to keep under the Scrap Metal Dealers Act 1964 ("the 1964 Act").[3] In this respect, section 2 of the 1964 Act requires every scrap metal dealer to keep, at each place occupied by him as a scrap metal store, a book[4] and to enter in the book specified particulars with respect to:—

(a) all scrap metal received at that place, and

(b) all scrap metal either processed at, or despatched from, that place.

**7.6.** Section 2(2) and (3) of the 1964 Act specifies the particulars to be entered in the book as follows:—

*In the case of scrap metal received at the place occupied by the dealer*

"(a) the description and weight of the scrap metal;

(b) the date and time of the receipt of the scrap metal;

(c) if the scrap metal is received from another person, the full name and address of that person;

(d) the price, if any, payable in respect of the receipt of the scrap metal, if that price has been ascertained at the time when the entry in the book relating to that scrap metal is to be made;

(e) where the last preceding paragraph does not apply, the value of the scrap metal at the time when the entry is to be made as estimated by the dealer;

(f) in the case of scrap metal delivered at the place in question by means of a mechanically propelled vehicle bearing a registration mark (whether the vehicle belongs to the dealer or not), the registration mark borne by the vehicle."

*In the case of scrap metal either Processed at, or despatched from. the place occupied by the dealer*

"(a) the description and weight of the scrap metal;

(h) the date of processing or, as the case may be, despatch of the scrap metal, and, if processed, the process applied;

(i) in the case of scrap metal despatched on sale or exchange, the full name and address of the person to whom the scrap metal is sold or with whom it is exchanged, and the consideration for which it is sold or exchanged;

(j) in the case of scrap metal processed or despatched otherwise than on sale or exchange, the value of the scrap metal immediately before its processing or dispatch as estimated by the dealer."

**7.7.** As indicated at paragraph 7.4 above, the form of the transfer note required for the purposes of the duty of care is not prescribed in the 1991 Regulations. The purpose of this was to allow each sector of industry to use or adapt its existing systems. This approach enables the scrap metal industry to use the records which dealers are required to keep under the 1964 Act[5] as a basis to fulfil the requirements of the 1991 Regulations.

---

[1] P.827 above.
[2] P.847 below.
[3] The equivalent provision in Scotland is section 30 of the Civic Government (Scotland) Act 1982 (the 1982 Act).

[4] Section 30(3)(b) of the 1982 Act provides that in Scotland records may alternatively be kept by "the use of a device for storing and processing information."
[5] In Scotland the Civic Government (Scotland) Act 1982.

**7.8.** The only other information required by the 1991 Regulations is:

    (a) how the material is contained on its transfer (ie whether it is loose or in a container and the kind of any container eg in sacks a skip or drums);

    (b) whether the person transferring the waste is the producer or importer of that material;

    (c) to which category of authorised persons[1] the person transferring the waste and the person receiving the waste belongs; and

    (d) the place of transfer[2]

**7.9. Annex C** paragraph C.8 provides guidance on the completion of transfer notes.[3]

*Keeping a record of transactions*

**7.10.** Section 2(5) of the 1964 Act[4] requires scrap metal dealers to retain the book containing records of dealings for two years beginning from the day on which the last entry was made in the book. This is similar to the requirement under the 1991 Regulations. The 1991 Regulations do not specify which of the two parties must complete the transfer note. It may be completed by either party. However, both parties are required to ensure that it is completed and must sign it and keep a copy.

**7.11.** Scrap metal dealers may wish, therefore, to assist those who transfer scrap metal to them by providing prepared documentation including the required information which the transferor may then complete and sign. If prepared documentation is provided the transferor should ensure that he is advised by the dealer that the details are correct.

*Records kept by itinerant traders*

**7.12.** Among other matters, section 3 of the 1964 Act makes provision for dealers who carry on their business as part of the business of an itinerant collector. This sets out the particular record keeping requirements for itinerant collectors, although it remains the case that transaction receipts should be kept for two years. From 1 October 1995 itinerant collectors are subject to the duty of care in the same way as anyone else who deals in scrap metal. Itinerant collectors must therefore ensure that a transfer note is completed and that they retain a copy when they collect or hand on scrap metal. An important exception to this relates to householders' own waste collected from their home (see paragraph 7.15 below).

**7.13.** In Scotland, the equivalent term for an itinerant collector is an itinerant metal dealer. Provisions covering itinerant metal dealers are contained in sections 32 and 33 of the Civic Government (Scotland) Act 1982 (the 1982 Act). Section 33 (3) of the 1982 Act provides that "... an itinerant metal dealer shall keep a record in respect of each sale to him of metal ..." section 33(4) goes on to say "any such records shall be kept by the dealer for a period of 6 months from the date of the sale to which it relates". Therefore, if itinerant metal dealers in Scotland wish to use these record for the purpose of the duty of care provisions they must keep them for two years.

*Records kept by motor vehicle dismantlers*

**7.14.** Any motor vehicle dismantler who falls outside the provisions of the 1964 Act because the materials in which he deals are not scrap metal, should follow the guidance on transfer notes provided in paragraphs 1.7–1.9 above and in **Annex C**[5] of this Code of Practice.[6]

---

[1] If the transfer is to a person for authorised transport purposes, it is necessary to specify which of those purposes.
[2] Regulation 2(2)(a)(iii) of the 1991 Regulations. In the case of scrap metal despatched from the place occupied by the dealer, the transfer note should also record the time of transfer.
[3] P.848 below.
[4] In Scotland section 30(4) of the 1982 Act.
[5] P.847 below.

[6] Section 9(1) of the Scrap Metal Dealers Act 1964 defines a scrap metal dealer as follows: "For the purposes of this Act a person carries on business as a scrap metal dealer if he carries on a business which consists wholly or partly of buying and selling scrap metal, whether the scrap metal sold is in the form in which it was bought or otherwise, other than a business in the course of which scrap metal is not bought except as materials for the manufacture of other articles and is not sold except as a by-product of such

*Householders*

**7.15.** Householders are exempt from the duty of care for their own household waste (**Annex A** paragraph A.9).[1] This means that a transfer note does not need to be completed when a householder brings his own household waste to a MRS; or when a householder's own scrap metal is collected from his home.

*Season tickets*

**7.16.** For regular customers and suppliers there is provision to agree a "season ticket". In other words, one transfer note which will cover multiple transfers over a given period of time. The use of a season ticket is, however, only permissible where the parties involved in the series of transfers do not change and where the description of the waste transferred remains the same (see **Annex C** paragraph C.4).[2]

*Transferring and receiving waste*

**7.17.** The guidance provided in **Section 3** (Transfer to the right person) and **Section 4** (Receiving waste) applies to anyone subject to the duty of care, including operators of MRSs. As those **Sections** explain, controlled waste may be transferred only to authorised persons or to persons for authorised transport purposes. A full list of authorised persons is at **Section 3**, paragraph 3.2.[3]

**7.18.** It is recognised that the scrap metal industry receives its material from diverse sources and that it could take considerable time to verify carriers' or suppliers' credentials at a site which undertakes a great number of transactions each day. The code is not intended to place dealers in the position where they have to seek excessive verification from their suppliers to an extent that in time, discourages them from transferring scrap metal for recovery.

**7.19.** As **Section 4** explains, checking back when waste is received need not be as thorough as checking forward. There is no explicit requirement for a person receiving waste from a waste carrier to check on whether or not the carrier is registered. In the Departments' view, it is not an offence under section 34(1) of the 1990 Act for a scrap metal dealer[4] to accept waste from an unregistered carrier. However, an offence might have been committed earlier in the chain. For example, a waste producer who transfers waste to someone who is not authorised to accept it. This may be a carrier who was required to be registered but was not. The carrier himself would also be in breach of the carrier registration legislation if he was required to be registered but was not.

**7.20.** However, the first time a carrier delivers waste, the recipient should satisfy himself that he is dealing with someone who is properly registered to transport the waste. In this case it would be reasonable to ask to see either the carrier's registration certificate or official copy certificate, or to request confirmation of the type of exemption under which the carrier is transporting the waste.

*Role of the Environment Agency and the Scottish Environment Protection Agency*

**7.21.** **Section 5** (paragraphs 5.10–5.11)[5] explains that, whilst the Agencies do not have a specific duty to enforce the duty of care, they have a major interest in breaches of the duty which might contribute to illegal waste management. The Agencies can, as can anyone else, bring a prosecution if they have evidence that the duty of care has been breached. In their dealings with the scrap metal industry, the Agencies have been asked to have regard to the considerations referred to in paragraph 7.2 above.

manufacture or as surplus materials bought but not required for such manufacture; and scrap metal dealer' (where that expression is used in this Act otherwise than in a reference to carrying on business as a scrap metal dealer) means a person who (in accordance with the preceding provisions of this subsection) carries on business as a scrap metal dealer."

[1] P.844 below.
[2] P.848 below.
[3] P.830 above.
[4] Or any other person subject to the duty of care.
[5] P.836 above.

SUMMARY CHECKLIST

This section draws together in one place a simple checklist of the main steps that are normally necessary to meet the duty of care. As with the code itself, *this does not mean that completing the steps listed here is all that needs to be done under the duty of care.* The checklist cross-refers to key sections of the code, to the introduction to the code and to the Appendix for fuller guidance. It should be noted that the introduction to the code and the Appendix do not form part of the code of practice itself.

|  |  | *Refer to paragraphs* |
|---|---|---|
| (a) | Is what you have waste? If yes, | Introduction and the Appendix |
| (b) | is it controlled waste? If yes, | 1.2 |
| (c) | while you have it, protect and store it properly, | 2.1–2.4 |
| (d) | write a proper description of the waste, covering:— | 1.7–1.9 |
| | —any problems it poses; | 1.3–1.6 & 1.10 |
| | and, *as necessary to others who might deal with it later,* one or more of: | |
| | —the type of premises the waste comes from; | 1.11–1.12 |
| | —what the waste is called; | 1.13 |
| | —the process that produced the waste; and | 1.14–1.15 |
| | —a full analysis; | 1.16–1.17 |
| (e) | select someone else to take the waste. They must be an authorised person or authorised for transport purposes. As such they should be one or more of the following and must prove that they are:— | |
| | —a registered waste carrier; | 3.6–3.8 |
| | —exempt from waste carrier registration; | 3.9–3.12 |
| | —a waste manager licensed to accept the waste; | 3.13–3 .16 |
| | —exempt from waste management licensing; | 3.17–3.18 |
| | —a waste collection authority; | 3.5 |
| | —In Scotland, a waste disposal authority operating under the terms of a resolution; | 3.20–3.21 |
| | —authorised transport purposes; | 3.3 |
| (f) | anyone arranging on behalf of another person for the disposal or recovery of controlled waste must be: | |
| | —a registered waste broker or | 3.4, 3.19, 4.10 |
| | —an exempt waste broker | 3.4 |
| (g) | pack the waste safely when transferring it and keep it in your possession until it is to be transferred; | 2.5–2.7 |
| (h) | check the next person's credentials when transferring waste to them; | 3.7–3.12, 3.15–3.19 |
| (i) | complete and sign a transfer note; | Annex C, C.3–C.4 |
| (j) | hand over the description and complete a transfer note when transferring the waste; | 1.7–1.9 Annex C, C.3–C.4 |
| (k) | keep a copy of the transfer note signed by the person the waste was given to, and a copy of the description, for two years; | Annex C, C. 5 |

*Refer to paragraphs*

(1) when *receiving* waste, check that the person who
hands it over is one of those listed in (e), or
the producer of the waste, obtain a description
from them, complete a transfer note and keep the        4.2–5.10,
documents for two years.        5.4

(m) whether transferring or receiving waste, be alert
for any evidence or suspicion that the waste you
handle is being dealt with illegally at any stage,
in case of doubt question the person involved and
if not satisfied, alert the Environment Agency
or the Scottish Environment Protection Agency.        5.5–5.11

(n) supplementary guidance for holders of scrap metal        Section 7

ANNEX A

THE LAW ON THE DUTY OF CARE

*What the duty requires*

**A.1.** The duty of care is set out in section 34 of the 1990 Act.[1] Those subject to the duty must try to achieve the following four things:—

(a) to prevent any other person committing the offences of depositing, disposing of or recovering controlled waste without a waste management licence;[2] contrary to the conditions of a licence;[3] or in a manner likely to cause environmental pollution or harm to health[4] (It should also be noted that, where a person purports to be carrying on an activity which is exempt from licensing but he fails to comply with the terms and conditions of the exemption, he may be prosecuted under section 33(1) of the 1990 Act for carrying out a licensable activity without a licence.);

(b) to prevent the escape of waste, that is, to contain it;

(c) to ensure that, if the waste is transferred, it goes only to an "authorised person" or to a person for "authorised transport purposes". **A list of authorised persons is provided at paragraph 3.2.** The list of authorised transport purposes is set out in section 34(4) of the 1990 Act;

(d) when waste is transferred, to make sure that there is also transferred a written description of the waste, a description good enough to enable each person receiving it to avoid committing any of the offences under (a) above; and to comply with the duty at (b) above to prevent the escape of waste.

**A.2.** Those subject to the duty must also comply with the 1991 Regulations which require them to keep records and make them available to the Agencies. The 1991 Regulations[5] are additional to the code of practice and are summarised at **Annex C**.[6]

**A.3. Failing to observe the duty of care or the 1991 Regulations is a criminal offence.**

*Amendments to section 34*

**A.4.** Since section 34 of the 1990 Act was originally brought into force there have been two amendments to it:—

(a) section 33 of the Deregulation and Contracting Out Act 1994 clarifies the transfer note requirements relating to multiple transfers of waste (the "season ticket" arrangements—see also **Annex C** paragraph C.4 and **Section 7** paragraph 7.16). This amendment was made because section 34 of the 1990 Act might have been construed as requiring a separate

---

[1] P.117 above.
[2] Section 33(1)(a) and (b) of the 1990 Act as modified by paragraph 9 of Schedule 4 to the 1994 Regulations.
[3] Section 33(6) of the 1990 Act.
[4] Section 33(1)(c) of the 1990 Act.
[5] P.650 above.
[6] P.847 below.

844 Waste Management: A Code of Practice

description to be supplied with each load of waste. Section 33 (4A) of the 1994 Act therefore provides that:—

"(a) a transfer of waste in stages shall be treated as taking place when the first stage of the transfer takes place; and

(b) a series of transfers between the same parties of waste of the same description shall be treated as a single transfer taking place when the first of the transfers in the series takes place".

(b) Paragraph 65 of Schedule 22 of The Environment Act 1995 amends section 34 of the 1990 Act to allow the Secretary of State to make regulations to specify persons as authorised persons under the duty of care as follows:

"(3A) The Secretary of State may by regulations amend subsection (3) above so as to add, whether generally or in such circumstances as may be prescribed in the regulations, any person specified in the regulations, or any description of person so specified, to the persons who are authorised persons for the purposes of subsection (1)(c) above."

*Who is under the duty?*

**A.5.** The duty and therefore this code apply to any person who:—

(a) imports, produces or carries controlled waste;

(b) keeps, treats or disposes of controlled waste (a "waste manager"); or

(c) as a broker has control of controlled waste.

**A.6.** In this code and its **Annexes** all the persons referred to in paragraph A.5 above are referred to as "holders" of waste. Brokers are included in this term for convenience. However, the description in paragraph A.7 below should be borne in mind by users of the code.

**A.7.** Section 34 of the 1990 Act does not define "broker". However regulation 20 of the 1994 Regulations describes a broker as a person who arranges "for the disposal or recovery of controlled waste on behalf of another person". A broker does not handle waste himself or have it in his own physical possession but he controls what happens to it.

**A.8.** Employers are responsible for the acts and omissions of their employees. They therefore should provide adequate equipment, training and supervision to ensure that their employees observe the duty of care.

*Exemption for householders*

**A.9.** The only exception to the duty is for occupiers of domestic property for "household waste" (see entry for "controlled waste" in the Glossary of terms) from the property. Note that this does *not* exempt:—

(a) a householder disposing of waste that is not from his property (for example, waste from his workplace; or waste from his neighbour's property); or

(b) someone who is not the occupier of the property (for example, a builder carrying out works to a house he does not occupy is subject to the duty for the waste he produces).

*Exemption for animal by-products*

**A.10.** Animal waste which is collected and transported in accordance with Schedule 2 to the Animal By-Products Order 1992 is not subject to the duty of care. The 1994 regulations amend the Controlled Waste Regulations 1992 so that this type of waste is not treated as controlled waste for the purposes of the duty of care.[1] Schedule 2 of the Animal By-Products Order contains a system of control on the transfer of waste which achieves broadly the same objective as the duty of care.

---

[1] Regulation 24(7) of the Waste Management Licensing Regulations 1994 amends regulation 7 of the Controlled Waste Regulations 1992 (S.I. 1992 No.588), p.664 above.

*What each waste holder has to do*

**A.11.** A waste holder is not responsible for ensuring that all the aims of the duty of care (listed in paragraph A.1) are fulfilled. A holder is only expected to take measures that are:—

(a) reasonable in the circumstances, *and*

(b) applicable to him in his capacity.

**A.12.** The *circumstances* that affect what is reasonable include:—

(a) what the waste is;

(b) the dangers it presents in handling and treatment;

(c) how it is dealt with; and

(d) what the holder might reasonably be expected to know or foresee.

**A.13.** The *capacity* of the holder is who he is, how much control he has over what happens to the waste and in particular what his connection with the waste is. Different measures will be reasonable depending on whether his connection with the waste is as an importer, producer, carrier, keeper, treater, disposer, dealer or broker.

**A.14.** Waste holders can be responsible only for waste which is at some time under their control. It is not a breach of the duty to fail to take steps to prevent someone else from mishandling any other waste. However, a holder' s responsibility for waste which he at any stage controls extends to what happens to it at other times, insofar as he knows or might reasonably foresee. Further guidance on the reasonable limits of responsibilities is in **Annex B**.

*Offences and penalties*

**A.15.** Breach of the duty of care is a criminal offence. It is an offence irrespective of whether or not there has been any other breach of the law or any consequent environmental pollution or harm to human health. The offence is punishable by a fine of up to £5,000 on summary conviction or an unlimited fine on conviction on indictment.

*The Code of Practice*

**A.16.** This code of practice has statutory standing. The Secretary of State is obliged by section 34 of the 1990 Act to issue practical guidance on how to discharge the duty. This code constitutes that guidance. The code is admissible in evidence in court. Section 34(10) of the 1990 Act provides that if a provision of the code appears to the court to be relevant to any question arising in the proceedings, it must be taken into account in determining that question. The code may therefore be used by a Court in deciding whether or not an accused has complied with his duty of care.

ANNEX B

RESPONSIBILITIES UNDER THE DUTY OF CARE

**B.1.** The main **Sections** of the code address all waste holders who are subject to the duty of care. In law all the responsibilities for waste under the duty are spread among all those who hold that waste at any stage. But responsibilities are not spread evenly. Some holders will have greater or less responsibility for some aspects of the duty, according to their connection with the waste (see **Annex A** paragraphs A.11–A.14). This **Annex** offers guidance for each category of waste holder on their particular responsibilities. This **Annex** is neither comprehensive nor self-contained guidance for particular categories of waste holder. It only draws out questions of the allocation of responsibility. All waste holders should follow the guidance in the main sections of the code of practice.

*Waste producers*

**B.2.** The duty of care applies to a person who "produces" waste. Section 34 of the 1990 Act[1] does not define this term. However, in relation to the definition of waste, regulation 1(3) of the 1994

[1] P.117 above.

Regulations provides that "'producer' means anyone whose activities produce [Directive] waste or who carries out preprocessing, mixing or other operations resulting in a change in its nature or composition". This definition is also reflected in paragraph 88 of Schedule 22 of the Environment Act 1995.

**B.3.** Waste producers are solely responsible for the care of their waste while they hold it. Waste producers are normally best placed to know what their waste is and to choose the disposal, treatment or recovery method, if necessary with expert help and advice. They bear the main responsibility for ensuring that the description of the waste which leaves them is accurate and contains all the information necessary for safe handling, disposal, treatment or recovery. If they also select a final disposal, treatment or recovery destination then they share with the waste manager of that destination responsibility for ensuring that the waste falls within the terms of any licence or exemption relevant to that final destination.

**B.4.** Producers bear the main responsibility for packing waste to prevent its escape in transit. Waste leaving producers should be packed in a way that subsequent holders can rely on.

**B.5.** Using a registered or exempt carrier does not necessarily let a producer out of all responsibility for checking the later stages of the disposal of his waste. The producer and the disposer may sometimes make all the arrangements for the disposal or recovery of waste, and then contract with a carrier simply to convey the waste from one to the other. Such a case is very little different in practice from that where there is no intermediate carrier involved. If a producer arranges disposal or recovery then he should exercise the same care in selecting the disposer or recoverer as if he were delivering the waste himself.

**B.6.** It is not possible to draw a line at the gate of producers' premises and say that their responsibility for waste ends there. A producer is responsible according to what he knows or should have foreseen. So if he hands waste to a carrier not only should it be properly packed when transferred, but the producer should take account of anything he sees or learns about the way in which the carrier is subsequently handling it. The producer would not be expected to follow the carrier but he should be able to see whether the waste is loaded securely for transport when it leaves, and he may come to learn or suspect that it is not ending up at a legitimate destination. A producer may notice a carrier's lorries returning empty for further loads in a shorter time than they could possibly have taken to reach and return from the nearest lawful disposal site; or a producer may notice his carrier apparently engaged in the unlawful dumping of someone else's waste. These would be grounds for suspecting illegal disposal of his own waste. The same reasoning applies when a producer makes arrangements with a waste manager for the disposal, treatment or recovery of waste. The producer shares the blame for illegal treatment of his waste if he ignores evidence of mistreatment. A producer should act on knowledge to stop the illegal handling of waste (see paragraphs 5.5–5.12[1]).

*Waste importers*

**B.7.** Revised legislative requirements mean that waste importers and exporters face stringent controls and in some cases, prohibitions on transfrontier shipments of waste. Consent to movements of waste must be obtained from the competent authorities involved and full details about each shipment must be given on a consignment note (**Annex D** vi. D.21–D.22[2]).

*Waste carriers*

**B.8.** A waste carrier is responsible for the adequacy of packaging while waste is under his control. He should not rely totally on how it is packed or handed over by the previous holder. He should at least look at how it is contained to ensure that it is not obviously about to escape. His own handling in transferring and transporting waste should take account of how it is packed, or if necessary he may need to repack it or have it repacked to withstand handling.

---

[1] P.835 above.  [2] P.852 below.

**B.9.** A waste carrier would not normally be expected to take particular measures to provide a new description of the waste he carried unless he altered it in some way. The description would normally be provided by the waste producer, unless the producer is a householder not subject to the duty, in which case the person first taking waste from the householder would have to ensure that a description was furnished to the next holder. When accepting any waste a carrier should make at least a quick visual inspection to see that it appears to match the description, but he need not analyse the waste unless there is reason to suspect an anomaly or the waste is to be treated in some way not foreseen by the producer.

**B.10.** If a carrier or any other intermediate holder does alter waste in any way, by mixing, treating or repacking it, he will need to consider whether a new description is necessary. The description received may continue to serve for waste that is merely compacted or mixed with similar waste, but if it has deteriorated or decomposed or if it has been altered in any way that matters for handling and disposal then a new description should be written.

**B.11.** Where there is a contract between the producer and the waste manager and a carrier is contracted solely to provide transport, he may rely on the producer checking the scope of the licence or exemption of the waste manager to whom the waste is delivered. In other cases the carrier should check this himself.

*Waste brokers*

**B.12.** A waste broker arranging the transfer of waste between a producer and a waste manager, to such an extent that he controls what happens to the waste, is taking responsibility for the legality of the arrangement. He should ensure that he is as well informed about the nature of the waste as if he were discharging the responsibilities of both producer and waste manager. He is as responsible as either for ensuring that a correct and adequate description is transferred, that the waste is within the scope of any waste licence or exemption, that it is carried only by a registered or exempt carrier and that documentation is properly completed. As he does not directly handle the waste, he cannot be held responsible for its packaging. However, he may be in a position to advise producers on appropriate methods of packaging or containment if he has greater knowledge of how the waste will be handled once it is removed from the producers premises. He should also undertake the same level of checks after transfer, and the same action on any cause for suspicion, as a waste holder.

*Waste managers*

**B.13.** Waste managers, like waste carriers, should normally be able to rely on the description of waste supplied to them. However in disposing, treating or recovering waste they are in a stronger position to notice discrepancies between the description and the waste and therefore bear a greater responsibility for checking descriptions of waste they receive. Sample checks on the composition of waste received would be good practice.

**B.14.** Waste managers are also in a good position to notice that waste has not been properly dealt with or falsely documented before it reaches them . For example, a waste manager may receive waste which is documented as coming directly from one producer but which shows signs of having been mixed or treated at some intermediate stage. A manager is to some extent responsible for following up evidence of previous misconduct just as he is for subsequent mismanagement of waste, that is to the extent that he knew or should have foreseen it and to the extent that he can control what happens.

ANNEX C

REGULATIONS ON KEEPING RECORDS

**C.1.** The 1991 Regulations[1] are made under section 34(5) of the 1990 Act[2] and require all those subject to the duty to make records of waste they receive and consign, to keep the records and to make them available to the Environment Agency or to the Scottish Environment Protection Agency.

---

[1] P.650 above.     [2] P.118 above.

**C.2.** The 1991 Regulations require each party to any transfer to keep a copy of the description which is transferred. An individual holder might transfer onward the description of the waste that he received unchanged in which case it would be advisable for the sake of clarity to endorse the description for onward transfer to the effect that the waste was sent onwards as received. If a different description of waste is transferred onwards, whether or not this reflects any change in the nature or composition of the waste, then copies of both descriptions must be made. The holder making the copy need not be the author of the description, which will often be written only by the producer or broker and reused unchanged by each subsequent holder.

**C.3.** The Regulations also require the parties to complete, sign and keep a transfer note. The transfer note contains information about the waste and about the parties to the transfer.

*Season ticket provisions*

**C.4.** While all transfers of waste must be documented, the 1991 Regulations do not require *each* individual transfer to be separately documented. Where a series of transfers of waste of the same description is being made between the same parties, provision is made for the parties to agree a "season ticket"—ie one transfer note covering a series of transfers (see paragraph A.4 above[1]). A season ticket might be used, for example, for the weekly or daily collections of waste from shops or commercial premises, or the removal of a large heap of waste by multiple lorry trips. In the Departments' view, however, a season ticket should not extend for a period of more than 12 months from the date on which the first of the transfers subject to the arrangements takes place.

*Duty of care: Controlled waste transfer note*

**C.5.** The 1991 Regulations require these records (both the descriptions and the transfer notes) to be kept for at least two years. Holders (which includes where relevant, brokers) must provide copies of these records if requested by the Agencies.

**C.6.** One purpose of documentation is to create an information source of use to other holders. It is open to holders (including where relevant, brokers) to ask each other for details from records, especially to check what happened to waste after it was consigned. A holder or broker might draw conclusions and alert the Agencies to any suspected breach of the duty if such a request were refused.

*Format of the record*

**C.7.** There is no compulsory form for keeping these records. It is recognised that a number of holders already keep records of waste in a manner that meets the requirements of the 1991 Regulations with little or no further adaptation. For example, scrap metal dealers may adapt the system of books they are obliged to keep under the Scrap Metal Dealers Act 1964 or in Scotland the Civic Government (Scotland) Act 1982 (see **Section** 7 paragraphs 7.5–7.13[2]). The consignment note for special waste can be properly completed so as to fulfil the duty of care requirements (**Annex D** paragraphs D.16–D.18[3]). Similarly, the consignment note system for transfrontier shipments of waste which involves the use of movement and tracking forms should, if properly completed satisfy the duty of care arrangements (**Annex D** paragraphs D.21–D.22).

**C.8.** A suggested standard form for voluntary use is included in this **Annex.** It should be noted that the boxes on the model form are consistent with the requirements of section 34(1) of the 1990 Act and with the requirements of the 1991 Regulations. This means that where existing documentation systems are adapted to meet the transfer note requirements of the duty of care, all of this information should be included.

**C.9. Breach of any provision of the 1991 Regulations is an offence.**

---

[1] P.843 above.     [2] P.839 above.     [3] P.852 below.

**Duty of Care: Controlled Waste Transfer Note**

**Section A—Description of Waste**

1. Please describe the waste being transferred:

2. How is the waste contained?

   *Loose* ☐ *Sacks* ☐ *Skip* ☐ *Drum* ☐ *Other* ☐ → *please describe:*

3. What is the quantity of waste (number of sacks, weight etc):

**Section B—Current holder of the waste (Transferor)**

1. Full Name (BLOCK CAPITALS):

2. Name and address of Company:

3. Which of the following are you? (Please ✓ one or more boxes)

   *producer of the waste* ☐    *holder of waste disposal or waste management licence* ☐→    *Licence number: Issued by:*

   *importer of the waste* ☐    *exempt from requirerment to have a waste disposal or waste management licence* ☐→    *Give reason:*

   *waste collection authority* ☐    *registered waste carrier* ☐→    *Registration number: Issued by:*

   *waste disposal authority (Scotland only)* ☐    *exempt from requirement to register* ☐→    *Give reason:*

**Section C—Person collecting the waste (Transferee)**

1. Full Name (BLOCK CAPITALS):

2. Name and address of Company:

3. Which of the following are you? (Please ✓ one or more boxes)

   *authorised for transport purposes* ☐→    *Specify which of those purposes:*

   *waste collection authority* ☐    *holder of waste disporal or waste management licence* ☐→    *Licence number: Issued by:*

   *waste disposal authority (Scotland only)* ☐    *exempt from requirement to have a waste management licence* ☐→    *Give reason:*

   *registered waste carrier* ☐→    *Registration number: Issued by:*

   *exempt from requirement to register* ☐→    *Give reason:*

**Section D**

1. Address of place of transfer/collection point:

2. Date of transfer:       3. Time(s) of transfer (for multiple consignments, give "between" dates):

4. Name and address of broker who arranged this waste transfer (if applicable):

|    **Transferor**    |    **Transferee**    |
|---|---|
| 5. Signed: | Signed: |
| Full name: | Full Name: |
| (BLOCK CAPITALS) | (BLOCK CAPITALS) |
| Representing | Representing: |

FED 0443 (02/96 DDP)

ANNEX D

OTHER LEGAL CONTROLS

**D.1.** This code offers guidance on the discharge of a waste holder's duty of care under section 34 of the 1990 Act.[1] Holders are also subject to other statutory requirements, some of the most important of which are set out here.

*i. Waste management licensing*

**D.2.** In *England, Wales* and *Scotland* a new system of waste management licensing under Part II of the 1990 Act came into force on 1 May 1994 and replaced the system of licensing set up under the Control of Pollution Act 1974. (The new system applied to the recovery of scrap metal and waste motor vehicle dismantling from 1 April 1995). The new system is the main means by which the Government's obligations under the amended EC Framework Directive on waste are fulfilled.

**D.3.** Under the 1990 Act *waste management licences* are required to authorise the:—

(a) deposit of controlled waste in or on land;

(b) the disposal or recovery of controlled waste (ie a disposal operation or a recovery operation);

(c) the use of certain mobile plant to dispose of or recover controlled waste.

**D.4.** Exemptions from the requirement to have a waste management licence for any of the activities listed above are to be found in regulations 16 and 17 of[2] and Schedule 3 to[3] the 1994 Regulations.

*New controls*

**D.5.** The Environment Act 1995 transfers waste regulation functions in *England and Wales* from waste regulation authorities to the Environment Agency, and in *Scotland* to the Scottish Environment Protection Agency on 1 April 1996.

**D.6.** Paragraph 65 of Schedule 22 of the Environment Act 1995 also provides that additions may be made to the list of "authorised persons" (listed in **Section** 3 paragraph 3.2[4]), for the purpose of the duty of care.

*ii. The registration of waste carriers*

**D.7.** Subject to certain provisions, section 1(1) of the Control of Pollution (Amendment) Act 1989[5] ("the 1989 Act") makes it an offence to transport controlled waste without being registered as a

---

[1] P.117 above.
[2] P.688 above.
[3] P.697 above.

[4] P.830 above.
[5] P.72 above.

waste carrier. The requirement to register applies to any person who transports controlled waste which that person has not produced themselves, to or from any place in Great Britain in the course of any business of his or otherwise with a view to profit. For this purpose, "transport" includes the transport of waste by road, rail, air, sea or inland waterway. It should be noted that construction (which includes improvement, repair or alteration) and demolition contractors would have to be registered as carriers if they wished to transport such waste, even if they had produced it themselves, and the transport of such waste when not registered would constitute a breach of the duty of care. The Controlled Waste (Registration of Carriers and Seizure of Vehicles) Regulations 1991[1] require the Agencies to establish and maintain a register of waste carriers; and set out the basis on which the registration system operates. Guidance on registration is provided in DOE Circular 11/91.[2]

**D.8.** Paragraph 12 of Schedule 4 to the 1994 Regulations[3] requires any waste carrier exempted from the waste carrier registration requirements (ie charities, voluntary organisations, waste collection/ British Rail subsidiaries and the Agencies) to register as an exempt carrier with the Environment Agency or with the Scottish Environment Protection Agency.

**D.9.** Anyone subject to the duty of care must ensure that, if waste is transferred, it is transferred only to an authorised person or to a person for authorised transport purposes. Among those who are "authorised persons" are:—

    (a) any person registered with the Agencies as a carrier of controlled waste; and

    (b) any person who is exempt from registration by virtue of regulations made under section 1(3) of the 1989 Act. The exemptions at present in force are set out in regulation 2 of the Controlled Waste (Registration of Carriers and Seizure of Vehicles) Regulations 1991.[4]

**D.10.** It is not an offence under section 1(1) the 1989 Act to transport controlled waste without being registered in the circumstances set out in (a)–(c) below. The following are also "authorised transport purposes" for the duty of care:

    (a) the transport of controlled waste between different places within the same premises;

    (b) the transport to a place in Great Britain of controlled waste which has been brought from a country or territory outside Great Britain and is not landed in Great Britain until it arrives at that place. This means that the requirement to register as a carrier applies only from the point at which imported waste is landed in Great Britain; and

    (c) the transport by air or sea of controlled waste being exported from Great Britain.

*iii. The registration of waste brokers*

**D.11.** Subject to various provisions, regulation 20 of the 1994 Regulations[5] makes it an offence for anyone to arrange on behalf of another person for the disposal or recovery of controlled waste if he is not registered as a broker. Anyone subject to the duty of care must ensure that, insofar as they use a broker when transferring waste, they use a registered broker or one exempt from the registration requirements.

**D.12.** The Transfrontier Shipment of Waste Regulations 1994 (S.I. 1994 No.1137)[6] require waste brokers making international arrangements for the disposal or recovery of controlled waste within Great Britain or abroad to be registered.

**D.13.** Registered waste carriers transporting waste to or from any place in Great Britain as part of the arrangement do not need to be registered as a broker.

**D.14.** Paragraph 12 of Schedule 4 to the 1994 Regulations[7] requires any undertaking which acts as a waste broker or dealer, is exempted under regulation 20 (ie a charity, voluntary organisation, waste collection/disposal/regulation authority) and possesses no other relevant permit for carrying on this activity, to register with the Agencies.

---

[1] P.630 above.
[2] Welsh Office Circular 34/91 and The Scottish Office Environment Department Circular 18/91.
[3] P.718 above.

[4] P.631 above.
[5] P.692 above.
[6] P.741 above.
[7] P.718 above.

**D.15.** Anyone subject to the duty of care must ensure that, if waste is transferred, it is transferred only to an authorised person or to a person for authorised transport purposes. Authorised persons are discussed and listed in **Section 3** paragraph 3.2[1] and at **Annex A.**[2]

*iv. Special waste*

**D.16.** Certain particularly difficult or dangerous wastes ("special wastes") are subject to additional requirements in The Control of Pollution (Special Waste) Regulations 1980 (S.I. 1980 No.1709) made under the Control of Pollution Act 1974. The 1980 Regulations will be replaced by new Special Waste Regulations made under section 62 of the 1990 Act. The new Regulations are planned to come into force in 1996.[3]

**D.17.** Special waste is subject to the duty of care, including the guidance in the code of practice and the requirements of the 1991 Regulations,[4] in the same way as other controlled waste. Compliance with the duty of care does not in any way discharge the need also to comply with the Special Waste Regulations.

**D.18.** The consignment note for special waste can be properly completed so as to fulfil the duty of care requirements; a separate transfer note is not then required.

*v. Road transport of dangerous substances*

**D.19.** Waste holders have obligations in respect of the regulations and associated codes of practice concerned with the transport of dangerous substances. For national transport the primary regulations are:—

(a) The Road Traffic (Carriage of Dangerous Substances in Road Tankers and Tank Containers) Regulations 1992 (S.I. 1992 No.743 as amended by S.I. 1992 No.1213, S.I. 1993 No.1746 and S.I. 1994 No.669;

(b) The Carriage of Dangerous Goods by Road and Rail (Classification, Packaging and Labelling) Regulations 1994 (S.I. 1994 No.669);

(c) The Road Traffic (Carriage of Dangerous Substances in Packages etc.) Regulations 1992 (S.I. 1992 No.742 as amended by S.I. 1992 No.1213, S.I. 1993 No.1746 and S.I. 1994 No.669);

(d) The Road Traffic (Training of Drivers of Vehicles Carrying Dangerous Goods) Regulations 1992 (S.I. 1992 No.744 as amended by S.I. 1992 No.1213, S.I. 1993 No.1122, S.I. 1993 No.1746, S.I. 1994 No.397 and S.I. 1994 No.669);

(e) The Dangerous Substances in Harbour Areas Regulations 1987 (S.I. 1987 No.37).

**D.20.** The regulations listed above are supplemented by the Approved Carriage List—Information approved for the classification, packaging and labelling of dangerous goods for carriage by road and rail (ISBN 0 7176 0745 3, available from Health and Safety Executive (HSE) Books.) The regulations are also supplemented by the Approved Methods for the Classification and Packaging of Dangerous Goods for Carriage by Road and Rail (ISBN 0 7176 0744 5, available from HSE Books).

*vi. International waste transfers*

**D.21.** Waste importers or exporters must act according to the requirements of the EC Waste Shipments Regulation (259/93/EEC) and the associated Transfrontier Shipment of Waste Regulations 1994 (S.I. 1994 No 1137).

**D.22.** The EC Regulation requires pre-notification of and consent to movements of waste, with the details of each shipment set out on a consignment note. (Non-hazardous waste moving for recovery does not need to be pre-notified). The consignment note adopted by the EC is the OECD notification and movement/tracking form. It is generally agreed in the UK that copies of both documents should accompany each shipment. These two documents together should

---

[1] P.830 above.    [2] P.843 above.    [3] See S.I. 1996/972, p.763 above.    [4] P.650 above.

satisfy the duty of care requirements. Forms are issued by UK/EC competent authorities of dispatch or destination, except for imports of waste for recovery into the EC from an OECD country where they are issued by the competent authority of dispatch in that country.

*vii. Health and safety*

**D.23.** Waste holders have a duty to ensure, so far as is reasonably practicable, the health and safety of their employees and other persons who may be affected by their actions in connection with the use, handling, storage or transport of waste, by virtue of sections 2 and 3 of the Health and Safety at Work etc Act 1974.

**D.24.** Holders also have specific duties under health and safety regulations, including the Control of Substances Hazardous to Health Regulations 1994 (S.I. 1994 No.3246), and in particular the requirement to carry out an assessment of the risks of their activities as required by the Management of Health and Safety at Work Regulations 1992 (S.I. 1992 No 2051).

ANNEX E

GLOSSARY OF TERMS USED IN THIS CODE OF PRACTICE

**The 1995 Act:** The Environment Act 1995.[1]

**The 1990 Act:** the Environmental Protection Act 1990.[2]

**The 1989 Act:** the Control of Pollution (Amendment) Act 1989.[3]

**The 1982 Act:** The Civic Government (Scotland) Act 1982.

**The 1964 Act:** The Scrap Metal Dealers Act 1964.

**The Agencies:** The Environment Agency and the Scottish Environment Protection Agency. These are the waste regulation authorities in Great Britain from 1 April 1996.

**Broker:** a person who arranges for the disposal or recovery of controlled waste on behalf of another. Such arrangements will include those for the transfer of waste. He does not handle waste himself or have it in his own physical possession, but he controls what happens to it. However, for convenience, brokers are included within the term "waste holder" as it is used in the code of practice.

**A registered broker** is registered with a waste regulation authority in accordance with regulation 20 of the Waste Management Licensing Regulations 1994.[4]

**An exempt broker** is a waste broker who by virtue of regulation 20(2), (3) or (4) of the Waste Management Licensing Regulations 1994 is not required to be registered under regulation 20.

**Carrier:** a person who transports controlled waste, within Great Britain, including journeys into and out of Great Britain.

**A registered carrier** is registered with a waste regulation authority under the 1989 Act.

**An exempt carrier** is a waste carrier who is not required to register under the 1989 Act because:

(a) he is exempt from registration by virtue of regulation 2 of the Controlled Waste (Registration of Carriers and Seizure of Vehicles) Regulations 1991;[5] or

(b) he is transporting waste in the circumstances set out in section 1(2) of the 1989 Act.[6] These circumstances are also "authorised transport purposes" as defined in section 34(4) of the 1990 Act.[7]

**Controlled waste:** as defined in section 30 of the Control of Pollution Act 1974, section 75 of the 1990 Act and the Controlled Waste Regulations 1992 (as amended).[8] That is, household, commercial and industrial waste. Paragraphs 9(2) and 10(3) to Schedule 4 of the Waste Management Licensing Regulations 1994[9] provides that any reference to "waste" in Part I of the 1974 Act or Part II of the 1990 Act includes a reference to Directive Waste.

[1] P.415 above.
[2] P.83 above.
[3] P.71 above.
[4] P.692 above.
[5] P.630 above.
[6] P.72 above.
[7] P.118 above.
[8] P.662 above.
[9] P.717 above.

**Dealer:** a dealer in controlled waste acquires waste and sells it on. He may be a holder of the waste, or he may (as a broker does) make arrangements for its transfer without holding it.

**A registered dealer** is registered with a waste regulation authority in accordance with regulation 20 of the Waste Management Licensing Regulations 1994.[1]

**A registered dealer in scrap metal:** A scrap metal dealer registered with the local authority in accordance with the Scrap Metal Dealers Act 1964. For the purposes of that Act a scrap metal dealer is defined as a person who "carries on a business which consists wholly or partly of buying and selling scrap metal. . . ."

**Directive waste:** as defined in regulation 1(3) of the Waste Management Licensing Regulations 1994.[2] Directive waste is subject to control as household, industrial or commercial waste (ie as "controlled waste").

**Disposal operation:** "disposal" as defined in Regulation 1(3) of the Waste Management Licensing Regulations 1994. A list of disposal operations is set out at Part III of Schedule 4 to those Regulations.

**The Framework Directive on waste:** Council Directive 75/442/EEC as amended by Directives 91/156/EEC and 91/6921EEC. The Framework Directive provides a common European definition of waste; it requires the control through licensing of waste recovery and disposal operations; and defines the circumstances under which exemptions from licensing may be made.

**Holder:** means a person who imports, produces, carries, keeps, treats, or disposes of controlled waste or, as a broker, has control of it.

**Licensed waste manager** is one in possession of a licence under section 35 of the 1990 Act or,[3] for a transitional period, under section 5 of the Control of Pollution Act 1974.

**An exempt waste manager** is one exempted from licensing by regulations under section 33(3) of the 1990 Act.

**Metal recycling site (MRS):** a site for the recovery scrap metal or waste motor vehicle dismantling. The site may either be subject to waste management licensing or operated under the terms and conditions of an exemption from licensing.

**Producer:** means anyone whose activities produce [Directive] waste or who carries out preprocessing, mixing or other operations resulting in a change in its nature or composition (regulation 1(3) of the Waste Management Licensing Regulations 1994 (S.I. 1994 No.1056)).

**Recovery operation:** "recovery" as defined in regulation 1(3) of the Waste Management Licensing Regulations 1994.[4] A list of recovery operations is set out in Part 1V of Schedule 4 to the Waste Management Licensing Regulations 1994.[5]

**The 1991 Regulations:** The Environmental Protection (Duty of Care) Regulations 1991[6] (S.I. 1991 No 2839).

**The 1994 Regulations:** The Waste Management. Licensing Regulations 1994[7] (S.I. 1994 No 1056).

**The 1995 Regulations:** The Waste Management Licensing (Amendment etc) Regulations 1995[8] (S.I. 1995 No 288).

**Transferee:** The person to whom waste is transferred.

**Transferor:** The person transferring the waste to another person.

**Waste collection authority:** local authority responsible for collecting waste; as defined in section 30(3) of the 1990 Act.[9]

**Waste disposal authority:** as defined in section 30(2) of the 1990 Act. That is a local authority responsible for arranging the disposal of publicly collected waste. **In Scotland,** a waste disposal authority may itself act as a waste manager.

---

[1] P.692 above.
[2] P.676 above.
[3] P.119 above.
[4] P.677 above.
[5] P.722 above.
[6] P.650 above.
[7] P.675 above.
[8] P.751 above.
[9] P.113 above.

**Waste regulation authority:** as defined in section 30(1) of the 1990 Act. The authority formerly charged with the issue of waste management licences under section 35 of the 1990 Act. Section 30(1) of the 1990 Act originally designated waste regulation as a local authority function. The 1995 Act transfers on 1 April 1996, responsibility for waste regulation to two new Agencies—the Environment Agency in England and Wales and the Scottish Environment Protection Agency in Scotland. Section 30(1) of the 1990 Act is amended accordingly.

APPENDIX

THE DEFINITION OF WASTE

The following is re-produced from DOE Circular 11/94.[1] The highlighted paragraph references are references to paragraphs of DOE Circular 11/94. This Appendix is not part of the code of practice.

"*SUMMARY*

*What Is Waste?*

2.53. The following paragraphs are intended to provide a helpful summary of the Departments' guidance on the definition of waste; and to draw attention to some of the main questions which should be addressed in reaching a view on whether a particular substance or object is waste. *However, the Departments caution against reaching a view on whether any particular substance or object is waste until all of the relevant issues have been considered.* The main questions are:—

(a) does the substance or object fall into one of the categories set out in Part II of Schedule 4 to the Regulations; *and*

(b) if so, has it been discarded by its holder, does he have any intention of discarding it or is he required to discard it (**paragraphs 2.18 and 2.19**)?

*When Is A Substance Or Object Discarded?*

2.54. Waste appears to be perceived in the Directive as posing a threat to human health or the environment which is different from the threat posed by substances or objects which are not waste. This threat arises from the particular propensity of waste to be disposed of or recovered in ways which are potentially harmful to human health or the environment *and from the fact that the producers of the substances or objects concerned may no longer have the self interest necessary to ensure the provision of appropriate safeguards.* The purpose of the Directive, therefore, is to treat as waste those substances or objects which fall out of the normal commercial cycle or out of the chain of utility (**paragraph 2.14**). To determine whether a substance or object has been discarded the following question should be asked:—

- has the substance or object been discarded so that it is no longer part of the normal commercial cycle or chain of utility?

2.55. An answer of "no" to this question should provide a reasonable indication that the substance or object concerned is not waste (**paragraphs 2.20 and 2.21**). A substance or object should *not* be regarded as waste:

(a) solely on the grounds that it falls into one of the categories listed in Part II of Schedule 4 to the Regulations (**paragraph 2.19**);

(b) solely on the grounds that it has been consigned to a recovery operation listed in Part IV of Schedule 4 to the Regulations (**paragraphs 2.25 and 2.26**);

(c) if it is sold or given away and can be used in its present form (albeit after repair) or in the same way as any other raw material without being subjected to *a specialised recovery operation* (**paragraphs 2.28(a), 2.30–2.31, 2.32, 2.33(a), 2.33(b)(I), 2.35 and 2.36**);

(d) if its producer puts it to beneficial use (**paragraph 2.40**); or

---

[43] Welsh Office Circular 26/94 and The Scottish Office Environment Department Circular 10/94.

(e) solely on the grounds that its producer would be unlikely to seek a substitute for it if it ceased to become available to him as, say a by-product (**paragraph 2.42**)

**2.56.** A substance or object *should be* regarded as waste if it falls into one of the categories listed in Part II of Schedule 4 to the Regulations and:—

(a) it is consigned to a disposal operation listed in Part III of Schedule 4 to the Regulations (**paragraph 2.33**);

(b) it can be used only after it has been consigned to *a specialised recovery operation* (**paragraphs 2.28(b), 2.30–2.31 and 2.33(c)**);

(c) the holder pays someone to provide him with a service and that service is the collection [and taking away] of a substance or object which the holder does not want and wishes to get rid of (**paragraph 2.33(d)**);

(d) the purpose of any [beneficial] use is wholly or mainly to relieve the holder of the burden of disposing of it and the user would be unlikely to seek a substitute for it if it ceased to become available to him as, say a by-product (**paragraphs 2.37, 2.38, 2.41 and 2.42**);

(e) it is discarded or otherwise dealt with as if it were waste (**paragraphs 2.33(b)(ii) and 2.52**); or

(f) it is abandoned or dumped (**paragraph 2.24**).

*Can Waste Cease To Be Waste?*

**2.57.** A substance or object which is waste *does not* cease to be waste as soon as it is transferred for collection, transport, storage, *specialised recovery* or disposal; or as soon as it reaches a *specialised recovery establishment or undertaking*. A substance or object which is waste and is not fit for use in its present form or in the same way as any other raw material may cease to be waste when it has been recovered within the meaning of the Directive (**paragraphs 2.46–2.49**)

**2.58.** The recovery of waste occurs when its processing produces a material of sufficient beneficial use to eliminate or sufficiently diminish the threat posed by the original production of the waste This will generally take place when the recovered material can be used as a raw material in the same way as raw materials of non-waste origin by a natural or legal person other than *a specialised recovery establishment or undertaking* (**paragraphs 2.47–2.49**)

**2.59.** In a few cases, a change of intention by the person to whom waste has been transferred may be sufficient to result in the substance or object concerned ceasing to be waste This is likely to occur only where it transpires that the substance or object which has been transferred as waste is in fact fit for use in its present form (albeit after repair) or in the same way as any other raw material without being subjected to *a specialised recovery operation* (**paragraph 2.50**)."

# Index

agricultural practice:
  good, codes of 288
    Scotland 48
agriculture:
  meaning 547
  sludge, use of *see* sludge
air pollution:
  cable burning, offence of 354
  colliery spoilbanks, burning of refuse 359–60
  control, transfer of functions 88
  Crown premises 362
  information:
    local authorities obtaining 355–6
    local authority functions, regulations 358
    notices requiring 356–7
      appeals 357
    provision to Secretary of State 359
  inquiries 368
  investigations and research, exemptions for
    purposes of 361
  local control, guidance notes 818–21
  motor fuel, regulations 352–4
  oil fuel, regulations 353–4
  prescribed processes, provisions not applying
    to 359
  research and publicity 355
air quality:
  Agencies having regard to 466
  consultation requirements 520–1
  county councils in areas of district councils,
    functions of 469–71
  exchange of information 521
  fixed penalty offences 522–4
  guidance, issue of 473
  interpretation of provisions 474–5
  Isles of Scilly, application of provisions 474
  local authority functions, joint exercise of 521
  local authority reviews 467
  management areas:
    action plan 468, 470
    designation of 467
    local authorities, duties of 467–8
  national strategy 465–6
  public access to information 522
  regulations 471–3
  Scottish Environment Protection Agency,
    reserve powers of 468–9
  Secretary of State, reserve powers of 468–9
Atomic Energy Authority
  disposal of waste by 59

borrowing powers:
  Environment Agency and Scottish
    Environment Protection Agency, of 458

government guarantees 459

cable burning:
  offence of 354
chimneys:
  dark smoke, prohibition of 336–7
  height of:
    approval, application for 344–5
    plans for 345–6
    requirements 343–4
  meaning 371
clean air *see also* air pollution; dark smoke;
    furnaces; smoke control areas
  Crown premises 362
  default powers 368
  enforcement of provisions 365
  entry and inspection, powers of 366–7
  European Communities Act, regulations
    under 802
  information:
    power of local authority to obtain 367
    unjustified disclosure of 363
  interpretation of provisions 371–3
  Isles of Scilly, provisions applying 373
  local authority functions, joint exercise of
    369
  offences:
    act or default of another, due to 365
    body corporate, by 365
    cumulative penalties 364
    occupiers, duty to notify 364
  Public Health Act provisions, application of
    370
  regulations and orders 371
  statutory instruments, list of 799–801
  transitory provisions 373, 376–80
  works, power of county court to authorise
    365
Community obligations:
  power to give effect to 205–6
compulsory purchase of land:
  Scottish Environment Protection Agency, by
    442
contaminated land:
  Agency:
    guidance by Secretary of State, having
      regard to 184
    meaning 164
    site-specific guidance on 183–4
    state of land, reports 183
  contaminating substances escaping to other
    land, liability for 173–4
  controlled waters:
    affected by 164

contaminated land (*cont.*):
  controlled waters (*cont.*):
    meaning 164
    pollution of:
      liability, restrictions on 173
      meaning 165
  enforcing authority:
    land adjoining or adjacent to area,
      functions relating to 184
    meaning 164
  registers:
    confidential information, exclusion of
      182–3
    contents of 180–1
    information affecting national security,
      exclusion of 181–2
    maintenance of 180–1
  remediation, carrying out:
    charging notice 178
    costs, recovery of and security for 177–9
    powers of 176–7
  remediation, duty as to 168
  harm, meaning 163
  identification of 165
  interaction of provisions 186
  interpretation of terms 162–5
  Isles of Scilly, provisions applied to 185
  meaning 163
  notice of 165
  owner, meaning 164
  radioactivity, harm or pollution attributable
    to 187
  remediation:
    costs of 185
    enforcing authority carrying out
      charging notice 178
      costs, recovery of and security for 177–9
      powers of 176–7
    enforcing authority, duty of 168
    meaning 163
    notice:
      appeals 175
      contaminating substances escaping to
        other land, for 174
      contents of 170
      failure to comply with 176
      prohibitions 170–2
      restrictions on 170–2, 186
      special site, for 179
    responsibility for 169
    rights of entry 170
    statement 172
  Secretary of State, guidance by 184, 186
  special site:
    decisions referred to Secretary of State 167
    designation of 166–7
    identification of 166
    meaning 163
    remediation notice, adoption of 179
    review of condition 179
    termination of designation 180

two or more sites considered together 184
Court of Session:
  appeals to 51
Crown:
  Environment Act, application of 490–1
  premises, prevention of air pollution 362
  radioactive substances, application of
    provisions 406
  sewerage provisions, application of 262–3
  water pollution provisions, application of
    317
Crown Court:
  appeals to 51

dams:
  destruction of 68
dark smoke:
  chimneys, prohibition from 336–7
  Crown premises 362
  enforcement of provisions 365
  industrial or trade premises, prohibition from
    337
  investigations and research, exemptions for
    purposes of 361
  meaning 338
  railway engines, from 360
  vessels, from 360–1
dust:
  furnaces, emission from *see* furnaces

effluent:
  application of trade effluent provisions
    246–7
  samples:
    conditions of taking, presumption as to 9
    Scottish Environment Protection Agency,
      taken by 5, 9–10
  sewage:
    consents for discharges
      Scotland *see* water pollution, Scotland
    discharge of 275
    meaning 6, 49
  trade *see* trade effluent
environment:
  appeals, delegation of functions of Secretary
    of State 489–90, 527–9
  Crown, application of provisions to 490–1
  directions 494
  documents, service of 494–5
  enforcing authorities, powers of 481–6
  information, disclosure of 488–9
  interpretation of provisions 495
  Isles of Scilly, application of provisions 491
  local statutory provisions, amendment of
    493
  notices, service of 207
  offences:
    body corporate, by 206
    fault of another, due to 207
  powers of entry on premises 481–6, 535–6
  regulations, orders and directions 208

release of substance into 90
transitional provisions 539–35
Environment Agency:
accounts and records 456
addresses 811–13
advisory committees:
environment protection 431–2
members 507–8
membership schemes 506–7
regional and local fisheries 432–3
Wales, for 431
air quality strategy, having regard to 466
annual report 460
audit 457
borrowing, government guarantees 459
borrowing powers 458
chairman and deputy chairman 497
charges, incidental power to impose 455
charging schemes:
approval of 454–5
environmental licences, for 452–3
making 452–3
transitional provisions 530
continuity of exercise of functions 461–2
costs and benefits, having regard to 451
delegation of functions to 449–50
delegation of powers 498
documents, service of 499
enforcing authority, as 90
environmental and recreational duties 427–8
codes of practice 429–30
establishment of 420
financial duties, general 455–6
fisheries functions 426
flood defence committee see flood defence
general duties 271
government loans to 458–9
grants to 458
guidance to 823
incidental functions 430–1, 448–9
information, provision of 459–60
inquiries as to 460–1
instruments, proof of 499
interpretation of provisions 462–4
Isles of Scilly, functions in 792
legal proceedings, appearance in 461
members 420, 497
defective appointments 499
interests of 498
remuneration and pensions 497
vacancies 499
Ministerial directions to 451
minutes 499
objectives 424
pollution control functions 424–5
principal aim of 424
proceedings 498
property, rights and liabilities transferred to
422–4
consideration 505
continuity 505

contracts of employment 501–3
foreign, vesting 505–6
interpretation of provisions 500
remedies 505
transfer schemes:
approval or rejection of 423
division of property 503
duty to make 423
incidental, supplemental and consequential provision 503
information and assistance, provision of
504
modification of 423, 504
property, description of 503
Secretary of State, by 423
types of 501
seal, application of 499
sites of special scientific interest, duties with
respect to 428–9
special waste, responsibility for 776
staff 497–8
transfer of functions to 421–2
waste, functions as to 111
water, duties relating to 425–7
water pollution, provisions applying see water
pollution
environmental licence:
holder, meaning 757
meaning 461
notice demanding payment 757
revocation, notice of 757–8
suspension, notice of 757–8
Environmental Protection Act 1990:
commencement 738–40

fish:
border rivers, in 69
offences relating to 69
River Esk, in 69
Solway Firth, in 69–70
water containing:
dams, destruction of 68
explosives, poisons or electrical devices,
use of 68
pollution of 67
fisheries:
advisory committees 432–3
Environment Agency, duties of 426
regional and local committees 530
flood defence:
Environment Agency, functions of 426
local committees:
authentication of documents 516
composition 437–8
consultations 437
functions of 436–7
members:
casual vacancies 513
declarations of interest 515
deputies 513
payments to 514

flood defence (*cont.*):
  local committees (*cont.*):
    members (*cont.*):
      re-appointment 513
      resignation 513
    membership:
      constituent council, of 511
      disqualification 511–12
      terms of 511
    proceedings 514–16
    sub-committees 514–15
  local district 437
  local schemes 436–7
  regional committees:
    areas 508–10
    authentication of documents 516
    composition 434
      change of 435–6
    functions of 433
    members:
      casual vacancies 513
      declarations of interest 515
      deputies 513
      payments to 514
      re-appointment 513
      resignation 513
    membership:
      constituent council, of 511
      disqualification 511–12
      terms of 511
    proceedings 514–16
    sub-committees 514–15

fumes:
  meaning 371
  provisions applied to 363
furnaces:
  arrestment plant
    approval, appeals 341
    domestic furnace, for 341
    non-domestic furnace, for 339–40
    exemptions 340
  chimneys, height of:
    approval, application for 344–5
    requirements 343–4
  domestic, meaning 371
  grit and dust:
    emission of 339
    measurement of:
      local authorities, by 342
      occupiers, by 341–2
    outdoor furnaces, from 343
  information, requirement to furnish 343
  investigations and research, exemptions for
    purposes of 361
  new, requirement to be smokeless 338–9
  oil fuel, regulations 353–4
  outdoor 343

gases:
  provisions applied to 363

grit:
  furnaces, emission from *see* furnaces
groundwater:
  waste management licence, provisions of 686–8
hazardous substances:
  Advisory Committee 227–8
  potential, power to obtain information about
    203–4

industrial or trade premises:
  dark smoke, prohibition of 337
  meaning 338
information:
  air pollution, concerning:
    local authorities obtaining 355–6
    local authority functions, regulations 358
    notices requiring 356–7
      appeals 357
    provision to Secretary of State 359
  clean air, as to:
    power of local authority to obtain 367
    unjustified disclosure of 363
  disclosure, prohibition of 56–7
  Environment Agency, provision by 459–60
  environment, disclosure relating to 488–9
  environmental:
    construction of regulations 671
    meaning 671
    obligation to make available 672
    right to:
      exceptions 672–3
      existing 673–4
      obligation to make available 672
  furnaces and fuel, about 343
  hazardous substances, in respect of 203–4
  power of authorities to obtain 56
  Scottish Environment Protection Agency :
    obtaining 442–3
    provision by 459–60
  sludge, about 549
  trade effluent, as to *see* trade effluent
  waste regulation authority obtaining 156
  water pollution, as to 304–6
injurious substances or articles:
  Advisory Committee 227–8
  importation, use, supply or storage, power to
    prohibit or restrict 200–2
  list of regulations relating to 797–8
integrated pollution control:
  definitions 89–90
  enforcing authority:
    authorisations *see* prescribed processes
    discharge and scope of functions 93–4
    High Court, enforcement of provisions by
      109
    information, obtaining or supply of 104–5
    meaning 90
    registers:
      appeals 612–615
      confidential information, exclusion of
      107–8

contents of 105–6, 615–17
determination periods 619–21
inspection of 106
maintenance of 105–6
matters affecting national security,
    exclusion of 106
monitoring data 617
guidance notes 815–18
harm, remedying 110
High Court, enforcement of provisions by
    109
offences 108–9
transfer of functions 88
international agreements:
power to give effect to 60
    air pollution 363
international obligations:
power to give effect to 205–6
Isles of Scilly:
air quality provisions, application of 474
Clean Air Act, application of 373
contaminated land provisions applying to
    185
Control of Pollution (Amendment) Act 1989,
    application of 81
Control of Pollution Act 1974, application of
    63
Environment Act, application of 491
Environment Agency, functions of 792
waste provisions applying to 160
Water Industry Act provisions, application of
    263
Water Resources Act, application of provi-
    sions 318

land:
right of entry on 54–6
legal proceedings:
act or default of other person, offence due to
    52
appeal, notice as to 52
body corporate, against 51–2
Crown Court or Court of Session, appeals to
    51
Environment Agency appearing in 461
integrated pollution control:
    cause of offence, order for remedy of 110
    High Court, enforcement of provisions by
        109
    onus of proof 110
Scottish Environment Protection Agency
    appearing in 461
summary, in Scotland 52
waste, concerning 157
litter:
application of provisions to 664–5
local inquiries:
air pollution, as to 368
environment, as to 527–8
power to hold 57
sewerage provisions, under 255

mines:
abandonment:
    meaning 282
    notice of 283
    Scotland, in see Scotland
air pollution, prevention of 359–60
mobile radioactive apparatus:
meaning 384
registration:
    appeals 398–9
    application for 387–8
        determinations of Secretary of State
            396
        directions of Secretary of State 395–6
        knowledge, restriction of 397
    authorisations:
        site or disposal records, retention and
            production of 393–4, 401
    cancellation 388
    display of documents 301, 393
    enforcement notices 394
    exemptions 388
    notices 398
    offences 401
    prohibition notices 395
    prohibition of use without 387
    variation 388
motor fuel:
regulations 352–4

National Heritage Areas:
Scottish Environment Protection Agency,
    duties of 447
National Rivers Authority:
Environment Agency, transfer of functions to
    421
national security:
directions in interest of 251–2, 306–7
registers, information excluded from see
    contaminated land, etc
nitrates:
controlled waters, prevention or control of
    entry into 285–7
Scotland:
    agreements, registration of 28
    nitrate sensitive areas 27–8, 64–6
noise:
provisions relating to 51
statutory nuisance, as 192–3
nuisance:
statutory see statutory nuisance

offensive trades:
existing controls, termination of 198–9
statutory nuisance, as see statutory nuisance
oil fuel:
meaning 354
regulations 353–4

pollution:
air see air pollution

pollution (*cont.*):
  authorities:
    default, in 58
    establishment charges and interest 53–4
    information, power to obtain 56
    relevant 58–9
  Environment Agency, functions of 424–5
  environment, of 89
  integrated control *see* integrated pollution
    control
  interpretation of terms 61
  offences 486–7
    evidence 487–8
  orders and regulations 60
  rivers and other waters, of, Scotland 4
  Scottish Environment Protection Agency,
    duties of 445–6
  serious, dealing with imminent danger of 486
  water *see* water pollution
prescribed processes:
  acid 580
  air pollution provisions not applying 359
  animal or vegetable matter, treatment and
    processing 588–9
  asbestos, involving 575–6
  authorisations:
    advertisements 610, 617
    appeals 103–4
      action of receipt of notice 613–14
      determination, notification of 615
      hearings 614–15
      notice of 612
      time limit for bringing 612–13
      written representations 614
    application for 95, 211, 605–7
      transmitted 612
    conditions 95–7
      variation of 100–2, 607–8
    consultations 608–10
    controlled waste, condition not to regulate
      deposit of 111
    date from which required 594–8
    determination of 211–12
    determination periods 619–21
    fees and charges 97–8
    offences 108–9
    onus of proof 110
    requirement of 95
    review of 95
    revocation 102
    statutory controls 111
    transfer of 98
    variation 99–100
      application for 213–15
      enforcing authority, by 213
    waste oil burners, exemption for 611
  authority, functions of 93–4
  best available techniques not entailing
    excessive cost, use of 96
  carbonisation 569–71
  cement and lime manufacture 575

  ceramic production 578
  chemical fertiliser production 582
  chemicals, storage in bulk 583
  coating and printing 586
  di-isocyanate 585
  dyestuffs, printing ink and coating materials,
    manufacture of 587
  enforcement notices 102
    appeals 103–4
      action of receipt of notice 613–14
      determination, notification of 615
      hearings 614–15
      notice of 612
      time limit for bringing 612–13
      written representations 614
    offences 109
  exceptions 567–8
  fuel, production from waste 584
  gasification 569
  glass manufacture and production 577
  halogens, involving 580–2
  interpretation of schedule 590–2
  iron and steel 571–2
  local control 93
  meaning 91
  mineral fibres 576–7
  non-ferrous metals 573–4
  organic chemicals, manufacture and use of
    579
  paper and pulp manufacture 584
  Part A:
    central control 568
    characteristics 567
    meaning 566
  Part B:
    local control 568
    meaning 566
    processes taken to be 567
  petrochemical, 578
  petroleum 571
  pharmaceutical production 582
  prohibition notices 103
    appeals 103–4
      action of receipt of notice 613–14
      determination, notification of 615
      hearings 614–15
      notice of 612
      time limit for bringing 612–13
      written representations 614
    offences 109
  registers:
    appeals:
      action of receipt of notice 613–14
      determination, notification of 615
      hearings 614–15
      notice of 612
      time limit for bringing 612–13
      written representations 614
    confidential information, exclusion of
      107–8, 611–12
    contents of 105–6, 615–17

determination periods 619–21
inspection of 106
maintenance of 105–6
matters affecting national security,
    exclusion of 106, 611–12
monitoring data 617
rubber, involving 588
schedule of 567, 569–89
smelting 574
standards, objectives or requirements 92
statutory controls 111
tar and bitumen 585
timber 587–8
trade effluents derived from 543–4, 656
transitional provisions 598–603
uranium, involving 586
waste incineration 583–4
waste recovery 584
process:
meaning 89
prescribed *see* prescribed processes

quarry:
air pollution, prevention of 359–60

radioactive material:
meaning 383–4
registration:
    appeals 398–9
    applications
        determinations of Secretary of State 396
        directions of Secretary of State 395–6
        knowledge, restriction of 397
    authorisations:
        site or disposal records, retention and
            production of 393–4, 401
    display of documents 301, 393
    enforcement notices 394
    notices 398
    offences 401
    prohibition notices 395
    prohibition of use without 384–5
    users, of 385–6
        exemptions 386–7
        nuclear site licence in force, where
            386–7
radioactive substances:
appeals:
    determination, notification of 565
    hearings 565
    notice of 563
        receipt, action on 564
    time limit for bringing 563
    written representations 564
Crown, application of provisions to 406
documents and records, public access to
    403–4
documents, service of 405
interpretation of provisions 407–10
offences:
    another's fault, due to 403

authorisation, as top 401
body corporate, by 403
documents or records, as to 401
false entries or records, making 402
false or misleading statements, making,
    402
prosecutions, restriction on 403
registration, as to 401
trade secrets, disclosure of 402
radioactivity to be disregarded 404–5, 411
regulations and orders 407
specified elements 410
statutory instruments, list of 803–7
transfer of functions 383
transitional provisions 412–14
radioactive waste:
accumulation of 389
authorisations:
    appeals 398–9
    application for 390–1
    determinations of Secretary of State 396
    directions of Secretary of State 395–6
    display of documents 393, 301
    enforcement notices 394
    grant of 390–1
    knowledge of applications, restriction of
        397
    meaning 390
    notices 398
    offences 401
    prohibition notices 395
    public and local authorities, functions of
        392–3
    revocation 392
    site or disposal records, retention and
        production of 393–4, 401
    variation 392
exemptions from provisions 390
provision of facilities for 400
disposal of 389
authorisations:
    appeals 398–9
    application for 390–1
    determinations of Secretary of State 396
    directions of Secretary of State 395–6
    display of documents 301, 393
    enforcement notices 394
    grant of 390–1
    knowledge of applications, restriction of
        397
    meaning 390
    notices 398
    offences 401
    prohibition notices 395
    public and local authorities, functions of
        392–3
    revocation 392
    site or disposal records, retention and
        production of 393–4, 401
    variation 392
exemptions from provisions 390

radioactive waste (*cont.*):
  disposal of (*cont.*):
    provision of facilities for 400
    Secretary of State, powers of 400
  meaning 384
  provisions applying to 162
  Radioactive Substances Act 1960, application
      of 545–6
  Scotland, provisions applying in 648–9
  special waste, as 766
  Water Act 1989, provisions applying 545
railway engines:
  dark smoke, prohibition of emissions 360
refuse:
  application of provisions to 664–5
River Esk:
  fish, provisions relating to 69
river purification authorities:
  operations remedying or forestalling
      pollution by, Scotland 41–2
  Scottish Environment Protection Agency,
      transfer of functions to 439
  unregistered vessels, exclusion from inland
      waters 46
  waste from vessels, dealing with, Scotland 45
rivers:
  deposits and vegetation in 46, 278
  ecosystem, classification of waters 735–7
  freshwater limits, maps of 302
  pollution, prevention of:
    Scotland 4–9, 25–6
    Scottish Environment Protection Agency
        *see* Scottish Environment Protection
        Agency
    unregistered vessels, exclusion from inland
        waters 46

sanitary appliances:
  meaning 29
  vessels, control on, Scotland 29
scientific purposes:
  acts done for 10
Scotland:
  abandoned mines:
    abandonment:
      meaning 15
      notice to SEPA 15–16
    official receiver:
      acting in compulsory capacity, meaning
          15
      meaning 15
    provisions on 14
    water pollution problems arising from 48
  bathing waters, classification 626–9
  Control of Pollution Act 1974, application of
      62
  directions to accept, treat, dispose of or
      deliver waste 148
  national waste strategy 136–7
  pollution of rivers and other waters, preven-
      tion of 4

radioactive waste, provisions applying 648–9
recycling waste, powers of 148
statutory nuisance, appeals 793–6
summary proceedings in 52
surface waters, classification of 558–9
  dangerous substances 560–1, 659–60
water pollution *see* water pollution
Scottish Environment Protection Agency:
  abandonment of mines, notice of 15–16
  accounts and records 456
  addresses 813–14
  aims and objectives, guidance on 444–5
  air quality strategy, having regard to 466
  annual report 460
  anti-pollution operations, notices requiring
      42–3
  audit 457
  borrowing, government guarantees 459
  borrowing powers 458
  byelaws, making 443
  chairman and deputy chairman 517
  charges, incidental power to impose 455
  charging schemes:
    approval of 454–5
    environmental licences, for 452–3
    making 452–3
    transitional provisions 530
  closure of mines, investigation of problems
      arising from 48
  compulsory purchase of land by 442
  consents for discharges:
    alteration and imposition of conditions 33
    appeals 35–7
    application for 29
    conditional 30
    enforcement notices 47
      appeals 47–8
    general review of 34–5
    grant or refusal of 30
    notice of application 31–3
    revocation 33
    Secretary of State, reference to 31
    transitional provisions 37
    variation, restrictions on 34
  consultation and collaboration 21
  continuity of exercise of functions 461–2
  costs and benefits, having regard to 451
  delegation of functions to 449–50
  delegation of powers 518
  drainage works, consultation on 442
  environmental and recreational duties 445
    codes of practice 448
  establishment charges, recovery of 53
  establishment of 438
  expenses, interest on 54
  financial duties, general 455–6
  flood risk, assessment of 442
  government loans to 458–9
  grants to 458
  guidance to 823
  incidental general functions 448–9

information:
  obtaining 4, 442–3
  provision of 4, 459–60
inquiries as to 460–1
interpretation of provisions 462–4
legal proceedings, appearance in 461
members of 517
  interests of 519
  remuneration and pensions 517
Ministerial directions to 451
minutes 519
National Heritage Areas, duties as to 447
operations remedying or forestalling
      pollution by 41–2
pollution control, duties as to 445–6
private legislation, promotion or opposition
      443
proceedings 518
property, rights and liabilities transferred to
      440–1
  consideration 505
  continuity 505
  contracts of employment 501–3
  foreign, vesting 505–6
  interpretation of provisions 500
  remedies 505
  transfer schemes:
    approval or rejection of 441
    division of property 503
    duty to make 440
    incidental, supplemental and conse-
      quential provision 503
    information and assistance, provision of
      504
    modification of 441, 504
    property, description of 503
    Secretary of Satte, by 441
  types of 501
records held by 444
regional boards 518–19
registers:
  confidential information, exclusion of
      39–41
  maintenance of 38
  national security, exclusion of matters
      affecting 39
  particulars in 38
samples of effluents, taking 5, 9–10
sites of special scientific interest, duties with
      respect to 447
special waste, responsibility for 776
staff 518
staff commission, functions of 441
status of 516
sustainable development, guidance on 444
transfer of functions to 3, 17, 438–40
water, duties relating to 446–7
works notice:
  anti-pollution operations, requiring 42–3
  appeals 44
  compensation under 44

  entitlement to carry out works 43–4
  failure to comply with 45
  rights of entry 43–4
sewerage:
  documents, service of 255–6
  forms, power to prescribe 255
  interpretation of provisions 257–62
  local inquiries 255
  offences:
    body corporate, by 253
    limitation on right to prosecute 253
  regulations, power to make 254
  trade effluent, discharge of see trade effluent
sewerage undertakers:
  Crown, provisions binding 262–3
  functions conferred on, construction 256–7
  interpretation of provisions 257–62
  Isles of Scilly, provisions applying to 263
  local Acts, effect of 262
  service of documents on 57
sewers:
  discharges into and from, Scotland 22–3
sites of special scientific interest:
  Environment Agency, duties of 428–9
  Scottish Environment Protection Agency,
      duties of 447
sludge:
  agriculture, use in:
    dedicated sites 550
    interpretation of provisions 547
    precautions 548
    prohibition on 547–8
    soil, testing 551–2
    use, meaning 547
  information, supply of 549
  meaning 547
  producer:
    information to be supplied to 548
    meaning 547
    register kept by 549
  septic tank, meaning 547
  table 547, 551
  testing 550–1
  treated, meaning 547
smoke:
  control areas see smoke control areas
  dark see dark smoke
  meaning 372
smoke control areas:
  creation of 346
  emission of smoke in, prohibition of 348
  exemptions 348
  expenditure incurred on execution of works
    351
  fireplaces in:
    adaptation of:
      church, chapel and charity buildings,
        grants for 350
      contraventions of provisions, avoiding
        351
      expenditure incurred 350

smoke control areas (*cont.*):
  fireplaces in (*cont.*):
    expenditure incurred, grants for 374–6
    power of local authority to require
      349–50
    unsuitable appliances, exclusion of
      grants 375
    exempted from control 348
  interpretation of provisions 352
  local authority, declaration by 346
  orders:
    coming into operation 374
    contents of 346
    meaning 346
    transitional provisions 379–80
  Secretary of State requiring creation of 347
  unauthorised fuel, acquisition and sale of
    348–9
Solway Firth:
  fish, provisions relating to 69–70
stamp duty:
  exemptions 491
statutory nuisance:
  abatement notice:
    appeals 191, 224–5, 753–5
    failure to comply with 191
    meaning 190
    noise in street, in respect of 192–3
    requirements 191
    service of 191
    suspension 755–6
      Scotland 795–6
  abatement of 193–4
  act outside area of local authority, caused by
    193
  appeals, Scotland 793–6
  contaminated state, land in 187–8
  default powers 226–7
  exclusions 188
  expenses:
    abatement, of 194
    payment by instalments 195
    recovery of 194–5
  High Court proceedings 194
  inspections 187
  interpretation of terms 188–90
  matters constituting 187
  more than one person responsible for 193
  notices, statement of right of appeal in 227
  offences 191–2
  person responsible 189
  personal liability, protection of local
    authority members from 227
  powers of entry 225–6
  summary proceedings:
    institution of 190–2
    person aggrieved, by 196–8
substances:
  prescribed 90
  release of:
    air, into 592

best available techniques not entailing
  excessive cost, use of 96
control of 568
land, into 593
meaning 90
standard requirements 92
water, into 593
trade effluent:
  agreement for disposal:
    carrying into effect 240
    entry into 240
    special category effluent, for:
      reference to Secretary of State 240–1
      review of 241–2
    transitional authority 264–6
  appeals, statement of case on 245
  consents for discharges:
    appeals 235–6
    application for 233
    charges 242–5
    conditions of 234–5
    requirement of 232–1
    Scotland *see* water pollution, Scotland
    special category effluent, for 233–4
      appeals 236
      review by Secretary of State 239
    time for discharge, application for variation
      of 239–8
    transitional authority 264–6
    variations 543
      appeals 238
      directions 237
      time limit, within 237–8
  disclosure of information, restriction on
    249–51, 266
  false information, provision of 251
  interpretation of provisions 247, 542
  meaning 7, 49–50, 61, 247
  meters, evidence from 245
  other effluents, application of provisions to
    246–7
  pre-1989 Act authority 247
  prescribed processes, derived from 543–4,
    656
  prescribed substances, containing 542–4
  registers 248
  sewerage undertakers, provision of informa-
    tion to 248
  special category:
    agreement for disposal:
      reference to Secretary of State 240–1
      review of 241–2
    consents for discharges 233–4
      appeals 238
      directions 237
      review by Secretary of State 239
      time limit, within 237–8
    Environment Agency, power to acquire
      information 245
    meaning 246

references and reviews:
  compensation for loss or damage  244
  determination, effect of  243–4
  procedure on  242–3

vessels:
  dark smoke, prohibition of emissions  360–1
  right of entry on  54–6
  sanitary appliances, control of, Scotland  29
  unregistered, exclusion from inland waters
    46
  waste from, dealing with, Scotland  45

waste:
  appeals  157
  Atomic Energy Authority, disposal by  59
  brokers:
    registration:
      amendments  725–6
      appeals  727
      applications  724–5, 729–32
      cessation of  729
      duration of  728
      Framework Direction provisions  718–19
      grant of  725–6
      interpretation of provisions  723
      registers  724
      renewal, form for  732–3
      revocation  726
      transfrontier shipment  748
  categories of  223–4
  civil liability  157
  collection authority see waste collection
    authority
  commercial:
    collection of  137–9
    meaning  159
    receptables for  140–1
    treatment as  160
    waste not treated as  664
    waste treated as  664, 669–70
  controlled:
    brokers, registration of  692–3
    carriers, registration of:
      additional partners, of  635
      amendment of entries  635
      appeals  75–6, 638
      applications  633, 642–4
      certificate, form of  646–7
      certificates, copies of  636
      cessation, alteration of register to  reflect
        637
      change of circumstances  635
      duration  636–7
      duty to return certificates  637
      entry in register  634
      exemption  631–2
      interpretation of provisions  631
      partnership, of  74
      prescribed information  639
      prescribed offences  75, 641

production of authority  637
refusal of application  74, 633–4
registered  632
regulations  73–4
renewal, application for  645–6
revocation  74–5, 636
checking procedures  835–6
collection of  137–9
commercial see commercial, above
directions to accept, treat, dispose of or
  deliver  148
duty of care  117–19, 650–1
  Code of Practice  824–56
  law on  843–5
  responsibilities under  845–7
enforcement provisions  79
expert help and guidance  837
glossary of terms  853–5
household see household, below
identification and description  826–9
illegal disposal, seizure and disposal of
  vehicles used for  75–9, 639–41
industrial see industrial, below
interpretation of provisions  662
legal controls  850–3
meaning  159
receipt of  833–5
records, keeping  847–9
regulations  80
safe keeping of  829
scrap metal  838–41
summary checklist  842
transfer of  830–3
transport of:
  authority, production of  76–7
  registering, without  72
unlawfully deposited, powers to require
  removal of  149–50
dangerous or intractable  151
dealers, registration:
  Framework Direction provisions  718–19
  transfrontier shipment  748
definition  855–6
deposit on land, civil liability for  52–3
Directive:
  meaning  662
  reference to  718
  treatment of  664
disposal:
  authority see waste disposal authority
  company see waste disposal company
  contractor, meaning  114
  costs savings  657–8
  meaning  112
  operations  721–2
  unauthorised or harmful, prohibition on
    116–15
duty of care  117–19, 650–1
  Code of Practice  824–56
  law on  843–5
  responsibilities under  845–7

waste (*cont.*):
  Framework Directive:
    appropriate periodic inspections, carrying
      out 719–20
    competent authority:
      duties of 714
      meaning 714–15
    development plans, modification of
      provisions 717
    Directive waste, reference to 718
    interpretation of provisions 712–14
    modification of provisions 717–18
    offshore waste management plan,
      preparation of 716
    permits, matters covered by 717
    record keeping 720
    relevant objectives 715–16
    substances or objects being waste when
      discarded 721
    waste disposal operations 721–2
    waste recovery operations 722
  hazardous 781–90
  household:
    collection of 137–9
      charges for 663, 666–7
    deposit, arrangements for 144
    meaning 159, 765
    receptables for 139–40
    treatment as 160
    waste not treated as 663
    waste treated as 663, 665–6
  importation or exportation, power to prohibit
    or restrict 202–3
  industrial:
    collection of 137–9
    meaning 159
    receptables for 140–1
    treatment as 160
    waste not treated as 664
    waste treated as 663, 667–9
  interpretation of provisions 112
  Isles of Scilly, provisions applied to 160
  legal proceedings 157
  management licences *see* waste management
    licences
  management papers 822
  meaning 159
  mobile plant licence *see also* waste manage-
    ment licences
    application for 121
    grant of 121–4
    meaning 120, 685–6
    relevant land 124
  national strategy:
    England and Wales 134–6
    objectives 222–3
    Scotland 136–7
  other than controlled, regulations for 152
  producer responsibility obligations:
    imposition of 475–7
    offences 480

    regulations, content of 476–80
  professional collectors and transported,
    registration of 718–19
  radioactive *see* radioactive waste
  receptacles, interference with 150
  recovery operations 722
  recycling and disposal, payments for 145–6
  recycling payments 657–8
  recycling plans 142–3
  regulation authority *see* waste regulation
    authority
  sea, deposits in 693
  site licence *see also* waste management
    licences
    application for 121
    grant of 121–4
    meaning 120
    relevant land 124
    surrender 129–31
      application for 678, 695
  sites, interference with 150
  special:
    Agencies, responsibility of 776
    amendment of provisions 777
    consignment notes:
      Agencies, duties of 771–2
      carrier's rounds 769–70, 779–80
      consignee not accepting delivery, duty of
        771
      form of 778
      furnishing, duties as to 772
      importers and exporters 772
      pre-notification not required 766–9
      reception facilities, removal of ship's
        waste to 770
      standard procedure 766
    consignments, coding 766
    environmental effects, assessment of 777
    fees 773
    hazardous waste list 781–90
    interpretation of provisions 764–6
    legal controls 852
    meaning 151, 160, 766
    mixing, restrictions on 775
    offences 775–6
    radioactive waste being 766
    registers 774
    site records 774–5
    technical competence, certificates of 776–7
    treatment, keeping or disposal of 151
  substances or objects being discarded 721
  transfrontier shipment:
    competent authority of destination:
      authorities being 742
      disposal of waste, ensuring 744
    competent authority of dispatch:
      authorities being 742
      notification, transmission of 742
      return of waste, power to ensure 743
    competent authority of transit, authority
      being 742

correspondent, Secretary of State as 742
dealers and brokers, registration of 748
defences 746–7
financial guarantees 743
information, provision of 747
interpretation of provisions 741
notices 747
objections to 745
offences 745–4
penalties 747
power of customs to detain 745
transitional provisions 161–2
unauthorised or harmful depositing or
      treatment, prohibition on 116–15
vessels, from 45
waste collection authority:
controlled waste, collection of 137–9
disposal of waste 141–2, 146–7
meaning 113
receptacles, interference with 150
recycling and disposal, payments for 145–6
recycling, powers of 147
    Scotland 148
sites, interference with 150
waste recycling plans 142–3
waste disposal authority:
constitution as 114
contracts:
    putting out to tender 221
    terms of 221
    variation 222
disposal of waste 141–2, 146–7
existing, meaning 114
functions of 144–5
meaning 113
receptacles, interference with 150
recycling and disposal, payments for 145–6
recycling, powers of 147
    Scotland 148
sites, interference with 150
waste disposal company, transition to
      114–15, 215–20
waste disposal company:
contracts:
    putting out to tender 221
    terms of 221
    variation 222
formation and status of 216
tax and company provisions 218
transfer of securities 222
transition to 114–15, 215–20
waste management licences:
appeals:
    determination, notification of 683
    hearings, report of 682
    notice of 681–2
    time limit for 682
application for 678
conditions 119–20
decisions relating to, appeals 133–4
exempt activities:

activities under other control regimes
    688–9
establishment and operations, registration
    of 694
licensing, from 689, 697–712
registration 690–3
false entries of information 134
false or misleading statements 134
fit and proper person to hold 158
grant of 119, 121–4
consultation before 124–5
groundwater, relating to 686–8
health of persons at work, conditions not
    imposed for 686
holder, directions to accept, treat, dispose of
    or deliver waste by 148
interpretation of provisions 676–8
licensing provisions 14
meaning 119
registers:
information excluded or removed from
    685
particulars to be entered in 683–5
relevant offences 678
revocation 125, 127–9
rights, compensation for 120–1
Scotland, application of provisions to 677
supervision 131–2
surrender 120, 129–31
suspension 127–9
technical competence 679–81, 751–2
pre-qualification 759–60
Scotland 762–3
waste treatment plants 761
transfer 120, 131
application for 678, 696
variation 125–6
consultation before 126–7
waste oils, relating to 686
waste regulation authority, functions of 120
waste regulation authority:
Environment Agency, transfer of functions to
    421
importation or exportation of waste,
    functions as to 202–3
information, obtaining 156
meaning 113
public registers:
confidential information, exclusion of
    154–6
contents of 152–4
information affecting national security,
    exclusion of 154
maintenance of 152–4
references to 113
Scottish Environment Protection Agency,
    transfer of functions to 439
transfer of functions 111
waste management licences, functions as to
    120
water see also waters

water (*cont.*):
  Environment Agency, duties of  425–7
  escapes, civil liability for  252–3
  foul, power to deal with  296–7
  interpretation of provisions  311–17
  Isles of Scilly, application of provisions to
    318
  pollution *see* water pollution
  protection zones  284–5
  quality:
    classification  271
    objectives  272–3
  Scottish Environment Protection Agency,
    duties of 446–7
  visiting forces, provisions not applying to  318
water bailiffs:
  powers of  69
water pollution:
  anti-pollution works and operations:
    Environment Agency, powers of  292–3
    notices requiring  293–4
    rights of entry  294–5
    works notice:
      appeals  295–6
      contents of  293
      failure to comply with  296
      regulations  294
      service of  293
  byelaws  308–9
  civil liability  289
  controlled waters:
    meaning  290–1
    nitrates, entry of  285–7
    Scotland  27–9
  Crown, provisions binding  317
  discharge consents:
    appeals  280–81
    application for  278
      consideration and determination of  320
      consultations  319
      making  319
      Secretary of State, reference to  321
    application, without  321
    conditions  322
    enforcement notices  279
    general review of  323
    revocation  322
    transfer of  324
    variation:
      application for  323
      restriction on  322–3
  discharges, prohibition of  274
  disclosure of information, restriction on
    304–6, 330–1
  documents, service of  310–11
  Environment Agency:
    anti-pollution works and operations by
      292–3
    consents required by  289
    enforcement powers and duties  309
    escapes of water, civil liability for  307–8

exchange of information  303
foul water, power to deal with  296–7
information and assistance, requiring  303
pollution control register:
  confidential information, exclusion of
    300–2
  contents of  298–9
  maintenance of  298–90
  national security, exclusion of informa-
    tion affecting  300
  powers of  296–7
false statements, making  306
fish, injurious to  67
good agricultural practice, codes of  288
  Scotland  48
international obligations, giving effect to  290
interpretation of provisions  311–17
nitrate sensitive areas:
  agreements in  287
  consents required  287–8
  designation of  285–7
    Scotland  27–8, 64–6
  orders:
    application for  326
    mandatory provisions  436–8
offences:
  authorised discharges, defence in respect
    of  276
  controlled waters, polluting  273
  defences  277
  deposits and vegetation in rivers, as to  278
  directors and other third parties, criminal
    liabilities of  309
  enforcement powers and duties  309
  public sewers, discharges into and from
    275
  summary, limitation  290
radioactive waste, by  289
regulations, power to make  310
requirement to take precautions against  284
samples and extractions, evidence of  308
Scotland:
  amended provisions  17
  anti-pollution operations, notices
    requiring  42–3
  closure of mines, problems arising from  48
  consents for discharges:
    alteration and imposition of conditions
      33
    appeals  35–7
    application for  29
    conditional  30
    enforcement notices  47–8
    general review of  34–5
    grant or refusal of  30
    notice of application  31–3
    revocation  33
    Secretary of State, reference to  31
    transitional provisions  37
    variation, restrictions on  34
  consultation and collaboration  21

controlled waters:
  matter entering, offences  21
  meaning  18
  nitrates, entry of  27–9
  vessels, control of sanitary appliances on
    29
definitions  18–19
discharges:
  authorised, defences in respect of  23–4
  defences  24–5
  prohibition by notice or regulation  22
  sewers, to and from  22–3
good agricultural practice, codes of  48
interpretation of provisions  49–50
nitrate sensitive areas:
  agreements, registration of  28
  designation of  27–8, 64–6
offences  21
precautions against  26–7
radioactive waste, provisions relating to  18
registers relating to:
  confidential information, exclusion of
    39–41
  maintenance of  38
  national security, exclusion of matters
    affecting  39
  particulars in  38
regulations  49
river purification authorities:
  operations remedying or forestalling
    pollution by  41–2
  waste from vessels, dealing with  45
rivers and coastal waters  25–6
rivers, deposits and vegetation in  46
transfer of functions  17
unregistered vessels, exclusion from inland
    waters  46
vessels, control of sanitary appliances on
    29
water quality:
  achievement and maintenance of
    objectives  21
  classification  19
  objectives  20
waters to which provisions applying  18
works notice:
  anti-pollution operations, requiring
    42–3
  appeals  44
  compensation under  44

entitlement to carry out works  43–4
failure to comply with  45
meaning  42
rights of entry  43–4
transitional provisions  290, 328–30
water protection zones:
  designation of  284–5
  orders:
    application for  324–5
    draft, supply of copies of  325
    modification of proposals  325
    objections, consideration of  325
  provisions for  284–5
water supply:
  domestic purposes, meaning  257
water undertakers:
  service of documents on  57
watercourses:
  freshwater limits, maps of  302
waters:
  bathing:
    classification  622–5
      Scotland  626–9
    sampling requirements  623–5
      Scotland  627–9
  controlled:
    lakes and ponds  541
    lochs and ponds  557
    meaning  290–1
    nitrates, entry of  285–7
      Scotland  27–9
    polluting  273
    reservoirs:
      lakes and ponds, treated as  541
      lochs and ponds, treated as  557
    Scotland:
      matter entering, offences  21
      meaning  18
      nitrates, entry of  27–9
      vessels, control of sanitary appliances on
        29
  surface:
    classification of  539–40, 554
      coastal  555, 654
      dangerous substances  554–6, 560–1,
        653–4, 659–60
      inland  555, 654
      river ecosystem  735–7
      Scotland  558–9
      territorial  555, 654